THE VOICE OF TOIL

THE VOICE OF TOIL

Nineteenth-Century British Writings about Work

Edited by David J. Bradshaw & Suzanne Ozment

Ohio University Press   Athens

Publication of this book was made possible in part by the
support of the Citadel Development Foundation.

Ohio University Press, Athens, Ohio 45701
© 2000 by David J. Bradshaw and Suzanne Ozment
Printed in the United States of America

Ohio University Press books are printed on acid-free paper ∞ ™
09 08 07 06 05 04 03 02 01 00   5 4 3 2 1

Library of Congress Cataloging-in-Publication Data
The voice of toil : nineteenth-century British writings
    about work / edited by David J. Bradshaw,
    Suzanne Ozment.
        p.   cm.
    Includes bibliographical references.
    ISBN 0-8214-1292-2 (cloth : alk. paper). —
    ISBN 0-8214-1293-0 (pbk. : alk. paper)
    1. Working class—History—19th century—
Sources. 2. Working class—Great Britain—History—
19th century—Sources. 3. Working class in literature.
I. Bradshaw, David J. II. Ozment, Suzanne.
HD4853.V65 1999 2000
305.5'62'   094109034—dc21   99-33101

Cover: Walter Crane, *Work*. Courtesy of Liverpool City Libraries.
    A disciple of W. J. Linton and John Ruskin, the artist Walter Crane (1845–1894)
was influenced by William Morris to convert to socialism in the early 1880s. Like Morris, Crane believed worthwhile work was essential to the health and happiness of the
individual. He promoted this view through weekly cartoons created for socialist magazines such as *Justice* and *Commonweal*. This 1889 heading for the newspaper *Work*
celebrates the labor of ordinary craftspeople.

This book is dedicated to
Leslie, Nathan, Andrew, Peter, and Meredith

Man is sent hither not to question, but to work: "the end of man," it was long ago written, "is an Action, not a Thought."

—Thomas Carlyle, "Characteristics"

Contents

Part 3: Work as Oppression

Illustrations

Part 4: (Separate) Spheres of Work

Acknowledgments

David J. Bradshaw's research was underwritten both by a sabbatical leave awarded by Warren Wilson College and by a grant from the Andrew W. Mellon Foundation conferred by the Faculty Scholars Program at the University of Kentucky and administered through the Department of English at the University of Virginia. At the University of Virginia, Herbert F. Tucker offered the very best collegial support, steady encouragement, and judicious critical comment. David Bradshaw also expresses his gratitude to other scholars whose assistance was essential to the completion of this project: Patricia Meyer Spacks, Barbara Smith, Andrew Stauffer, Amanda French, Patrick Scott, Lawrence F. Rhu, Joy Pastucha, David A. Mycoff, Brandy Steinhilber, and Kelly Graben.

Suzanne Ozment's research was underwritten both by a sabbatical leave awarded by The Citadel and by generous grants from The Citadel Development Foundation. Suzanne Ozment expresses her gratitude to the following individuals whose assistance proved invaluable at various stages of the project: Patrick Scott, Sandra Young, Debbie Causey, Julie Steer, Daphne Thompson, Judy Hagen, and Libby Walker.

Editors' Note

In preparing the selections included in this anthology, we have, in most cases, used original publications or authoritative nineteenth-century editions of primary texts. For certain selections ("Lilies: Of Queens' Gardens" and the chapter from *The Condition of the Working Class in England,* for example), we have used reliable nineteenth-century American editions. We have adapted the sources slightly so that they would conform to a uniform system for presenting quotations; otherwise, we have represented the original punctuation and spellings, making silent corrections of obvious misprints in the sources. At the specific request of the executors of the Bernard Shaw estate, we have retained in *Mrs Warren's Profession* Bernard Shaw's distinctive practices for punctuating and spelling and for the extended printing of particular words.

Insofar as has been practical to do so, we have presented selections (whether chapters from books, magazine or newspaper articles, poems, or essays) in their entirety, preferring not to disrupt the context of presentations by abridging them.

Mrs Warren's Profession is reprinted here courtesy of The Society of Authors on behalf of the Estate of Bernard Shaw. © Copyright 1898, 1913, 1926, 1930, 1941, George Bernard Shaw. © Copyright 1957 The Public Trustee as Executor of the Estate of George Bernard Shaw.

General Introduction

One way to approach the study of nineteenth-century English literature and culture is to explore the diversity of attitudes toward work which characterized the period. As did earnestness, work—the distinctive expression of earnestness—came to define the era. Concern with work was pervasive, so much so that it seemed imperative to address the subject and to address it with passion and conviction. Indeed, the topic of work became a polemical filter through which various social and political controversies were screened and refined.

The social activism of prominent upper-class individuals found its most characteristic expression in enterprises associated with work. Protecting workers from exploitation, ensuring improved working conditions for oppressed groups and adequate living conditions for laborers, establishing new educational and vocational opportunities for the underprivileged or marginalized—these were the causes to which idealists such as Angela Burdett-Coutts, Anthony Ashley Cooper, Emily Davies, and William Morris committed their impressive energies as well as substantial financial resources. The ventures undertaken by such people were calculated not to devalue national industry but rather to increase possibilities for a general enhanced productivity through the cultivation of expert trades craftsmanship, practical skills, and professional talents. While the debilitating aspects of repetitive and onerous work were to be eliminated, work itself was conceived of as both necessary and good, a conception vividly realized in the exertions of these philanthropists themselves, who, in their own devotion to various projects, rejected the lives of casual leisure that their wealth would have made possible.

Idealization of and nearly obsessive devotion to work also distinguished the dominant middle-class moral tone of the period, an attitude made abundantly clear in the novels and poems to which the literate public turned as much for instruction as for enjoyment. That work is essential rather than inappropriate to true gentlemanliness is the lesson William Makepeace Thackeray, Charles Dickens, and George Eliot were at pains to inculcate in their readers through the experiences of characters as varied as Dobbins, Pip, and Fred Vincy. Once distinguished by his not needing to work, the gentleman came to be defined by his commitment to labor responsibly undertaken both to fulfill duties to others and to sustain himself and those dependent upon him. Fitzwilliam Darcy as a social figure stimulates little beyond contempt in Elizabeth Bennett, the heroine of Jane Austen's *Pride and Prejudice,* but, when Elizabeth comes to learn of the industrious and punctilious care with which he manages his estate, she begins to admire him as an example of genuine manliness. In Barrett Browning's *Aurora Leigh,* mid-century readers encountered the heroine's wealthy cousin Romney, who, in his passionate resolution to work for and with unemployed laborers, destitute slum dwellers, and only partially reclaimed criminals, offered a reflection of a number of Victorian individuals devoted to unceasing work to serve others, whether in settlement houses, mechanics' institutes, reformatories, or cooperative societies. And at the latter end of the century, Mary Augusta Ward advanced as the hero of her best-selling novel *Robert Elsmere* a priest who, having left the church because of his honest doubt, finds his true mission serving in the slums of London's East End, where he quite literally works himself to a happy death.

Indeed, no longer to be construed as demeaning, work was configured, throughout the century, as spiritually uplifting, an attitude made clear in the assertion by Carlyle that "there is a perennial nobleness, and even sacredness, in Work." If such a view of work as ennobling was stressed most when labor was understood as involving a commitment to the good of others, Cardinal Newman summarized the dominant ideal by posing work and mission as veritable synonyms: everyone, he asserted, "has a mission, has a work." And behind the endorsement of earnest work that both of these Victorian sages offered lay the authority of Evangelicalism and John Wesley. For Wesley, whose influence upon the nineteenth century was enormous, had, in his famous exhortation concerning wealth, linked both a traditional work ethic and frugality to the enlightened service of others: "Make all you can. . . . Save all you can. . . . Give all you can." The expatriate philanthropist Andrew Carnegie boasted that he had followed Wesley's entire admonition, especially the third injunction, and Carnegie's working-class origins suggest that it was not just among middle- and upper-class individuals that work had assumed an elevated spiritual dignity. Yet for most in the lower class as well as for many in the middle class, work provided the means for material advancement and psychological fulfillment as well as religiously based self-satisfaction.

For if one aspiration was to establish, through work, the self-respect that derives from committing oneself to the service of higher social and moral causes, there was also a more practical concern to achieve, through work, a measure of personal independence and security. Work of widely varying sorts came to be regarded not as a curse to be avoided but instead as an opportunity to be embraced. Work was seen as promoting the worker's health, as enabling an individual to escape intellectual despair, emotional disorder, and spiritual anomie. Here again, Carlyle's unhesitating rhetoric encapsulates the idea: "Older than all preached Gospels was this unpreached, inarticulate, but ineradicable, forever-enduring Gospel: Work, and therein have well-being." More sedately yet no less seriously articulated is an anonymous commendation of work that appeared in the *Pall Mall Gazette,* an endorsement of labor as the means of developing moral character:

There can be no question nowadays, that application to work, absorption in affairs, contact with men, and all the stress which business imposes on us, gives a noble training to the intellect, and splendid opportunity for discipline of character. It is an utterly low view of business which regards it as only a means of getting a living. A man's business is his part of the world's work, his share of the great activities which render society possible. . . . [T]he perpetual call on a man's readiness, self-control, and vigor which business makes, the constant appeal to the intellect, the stress upon the will, the necessity for rapid and responsible exercise of judgment—all these things constitute a high culture.

Work effected not simply spiritual well-being but the social recognition that was most prized: respectability. Moreover, in a period that encompassed major redefinitions of class, success in different forms of work often led to the improving and actual redefining of one's social as well as economic status. The industrial revolution and the development of new professions, while destabilizing in many of their effects, presented new possibilities for individuals to become economically self-sufficient. The sense that the age was one not just of transition but of improvement ensured that people could construe their self-interested pragmatism within an exalted ideal of participation in cultural progress ("the great activities which render society possible"), making work seem all the more honorable and commendable.

Among those for whom labor signified personal security and much needed material advancement, this concern with the "world's work" remained telling. Books emphasizing the connections between hard work and success were immensely popular throughout the century, none more so than those written by Samuel Smiles, who became known as "Self-Help Smiles" after the title of his most popular book. Smiles wrote in *Thrift* that "Without work, life is worthless; it becomes a mere state of moral coma." Yet he went on to insist that, for everyone, truly significant labor must transcend the physical toil that leads to material gain: "There is a great deal of higher work—the work of action and endurance, of trial and patience, of enterprise and philanthropy, of spreading truth and civilization, of diminishing suffering and relieving the poor, of helping the weak, and enabling them to help themselves." During the last third of the century, Smiles's books sold in the hundreds of thousands, and the evidence suggests that most purchasers were lower-middle-class workers. But if such popularity is a register of their identification with Smiles's principles, their aspirations to personal improvement were never divorced from a complementary sense of social duty.

This sense of social duty also involved individuals from all segments of society in a rather different conversation concerning work. Satisfaction with what work could do for individuals had its counterbalance in the anger and dismay expressed at the conditions of those whom Robert Owen, in 1817, first called the "working class." What working-class people confronted both at the work site and in their lodgings was recognized as oppressive, and the misery of their lives became the subject of sentimental poetry, government report, popular fiction, and journalistic exposé. Conditions in factories, small home-shops and sweatshops, mines, farms, and the workhouse—the "poor man's Bastille"—were bitterly deplored and also blamed for the absence of genuine culture and compassionate morality in workers. Much of the discourse concerning work in the nineteenth century was distin-

guished by calls for reformation of attitudes toward workers and relationships between classes. Paintings, engravings, and cartoons, readily reproduced and widely
available, reinforced consciousness of workers' often desperate situations, while
photography added a documentary realism to considerations of what Engels called
"the condition of the working class."

Although conditions for farm laborers were quite bad, especially during the
middle third of the century, more sustained attention was given to the plight of
urban workers. Indeed, often rural work was falsely idealized in order to point the
newer distresses that distinguished mill workers or miners. Engels's register of the
general situation in the mines in 1844 was horrifying, but the English reading public
did not find *The Condition of the Working Class* in translation until the end of the
century; the official government reports ("blue books") that informed Engels's
writing were sensational enough in themselves, revealing terrible abuses of young
children and appalling readers with descriptions of the dangers and oppressive
circumstances faced by adult workers, especially women. The so-called industrial
novel of the 1840s and 1850s, however, gave greatest prominence to the exploitation
of workers in small handwork shops ("manufactories") and in the larger mills and
factories powered by water and steam. Writers such as Dickens, Charles Kingsley,
and Elizabeth Gaskell emphasized the deadening effect that mechanized work had
upon such laborers, the tensions generated between owners and operatives by
obsessive adherence to *laissez-faire* practice, the abuses that seemed inevitable when
one group exerted almost total control over a laboring class so numerous as to
become faceless, and the pernicious living conditions of intensely concentrated
populations of urban workers.

Perhaps as heated as the discussion about the conditions of lower-class workers
was the conversation about separate spheres of work for men and women. The
contentious issues comprising what nineteenth-century writers called "the Woman
Question" found their natural expression in the debate over possibilities for wom-
en's work and the way those possibilities served to define familial, social, and
political roles for both men and women. Of course, however many prescriptive
definitions of women's work were advanced, they pertained only to the reasonably
well-off: those millions of women who labored in domestic service, farms, and
factories were not the focus of this controversy, which related to men and women
of the middle and upper classes. For those women who did enjoy some measure of
financial security, however, efforts to redefine political and economic status necessarily involved consideration of what work women might do—for there was no
question in this society that idleness was wrong and that even moderate leisure
represented a temptation. Whether women should function at all in the workplace
or instead remain moral guardians of the home was the key issue, but the discussion radiated outward to include education for women, distinctive talents that
women should cultivate, and efforts for those described as "redundant women":
women uneducated to work who found themselves, as widows or spinsters, without financial support.

The selections in this anthology have been arranged to reflect four prominent ways in which the subject of work was addressed in the nineteenth century: Work as Mission, Work as Opportunity, Work as Oppression, and (Separate) Spheres of Work. Notes throughout will help direct readers to instructive interrelations with selections included in other sections, while introductions to each selection offer brief biographical notes concerning authors. The selections are intended to be suggestive rather than exhaustive: the effort has been to provide readings that will provoke thought and discussion about one of the most recurrent and controversial topics of nineteenth-century discourse.

PART 1

Work as Mission

What is the great idea that has seized the mind of this
age? It is the grand idea of *man*—of the importance of
man as man; that every human being has a great mission
to perform—has noble faculties to cultivate, great ideas
to assert, a vast destiny to accomplish.

—Samuel Smiles, *Autobiography*

Introduction

Two scenes in *Middlemarch* prove particularly instructive about the conception of work that George Eliot advances as normative. Fred Vincy serendipitously encounters Caleb Garth when Caleb is most in need of assistance in his surveying and assessing of lands, and, having labored throughout the day with the older man, Fred asks whether such work might be possible for him on a permanent basis: "You do think I could do some good at it, if I were to try?" he inquires of Caleb. In the larger scheme of the novel, this occasion is the turning point for Fred, who changes from being feckless and irresponsibly self-centered to become directed, reliable, and sensitive to others' needs and limitations. The framing of his question points the essential reorientation in his life: he will embrace work but needs to understand such work as productive of "some good." A similar emphasis informs an interchange between two other figures. Lydgate, the idealistic young doctor who has run into overwhelming debt, has been granted a substantial loan by the banker Bulstrode, a loan that will enable him to repay his most pressing creditors. Lydgate's expression of thanks defines the values that he holds most dear, that establish him, in the midst of his troubles, as clearly sympathetic to readers: "I am deeply grateful to you. . . . You have restored to me the prospect of working with some happiness and some chance of good." Lydgate values the financial assistance not because it enables him to escape responsibilities but because it ensures his ability to work, to work with "some chance of good."

Eliot certainly was not alone among nineteenth-century writers in offering an endorsement of work that associated and sometimes identified work with the earnest pursuit of doing good. Indeed, the pervasive concern in *Middlemarch* to construe genuine work as synonymous with the pursuit of a higher moral mission may explain why so many regard it as the novel most representative of Victorian values, and in Eliot's delineation of the normative character of Caleb Garth readers find perhaps the most strongly articulated summation of the work ethic.

> Caleb Garth often shook his head in meditation on the value, the indispensable might of that myriad-headed, myriad-handed labour by which the social body is fed, clothed, and housed. It had laid hold of his imagination in boyhood. The echoes of the great hammer where roof or keel were a-making, the signal-shouts of the workmen, the roar of the furnace, the thunder and plash of the engine, were a sublime music to him; the felling and lading of timber, and the huge trunk vibrating star-like in the distance along the highway, the crane at work on the wharf, the

piled-up produce in warehouses, the precision and variety of muscular effort wherever exact work had to be turned out,—all these sights of his youth had acted on him
as poetry without the aid of the poets, had made a philosophy for him without the
aid of philosophers, a religion without the aid of theology. His early ambition had
been to have as effective a share as possible in this sublime labour, which was
peculiarly dignified by him with the name of "business."

Labor that serves the social body is "sublime," and imaginative involvement with it
substitutes for and comprises poetry, philosophy, and religion. Caleb's articulation of this attitude makes even more clear the religious nature of his conception
of work.

> " . . . [the opportunity to work is] a fine thing to come to a man when he's seen into
> the nature of business: to have the chance of getting a bit of the country into good
> fettle, as they say, and putting men into the right way with their farming and getting
> a bit of good contriving and solid building done—that those who are living and
> those who come after will be the better for. I'd sooner have it than a fortune. I hold it
> the most honourable work that is." Here Caleb laid down his letters, thrust his
> fingers between the buttons of his waistcoat, and sat upright, but presently pro-
> ceeded with some awe in his voice and moving his head slowly aside—"It's a great
> gift of God, Susan."

Not the curse accompanying exile from Eden but rather a "great gift of God," work
is a mission entailing a commitment to serve others and promote a better future.

Yet such an understanding of the nature of work was not original with Eliot,
however memorably she may have given it expression. Behind her highly charged
language is her own strongly religious background and the pervasive influence of
Evangelicalism on the nineteenth century. In selections below from John Wesley's
eighteenth-century sermon, one can sense the fervor of which Caleb's words are a
not-too-distant echo, and in Wesley one finds expressly proposed the notion that
true work is the activity of stewardship, of caring for, developing, and perfecting
things in order that they might better serve the higher purposes that God wills.
However secularized this idea subsequently became, there remained the insistent
effort to discriminate between the steward's ennobling consummation of duty and
the timeserver's enthrallment to debasing work; even Morris's largely socialist
"Useful Work versus Useless Toil" carries the religious overtone that work must be
understood as mission or it becomes the very opposite of a blessing.

The selections in the "Work as Mission" section reflect, in varying ways, this
attitude that appropriate human labor involves fulfillment of a steward's responsibilities. For Thomas Carlyle, carefully recalling Milton, "All men, if they work
not as in a Great Taskmaster's eye, will work wrong, work unhappily for themselves and you" (*Past and Present*). Tennyson's Arthur, reflecting on his decision
not to go in quest of the Grail, assesses a king as simply another steward whose
responsibilities bind him in sacred duty to quotidian work in an ostensibly non-
heroic world:

> the King must guard
> That which he rules, and is but as the hind
> To whom a space of land is given to plow,
> Who may not wander from the allotted field
> Before his work be done, but, being done,
> Let visions of the night or of the day
> Come as they will; and many a time they come,
> Until this earth he walks on seems not earth,
> This light that strikes his eyeball is not light,
> This air that smites his forehead is not air
> But vision— (*The Holy Grail* 901–11)

Tennyson's king sees the reward of lowly-wise labor as a translation into another, more spiritual world, an "earth . . . that seems not earth." The hope-filled vision is not very far from that adumbrated by Matthew Arnold in "Rugby Chapel," the poem in which he celebrates the commitment to serve others that distinguished his father and the other "noble and great who are gone":

> souls temper'd with fire,
> Fervent, heroic, and good,
> Helpers and friends of mankind. (159–61)

Hero-worship of that same Thomas Arnold inspired the former Rugby schoolboy Thomas Hughes; the selection from his best-selling boys' novel *Tom Brown's School-days* offers a vision of Heaven in which the communion of saints actually continues to struggle in common enterprise with those still living on earth: eternal labor, joyously eternal labor rather than eternal rest is the reward of the just. What is perhaps most remarkable about Hughes's redefining of Heaven as a place of unceasing work is that no one found such a transvaluation worthy of remark, let alone objection. That work was a mission and that this mission would be carried on in Heaven was nothing strange to the mid-Victorian imagination, and Barrett Browning's Christian socialist Romney Leigh puts the case most directly: "I count that Heaven itself is only work / To a surer issue" (*Aurora Leigh* 8:724–25).

If labor was seen as an expression of spiritual and psychic strength, it was also regarded as a means to secure such strength. Wordsworth's Michael, working at the unfinished sheepfold for seven years, dwells with and upon his grief for his lost son Luke, deriving from the action of labor and memory a solace that sustains him. Carlyle insists that spiritual peace and mental health are possible only for those who work, that sanity is a by-product of industry: "All Works, each in their degree, are a making of Madness sane" (*Past and Present*). Florence Nightingale validated Carlyle's vision by seeing in the inactivity of her early life the source of melancholy and mental instability bordering on despair; what is needed for her as for Carlyle is a mission, a work, to which she might commit her energies and her very self. Nightingale, of course, found first one such mission and then several others. For all of these thinkers, *purposeful* work was a realization of transcendent energy in the form of human endeavor, but work without a purpose, without a mission, degenerated into an oppression that was spiritually enervating. Everyone, as Cardinal Newman insisted, "has a mission, has a work" (*Discourses to Mixed Congregations*); for individuals of all classes in the nineteenth century, this assertion carried the conviction of a self-evident truth and the force of a divine injunction.

JOHN WESLEY

J OHN WESLEY (1703–1791) was the principal motivating force behind the evangelical movement that, in the eighteenth and early nineteenth centuries, swept through the Established Church and Nonconformist sects alike. Born into a religious family and educated at Oxford, he was already a devout believer when, in his early thirties, he experienced an intense spiritual awakening and committed himself fully to a zealous preaching of the Christian gospel. With his brother Charles (1707–1788) and George Whitefield (1714–1770), Wesley made popular the practice of itinerant preaching, reaching with his message many in rural areas and newly developed towns who were inadequately served by the traditional parish systems. His ardent religious revival attracted the sympathies of those who felt estranged from a dormant and distant Church, and his influence spread well beyond formal ecclesiastical communities of his own day into the broader culture, sanctioning Romantic emphasis upon the noble virtues of the good of heart and shaping Victorian preoccupation with earnest fulfillment of duty. That Wesley was such a strong influence upon nineteenth-century culture is the reason that his sermon, given final form in the 1770s, is included in this anthology with nineteenth-century documents. (Rigorously annotated versions of Wesley's sermons may be consulted in the bicentennial edition of *The Works of John Wesley*, edited by Albert C. Outler.)

The subject of "The Use of Money" was popular with Wesley's late-eighteenth-century audiences and with evangelical activists throughout the Victorian period. "Gain all you can; save all you can; give all you can": the Scots-American industrialist and philanthropist Andrew Carnegie, in "The Gospel of Wealth," cited Wesley's three-part counsel about money as the foundation for his life's work and mission. German sociologist Max Weber, quoting Wesley but conveniently leaving off the third element in this admonition, employs Wesley's exhortation as part of the concluding negative analysis in *The Protestant Ethic and the Spirit of Capitalism* (1904–5), a critique anticipated by Ernst Troeltsch, a nineteenth-century theologian and Weber's friend. Wesley was aware that his endorsement of self-restraint and frugality accorded well with materialistic attitudes that underlay the expanding English economy, and he made clear efforts to give to these potentially worldly qualities a specifically Christian pointing. Indeed, Wesley's sermon summarizes certain Victorian moral attitudes toward work, attitudes for which it was, in fact, a source:

Gain all you can by honest industry: use all possible diligence in your calling. Lose no time. . . . Every business will afford some employment sufficient for every day and every hour. That wherein *you* are placed, if you follow it in earnest, will leave you no leisure for silly, unprofitable diversions. . . . And "whatsoever thy hand findeth to do, do it with all thy might." Do it *as soon* as possible. . . . And do it *as well* as possible. Do not sleep or yawn over it. Put your whole strength to the work.

The Victorian work ethic also owed to Wesleyan emphasis upon social mission the ideal of stewardship, the belief that a person's conduct in the economic and social realms should be governed by awareness that he or she has been "placed . . . here not as a proprietor, but a steward"; the righteous (and sometimes self-righteous) enthusiasm with which many in the nineteenth century approached work is grounded in this understanding of proper mission advanced in Wesley's sermon.

The Use of Money

Luke 16:9
I say unto you, Make unto yourselves friends of the mammon of unrighteousness, that when ye fail, they may receive you into the everlasting habitations.

1. Our Lord, having finished the beautiful parable of the Prodigal Son, which he had particularly addressed to those who murmured at his receiving publicans and sinners, adds another relation of a different kind, addressed rather to the children of God.[1] "He said unto his disciples"—not so much to the scribes and Pharisees to whom he had been speaking before—"There was a certain rich man, who had a steward, and he was accused to him of wasting his goods. And calling him he said, Give an account of thy stewardship, for thou canst be no longer steward." After reciting the method which the bad steward used to provide against the day of necessity, our Saviour adds, "His lord commended the unjust steward"—namely in this respect, that he used timely precaution—and subjoins this weighty reflection, "The children of this world are wiser in their generation than the children of light." Those who seek no other portion than "this world are wiser" (not absolutely; for they are one and all the veriest fools, the most egregious madmen under heaven, but) "in

---

1. The Parable of the Prodigal Son is offered in Luke 15:11–32, and the Parable of the Unjust Steward follows in Luke 16:1–13; Wesley quotes extensively from the Parable of the Unjust Steward in the initial segments of the sermon.

their generation," in their own way; they are more consistent with themselves, they are truer to their acknowledged principles, they more steadily pursue their end, "than the children of light," than they who see "the light of the glory of God in the face of Jesus Christ."[2] Then follow the words above recited: "And I"—the only-begotten Son of God, the Creator, Lord and Possessor of heaven and earth, and all that is therein; the Judge of all, to whom ye are to "give an account of your stewardship" when ye "can be no longer stewards"—"I say unto you" (learn in this respect even of the unjust steward), "make yourselves friends," by wise, timely precaution, "of the mammon of unrighteousness." "Mammon" means riches or money. It is termed "the mammon of unrighteousness" because of the unrighteous manner wherein it is frequently procured, and wherein even that which was honestly procured is generally employed. "Make yourselves friends" of this by doing all possible good, particularly to the children of God; "that when ye fail," when ye return to dust, when ye have no more place under the sun, those of them who are gone before "may receive you," may welcome you "into the everlasting habitations."

2. An excellent branch of Christian wisdom is here inculcated by our Lord on all his followers, namely, the right use of money—a subject largely spoken of, after their manner, by men of the world, but not sufficiently considered by those whom God hath chosen out of the world. These generally do not consider as the importance of the subject requires the use of this excellent talent. Neither do they understand how to employ it to the greatest advantage; the introduction of which into the world is one admirable instance of the wise and gracious providence of God. It has indeed been the manner of poets, orators, and philosophers, in almost all ages and nations, to rail at this as the grand corrupter of the world, the bane of virtue, the pest of human society. Hence nothing so commonly heard as:

Ferrum, ferroque nocentius aurum—

"And gold, more mischievous than keenest steel." Hence the lamentable complaint,

Effodiuntur opes, irritamenta malorum.[3]

Nay, one celebrated writer gravely exhorts his countrymen, in order to banish all vice at once, to "throw all their money into the sea":

. . . in mare proximum [. . .]
Summi materiem mali![4]

But is not all this mere empty rant? Is there any solid reason therein? By no means. For let the world be as corrupt as it will, is gold or silver to blame? "The love of

---

2. 2 Corinthians 4:6.

3. The lines, quoted in reverse order, are taken from Ovid's description of the ages of man (*Metamorphoses* 1.140–41): "Wealth is dug out, an incitement to evils, / iron, and more harmful than iron, gold."

4. Wesley quotes fragmentarily from Horace's *Odes* (3.24.47–50), leaving out an intervening line and the governing verb. The full context reads, *"vel nos in mare proximum / gemmas et lapides aurum et inutile / summi materiem mali / mittamus"* (Or let us into the nearest sea / our gems and stones and useless gold / the substance of our ill, / sink).

money," we know, "is the root of all evil;"[5] but not the thing itself. The fault does not lie in the money, but in them that use it. It may be used ill; and what may not? But it may likewise be used well; it is full as applicable to the best as to the worst uses. It is of unspeakable service to all civilized nations in all the common affairs of life. It is a most compendious instrument of transacting all manner of business, and (if we use it according to Christian wisdom) of doing all manner of good. It is true, were man in a state of innocence, or were all men "filled with the Holy Ghost," so that, like the infant church at Jerusalem, "no man counted anything he had his own," but "distribution was made to everyone as he had need,"[6] the use of it would be superseded; as we cannot conceive there is anything of the kind among the inhabitants of heaven. But in the present state of mankind it is an excellent gift of God, answering the noblest ends.[7] In the hands of his children it is food for the hungry, drink for the thirsty, raiment for the naked. It gives to the traveller and the stranger where to lay his head. By it we may supply the place of an husband to the widow, and of a father to the fatherless; we may be a defence for the oppressed, a means of health to the sick, of ease to them that are in pain. It may be as eyes to the blind, as feet to the lame; yea, a lifter up from the gates of death.

3. It is therefore of the highest concern that all who fear God know how to employ this valuable talent; that they be instructed how it may answer these glorious ends, and in the highest degree. And perhaps all the instructions which are necessary for this may be reduced to three plain rules, by the exact observance whereof we may approve ourselves faithful stewards of "the mammon of unrighteousness."

I. 1. The first of these is (he that heareth let him understand!) *Gain all you can.* Here we may speak like the children of the world. We meet them on their own ground. And it is our bounden duty to do this. We ought to gain all we can gain without buying gold too dear, without paying more for it than it is worth. But this it is certain we ought not do: we ought not to gain money at the expense of life; nor (which is in effect the same thing) at the expense of our health. Therefore no gain whatsoever should induce us to enter into, or to continue in, any employ which is of such a kind, or is attended with so hard or so long labour, as to impair our constitution. Neither should we begin or continue in any business which necessarily deprives us of proper seasons for food and sleep in such a proportion as our nature requires. Indeed there is a great difference here. Some employments are absolutely and totally unhealthy—as those which imply the dealing much with arsenic or other equally hurtful minerals, or the breathing an air tainted with steams of melting lead, which must at length destroy the firmest constitution. Others may not be absolutely unhealthy, but only to persons of a weak constitution. Such are those which require many hours to be spent in writing, especially if a person write sitting, and lean upon his stomach, or remain long in an uneasy

5. 1 Timothy 6:10.
6. Acts 4:31–32.
7. Wesley goes on to describe what are termed the corporal works of mercy.

posture. But whatever it is which reason or experience shows to be destructive of health or strength, that we may not submit to; seeing "the life is more" valuable "than meat, and the body than raiment."[8] And if we are already engaged in such an employ, we should exchange it as soon as possible for some which, if it lessen our gain, will however not lessen our health.

2. We are, secondly, to gain all we can without hurting our mind any more than our body. For neither may we hurt this. We must preserve, at all events, the spirit of an healthful mind. Therefore we may not engage or continue in any sinful trade, any that is contrary to the law of God, or of our country. Such are all that necessarily imply our robbing or defrauding the king of his lawful customs. For it is at least as sinful to defraud the king of his right as to rob our fellow subjects. And the king has full as much right to his customs as we have to our houses and apparel. Other businesses there are, which however innocent *in themselves,* cannot be followed with innocence *now* (at least, not in England): such, for instance, as will not afford a competent maintenance without cheating or lying, or conformity to some custom which is not consistent with a good conscience. These likewise are sacredly to be avoided, whatever gain they may be attended with provided we follow the custom of the trade; for to gain money we must not lose our souls. There are yet others which many pursue with perfect innocence without hurting either their body or mind. And yet perhaps *you* cannot: either they may entangle you in that company which would destroy your soul—and by repeated experiments it may appear that you cannot separate the one from the other—or there may be an idiosyncrasy, a peculiarity in your constitution of soul (as there is in the bodily constitution of many) by reason whereof that employment is deadly to *you* which another may safely follow. So I am convinced, from many experiments, I could not study to any degree of perfection either mathematics, arithmetic, or algebra, without being a deist, if not an atheist. And yet others may study them all their lives without sustaining any inconvenience. None therefore can here determine for another, but every man must judge for himself, and abstain from whatever he in particular finds to be hurtful to his soul.

3. We are, thirdly, to gain all we can without hurting our neighbour. But this we may not, cannot do, if we love our neighbour as ourselves. We cannot, if we love everyone as ourselves, hurt anyone *in his substance.* We cannot devour the increase of his lands, and perhaps the lands and houses themselves, by gaming, by overgrown bills (whether on account of physic, or law, or anything else), or by requiring or taking such interest as even the laws of our country forbid. Hereby all *pawnbroking* is excluded, seeing whatever good we might do thereby all unprejudiced men see with grief to be abundantly overbalanced by the evil. And if it were otherwise, yet we are not allowed to "do evil that good may come."[9] We cannot, consistent with brotherly love, sell our goods below the market price. We cannot study to ruin our neighbour's trade in order to advance our own. Much less can we

8. Matthew 6:25.
9. Romans 3:8.

entice away or receive any of his servants or workmen whom he has need of. None can gain by swallowing up his neighbour's substance, without gaining the damnation of hell.

4. Neither may we gain by hurting our neighbour *in his body*. Therefore we may not sell anything which tends to impair health. Such is, eminently, all that liquid fire commonly called "drams" or "spirituous liquor." It is true, these may have a place in medicine; they may be of use in some bodily disorders (although there would rarely be occasion for them were it not for the unskillfulness of the practitioner). Therefore such as prepare and sell them *only for this end* may keep their conscience clear. But who are they? Who prepare and sell them *only for this end*? Do you know ten such distillers in England? Then excuse these. But all who sell them in the common way, to any that will buy, are poisoners-general. They murder his Majesty's subjects by wholesale, neither does their eye pity or spare. They drive them to hell like sheep. And what is their gain? Is it not the blood of these men? Who then would envy their large estates and sumptuous palaces? A curse is in the midst of them: the curse of God cleaves to the stones, the timber, the furniture of them. The curse of God is in their gardens, their walks, their groves; a fire that burns to the nethermost hell. Blood, blood is there—the foundation, the floor, the walls, the roof are stained with blood! And canst thou hope, O thou man of blood, though thou art "clothed in scarlet and fine linen, and farest sumptuously every day,"[10] canst thou hope to deliver down thy "fields of blood" to the third generation?[11] Not so; for there is a God in heaven. Therefore thy name shall soon be rooted out. Like as those whom thou hast destroyed, body and soul, "thy memorial shall perish with thee."[12]

5. And are not they partakers of the same guilt, though in a lower degree, whether surgeons, apothecaries, or physicians, who play with the lives or health of men to enlarge their own gain? Who purposely lengthen the pain or disease which they are able to remove speedily? Who protract the cure of their patient's body in order to plunder his substance? Can any man be clear before God who does not shorten every disorder *as much as he can,* and remove all sickness and pain *as soon as he can.* He cannot. For nothing can be more clear than that he does not "love his neighbour as himself";[13] than that he does not "do unto others as he would they should do unto himself."[14]

6. This is dear-bought gain. And so is whatever is procured by hurting our neighbour *in his soul:* by ministering, suppose either directly or indirectly, to his unchastity or intemperance, which certainly none can do who has any fear of God, or any real desire of pleasing him. It nearly concerns all those to consider this who have anything to do with taverns, victualling-houses, opera-houses, playhouses, or

---

10. Luke 16:19; Wesley quotes here from the story of Dives and Lazarus which follows the Parable of the Unjust Steward.
11. Acts 1:15–20.
12. Adapted from Psalm 9:6.
13. Matthew 22:39.
14. Luke 6:31.

any other places of public, fashionable diversion. If these profit the souls of men, you are clear; your employment is good, and your gain innocent. But if they are either sinful in themselves, or natural inlets to sin of various kinds, then it is to be feared you have a sad account to make. O beware lest God say in that day, "These have perished in their iniquity, but their blood do I require at thy hands!"[15]

7. These cautions and restrictions being observed, it is the bounden duty of all who are engaged in worldly business to observe that first and great rule of Christian wisdom with respect to money, "Gain all you can." Gain all you can by honest industry: use all possible diligence in your calling. Lose no time. If you understand yourself and your relation to God and man, you know you have none to spare. If you understand your particular calling as you ought, you will have no time that hangs upon your hands. Every business will afford some employment sufficient for every day and every hour. That wherein *you* are placed, if you follow it in earnest, will leave you no leisure for silly, unprofitable diversions. You have always something better to do, something that will profit you, more or less. And "whatsoever thy hand findeth to do, do it with thy might."[16] Do it *as soon* as possible. No delay! No putting off from day to day, or from hour to hour. Never leave anything till tomorrow which you can do today. And do it *as well* as possible. Do not sleep or yawn over it. Put your whole strength to the work. Spare no pains. Let nothing be done by halves, or in a slight and careless manner. Let nothing in your business be left undone if it can be done by labour or patience.

8. Gain *all* you can, by common sense, by using in your business all the understanding which God has given you. It is amazing to observe how few do this; how men run on in the same dull track with their forefathers. But whatever they do who know not God, this is no rule for *you*. It is a shame for a Christian not to improve upon *them* in whatever he takes in hand. *You* should be continually learning from the experience of others or from your own experience, reading, and reflection, to do everything you have to do better today than you did yesterday. And see that you practise whatever you learn, that you may make the best of all that is in your hands.

II. 1. Having gained all you can, by honest wisdom and unwearied diligence, the second rule of Christian prudence is, *Save all you can.* Do not throw the precious talent into the sea: leave that folly to heathen philosophers. Do not throw it away in idle expenses, which is just the same as throwing it into the sea. Expend no part of it merely to gratify the desire of the flesh, the desire of the eye, or the pride of life.

2. Do not waste any part of so precious a talent merely in gratifying the desires of the flesh; in procuring the pleasures of sense of whatever kind; particularly, in enlarging the pleasure of tasting. I do not mean, avoid gluttony and drunkenness only: an honest heathen would condemn these. But there is a regular, reputable kind of sensuality, an elegant epicurism, which does not immediately disorder the

---

15. Adapted from Ezekiel 3:18.
16. Ecclesiastes 9:10. This verse was frequently quoted and paraphrased by Thomas Carlyle.

stomach, nor (sensibly, at least) impair the understanding. And yet (to mention no other effects of it now) it cannot be maintained without considerable expense. Cut off all this expense. Despise delicacy and variety, and be content with what plain nature requires.

3. Do not waste any part of so precious a talent merely in gratifying the desire of the eye by superfluous or expensive apparel, or by needless ornaments. Waste no part of it in curiously adorning your houses in superfluous or expensive furniture; in costly pictures, painting, gilding, books; in elegant (rather than useful) gardens. Let your neighbours, who know nothing better, do this: "Let the dead bury their dead." But "What is that to thee?" says our Lord: "Follow thou me."[17] Are you willing? Then you are able so to do.

4. Lay out nothing to gratify the pride of life, to gain the admiration or praise of men. This motive of expense is frequently interwoven with one or both of the former. Men are expensive in diet, or apparel, or furniture, not barely to please their appetite, or to gratify their eye, their imagination, but their vanity too. "So long as thou dost well unto thyself, men will speak good of thee."[18] So long as thou art "clothed in purple and fine linen, and farest sumptuously every day,"[19] no doubt many will applaud thy elegance of taste, thy generosity and hospitality. But do not buy their applause so dear. Rather be content with the honour that cometh from God.

5. Who would expend anything in gratifying these desires if he considered that to gratify them is to increase them? Nothing can be more certain than this: daily experience shows, the more they are indulged, they increase the more. Whenever therefore you expend anything to please your taste or other senses, you pay so much for sensuality. When you lay out money to please your eye, you give so much for an increase of curiosity, for a stronger attachment to these pleasures, which perish in the using. While you are purchasing anything which men use to applaud, you are purchasing more vanity. Had you not then enough of vanity, sensuality, curiosity before? Was there need of any addition? And would you pay for it, too? What manner of wisdom is this? Would not the literally throwing your money into the sea be a less mischievous folly?

6. And why should you throw away money upon your children, any more than upon yourself, in delicate food, in gay or costly apparel, in superfluities of any kind? Why should you purchase for them more pride or lust, more vanity, or foolish and hurtful desires? They do not want any more; they have enough already; nature has made ample provision for them. Why should you be at farther expense to increase their temptations and snares, and to "pierce them through with more sorrows"?[20]

7. Do not *leave it* to them, to throw away. If you have good reason to believe that

17. Luke 9:59–60.
18. Adapted from Psalm 49:18.
19. See note 10.
20. 1 Timothy 6:10; this phrasing is the completion of the verse in which the "love of money" is described as "the root of all evil": see note 5.

they would waste what is now in your possession in gratifying and thereby increasing the desire of the flesh, the desire of the eye, or the pride of life (at the peril of theirs and your own soul), do not set these traps in their way. Do not offer your sons or your daughters unto Belial any more than unto Moloch.[21] Have pity upon them, and remove out of their way what you may easily foresee would increase their sins, and consequently plunge them deeper into everlasting perdition. How amazing then is the infatuation of those parents who think they can never leave their children enough? What! cannot you leave them enough of arrows, firebrands, and death? Not enough of foolish and hurtful desires? Not enough of pride, lust, ambition, vanity? Not enough of everlasting burnings! Poor wretch! Thou fearest where no fear is. Surely both thou and they, when ye are lifting up your eyes in hell, will have enough both of the "worm that never dieth," and of "the fire that never shall be quenched."[22]

8. "What then would you do if you was in my case? If you had a considerable fortune to leave?" Whether I *would* do it or no, I know what I *ought* to do: this will admit of no reasonable question. If I had one child, elder or younger, who knew the value of money, one who I believed would put it to the true use, I should think it my absolute, indispensable duty to leave that child the bulk of my fortune; and to the rest just so much as would enable them to live in the manner they had been accustomed to do. "But what if all your children were equally ignorant of the true use of money?" I ought then (hard saying! Who can hear it?) to give each what would keep him above want, and to bestow all the rest in such a manner as I judged would be most for the glory of God.

III. 1. But let not any man imagine that he has done anything barely by going thus far, by *gaining and saving all he can,* if he were to stop here. All this is nothing if a man go not forward, if he does not point all this at a farther end. Nor indeed can a man properly be said to *save* anything if he only *lays it up.* You may as well throw your money into the sea as bury it in the earth. And you may as well bury it in the earth as in your chest, or in the Bank of England. Not to use, is effectually to throw it away. If therefore you would indeed "make yourselves friends of the mammon of unrighteousness," add the third rule to the two preceding. Having first gained all you can, and secondly saved all you can, then give all you can.

2. In order to see the ground and reason of this, consider: when the possessor of heaven and earth brought you into being and placed you in this world, he placed you here not as a proprietor, but a steward. As such he entrusted you for a season with goods of various kinds. But the sole property of these still rests in him, nor can ever be alienated from him. As you yourself are not your own, but his, such is

21. Belial is a name associated with Satan, with whom Belial is sometimes identified, while Moloch is a Canaanite god associated with child sacrifice. In *Paradise Lost* II, Milton makes them principal confederates of Satan, casting Belial as a perverse voluptuary and Moloch as a wrathful aggressor, thereby linking the concupiscent and irascible passions. Wesley may have been led to speak of them here because the third spirit associated by Milton with these two is Mammon.

22. A coupled phrasing that is repeated three times in Mark 9:43–48.

likewise all that you enjoy. Such is your soul, and your body—not your own, but God's. And so is your substance in particular. And he has told you in the most clear and express terms how you are to employ it for him, in such a manner that it may be all an holy sacrifice, acceptable through Christ Jesus. And this light, easy service he has promised to reward with an eternal weight of glory.

3. The directions which God has given us touching the use of our worldly substance may be comprised in the following particulars. If you desire to be a faithful and a wise steward, out of that portion of your Lord's goods which he has for the present lodged in your hands, but with the right of resuming whenever it pleases him, first, provide things needful for yourself—food to eat, raiment to put on, whatever nature moderately requires for preserving the body in health and strength. Secondly, provide these for your wife, your children, your servants, or any others who pertain to your household. If when this is done there be an overplus left, then "do good to them that are of the household of faith." If there be an overplus still, "as you have opportunity, do good unto all men."[23] In so doing, you *give all you can*; nay, in a sound sense, all you have. For all that is laid out in this manner is really given to God. You "render unto God the things that are God's,"[24] not only by what you give to the poor, but also by that which you expend in providing things needful for yourself and your household.

4. If then a doubt should at any time arise in your mind concerning what you are going to expend, either on yourself or any part of your family, you have an easy way to remove it. Calmly and seriously inquire: (1). In expending this, am I acting according to my character? Am I acting herein, not as a proprietor, but as a steward of my Lord's goods? (2). Am I doing this in obedience to his Word? In what Scripture does he require me so to do? (3). Can I offer up this action, this expense, as a sacrifice to God through Jesus Christ? (4). Have I reason to believe that for this very work I shall have a reward at the resurrection of the just? You will seldom need anything more to remove any doubt which arises on this head; but by this fourfold consideration you will receive clear light as to the way wherein you should go.

5. If any doubt still remain, you may farther examine yourself by prayer according to those heads of inquiry. Try whether you can say to the Searcher of hearts, your conscience not condemning you: "Lord, thou seest I am going to expend this sum on that food, apparel, furniture. And thou knowest I act herein with a single eye as a steward of thy goods, expending this portion of them thus in pursuance of the design thou hadst in entrusting me with them. Thou knowest I do this in obedience to thy Word, as thou commandest, and because thou commandest it. Let this, I beseech thee, be an holy sacrifice, acceptable through Jesus Christ! And give me a witness in myself that for this labour of love I shall have a recompense when thou rewardest every man according to his works." Now if your conscience bear you witness in the Holy Ghost that this prayer is well-pleasing to God, then have you no reason to doubt but that expense is right and good, and such as will never make you ashamed.

23. Galatians 6:10.
24. Mark 12:17.

6. You see then what it is to "make [to] yourselves friends of the mammon of unrighteousness," and by what means you may procure "that when ye fail they may receive you into the everlasting habitations." You see the nature and extent of truly Christian prudence so far as it relates to the use of that great talent—money. *Gain all you can,* without hurting either yourself or your neighbour, in soul or body, by applying hereto with unintermitted diligence, and with all the understanding which God has given you. *Save all you can,* by cutting off every expense which serves only to indulge foolish desire, to gratify either the desire of the flesh, the desire of the eye, or the pride of life. Waste nothing, living or dying, on sin or folly, whether for yourself or your children. And then, *Give all you can,* or in other words give all you have to God. Do not stint yourself, like a Jew rather than a Christian, to this or that proportion. "Render unto God," not a tenth, not a third, not half, but "all that is God's,"[25] be it more or less, by employing all on yourself, your household, the household of faith, and all mankind, in such a manner that you may give a good account of your stewardship when ye can be no longer stewards; in such a manner as the oracles of God direct, both by general and particular precepts; in such a manner that whatever ye do may be "a sacrifice of a sweet-smelling savour to God,"[26] and that every act may be rewarded in that day when the Lord cometh with all his saints.

Brethren, can we be either wise or faithful stewards unless we thus manage our Lord's goods? We cannot, as not only the oracles of God, but our own conscience beareth witness. Then why should we delay? Why should we confer any longer with flesh and blood, or men of the world? Our kingdom, our wisdom "is not of this world."[27] Heathen custom is nothing to us. We follow no men any farther than they are followers of Christ. Hear ye him. Yea, today, while it is called today, hear and obey his voice. At this hour and from this hour, do his will; fulfil his word in this and in all things. I entreat you, in the name of the Lord Jesus, act up to the dignity of your calling. No more sloth! Whatsoever your hand findeth to do, do it with your might. No more waste! Cut off every expense which fashion, caprice, or flesh and blood demand. No more covetousness! But employ whatever God has entrusted you with in doing good, all possible good, in every possible kind and degree, to the household of faith, to all men. This is no small part of "the wisdom of the just."[28] Give all ye have, as well as all ye are, a spiritual sacrifice to him who withheld not from you his Son, his only Son; so "laying up in store for yourselves a good foundation against the time to come, that ye may attain eternal life."[29]

25. Ibid.
26. Ephesians 5:2.
27. John 18:36.
28. Luke 1:17.
29. 1 Timothy 6:19.

WILLIAM WORDSWORTH

I N THE 1800 Preface to his highly innovative *Lyrical Ballads,* William Wordsworth (1770–1850) declared his intention to inaugurate a major change in the practice of writing poetry by shifting the focus of verse from stylized portrayals of human activity to a concentration on "incidents and situations from common life." Although his rationale for this emphasis upon "[l]ow and rustic life" derived from Enlightenment discussions of primitivism, his pronounced change in subject matter was both thoroughgoing and revolutionary; it also led his growing readership to give serious consideration to the laboring (and often unemployed) poor. Over the next twenty years, he enjoyed substantial success in publishing verse, and, though some decried his seeming abandonment of an early political radicalism, he was held in increasing respect, almost veneration, throughout the remainder of the century.

Michael represents Wordsworth's revision of the traditional pastoral, which had been distinguished by its artificiality and unrealistic prettiness. In the place of poetic swains piping tunes on oaten flutes while tending picturesque sheep, Wordsworth supplies a family of quite real country shepherds who, through hard, tedious labor, have first secured their landhold from mortgage and then try to retain it through the strategy of sending the son from the country to the city to work in trade. Described as "a proverb" "for endless industry" and as "[l]iving a life of eager industry," the elderly Michael, his wife Isabel, and their young son Luke exemplify the struggle of rural people to acquire, through steady toil and thrift, a modest independence. Work for them represents an opportunity to secure property, but, more important, it embodies for them the morally principled life. Here, Wordsworth modulates from the stylized pastoral to the more realistic rusticity of the georgic, as he has work define real virtue, giving dignity and purpose to simple lives. Michael establishes as a covenant between himself and his son the shared labor of building a sheepfold. His participation in the initial stages of this project is to serve Luke, when he leaves to work in the city, as a hallowed reminder of necessary commitment to family and virtues, safeguarding him against the enticements of the dissolute city: in times of temptation, Michael urges as Luke lays the cornerstone of the sheepfold,

> think of me, my Son,
> And of this moment; hither turn thy thoughts,
> And God will strengthen thee: amid all fear

> And all temptation, Luke, I pray that thou
> May'st bear in mind the life thy Fathers lived,
> Who, being innocent, did for that cause
> Bestir them in good deeds.

The simple tragedy of the story is that, in spite of this commitment to consecrate his efforts in trade through their association with the family tradition of honorable work, Luke does "g[i]ve himself / To evil courses; ignominy and shame / F[a]ll on him." Michael's sad triumph is that, having learned of Luke's degeneracy, he continues to find meaning and a strange consolation in his own work on the sheepfold, work that sustains him but that he can never carry to completion. Though less happy in tone, *Michael* might be profitably compared with Elizabeth Gaskell's "Cumberland Sheep-Shearers" (see part 2) for a positive yet realistic portrayal of rural work.

Michael
A Pastoral Poem

> If from the public way you turn your steps
> Up the tumultuous brook of Greenhead Ghyll,[1]
> You will suppose that with an upright path
> Your feet must struggle; in such bold ascent
> The pastoral mountains front you, face to face.　　　　5
> But, courage! for around that boisterous brook
> The mountains have all opened out themselves,
> And made a hidden valley of their own.
> No habitation can be seen; but they
> Who journey thither find themselves alone　　　　10
> With a few sheep, with rocks and stones, and kites[2]
> That overhead are sailing in the sky.
> It is in truth an utter solitude;
> Nor should I have made mention of this Dell

1. A *ghyll* or *gill* is a narrow stream bed.
2. Hawks distinguished for hunting small prey.

But for one object which you might pass by,   15
Might see and notice not. Beside the brook
Appears a straggling heap of unhewn stones!
And to that simple object appertains
A story—unenriched with strange events,
Yet not unfit, I deem, for the fireside,   20
Or for the summer shade. It was the first
Of those domestic tales that spake to me
Of shepherds, dwellers in the valleys, men
Whom I already loved;—not verily
For their own sakes, but for the fields and hills   25
Where was their occupation and abode.
And hence this Tale, while I was yet a Boy
Careless of books, yet having felt the power
Of Nature, by the gentle agency
Of natural objects, led me on to feel   30
For passions that were not my own, and think
(At random and imperfectly indeed)
On man, the heart of man, and human life.
Therefore, although it be a history
Homely and rude, I will relate the same   35
For the delight of a few natural hearts;
And, with yet fonder feeling, for the sake
Of youthful Poets, who among these hills
Will be my second self when I am gone.

　　　Upon the forest-side in Grasmere Vale   40
There dwelt a Shepherd, Michael was his name;
An old man, stout of heart, and strong of limb.
His bodily frame had been from youth to age
Of an unusual strength: his mind was keen,
Intense, and frugal, apt for all affairs,   45
And in his shepherd's calling he was prompt
And watchful more than ordinary men.
Hence had he learned the meaning of all winds,
Of blasts of every tone; and oftentimes,
When others heeded not, he heard the South   50
Make subterraneous music, like the noise
Of bagpipers on distant Highland hills.
The Shepherd, at such warning, of his flock
Bethought him, and he to himself would say,
"The winds are now devising work for me!"   55
And, truly, at all times, the storm, that drives
The traveller to a shelter, summoned him

Up to the mountains: he had been alone
Amid the heart of many thousand mists,
That came to him, and left him, on the heights.   60
So lived he till his eightieth year was past.
And grossly that man errs, who should suppose
That the green valleys, and the streams and rocks,
Were things indifferent to the Shepherd's thoughts.
Fields, where with cheerful spirits he had breathed   65
The common air; hills, which with vigorous step
He had so often climbed; which impressed
So many incidents upon his mind
Of hardship, skill or courage, joy or fear;
Which, like a book, preserved the memory   70
Of the dumb animals, whom he had saved,
Had fed or sheltered, linking to such acts
The certainty of honourable gain;
Those fields, those hills—what could they less? had laid
Strong hold on his affections, were to him   75
A pleasurable feeling of blind love,
The pleasure which there is in life itself.

    His days had not been passed in singleness.
His Helpmate was a comely matron, old—
Though younger than himself full twenty years.   80
She was a woman of a stirring life,
Whose heart was in her house: two wheels she had
Of antique form; this large, for spinning wool;
That small, for flax; and, if one wheel had rest
It was because the other was at work.   85
The Pair had but one inmate in their house,
An only Child, who had been born to them
When Michael, telling o'er his years, began
To deem that he was old—in shepherd's phrase,
With one foot in the grave. This only Son,   90
With two brave sheep-dogs tried in many a storm,
The one of an inestimable worth,
Made all their household. I may truly say,
That they were as a proverb in the vale
For endless industry. When day was gone,   95
And from their occupations out of doors
The Son and Father were come home, even then,
Their labour did not cease; unless when all
Turned to the cleanly supper-board, and there,
Each with a mess of pottage and skimmed milk,   100

Sat round the basket piled with oaten cakes,
And their plain home-made cheese. Yet when the meal
Was ended, Luke (for so the Son was named)
And his old Father both betook themselves
To such convenient work as might employ   105
Their hands by the fireside; perhaps to card
Wool for the Housewife's spindle, or repair
Some injury done to sickle, flail, or scythe,
Or other implement of house or field.

    Down from the ceiling, by the chimney's edge,   110
That in our ancient uncouth country style
With huge and black projection overbrowed
Large space beneath, as duly as the light
Of day grew dim the Housewife hung a lamp;
An aged utensil, which had performed   115
Service beyond all others of its kind.
Early at evening did it burn—and late,
Surviving comrade of uncounted hours,
Which, going by from year to year, had found,
And left, the couple neither gay perhaps   120
Nor cheerful, yet with objects and with hopes,
Living a life of eager industry.
And now, when Luke had reached his eighteenth year,
There by the light of this old lamp they sate,
Father and Son, while far into the night   125
The Housewife plied her own peculiar work,
Making the cottage through the silent hours
Murmur as with the sound of summer flies.
This light was famous in its neighbourhood,
And was a public symbol of the life   130
That thrifty Pair had lived. For, as it chanced,
Their cottage on a plot of rising ground
Stood single, with large prospect, north and south,
High into Easedale, up to Dunmail-Raise,
And westward to the village near the lake;   135
And from this constant light, so regular
And so far seen, the House itself, by all
Who dwelt within the limits of the vale,
Both old and young, was named THE EVENING STAR.

    Thus living on through such a length of years,   140
The Shepherd, if he loved himself, must needs
Have loved his Helpmate; but to Michael's heart

This son of his old age was yet more dear—
Less from instinctive tenderness, the same
Fond spirit that blindly works in the blood of all—   145
Than that a child, more than all other gifts
That earth can offer to declining man,
Brings hope with it, and forward-looking thoughts,
And stirrings of inquietude, when they
By tendency of nature needs must fail.   150
Exceeding was the love he bare to him,
His heart and his heart's joy! For oftentimes
Old Michael, while he was a babe in arms,
Had done him female service, not alone
For pastime and delight, as is the use   155
Of fathers, but with patient mind enforced
To acts of tenderness; and he had rocked
His cradle, as with a woman's gentle hand.

    And in a later time, ere yet the Boy
Had put on boy's attire, did Michael love,   160
Albeit of a stern unbending mind,
To have the Young-one in his sight, when he
Wrought in the field, or on his shepherd's stool
Sate with a fettered sheep before him stretched
Under the large old oak, that near his door   165
Stood single, and, from matchless depth of shade,
Chosen for the Shearer's covert from the sun,
Thence in our rustic dialect was called
The CLIPPING TREE, a name which yet it bears.
There, while they two were sitting in the shade,   170
With others round them, earnest all and blithe,
Would Michael exercise his heart with looks
Of fond correction and reproof bestowed
Upon the Child, if he disturbed the sheep
By catching at their legs, or with his shouts   175
Scared them, while they lay still beneath the shears.

    And when by Heaven's good grace the boy grew up
A healthy Lad, and carried in his cheek
Two steady roses that were five years old;
Then Michael from a winter coppice³ cut   180
With his own hand a sapling, which he hooped
With iron, making it throughout in all

---

3. A shaw or stand of trees; a thicket.

Due requisites a perfect shepherd's staff,
And gave it to the Boy; wherewith equipt
He as a watchman oftentimes was placed   185
At gate or gap, to stem or turn the flock;
And, to his office prematurely called,
There stood the urchin, as you will divine,
Something between a hindrance and a help;
And for this cause not always, I believe,   190
Receiving from his Father hire[4] of praise;
Though nought was left undone which staff, or voice,
Or looks, or threatening gestures, could perform.

But soon as Luke, full ten years old, could stand
Against the mountain blasts; and to the heights,   195
Not fearing toil, nor length of weary ways,
He with his Father daily went, and they
Were as companions, why should I relate
That objects which the Shepherd loved before
Were dearer now? that from the Boy there came   200
Feelings and emanations—things which were
Light to the sun and music to the wind;
And that the old Man's heart seemed born again?

Thus in his Father's sight the Boy grew up:
And now, when he had reached his eighteenth year,   205
He was his comfort and his daily hope.

While in this sort the simple household lived
From day to day, to Michael's ear there came
Distressful tidings. Long before the time
Of which I speak, the Shepherd had been bound   210
In surety for his brother's son, a man
Of an industrious life, and ample means;
But unforeseen misfortunes suddenly
Had prest upon him; and old Michael now
Was summoned to discharge the forfeiture,   215
A grievous penalty, but little less
Than half his substance. This unlooked-for claim,
At the first hearing, for a moment took
More hope out of his life than he supposed
That any old man ever could have lost.   220
As soon as he had armed himself with strength
To look his trouble in the face, it seemed

4. The wage of praise: notably, what the boy works for is the father's express approbation.

The Shepherd's sole resource to sell at once
A portion of his patrimonial fields.
Such was his first resolve; he thought again,   225
And his heart failed him. "Isabel," said he,
Two evenings after he had heard the news,
"I have been toiling more than seventy years,
And in the open sunshine of God's love
Have we all lived; yet, if these fields of ours   230
Should pass into a stranger's hand, I think
That I could not lie quiet in my grave.
Our lot is a hard lot; the sun himself
Has scarcely been more diligent than I;
And I have lived to be a fool at last   235
To my own family. An evil man
That was, and made an evil choice, if he
Were false to us; and if he were not false,
There are ten thousand to whom loss like this
Had been no sorrow. I forgive him;—but   240
'Twere better to be dumb than to talk thus.

        "When I began, my purpose was to speak
Of remedies and of a cheerful hope.
Our Luke shall leave us, Isabel; the land
Shall not go from us, and it shall be free;   245
He shall possess it, free as is the wind
That passes over it. We have, thou know'st,
Another kinsman—he will be our friend
In this distress. He is a prosperous man,
Thriving in trade—and Luke to him shall go,   250
And with his kinsman's help and his own thrift
He quickly will repair this loss, and then
He may return to us. If here he stay,
What can be done? Where everyone is poor,
What can be gained?"
                        At this the old Man paused,   255
And Isabel sat silent, for her mind
Was busy, looking back into past times.
There's Richard Bateman, thought she to herself,
He was a parish-boy—at the church-door
They made a gathering for him, shillings, pence,   260
And halfpennies, wherewith the neighbors bought
A basket, which they filled with pedlar's wares;
And, with this basket on his arm, the lad
Went up to London, found a master there,

Who, out of many, chose the trusty boy   265
To go and overlook his merchandise
Beyond the seas; where he grew wondrous rich,
And left estates and monies to the poor,
And, at his birth-place, built a chapel, floored
With marble, which he sent from foreign lands.[5]   270
These thoughts, and many others of like sort,
Passed quickly through the mind of Isabel,
And her face brightened. The old Man was glad,
And thus resumed;—"Well, Isabel! this scheme
These two days, has been meat and drink to me.   275
Far more than we have lost is left us yet.
—We have enough—I wish indeed that I
Were younger;—but this hope is a good hope.
Make ready Luke's best garments, of the best
Buy for him more, and let us send him forth   280
To-morrow, or the next day, or to-night:
—If he *could* go, the Boy should go tonight."

        Here Michael ceased, and to the fields went forth
With a light heart. The Housewife for five days
Was restless morn and night, and all day long   285
Wrought on with her best fingers to prepare
Things needful for the journey of her son.
But Isabel was glad when Sunday came
To stop her in her work: for, when she lay
By Michael's side, she through the last two nights   290
Heard him, how he was troubled in his sleep:
And when they rose at morning she could see
That all his hopes were gone. That day at noon
She said to Luke, while they two by themselves
Were sitting at the door, "Thou must not go: 295
We have no other Child but thee to lose,
None to remember—do not go away,
For if thou leave thy Father he will die."
The Youth made answer with a jocund voice;
And Isabel, when she had told her fears,   300
Recovered her heart. That evening her best fare
Did she bring forth, and all together sat
Like happy people round a Christmas fire.

        With daylight Isabel resumed her work;
And all the ensuing week the house appeared   305

---

5. Wordsworth notes that the Richard Bateman story was both true and widely known.

As cheerful as a grove in Spring: at length
The expected letter from their kinsman came,
With kind assurances that he would do
His utmost for the welfare of the Boy;
To which, requests were added, that forthwith   310
He might be sent to him. Ten times or more
The letter was read over; Isabel
Went forth to show it to the neighbors round;
Nor was there at that time on English land
A prouder heart than Luke's. When Isabel   315
Had to her house returned, the old Man said,
"He shall depart to-morrow." To this word
The Housewife answered, talking much of things
Which, if at such short notice he should go,
Would surely be forgotten. But at length   320
She gave consent, and Michael was at ease.

    Near the tumultuous brook of Greenhead Ghyll,
In that deep valley, Michael had designed
To build a Sheepfold; and, before he heard
The tidings of his melancholy loss,   325
For this same purpose he had gathered up
A heap of stones, which by the streamlet's edge
Lay thrown together, ready for the work.
With Luke that evening thitherward he walked:
And soon as they had reached the place he stopped,   330
And thus the old Man spake to him:—"My son,
To-morrow thou wilt leave me: with full heart
I look upon thee, for thou art the same
That wert a promise to me ere thy birth,
And all thy life hast been my daily joy.   335
I will relate to thee some little part
Of our two histories; 'twill do thee good
When thou art from me, even if I should touch
On things thou canst not know of.—After thou
First cam'st into the world—as oft befalls   340
To new-born infants—thou didst sleep away
Two days, and blessings from thy Father's tongue
Then fell upon thee. Day by day passed on,
And still I loved thee with increasing love.
Never to living ear came sweeter sounds   345
Than when I heard thee by our own fireside
First uttering, without words, a natural tune;
While thou, a feeding babe, didst in thy joy
Sing at thy Mother's breast. Month followed month,

And in the open fields my life was passed   350
And on the mountains; else I think that thou
Hadst been brought up upon thy Father's knees.
But we were playmates, Luke: among these hills,
As well thou knowest, in us the old and young
Have played together, nor with me didst thou   355
Lack any pleasure which a boy can know."
Luke had a manly heart; but at these words
He sobbed aloud. The old Man grasped his hand,
And said, "Nay, do not take it so—I see
That these are things of which I need not speak.   360
—Even to the utmost I have been to thee
A kind and a good Father: and herein
I but repay a gift which I myself
Received at others' hands; for, though now old
Beyond the common life of man, I still   365
Remember them who loved me in my youth.
Both of them sleep together: here they lived,
As all their Forefathers had done; and, when
At length their time was come, they were not loth
To give their bodies to the family mould.   370
I wished that thou shouldst live the life they lived,
But, 'tis a long time to look back, my Son,
And see so little gain from threescore years.
These fields were burthened when they came to me;[6]
Till I was forty years of age, not more   375
Than half of my inheritance was mine.
I toiled and toiled; God blessed me in my work,
And till these three weeks past the land was free.
—It looks as if it never could endure
Another Master. Heaven forgive me, Luke,   380
If I judge ill for thee, but it seems good
That thou shouldst go."
                    At this the old Man paused;
Then, pointing to the stones near which they stood,
Thus after a short silence, he resumed:
"This was a work for us; and now, my Son,   385
It is a work for me. But, lay one stone—
Here, lay it for me, Luke, with thine own hands.
Nay, Boy, be of good hope;—we both may live
To see a better day. At eighty-four
I still am strong and hale;—do thou thy part;   390

---

6. The lands were mortgaged when Michael first inherited them, and he labored for years to pay off this mortgage and secure his full patrimony.

I will do mine.—I will begin again
With many tasks that were resigned to thee:
Up to the heights, and in among the storms,
Will I without thee go again, and do
All works which I was wont to do alone,   395
Before I knew thy face.—Heaven bless thee, Boy!
Thy heart these two weeks has been beating fast
With many hopes; it should be so—yes—yes—
I knew that thou couldst never have a wish
To leave me, Luke: thou hast been bound to me   400
Only by links of love: when thou art gone,
What will be left to us!—But I forget
My purposes. Lay now the corner-stone,
As I requested; and hereafter, Luke,
When thou art gone away, should evil men   405
Be thy companions, think of me, my Son
And of this moment; hither turn thy thoughts,
And God will strengthen thee: amid all fear
And all temptation, Luke, I pray that thou
May'st bear in mind the life thy Fathers lived,   410
Who, being innocent, did for that cause
Bestir them in good deeds. Now, fare thee well—
When thou return'st, thou in this place wilt see
A work which is not here: a covenant
'Twill be between us; but, whatever fate   415
Befall thee, I shall love thee to the last,
And bear thy memory with me to the grave."

    The Shepherd ended here; and Luke stooped down,
And, as his Father had requested, laid
The first stone of the Sheepfold. At the sight   420
The old Man's grief broke from him; to his heart
He pressed his Son, he kissed him and wept;
And to the house together they returned.
—Hushed was that House in peace, or seeming peace,
Ere the night fell:—with morrow's dawn the Boy   425
Began his journey, and, when he had reached
The public way, he put on a bold face;
And all the neighbors, as he passed their doors,
Came forth with wishes and with farewell prayers,
That followed him till he was out of sight.   430

    A good report did from their Kinsman come,
Of Luke and his well-doing: and the Boy
Wrote loving letters, full of wondrous news,

Which, as the Housewife phrased it, were throughout
"The prettiest letters that were ever seen."   435
Both parents read them with rejoicing hearts.
So, many months passed on: and once again
The Shepherd went about his daily work
With confident and cheerful thoughts; and now
Sometimes when he could find a leisure hour   440
He to that valley took his way, and there
Wrought at the Sheepfold. Meantime Luke began
To slacken in his duty; and, at length,
He in the dissolute city gave himself
To evil courses: ignominy and shame   445
Fell on him, so that he was driven at last
To seek a hiding-place beyond the seas.[7]

      There is a comfort in the strength of love;
'Twill make a thing endurable, which else
Would overset the brain, or break the heart: 450
I have conversed with more than one who well
Remember the old Man, and what he was
Years after he had heard this heavy news.
His bodily frame had been from youth to age
Of an unusual strength. Among the rocks   455
He went, and still looked up to sun and cloud,
And listened to the wind; and, as before,
Performed all kinds of labour for his sheep,
And for the land, his small inheritance.
And to that hollow dell from time to time   460
Did he repair, to build the Fold of which
His flock had need. 'Tis not forgotten yet
The pity which was then in every heart
For the old Man—and 'tis believed by all
That many and many a day he thither went,   465
And never lifted up a single stone.

      There, by the Sheepfold, sometimes was he seen
Sitting alone, or with his faithful Dog,
Then old, beside him, lying at his feet.
The length of full seven years, from time to time,   470
He at the building of this Sheepfold wrought,
And left the work unfinished when he died.

---

7. That country youth would suffer corruption in the city was already a literary cliché when Oliver Goldsmith (1730–1774), in *The Deserted Village* (1770), made it almost prescriptive in portraying rural populations displaced into the city.

Three years, or little more, did Isabel
Survive her Husband: at her death the estate
Was sold, and went into a stranger's hand.   475
The Cottage which was named the EVENING STAR
Is gone—the ploughshare has been through the ground
On which it stood; great changes have been wrought
In all the neighborhood:—yet the oak is left
That grew beside the door; and the remains   480
Of the unfinished Sheepfold may be seen
Beside the boisterous brook of Greenhead Ghyll.

THOMAS CARLYLE

THOMAS CARLYLE (1795–1881), judged by George Eliot to be the most influential thinker of the Victorian era, was also the most assertive advocate of the value of work. His exhortations to regard work as a means to psychological well-being and social sanity echoed throughout the century.

Scots by birth, Carlyle attended Edinburgh University to prepare for the ministry. While there, however, he became an "honest doubter," and his struggle to overcome an arid skepticism that seemed the logical alternative to his lost faith was given voice in essays on German idealism and, at greater length, in *Sartor Resartus* (1833–34). This playful and deliberately eccentric discourse includes a description of his own spiritual crisis of immobilizing doubt and self-alienation and sets forth a commitment to dutiful work as the solution to the despondency that can derange an individual or a society. The "Gospel of Freedom" is grounded in the "God-given mandate, *Work thou in Welldoing*," Carlyle insists, and, in a Scriptural phrase repeated in *Past and Present* (1843), he admonishes his reader to work productively: "Whatsoever thy hand findeth to do, do it with thy whole might: Work while it is called Today; for the Night cometh, wherein no man can work."

Past and Present, composed a decade after *Sartor Resartus*, is characterized by the declamatory and hyperbolic rhetoric that Carlyle cultivated. The "past" of the title is a medieval one, favorably contrasted with the "present" of nineteenth-century England. In the past, people led meaningful, self-confident lives informed by faith, devotion to ideals, and responsible commitment to others; in the present, people lead trivial, doubt-ridden lives characterized by melancholy, absence of conviction, and estrangement from self and others. Carlyle attacks the "moral calculus" of Utilitarian thought as well as laissez-faire economic practice for causing many of the woes besetting his contemporary England. In the chapters presented below, he insists that what people need in order to restore them to mental and moral health is the opportunity to engage in work that can provide both self-respect and a sense of duty completed.

From *Past and Present,* Book 3—*The Modern Worker*

Chapter 4
Happy

All work, even cotton-spinning, is noble; work is alone noble: be that here said and asserted once more. And in like manner, too, all dignity is painful; a life of ease is not for any man, nor for any god. The life of all gods figures itself to us as a Sublime Sadness,—earnestness of Infinite Battle against Infinite Labour. Our highest religion is named the "Worship of Sorrow." For the son of man there is no noble crown, well worn or even ill worn, but is a crown of thorns!—These things, in spoken words, or still better, in felt instincts alive in every heart, were once well known.

Does not the whole wretchedness, the whole *Atheism* as I call it, of man's ways, in these generations, shadow itself for us in that unspeakable Life-philosophy of his: The pretension to be what he calls "happy"? Every pitifulest whipster that walks within a skin has his head filled with the notion that he is, shall be, or by all human and divine laws ought to be "happy." His wishes, the pitifulest whipster's, are to be fulfilled for him; his days, the pitifulest whipster's, are to flow on in ever-gentle current of enjoyment, impossible even for the gods. The prophets preach to us, Thou shalt be happy; thou shalt love pleasant things, and find them. The people clamour, Why have we not found pleasant things?

We construct our theory of Human Duties, not on any Greatest-Nobleness Principle, never so mistaken; no, but on a Greatest-Happiness Principle.[1] "The word *Soul* with us, as in some Slavonic dialects, seems to be synonymous with *Stomach.*"[2] We plead and speak, in our Parliaments and elsewhere, not as from the Soul, but from the Stomach;—wherefore indeed our pleadings are so slow to profit. We plead not for God's Justice; we are not ashamed to stand clamouring and pleading for our own "interests," our own rents and trade-profits; we say, They are the "interests" of so many; there is such an intense desire in us for them! We demand Free-Trade, with much just vociferation and benevolence, That the poorer classes, who are terribly ill-off at present, may have cheaper New-Orleans bacon. Men ask on Free-trade platforms, How can the indomitable spirit of Englishmen be kept up without plenty of bacon? We shall become a ruined Nation!—Surely, my friends, plenty of bacon is good and indispensable: but, I doubt, you will never get even bacon by aiming only at that. You are men, not animals of prey, well-used

---

1. A general goal of Utilitarian reformers was to secure the greatest happiness for the greatest number of people. Throughout his writings, Carlyle repudiated Utilitarianism, finding in this philosophy one of the principal causes of the spiritual enervation of his age.

2. Here Carlyle, as he often does, quotes or paraphrases an earlier pronouncement of his own; in this case, he returns to an assertion in *Sartor Resartus* that reflective individuals have "discovered, in contradiction to much Profit-and-Loss Philosophy, speculative and practical, that Soul is *not* synonymous with Stomach."

Figure 1.1. Ford Madox Brown, *Work.* Courtesy of Manchester City Art Galleries.

Inspired by the writings of Thomas Carlyle, especially *Past and Present,* Ford Madox Brown (1821–1893) began *Work* in 1852 but did not finish the painting until 1863. Central to the picture is a group of manual laborers excavating a sewer system. According to the description given in the catalog when the painting was exhibited in 1865, these men present "the outward and visible type of *Work.*" To the left is a flower seller, a "ragged wretch who has never been *taught* to *work.*" The two ladies behind him, one of whom has been distributing religious tracts, represent "the *rich* who have no need to work." Beyond the construction workers, on horseback, are the leisured gentry, while in front of them stands a group of ragged children who are cared for and disciplined by the eldest. On the right, beneath the trees, rest haymakers in need of work. Leaning against the railing and looking on approvingly are the intellectual workers, Thomas Carlyle (bearded) and F. D. Maurice (see part 2), "who, seeming to be idle, work, and are the cause of well-ordained work and happiness in others." Brown symbolizes the human conflict between rich and poor, idlers and laborers, in the canine confrontation shown in the foreground between the sturdy mongrel and the sleek, jacketed whippet.

or ill-used! Your Greatest-Happiness Principle seems to me fast becoming a rather unhappy one.—What if we should cease babbling about "happiness," and leave *it* resting on its own basis, as it used to do!

A gifted Byron[3] rises in his wrath; and feeling too surely that he for his part is not "happy," declares the same in very violent language, as a piece of news that may

3. George Gordon, Lord Byron (1788–1824) was the English poet who, in *Childe Harold's Pil- grimage,* gave definitive expression to the spirit of romantic melancholy by passionately bemoaning

be interesting. It evidently has surprised him much. One dislikes to see a man and poet reduced to proclaim on the streets such tidings, but on the whole, as matters go, that is not the most dislikable. Byron speaks the *truth* in this matter. Byron's large audience indicates how true it is felt to be.

"Happy," my brother? First of all, what difference is it whether thou art happy or not! Today becomes Yesterday so fast, all Tomorrows become Yesterdays; and then there is no question whatever of the "happiness," but quite another question. Nay, thou hast such a sacred pity left at least for thyself, thy very pains, once gone over into Yesterday, become joys to thee. Besides, thou knowest not what heavenly blessedness and indispensable sanative virtue was in them; thou shalt only know it after many days, when thou art wiser!—A benevolent old Surgeon sat once in our company, with a Patient fallen sick by gourmandising, whom he had just, too briefly in the Patient's judgment, been examining. The foolish Patient still at intervals continued to break in on our discourse, which rather promised to take a philosophic turn: "But I have lost my appetite," said he, objurgatively,[4] with a tone of irritated pathos; "I have no appetite; I can't eat!"—"My dear fellow," answered the Doctor in mildest tone, "it isn't of the slightest consequence";—and continued his philosophical discoursings with us!

Or does the reader not know the history of that Scottish iron Misanthrope? The inmates of some town-mansion, in those Northern parts, were thrown into the fearfulest alarm by indubitable symptoms of a ghost inhabiting the next house, or perhaps even the partition-wall! Ever at a certain hour, with preternatural gnar-ring, growling, and screeching, which attended as running bass, there began, in a horrid, semi-articulate, unearthly voice, this song: "Once I was hap-hap-happy, but now I am *meese*rable! Clack-clack-clack, gnarr-r-r, whuz-z: Once I was hap-hap-happy, but now I'm *meese*rable!"—Rest, rest, perturbed spirit;[5]—or indeed, as the good old Doctor said: My dear fellow, it isn't of the slightest consequence! But no; the perturbed spirit could not rest; and to the neighbours, fretted, affrighted, or at least insufferably bored by him, it *was* of such consequence that they had to go and examine in his haunted chamber. In his haunted chamber, they find that the perturbed spirit is an unfortunate—Imitator of Byron? No, is an unfortunate rusty Meat-jack, gnarring and creaking with rust and work; and this, in Scottish dialect, is *its* Byronian musical Life-philosophy, sung according to ability!

Truly, I think the man who goes about pothering and uproaring for his "happi-ness,"—pothering, and were it ballot-boxing, poem-making, or in what way soever fussing and exerting himself,—he is not the man that will help us to "get our knaves and dastards arrested!" No; he rather is on the way to increase the number,—by at

---

the experience of loss and pain that the sensitive soul must endure. In the earlier nineteenth century, Byron was the most popular of poets, and he was celebrated throughout Europe. Carlyle found By-ron's melancholy compelling but finally unproductive; in *Sartor Resartus*, he offers the famous admo-nition: "Close thy *Byron*; open thy *Goethe*."

4. Reprovingly.

5. Carlyle quotes Hamlet's words to the Ghost: *Hamlet*, 1.5.182.

least one unit and his tail! Observe, too, that this is all a modern affair; belongs not to the old heroic times, but to these dastard new times. "Happiness our being's end and aim,"[6] all that very paltry speculation is at bottom, if we will count well, not yet two centuries old in the world.

The only happiness a brave man ever troubled himself with asking much about was, happiness enough to get his work done. Not "I can't eat!" but "I can't work!" that was the burden of all wise complaining among men. It is, after all, the one unhappiness of a man, That he cannot work; that he cannot get his destiny as a man fulfilled. Behold, the day is passing swiftly over, our life is passing swiftly over; and the night cometh, wherein no man can work.[7] The night once come, our happiness, our unhappiness,—it is all abolished; vanished, clean gone; a thing that has been: "not of the slightest consequence" whether we were happy as eupeptic Curtis,[8] as the fattest pig of Epicurus,[9] or unhappy as Job with potsherds,[10] as musical Byron with Giaours[11] and sensibilities of the heart; as the unmusical Meat-jack with hard labour and rust! But our work,—behold that is not abolished, that has not vanished: our work, behold, it remains, or the want of it remains;—for endless Times and Eternities, remains; and that is now the sole question with us for evermore! Brief brawling Day, with its noisy phantasms, its poor paper-crowns tinsel-gilt, is gone; and divine everlasting Night, with her star-diadems, with her silences and her veracities, is come! What hast thou done, and how? Happiness, unhappiness: all that was but the *wages* thou hadst; thou hast spent all that, in sustaining thyself hitherward; not a coin of it remains with thee, it is all spent, eaten: and now thy work, where is thy work? Swift, out with it; let us see thy work!

Of a truth, if man were not a poor hungry dastard, and even much of a blockhead withal, he would cease criticising his victuals to such extent; and criticise himself rather, what he does with his victuals!

Chapter 11
Labour

For there is a perennial nobleness, and even sacredness, in Work. Were he never so benighted, forgetful of his high calling, there is always hope in a man that

---

6. The quotation is from Pope's *An Essay on Man*, Epistle 4, line 1. Carlyle was troubled by the assumption made by numerous writers of the eighteenth century—not just Pope—that man's essential *happiness* should be the prime concern of a benevolent Creator.

7. The phrasing, which Carlyle repeats and varies throughout his writings, is taken from John 9:4: "I must work the works of him that sent me, while it is day: the night cometh, when no man can work."

8. Sir William Curtis (1752–1829) was Lord Mayor of London and a prominent Tory politician. A staunch supporter and companion of George IV, he is associated with an easy and, indeed, opulent lifestyle and therefore is given the descriptive "eupeptic."

9. Epicurus (340–270 B.C.E.) was the philosopher whose principal axiom was that the attainment of happiness was the highest goal in life.

10. In the Book of Job, God afflicts Job with many evils, among which are sores that he scrapes with a potsherd, or broken piece of pottery (Job 2:7–8).

11. One of Byron's most successful narrative poems is titled *The Giaour*.

actually and earnestly works: in Idleness alone is there perpetual despair. Work, never so Mammonish,[12] mean, *is* in communication with Nature; the real desire to get Work done will itself lead one more and more to truth, to Nature's appointments and regulations, which are truth.

The latest Gospel in this world is, Know thy work and do it. "Know thyself":[13] long enough has that poor "self" of thine tormented thee; thou wilt never get to "know" it, I believe! Think it not thy business, this of knowing thyself; thou art an unknowable individual: know what thou canst work at; and work at it, like a Hercules![14] That will be thy better plan.

It has been written, "an endless significance lies in Work";[15] a man perfects himself by working. Foul jungles are cleared away, fair seedfields rise instead, and stately cities; and withal the man himself first ceases to be a jungle and foul unwholesome desert thereby. Consider how, even in the meanest sorts of Labour, the whole soul of a man is composed into a kind of real harmony, the instant he sets himself to work! Doubt, Desire, Sorrow, Remorse, Indignation, Despair itself, all these like helldogs lie beleaguering the soul of the poor dayworker, as of every man: but he bends himself with free valour against his task, and all these are stilled, all these shrink murmuring far off into their caves. The man is now a man. The blessed glow of Labour in him, is it not as purifying fire, wherein all poison is burnt up, and of sour smoke itself there is made bright blessed flame!

Destiny, on the whole, has no other way of cultivating us. A formless Chaos, once set it *revolving*, grows round and ever rounder; ranges itself, by mere force of gravity, into strata, spherical courses; is no longer a Chaos, but a round compacted World.[16] What would become of the Earth, did she cease to revolve? In the poor old Earth, so long as she revolves, all inequalities, irregularities disperse themselves; all irregularities are incessantly becoming regular. Hast thou looked on the Potter's wheel,—one of the venerablest objects; old as the Prophet Ezechiel and far older? Rude lumps of clay, how they spin themselves up, by mere quick whirling, into beautiful circular dishes. And fancy the most assiduous Potter, but without his wheel; reduced to make dishes, or rather amorphous botches, by mere kneading and baking! Even such a Potter were Destiny, with a human soul that would rest

12. Given to the pursuit of material wealth rather than to the service of God. "Ye cannot serve God and mammon" (Luke 16:13). See John Wesley's sermon in this section.

13. *Gnothi seauton*, "know thyself," was inscribed over the temple dedicated to Apollo at Delphi. The phrase is often associated, although not exclusively, with Socrates. That work would lead both to self-discovery and to self-definition is a matter that Carlyle addresses in almost identical fashion in *Sartor Resartus:* "A certain inarticulate Self-consciousness dwells dimly in us; which only our Works can render articulate and decisively discernible. Our Works are the mirror wherein the spirit first sees its natural lineaments. Hence, too, the folly of that impossible Precept, *Know thyself;* till it be translated into this partially possible one, *Know what thou canst work at.*"

14. Hercules (Heracles) is the Greek hero celebrated for completing twelve difficult *athloi* or contests, usually translated as "labors."

15. Here, again, Carlyle may be quoting himself or loosely paraphrasing Goethe's pronouncements in *Wilhelm Meister.*

16. Carlyle seems to be offering here a popularized version of the so-called nebular theory of Pierre Simon de Laplace (1749–1827) concerning the formation of the solar system. Laplace's nebular hypothesis, articulated in *Mécanique Céleste,* remained popular well into the latter nineteenth century.

and lie at ease, that would not work and spin! Of an idle unrevolving man the kindest Destiny, like the most assiduous Potter without wheel, can bake and knead nothing other than a botch; let her spend on him what expensive colouring, what gilding and enamelling she will, he is but a botch. Not a dish; no, a bulging, kneaded, crooked, shambling, squint-cornered, amorphous botch,—a mere enamelled vessel of dishonour! Let the idle think of this.

Blessed is he who has found his work; let him ask no other blessedness. He has a work, a life-purpose; he has found it, and will follow it! How, as a free-flowing channel, dug and torn by noble force through the sour mud-swamp of one's existence, like an ever-deepening river there, it runs and flows;—draining-off the sour festering water, gradually from the root of the remotest grass-blade; making, instead of pestilential swamp, a green fruitful meadow with its clear-flowing stream. How blessed for the meadow itself, let the stream and *its* value be great or small! Labour is Life: from the inmost heart of the Worker rises his god-given Force, the sacred celestial Life-essence breathed into him by Almighty God; from his inmost heart awakens him to all nobleness,—to all knowledge, "self-knowledge" and much else, as soon as Work fitly begins. Knowledge? The knowledge that will hold good in working, cleave thou to that; for Nature herself accredits that, says Yea to that. Properly thou hast no other knowledge but what thou hast got by working: the rest is yet all a hypothesis of knowledge; a thing to be argued of in schools, a thing floating in the clouds, in endless logic-vortices, till we try it and fix it. "Doubt, of whatever kind, can be ended by Action alone."[17]

And again, hast thou valued Patience, Courage, Perseverance, Openness to light; readiness to own thyself mistaken, to do better next time? All these, all virtues, in wrestling with the dim brute Powers of Fact, in ordering of thy fellows in such wrestle, there and elsewhere not at all, thou wilt continually learn. Set down a brave Sir Christopher[18] in the middle of black ruined Stone-heaps, of foolish unarchitectural Bishops, redtape Officials, idle Nell-Gwyn Defenders of the Faith; and see whether he will ever raise a Paul's Cathedral out of all that, yea or no! Rough, rude, contradictory are all things and persons, from the mutinous masons and Irish hodmen,[19] up to the idle Nell-Gwyn Defenders, to blustering redtape Officials, foolish unarchitectural Bishops. All these things and persons are there not for Christopher's sake and his Cathedral's; they are there for their own sake mainly! Christopher will have to conquer and constrain all these,—if he be able.

17. Carlyle directly translates Goethe's assertion in *Wilhelm Meister*.

18. Sir Christopher Wren (1632–1723) was the architect who redesigned and rebuilt a number of churches in London following the Great Fire of 1666. His most impressive work is Saint Paul's Cathedral ("Paul's Edifice"), to which Carlyle refers. The subsequent phrasing "Nell-Gwyn Defenders of the Faith" reflects the popularity of actress Nell Gwyn, mistress of Charles II. Many Londoners indifferent to more important matters such as the reconstruction of the burned city became fixated on Nell Gwyn because, unlike Charles's other mistresses, she was not Catholic; they turned out to cheer her as she rode through the streets, hailing her with approbation as "the Protestant whore."

19. During the economically depressed 1840s (the "Hungry Forties"), manufacturers tried to undermine the resolve of union activists by replacing striking laborers with Irish workers.

All these are against him. Equitable Nature herself, who carries her mathematics and architectonics not on the face of her, but deep in the hidden heart of her,—Nature herself is but partially for him; will be wholly against him, if he constrain her not! His very money, where is it to come from? The pious munificence of England lies far-scattered, distant, unable to speak, and say, "I am here";—must be spoken to before it can speak. Pious munificence, and all help, is so silent, invisible like the gods; impediment, contradictions manifold are so loud and near! O brave Sir Christopher, trust thou in those notwithstanding, and front all these; understand all these; by valiant patience, noble effort, insight, by man's-strength, vanquish and compel all these,—and, on the whole, strike down victoriously the last topstone of that Paul's Edifice; thy monument for certain centuries, the stamp "Great Man" impressed very legibly on Portland-stone there!—[20]

Yes, all manner of help, and pious response from Men or Nature, is always what we call silent; cannot speak or come to light, till it be seen, till it be spoken to. Every noble work is at first "impossible." In very truth, for every noble work the possibilities will lie diffused through Immensity; inarticulate, undiscoverable except to faith. Like Gideon thou shalt spread out thy fleece at the door of thy tent;[21] see whether under the wide arch of Heaven there be any bounteous moisture, or none. Thy heart and life-purpose shall be as a miraculous Gideon's fleece, spread out in silent appeal to Heaven: and from the kind Immensities, what from the poor unkind Localities and town and country Parishes there never could, blessed dew-moisture to suffice thee shall have fallen!

Work is of a religious nature:—work is of a *brave* nature; which it is the aim of all religion to be. All work of man is as the swimmer's: a waste ocean threatens to devour him; if he front it not bravely, it will keep its word. By incessant wise defiance of it, lusty rebuke and buffet of it, behold how it loyally supports him, bears him as its conqueror along. "It is so," says Goethe,[22] "with all things that man undertakes in this world."

Brave Sea-captain, Norse Sea-King,—Columbus, my hero, royalest Sea-king of all! it is no friendly environment this of thine, in the waste deep waters; around thee mutinous discouraged souls, behind thee disgrace and ruin, before thee the

---

20. Stone quarried from the Isle of Portland.

21. In Judges 6:37–40, Gideon twice asks for signs that he might defeat the Midianites:

Behold, I will put a fleece of wool on the floor; and if the dew be on the fleece only, and it be dry upon all the earth beside, then shall I know that thou wilt save Israel by mine hand, as thou hast said.

And it was so: for he rose up early on the morrow, and thrust the fleece together, and wringed the dew out of the fleece, a bowl full of water.

And Gideon said unto God, Let not thine anger be hot against me, and I will speak but this once: let me prove, I pray thee, but this once with the fleece; let it now be dry only upon the fleece, and upon the ground let there be dew.

And God did so that night: for it was dry upon the fleece only, and there was dew on all the ground.

22. Johann Wolfgang von Goethe (1749–1832) was the German thinker who most strongly influenced Carlyle. Carlyle translated both parts of Goethe's *Wilhelm Meister* and quotes from it frequently in all of his earlier writings. See note 3 above.

unpenetrated veil of Night. Brother, these wild water-mountains, bounding from their deep bases (ten miles deep, I am told), are not entirely there on thy behalf! Meseems *they* have other work than floating thee forward:—and the huge Winds, that sweep from Ursa Major to the Tropics and Equators, dancing their giant-waltz through the kingdoms of Chaos and Immensity, they care little about filling rightly or filling wrongly the small shoulder-of-mutton sails in this cockle-skiff of thine! Thou art not among articulate-speaking friends, my brother; thou art among immeasurable dumb monsters, tumbling, howling wide as the world here. Secret, far off, invisible to all hearts but thine, there lies a help in them: see how thou wilt get at that. Patiently thou wilt wait till the mad Southwester spend itself, saving thyself by dextrous science of defence, the while: valiantly, with swift decision, wilt thou strike in, when the favouring East, the Possible, springs up. Mutiny of men thou wilt sternly repress; weakness, despondency, thou wilt cheerily encourage: thou wilt swallow down complaint, unreason, weariness, weakness of others and thyself;—how much wilt thou swallow down! There shall be a depth of Silence in thee, deeper than this Sea, which is but ten miles deep: a Silence unsoundable; known to God only. Thou shalt be a Great Man. Yes, my World-Soldier, thou of the World Marine-service,—thou wilt have to be *greater* than this tumultuous un-measured World here round thee is: thou, in thy strong soul, as with wrestler's arms, shalt embrace it, harness it down; and make it bear thee on,—to new Americas, or whither God wills!

Chapter 12
Reward

"RELIGION" I said; for, properly speaking, all true Work is Religion: and what-soever Religion is not Work may go and dwell among the Brahmins, Antinomians, Spinning Dervishes,[23] or where it will; with me it shall have no harbour. Admirable was that of the old Monks, *"Laborare est Orare,* Work is Worship."

Older than all preached Gospels was this unpreached, inarticulate, but ineradi-cable, forever-enduring Gospel: Work, and therein have wellbeing. Man, Son of Earth and of Heaven, lies there not, in the innermost heart of thee, a Spirit of active Method, a Force for Work;—and burns like a painfully-smouldering fire, giving thee no rest till thou unfold it, till thou write it down in beneficent Facts around thee! What is immethodic, waste, thou shalt make methodic, regulated, arable; obedient and productive to thee. Wheresoever thou findest Disorder, there is thy eternal enemy; attack him swiftly, subdue him; make Order of him, the subject not of Chaos, but of Intelligence, Divinity and Thee! The thistle that grows in thy path, dig it out, that a blade of useful grass, a drop of nourishing milk, may grow there

23. Brahmins are members of the highest caste of Hindus; Antinomians are Christians who believe that faith only is necessary for salvation; Spinning Dervishes are Muslims who strive for spiritual ec-stacy by chanting and engaging in twirling, dizzying dances.

instead. The waste cotton-shrub, gather its waste white down, spin it, weave it; that, in place of idle litter, there may be folded webs, and the naked skin of man be covered.

But above all, where thou findest Ignorance, Stupidity, Brute-mindedness,— yes, there, with or without Church-tithes and Shovel-hat,[24] with or without Talfourd-Mahon Copyrights,[25] or were it with mere dungeons and gibbets and crosses, attack it, I say; smite it wisely, unweariedly, and rest not while thou livest and it lives; but smite, smite, in the name of God! The Highest God, as I understand it, does audibly so command thee; still audibly, if thou have ears to hear. He, even He, with his *un*spoken voice, awfuler than any Sinai thunders or syllabled speech of Whirlwinds; for the SILENCE of deep Eternities, of Worlds from beyond the morning-stars,[26] does it not speak to thee? The unborn Ages; the old Graves, with their long-mouldering dust, the very tears that wetted it now all dry,—do not these speak to thee, what ear hath not heard? The deep Death-kingdoms, the Stars in their never-resting courses, all Space and all Time, proclaim it to thee in continual silent admonition. Thou too, if ever man should, shalt work while it is called Today. For the Night cometh, wherein no man can work.

All true Work is sacred; in all true Work, were it but true hand-labour, there is something of divineness. Labour, wide as the Earth, has its summit in Heaven. Sweat of the brow; and up from that to sweat of the brain, sweat of the heart; which includes all Kepler[27] calculations, Newton[28] meditations, all Sciences, all spoken Epics, all acted Heroisms, Martyrdoms,—up to that "Agony of bloody sweat,"[29] which all men have called divine! O brother, if this is not "worship," then I say, the more pity for worship; for this is the noblest thing yet discovered under God's sky. Who art thou that complainest of thy life of toil? Complain not. Look up, my wearied brother; see thy fellow Workmen there, in God's Eternity; surviving there, they alone surviving: sacred Band of the Immortals, celestial Bodyguard of the Empire of Mankind. Even in the weak Human Memory they survive so long, as saints, as heroes, as gods; they alone surviving; peopling, they alone, the unmeasured solitudes of Time! To thee Heaven, though severe, is *not* unkind; Heaven is

24. The shovel-hat was a wide-brimmed hat worn by the Anglican clergy in the eighteenth and nineteenth centuries. Church-tithes were the "tenths" paid by parishioners, either in produce or money, to the rector of the church.

25. Sir Thomas Noon Talfourd (1795–1854) and Sir Philip Stanhope, Lord Mahon (1805–1875) were instrumental in securing passage of the Copyright Act (1842).

26. In this sentence, Carlyle echoes phrases from chapters 37 and 38 of the Book of Job. The voice of the Lord thunders (Job 37:4–5) as it does after He gives Moses the commandments on Mount Sinai (Exodus 20:18). The Lord answers Job out of the whirlwind (Job 38:1), and the Lord asks Job where he was "when the morning stars sang together, and all the sons of God shouted for joy" (Job 38:7).

27. Johannes Kepler (1571–1630), a German astronomer who traced the elliptical movement of the planets.

28. Sir Isaac Newton (1642–1727), English scientist whose theory of gravitation revolutionized physics and astronomy.

29. In the Garden of Gethsemane, on the night before his death, foreseeing what he must endure, Jesus "being in an agony . . . prayed more earnestly: and his sweat was as it were great drops of blood falling down to the ground" (Luke 22:44).

kind,—as a noble Mother; as that Spartan Mother, saying while she gave her son his shield, "With it, my son, or upon it!"[30] Thou too shalt return *home* in honour; to thy far-distant Home, in honour; doubt it not,—if in the battle thou keep thy shield! Thou, in the Eternities and deepest Death-kingdoms, art not an alien; thou everywhere art a denizen! Complain not; the very Spartans did not *complain.*

And who art thou that braggest of thy life of Idleness; complacently showest thy bright gilt equipages; sumptuous cushions; appliances for folding of the hands to mere sleep? Looking up, looking down, around, behind or before, discernest thou, if it be not in Mayfair[31] alone, any *idle* hero, saint, god, or even devil? Not a vestige of one. In the Heavens, in the Earth, in the Waters under the Earth, is none like unto thee. Thou art an original figure in this Creation; a denizen in Mayfair alone, in this extraordinary Century or Half-Century alone! One monster there is in the world: the idle man. What is his "Religion"? That Nature is a Phantasm, where cunning beggary or thievery may sometimes find good victual. That God is a lie; and that Man and his Life are a lie.—Alas, alas, who of us *is* there that can say, I have worked? The faithfulest of us are unprofitable servants;[32] the faithfulest of us know that best. The faithfulest of us may say, with sad and true old Samuel, "Much of my life has been trifled away!"[33] But he that has, and except "on public occasions" professes to have, no function but that of going idle in a graceful or graceless manner; and of begetting sons to go idle; and to address Chief Spinners and Diggers, who at least *are* spinning and digging, "Ye scandalous persons who produce too much"—My Corn-Law[34] friends, on what imaginary still richer Eldorados,[35] and true iron-spikes with law of gravitation, are ye rushing!

As to the Wages of Work there might innumerable things be said; there will and must yet innumerable things be said and spoken, in St. Stephen's and out of St. Stephen's;[36] and gradually not a few things be ascertained and written, on Law-parchment, concerning this very matter:—"Fair day's-wages for a fair day's-work" is the most unrefusable demand! Money-wages "to the extent of keeping your worker alive that he may work more"; these, unless you mean to dismiss him straightway out of this world, are indispensable alike to the noblest Worker and to the least noble!

One thing only I will say here, in special reference to the former class, the noble

30. The traditional exhortation by the Spartan mother was that her son was to return victorious ("with his shield") or dead ("on his shield"); there could be no other option.

31. Fashionable area of London.

32. See Luke 17:10.

33. The reference may be to Samuel Johnson (1709–1784), whose obsessive fear of death was associated, in spite of his exceptional productivity, with anxiety that he had been idle and frivolous with his time.

34. Corn Laws were protectionist tariffs on grain; such regulation was opposed by manufacturing interests because it raised the cost of bread for workers and made foreign trade more difficult.

35. Eldorado was a legendary city of gold.

36. The House of Commons met in St. Stephen's Chapel in Wetsminister until St. Stephen's was destroyed by fire in 1834.

and noblest; but throwing light on all the other classes and their arrangements of this difficult matter: The "wages" of every noble Work do yet lie in Heaven or else Nowhere. Not in Bank-of-England bills, in Owen's Labour-bank,[37] or any the most improved establishment of banking and money-changing, needest thou, heroic soul, present thy account of earnings. Human banks and labour-banks know thee not; or know thee after generations and centuries have passed away, and thou art clean gone from "rewarding,"—all manner of bank-drafts, shop-tills, and Downing-street Exchequers[38] lying very invisible, so far from thee! Nay, at bottom, dost thou need any reward? Was it thy aim and life-purpose to be filled with good things for thy heroism; to have a life of pomp and ease, and be what men call "happy," in this world, or in any other world? I answer for thee deliberately, No. The whole spiritual secret of the new epoch lies in this, that thou canst answer for thyself, with thy whole clearness of head and heart, deliberately, No!

My brother, the brave man has to give his Life away. Give it, I advise thee;—thou dost not expect to *sell* thy Life in an adequate manner? What price, for example, would content thee? The just price of thy LIFE to thee,—why, God's entire Creation to thyself, the whole Universe of Space, the whole Eternity of Time, and what they hold: that is the price which would content thee; that, and if thou wilt be candid, nothing short of that! It is thy all; and for it thou wouldst have all. Thou art an unreasonable mortal;—or rather thou art a poor *infinite* mortal, who, in thy narrow clay-prison here, *seemest* so unreasonable! Thou wilt never sell thy Life, or any part of thy Life, in a satisfactory manner. Give it, like a royal heart; let the price be Nothing: thou *hast* then, in a certain sense, got All for it! The heroic man,—and is not every man, God be thanked, a potential hero?—has to do so, in all times and circumstances. In the most heroic age, as in the most unheroic, he will have to say, as Burns[39] said proudly and humbly of his little Scottish Songs, little dewdrops of Celestial Melody in an age when so much was unmelodious: "By Heaven, they shall either be invaluable or of no value; I do not need your guineas for them!" It is an element which should, and must, enter deeply into all settlements of wages here below. They never will be "satisfactory" otherwise; they cannot, O Mammon Gospel, they never can! Money for my little piece of work "to the extent that will allow me to keep working"; yes, this,—unless you mean that I shall go my ways *before* the work is all taken out of me: but as to "wages"—!—

On the whole, we do entirely agree with those old Monks, *Laborare est Orare*. In a thousand senses, from one end of it to the other, true Work *is* Worship. He that

37. Robert Owen (1771–1858) was an industrial reformer who actively promoted a labor-oriented theory that one's hours worked should determine the value of one's product. In the early 1830s, Owen put this theory into limited practice in London with the "Equitable Labour Exchange." (Owen's "Observations on the Effect of the Manufacturing System" is included in part 2.)

38. The official residence of the Chancellor of the Exchequer is in Downing Street. Number 10 Downing Street is the official residence of the English Prime Minister and the site for Cabinet meetings. "Downing Street," accordingly, generally stands for "governmental."

39. Robert Burns (1759–1796) was the Scots poet whom Carlyle had celebrated in Lecture 5 of *On Heroes and Hero-Worship:* "The Hero as Man of Letters" (1840).

works, whatsoever be his work, he bodies forth the form of Things Unseen; a small Poet every Worker is.[40] The idea, were it but of his poor Delf Platter, how much more of his Epic Poem, is as yet "seen," half-seen, only by himself; to all others it is a thing unseen, impossible; to Nature herself it is a thing unseen, a thing which never hitherto was;—very "impossible," for it is as yet a No-thing! The Unseen Powers had need to watch over such a man; he works in and for the Unseen. Alas, if he look to the Seen Powers only, he may as well quit the business; his No-thing will never rightly issue as a Thing, but as a Deceptivity, a Sham-thing,—which it had better not do!

Thy No-thing of an Intended Poem, O Poet who hast looked merely to review-ers, copyrights, booksellers, popularities, behold it has not yet become a Thing; for the truth is not in it! Though printed, hotpressed,[41] reviewed, celebrated, sold to the twentieth edition: what is all that? The Thing, in philosophical uncommercial language, is still a No-thing, mostly semblance and deception of the sight;—benign Oblivion incessantly gnawing at it, impatient till Chaos, to which it belongs, do reabsorb it!—

He who takes not counsel of the Unseen and Silent, from him will never come real visibility and speech. Thou must descend to the *Mothers*, to the *Manes*,[42] and Hercules-like long suffer and labour there, wouldst thou emerge with victory into the sunlight. As in battle and the shock of war,—for is not this a battle?—thou too shalt fear no pain or death, shalt love no ease or life; the voice of festive Lubber-lands,[43] the noise of greedy Acheron[44] shall alike lie silent under thy victorious feet. Thy work, like Dante's, shall "make thee lean for many years."[45] The world and its wages, its criticisms, counsels, helps, impediments, shall be as a waste ocean-flood; the chaos through which thou art to swim and sail. Not the waste waves and their weedy gulf-streams, shalt thou take for guidance: thy star alone,— "*Se tu segui tua stella!*"[46] Thy star alone, now clear-beaming over Chaos, nay now by fits gone out, disastrously eclipsed: this only shalt thou strive to follow. O, it is a business, as I fancy, that of weltering your way through Chaos and the murk of Hell! Green-eyed dragons watching you, three-headed Cerberuses,[47]—not without sympathy of *their* sort! "*Eccovi l'uom ch' è stato all' Inferno.*"[48] For in fine, as Poet Dryden says, you do

---

40. Carlyle here echoes Theseus's famous speech about the poet in Shakespeare's *A Midsummer Night's Dream*: 5.1.12–17.

41. Hotpressing is a process for supplying a glossy finish to paper.

42. In Roman culture, the *manes* were the shades of the ancestors.

43. Lubberland is the traditional land of wish-fulfillment, where, as the proverb runs, "Pigs run about ready roasted and cry, 'Come eat me.'"

44. The "river of woe," the Acheron is the river of the classical underworld over which Charon fer-ries the dead.

45. From Dante's *Paradiso* xxv.

46. "If you follow your star."

47. Cerberus is the three-headed dog guarding the entry into the classical underworld.

48. "Behold the man who has been through Hell." The tradition is that, following his completion of the *Inferno*, as Dante would walk through the streets, people would point at him and repeat this sentence.

walk hand in hand with sheer Madness, all the way,[49]—who is by no means pleasant company! You look fixedly into Madness, and *her* undiscovered, boundless, bottomless Night-empire; that you may extort new Wisdom out of it, as an Eurydice from Tartarus.[50] The higher the Wisdom, the closer was its neighbourhood and kindred with mere Insanity; literally so;—and thou wilt, with a speechless feeling, observe how highest Wisdom, struggling up into this world, has oftentimes carried such tinctures and adhesions of Insanity still cleaving to it hither!

All Works, each in their degree, are a making of Madness sane;—truly enough a religious operation; which cannot be carried on without religion. You have not work otherwise; you have eye-service, greedy grasping of wages, swift and ever swifter manufacture of semblances to get hold of wages. Instead of better felt-hats to cover your head, you have bigger lath-and-plaster hats set travelling the streets on wheels. Instead of heavenly and earthly Guidance for the souls of men, you have "Black or White Surplice" Controversies,[51] stuffed hair-and-leather Popes;[52]—terrestrial *Law-wards,* Lords and Law-bringers, "organising Labour" in these years, by passing Corn-Laws. With all which, alas, this distracted Earth is now full, nigh to bursting. Semblances most smooth to the touch and eye; most accursed, nevertheless, to body and soul. Semblances, be they of Sham-woven Cloth or of Dilettante Legislation, which are *not* real wool or substance, but Devil's dust, accursed of God and man! No man has worked, or can work, except religiously; not even the poor day-labourer, the weaver of your coat, the sewer of your shoes. All men, if they work not as in a Great Taskmaster's eye,[53] will work wrong, work unhappily for themselves and you.

Industrial work, still under bondage to Mammon, the rational soul of it not yet awakened, is a tragic spectacle. Men in the rapidest motion and self-motion; restless, with convulsive energy, as if driven by Galvanism,[54] as if possessed by a Devil; tearing asunder mountains,—to no purpose, for Mammonism is always Midas-eared![55] This is sad, on the face of it. Yet courage: the beneficent Destinies, kind in their sternness, are apprising us that this cannot continue. Labour is not a

49. Carlyle refers to the following lines from *Absalom and Achitophel* by John Dryden (1631–1700): "Great wits are sure to madness near allied, / And thin partitions do their bounds divide" (163–64).

50. The poet Orpheus redeemed Eurydice from Tartarus, the underworld, winning her freedom by the sweetness of his song. However, because he looked back to assure himself that she was following him up from Tartarus, Orpheus was condemned to see Eurydice descend again into death.

51. References to nineteenth-century debate about ecclesiastical rituals.

52. In "Phenomena," chapter 1 of book 3 of *Past and Present,* Carlyle provides the story of a rheumatic pope who finds it difficult to kneel as he rides through the streets on the feast of Corpus Christi. Accordingly, his cardinals make a kneeling figure within which the pope may sit so that his own hands and face will be visible through the "stuffed hair and leather."

53. Carlyle quotes in truncated fashion the last line of Milton's sonnet "How soon hath Time, the subtle thief of youth," a poem in which Milton addresses his anxiety to be productive and the necessity of realizing that an individual's industry is valuable only as it is valued in God's eyes.

54. Galvanism, named after Luigi Galvani (1737–1798), was the process of passing an electrical current through organic tissue in the hope of (re)vitalizing the tissue.

55. Because Midas misjudged a musical competition, declaring Apollo's music to be inferior to Pan's, Apollo changed his ears to those of an ass, a beast presumably insensitive to music.

devil, even while encased in Mammonism; Labour is ever an imprisoned god, writhing unconsciously or consciously to escape out of Mammonism! Plugson of Undershot, like Taillefer of Normandy,[56] wants victory; how much happier will even Plugson be to have a Chivalrous victory than a Chactaw one! The unredeemed ugliness is that of a slothful People. Show me a People energetically busy; heaving, struggling, all shoulders at the wheel; their heart pulsing, every muscle swelling, with man's energy and will;—I show you a People of whom great good is already predicable; to whom all manner of good is yet certain, if their energy endure. By very working, they will learn; they have, Antaeus-like,[57] their foot on Mother Fact: how can they but learn?

The vulgarest Plugson of a Master-Worker, who can command Workers, and get work out of them, is already a considerable man. Blessed and thrice-blessed symptoms I discern of Master-Workers who are not vulgar men; who are Nobles, and begin to feel that they must act as such: all speed to these, they are England's hope at present! But in this Plugson himself, conscious of almost no nobleness whatever, how much is there! Not without man's faculty, insight, courage, hard energy, is this rugged figure. His words none of the wisest; but his actings cannot be altogether foolish. Think, how were it, stoodst thou suddenly in his shoes! He has to command a thousand men. And not imaginary commanding; no, it is real, incessantly practical. The evil passions of so many men (with the Devil in them, as in all of us) he has to vanquish; by manifold force of speech and of silence, to repress or evade. What a force of silence, to say nothing of the others, is in Plugson! For these his thousand men he has to provide raw-material, machinery, arrangement, house-room; and ever at the week's end, wages by due sale. No Civil-List, or Goulburn-Baring Budget[58] has he to fall back upon, for paying of his regiment; he has to pick his supplies from the confused face of the whole Earth and Contemporaneous History, by his dexterity alone. There will be dry eyes if he fail to do it!—He exclaims, at present, "black in the face," near strangled with Dilettante Legislation; "Let me have elbow-room, throat-room, and I will not fail! No, I will spin yet, and conquer like a giant: what 'sinews of war' lie in me, untold resources towards the

---

56. Plugson of Undershot, introduced in the chapter preceding "Labour," is a fictional cotton manufacturer whom Carlyle wishes to become a "Captain of Industry" in the "battle" of transforming raw cotton into clothing for men. Carlyle sees the commercial success that enriched Plugson but left his workers still impoverished as a "Chactaw [or Choctaw] Indian" or savagely pointless victory, a taking of thousand-pound notes as though they were so many scalps; Carlyle sets against such foolish greed what he sees as the chivalrous action of William the Conqueror and his Taillefers or Ironcutters, who shared with their followers the responsibilities of governing the English lands they had conquered.

57. Antaeus is the offspring of Poseidon and Gaia, the earth mother, and his strength is reinforced through contact with his mother earth. When Heracles wrestles with him, Antaeus becomes more formidable each time he is thrown to the ground; Heracles finally must hold him in the air to strangle him.

58. The Civil List was the funding Parliament provided to support the Royal Family. Sir Francis Thornhill Baring was Chancellor of the Exchequer from 1839 to 1841; Henry Goulburn held the office from 1841 to 1846.

Conquest of this Planet, if instead of hanging me, you husband them, and help me!"—My indomitable friend, it is *true;* and thou shalt and must be helped.

This is not a man I would kill and strangle by Corn-Laws, even if I could! No, I would fling my Corn-Laws and Shot-belts to the Devil; and try to help this man. I would teach him, by noble precept and law-precept, by noble example most of all, that Mammonism was not the essence of his or of my station in God's Universe; but the adscititious[59] excrescence of it; the gross, terrene, godless embodiment of it; which would have to become, more or less, a godlike one. By noble *real* legislation, by true *noble's*-work, by unwearied, valiant, and were it wageless effort, in my Parliament and in my Parish, I would aid, constrain, encourage him to effect more or less this blessed change. I should know that it would have to be effected; that unless it were in some measure effected, he and I and all of us, I first and soonest of all, were doomed to perdition!—Effected it will be; unless it were a Demon that made this Universe; which I, for my own part, do at no moment, under no form, in the least believe.

May it please your Serene Highnesses, your Majesties, Lordships and Law-wardships, the proper Epic of this world is not now "Arms and the Man";[60] how much less, "Shirt-frills and the Man": no, it is now "Tools and the Man": that, henceforth to all time, is now our Epic;—and you, first of all others, I think, were wise to take note of that!

In "Occasional Discourse on the Nigger Question," first published in *Fraser's Magazine* in 1849, six years after *Past and Present,* Carlyle's impassioned rhetoric verges on strident polemic concerning work as mission. In 1833, William Wilberforce and others had finally succeeded in a lengthy campaign to secure, with the Emancipation Act, the abolition of slavery within all British territories, and, in the late thirties and especially in the forties, plantation owners in British Caribbean possessions encountered difficulties in changing from a system of cultivation and marketing based upon slave labor to one in which emancipated slaves were to be treated for the first time as salaried workers. As productivity in the Caribbean fell off and as reports concerning the indolence of freed slaves spread, Carlyle seized upon what was then called "the West India Question" to advance major themes from his earlier writing: his complaint that laissez-faire economists demeaned workers by reducing human relationships to financial negotiations; his criticism that philanthropic endeavors to improve the material well-being of poor laborers disregarded the more fundamental issue of the moral and spiritual condition of workers; his conviction that work is humanity's prime mission, that "the everlasting

59. "Derived from the outside."
60. *"Arma virumque cano"* are the opening words of Virgil's *Aeneid,* which had become the standard for all epics.

duty of all men, black or white, who are born into this world" is to "do competent work, to labour honestly according to the ability given them; for that and for no other purpose was each one of us sent into this world."

As Carlyle lodged his grievances, however, he cultivated even more fully than in his earlier writings the pose of the controversialist idiosyncratically at odds with his society, creating a voice and a stance calculated to irritate his audience. Construing the humanitarianism of public reformers as a shallow and smug self-righteousness, he assaults it as Exeter Hall Christian Sentimentalism. Genuinely opposed to slavery, which he declares a "contradiction of the Laws of this Universe," he nonetheless self-consciously plays with the terms *slave* and *free*, suggesting that there is a debasement of the noble nature of work which leads to a subjection more demoralizing than actual slavery. In challenging egalitarian principles he expresses doubt about the common citizen's capacity for self-government. Further, he deliberately voices an overt racism that was implicit but disguised in British philanthropic efforts to arrange the affairs of non-white colonials for them: white Europeans, especially Anglo-Saxons, are superior to dark-skinned Africans or West Indians because Europeans display heroic self-discipline and a commitment to work that enables them to transform waste wildernesses into productive islands. With uncompromising bluntness, Carlyle endorses a sense of cultural and racial supremacy that is tied to a belief that dedication to work defines one people as superior to another, a configuration of attitudes that is one of the most significant elements of British imperial and colonial discourse. Imperial rule itself is legitimized as a mission defined by a combination of work and self-sacrifice, a political perspective still strong at the end of the century and given popular expression in Rudyard Kipling's "The White Man's Burden" (included as the final selection in part 1).

"Occasional Discourse on the Nigger Question" is, in many ways, an offensive harangue. Disturbed by the racism apparent in its title and prominent in its argument, John Stuart Mill (see part 4) ended his friendship with Carlyle after answering Carlyle's essay with his own analysis of the situation. The most favorable responses Carlyle received were from proponents of the slave system in the American South, although his tract was attacked in the Abolitionist press, notably by John Greenleaf Whittier. And Carlyle scholars today remain embarrassed by the piece, refraining from critical analysis and republication. Few other documents, however, provide such a straightforward articulation of the nineteenth-century belief that work is at once the essential duty of all people and the distinct expression of the moral and political superiority of some over others.

The Nigger Question
[Precursor to Latter-day Pamphlets.]
[1849]

Occasional Discourse on the Nigger Question

The following Occasional Discourse, delivered by we know not whom, and of date seemingly above a year back, may perhaps be welcome to here and there a speculative reader. It comes to us,—no speaker named, no time or place assigned, no commentary of any sort given,—in the handwriting of the so-called "Doctor," properly "Absconded Reporter," Dr. Phelim M'Quirk, whose singular powers of reporting, and also whose debts, extravagancies and sorrowful insidious finance-operations, now winded-up by a sudden disappearance, to the grief of many poor tradespeople, are making too much noise in the police-offices at present! Of M'Quirk's composition we by no means suppose it to be; but from M'Quirk, as the last traceable source, it comes to us;—offered, in fact, by his respectable unfortunate landlady, desirous to make-up part of her losses in this way.

To absconded reporters who bilk their lodgings,[1] we have of course no account to give; but if the Speaker be of any eminence or substantiality, and feel himself aggrieved by the transaction, let him understand that such, and such only, is our connection with him or his affairs. As the Colonial and Negro Question is still alive, and likely to grow livelier for some time, we have accepted the Article, at a cheap market-rate; and give it publicity, without in the least committing ourselves to the strange doctrines and notions shadowed forth in it. Doctrines and notions which, we rather suspect, are pretty much in a "minority of one," in the present era of the world! Here, sure enough, are peculiar views of the Rights of Negroes; involving, it is probable, peculiar ditto[2] of innumerable other rights, duties, expectations, wrongs and disappointments, much argued of, by logic and by grape-shot,[3] in these emancipated epochs of the human mind!—Silence now, however; and let the Speaker himself enter.

MY PHILANTHROPIC FRIENDS,—It is my painful duty to address some words to you, this evening, on the Rights of Negroes. Taking, as we hope we do, an

1. Evade payment for.
2. Repetition.
3. Type of cannon ammunition consisting of three layers of cast-iron balls separated by four iron disks.

extensive survey of social affairs, which we find all in a state of the frightfulest embroilment, and as it were of inextricable final bankruptcy, just at present; and being desirous to adjust ourselves in that huge upbreak, and unutterable welter of tumbling ruins, and to see well that our grand proposed Association of Associations, the UNIVERSAL ABOLITION-OF-PAIN ASSOCIATION, which is meant to be the consummate golden flower and summary of modern Philanthropisms all in one, do *not* issue as a universal "Sluggard-and-Scoundrel Protection Society,"—we have judged that, before constituting ourselves, it would be very proper to commune earnestly with one another, and discourse together on the leading elements of our great Problem, which surely is one of the greatest. With this view the Council has decided, both that the Negro Question, as lying at the bottom, was to be the first handled, and if possible the first settled; and then also, what was of much more questionable wisdom, that—that, in short, I was to be Speaker on the occasion. An honourable duty; yet, as I said, a painful one!—Well, you shall hear what I have to say on the matter; and probably you will not in the least like it.

West-Indian affairs, as we all know, and as some of us know to our cost, are in a rather troublous condition this good while. In regard to West-Indian affairs, however, Lord John Russell[4] is able to comfort us with one fact, indisputable where so many are dubious, That the Negroes are all very happy and doing well. A fact very comfortable indeed. West-Indian Whites, it is admitted, are far enough from happy; West-Indian Colonies not unlike sinking wholly into ruin: at home too, the British Whites are rather badly off; several millions of them hanging on the verge of continual famine; and in single towns, many thousands of them very sore put to it, at this time, not to live "well" or as a man should, in any sense temporal or spiritual, but to live at all:—these, again, are uncomfortable facts; and they are extremely extensive and important ones. But, thank Heaven, our interesting Black population,—equalling almost in number of heads one of the Ridings[5] of Yorkshire, and in *worth* (in quantity of intellect, faculty, docility, energy, and available human valour and value) perhaps one of the streets of Seven Dials,[6]—are all doing remarkably well. "Sweet blighted lilies,"—as the American epitaph on the Nigger child has it,—sweet blighted lilies, they are holding-up their heads again! How pleasant, in the universal bankruptcy abroad, and dim dreary stagnancy at home, as if for England too there remained nothing but to suppress Chartist riots,[7]

4. Lord John Russell (1792–1878), British statesman who held the offices of Home Secretary and Colonial Secretary in the late 1830s. He served as Prime Minister from 1846 to 1852 and from 1865 to 1866, being in office while Carlyle was composing "Occasional Discourse." Russell was a firm believer in the laissez-faire economics that Carlyle so adamantly opposed.

5. Yorkshire is divided into three administrative jurisdictions, each of which is called a riding.

6. The Dials was a London district known for crime and immorality. It was named for a pillar with six sun dials surrounded by seven streets.

7. "Chartists" was the name given to supporters of The People's Charter (included in part 3), a proposal for reforms such as universal male suffrage and voting by secret ballot. In the 1830s and 1840s, Chartist organizers held conventions, rallies, and meetings. Riots associated with the Chartist movement had occurred in 1839 in Birmingham and Newport and, in 1848, the year prior to Carlyle's composition of "Occasional Discourse," in Glasgow.

banish united Irishmen,[8] vote the supplies, and *wait* with arms crossed till black Anarchy and Social Death devoured us also, as it has done the others; how pleasant to have always this fact to fall-back upon: Our beautiful Black darlings are at last happy; with little labour except to the teeth, *which* surely, in those excellent horse-jaws of theirs, will not fail!

Exeter Hall,[9] my philanthropic friends, has had its way in this matter. The Twenty Millions, a mere trifle despatched with a single dash of the pen, are paid; and far over the sea, we have a few black persons rendered extremely "free" indeed. Sitting yonder with their beautiful muzzles up to the ears in pumpkins, imbibing sweet pulps and juices; the grinder and incisor teeth ready for ever new work, and the pumpkins cheap as grass in those rich climates: while the sugar-crops rot round them uncut, because labour cannot be hired, so cheap are the pumpkins;—and at home we are but required to rasp[10] from the breakfast-loaves of our own English labourers some slight "differential sugar-duties," and lend a poor half-million or a few poor millions now and then, to keep that beautiful state of matters going on. A state of matters lovely to contemplate, in these emancipated epochs of the human mind; which has earned us not only the praises of Exeter Hall, and loud long-eared hallelujahs of laudatory psalmody from the Friends of Freedom every-where, but lasting favour (it is hoped) from the Heavenly Powers themselves;—and which may, at least, justly appeal to the Heavenly Powers, and ask them, If ever in terrestrial procedure they saw the match of it? Certainly in the past history of the human species it has no parallel: nor, one hopes, will it have in the future. [*Some emotion in the audience; which the Chairman suppressed.*]

Sunk in deep froth-oceans of "Benevolence," "Fraternity," "Emancipation-principle," "Christian Philanthropy," and other most amiable-looking, but most baseless, and in the end baleful and all bewildering jargon,—sad product of a sceptical Eighteenth Century, and of poor human hearts left *destitute* of any ear-nest guidance, and disbelieving that there ever was any, Christian or Heathen, and reduced to believe in rosepink Sentimentalism alone, and to cultivate the same under its Christian, Antichristian, Broad-brimmed, Brutus-headed,[11] and other forms,—has not the human species gone strange roads, during that period? And poor Exeter Hall, cultivating the Broad-brimmed form of Christian Sentimental-ism, and long talking and bleating and braying in that strain, has it not worked-out results? Our West-Indian Legislatings, with their spouting, anti-spoutings, and

8. The United Irishmen were radical political societies composed of Presbyterians and middle-class Catholics who supported Catholic emancipation, Parliamentary reform, and Ireland's indepen-dence. They had been involved in unsuccessful rebellions in 1798 and 1803.

9. Exeter Hall was a meeting place in the Strand in London that had opened in 1831 and was used by religious and philanthropic groups. The leverage of these organizations with respect to colonial policy and humanitarian causes became known as the Exeter Hall influence.

10. Grate or scrape.

11. "Broad-brimmed" is a term associated with the Anglican Church, particularly the Evangelical party; the reference is to the shovel-hat, a wide-brimmed hat worn by the Anglican clergy in the eighteenth and nineteenth centuries. "Brutus-headed" may refer to a sentimentalism associated with a general stoicism and a concern for civic duty.

interminable jangle and babble; our Twenty millions down on the nail for Blacks of our own; Thirty gradual millions more, and many brave British lives to boot, in watching Blacks of other people's; and now at last our ruined sugar-estates, differential sugar-duties, "immigration loan," and beautiful Blacks sitting there up to the ears in pumpkins, and doleful Whites sitting here without potatoes to eat: never till now, I think, did the sun look-down on such a jumble of human non-senses;—of which, with the two hot nights of the Missing-Despatch Debate,[12] God grant that the measure might now at last be full! But no, it is not yet full; we have a long way to travel back, and terrible flounderings to make, and in fact an immense load of nonsense to dislodge from our poor heads, and manifold cobwebs to rend from our poor eyes, before we get into the road again, and can begin to act as serious men that have work to do in this Universe, and no longer as windy sentimentalists that merely have speeches to deliver and despatches to write. O Heaven, in West-Indian matters, and in all manner of matters, it is so with us: the more is the sorrow!—

The West Indies, it appears, are short of labour; as indeed is very conceivable in those circumstances. Where a Black man, by working about half-an-hour a-day (such is the calculation), can supply himself, by aid of sun and soil, with as much pumpkin as will suffice, he is likely to be a little stiff to raise into hard work! Supply and demand, which, science says, should be brought to bear on him, have an uphill task of it with such a man. Strong sun supplies itself gratis, rich soil in those unpeopled or half-peopled regions almost gratis; these are *his* "supply"; and half-an-hour a-day, directed upon these, will produce pumpkin, which is his "demand." The fortunate Black man, very swiftly does he settle *his* account with supply and demand:—not so swiftly the less fortunate White man of those tropical localities. A bad case, his, just now. He himself cannot work; and his black neighbour, rich in pumpkin, is in no haste to help him. Sunk to the ears in pumpkin, imbibing saccharine juices, and much at his ease in the Creation, he can listen to the less fortunate white man's "demand," and take his own time in supplying it. Higher wages, massa; higher, for your cane-crop cannot wait; still higher,—till no conceivable opulence of cane-crop will cover such wages. In Demerara,[13] as I read in the Blue-book[14] of last year, the cane-crop, far and wide, stands rotting; the fortunate black gentlemen, strong in their pumpkins, having all struck till the "demand" rise a little. Sweet blighted lilies, now getting-up their heads again!

Science, however, has a remedy still. Since the demand is so pressing, and the supply so inadequate (equal in fact to *nothing* in some places, as appears), increase the supply; bring more Blacks into the labour-market, then will the rate fall, says

12. Carlyle's note: "Does any reader now remember it? A cloudy reminiscence of some such thing, and of noise in the Newspapers upon it, remains with us,—fast hastening to abolition for everybody."

13. Demerara was a county in British Guiana that had large sugar and rice plantations. Carlyle follows a common practice of using the name of this county to refer to the entire colony of British Guiana.

14. Blue-books were official collections of statistics, testimony, and evidence gathered by select committees of Parliament and royal commissions studying social and economic issues.

science. Not the least surprising part of our West-Indian policy is this recipe of "immigration"; of keeping-down the labour-market in those islands by importing new Africans to labour and live there. If the Africans that are already there could be made to lay-down their pumpkins, and labour for their living, there are already Africans enough. If the new Africans, after labouring a little, take to pumpkins like the others, what remedy is there? To bring-in new and ever new Africans, say you, till pumpkins themselves grow dear; till the country is crowded with Africans; and black men there, like white men here, are forced by hunger to labour for their living? That will be a consummation. To have "emancipated" the West Indies into a *Black Ireland;* "free" indeed, but an Ireland, and Black! The world may yet see prodigies; and reality be stranger than a nightmare dream.

Our own white or sallow Ireland, sluttishly starving from age to age on its act-of-parliament "freedom," was hitherto the flower of mismanagement among the nations: but what will this be to a Negro Ireland, with pumpkins themselves fallen scarce like potatoes![15] Imagination cannot fathom such an object; the belly of Chaos never held the like. The human mind, in its wide wanderings, has not dreamt yet of such a "freedom" as that will be. Towards that, if Exeter Hall and science of supply-and-demand are to continue our guides in the matter, we are daily travelling, and even struggling, with loans of half-a-million and suchlike, to accelerate ourselves.

Truly, my philanthropic friends, Exeter-Hall Philanthropy is wonderful. And the Social Science,—not a "gay science," but a rueful,—which finds the secret of this Universe in "supply and demand," and reduces the duty of human governors to that of letting men alone, is also wonderful. Not a "gay science," I should say, like some we have heard of; no, a dreary, desolate, and indeed quite abject and distressing one; what we might call, by way of eminence, the *dismal science.*[16] These two, Exeter-Hall Philanthropy and the Dismal Science, led by any sacred cause of Black Emancipation, or the like, to fall in love and make a wedding of it,—will give birth to progenies and prodigies; dark extensive moon-calves,[17] unnamable abortions, wide-coiled monstrosities, such as the world has not seen hitherto! [*Increased emotion, again suppressed by the Chairman.*]

In fact, it will behove us of this English nation to overhaul our West-Indian procedure from top to bottom, and ascertain a little better what it is that Fact and Nature demand of us, and what only Exeter Hall wedded to the Dismal Science demands. To the former set of demands we will endeavour, at our peril,—and worse peril than our purse's, at our soul's peril,—to give all obedience. To the latter we will very frequently demur, and try if we cannot stop short where they contradict

15. The Great Famine (the "Great Hunger") in Ireland was caused by a blight that affected the potato crop. The initial failure of the potato crop in 1845 was addressed with programs of relief inaugurated by then Prime Minister Robert Peel. He was succeeded in 1846 by Lord John Russell (see note 4), whose obsession with laissez-faire theory led him to cut any substantial economic aid to Ireland.

16. Economics.

17. Monsters. The name was applied to calves born dead or deformed, the moon being the supposed cause of such births.

the former,—and especially *before* arriving at the black throat of ruin, whither they appear to be leading us. Alas, in many other provinces besides the West Indian, that unhappy wedlock of Philanthropic Liberalism and the Dismal Science has engendered such all-enveloping delusions, of the moon-calf sort, and wrought huge woe for us, and for the poor civilised world, in these days! And sore will be the battle with said moon-calves; and terrible the struggle to return out of our delusions, floating rapidly on which, not the West Indies alone, but Europe generally, is nearing the Niagara Falls.[18] [*Here various persons, in an agitated manner, with an air of indignation, left the room; especially one very tall gentleman in white trousers, whose boots creaked much. The President, in a resolved voice, with a look of official rigour, whatever his own private feelings might be, enjoined "Silence, Silence!" The meeting again sat motionless.*]

My philanthropic friends, can you discern no fixed headlands in this wide-weltering deluge, of benevolent twaddle and revolutionary grape-shot, that has burst-forth on us; no sure bearings at all? Fact and Nature, it seems to me, say a few words to us, if happily we have still an ear for Fact and Nature. Let us listen a little and try.

And first, with regard to the West Indies, it may be laid-down as a principle, which no eloquence in Exeter Hall, or Westminster Hall, or elsewhere, can invalidate or hide, except for a short time only, That no Black man who will not work according to what ability the gods have given him for working, has the smallest right to eat pumpkin, or to any fraction of land that will grow pumpkin, however plentiful such land may be; but has an indisputable and perpetual *right* to be compelled, by the real proprietors of said land, to do competent work for his living. This is the everlasting duty of all men, black or white, who are born into this world. To do competent work, to labour honestly according to the ability given them; for that and for no other purpose was each one of us sent into this world; and woe is to every man who, by friend or by foe, is prevented from fulfilling this the end of his being. That is the "unhappy" lot: lot equally unhappy cannot otherwise be provided for man. Whatsoever prohibits or prevents a man from this his sacred appointment to labour while he lives on earth,—that, I say, is the man's deadliest enemy; and all men are called upon to do what is in their power or opportunity towards delivering him from that. If it be his own indolence that prevents and prohibits him, then his own indolence is the enemy he must be delivered from: and the first "right" he has,—poor indolent blockhead, black or white,—is, That every *un*prohibited man, whatsoever wiser, more industrious person may be passing that way, shall endeavour to "emancipate" him from his indolence, and by some wise means, as I said, compel him, since inducing will not serve, to do the work he is fit for. Induce him, if you can: yes, sure enough, by all means try what inducement will do; and indeed every coachman and carman knows that secret, without our preaching, and applies it to his very horses as the

18. In 1867, Carlyle would give the title "Shooting Niagara, and After?" to an essay questioning the wisdom of egalitarian emphasis in the Second Reform Bill.

true method:—but if your Nigger will not be induced? In that case, it is full certain, he must be compelled; should and must; and the tacit prayer he makes (unconsciously he, poor blockhead), to you, and to me, and to all the world who are wiser than himself, is, "Compel me!" For indeed he *must,* or else do and suffer worse,— he as well as we. It were better the work did come out of him! It was the meaning of the gods with him and with us, that his gift should turn to use in this Creation, and not lie poisoning the thoroughfares, as a rotten mass of idleness, agreeable to neither heaven nor earth. For idleness does, in all cases, inevitably *rot,* and become putrescent;—and I say deliberately, the very Devil is in *it.*

None of you, my friends, have been in Demerara lately, I apprehend? May none of you go till matters mend there a little! Under the sky there are uglier sights than perhaps were seen hitherto! Dead corpses, the rotting body of a brother man, whom fate or unjust men have killed, this is not a pleasant spectacle; but what say you to the dead soul of a man,—in a body which still pretends to be vigorously alive, and can drink rum? An idle White gentleman is not pleasant to me; though I confess the real work for him is not easy to find, in these our epochs; and perhaps he is seeking, poor soul, and may find at last. But what say you to an idle Black gentleman, with his rum-bottle in his hand (for a little additional pumpkin you can have red-herrings and rum, in Demerara),—rum-bottle in his hand, no breeches on his body, pumpkin at discretion, and the fruitfulest region of the earth going back to jungle round him? Such things the sun looks-down upon in our fine times; and I, for one, would rather have no hand in them.

Yes, this is the eternal law of Nature for a man, my beneficent Exeter-Hall friends; this, that he shall be permitted, encouraged, and if need be, compelled to do what work the Maker of him has intended by the making of him for this world! Not that he should eat pumpkin with never such felicity in the West-India Islands is, or can be, the blessedness of our Black friend; but that he should do useful work there, according as the gifts have been bestowed on him for that. And his own happiness, and that of others round him, will alone be possible by his and their getting into such a relation that this can be permitted him, and in case of need, that this can be compelled him. I beg you to understand this; for you seem to have a little forgotten it, and there lie a thousand inferences in it, not quite useless for Exeter Hall, at present. The idle Black man in the West Indies had, not long since, the right, and will again under better form, if it please Heaven, have the right (actually the first "right of man" for an indolent person) to be *compelled* to work as he was fit, and to *do* the Maker's will who had constructed him with such and such capabilities, and prefigurements of capability. And I incessantly pray Heaven, all men, the whitest alike and the blackest, the richest and the poorest, in other regions of the world, had attained precisely the same right, the divine right of being compelled (if "permitted" will not answer) to do what work they are appointed for, and not to go idle another minute, in a life which is so short, and where idleness so soon runs to putrescence! Alas, we had then a perfect world; and the Millennium, and true "Organisation of Labour," and reign of complete blessedness, for all workers and men, had then arrived,—which in these our own poor districts of the Planet, as we all lament to know, it is very far from having yet done. [*More withdrawals; but the rest sitting with increased attention.*]

Do I, then, hate the Negro? No; except when the soul is killed out of him, I decidedly like poor Quashee;[19] and find him a pretty kind of man. With a pennyworth of oil, you can make a handsome glossy thing of Quashee, when the soul is not killed in him! A swift, supple fellow; a merry-hearted, grinning, dancing, singing, affectionate kind of creature, with a great deal of melody and amenability in his composition. This certainly is a notable fact: The black African, alone of wild-men, can live among men civilised. While all manner of Caribs[20] and others pine into annihilation in presence of the pale faces, he contrives to continue; does not die of sullen irreconcilable rage, of rum, of brutish laziness and darkness, and fated incompatibility with his new place; but lives and multiplies, and evidently means to abide among us, if we can find the right regulation for him. We shall have to find it; we are now engaged in the search; and have at least discovered that of two methods, the old Demerara method, and the new Demerara method,[21] neither will answer.

Alas, my friends, I understand well your rage against the poor Negro's slavery; what said rage proceeds from; and have a perfect sympathy with it, and even know it by experience. Can the oppressor of my black fellow-man be of any use to me in particular? Am I gratified in my mind by the ill-usage of any two- or four-legged thing; of any horse or any dog? Not so, I assure you. In me too the natural sources of human rage exist more or less, and the capability of flying out into "fiery wrath against oppression," and of signing petitions; both of which things can be done very cheap. Good heavens, if signing petitions would do it, if hopping to Rome on one leg would do it, think you it were long undone!

Frightful things are continually told us of Negro slavery, of the hardships, bodily and spiritual, suffered by slaves. Much exaggerated, and mere exceptional cases, say the opponents. Exceptional cases, I answer; yes, and universal ones! On the whole, hardships, and even oppressions and injustices are not unknown in this world; I myself have suffered such, and have not you? It is said, Man, of whatever colour, is born to such, even as the sparks fly upwards.[22] For in fact labour, and this is properly what we call hardship, misery, etc. (meaning mere ugly labour not yet done), labour is not joyous but grievous; and we have a good deal of it to do among us here. We have, simply, to carry the whole world and its businesses upon our backs, we poor united Human Species; to carry it, and shove it forward, from day

19. Taken from the West African word *Kwasi*, a name commonly given to a child born on Sunday, "Quashee" is a term used by Carlyle to denote the generic emancipated black man in the West Indies. As in *Past and Present*, similar reductive, two-dimensional names occur with frequency in "Occasional Discourse": see, later in the essay, Tompkins and Jobson, the Duke of Trumps, Jellysnob, Farmer Hodge, and Hickory Buckskin.

20. Members of a native American tribe inhabiting the southern West Indies and the northern coast of South America.

21. The old method involved the slave system; the new method involved the inefficient production that Carlyle addresses in the essay.

22. "Yet man is born unto trouble, as the sparks fly upward" (Job 5:7).

to day, somehow or other, among us, or else be ground to powder under it, one and all. No light task, let me tell you, even if each did his part honestly, which each doesn't by any means. No, only the noble lift willingly with their whole strength, at the general burden; and in such a crowd, after all your drillings, regulatings, and attempts at equitable distribution, and compulsion, what deceptions are still practicable, what errors are inevitable! Many cunning ignoble fellows shirk the labour altogether; and instead of faithfully lifting at the immeasurable universal handbarrow with its thousand-million handles, contrive to get on some ledge of it, and be lifted!

What a story we have heard about all that, not from vague rumour since yesterday, but from inspired prophets, speakers and seers, ever since speech began! How the giant willing spirit, among white masters, and in the best-regulated families, is so often not loaded only but overloaded, crushed-down like an Enceladus;[23] and, all his life, has to have armies of pigmies building tabernacles on his chest; marching composedly over his neck, as if it were a highway; and much amazed if, when they run their straw spear into his nostril, he is betrayed into sudden sneezing, and oversets some of them. [*Some laughter, the speaker himself looking terribly serious.*] My friends, I have come to the sad conclusion that SLAVERY, whether established by law, or by law abrogated, exists very extensively in this world, in and out of the West Indies; and, in fact, that you cannot abolish slavery by act of parliament, but can only abolish the *name* of it, which is very little!

In the West Indies itself, if you chance to abolish Slavery to Men, and in return establish Slavery to the Devil (as we see in Demerara), what good is it? To save men's bodies, and fill them with pumpkins and rum, is a poor task for human benevolence, if you have to kill their soul, what soul there was, in the business! Slavery is not so easy to be abolished; it will long continue, in spite of acts of parliament. And shall I tell you which is the one intolerable sort of slavery; the slavery over which the very gods weep? That sort is not rifest in the West Indies; but, with all its sad fruits, prevails in nobler countries. It is the slavery of the strong to the weak; of the great and noble-minded to the small and mean! The slavery of Wisdom to Folly. When Folly all "emancipated," and become supreme, armed with ballot-boxes, universal suffrages, and appealing to what Dismal Sciences, Statistics, Constitutional Philosophies, and other Fool Gospels it has got devised for itself, can say to Wisdom: "Be silent, or thou shalt repent it! Suppress thyself, I advise thee; canst thou not contrive to cease, then?" That also, in some anarchic-constitutional epochs, has been seen. When, of high and noble objects, there remained, in the market-place of human things, at length none; and he that could not make guineas his pursuit, and the applause of flunkies[24] his reward, found himself in such a minority as seldom was before.

Minority, I know, there always was: but there are degrees of it, down to minority

---

23. In classical myth, Enceladus was a giant with a hundred arms who fought against the Olympian gods and was buried by Zeus under Mount Etna; the fiery breath of the buried giant was thought to cause the mountain to erupt.

24. Flunkies were individuals employed to perform menial duties, but the term came to indicate "yes-men" as well.

of one,—down to suppression of the unfortunate minority, and reducing it to zero, that the flunky-world may have peace from it henceforth. The flunky-world has peace; and descends, manipulating its ballot-boxes, Coppock[25] suffrages, and divine constitutional apparatus; quoting its Dismal Sciences, Statistics, and other satisfactory Gospels and Talmuds,[26]—into the throat of the Devil; not bothered by the importunate minority on the road. Did you never hear of "Crucify him! Crucify him!"[27] That was a considerable feat in the suppressing of minorities; and is still talked-of on Sundays,—with very little understanding, when I last heard of it. My friends, my friends, I fear we are a stupid people; and stuffed with such delusions, above all with such immense hypocrisies and self-delusions, from our birth upwards, as no people were before; God help us!—Emancipated? Yes, indeed, we are emancipated out of several things, and into several things. No man, wise or foolish, any longer can control you for good or for evil. Foolish Tomkins, foolish Jobson,[28] cannot now singly oppress you: but if the Universal Company of the Tomkinses and Jobsons, as by law established, can more than ever? If, on all highways and byways, that lead to other than a Tomkins-Jobson winning-post, you meet, at the second step, the big, dumb, universal genius of Chaos, and are so placidly yet peremptorily taught, "Halt here!" There is properly but one slavery in the world. One slavery, in which all other slaveries and miseries that afflict the earth are included; compared with which the worst West-Indian, white, or black, or yellow slaveries are a small matter. One slavery over which the very gods weep. Other slaveries, women and children and stump-orators weep over; but this is for men and gods! [*Sensation; some, however, took snuff.*]

If precisely the Wisest Man were at the top of society, and the next-wisest next, and so on till we reached the Demerara Nigger (from whom downwards, through the horse, etc., there is no question hitherto), then were this a perfect world, the extreme *maximum* of wisdom produced in it. That is how you might produce your maximum, would some god assist. And I can tell you also how the *minimum* were producible. Let no man in particular be put at the top; let all men be accounted equally wise and worthy, and the notion get abroad that anybody or nobody will do well enough at the top; that money (to which may be added success in stump-oratory) is the real symbol of wisdom, and supply-and-demand the all-sufficient substitute for command and obedience among two-legged animals of the unfeathered class: accomplish all those remarkable convictions in your thinking department; and then in your practical, as is fit, decide by count of heads, the vote of a Demerara Nigger equal and no more to that of a Chancellor Bacon:[29] this, I perceive, will (so soon as it is fairly under way, and *all* obstructions left behind) give the *minimum* of wisdom in your proceedings. Thus were your minimum

---

25. James Coppock (1798–1857) was an election agent.
26. Sacred Jewish Scriptures.
27. The cry of the Jews to the Roman governor Pilate when he finds no fault in Jesus: see John 19:6.
28. See note 19.
29. Sir Francis Bacon, later Lord Verulam (1561–1625), Lord Chancellor to James I, was a famous philosopher, scientist, and statesman.

producible,—with no God needed to assist, nor any Demon even, except the general Demon of *Ignavia* (Unvalour), lazy Indifference to the production or non-production of such things, which runs in our own blood. Were it beautiful, think you? Folly in such million-fold majority, at length peaceably supreme in this earth. Advancing on you as the huge buffalo-phalanx[30] does in the Western Deserts; or as, on a smaller scale, those bristly creatures did in the Country of the Gadarenes.[31] Rushing, namely, in wild *stampede* (the Devil being in them, some small fly having stung them), boundless,—one wing on that edge of your horizon, the other wing on that, and rearward whole tides and oceans of them:—so could Folly rush; the enlightened public one huge Gadarenes-swinery, tail cocked, snout in air, with joyful animating short squeak; fast and ever faster; down steep places,—to the sea of Tiberias, and the bottomless cloacas[32] of Nature: quenched there, since nowhere sooner. My friends, such sight is *too* sublime, if you are out in it, and are not of it!—

Well, *except* by Mastership and Servantship, there is no conceivable deliverance from Tyranny and Slavery. Cosmos is not Chaos, simply by this one quality, That it is governed. Where wisdom, even approximately, can contrive to govern, all is right, or is ever striving to become so; where folly is "emancipated," and gets to govern, as it soon will, all is wrong. That is the sad fact; and in other places than Demerara, and in regard to other interests than those of sugar-making, we sorrowfully experience the same.

I have to complain that, in these days, the relation of master to servant, and of superior to inferior, in all stages of it, is fallen sadly out of joint. As may well be, when the very highest stage and form of it, which should be the summary of all and the keystone of all, is got to such a pass. Kings themselves are grown sham-kings; and their subjects very naturally are sham-subjects; with mere lip-homage, insincere to their sham-kings;—sincere chiefly when they get into the streets (as is now our desperate case generally in Europe) to shoot them down as nuisances.[33] Royalty is terribly gone; and loyalty in consequence has had to go. No man reverences another; at the best, each man slaps the other good-humouredly on the shoulder, with, "Hail, fellow; well met:"—at the worst (which is sure enough to *follow* such unreasonable good-humour, in a world like ours), clutches him by the throat, with "Tyrannous son of perdition, shall I endure thee, then, and thy injustices forever?" We are not yet got to the worst extreme, we here in these Isles; but we are well half-way towards it, I often think.

Certainly, by any ballot-box, Jesus Christ goes just as far as Judas Iscariot; and with reason, according to the New Gospels, Talmuds and Dismal Sciences of these

30. American bison move in closely massed unison much as soldiers in the classical phalanx moved.

31. Jesus, while in the land of the Gadarenes, casts demons from a man and sends them into nearby swine. The pigs, possessed by the demons, run into the sea—the "sea of Tiberias" mentioned subsequently—and drown.

32. Sewers.

33. Carlyle refers here to the violence resulting from the political turmoil of the revolutions of 1848 on the continent.

days. Judas looks him in the face; asks proudly, "Am not I as good as thou? Better, perhaps!" slapping his breeches-pocket, in which is audible the cheerful jingle of thirty pieces of silver.[34] "Thirty of them here, thou cowering pauper!" My philanthropic friends, if there be a state of matters under the stars which deserves the name of damnable and damned, this I perceive is it! Alas, I know well whence it came, and how it could not help coming;—and I continually pray the gods its errand were done, and it had begun to go its way again. Vain hope, at least for a century to come! And there will be such a sediment of Egyptian mud to sweep away, and to fish all human things out of again, once this most sad though salutary deluge is well over, as the human species seldom had before. Patience, patience!—

In fact, without real masters you cannot have servants; and a master is not made by thirty pieces or thirty-million pieces of silver; only a sham-master is so made. The Dismal Science of this epoch defines him to be master good enough; but he is not such: you can see what kind of master he proves, what kind of servants he manages to have. Accordingly, the state of British servantship, of American help-ship—I confess to you, my friends, if looking out for what was *least* human and heroic, least lovely to the Supreme Powers, I should not go to Carolina[35] at this time; I should sorrowfully stay at home! Austere philosophers, possessed even of cash, have talked to me about the possibility of doing without servants; of trying somehow to serve yourself (boot-cleaning, etc., done by contract), and so escaping from a never-ending welter,[36] dirtier for your mind than boot-cleaning itself. Of which the perpetual *fluctuation,* and change from month to month, is probably the most inhuman element; the fruitful parent of all else that is evil, unendurable and inhuman. A poor Negro overworked on the Cuba sugar-grounds, he is sad to look upon; yet he inspires me with sacred pity, and a kind of human respect is not denied him; him, the hapless brother mortal, performing something useful in his day, and only suffering inhumanity, not doing it or being it. But with what feelings can I look upon an overfed White Flunky,[37] if I know his ways? Disloyal, unheroic, this one; *in*human in his character, and his work, and his position; more so no creature ever was. Pity is not for him, or not a soft kind of it; nor is any remedy visible, except abolition at no distant date! He is the flower of *nomadic* servitude, proceeding by month's warning, and free supply-and-demand; if obedience is not in his heart, if chiefly gluttony and mutiny are in his heart, and he has to be bribed by high feeding to do the shows of obedience,—what can await him, or be prayed for him, among men, except even "abolition"?

The Duke of Trumps,[38] who sometimes does me the honour of a little conversation, owned that the state of his domestic service was by no means satisfactory to

---

34. Judas was paid thirty pieces of silver for betraying Jesus to the authorities; see Matthew 26:14–50.

35. The antebellum Carolinas in the American South would have provided obvious instances of the oppression of slavery.

36. A rolling in turmoil.

37. See note 24.

38. As with Jellysnob mentioned in the Duke's speech, see note 19.

the human mind. "Five-and-forty of them," said his Grace; "really, I suppose, the cleverest in the market, for there is no limit to the wages: I often think how many quiet families, all down to the basis of society, I have disturbed, in attracting gradually, by higher and higher offers, that set of fellows to me; and what the use of them is when here! I feed them like aldermen, pay them as if they were sages and heroes:—Samuel Johnson's[39] wages, at the very last and best, as I have heard you say, were 300*l.* or 500*l.* a year; and Jellysnob, my butler, who indeed is clever, gets, I believe, more than the highest of these sums. And, shall I own it to you? In my young days, with one valet, I had more trouble saved me, more help afforded me to live,—actually more of my will accomplished,—than from these forty-five I now get, or ever shall. It is all a serious comedy; what you call a melancholy sham. Most civil, obsequious, and indeed expert fellows these; but bid one of them step-out of his regulated sphere on your behalf! An iron law presses on us all here; on them and on me. In my own house, how much of my will can I have done, dare I propose to have done? Prudence, on my side, is prescribed by a jealous and ridiculous point-of-honour attitude on theirs. They lie here more like a troop of foreign soldiers that had invaded me, than a body of servants I had hired. At free quarters; we have strict laws of war established between us; they make their salutes, and do certain bits of specified work, with many becks and scrapings; but as to *service,* properly so-called—!—I lead the life of a servant, sir; it is I that am a slave; and often I think of packing the whole brotherhood of them out of doors one good day, and retiring to furnished lodgings; but have never done it yet!"—Such was the confession of his Grace.

For, indeed, in the long-run, it is not possible to buy *obedience* with money. You may buy work done with money: from cleaning boots to building houses, and to far higher functions, there is much work bought with money, and got done in a supportable manner. But, mark withal, that is only from a class of supportably wise human creatures: from a huge and ever-increasing insupportably foolish class of human creatures you cannot buy work in that way; and the attempt in London itself, much more in Demerara, turns out a very "serious comedy" indeed! Who has not heard of the Distressed Needlewomen[40] in these days? We have thirty-thousand Distressed Needlewomen,—the most of whom cannot sew a reasonable stitch; for they are, in fact, Mutinous Serving-maids, who, instead of learning to work and to obey, learned to give warning: "Then suit yourself, Ma'am!"[41] Hapless enfranchised White Women, who took the "freedom" to serve the Devil with their faculties, instead of serving God or man; hapless souls, they were "enfranchised" to a most high degree, and had not the wisdom for so ticklish a predicament,—"Then suit yourself, Ma'am;"—and so have tumbled from one stage of folly to the other

39. Samuel Johnson (1709–1784) was an eighteenth-century British essayist and lexicographer, the extent of whose knowledge was legendary.

40. Women who earned their livings by sewing served as ready (and quite real) examples of abusive working conditions. See "The Slave of the Needle" and "The Song of the Shirt" in part 3.

41. Carlyle supplies the supposed petulant rejoinder of a servant to her mistress, a surly response that carries the implicit threat of her leaving the mistress's employ.

stage; and at last are on the street, with five hungry senses, and no available faculty whatever. Having finger and thumb, they do procure a needle, and call themselves Distressed Needlewomen, but cannot sew at all. I have inquired in the proper places, and find a quite passionate demand for women that can sew,—such being unattainable just now. "As well call them Distressed Astronomers as Distressed Needlewomen!" said a lady to me: "I myself will take three *sewing* Needlewomen, if you can get them for me today." Is not that a sight to set before the curious?

Distressed enough, God knows;—but it will require quite other remedies to get at the bottom of *their* complaint, I am afraid. O Brothers! O Sisters! It is for these White Women that my heart bleeds and my soul is heavy; it is for the sight of such mad notions and such unblessed doings now all-prevalent among mankind,—alas, it is for such life-theories and such life-practices, and ghastly clearstarched[42] life-hypocrisies, playing their part under high Heaven, as render these inevitable and unaidable,—that the world of today looks black and vile to me, and with all its guineas, in the nostril smells badly! It is not to the West Indies that I run first of all; and not thither with "enfranchisement" first of all, when I discern what "enfranchisement" has led to in hopefuler localities. I tell you again and again, he or she that will not work, and in the anger of the gods cannot be compelled to work, shall die! And not he or she only: alas, alas, were it the guilty only!—But as yet we cannot help it; as yet, for a long while, we must be patient, and let the Exeter-Hallery and other tragic Tomfoolery rave itself out. [*Deep silence in the small remnant of audience;—the gentleman in white trousers came in again, his creaking painfully audible in spite of efforts.*]

My friends, it is not good to be without a servant in this world; but to be without master, it appears, is a still fataler predicament for some. Without a master, in certain cases, you become a Distressed Needlewoman, and cannot so much as live. Happy he who has found his master, I will say; if not a good master, then some supportable approximation to a good one; for the worst, it appears, in some cases, is preferable to none!

Happy he who has found a master;—and now, farther I will say, having found, let him well keep him. In all human relations *permanency* is what I advocate; *nomadism*,[43] continual change, is what I perceive to be prohibitory of any good whatsoever. Two men that have got to coöperate will do well not to quarrel at the first cause of offence, and throw-up the concern in disgust, hoping to suit themselves better elsewhere. For the most part such hope is fallacious; and they will, on the average, not suit themselves better, but only about as well,—and have to begin again *bare*, which loss often repeated becomes immense, and is finally the loss of everything, and of their joint enterprise itself. For no mutual relation while it continues "bare," is yet a human one, or can bring blessedness, but is only waiting to become such,—mere new-piled crags, which, if you leave them, *will* at last

42. The starched collars associated with the philanthropists of Exeter Hall whom Carlyle consistently criticized.

43. Carlyle defines the status of a worker as nomadic in the laissez-faire system, thereby associating it with a lower state of cultural development.

"gather moss," and yield some verdure and pasture. O my friends, what a remedy is this we have fallen upon, for everything that goes wrong between one man and another: "Go, then; I give you a month's warning!" What would you think of a sacrament of marriage constructed on such principles? Marriage by the month,— why this too has been tried, and is still extensively practised in spite of Law and Gospel; but it is not found to do! The legislator, the preacher, all rational mortals, answer, "No, no!" You must marry for longer than a month, and the contract not so easily revocable, even should mistakes occur, as they sometimes do.

I am prepared to maintain against all comers, That in every human relation, from that of husband and wife down to that of master and servant, *nomadism* is the bad plan, and continuance the good. A thousand times, since I first had servants, it has occurred to me, How much better had I servants that were bound to me, and to whom I were bound! Doubtless it were not easy; doubtless it is now impossible: but if it could be done! I say, if the Black gentleman is born to be a servant, and, in fact, is useful in God's creation only as a servant, then let him hire not by the month, but by a very much longer term. That he be "hired for life,"— really here is the essence of the position he now holds! Consider that matter. All else is abuse in it, and this only is essence;—and the abuses must be cleared away. They must and shall! Yes; and the thing itself seems to offer (its abuses once cleared away) a possibility of the most precious kind for the Black man and for us. Servants hired for life, or by a contract for a long period, and not easily dissoluble; so and not otherwise would all reasonable mortals, Black and White, wish to hire and to be hired! I invite you to reflect on that; for you will find it true. And if true, it is important for us, in reference to this Negro Question and some others. The Germans say, "you must empty-out the bathing-tub, but not the baby along with it." Fling-out your dirty water with all zeal, and set it careering down the kennels;[44] but try if you can keep the little child!

How to abolish the abuses of slavery, and save the precious thing in it, alas, I do not pretend that this is easy, that it can be done in a day, or a single generation, or a single century: but I do surmise or perceive that it will, by straight methods or by circuitous, need to be done (not in the West-Indian regions alone); and that the one way of helping the Negro at present (Distressed Needlewomen etc. being quite out of our reach) were, by piously and strenuously beginning it. Begun it must be, I perceive; and carried on in all regions where servants are born and masters; and are *not* prepared to become Distressed Needlewomen, or Demerara Niggers, but to live in some human manner with one another. And truly, my friends, with regard to this world-famous Nigger Question,—which perhaps is louder than it is big, after all,—I would advise you to attack it on that side. Try against the dirty water, with an eye to *save* the baby! That will be a quite new point of attack; where, it seems to me, some real benefit and victory for the poor Negro, might before long be accomplished; and something else than Demerara freedom (with its rum-bottle and no breeches—"baby" quite *gone* down into the kennels!), or than American

44. Gutters in the street designed to drain off refuse.

stump-oratory, with mutual exasperation fast rising to the desperate pitch, might be possible for philanthropic men and women of the Anglo-Saxon type. Try this; perhaps the very Carolina planter will cooperate with you; he will, if he has any wisdom left in this exasperation! If he do not, he will do worse; and go a strange road with those Niggers of his.

By one means or another these enormities we hear of from the Slave States,— though I think they are hardly so hideous, any of them, as the sight our own Demerara now offers,—must be heard of no more. Men will and must summon "indignation-meetings" about them; and simple persons,—like Wilhelm Meister's[45] Felix flying at the cook's throat for plucking pigeons, yet himself seen shortly after pelting frogs to death with pebbles that lay handy,—will agitate their caucuses, ballot-boxes, dissever the Union, and, in short, play the very devil, if these things are not abated, and do not go on abating more and more towards perfect abolition. *Unjust* master over servant *hired for life* is, once for all, and shall be, unendurable to human souls. To *cut* the tie, and "fling Farmer Hodge's[46] horses quite loose" upon the supply-and-demand principle: that, I will believe, is not the method! But by some method, by hundredfold restrictions, responsibilities, laws, conditions, cunning methods, Hodge must be got to treat his horses *justly*, for we cannot stand it longer. And let Hodge think well of it,—I mean the American two-footed Hodge,—for there is no other salvation for him. And if he would avoid a consummation like our Demerara one, I would advise him to know this secret; which our poor Hodge did not know, or would not practise, and so is come to such a pass!—Here is part of my answer to the Hon. Hickory Buckskin,[47] a senator in those Southern States, and man of really respectable attainments and dimensions, who in his despair appears to be entertaining very violent projects now and then, as to uniting with our West Indies (under a *New Downing Street*),[48] forming a West-Indian empire, etc., etc.

"The *New Downing Street*, I take it, is at a great distance here; and we shall wait yet a while for it, and run good risk of losing all our Colonies before we can discover the way of managing them. On that side do not reckon upon help. At the same time, I can well understand you should 'publicly discuss the propriety of severing the Union,' and that the resolution should be general, 'you will rather die,' etc. A man, having certified himself about his trade and post under the sun, is actually called upon to 'die' in vindication of it, if needful; in defending the possibilities he has of carrying it on, and eschewing with it the belly of Perdition, when extraneous Insanity is pushing it thither. All this I presuppose of you, of men born of your lineage; and have not a word to say against it.

45. Wilhelm Meister is the main character in two works by Johann Wolfgang von Goethe (1749–1832): *Wilhelm Meister's Apprenticeship* (1795–96) and *Wilhelm Meister's Wanderings* (1821–29). Wilhelm abandons his illegitimate son Felix but later accepts his responsibilities as a father.

46. See note 19.

47. See note 19.

48. Downing Street was often used as a synonym for the British government. In 1725, George II made 10 Downing Street the official residence of the Prime Minister and the place where the cabinet holds its meetings. The Chancellor of the Exchequer resides at 11 Downing Street, and 12 Downing Street is the office of the government whip.

"Meanwhile suffer me to say this other thing. You will not find Negro Slavery defensible by the mere resolution, never so extensive, to defend it. No, there is another condition wanted: That your relation to the Negroes, in this thing called slavery (with such an emphasis upon the word) be actually fair, just and according to the facts;—fair, I say, not in the sight of New-England platforms,[49] but of God Almighty the Maker of both Negroes and you. That is the one ground on which men can take their stand; in the long-run all human causes, and this cause too, will come to be settled *there*. Forgive me for saying that I do not think you have yet got to that point of perfection with your Negro relations; that there is probably much in them *not* fair, nor agreeable to the Maker of us, and to the eternal laws of fact as written in the Negro's being and in ours.

"The advice of advices, therefore, to men so circumstanced were, With all diligence make them so! Otherwise than *so,* they are doomed by Earth and by Heaven. Demerara may be the maddest remedy, as I think it is a very mad one: but some remedy we must have; or if none, then destruction and annihilation, by the Demerara or a worse method. These things it would behove you of the Southern States, above all men, to be now thinking of. How to make the Negro's position among his White fellow-creatures a just one,—the real and genuine expression of what *commandment* the Maker has given to both of you, by making the one of you thus and the other so, and putting you in juxtaposition on this Earth of His? That you should *cut* the ligature, and say, 'He has made us equal,' would be saying a palpable falsity, big with hideous ruin for all concerned in it: I hope and believe, you, with our example before you, will say something much better than that. But something, very many things, do not hide from yourselves, will require to be said! And I do not pretend that it will be easy or soon done, to get a proper code of laws (and still more difficult, a proper system of habits, ways of thinking, for a basis to such 'code') on the rights of Negroes and Whites. But that also, you may depend upon it, has fallen to White men as a duty;—to you now in the first place, after our sad failure. And unless you can do it, be certain, neither will you be able to keep your Negroes; your portion too will be the Demerara or a worse one. This seems to me indubitable.

"Or perhaps you have already begun? Persist diligently, if so; but at all events, begin! For example, ought there not to be in every Slave State, a fixed legal sum, on paying which, any Black man was entitled to demand his freedom? Settle a fair sum; and let it stand fixed by law. If the poor Black can, by forethought, industry, self-denial, accumulate this sum, has he not proved the actual 'freedom' of his soul, to a fair extent: in God's name, why will you keep his body captive? It seems to me a well-considered law of this kind might do you invaluable service.—[M]ight it not be a real *safety-valve,* and ever-open *chimney,* for that down-pressed Slave-world with whatever injustices are still in it; whereby all the stronger and really worthier elements would escape peaceably, as they arose, instead of accumulating there, and convulsing you, as now? Or again, look at the Serfs of the Middle Ages: they married and gave in marriage, nay, they could not even be *divorced* from their natal

---

49. New England was the center of abolitionist activity.

soil; had home, family, and a treatment that was human. Many laws, and gradually a whole code of laws, on this matter could be made! And will have to be made; if you would avoid the ugly Demerara issue, or even uglier which may be in store. I can see no other road for you. This new question has arisen, million-voiced: 'What *are* the wages of a Black servant, hired for life by White men?' This question must be answered, in some not insupportably erroneous way: gods and men are warning you that you must answer it, if you would continue there!"—The Hon. Hickory never acknowledged my letter; but I hope he is getting on with the advice I gave him, all the same!

For the rest, I never thought the "rights of Negroes" worth much discussing, nor the rights of men in any form; the grand point, as I once said, is the *mights* of men,—what portion of their "rights" they have a chance of getting sorted out, and realised, in this confused world. We will not go deep into the question here about the Negro's rights. We will give a single glance into it, and see, for one thing, how complex it is.

West-India Islands, still full of waste fertility, produce abundant pumpkins: pumpkins, however, you will observe, are not the sole requisite for human well-being. No; for a pig they are the one thing needful: but for a man they are only the first of several things needful. The first is here; but the second and remaining, how are they to be got? The answer is wide as human society itself. Society at large, as instituted in each country of the world, is the answer such country has been able to give: Here, in this poor country, the rights of man and the mights of man are—such and such! An approximate answer to a question capable only of better and better solutions, never of any perfect, or absolutely good one. Nay, if we inquire, with much narrower scope, as to the right of chief management in cultivating those West-India lands: as to the "right of property" so-called, and of doing what you like with your own? Even this question is abstruse enough. Who it may be that has a right to raise pumpkins and other produce on those Islands, perhaps none can, except temporarily, decide. The Islands are good withal for pepper, for sugar, for sago, arrow-root, for coffee, perhaps for cinnamon and precious spices; things far nobler than pumpkins; and leading towards Commerces, Arts, Politics and Social Developments, which alone are the noble product, where men (and not pigs with pumpkins) are the parties concerned! Well, all this fruit too, fruit spicy and commercial, fruit spiritual and celestial, so far beyond the merely pumpkinish and grossly terrene, lies in the West-India lands: and the ultimate "proprietorship" of them,—why, I suppose, it will vest in him who can the *best* educe from them whatever of noble produce they were created fit for yielding. He, I compute, is the real "Vicegerent of the Maker"[50] there; in him, better and better chosen, and not in another, is the "property" vested by decree of Heaven's chancery itself![51]

---

50. A vicegerent is an administrative deputy, one who carries the power of the ruler.

51. In a tradition derived from Locke, Carlyle goes on to argue that property consists in what a person with freedom to act or work can produce from anything previously undeveloped. Property or wealth, in this sense, is the result of work. It is this understanding of possessions that enabled colonizing Europeans to regard vast lands as not the *property* of indigenous populations—the natives were

Up to this time it is the Saxon British mainly; they hitherto have cultivated with some manfulness: and when a manfuler class of cultivators, stronger, worthier to have such land, abler to bring fruit from it, shall make their appearance,—they, doubt it not, by fortune of war, and other confused negotiation and vicissitude, will be declared by Nature and Fact to *be* the worthier, and will become proprietors,—perhaps also only for a time. That is the law, I take it; ultimate, supreme, for all lands in all countries under this sky. The one perfect eternal proprietor is the Maker who created them: the temporary better or worse proprietor is he whom the Maker has sent on that mission; he who the best hitherto can educe from said lands the beneficent gifts the Maker endowed them with; or, which is but another definition of the same person, he who leads hitherto the manfulest life on that bit of soil, doing, better than another yet found can do, the Eternal Purpose and Supreme Will there.

And now observe, my friends, it was not Black Quashee, or those he represents, that made those West-India Islands what they are, or can, by any hypothesis, be considered to have the right of growing pumpkins there. For countless ages, since they first mounted oozy, on the back of earthquakes, from their dark bed in the Ocean deeps, and reeking saluted the tropical Sun, and ever onwards till the European white man first saw them some three short centuries ago, those Islands had produced mere jungle, savagery, poison-reptiles and swamp-malaria: till the white European first saw them, they were as if not yet created,—their noble elements of cinnamon, sugar, coffee, pepper black and grey, lying all asleep, waiting the white enchanter who should say to them, Awake! Till the end of human history and the sounding of the Trump of Doom,[52] they might have lain so, had Quashee and the like of him been the only artists in the game. Swamps[,] fever-jungles, man-eating Caribs, rattlesnakes, and reeking waste and putrefaction, this had been the produce of them under the incompetent Caribal (what we call Cannibal) possessors, till that time; and Quashee knows, himself, whether ever he could have introduced an improvement. Him, had he by a miraculous chance been wafted thither, the Caribals would have eaten, rolling him as a fat morsel under their tongue; for him, till the sounding of the Trump of Doom, the rattlesnakes and savageries would have held-on their way. It was not he, then; it was another than he! Never by art of his could one pumpkin have grown there to solace any human throat; nothing but savagery and reeking putrefaction could have grown there. These plentiful pumpkins, I say therefore, are not his: no, they are another's; they are his only under conditions. Conditions which Exeter Hall, for the present, has forgotten; but which Nature and the Eternal Powers have by no manner of means forgotten, but do at all moments keep in mind; and, at the right moment, will, with the due impressiveness, perhaps in a rather terrible manner, bring again to our mind also!

---

not doing anything with the lands, not working them, and, accordingly, the lands were not owned but rather free to become the property of the European developer.

52. The end of the world and beginning of the millennium were to be inaugurated by blasts from the trumpets of seven angels: see Revelations 8–11.

If Quashee will not honestly aid in bringing-out those sugars, cinnamons and nobler products of the West-Indian Islands, for the benefit of all mankind, then I say neither will the Powers permit Quashee to continue growing pumpkins there for his own lazy benefit; but will shear him out, by and by, like a lazy gourd overshadowing rich ground; him and all that partake with him,—perhaps in a very terrible manner. For, under favour of Exeter Hall, the "terrible manner" is not yet quite extinct with the Destinies in this Universe; nor will it quite cease, I apprehend, for soft sawder[53] or philanthropic stump-oratory now or henceforth. No; the gods wish besides pumpkins, that spices and valuable products be grown in their West Indies; thus much they have declared in so making the West Indies:— infinitely more they wish, that manful industrious men occupy their West Indies, not indolent two-legged cattle, however "happy" over their abundant pumpkins! Both these things, we may be assured, the immortal gods have decided upon, passed their eternal Act of Parliament for: and both of them, though all terrestrial Parliaments and entities oppose it to the death, shall be done. Quashee, if he will not help in bringing-out the spices, will get himself made a slave again (which state will be a little less ugly than his present one), and with beneficent whip, since other methods avail not, will be compelled to work.

Or, alas, let him look across to Haiti,[54] and trace a far sterner prophecy! Let him, by his ugliness, idleness, rebellion, banish all White men from the West Indies, and make it all one Haiti,—with little or no sugar growing, black Peter exterminating black Paul, and where a garden of the Hesperides[55] might be, nothing but a tropical dog-kennel and pestiferous jungle,—does he think that will forever continue pleasant to gods and men? I see men, the rose-pink cant all peeled away from them, land one day on those black coasts; men *sent* by the Laws of this Universe, and inexorable Course of Things; men hungry for gold, remorseless, fierce as the old Buccaneers were;—and a doom for Quashee which I had rather not contemplate! The gods are long-suffering; but the law from the beginning was, He that will not work shall perish from the earth; and the patience of the gods has limits!

Before the West Indies could grow a pumpkin for any Negro, how much European heroism had to spend itself in obscure battle; to sink, in mortal agony, before the jungles, the putrescences and waste savageries could become arable, and the Devils be in some measure chained there! The West Indies grow pine-apples, and sweet fruits, and spices; we hope they will one day grow beautiful Heroic human Lives too, which is surely the ultimate object they were made for: beautiful souls and brave; sages, poets, what not; making the Earth nobler round them, as their kindred from of old have been doing; true "splinters of the old Harz Rock";[56] heroic white men, worthy to be called old Saxons, browned with a mahogany tint

53. Flattery.
54. Haiti had been the first Caribbean territory to secure independence in 1804, but its subsequent history was marred by violent internal strife.
55. In classical myth, the Garden of the Hesperides was an Edenic region where the three sister Hesperides guarded the golden apples of Hera.
56. The northernmost mountain range in Germany settled by the Upper and the Lower Saxons.

in those new climates and conditions. But under the soil of Jamaica, before it could even produce spices or any pumpkin, the bones of many thousand British men had to be laid. Brave Colonel Fortescue, brave Colonel Sedgwick, brave Colonel Brayne,—the dust of many thousand strong old English hearts lies there; worn-down swiftly in frightful travail, chaining the Devils, which were manifold. Heroic Blake contributed a bit of his life to that Jamaica. A bit of the great Protector's[57] own life lies there; beneath those pumpkins lies a bit of the life that was Oliver Cromwell's. How the great Protector would have rejoiced to think, that all this was to issue in growing pumpkins to keep Quashee in a comfortably idle condition! No; that is not the ultimate issue; not that.

The West-Indian Whites, so soon as this bewilderment of philanthropic and other jargon abates from them, and their poor eyes get to discern a little what the Facts are and what the Laws are, will strike into another course, I apprehend! I apprehend they will, as a preliminary, resolutely *refuse* to permit the black man any privilege whatever of pumpkins till he agree for work in return. Not a square inch of soil in those fruitful Isles, purchased by British blood, shall any Black man hold to grow pumpkins for him, except on terms that are fair towards Britain. Fair; see that they be not unfair, not towards ourselves, and still more, not towards him. For injustice is *forever* accursed: and precisely our unfairness towards the enslaved Black man has,—by inevitable revulsion and fated turn of the wheel,—brought about these present confusions.

Fair towards Britain it will be, that Quashee give work for privilege to grow pumpkins. Not a pumpkin, Quashee, not a square yard of soil, till you agree to do the State so many days of service. Annually that soil will grow you pumpkins; but annually also, without fail, shall you, for the owner thereof, do your appointed days of labour. The State has plenty of waste soil; but the State will religiously give you none of it on other terms. The State wants sugar from these Islands, and means to have it; wants virtuous industry in these Islands, and must have it. The State demands of you such service as will bring these results, this latter result which includes all. Not a Black Ireland, by immigration, and boundless black supply for the demand;—not that, may the gods forbid!—but a regulated West Indies, with black working population in adequate numbers; all "happy," if they find it possible; and *not* entirely unbeautiful to gods and men, which latter result they *must* find possible! All "happy," enough; that is to say, all working according to the faculty they have got, making a little more divine this Earth which the gods have given them. Is there any other "happiness,"—if it be not that of pigs fattening daily to the slaughter? So will the State speak by and by.

Any poor idle Black man, any idle White man, rich or poor, is a mere eye-sorrow to the State; a perpetual blister on the skin of the State. The State is taking

---

57. The Great Protector was Oliver Cromwell (1599–1658), who ruled over England as Lord Protector from 1653 until his death. England acquired Jamaica (in May 1655) while Cromwell was in power; the other men Carlyle mentions were prominent in the early history of British rule in the Caribbean, Robert Blake (1599–1657) most notably as the commander of the British fleet that took possession of Jamaica.

measures, some of them rather extensive, in Europe at this very time, and already, as in Paris, Berlin and elsewhere, rather tremendous measures, to *get* its rich white men set to work; for alas, they also have long sat Negro-like up to the ears in pumpkin, regardless of "work," and of a world all going to waste for their idleness! Extensive measures, I say; and already (as, in all European lands, this scandalous Year of street-barricades and fugitive sham-kings exhibits) *tremendous* measures; for the thing is urgent to be done.[58]

The thing must be done everywhere; *must* is the word. Only it is so terribly difficult to do; and will take generations yet, this of getting our rich European white men "set to work"! But yours in the West Indies, my obscure black friends, your work, and the getting of you set to it, is a simple affair; and by diligence, the West-Indian legislatures, and Royal governors, setting their faces fairly to the problem, will get it done. You are not "slaves" now; nor do I wish, if it can be avoided, to see you slaves again: but decidedly you have to be servants to those that are born *wiser* than you, that are born lords of you; servants to the Whites, if they *are* (as what mortal can doubt they are?) born wiser than you. That, you may depend on it, my obscure Black friends, is and was always the Law of the World, for you and for all men: To *be* servants, the more foolish of us to the more wise; and only sorrow, futility and disappointment will betide both, till both in some approximate degree get to conform to the same. Heaven's laws are not repealable by Earth, however Earth may try,—and it has been trying hard, in some directions, of late! I say, no well-being, and in the end no being at all, will be possible for you or us, if the law of Heaven is not complied with. And if "slave" mean essentially "servant hired for life,"—for life, or by a contract of long continuance and not easily dissoluble,—I ask once more, Whether, in all human things, the "contract of long continuance" is not precisely the contract to be desired, were the right terms once found for it? Servant hired for life, were the right terms once found, which I do not pretend they are, seems to me much preferable to servant hired for the month, or by contract dissoluble in a day. What that amounts to, we have known, and our thirty-thousand Distressed Astronomers have known; and we don't want that! [*Some assent in the small remnant of an audience. "Silence!" from the Chair.*]

To state articulately, and put into practical Lawbooks, what on all sides is *fair* from the West-Indian White to the West-Indian Black; what relations the Eternal Maker *has* established between these two creatures of His; what He has written down with intricate but ineffaceable record, legible to candid human insight, in the respective qualities, strengths, necessities and capabilities of each of the two: this, as I told the Hon. Hickory my Carolina correspondent, will be a long problem; only to be solved by continuous human endeavour, and earnest effort gradually perfecting itself as experience successively yields new light to it. This will be to "*find* the right terms"; terms of a contract that will endure, and be sanctioned by Heaven, and obtain prosperity on Earth, between the two. A long problem, terribly

58. Carlyle again refers to the political unrest and violence of the revolutions of 1848 on the continent.

neglected hitherto;—whence these West-Indian sorrows, and Exeter-Hall monstrosities, just now! But a problem which must be entered upon, and by degrees be completed. A problem which, I think, the English People also, if they mean to retain human Colonies, and not Black Irelands in addition to the White, cannot begin too soon. What are the true relations between Negro and White, their mutual duties under the sight of the Maker of them both; what human laws will assist both to comply more and more with these? The solution, only to be gained by honest endeavour, and sincere reading of experience, such as have never yet been bestowed on it, is not yet here; the solution is perhaps still distant. But some approximation to it, various real approximations, could be made, and must be made:—this of declaring that Negro and White are *un*related, loose from one another, on a footing of perfect equality, and subject to no law but that of supply-and-demand according to the Dismal Science; this, which contradicts the palpablest facts, is clearly no solution, but a cutting of the knot asunder; and every hour we persist in this is leading us towards *dis*solution instead of solution!

What, then, is practically to be done by us poor English with our Demerara and other blacks? Well, in such a mess as we have made there, it is not easy saying what is first to be done! But all this of perfect equality, of cutting quite loose from one another; all this, with "immigration loan," "happiness of black peasantry," and the other melancholy stuff that has followed from it, will first of all require to be *un*done, and the ground cleared of it, by way of preliminary to "doing"! After that there may several things be possible.

Already one hears of Black *Adscripti glebae;*[59] which seems a promising arrangement, one of the first to suggest itself in such a complicacy. It appears the Dutch Blacks, in Java,[60] are already a kind of *Adscripts,* after the manner of the old European serfs; bound, by royal authority, to give so many days of work a year. Is not this something like a real approximation; the first step towards all manner of such? Wherever, in British territory, there exists a Black man, and needful work to the just extent is not to be got out of him, such a law, in defect of better, should be brought to bear upon said Black man! How many laws of like purport, conceivable some of them, might be brought to bear upon the Black man and the White, with all despatch by way of solution instead of dissolution to their complicated case just now! On the whole, it ought to be rendered possible, ought it not, for White men to live beside Black men, and in some just manner to command Black men, and produce West-Indian fruitfulness by means of them? West-Indian fruitfulness will need to be produced. If the English cannot find the method for that, they may rest assured there will another come (Brother Jonathan[61] or still another) who can. He

59. A slave to the earth: someone bound to an estate or lord. The English *adscript* that Carlyle uses in the next sentence derives from this legal Latin phrase.

60. The Dutch government needed to suppress a native revolt on Java during the years 1825–30, and tensions in Java remained high through the mid-century.

61. Brother Jonathan is the United States. The phrase originally meant a problem solver and supposedly derives from George Washington's saying, when he needed advice about his lack of ammunition, "we must consult Brother Jonathan." Washington consulted Jonathan Trumbull (1710–1785), Governor of Connecticut, who did find a solution to the problem.

it is whom the gods will bid continue in the West Indies; bidding us ignominiously, "Depart, ye quack-ridden, incompetent!"—

One other remark, as to the present Trade in Slaves, and to our suppression of the same. If buying of Black war-captives in Africa, and bringing them over to the Sugar Islands for sale again be, as I think it is, a contradiction of the Laws of this Universe, let us heartily pray Heaven to end the practice; let us ourselves help Heaven to end it, wherever the opportunity is given. If it be the most flagrant and alarming contradiction to the said Laws which is now witnessed on this Earth; so flagrant and alarming that a just man cannot exist, and follow his affairs, in the same Planet with it; why, then indeed— —But is it, quite certainly, such? Alas, look at that group of *un*sold, unbought, unmarketable Irish "free" citizens, dying there in the ditch, whither my Lord of Rackrent[62] and the constitutional sheriffs have evicted them; or at those "divine missionaries," of the same free country, now traversing, with rags on back, and child on each arm, the principal thoroughfares of London, to tell men what "freedom" really is;—and admit that there may be doubts on that point! But if it *is*, I say, the most alarming contradiction to the said Laws which is now witnessed on this earth; so flagrant a contradiction that a just man cannot exist, and follow his affairs, in the same Planet with it, then, sure enough, let us, in God's name, fling-aside all our affairs, and hasten out to put an end to it, as the first thing the Heavens want us to do. By all manner of means. This thing done, the Heavens will prosper all other things with us! Not a doubt of it,— provided your premiss be not doubtful.

But now, furthermore, give me leave to ask, Whether the way of doing it is this somewhat surprising one, of trying to blockade the continent of Africa itself, and to watch slave-ships along that extremely extensive and unwholesome coast?[63] The enterprise is very gigantic; and proves hitherto as futile as any enterprise has lately done. Certain wise men once, before this, set about confining the cuckoo by a big circular wall; but they could not manage it!—Watch the coast of Africa? That is a very long Coast; good part of the Coast of the terraqueous[64] Globe! And the living centres of this slave mischief, the live coals that produce all this world-wide smoke, it appears, lie simply in two points, Cuba and Brazil, which *are* perfectly accessible and manageable.

If the Laws of Heaven do authorise you to keep the whole world in a pother about this question; if you really can appeal to the Almighty God upon it, and set common interests, and terrestrial considerations, and common sense, at defiance in behalf of it,—why, in Heaven's name, not go to Cuba and Brazil with a sufficiency of Seventy-fours;[65] and signify to those nefarious countries: "Nefarious

---

62. A character in the novel *Castle Rackrent*, published in 1800 by Maria Edgeworth (1767–1849).

63. British concern about the ongoing slave trade led to patrolling of the African coast. The greater part of the remaining slave trade at this time actually was directed internally within Africa and over-land to the Ottoman Empire.

64. Made up of land and water.

65. Battleships armed with seventy-four guns.

countries, your procedure on the Negro Question is too bad; see, of all the sole-cisms now submitted to on Earth, it is the most alarming and transcendent, and, in fact, is such that a just man cannot follow his affairs any longer in the same Planet with it. You clearly will not, you nefarious populations, for love or fear, watching or entreaty, respect the rights of the Negro enough;—wherefore we here, with our Seventy-fours, are come to be King over you, and will on the spot henceforth see for ourselves that you do it!"

Why not, if Heaven do send us? The thing can be done; easily, if you are sure of that proviso.[66] It can be done: it is the way to "suppress the Slave-trade"; and so far as yet appears, the only way.

Most thinking people,—if hen-stealing prevail to a plainly unendurable extent, will you station police-officers at every hen-roost; and keep them watching and cruising incessantly to and fro over the Parish, in the unwholesome dark, at enormous expense, with almost no effect? Or will you not try rather to discover where the fox's den is, and kill the fox! Which of those two things will you do? Most thinking people, you know the fox and his den; there he is,—kill him, and discharge your cruisers and police-watchers!—[*Laughter.*]

O my friends, I feel there is an immense fund of Human Stupidity circulating among us, and much clogging our affairs for some time past! A certain man has called us, "of all peoples the wisest in action"; but he added, "the stupidest in speech":—and it is a sore thing, in these constitutional times, times mainly of universal Parliamentary and other Eloquence, that the "speakers" have all first to emit, in such tumultuous volumes, their human stupor, as the indispensable pre-liminary, and everywhere we must first see that and its results *out,* before begin-ning any business.—(*Explicit MS.*)[67]

66. An introductory stipulation, in this case the premise that the British ought to "keep the whole world in a pother about" the question of the slave trade.

67. *Explicit* is an abbreviation of *explicitus est liber*, Latin for "the book is unfolded or ended," a phrase used for books written on manuscript (MS) rolls.

JOHN HENRY NEWMAN

J OHN HENRY CARDINAL NEWMAN (1801–1890) was perhaps the most controversial religious figure of the nineteenth century in England. Raised as an
Evangelical within the Church of England, Newman attended Oxford and, soon
after graduation, became a university fellow, a position that enabled him to pursue, with friends and followers, an earnest examination of church history and doctrine. Ordained within the Anglican communion, he became vicar at St. Mary's,
the University Church, and, in the early 1830s, helped inaugurate what became
known as the Oxford or Tractarian Movement, a sustained effort to (re)establish
the authority of the English Church through an appeal to dogmatic history and an
emphasis upon liturgical ritualism and the sacraments. With others, Newman
developed the practice of composing and issuing tracts—statements on theological
issues—to foster opinions adopted by those within the movement; as he preached
and wrote about the Church of England, however, he found himself drawing
nearer to the Roman Catholic Church, and, in Tract 90, he argued that the Thirty-
Nine Articles (the principal points of the Anglican faith) were not in essential
disagreement with Roman Catholic doctrine. This tract was condemned by the
Anglican bishops and leaders at Oxford, and shortly thereafter Newman entered
into a two-year period of intense reflection about his own beliefs, subsequently
resigning his posts at Oxford in 1845 and converting to Roman Catholicism.

His conversion was a *cause célèbre,* the more so because many followed his
example. He soon took Holy Orders as a Catholic priest, founded the Oratory of
Saint Philip Neri in Birmingham, was appointed rector of the Catholic University
of Ireland in Dublin, and, shortly before his death, was elevated to become a
cardinal of the Roman Church. However, it was only in 1864, when the Anglican
rector Charles Kingsley falsely and maliciously attacked him for endorsing un-
truthfulness, that Newman began a series of writings, eventually published as
Apologia Pro Vita Sua, that constituted an explanation of his movement toward the
Roman faith. The work more than discredited Kingsley, earning Newman universal respect and prompting yet more believers to abandon the Anglican for the
Roman communion. The *Apologia* is considered a classic of spiritual autobiography and, with the unjustly ignored *The Idea of a University* (1852; rev. 1873) and the
philosophical *An Essay in Aid of a Grammar of Assent* (1870), stands as Newman's
chief contribution to nineteenth-century literature. He was also, however, a poet
and a novelist as well as a prolific writer of sermons.

"God's Will the End of Life," composed shortly after his conversion and published in 1849, provides a good example of the nineteenth-century sermon and of Newman's homiletic style: conversational yet tenacious, intellectually supple yet strongly emotional. Defining the active ministry of Christ as a work and a mission undertaken to serve God, Newman maintains that "every one . . . has a mission, has a work," asking his congregation, "is your religion a work? for if it be not, it is not religion at all." Finding the specific nature of this work, different for each person, is the spiritual task that Newman urges his listeners to address, entreating them to recognize that this endeavor is their prime business in life.

From *Discourses Addressed to Mixed Congregations*

Discourse VI
God's Will the End of Life

I am going to ask you a question, my dear brethren, so trite, and therefore so uninteresting at first sight, that you may wonder why I put it, and may object that it will be difficult to fix the mind on it, and may anticipate that nothing profitable can be made of it. It is this:—"Why were you sent into the world?" Yet, after all, it is perhaps a thought more obvious than it is common, more easy than it is familiar; I mean it ought to come into your minds, but it does not, and you never had more than a distant acquaintance with it, though that sort of acquaintance with it you have had for many years. Nay, once or twice, perhaps you have been thrown across the thought somewhat intimately, for a short season, but this was an accident which did not last. There are those who recollect the first time, as it would seem, when it came home to them. They were but little children, and they were by themselves, and they spontaneously asked themselves, or rather God spake in them, "Why am I here? how came I here? who brought me here? What am I to do here?" Perhaps it was the first act of reason, the beginning of their real responsibility, the commencement of their trial; perhaps from that day they may date their capacity, their awful power, of choosing between good and evil, and of committing mortal sin. And so, as life goes on, the thought comes vividly, from time to time, for a short season across their conscience; whether in illness, or in some anxiety, or at some season of solitude, or on hearing some preacher, or reading some religious work. A vivid feeling comes over them of the vanity and unprofitableness of the world, and then the question recurs, "Why then am I sent into it?"

And a great contrast indeed does this vain, unprofitable, yet overbearing world present with such a question as that. It seems out of place to ask such a question in so magnificent, so imposing a presence, as that of the great Babylon.[1] The world professes to supply all that we need, as if we were sent into it for the sake of being sent here, and for nothing beyond the sending. It is a great favour to have an introduction to this august world. This is to be our exposition, forsooth, of the mystery of life. Every man is doing his own will here, seeking his own pleasure, pursuing his own ends, and that is why he was brought into existence. Go abroad into the streets of the populous city, contemplate the continuous outpouring there of human energy, and the countless varieties of human character, and be satisfied! The ways are thronged, carriage-way and pavement; multitudes are hurrying to and fro, each on his own errand, or are loitering about from listlessness, or from want of work, or have come forth into the public concourse, to see and to be seen, for amusement or for display, or on the excuse of business. The carriages of the wealthy mingle with the slow wains[2] laden with provisions or merchandise, the productions of art or the demands of luxury. The streets are lined with shops, open and gay, inviting customers, and widen now and then into some spacious square or place, with lofty masses of brickwork or of stone, gleaming in the fitful sun-beam, and surrounded or fronted with what simulates a garden's foliage. Follow them in another direction, and you find the whole groundstead[3] covered with large buildings, planted thickly up and down, the homes of the mechanical arts. The air is filled, below, with a ceaseless, importunate, monotonous din, which penetrates even to your innermost chamber, and rings in your ears, even when you are not conscious of it; and overhead, with a canopy of smoke, shrouding God's day from the realms of obstinate sullen toil. This is the end of man!

Or stay at home, and take up one of those daily prints, which are so true a picture of the world; look down the columns of advertisements, and you will see the catalogue of pursuits, projects, aims, anxieties, amusements, indulgences which occupy the mind of man. He plays many parts:[4] here he has goods to sell, there he wants employment; there again he seeks to borrow money, here he offers you houses, great seats or small tenements; he has food for the million, and luxuries for the wealthy, and sovereign medicines for the credulous, and books, new and cheap, for the inquisitive. Pass on to the news of the day, and you will learn what great men are doing at home and abroad: you will read of wars and rumours of wars;[5] of debates in the Legislature; of rising men, and old statesmen going off the scene; of political contests in this city or that county; of the collision of rival interests. You will read of the money market, and the provision market,

---

1. Babylon was the city that, during certain eras of the first two millennia B.C.E., came to exercise temporary hegemony in Mesopotamia. Associated with the story of the tower of Babel (Genesis 11:1–9), Babylon early on in Hebrew Scripture assumed the role of the wickedly degenerate city, an identity preserved in the New Testament (see Revelations 17 and 18).

2. Wagons.

3. An area, usually fairly level, established as a building site.

4. From Shakespeare's *As You Like It,* 2.7.142.

5. Matthew 24:6.

and the market for metals; of the state of trade, the call for manufactures, news of ships arrived in port, of accidents at sea, of exports and imports, of gains and losses, of frauds and their detection. Go forward, and you arrive at discoveries in art and science, discoveries (so-called) in religion, the court and royalty, the entertainments of the great, places of amusement, strange trials, offences, accidents, escapes, exploits, experiments, contests, ventures. O this curious, restless, clamorous, panting being, which we call life!—and is there to be no end to all this? Is there no object in it? It never has an end, it is forsooth its own object!

And now, once more, my brethren, put aside what you see and what you read of the world, and try to penetrate into the hearts, and to reach the ideas and the feelings of those who constitute it; look into them as closely as you can; enter into their houses and private rooms; strike at random through the streets and lanes; take as they come, palace and hovel, office or factory, and what will you find? Listen to their words, witness, alas! their works; you will find in the main the same lawless thoughts, the same unrestrained desires, the same ungoverned passions, the same earthly opinions, the same wilful deeds, in high and low, learned and unlearned; you will find them all to be living for the sake of living; they one and all seem to tell you, "We are our own centre, our own end." Why are they toiling? why are they scheming? for what are they living? "We live to please ourselves; life is worthless except we have our own way; we are not *sent* here at all, but we find ourselves here, and we are but slaves unless we can think what we will, believe what we will, love what we will, hate what we will, do what we will. We detest interference on the part of God or man. We do not bargain to be rich or to be great; but we do bargain, whether rich or poor, high or low, to live for ourselves, to live for the lust of the moment, or, according to the doctrine of the hour, thinking of the future and the unseen just as much or as little as we please."

O my brethren, is it not a shocking thought, but who can deny its truth? The multitude of men are living without any aim beyond this visible scene; they may from time to time use religious words, or they may profess a communion or a worship, as a matter of course, or of expedience, or of duty, but, if there was any sincerity in such profession, the course of the world could not run as it does. What a contrast is all this to the end of life, as it is set before us in our most holy Faith! If there was one among the sons of men, who might allowably have taken His pleasure, and have done His own will here below, surely it was He who came down on earth from the bosom of the Father, and who was so pure and spotless in that human nature which He put on Him, that He could have no human purpose or aim inconsistent with the will of His Father. Yet He, the Son of God, the Eternal Word, came, not to do His own will, but His who sent Him, as you know very well is told us again and again in Scripture. Thus the Prophet in the Psalter,[6] speaking in His person, says, "Lo, I come to do Thy will, O God." And He says in the Prophet Isaias, "The Lord God hath opened Mine ear, and I do not resist; I have not gone back." And in the Gospel, when He had come on earth, "My food is to do the will

---

6. A collection of Psalms for liturgical use.

of Him that sent Me, and to finish His work." Hence, too, in His agony, He cried out, "Not My will, but Thine, be done"; and St. Paul, in like manner, says, that "Christ pleased not Himself"; and elsewhere, that, "though He was God's Son, yet learned He obedience by the things which He suffered."[7] Surely so it was; as being indeed the Eternal Co-equal Son, His will was one and the same with the Father's will, and He had no submission of will to make; but He chose to take on Him man's nature, and the will of that nature; He chose to take on Him affections, feelings, and inclinations proper to man, a will innocent indeed and good, but still a man's will, distinct from God's will; a will, which, had it acted simply according to what was pleasing to its nature, would, when pain and toil were to be endured, have held back from an active co-operation with the will of God. But, though He took on Himself the nature of man, He took not on Him that selfishness, with which fallen man wraps himself round, but in all things He devoted Himself as a ready sacrifice to His Father. He came on earth, not to take His pleasure, not to follow His taste, not for the mere exercise of human affection, but simply to glorify His Father and to do His will. He came charged with a mission, deputed for a work; He looked not to the right nor to the left, He thought not of Himself, He offered Himself up to God.

Hence it is that He was carried in the womb of a poor woman, who, before His birth, had two journeys to make, of love and of obedience, to the mountains and to Bethlehem.[8] He was born in a stable, and laid in a manger. He was hurried off to Egypt to sojourn there; then He lived till He was thirty years of age in a poor way, by a rough trade, in a small house, in a despised town. Then, when He went out to preach, He had not where to lay His head; He wandered up and down the country, as a stranger upon earth. He was driven out into the wilderness, and dwelt among the wild beasts. He endured heat and cold, hunger and weariness, reproach and calumny. His food was coarse bread, and fish from the lake, or depended on the hospitality of strangers. And as He had already left His Father's greatness on high, and had chosen an earthly home; so again, at that Father's bidding, He gave up the sole solace given Him in this world, and denied Himself His Mother's presence. He parted with her who bore Him; He endured to be strange to her; He endured to call her coldly "woman,"[9] who was His own undefiled one, all beautiful, all gracious, the best creature of His hands, and the sweet nurse of His infancy. He put her aside, as Levi,[10] His type, merited the sacred ministry, by saying to His parents and kinsmen, "I know you not." He exemplified in His own person the severe

---

7. The series of Scriptural quotations involves these passages: Psalms 40:8; Isaiah 50:5; John 4:34; Luke 22:42; Romans 15:3; Hebrews 5:8.

8. Following her conception of the Savior, Mary journeyed to the hill country to visit Zacharias and Elizabeth, who was pregnant with John the Baptist; this is the voyage of love. She traveled to Bethlehem in obedience to "the decree from Caesar Augustus that all the world should be taxed." See Luke 1:26–80; 2:1–20.

9. The reference is to the story of the wedding feast at Cana when Jesus turns to his mother and says, "Woman, what have I to do with thee? mine hour is not yet come." See John 2:1–11.

10. See Exodus 32:26–35 wherein the sons of Levi volunteer to slay for Moses all those who have worshipped the golden calf, even those who are brothers, companions, and neighbors to the Levites.

maxim, which He gave to His disciples, "He that loveth mother more than Me is not worthy of Me."[11] In all these many ways He sacrificed every wish of His own; that we might understand, that, if He, the Creator, came into His own world, not for His own pleasure, but to do His Father's will, we too have most surely some work to do, and have seriously to bethink ourselves what that work is.

Yes, so it is; realise it, my brethren;—every one who breathes, high and low, educated and ignorant, young and old, man and woman, has a mission, has a work. We are not sent into this world for nothing; we are not born at random; we are not here, that we may go to bed at night, and get up in the morning, toil for our bread, eat and drink, laugh and joke, sin when we have a mind, and reform when we are tired of sinning, rear a family and die. God sees every one of us; He creates every soul, He lodges it in the body, one by one, for a purpose. He needs, He deigns to need, every one of us. He has an end for each of us; we are all equal in His sight, and we are placed in our different ranks and stations, not to get what we can out of them for ourselves, but to labour in them for Him. As Christ has His work, we too have ours; as He rejoiced to do His work, we must rejoice in ours also.

St. Paul on one occasion speaks of the world as a scene in a theatre. Consider what is meant by this. You know, actors on a stage are on an equality with each other really, but for the occasion they assume a difference of character; some are high, some are low, some are merry, and some sad. Well, would it not be a simple absurdity in any actor to pride himself on his mock diadem, or his edgeless sword, instead of attending to his part? what, if he did but gaze at himself and his dress? what, if he secreted, or turned to his own use, what was valuable about it? Is it not his business, and nothing else, to act his part well? common sense tells us so. Now we are all but actors in this world; we are one and all equal, we shall be judged as equals as soon as life is over; yet, equal and similar in ourselves, each has his special part at present, each has his work, each has his mission,—not to indulge his passions, not to make money, not to get a name in the world, not to save himself trouble, not to follow his bent, not to be selfish and self-willed, but to do what God puts on him to do.

Look at that poor profligate in the Gospel, look at Dives;[12] do you think he understood that his wealth was to be spent, not on himself, but for the glory of God?—yet for forgetting this, he was lost for ever and ever. I will tell you what he thought, and how he viewed things:—he was a young man, and had succeeded to a good estate, and he determined to enjoy himself. It did not strike him that his wealth had any other use than that of enabling him to take his pleasure. Lazarus lay at his gate; he might have relieved Lazarus; *that* was God's will; but he managed to put conscience aside, and he persuaded himself he should be a fool, if he did not make the most of this world, while he had the means. So he resolved to have his fill of pleasure; and feasting was to his mind a principal part of it. "He fared sumptuously

11. Matthew 10:37.

12. See Luke 16:19–31 for the story of Dives and Lazarus. Newman's sense of the social work or mission of Christians as consisting in the relief of those suffering is foregrounded in his emphasis of this gospel story.

every day";[13] everything belonging to him was in the best style, as men speak; his house, his furniture, his plate of silver and gold, his attendants, his establishments. Everything was for enjoyment, and for show too; to attract the eyes of the world, and to gain the applause and admiration of his equals, who were the companions of his sins. These companions were doubtless such as became a person of such pretensions; they were fashionable men; a collection of refined, high-bred, haughty men, eating, not gluttonously, but what was rare and costly; delicate, exact, fastidious in their taste, from their very habits of indulgence; not eating for the mere sake of eating, or drinking for the mere sake of drinking, but making a sort of science of their sensuality; sensual, carnal, as flesh and blood can be, with eyes, ears, tongue, steeped in impurity, every thought, look, and sense, witnessing or ministering to the evil one who ruled them; yet, with exquisite correctness of idea and judgment, laying down rules for sinning;—heartless and selfish, high, punctilious, and disdainful in their outward deportment, and shrinking from Lazarus, who lay at the gate, as an eye-sore, who ought for the sake of decency to be put out of the way. Dives was one of such, and so he lived his short span, thinking of nothing, loving nothing, but himself, till one day he got into a fatal quarrel with one of his godless associates, or he caught some bad illness; and then he lay helpless on his bed of pain, cursing fortune and his physician, that he was no better, and impatient that he was thus kept from enjoying his youth, trying to fancy himself mending when he was getting worse, and disgusted at those who would not throw him some word of comfort in his suspense, and turning more resolutely from his Creator in proportion to his suffering;—and then at last his day came, and he died, and (oh! miserable!) "was buried in hell." And so ended he and his mission.

This was the fate of your pattern and idol, O ye, if any of you be present, young men, who, though not possessed of wealth and rank, yet affect the fashions of those who have them. You, my brethren, have not been born splendidly or nobly; you have not been brought up in the seats of liberal education; you have no high connexions; you have not learned the manners nor caught the tone of good society; you have no share of the largeness of mind, the candour, the romantic sense of honour, the correctness of taste, the consideration for others, and the gentleness which the world puts forth as its highest type of excellence; you have not come near the courts or the mansions of the great; yet you ape the sin of Dives, while you are strangers to his refinement. You think it the sign of a gentleman to set yourselves above religion, to criticise the religious and professors of religion, to look at Catholic and Methodist with impartial contempt, to gain a smattering of knowledge on a number of subjects, to dip into a number of frivolous publications, if they are popular, to have read the latest novel, to have heard the singer and seen the actor of the day, to be well up with the news, to know the names and, if so be, the persons of public men, to be able to bow to them, to walk up and down the street with your heads on high, and to stare at whatever meets you;—and to say and

13. Luke 16:19.

do worse things, of which these outward extravagances are but the symbol. And this is what you conceive you have come upon earth for! The Creator made you, it seems, O my children, for this work and office, to be a bad imitation of polished ungodliness, to be a piece of tawdry and faded finery, or a scent which has lost its freshness, and does but offend the sense! O! that you could see how absurd and base are such pretences in the eyes of any but yourselves! No calling of life but is honourable; no one is ridiculous who acts suitably to his calling and estate; no one, who has good sense and humility, but may, in any station of life, be truly well-bred and refined; but ostentation, affectation, and ambitious efforts are, in every station of life, high or low, nothing but vulgarities. Put them aside, despise them your-selves, O my very dear sons, whom I love, and whom I would fain serve;—oh! that you could feel that you have souls! oh, that you would have mercy on your souls! oh, that, before it is too late, you would betake yourselves to Him who is the Source of all that is truly high and magnificent and beautiful, all that is bright and pleasant, and secure what you ignorantly seek, in Him whom you so wilfully, so awfully despise!

He alone, the Son of God, "the brightness of the Eternal Light, and the spotless mirror of His Majesty," is the source of all good and all happiness to rich and poor, high and low. If you were ever so high, you would need Him; if you were ever so low, you could offend Him. The poor can offend Him; the poor man can neglect his divinely appointed mission as well as the rich. Do not suppose, my brethren, that what I have said against the upper or the middle class, will not, if you happen to be poor, also lie against you. Though a man were as poor as Lazarus, he could be as guilty as Dives. If you are resolved to degrade yourselves to the brutes of the field, who have no reason and no conscience, you need not wealth or rank to enable you to do so. Brutes have no wealth; they have no pride of life; they have no purple and fine linen, no splendid table, no retinue of servants, and yet they are brutes. They are brutes by the law of their nature: they are the poorest among the poor; there is not a vagrant and outcast who is so poor as they; they differ from him, not in their possessions, but in their want of a soul, in that he has a mission and they have not, he can sin and they can not. O my brethren, it stands to reason, a man may intoxicate himself with a cheap draught, as well as with a costly one; he may steal another's money for his appetites, though he does not waste his own upon them; he may break through the natural and social laws which encircle him, and profane the sanctity of family duties, though he be, not a child of nobles, but a peasant or artisan,—nay, and perhaps he does so more frequently than they. This is not the poor's blessedness, that he has less temptations to self-indulgence, for he has as many, but that from his circumstances he receives the penances and correc-tions of self-indulgence. Poverty is the mother of many pains and sorrows in their season, and these are God's messengers to lead the soul to repentance; but, alas! if the poor man indulges his passions, thinks little of religion, puts off repentance, refuses to make an effort, and dies without conversion, it matters nothing that he was poor in this world, it matters nothing that he was less daring than the rich, it matters not that he promised himself God's favour, that he sent for the Priest when death came, and received the last Sacraments; Lazarus too, in that case, shall be buried with Dives in hell, and shall have had his consolation neither in this world nor in the world to come.

My brethren, the simple question is, whatever a man's rank in life may be, does he in that rank perform the work which God has given him to do? Now then, let me turn to others of a very different description, and let me hear what they will say, when the question is asked them;—why, they will parry it thus:—"You give us no alternative," they will say to me, "except that of being sinners or Saints. You put before us our Lord's pattern, and you spread before us the guilt and the ruin of the deliberate transgressor; whereas we have no intention of going so far one way or the other; we do not aim at being Saints, but we have no desire at all to be sinners. We neither intend to disobey God's will, nor to give up our own. Surely there is a middle way, and a safe one, in which God's will and our will may both be satisfied. We mean to enjoy both this world and the next. We will guard against mortal sin; we are not obliged to guard against venial;[14] indeed it would be endless to attempt it. None but Saints do so; it is the work of a life; we need have nothing else to do. We are not monks, we are in the world, we are in business, we are parents, we have families; we must live for the day. It is a consolation to keep from mortal sin; that we do, and it is enough for salvation. It is a great thing to keep in God's favour; what indeed can we desire more? We come at due times to the Sacraments; this is our comfort and our stay; did we die, we should die in grace, and escape the doom of the wicked. But if we once attempted to go further, where should we stop? how will you draw the line for us? the line between mortal and venial sin is very distinct; we understand that; but do you not see that, if we attended to our venial sins, there would be just as much reason to attend to one as to another? If we began to repress our anger, why not also repress vainglory? why not also guard against niggardliness? why not also keep from falsehood? from gossiping, from idling, from excess in eating? And, after all, without venial sin we never can be, unless indeed we have the prerogative of the Mother of God, which it would be almost heresy to ascribe to any one but her.[15] You are not asking us to be converted; that we understand; we *are* converted, we were converted a long time ago. You bid us aim at an indefinite vague something, which is less than perfection, yet more than obedience, and which, without resulting in any tangible advantage, debars us from the pleasures and embarrasses us in the duties of this world."

This is what you will say; but your premises, my brethren, are better than your reasoning, and your conclusions will not stand. You have a right view why God has sent you into the world, viz., in order that you may get to heaven; it is quite true also that you would fare well indeed if you found yourselves there, you could desire

---

14. A mortal sin damns one to Hell from which there is no release; a venial sin relegates one to Purgatory from which there is eventual release.

15. Newman refers here to the doctrine of the Immaculate Conception, the belief that Mary, the mother of Jesus, was free both from actual sin and original sin. This traditional belief was made official doctrine only in 1854.

nothing better; nor, it is true, can you live any time without venial sin. It is true also that you are not obliged to aim at being Saints; it is no sin not to aim at perfection. So much is true and to the purpose; but it does not follow from it that you, with such views and feelings as you have expressed, are using sufficient exertions even for attaining to purgatory.[16] Has your religion any difficulty in it, or is it in all respects easy to you? Are you simply taking your own pleasure in your mode of living, or do you find your pleasure in submitting yourself to God's pleasure? In a word, is your religion a work? for if it be not, it is not religion at all. Here at once, before going into your argument, is a proof that it is an unsound one, because it brings you to the conclusion that, whereas Christ came to do a work, and all Saints, nay, nay, and sinners do a work too, you, on the contrary, have no work to do, because, forsooth, you are neither sinners nor Saints; or, if you once had a work, at least that you have despatched it already, and you have nothing upon your hands. You have attained your salvation, it seems, before your time, and have nothing to occupy you, and are detained on earth too long. The workdays are over, and your perpetual holiday is begun. Did then God send you, above all other men, into the world to be idle in spiritual matters? Is it your mission only to find pleasure in this world, in which you are but as pilgrims and sojourners? Are you more than sons of Adam, who, by the sweat of their brow, are to eat bread till they return to the earth out of which they are taken? Unless you have some work in hand, unless you are struggling, unless you are fighting with yourselves, you are no followers of those who "through many tribulations entered into the kingdom of God."[17] A fight is the very token of a Christian. He is a soldier of Christ;[18] high or low, he is this and nothing else. If you have triumphed over all mortal sin, as you seem to think, then you must attack your venial sins; there is no help for it; there is nothing else to do, if you would be soldiers of Jesus Christ. But, O simple souls! to think you have gained any triumph at all! No: you cannot safely be at peace with any, even the least malignant, of the foes of God; if you are at peace with venial sins, be certain that in their company and under their shadow mortal sins are lurking. Mortal sins are the children of venial, which, though they be not deadly themselves, yet are prolific of death. You may think that you have killed the giants who had possession of your hearts, and that you have nothing to fear, but may sit at rest under your vine and under your fig-tree;[19] but the giants will live again, they will rise from the dust, and, before you know where you are, you will be taken captive and slaughtered by the fierce, powerful, and eternal enemies of God.

The end of a thing is the test. It was our Lord's rejoicing in His last solemn hour, that He had done the work for which He was sent. "I have glorified Thee on earth," He says in His prayer, "I have finished the work which Thou gavest Me to do; I have

16. See note 14.
17. Acts 14:22.
18. 2 Timothy 2:3; see also Ephesians 6:10–18.
19. In Hebrew Scripture, vines and fig trees are traditional symbols of peaceful prosperity, and the great threat is their destruction: see Psalms 105:33; Jeremiah 5:17; Hosea 2:12; Joel 1:7.

manifested Thy name to the men whom Thou hast given Me out of the world."[20] It was St. Paul's consolation also; "I have fought the good fight, I have finished the course, I have kept the faith; henceforth there is laid up for me a crown of justice, which the Lord shall render to me in that Day, the just Judge."[21] Alas! alas! how different will be our view of things when we come to die, or when we have passed into eternity, from the dreams and pretences with which we beguile ourselves now! What will Babel[22] do for us then? Will it rescue our souls from the purgatory or the hell to which it sends them? If we were created, it was that we might serve God; if we have His gifts, it is that we may glorify Him; if we have a conscience, it is that we may obey it; if we have the prospect of heaven, it is that we may keep it before us; if we have light, that we may follow it; if we have grace, that we may save ourselves by means of it. Alas! alas! for those who die without fulfilling their mission! who were called to be holy, and lived in sin; who were called to worship Christ, and who plunged into this giddy and unbelieving world; who were called to fight, and who remained idle; who were called to be Catholics, and who did but remain in the religion of their birth! Alas for those who have had gifts and talent, and have not used, or have misused, or abused them; who have had wealth, and have spent it on themselves; who have had abilities, and have advocated what was sinful, or ridiculed what was true, or scattered doubts against what was sacred; who have had leisure, and have wasted it on wicked companions, or evil books, or foolish amusements! Alas! for those, of whom the best that can be said is, that they are harmless and naturally blameless, while they never have attempted to cleanse their hearts or to live in God's sight!

The world goes on from age to age, but the holy Angels and blessed Saints are always crying, alas, alas! and woe, woe! over the loss of vocations, and the disappointment of hopes, and the scorn of God's love, and the ruin of souls. One generation succeeds another, and whenever they look down upon earth from their golden thrones, they see scarcely anything but a multitude of guardian spirits, downcast and sad, each following his own charge, in anxiety, or in terror, or in despair, vainly endeavouring to shield him from the enemy, and failing because he will not be shielded. Times come and go, and man will not believe, that that is to be which is not yet, or that what now is only continues for a season, and is not eternity. The end is the trial; the world passes; it is but a pageant and a scene; the lofty palace crumbles, the busy city is mute, the ships of Tarshish[23] have sped away. On heart and flesh death is coming; the veil is breaking. Departing soul, how hast thou used thy talents, thy opportunities, the light poured around thee, the warnings given thee, the grace inspired into thee? O my Lord and Saviour, support me in that hour in the strong arms of Thy Sacraments, and by the fresh fragrance of Thy consolations. Let the absolving words be said over me, and the holy oil sign

20. John 17:1–6.

21. 2 Timothy 4:7–8.

22. See note 1.

23. A seaport frequently mentioned in Hebrew Scripture but most notable as the port to which Jonah sailed.

and seal me, and Thy own Body be my food, and Thy Blood my sprinkling; and let my sweet Mother Mary breathe on me, and my Angel whisper peace to me, and my glorious Saints, and my own dear Father, Philip,[24] smile on me; that in them all, and through them all, I may receive the gift of perseverance, and die, as I desire to live, in Thy faith, in Thy Church, in Thy service, and in Thy love.

24. Newman established the order of Saint Philip Neri (1515–1595) in England and founded at Birmingham the Oratory of Saint Philip Neri.

JOHN RUSKIN

JOHN RUSKIN (1819–1900) began writing as a critic of painting and architecture, yet even in commentary about the arts he consistently concerned himself with the nature of work. For him, the conditions and attitudes of the artisan who helped construct a cathedral were of greater importance in determining the significance of the structure than was the final consummation of some artistic design. Distressed by the dehumanization of workers in his own society, he insisted upon the dignity that workers gain when they are thoughtfully engaged in the shaping of products that are meaningful to them.

From the 1850s through the 1880s, he devoted much of his intellectual energy to direct scrutiny of social and economic aspects of Victorian culture, becoming as vehement as Carlyle in denouncing laissez-faire economics and industrialism. That workers should enjoy opportunity for original expression and that they should derive pleasure from their labors were fundamental tenets for Ruskin, and his writings influenced the general Arts and Crafts Movement and William Morris in particular (see selections by Morris in parts 1, 2, and 3). A worker's involvement with a task Ruskin considered in an ideal light, construing it as an aspiration to act creatively and thereby cultivate what is most noble in the soul. Those directing and employing workers he believed to have a great responsibility to serve the spiritual and psychological well-being of people under them, an attitude that remained consistent in his writing from *The Seven Lamps of Architecture* (1849) to *Unto This Last* (1860) to *Munera Pulveris* (1872) and throughout the writings (1871–1884) that came to compose *Fors Clavigera*. Ruskin saw himself as both prophet to and interpreter of his culture, and his writing is distinguished by the admonitory tone of the prophet remonstrating with a people fallen from spiritual to worldly concerns as they degrade work from an essentially religious activity to a base transaction designed to secure food for the body only and not for the spirit.

Volume 1 of *Stones of Venice* was published in 1851, volumes 2 and 3 in 1853. In *Stones*, as in the earlier *The Seven Lamps of Architecture*, Ruskin sees political unrest as being tied to people's dissatisfaction with work: "It is verily this degradation of the operative into a machine, which more than any other evil of the times, is leading the mass of nations everywhere into vain, incoherent, destructive struggling for a freedom of which they cannot explain the nature to themselves" (*The Stones of Venice*). In both studies, he emphasizes the interrelation of social ethics with aesthetics, focusing upon the ways in which a culture understands laborers, either validating or denigrating them: "It is not enough to find men absolute subsistence; we should think of the manner of life which our demands necessitate;

and endeavor, as far as may be, to make all our needs such as may, in the supply of them, raise, as well as feed, the poor" ("The Lamp of Obedience," *Seven Lamps*). Such responsibility to the laboring class he defines more fully by arguing, against the nineteenth-century concern with efficiency and precision, that people must accept and, indeed, value the incompleteness and imperfections of an artifact as an indication of the essential humanity of the craftsman. The value of any product he sees as derived from the fully human labor that goes into the making of it, and he denies that machines or mechanized workers impart any significant value to a product. The purpose of work, then, is to develop the individual creative person-ality of the worker. Each person has the responsibility to make his or her own work an expression of distinctive identity, and, in language that recalls his evangelical upbringing, Ruskin echoes John Wesley and concurs with John Henry Cardinal Newman about work as a divinely appointed mission: "For we are not sent into this world to do anything into which we cannot put our hearts. We have certain work to do for our bread, and that is to be done strenuously; other work to do for our delight, and that is to be done heartily: neither is to be done by halves or shifts, but with a will; and what is not worth this effort is not to be done at all" ("The Lamp of Life," *Seven Lamps*). Further, as do Wesley and Newman, Ruskin sees the worker's relationship to the earth and to culture as one of stewardship—laborers discover, express, and affirm their unique spirits through work, but they also have a duty to those who will succeed them, a commitment to leave an improved world.

The selection from *The Stones of Venice* is from "The Nature of Gothic," the most celebrated chapter in volume 2.

From *The Stones of Venice,* Vol. 2

From Chapter 6, The Nature of Gothic

I shall endeavour therefore to give the reader in this chapter an idea, at once broad and definite, of the true nature of *Gothic* architecture, properly so called; not of that of Venice only, but of universal Gothic: for it will be one of the most interesting parts of our subsequent inquiry, to find out how far Venetian architec-ture reached the universal or perfect type of Gothic, and how far it either fell short of it, or assumed foreign and independent forms.

The principal difficulty in doing this arises from the fact that every building of the Gothic period differs in some important respect from every other; and many include features which, if they occurred in other buildings, would not be considered

Gothic at all; so that all we have to reason upon is merely, if I may be allowed so to express it, a greater or less degree of Gothicness in each building we examine. And it is this Gothicness,—the character which, according as it is found more or less in a building, makes it more or less Gothic,—of which I want to define the nature; and I feel the same kind of difficulty in doing so which would be encountered by any one who undertook to explain, for instance, the nature of Redness, without any actually red thing to point to, but only orange and purple things. Suppose he had only a piece of heather and a dead oak-leaf to do it with. He might say, the colour which is mixed with the yellow in this oak-leaf, and with the blue in this heather, would be red, if you had it separate; but it would be difficult, nevertheless, to make the abstraction perfectly intelligible: and it is so in a far greater degree to make the abstraction of the Gothic character intelligible, because that character itself is made up of many mingled ideas, and can consist only in their union. That is to say, pointed arches do not constitute Gothic, nor vaulted roofs, nor flying buttresses, nor grotesque sculptures; but all or some of these things, and many other things with them, when they come together so as to have life. . . .

We have, then, the Gothic character submitted to our analysis, just as the rough mineral is submitted to that of the chemist, entangled with many other foreign substances, itself perhaps in no place pure, or ever to be obtained or seen in purity for more than an instant; but nevertheless a thing of definite and separate nature, however inextricable or confused in appearance. Now observe: the chemist defines his mineral by two separate kinds of character; one external, its crystalline form, hardness, lustre, &c.; the other internal, the proportions and nature of its constituent atoms. Exactly in the same manner, we shall find that Gothic architecture has external forms, and internal elements. Its elements are certain mental tendencies of the builders, legibly expressed in it; as fancifulness, love of variety, love of richness, and such others. Its external forms are pointed arches, vaulted roofs, &c. And unless both the elements and the forms are there, we have no right to call the style Gothic. It is not enough that it has the Form, if it have not also the power and life. It is not enough that it has the Power, if it have not the form. We must therefore inquire into each of these characters successively; and determine first, what is the Mental Expression, and secondly, what the Material Form, of Gothic architecture, properly so called. . . .

I believe, then, that the characteristic or moral elements of Gothic are the following, placed in the order of their importance:

1. Savageness.	4. Grotesqueness.
2. Changefulness.	5. Rigidity.
3. Naturalism.	6. Redundance.

These characters are here expressed as belonging to the building; as belonging to the builder, they would be expressed thus:—1. Savageness, or Rudeness. 2. Love of Change. 3. Love of Nature. 4. Disturbed Imagination. 5. Obstinacy. 6. Generosity. And I repeat, that the withdrawal of any one, or any two, will not at once destroy the Gothic character of a building, but the removal of a majority of them will. I shall proceed to examine them in their order.

SAVAGENESS. I am not sure when the word "Gothic" was first generically applied to the architecture of the North; but I presume that, whatever the date of its original usage, it was intended to imply reproach, and express the barbaric character of the nations among whom that architecture arose. It never implied that they were literally of the Gothic lineage, far less that their architecture had been originally invented by the Goths themselves; but it did imply that they and their buildings together exhibited a degree of sternness and rudeness, which, in contra-distinction to the character of Southern and Eastern nations, appeared like a perpetual reflection of the contrast between the Goth and the Roman in their first encounter. And when that fallen Roman, in the utmost impotence of his luxury, and insolence of his guilt, became the model for the imitation of civilised Europe, at the close of the so-called Dark ages, the word Gothic became a term of unmiti-gated contempt, not unmixed with aversion. From that contempt, by the exertion of the antiquaries and architects of this century, Gothic architecture has been sufficiently vindicated; and perhaps some among us, in our admiration of the magnificent science of its structure, and sacredness of its expression, might desire that the term of ancient reproach should be withdrawn, and some other, of more apparent honourableness, adopted in its place. There is no chance, as there is no need, of such a substitution. As far as the epithet was used scornfully, it was used falsely; but there is no reproach in the word, rightly understood; on the contrary, there is a profound truth, which the instinct of mankind almost unconsciously recognises. It is true, greatly and deeply true, that the architecture of the North is rude and wild; but it is not true, that, for this reason, we are to condemn it, or despise. Far otherwise: I believe it is in this very character that it deserves our profoundest reverence. . . .

If, however, the savageness of Gothic architecture, merely as an expression of its origin among Northern nations, may be considered, in some sort, a noble charac-ter, it possesses a higher nobility still, when considered as an index, not of climate, but of religious principle.

In the 13th and 14th paragraphs of Chapter XXI. of the first volume of this work, it was noticed that the systems of architectural ornament, properly so called, might be divided into three:—1. Servile ornament, in which the execution or power of the inferior workman is entirely subjected to the intellect of the higher;—2. Constitu-tional ornament, in which the executive inferior power is, to a certain point, emancipated and independent, having a will of its own, yet confessing its in-feriority and rendering obedience to higher powers;—and 3. Revolutionary orna-ment, in which no executive inferiority is admitted at all. I must here explain the nature of these divisions at somewhat greater length.

Of Servile ornament, the principal schools are the Greek, Ninevite,[1] and Egyptian;

---

1. Ninevah was an ancient city of Assyria situated on the Tigris River. Ruskin uses *Ninevah* and *Ninevite* interchangeably with *Assyria* and *Assyrian.*

but their servility is of different kinds. The Greek master-workman was far advanced in knowledge and power above the Assyrian or Egyptian. Neither he nor those for whom he worked could endure the appearance of imperfection in anything; and, therefore, what ornament he appointed to be done by those beneath him was composed of mere geometrical forms,—balls, ridges, and perfectly symmetrical foliage,—which could be executed with absolute precision by line and rule, and were as perfect in their way, when completed, as his own figure sculpture. The Assyrian and Egyptian, on the contrary, less cognisant of accurate form in anything, were content to allow their figure sculpture to be executed by inferior workmen, but lowered the method of its treatment to a standard which every workman could reach, and then trained him by discipline so rigid, that there was no chance of his falling beneath the standard appointed. The Greek gave to the lower workman no subject which he could not perfectly execute. The Assyrian gave him subjects which he could only execute imperfectly, but fixed a legal standard for his imperfection. The workman was, in both systems, a slave.[2]

But in the mediaeval, or especially Christian, system of ornament, this slavery is done away with altogether; Christianity having recognised, in small things as well as great, the individual value of every soul.[3] But it not only recognises its value; it confesses its imperfection, in only bestowing dignity upon the acknowledgment of unworthiness. That admission of lost power and fallen nature, which the Greek or Ninevite felt to be intensely painful, and, as far as might be, altogether refused, the Christian makes daily and hourly, contemplating the fact of it without fear, as tending, in the end, to God's greater glory. Therefore, to every spirit which Christianity summons to her service, her exhortation is: Do what you can, and confess frankly what you are unable to do; neither let your effort be shortened for fear of failure, nor your confession silenced for fear of shame. And it is, perhaps, the principal admirableness of the Gothic schools of architecture, that they thus receive the results of the labour of inferior minds; and out of fragments full of imperfection, and betraying that imperfection in every touch, indulgently raise up a stately and unaccusable whole.

But the modern English mind has this much in common with that of the Greek, that it intensely desires, in all things, the utmost completion or perfection compatible with their nature. This is a noble character in the abstract, but becomes ignoble when it causes us to forget the relative dignities of that nature itself, and to

2. Ruskin's note: "The third kind of ornament, the Renaissance, is that in which the inferior detail becomes principal, the executor of every minor portion being required to exhibit skill and possess knowledge as great as that which is possessed by the master of the design; and in the endeavour to endow him with this skill and knowledge, his own original power is overwhelmed, and the whole building becomes a wearisome exhibition of well-educated imbecility. We must fully inquire into the nature of this form of error, when we arrive at the examination of the Renaissance schools."

3. Ruskin's emphasis on the importance of the distinctive individuality of each person and his relation of such authentic integrity to Christian beliefs bears comparison with Gerard Manley Hopkins's insistence upon the *haecceitas* or "this-ness" of every aspect of nature and Hopkins's insistence that *haecceitas* results from the creative action of a providential God who is "past change." See especially Hopkins's poems "As kingfishers catch fire" and "Pied Beauty."

prefer the perfectness of the lower nature to the imperfection of the higher, not considering that as, judged by such a rule, all the brute animals would be preferable to man, because more perfect in their functions and kind, and yet are always held inferior to him, so also in the works of man, those which are more perfect in their kind are always inferior to those which are, in their nature, liable to more faults and shortcomings. For the finer the nature, the more flaws it will show through the clearness of it; and it is a law of this universe, that the best things shall be seldomest seen in their best form. The wild grass grows well and strongly, one year with another; but the wheat is, according to the greater nobleness of its nature, liable to the bitterer blight. And therefore, while in all things that we see, or do, we are to desire perfection, and strive for it, we are nevertheless not to set the meaner thing, in its narrow accomplishment, above the nobler thing, in its mighty progress; not to esteem smooth minuteness above shattered majesty; not to prefer mean victory to honourable defeat; not to lower the level of our aim, that we may the more surely enjoy the complacency of success. But above all, in our dealings with the souls of other men, we are to take care how we check, by severe requirement or narrow caution, efforts which might otherwise lead to a noble issue; and, still more, how we withhold our admiration from great excellencies, because they are mingled with rough faults. Now, in the make and nature of every man, however rude or simple, whom we employ in manual labour, there are some powers for better things: some tardy imagination, torpid capacity of emotion, tottering steps of thought, there are, even at the worst; and in most cases it is all our own fault that they *are* tardy or torpid. But they cannot be strengthened, unless we are content to take them in their feebleness, and unless we prize and honour them in their imperfection above the best and most perfect manual skill. And this is what we have to do with all our labourers; to look for the *thoughtful* part of them, and get that out of them, whatever we lose for it, whatever faults and errors we are obliged to take with it. For the best that is in them cannot manifest itself, but in company with much error. Understand this clearly: You can teach a man to draw a straight line, and to cut one; to strike a curved line, and to carve it; and to copy and carve any number of given lines or forms, with admirable speed and perfect precision; and you find his work perfect of its kind: but if you ask him to think about any of those forms, to consider if he cannot find any better in his own head, he stops; his execution becomes hesitating; he thinks, and ten to one he thinks wrong; ten to one he makes a mistake in the first touch he gives to his work as a thinking being. But you have made a man of him for all that. He was only a machine before, an animated tool.

And observe, you are put to stern choice in this matter. You must either make a tool of the creature, or a man of him. You cannot make both. Men were not intended to work with the accuracy of tools, to be precise and perfect in all their actions. If you will have that precision out of them, and make their fingers measure degrees like cog-wheels, and their arms strike curves like compasses, you must unhumanise them. All the energy of their spirits must be given to make cogs and compasses of themselves. All their attention and strength must go to the accomplishment of the mean act. The eye of the soul must be bent upon the finger-point, and the soul's force must fill all the invisible nerves that guide it, ten hours a day, that it may not err from its steely precision, and so soul and sight be worn away, and the whole human being lost at last—a heap of sawdust, so far as its intellectual work in this world is concerned; saved only by its Heart, which cannot go into the form of cogs and compasses, but expands, after the ten hours are over, into fireside humanity. On the other hand, if you will make a man of the working creature, you cannot make a tool. Let him but begin to imagine, to think, to try to do anything worth doing; and the engine-turned precision is lost at once. Out come all his roughness, all his dulness, all his incapability; shame upon shame, failure upon failure, pause after pause: but out comes the whole majesty of him also; and we know the height of it only, when we see the clouds settling upon him. And, whether the clouds be bright or dark, there will be transfiguration behind and within them.

And now, reader, look round this English room of yours, about which you have been proud so often, because the work of it was so good and strong, and the ornaments of it so finished. Examine again all those accurate mouldings, and perfect polishings, and unerring adjustments of the seasoned wood and tempered steel. Many a time you have exulted over them, and thought how great England was, because her slightest work was done so thoroughly. Alas! if read rightly, these perfectnesses are signs of a slavery in our England a thousand times more bitter and more degrading than that of the scourged African, or helot[4] Greek. Men may be beaten, chained, tormented, yoked like cattle, slaughtered like summer flies, and yet remain in one sense, and the best sense, free. But to smother their souls within them, to blight and hew into rotting pollards[5] the suckling branches of their human intelligence, to make the flesh and skin which, after the worm's work on it, is to see God, into leathern thongs to yoke machinery with,—this is to be slave-masters indeed; and there might be more freedom in England, though her feudal lords' lightest words were worth men's lives, and though the blood of the vexed husbandman dropped in the furrows of her fields, than there is while the anima-tion of her multitudes is sent like fuel to feed the factory smoke, and the strength of them is given daily to be wasted into the fineness of a web, or racked into the exactness of a line.

And, on the other hand, go forth again to gaze upon the old cathedral front, where you have smiled so often at the fantastic ignorance of the old sculptors: examine once more those ugly goblins, and formless monsters, and stern statues, anatomiless and rigid; but do not mock at them, for they are signs of the life and liberty of every workman who struck the stone; a freedom of thought, and rank in scale of being, such as no laws, no charters, no charities can secure; but which it must be the first aim of all Europe at this day to regain for her children.

4. Unlike most slaves in ancient Greek culture, who were foreign to the city-states, a helot was an indigenous person subjected to the rule of the citizen families. Although genuine evidence is scanty, literary tradition emphasizes the cruelty of Spartan citizens to their helots.

5. A pollard is a tree or bush that has been severely cut back in order to create a dense foliage that is then often trimmed into a shape.

Let me not be thought to speak wildly or extravagantly. It is verily this degradation of the operative into a machine, which, more than any other evil of the times, is leading the mass of the nations everywhere into vain, incoherent, destructive struggling for a freedom of which they cannot explain the nature to themselves.[6] Their universal outcry against wealth, and against nobility, is not forced from them either by the pressure of famine, or the sting of mortified pride. These do much, and have done much in all ages; but the foundations of society were never yet shaken as they are at this day. It is not that men are ill fed, but that they have no pleasure in the work by which they make their bread, and therefore look to wealth as the only means of pleasure. It is not that men are pained by the scorn of the upper classes, but they cannot endure their own; for they feel that the kind of labour to which they are condemned is verily a degrading one, and makes them less than men. Never had the upper classes so much sympathy with the lower, or charity for them, as they have at this day, and yet never were they so much hated by them: for, of old, the separation between the noble and the poor was merely a wall built by law; now it is a veritable difference in level of standing, a precipice between upper and lower grounds in the field of humanity, and there is pestilential air at the bottom of it. I know not if a day is ever to come when the nature of right freedom will be understood, and when men will see that to obey another man, to labour for him, yield reverence to him or to his place, is not slavery. It is often the best kind of liberty,—liberty from care. The man who says to one, Go, and he goeth, and to another, Come, and he cometh,[7] has, in most cases, more sense of restraint and difficulty than the man who obeys him. The movements of the one are hindered by the burden on his shoulder; of the other, by the bridle on his lips: there is no way by which the burden may be lightened; but we need not suffer from the bridle if we do not champ at it. To yield reverence to another, to hold ourselves and our lives at his disposal, is not slavery; often, it is the noblest state in which a man can live in this world. There is, indeed, a reverence which is servile, that is to say irrational or selfish: but there is also noble reverence, that is to say, reasonable and loving; and a man is never so noble as when he is reverent in this kind; nay, even if the feeling pass the bounds of mere reason, so that it be loving, a man is raised by it.[8] Which had, in reality, most of the serf nature in him,—the Irish peasant who was lying in wait yesterday for his landlord, with his musket muzzle thrust through the ragged hedge; or that old mountain servant, who, 200 years ago, at Inverkeithing, gave up his own life and the lives of his seven sons for his chief?—as each fell, calling forth his brother to the death, "Another for Hector!" And therefore, in all ages and all countries, reverence has been paid and sacrifice made by men to each other, not only without complaint, but rejoicingly; and famine, and peril, and sword, and all evil, and all shame, have been borne willingly in the causes of masters and kings; for

6. Ruskin refers here to the various revolutions of 1848 that had threatened political stability on the continent and also to the final defeat of Chartism in April of 1848 with the subsequent social unrest and fear of a workers' revolt in England.

7. See Matthew 8:5–13.

8. Ruskin seems to echo here the notions of hero-worship advanced throughout Carlyle's writings but pointedly summarized in *On Heroes, Hero-Worship, and the Heroic in History* (1841).

all these gifts of the heart ennobled the men who gave, not less than the men who received them, and nature prompted and God rewarded the sacrifice. But to feel their souls withering within them, unthanked, to find their whole being sunk into an unrecognised abyss, to be counted off into a heap of mechanism, numbered with its wheels, and weighed with its hammer strokes;—this nature bade not,—this God blesses not,—this humanity for no long time is able to endure.

We have much studied and much perfected, of late, the great civilised invention of the division of labour; only we give it a false name. It is not, truly speaking, the labour that is divided; but the men:—Divided into mere segments of men—broken into small fragments and crumbs of life; so that all the little piece of intelligence that is left in a man is not enough to make a pin, or a nail, but exhausts itself in making the point of a pin, or the head of nail. Now it is a good and desirable thing, truly, to make many pins in a day; but if we could only see with what crystal sand their points were polished,—sand of human soul, much to be magnified before it can be discerned for what it is,—we should think there might be some loss in it also. And the great cry that rises from all our manufacturing cities, louder than their furnace blast, is all in very deed for this,—that we manufacture everything there except men; we blanch cotton, and strengthen steel, and refine sugar, and shape pottery; but to brighten, to strengthen, to refine, or to form a single living spirit, never enters into our estimate of advantages. And all the evil to which that cry is urging our myriads can be met only in one way; not by teaching nor preaching, for to teach them is but to show them their misery, and to preach to them, if we do nothing more than preach, is to mock at it. It can be met only by a right understanding, on the part of all classes, of what kinds of labour are good for men, raising them, and making them happy; by a determined sacrifice of such convenience, or beauty, or cheapness as is to be got only by the degradation of the workman; and by equally determined demand for the products and results of healthy and ennobling labour.

And how, it will be asked, are these products to be recognised, and this demand to be regulated? Easily: by the observance of three broad and simple rules:

1. Never encourage the manufacture of any article not absolutely necessary, in the production of which *Invention* has no share.

2. Never demand an exact finish for its own sake, but only for some practical or noble end.

3. Never encourage imitation or copying of any kind, except for the sake of preserving record of great works.

The second of these principles is the only one which directly rises out of the consideration of our immediate subject; but I shall briefly explain the meaning and extent of the first also, reserving the enforcement of the third for another place.

1. Never encourage the manufacture of anything not necessary, in the production of which invention has no share.

For instance. Glass beads are utterly unnecessary, and there is no design or thought employed in their manufacture. They are formed by first drawing out the glass into rods; these rods are chopped up into fragments of the size of beads by the human hand, and the fragments are then rounded in the furnace. The men who chop up the rods sit at their work all day, their hands vibrating with a perpetual and exquisitely timed palsy, and the beads dropping beneath their vibration like hail. Neither they, nor the men who draw out the rods or fuse the fragments, have the smallest occasion for the use of any single human faculty; and every young lady, therefore, who buys glass beads is engaged in the slave-trade, and in a much more cruel one than that which we have so long been endeavouring to put down.

But glass cups and vessels may become the subjects of exquisite invention; and if in buying these we pay for the invention, that is to say for the beautiful form, or colour, or engraving, and not for mere finish of execution, we are doing good to humanity.

So again, the cutting of precious stones, in all ordinary cases, requires little exertion of any mental faculty; some tact and judgment in avoiding flaws, and so on, but nothing to bring out the whole mind. Every person who wears cut jewels merely for the sake of their value is, therefore, a slave-driver.

But the working of the goldsmith, and the various designing of grouped jewellery and enamel-work, may become the subject of the most noble human intelligence. Therefore, money spent in the purchase of well-designed plate, of precious engraved vases, cameos, or enamels, does good to humanity; and, in work of this kind, jewels may be employed to heighten its splendour; and their cutting is then a price paid for the attainment of a noble end, and thus perfectly allowable.

I shall perhaps press this law farther elsewhere, but our immediate concern is chiefly with the second, namely, never to demand an exact finish, when it does not lead to a noble end. For observe, I have only dwelt upon the rudeness of Gothic, or any other kind of imperfectness, as admirable, where it was impossible to get design or thought without it. If you are to have the thought of a rough and untaught man, you must have it in a rough and untaught way; but from an educated man, who can without effort express his thoughts in an educated way, take the graceful expression, and be thankful. Only *get* the thought, and do not silence the peasant because he cannot speak good grammar, or until you have taught him his grammar. Grammar and refinement are good things, both, only be sure of the better thing first. And thus in art, delicate finish is desirable from the greatest masters, and is always given by them. In some places Michael Angelo, Leonardo, Phidias, Perugino, Turner,[9] all finished with the most exquisite care; and the finish they give always leads to the fuller accomplishment of their noble purposes. But lower men than these cannot finish, for it requires consummate knowledge to finish consummately, and then we must take their thoughts as they are able to give them. So the rule is simple: Always look for invention first, and after that, for such execution as will help the invention, and as the inventor is capable of

---

9. Michelangelo Buonarroti (1475–1564); Leonardo da Vinci (1452–1519); Phidias (fifth century B.C.E.); Pietro Vannucci Perugino (1446–1523); Joseph Mallord William Turner (1775–1851): all were sculptors or painters. Ruskin had begun his famous five-volume *Modern Painters* as a defense of Turner, and, following Turner's death, Ruskin acted to organize and preserve the many drawings left to the nation in the Turner Bequest.

without painful effort, and *no more*. Above all, demand no refinement of execution where there is no thought, for that is slaves' work, unredeemed. Rather choose rough work than smooth work, so only that the practical purpose be answered, and never imagine there is reason to be proud of anything that may be accomplished by patience and sand-paper.

I shall only give one example, which however will show the reader what I mean, from the manufacture already alluded to, that of glass. Our modern glass is exquisitely clear in its substance, true in its form, accurate in its cutting. We are proud of this. We ought to be ashamed of it. The old Venice glass was muddy, inaccurate in all its forms, and clumsily cut, if at all. And the old Venetian was justly proud of it. For there is this difference between the English and Venetian workman, that the former thinks only of accurately matching his patterns, and getting his curves perfectly true and his edges perfectly sharp, and becomes a mere machine for rounding curves and sharpening edges, while the old Venetian cared not a whit whether his edges were sharp or not, but he invented a new design for every glass that he made, and never moulded a handle or a lip without a new fancy in it. And therefore, though some Venetian glass is ugly and clumsy enough, when made by clumsy and uninventive workmen, other Venetian glass is so lovely in its forms that no price is too great for it; and we never see the same form in it twice. Now you cannot have the finish and the varied form too. If the workman is thinking about his edges, he cannot be thinking of his design; if of his design, he cannot think of his edges. Choose whether you will pay for the lovely form or the perfect finish, and choose at the same moment whether you will make the worker a man or a grindstone.

Nay, but the reader interrupts me,—"If the workman can design beautifully, I would not have him kept at the furnace. Let him be taken away and made a gentleman, and have a studio, and design his glass there, and I will have it blown and cut for him by common workmen, and so I will have my design and my finish too."

All ideas of this kind are founded upon two mistaken suppositions: the first, that one man's thoughts can be, or ought to be, executed by another man's hands; the second, that manual labour is a degradation, when it is governed by intellect.

On a large scale, and in work determinable by line and rule, it is indeed both possible and necessary that the thoughts of one man should be carried out by the labour of others; in this sense I have already defined the best architecture to be the expression of the mind of manhood by the hands of childhood. But on a smaller scale, and in a design which cannot be mathematically defined, one man's thoughts can never be expressed by another: and the difference between the spirit of touch of the man who is inventing, and of the man who is obeying directions, is often all the difference between a great and a common work of art. How wide the separation is between original and second-hand execution, I shall endeavour to show elsewhere; it is not so much to our purpose here as to mark the other and more fatal error of despising manual labour when governed by intellect; for it is no less fatal an error to despise it when thus regulated by intellect, than to value it for its own sake. We are always in these days endeavouring to separate the two; we want one man to be always thinking, and another to be always working, and we call one a gentleman, and the other an operative; whereas the workman ought often to be thinking, and the thinker often to be working, and both should be gentlemen, in the best sense. As it is, we make both ungentle, the one envying, the other despising, his brother; and the mass of society is made up of morbid thinkers, and miserable workers. Now it is only by labour that thought can be made healthy, and only by thought that labour can be made happy, and the two cannot be separated with impunity. It would be well if all of us were good handi-craftsmen in some kind, and the dishonour of manual labour done away with altogether; so that though there should still be a trenchant distinction of race between nobles and commoners, there should not, among the latter, be a tren-chant distinction of employment, as between idle and working men, or between men of liberal and illiberal professions. All professions should be liberal, and there should be less pride felt in peculiarity of employment, and more in excellence of achievement. And yet more, in each several profession, no master should be too proud to do its hardest work. The painter should grind his own colours; the architect work in the mason's yard with his men; the master-manufacturer be himself a more skilful operative than any man in his mills; and the distinction between one man and another be only in experience and skill, and the authority and wealth which these must naturally and justly obtain.

I should be led far from the matter in hand, if I were to pursue this interesting subject. Enough, I trust, has been said to show the reader that the rudeness or imperfection which at first rendered the term "Gothic" one of reproach is indeed, when rightly understood, one of the most noble characters of Christian architec-ture, and not only a noble but an *essential* one. It seems a fantastic paradox, but it is nevertheless a most important truth, that no architecture can be truly noble which is *not* imperfect. And this is easily demonstrable. For since the architect, whom we will suppose capable of doing all in perfection, cannot execute the whole with his own hands, he must either make slaves of his workmen in the old Greek, and present English fashion, and level his work to a slave's capacities, which is to degrade it; or else he must take his workmen as he finds them, and let them show their weaknesses together with their strength, which will involve the Gothic imper-fection, but render the whole work as noble as the intellect of the age can make it.

But the principle may be stated more broadly still. I have confined the illustra-tion of it to architecture, but I must not leave it as if true of architecture only. Hitherto I have used the words imperfect and perfect merely to distinguish be-tween work grossly unskilful, and work executed with average precision and sci-ence; and I have been pleading that any degree of unskilfulness should be admitted, so only that the labourer's mind had room for expression. But, accurately speaking, no good work whatever can be perfect, and *the demand for perfection is always a sign of a misunderstanding of the ends of art.*

This for two reasons, both based on everlasting laws. The first, that no great man ever stops working till he has reached his point of failure; that is to say, his mind is always far in advance of his powers of execution, and the latter will now and then give way in trying to follow it; besides that he will always give to the inferior portions of his work only such inferior attention as they require; and according to his greatness he becomes so accustomed to the feeling of dissatisfaction with the best he can do, that in moments of lassitude or anger with himself he will not care though the beholder be dissatisfied also. I believe there has only been one man who would not acknowledge this necessity, and strove always to reach perfection, Leonardo;[10] the end of his vain effort being merely that he would take ten years to a picture, and leave it unfinished. And therefore, if we are to have great men working at all, or less men doing their best, the work will be imperfect, however beautiful. Of human work none but what is bad can be perfect, in its own bad way.

The second reason is, that imperfection is in some sort essential to all that we know of life. It is the sign of life in a mortal body, that is to say, of a state of progress and change. Nothing that lives is, or can be, rigidly perfect; part of it is decaying, part nascent. The foxglove blossom,—a third part, bud, a third part past, a third part in full bloom,—is a type of the life of this world. And in all things that live there are certain irregularities and deficiencies which are not only signs of life, but sources of beauty. No human face is exactly the same in its lines on each side, no leaf perfect in its lobes, no branch in its symmetry. All admit irregularity as they imply change; and to banish imperfection is to destroy expression, to check exertion, to paralyse vitality. All things are literally better, lovelier, and more beloved for the imperfections which have been divinely appointed, that the law of human life may be Effort, and the law of human judgment, Mercy.

Accept this then for a universal law, that neither architecture nor any other noble work of man can be good unless it be imperfect; and let us be prepared for the otherwise strange fact, which we shall discern clearly as we approach the period of the Renaissance, that the first cause of the fall of the arts of Europe was a relentless requirement of perfection, incapable alike either of being silenced by veneration for greatness, or softened into forgiveness of simplicity.

Thus far then of the Rudeness or Savageness, which is the first mental element of Gothic architecture. It is an element in many other healthy architectures also, as in Byzantine and Romanesque; but true Gothic cannot exist without it.

10. Leonardo da Vinci (1452–1519) was the quintessential Renaissance genius: painter, sculptor, inventor, architect, engineer, writer.

ROBERT BROWNING

T HE SON OF a bank clerk, Robert Browning (1812–1889) belonged to a small, close-knit family. Browning was educated at home where he felt the influence of his father's interest in history and art and his mother's love of music, subjects he examined in his poems. In 1845, Browning met and fell in love with Elizabeth Barrett. They married the following year and moved to Italy, where they resided until Elizabeth's death fifteen years later. Although he published his first poem in 1832, Browning did not secure critical and popular acclaim until the 1860s. From then until his death, he was lionized in England and America.

Browning excelled in the dramatic monologue, the form in which *Fra Lippo Lippi* is written. The dramatic monologue presents a character in a dramatic situation, allowing Browning to create in-depth psychological profiles of a range of fascinating and complex personalities. *Fra Lippo Lippi*, published in *Men and Women* in 1855, is about an Italian Renaissance artist whose biography Browning read in Giorgio Vasari's *The Lives of the Painters*. Filippo Lippi (1406–1469), a libertine and accomplished Florentine painter, belonged to the Carmelite order ("Fra" meaning brother). Browning presents him as a bold, innovative artist, true to his own creative genius and convinced that the artist's mission is, through his work, to "[i]nterpret God to all."

Fra Lippo Lippi

I am poor brother Lippo, by your leave!
You need not clap your torches to my face.
Zooks,[1] what's to blame? you think you see a monk!
What, 't is past midnight, and you go the rounds,

1. A mild oath.

And here you catch me at an alley's end   5
Where sportive ladies leave their doors ajar?
The Carmine's[2] my cloister: hunt it up,
Do,—harry out, if you must show your zeal,
Whatever rat, there, haps on his wrong hole,
And nip each softling of a wee white mouse,   10
Weke, weke, that's crept to keep him company!
Aha, you know your betters? Then, you'll take
Your hand away that's fiddling on my throat,
And please to know me likewise. Who am I?
Why, one, sir, who is lodging with a friend   15
Three streets off—he's a certain . . . how d'ye call?
Master—a . . . Cosimo of the Medici,[3]
I' the house that caps the corner. Boh! you were best!
Remember and tell me, the day you're hanged,
How you affected such a gullet's-gripe![4]   20
But you, sir, it concerns you that your knaves
Pick up a manner nor discredit you:
Zooks, are we pilchards,[5] that they sweep the streets
And count fair prize what comes into their net?
He's Judas to a tittle, that man is!   25
Just such a face! Why, sir, you make amends.
Lord, I'm not angry! Bid your hangdogs go
Drink out this quarter-florin to the health
Of the munificent House that harbours me
(And many more beside, lads! more beside!)   30
And all's come square again. I'd like his face—
His, elbowing on his comrade in the door
With the pike and lantern,—for the slave that holds
John Baptist's head a-dangle by the hair
With one hand ("Look you, now," as who should say)   35
And his weapon in the other, yet unwiped!
It's not your chance to have a bit of chalk,
A wood-coal or the like? or you should see!
Yes, I'm the painter, since you style me so.
What, brother Lippo's doings, up and down,   40
You know them and they take you? like enough!
I saw the proper twinkle in your eye—
'Tell you, I liked your looks at very first.
Let's sit and set things straight now, hip to haunch.

2. Monastery of the Carmelite friars.
3. Cosimo de Medici (1389–1464) was a wealthy and powerful banker and art patron.
4. Grip on the throat or gullet.
5. Small fish.

Here's spring come, and the nights one makes up bands 45
To roam the town and sing out carnival,
And I've been three weeks shut within my mew,[6]
A-painting for the great man, saints and saints
And saints again. I could not paint all night—
Ouf! I leaned out of window for fresh air. 50
There came a hurry of feet and little feet,
A sweep of lute-strings, laughs, and whifts of song,—
Flower o' the broom,
Take away love, and our earth is a tomb!
Flower o' the quince, 55
I let Lisa go, and what good in life since?
Flower o' the thyme—and so on. Round they went.
Scarce had they turned the corner when a titter
Like the skipping of rabbits by moonlight,—three slim shapes,
And a face that looked up . . . zooks, sir, flesh and blood, 60
That's all I'm made of! Into shreds it went,
Curtain and counterpane and coverlet,
All the bed furniture,—a dozen knots,
There was a ladder! Down I let myself,
Hands and feet, scrambling somehow, and so dropped, 65
And after them. I came up with the fun
Hard by St. Laurence,[7] hail fellow, well met.—
Flower o' the rose,
If I've been merry, what matter who knows?
And so as I was stealing back again 70
To get to bed and have a bit of sleep
Ere I rise up to-morrow and go work
On Jerome[8] knocking at his poor old breast
With his great round stone to subdue the flesh,
You snap me of the sudden. Ah, I see! 75
Though your eye twinkles still, you shake your head—
Mine's shaved,—a monk, you say—the sting's in that!
If Master Cosimo announced himself,
Mum's the word naturally; but a monk!
Come, what am I a beast for? tell us, now! 80
I was a baby when my mother died
And father died and left me in the street.
I starved there, God knows how, a year or two
On fig-skins, melon-parings, rinds and shucks,

6. A pen.
7. San Lorenzo, a church in Florence.
8. St. Jerome (?340–420), Christian ascetic who prepared a Latin translation of the Bible. He is usually portrayed in paintings gazing at a skull and beating his breast with a rock.

Refuse and rubbish. One fine frosty day,   85
My stomach being empty as your hat,
The wind doubled me up and down I went.
Old Aunt Lapaccia trussed me with one hand,
(Its fellow was a stinger as I knew)
And so along the wall, over the bridge,   90
By the straight cut to the convent. Six words there,
While I stood munching my first bread that month:
"So, boy, you're minded," quoth the good fat father
Wiping his own mouth, 'twas refection-time,—[9]
"To quit this very miserable world?   95
"Will you renounce" . . . "the mouthful of bread?" thought I;
By no means! Brief, they made a monk of me;
I did renounce the world, its pride and greed,
Palace, farm, villa, shop and banking-house,
Trash, such as these poor devils of Medici   100
Have given their hearts to—all at eight years old.
Well, sir, I found in time, you may be sure,
'Twas not for nothing—the good bellyful,
The warm serge and the rope that goes all round,
And day-long blessed idleness beside!   105
"Let's see what the urchin's fit for"—that came next.
Not overmuch their way, I must confess.
Such a to-do! they tried me with their books:
Lord, they'd have taught me Latin in pure waste!
Flower o' the clove,   110
All the Latin I construe is, "amo" I love!
But, mind you, when a boy starves in the streets
Eight years together, as my fortune was,
Watching folk's faces to know who will fling
The bit of half-stripped grape-bunch he desires,   115
And who will curse or kick him for his pains,—
Which gentleman processional and fine,
Holding a candle to the Sacrament,
Will wink and let him lift a plate and catch
The droppings of the wax to sell again,   120
Or holla for the Eight[10] and have him whipped,—
How say I?—nay, which dog bites, which lets drop
His bone from the heap of offal in the street,—
Why, soul and sense of him grow sharp alike,
He learns the look of things, and none the less   125

9. Mealtime.
10. Magistrates of Florence.

For admonition from the hunger-pinch.
I had a store of such remarks, be sure,
Which, after I found leisure, turned to use.
I drew men's faces on my copy-books,
Scrawled them within the antiphonary's[11] marge,   130
Joined legs and arms to the long music-notes,
Found eyes and nose and chin for A's and B's,
And made a string of pictures of the world
Betwixt the ins and outs of verb and noun,
On the wall, the bench, the door. The monks looked black.   135
"Nay," quoth the Prior, "turn him out, d' ye say?
In no wise. Lose a crow and catch a lark.
What if at last we get our man of parts,
We Carmelites, like those Camaldolese[12]
And Preaching Friars,[13] to do our church up fine   140
And put the front on it that ought to be!"
And hereupon he bade me daub away.
Thank you! my head being crammed, the walls a blank,
Never was such prompt disemburdening.
First, every sort of monk, the black and white,   145
I drew them, fat and lean: then, folk at church,
From good old gossips waiting to confess
Their cribs[14] of barrel-droppings, candle-ends,—
To the breathless fellow at the altar-foot,
Fresh from his murder, safe and sitting there   150
With the little children round him in a row
Of admiration, half for his beard and half
For that white anger of his victim's son
Shaking a fist at him with one fierce arm,
Signing himself with the other because of Christ   155
(Whose sad face on the cross sees only this
After the passion of a thousand years)
Till some poor girl, her apron o'er her head,
(Which the intense eyes looked through) came at eve
On tiptoe, said a word, dropped in a loaf,   160
Her pair of earrings and a bunch of flowers
(The brute took growling), prayed, and so was gone.
I painted all, then cried, "'T is ask and have;
Choose, for more's ready!"—laid the ladder flat,
And showed my covered bit of cloister-wall.   165

11. A book of antiphons, verses or prayers to be chanted or sung in response.
12. Religious order established c. 1012.
13. Dominicans, named for St. Dominic (1170–1221), were devoted to preaching and study.
14. Petty thefts.

The monks closed in a circle and praised loud
Till checked, taught what to see and not to see,
Being simple bodies,—"That's the very man!
Look at the boy who stoops to pat the dog!
That woman's like the Prior's niece who comes   170
To care about his asthma: it's the life!"
But there my triumph's straw-fire flared and funked;
Their betters took their turn to see and say:
The Prior and the learned pulled a face
And stopped all that in no time. "How? what's here?   175
Quite from the mark of painting, bless us all!
Faces, arms, legs and bodies like the true
As much as pea and pea! it's devil's-game!
Your business is not to catch men with show,
With homage to the perishable clay,   180
But lift them over it, ignore it all,
Make them forget there's such a thing as flesh.
Your business is to paint the souls of men—
Man's soul, and it's a fire, smoke . . . no, it's not . . .
It's vapour done up like a new-born babe—   185
(In that shape when you die it leaves your mouth)
It's . . . well, what matters talking, it's the soul!
Give us no more of body than shows soul!
Here's Giotto,¹⁵ with his Saint a-praising God,
That sets us praising,—why not stop with him?   190
Why put all thoughts of praise out of our head
With wonder at lines, colours, and what not?
Paint the soul, never mind the legs and arms!
Rub all out, try at it a second time.
Oh, that white smallish female with the breasts,   195
She's just my niece . . . Herodias,¹⁶ I would say,—
Who went and danced and got men's heads cut off!
Have it all out!" Now, is this sense, I ask?
A fine way to paint soul, by painting body
So ill, the eye can't stop there, must go further   200
And can't fare worse! Thus, yellow does for white
When what you put for yellow's simply black,
And any sort of meaning looks intense
When all beside itself means and looks nought.
Why can't a painter lift each foot in turn,   205

---

15. Giotto di Bondone (1276–1337), a noted Florentine painter, architect, and sculptor.
16. Another name for Salome. Matthew 14:1–11 tells of King Herod's fulfillment of her request that John the Baptist's head be brought to her on a charger.

Left foot and right foot, go a double step,
Make his flesh liker and his soul more like,
Both in their order? Take the prettiest face,
The Prior's niece . . . patron-saint—is it so pretty
You can't discover if it means hope, fear,   210
Sorrow or joy? won't beauty go with these?
Suppose I've made her eyes all right and blue,
Can't I take breath and try to add life's flash,
And then add soul and heighten them threefold?
Or say there's beauty with no soul at all—   215
(I never saw it—put the case the same—)
If you get simple beauty and nought else,
You get about the best thing God invents:
That's somewhat: and you'll find the soul you have missed,
Within yourself, when you return him thanks.   220
"Rub all out!" Well, well, there's my life, in short,
And so the thing has gone on ever since.
I'm grown a man no doubt, I've broken bounds:
You should not take a fellow eight years old
And make him swear to never kiss the girls.   225
I'm my own master, paint now as I please—
Having a friend, you see, in the Corner-house!
Lord, it's fast holding by the rings in front—
Those great rings serve more purposes than just
To plant a flag in, or tie up a horse!   230
And yet the old schooling sticks, the old grave eyes
Are peeping o'er my shoulder as I work,
The heads shake still—"It's art's decline, my son!
You're not of the true painters, great and old;
Brother Angelico's[17] the man, you'll find;   235
Brother Lorenzo[18] stands his single peer:
Fag on at flesh,[19] you'll never make the third!"
Flower o' the pine,
You keep your mistr . . .[20] manners, and I'll stick to mine!
I'm not the third, then: bless us, they must know!   240
Don't you think they're the likeliest to know,
They with their Latin? So, I swallow my rage,
Clench my teeth, suck my lips in tight, and paint

17. Giovanni da Fiesole (1387–1455), medieval religious artist.
18. Lorenzo Monaco (1370–1425), an artist who belonged to the Camaldolese order.
19. In other words, "Work on [fag on] at painting flesh; you will never be among the three greatest painters."
20. Lippi sings the next couple of lines of the song he has been singing snatches of since line 53. This time, he tactfully emends a verse, substituting "manners" for "mistress."

To please them—sometimes do and sometimes don't;
For, doing most, there's pretty sure to come   245
A turn, some warm eve finds me at my saints—
A laugh, a cry, the business of the world—
(*Flower o' the peach,*
Death for us all, and his own life for each!)
And my whole soul revolves, the cup runs over,   250
The world and life's too big to pass for a dream,
And I do these wild things in sheer despite,
And play the fooleries you catch me at,
In pure rage! The old mill-horse, out at grass
After hard years, throws up his stiff heels so,   255
Although the miller does not preach to him
The only good of grass is to make chaff.
What would men have? Do they like grass or no—
May they or mayn't they? all I want's the thing
Settled for ever one way. As it is,   260
You tell too many lies and hurt yourself:
You don't like what you only like too much,
You do like what, if given you at your word,
You find abundantly detestable.
For me, I think I speak as I was taught;   265
I always see the garden and God there
A-making man's wife: and, my lesson learned,
The value and significance of flesh,
I can't unlearn ten minutes afterwards.

You understand me: I'm a beast, I know.   270
But see, now—why, I see as certainly
As that the morning-star's about to shine,
What will hap some day. We've a youngster here
Comes to our convent, studies what I do,
Slouches and stares and lets no atom drop: 275
His name is Guidi[21]—he'll not mind the monks—
They call him Hulking Tom, he lets them talk—
He picks my practice up—he'll paint apace,
I hope so—though I never live so long,
I know what's sure to follow. You be judge!   280
You speak no Latin more than I, belike,
However, you're my man, you've seen the world
—The beauty and the wonder and the power,
The shapes of things, their colours, lights and shades,

21. Guidi or Masaccio (1401–1428), an artist who painted frescoes in the chapel of Santa Maria del Carmine, the cloister where Lippi resided. It is unclear, given their dates, whether Guidi studied under Lippi or vice versa.

Changes, surprises,—and God made it all! 285
—For what? Do you feel thankful, ay or no,
For this fair town's face, yonder river's line,
The mountain round it and the sky above,
Much more the figures of man, woman, child,
These are the frame to? What's it all about? 290
To be passed over, despised? or dwelt upon,
Wondered at? oh, this last of course!—you say.
But why not do as well as say,—paint these
Just as they are, careless what comes of it?
God's works—paint anyone, and count it crime 295
To let a truth slip. Don't object, "His works
Are here already; nature is complete:
Suppose you reproduce her—(which you can't)
There's no advantage! you must beat her, then."
For, don't you mark? we're made so that we love 300
First when we see them painted, things we have passed
Perhaps a hundred times nor cared to see;
And so they are better, painted—better to us,
Which is the same thing. Art was given for that;
God uses us to help each other so, 305
Lending our minds out. Have you noticed, now,
Your cullion's[22] hanging face? A bit of chalk,
And trust me but you should, though! How much more,
If I drew higher things with the same truth!
That were to take the Prior's pulpit-place, 310
Interpret God to all of you! Oh, oh,
It makes me mad to see what men shall do
And we in our graves! This world's no blot for us,
Nor blank; it means intensely, and means good:
To find its meaning is my meat and drink. 315
"Ay, but you don't so instigate to prayer!"
Strikes in the Prior: "when your meaning's plain
It does not say to folk—remember matins,
Or, mind you fast next Friday!" Why, for this
What need of art at all? A skull and bones, 320
Two bits of stick nailed crosswise, or, what's best,
A bell to chime the hour with, does as well.
I painted a Saint Laurence[23] six months since
At Prato,[24] splashed the fresco[25] in fine style:
"How looks my painting, now the scaffold's down?" 325

22. Rascal.
23. Roman martyred by being burned alive in 258.
24. City near Florence.
25. Painting on fresh, moist plaster.

I ask a brother: "Hugely," he returns—
"Already not one phiz[26] of your three slaves
Who turn the Deacon off his toasted side,
But's scratched and prodded to our heart's content,
The pious people have so eased their own   330
With coming to say prayers there in a rage:
We get on fast to see the bricks beneath.
Expect another job this time next year,
For pity and religion grow i' the crowd—
Your painting serves its purpose!" Hang the fools!   335
—That is—you'll not mistake an idle word
Spoke in a huff by a poor monk, God wot,
Tasting the air this spicy night which turns
The unaccustomed head like Chianti wine!
Oh, the church knows! don't misreport me, now!   340
It's natural a poor monk out of bounds
Should have his apt word to excuse himself:
And hearken how I plot to make amends.
I have bethought me: I shall paint a piece
... There's for you! Give me six months, then go, see   345
Something in Sant' Ambrogio's![27] Bless the nuns!
They want a cast o' my office. I shall paint
God in the midst, Madonna and her babe,
Ringed by a bowery flowery angel-brood,
Lilies and vestments and white faces, sweet   350
As puff on puff of grated orris-root
When ladies crowd to Church at midsummer.[28]
And then i' the front, of course a saint or two—
Saint John, because he saves the Florentines,
Saint Ambrose,[29] who puts down in black and white   355
The convent's friends and gives them a long day,
And Job,[30] I must have him there past mistake,
The man of Uz[31] (and Us without the z,
Painters who need his patience). Well, all these
Secured at their devotion, up shall come   360
Out of a corner when you least expect,
As one by a dark stair into a great light,

26. Face.
27. Convent church in Florence.
28. The painting described is Lippi's *Coronation of the Virgin*, which Browning saw in Florence.
29. Ambrose (c. 339–397) carried out a dedicated pastoral mission. His most famous convert was
Augustine (354–430).
30. Long-suffering Old Testament figure.
31. Job's birthplace.

Music and talking, who but Lippo! I!—
Mazed, motionless and moonstruck—I'm the man!
Back I shrink—what is this I see and hear? 365
I, caught up with my monk's things by mistake,
My old serge gown and rope that goes all round,
I, in this presence, this pure company!
Where's a hole, where's a corner for escape?
Then steps a sweet angelic slip of a thing 370
Forward, puts out a soft palm—"Not so fast!"
—Addresses the celestial presence, "nay—
He made you and devised you, after all,
Though he's none of you! Could Saint John there draw—
His camel-hair[32] make up a painting brush? 375
We come to brother Lippo for all that,
'*Iste perfecit opus!*'"[33] So, all smile—
I shuffle sideways with my blushing face
Under the cover of a hundred wings
Thrown like a spread of kirtles[34] when you're gay 380
And play hot cockles,[35] all the doors being shut,
Till, wholly unexpected, in there pops
The hothead husband! Thus I scuttle off
To some safe bench behind, not letting go
The palm of her, the little lily thing 385
That spoke the good word for me in the nick,
Like the Prior's niece . . . Saint Lucy,[36] I would say.
And so all's saved for me, and for the church
A pretty picture gained. Go, six months hence!
Your hand, sir, and good-bye: no lights, no lights! 390
The street's hushed, and I know my own way back,
Don't fear me! There's the grey beginning. Zooks!

32. According to Mark 1:6, John was clothed in camel's hair.
33. "This man made the work."
34. Skirts.
35. A game in which one player is blindfolded.
36. Fourth-century Sicilian virgin martyr.

THOMAS HUGHES

In 1854, Thomas Hughes (1822–1896) helped establish and then administered F. D. Maurice's Working Men's College, serving from 1872 to 1883 as principal of this institution (see the introductory essay on Maurice in part 2); he also served as a radical member of Parliament devoted to labor reform and union rights. He is best known as the proponent of Victorian "muscular Christianity," although in *The Manliness of Christ* (1879) he suggested that this phrase comprised an unfairly reductive assessment of his moral philosophy. By whatever name it was known, however, the type of virtue that he extolled—a clean-living and combative devotion to social justice enacted within a Christian commonwealth—became familiar to the Victorian public through his immensely popular *Tom Brown's Schooldays* (1857) and the sequel *Tom Brown at Oxford* (1859–61).

Tom Brown's Schooldays depicts the Rugby that Hughes attended from 1834 to 1841 while Thomas Arnold was remolding this public school so that every student "felt that he, young as he might be, was of some use in the little school world, and had a work to do there." Tom Brown is sent to Rugby so that he might "turn out a brave, helpful, truth-telling Englishman, and a gentleman, and a Christian." He does so, becoming a hero-worshipper of the Doctor, the inspiring headmaster who, "with all his heart and soul and strength, [was] striving against whatever was mean and unmanly and unrighteous . . . , fighting for us and by our sides, and calling on us to help him and ourselves and one another." Tom needs more than this fictionalized figure of Thomas Arnold to shape him up to true Christian manliness, however; the influence of a schoolfellow named George Arthur is the decisive factor in turning Tom toward full acceptance of both religious and social responsibilities.

In the first of the following two excerpts from *Tom Brown's Schooldays*, the history of George Arthur's deceased clergyman father is given, and Hughes valorizes the understanding of work as a divine mission best realized in the service of others. In the second passage, young George, recovering from a near-fatal fever, recounts a dream that he has had during his illness. Here, even heaven itself is conceived as a place ennobled by unceasing work, for the vision that George is granted involves both the living and the dead laboring together to establish some greater, if not fully discerned, good.

From *Tom Brown's Schooldays*

From Part 2, Chapter 2: The New Boy

From this time Arthur constantly spoke of his home, and, above all, of his father, who had been dead about a year, and whose memory Tom soon got to love and reverence almost as much as his own son did.

Arthur's father had been the clergyman of a parish in the Midland Counties, which had risen into a large town during the war, and upon which the hard years which followed had fallen with fearful weight. The trade had been half ruined: and then came the old sad story, of masters reducing their establishments, men turned off and wandering about, hungry and wan in body, and fierce in soul, from the thought of wives and children starving at home, and the last sticks of furniture going to the pawn-shop; children taken from school, and lounging about the dirty streets and courts, too listless almost to play, and squalid in rags and misery. And then the fearful struggle between the employers and men; lowerings of wages, strikes, and the long course of oft-repeated crime, ending every now and then with a riot, a fire, and the county yeomanry.[1] There is no need here to dwell upon such tales; the Englishman into whose soul they have not sunk deep, is not worthy the name; you English boys for whom this book is meant (God bless your bright faces and kind hearts!) will learn it all soon enough.

Into such a parish and state of society, Arthur's father had been thrown at the age of twenty-five, a young married parson, full of faith, hope, and love. He had battled with it like a man, and had lots of fine Utopian ideas about the perfectibility of mankind, glorious humanity, and such-like knocked out of his head; and a real wholesome Christian love for the poor struggling, sinning men, of whom he felt himself one, and with and for whom he spent fortune and strength and life, driven into his heart. He had battled like a man, and gotten a man's reward. No silver teapots or salvers, with flowery inscriptions, setting forth his virtues and the appreciation of a genteel parish; no fat living or stall,[2] for which he never looked, and didn't care; no sighs and praises of comfortable dowagers and well got-up young women, who worked him slippers, sugared his tea, and adored him as "a devoted man"; but a manly respect, wrung from the unwilling souls of men who fancied his order their natural enemies; the fear and hatred of every one who was false or unjust in the district, were he master or man; and the blessed sight of

---

1. Ostensibly, Hughes is describing the mid-thirties, the time when George Arthur arrives at Rugby. Hughes's real concern, however, both here and in his commitment to F. D. Maurice's Working Men's College, relates to the low employment and labor unrest of the "Hungry Forties," conditions that obtained at the time Hughes was composing the novel.

2. A living is a position granted to a clergyman that carries with it a fixed amount of property and income. A stall is a fixed seat on either side of the chancel of a cathedral that serves as the official seat of a dignitary.

women and children daily becoming more human and more homely, a comfort to themselves and to their husbands and fathers.

These things of course took time, and had to be fought for with toil and sweat of brain and heart, and with the life-blood poured out. All that, Arthur had laid his account to give, and took as a matter of course; neither pitying himself, or looking on himself as a martyr, when he felt the wear and tear making him feel old before his time, and the stifling air of fever dens telling on his health. His wife seconded him in everything. She had been rather fond of society, and much admired and run after before her marriage; and the London world to which she had belonged, pitied poor Fanny Evelyn when she married the young clergyman, and went to settle in that smoky hole Turley, a very nest of Chartism and Atheism, in a part of the county which all the decent families had had to leave for years. However, somehow or other she didn't seem to care. If her husband's living had been amongst green fields and near pleasant neighbours, she would have liked it better,—that she never pretended to deny. But there they were: the air wasn't bad after all; the people were very good sort of people, civil to you if you were civil to them, after the first brush; and they didn't expect to work miracles, and convert them all off-hand into model Christians. So he and she went quietly among the folk, talking to and treating them just as they would have done people of their own rank. They didn't feel that they were doing anything out of the common way, and so were perfectly natural, and had none of that condescension or consciousness of manner which so outrages the independent poor. And thus they gradually won respect and confidence; and after sixteen years he was looked up to by the whole neighbourhood as *the* just man, *the* man to whom masters and men could go in their strikes, and all in their quarrels and difficulties, and by whom the right and true word would be said without fear or favour. And the women had come round to take her advice, and go to her as a friend in all their troubles; while the children all worshipped the very ground she trod on.

They had three children, two daughters and a son, little Arthur, who came between his sisters. He had been a very delicate boy from his childhood; they thought he had a tendency to consumption, and so he had been kept at home and taught by his father, who had made a companion of him, and from whom he had gained good scholarship, and a knowledge of and interest in many subjects which boys in general never come across till they are many years older.

Just as he reached his thirteenth year, and his father had settled that he was strong enough to go to school, and, after much debating with himself, had resolved to send him there, a desperate typhus-fever broke out in the town; most of the other clergy, and almost all the doctors, ran away; the work fell with tenfold weight on those who stood to their work. Arthur and his wife both caught the fever, of which he died in a few days, and she recovered, having been able to nurse him to the end, and store up his last words. He was sensible to the last, and calm and happy, leaving his wife and children with fearless trust for a few years in the hands of the Lord and Friend who had lived and died for him, and for whom he, to the best of his power, had lived and died. His widow's mourning was deep and gentle; she was more affected by the request of the Committee of a Freethinking club, established in the town by some of the factory hands (which he had striven against with might and main, and nearly suppressed), that some of their number might be allowed to help bear the coffin, than by anything else. Two of them were chosen, who with six other labouring men, his own fellow-workmen and friends, bore him to his grave—a man who had fought the Lord's fight even unto the death. The shops were closed and the factories shut that day in the parish, yet no master stopped the day's wages; but for many a year afterwards the townsfolk felt the want of that brave, hopeful, loving parson, and his wife, who had lived to teach them mutual forbearance and helpfulness, and had *almost* at last given them a glimpse of what this old world would be, if people would live for God and each other, instead of for themselves.[3]

From Part 2, Chapter 6: Fever in the School

Arthur paused a moment, and then said quickly, "I'll tell you how it all happened. At first, when I was sent to the sick-room, and found I had really got the fever, I was terribly frightened. I thought I should die, and I could not face it for a moment. I don't think it was sheer cowardice at first, but I thought how hard it was to be taken away from my mother and sisters, and you all, just as I was beginning to see my way to many things, and to feel that I might be a man and do a man's work. To die without having fought, and worked, and given one's life away, was too hard to bear. I got terribly impatient, and accused God of injustice, and strove to justify myself; and the harder I strove the deeper I sank. Then the image of my dear father often came across me, but I turned from it. Whenever it came, a heavy numbing throb seemed to take hold of my heart, and say, 'Dead—dead—dead.' And I cried out, 'The living, the living shall praise Thee, O God; the dead cannot praise Thee.[4] There is no work in the grave;[5] in the night no man can work.[6] But I can work. I can do great things. I *will* do great things. Why wilt Thou slay me?' And so I struggled and plunged, deeper and deeper, and went down into a living black tomb. I was alone there, with no power to stir or think; alone with myself; beyond the reach of all human fellowship; beyond Christ's reach, I thought, in my nightmare. You, who are brave and bright and strong, can have no idea of that agony. Pray to God you never may. Pray as for your life."

3. Hughes's depiction of how lower-class resentment and prejudices may be overcome by the dedicated work of a caring pastor and his wife received much fuller treatment from the granddaughter of Rugby headmaster Thomas Arnold, Mrs. Humphrey Ward; the hero of her *Robert Elsmere* (1888) is, in his devotion to the working class if not in his theological convictions, the embodiment of ideals set forth by Hughes, F. D. Maurice, Charles Kingsley, and other Christian Socialists.

4. George Arthur's speech is replete with echoes of well-known Scriptural verses. See Isaiah 38:16–19.

5. See Ecclesiastes 9:10.

6. See John 9:4. Carlyle, whose worship of work may be seen throughout Hughes's writings, gave repeated emphasis to this particular biblical verse, using it in *Sartor Resartus* to conclude the crucial chapter "The Everlasting Yea."

Arthur stopped—from exhaustion, Tom thought; but what between his fear lest Arthur should hurt himself, his awe, and longing for him to go on, he couldn't ask, or stir to help him.

Presently he went on, but quite calm and slow. "I don't know how long I was in that state. For more than a day, I know; for I was quite conscious, and lived my outer life all the time, and took my medicines, and spoke to my mother, and heard what they said. But I didn't take much note of time; I thought time was over for me, and that the tomb was what was beyond. Well, on last Sunday morning, as I seemed to lie in that tomb, alone, as I thought, for ever and ever, the black dead wall was cleft in two, and I was caught up and borne through into the light by some great power, some living mighty spirit. Tom, do you remember the living creatures and the wheels in Ezekiel? It was just like that: 'When they went I heard the noise of their wings, like the noise of great waters, as the voice of the Almighty, the voice of speech, as the noise of an host; when they stood they let down their wings' . . . 'and they went every one straight forward; whither the spirit was to go they went, and they turned not when they went.'[7] And we rushed through the bright air, which was full of myriads of living creatures, and paused on the brink of a great river. And the power held me up, and I knew that that great river was the grave, and death dwelt there; but not the death I had met in the black tomb—that I felt was gone for ever. For on the other bank of the great river I saw men and women and children rising up pure and bright, and the tears were wiped from their eyes, and they put on glory and strength, and all weariness and pain fell away.[8] And beyond were a multitude which no man could number, and they worked at some great work; and they who rose from the river went on and joined in the work. They all worked, and each worked in a different way, but all at the same work. And I saw there my father, and the men in the old town whom I knew when I was a child; many a hard stern man, who never came to church, and whom they called atheist and infidel. There they were, side by side with my father, whom I had seen toil and die for them, and women and little children, and the seal was on the foreheads of all. And I longed to see what the work was, and could not; so I tried to plunge in the river, for I thought I would join them, but I could not. Then I looked about to see how they got into the river. And this I could not see, but I saw myriads on this side, and they too worked, and I knew that it was the same work; and the same seal was on their foreheads.[9] And though I saw that there was toil and anguish in the work of these, and that most that were working were blind and feeble, yet I longed no more to plunge into the river, but more and more to know what the work was. And as I looked I saw my mother and my sisters, and I saw the Doctor, and you, Tom, and hundreds more whom I knew; and at last I saw myself too, and I was toiling and doing ever so little a piece of the great work. Then it all melted away, and the power left me, and as it left me I thought I heard a voice say, 'The vision is

7. See the first chapter of Ezekiel.

8. The reference here is to the promised New Jerusalem of Christian eschatology: see Revelation 21: 1–5.

9. The seal is the seal of God: see Revelation 9:4.

for an appointed time; though it tarry, wait for it, for in the end it shall speak and not lie, it shall surely come, it shall not tarry.' It was early morning I know then, it was so quiet and cool, and my mother was fast asleep in the chair by my bedside; but it wasn't only a dream of mine. I know it wasn't a dream. Then I fell into a deep sleep, and only woke after afternoon chapel; and the Doctor came and gave me the Sacrament, as I told you. I told him and my mother I should get well—I knew I should; but I couldn't tell them why. Tom," said Arthur, gently, after another minute, "do you see why I could not grieve now to see my dearest friend die? It can't be—it isn't all fever or illness. God would never have let me see it so clear if it wasn't true. I don't understand it all yet—it will take me my life and longer to do that—to find out what the work is."

FLORENCE NIGHTINGALE

N O OTHER FIGURE could more fully exemplify the Victorian enthusiasm for self-denial and unremitting work to serve others than Florence Nightingale (1820–1910). Throughout her long career as an activist following the Crimean War, she worked obsessively, refusing any release, however temporary, from work and denying herself a social or personal life while becoming harshly angry when any of her collaborators sought to have one. The results of her efforts are impressive, the more so because she never held an official position that accorded her authority to do anything: by means of moral suasion, public bullying, behind-the-scenes diplomacy, and sheer tenacity of will, she brought about reform in military operations, not alone in health and sanitation but also in systems of supply, professional appointments, and training; she also argued successfully for the acceptance of district health inspectors; she helped reform the practice of nursing and promoted schooling for professional nurses; and she lobbied for important changes in England's system of public sanitation. She is best known, however, as the Lady of the Lamp, the woman whose shadow the wounded soldiers of the Crimean War would kiss as she moved through the wards to tend to them.

Born to wealth and privilege, gifted with superior intelligence and personal beauty, Nightingale became, in her twenties, determined to create for herself a life of meaningful activity rather than the vapid social existence of the idle upper-class woman. (Nightingale, however, was distrustful of the burgeoning woman's movement and consistently declined to associate herself with it.) Struggling against familial opposition as well as widespread social prejudice, she managed, in 1854, to secure an appointment as director of the first official group of women nurses to be employed for the British army at the front lines. For two years, she worked tirelessly in the Crimea, laboring to change what she publicly denounced in letters and reports sent home: the filth, chaotic administration, lack of appropriate supplies, carelessness about basic hygiene, and indifference to safeguards against disease, all of which characterized the military hospitals of the time. Her devotion to the common soldiers (a commitment that continued when she returned home), her manifest integrity, and the simple heroism of her decision to put herself into danger to serve the men fighting for England gave her legendary status. When she returned to London, she was consulted (and she made certain that she was consulted) about governmental decisions concerning both military matters and issues of public health in England and in the overseas Empire. She remained, for the next half century, the only woman whose popularity and moral authority could rival the queen's.

Figure 1.2. Jerry Barrett, *Florence Nightingale Receiving the Wounded at Scutari in 1856.*
Courtesy of The Forbes Magazine Collection, New York. © All rights reserved.

Jerry Barrett (1814–1906) worked on site in Turkey to produce this image of *Florence Nightingale Receiving the Wounded at Scutari in 1856;* Barrett himself is pictured in the window. In 1854, Florence Nightingale agreed to serve as superintendent of nurses for the English General Military Hospitals in Turkey where England was engaged in the Crimean War against Russia. She succeeded in improving nursing practices and sanitary conditions in the army hospitals and came to be revered as a patriot for her support of English soldiers.

Cassandra, however, composed in 1852 and privately printed in 1860 in the second volume of *Suggestions for Thought to Searchers after Religious Truth,* is a record not of triumph but of the desperation and depression that confronted Nightingale as a young woman of leisure whose life lacked purpose. Autobiographical in substance, this essay of sorts describes the vacuous emotional and intellectual life generally led by privileged women. What was supposed to define this existence—freedom from civic responsibility and work in the public sphere— was what Nightingale found stultifying. Assessing her life as sterile and futile, largely because of the constraints placed upon her as a woman, she craved a work, a mission that might endow her life with significance and meaning. Only in purposeful activity could a woman discover or create a distinctive identity, a true self: "how different would be [our] success, if we learnt our work as a serious study, and followed it out steadily as a profession!" The irony implicit in the title of the piece is that, in classical mythology, Cassandra is a woman gifted with the ability to divine truths but burdened with the curse that no one will believe her. This irony is modulated somewhat in Nightingale's epigraph echoing Luke 3:4, suggesting that her crying in the wilderness may precede social renewal. *Cassandra* bears close relation to the selections included in part 4 of the anthology, "(Separate) Spheres of Work"; in particular, Nightingale's essay offers parallels to the tensions between gendered spheres of work and mission that Tennyson analyzes in *The Princess* and to the assessment of woman's work and life set forth in Barrett Browning's *Aurora Leigh* (both of which are excerpted in part 4), the first published some four years before and the second some four years after Nightingale composed *Cassandra*.

Cassandra

I

"The voice of one crying in the" crowd,

"Prepare ye the way of the Lord."

One often comes to be thus wandering alone in the bitterness of life without. It might be that such an one might be tempted to seek an escape in hope of a more congenial sphere. Yet, perhaps, if prematurely we dismiss ourselves from this world, all may even have to be suffered through again—the premature birth may not contribute to the production of another being, which must be begun again from the beginning.

Such an one longs to replunge into the happy unconscious sleep of the rest of the race! they slumber in one another's arms—they are not yet awake. To them evil and suffering are not, for they are not conscious of evil. While one alone, awake and prematurely alive to it, must wander out in silence and solitude—such an one has awakened too early, has risen up too soon, has rejected the companionship of the race, unlinked to any human being. Such an one sees the evil they do not see, and yet has no power to discover the remedy for it.

Why have women passion, intellect, moral activity—these three—and a place in society where no one of the three can be exercised? Men say that God punishes for complaining. No, but men are angry with misery. They are irritated with women for not being happy. They take it as a personal offence. To God alone may women complain, without insulting Him!

And women, who are afraid, while in words they acknowledge that God's work is good, to say, Thy will be *not* done (declaring another order of society from that which He has made), go about maudling[1] to each other and teaching to their daughters that "women have no passions." In the conventional society, which men have made for women, and women have accepted, they *must* have none, they *must* act the farce of hypocrisy, the lie that they are without passion—and therefore what else can they say to their daughters, without giving the lie to themselves?

"Suffering, sad" female "humanity!"[2] What are these feelings which they are taught to consider as disgraceful, to deny to themselves? What form do the Chinese feet assume when denied their proper development?[3] If the young girls of the "higher classes," who never commit a false step, whose justly earned reputations were never sullied even by the stain which the fruit of mere "knowledge of good and evil"[4] leaves behind, were to speak, and say what are their thoughts employed upon, their *thoughts*, which alone are free, what would they say?

That, with the phantom companion of their fancy, they talk (not love, they are too innocent, too pure, too full of genius and imagination for that, but) they talk, in fancy, of that which interests them most; they seek a companion for their every thought; the companion they find not in reality they seek in fancy, or, if not that, if not absorbed in endless conversations, they see themselves engaged with him in stirring events, circumstances which call out the interest wanting to them. Yes, fathers, mothers, you who see your daughter proudly rejecting all semblance of flirtation, primly engaged in the duties of the breakfast table, you little think how her fancy compensates itself by endless interviews and sympathies (sympathies either for ideas or events) with the fancy's companion of the hour! And you say, "She is not susceptible. Women have no passion." Mothers, who cradle yourselves in visions about the domestic hearth, how many of your sons and daughters are *there*, do you think, while sitting round under your complacent maternal eye? Were you there yourself during your own (now forgotten) girlhood?

What are the thoughts of these young girls while one is singing Schubert,[5] another is reading the Review,[6] and a third is busy embroidering? Is not one fancying herself the nurse of some new friend in sickness; another engaging in

1. Engaging in excessive and intellectually vapid sentimental conversation.

2. The quotation is from American poet Henry W. Longfellow (1807–1882), "The Goblet of Life":

O suffering, sad humanity!
O ye afflicted ones, who lie
Steeped to the lips in misery,
Longing, yet afraid to die,
Patient, though sorely tried!

3. Upper-class Chinese women had their feet bound in such fashion that they became incapable of walking regularly or of using their lower limbs to work. The practice at once demonstrated the women's subservience to men and the economic privilege of the fathers and husbands who would not need their women to engage in hard labor. There is a pointed comparison to the ways in which Victorian women were, by the emptiness of their daily activities, physically and emotionally incapacitated, excluded from control of their own lives, and exploited as validations of the economic power of their fathers, brothers, and husbands.

4. Genesis 2:16–17.

5. Franz Peter Schubert (1797–1828) was an Austrian composer.

6. Either *The Edinburgh Review* or *The Quarterly Review*, respectively the Whig and Tory journals most prominent in the nineteenth century.

romantic dangers with him, such as call out the character and afford more food for sympathy than the monotonous events of domestic society; another undergoing unheard-of trials under the observation of someone whom she has chosen as the companion of her dream? another having a loving and loved companion in the life she is living, which many do not want to change?

And is not all this most natural, inevitable? Are they, who are too much ashamed of it to confess it even to themselves, to be blamed for that which cannot be otherwise, the causes of which stare one in the face, *if one's eyes were not closed?* Many struggle against this as a "snare." No Trappist[7] ascetic watches or fasts more in the body than these do in the soul! They understand the discipline of Thebaid[8]— the life-long agonies to which those strong moral Mohicans[9] subjected themselves. How cordially they could do the same, in order to escape the worse torture of wandering "vain imaginations." But the laws of God for moral well-being are not thus to be obeyed. We fast mentally, scourge ourselves morally, use the intellectual hair-shirt, in order to subdue the perpetual day-dreaming, which is so dangerous! We resolve "this day month I will be free from it"; twice a day with prayer and written record of the times when we have indulged in it, we endeavour to combat it. Never, with the slightest success. By mortifying vanity we do ourselves no good. It is the want of interest in our life which produces it; by filling up that want of interest in our life we can alone remedy it. And, did we even see this, how can we make the difference? How obtain the interest which Society declares *she* does not want, and *we* cannot want?

What are novels? What is the secret of the charm of every romance that ever was written? The first thing in a good novel is to place the persons together in circumstances which naturally call out the high feelings and thoughts of the character, which afford food for sympathy between them on these points—romantic events they are called. The second is that the heroine has *generally* no family ties (almost *invariably* no mother), or, if she has, these do not interfere with her entire independence.

These two things constitute the main charm of reading novels. Now, in as far as these are good and not spurious interests, let us see what we have to correspond with them in real life. Can high sympathies be fed upon the opera, the exhibitions, the gossip of the House of Commons, and the political caricature? If, together, man and woman approach any of the high questions of social, political, or religious life, they are said (and justly—under our present disqualifications) to be going "too far." That such things can be!

"Is it Thou, Lord?" And He said, "It is I."[10] Let our hearts be still.

---

7. A particularly ascetic branch of the Roman Catholic Cistercian Order, the Trappists were established in the seventeenth century at La Trappe in Normandy.

8. The Theban Legion of the Roman Empire (also known as the Thundering Legion), made up of Christian soldiers and led by Saint Maurice, was noted for its discipline and success.

9. An American Indian tribe whom Nightingale construes as Spartan in virtue and discipline.

10. See Matthew 14:22–33 for the story of Jesus' walking on the water. For Nightingale, both the possibility of miracles happening and the importance of faith in sustaining the miraculous are emphasized as the apostle Peter, being assured that it is the Lord who walks on the water before him, first

II

> "Yet I would spare no pang,
> Would wish no torture less,
> The more that anguish racks,
> The earlier it will bless."[11]

Give us back our suffering, we cry to Heaven in our hearts—suffering rather than indifferentism; for out of nothing comes nothing.[12] But out of suffering may come the cure. Better have pain than paralysis! A hundred struggle and drown in the breakers. One discovers the new world. But rather, ten times rather, die in the surf, heralding the way to that new world, than stand idly on the shore!

Passion, intellect, moral activity—these three have never been satisfied in woman. In this cold and oppressive conventional atmosphere, they cannot be satisfied. To say more on this subject would be to enter into the whole history of society, of the present state of civilization.

Look at that lizard—"it is not hot," he says, "I like it. The atmosphere which enervates you is life to me." The state of society which some complain of makes others happy. Why should these complain to those? *They* do not suffer. *They* would not understand it, any more than that lizard would comprehend the sufferings of a Shetland sheep.

The progressive world is necessarily divided into two classes—those who take the best of what there is and enjoy it—those who wish for something better and try to create it. Without these two classes, the world would be badly off. They are the very conditions of progress, both the one and the other. Were there none who were discontented with what they have, the world would never reach anything better. And, through the other class, which is constantly taking the best of what the first is creating for them, a balance is secured, and that which is conquered is held fast. But with neither class must we quarrel for not possessing the privileges of the other. The laws of the nature of each make it impossible.

Is discontent a privilege?

Yes, it is a privilege to suffer for your race—a privilege not reserved to the Redeemer and the martyrs alone, but one enjoyed by numbers in every age.

---

steps confidently on the waves and himself walks on water but then doubts and immediately begins to sink.

11. The epigraph is a slightly altered version of two lines from the penultimate stanza of "The Prisoner. A Fragment" by Emily Brontë (1818–1848), which in their original context read:

> "Yet I would lose no sting, would wish no torture less;
> The more that anguish racks the earlier it will bless;
> And robed in fires of Hell, or bright with heavenly shine,
> If it but herald Death, the vision is divine."

An excerpt from a longer manuscript poem titled "Julian M. and A. G. Rochelle," "The Prisoner" was first published in 1846 in the Brontë sisters' pseudonymous collection *Poems by Currer, Ellis, and Acton Bell.*

12. Nightingale echoes Lear's words to Cordelia: Shakespeare's *King Lear* 1.1.90.

The common-place lives of thousands; and in that is its only interest—its only merit as a history: vis., that it *is* the type of common sufferings—the story of one who has not the courage to resist nor to submit to the civilization of her time—is this.

Poetry and imagination begin life. A child will fall on its knees on the gravel walk at the sight of a pink hawthorn in full flower, when it is by itself, to praise God for it.

Then comes intellect. It wishes to satisfy the wants which intellect creates for it. But there is a physical, not moral, impossibility of supplying the wants of the intellect in the state of civilization at which we have arrived. The stimulus, the training, the time, are all three wanting to us; or, in other words, the means and inducements are not there.

Look at the poor lives which we lead. It is a wonder that we are so good as we are, not that we are so bad. In looking round we are struck with the power of the organizations we see, not with their want of power. Now and then, it is true, we are conscious that *there* is an inferior organization, but, in general, just the contrary. Mrs. A. has the imagination, the poetry of a Murillo,[13] and has sufficient power of execution to show that she might have had a great deal more. Why is she not a Murillo? From a material difficulty, not a mental one. If she has a knife and fork in her hands during three hours of the day, she cannot have a pencil or brush. Dinner is the great sacred ceremony of this day, the great sacrament. To be absent from dinner is equivalent to being ill. Nothing else will excuse us from it. Bodily incapacity is the only apology valid.[14] If she has a pen and ink in her hands during other three hours, writing answers for the penny post; again, she cannot have her pencil, and so *ad infinitum* through life. People have no type before them in their lives, neither fathers and mothers, nor the children themselves. They look at things in detail. They say, "It is very desirable that A., my daughter, should go to such a party, should know such a lady, should sit by such a person." It is true. But what standard have they before them? of the nature and destination of man? The very words are rejected as pedantic. But might they not, at least, have a type in their minds that such an one might be a discoverer through her intellect, such another through her art, a third through her moral power?

Women often try one branch of intellect after another in their youth, *e.g.,* mathematics. But that, least of all, is compatible with the life of "society." It is impossible to follow up anything systematically. Women often long to enter some man's profession where they would find direction, competition (or rather opportunity of measuring the intellect with others), and, above all, time.

In those wise institutions, mixed as they are with many follies, which will last as long as the human race lasts, because they are adapted to the wants of the human race; those institutions which we call monasteries, and which, embracing much

---

13. Bartolume Esteban Murillo (1617–1682) was a Spanish painter.

14. After she had returned from the Crimea, for several years Nightingale adopted the pretence of being ill—confined to her bed—so that she might work undisturbed by family and friends; much of her voluminous professional correspondence was composed while she lay a-bed, an ostensible invalid, throughout the day.

that is contrary to the laws of nature, are yet better adapted to the union of the life of action and that of thought than any other mode of life with which we are acquainted; in many such, four and a half hours, at least, are daily set aside for thought, rules are given for thought, training and opportunity afforded. Among us, there is *no* time appointed for this purpose, and the difficulty is that, in our social life, we must be always doubtful whether we ought not to be with somebody else or be doing something else.

Are men better off than women in this?

If one calls upon a friend in London and sees her son in the drawing-room, it strikes one as odd to find a young man sitting idling in his mother's drawing-room in the morning. For men, who are seen much in those haunts, there is no end of the epithets we have; "knights of the carpet," "drawing-room heroes," "ladies' men." But suppose we were to see a number of men in the morning sitting round a table in the drawing-room, looking at prints, doing worsted work,[15] and reading little books, how we should laugh! A member of the House of Commons was once known to do worsted work. Of another man was said, "His only fault is that he is too good; he drives out with his mother every day in the carriage, and if he is asked anywhere he answers that he must dine with his mother, but, if she can spare him, he will come in to tea, and he does not come."

Now, why is it more ridiculous for a man than for a woman to do worsted work and drive out every day in the carriage? Why should we laugh if we were to see a parcel of men sitting round a drawing-room table in the morning, and think it all right if they were women?

Is man's time more valuable than woman's? or is the difference between man and woman this, that woman has confessedly nothing to do?

Women are never supposed to have any occupation of sufficient importance *not* to be interrupted, except "suckling their fools";[16] and women themselves have accepted this, have written books to support it, and have trained themselves so as to consider whatever they do as *not* of such value to the world or to others, but that they can throw it up at the first "claim of social life." They have accustomed themselves to consider intellectual occupation as a merely selfish amusement, which it is their "duty" to give up for every trifler more selfish than themselves.

A young man (who was afterwards useful and known in his day and generation) when busy reading and sent for by his proud mother to shine in some morning visit, came; but, after it was over, he said, "Now, remember, this is not to happen again. I came that you might not think me sulky, but I shall not come again." But for a young woman to send such a message to her mother and sisters, how impertinent it would be! A woman of great administrative powers said that she never undertook anything which she "could not throw by at once, if necessary."

How do we explain then the many cases of women who have distinguished themselves in classics, mathematics, even in politics?

Widowhood, ill-health, or want of bread, these three explanations or excuses

15. Knitting, crocheting, tatting.
16. *Othello* 2.1.160: "To suckle fools and chronicle small beer."

are supposed to justify a woman in taking up an occupation. In some cases, no doubt, an indomitable force of character will suffice without any of these three, but such are rare.

But see how society fritters away the intellects of those committed to her charge! It is said that society is necessary to sharpen the intellect. But what do we seek society for? It does sharpen the intellect, because it is a kind of *tour-de-force* to say something at a pinch—unprepared and uninterested with any subject, to improvise something under difficulties. But what "go we out for to seek?"[17] To take the chance of some one having something to say which we want to hear? or of our finding something to say which *they* want to hear? You have a little to say, but not much. You often make a stipulation with some one else, "Come in ten minutes, for I shall not be able to find enough to spin out longer than that." You are not to talk of anything very interesting, for the essence of society is to prevent any long conversations and all *tête-à-têtes*. "Glissez, n'appuyez pas"[18] is its very motto. The praise of a good *"maîtresse de maison"*[19] consists in this, that she allows no one person to be too much absorbed in, or too long about, a conversation. She always recalls them to their "duty." People do not go into the company of their fellow-creatures for what would seem a very sufficient reason, namely, that they have something to say to them, or something that they want to hear from them; but in the vague hope that they may find something to say.

Then as to solitary opportunities. Women never have half an hour in all their lives (excepting before or after anybody is up in the house) that they can call their own, without fear of offending or of hurting some one. Why do people sit up so late, or, more rarely, get up so early? Not because the day is not long enough, but because they have "no time in the day to themselves."

If we do attempt to do anything in company, what is the system of literary exercise which we pursue? Everybody reads aloud out of their own book or newspaper—or, every five minutes, something is said. And what is it to be "read aloud to?" The most miserable exercise of the human intellect. Or rather, is it any exercise at all? It is like lying on one's back, with one's hands tied and having liquid poured down one's throat. Worse than that, because suffocation would immediately ensue and put a stop to this operation. But no suffocation would stop the other.

So much for the satisfaction of the intellect. Yet for a married woman in society, it is even worse. A married woman was heard to wish that she could break a limb that she might have a little time to herself. Many take advantage of the fear of "infection" to do the same.

It is a thing *so* accepted among women that they have nothing to do, that one woman has not the least scruple in saying to another, "I will come and spend the

17. Luke 12:27–31.
18. "Slide along; don't press the point."
19. "Mistress of the home." Nightingale had particularly strained relations with her mother and her sister, both of whom feared and resented her wishes to step outside the boundaries of decorous activity prescribed for young women.

morning with you." And you would be thought quite surly and absurd, if you were to refuse it on the plea of occupation. Nay, it is thought a mark of amiability and affection, if you are "on such terms" that you can "come in" "any morning you please."

In a country house, if there is a large party of young people, "You will spend the morning with us," they say to the neighbours, "we will drive together in the afternoon," "tomorrow we will make an expedition, and we will spend the evening together." And this is thought friendly, and spending time in a pleasant manner. So women play through life. Yet time is the most valuable of all things. If they had come every morning and afternoon and robbed us of half-a-crown we should have had redress from the police. But it is laid down, that our time is of no value. If you offer a morning visit to a professional man, and say, "I will just stay an hour with you, if you will allow me, till so and so comes back to fetch me"; it costs him the earnings of an hour, and therefore he has a right to complain. But women have no right, because it is "*only* their time."

Women have no means given them, whereby they *can* resist the "claims of social life." They are taught from their infancy upwards that it is wrong, ill-tempered, and a misunderstanding of "a woman's mission" (with a great M.) if they do not allow themselves *willingly* to be interrupted at all hours. If a woman has once put in a claim to be treated as a man by some work of science or art or literature, which she can *show* as the "fruit of her leisure," then she will be considered justified in *having* leisure (hardly, perhaps, even then). But if not, not. If she has nothing to show, she must resign herself to her fate.

III

"I like riding about this beautiful place, why don't you? I like walking about the garden, why don't you?" is the common expostulation—as if we were children, whose spirits rise during a fortnight's holidays, who think that they will last for ever—and look neither backwards nor forwards.

Society triumphs over many. They wish to regenerate the world with their institutions, with their moral philosophy, with their love. Then they sink to living from breakfast till dinner, from dinner till tea, with a little worsted work, and to looking forward to nothing but bed.

When shall we see a life full of steady enthusiasm, walking straight to its aim, flying home, as that bird is now, against the wind—with the calmness and the confidence of one who knows the laws of God and can apply them?

What *do* we see? We see great and fine organizations deteriorating. We see girls and boys of seventeen, before whose noble ambitions, heroic dreams, and rich endowments we bow our heads, as before *God incarnate in the flesh*. But, ere they are thirty, they are withered, paralysed, extinguished. "We have forgotten our visions," they say themselves.

The "dreams of youth" have become a proverb. That organizations, early rich, fall far short of their promise has been repeated to satiety. But is it extraordinary that it should be so? For do we ever *utilize* this heroism? Look how it lives upon itself and perishes for lack of food. We do not know what to do with it. We had rather that it should not be there. Often we laugh at it. Always we find it troublesome. Look at the poverty of our life! Can we expect anything else but poor creatures to come out of it? Did Michael Angelo's genius fail, did Pascal's die in its bud, did Sir Isaac Newton[20] become a common-place sort of man? In two of these cases the knife wore out the sheath. But the knife itself did not become rusty, till the body was dead or infirm.

Why cannot we *make use* of the noble rising heroisms of our own day, instead of leaving them to rust?

They have nothing to do.

Are they to be employed in sitting in the drawing-room, saying words which may as well not be said, which could be said as well if *they* were not there?

Women often strive to live by intellect. The clear, brilliant, sharp radiance of intellect's moonlight rising upon such an expanse of snow is dreary, it is true, but some love its solemn desolation, its silence, its solitude—if they are but *allowed* to live in it; if they are not perpetually baulked and disappointed. But a woman cannot live in the light of intellect. Society forbids it. Those conventional frivolities, which are called her "duties," forbid it. Her "domestic duties," high-sounding words, which, for the most part, are but bad habits (which she has not the courage to enfranchise herself from, the strength to break through) forbid it. What are these duties (or bad habits)?—Answering a multitude of letters which lead to nothing, from her so-called friends—keeping herself up to the level of the world that she may furnish her quota of amusement at the breakfast-table; driving out her company in the carriage. And all these things are exacted from her by her family which, if she is good and affectionate, will have more influence with her than the world.

What wonder if, wearied out, sick at heart with hope deferred, the springs of will broken, not seeing clearly *where* her duty lies, she abandons intellect as a vocation and takes it only, as we use the moon, by glimpses through her tight-closed window-shutters?

The family? It is too narrow a field for the development of an immortal spirit, be that spirit male or female. The chances are a thousand to one that, in that small sphere, the task for which that immortal spirit is destined by the qualities and the gifts which its Creator has placed within it, will not be found.

The family uses people, *not* for what they are, not for what they are intended to be, but for what it wants them for—for its own uses. It thinks of them not as what God has made them, but as the something which *it* has arranged that they shall be. If it wants some one to sit in the drawing-room, *that* some one is to be supplied by

---

20. Michelangelo Buonarroti (1475–1564) was an Italian painter and sculptor. Blaise Pascal (1623–1662) was a French philosopher and theologian. Sir Isaac Newton (1642–1727) was an English mathematician and scientist.

the family, though that member may be destined for science, or for education, or for active superintendence by God, *i.e.*, by the gifts within.

This system dooms some minds to incurable infancy, others to silent misery.

And family boasts that it has performed its mission well, in as far as it has enabled the individual to say, "I have *no* peculiar work, nothing but what the moment brings me, nothing that I cannot throw up at once at anybody's claim"; in as far, that is, as it has *destroyed* the individual life. And the individual thinks that a great victory has been accomplished, when, at last, she is able to say that she has "no personal desires or plans." What is this but throwing the gifts of God aside as worthless, and substituting for them those of the world?

Marriage is the only chance (and it is but a chance) offered to women for escape from this death; and how eagerly and how ignorantly it is embraced!

At present we live to impede each other's satisfactions; competition, domestic life, society, what is it all but this? We go somewhere where we are not wanted and where we don't want to go. What else is conventional life? *Passivity* when we want to be active. So many hours spent every day in passively doing what conventional life tells us, when we would so gladly be at work.

And is it a wonder that all individual life is extinguished?

Women dream of a great sphere of steady, not sketchy benevolence, of moral activity, for which they would fain be trained and fitted, instead of working in the dark, neither knowing nor registering whither their steps lead, whether farther from or nearer to the aim.

For how do people exercise their moral activity now? We visit, we teach, we talk, among "the poor"; we are told, "don't look for the fruits, cast thy bread upon the waters: for thou shalt find it after many days."[21] Certainly "don't look," for you won't see. You will *not* "find it," and then you would "strike work."

How different would be the heart for the work, and how different would be the success, if we learnt our work as a serious study, and followed it out steadily as a profession!

Were the physician to set to work at *his* trade, as the philanthropist does at his, how many bodies would he not spoil before he cured one?

We set the treatment of bodies so high above the treatment of souls, that the physician occupies a higher place in society than the schoolmaster. The governess is to have every one of God's gifts; she is to do that which the mother herself is incapable of doing; but our son must not degrade himself by marrying the governess, nor our daughter the tutor, though she might marry the medical man.

But my medical man does do something for me, it is said, my tutor has done nothing.

This is true, this is the real reason. And what a condemnation of the state of mental science it is! Low as is physical science, that of the mind is still lower.

Women long for an education to teach them *to teach*, to teach them the laws of the human mind and how to apply them—and knowing how imperfect, in the

---

21. Ecclesiastes 11:1.

present state of the world, such an education must be, they long for experience, not patch-work experience, but experience followed up and systematized, to enable them to know what they are about and *where* they are "casting their bread" and whether it is *"bread"* or a stone.[22]

How should we learn a language if we were to give to it an hour a week? A fortnight's steady application would make more way in it than a year of such patch-work. A "lady" can hardly go to "her school" two days running. She cannot leave the breakfast-table—or she must be fulfilling some little frivolous "duty," which others ought not to exact, or which might just as well be done some other time.

Dreaming always—never accomplishing; thus women live—too much ashamed of their dreams, which they think "romantic," to tell them where they will be laughed at, even if not considered wrong.

With greater strength of purpose they might accomplish something. But if they were strong, all of them, they would not need to have their story told, for all the world would read it in the mission they have fulfilled. It is for common place, every-day characters that we tell our tale—because it is the sample of hundreds of lives (or rather deaths) of persons who cannot fight with society, or who, unsupported by the sympathies about them, give up their own destiny as not worth the fierce and continued struggle necessary to accomplish it. *One* struggle they *could* make and be free (and, in the Church of Rome, many, many, unallured by any other motive, make this one struggle to enter a convent);[23] but the perpetual series of petty spars,[24] with discouragements between, and doubts as to whether they are right—these wear out the very life necessary to make them.

If a man were to follow up his profession or occupation at odd times, how would he do it? Would he become skilful in that profession? It is acknowledged by women themselves that they are inferior in every occupation to men. Is it wonderful? *They* do *everything* at "odd times."

And if a woman's music and drawing are only used by her as an amusement (a *pass-time*, as it is called), is it wonderful that she tires of them, that she becomes disgusted with them?

In every dream of the life of intelligence or that of activity, women are accompanied by a phantom—the phantom of sympathy, guiding, lighting the way—even if they do not marry. Some few sacrifice marriage, because they must sacrifice all other life if they accept that. That man and woman have an equality of duties and rights is accepted by woman even less than by man. Behind *his* destiny woman must annihilate herself, must be only his complement. A woman dedicates herself to the vocation of her husband; she fills up and performs the subordinate parts in

22. See Matthew 7:9, where Jesus asks, "Or what man of you, if his son ask for bread, will give him a stone?"

23. Nightingale seriously considered conversion to Roman Catholicism and held extensive conversations with Henry Edward Cardinal Manning (before he was elevated to cardinal or even ordained bishop) concerning this possibility. Manning advised against her converting because she lacked the requisite humility and faith, but he remained her friend and supporter and arranged, just prior to her expedition to the Crimea, for her training in a French Catholic hospital administered by nuns.

24. Sparrings or moves (jabs, feints, or blocks) in boxing.

it. But if she has any destiny, any vocation of her own, she must renounce it, in nine cases out of ten. Some few, like Mrs. Somerville, Mrs. Chisholm, Mrs. Fry,[25] have not done so; but these are exceptions. The fact is that woman has so seldom any vocation of her own, that it does not much signify; she has none to renounce. A man gains everything by marriage: he gains a "helpmate," but a woman does not.

But if ever women come into contact with sickness, and crime, and poverty in masses, how the practical reality of life revives them! They are exhausted, like those who live on opium or on novels, all their lives—exhausted with feelings which lead to no action. If they see and enter into a continuous line of action, with a full and interesting life, with training constantly kept up to the occupation, occupation constantly testing the training—it is the *beau-idéal* of practical, not theoretical, education—they are re-tempered, their life is filled, they have found their work, and the means to do it.

Women, while they are young, sometimes think that an actress's life is a happy one—not for the sake of the admiration, not for the sake of the fame; but because in the morning she studies, in the evening she embodies those studies: she has the means of testing and correcting them by practice, and of resuming her studies in the morning, to improve the weak parts, remedy the failures, and in the evening try the corrections again. It is, indeed, true that, even after middle age, with such exercise of faculty, there is no end to the progress which may be made.

Some are only deterred from suicide because it is in the most distinct manner to say to God: "I will not, I will not do as Thou wouldst have me," and because it is "no use."

To have no food for our heads, no food for our hearts, no food for our activity, is that nothing? If we have no food for the body, how do we cry out, how all the world hears of it, how all the newspapers talk of it, with a paragraph headed in great capital letters, DEATH FROM STARVATION! But suppose one were to put a paragraph in the "Times," *Death of Thought from Starvation,* or *Death of Moral Activity from Starvation,* how people would stare, how they would laugh and wonder! One would think we had no heads or hearts, by the total indifference of the public towards them. Our bodies are the only things of any consequence.

We have nothing to do which raises us, no food which agrees with us. We can never pursue any object for a single two hours, for we can never command any regular leisure or solitude; and in social or domestic life one is bound, under pain of being thought sulky, to make a remark every two minutes.

Men are on the side of society; they blow hot and cold; they say, "Why can't you employ yourself in society?" and then, "Why don't you talk in society?" I can pursue a connected conversation, or I can be silent; but to drop a remark, as it is called, every two minutes, how wearisome it is! It is impossible to pursue the current of

25. Mary Fairfax Somerville (1780–1872), a writer on scientific matters, was regarded as one of the most brilliant minds of the era. Caroline Jones Chisholm (1808–1877) was known as "the emigrant's friend" for her work in helping female emigrants to Australia secure safe lodgings and become settled in respectable positions. Elizabeth Gurney Fry (1780–1845) was a prominent British Quaker who worked for prison reforms, especially reforms affecting women.

one's own thoughts, because one must keep oneself ever on the alert "to say something"; and it is impossible to say what one is thinking, because the essence of a remark is not to be a thought, but an impression. With what labour women have toiled to break down all individual and independent life, in order to fit themselves for this social and domestic existence, thinking it right! And when they have killed themselves to do it, they have awakened (too late) to think it wrong.

For, later in life, women could not make use of leisure and solitude if they had it! Like the Chinese woman, who could not make use of her feet, if she were brought into European life.

Some have an attention like a battering-ram, which, slowly brought to bear, can work upon a subject for any length of time. They can work ten hours just as well as two upon the same thing. But this age would have men like the musket, which you can load so fast that nothing but its heating in the process puts any limit to the number and frequency of times of firing, and at as many different objects as you please.

So, later in life, people cannot use their battering-ram. Their attention, like society's, goes off in a thousand different directions. They are an hour before they can fix it; and by the time it is fixed, the leisure is gone. They become incapable of con-secutive or strenuous work.

What these suffer—even physically—from the want of such work no one can tell. The accumulation of nervous energy, which has had nothing to do during the day, makes them feel every night, when they go to bed, as if they were going mad; and they are obliged to lie long in bed in the morning to let it evaporate and keep it down.

At last they suffer at once from disgust of the one and incapacity for the other—from loathing of conventional idleness and powerlessness to do work when they have it. "Now go, you have several hours," say people, "you have all the afternoon to yourself." When they are all frittered away, they are to begin to work. When they are broken up into little bits, they are to hew away.

IV

Moral activity? There is scarcely such a thing possible! Everything is sketchy. The world does nothing but sketch. One Lady Bountiful sketches a school, but it never comes to a finished study; she can hardly work at it two weeks consecutively. Here and there a solitary individual, it is true, makes a really careful study,—as Mrs. Chisholm of emigration—as Miss Carpenter of reformatory discipline.[26] But, in general, a "lady" has too many sketches on hand. She has a sketch of society, a

---

26. Lady Bountiful is a character from *The Beaux' Strategem* (1707), a comic play by George Far-quhar (1678–1707). Amiable and well-intentioned, she dispenses various medicinal remedies to her neighbors and interests herself in their general well-being. For Mrs. Chisholm, see note 25. Mary Car-penter (1807–1877) was an educational reformer who organized, taught in, and promoted "ragged schools" (schools for indigent children) and who also argued for reform in the establishment of both vocational and reformatory schools for youth. Like Nightingale, she was suspicious of and refused sig-nificant involvement in the nascent women's movement.

sketch of her children's education, sketches of her "charities," sketches of her reading. She is like a painter who should have five pictures in his studio at once, and giving now a stroke to one, and now a stroke to another, till he had made the whole round, should continue this routine to the end.

All life is sketchy,—the poet's verse (compare Tennyson, Milnes, and Mrs. Browning with Milton or even Byron:[27] it is not the difference of genius which strikes one so much as the unfinished state of these modern sketches compared with the studies of the old masters),—the artist's picture, the author's composition—all are rough, imperfect, incomplete, even as works of art.

And how can it be otherwise? A "leader"[28] out of a newspaper, an article out of a review, five books read aloud in the course of an evening, such is our literature. What mind can stand three leading articles every morning as its food?

When shall we see a woman making a *study* of what she does? Married women cannot; for a man would think, if his wife undertook any great work with the intention of carrying it out,—of making anything but a sham of it—that she would "suckle his fools and chronicle his small beer" less well for it,—that he would not have so good a dinner—that she would destroy, as it is called, his domestic life.

The intercourse of man and woman—how frivolous, how unworthy it is! Can we call *that* the true vocation of woman—her high career? Look round at the marriages which you know. The true marriage—that noble union, by which a man and woman become together the one perfect being—probably does not exist at present upon earth.

It is not surprising that husbands and wives seem so little part of one another. It is surprising that there is so much love as there is. For there is no food for it. What does it live upon—what nourishes it? Husbands and wives never seem to have anything to say to one another. What do they talk about? Not about any great religious, social, political questions or feelings. They talk about who shall come to dinner, who is to live in this lodge and who in that, about the improvement of the place, or when they shall go to London. If there are children, they form a common subject of some nourishment. But, even then, the case is oftenest thus,—the husband is to think of how they are to get on in life; the wife of bringing them up at home.

27. Alfred, Lord Tennyson (1809–1892) was the most popular and well-known Victorian poet; for selections from Tennyson's work, see parts 1 and 4. Richard Monckton Milnes, Lord Houghton (1809–1885) was a minor poet, social celebrity, philanthropist, and politician; he probably would not have been included with Tennyson and Barrett Browning were it not for the fact that he courted (for nine years) and proposed to Florence Nightingale, who declined his offer of marriage but never quite overcame her involvement with him—see note 29 below. Elizabeth Barrett Browning (1806–1861) was a poet who, at the time Nightingale was composing *Cassandra,* was more famous than her husband Robert; see parts 3 and 4 for selections from her work. John Milton (1608–1674) was the author of *Paradise Lost* and *Paradise Regained,* the great English religious epics; in the nineteenth century, his reputation as the truly sublime poet was unquestioned. George Gordon, Lord Byron (1788–1824) was, during the early nineteenth century, the most famous of the Romantics, and his reputation as the most poignantly passionate of poets had, at mid-century, only begun to fade a little in England while it remained secure on the continent; although he was in fact quite meticulous in his poetic composition, he cultivated a reputation of being carelessly spontaneous, a fact that makes Nightingale's assessment of him peculiar.

28. A leading or front-page article.

But any real communion between husband and wife—any descending into the depths of their being, and drawing out thence what they find and comparing it—do we ever dream of such a thing? Yes, we may dream of it during the season of "passion"; but we shall not find it afterwards. We even *expect* it to go off, and lay our account that it will. If the husband has, by chance, gone into the depths of *his* being, and found anything there unorthodox, he, oftenest, conceals it carefully from his wife,—he is afraid of "unsettling her opinions."

What is the mystery of passion, spiritually speaking? For there *is* a passion of the Spirit. *Blind* passion, as it has most truly been called, seems to come on in man without his exactly knowing why, without his *at all* knowing why for *this* person rather than for *that,* and (whether it has been satisfied or unsatisfied) to go off again after a while, as it came, also without his knowing why.

The woman's passion is generally more lasting.

It is possible that this difference may be, because there is really more in man than in woman. There is nothing in her for him to have this intimate communion *with.* He cannot impart to her his religious beliefs, if he have any, because she would be "shocked." Religious men are and must be heretics now—for we must not pray, except in a "form" of words, made beforehand—or think of God but with a prearranged idea.

With the man's political ideas, if they extend beyond the merest party politics, she has no sympathy.

His social ideas, if they are "advanced," she will probably denounce without knowing why, as savouring of "socialism" (a convenient word, which covers a multitude of new ideas and offences). For woman is "by birth a Tory,"—has been often said—by education a "Tory," we mean.

Woman has nothing but her affections,—and this makes her at once more loving and less loved.

But is it surprising that there should be so little real marriage, when we think what the process is which leads to marriage?

Under the eyes of an always present mother and sisters (of whom even the most refined and intellectual cannot abstain from a jest upon the subject, who think it their *duty* to be anxious, to watch every germ and bud of it) the acquaintance begins. It is fed—upon what?—the gossip of art, musical and pictorial, the party politics of the day, the chit-chat of society, and people marry or sometimes they don't marry, discouraged by the impossibility of knowing any more of one another than this will furnish.

They prefer to marry in *thought,* to hold imaginary conversations with one another in idea, rather than, on such a flimsy pretext of communion, to take the chance (*certainly* it cannot be) of having more to say to one another in marriage.

Men and women meet now *to be idle.* Is it extraordinary that they do not know each other, and that, in their mutual ignorance, they form no surer friendships? Did they meet to *do* something together, then indeed they might form some real tie.

But, as it is, *they* are not there, it is only a mask which is there—a mouth-piece of ready-made sentences about the "topics of the day"; and then people rail against men for choosing a woman "for her face"—why, what else do they see?

It is very well to say "be prudent, be careful, try to know each other." But how are you to know each other?

Unless a woman has lost all pride, how is it possible for her, under the eyes of all her family, to indulge in long exclusive conversations with a man? "Such a thing" must not take place till after her "engagement." And how is she to make an engagement, if "such a thing" has not taken place?

Besides, young women at home have so little to occupy and to interest them—they have so little reason for *not* quitting their home, that a young and independent man cannot look at a girl without giving rise to "expectations," if not on her own part, on that of her family. Happy he, if he is not said to have been "trifling with her feelings," or "disappointing her hopes!" Under these circumstances, how can a man, who has any pride or any principle, become acquainted with a woman in such a manner as to *justify* them in marrying?

There are four ways in which people marry. First, accident or relationship has thrown them together in their childhood, and acquaintance has grown up naturally and unconsciously. Accordingly, in novels, it is generally cousins who marry; and *now* it seems the only natural thing—the only possible way of making an intimacy. And yet, we know that intermarriage between relations is in direct contravention of the laws of nature for the well-being of the race; witness the Quakers, the Spanish grandees, the royal races, the secluded valleys of mountainous countries, where madness, degeneration of race, defective organization and cretinism flourish and multiply.

The second way, and by far the most general, in which people marry, is this. A woman, thoroughly uninterested at home, and having formed a slight acquaintance with some accidental person, accepts him, if he "falls in love" with her, as it is technically called, and takes the chance. Hence the vulgar expression of marriage being a lottery, which it most truly is, for that the *right* two should come together has as many chances against it as there are blanks in any lottery.

The third way is, that some person is found sufficiently independent, sufficiently careless of the opinions of others, or sufficiently without modesty to speculate thus:—"It is worth while that I should become acquainted with so and so. I do not care what his or her opinion of me is, if, *after* having become acquainted, to do which can bear no other construction in people's eyes than a desire of marriage, I retreat." But there is this to be said, that it is doubtful whether, under this unnatural tension, which, to all susceptible characters, such a disregard of the opinions which they care for must be, a healthy or a natural feeling can grow up.

And now they are married—that is to say, two people have received the licence of a man in a white surplice. But they are no more man and wife for that than Louis XIV and the Infanta of Spain, married by proxy, were man and wife. The woman who has sold herself for an establishment, in what is she superior to those we may not name?

Lastly, in a few rare, very rare, cases, such as circumstances, always provided in novels, but seldom to be met with in real life, present—whether the accident of parents' neglect, or of parents' unusual skill and wisdom, or of having no parents at all, which is generally the case in novels—or marrying out of the person's rank of life, by which the usual restraints are removed, and there is room and play left for attraction—or extraordinary events, isolation, misfortunes, which many wish for, even though their imaginations be not tainted by romance-reading; such alternatives as these give food and space for the development of character and mutual sympathies.

But a girl, if she has any pride, is so ashamed of having any thing she wishes to say out of the hearing of her own family, she thinks it must be something so very wrong, that it is ten to one, if she has the opportunity of saying it, that she will not.

And yet she is spending her life, perhaps, in dreaming of accidental means of unrestrained communion.

And then it is thought pretty to say that "Women have no passion." If passion is excitement in the daily social intercourse with men, women think about marriage much more than men do; it is the only event of their lives. It ought to be a sacred event, but surely not the only event of a woman's life, as it is now. Many women spend their lives in asking men to marry them, in a refined way. Yet it is true that women are seldom in love. How can they be?

How cruel are the revulsions which high-minded women suffer! There was one who loved, in connexion with great deeds, noble thoughts, devoted feelings. They met after an interval. It was at one of those crowded parties of Civilization which we call Society. His only careless passing remark was, "The buzz to-night is like a manufactory." Yet he loved her.[29]

V

"L'enthousiasme et la faiblesse d'un temps où l'intelligence monte très haut, entrainée par l'imagination, et tombe très bas, écrasée par une réalité, sans poésie et sans grandeur."[30]

Women dream till they have no longer the strength to dream; those dreams against which they so struggle, so honestly, vigorously, and conscientiously, and so in vain, yet which are their life, without which they could not have lived; those dreams go at last. All their plans and visions seem vanished, and they know not where; gone and they cannot recall them. They do not even remember them. And they are left without the food either of reality or of hope.

Later in life, they neither desire nor dream, neither of activity, nor of love, nor of intellect. The last often survives the longest. They wish, if their experiences would benefit anybody, to give them to some one. But they never find an hour free

29. Perhaps the only matter more pointedly autobiographical than this commentary in the concluding paragraph to section IV is the reiterated concern about young women's daydreaming, a habit that had become all-consuming for Nightingale and had filled her with guilt about dissipating and squandering her energies. The situation described in this concluding paragraph, however, is quite personalized and particular. Having declined, in 1849, Monckton Milnes's proposal of marriage, Nightingale encountered him at an evening party two years later and was profoundly disturbed when he came to speak with her and remarked, "The noise of this room is like a cotton-mill."

30. "The enthusiasm and weakness of an era when intelligence mounts high, brought along by imagination, and sinks low, squelched by a reality, without poetry and without grandeur."

in which to collect their thoughts, and so discouragement becomes ever deeper and deeper, and they less and less capable of undertaking anything.

It seems as if the female spirit of the world were mourning everlastingly over blessings, *not* lost, but which she has never had, and which, in her discouragement, she feels that she never will have, they are so far off.

The more complete a woman's organization, the more she will feel it, till at last there shall arise a woman, who will resume, in her own soul, all the sufferings of her race, and that woman will be the Saviour of her race.

Jesus Christ raised women above the condition of mere slaves, mere ministers to the passions of the man, raised them by this sympathy, to be ministers of God. He gave them moral activity. But the Age, the World, Humanity, must give them the means to exercise this moral activity, must give them intellectual cultivation, spheres of action.

There is perhaps no century where the woman shows so meanly as in this.[31] Because her education seems entirely to have parted company with her vocation; there is no longer unity between the woman as inwardly developed, and as outwardly manifested.

In the last century it was not so. In the succeeding one let us hope that it will no longer be so.

But now she is like the Archangel Michael as he stands upon Saint Angelo at Rome. She has an immense provision of wings, which seem as if they would bear her over earth and heaven; but when she tries to use them, she is petrified into stone, her feet are grown into the earth, chained to the bronze pedestal.

Nothing can well be imagined more painful than the present position of woman, unless, on the one hand, she renounces all outward activity and keeps herself within the magic sphere, the bubble of her dreams; or, on the other, surrendering all aspiration, she gives herself to her real life, soul and body. For those to whom it is possible, the latter is best; for out of activity may come thought, out of mere aspiration can come nothing.

But now—when the young imagination is so high and so developed, and reality is so narrow and conventional—there is no more parallelism between life in the thought and life in the actual than between the corpse, which lies motionless in its narrow bed, and the spirit, which, in our imagination, is at large among the stars.

The ideal life is passed in noble schemes of good consecutively followed up, of devotion to a great object, of sympathy given and received for high ideas and generous feelings. The actual life is passed in sympathy given and received for a dinner, a party, a piece of furniture, a house built or a garden laid out well, in devotion to your guests—(a too real devotion, for it implies that of all your time)—in schemes

31. Nightingale's note: "At almost every period of social life, we find, as it were, two under currents running different ways. There is the noble woman who dreams the following out her useful vocation; but there is also the selfish dreamer now, who is ever turning to something new, regardless of the expectations she has voluntarily excited, who is ever talking about 'making a life for herself,' heedless that she is spoiling another life, undertaken, perhaps, at her own bidding. This is the ugly reverse of the medal."

of schooling for the poor, which you follow up perhaps in an odd quarter of an hour, between luncheon and driving out in the carriage—broth and dripping are included in the plan—and the rest of your time goes in ordering the dinner, hunting for a governess for your children, and sending pheasants and apples to your poorer relations. Is there anything in *this* life which can be called an Incarnation of the ideal life within? Is it a wonder that the unhappy woman should prefer to keep them entirely separate? not to take the bloom off her Ideal by mixing it up with her Actual; not to make her Actual still more unpalatable by trying to *inform* it with her Ideal? And then she is blamed, and her own sex unites against her, for not being content with the "day of small things." She is told that "trifles make the sum of human things"; they do indeed. She is contemptuously asked, "Would she abolish domestic life?" Men are afraid that their houses will not be so comfortable, that their wives will make themselves "remarkable"—women, that they will make themselves distasteful to men; they write books (and very wisely) to teach themselves to dramatize "little things," to persuade themselves that "domestic life is their sphere" and to idealize the "sacred hearth." Sacred it is indeed. Sacred from the touch of their sons almost as soon as they are out of childhood—from its dulness and its tyrannous trifling *these* recoil. Sacred from the grasp of their daughters' affections, upon which it has so light a hold that they seize the first opportunity of marriage, *their* only chance of emancipation. The "sacred hearth"; sacred to their husband's sleep, their sons' absence in the body and their daughters' in mind.

Oh! mothers, who talk about this hearth, how much do you know of your sons' real life, how much of your daughters' imaginary one? Awake, ye women, all ye that sleep, awake! If this domestic life were so very good, would your young men wander away from it, your maidens think of something else?

The time is come when women must do something more than the "domestic hearth," which means nursing the infants, keeping a pretty house, having a good dinner and an entertaining party.

You say, "it is true, our young men see visions, and our maidens dream dreams,[32] but what of? Does not the woman intend to marry, and have over again what she has at home? and the man ultimately too?" Yes, but not the same; she *will* have the same, that is, if circumstances are not altered to prevent it; but her *idéal* is very different, though that *idéal* and the reality will never come together to mould each other. And it is not only the unmarried woman who dreams. The married woman also holds long imaginary conversations but too often.

VI

We live in the world, it is said, and must walk in its ways.

Was Christ called a complainer against the world? Yet all these great teachers and preachers must have had a most deep and ingrained sense, a continual gnaw-

---

32. See Joel 2:28: "And it shall come to pass afterward, that I will pour out my spirit upon all flesh; and your sons and your daughters shall prophesy, your old men shall dream dreams, and your young men shall see visions."

ing feeling of the miseries and wrongs of the world. Otherwise they would not have been impelled to devote life and death to redress them. Christ, Socrates, Howard,[33] they must have had no ear for the joys, compared to that which they had for the sorrows of the world.

They acted, however, and we complain. The great reformers of the world turn into the great misanthropists, if circumstances or organisation do not permit them to act. Christ, if He had been a woman, might have been nothing but a great complainer. Peace be with the misanthropists! They have made a step in progress; the next will make them great philanthropists; they are divided but by a line.

The next Christ will perhaps be a female Christ. But do we see one woman who looks like a female Christ? or even like "the messenger before" her "face," to go before her and prepare the hearts and minds for her?[34]

To this will be answered that half the inmates of Bedlam begin in this way, by fancying that they are "the Christ."[35]

People talk about imitating Christ, and imitate Him in the little trifling formal things, such as washing the feet, saying his prayer, and so on; but if any one attempts the real imitation of Him, there are no bounds to the outcry with which the presumption of that person is condemned.

For instance, Christ was saying something to the people one day, which interested Him very much, and interested them very much; and Mary and his brothers came in the middle of it, and wanted to interrupt Him, and take Him home to dinner, very likely—(how natural that story is! does it not speak more home than any historic evidences of the Gospel's reality?), and He instead of being angry with their interruption of Him in such an important work for some trifling thing, answers, "Who is my mother? and who are my brethren? Whosoever shall do the will of my Father which is in heaven, the same is my brother and sister and mother."[36] But if *we* were to say that, we should be accused of "destroying the family tie," of diminishing the obligation of the home duties.

33. The prison reformer John Howard (1726–1790) may seem a curious figure to link with the Christian Savior and the idealist Greek philosopher Socrates (470–399 B.C.E.), but the selection accords with Nightingale's references, earlier in *Cassandra*, to Elizabeth Fry and Mary Carpenter, both of whom also were prominent in prison reform, Fry focusing upon adult women and Carpenter upon youthful offenders.

34. The reference here is to John the Baptist, of whom Jesus says, "For this is he, of whom it is written, Behold, I send my messenger before thy face, which shall prepare thy way before thee" (Matthew 11:10).

35. Nightingale's note: "It is quite true that insanity, sensuality, and monstrous fraud have constantly assumed to be 'the Christ,' *vide* [see] the *Agapemone,* and the Mormons. 'Believing' a man of the name of Prince 'to be the tabernacle of God on earth,' poor deluded women transfer to him all their stock in the Three per Cents. We hear of the Mormons, &c., being the 'recipients and mouthpieces of God's spirit.' They profess to be 'incarnations of the Deity,' 'witnesses of the Almighty, solely knowing God's will, and being the medium of communicating it to man,' and so forth. It does not appear to us that this blasphemy is very dangerous to the cause of true religion in general, any more than forgery is very dangerous to commerce in general. It is the universal dishonesty in religion, as in trade, which is really dangerous."

The Agapemone was a commune founded about 1849 in Spaxton, England, which had a reputation for immorality. The name came to refer to free-love institutions. For Nightingale, the Mormons are also guilty of sensuality because of their practice of polygamy.

36. Matthew 12:46–50.

He might well say, "Heaven and earth shall pass away, but my words shall not pass away."[37] His words will never pass away. If He had said, "Tell them I am engaged at this moment in something very important; that the instruction of the multitude ought to go before any personal ties; that I will remember to come when I have done," no one would have been impressed by His words; but how striking is that, "Behold my mother and my brethren!"

VII

The dying woman to her mourners:—"Oh! if you knew how gladly I leave this life, how much more courage I feel to take the chance of another, than of anything I see before me in this, you would put on your wedding-clothes instead of mourning for me!"

"But," they say, "so much talent! so many gifts! such good which you might have done!"

"The world will be put back some little time by my death," she says; "you see I estimate my powers at least as highly as you can; but it is by the death which has taken place some years ago in me, not by the death which is about to take place now." And so is the world put back by the death of every one who has to sacrifice the development of his or her peculiar gifts (which were meant, not for selfish gratification, but for the improvement of that world) to conventionality.

"My people were like children playing on the shore of the eighteenth century. I was their hobby-horse, their plaything; and they drove me to and fro, dear souls! never weary of the play themselves, till I, who had grown to woman's estate and to the ideas of the nineteenth century, lay down exhausted, my mind closed to hope, my heart to strength.

"Free—free—oh! divine freedom, art thou come at last? Welcome, beautiful death!"

Let neither name nor date be placed on her grave, still less the expression of regret or of admiration; but simply the words, "I believe in God."

37. Luke 22:33.

MATTHEW ARNOLD

E MPLOYED FOR thirty-five years as an inspector of schools, Matthew Arnold (1822–1888) is best known as one of the most accomplished Victorian poets and prose writers. While his essays argue vigorously for intellectual and cultural enlightenment, his poems take a very different tone. Often melancholy or nostalgic, Arnold's poems focus on the isolation and alienation of modern men and women, a condition that he believed resulted from increasing mechanization and materialism and the diminishing power of social and religious institutions.

"Rugby Chapel," an elegy for the poet's father, Dr. Thomas Arnold (1795–1842), was written in 1857 and published in 1867. Thomas Arnold, headmaster of Rugby from 1828 until his death in 1842, instituted a number of reforms in living conditions, school governance, and curricula consistent with his goal of molding Christian gentlemen. In his son's poem, Dr. Arnold, unlike the majority of his contemporaries, does not suffer from debilitating doubt and disorientation. Strong and purposeful, he finds, in his work, fulfillment of his mission to direct and influence others.

See the excerpts earlier in part 1 from Thomas Hughes's novel *Tom Brown's Schooldays* (1857), a story set at Rugby during Dr. Arnold's term as headmaster.

Rugby Chapel
November, 1857

Coldly, sadly descends
The autumn-evening. The field
Strewn with its dank yellow drifts
Of wither'd leaves, and the elms,
Fade into dimness apace,   5

Silent;—hardly a shout
From a few boys late at their play!
The lights come out in the street,
In the school-room windows—but cold,
Solemn, unlighted, austere,   10
Through the gathering darkness, arise
The chapel-walls, in whose bound
Thou, my father! art laid.[1]

There thou dost lie, in the gloom
Of the autumn evening. But ah!   15
That word, *gloom,* to my mind
Brings thee back, in the light
Of thy radiant vigour again;
In the gloom of November we pass'd
Days not dark at thy side;   20
Seasons impair'd not the ray
Of thy buoyant cheerfulness clear.
Such thou wast! and I stand
In the autumn evening, and think
Of bygone autumns with thee.   25

Fifteen years have gone round
Since thou arosest to tread,
In the summer-morning, the road
Of death, at a call unforeseen,
Sudden. For fifteen years,   30
We who till then in thy shade
Rested as under the boughs
Of a mighty oak, have endured
Sunshine and rain as we might,
Bare, unshaded, alone,   35
Lacking the shelter of thee.

O strong soul, by what shore
Tarriest thou now? For that force,
Surely, has not been left vain!
Somewhere, surely, afar,   40
In the sounding labour-house vast
Of being, is practised that strength,
Zealous, beneficent, firm!

1. Dr. Arnold was buried beneath the altar in the campus chapel.

Yes, in some far-shining sphere,
Conscious or not of the past,   45
Still thou performest the word
Of the Spirit in whom thou dost live—
Prompt, unwearied, as here!
Still thou upraisest with zeal
The humble good from the ground,   50
Sternly repressest the bad!
Still, like a trumpet, dost rouse
Those who with half-open eyes
Tread the border-land dim
'Twixt vice and virtue; reviv'st,   55
Succourest!—this was thy work,
This was thy life upon earth.

What is the course of the life
Of mortal men on the earth?—
Most men eddy about   60
Here and there—eat and drink,
Chatter and love and hate,
Gather and squander, are raised
Aloft, are hurl'd in the dust,
Striving blindly, achieving   65
Nothing; and then they die—
Perish—and no one asks
Who or what they have been,
More than he asks what waves,
In the moonlit solitudes mild   70
Of the midmost Ocean, have swell'd.
Foam'd for a moment, and gone.

And there are some, whom a thirst
Ardent, unquenchable, fires,
Not with the crowd to be spent,   75
Not without aim to go round
In an eddy of purposeless dust,
Effort unmeaning and vain.
Ah yes! some of us strive
Not without action to die   80
Fruitless, but something to snatch
From dull oblivion, nor all
Glut the devouring grave!
We, we have chosen our path—

Path to a clear-purposed goal,   85
Path of advance!—but it leads
A long, steep journey, through sunk
Gorges, o'er mountains in snow.
Cheerful, with friends, we set forth—
Then, on the height, comes the storm.   90
Thunder crashes from rock
To rock, the cataracts reply;
Lightnings dazzle our eyes;
Roaring torrents have breach'd
The track, the stream-bed descends   95
In the place where the wayfarer once
Planted his footstep—the spray
Boils o'er its borders! aloft
The unseen snow-beds dislodge
Their hanging ruin;—alas,   100
Havoc is made in our train!
Friends, who set forth at our side,
Falter, are lost in the storm.
We, we only are left!—
With frowning foreheads, with lips   105
Sternly compress'd, we strain on,
On—and at nightfall at last
Come to the end of our way,
To the lonely inn 'mid the rocks;
Where the gaunt and taciturn host   110
Stands on the threshold, the wind
Shaking his thin white hairs—
Holds his lantern to scan
Our storm-beat figures, and asks:
Whom in our party we bring?   115
Whom we have left in the snow?

Sadly we answer: We bring
Only ourselves! we lost
Sight of the rest in the storm.
Hardly ourselves we fought through,   120
Stripp'd, without friends, as we are.
Friends, companions, and train,
The avalanche swept from our side.

But thou would'st not *alone*
Be saved, my father! *alone*   125
Conquer and come to thy goal,

Leaving the rest in the wild.
We were weary, and we
Fearful, and we in our march
Fain to drop down and to die. 130
Still thou turnedst, and still
Beckonedst the trembler, and still
Gavest the weary thy hand.

If, in the paths of the world,
Stones might have wounded thy feet, 135
Toil or dejection have tried
Thy spirit, of that we saw
Nothing—to us thou wast still
Cheerful, and helpful, and firm!
Therefore to thee it was given 140
Many to save with thyself;
And, at the end of thy day,
O faithful shepherd! to come,
Bringing thy sheep in thy hand.

And through thee I believe 145
In the noble and great who are gone;
Pure souls honour'd and blest
By former ages, who else—
Such, so soulless, so poor,
Is the race of men whom I see— 150
Seem'd but a dream of the heart,
Seem'd but a cry of desire.
Yes! I believe that there lived
Others like thee in the past,
Not like the men of the crowd 155
Who all round me to-day
Bluster or cringe, and make life
Hideous, and arid, and vile;
But souls temper'd with fire,
Fervent, heroic, and good, 160
Helpers and friends of mankind.

Servants of God!—or sons
Shall I not call you? because
Not as servants ye knew
Your Father's innermost mind, 165
His, who unwillingly sees
One of his little ones lost—

Yours is the praise, if mankind
Hath not as yet in its march
Fainted, and fallen, and died!   170

See! In the rocks of the world
Marches the host of mankind,
A feeble, wavering line.
Where are they tending?—A God
Marshall'd them, gave them their goal.—   175
Ah, but the way is so long!
Years they have been in the wild!
Sore thirst plagues them, the rocks,
Rising all round, overawe;
Factions divide them, their host   180
Threatens to break, to dissolve.—
Ah, keep, keep them combined!
Else, of the myriads who fill
That army, not one shall arrive;
Sole they shall stray; on the rocks   185
Batter for ever in vain,
Die one by one in the waste.

Then, in such hour of need
Of your fainting, dispirited race,
Ye, like angels, appear,   190
Radiant with ardour divine.
Beacons of hope, ye appear!
Languor is not in your heart,
Weakness is not in your word,
Weariness not on your brow.   195
Ye alight in our van! at your voice,
Panic, despair, flee away.
Ye move through the ranks, recall
The stragglers, refresh the outworn,
Praise, re-inspire the brave.   200
Order, courage, return;
Eyes rekindling, and prayers,
Follow your steps as ye go.
Ye fill up the gaps in our files,
Strengthen the wavering line,   205
Stablish, continue our march,
On, to the bound of the waste,
On, to the City of God.

JEAN INGELOW

B EST-SELLING author of poems, novels, and children's stories in England and the United States, Jean Ingelow (1820–1897) was acquainted with most of the great writers and artists of her day. Ingelow was influenced by Wordsworth and Tennyson, highly regarded by Christina Rossetti, and friendly with John Ruskin and Robert Browning. Her sonnet "Work" echoes the conventional morality that work is its own reward.

Figure 1.3. The Crystal Palace.
In 1851, England hosted a world's fair to showcase its industrial superiority. The Great Exhibition of the Works of Industry of All Nations was housed in the Crystal Palace, a grand structure of metal and glass, designed by Joseph Paxton (1803–1865) and erected in London's Hyde Park. On display were objects from four categories: raw materials, manufactures, fine arts, and machinery, with the latter proving the most popular to visitors. Shown here is the Crystal Palace from the south side.

Work

Like coral insects multitudinous
    The minutes are whereof our life is made.
    They build it up as in the deep's blue shade
It grows; it comes to light, and then, and thus
For both there is an end. The populous   5
    Sea-blossoms close, our minutes that have paid
    Life's debt of work are spent; the work is laid
Before their feet that shall come after us.
We may not stay to watch if it will speed;
    The bard if on some luter's string his song   10
    Live sweetly yet; the hero if his star
Doth shine. Work is its own best earthly meed,
    Else have we none more than the sea-born throng
    Who wrought these marvellous isles that bloom afar.

ANNIE MATHESON

Annie Matheson (1853–1924) wrote poetry, children's literature, and a biography of Florence Nightingale. The message of Christian Socialism—of the Church's responsibility to work for social justice—figures in many of her poems. In "A Song of Handicrafts," Matheson presents the voices of three artisans who recognize themselves as the agents of the "Mighty Craftsman," God.

A Song of Handicrafts

The Weaver

Sunlight from the sky's own heart,
    Flax unfolded to receive:
Out of sky and flax and art,
    Lovely raiment I achieve—
Earth a part and heaven a part,
    God in all, for Whom I weave!

The Carpenter

Deep into the wood I hew,
    A message fell from the sun's lip;
Fire and strength it downward drew
    For the faggot and the ship:
God's own, in the forest, grew
    Timber that I hew and chip.

The Mason

Out of clay or living rock
    I will make my brick or stone:
At the door of God I knock,
    Builder whose command I own,
Who can birth and death unlock,
    And in dust can find a throne.

Chorus

Mighty Craftsman! craftsmen, we,
    Feel Thy spirit in our hands:
All the worlds are full of Thee—
    Wake our eyes and break our bands—
Servants, and for ever free,
    Sons, and heirs of all thy lands!

ALFRED, LORD TENNYSON

A LFRED, LORD TENNYSON (1809–1892) became poet laureate in 1850, succeeding William Wordsworth. The 1830s and 1840s had been for him a
period of personal, artistic, and financial insecurity, but, by mid-century, his
reputation had been established by the publication of new and revised verses in his
two-volume *Poems* (1842), *The Princess* (1847), and *In Memoriam* (1850); he enjoyed increasing success with later publications, most notably *Maud, and Other
Poems* (1855) and the twelve lengthy poems subsequently collected under the title
Idylls of the King (1872; 1888), the title that he had first employed in 1859 to present
four of these narratives. Once he had been appointed poet laureate, he assumed for
the public almost vatic status—he was, for them, the voice of England, brooding
over the doubts and conflicts of the age, offering consoling comment that resolved
anxieties and answered unsettling skepticism. Their sense of him as someone
sensitive to but finally confident in dealing with the distinctive apprehensions of
the culture disregarded his dysfunctional family background troubled by his father's violent alcoholism and mental illness, his own early bohemian lifestyle, the
financial instability that prevented his marrying until he had reached his early
forties, the often incapacitating melancholia that seemed to him akin to madness,
the recurring and intense personal self-doubt from which a nation's adulation
could never fully deliver him. He was not the assured and remote figure many
thought him to be, but, if people found solace and settled answers in his poetry,
they did so because he confronted misgivings about the culture without despairing
of some resolution.

Consistently attentive to the problems of a period notable for its concern with
work, Tennyson offered varied considerations of work as a social responsibility to
be assumed, a mission to be fulfilled. Apprehensive that aesthetic endeavors or
spiritual yearnings might divorce people from their duty to work for the betterment of society, Tennyson recapitulated, in different poems, his vision of the
disorder that results from too exclusive a focus upon art or upon other-worldly
spirituality. Commitment to art and artwork needed to be yoked to the work of
social responsibility and service to others, but, even more urgently, religious aspiration needed such attachment to public-minded goals. Aware that religious fervor could lead people to direct their energies away from a world that threatened
confusion to an intangible spiritual realm that offered comforting certainties,
Tennyson insisted, in *The Holy Grail* (1869; published 1870), that the work of
secular stewardship is, for all but a very select few, the appropriate way to enact

genuine religious commitment. Love of God is to be made manifest in love of and care for humankind. At the very point when the knights of the Round Table are misled to pledge themselves to seek the Holy Grail, the exemplary King Arthur is faithfully discharging his trust by redressing the plight of an "outraged maiden" who has been victimized by outlaws: his is the normative labor of service to others set against the self-absorbed quests pursued by his knights. Nor is the King's chivalrous gallantry the only example of proper moral orientation to the needs of others. Sir Percivale, withdrawn from courtly life into an abbey and "leaving human wrongs to right themselves," recounts the tale of the Grail to the simple monk Ambrosius, whose deprecation of his own helpful involvement with the quotidian lives of abbey parishioners contrasts with the abandonment of their communal responsibilities by the questing knights:

> [I] then go forth and pass
> Down to the little thorpe that lies so close,
> And almost plastered like a martin's nest
> To these old walls—and mingle with our folk;
> And knowing every honest face of theirs
> As well as ever shepherd knew his sheep,
> And every homely secret in their hearts,
> Delight myself with gossip and old wives,
> And ills and aches, and teethings, lyings-in,
> And mirthful sayings, children of the place,
> That have no meaning half a league away;
> Or lulling random squabbles when they rise,
> Chafferings and chatterings at the market-cross,
> Rejoice, small man, in this small world of mine,
> Yea, even in their hens and in their eggs.

Ambrosius is the faithful shepherd who knows and cares for his congregation, realizing, by being "lowly wise," the Miltonic virtue that Wordsworth celebrated in the "Ode to Duty" as the unassuming "spirit of self-sacrifice"; Tennyson juxtaposes Ambrosius's modest pastoral care with the competitive ambitions of the knights who, in seeking the Grail, ignore their appropriate work as "men / With strength and will to right the wronged, of power / To lay the sudden heads of violence flat." The upshot of the knights' "leaving human wrongs to right themselves" is that the wrongs go unrighted and the great civilizing work of Camelot is nullified. The images of the ruined court with which the poem concludes represent the social anomie that Tennyson saw as the consequence of a religious disposition whose endeavors are divorced from a commitment to work for the larger commonwealth.

The Holy Grail

From noiseful arms, and acts of prowess done
In tournament or tilt, Sir Percivale[1]
Whom Arthur and his knighthood called the Pure,
Had past into the silent life of prayer,
Praise, fast, and alms; and leaving for the cowl   5
The helmet in an abbey far away
From Camelot, there, and not long after, died.

And one, a fellow-monk among the rest,
Ambrosius, loved him much beyond the rest,
And honored him, and wrought into his heart   10
A way by love that wakened love within,
To answer that which came; and as they sat
Beneath a world-old yew-tree, darkening half
The cloisters, on a gustful April morn
That puffed the swaying branches into smoke[2]   15
Above them, ere the summer when he died,
The monk Ambrosius questioned Percivale:

"O brother, I have seen this yew-tree smoke,
Spring after spring, for half a hundred years;
For never have I known the world without,   20
Nor ever strayed beyond the pale.[3] But thee,
When first thou camest—such a courtesy
Spake through thy limbs and in thy voice—I knew
For one of those who eat in Arthur's hall;
For good ye are and bad, and like to coins,   25
Some true, some light, but every one of you
Stamped with the image of the King; and now
Tell me, what drove thee from the Table Round,
My brother? Was it earthly passion crossed?"

"Nay," said the knight; "for no such passion mine.   30
But the sweet vision of the Holy Grail[4]

1. In some versions of the Grail story, notably Chrétien de Troyes's *Perceval* and Wolfram von Eschenbach's *Parzival*, Percival is the knight whose quest for the Holy Grail succeeds.
2. Pollen from the yew tree.
3. "Beyond the pale" means, literally, beyond the fence or palisade; the phrase generally means outside the boundaries of an established jurisdiction or set of rules.
4. The Grail, in later versions of the story, is the chalice used by Christ at the Passover meal. Joseph

Drove me from all vainglories, rivalries,
And earthly heats that spring and sparkle out
Among us in the jousts while women watch
Who wins, who falls, and waste the spiritual strength   35
Within us, better offered up to heaven."

    To whom the monk: "The Holy Grail!—I trust
We are green in Heaven's eyes; but here too much
We moulder—as to things without, I mean—
Yet one of your own knights, a guest of ours,   40
Told us of this in our refectory,
But spake with such a sadness and so low
We heard not half of what he said. What is it?
The phantom of a cup that comes and goes?"

    "Nay, monk! what phantom?" answered Percivale.   45
"The cup, the cup itself, from which our Lord
Drank at the last sad supper with his own.
This, from the blessed land of Aromat[5]—
After the day of darkness, when the dead
Went wandering o'er Moriah[6]—the good saint   50
Arimathæan Joseph, journeying brought
To Glastonbury, where the winter thorn
Blossoms at Christmas, mindful of our Lord.
And there awhile it bode; and if a man
Could touch or see it, he was healed at once,   55
By faith, of all his ills. But then the times
Grew to such evil that the holy cup
Was caught away to heaven, and disappeared."

    To whom the monk: "From our old books I know
That Joseph came of old to Glastonbury,   60
And there the heathen Prince, Arviragus,
Gave him an isle of marsh wheron to build;
And there he built with wattles from the marsh
A little lonely church in days of yore,
For so they say, these books of ours, but seem   65
Mute of this miracle, far as I have read.
But who first saw the holy thing today?"

---

of Arimathea is said to have taken this chalice to Glastonbury in northern Wales: see lines 50–53. In the Gospels, Joseph of Arimathea is the one who claims the body of the crucified Jesus and entombs it.
    5. Arimathea, a town in Palestine.
    6. A hill in east Jerusalem. The "dead" who "[w]ent wandering o'er Moriah" did so following the resurrection of Christ: they "came out of the graves after his resurrection, and went into the holy city, and appeared unto many" (Matthew 27:53).

"A woman," answered Percivale, "a nun,
And one no further off in blood from me
Than sister; and if ever holy maid   70
With knees of adoration wore the stone,
A holy maid; though never maiden glowed,
But that was in her earlier maidenhood,
With such a fervent flame of human love,
Which, being rudely blunted, glanced and shot   75
Only to holy things; to prayer and praise
She gave herself, to fast and alms. And yet,
Nun as she was, the scandal of the Court,
Sin against Arthur and the Table Round,
And the strange sound of an adulterous race,   80
Across the iron grating of her cell
Beat, and she prayed and fasted all the more.

  "And he to whom she told her sins, or what
Her all but utter whiteness held for sin,
A man wellnigh a hundred winters old,   85
Spake often with her of the Holy Grail,
A legend handed down through five or six,
And each of these a hundred winters old,
From our Lord's time. And when King Arthur made
His Table Round, and all men's hearts became   90
Clean for a season, surely he had thought
That now the Holy Grail would come again;
But sin broke out. Ah, Christ, that it would come,
And heal the world of all their wickedness!
'O Father!' asked the maiden, 'might it come   95
To me by prayer and fasting?' 'Nay,' said he,
'I know not, for thy heart is pure as snow.'
And so she prayed and fasted, till the sun
Shone, and the wind blew, through her, and I thought
She might have risen and floated when I saw her.   100

  "For on a day she sent to speak with me.
And when she came to speak, behold her eyes
Beyond my knowing of them, beautiful,
Beyond all knowing of them, wonderful,
Beautiful in the light of holiness!   105
And 'O my brother Percivale,' she said,
'Sweet brother, I have seen the Holy Grail;
For, waked at dead of night, I heard a sound
As of a silver horn from o'er the hills

Blown, and I thought, "It is not Arthur's use   110
To hunt by moonlight." And the slender sound
As from a distance beyond distance grew
Coming upon me—O never harp nor horn,
Nor aught we blow with breath, or touch with hand,
Was like that music as it came; and then   115
Streamed through my cell a cold and silver beam,
And down the long beam stole the Holy Grail,
Rose-red with beatings in it, as if alive,
Till all the white walls of my cell were dyed
With rosy colors leaping on the wall;   120
And then the music faded, and the Grail
Past, and the beam decayed, and from the walls
The rosy quiverings died into the night.
So now the Holy Thing is here again
Among us, brother; fast thou too and pray,   125
And tell the brother knights to fast and pray,
That so perchance the vision may be seen
By thee and those, and all the world be healed.'

    "Then leaving the pale nun, I spake of this
To all men; and myself fasted and prayed   130
Always, and many among us many a week
Fasted and prayed even to the uttermost,
Expectant of the wonder that would be.

    "And one there was among us, ever moved
Among us in white armor, Galahad.[7]   135
'God make thee good as thou art beautiful!'
Said Arthur, when he dubbed him knight, and none
In so young youth was ever made a knight
Till Galahad; and this Galahad, when he heard
My sister's vision, filled me with amaze;   140
His eyes became so like her own, they seemed
Hers, and himself her brother more than I.

    "Sister or brother none had he; but some
Called him a son of Lancelot, and some said
Begotten by enchantment—chatterers they,   145
Like birds of passage piping up and down,
That gape for flies—we know not whence they come;
For when was Lancelot wanderingly lewd?

---

7. Galahad is the son of Lancelot and the Lady Elaine, daughter of King Pelleas.

"But she, the wan sweet maiden, shore away
Clean from her forehead all that wealth of hair 150
Which made a silken mat-work for her feet;
And out of this she plaited broad and long
A strong sword-belt, and wove with silver thread
And crimson in the belt a strange device,
A crimson grail within a silver beam; 155
And saw the bright boy-knight, and bound it on him,
Saying, 'My knight, my love, my knight of heaven,
O thou, my love, whose love is one with mine,
I, maiden, round thee, maiden, bind my belt.
Go forth, for thou shalt see what I have seen, 160
And break through all, till one will crown thee king
Far in the spiritual city'; and as she spake
She sent the deathless passion in her eyes
Through him, and made him hers, and laid her mind
On him, and he believed in her belief. 165

"Then came a year of miracle. O brother,
In our great hall there stood a vacant chair,
Fashioned by Merlin[8] ere he passed away,
And carven with strange figures; and in and out
The figures, like a serpent, ran a scroll 170
Of letters in a tongue no man could read.
And Merlin called it 'the Siege Perilous,'
Perilous for good and ill; for there, he said,
No man could sit but he should lose himself.
And once by misadvertence Merlin sat 175
In his own chair, and so was lost; but he,
Galahad, when he heard of Merlin's doom,
Cried, 'If I lose myself, I save myself!'[9]

"Then on a summer night it came to pass,
While the great banquet lay along the hall, 180
That Galahad would sit down in Merlin's chair.

"And all at once, as there we sat, we heard
A cracking and a riving of the roofs,
And rending, and a blast, and overhead
Thunder, and in the thunder was a cry. 185
And in the blast there smote along the hall

8. Merlin is the seer and sorcerer of the Round Table.
9. Galahad paraphrases Scripture: "He that findeth his life shall lose it; and he that loseth his life for my sake shall find it" (Matthew 10:39).

A beam of light seven times more clear than day;
And down the long beam stole the Holy Grail
All over covered with a luminous cloud,
And none might see who bare it, and it past.　　　　　190
But every knight beheld his fellow's face
As in a glory, and all the knights arose,
And, staring each at other like dumb men,
Stood, till I found a voice and sware a vow.

"I sware a vow before them all, that I,　　　　　195
Because I had not seen the Grail, would ride
A twelvemonth and a day in quest of it,
Until I found and saw it, as the nun
My sister saw it; and Galahad sware the vow,
And good Sir Bors, our Lancelot's cousin, sware,　　　　　200
And Lancelot sware, and many among the knights,
And Gawain sware, and louder than the rest."

Then spake the monk Ambrosius, asking him,
"What said the King? Did Arthur take the vow?"

"Nay, for my lord," said Percivale, "the King,　　　　　205
Was not in hall; for early the same day,
Scaped through a cavern from a bandit bold,
An outraged maiden sprang into the hall
Crying on help; for all her shining hair
Was smeared with earth, and either milky arm　　　　　210
Red-rent with hooks of bramble, and all she wore
Torn as a sail that leaves the rope is torn
In tempest. So the King arose and went
To smoke the scandalous hive of those wild bees
That made such honey in his realm.[10] Howbeit　　　　　215
Some little of this marvel he too saw,
Returning o'er the plain that then began
To darken under Camelot; whence the King
Looked up, calling aloud, 'Lo, there! the roofs
Of our great hall are rolled in thunder-smoke!　　　　　220
Pray heaven, they be not smitten by the bolt!'
For dear to Arthur was that hall of ours,
As having there so oft with all his knights
Feasted, and as the stateliest under heaven.

---

10. Notably, King Arthur is fulfilling his obligation to work for the common good at the very time when his principal knights are swearing oaths that will take them from their commitment to a similar mission.

"O brother, had you known our mighty hall,   225
Which Merlin built for Arthur long ago!
For all the sacred mount of Camelot,
And all the dim rich city, roof by roof,
Tower after tower, spire beyond spire,
By grove, and garden-lawn, and rushing brook,   230
Climbs to the mighty hall that Merlin built.
And four great zones of sculpture, set betwixt
With many a mystic symbol, gird the hall;
And in the lowest beasts are slaying men,
And in the second men are slaying beasts,   235
And on the third are warriors, perfect men,
And on the fourth are men with growing wings,
And over all one statue in the mould
Of Arthur, made by Merlin, with a crown,
And peaked wings pointed to the Northern Star.   240
And eastward fronts the statue, and the crown
And both the wings are made of gold, and flame
At sunrise till the people in far fields
Wasted so often by the heathen hordes,
Behold it, crying 'We have still a king.'   245

"And, brother had you known our hall within,
Broader and higher than any in all the lands!
Where twelve great windows blazon Arthur's wars,
And all the light that falls upon the board
Streams through the twelve great battles of our King.   250
Nay, one there is, and at the eastern end,
Wealthy with wandering lines of mount and mere,[11]
Where Arthur finds the brand Excalibur.
And also one to the west, and counter to it,
And blank; and who shall blazon it? when and how?—   255
O there, perchance, when all our wars are done,
The brand Excalibur will be cast away!

"So to this hall full quickly rode the King,
In horror lest the work by Merlin wrought,
Dreamlike, should on the sudden vanish, wrapped   260
In unremorseful folds of rolling fire.
And in he rode, and up I glanced, and saw
The golden dragon sparkling over all;
And many of those who burned the hold, their arms
Hacked, and their foreheads grimed with smoke and seared,   265

11. A lake or any somewhat extensive body of standing water.

Followed, and in among bright faces, ours,
Full of the vision, pressed; and then the King
Spake to me, being nearest, 'Percivale'—
Because the hall was all in tumult—some
Vowing, and some protesting—'what is this?'   270

"O brother, when I told him what had chanced,
My sister's vision and the rest, his face
Darkened as I have seen it more than once,
When some brave deed seemed to be done in vain,
Darken; and 'Woe is me, my knights,' he cried,   275
'Had I been here, ye had not sworn the vow.'
Bold was mine answer, 'Had thyself been here,
My King, thou woulds't have sworn.' 'Yea, yea,' said he,
'Art thou so bold and hast not seen the Grail?'

" 'Nay, lord, I heard the sound, I saw the light,   280
But since I did not see the holy thing,
I sware a vow to follow it till I saw.'

"Then when he asked us, knight by knight, if any
Had seen it, all their answers were as one:
'Nay, lord, and therefore have we sworn our vows.'   285

" 'Lo, now,' said Arthur, 'have ye seen a cloud?
What go ye into the wilderness to see?'

"Then Galahad on the sudden, and in a voice
Shrilling along the hall to Arthur, called,
'But I, Sir Arthur, saw the Holy Grail,   290
I saw the Holy Grail and heard a cry—
"O Galahad, and O Galahad, follow me!" ' "

" 'Ah, Galahad, Galahad,' said the King, 'for such
As thou art is the vision, not for these.
Thy holy nun and thou have seen a sign—   295
Holier is none, my Percivale, than she—
A sign to maim this Order which I made.
But ye that follow but the leader's bell'—
Brother, the King was hard upon his knights—
'Taliessin[12] is our fullest throat of song,   300
And one hath sung and all the dumb will sing.

12. Taliessin refers to Taliesin, a Welsh singer and teller of tales from the sixth century, the supposed time of Arthur's activity. *The Book of Taliesin* is a medieval collation of poems by various writers, all of which have been ascribed to Taliesin.

Lancelot is Lancelot, and hath overborne
Five knights at once, and every younger knight,
Unproven, holds himself as Lancelot,
Till overborne by one, he learns—and ye,   305
What are ye? Galahads?—no, nor Percivales'—
For thus it pleased the King to range me close
After Sir Galahad;—'nay,' said he, 'but men
With strength and will to right the wronged, of power
To lay the sudden heads of violence flat,[13]   310
Knights that in twelve great battles splashed and dyed
The strong White Horse[14] in his own heathen blood—
But one hath seen, and all the blind will see.
Go, since your vows are sacred, being made.
Yet—for ye know the cries of all my realm   315
Pass through this hall—how often, O my knights,
Your places being vacant at my side.
This chance of noble deeds will come and go
Unchallenged, while ye follow wandering fires
Lost in the quagmire! Many of you, yea most,   320
Return no more. Ye think I show myself
Too dark a prophet. Come now, let us meet
The morrow morn once more in one full field
Of gracious pastime, that once more the King,
Before ye leave him for this quest, may count   325
The yet-unbroken strength of all his knights,
Rejoicing in that Order which he made.'

  "So when the sun broke next from underground,
All the great Table of our Arthur closed
And clashed in such a tourney and so full,   330
So many lances broken—never yet
Had Camelot seen the like since Arthur came;
And I myself and Galahad, for a strength
Was in us from the vision, overthrew
So many knights that all the people cried,   335
And almost burst the barriers in their heat,
Shouting, 'Sir Galahad and Sir Percivale!'

  "But when the next day brake from underground—
O brother, had you known our Camelot,
Built by old kings, age after age, so old   340
The King himself had fears that it would fall,

13. Arthur defines here the specific mission of the Round-Table knights; by going in quest of the Grail, they abandon the public duty that has defined their moral character.
14. The White Horse was the insignia of the Saxons against whom Arthur has conducted his battles.

So strange, and rich, and dim; for where the roofs
Tottered toward each other in the sky,
Met foreheads all along the street of those
Who watched us pass; and lower, and where the long   345
Rich galleries, lady-laden, weighed the necks
Of dragons clinging to the crazy walls,
Thicker than drops from thunder, showers of flowers
Fell as we passed; and men and boys astride
On wyvern, lion, dragon, griffin, swan,[15]   350
At all the corners, named us each by name,
Calling 'God speed!' but in the ways below
The knights and ladies wept, and rich and poor
Wept, and the King himself could hardly speak
For grief, and all in middle street the Queen,   355
Who rode by Lancelot, wailed and shrieked aloud,
'This madness has come upon us for our sins.'[16]
So to the Gate of the Three Queens we came,
Where Arthur's wars are rendered mystically,
And thence departed every one his way.   360

    "And I was lifted up in heart, and thought
Of all my late-shown prowess in the lists,
How my strong lance had beaten down the knights,
So many and famous names; and never yet
Had heaven appeared so blue, nor earth so green,   365
For all my blood danced in me, and I knew
That I should light upon the Holy Grail.

    "Thereafter, the dark warning of our King,
That most of us would follow wandering fires,
Came like a driving gloom across my mind.   370
Then every evil word I had spoken once,
And every evil thought I had thought of old,
And every evil deed I ever did,
Awoke and cried, 'This quest is not for thee.'
And lifting up mine eyes, I found myself   375
Alone, and in a land of sand and thorns,

15. The men and boys sit astride carved figures similar to the necks of dragons mentioned in lines 346–47. A wyvern is a winged dragon; a griffin is a hybrid animal, half-lion and half-eagle. Note, in, lines 712–17, that such carved figures, following the knights' abandonment of the mission of the Round Table as they turn to seek the Grail, have fallen from the walls that they had graced—a visible sign of the moral disintegration of Camelot.

16. Arthur's Queen Guinevere refers here to her adulterous relationship with Sir Lancelot, the prime cause of the strife that ultimately destroys Arthur's rule. See lines 763–77 for Lancelot's anxiety about the fact that his chivalric championing of the queen has degenerated into simple adultery.

And I was thirsty even unto death;
And I, too, cried, 'This quest is not for thee.'

"And on I rode, and when I thought my thirst
Would slay me, saw deep lawns, and then a brook,   380
With one sharp rapid, where the crisping white
Played ever back upon the sloping wave
And took both ear and eye; and o'er the brook
Were apple-trees, and apples by the brook
Fallen, and on the lawns. 'I will rest here,'   385
I said; 'I am not worthy of the quest';
But even while I drank the brook, and ate
The goodly apples, all these things at once
Fell into dust, and I was left alone
And thirsting in a land of sand and thorns.   390

"And then behold a woman at a door
Spinning; and fair the house whereby she sat,
And kind the woman's eyes and innocent,
And all her bearing gracious; and she rose,
Opening her arms to meet me, as who should say,   395
'Rest here'; but when I touched her, lo! she, too,
Fell into dust and nothing, and the house
Became no better than a broken shed,
And in it a dead babe; and also this
Fell into dust, and I was left alone.   400

"And on I rode, and greater was my thirst.
Then flashed a yellow gleam across the world,
And where it smote the plowshare in the field
The plowman left his plowing and fell down
Before it; where it glittered on her pail   405
The milkmaid left her milking and fell down
Before it, and I knew not why, but thought
'The sun is rising,' though the sun had risen.
Then was I ware of one that on me moved
In golden armor with a crown of gold   410
About a casque[17] all jewels, and his horse
In golden armor jewelled everywhere;
And on the splendor came, flashing me blind,
And seemed to me the lord of all the world,
Being so huge. But when I thought he meant   415
To crush me, moving on me, lo! he, too,

17. Helmet.

Opened his arms to embrace me as he came,
And up I went and touched him, and he, too,
Fell into dust, and I was left alone
And wearying in a land of sand and thorns.   420

     "And I rode on and found a mighty hill,
And on the top a city walled; the spires
Pricked with incredible pinnacles into heaven.
And by the gateway stirred a crowd; and these
Cried to me climbing, 'Welcome, Percivale!   425
Thou mightiest and thou purest among men!'
And glad was I and clomb, but found at top
No man, nor any voice. And thence I passed
Far through a ruinous city, and I saw
That man had once dwelt there; but there I found   430
Only one man of an exceeding age.
'Where is that goodly company,' said I,
'That so cried out upon me?' And he had
Scarce any voice to answer, and yet gasped,
'Whence and what art thou?' and even as he spoke   435
Fell into dust and disappeared, and I
Was left alone once more and cried in grief,
'Lo, if I find the Holy Grail itself
And touch it, it will crumble into dust!'

     "And thence I dropped into a lowly vale,   440
Low as the hill was high, and where the vale
Was lowest found a chapel, and thereby
A holy hermit in a hermitage,
To whom I told my phantoms, and he said:

     " 'O son, thou hast not true humility,   445
The highest virtue, mother of them all;
For when the Lord of all things made Himself
Naked of glory for His mortal change,
"Take thou my robe," she[18] said, "for all is thine,"
And all her form shone forth with sudden light   450
So that the angels were amazed, and she
Followed Him down, and like a flying star
Led on the gray-haired wisdom of the East.[19]
But her thou hast not known; for what is this

18. The "true humility" of line 445.
19. The "grey-haired wisdom" refers to the Magi who traveled from the East to Bethlehem to see the new-born Christ.

Thou thoughtest of thy prowess and thy sins? 455
Thou hast not lost thyself to save thyself
As Galahad.' When the hermit made an end,
In silver armor suddenly Galahad shone
Before us, and against the chapel door
Laid lance and entered, and we knelt in prayer. 460
And there the hermit slaked my burning thirst,
And at the sacring[20] of the Mass I saw
The holy elements alone; but he,
'Saw ye no more? I, Galahad, saw the Grail,
The Holy Grail, descend upon the shrine. 465
I saw the fiery face as of a child
That smote itself into the bread and went;
And hither am I come; and never yet
Hath what thy sister taught me first to see,
This holy thing, failed from my side, nor come 470
Covered, but moving with me night and day,
Fainter by day, but always in the night
Blood-red, and sliding down the blackened marsh
Blood-red, and on the naked mountain top
Blood-red, and in the sleeping mere below 475
Blood-red. And in the strength of this I rode,
Shattering all evil customs everywhere,
And passed through Pagan realms, and made them mine,
And clashed with Pagan hordes, and bore them down,
And broke through all, and in the strength of this 480
Come victor. But my time is hard at hand,
And hence I go, and one will crown me king
Far in the spiritual city; and come thou, too,
For thou shalt see the vision when I go.'

"While thus he spake, his eye, dwelling on mine, 485
Drew me, with power upon me, till I grew
One with him, to believe as he believed.
Then, when the day began to wane, we went.

"There rose a hill that none but man could climb,
Scarred with a hundred wintry watercourses— 490
Storm at the top, and when we gained it, storm
Round us and death; for every moment glanced
His silver arms and gloomed, so quick and thick
The lightnings here and there to left and right

20. The Consecration, that part of the Mass wherein bread and wine become the body and blood of Christ. See lines 464–67.

Struck, till the dry old trunks about us, dead,   495
Yea, rotten with a hundred years of death,
Sprang into fire. And at the base we found
On either hand, as far as eye could see,
A great black swamp and of an evil smell,
Part black, part whitened with the bones of men,   500
Not to be crossed, save that some ancient king
Had built a way, where, linked with many a bridge,
A thousand piers ran into the great Sea.
And Galahad fled along them bridge by bridge,
And every bridge as quickly as he crossed   505
Sprang into fire and vanished, though I yearned
To follow; and thrice above him all the heavens
Opened and blazed with thunder such as seemed
Shoutings of all the sons of God. And first
At once I saw him far on the great Sea,   510
In silver-shining armor starry-clear;
And o'er his head the Holy Vessel hung
Clothed in white samite[21] or a luminous cloud.
And with exceeding swiftness ran the boat,
If boat it were—I saw not whence it came.   515
And when the heavens opened and blazed again
Roaring, I saw him like a silver star—
And had he set the sail, or had the boat
Become a living creature clad with wings?
And o'er his head the Holy Vessel hung   520
Redder than any rose, a joy to me,
For now I knew the veil had been withdrawn.
Then in a moment when they blazed again
Opening, I saw the least of little stars
Down on the waste, and straight beyond the star   525
I saw the spiritual city and all her spires
And gateways in a glory like one pearl—
No larger, though the goal of all the saints—
Strike from the sea; and from the star there shot
A rose-red sparkle to the city, and there   530
Dwelt, and I knew it was the Holy Grail,
Which never eyes on earth again shall see.
Then fell the floods of heaven drowning the deep,
And how my feet recrossed the deathful ridge
No memory in me lives; but that I touched   535
The chapel-doors at dawn I know, and thence

---

21. Silk material interwoven with gold thread.

Taking my war-horse from the holy man,
Glad that no phantom vexed me more, returned
To whence I came, the gate of Arthur's wars."

"O brother," asked Ambrosius,—"for in sooth   540
These ancient books—and they would win thee—teem,
Only I find not there this Holy Grail,
With miracles and marvels like to these,
Not all unlike; which oftentime I read,
Who read but on my breviary with ease,   545
Till my head swims, and then go forth and pass
Down to the little thorpe[22] that lies so close,
And almost plastered like a martin's nest
To these old walls—and mingle with our folk;
And knowing every honest face of theirs   550
As well as ever shepherd knew his sheep,
And every homely secret in their hearts,
Delight myself with gossip and old wives,
And ills and aches, and teethings, lyings-in,
And mirthful sayings, children of the place,   555
That have no meaning half a league away;
Or lulling random squabbles when they rise,
Chafferings and chatterings at the market-cross,[23]
Rejoice, small man, in this small world of mine,
Yea, even in their hens and in their eggs—   560
O brother, saving this Sir Galahad,
Came ye on none but phantoms in your quest,
No man, no woman?"

            Then Sir Percivale:
"All men, to one so bound by such a vow,
And women were as phantoms. O my brother,   565
Why wilt thou shame me to confess to thee
How far I faltered from my quest and vow?
For after I had lain so many nights,
A bed-mate of the snail and eft[24] and snake,
In grass and burdock, I was changed to wan   570
And meagre, and the vision had not come;
And then I chanced upon a goodly town
With one great dwelling in the middle of it.

22. A thorpe is a small hamlet or gathering of houses.
    23. A cross erected in the central part of a town, the place where any commerce would be
conducted.
    24. Newt.

Thither I made, and there was I disarmed
By maidens each as fair as any flower;   575
But when they led me into hall, behold,
The princess of that castle was the one,
Brother, and that one only, who had ever
Made my heart leap; for when I moved of old
A slender page about her father's hall,   580
And she a slender maiden, all my heart
Went after her with longing, yet we twain
Had never kissed a kiss or vowed a vow.
And now I came upon her once again,
And one had wedded her, and he was dead,   585
And all his land and wealth and state were hers.
And while I tarried, every day she set
A banquet richer than the day before
By me, for all her longing and her will
Was toward me as of old; till one fair morn,   590
I walking to and fro beside a stream
That flashed across her orchard underneath
Her castle-walls, she stole upon my walk,
And calling me the greatest of all knights,
Embraced me, and so kissed me the first time,   595
And gave herself and all her wealth to me.
Then I remembered Arthur's warning word,
That most of us would follow wandering fires,
And the quest faded in my heart. Anon,
The heads of all her people drew to me,   600
With supplication both of knees and tongue:
'We have heard of thee; thou art our greatest knight;
Our Lady says it, and we well believe.
Wed thou our Lady, and rule over us,
And thou shalt be as Arthur in our land.   605
O me, my brother! but one night my vow
Burned me within, so that I rose and fled,
But wailed and wept, and hated mine own self,
And even the holy quest, and all but her;
Then after I was joined with Galahad   610
Cared not for her nor anything upon earth."

Then said the monk: "Poor men, when yule[25] is cold,
Must be content to sit by little fires.
And this am I, so that ye care for me

25. The yule log set to burn during Christmastide.

Ever so little; yea, and blest be heaven   615
That brought thee here to this poor house of ours
Where all the brethren are so hard, to warm
My cold heart with a friend; but O the pity
To find thine own first love once more—to hold,
Hold her a wealthy bride within thine arms,   620
Or all but hold, and then—cast her aside,
Foregoing all her sweetness, like a weed!
For we that want the warmth of double life,
We that are plagued with dreams of something sweet
Beyond all sweetness in a life so rich,—   625
Ah, blessed Lord, I speak too earthly-wise,
Seeing I never strayed beyond the cell,
But live like an old badger in his earth,
With earth about him everywhere, despite
All fast and penance. Saw ye none beside,   630
None of your knights?"

    "Yea, so," said Percivale.
"One night my pathway swerving east, I saw
The pelican on the casque of our Sir Bors
All in the middle of the rising moon,
And toward him spurred, and hailed him, and he me,   635
And each made joy of either. Then he asked,
'Where is he? Hast thou seen him—Lancelot?—Once,'
Said good Sir Bors, 'he dashed across me—mad,
And maddening what he rode; and when I cried,
"Ridest thou then so hotly on a quest   640
So holy?" Lancelot shouted, "Stay me not!
I have been the sluggard, and I ride apace,
For now there is a lion in the way!"
So vanished.'

    "Then Sir Bors had ridden on
Softly, and sorrowing for our Lancelot,   645
Because his former madness, once the talk
And scandal of our table, had returned;
For Lancelot's kith and kin so worship him
That ill to him is ill to them, to Bors
Beyond the rest. He well had been content   650
Not to have seen, so Lancelot might have seen,
The Holy Cup of healing; and, indeed,
Being so clouded with his grief and love,
Small heart was his after the holy quest.

If God would send the vision, well; if not,   655
The quest and he were in the hands of Heaven.

    "And then, with small adventure met, Sir Bors
Rode to the lonest tract of all the realm,
And found a people there among their crags,
Our race and blood, a remnant that were left   660
Paynim amid their circles, and the stones
They pitch up straight to heaven;[26] and their wise men
Were strong in that old magic which can trace
The wandering of the stars, and scoffed at him
And this high quest as at a simple thing,   665
Told him he followed—almost Arthur's words—
A mocking fire: 'What other fire than he[27]
Whereby the blood beats, and the blossom blows,
And the sea rolls, and all the world is warmed?'
And when his answer chafed them, the rough crowd,   670
Hearing he had a difference with their priests,
Seized him, and bound and plunged him into a cell
Of great piled stones; and lying bounden there
In darkness through innumerable hours
He heard the hollow-ringing heavens sweep   675
Over him till by miracle—what else?—
Heavy as it was, a great stone slipped and fell,
Such as no wind could move; and through the gap
Glimmered the streaming scud.[28] Then came a night
Still as the day was loud, and through the gap   680
The seven clear stars of Arthur's Table Round—
For, brother, so one night, because they roll
Through such a round in heaven, we named the stars,
Rejoicing in ourselves and in our King—
And these, like bright eyes of familiar friends,   685
In on him shone: 'And then to me, to me,'
Said good Sir Bors, 'beyond all hopes of mine,
Who scarce had prayed or asked it for myself—
Across the seven clear stars—O grace to me!—
In color like the fingers of a hand   690
Before a burning taper, the sweet Grail
Glided and past, and close upon it pealed

---

26. The circles would be the barrow-fortresses associated with early inhabitants of Britain, the pagans or "Paynim" remnants of line 661; the stones pitched upright would be monoliths and dolmens similar to those at Stonehenge.

27. The sun, the object of pagan worship.

28. Sleet or heavy rain driven by the wind.

A sharp quick thunder.' Afterwards, a maid,
Who kept our holy faith among her kin
In secret, entering, loosed and let him go." 695

    To whom the monk: "And I remember now
That pelican on the casque. Sir Bors it was
Who spake so low and sadly at our board,
And mighty reverent at our grace was he;
A square-set man and honest, and his eyes, 700
An outdoor sign of all the warmth within,
Smiled with his lips—a smile beneath a cloud,
But heaven had meant it for a sunny one.
Aye, aye, Sir Bors, who else? But when ye reached
The city, found ye all your knights returned, 705
Or was there sooth in Arthur's prophecy,
Tell me, and what said each, and what the King?"

    Then answered Percivale: "And that can I,
Brother, and truly; since the living words
Of so great men as Lancelot and our King 710
Pass not from door to door and out again,
But sit within the house. O when we reached
The city, our horses stumbling as they trode
On heaps of ruin, hornless unicorns,
Cracked basilisks, and splintered cockatrices, 715
And shattered talbots,[29] which had left the stones
Raw that they fell from, brought us to the hall.

    "And there sat Arthur on the dais-throne,
And those that had gone out upon the quest,
Wasted and worn, and but a tithe[30] of them, 720
And those that had not, stood before the King,
Who, when he saw me, rose and bade me hail,
Saying, 'A welfare in thine eyes reproves
Our fear of some disastrous chance for thee
On hill or plain, at sea or flooding ford. 725
So fierce a gale made havoc here of late
Among the strange devices of our kings,
Yea, shook this newer, stronger hall of ours,
And from the statue Merlin moulded for us

29. A basilisk is a legendary lizard that killed with its gaze; a cockatrice, another serpent-like creature with a mortal glance, is said to be hatched from a cock's egg by a serpent's brooding on it; a
talbot—an actual rather than a legendary animal—is a hunting dog.
    30. A tenth.

Half-wrenched a golden wing; but now—the quest,   730
This vision—hast thou seen the Holy Cup
That Joseph brought of old to Glastonbury?'

"So when I told him all thyself hast heard,
Ambrosius, and my fresh but fixed resolve
To pass away into the quiet life,   735
He answered not, but, sharply turning, asked
Of Gawain, 'Gawain, was this quest for thee?'

" 'Nay, lord,' said Gawain, 'not for such as I.
Therefore I communed with a saintly man,
Who made me sure the quest was not for me;   740
For I was much a-wearied of the quest,
But found a silk pavilion in a field,
And merry maidens in it; and then this gale
Tore my pavilion from the tenting-pin,
And blew my merry maidens all about   745
With all discomfort; yea, and but for this,
My twelvemonth and a day were pleasant to me.'

"He ceased; and Arthur turned to whom at first
He saw not, for Sir Bors, on entering, pushed
Athwart the throng to Lancelot, caught his hand,   750
Held it, and there, half-hidden by him, stood,
Until the King espied him, saying to him,
'Hail, Bors! If ever loyal man and true
Could see it, thou hast seen the Grail'; and Bors,
'Ask me not, for I may not speak of it;   755
I saw it'; and the tears were in his eyes.

"Then there remained but Lancelot, for the rest
Spake but of sundry perils in the storm.
Perhaps, like him of Cana in Holy Writ,
Our Arthur kept his best until the last;[31]   760
'Thou, too, my Lancelot,' asked the King, 'my friend,
Our mightiest, hath this quest availed for thee?'

" 'Our mightiest!' answered Lancelot, with a groan;
'O King!'—and when he paused methought I spied
A dying fire of madness in his eyes—   765

31. The story of the wedding feast at Cana (John 2:1–11) involves Jesus's changing water into wine.
When this wine is served last, the "ruler of the feast" upbraids the bridegroom for having served the
best wine last, the ordinary course being to serve the best wine first.

'O King, my friend, if friend of thine I be,
Happier are those that welter in their sin,
Swine in the mud, that cannot see for slime,
Slime of the ditch; but in me lived a sin
So strange, of such a kind, that all of pure,   770
Noble, and knightly in me twined and clung
Round that one sin, until the wholesome flower
And poisonous grew together, each as each,
Not to be plucked asunder; and when thy knights
Sware, I sware with them only in the hope   775
That could I touch or see the Holy Grail
They might be plucked asunder. Then I spake
To one most holy saint, who wept and said
That, save they could be plucked asunder, all
My quest were but in vain; to whom I vowed   780
That I would work according as he willed.
And forth I went, and while I yearn'd and strove
To tear the twain asunder in my heart,
My madness came upon me as of old,
And whipped me into waste fields far away.   785
There was I beaten down by little men,
Mean knights, to whom the moving of my sword
And shadow of my spear had been enow
To scare them from me once; and then I came
All in my folly to the naked shore,   790
Wide flats, where nothing but coarse grasses grew;
But such a blast, my King, began to blow,
So loud a blast along the shore and sea,
Ye could not hear the waters for the blast,
Though heaped in mounds and ridges all the sea   795
Drove like a cataract, and all the sand
Swept like a river, and the clouded heavens
Were shaken with the motion and the sound.
And blackening in the sea-foam swayed a boat,
Half-swallowed in it, anchored with a chain;   800
And in my madness to myself I said,
"I will embark and I will lose myself,
And in the great sea wash away my sin."
I burst the chain; I sprang into the boat.
Seven days I drove along the dreary deep,   805
And with me drove the moon and all the stars;
And the wind fell, and on the seventh night
I heard the shingle grinding in the surge,
And felt the boat shock earth, and looking up,

Behold, the enchanted towers of Carbonek,[32]   810
A castle like a rock upon a rock,
With chasm-like portals open to the sea,
And steps that met the breaker! There was none
Stood near it but a lion on each side
That kept the entry, and the moon was full.   815
Then from the boat I leapt, and up the stairs,
There drew my sword. With sudden-flaring manes
Those two great beasts rose upright like a man,
Each gripped a shoulder, and I stood between,
And, when I would have smitten them, heard a voice,   820
"Doubt not, go forward; if thou doubt, the beasts
Will tear thee piecemeal." Then with violence
The sword was dashed from out my hand, and fell.
And up into the sounding hall I passed;
But nothing in the sounding hall I saw—   825
No bench nor table, painting on the wall
Or shield of knight, only the rounded moon
Through the tall oriel on the rolling sea.
But always in the quiet house I heard,
Clear as a lark, high o'er me as a lark,   830
A sweet voice singing in the topmost tower
To the eastward. Up I climbed a thousand steps
With pain; as in a dream I seemed to climb
Forever. At the last I reached a door,
A light was in the crannies, and I heard,   835
"Glory and joy and honor to our Lord
And to the Holy Vessel of the Grail!"
Then in my madness I essayed the door;
It gave, and through a stormy glare, a heat
As from a seven-times-heated furnace, I,   840
Blasted and burnt, and blinded as I was,
With such a fierceness that I swooned away—
O yet methought I saw the Holy Grail,
All palled in crimson samite, and around
Great angels, awful shapes, and wings and eyes!   845
And but for all my madness and my sin,
And then my swooning, I had sworn I saw
That which I saw; but what I saw was veiled
And covered, and this quest was not for me.'

    "So speaking, and here ceasing, Lancelot left   850
The hall long silent, till Sir Gawain—nay,

32. Carbonek or Corbenic is the castle where the Grail is kept.

Brother, I need not tell thee foolish words—
A reckless and irreverent knight was he,
Now boldened by the silence of his King—
Well, I will tell thee: 'O King, my liege,' he said,   855
'Hath Gawain failed in any quest of thine?
When have I stinted stroke in foughten field?
But as for thine, my good friend Percivale,
Thy holy nun and thou have driven men mad,
Yea, made our mightiest madder than our least.   860
But by mine eyes and by mine ears I swear,
I will be deafer than the blue-eyed cat,
And thrice as blind as any noonday owl,
To holy virgins in their ecstasies,
Henceforward.'

         " 'Deafer,' said the blameless King,   865
'Gawain, and blinder unto holy things,
Hope not to make thyself by idle vows,
Being too blind to have desire to see.
But if indeed there came a sign from heaven,
Blessed are Bors, Lancelot, and Percivale,   870
For these have seen according to their sight.
For every fiery prophet in old times,
And all the sacred madness of the bard,
When God made music through them, could but speak
His music by the framework and the chord;   875
And as ye saw it ye have spoken truth.

     " 'Nay—but thou errest, Lancelot; never yet
Could all of true and noble in knight and man
Twine round one sin, whatever it might be,
With such a closeness but apart there grew,   880
Save that he were the swine thou spakest of,
Some root of knighthood and pure nobleness;
Whereto see thou, that it may bear its flower.

     " 'And spake I not too truly, O my knights?
Was I too dark a prophet when I said   885
To those who went upon the Holy Quest,
That most of them would follow wandering fires,
Lost in the quagmire?—lost to me and gone,
And left me gazing at a barren board,
And a lean Order—scarce returned a tithe—   890
And out of those to whom the vision came
My greatest hardly will believe he saw.

Another hath beheld it afar off,
And, leaving human wrongs to right themselves,
Cares but to pass into the silent life.   895
And one hath had the vision face to face,
And now his chair desires him here in vain,
However they may crown him otherwhere.

   " 'And some among you held that if the King
Had seen the sight he would have sworn the vow.   900
Not easily, seeing that the King must guard
That which he rules, and is but as the hind[33]
To whom a space of land is given to plow,
Who may not wander from the allotted field
Before his work be done, but, being done,   905
Let visions of the night or of the day
Come as they will; and many a time they come,
Until this earth he walks on seems not earth,
This light that strikes his eyeball is not light,
This air that smites his forehead is not air   910
But vision—yea, his very hand and foot—
In moments when he feels he cannot die,
And knows himself no vision to himself,
Nor the high God a vision, nor that One
Who rose again. Ye have seen what ye have seen.'   915

   "So spake the King; I knew not all he meant."

33. A farm laborer.

WILLIAM MORRIS

W ILLIAM MORRIS (1834–1896), the son of a well-to-do London stockbroker, attended Marlborough College and entered Oxford intending to pursue a career in the church. While he was there, his interest in medieval history and culture intensified, and he determined to devote himself to the arts instead. Morris's friendship with the Pre-Raphaelite painter Edward Burne-Jones brought him into contact with a circle of artists who encouraged his early writing of poetry and prose romances.

Morris's developing views of art and society were profoundly influenced by those of John Ruskin. He was particularly impressed by "On the Nature of Gothic" from volume 2 of *The Stones of Venice*, published in 1853. Like Ruskin, Morris believed that workers should take pleasure and find satisfaction in meaningful labor and that art and craftsmanship should invest ordinary life with beauty. Distressed by the inferior quality and the ugliness of mass-produced articles and eager to put his principles into practice, Morris, in 1861, opened the decorating firm of Morris, Marshall, Faulkner and Company (after 1874, Morris and Company) and began to design and produce furniture, tapestries, wallpaper, tiles, carpets, and stained-glass windows. The business was ultimately so successful that Morris and Company was commissioned to redecorate the Throne and Reception rooms of St. James's Palace in 1880. The late-nineteenth-century Arts and Crafts movements in England and the United States to a large extent drew their inspiration from Morris's efforts.

Morris's concerns extended beyond furnishings to encompass the artistic integrity of the buildings that held them. In 1877, he founded the Society for the Preservation of Ancient Buildings, which saved hundreds of historic structures from clumsy attempts at "restoration."

In 1883, Morris joined England's earliest socialist organization, the Democratic Federation, and began reading a French translation of *Capital* by Karl Marx (1818–1883). At the end of the following year, he led a large group that withdrew from the Federation to form the Socialist League and became the editor of the League's Marxist journal, *Commonweal*. By 1890, the League had come to be dominated by anarchists, and Morris left to found the Hammersmith Socialist Society. Throughout the 1880s and '90s, Morris contributed his time, talents, and money to Socialist causes. He delivered dozens of lectures to working men and submitted essays to a wide range of periodicals on the relationships among art, work, and society. Confident of the creative capabilities of ordinary people, he believed that employers and employees should labor together to produce articles of which they all could be proud. Morris was sensitive to the contradictions between his socialist principles and his position as a prosperous businessman and tried, with some measure of success, to create between himself and his own workers the ideal relationship he advocated.

Even as he immersed himself in politics, Morris continued his work as writer and designer. *News from Nowhere,* his influential utopian novel, appeared in 1890, and, in the following year, the Kelmscott Press, which Morris established, began printing beautifully crafted books, the most famous of which is the sumptuous edition of Chaucer's *The Canterbury Tales.*

When he died in 1896, a physician told his biographer, J. W. Mackail, that in his estimation, the cause of death was "simply being William Morris, and having done more work than most ten men."

Originally delivered as a lecture to the Hampstead Liberal Club in January 1884, "Useful Work *versus* Useless Toil" was published the following year by the Socialist League Office as *The Socialist Platform—No. 2.*

In a letter to the editor of *The Manchester Examiner* in March 1883, Morris explains his attitude toward work, his own and that of the common man. "I could never forget," he wrote, "that in spite of all drawbacks my work is little else than pleasure to me; that under no conceivable circumstances would I give it up even if I could. Over and over again have I asked myself why should not my lot be the common lot? My work is simple enough; much of it, nor that the least pleasant, any man of decent intelligence could do, if he could but get to care about the work and its results. Indeed I have been ashamed when I have thought of the contrast between my happy working hours and the unpraised, unrewarded, monotonous drudgery which most men are condemned to. Nothing shall convince me that such labour as this is good or necessary to civilization."

In "Useful Work *versus* Useless Toil," Morris explores the conditions under which all work may be genuinely useful and pleasurable. The influence of John Ruskin's "The Nature of Gothic" (see excerpt earlier in part 1) is readily apparent.

Useful Work *versus* Useless Toil

The above title may strike some of my readers as strange. It is assumed by most people nowadays that all work is useful, and by most *well-to-do* people that all work is desirable. Most people, well-to-do or not, believe that, even when a man is

Figure 1.4. Peter Henry Emerson, *During the Reed Harvest.* Platinotype 8⅝ × 11¼.
Courtesy of The J. Paul Getty Museum, Los Angeles.

Rural labor was the subject of many of the photographs taken by Peter Henry
Emerson (1856–1936). While Emerson's naturalistic pictures avoid the artificiality of
many posed photographs of workers, their aim was more aesthetic than documentary.
During the Reed Harvest is taken from his first published collection of photographs,
Life and Landscape on the Norfolk Broads (1886). The rather passive workers bow their
heads or turn their backs to the viewer and seem to merge with the quiet landscape.
Emerson makes no attempt to individualize them or present the hardship of their lot.

doing work which appears to be useless, he is earning his livelihood by it—he is
"employed," as the phrase goes; and most of those who are well-to-do cheer on the
happy worker with congratulations and praises, if he is only "industrious" enough
and deprives himself of all pleasure and holidays in the sacred cause of labour.[1] In
short, it has become an article of the creed of modern morality that all labour is
good in itself—a convenient belief to those who live on the labour of others. But as
to those on whom they live, I recommend them not to take it on trust, but to look
into the matter a little deeper.

Let us grant, first, that the race of man must either labour or perish. Nature
does not give us our livelihood gratis; we must win it by toil of some sort or degree.
Let us see, then, if she does not give us some compensation for this compulsion to
labour, since certainly in other matters she takes care to make the acts necessary to
the continuance of life in the individual and the race not only endurable, but even
pleasurable.

You may be sure that she does so, that it is of the nature of man, when he is not

1. Thomas Carlyle opens chapter 11 in book 3 of *Past and Present* (1843) with the proclamation,
"For there is a perennial nobleness, and even sacredness, in Work" (see "Labour" earlier in part 1).

diseased, to take pleasure in his work under certain conditions. And, yet, we must say in the teeth of the hypocritical praise of all labour, whatsoever it may be, of which I have made mention, that there is some labour which is so far from being a blessing that it is a curse; that it would be better for the community and for the worker if the latter were to fold his hands and refuse to work, and either die or let us pack him off to the workhouse[2] or prison—which you will.

Here, you see, two kinds of work—one good, the other bad; one not far removed from a blessing, a lightening of life; the other a mere curse, a burden to life.

What is the difference between them, then? This: one has hope in it, the other has not. It is manly to do the one kind of work, and manly also to refuse to do the other.

What is the nature of the hope which, when it is present in work, makes it worth doing?

It is threefold, I think—hope of rest, hope of product, hope of pleasure in the work itself; and hope of these also in some abundance and of good quality; rest enough and good enough to be worth having; product worth having by one who is neither a fool nor an ascetic; pleasure enough for all for us to be conscious of it while we are at work; not a mere habit, the loss of which we shall feel as a fidgety man feels the loss of the bit of string he fidgets with.

I have put the hope of rest first because it is the simplest and most natural part of our hope. Whatever pleasure there is in some work, there is certainly some pain in all work, the beast-like pain of stirring up our slumbering energies to action, the beast-like dread of change when things are pretty well with us; and the compensation for this animal pain is animal rest. We must feel while we are working that the time will come when we shall not have to work. Also the rest, when it comes, must be long enough to allow us to enjoy it; it must be longer than is merely necessary for us to recover the strength we have expended in working, and it must be animal rest also in this, that it must not be disturbed by anxiety, else we shall not be able to enjoy it. If we have this amount and kind of rest we shall, so far, be no worse off than the beasts.

As to the hope of product, I have said that Nature compels us to work for that. It remains for *us* to look to it that we *do* really produce something, and not nothing, or at least nothing that we want or are allowed to use. If we look to this and use our wills we shall, so far, be better than machines.

The hope of pleasure in the work itself: how strange that hope must seem to some of my readers—to most of them! Yet I think that to all living things there is a pleasure in the exercise of their energies, and that even beasts rejoice in being lithe and swift and strong. But a man at work, making something which he feels will exist because he is working at it and wills it, is exercising the energies of his mind and soul as well as of his body. Memory and imagination help him as he works.

---

2. The New Poor Law of 1834 eliminated outdoor relief (in other words, assistance to those who lived outside charitable organizations) and mandated that welfare recipients live and, if they were able, work in government-run institutions.

Not only his own thoughts, but the thoughts of the men of past ages guide his hands; and, as a part of the human race, he creates. If we work thus we shall be men, and our days will be happy and eventful.

Thus worthy work carries with it the hope of pleasure in rest, the hope of the pleasure in our using what it makes, and the hope of pleasure in our daily creative skill.

All other work but this is worthless; it is slaves' work—mere toiling to live, that we may live to toil.

Therefore, since we have, as it were, a pair of scales in which to weigh the work now done in the world, let us use them. Let us estimate the worthiness of the work we do, after so many thousand years of toil, so many promises of hope deferred, such boundless exultation over the progress of civilization and the gain of liberty.

Now, the first thing as to the work done in civilization and the easiest to notice is that it is portioned out very unequally amongst the different classes of society. First, there are people—not a few—who do no work, and make no pretense of doing any. Next, there are people, and very many of them, who work fairly hard, though with abundant easements and holidays, claimed and allowed; and lastly, there are people who work so hard that they may be said to do nothing else than work, and are accordingly called "the working classes," as distinguished from the middle classes and the rich, or aristocracy, whom I have mentioned above.

It is clear that this inequality presses heavily upon the "working" class, and must visibly tend to destroy their hope of rest at least, and so, in that particular, make them worse off than mere beasts of the field; but that is not the sum and end of our folly of turning useful work into useless toil, but only the beginning of it.

For first, as to the class of rich people doing no work, we all know that they consume a great deal while they produce nothing.[3] Therefore, clearly, they have to be kept at the expense of those who do work, just as paupers have, and are a mere burden on the community.

In these days there are many who have learned to see this, though they can see no further into the evils of our present system, and have formed no idea of any scheme for getting rid of this burden; though perhaps they have a vague hope that changes in the system of voting for members of the House of Commons may, as if by magic, tend in that direction.[4] With such hopes or superstitions we need not trouble ourselves. Moreover, this class, the aristocracy, once thought most necessary to the State, is scant of numbers, and has now no power of its own, but depends on the support of the class next below it—the middle class. In fact, it is really composed either of the most successful men of that class, or of their immediate descendants.

3. Morris echoes other eminent Victorians in his condemnation of the idle rich. See, for instance, Thomas Carlyle's *Past and Present*, especially book 3, chapter 3, "Gospel of Dilettantism." In virtually every novel of Charles Dickens, those who do no work are also condemned.

4. The 1884 Reform Act was the third and final voting reform bill passed in the nineteenth century. It enfranchised two million agricultural workers and included a redistricting plan to improve voter representation.

As to the middle class, including the trading, manufacturing, and professional people of our society, they do, as a rule, seem to work quite hard enough, and so at first sight might be thought to help the community, and not burden it. But by far the greater part of them, though they work, do not produce, and even when they do produce, as in the case of those engaged (wastefully indeed) in the distribution of goods, or doctors, or (genuine) artists and literary men, they consume out of all proportion to their due share. The commercial and manufacturing part of them, the most powerful part, spend their lives and energies in fighting amongst themselves for their respective shares of the wealth which they *force* the genuine workers to provide for them; the others are almost wholly the hangers-on of these; they do not work for the public, but a privileged class: they are the parasites of property, sometimes, as in the case of lawyers, undisguisedly so; sometimes, as the doctors and others above mentioned, professing to be useful, but too often of no use save as supporters of the system of folly, fraud, and tyranny of which they form a part. And all these we must remember have, as a rule, one aim in view; not the production of utilities, but the gaining of a position either for themselves or their children in which they will not have to work at all. It is their ambition and the end of their whole lives to gain, if not for themselves yet at least for their children, the proud position of being obvious burdens on the community. For their work itself, in spite of the sham dignity with which they surround it, they care nothing: save a few enthusiasts, men of science, art, or letters, who, if they are not the salt of the earth, are at least (and oh, the pity of it!) the salt of the miserable system of which they are the slaves, which hinders and thwarts them at every turn, and even sometimes corrupts them.

Here then is another class, this time very numerous and all-powerful, which produces very little and consumes enormously, and is therefore in the main supported, as paupers are, by the real producers. The class that remains to be considered produces all that is produced, and supports both itself and the other classes, though it is placed in a position of inferiority to them; real inferiority, mind you, involving a degradation both of mind and body. But it is a necessary consequence of this tyranny and folly that again many of these workers are not producers. A vast number of them once more are merely parasites of property, some of them openly so, as the soldiers by land and sea who are kept on foot for the perpetuating of national rivalries and enmities, and for the purposes of the national struggle for the share of the product of unpaid labour. But besides this obvious burden on the producers and the scarcely less obvious one of domestic servants, there is first the army of clerks, shop-assistants, and so forth, who are engaged in the service of the private war for wealth, which, as above said, is the real occupation of the well-to-do middle class. This is a larger body of workers than might be supposed, for it includes amongst others all those engaged in what I should call competitive salesmanship, or, to use a less dignified word, the puffery of wares, which has now got to such a pitch that there are many things which cost far more to sell than they do to make.

Next there is the mass of people employed in making all those articles of folly and luxury, the demand for which is the outcome of the existence of the rich non-producing classes; things which people leading a manly and uncorrupted life would not ask for or dream of. These things, whoever may gainsay me, I will for ever refuse to call wealth: they are not wealth, but waste. Wealth is what Nature gives us and what a reasonable man can make out of the gifts of Nature for his reasonable use. The sunlight, the fresh air, the unspoiled face of the earth, food, raiment and housing necessary and decent; the storing up of knowledge of all kinds, and the power of disseminating it; means of free communication between man and man; works of art, the beauty which man creates when he is most a man, most aspiring and thoughtful—all things which serve the pleasure of people, free, manly, and uncorrupted. This is wealth. Nor can I think of anything worth having which does not come under one or other of these heads. But think, I beseech you, of the product of England, the workshop of the world, and will you not be bewildered, as I am, at the thought of the mass of things which no sane man could desire, but which our useless toil makes—and sells?

Now, further, there is even a sadder industry yet, which is forced on many, very many, of our workers—the making of wares which are necessary to them and their brethren, *because they are an inferior class.* For if many men live without producing, nay, must live lives so empty and foolish that they *force* a great part of the workers to produce wares which no one needs, not even the rich, it follows that most men must be poor; and living as they do on wages from those whom they support, cannot get for their use the *goods* which men naturally desire, but must put up with miserable makeshifts for them, with coarse food that does not nourish, with rotten raiment which does not shelter, with wretched houses which may well make a town-dweller in civilization look back with regret to the tent of the nomad tribe, or the cave of the prehistoric savage. Nay, the workers must even lend a hand to the great industrial invention of the age—adulteration, and by its help produce for their own use shams and mockeries of the luxury of the rich; for the wage-earners must always live as the wage-payers bid them, and their habits of life are *forced* on them by their masters.

But it is waste of time to try to express in words due contempt of the productions of the much-praised cheapness of our epoch. It must be enough to say that this cheapness is necessary to the system of exploiting on which modern manufacture rests. In other words, our society includes a great mass of slaves, who must be fed, clothed, housed and amused as slaves, and that their daily necessity compels them to make the slave-wares whose use is the perpetuation of their slavery.

To sum up, then, concerning the manner of work in civilized States, these States are composed of three classes—a class which does not even pretend to work, a class which pretends to work but which produces nothing, and a class which works, but is compelled by the other two classes to do work which is often unproductive.

Civilization therefore wastes its own resources, and will do so as long as the present system lasts. These are cold words with which to describe the tyranny under which we suffer; try then to consider what they mean.

There is a certain amount of natural material and of natural forces in the world, and a certain amount of labour-power inherent in the persons of the men that inhabit it. Men urged by their necessities and desires have laboured for many thousands of years at the task of subjugating the forces of Nature and of making the natural material useful to them. To our eyes, since we cannot see into the future, that struggle with Nature seems nearly over, and the victory of the human race over her nearly complete. And, looking backwards to the time when history first began, we note that the progress of that victory has been far swifter and more startling within the last two hundred years than ever before. Surely therefore, we moderns ought to be in all ways vastly better off than any who have gone before us. Surely we ought, one and all of us, to be wealthy, to be well furnished with the good things which our victory over Nature has won for us.

But what is the real fact? Who will dare to deny that the great mass of civilized men are poor?[5] So poor are they that it is mere childishness troubling ourselves to discuss whether perhaps they are in some ways a little better off than their fore-fathers. They are poor; nor can their poverty be measured by the poverty of a resourceless savage, for he knows of nothing else than his poverty; that he should be cold, hungry, houseless, dirty, ignorant, all that is to him as natural as that he should have a skin. But for us, for the most of us, civilization has bred desires which she forbids us to satisfy, and so is not merely a niggard but a torturer also.

Thus then have the fruits of our victory over Nature been stolen from us, thus has compulsion by Nature to labour in hope of rest, gain, and pleasure been turned into compulsion by man to labour. in hope—of living to labour!

What shall we do then, can we mend it?

Well, remember once more that it is not our remote ancestors who achieved the victory over Nature, but our fathers, nay, our very selves. For us to sit hopeless and helpless then would be a strange folly indeed: be sure that we can amend it. What, then, is the first thing to be done?

We have seen that modern society is divided into two classes, one of which is *privileged* to be kept by the labour of the other—that is, it forces the other to work for it and takes from this inferior class everything that it *can* take from it, and uses the wealth so taken to keep its own members in a superior position, to make them beings of a higher order than the others: longer lived, more beautiful, more honoured, more refined than those of the other class. I do not say that it troubles itself about its members being *positively* long lived, beautiful or refined, but merely insists that they shall be so *relatively* to the inferior class. As also it cannot use the labour-power of the inferior class fairly in producing real wealth, it wastes it wholesale in the production of rubbish.

It is this robbery and waste on the part of the minority which keeps the majority poor; if it could be shown that it is necessary for the preservation of society that this should be submitted to, little more could be said on the matter, save that the

5. Six years after Morris published this essay, the early sociologist Charles Booth (1840–1916) reported in his monumental study *Life and Labour of the People in London* that over 30 percent of Londoners lived in poverty. See excerpt in part 3.

despair of the oppressed majority would probably at some time or other destroy Society. But it has been shown, on the contrary, even by such incomplete experiments, for instance, as Co-operation[6] (so called), that the existence of a privileged class is by no means necessary for the production of wealth, but rather for the "government" of the producers of wealth, or, in other words, for the upholding of privilege.

The first step to be taken then is to abolish a class of men privileged to shirk their duties as men, thus forcing others to do the work which they refuse to do. All must work according to their ability, and so produce what they consume—that is, each man should work as well as he can for his own livelihood, and his livelihood should be assured to him; that is to say, all the advantages which society would provide for each and all of its members.

Thus, at last, would true Society be founded. It would rest on equality of condition. No man would be tormented for the benefit of another—nay, no one man would be tormented for the benefit of Society. Nor, indeed, can that order be called Society which is not upheld for the benefit of every one of its members.

But since men live now, badly as they live, when so many people do not produce at all, and when so much work is wasted, it is clear that, under conditions where all produced and no work was wasted, not only would every one work with the certain hope of gaining a due share of wealth by his work, but also he could not miss his due share of rest. Here, then, are two out of the three kinds of hope mentioned above as an essential part of worthy work assured to the worker. When class-robbery is abolished, every man will reap the fruits of his labour, every man will have due rest—leisure, that is. Some Socialists might say we need not go any further than this; it is enough that the worker should get the full produce of his work, and that his rest should be abundant. But though the compulsion of man's tyranny is thus abolished, I yet demand compensation for the compulsion of Nature's necessity. As long as the work is repulsive it will still be a burden which must be taken up daily, and even so would mar our life, even though the hours of labour were short. What we want to do is to add to our wealth without diminishing our pleasure. Nature will not be finally conquered till our work becomes a part of the pleasure of our lives.

That first step of freeing people from the compulsion to labour needlessly will at least put us on the way towards this happy end; for we shall then have time and opportunities for bringing it about. As things are now, between the waste of labour-power in mere idleness and its waste in unproductive work, it is clear that the world of civilization is supported by a small part of its people; when *all* were working *usefully* for its support, the share of work which each would have to do would be but small, if our standard of life were about on the footing of what well-to-do and refined people now think desirable. We shall have labour-power to

6. Robert Owen (1771–1858) advocated cooperation (in production and the sharing of profits) rather than competition. The first cooperative societies were established in 1821; by 1880, the cooperative movement had 600,000 members, though their goals were hardly uniform. See entry on Owen in part 2.

spare, and shall, in short, be as wealthy as we please. It will be easy to live. If we were to wake up some morning now, under our present system, and find it "easy to live," that system would force us to set to work at once and make it hard to live; we should call that "developing our resources," or some such fine name. The multiplication of labour has become a necessity for us, and as long as that goes on no ingenuity in the invention of machines will be of any real use to us. Each new machine will cause a certain amount of misery among the workers whose special industry it may disturb; so many of them will be reduced from skilled to unskilled workmen, and then gradually matters will slip into their due grooves, and all will work apparently smoothly again; and if it were not that all this is preparing revolution, things would be, for the greater part of men, just as they were before the new wonderful invention.

But when revolution has made it "easy to live," when all are working harmoniously together and there is no one to rob the worker of his time, that is to say, his life; in those coming days there will be no compulsion on us to go on producing things we do not want, no compulsion on us to labour for nothing; we shall be able calmly and thoughtfully to consider what we shall do with our wealth of labour-power. Now, for my part, I think the first use we ought to make of that wealth, of that freedom, should be to make all our labour, even the commonest and most necessary, pleasant to everybody; for thinking over the matter carefully I can see that the one course which will certainly make life happy in the face of all accidents and troubles is to take a pleasurable interest in all the details of life. And lest perchance you think that an assertion too universally accepted to be worth making, let me remind you how entirely modern civilization forbids it; with what sordid, and even terrible, details it surrounds the life of the poor, what a mechanical and empty life she forces on the rich; and how rare a holiday it is for any of us to feel ourselves a part of Nature, and unhurriedly, thoughtfully, and happily to note the course of our lives amidst all the little links of events which connect them with the lives of others, and build up the great whole of humanity.

But such a holiday our whole lives might be, if we were resolute to make all our labour reasonable and pleasant. But we must be resolute indeed; for no half measures will help us here. It has been said already that our present joyless labour, and our lives scared and anxious as the life of a hunted beast, are forced upon us by the present system of producing for the profit of the privileged classes. It is necessary to state what this means. Under the present system of wages and capital the "manufacturer" (most absurdly so called, since a manufacturer means a person who makes with his hands), having a monopoly of the means whereby the power to labour inherent in every man's body can be used for production, is the master of those who are not so privileged; he, and he alone, is able to make use of this labour-power, which, on the other hand, is the only commodity by means of which his "capital," that is to say, the accumulated product of past labour, can be made productive to him. He therefore buys the labour-power of those who are bare of capital and can only live by selling it to him; his purpose in this transaction is to increase his capital, to make it breed. It is clear that if he paid those with whom he makes his bargain the full value of their labour, that is to say, all that they produced, he would fail in his purpose. But since he is the monopolist of the means of productive labour, he can *compel* them to make a bargain better for him and worse for them than that; which bargain is that after they have earned their livelihood, estimated according to a standard high enough to ensure their peaceable submission to his mastership, the rest (and by far the larger part as a matter of fact) of what they produce shall belong to him, shall be his *property* to do as he likes with, to use or abuse at his pleasure; which property is, as we all know, jealously guarded by army and navy, police and prison; in short, by that huge mass of physical force which superstition, habit, fear of death by starvation—IGNORANCE, in one word, among the propertyless masses, enables the propertied classes to use for the subjection of—their slaves.

Now, at other times, other evils resulting from this system may be put forward. What I want to point out now is the impossibility of our attaining to attractive labour under this system, and to repeat that it is this robbery (there is no other word for it) which wastes the available labour-power of the civilized world, forcing many men to do nothing, and many, very many more to do nothing useful; and forcing those who carry on really useful labour to most burdensome overwork. For understand once for all that the "manufacturer" aims primarily at producing, by means of the labour he has stolen from others, not goods but profits, that is, the "wealth" that is produced over and above the livelihood of his workmen, and the wear and tear of his machinery. Whether that "wealth" is real or sham matters nothing to him. If it sells and yields him a "profit" it is all right. I have said that, owing to there being rich people who have more money than they can spend reasonably, and who therefore buy sham wealth, there is waste on that side; and also that, owing to there being poor people who cannot afford to buy things which are worth making, there is waste on that side. So that the "demand" which the capitalist "supplies" is a false demand. The market in which he sells is "rigged" by the miserable inequalities produced by the robbery of the system of Capital and Wages.

It is this system, therefore, which we must be resolute in getting rid of, if we are to attain to happy and useful work for all. The first step towards making labour attractive is to get the means of making labour fruitful, the Capital, including the land, machinery, factories &c., into the hands of the community, to be used for the good of all alike, so that we might all work at "supplying" the real "demands" of each and all—that is to say, work for livelihood, instead of working to supply the demand of the profit market—instead of working for profit—*i.e.*, the power of compelling other men to work against their will.

When this first step has been taken and men begin to understand that Nature wills all men either to work or starve, and when they are no longer such fools as to allow some the alternative of stealing, when this happy day is come, we shall then be relieved from the tax of waste, and consequently shall find that we have, as aforesaid, a mass of labour-power available, which will enable us to live as we please within reasonable limits. We shall no longer be hurried and driven by the fear of starvation, which at present presses no less on the greater part of men in civilized communities than it does on mere savages. The first and most obvious necessities will be so easily provided for in a community in which there is no waste of labour, that we shall have time to look round and consider what we really do want, that can be obtained without over-taxing our energies; for the often-expressed fear of mere idleness falling upon us when the force supplied by the present hierarchy of compulsion is withdrawn, is a fear which is but generated by the burden of excessive and repulsive labour, which we most of us have to bear at present.

I say once more that, in my belief, the first thing which we shall think so necessary as to be worth sacrificing some idle time for, will be the attractiveness of labour. No very heavy sacrifice will be required for attaining this object, but some *will* be required. For we may hope that men who have just waded through a period of strife and revolution will be the last to put up long with a life of mere utilitarianism,[7] though Socialists are sometimes accused by ignorant persons of aiming at such a life. On the other hand, the ornamental part of modern life is already rotten to the core, and must be utterly swept away before the new order of things is realized. There is nothing of it—there is nothing which could come of it that could satisfy the aspirations of men set free from the tyranny of commercialism.

We must begin to build up the ornamental part of life—its pleasures, bodily and mental, scientific and artistic, social and individual—on the basis of work undertaken willingly and cheerfully, with the consciousness of benefiting ourselves and our neighbours by it. Such absolutely necessary work as we should have to do would in the first place take up but a small part of each day, and so far would not be burdensome; but it would be a task of daily recurrence, and therefore would spoil our day's pleasure unless it were made at least endurable while it lasted. In other words, all labour, even the commonest, must be made attractive.

How can this be done?—is the question the answer to which will take up the rest of this paper. In giving some hints on this question, I know that, while all Socialists will agree with many of the suggestions made, some of them may seem to some strange and venturesome. These must be considered as being given without any intention of dogmatizing, and as merely expressing my own personal opinion.

From all that has been said already it follows that labour, to be attractive, must be directed towards some obviously useful end, unless in cases where it is undertaken voluntarily by each individual as a pastime. This element of obvious usefulness is all the more to be counted on in sweetening tasks otherwise irksome, since social morality, the responsibility of man towards the life of man, will, in the new order of things, take the place of theological morality, or the responsibility of man to some abstract idea. Next, the day's work will be short. This need not be insisted

7. Also known as Benthamism, after Jeremy Bentham (1748–1832), utilitarianism was based on the assumption that humans are motivated by self-interest. Given this premise, the utilitarians argued that economic, social, and political conflicts should be resolved rationally by calculating what would produce "the greatest happiness for the greatest number" of people.

on. It is clear that with work unwasted it *can* be short. It is clear also that much work which is now a torment, would be easily endurable if it were much shortened.

Variety of work is the next point, and a most important one. To compel a man to do day after day the same task, without any hope of escape or change, means nothing short of turning his life into a prison-torment. Nothing but the tyranny of profit-grinding makes this necessary. A man might easily learn and practise at least three crafts, varying sedentary occupation with outdoor—occupation calling for the exercise of strong bodily energy for work in which the mind had more to do. There are few men, for instance, who would not wish to spend part of their lives in the most necessary and pleasantest of all work—cultivating the earth. One thing which will make this variety of employment possible will be the form that education will take in a socially ordered community. At present all education is directed towards the end of fitting people to take their places in the hierarchy of commerce—these as masters, those as workmen. The education of the masters is more ornamental than that of the workmen, but it is commercial still; and even at the ancient universities learning is but little regarded unless it can in the long run be made *to pay*. Due education is a totally different thing from this, and concerns itself in finding out what different people are fit for, and helping them along the road which they are inclined to take. In a duly ordered society, therefore, young people would be taught such handicrafts as they had a turn for as a part of their education, the discipline of their minds and bodies; and adults would also have opportunities of learning in the same schools, for the development of individual capacities would be of all things chiefly aimed at by education, instead, as now, the subordination of all capacities to the great end of "money-making" for oneself—or one's master. The amount of talent, and even genius, which the present system crushes, and which would be drawn out by such a system, would make our daily work easy and interesting.

Under this head of variety I will note one product of industry which has suffered so much from commercialism that it can scarcely be said to exist, and is, indeed, so foreign from our epoch that I fear there are some who will find it difficult to understand what I have to say on the subject, which I nevertheless must say, since it is really a most important one. I mean that side of art which is, or ought to be, done by the ordinary workman while he is about his ordinary work, and which has got to be called, very properly, Popular Art. This art, I repeat, no longer exists now, having been killed by commercialism. But from the beginning of man's contest with Nature till the rise of the present capitalistic system, it was alive, and generally flourished. While it lasted, everything that was made by man was adorned by man, just as everything made by Nature is adorned by her. The craftsman, as he fashioned the thing he had under his hand, ornamented it so naturally and so entirely without conscious effort, that it is often difficult to distinguish where the mere utilitarian part of his work ended and the ornamental began. Now the origin of this art was the necessity that the workman felt for variety in his work, and though the beauty produced by this desire was a great gift to the world, yet the obtaining variety and pleasure in the work by the workman was a matter of more importance still, for it stamped all labour with the impress of pleasure. All this has now quite disappeared from the work of civilization. If you wish to have ornament, you must pay specially for it, and the workman is compelled to produce ornament, as he is to produce other wares. He is compelled to pretend happiness in his work, so that the beauty produced by man's hand, which was once a solace to his labour, has now become an extra burden to him, and ornament is now but one of the follies of useless toil, and perhaps not the least irksome of its fetters.

Besides the short duration of labour, its conscious usefulness, and the variety which should go with it, there is another thing needed to make it attractive, and that is pleasant surroundings. The misery and squalor which we people of civilization bear with so much complacency as a necessary part of the manufacturing system, is just as necessary to the community at large as a proportionate amount of filth would be in the house of a private rich man. If such a man were to allow the cinders to be raked all over his drawing room, and a privy to be established in each corner of his dining-room, if he habitually made a dust and refuse heap of his once beautiful garden, never washed his sheets or changed his tablecloth, and made his family sleep five in bed, he would surely find himself in the claws of a commission *de lunatico*. But such acts of miserly folly are just what our present society is doing daily under the compulsion of a supposed necessity, which is nothing short of madness. I beg you to bring your commission of lunacy against civilization without more delay.

For all our crowded towns and bewildering factories are simply the outcome of the profit system. Capitalistic manufacture, capitalistic land-owning, and capitalistic exchange force men into big cities in order to manipulate them in the interests of capital; the same tyranny contracts the due space of the factory so much that (for instance) the interior of a great-weaving shed is almost as ridiculous a spectacle as it is a horrible one. There is no other necessity for all this, save the necessity for grinding profits out of men's lives, and of producing cheap goods for the use (and subjection) of the slaves who grind. All labour is not yet driven into factories; often where it is there is no necessity for it, save again the profit-tyranny. People engaged in all such labour need by no means be compelled to pig together in close city quarters. There is no reason why they should not follow their occupations in quiet country homes, in industrial colleges, in small towns, or, in short, where they find it happiest for them to live.

As to that part of labour which must be associated on a large scale, this very factory system, under a reasonable order of things (though to my mind there might still be drawbacks to it), would at least offer opportunities for a full and eager social life surrounded by many pleasures. The factories might be centres of intellectual activity also, and work in them might well be varied very much: the tending of the necessary machinery might to each individual be but a short part of the day's work. The other work might vary from raising food from the surrounding country to the study and practice of art and science. It is a matter of course that people engaged in such work, and being the masters of their own lives, would not allow any hurry or want of foresight to force them into enduring dirt, disorder, or want of room. Science duly applied would enable them to get rid of refuse, to minimize, if not wholly to destroy, all the inconveniences which at present attend the use of elaborate machinery, such as smoke, stench, and noise; nor would they endure that the buildings in which they worked or lived should be ugly blots on the fair face of the earth. Beginning by making their factories, buildings and sheds decent and convenient like their homes, they would infallibly go on to make them not merely negatively good, inoffensive merely, but even beautiful, so that the glorious art of architecture, now for some time slain by commercial greed, would be born again and flourish.

So, you see, I claim that work in a duly ordered community should be made attractive by the consciousness of usefulness, by its being carried on with intelligent interest, by variety, and by its being exercised amidst pleasurable surroundings. But I have also claimed, as we all do, that the day's work should not be wearisomely long. It may be said, "How can you make this last claim square with the others? If the work is to be so refined, will not the goods made be very expensive?"

I do admit, as I have said before, that some sacrifice will be necessary in order to make labour attractive. I mean that if we *could* be contented in a free community to work in the same hurried, dirty, disorderly, heartless way as we do now, we might shorten our day's labour very much more than I suppose we shall do, taking all kinds of labour into account. But if we did, it would mean that our new-won freedom of condition would leave us listless and wretched, if not anxious, as we are now, which I hold is simply impossible. We should be contented to make the sacrifices necessary for raising our condition to the standard called out for as desirable by the whole community. Nor only so. We should, individually, be emulous to sacrifice quite freely still more of our time and our ease towards the raising of the standard of life. Persons, either by themselves, or associated for such purposes, would freely, and for the love of the work and for its results—stimulated by the hope of the pleasure of creation—produce those ornaments of life for the service of all, which they are now bribed to produce (or pretend to produce) for the service of a few rich men. The experiment of a civilized community living wholly without art or literature has not yet been tried. The past degradation and corruption of civilization may force this denial of pleasure upon the society which will arise from its ashes. If that must be, we must accept the passing phase of utilitarianism as a foundation for the art which is to be. If the cripple and the starveling disappear from our streets, if the earth nourish us all alike, if the sun shine for all of us alike, if to one and all of us the glorious drama of the earth—day and night, summer and winter—can be presented as a thing to understand and love, we can afford to wait awhile till we are purified from the shame of the past corruption, and till art arises again amongst people freed from the terror of the slave and the shame of the robber.

Meantime, in any case, the refinement, thoughtfulness, and deliberation of labour must indeed be paid for, but not by compulsion to labour long hours. Our epoch has invented machines which would have appeared wild dreams to the men of past ages, and of those machines we have as yet *made no use.*

They are called "labour-saving" machines—a commonly used phrase which implies what we expect of them; but we do not get what we expect.[8] What they really do is to reduce the skilled labourer to the ranks of the unskilled, to increase the number of the "reserve army of labour"—that is, to increase the precariousness of life among the workers and to intensify the labour of those who serve the machines (as slaves their masters). All this they do by the way, while they pile up the profits of the employers of labour, or force them to expend those profits in bitter commercial war with each other. In a true society these miracles of ingenuity would be for the first time used for minimizing the amount of time spent in unattractive labour, which by their means might be so reduced as to be but a very light burden on each individual. All the more as these machines would most certainly be very much improved when it was no longer a question as to whether their improvement would "pay" the individual, but rather whether it would bene-fit the community.

So much for the ordinary use of machinery, which would probably, after a time, be somewhat restricted when men found out that there was no need for anxiety as to mere subsistence, and learned to take an interest and pleasure in handiwork which, done deliberately and thoughtfully, could be made more attractive than machine work.

Again, as people freed from the daily terror of starvation find out what they really wanted, being no longer compelled by anything but their own needs, they would refuse to produce the mere inanities which are now called luxuries, or the poison and trash now called cheap wares. No one would make plush breeches when there were no flunkies[9] to wear them, nor would anybody waste his time over making oleomargarine when no one was *compelled* to abstain from real butter. Adulteration laws are only needed in a society of thieves—and in such a society they are a dead letter.

Socialists are often asked how work of the rougher and more repulsive kind could be carried out in the new condition of things. To attempt to answer such questions fully or authoritatively would be attempting the impossibility of con-structing a scheme of a new society out of the materials of the old, before we knew which of those materials would disappear and which endure through the evolu-tion which is leading us to the great change. Yet it is not difficult to conceive of some arrangement whereby those who did the roughest work should work for the shortest spells. And again, what is said above of the variety of work applies spe-cially here. Once more I say, that for a man to be the whole of his life hopelessly engaged in performing one repulsive and never-ending task, is an arrangement fit enough for the hell imagined by theologians, but scarcely fit for any other form of

8. See W. Cooke Taylor's defense of mechanized industry in part 2.
9. A liveried, or uniformed, manservant. Also one who performs menial or trivial labor.

society. Lastly, if this rougher work were of any special kind, we may suppose that special volunteers would be called on to perform it, who would surely be forthcoming, unless men in a state of freedom should lose the sparks of manliness which they possessed as slaves.

And yet if there be any work which cannot be made other than repulsive, either by the shortness of its duration or the intermittency of its recurrence, or by the sense of special and peculiar usefulness (and therefore honour) in the mind of the man who performs it freely—if there be any work which cannot be but a torment to the worker, what then? Well, then, let us see if the heavens will fall on us if we leave it undone, for it were better that they should. The produce of such work cannot be worth the price of it.

Now we have seen that the semi-theological dogma that all labour, under any circumstances, is a blessing to the labourer, is hypocritical and false; that, on the other hand, labour is good when due hope of rest and pleasure accompanies it. We have weighed the work of civilization in the balance and found it wanting, since hope is mostly lacking to it, and therefore we see that civilization has bred a dire curse for men. But we have seen also that the work of the world might be carried on in hope and with pleasure if it were not wasted by folly and tyranny, by the perpetual strife of opposing classes.

It is Peace, therefore, which we need in order that we may live and work in hope and with pleasure. Peace so much desired, if we may trust men's words, but which has been so continually and steadily rejected by them in deeds. But for us, let us set our hearts on it and win it at whatever cost.

What the cost may be, who can tell? Will it be possible to win peace peaceably? Alas, how can it be? We are so hemmed in by wrong and folly, that in one way or other we must always be fighting against them: our own lives may see no end to the struggle, perhaps no obvious hope of the end. It may be that the best we can hope to see is that struggle getting sharper and bitterer day by day, until it breaks out openly at last into the slaughter of men by actual warfare instead of by the slower and crueller methods of "peaceful" commerce. If we live to see that, we shall live to see much; for it will mean the rich classes grown conscious of their own wrong and robbery, and consciously defending them by open violence; and then the end will be drawing near.

But in any case, and whatever the nature of our strife for peace may be, if we only aim at it steadily and with singleness of heart, and ever keep it in view, a reflection from that peace of the future will illumine the turmoil and trouble of our lives, whether the trouble be seemingly petty, or obviously tragic; and we shall, in our hopes at least, live the lives of men: nor can the present times give us any reward greater than that.

RUDYARD KIPLING

RUDYARD KIPLING (1865–1936) achieved great popularity with his fiction and poetry in the latter decades of the nineteenth century and the pre–World War I period. Born in India and then educated in England away from his parents, Kipling returned to India when he was seventeen and worked for several years as an editor and journalist. In India, he published fiction and poetry, enjoying a moderate success. When *Plain Tales from the Hills* (1888), a collection of realistic stories concerning life in India, received, locally, highly favorable reviews, he moved back to England where William Ernest Henley (see part 2) published certain of his poems and promoted his reputation. Quite soon, Kipling became exceedingly popular with the English reading public, a popularity that he continued to enjoy throughout his lifetime, coming to be regarded as the voice of the common man. Writing with first-hand knowledge of the colonial experience, Kipling fed a growing public appetite for fiction and verse concerned with descriptive analyses of the great imperial ventures in which Britain was caught up. Disparaged by some of his contemporaries and castigated by modern commentators for being simplistically imperialist in his outlook, Kipling has survived righteously indignant critical attacks to remain, a century after his first popularity, a best-selling author whose depictions of engagements between the English and those colonial peoples over whom they ruled are being reassessed as more complex, shrewd, and even-handed than naive and reductionist.

No other poem of Kipling has come under more virulent censure for propagandistic imperialism than has "The White Man's Burden," originally published in the *Times* (February 4, 1899) and in *McClure's Magazine* (February 1899). That it was immensely popular in its own time and remained so throughout much of the twentieth century may indicate how completely Kipling gave popular sentimental expression to an idealized understanding of the responsibilities of guardianship over colonized peoples. Written in response to the American acquisition of Cuba and the Philippines in 1898 and addressed to Americans, the poem affords a very clear example of how the English construed the administration of the Empire as a great moral trust to be discharged. Here the preeminent Victorian ideals of duty and work are united: the labor of custodianship—disinterested, patient, thankless, and arduous—is presented as the imperial mission to be assumed with clear-sighted responsibility and self-sacrificing determination to serve, through commitment to work, the higher good.

The White Man's Burden

Take up the White Man's burden—
    Send forth the best ye breed—
Go bind your sons to exile
    To serve your captives' need;
To wait in heavy harness,   5
    On fluttered folk and wild—
Your new-caught, sullen peoples,
    Half-devil and half-child.

Take up the White Man's burden—
    In patience to abide,   10
To veil the threat of terror
    And check the show of pride;
By open speech and simple,
    An hundred times made plain,
To seek another's profit,   15
    And work another's gain.[1]

Take up the White Man's burden—
    The savage wars of peace—
Fill full the mouth of Famine
    And bid the sickness cease;   20
And when your goal is nearest
    The end for others sought,
Watch Sloth and heathen Folly
    Bring all your hope to nought.

Take up the White Man's burden—   25
    No tawdry rule of kings,
But toil of serf and sweeper—
    The tale of common things.
The ports ye shall not enter,
    The roads ye shall not tread,   30
Go make them with your living,
    And mark them with your dead.

Take up the White Man's burden—
    And reap his old reward:

1. Lines 15 and 16 may reflect the growing perplexity of the English at the fact that their most recent colonial ventures in Africa were, with few exceptions, not economically profitable.

The blame of those ye better,   35
    The hate of those ye guard—
The cry of hosts ye humour
    (Ah, slowly!) toward the light:—
"Why brought ye us from bondage,
    Our loved Egyptian night?"[2]   40

Take up the White Man's burden—
    Ye dare not stoop to less—
Nor call too loud on Freedom
    To cloak your weariness;
By all ye cry or whisper,   45
    By all ye leave or do,
The silent, sullen peoples
    Shall weigh your Gods and you.

Take up the White Man's burden—
    Have done with childish days—   50
The lightly proffered laurel,
    The easy, ungrudged praise.
Comes now, to search your manhood
    Through all the thankless years,
Cold, edged with dear-bought wisdom,   55
    The judgment of your peers!

2. When Moses led the Israelites through the wilderness, they complained bitterly at the difficulties of the journey toward the Promised Land, wishing to return to their menial yet secure status in
Egypt: see Exodus 16 and 32. Kipling's "Egyptian night" refers not to the plague of darkness that had
been visited upon Pharaoh but instead to the preference of the Israelites (and of the "sullen peoples"
under colonial care) for the oblivion of moral and spiritual bondage rather than the enlightenment of
civilized liberty and political responsibility.

PART 2

Work as Opportunity

Without work, life is worthless; it becomes a mere state of moral coma. We do not mean merely physical work. There is a great deal of higher work—the work of action and endurance, of trial and patience, of enterprise and philanthropy, of spreading truth and civilization, of diminishing suffering and relieving the poor, of helping the weak, and enabling them to help themselves.

—Samuel Smiles, *Thrift*

Introduction

IT HAS BECOME a commonplace to note the consciousness that people in the nineteenth century had of their living in an age of transition and to comment further that such consciousness often generated a debilitating if not disabling anxiety. The complementary reading of the situation receives less studied attention, perhaps because this reading is too obvious: If the era was an age of transition, it was necessarily one of great opportunity as well, opportunity for individuals to redefine their social and political status, to assume control over an expanding economy and an unceasingly diversifying industry, to come to new understandings of the physical environment and their place in it. Above all, people had multiple opportunities for material self-advancement through new and varied forms of work. Success in different modes of work ensured economic well-being and, of equal importance to all classes, a reputation for respectability—good workers, whatever they might earn, were eminently respectable, for they were assumed to have all the other virtues seen naturally to accompany industriousness: sobriety, prudence, honesty, frugality, steadiness, and a respect for property and tradition. That work afforded some individuals the social reputation and the self-respect that derive from economic independence and emotional self-reliance did not, however, preclude these same people from seeing work also as part of some larger social or spiritual mission. The utilitarian discourse about work as a demonstration of self-reliance frequently did involve the rhetoric of mission and higher duties explored in the first part of this anthology. In the exhortations of Samuel Smiles and others, the self-interested pragmatism evidenced by the industrious was usually connected with and often subordinated to an exalted ideal of participation in cultural progress, development of character, and service to society, an association of ideas tending to confirm Thomas Carlyle's pronouncement that, "properly speaking, all true Work is Religion" (*Past and Present*).

Smiles was the great retailer of Victorian success stories, notably stories involving the triumph of individuals who persevered in their work and thereby attained both independence and a measure of dignity; his prominence as a cultural spokesman accounts for the substantial selection from *Character* included here. Yet for Smiles and the hundreds of thousands who read his books, opportunities afforded by work were not just commercial in nature; self-culture was as important a goal as economic self-advancement. Smiles often enough adopts the style of common how-to-succeed tracts, as his subtitle for his late book *Thrift* indicates: *Thrift; or How to Get On in the World.* Yet his message and his language more frequently reflect a homiletic tradition reminiscent of Carlyle or John Ruskin, as when he asserts that "we are but as stewards, appointed to employ the means entrusted to us for our own and for others' good." For him, commercial success by itself was contemptible unless such an outward and visible sign confirmed an inward and spiritual graciousness directed toward others. Consider this selection from the 1845 lecture on the education of the working class which became the germ of *Self-Help*, published fourteen years later:

> I regard it as discreditable to this country that, while so much has been done to draw forth the resources of its soil, so little has been done to develop the character of its people. What signifies to me the richness of our territory, if it do not produce good and wise men? . . . What is the great idea that has seized the mind of this age? It is the grand idea of *man*—of the importance of man as man; that every human being has a great mission to perform—has noble faculties to cultivate, great ideas to assert, a vast destiny to accomplish.

Once again, *mission* is the key word, yet in Smiles there is the comfortable assumption that duty and mission are fulfilled through the realization of those opportunities in the workplace that assure personal prosperity.

Such sanguine expectations were less easy to entertain for those who both looked for and tried to create opportunities for women in the varied worlds of work. For women even more than for men, much of the work available was physically exhausting and intellectually deadening; in the nineteenth century, the greatest number of women in paying positions worked on farms or as domestic servants, while somewhat fewer worked in factories. However, for some women in the middle class there were new possibilities for employment, hard fought for and not always clearly won, and therefore all the more significant in nature. Women were seen as having special missions particularly suited to the strengths of their sex, a view explored more fully in the fourth section of the anthology, "(Separate) Spheres of Work." Angela Burdett-Coutts, Harriet Martineau, and Octavia Hill, all indefatigable workers, proposed specific employment for women and argued convincingly that such work be acknowledged and respected. Perhaps more successfully than anyone else, Emily Davies established clear objectives for women seeking higher education, shaping the defense of her educational philosophy to demonstrate the practicality of having well-educated women serve specific needs of the society.

As had the middle-class woman, the common working-class man had long been hindered from securing a liberal and practical education. The creation of mechanics' institutes and working men's colleges in large towns as well as in London changed the ways in which working men regarded themselves and looked to their future. What is striking from a modern perspective is that the educational programs proposed for these workers were considerably less "practical" or "vocational" in nature than one might have expected. The course of studies and, more tellingly, the methodology of instruction proposed by F. D. Maurice for the Working Men's College at Red Lion Square, which he had helped to establish, reveal much about increased respect and concern for working-class individuals. Maurice's followers actively supported the cooperative movement, which hearkened back to the ideals set forth by Robert Owen in the selection from *The Revolution in the Mind and Practice of the Human Race* included in this section. These readings indicate how vital was the intellectual life of the working class.

Such vitality is striking, but the variety of new opportunities for work is what distinguishes the nineteenth century. How writers viewed both workers and work is suggested by the selection of readings from poets, fiction writers, and journalists included below. Common in the selections is a delight in the existence of new work opportunities as well as a nostalgia for (and possible over-idealization of) traditional types and experiences of work. Such expression of a positive attitude toward work must have become, if one may trust the final confession of Dickens's Uriah Heep, almost as formulaic as the contrasting understanding of work as a curse:

> ". . . they used to teach at school (the same school where I picked up so much umbleness), from nine o'clock to eleven, that labour was a curse; and from eleven o'clock to one, that it was a blessing and a cheerfulness, and a dignity, and I don't know what all . . ." (*David Copperfield*)

Heep's myopic egocentricity prevents him from seeing work as a means of genuine liberation or self-affirmation; it is his nemesis—and Dickens's favorite creation—David Copperfield whose life assumes meaning ("blessing," "cheerfulness," "dignity") because he finds the work that gives him both purpose and identity. The self-actualization that comes to David through his vocation as a writer constitutes Dickens's own endorsement of the worth of work, for the oppressive situations Dickens opposed in so many of his novels were perversions of the work ethic rather than work itself. The most striking nineteenth-century model for success through enterprising work, Dickens shared the basic assumptions underlying almost all the selections below: that work is, generally, good and that workers are to be respected for their individuality and intrinsic worth.

WILLIAM WORDSWORTH

W ILLIAM WORDSWORTH (1770–1850) was the most famous poet of the nineteenth century, a culturally dominant figure whom Matthew Arnold, at mid-century, extolled for his ability to "loose[ ] our heart in tears," to resolve the angst of those who felt intellectually and emotionally incapacitated by having fallen upon an "iron time / Of doubts, disputes, distractions, fears." Such a view of Wordsworth as the compassionate philosopher who soothed anxieties and restored the doubt-ridden to "primal joy" was not uncommon among the Victorians, but it obscured the distinctively revolutionary turn of Wordsworth's poetry that, in form and subject matter, is marked by a critical exploration of and challenge to established norms. Even in 1814, when many critics feel that he had become prosaically conventional in his views, Wordsworth was probing the potential effects of industrialization in England, finding in the growth of systematized, mechanical manufactories both opportunities and dangers.

The excerpts below derive from *The Excursion,* a lengthy work that Wordsworth published in 1814. The poem is largely conversational, consisting of interchanges among a very few figures: the Poet, an essentially reclusive person whose general outlook was to comprise the subject matter for a yet larger (never completed) composition embracing *The Excursion;* the Wanderer, a former peddler of a philosophically reflective bent whose wisdom, bred of age and wide-ranging experience, shapes the more youthful opinions of the Poet with whom he traverses the countryside; the Solitary, a gifted yet disillusioned man who feeds his misanthropy and skepticism in isolation; and the Pastor, whose home they visit and the lives of whose parishioners, living and dead, provide subjects for moral commentary and philosophic speculation. In the latter books of *The Excursion,* Wordsworth has these individuals appraise the worth of the nascent factory system whose growth would soon transform the nation. Among the issues touched upon are the role of industry in socializing (and thereby culturing) the populace, the corresponding role of trade in nurturing civilization, the disruption by the factory system of traditional and healthy familial relations, the deleterious effects of some aspects of factory work, the assessment of whether the traditional ideal of rural work is oversentimentalized, the importance of education for the working classes, the security of England from violent action by the working classes, and the "safety valve" of emigration to colonial domains for unemployed workers. What may surprise many is not Wordsworth's criticism of factory life but rather his initial hopeful reading of manufactory systems as providing beneficial opportunities to individuals and the nation.

The initial selection below (book 8, lines 82–440) includes the Wanderer's endorsement of the economic benefits gained through increasing industrialization, an approval almost immediately tempered by misgivings about that disruption of the "old domestic morals of the land" occasioned by the "unnatural light / Prepared for never-resting Labour's eyes"—the system of day and night working shifts that segregate family members from one another and from healthful engagement with the natural world. The Solitary directly takes up the argument, pointing out that the traditions of agrarian labor have also produced degenerate lifestyles characterized by poverty, beggary, ignorance, and moral torpor unenlightened by education. In the second selection (book 9, lines 254–415), Wordsworth develops further the theme of education as the Wanderer endorses universal instruction for the working classes, seeing the continued prosperity of England as dependent upon such schooling; inspired by the happy sense of domestic security, the Wanderer proceeds with an interesting linkage of the civilizing efficacy of British imperial dominion to "the faithful care of unambitious schools / Instructing simple childhood's ready ear."

See the introduction to Wordsworth in part 1 for more biographical information.

From *The Excursion*

From Book VIII

"Happy," rejoined the Wanderer, "they who gain
A panegyric from your[1] generous tongue!
But, if to these Wayfarers once pertained
Aught of romantic interest, it is gone.   85
Their purer service, in this realm at least,
Is past for ever.—An inventive Age
Has wrought, if not with speed of magic, yet
To most strange issues. I have lived to mark

---

1. The Wanderer is addressing the Solitary, who has just offered a more than half-playful analogy between knights errant and the itinerant Peddlers (the "Wayfarers" of line 84) whose work in carrying commerce to provincial areas has helped refine and civilize uncouth rural populations.

A new and unforeseen creation rise   90
From out the labours of a peaceful Land
Wielding her potent enginery to frame
And to produce, with appetite as keen
As that of war, which rests not night or day,
Industrious to destroy! With fruitless pains   95
Might one like me *now* visit many a tract
Which, in his youth, he trod, and trod again,
A lone pedestrian with a scanty freight,
Wished-for, or welcome, wheresoe'er he came—
Among the tenantry of thorpe² and vill;   100
Or straggling burgh, of ancient charter proud,
And dignified by battlements and towers
Of some stern castle, mouldering on the brow
Of a green hill or bank of rugged stream.
The foot-path faintly marked, the horse-track wild,   105
And formidable length of plashy lane,
(Prized avenues ere others had been shaped
Or easier links connecting place with place)
Have vanished—swallowed up by stately roads
Easy and bold, that penetrate the gloom   110
Of Britain's farthest glens. The Earth has lent
Her waters, Air her breezes; and the sail
Of traffic glides with ceaseless intercourse,
Glistening along the low and woody dale;
Or, in its progress, on the lofty side,   115
Of some bare hill, with wonder kenned from far.

    "Meanwhile, at social Industry's command,
How quick, how vast an increase! From the germ
Of some poor hamlet, rapidly produced
Here a huge town, continuous and compact,   120
Hiding the face of earth for leagues—and there,
Where not a habitation stood before,
Abodes of men irregularly massed
Like trees in forests,—spread through spacious tracts,
O'er which the smoke of unremitting fires   125
Hangs permanent, and plentiful as wreaths
Of vapour glittering in the morning sun.
And, wheresoe'er the traveller turns his steps,
He sees the barren wilderness erased,

---

2. A *thorpe* is a small hamlet or gathering of houses. A *vill* (line 100) is a village, and a *burgh* (line 101) is a somewhat larger entity approximating the consequence of an incorporated town.

Or disappearing; triumph that proclaims   130
How much the mild Directress of the plough
Owes to alliance with these new-born arts!
—Hence is the wide sea peopled,—hence the shores
Of Britain are resorted to by ships
Freighted from every climate of the world   135
With the world's choicest produce. Hence that sum
Of keels that rest within her crowded ports,
Or ride at anchor in her sounds and bays;
That animating spectacle of sails
That, through her inland regions, to and fro   140
Pass with the respirations of the tide,
Perpetual, multitudinous! Finally,
Hence a dread arm of floating power, a voice
Of thunder daunting those who would approach
With hostile purposes the blessed Isle,   145
Truth's consecrated residence, the seat
Impregnable of Liberty and Peace.

    "And yet, O happy Pastor of a flock
Faithfully watched, and, by that loving care
And Heaven's good providence, preserved from taint!   150
With you I grieve, when on the darker side
Of this great change I look; and there behold
Such outrage done to nature as compels
The indignant power to justify herself;
Yea, to avenge her violated rights,   155
For England's bane.—When soothing darkness spreads
O'er hill and vale," the Wanderer thus expressed
His recollections, "and the punctual stars,
While all things else are gathering to their homes,
Advance, and in the firmament of heaven   160
Glitter—but undisturbing, undisturbed;
As if their silent company were charged
With peaceful admonitions for the heart
Of all-beholding Man, earth's thoughtful lord;
Then, in full many a region, once like this   165
The assured domain of calm simplicity
And pensive quiet, an unnatural light
Prepared for never-resting Labour's eyes
Breaks from a many-windowed fabric huge;
And at the appointed hour a bell is heard—   170
Of harsher import than the curfew-knoll

That spake the Norman Conqueror's stern behest[3]—
A local summons to unceasing toil!
Disgorged are now the ministers of day;
And, as they issue from the illumined pile,   175
A fresh band meets them, at the crowded door—
And in the courts—and where the rumbling stream,
That turns the multitude of dizzy wheels,
Glares, like a troubled spirit, in its bed
Among the rocks below. Men, maidens, youths,   180
Mother[s] and little children, boys and girls,
Enter, and each the wonted task resumes
Within this temple, where is offered up
To Gain, the master idol of the realm,
Perpetual sacrifice. Even thus of old   185
Our ancestors, within the still domain
Of vast cathedral or conventual church,
Their vigils kept; where tapers day and night
On the dim altar burned continually,
In token that the House was evermore   190
Watching to God. Religious men were they;
Nor would their reason, tutored to aspire
Above this transitory world, allow
That there should pass a moment of the year,
When in their land the Almighty's service ceased.[4]   195

    "Triumph who will in these profaner rites
Which we, a generation self-extolled,
As zealously perform! I cannot share
His proud complacency:—yet do I exult,
Casting reserve away, exult to see   200
An intellectual mastery exercised
O'er the blind elements; a purpose given,
A perseverance fed; almost a soul
Imparted—to brute matter. I rejoice,
Measuring the force of those gigantic powers   205
That, by the thinking mind, have been compelled

---

3. The curfew, or covering of the fire, was a regulation instituted in England by the newly established Norman overlords to ensure that no indigenous groups could meet in the night to plan resistance. The curfew time was indicated by the tolling of the church bells.

4. The comparison traced in lines 185–95 between modern and medieval times became commonplace in the nineteenth century, with medieval culture consistently being cast as more stable, more humane, and more spiritually vital. See part 1 for selections from *Past and Present,* a later prose work in which Thomas Carlyle offers extended comparison between his own times and those of the middle ages.

To serve the will of feeble-bodied Man.
For with the sense of admiration blends
The animating hope that time may come
When, strengthened, yet not dazzled, by the might   210
Of this dominion over nature gained,
Men of all lands shall exercise the same
In due proportion to their country's need;[5]
Learning, though late, that all true glory rests,
All praise, all safety, and all happiness,   215
Upon the moral law. Egyptian Thebes,
Tyre, by the margin of the sounding waves,
Palmyra,[6] central in the desert, fell;
And the Arts died by which they had been raised.
—Call Archimedes[7] from his buried tomb   220
Upon the grave of vanished Syracuse,
And feelingly the Sage shall make report
How insecure, how baseless in itself,
Is the Philosophy whose sway depends
On mere material instruments;—how weak   225
Those arts, and high inventions, if unpropped
By virtue.—He, sighing with pensive grief,
Amid his calm abstractions, would admit
That not the slender privilege is theirs
To save themselves from blank forgetfulness!"   230

    When from the Wanderer's lips these words had fallen,
I said,[8] "And, did in truth those vaunted Arts
Possess such privilege, how could we escape
Sadness and keen regret, we who revere,
And would preserve as things above all price,   235
The old domestic morals of the land,
Her simple manners, and the stable worth

5. For the Wanderer—and, indeed, for Wordsworth himself—neither machinery nor manufactories were themselves problematic; as he made clear in comments about *The Fleece*, a poem by John Dyer (1699–1757) celebrating the very beginnings of industrialization, Wordsworth took issue with the *management* of innovative use of machinery, what he called "the ill-regulated and excessive application of powers so admirable in themselves."

6. Thebes was, for a while, the capital of Egypt; Tyre was the center of Phoenician trade for several centuries; Palmyra was a famous trading center at an oasis between Babylon and Syria. Like Syracuse, the Greek colony on Sicily mentioned in line 221, each of these cities was noted for its material wealth based upon industry and trade, and each had associations of a morally decadent opulence.

7. Archimedes (287–212 B.C.E.) was the great practical inventor and mathematical theoretician who was native to Syracuse; he purportedly invented machines used in the defense of Syracuse against the Romans, and he died when the Romans sacked the city.

8. The "I" who interposes here is the young Poet who accompanies the Wanderer and serves as general narrator for the entire poem.

That dignified and cheered a low estate?
Oh! where is now the character of peace,
Sobriety, and order, and chaste love,   240
And honest dealing, and untainted speech,
And pure good-will, and hospitable cheer;
That made the very thought of country-life
A thought of refuge, for a mind detained
Reluctantly amid the bustling crowd?   245
Where now the beauty of the sabbath kept
With conscientious reverence, as a day
By the almighty Lawgiver pronounced
Holy and blest? and where the winning grace
Of all the lighter ornaments attached   250
To time and season, as the year rolled round?"

      "Fled!" was the Wanderer's passionate response,
"Fled utterly! or only to be traced
In a few fortunate retreats like this;
Which I behold with trembling, when I think   255
What lamentable change, a year—a month—
May bring; that brook converting as it runs
Into an instrument of deadly bane
For those, who, yet untempted to forsake
The simple occupations of their sires,   260
Drink the pure water of its innocent stream
With lip almost as pure.—Domestic bliss
(Or call it comfort, by a humbler name,)
How art thou blighted for the poor Man's heart!
Lo! in such neighbourhood, from morn to eve,   265
The habitations empty! or perchance
The Mother left alone,—no helping hand
To rock the cradle of her peevish babe;
No daughters round her, busy at the wheel,
Or in dispatch of each day's little growth   270
Of household occupation; no nice arts
Of needle-work; no bustle at the fire,
Where once the dinner was prepared with pride;
Nothing to speed the day, or cheer the mind;
Nothing to praise, to teach, or to command!   275

      "The Father, if perchance he still retain
His old employments, goes to field or wood,
No longer led or followed by the Sons;
Idlers perchance they were,—but in *his* sight;

Breathing fresh air, and treading the green earth: 280
'Till their short holiday of childhood ceased,
Ne'er to return! That birthright now is lost.
Economists will tell you that the State
Thrives by the forfeiture—unfeeling thought,
And false as monstrous! Can the mother thrive   285
By the destruction of her innocent sons
In whom a premature necessity
Blocks out the forms of nature, preconsumes
The reason, famishes the heart, shuts up
The infant Being in itself, and makes   290
Its very spring a season of decay!
The lot is wretched, the condition sad,
Whether a pining discontent survive,
And thirst for change; or habit hath subdued
The soul deprest, dejected—even to love   295
Of her close tasks, and long captivity.

      "Oh, banish far such wisdom as condemns
A native Briton to these inward chains,
Fixed in his soul, so early and so deep;
Without his own consent, or knowledge, fixed!   300
He is a slave to whom release comes not,
And cannot come. The boy, where'er he turns,
Is still a prisoner; when the wind is up
Among the clouds, and roars through the ancient woods;
Or when the sun is shining in the east,   305
Quiet and calm. Behold him—in the school
Of his attainments? no; but with the air
Fanning his temples under heaven's blue arch.
His raiment, whitened o'er with cotton-flakes
Or locks of wool, announces whence he comes.   310
Creeping his gait and cowering, his lip pale,
His respiration quick and audible;
And scarcely could you fancy that a gleam
Could break from out those languid eyes, or a blush
Mantle upon his cheek. Is this the form,   315
Is that the countenance, and such the port,
Of no mean Being? One who should be clothed
With dignity befitting his proud hope;
Who, in his very childhood, should appear
Sublime from present purity and joy!   320
The limbs increase; but liberty of mind
Is gone for ever; and this organic frame,

So joyful in its motions, is become
Dull, to the joy of her own motions dead;
And even the touch, so exquisitely poured   325
Through the whole body, with a languid will
Performs its functions; rarely competent
To impress a vivid feeling on the mind
Of what there is delightful in the breeze,
The gentle visitations of the sun,   330
Or lapse of liquid element—by hand,
Or foot, or lip, in summer's warmth—perceived.
—Can hope look forward to a manhood raised
On such foundations?"
                          "Hope is none for him!"
The pale Recluse[9] indignantly exclaimed,   335
"And tens of thousands suffer wrong as deep.
Yet be it asked, in justice to our age,
If there were not, before those arts appeared,
These structures rose, commingling old and young,
And unripe sex with sex, for mutual taint;   340
If there were not, *then,* in our far-famed Isle,
Multitudes, who from infancy had breathed
Air unimprisoned, and had lived at large;
Yet walked beneath the sun, in human shape,
As abject, as degraded? At this day,   345
Who shall enumerate the crazy huts
And tottering hovels, whence do issue forth
A ragged Offspring, with their upright hair
Crowned like the image of fantastic Fear;
Or wearing, (shall we say?) in that white growth   350
An ill-adjusted turban, for defence
Or fierceness, wreathed around their sunburnt brows,
By savage Nature? Shrivelled are their lips,
Naked, and coloured like the soil, the feet
On which they stand; as if thereby they drew   355
Some nourishment, as trees do by their roots,
From earth, the common mother of us all.
Figure and mien, complexion and attire,
Are leagued to strike dismay; but out-stretched hand
And whining voice denote them supplicants   ·   360
For the least boon that pity can bestow.

9. The embittered and misanthropic Solitary speaks here, pointing out that it is not the factory boy alone who is degraded by work divorced from meaningful human intercourse and genuine purpose: such abasement he sees as the lot of the rural dweller and the agrarian laborer.

Such on the breast of darksome heaths are found;
And with their parents occupy the skirts
Of furze-clad commons; such are born and reared
At the mine's mouth under impending rocks;   365
Or dwell in chambers of some natural cave;
Or where their ancestors erected huts,
For the convenience of unlawful gain,
In forest purlieus; and the like are bred,
All England through, where nooks and slips of ground   370
Purloined, in times less jealous than our own,
From the green margin of the public way,
A residence afford them, 'mid the bloom
And gaiety of cultivated fields.
Such (we will hope the lowest in the scale)   375
Do I remember oft-times to have seen
'Mid Buxton's dreary heights. In earnest watch,
Till the swift vehicle approach, they stand;
Then, following closely with the cloud of dust,
An uncouth feat exhibit, and are gone   380
Heels over head, like tumblers on a stage.
—Up from the ground they snatch the copper coin,
And, on the freight of merry passengers
Fixing a steady eye, maintain their speed;
And spin—and pant—and overhead again,   385
Wild pursuivants![10] until their breath is lost,
Or bounty tires—and every face, that smiled
Encouragement, hath ceased to look that way.
—But, like the vagrants of the gipsy tribe,
These, bred to little pleasure in themselves,   390
Are profitless to others.
                    "Turn we then
To Britons born and bred within the pale
Of civil polity, and early trained
To earn, by wholesome labour in the field,
The bread they eat. A sample should I give   395
Of what this stock hath long produced to enrich
The tender age of life, ye would exclaim,
'Is this the whistling plough-boy whose shrill notes
Impart new gladness to the morning air!'
Forgive me if I venture to suspect   400
That many, sweet to hear of in soft verse,

10. Followers or attendants.

Are of no finer frame. Stiff are his joints;
Beneath a cumbrous frock, that to the knees
Invests the thriving churl, his legs appear,
Fellows to those that lustily upheld   405
The wooden stools for everlasting use,
Whereon our fathers sate. And mark his brow
Under whose shaggy canopy are set
Two eyes—not dim, but of a healthy stare—
Wide, sluggish, blank, and ignorant, and strange—   410
Proclaiming boldly that they never drew
A look or motion of intelligence
From infant-conning of the Christ-cross-row,[11]
Or puzzling through a primer, line by line,
Till perfect mastery crown the pains at last.   415
—What kindly warmth from touch of fostering hand,
What penetrating power of sun or breeze,
Shall e'er dissolve the crust wherein his soul
Sleeps, like a caterpillar sheathed in ice?
This torpor is no pitiable work   420
Of modern ingenuity; no town
Nor crowded city can be taxed with aught
Of sottish vice or desperate breach of law,
To which (and who can tell where or how soon?)
He may be roused. This Boy the fields produce: 425
His spade and hoe, mattock and glittering scythe,
The carter's whip that on his shoulder rests
In air high-towering with a boorish pomp,
The sceptre of his sway; his country's name,
Her equal rights, her churches and her schools—   430
What have they done for him? And, let me ask,
For tens of thousands uninformed as he?
In brief, what liberty of *mind* is here?"

      This ardent sally pleased the mild good Man,
To whom the appeal couched in its closing words   435
Was pointedly addressed; and to the thoughts
That, in assent or opposition, rose
Within his mind, he seemed prepared to give
Prompt utterance; but the Vicar interposed
With invitation urgently renewed.   440

11. In traditional children's primers, the letters of the alphabet were arranged in a cross so that, as
they learned their ABC's, children would be reminded of the Savior's sacrifice.

From Book IX

Then let us rather fix our gladdened thoughts   255
Upon the brighter scene.[12] How blest that pair
Of blooming Boys[13] (whom we beheld even now)
Blest in their several and their common lot!
A few short hours of each returning day
The thriving prisoners of their village-school: 260
And thence let loose, to seek their pleasant homes
Or range the grassy lawn in vacancy;
To breathe and to be happy, run and shout
Idle,—but no delay, no harm, no loss;
For every genial power of heaven and earth,   265
Through all the seasons of the changeful year,
Obsequiously doth take upon herself
To labour for them; bringing each in turn
The tribute of enjoyment, knowledge, health,
Beauty, or strength! Such privilege is theirs,   270
Granted alike in the outset of their course
To both; and, if that partnership must cease,
I grieve not," to the Pastor here he turned,
"Much as I glory in that child of yours,
Repine not for his cottage-comrade, whom   275
Belike no higher destiny awaits
Than the old hereditary wish fulfilled;
The wish for liberty to live—content
With what Heaven grants, and die—in peace of mind,
Within the bosom of his native vale.   280
At least, whatever fate the noon of life
Reserves for either, sure it is that both
Have been permitted to enjoy the dawn;
Whether regarded as a jocund time,
That in itself may terminate, or lead   285
In course of nature to a sober eve.
Both have been fairly dealt with; looking back
They will allow that justice has in them
Been shown, alike to body and to mind."

12. The Wanderer speaks here, responding to the observations by the Solitary that rural ignorance and subsequent moral degradation comprise as real an evil as does the moral retardation linked to factory work.

13. The Pastor's son and this son's companion, a cottage boy who is not his social equal and will not enjoy the educational and social opportunities afforded to a cleric's child. The two boys have just returned from a fishing expedition.

He paused, as if revolving in his soul   290
Some weighty manner; then, with fervent voice
And an impassioned majesty, exclaimed—

"O for the coming of that glorious time
When, prizing knowledge as her noblest wealth
And best protection, this imperial Realm,   295
While she exacts allegiance, shall admit
An obligation, on her part, to *teach*
Them who are born to serve her and obey;
Binding herself by statute to secure
For all the children whom her soil maintains   300
The rudiments of letters, and inform
The mind with moral and religious truth,
Both understood and practised,—so that none,
However destitute, be left to droop
By timely culture unsustained; or run   305
Into a wild disorder; or be forced
To drudge through a weary life without the help
Of intellectual implements and tools;
A savage horde among the civilised,
A servile band among the lordly free!   310
This sacred right, the lisping babe proclaims
To be inherent in him, by Heaven's will,
For the protection of his innocence;
And the rude boy—who, having overpast
The sinless age, by conscience is enrolled,   315
Yet mutinously knits his angry brow,
And lifts his wilful hand on mischief bent,
Or turns the godlike faculty of speech
To impious use—by process indirect
Declares his due, while he makes known his need.   320
—This sacred right is fruitlessly announced,
This universal plea in vain addressed,
To eyes and ears of parents who themselves
Did, in the time of their necessity,
Urge it in vain; and, therefore, like a prayer   325
That from the humblest floor ascends to heaven,
It mounts to reach the State's parental ear;
Who, if indeed she own a mother's heart,
And be not most unfeelingly devoid
Of gratitude to Providence, will grant   330
The unquestionable good—which, England, safe

From interference of external force,
May grant at leisure; without risk incurred
That what in wisdom for herself she doth,
Others shall e'er be able to undo.   335

    "Look! and behold, from Calpe's[14] sunburnt cliffs
To the flat margin of the Baltic sea,
Long-reverenced titles cast away as weeds;
Laws overturned; and territory split,
Like fields of ice rent by the polar wind,   340
And forced to join in less obnoxious shapes
Which, ere they gain consistence, by a gust
Of the same breath are shattered and destroyed.
Meantime the sovereignty of these fair Isles
Remains entire and indivisible: 345
And, if that ignorance were removed, which breeds
Within the compass of their several shores
Dark discontent, or loud commotion, each
Might still preserve the beautiful repose
Of heavenly bodies shining in their spheres.   350
—The discipline of slavery is unknown
Among us,—hence the more do we require
The discipline of virtue; order else
Cannot subsist, nor confidence, nor peace.
Thus, duties rising out of good possest   355
And prudent caution needful to avert
Impending evil, equally require
That the whole people should be taught and trained.
So shall licentiousness and black resolve
Be rooted out, and virtuous habits take   360
Their place; and genuine piety descend,
Like an inheritance, from age to age.

    "With such foundations laid, avaunt[15] the fear
Of numbers crowded on their native soil,
To the prevention of all healthful growth   365
Through mutual injury! Rather in the law
Of increase and the mandate from above
Rejoice!—and ye have special cause for joy.
—For, as the element of air affords
An easy passage to the industrious bees   370

14. Gibraltar. Wordsworth refers, in lines 336–43, to the reorganization of Europe during the Napoleonic wars, a transformation in the process of reversal as Napoleon sustained repeated defeats.
15. Take hence.

Fraught with their burthens; and a way as smooth
For those ordained to take their sounding flight
From the thronged hive, and settle where they list
In fresh abodes—their labour to renew;
So the wide waters, open to the power,   375
The will, the instincts, and appointed needs
Of Britain, do invite her to cast off
Her swarms, and in succession send them forth;
Bound to establish new communities
On every shore whose aspect favours hope   380
Or bold adventure; promising to skill
And perseverance their deserved reward.

"Yes," he continued, kindling as he spake,
"Change wide, and deep, and silently performed,
This Land shall witness; and as days roll on,   385
Earth's universal frame shall feel the effect;
Even till the smallest habitable rock,
Beaten by lonely billows, hear the songs
Of humanised society; and bloom
With civil arts, that shall breathe forth their fragrance,   390
A grateful tribute to all-ruling Heaven.[16]
From culture, unexclusively bestowed
On Albion's noble Race in freedom born,
Expect these mighty issues: from the pains
And faithful care of unambitious schools   395
Instructing simple childhood's ready ear:
Thence look for these magnificent results!
—Vast the circumference of hope—and ye
Are at its centre, British Lawgivers;
Ah! sleep not there in shame! Shall Wisdom's voice   400
From out the bosom of these troubled times
Repeat the dictates of her calmer mind,
And shall the venerable halls ye fill
Refuse to echo the sublime decree?
Trust not to partial care a general good;   405
Transfer not to futurity a work
Of urgent need.—Your Country must complete
Her glorious destiny. Begin even now,
Now, when oppression, like the Egyptian plague

16. The idea, traced in lines 363–91, that colonial territories would absorb the superfluous workers of the mother country and that otherwise troublesome energies would transform waste wildernesses into profitable imperial dominions was popular in the late eighteenth and early nineteenth centuries, and it remained an accepted principle of some economic theorists until the early twentieth century.

Of darkness,[17] stretched o'er guilty Europe, makes   410
The brightness more conspicuous that invests
The happy Island where ye think and act;
Now, when destruction is a prime pursuit,
Show to the wretched nations for what end
The powers of civil polity were given."   415

17. One of the ten plagues that are visited upon Egypt in order to convince Pharaoh to let Moses lead the chosen people out of the land of Goshen (Exodus 7:14–12:36). The plague of darkness, "even darkness which may be felt," lasts for three days (Exodus 10:21–23), during which time the Israelites have light.

ROBERT OWEN

Born in Wales, the son of a saddler and ironmonger, Robert Owen (1771–1858) left school at age nine to become a shop-boy. The following year he moved to England where, for the next few years, he worked for haberdashers and drapers. An ambitious young man, he was at age nineteen made manager of a Lancashire spinning mill employing five hundred people. Under his supervision, the efficiency and productivity of the mill increased significantly, and the conduct and attitudes of the workers improved. He soon went into business for himself and met with considerable success.

In 1800, he and his business partners acquired the New Lanark Mills, a large, well-equipped enterprise in Scotland. Long convinced of the oppressive and dehumanizing nature of the manufacturing system, Owen sought to transform New Lanark into a model factory and a model community. His commitment to providing a wholesome living and working environment led to better pay and shorter hours for his laborers and to his refusal to employ children under age ten or to engage pauper apprentices. A percentage of the profits realized by the business was reinvested in the community. Owen built parks, opened schools, and established stores that stocked quality goods at reasonable prices. Guided by his conviction that circumstances determine character, Owen administered what he referred to as a "rational" program designed to mold working-class individuals into responsible, industrious citizens.

Owen spent over twenty-five years at New Lanark and attracted widespread public notice with his innovative system. In 1825, he established another model community in the United States, at New Harmony, Indiana, but the experiment failed within a few years.

Robert Owen was one of the earliest champions of factory reform legislation and an outspoken promoter of trade unionism and of the cooperative movement, arguing for profit shares to be distributed among masters, laborers, and consumers. Firmly persuaded of the rightness of his theories, Owen worked tirelessly to win adherents to his system and invested his considerable wealth in projects for the betterment of society. His principal views were set forth in *A New View of Society* (1813–16) and repeated in countless public addresses, journal articles, pamphlets, and books.

The following essay was written in 1815.

Observations on the Effect of the
Manufacturing System:
With Hints for the Improvement of those parts of it which
are most injurious to Health and Morals.

Those who were engaged in the trade, manufactures, and commerce of this country thirty or forty years ago formed but a very insignificant portion of the knowledge, wealth, influence, or population of the Empire.

Prior to that period, Britain was essentially agricultural. But, from that time to the present, the home and foreign trade have increased in a manner so rapid and extraordinary as to have raised commerce to an importance, which it never previously attained in any country possessing so much political power and influence.

(By the returns to the Population Act in 1811, it appears that in England, Scotland and Wales, there are 895,998 families chiefly employed in agriculture—1,129,049 families chiefly employed in trade and manufactures—640,500 individuals in the army and navy—and 519,168 families not engaged in any of these employments. It follows that nearly half as many more persons are engaged in trade as in agriculture—and that of the whole population the agriculturists are about 1 to 3.)

This change has been owing chiefly to the mechanical inventions which introduced the cotton trade into this country, and to the cultivation of the cotton tree in America.[1] The wants which this trade created for the various materials requisite to forward its multiplied operations, caused an extraordinary demand for almost all the manufactures previously established, and, of course, for human labour. The numerous fanciful and useful fabrics manufactured from cotton soon became objects of desire in Europe and America: and the consequent extension of the British foreign trade was such as to astonish and confound the most enlightened statesmen both at home and abroad.

The immediate effects of this manufacturing phenomenon were a rapid increase of the wealth, industry, population, and political influence of the British Empire; and by the aid of which it has been enabled to contend for five-and-twenty

---

1. The mechanical advances to which Owen refers include the following: invention of the steam engine by the Scots engineer, James Watt (1763–1819); development of the spinning jenny, a machine that could spin several threads simultaneously, by an Englishman, James Hargreaves (sometimes spelled Hargraves, d. 1778); construction of the spinning frame, a water-powered machine that had a much larger capacity than the jenny but could spin only coarse thread, by an English manufacturer, Sir Richard Arkwright (1732–1792); and invention of the spinning mule, a machine that made possible large-scale production of high-quality thread and yarn, by an Englishman, Samuel Crompton (1753–1827). North American cotton was first processed with the newly-developed English equipment in 1791. Owen, then the manager of a large cotton mill, was one of the first Britons to use it.

years against the most formidable military and *immoral* power that the world perhaps ever contained.

These important results, however, great as they really are, have not been obtained without accompanying evils of such a magnitude as to raise a doubt whether the latter do not preponderate over the former.

Hitherto, legislators have appeared to regard manufactures only in one point of view, as a source of national wealth.

The other mighty consequences which proceed from extended manufactures *when left to their natural progress,* have never yet engaged the attention of any legislature. Yet the political and moral effects to which we allude, well deserve to occupy the best faculties of the greatest and the wisest statesmen.

The general diffusion of manufactures throughout a country generates a new character in its inhabitants; and as this character is formed upon a principle quite unfavourable to individual or general happiness, it will produce the most lamentable and permanent evils, unless its tendency be counteracted by legislative interference and direction.

The manufacturing system has already so far extended its influence over the British Empire, as to effect an essential change in the general character of the mass of the people. This alteration is still in rapid progress; and ere long, the comparatively happy simplicity of the agricultural peasant will be wholly lost amongst us. It is even now scarcely anywhere to be found without a mixture of those habits which are the offspring of trade, manufactures, and commerce.

The acquisition of wealth, and the desire which it naturally creates for a continued increase, have introduced a fondness for essentially injurious luxuries among a numerous class of individuals who formerly never thought of them, and they have also generated a disposition which strongly impels its possessors to sacrifice the best feelings of human nature to this love of accumulation. To succeed in this career, the industry of the lower orders, from whose labour this wealth is now drawn, has been carried by new competitors striving against those of longer standing, to a point of real oppression, reducing them by successive changes, as the spirit of competition increased and the ease of acquiring wealth diminished, to a state more wretched than can be imagined by those who have not attentively observed the changes as they have gradually occurred. In consequence, they are at present in a situation infinitely more degraded and miserable than they were before the introduction of these manufactories, upon the success of which their bare subsistence now depends.

To support the additional population which this increased demand for labour has produced, it now becomes necessary to maintain the present extent of our foreign trade, or, under the existing circumstances of our population, it will become a serious and alarming evil.

It is highly probable, however, that the export trade of this country has attained its utmost height, and that by the competition of other states, possessing equal or greater local advantages, it will now gradually diminish.

The direct effect of the Corn Bill lately passed will be to hasten this decline and prematurely to destroy that trade. In this view it is deeply to be regretted that the Bill passed into a law; and I am persuaded its promoters will ere long discover the absolute necessity for its repeal, to prevent the misery which must ensue to the great mass of the people.[2]

The inhabitants of every country are trained and formed by its great leading existing circumstances, and the character of the lower orders in Britain is now formed chiefly by circumstances arising from trade, manufactures, and commerce; and the governing principle of trade, manufactures, and commerce is immediate pecuniary gain, to which on the great scale every other is made to give way. All are sedulously trained to buy cheap and to sell dear; and to succeed in this art, the parties must be taught to acquire strong powers of deception; and thus a spirit is generated through every class of traders, destructive of that open, honest sincerity, without which man cannot make others happy, nor enjoy happiness himself.

Strictly speaking, however, this defect of character ought not to be attributed to the individuals possessing it, but to the overwhelming effect of the system under which they have been trained.

But the effects of this principle of gain, unrestrained, are still more lamentable on the working classes, those who are employed in the operative parts of the manufactures; for most of these branches are more or less unfavourable to the health and morals of adults. Yet parents do not hesitate to sacrifice the well-being of their children by putting them to occupations by which the constitution of their minds and bodies is rendered greatly inferior to what it might and ought to be under a system of common foresight and humanity.

Not more than thirty years since, the poorest parents thought the age of fourteen sufficiently early for their children to commence regular labour: and they judged well; for by that period of their lives they had acquired by play and exercise in the open air, the foundation of a sound robust constitution; and if they were not all initiated in book learning, they had been taught the far more useful knowledge of domestic life, which could not but be familiar to them at the age of fourteen, and which, as they grew up and became heads of families, was of more value to them (as it taught them economy in the expenditure of their earnings) than one half of their wages under the present circumstances.

It should be remembered also that twelve hours per day, including the time for regular rest and meals, were then thought sufficient to extract all the working strength of the most robust adult; when it may be remarked local holidays were much more frequent than at present in most parts of the kingdom.

At this period, too, they were generally trained by the example of some landed proprietor, and in such habits as created a mutual interest between the parties, by which means even the lowest peasant was generally considered as belonging to,

---

2. The Corn Laws, protective legislation passed in 1815, levied a tariff on imported grain. Opponents maintained that this regulation made the price of bread prohibitive for the poor. The Corn Laws were not permanently abolished until 1849.

and forming somewhat of a member of, a respectable family. Under these circumstances the lower orders experienced not only a considerable degree of comfort, but they had also frequent opportunities of enjoying healthy rational sports and amusements; and in consequence they became strongly attached to those on whom they depended; their services were willingly performed; and mutual good offices bound the parties by the strongest ties of human nature to consider each other as friends in somewhat different situations; the servant indeed often enjoying more solid comfort and ease than his master.

Contrast this state of matters with that of the lower orders of the present day;—with human nature trained as it now is, under the new manufacturing system.

In the manufacturing districts it is common for parents to send their children of both sexes at seven or eight years of age, in winter as well as summer, at six o'clock in the morning, sometimes of course in the dark, and occasionally amidst frost and snow, to enter the manufactories, which are often heated to a high temperature, and contain an atmosphere far from being the most favourable to human life, and in which all those employed in them very frequently continue until twelve o'clock at noon, when an hour is allowed for dinner, after which they return to remain, in a majority of cases, till eight o'clock at night.

The children now find they must labour incessantly for their bare subsistence: they have not been used to innocent, healthy, and rational amusements; they are not permitted the requisite time, if they had been previously accustomed to enjoy them. They know not what relaxation means, except by the actual cessation from labour. They are surrounded by others similarly circumstanced with themselves; and thus passing on from childhood to youth, they become gradually initiated, the young men in particular, but often the young females also, in the seductive pleasure of the pot-house and inebriation: for which their daily hard labour, want of better habits, and the general vacuity of their minds, tend to prepare them.

Such a system of training cannot be expected to produce any other than a population weak in bodily and mental faculties, and with habits generally destructive of their own comforts, of the well-being of those around them, and strongly calculated to subdue all the social affections. Man so circumstanced sees all around him hurrying forward, at a mail-coach speed, to acquire individual wealth, regardless of him, his comforts, his wants, or even his sufferings, except by way of a *degrading parish charity,* fitted only to steel the heart of man against his fellows, or to form the tyrant and the slave. To-day he labours for one master, to-morrow for a second, then for a third, and a fourth, until all ties between employers and employed are frittered down to the consideration of what immediate gain each can derive from the other.

The employer regards the employed as mere instruments of gain, while these acquire a gross ferocity of character, which, if legislative measures shall not be judiciously devised to prevent its increase, and ameliorate the condition of this class, will sooner or later plunge the country into a formidable and perhaps inextricable state of danger.

The direct object of these observations is to effect the amelioration and avert the danger. The only mode by which these objects can be accomplished is to obtain an Act of Parliament—

First,—To limit the regular hours of labour in mills of machinery to twelve per day, including one hour and a half for meals.

Second,—To prevent children from being employed in mills of machinery until they shall be ten years old, or that they shall not be employed more than six hours per day until they shall be twelve years old.

Third,—That children of either sex shall not be admitted into any manufactory,—after a time to be named,—until they can read and write in an useful manner, understand the first four rules of arithmetic, and the girls be likewise competent to sew their common garments of clothing.[3]

These measures, when influenced by no party feelings or narrow mistaken notions of immediate self-interest, but considered solely in a national view, will be found to be beneficial to the child, to the parent, to the employer, and to the country. Yet, as we are now trained, many individuals cannot detach general subjects from party considerations, while others can see them only through the medium of present pecuniary gain. It may thence be concluded, that individuals of various descriptions will disapprove of some or all of these measures. I will therefore endeavour to anticipate their objections, and reply to them.

The child cannot be supposed to make any objection to the plans proposed: he may easily be taught to consider them, as they will prove to be by experience, essentially beneficial to him in childhood, youth, manhood, and old age.

Parents who have grown up in ignorance and bad habits, and who consequently are in poverty, may say "We cannot afford to maintain our children until they shall be twelve years of age, without putting them to employment by which they may earn wages, and we therefore object to that part of the plan which precludes us from sending them to manufactories until they shall be of that age."

If the poorest and most miserable of the people formerly supported their children without regular employment until they were fourteen, why may they not now support them until they shall be twelve years old? If parents who decline this duty had not been ignorant and trained in bad habits which render their mental faculties inferior to the instinct of many animals, they would understand that by forcing their children to labour in such situations at a premature age, they place their offspring in circumstances calculated to retard their growth, and make them peculiarly liable to bodily disease and mental injury, while they debar them the chance of acquiring that sound robust constitution which otherwise they would

3. Sir Robert Peel (1788–1850), a Tory leader, introduced restrictive factory legislation in 1815. Testifying before the committee appointed to study the feasibility of the bill, Robert Owen used his own mill as an example of a successful enterprise where no child under age ten was employed and the maximum number of hours worked was twelve with an hour and a quarter allowed for meals. To Owen's great disappointment, the bill was defeated. In 1819, Parliament passed a much weaker piece of legislation that was limited to cotton mills and devoid of an effective oversight and enforcement system. The bill, an Act for the Regulation of Cotton Mills and Factories, set the age limit at nine and restricted those under age sixteen to twelve-hour days, exclusive of meals.

possess, and without which they cannot enjoy much happiness, but must become a burthen to themselves, their friends, and their country. Parents by so acting also deprive their children of the opportunity of acquiring the habits of domestic life, without a knowledge of which high nominal wages can procure them but few comforts, and without which among the working classes very little domestic happiness can be enjoyed.

Children thus prematurely employed are prevented from acquiring any of the common rudiments of book learning; but in lieu of this useful and valuable knowledge, they are likely to acquire the most injurious habits by continually associating with those as ignorant and as ill instructed as themselves. And thus it may be truly said, that for every penny gained by parents from the premature labour of their offspring, they sacrifice not only future pounds, but also the future health, comfort, and good conduct of their children; and unless this pernicious system shall be arrested by the introduction of a better, the evil is likely to extend, and to become worse through every succeeding generation.

I do not anticipate any objection from employers to the age named for the admittance of children into their manufactories; or to children being previously trained in good habits and the rudiments of common learning; for, upon an experience abundantly sufficient to ascertain the fact, I have uniformly found it to be more profitable to admit children to constant daily employment at ten years old, than at any earlier period; and that those children, or adults, who had been the best taught, made the best servants, and were by far the most easily directed to do every thing that was right and proper for them to perform. The proprietors of expensive establishments may object to the reduction of the *now* customary hours of labour. The utmost extent, however, of their argument is, that the rent or interest of the capital expended in forming the establishment is chargeable on the quantity of its produce;—and if, instead of being permitted to employ their work-people within their manufactories so long as human nature can be tempted to continue its exertions, say for fourteen or fifteen hours per day, they shall be restricted to twelve hours of labour per day from their work-people, then the prime cost of the article which they manufacture will be increased by the greater proportion of rent or interest which attaches to the smaller quantity produced. If, however, this law shall be, as it is proposed, general over England, Scotland, and Ireland, whatever difference may ultimately arise in the prime cost of the articles produced in these manufactories, will be borne by the consumers, and not by the proprietors of such establishments. And, in a national view, the labour which is exerted twelve hours per day will be obtained more economically than if stretched to a longer period.

I doubt, however, whether any manufactory, so arranged as to occupy the hands employed in it twelve hours per day, will not produce its fabric, even to the immediate proprietor, nearly if not altogether as cheap as those in which the exertions of the employed are continued to fourteen or fifteen hours per day.

Should this, however, not prove to be the case to the extent mentioned, the improved health, the comforts, useful acquirements of the population, and the diminution of poor-rates,[4] naturally consequent on this change in the manners and habits of the people, will amply compensate to the country for a mere fractional addition to the prime cost of any commodity.

And is it to be imagined that the British Government will ever put the chance of a trivial pecuniary gain of a few, in competition with the solid welfare of so many millions of human beings?

The employer cannot be injured by being obliged to act towards his labourers as, for the interest of the country, he should act. Since the general introduction of expensive machinery, human nature has been forced far beyond its average strength; and much, very much private misery and public injury are the consequences.

It is indeed a measure more to be deplored in a national view than almost any other that has occurred for many centuries past. It has deranged the domestic habits of the great mass of the people. It has deprived them of the time in which they might acquire instruction, or enjoy rational amusements. It has robbed them of their substantial advantages, and, by leading them into habits of the pot-house and inebriation, it has poisoned all their social comforts.

Shall we then make laws to imprison, transport, or condemn to death those who purloin a few shillings of our property, injure any of our domestic animals, or even a growing twig;[5] and shall we *not* make laws to restrain those who otherwise will not be restrained in their desire for gain, from robbing, in the pursuit of it, millions of our fellow-creatures of their health,—their time for acquiring knowledge and future improvement,—of their social comforts,—and of every rational enjoyment? This system of proceeding cannot continue long;—it will work its own cure by the practical evils which it creates, and that in a most dangerous way to the public welfare, if the Government shall not give it a proper direction.

The public, however, are perhaps most interested in that part of the plan which recommends the training and educating of the lower orders under the direction and at the expense of the country.[6] And it is much to be wished that the extended substantial advantages to be derived from this measure were more generally considered and understood, in order that the mistaken ideas which now exist regarding it, in the most opposite quarters, may be entirely removed.

A slight general knowledge of the past occurrences of the world, with some experience of human nature as it appears in the little sects and parties around us, is sufficient to make it evident to those not very much mis-instructed from infancy, that children may be taught any habits and any sentiments; and that these, with the bodily and mental propensities and faculties existing at birth in each individual, combined with the general circumstances in which he is placed, constitute the whole character of man.

It is thence evident that human nature can be improved and formed into the

---

4. Taxes collected from landholders and used for the support of those unable to support themselves.

5. In the early nineteenth century in England, over two hundred crimes were punishable by death.

6. It was not until 1870 with the Elementary Education Act, sponsored by William Edward Forster (1818–1886), that government-supported education was available to all children.

character which it is for the interest and happiness of all it should possess, solely by directing the attention of mankind to the adoption of legislative measures judiciously calculated to give the best habits and most just and useful sentiments to the rising generation; and in an especial manner to those who are placed in situations which, without such measures, render them liable to be taught the worst habits and the most useless and injurious sentiments.

I ask those who have studied the science of government upon those enlightened principles which alone ought to influence the statesman—What is the difference, in a national view, between an individual trained in habits which give him health, temperance, industry, correct principles of judging, foresight, and general good conduct; and one trained in ignorance, idleness, intemperance, defective powers of judging, and in general vicious habits? Is not one of the former of more real worth and political strength to the State than many of the latter?

Are there not many millions in the British dominions in whom this difference can be made? And if a change which so essentially affects the well-being of those individuals, and, through them, of every member of the empire, *may* be made, is it not the first duty of the Government and the country to put into immediate practice the means which *can* effect the change?

Shall then such important measures be waived, and the best interests of this country compromised, because one party wishes its own peculiar principles to be forced on the young mind; or because another is afraid that the advantages to be derived from this improved system of legislation will be so great as to give too much popularity and influence to the Ministers who shall introduce it?

The termination of such errors in practice is, I trust, near at hand, and then Government will be no longer compelled to sacrifice the well-doing and the well-being of the great mass of the people and of the empire, to the prejudices of comparatively a few individuals, trained to mistake even their own security and interests.

Surely a measure most obviously calculated to render a greater benefit to millions of our fellow-creatures than any other ever yet adopted, cannot be much longer suspended because one party in the State may erroneously suppose it would weaken their influence over the public mind unless that party shall alone direct that plan; but which direction, it is most obvious, the intelligence of the age will not commit to any party exclusively. Or because others, trained in very opposite principles, may imagine that a national system of education for the poor and lower orders, under the sanction of Government, but superintended and directed in its details by the country, would place a dangerous power in the hands of Ministers of the Crown.

Such sentiments as these cannot exist in minds divested of party considerations, who sincerely desire to benefit their fellow-men, who have no private views to accomplish, and who wish to support and strengthen the Government, that the Government may be the better enabled to adopt decisive and effectual measures for the general amelioration of the people.

I now therefore, in the name of the millions of the neglected poor and ignorant, whose habits and sentiments have been hitherto formed to render them wretched, call upon the British Government and the British Nation to unite their efforts to arrange a system to train and instruct those who, for any good or useful purpose, are now untrained and uninstructed; and to arrest by a clear, easy, and practical system of prevention, the ignorance and consequent poverty, vice, and misery which are rapidly increasing throughout the empire; for, "Train up a child in the way he should go, and when he is old he will not depart from it."[7]

7. Proverbs 22:6.

W. COOKE TAYLOR

WILLIAM COOKE TAYLOR (1800–1849) was born in Ireland, the son of a manufacturer, and graduated from Trinity College in Dublin. He was a prolific author of history and biography as well as of political pamphlets and analyses of education and industry. In the early 1840s, Taylor spent some time in Lancashire in northwest England studying the factory system and came away a wholehearted supporter of free-trade economics and industrialization. The following two chapters—"Factories and Machinery" and "Infant Labour"—are taken from Taylor's book, *Factories and the Factory System from Parliamentary Documents and Personal Examination,* published in 1844. Taylor's arguments offer a striking counterpoint to those advanced by Friedrich Engels in "Single Branches of Industry: Factory-Hands" from *The Condition of the Working Class in England,* published in German two years later (see part 3).

From *Factories and the Factory System from Parliamentary Documents and Personal Examination*

Chapter III
Factories and Machinery

It would be a great blessing to the community if those who take upon them to discuss the factory system, and to legislate respecting it, were compelled to visit the places which they pretend to describe, and to examine the system which they are ambitious of regulating. The large factories, improperly called "mills," are described with most vehemence by those who have never been inside such an establishment in their lives, but who have conjectured its arrangements from viewing its outside, or, without ever visiting the localities where they are situated, have put together, in a strange jumble, all the notions which the vague term "mill" has suggested to their minds. It is already notorious that Lord Ashley, the leading patron of factory legislation, deems it a necessary qualification for his task to take a one-sided view of the entire matter, and that he declined an offer to guide him through the principal spinning establishments as gratuitous and unnecessary.[1] But Lord Ashley is not alone in this apparent determination to form a judgment without impartially examining evidence; in spite of Aristotle,[2] there is a constant tendency to pass sentence on a conclusion after having adjourned the consideration of the premises, and nowhere is this more apparent than in the opinions set forth respecting the bearings of machinery on the factory question. Hence, the facts which are to be now laid before the public will be received by persons unacquainted with factories as startling novelties, whilst those who know anything about the subject will regard them as trite truisms, of which the general world has as little reason to be told as that the sun shines at noon, or that cows have horns. In fact, the master-manufacturers of northern England have allowed countless calumnies to pass unnoticed, because they were persuaded that such gross absurdities could not for a moment be credited; and their reward for thus trusting to the common sense of their countrymen is, that their silence has been taken for a tacit confession of guilt.

It is not, however, surprising that many false notions should prevail respecting the influence of machinery; the tourist, visiting a factory-district for the first time, cannot contemplate, without wonder and even some emotions of involuntary fear, the lofty chimneys emitting clouds of smoke that obscure the sky, the immense water-wheel revolving with a weight and velocity which cannot be witnessed without a shudder, or the mighty steam-engine performing its functions with a monotonous regularity not less impressive than the enormous force which it sets in motion. His earliest impression is that fire and water—proverbially the best servants and the worst masters—have here established despotic dominion over man, and that here matter has acquired undisputed empire over mind. It requires time and patience, repeated observation, and calm reflection, to discover that the giant, steam, is not the tyrant but the slave of the operatives; not their rival but their fellow-labourer, employed as a drudge to do all the heavy work, leaving to them the lighter and more delicate operations.

1. Anthony Ashley Cooper (1801–1885) became the seventh earl of Shaftesbury in 1851. Ashley was elected a Tory member of Parliament in 1826 and quickly made a name for himself as a social reformer. In 1833, he submitted a Ten Hours Bill for textile mill employees. A weaker version of the bill which became law prohibited the employment of children under age nine and limited to eight hours a day, six days a week, the employment of those between the ages of nine and thirteen. Lord Ashley, who continued to pursue legislation restricting working hours, made a tour of the manufacturing districts in 1842 in order to interview workers and acquire information.

In 1844, the year Taylor's book on the factory system appeared, Parliament passed another Factory Act which lowered the allowable age of child workers to eight but limited their daily hours to six and a half and restricted women to a twelve-hour workday. It was not until 1847 that the working hours for women and youth were reduced to ten. This effectively reduced the working hours for men as well since they could not perform their jobs in isolation.

2. The Greek philosopher Aristotle (384–322 B.C.E.) contended that truth could be arrived at only through scientific demonstration and formal logic.

No popular error is more common than the belief that the operatives in a factory, which has its machinery set in motion by a water-wheel or a steam-engine, have no more repose than the wheels and shafts of the mill in which they are employed, and that they must, consequently, be worn down by incessant fatigue, unrelieved by a moment's relaxation. It is necessary only to go through a factory, and pay ordinary attention to its operations, in order to discover that this is an error. In the first place, the machines themselves are not in constant operation, to say nothing of the whole being suspended at meal times; the different parts of the machinery are not of necessity in motion together. Motion is communicated to the several frames of machinery by a driving-strap, which passes over a principal wheel attached to each frame, and connects it with a turning-shaft, set in motion by the water-wheel or the steam-engine. To stop the motion of any separate frame it is only necessary to take off the driving-strap; and this has to be done very frequently by the tenter, or operative, who superintends the frame in which the particular process for which it was constructed is carried on. In most of the processes employed in spinning wool, flax, or cotton, or in throwing silk, the chief occupations of the operatives are to feed the machine with a proper supply of material, to remove what has received so much finish as the process of manufacture under their charge confers, and to watch the machine so as to be sure that it performs its work aright. So long as the machine works on without error, its tenter, or the operative, who is its fellow-labourer, has absolutely nothing to do; it is only when the machine goes wrong that the operative compels his drudge to stop, by removing the driving-strap, corrects the error, and then sets his unwearied assistant to work again. Thus the motion of machinery is the rest of the operative, and what the ignorant spectator sets down as the source of endless fatigue is, in fact, the great source of his relaxation. Even the spinners and piecers, whose labours are the most incessant, have frequently-recurring intervals of relaxation: the latter, indeed, whose duty it is to piece or mend any yarns that may be broken while in the process of being elongated or twisted by the mule frame,[3] effect this object at the moment that the mule carriage begins to be drawn out, and have a respite from labour during the remaining time of the carriage being drawn out and the whole period of its return.

No process in the spinning factories, whether of flax, wool, or cotton, or in power-loom establishments, requires the operatives to fix themselves in a constrained or painful attitude, or to remain for any time in an unnatural position. This is a point on which every man can satisfy himself by visiting a cotton or woollen factory; he will see that there are no processes involving more distortion than ordinary standing or walking, and that there are none which at all require such fatiguing attitudes and painful positions as are common in those trades where little or no aid is derived from machinery. It would be interesting to compare some of the mechanical processes in the spinning establishments with those

3. The spinning mule, a machine that made possible large-scale production of high-quality thread and yarn, was invented by Sir Richard Arkwright (1732–1792).

used when similar results were sought to be attained by unaided manual labour. Let us, for instance, compare the cleaning of cotton by the manual process called *batting*, and the machine called "the willow."[4] In the first case the cotton is beaten with switches or rattans, the use of which requires such strenuous and incessant exertion that perspiration streams from every pore, and the fatigue of the arm produces the most acute pain and suffering; the particles of dust and flue[5] that are thrown about clog the mouth and nostrils, and irritate the eyes of the persons engaged in the task; it is as dirty as it is laborious. Cleaning cotton with the willow involves no more labour than feeding the machine with raw cotton and removing that which is cleaned; the dirt and flue are prevented from escaping, and do not produce any inconvenience to the operatives.

It would be easy to carry this comparison further, and to show that in every instance mechanical invention has lightened the toil of man; but we are here met with the assertion that this is its greatest condemnation, for that, by thus superseding human labour, it diminishes the demand for human labour, thus throwing many out of employment and lowering the wages of the rest. We have already given a general answer to this objection, but many people, otherwise sensible, cling to it with so much obstinacy that it is worth while to consider it more particularly. We shall take a case where the introduction of machinery bears the strongest aspect of grievance: it is one which actually occurred. A certain part of a gun-lock, when prepared by manual labour, required such minute attention to its proportions that many workmen were induced to make it the special object of their attention: by practice they acquired a dexterity and mechanical skill in preparing the article which enabled them to defy the competition of untrained workmen, and thus to obtain their own price for the manufacture of the article. A machine was invented by which the most unskilled artificer was enabled to produce this very article even more perfect than the best trained workmen with unaided skill, and the whole of those previously engaged in its production were deprived of all the advantages which they had previously acquired by a long and laborious course of training and practice. Now there can be no doubt that the introduction of this machine, in its first and immediate operation did injure these men; it compelled them to accept lower wages, and to turn to other less lucrative branches of the trade in which their previous training was a disadvantage instead of a gain.

It does not mend the matter much to state, what in this case happens to be a fact, that the mechanical invention would in all human probability never have been made, had not the artisans in question made an unfair use of the monopoly which their skill and dexterity conferred upon them; the extravagant price which they set on their work induced the master-manufacturers to exercise their ingenuity in devising a plan for getting rid of the workmen. This may serve to show the dangers to which artisans sometimes expose themselves by combinations and

4. A machine featuring a spiked drum revolving inside a spiked chamber used to open and clean unprocessed cotton or wool.

5. A woolly or downy substance.

trades-unions;[6] but it is scarcely a set-off against the direct injury which a division of workers in iron suffered by mechanical invention. The discovery did, in this instance, inflict a sensible injury on a class of men who were not adequately remunerated by the general advantage which the invention conferred upon the community.

But while we confess this grievance we must, on the other hand, state that such an event is one of exceedingly rare occurrence; that the evil it produces is very partial in its extent, and very limited in its duration. There is no greater mistake than to suppose that mechanical improvements are immediately and all at once adopted. When a man has invested an immense capital in furnishing a mill with machinery, it must be some very striking advantage indeed which will induce him to derange the whole economy of his apparatus for the purpose of introducing some new improvement. Years elapse before improvements become general throughout a trade. Each improvement affects only a single and limited class of operatives; during the process of its introduction the persons whom it will affect have breathing time afforded them, and can avail themselves of the interval to seek some other means of employment. And such means of employment are not difficult to be found; for each mechanical improvement, however it may affect a particular set of workmen, has always extended the demand for labour amongst the general body of operatives engaged in the trade. No other proof of this need be quoted than the notorious fact, that population has increased most rapidly in those districts where mechanical ingenuity has been exerted to the utmost, and where the improvements in machinery have been brought into most extensive use; so that it is an undeniable fact that machinery has multiplied the demand for those arms which vulgar error asserts that it must have superseded.

Those who declare against machinery must not altogether escape from examining their own alternative. We are justified in asking them to name the machinery with which they would dispense;—to tell us whether the whole steam apparatus should be banished from mills, or whether manufacturers should only be compelled to dispense with certain parts of it. We have found but one instance of human power being used instead of the steam-engine or water-wheel to give impulse to cotton-spinning machinery. We take the description of the experiment from one who witnessed it, M. de Villerme, author of a "Report on the Physical and Moral Condition of the Working Classes in France."[7]

"I could never have formed an idea of the humane influence of machinery had I not seen, in November, 1835, at the central prison of Loos, near Lille, unfortunate men compelled to exert almost incredible efforts for the purpose of giving motion to the machinery used in the spinning of cotton. These wretched beings, absolutely naked from the waist upwards, panting, exhausted, and covered with sweat, had all

6. Considerable union activity occurred among miners and textile workers in the north of England in the 1840s.

7. French physician Louis-René de Villermé (1782–1863) authored *Tableau de l'état physique et moral des ouvriers dans les fabriques de coton, de laine et de soie* (1840), which led to the passage of protective legislation for children laboring in French factories.

the muscles of their body in a state of constant agitation; they were degraded to the level of beasts of burthen; the very sight of them was revolting. Luckily the introduction of the steam-engine has put an end to this barbarity, worthy only of the ages when the lords of the soil harnessed their peasants like beasts to the drags with which it was the custom to separate the grain from the ear before threshing-machines were invented."

This is a specimen of the sort of humanity which dictates the senseless clamour against machinery. But, even if this degradation of man could be attained by superseding the steam-engine, it still remains to be determined whether, after all, a greater amount of employment would be provided for the working population. To answer this question we must first inquire whether the cost of production would not be increased if human force should be substituted for steam power. Every one knows that it would, and every one also knows that a very small increase in the cost of production, and consequently in the price of the article, would produce a very large and a very disproportionate diminution in the consumption. There would thus be far less demand for the finished article, and consequently a similar falling off in the demand for the labour by which it is produced. Were the price of printed calicoes raised, many thousands who now wear decent gowns would be doomed to patched and picturesque rags; and the spinners, weavers, and printers, employed in the production of these gowns, would be left without work, and consequently without wages.

But this is not all: we may, in the wisdom of insanity, reject machinery; but can we persuade other nations to follow our example? Unless this conspiracy against mechanical improvements be made general, we shall be doing nothing better than making a present of our manufacturing industry and all its profits to rival nations. It is utterly impossible for us to sustain manufactures on dearer terms than those on which they can be supported in other countries. Our entire export trade would be demolished at one blow, for those who sell at the cheapest rate must ever command foreign and neutral markets. It would soon be impossible to keep even our own market, for all the legal prohibitions and protections in the world are beaten down before decided cheapness; the smuggler's straightforward mode of proceeding baffles all the complicated checks and precautions of the custom-house officer. The whole question of machinery then resolves itself into this: whether we shall retain our largest branches of manufacturing industry at home for the employment of our own countrymen, or whether we shall abandon them to foreigners, and consign our own people to idleness and starvation.

Nothing is more common than to hear people, who are utterly ignorant of the matter, express their astonishment at the rapidity with which new improvements are introduced; the fact is, that the slowness with which they are adopted is nearly the most wondrous thing about them. The history of the power-loom in England and the Jacquard-loom in France affords abundant proof of the tardiness with which men introduce new systems of machinery,[8] even when they are not deterred

8. The power loom, patented in the 1780s by a clergyman, Edmund Cartwright (1743–1823), was sufficiently improved by 1815 to be in widespread use. The Jacquard-loom, invented in 1801 by the

from using it by having a large amount of capital already invested in old machines. The very delay which the re-stocking of a mill with new machinery would involve, added to the cost and the loss by old machinery, is a sufficient guarantee to the operative against being suddenly and hastily placed in collision with new machinery.

That there is a jealousy of machinery diffused amongst the operative class is unfortunately true; but this feeling is neither so strong nor so general as it was some years ago. For the most part the hostility is directed only against the latest improvements; and even in this case it rarely amounts to direct hostility. A man sees a new demand created in a branch of labour to which he has been trained, and he is surprised to find that there is not a proportionate demand for labourers: he rightly attributes this difference between the two demands to the increased powers of production derived from machinery; but he does not see that this increased power of production, by lowering the price of the manufactured article, is the principal element in the new demand which has excited his jealousy.[9] Were the labourers to be multiplied in the same proportion as the labour, cheapness of production would be unattainable. But, though the demand produced by cheapness does not increase the demand for labour in proportion to the work done, yet it generally increases that demand very largely in relation to the demand for hands in that particular branch of trade previous to the period when lowering the cost of production greatly extended the consumption.

Before quitting this subject it may be necessary to notice an objection to machinery, which will appear ludicrously absurd to those who are acquainted with factories, but which has some weight with those who have never paid any attention to the subject. We allude to the accidents which are supposed to be of common occurrence from machinery. Any one who reflected for a moment could not fail to discover that an accident which destroyed life or limb must also derange the machinery, and, however careless he might suppose master manufacturers to be of their workmen, he cannot imagine them to be equally regardless of their own property. Now, however true it may be, that accidents were of frequent occurrence when machinery was a novelty, it is certainly untrue that they are equally common now. Experience has taught the mode of managing machines with safety, and, in fact, the accidents of collision from cabs, carriages, waggons, &c, in the city of London, far exceed in number, and in the amount of injury sustained, all the serious accidents which occur from machinery throughout England. No one can examine a cotton-mill without seeing, not only that its operations can be conducted with perfect safety to the operatives, but that there must be an utter disregard of ordinary precautions—a total want of prudence, and not a little perverted ingenuity, to get into danger.

Frenchman Joseph Marie Jacquard (1752–1834), was the earliest machine to include all weaving motions and the earliest capable of weaving figured designs.

9. Desperate craftsmen reacted violently to the introduction of the first textile machines, with attacks on mills and destruction of the machines themselves. For example, in 1811–1812, the Luddite riots, named for Ned Ludlam, one of the participants, resulted in damage to dozens of factories. Such instances of machine breaking proved largely ineffective, however, in impeding the growth of mechanized industry.

It is not necessary to dwell upon the advantages which the introduction of machinery, by lowering the price of manufactured articles, has conferred upon consumers; we need only look around us to discover that the middle and lower classes in Great Britain are far better clothed than they were within the memory of many still living amongst us; and it requires no very deep knowledge of history to discover, that the wardrobe of the wife of an humble tradesman of the present day would have excited the envy of a Saxon queen[10] or even a Plantagenet princess.[11] This abundance of cheap clothing has not only increased the comfort, but it has tended to promote the moral advancement of the people. He was a shrewd observer of mankind, who declared that "cleanliness was next to godliness"; for the experience of all ages has proved that decency and its companion, delicacy, are the best preservatives of chastity. But as no person has contested the benefits which machinery has conferred on the general community, we shall once more advert to the advantages it has conferred on the operatives taken as a class.

A question often asked by the ignorant and unthinking deserves some portion of our consideration; they ask whether the demand for labour would not be greatly increased if the operations of machinery were suspended and hand-labour employed to produce the present amount of fabrics. The plain answer is, that in such a case nothing like the same amount of fabrics would be produced in England, for their price would not remunerate the manufacturer, even though he should pay his workmen the lowest possible rate of wages. The English hand-spinners of cotton could never compete with the Hindoos in the production of fine yarn; with the Egyptian Fellahs[12] in the manufacture of coarse threads; with the African negroes in common products of the loom; or with the Indians of North America in cheap articles of dress. English artisans would starve on the same rate of wages which would support life in a country less heavily taxed, and no higher rate of wages could they obtain so long as there existed one foreign competitor to meet them in the market. It is a great, but a neglected truth, that machinery sustains wages; for it is by means of machinery that so large an amount of spun and woven fabrics is produced; it is in consequence of the magnitude of this amount that British manufactures can be sold so cheap; and it is in consequence of their superior cheapness that these articles find purchasers. The sad example of the hand-loom weavers, to which we have already referred, shows the utter inability of British artisans to sustain competition with the foreigners when they are not backed by the support of machinery.

It is then clear, that the prosperity of British manufacturers depends on the continued concentration of mechanical power in mills and factories, by which British operatives are enabled to compete with those who, like the Hindoos, possessing a more delicate organization, could with the unaided fingers produce a finer texture; and still more to meet those in the market who, from a cheaper and

---

10. Saxon queen: a reference to the West Germanic tribes that invaded England in the fifth century.
11. The Plantagenets were the ruling family in England from 1154 to 1485.
12. Arab peasants or agricultural laborers.

more extensive command of the necessaries of life, can afford to work at a lower rate of wages, and, therefore, enable employers to bring goods into the market with less cost of production, and, consequently, with ability to sell at a cheaper rate. Thus viewed, machinery appears to be absolutely necessary to the continuance of employment in Great Britain; without it our workmen would be unable to produce goods at a price which would bear competition with the manufactures of other countries in the foreign market; and thus it appears that machinery, instead of limiting the demand for labour, is the real cause why the demand for the trained labour of operatives is greater in England than in any other part of the world, and the only means by which the continuance of such employment can be secured.

The last objection to machinery which we have to notice is, that it tends to "over-production." This newly-invented term is not very intelligible, because so long as there are persons in the world destitute of clothing, but willing to work in order that they might purchase proper covering, it is sheer absurdity to say that too large a quantity of cloth is manufactured. If, however, "over-production" be used as a relative term, and the meaning be that too much has been produced in proportion to the markets, we have to inquire, before we condemn machinery, what are the causes that limit the amount of our foreign markets, and diminish the means or the number of customers in the domestic markets? It is perfectly obvious that a limit placed on production, would be also a limit on the employment of capital and the consequent demand for labour.

It is rather singular to find that those who complain of machinery as an artificial means of creating too large a manufacturing production, are at the same moment engaged in devising artificial means to increase agricultural production. Throughout the country there is fast spreading a conviction of the vast importance of increasing the productiveness of the soils by the application of chemical and mechanical science: now such aids are in effect the same advantages to the farm that the steam-engine is to the factory; the increase of fertility leads to the same end in one case that the increase of power does in the other. In fact, it is now universally acknowledged, that the best farm system is the one which most nearly approximates to the factory system; that efficient agriculture, like efficient manufacture, requires a large investment of capital, an extensive application of mechanical and chemical aids to the powers of nature, and free markets for the sale of produce.

Chapter IV
Infant Labour

Although the subject about to be discussed in this chapter is far from being the most important question connected with the factory-system, yet it has from recent discussions acquired such factitious interest, and has been so studiously misrepresented by ignorance, by prejudice, and by still worse motives, that we deem it necessary to examine it thus early, and to bestow upon it more attention than, under other circumstances, its merits would require. Much evil has arisen to the cause of truth from the use of the term "Infant Labour"; there neither is nor can be any such thing; the point we have really to examine is, whether children should be employed in tasks suitable to their age, and enabled by their industry to contribute to their own support. It requires very little argument to show that manufacturers can employ children only in tasks suitable to their age, for if they employed them at any other they would be guilty of the folly of paying wages for having their materials spoiled. It is so clearly the interest of manufacturers not to employ children in tasks beyond the limits of their physical strength that not a word more need be said on the subject. It is, however, obvious that children may be engaged in employments injurious to health or morals, and that even unobjectionable occupation may be protracted to such a length as to produce injurious consequences; while, therefore, we contend that the general employment of children is not an evil, it must ever be borne in mind that we as strongly declare that there may be, and are, circumstances of labour to which it is a crying sin that childhood and youth should be subjected.

Every man acquainted with the political history of the last half century must know, that the labour of children was actually pointed out to the manufacturers by Mr. William Pitt,[13] as a new resource by which they might be enabled to bear the additional load of taxation which the necessities of the state compelled him to impose. The necessity for labour created by this taxation has not yet abated; because the immense capital taken away by the enormous expenditure of the great wars arising out of the French Revolution[14]—an expenditure which was mainly supported out of the industrial resources of the country—has not been replaced. But even independent of these considerations, and irrespective of a past which can never be recalled, we mean to assert, as we have done elsewhere, in broad terms and the plainest language, that the infant labour, as it is erroneously called,—or the juvenile labour, as it should be called,—in factories, is in fact a national blessing, and absolutely necessary for the support of the manifold fiscal burthens which have been placed upon the industry of this country. It is quite sufficient to say that the children of the operatives have mouths, and must be fed; they have limbs, and must be clothed; they have minds, which ought to be instructed; and they have passions, which must be controlled. Now, if the parents are unable to provide these requisites—and their inability to do so is just as notorious as their existence—it becomes absolutely necessary that the children should aid in obtaining them for themselves. To abolish juvenile labour, is plainly nothing else than to abolish juvenile means of support; and to confine it within very narrow limits, is just to subtract a dinner or a supper from the unhappy objects of mistaken benevolence.

This is not a mere conjecture: we find it asserted in the broadest terms by the factory inspectors, when they remonstrated against the clause of the Factory Act of

13. William Pitt (1759–1806) was the Conservative Prime Minister from 1783–1801 and 1804–1806.
14. England was at war with France off and on from 1793 until the Battle of Waterloo in 1815.

1833, which placed a less restriction on juvenile labour than was sought by the party opposed to the manufacturers.[15] We beg attention to the following extracts:—

"To avoid these inconveniences, and other lesser ones which are apprehended, and have indeed been experienced, in cases where working by relays have been resorted to from necessity, great numbers of children, under eleven years of age, have been discharged in various parts of the country, and great distress has in many instances been the unavoidable result. The children thus discharged, if unable to find other employment, are left to wander about the streets in idleness. In addition to the loss of their weekly wages, the benefit of that education which the Act proposed to extend to them is thus also completely lost; and parish relief[16] must necessarily, in this case, be sought as their only alternative. The injury and inconvenience thus sustained from the operation of the clauses here alluded to, will, it is said, and I fear with truth, be greatly enhanced after the 1st March, 1835, when these provisions shall apply to children under twelve years of age; and after the 1st March, 1836, when embracing children under thirteen years of age, the evil, it is apprehended, will be intolerable."—*Report of R. Rickards, Esq., 15th April, 1834*—*Reports of Inspectors of Factories, p. 36.*

"I have now found, as I then anticipated, that, in the majority of instances, children under the age of eleven years have been discharged from their employment for the reasons stated in that report."—*Report of Inspectors of Factories, p. 23.*—*T.J. Howell, Esq., 28th July, 1834.*

"Where schools can be established, or a disposition shown to do so, I invariably encourage it; but here at least the necessity for the schooling prescribed by the Act is superseded, I regret to say, by the mill-owners having already very generally dismissed all their working hands under eleven years of age, and many of these cases, with pain I relate it, are truly distressing. *Both masters and operatives have represented to me, in strong colours, the suffering thus endured, and, hard and heart-rending as these cases are, I have been obliged to answer that I had no power of relief.*"—*Report of R. Rickards, Esq., 10th February, 1834.*—*Report of Inspectors of Factories, p. 29.*

"The limitations of eight hours' work to children under eleven years of age has already occasioned a revolution in the trade by the discharge of vast numbers under 11. When the limitation comes to be extended to children under twelve years, and ultimately under thirteen, it is very generally dreaded in this quarter, as likely to prove fatal to manufacturing prosperity."—*Report of R. Rickards, Esq., 15th April, 1834.*—*Reports of Inspectors of Factories, p. 38.*

It comes within our knowledge that children who were deprived of the easy work of the factories have been sent to toil in the coal-mines, and to other avocations

15. Factory Act of 1833: as its name indicated, the *original* Ten Hours Bill called for prohibiting the employment of children under age nine and restricting the hours of those between the ages of nine and eighteen to ten hours each weekday and eight hours on Saturday. See note 1 above for the provisions of the revised bill that was passed by Parliament.

16. Charitable assistance provided at the local, or parish, level.

equally injurious to health, and far more ruinous to morals. The parents are compelled by sheer necessity to send their children to work; they could not otherwise support them in comfort, and in many instances they could not keep them from contact with perilous pollution. It is easy to sneer at political economy; perhaps more favour may be shown to an examination of the domestic economy of the working man.

The house-accommodations of the operatives in large towns are necessarily very limited; if the children were excluded from factories and workshops it is not very clear what would become of them. At home they could not remain even if they were disposed to do so; there is no legal provision for compelling them to attend schools—their only resource would be the street, with all its perils and temptations. If juvenile labour were in itself an evil, which we emphatically deny, it would still be preferable as the choice of evils, for juvenile vagrancy and juvenile delinquency are infinitely worse; and both have increased in Manchester since the Factory Act has been brought into operation. In May, 1835, the number of children between the age of nine and thirteen employed in factories was 21,977; in February, 1839, the number was reduced to 10,627. The factory law, in the name of philanthrophy, swept away the means of subsistance from 11,000 young persons, and took no further care about their destiny. Would it not be well to inquire whether the physical and moral condition of these children was improved by depriving them of work and wages? It would be well if those who swell the senseless cry against what they are pleased to term infant labour would set themselves to discover the solution of this question.

It is confessed on all hands that the education of the young should be such as would prepare them for the functions they have to discharge in active life. He who is to live by labour must early be trained to labour, and hence industrial education has been wisely united with literary education by the most enlightened philanthropists. Manual labour or bodily employment is seldom irksome to the young, but we all know that learning is irksome to the great majority of them; the question, however, which we have to discuss is not what would please but what would benefit; the question, in fact, lies between juvenile labour and juvenile destitution.

Were a North American Indian or New Zealand chieftain introduced into one of our highest schools, he would waste much pity and compassion on the poor boys condemned to pore over books and con[17] disagreeable tasks instead of taking healthful exercise in the open air, enjoying the excitement of the chase, or freely sporting over the plain. Were he able to write, and a rival of Mrs. Trollope in imaginative invective, his "English School Boy" would beat that lady's "Factory Boy," or, as it was more appropriately designated, her "Unsatisfactory Boy," all to nothing.[18] Weeping squaws in the forests and prairies would thank heaven that

---

17. Study; learn.

18. Hoping to stimulate further reform legislation, Frances Trollope (1779–1863) published *The Life and Adventures of Michael Armstrong, the Factory Boy* in 1839.

their babes were not destined to the thraldom of English academies; every school-master would be described as an exaggerated Squeers without the chance of a Nickleby interfering with his tyranny.[19] Now, this imaginative case has been surpassed in the views taken of manufacturers and the children in their employment. Persons enter a mill, or suppose that they have done so, they see, or imagine to themselves, the figures of the little piecers and cleaners employed in their monotonous routine, when the sun is high in heaven, when the skies look smilingly upon earth, and earth answers again with its own laughing aspect of loveliness and fertility; and they think how much more delightful would have been the gambol of the free limbs on the hill-side, the inhaling of the fresh breeze, the sight of the green mead, with its spangles of butter-cups and daisies, the song of the bird, and the humming of the bee![20] But they should compare the aspect of the youthful operatives with other sights which they must have met in the course of their experience, as we too often have in ours: we have seen children perishing from sheer hunger in the mud-hovel, or in the ditch by the way-side, where a few sods and withered boughs had formed a hut, compared with which a wigwam were a palace. We have seen the juvenile mendicant, and the juvenile vagrant, with famine in their cheeks and despair in their hearts. We have seen the juvenile delinquent, his conscience seared by misery, his moral nature destroyed by suffering, his intellectual powers trained to perversity by the irresistible force of the circumstances that surrounded him. It is a sad confession to make, but owing, perhaps, to some peculiar obliquity of intellect or hardness of heart,—we would rather see boys and girls earning the means of support in the mill than starving by the road-side, shivering on the pavement, or even conveyed in an omnibus to Bridewell.[21]

Some of the operatives, and many people of higher pretensions, object to juvenile labour, because they believe that it diminishes the demand for the labour of full grown people. They imagine, that if the boys and girls were withdrawn from the mills, there would necessarily be an increased demand for men and women, that employment would be more abundant, and that wages would consequently rise.

It is no difficult matter to expose the fallacy of this expectation in the remarks already made on the condition of the hand-loom weavers,—the system of juvenile labour is actually beneficial to the operatives, taken as a class. The three elements for which an employer pays are time, skill, and strength; the labourer who exerts

---

19. Nicholas Nickleby is the hero of Charles Dickens's (1812–1870) third novel, *The Life and Adventures of Nicholas Nickleby* (1838). When his father dies leaving him penniless and responsible for the support of his mother and sister, young, naive Nicholas accepts a situation as a teacher at Dotheboys Hall, a Yorkshire school run by the sadistic Wackford Squeers, where unwanted boys suffer extreme physical and psychological abuse and receive no education at all.

20. Caroline Norton's *A Voice from the Factories,* Elizabeth Barrett Browning's "The Cry of the Children," and Eliza Cook's "Our Father!" all present an idyllic life in the countryside as an alternative to factory labor for children (see part 3).

21. Under the reign of King Edward VI (1537–1553; ruled 1547–53), the Royal Palace at Bridewell became an institution where vagrants and petty offenders were put to work. The term "bridewell" came to be applied generically to similar institutions.

only the skill and the strength of a child will, in the long run, even leaving out of view the competition of foreign nations, obtain only the wages of a child, because he has nothing on which to rely for obtaining his value in the market. Were the manufacturers compelled to dismiss the children, they would not supply their places with trained and skilled workmen, because the training and skill would be worthless; but they would import an abundant supply of untrained labourers from Wales, from Scotland, and from Ireland, to whom the wages of the children, small as they are, would be a desirable object. Many of these would in time begin to compete with the superior operatives; they would draw them down faster than they would raise themselves up, and the rate of wages would sink rapidly below its present level. The example of the hand-loom weavers should teach the spinners the danger of a trade being inundated by operatives who require little or no preparatory training to make a commencement.[22] It is their good fortune that the employments in the mill, which require but little skill, also demand but little strength, for it has saved them from being reduced to the level of agricultural labourers by the appearance of untrained hordes mingling in their ranks.

In truth the Factory Act has, in this respect, injured the operatives, and they know it. When children under thirteen years of age were dismissed from the mills, young persons above that age came readily to supply their places from Wales, Scotland, Ireland, and the agricultural counties, because the wages of factory labour are far above those of farm labour. We have conversed with many of these persons, and we never found one of them that regretted abandoning agricultural labour, or had the slightest intention of returning to farming pursuits. The operatives who had been deluded into raising a clamour for the Factory Bill found, to their great mortification, that they had deprived their own children of employment to give it to strangers, and that they had besides brought in a new generation of operatives, who would soon compete with themselves in the labour-market.

Juvenile labour, then, is demonstrably beneficial to the parents of the children by contributing to their support, and by placing them in a position where they are safer from the allurements of vice; it is advantageous to the children, by training them to those habits of industry by which they are to gain support in future life; and it is beneficial to the class of operatives, by preventing the influx of imperfect adult labour, which would be the inevitable result of throwing the children out of employment. We have, as far as possible, confined ourselves to generalities, and viewed the question of the employment of children without any special reference to factories. Before, however, we enter upon the special conditions of factory labour, it is proper to mention a fact which is generally neglected in all the discussions on the subject, and that is, that the children of the poor in every part of England are compelled to work, if they can get employment, so soon as they are able to turn their hands to anything. It seems, for a time, to have been assumed that children worked no where but in factories; a very little inquiry would have shown that there is no place where they work less, and that the toils of a cotton-

22. The perfection of the power loom had put hand-loom weavers out of business by the 1820s.

mill are nothing when compared to the extremes in which gaping poverty in most instances, and grasping avarice in some, may drive their parents.[23]

The occupations of children in spinning-mills are chiefly piecing, cleaning, and feeding the carding and cleansing machines. The labour of the piecer is, as has already been stated, nothing more than to reunite yarns which have been broken during the process of stretching by the mule. This is done when the carriage is close to the frame, and there is a space for rest while the carriage traverses backwards and forwards. The piecing does not require the young operative to put himself in any painful position; neither does it compel him to continue long in any position. On the contrary, as a thread breaks he has to move from spindle to spindle to repair the damage, and is thus forced to take that moderate exercise which is most conducive to health. The business of the cleaner is to sweep away any particles of flue or loose cotton which may be disengaged in the process of spinning; the nature of this occupation is so very easily comprehended that it is unnecessary to say one word to prove that it is not prejudicial. The bringing of the cotton to the willow or the carding machine, and the removal of the cans in which the article is placed after the process is completed, are occupations which involve no painful posture and no heavy toil. It is undeniable that the mill is a far better place than the mine, the forge, and the great majority of private workshops; and from personal inquiry we can state, that the children of hand-loom weavers far prefer employment in the factories to working at home for their parents. We have also inquired of those who have tried farm or field work, and have never found an instance in which the mill was not preferred to either.

There are many who will doubt or disbelieve the fact that mill-work is preferred to agricultural labour by young persons; their imaginations have been too long dazzled by Arcadian pictures of rural life, for them to take the trouble of attending to sober realities.[24] One great cause of the prevalent delusion is, that agricultural labour is rarely witnessed by casual spectators except during fine weather. Persons taking an excursion for pleasure on a summer's day, when their own spirits are exhilarated and their own hearts cheered, naturally associate the pleasurable feelings of which they are conscious with all the objects around them. But if they were compelled to take the same journey under heavy rain, during sleet, or during a very severe frost, they would form very different notions of the dripping and shivering beings in the fields around them. The tenters, piecers, and cleaners escape that exposure to the vicissitudes of the season under which the agricultural children suffer; and such young persons as have tried both invariably assign their protection from wet and cold as the chief reason for their preferring factory labour.

23. The Lancashire mills alone, those Taylor himself studied and on which his book is largely based, employed 30,000 children a year from 1830 on. Even so, many more children entered service or worked on farms and in cottage industries while significant numbers were employed in nontextile factories and in mines.

24. Reference to Arcadia, a region in ancient Greece celebrated by poets for its pastoral beauty and tranquility. Such an "Arcadian picture[ ] of rural life" is given in Elizabeth Gaskell's story "Cumberland Sheep-Shearers," also in part 2.

The children engaged in the mills are better paid, and work less. It appears from the "Agricultural Report on the Labour of Women and Children," that the wages of children from nine to fifteen, employed in farms, range from one to three shillings per week; persons above thirteen, employed in a cotton-mill, would receive from four to nine shillings per week, and, though their hours of work would be longer than on a farm, their toil would be less continuous.[25] There are no tasks imposed on young persons in factories that are anything near so laborious as hand-weeding corn, hay-making, stone-picking, potato-planting, potato-picking, or bean-chopping. It is only necessary for a person to see the processes with his own eyes to be perfectly satisfied on the point.

As a further confirmation of the account here given of the nature of juvenile employment in factories, it deserves to be noticed, that the operatives of Lancashire and the overseers of mills, the persons who must be best acquainted with the nature of such occupations, evince the greatest anxiety to get their children into the mills at as early an age as the law will allow. Now, the overseers of mills generally occupy the same rank in the social scale as the retail shopkeepers of our large towns, and no one would believe, if he only stopped to consider, that such persons would condemn their children to a course of life which they knew to be injurious or deleterious.

This subject has been usually discussed in utter forgetfulness of the parents of the children employed in the factories. Those who exclaim against what they are pleased to portray as little better than a system of child-murder, seem quite unconscious that they are accusing fathers and mothers of being accessories to the homicide. They speak as if mill-owners and master-manufacturers employed regular troops of kidnappers and child-hunters to collect boys and girls, as negroes are obtained by slave-dealers, and bring them to the mills in slave-gangs. The fact notoriously is, that the children are brought thither by their parents, that great anxiety is manifested to obtain admission, and great disappointment both felt and expressed when they are rejected. It is not at all uncommon to find them misrepresenting the ages of their children in order that they may be admitted before the period fixed by Act of Parliament. Now, it would be one of the most false and atrocious libels ever uttered to represent the operatives of Lancashire as unnatural parents, insensible to the condition of their offsprings, reckless of the sufferings of their children, or patient spectators of the wrongs inflicted upon them. They are the very contrary of all this; no division of the nation has less of the attributes of a slave-class, or would less patiently endure any wrong offered to themselves or to their children. It has been said of yore, "Tread upon a worm and it will turn;" but he that would venture to tread upon a Lancashire operative had much better make some preliminary experiment with a rattle-snake or a cobra-capella.[26]

It is impossible to pay the slightest attention to this subject without discovering

---

25. A report on the "Employment of Women and Children in Agriculture" was issued by the government in 1843.

26. *Cobra de capello* is Portuguese for "snake with a hood."

that factory labour supplies the children with food, clothing, shelter, and protection; and that it is impossible to discover how they could procure these requisites without the factory. Everybody has laughed at the French princess,[27] who, hearing that the poor had an insufficiency of bread, proposed to feed them with plumcake; but her proposition was absolute wisdom when compared with that of some of the humanity-mongers of the present day;—she at least thought of an alternative, but such a matter of fact has been left wholly out of their sublime consideration. They have not even condescended to inquire whether the factory children do not receive a more sound and efficient education than, in proportion to their position, is enjoyed by any other class in the community, as we shall hereafter demonstrate.[28] Their only cry is "Abolish the labour of children," but they forget that labour brings wages, and that wages bring bread: their charity is starvation; their humanity a little better than absolute ruin. How glorious is the philanthropy which closes the mill in order to throw open the workhouse, the prison, and the grave!

In the present state of the operative population, the labour of children is necessary to their support; is a relief to their parents; is, under reasonable restrictions, advantageous rather than injurious to their health; and is, as Mr. Pitt wisely showed, a large addition to the economic resources of the nation. Inquiry is not merely challenged but courted into the evidence on which these conclusions are founded; the reports of the commissioners, who made the first inquiries into the factory system, and by the subsequent reports of the inspectors appointed by act of Parliament.[29] To the latter documents particular attention is due, because they are the testimonies of witnesses who must be regarded as hostile to the manufacturers, inasmuch as their occupation would be gone if manufacturers and mill-owners held that place in the confidence of the country which they merit. It may very reasonably be asked, how it happened that so unjust and injurious a clamour was ever raised, and how it happened to obtain even a temporary success? The factory commissioners have decisively established its origin; it was raised by those who joined in what was once a most formidable combination, and perhaps in some respects the most desperate body which the dark history of trades-unions could exhibit—the old cotton-spinners' union[30]—in the hope that the limitation of juvenile labour would compel the masters to submit to the rate of wages which the

---

27. The French philosopher Jean Jacques Rousseau (1712–1778) tells this story in his autobiography, *Confessions.* The saying is often incorrectly attributed to Marie Antoinette, Queen of France from 1774 to 1793.

28. The 1833 Factory Act mandated that children receive two hours' schooling each day in the factory.

29. Parliamentary debate on the factory question was largely based on the reports of several investigatory commissions appointed in 1832 and 1833. Enforcement of the 1833 Factory Act was to be provided by four itinerant inspectors who were to visit industries to check for compliance and make semi-annual reports to Parliament. Taylor contends that these inspectors justify their positions by reporting problems and abuses.

30. In 1829, John Doherty, a Lancashire union leader, brought together most British unionized spinners into the first genuinely national trade union, the Grand General Union of all the Operative Spinners of the United Kingdom. Support of the spinners in Scotland and Ireland proved tenuous, however, and the Grand General Union had largely disappeared by 1831.

union would please to dictate. It was intended as a blind to the ulterior project of a Ten-hours' Bill, by which the operatives absurdly hoped to compel the masters to give them the same wages for the labour of ten hours that they usually received for twelve; and it was altogether based on the delusion that the workmen, by limiting the supply of labour, could compel the masters to submit to whatever terms they pleased to dictate.

We have before said that there are many people in the world who think that wages are discretionary, and that the price of labour may be regulated by something independent of demand and supply. In fact the cry for "protection to labour," and the variety of a "protection to native industry," not unfrequently meet our ears at the present hour. At the risk of being charged with repetition, we must be permitted again to show, that what is called "protection to labour" would lead by a certain and direct process to the ruin of the operative. A capitalist, or master-manufacturer, must either pay wages out of his capital or his profits; if he is forced to pay it out of his capital, his ability to give employment must rapidly diminish, until it is finally exhausted, and then his factory must close, for no other capitalist will embark in a business which yields no return. Wages then must be legitimately derived from profits, and profits can only be obtained from sales. The extent of sale will depend on the ability of consumers to buy, and on the ability of the seller to meet other sellers in the market, and dispose of his goods at as low a price as his competitors. Even if all foreign competition was excluded, a small rise in the price of an article would greatly limit its consumption, or, in other words, diminish the sales, which sales are to give the profits, which profits are to give the wages. An instance of this occurred during the war when a stamp-duty was imposed upon hats; though it was small in amount, we have been assured by persons engaged in the trade that it diminished the consumption of hats more than one-half; and that even persons of fortune made it a subject of boast that they could wear "a shocking bad hat" for months without being tempted to purchase a new one. The number of hatters thrown out of employment was consequently very great, and we are assured that in one town two-thirds of the journeymen hatters enlisted for soldiers within a single year. Now, precisely the same result would follow if, by any combination of workmen, an addition was made to the cost of production, and, consequently, to the selling price of printed calicoes, muslins, ginghams, &c.; patched and mended gowns would multiply; new dresses would be diminished in the same proportion; and even if the trades-unions succeeded in maintaining the rate of wages, they would greatly diminish the amount of employment, for in their worst madness they never dreamed of anything so preposterous as asking for an act of Parliament to compel manufacturers to engage or keep more workmen than they could profitably employ.

But the evil would be incalculably aggravated if foreign competitors appeared in the market able to undersell the English manufacturer; and to this danger there is generally a wilful and obstinate blindness equally astonishing and deplorable. It has been hinted that the master-manufacturer could be "protected." But is there any conceivable system of protection which would give them superiority in foreign markets? Will a Brazilian pay a higher price for the same article to an Englishman than to a Frenchman, a German, or an American? Here the rise of price would put an end to sales profits, and wages, in a single blow.

In fact, the amount of profits will determine the number of masters that can be tempted to enter into any given business, and, consequently, it will determine the amount for the specific labour which that business requires in the labour-market; and thus the whole question comes to the plain common-sense principle, "when two masters are looking for a man wages will be high, and when two men are looking for a master wages will be low."

If these plain truths had been understood by the members of combinations and trades-unions, we should never have heard one word concerning infant slavery, factory bills, and ten-hours' bills. But, unfortunately, the operatives were flattered with the idea that the masters could not do without them, which was to some extent true; but they quite forgot they could not do without the masters, and that they were destroying the competition which alone could raise wages, when they frightened some capitalists out of business, and deterred others from coming into it. This, in fact, is the obvious and undeniable cause of the misery of the Spital-fields weavers;[31] and it is to be lamented that the example of their perverse system has not had sufficient influence on the working classes throughout the country.

That the factory cry was raised by those ignorant and self-constituted legisla-tors, who supposed that they could accomplish what acts of Parliament had failed to effect—the fixing of the rate of wages, is abundantly proved by the reports of the commissioners. We extract the following out of numberless passages to the same effect.[32]

["]In support of these indications, that the interest of the children is not really at the root of the agitation of this question, excepting amongst benevolent individ-uals in a higher sphere, we might cite innumerable cases extracted from the evi-dence. It appears that although the case of the children is invariably put forward as the plea for restriction in all appeals to the public, it is hardly so much as men-tioned in the meetings or discussions of the operative body themselves, or if mentioned, it is only in connection with the anticipated curtailment of the work-ing time for adults.

["]The men who have placed themselves at the head of the agitation of this question, are the same men who, in every instance of rash and headlong strikes, have assumed the command of the discontented members of the operative body, and who have used the grossest means of intimidation to subjugate the quiet and contented part of the work-people. It appears that agitation is the trade by which they live, and that success in the attainment of the objects at which they profess to

---

31. Spitalfields was the name of a notorious section of east London where impoverished weavers labored in sweatshops under appalling conditions.

32. The first and second reports of the Factory Commission were issued in 1833. Supplementary reports appeared in the following year.

aim would involve the loss of their actual occupation, which consists in keeping up discontent at such a height as to secure distinction and profit for themselves, at the expense of their fellows.["]—*Factory Commission, Report* 1, *page* 47.

The fact that struck me most, in the course of my investigation, was the different grounds on which the proposed Factory Bill of Lord Ashley is advocated in Parliament, and I believe everywhere out of the manufacturing districts, and in them. The cruelty of employing young children during the long hours of factory labour, and the ill-usage to which they are subjected in keeping them to their work, is the parliamentary and public ground for supporting the bill,—the ground on which the philanthropists take their stand. Now, not a single witness that came before me to give evidence in favour of the Ten Hours' Bill,—and I made it a rule never to turn away any of the class (besides summoning many who otherwise would not have come forward at all),—not a single witness who advocated the bill, of whatever trade or station he may have been, supported it on the above grounds. This reason was of course mentioned to me by some of them, as influencing their determinations; but by cross-questioning them, and by means of circumstances which came to my knowledge, I am perfectly satisfied that motives of humanity have not the smallest weight in inducing them to uphold the Ten Hours' Bill. I made this fact out with a degree of certainty which I am confident leaves no room whatever for doubt upon the subject.

The following are a few of the quotations from the evidence that establish this point:—

["]Do you know the reason why some operatives advocate the Ten Hours' Bill?—I believe it is principally owing to the want of due consideration in them. I think they indulge an idea that the articles manufactured will get up to a better price in the market, so that in a short time they will be able to demand their present wages; but we think that is not likely to be the case at all.

["]Did you ever hear any other reason for their advocating it?—I don't know that they had any other reasons, but I believe not. There was a man from Manchester, who came into our meeting, an advocate for the Ten Hours' Bill, and he told us that we should receive no less wages in twelve months' time than we do now, provided it was dropped to ten.

["]Did he give any other reasons for wishing you to agree to his opinions?—No, he did not.

["]Did he say nothing about the cruelty of employing young children in mills twelve hours daily?—No, he did not say anything about it. I often heard statements of this sort, of persons being deformed by working so long, but I never saw anything of the sort.["]—*Suppl. Factory Report,* D.II.

["]I do not mean to say but that the men are perfectly justified in attempting to raise their wages, so long as they do so by honest means. I am only animadverting on the deceit which they practised, by pretending that the good of the children was their motive for wishing the Ten Hours' Bill, and supporting their statements by the most unparalleled falsehoods and calumnies against the masters. All this is so perfectly notorious in Lancashire, that it must be superfluous to any one who has visited that great manufacturing district; but the fraud was so long successful elsewhere, and perhaps still is, that it cannot be too often repeated, that the whole and sole view with which the working classes advocated Lord Ashley's Bill, was to get the wages of twelve hours with the work of ten.["]—*Factory Commission Report, by Mr. Tuffnell, page* 209.

It may yet be inquired, how it happened that this cry against factory-labour obtained patronage in high quarters? Unfortunately, this is of no more difficult solution than to discover why the preposterous fictions of Titus Oates were taken up by influential persons, and sedulously trumpeted into popularity.[33] At all times a cry can be made subservient to party purposes, and consequently when once raised, it is sure to be echoed until people begin to believe it from constant repetition. Such tactics have been so often employed by political parties, that we have long since ceased to view them with wonder. There never was any story devised which was in all its parts so utterly absurd as that James II[34] caused a false heir to the English throne to be smuggled into his queen's bed in a warming-pan, and then exhibited the infant as his legitimate offspring; but this monstrous fiction when propagated by party received all but universal evidence, and it was for many years scarcely possible to deny it without running the risk of a trial for high treason. The history of the success of the factory cry is precisely similar; it came at a moment when it was likely to be serviceable to a powerful and well-organized party; it was adopted without any inquiry, for it was convenient that it should be true, and in party logic convenience is a far stronger argument for truth than the most substantial reality. There is no imputation designed or conveyed against those who so eagerly availed themselves of what appeared to be a ready-made argument; they were so very anxious to believe, that it is probable in the majority of instances that they *did* believe. Neither philosophy nor history records many examples of persons being over careful in sifting the evidence which was brought to support an advantageous theory.

The mill-owners and manufacturers had no available means of meeting this clamour; they never formed a united and organized body; a rope of sand exhibits perfect cohesion when compared with their class; there were countless elements of repulsion which kept them apart from each other, and prevented them from ever regarding themselves as a distinct order of society. A few individuals protested against the calumnies; they were regarded as the exceptions which proved the rule: it was immediately said, "If these statements were generally untrue, they would have been generally denied." Silence was thus not unreasonably regarded as something like a confession of guilt, until the diligence with which misrepresentation was circulated, and the apathy shown by those interested in its exposure, gave

---

33. Titus Oates (1649–1705) concocted the Popish Plot in 1678. In perjured testimony, he claimed that Roman Catholics planned to massacre Protestants, set fire to London, and assassinate King Charles II.

34. James II (1633–1701), a Catholic, was King of England from 1685 until his abdication in 1688.

temporary success to the most extraordinary popular delusion which the present generation has witnessed.

"Words," says an eminent writer, "are often things,"[35] and the authors of the factory-cry gave very strong proofs of the aphorism; they carried the abuse of words to the utmost; their category of "infants of tender years" included, and still includes, all persons under eighteen years of age! They have actually assailed the Factory Commissioners for making a distinction between the juvenile operatives of from nine to fourteen, and those from fourteen to eighteen years of age. The reasons for drawing the line are thus stated by the commissioners:—"The grounds on which we recommend the above restriction on hours of labour to be limited to the commencement of the fourteenth year are: 1. That at that age the period of childhood, properly so called, ceases, and that of puberty is established, when the body becomes more capable of enduring protracted labour. It appears in evidence from the statements and depositions of all classes of witnesses, including the young persons themselves, that the same labour which was fatiguing and exhausting at an earlier period is in general comparatively easy after the age in question. 2. That from the comparative infrequency with which serious and permanent disease appears to have been produced when labour did not commence before the ninth year, and was not immoderate, there is reason to conclude that the restriction now suggested will afford an adequate protection. 3. That in general at or about the fourteenth year young persons are no longer treated as children; they are not usually chastised by corporal punishment, and at the same time an important change takes place in what may be termed their domestic condition. For the most part they cease to be under the complete control of their parents and guardians. They begin to retain a part of their wages. They frequently pay for their own lodgings, board, and clothing. They usually make their own contracts, and are, in the proper sense of the words, free agents. For all these reasons we conceive that this is the natural period when young persons may be placed on the same footing as adults, as far as regards the disposal of their labour."

Now, this is actually described by a very influential adviser of the factory legislators as "protecting one portion of the *infantile* labourers at the expense of another." In fact, as Mr. Nassau W. Senior[36] has ably shown, the restraints imposed upon juvenile labour by the Factory Act, which was conceded to the popular clamour, have produced the most bitter feelings of disappointment amongst the leaders of the operative combinations, who hoped to have obtained a legislation of a very different kind:—

"The usual plan pursued by manufacturers since the passing of the Factory Act

---

35. Taylor may have in mind the following lines from Lord Byron's *Don Juan:*
    But words are things; and a small drop of ink,
    Falling, like dew, upon a thought, produces
    That which makes thousands, perhaps millions, think. (canto 3, stanza 88)

36. Nassau William Senior (1790–1864) was an influential political economist who served on government commissions investigating factories in 1837 and the conditions of handloom weavers in 1841.

is to employ one set of children for the first eight hours of the day, and to get them on as well as may be during the remaining four without them.

The consequences are—

1st. Loss to the parents who have children under thirteen, by the non-employment of those under nine, and by the reduced wages of those between ten and thirteen.

2nd. Loss to the operatives, who are the *direct* employers of the children as their assistants; first, by their having to employ more assistants above thirteen, and at higher wages; and secondly, by their being able to get through less work after they lose the assistance of the younger children.

3rd. Loss to the millowner, whose produce during the last four hours of each day is diminished in quantity, and deteriorated in quality, and who has sometimes to repay to his operatives a part of their loss.

The gainers are the children above thirteen, whose wages have risen, and the children under thirteen, so far as they are better educated and have less fatigue than before.

As to the value of this gain, however, as far as education is concerned, I am sceptical. If good schools and a good system of instruction were established, no doubt much could be learned in the two hours a-day of compulsory schooling.

But those portions of the bill which provided for the establishment of schools having been thrown out by the Lords, the school appears to be generally rather a place for detaining and annoying the children than of real instruction. Instead of the vast and airy apartments of a well-regulated factory, they are kept in a small, low, close room; and instead of the light work, or rather attendance, of a factory, which really is not more exercise than a child voluntarily takes, they have to sit on a form, supposed to be studying a spelling-book. We found a universal statement that the children could not be got into the school except by force; that they tried every means to remain in the factory, or, if excluded, to ramble over the fields or the streets.

It may easily be supposed that the *operatives* are outrageous against this state of things. Their original object was to raise the price of their *own* labour. For this purpose the spinners, who form, as I stated in my first letter, a very small (about one-twentieth) but a powerful body among them, finding that they could not obtain a limitation of the hours of work to ten by combination, tried to effect it through the Legislature. They knew that Parliament would not legislate for adults. They got up, therefore, a frightful and (as far as we have heard and seen) an utterly unfounded picture of the ill-treatment of the children, in the hope that the Legislature would restrain all persons under eighteen years old to ten hours, which they knew would, in fact, restrict the labour of adults to the same period. The act having not only defeated this attempt, but absolutely turned it against them,—having, in fact, increased their labour and diminished their pay,—they are far more vehement for a ten-hours' bill than before, and are endeavouring by every means to impede the working of the existing act, and to render its enactments vexatious or nugatory."—(*Senior's Letters on the Factory Act*, 18–20).

It would be a mere waste of time to show, from physiological and other considerations, that young persons between the age of fourteen and eighteen cannot be called "infants," and that it is utterly absurd to require that they be treated as such. Yet this is really the object for which the factory-cry is perversely continued to the present moment, and operatives of a marriageable age are the *infants* for whom public sympathy is now invoked.

The word "mill" has undesignedly lent considerable aid to swell the amount of popular delusion on the subject of factory labour. To those who have not visited the northern counties it suggests the notions of the corn-mill, or the tread-mill;[37] and there are thousands whom it would be difficult to persuade that a spinning-mill has not some resemblance either to one or the other. They cannot, from the name, frame to themselves the notion of a large and spacious edifice, kept scrupulously clean, having a uniform temperature maintained in all of its apartments, and where it is impossible that persons should be crowded together, for the very simple reason that the greater proportion of the space is occupied by machinery.

"It would be an outrageous falsehood to assert, that any part of a cotton-mill is one-tenth part as crowded, or the air one-tenth part so impure, *as the House of Commons with a moderate attendance of members.*"—(*Factory Commission Report*, D.2 page 200).

It is not necessary to pursue this subject farther, but there has been recently put forward an argument for believing that there is something wrong in the factory system which is not destitute of a semblance of plausibility, and which, therefore, merits brief notice. It is asked, "If millowners were not conscious of some unsoundness in their system, would they have patiently submitted to a legalised inspection and espionage, such as exists over no other class of the community?" The answer to this has been already given; the master-manufacturers never organized themselves into a body, never acted together, and never looked upon themselves as forming a class or order. However annoyed they may have been individually, they had no means of protesting collectively; they had no influence in the Legislature, and no available means of making an appeal to their fellow-countrymen. Many of them, in the full consciousness of innocence, courted inspection, being convinced that the results of every inquiry would only tend to restore them to that place in the estimation of their countrymen of which they had been unjustly deprived. They forgot that inspectors once appointed would have substantial reasons for endeavouring to procure the continuance of their office, and would, therefore, be interested in keeping up the belief that there was something peculiar to the factory system which required authoritative supervision and parliamentary interference. That they are no more satisfied with the results than the operatives are is pretty apparent, but no small portion of the blame rests upon themselves. The reports of the commissioners appointed to inquire into the condi-

---

37. Machine powered by people or animals treading on a set of moving steps or a beltline.

Figure 2.1. *Once a Little Vagrant; Now a Little Workman.* Courtesy of Barnardo's Photographic Archive.

Dr. Thomas Barnardo (1845–1905), a physician and social reformer, was especially known for his efforts on behalf of impoverished children. He established his first Home for Working and Destitute Lads in 1870 and went on to found many more homes for boys and girls alike. The companion photographs shown here—*Once a Little Vagrant* and *Now a Little Workman*—were among many sold by Dr. Barnardo's homes to raise funds.

tion of children in mines and metal-manufactures *establish* a case of greater hardship and suffering to the children engaged in these pursuits than the assailants of factories ever *invented;* but, in these cases, no attempt has been made to establish a system of inspection, for reasons which need not here be discussed, as they are perfectly obvious to every person of common understanding.*[38]

38. The first report from the commissioners appointed to investigate children's employment in mines appeared in 1842, prompting the passage of protective legislation in the same year. At about the same time, 1842–43, a Commission of Inquiry into the Employment of Children in Trades and Manufactures made its report, but no legislation was passed to protect workers in non-textile industries until the 1867 Factory Acts Extension Bill.

*[Taylor's note:] As this work is likely to fall into the hands of many persons who have not had an opportunity of learning the nature of mule-spinning, we deem it right to insert here a description of the process, illustrated by a wood-cut.

Mule-spinning belongs both to the cotton and to the short-wool manufacture, but in the former is both more extensive and more interesting.

Let the reader imagine himself in the room, a part of which is represented in the accompanying

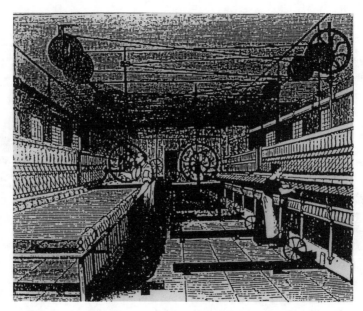

Figure 2.2. Mule-spinning.

cut . . . and it is probable that the circumstances worthy of his notice will present themselves in nearly the following order. He will see a carriage about a yard in height, and of very considerable length, varying in different mills, bearing a row of spindles between its upper rails; it has generally three wheels, which traverse on the same number of iron guiding bars, so as to allow of its drawing on, to a distance of more than four feet from the stationary frame; as it recedes from the frame, it draws with it and elongates the threads or rather rovings delivered to it through rollers, by a series of bobbins in the creels or stationary rails. The threads as they are elongated are twisted by the spindles, and, should any of them break, it is the duty of a boy or girl, called a piecener, to join the disunited ends as the carriage moves from the upright frame. A girl in the act of piecing the yarn is represented in the cut. When the carriage has receded to its full extent, the spindles continue to revolve until the requisite quantity of twist is communicated to the yarn. The spinner then causes the spindles to revolve backwards until he has unwound the portion of thread which has coiled spirally round it from the point to the nose of the cop, and at the same time he lowers a faller wire, supported by hooks, as seen in the cut, so as to regulate the winding of the yarn on the cop in a proper spiral. There is great nicety required in regulating the pushing back of the carriage, for it is necessary that its rate of travelling should be commensurate with the revolution of the spindles. Three simultaneous and delicate movements have thus to be effected by the spinner as the carriage returns; he must guide the faller wire so as to ensure the regular winding of the yarn on the cop; he must regulate the rotation of the spindles, of which there are often a thousand to one mule; and he must push the carriage at such a rate as to supply precisely the exact amount of yarn that the spindles can take up.

The little pieceners can only take up the ends when the carriage is within a foot or two of the delivering roller, and they have therefore an interval of rest while the carriages traverse backwards and forwards. The spinner, too, has a brief respite while the carriage is moving outwards from the frame. The time taken to make a stretch, that is, to draw out a thread equal in length to the range of the carriage, increases with the fineness of the yarn, and varies also according to the completeness of the machinery and the skill of the operative. The breaking of the threads depends not merely on the machinery, but to a very great extent on the atmosphere and temperature. We were in a mill during the prevalence of a sharp drying east wind, and found that it produced such an effect on the fibres of the cotton, that the threads broke faster than the pieceners could mend them, and that the spinning of very high numbers at such a time was all but impossible.

JOANNA BAILLIE

JOANNA BAILLIE (1762–1851) was born in Scotland but moved to England in 1783. Sister to the well-known physician and anatomist Matthew Baillie and friend of Sir Walter Scott, Baillie became a popular poet and playwright. Elizabeth Barrett Browning considered her "the first female poet in all senses in England."[1] In "Hay-Making," Baillie idealizes rural life in her bright picture of "the cheerful work" of the hay-makers.

Hay-Making

Upon the grass no longer hangs the dew;
Forth hies the mower with his glittering scythe,
In snowy shirt bedight, and all unbraced,
He moves athwart the mead with sideling bend.
And lays the grass in many a swarthy line;   5
In every field, in every lawn and mead,
The rousing voice of industry is heard;
The haycock rises, and the frequent rake
Sweeps on the fragrant hay in heavy wreaths.
The old and young, the weak and strong are there,   10
And, as they can, help on the cheerful work.
The father jeers his awkward half-grown lad,
Who trails his tawdry armful o'er the field,
Nor does he fear the jeering to repay.

1. Frederic G. Kenyon, ed., *The Letters of Elizabeth Barrett Browning*, 2 vols. (London: Smith, Elder, 1898), 1:230.

Figure 2.3. Myles Birket Foster, *The Hayrick*. Courtesy of Yale Center for British Art, Paul Mellon Collection.

Illustrator and painter Myles Birket Foster (1825–1899) created hundreds of sunny rural landscapes such as the idyllic watercolor *The Hayrick*, c. 1862.

> The village oracle and simple maid   15
> Jest in their turns and raise the ready laugh;
> All are companions in the general glee;
> Authority, hard favoured, frowns not there.
> Some, more advanced, raise up the lofty rick,
> Whilst on its top doth stand the parish toast   20

In loose attire and swelling ruddy cheek.
With taunts and harmless mockery she receives
The tossed-up heaps from fork of simple youth,
Who, staring on her, takes his arm away,
While half the load falls back upon himself.   25
Loud is her laugh, her voice is heard afar:
The mower busied on the distant lawn,
The carter trudging on his dusty way,
The shrill sound know, their bonnets tossed in air,
And roar across the field to catch the notice: 30
She waves her arm to them, and shakes her head,
And then renews her work with double spirit.
Thus do they jest and laugh away their toil,
Till the bright sun, now past its middle course,
Shoots down his fiercest beams which none may brave.   35
The stoutest arm feels listless, and the swart
And brawny-shouldered clown begins to fail.
But to the weary, lo—there comes relief!
A troop of welcome children, o'er the lawn,
With slow and wary steps approach: some bear   40
In baskets, oaten cakes or barley scones,
And gusty² cheese and stoups³ of milk or whey:⁴
Beneath the branches of a spreading tree,
Or by the shady side of the tall rick,
They spread their homely fare, and seated round,   45
Taste every pleasure that a feast can give.

2. Tasty.
3. Tankards.
4. Watery part of the milk that separates from the curds, or coagulated part.

ELIZABETH GASKELL

E LIZABETH CLEGHORN GASKELL (1810–1865) balanced a demanding life as a clergyman's wife with an increasingly active career as a professional writer. Her husband's ministry was in the rapidly expanding manufacturing city of Manchester, and she developed a sensitive awareness of the estrangement of management from working people, an awareness that informs much of her writing, notably *Mary Barton: A Tale of Manchester Life* (1848) and *North and South* (1854–55), industrial novels that enjoyed marked success in the nineteenth century and are popular again today with an audience that reaches beyond the academic community. While she is best known for her writings on the industrial scene and her biography of her friend Charlotte Brontë, she addressed a variety of subjects both in her sustained fiction writing and in the shorter works for which she was also known and respected. She contributed novels in serialized form as well as short stories, vignettes, and essays to Charles Dickens's journals *Household Words* and *All the Year Round*.

"Cumberland Sheep-Shearers" is one such piece published in *Household Words* in 1853. In this narrative, Gaskell focuses upon the agricultural rather than the manufacturing worker, and her tone has an elegiac cast as she invests her detailed description of activities and scenes with archetypal significance. Neither work nor provincial life is prettified into pastoral, but common labor within the rhythms of rural culture is portrayed as physically wholesome and psychologically assuring. Prudent care and responsible attention to both nature and custom, homely living, unremitting yet not enervating toil, the honoring of social obligations: all are celebrated in a candid expression of a nineteenth-century georgic ideal reminiscent of Wordsworth's praise of similar scenes from this same area. Gaskell sees rural labor as an enterprise that unites community while giving the individual dignity; such a perspective differs sharply from common nineteenth-century portrayals of industrial work as disruptive of community and demeaning to individual laborers. This attitude that agricultural life and labor were intrinsically superior to the urban manufacturing experience was a staple of nineteenth-century British commentary and received increased nostalgic emphasis in the second half of the century.

Cumberland Sheep-Shearers

Three or four years ago we spent part of a summer in one of the dales in the neighbourhood of Keswick. We lodged at the house of a small Statesman,[1] who added to his occupation of a sheep-farmer that of a woollen manufacturer. His own flock was not large, but he bought up other people's fleeces, either on commission, or for his own purposes; and his life seemed to unite many pleasant and various modes of employment, and the great jolly burly man throve upon all, both in body and mind.

One day, his handsome wife proposed to us that we should accompany her to a distant sheep-shearing, to be held at the house of one of her husband's customers, where she was sure we should be heartily welcome, and where we would see an old-fashioned shearing, such as was not often met with now in the Dales. I don't know why it was, but we were lazy, and declined her invitation. It might be that the day was a broiling one, even for July, or it might be a fit of shyness; but whichever was the reason, it very unaccountably vanished soon after she was gone, and the opportunity seemed to have slipped through our fingers. The day was hotter than ever; and we should have twice as much reason to be shy and self-conscious, now that we should not have our hostess to introduce and chaperone us. However, so great was our wish to go, that we blew these obstacles to the winds, if there were any that day; and, obtaining the requisite directions from the farm-servant, we set out on our five mile walk, about one o'clock on a cloudless day in the first half of July.

Our party consisted of two grown up persons and four children, the youngest almost a baby, who had to be carried the greater part of that weary length of way. We passed through Keswick, and saw the groups of sketching, boating tourists, on whom we, as residents for a month in the neighbourhood, looked down with some contempt as mere strangers, who were sure to go about blundering, or losing their way, or being imposed upon by guides, or admiring the wrong things, and never seeing the right things. After we had dragged ourselves through the long straggling town, we came to a part of the highway where it wound between copses sufficiently high to make a green gloom in a green shade;[2] the branches touched and interlaced overhead, while the road was so straight, that all the quarter-of-an-hour that we were walking we could see the opening of blue light at the other end, and note the quivering of the heated luminous air beyond the dense shade in which we moved. Every now and then, we caught glimpses of the silver lake that shimmered through

---

1. An independent landowner who farmed his own acres or "estate" rather than working the land for another.

2. Gaskell deliberately echoes "The Garden" by Andrew Marvell (1621–1678), a lyric wherein the speaker celebrates the autonomy of the imaginative mind that "creates" "other worlds, and other seas," than the physical ones, "Annihilating all that's made / To a green thought in a green shade."

Figure 2.4. Arthur Hughes, *Home from Work.* Courtesy of The Forbes Magazine Collection, New York. © All rights reserved.

Pre-Raphaelite painter and illustrator Arthur Hughes (1832–1915) produced many of his most famous paintings (including *April Love, The Long Engagement,* and *Home from Sea*) in the 1850s. This picture, *Home from Work,* was exhibited in 1861. Painted in rich, warm tones, this tender domestic scene shows a woodcutter returning from his day's labor to an ivy-clad cottage and the embrace of an angelic little girl and, thus, presents a reassuring image of working-class life.

the trees; and, now and then, in the dead noon-tide stillness, we could hear the gentle lapping of the water on the pebbled shore—the only sound we heard, except the low deep hum of myriads of insects revelling out their summer lives. We had all agreed that talking made us hotter, so we and the birds were very silent. Out again into the hot bright sunny dazzling road, the fierce sun above our heads made us long to be at home, but we had passed the half-way, and to go on was shorter than to return. Now we left the highway, and began to mount. The ascent looked disheartening, but at almost every step we gained increased freshness of air; and the crisp short mountain grass was soft and cool in comparison with the high road. The little wandering breezes, that came every now and then athwart us, were laden with fragrant scents—now of wild thyme—now of the little scrambling creeping white rose, which ran along the ground and pricked our feet with its sharp thorns; and now we came to a trickling streamlet, on whose spongy banks grew great bushes of the bog-myrtle, giving a spicy odour to the air. When our breath failed us during that steep ascent, we had one invariable dodge by which we hoped to escape the "fat and scant of breath" quotation;[3] we turned round and admired the lovely views, which from each succeeding elevation became more and more beautiful.

At last, perched on a level which seemed nothing more than a mere shelf of rock, we saw our destined haven—a grey stone farmhouse, high over our heads, high above the lake as we were—with out-buildings enough around it to justify the Scotch name of a 'town';[4] and near it one of those great bossy sycamores, so common in similar situations all through Cumberland and Westmoreland. One more long tug and then we should be there. So, cheering the poor tired little ones, we set off bravely for that last piece of steep rocky path; and we never looked behind till we stood in the coolness of the deep porch, looking down from our natural terrace on the glassy Derwent Water, far, far below, reflecting each tint of the blue sky, only in darker fuller colours every one. We seemed on a level with the top of Cat Bell; and the tops of great trees lay deep down—so deep that we felt as if they were close enough together and solid enough to bear our feet if we chose to spring down and walk upon them. Right in front of where we stood, there was a ledge of the rocky field that surrounded the house. We had knocked at the door, but it was evident that we were unheard in the din and merry clatter of voices within, and our old original shyness returned. By and by, someone found us out, and a hearty burst of hospitable welcome ensued. Our coming was all right; it was understood in a minute who we were; our real hostess was hardly less urgent in her civilities than our temporary hostess, and both together bustled us out of the room upon which the outer door entered, into a large bedroom which opened out of it— the state apartment, in all such houses in Cumberland—where the children make their first appearance, and where the heads of the household lie down to die if the Great Conqueror gives them sufficient warning for such decent and composed submission as is best in accordance with the simple dignity of their lives.

Into this chamber we were ushered, and the immediate relief from its dark coolness to our overheated bodies and dazzled eyes was inexpressibly refreshing. The walls were so thick that there was room for a very comfortable window-seat in them, without there being any projection into the room; and the long low shape prevented the sky-line from being unusually depressed, even at that height, and so

---

3. See Shakespeare's *Hamlet* 5.2.287 where, during his duel with Laertes, Gertrude says of Hamlet that "He's fat, and scant of breath."

4. Originally, a "town" would have consisted of households and outbuildings related to a central home, the combined areas being enclosed by a wall and usually some natural boundary such as a stream.

the light was subdued, and the general tint through the room deepened into darkness, where the eye fell on that stupendous bed, with its posts, and its head-piece, and its foot-board, and its trappings of all kinds of the deepest brown; and the frame itself looked large enough for six or seven people to lie comfortably therein, without even touching each other. In the hearth-place, stood a great pitcher filled with branches of odorous mountain flowers; and little bits of rose-mary and lavender were strewed about the room; partly as I afterwards learnt to prevent incautious feet from slipping about on the polished oak floor. When we had noticed everything, and rested, and cooled (as much as we could do before the equinox), we returned to the company assembled in the house-place.

This house-place was almost a hall in grandeur. Along one side ran an oaken dresser, all decked with the same sweet evergreens, fragments of which strewed the bedroom floor. Over this dresser were shelves, bright with most exquisitely pol-ished pewter. Opposite to the bedroom door was the great hospitable fireplace, ensconced within its proper chimney corners, and having the "master's cupboard" on its right hand side. Do you know what a "master's cupboard" is? Mr Words-worth[5] could have told you; ay, and have shown you one at Rydal Mount, too. It is a cupboard about a foot in width, and a foot and a half in breadth, expressly reserved for the use of the master of the household. Here he may keep pipe and tankard, almanac, and what not; and although no door bars the access of any hand, in this open cupboard his peculiar properties rest secure, for is it not "the master's cupboard"? There was a fire in the house-place, even on this hot day; it gave a grace and vividness to the room, and being kept within proper limits, it seemed no more than was requisite to boil the kettle. For, I should say, that the very minute of our arrival, our hostess (so I shall designate the wife of the farmer at whose house the sheep-shearing was to be held) proposed tea; and although we had not dined, for it was but little past three, yet, on the principle of "Do at Rome as the Romans do," we assented with a good grace, thankful to have any refresh-ment offered us short of water-gruel, after our long and tiring walk, and rather afraid of our children "cooling too quickly."

While the tea was preparing, and it took six comely matrons to do it justice, we proposed to Mrs C. (our real hostess), that we should go and see the sheep-shearing. She accordingly led us away into a back yard, where the process was going on. By a back yard I mean a far different place from what a Londoner would so designate; our back yard, high up on the mountainside was a space about forty yards by twenty, overshadowed by the noble sycamore, which might have been the very one that suggested to Coleridge—

> This sycamore (oft musical with bees—
> Such tents the Patriarchs loved) &c., &c.[6]

5. William Wordsworth (1770–1850) was, when Gaskell composed this narrative, recently deceased and widely revered as England's finest poet. Gaskell had met Wordsworth at his home of Rydal Mount in the year before the poet died.

6. Samuel Taylor Coleridge (1772–1834) was a well-known Romantic poet. In "Inscription for a Fountain on a Heath," from which Gaskell quotes, he praised a sycamore that provided "a deep and ample shade."

And in this deep, cool, green shadow sat two or three grey-haired sires, smoking their pipes, and regarding the proceedings with a placid complacency, which had a savour of contempt in it for the degeneracy of the present times—a sort of "Ah! they don't know what good shearing is nowadays" look in it. That round shadow of the sycamore tree, and the elders who sat there looking on, were the only things not full of motion and life in the yard. The yard itself was bounded by a grey stone wall, and the moors rose above it to the mountain top; we looked over the low walls on to the spaces bright with the yellow asphodel, and the first flush of the purple heather. The shadow of the farmhouse fell over this yard, so that it was cool in aspect, save for the ruddy faces of the eager shearers, and the gay-coloured linsey petticoats of the women, folding the fleeces with tucked-up gowns.

When we first went into the yard, every corner of it seemed as full of motion as an antique frieze, and, like that had to be studied before I could ascertain the different actions and purposes involved. On the left hand was a walled-in field of small extent, full of sunshine and light, with the heated air quivering over the flocks of panting bewildered sheep, who were penned up therein, awaiting their turn to be shorn. At the gate by which this field was entered from the yard stood a group of eager-eyed boys, panting like the sheep, but not like them from fear, but from excitement and joyous exertion. Their faces were flushed with brown-crimson, their scarlet lips were parted into smiles, and their eyes had that peculiar blue lustre in them, which is only gained by a free life in the pure and blithesome air. As soon as these lads saw that a sheep was wanted by the shearers within, they sprang towards one in the field—the more boisterous and stubborn an old ram the better—and tugging, and pulling, and pushing, and shouting—sometimes mounting astride of the poor obstreperous brute, and holding his horns like a bridle—they gained their point and dragged their captive up to the shearer, like little victors as they were, all glowing and ruddy with conquest. The shearers sat each astride on a long bench, grave and important—the heroes of the day. The flock of sheep to be shorn on this occasion consisted of more than a thousand, and eleven famous shearers had come, walking in from many miles' distance to try their skill one against the other; for sheep-shearings are a sort of rural Olympics. They were all young men in their prime, strong, and well-made; without coat or waistcoat, and with upturned shirt-sleeves. They sat each across a long bench or narrow table, and caught up the sheep from the attendant boys, who had dragged it in; they lifted it on to the bench, and placing it by a dexterous knack on its back, they began to shear the wool off the tail and under parts; then they tied the two hind legs and the two fore legs together, and laid it first on one side and then on the other, till the fleece came off in one whole piece; the art was to shear all the wool off, and yet not to injure the sheep by any awkward cut: if such an accident did occur, a mixture of tar and butter was immediately applied; but every wound was a blemish on the shearer's fame. To shear well and completely, and yet to do it quickly, shows the perfection of the clippers. Some can finish off as many as six score sheep in a summer's day; and if you consider the weight and uncouthness of the animal, and the general heat of the weather, you will see that, with justice, clipping or shearing is regarded as harder work than mowing. But most good shearers are content with despatching four or five score; it is only on unusual occasions, or when Greek meets Greek, that six score are attempted or accomplished.

When the sheep is divided into its fleece and itself, it becomes the property of two persons. The women seize the fleece, and, standing by the side of a temporary dresser (in this case made of planks laid across barrels, beneath what sharp scant shadow could be obtained from the eaves of the house), they fold it up. This again is an art, simple as it may seem; and the farmer's wives and daughters about Langdale Head are famous for it. They begin with folding up the legs, and then roll the whole fleece up, tying it with the neck; and the skill consists not merely in doing this quickly and firmly, but in certain artistic pulls of the wool so as to display the finer parts, and not, by crushing up the fibre, to make it appear coarse to the buyer. Six comely women were thus employed; they laughed, and talked, and sent shafts of merry satire at the grave and busy shearers, who were too earnest in their work to reply, although an occasional deepening of colour, or twinkle of the eye, would tell that the remark had hit. But they reserved their retorts, if they had any, until the evening, when the day's labour would be over, and when, in the license of country humour, I imagine, some of the saucy speakers would meet with their match. As yet, the applause came from their own party of women; though now and then one of the old men, sitting under the shade of a sycamore, would take his pipe out of his mouth to spit, and, before beginning again to send up the softly curling white wreaths of smoke, he would condescend on a short deep laugh, and a "Well done, Maggie!" "Give it him, lass!" for with the not unkindly jealousy of age towards youth, the old grandfathers invariably took part with the women against the young men. These sheared on, throwing the fleeces to the folders, and casting the sheep down on the ground with gentle strength, ready for another troop of boys to haul it to the right hand side of the farmyard, where the great out-buildings were placed; where all sorts of country vehicles were crammed and piled, and seemed to throw up their scarlet shafts into the air, as if imploring relief from the crowd of shandries[7] and market carts that pressed upon them. Out of the sun, in the dark shadow of the cart-house, a pan of red-hot coals glowed in a trivet; and upon them was placed an iron basin holding tar and raddle, or ruddle.[8] Hither the right hand troop of boys dragged the poor naked sheep to be "smitten"—that is to say, marked with the initials or cypher of the owner. In this case, the sign of the possessor was a circle or spot on one side, and a straight line on the other; and after the sheep were thus marked, they were turned out to the moor, and the crowd of bleating lambs that sent up an incessant moan for their lost mothers; each found out the ewe to which it belonged the moment she was turned out of the yard, and the placid contentment of the sheep that wandered away up the hillside, with their little lambs trotting by them, gave just the necessary touch of peace and repose to

7. A shandry is a small cart.

8. Ruddle (or reddle or raddle or redden) is red ochre; it was used to mark livestock. Later in the century, Thomas Hardy (1840–1928) would create as one of his most sympathetic characters in *The Return of the Native* Diggory Venn, a reddleman or supplier of reddle to the sheep farmers of his district.

the scene. There were all the classical elements for the representation of life; there were the "Old men and maidens, young men and children" of the Psalmist;[9] there were all the stages and conditions of being that sing forth their farewell to the departing crusaders in the "Saint's Tragedy."[10]

We were very glad indeed that we had seen the sheep-shearing, though the road had been hot, and long, and dusty, and we were as yet unrefreshed and hungry. When we had understood the separate actions of the busy scene, we could begin to notice individuals. I soon picked out a very beautiful young woman as an object of admiration and interest. She stood by a buxom woman of middle age, who had just sufficient likeness to point her out as the mother. Both were folding fleeces, and folding them well; but the mother talked all the time with a rich-toned voice, and a merry laugh and eye, while the daughter hung her head silently over her work; and I could only guess at the beauty of her eyes by the dark sweeping shadow of her eyelashes. She was well dressed, and had evidently got on her Sunday gown, although a good deal for the honour of the thing, as the flowing skirt was tucked up in a bunch behind, in order to be out of her way: beneath the gown, and far more conspicuous—and, possibly, far prettier—was a striped petticoat of full deep blue and scarlet, revealing the blue cotton stockings common in that part of the country, and the pretty, neat leather shoes. The girl had tucked her brown hair back behind her ears; but if she had known how often she would have had occasion to blush, I think she would have kept that natural veil more over her delicate cheek. She blushed deeper and ever deeper, because one of the shearers, in every interval of his work, looked at her and sighed. Neither of them spoke a word, though both were as conscious of the other as could be; and the buxom mother, with a sidelong glance, took cognizance of the affair from time to time, with no unpleased expression.

I had got thus far in my career of observation when our hostess for the day came to tell us that tea was ready, and we arose stiffly from the sward on which we had been sitting, and went indoors to the house-place. There, all round were ranged rows of sedate matrons; some with babies, some without; they had been summoned from over mountains, and beyond wild fells, and across deep dales, to the shearing of that day, just as their ancestors were called out by the Fiery Cross.[11] We were conducted to a tea-table, at which, in spite of our entreaties, no one would sit down except our hostess, who poured out tea, of which more by-and-by. Behind us, on the dresser, were plates piled up with "berry-cake" (puff-paste with gooseberries inside), currant and plain bread and butter, hot cakes buttered with honey (if that is not Irish), and great pieces of new cheese to be put in between the honeyed slices, and so toasted impromptu. There were two black teapots on the

9. Gaskell inverts somewhat the order in which these groups are mentioned in Psalms 148:11–12.

10. Charles Kingsley (1819–1875) was an Anglican cleric who was a friend of Gaskell and an admirer of her writing. (Her *Mary Barton* influenced Kingsley's most famous work, *Alton Locke, Tailor and Poet: An Autobiography*, a novel concerned with the Chartist movement.) In 1848, Kingsley had published *The Saint's Tragedy*, a play about Saint Elizabeth of Hungary.

11. A cross or T-shaped staff, which seems to have antedated the Christian period but which readily merged with Christian traditions, was used to signal the calling of clan members together.

tray, and taking one of these in her left hand, and one in her right, our hostess held them up both on high, and skilfully poured from each into one and the same cup; the teapots contained green and black tea, and this was her way of mixing them, which she considered far better, she told us, than if both the leaves had been "masked" together. The cups of tea were dosed with lump upon lump of the finest sugar, but the rich yellow fragrant cream was dropped in but very sparingly. I reserved many of my inquiries, suggested by this Dale tea-drinking, to be answered by Mrs C., with whom we were lodging: and I asked her why I could neither get cream enough for myself, nor milk sufficient for the children, when both were evidently so abundant, and our entertainers so profusely hospitable. She told me, that my request for each was set down to modesty and a desire to spare the "grocer's stuff," which, as costing money, was considered the proper thing to force upon visitors, while the farm produce was reckoned too common and everyday for such a choice festivity and such honoured guests. So I drank tea as strong as brandy and as sweet as syrup, and had to moan in secret over my children's nerves. My children found something else to moan over before the meal was ended; the good farmer's wife would give them each "sweet butter" on their oat-cake or "clap-bread"; and sweet butter is made of butter, sugar, and rum melted together and potted, and is altogether the most nauseous compound in the shape of a dainty I ever tasted. My poor children thought it so, as I could tell by their glistening piteous eyes and trembling lips, as they vainly tried to get through what their stomachs rejected. I got it from them by stealth and ate it myself, in order to spare the feelings of our hostess, who, evidently, considered it as a choice delicacy. But no sooner did she perceive that they were without sweet butter than she urged them to take some more, and bade me not scrimp it, for they had enough and to spare for everybody. This "sweet butter" is made for express occasions—the clippings, and Christmas; and for these two seasons all christenings in a family are generally reserved. When we had eaten and eaten—and, hungry as we were, we found it difficult to come up to our hostess's ideas of the duty before us—she took me into the real working kitchen, to show me the preparations going on for the refreshment of the seventy people there and then assembled. Rounds of beef, hams, fillets of veal, and legs of mutton bobbed, indiscriminately with plum puddings, up and down in a great boiler, from which a steam arose, when she lifted up the lid, reminding one exceedingly of Camacho's wedding.[12] The resemblance was increased when we were shown another boiler out of doors, placed over a temporary framework of brick, and equally full with the other, if, indeed, not more so.

Just at this moment—as she and I stood on the remote side of the farmbuildings, within sound of all the pleasant noises which told of merry life so near, and yet out of sight of any of them, gazing forth on the moorland and the rocks, and the purple crest of the mountain, the opposite base of which fell into Watendlath—

---

12. In *Don Quixote* by Miguel Cervantes (1547–1616), Camacho is a very wealthy farmer who sets forth a sumptuous wedding banquet to celebrate his marriage; his bride, however, is stolen by another.

the gate of the yard was opened, and my rustic beauty came rushing in, her face all a-fire. When she saw us she stopped suddenly, and was about to turn, when she was followed, and the entrance blocked up by the handsome young shearer. I saw a knowing look on my companion's face, as she quietly led me out by another way.

"Who is that handsome girl?" asked I.

"It's just Isabel Crosthwaite," she replied. "Her mother is a cousin of my master's, widow of a statesman near Appleby. She is well to do, and Isabel is her only child."

"Heiress, as well as beauty," thought I; but all I said was, "And who is the young man with her?"

"That," said she, looking up at me with surprise. "That's our Tom. You see, his father and me and Margaret Crosthwaite have fixed that these young ones are to wed each other; and Tom is very willing—but she is young and skittish; but she'll come to—she'll come to. He'll not be the best shearer this day anyhow, as he was last year down in Buttermere; but he'll maybe come round for next year."

So spoke middle age of the passionate loves of the young. I could fancy that Isabel might resent being so calmly disposed of, and I did not like or admire her the less because by-and-by she plunged into the very midst of the circle of matrons, as if in the Eleusinian circle[13] she could alone obtain a sanctuary against her lover's pursuit. She looked so much and so truly annoyed that I disliked her mother, and thought the young man unworthy of her, until I saw the mother come and take into her arms a little orphan child, whom I learnt she had bought from a beggar on the roadside that was ill-using her. This child hung about the woman, and called her "Mammy" in such pretty trusting tones, that I became reconciled to the matchmaking widow, for the sake of her warm heart; and as for the young man— the woe-begone face that he presented from time to time at the open door, to be scouted and scolded thence by all the women, while Isabel resolutely turned her back upon him, and pretended to be very busy cutting bread and butter, made me really sorry for him; though we—experienced spectators—could see the end of all this coyness and blushing as well as if we were in church at the wedding.

From four to five o'clock on a summer's day is a sort of second noon for heat; and now that we were up on this breezy height, it seemed so disagreeable to think of going once more into the close woods down below, and to brave the parched and dusty road, that we gladly and lazily resigned ourselves to stay a little later, and to make our jolly three o'clock tea serve for dinner.

So I strolled into the busy yard once more, and by watching my opportunity, I crossed between men, women, boys, sheep, and barking dogs, and got to an old man, sitting under the sycamore, who had been pointed out to me as the owner of the sheep and the farm. For a few minutes he went on, doggedly puffing away; but I knew that this reserve on his part arose from no want of friendliness, but from the

---

13. Gaskell refers here to the ancient mystery religion of the Greeks, the Eleusinian rites. That the rites were sacred to the earth goddess Demeter and her daughter Persephone, recovered from the underworld, would seem pertinent here in light of the concern with Mrs. Crosthwaite and her daughter Isabel; whatever other connection Gaskell might have had in mind is not apparent.

shy reserve which is the characteristic of most Westmoreland and Cumberland people. By-and-by he began to talk, and he gave me much information about his sheep. He took a "walk" from a landowner with so many sheep upon it; in his case one thousand and fifty, which was a large number, about six hundred being the average. Before taking the "walk," he and his landlord each appointed two "knowledgeable people" to value the stock. The "walk" was taken on lease of five or seven years, and extended ten miles over the Fells in one direction—he could not exactly say how far in another, but more; yes! certainly more. At the expiration of the lease, the stock are again numbered, and valued in the same way. If the sheep are poorer, and gone off, the tenant has to pay for their depreciation in money; if they have improved in quality, the landlord pays him; but one way or another the same number must be restored, while the increase of each year, and the annual fleeces form the tenant's profit. Of course they were all of the black-faced or mountain breed, fit for scrambling and endurance, and capable of being nourished by the sweet but scanty grass that grew on the Fells. To take charge of his flock he employed three shepherds, one of whom was my friend Tom. They had other work down on the farm, for the farm was "down" compared with the airy heights to which these sheep will scramble. The shepherd's year begins before the twentieth of March, by which time the ewes must be all safely down in the home pastures, at hand in case they or their lambs require extra care at yeaning time.[14] About the sixteenth of June the sheep washing begins. Formerly, said my old man, men stood barelegged in a running stream, dammed up so as to make a pool, which was more cleansing that any still water, with its continual foam, and fret, and struggle to overcome the obstacle that impeded its progress: and these men caught the sheep, which were hurled to them by the people on the banks, and rubbed them and soused them well; but now (alas! for these degenerate days) folk were content to throw them in head downwards, and thought that they were washed enough with swimming to the bank. However, this proceeding was managed in a fortnight after the shearing or clipping came on; and people were bidden to it from twenty miles off or better; but not as they had been fifty years ago. Still, if a family possessed a skilful shearer in the person of a son, or if the good wife could fold fleeces well and deftly, they were sure of a gay week in clipping time, passing from farm to farm in merry succession, giving their aid, feasting on the fat of the land ("sweet butter" amongst other things, and much good may it do them!) until they in their turn called upon their neighbours for help. In short, good old-fashioned sheep-shearings are carried on much in the same sort of way as an American Bee.[15]

As soon as the clipping is over, the sheep are turned out upon the Fells, where their greatest enemy is the fly. The ravens do harm to the young lambs in May and June, and the shepherds scale the steep grey rocks to take a raven's nest with infinite zest and delight; but no shepherd can save his sheep from the terrible fly—the

---

14. Yeaning is giving birth; the word is used almost exclusively for goats and sheep.

15. A "bee" or "been" was a response (or "boon") to a request for assistance. The word developed to mean a gathering of individuals to help others through cooperative work.

common flesh fly—which burrows in the poor animal, and lays its obscene eggs, and the maggots eat it up alive. To obviate this as much as ever they can, the shepherds go up on the Fells about twice a week in summer, and, sending out their faithful dogs, collect the sheep into great circles, the dogs running on the outside and keeping them in. The quick-eyed shepherd stands in the midst, and, if a sheep make an effort to scratch herself, the dog is summoned, and the infected sheep brought up to be examined, the piece cut out, and salved. But, notwithstanding this, in some summers scores of sheep are killed in this way: thundery and close weather is peculiarly productive of this plague. The next operation which the shepherd has to attend to is about the middle or end of October, when the sheep are brought down to be salved, and an extra man is usually hired on the farm for this week. But it is no feasting or merry-making time like a clipping. Sober business reigns. The men sit astride on their benches and besmear the poor helpless beast with a mixture of tar and bad butter, or coarse grease, which is supposed to promote the growth and fineness of the wool, by preventing skin diseases of all kinds, such as would leave a patch bare. The mark of ownership is renewed with additional tar and raddle, and they are sent up once more to their breezy walk, where the winter winds begin to pipe and blow, and to call away their brethren from the icy North. Once a week the shepherds go up and scour the Fells, looking over the sheep, and seeing how the herbage lasts. And this is the dangerous and wild time for the shepherds. The snows and the mists (more to be dreaded even than snow) may come on; and there is no lack of tales, about the Christmas hearth, of men who have gone up to the wild and desolate Fells and have never been seen more, but whose voices are yet heard calling on their dogs, or uttering fierce despairing cries for help; and so they will call till the end of time, till their whitened bones have risen again.

Towards the middle of January, great care is necessary, as by this time the sheep have grown weak and lean with lack of food, and the excess of cold. Yet as the mountain sheep will not eat turnips, but must be fed with hay, it is a piece of economy to delay beginning to feed them as long as possible; and to know the exact nick of time, requires as much skill as must have been possessed by Emma's father in Miss Austen's delightful novel,[16] who required his gruel "thin, but not too thin—thick, but not too thick." And so the Shepherd's Calendar[17] works round to yeaning time again! It must be a pleasant employment; reminding one of Wordsworth's lines—

> In that fair clime, the lonely herdsman stretched
> On the soft grass, through half the summer's day, &c.[18]

16. Jane Austen (1775–1817) published *Emma* the year before she died; the heroine's father is a querulous hypochondriac.

17. In 1579, Edmund Spenser (?1552–1599) dedicated *Shepheardes Calendar* to his fellow poet Sir Philip Sidney (1554–1586). The nineteenth-century "ploughman poet" John Clare (1793–1864) also published a work titled *The Shepherd's Calendar*.

18. The lines are from Wordsworth's *The Excursion* 4.851–52 and describe the response of an ancient Greek shepherd to "rural solitude."

and of shepherd boys with their reedy pipes, taught by Pan,[19] and of the Chaldean[20] shepherds studying the stars; of Poussin's[21] picture of the Good Shepherd, of the "Shepherds keeping watch by night!" and I don't know how many other things, not forgetting some of Cooper's[22] delightful pieces.

While I was thus rambling on in thought, my host was telling me of the prices of wool that year, for we had grown quite confidential by this time. Wool was sold by the stone; he expected to get ten or twelve shillings a stone; it took three or four fleeces to make a stone: before the Australian wool[23] came in, he had got twenty shillings, ay and more; but now—and again we sighed over the degeneracy of the times, till he took up his pipe (not Pandean) for consolation, and I bethought me of the long walk home, and the tired little ones, who must not be worried. So, with much regret, we took our leave; the fiddler had just arrived as we were wishing goodbye; the shadow of the house had overspread the yard; the boys were more in number than the sheep that remained to be shorn; the busy women were dishing up great smoking rounds of beef; and in addition to all the provision I had seen in the boilers, large-mouthed ovens were disgorging berry pies without end, and rice-puddings stuck full of almonds and raisins.

As we descended the hill, we passed a little rustic bridge with a great alder bush near it. Underneath sat Isabel, as rosy red as ever, but dimpling up with smiles, while Tom lay at her feet, and looked up into her eyes; his faithful sheep-dog sat by him, but flapped his tail vainly in hope of obtaining some notice. His master was too much absorbed for that. Poor Fly! Every dog has his day, and yours was not this tenth of July.

19. Pan is the primary woodland deity, the Greek god of wild nature and of shepherds; he is associated with the music of reeds and pipes, and, in traditional bucolic poems, shepherds play such pipes in contests.

20. The Chaldeans were an ancient culture based near the Euphrates river; they have traditionally been associated with both astronomical and astrological lore.

21. Nicholas Poussin (1594–1665) was a French painter who often took scriptural stories as his subjects.

22. Thomas Sidney Cooper (1803–1902) was a nineteenth-century landscape painter; he should not be confused with Thomas Cooper the Chartist activist and author (1805–1892); see his story "Seth Thompson, the Stockinger" in part 3.

23. By mid-century, wool exported by Australian colonists to England began to compete seriously with domestically grown wool, depressing the prices that British sheep farmers could get for their product.

F. D. MAURICE

F. D. Maurice—(John) Frederick Denison Maurice—(1805–1872) is recognized by students of Victorian painting as one of the two prominent contemplative figures (Thomas Carlyle is the other) in Ford Madox Brown's *Work* (see Figure 1.1); that he should figure so conspicuously in this painting suggests the honor in which his contemporaries held him for his championship of workers and their aspirations. Maurice was one of the more controversial clerics of the nineteenth century, partly because he voiced concern about overly literal understanding of Scriptural pronouncements and partly because he insisted upon the social responsibility of the Church to alleviate the distressed condition of the working classes. Sometimes credited with coining the phrase "Christian socialism," regarded at mid-century as an oxymoron, Maurice certainly was the best-known advocate of an activism that involved the fusion of socialist attitudes (usually construed as anti-religious) with Christian ethics (generally assumed to be at odds with socialism). In the late 1840s, during and after the final dismissal by Parliament of The People's Charter (see part 3), Maurice became the moral force behind a concerted effort to defuse workers' political dissatisfactions by demonstrating the benevolent interest of the upper classes in the lives of common laborers, employed and unemployed. He helped found Queen's College for Women, inaugurated a Society for Promoting Working Men's Associations, authored some and edited others of the *Tracts on Christian Socialism,* oversaw production of the short-lived journal *The Christian Socialist,* urged the creation of provident societies, and promoted the idea of settlement houses. Most notably, he founded, in 1854, the London Working Men's College, for which he served as the first principal.

The Working Men's College was designed to provide artisans and laborers with opportunities for humane and liberal education. Operated almost entirely on a volunteer basis and set forth as a cooperative venture between teachers and students, the college offered evening lecture series and discussion groups on a variety of subjects. Maurice, Ford Madox Brown, Frederic Harrison, John Ruskin, F. J. Furnival, Charles Kingsley, Dante Gabriel Rossetti, Thomas Hughes, and Leslie Stephen were among those who taught at the college. Desiring to have classes available also for women, Maurice appointed a young Octavia Hill as an additional teacher and administrator for women. The college was most pointedly not to be a trades school; the emphasis was to be entirely upon studies that would develop the intellectual and moral understanding of those working men involved in the project. In the dedication (to John Malcolm Ludlow, Maurice's fellow Christian Socialist) of

Learning and Working, a collection of lectures delivered in 1854 and published the following year, from which "The Studies of a Working College" is taken, Maurice articulates both his understanding of the importance of working-class education and his sense that such education should stress both the humanity and the social responsibility of workers and of all men:

> We have neither of us ever doubted that the whole country must look for its blessings through the elevation of its Working Class, that we all must sink if that is not raised. We have never dreamed that that class could be benefited by losing its working character, by acquiring habits of ease or self-indulgence. We have rather thought that *all* must learn the dignity of labour and the blessing of self-restraint. We could not talk to suffering men of intellectual or moral improvement, without first taking an interest in their physical conditions and their ordinary occupation; but we felt that any interest of this kind would be utterly wasted, that it would do harm and not good, if it were not the means of leading them to regard themselves as human beings made in the image of God. We have never thought that we could help them to be individually wise or individually good, if we forgot that they were social beings, bound to each other by the ties of family, neighbourhood, country, and by a common humanity.

The idealism evident in Maurice's comments about the goals for the college is reflected more particularly in his specification of what studies should define a working men's institution. Music, art, ethics, language—all should be the concern of the artisan and the laborer. Maurice had no gift for organization and sometimes regarded formal associations and parties as aberrations, complaining about them as "machinery"; the administration of the Working Men's College soon passed to others, but the vision of what such an institution might be and what working men might aspire to become was very much the product of Maurice's ardent moral convictions.

From *Learning and Working*

Lecture V
The Studies in a Working College

I said in my last Lecture[1] that the ends which we should propose to ourselves in the Education of working men, and of all men, were to give them Freedom and

1. The title of Maurice's previous lecture was "Learning the Ministry of Freedom and Order."

Order. Of course, I know how little worth there is in either of these words, so long as it is a mere word. Freedom and Order have become, may continue to be—symbols for stump orators and election placards. Either symbol may stand as a representative of most mischievous and hateful acts and principles. We all remember what Madame Roland said about the first as she went to execution; surely there are hundreds lying in Italian prisons[2] who could utter a still deeper groan about the crimes that have been perpetrated in the other name. To speak of them in connexion with Education, I assume that they can be redeemed from the service of the platform and the hustings;[3] that they can find a living, intelligible, practical signification; that they can be wrenched out of the hands of the anarchist and the despot, (perhaps it is a blunder to distinguish names which are always found at last to denote the same thing,) and can be turned against them. If we have that purpose in view, the more habitually we remember it, the more plainly we avow it, the better it will be for us and for those whom we teach. I say for myself, that I do not care for Education in the least except so far as I believe it will contribute to these results.

I tried to show you that our Grammar-schools and Universities nominally aim at these objects, much more than at communicating any greater or less amount of teaching; that this is the justification we commonly put forth for them; that all true and effectual reformers have laboured to bring them back to this standard, to make them real instruments in emancipating the spirits of the students, and in giving them a sense of Order. We have stated the case to ourselves thus:—"These boys will hereafter have to toil in some profession or other, as statesmen, as soldiers, as sailors, as landlords, as cultivators of the land, as lawyers, as physicians, as divines. God forbid that they should not toil! God forbid that they should become idlers in the land! But they may become drudges instead of workers. They will, unless they are men as well as workers. Then their work will be free, brave, intelligent. The practice of their professions will be honourable, the science of them will be expanded. If they are swallowed up in their work,—if they think of themselves only as landlords, as soldiers, as sailors, as physicians,—the profession will sink into a craft; its mercenary ends will be chiefly regarded. It will lose its old dignity, it will conquer no new regions of thought and experience. Therefore, for the sake of Work, let us have an education which has not merely a reference to Work."

We have been so vehement in these assertions, that we have even exaggerated the application of them, and so have weakened their effect. We have so much

2. Jeanne-Marie Roland (née Phlipon) (1754–1793), a socially and intellectually brilliant daughter of a Paris engraver, married an older courtier and became prominent (perhaps more so than her husband) in the early period of the French Revolution. She gathered around herself a politically significant salon of the moderate republican Girondists over whom she exercised considerable influence. In subsequent strife among leaders of different factions, she was denounced by the revolutionary leader Jean Paul Marat (1743–1793) and arrested at the order of the radical Maximilien Robespierre (1758–1794). She was condemned to the guillotine, and her last words reportedly were, "Liberty! What crimes are committed in your name." Maurice goes on to refer to repressions in Italy following the failure of the Revolution of 1848.

3. The term for the platform on which, until 1872, candidates for political office stood when they were being nominated to serve in Parliament.

dreaded to make the Education of our Schools and Universities professional, that we have kept it at a wide, almost hopeless, distance from professional life. So those effects have followed which I spoke of in my first Lecture. The higher adult Education, that which our ancestors described by the word Faculties, that from which our Universities started, and which is their proper characteristic, has been buried under the mere school education. The teaching of boys has given the tone and form to the discipline which should direct the thoughts of men, when they are about to plunge into the business of the world. Hence that business has become, unhappily, divorced from the previous study. It is in danger of becoming a mere absorbing practice. The springs which should have fed it have been choked up or diverted elsewhere. I rejoice to think that we have suffered less from these causes than we might reasonably have expected. There is, I am sure, among the professional men of England a manliness and nobleness that are scarcely to be found anywhere. Every one of us must have had proofs in his intercourse with physicians of their freedom from sordid feelings—proofs to be recollected with silent gratitude and humiliation.[4] Those who have conversed much with lawyers, will readily acknowledge that the generous and high-minded judge, who was as dear to the scholar as to the lawyer, and whose dying words entitle him to the love of the working-people as much as of either, was not an exception in his order, but a specimen of what it may produce. And yet I gather from the lamentations I have heard among the members of these noble professions, how much they fear lest the science of medicine or of law, being separated from other sciences, and from the studies which belong to humanity, should be crushed under the details of business, lest their own lives should yield to the same oppression. I have no doubt that some of these evils are counteracted by that which they often find very inconvenient, the grumbling of patients and suitors, whose demands, often ignorant no doubt, but expressing real wants, force them to reflect upon their traditional habits and rules in connexion with the general interests of mankind, and with the principles of their science, from which any reformation that is not hasty and mischievous must begin. Still greater benefits may arise to these professions—and to another that is liable to more flagrant abuses and perversions from the idols of the cave and of the market place—if the Universities, stimulated by the Legislature, make a serious effort to revive their adult lore, so carrying into effect their own true faith that all particular branches of knowledge should be subject to a comprehensive human culture. But the greatest good of all to Law, Physic, and Divinity, may be expected, as I think, if lawyers, physicians, and divines, determine in their hearts that the hand workers shall not be mere drudges more than themselves, that they also shall be taught how to work as men, that they shall have such Freedom and such an Order as no arrangements of society, without a spirit to direct them and the men who compose the society, can ever give.

When we had settled these to be ends of our teaching, we were less scandalised and discouraged than we should otherwise have been, by some discoveries which

4. Humility.

were made to us respecting the tastes and inclinations of the working people themselves. It was a curious, and at first a very startling fact, that they apparently preferred musical instruction to any other we could afford them. Almost any lessons would have seemed more practical, more suitable to their appointed tasks, than these. With the little time they have for acquiring information, how strange, how perplexing, that they should fix their affections upon a pursuit which, after considerable labour, could return them so little. But possibly their instinct is sounder than our criticism. They may have discovered the very truth which we have nearly forgotten; their welcoming of music may be a sign that they want something deeper and better than all mere indoctrination. The fact, it seemed to me, ought not to be overlooked. I was as much disposed to complain of it as any one could be: but it is of no use to complain of facts; we must adjust ourselves to them as we can. If we do not adjust ourselves to them, I believe our Education will not be worth having.

It would indeed be a very hasty inference from this observation, that music is the only study or the chief study which we are to offer our people facilities for learning. I have already told you that not a few of them, under every possible disadvantage, have devoted themselves to Mathematics, and that the works they were engaged in have given them an interest in the study which they would not otherwise have had. Cases of their giving themselves to languages may be rarer, but unquestionably they are to be found. The authoress of "Mary Barton,"[5] the most satisfactory of all witnesses, testifies to the existence of learned botanists and ento-mologists among the Manchester spinners. How many of those who have devised our greatest engineering wonders have begun in the workshop, I believe we are scarcely aware. The profoundest scientific chemists have been servants in the labor-atory. I believe the statistics of the most popular lecture rooms which the working people frequent, would show that history and poetry are subjects on which they es-pecially like to hear discourses. I need not speak of the impulse to oratory, which exists certainly as much in them as in any class of the community. And no one can have listened to any of their speeches, without seeing how many ethical and meta-physical as well as political theories are seething in their brains. What, therefore, I gather from the willingness they have shown to receive musical instruction, is (1.) That all the other instruction should speak to them as this does, less as distin-guished by particular occupations, than as sharers of a common humanity, and as capable of entering into the feeling of it, in spite of their different pursuits, or by means of them. (2.) That it being regarded as the great end of studies to raise and cultivate that which is human, the arbitrary division of them into useful and entertaining should be discarded as illogical and embarrassing. (3.) That they should have a considerable number of studies presented to them, out of which they may choose the one or two which have most attractions for them. (4.) That though

5. Writer Elizabeth Cleghorn Gaskell (1810–1865) addressed in some of her novels problems en-countered by the working classes. In 1848, she published *Mary Barton: A Tale of Manchester Life,* a novel dealing with social abuses endured by the working classes during the Hungry Forties. See the introduction to her "Cumberland Sheep-Shearers," immediately preceding in this section.

they never should be invited to devote more time to any studies than is compatible with their ordinary occupations, they should be led to perceive that there is a relation between all studies; that the boundary lines between them are often artificial and imaginary; that when they are most real, and when it is most needful to distinguish between their objects and their spheres, they again blend together when they are contemplated in reference to our lives and duties.

I could not even venture to speak of a course of studies for a College of Working Men, without making these preliminary remarks. For you will be ready to exclaim—"Course of studies! what a wild dream is this! Here are ignorant, untrained men, with an hour or two which they can with great difficulty snatch out of a day of extreme toil, and you fancy that you can give them a regular systematic indoctrination in a dozen or fifteen subjects, to understand any one of which would require all the wits of ordinary people of our class, who have had a preparatory discipline of many years." I am guilty of no such monstrous extravagances. I am going to speak of various branches of knowledge, between which I feel there is a close inward connexion. I wish the working man to understand that there is this connexion. But I would have him understand it, not by plunging into all these studies together, or even into one after another, but by learning under a teacher who feels the connexion himself; who is in friendly and continual intercourse with other teachers, each trying to initiate his pupils into the subject with which he is most familiar. I allow for the short time, the very short time, which the working man is able to give to any subject. I do not anticipate the day, which, nevertheless, I trust our children will see, if we do not, when Mr. Wilson's[6] principle will be carried out to its full extent, when the Factory shall become the College, when Working and Learning shall be regarded as inseparable. I take things as I find them. The hard won evening hours are all I ask for. I do not wish the married man—I do not expect the bachelor—to give up half or a third of these to the college. What I think he may do, if there is a subject which has already some hold upon him, or which he wishes for any reason to take hold of, is to come for the hour or hour and a half, when that subject is taught, week after week. He can, if he likes and if he lives, spread his lessons over a much wider tract of years than the ordinary student in a University; since he is not preparing for work, but in the midst of work. The Degree need not terminate his career, as it does that of the other; he may, therefore, make some amends for a little time at first, by the greater time afterwards. But he may make much better amends than this, if he is really awake and interested in that which he is about. He may speak of it at home with his wife and children; he may think of it, and even, as the mathematical students I alluded to are in the habit of doing, read about it, when his work is merely mechanical. And then when he feels that his mind is freer and more orderly for this part of learning, and if he has seen something on the right or left of it which is needed to bring out the full sense of it, he may betake himself to that, or he may work with dogged pertinacity in his own original mine, till he has brought out

6. George Wilson was an activist who, in the 1840s, served as head of the Anti-Corn-Law League.

some of its deeper and more hidden treasures. I have said thus much about the teachers, and the way in which I would have them think and work together, each keeping his own calling directly before him, each growing into a respect for his neighbour's calling and curing himself of his exclusiveness, because I could not well separate it from the topic which is before us now. But I reserve for my final Lecture the consideration of the class from which the teaching body should be taken, of the form which should be given to it, of the relation in which it should stand to the learners. My business now is to enumerate the subjects which I suppose we are warranted in offering to a body of working men, as being likely on one ground or another to engage their sympathies, and as fitted to elevate them individually and socially.

The first I shall speak of, is one which you might fancy I should keep to the last, as being very difficult and dangerous to handle, if I were not prudent enough to omit it altogether. There can be no doubt that the subject of Politics has an interest for a large body of English workmen which no other subject has. That is the reason why it is banished from many institutions which seek to do them good.[7] "We do not want," it is said, "questions which set men at war. Education is designed to make the mind calm and sober. Confine yourselves to physics; there is no excitement and passion. Once venture on the other ground, and you are in the midst of smoke; a smoke which betokens that there is fire if it has not yet burst out."

There are some who feel the force of this remark, and yet who half suspect that you do not clear away the smoke or put out the fire, by pretending not to observe them. They think political instruction should be given, but under another name. "Why may we not teach what is needful to be known of Politics in the form of History? We do in fact communicate much political information to school-boys when we read Livy or Tacitus[8] with them. Working men who are likely to frequent a college will learn what they want or can receive respecting the present from the newspaper; our business is to give them tidings respecting the past, of which they have as yet only a very loose and incorrect impression." I feel all the temptations to adopt this mode of escaping from the difficulty. I know what plausible and strong arguments there are for avoiding a name, which often alarms quiet people more than the most terrible things. But I am satisfied that these risks ought to be incurred, and that an Education such as I am proposing for men, will fail altogether of its object, if it does not teach Politics; if it does not give great prominence to them; if it attempts to disguise the purpose by any subterfuge whatever. Unquestionably I wish the working men to feel that they are studying Politics when they are studying History; I wish them to think of the past and to learn the

---

7. The practice of excluding politics from new institutions of learning continued late into the nineteenth century. Worth comparing with Maurice's ideas are those set forth by Thomas Henry Huxley (1825–1895) in "Science and Culture" (1880), wherein Huxley approves of the exclusion of certain studies from the new Scientific College at Birmingham: "Party politics are forbidden to enter the minds of either [administrators or teachers], so far as the work of the College is concerned; theology is as sternly banished from its precincts; and finally, it is especially declared that the College shall make no provision for 'mere literary instruction and education.'"

8. Livy (59 B.C.E.–17 C.E.) and Tacitus (55–117) were Roman historians.

lessons of the past. I rejoice to believe that our English boys are learning politics, and not merely Latin and Greek, from Tacitus and Thucydides;[9] they will learn still more of politics, I suspect, from the Bible, if they read it with open eyes. But I have to remark, once for all, that we never can teach men as we teach boys, let their previous deficiencies be what they may. You will all remember the passage in Guy Mannering,[10] where Dominie Sampson in his first rapture at receiving Mr. Henry Bertram, the pupil who had been lost at five years old and had come back at twenty-two, tells him how much his sister has been learning in the interval, and proposes to begin again with him from the first rudiments of grammar. Now there was nothing ridiculous in this proposition according to school notions. There was a reasonable presumption that Mr. Bertram, who had been roughing it in the world, was rather rusty in his accidence,[11] if he had been lucky enough to have meddled with it at all, after he fell among the smugglers. Since sound knowledge requires a sound foundation, the Dominie had a fair excuse for suggesting that he should resume his studies where he had left them off. Why then did the clear worldly sense of Sir Walter Scott perceive something exquisitely humorous in this scheme of the tutor? why has he made his readers laugh at it more even than at his exorcism of Meg Merrilies? Because we feel instinctively that a man has rights, has a knowledge, has a position, which must be taken for granted, and respected; that he must under no circumstances be put on a first form, and turned into a child. You cannot do it; you have no business to attempt it. The world has been teaching him—I must add with all reverence, God has been teaching him—whatever you have been doing. To overlook that fact, is simply to deprive yourself of the best opportunity of delivering him from the ignorance which cleaves to him.

I am not at all sure that we have not been too indifferent to the present, in our teaching of boys; that we have not far too much ignored the amount of incoherent information which they have received from conversation and newspapers, and have not failed to connect that with the work of the schoolroom. I find the most intelligent schoolmasters are beginning to adopt that opinion, and to alter their practice in conformity with it. And I think that by doing so, they will help to bring about one of the most desirable and necessary of all reforms.

It has become the fashion even at our public schools to give the pupils extracts from great authors, for the sake of the language, rather than the authors themselves. So they are driven to learn what is called their History from outlines and epitomes.[12] The moment we begin to regard History as the interpretation of the present by the past, these must prove utterly unavailing; Livy and Xenophon[13]

---

9. Thucydides (471–400 B.C.E.) was a Greek historian.

10. *Guy Mannering* is a novel published in 1815 by Sir Walter Scott (1771–1832); Meg Merrilies, mentioned subsequently, is the old gypsy woman in the novel.

11. *Accidence* refers to the placing of distinctive endings upon words in an inflected language such as Latin or Greek.

12. Abstracts.

13. Xenophon (434–355 B.C.E.) was a Greek historian.

must resume their place as teachers; Mr. Pinnock's Catechisms may be used to light our fires, since they have no light in themselves.

I think, then, that instead of binding ourselves by precedents drawn from the teaching of children, we may rather hope greatly to benefit that teaching by following out the method which is obviously the most suitable for men. To make our working people aware of the treasures which they possess in the history of the country, I would begin with the topics that are most occupying us in this day. No doubt these are party topics,—that is to say, each party in the country has its own views upon them. You may make that an excuse for passing them by, and for talking upon some subject upon which all people agree, or seem to agree. You may say, "There is a Tory tradition about this point, and a Whig tradition. I find these working people rather impatient of both, inclined to take up with some Radical opinion which they fancy is not traditional. It is much better to move the previous question, and discourse of air-pumps and gases." What is the effect? The most active and energetic thoughts of the minds with which you have to deal, are those which you do not meet, which you leave to the sport of any chance influence. You say to the most vigorous man,—"Your vigour is in our way; we had rather you were stupid or asleep; and we will try to find some part of you which is not alive, that we may address ourselves to that." It would be better to take any course, even what I should think the narrowest, than this. Give them your Tory traditions or your Whig traditions; enforce them by the most passionate declamation, by the most onesided exhibition of facts. Bring up your fierce Radicalism to confound both. In any of these ways you will do something; you will often irritate the man's faith, you will often outrage his conscience; perhaps you will find that you are not dealing very fairly with your own; but at least you will kindle some emotions, with which good will mix as well as evil. You will not leave the man to the thought which is the worst of all for him and for you, that there is nothing common between him and you; that you do not care for the same things, that you are indifferent whether you are fellow-citizens, or deadly foes.

I believe, indeed, that there is a more excellent way than either—one which those who care to educate working men and to educate thinking men, more than to propagate their opinions, will find. I believe that they will be able to point out the great and precious principles which have been vindicated by the Tory traditions and by the Whig traditions; the grievous loss which it would have been if either had been wanting to the land; the great and noble spirit which has gone forth in support of both. I believe that in justifying these, and in showing how, while apparently counteracting each other, they have nobly worked together for building up the nation, you would be able to point out far more clearly what have been the sins into which each party has fallen, and what reason each has afforded for the bitter complaints against it. You would then be able to explain, while confessing the good of both, while proving that good to be necessary for our time as well as for any past time, that there is a good which neither could effect, nor both together, and which we may effect if we profit by the wisdom of both, while we refuse to be bound by the exclusiveness of either. Thus a teacher may give the most cordial welcome to the convictions and hopes which he will find stirring in the hearts of the working men, and yet may bring the experience of history to remove their prejudices and diminish their asperities. This cannot be, if we do not come to the task with a willingness to have our own theories broken to pieces by facts; desirous to find men, better than we have supposed them to be; determined that what is right and true must be mightier and must show itself to be mightier than we and all other men are. This willingness, this determination, may grow weaker or firmer by practice. Nothing is so likely to weaken them as the habit of attacking others and apologising for ourselves. Nothing is so likely to strengthen them as the habit of bringing our thoughts into collision with those of men whom we wish to help, who will not take what we say for granted, who will often surprise us by their ignorance, often by showing us that they have got beyond our depth.

You may ask how I would begin with defining the subject which I propose should have such prominence; into how many portions I would divide it. I answer, I think if we begin with the topics to which we ordinarily give the name Political,—those topics that are most occupying our thoughts, foreign, domestic, economical, legal,—we shall arrive by degrees at the sense of the word; at the very sense of it which is indicated by its etymology; at the very sense which the greatest thinkers have seen in it, far more securely and satisfactorily than if we started with a formal definition, which would embarrass the student and separate the subject from his actual interests and sympathies. By the same method we shall get to perceive when Politics are dealing with human beings; when with the things which they work with or traffic with; when they are conversant about decrees; when with laws; when they are occupied with what is mutable, when with that which is fixed and eternal,—far better than if we introduced divisions at the outset which are likely to tie it down by maxims of ours, sometimes confounding what should be distinguished, sometimes separating what should be united. By this experimental course, we do justice to the ignorance and the knowledge both of ourselves and our pupils, and we may make a particular study the means of illustrating and cultivating the method which belongs to all studies.

That is one excuse for the disproportionate length at which I have spoken of this subject. Another is, that I have included in it much that I have to say on some other subjects which would else require a careful treatment. I shall not need to explain how I suppose the History of England, or of any other country in the modern or old world, ought to be presented to a body of workers; I have already shown that I look upon them all as deriving their interest and significance from the light which they throw upon our own noisy age, from the power which they give of looking into the heart of questions which we are all inclined to contemplate chiefly from the outside. And do not suppose that I am showing our forefathers any disrespect, or am forgetting that they had a life and battle of their own, because I claim them first of all as commentators upon us. On the contrary, I am sure they will come forth as living figures out of the canvass—they will put on flesh and blood again, and be seen, not merely in the costume of their own time, but surrounded with all its circumstances and interests, the actors in a true human drama, when we connect them with what we see and do and feel. Dr. Arnold,[14] in an admirable passage of his Lectures, dwells upon the good which he had got from Mitford's "Greece,"[15] not because the sentiments of the historian were just, or his statements of facts always credible, but because he wrote in a passion, because he denounced Pericles[16] with the same vehemence with which he would have denounced Mr. Fox.[17] So Dr. Arnold learnt that Pericles was not less an actual person, not more a shadow, than Mr. Fox. He could judge afterwards for himself what place he occupied among men, whether it was that which Mitford had assigned him or quite a different one; but hereafter a place he must have, not in a mausoleum, but among thinkers and workers. One ought to be thankful for the existence of the historical partisan, if he only produces one such actual believer in history as Arnold was. But the experience, I suspect, is not an uncommon one. We have all had to bless some one or other for making us know that we are reading of men and women when we are reading bound books. I think it is also Dr. Arnold who says that he owed much to the "Fortunes of Nigel"[18] for making him recollect that King James[19] talked broad Scotch. That is the kind of benefit which we have most of us derived from Sir Walter Scott. If we cannot always assure ourselves that his kings and queens, even that his ordinary ladies and gentlemen, had hearts beneath their robes, we have at least had one great difficulty removed. They did walk and talk; they had shoes and head-gear; they are not only to be found on coins. When we have got them so far brought into the region of humanity, Shakspeare will show us what they were, as well as what they wore; we begin to recognise with awe and almost trembling that nothing has departed or can depart; that words once spoken, thoughts once thought, have a permanence which man did not give them, and cannot take away from them.

To receive this impression even imperfectly, is to learn history,—to convey it, is to teach history. Englishmen can, I think, learn it and teach it in no other way; no men are more likely both to learn it and teach it again to us in that way, than our working people. It is one of the great blessings I expect from a free intercourse with them, that we shall be compelled to study all that we might look at as antiquarians

14. Thomas Arnold (1795–1842) was an historian and the noted educational reformer and headmaster of Rugby. As a prominent Broadchurchman, Arnold worked to secure within the Church of England ecumenical unity of Protestant denominations. See the selection from Thomas Hughes's *Tom Brown's Schooldays* in part 1.

15. William Mitford (1744–1827) was the author of *History of Greece*, quite popular in the first half of the nineteenth century.

16. Pericles (495–429 B.C.E.) was an Athenian statesman famous for his adroit political maneuvering and for his rhetorical eloquence; a more than able administrator, he suffered somewhat from scandalous stories spread about his personal life.

17. Charles James Fox (1749–1806) was a prominent and able late-eighteenth-century Whig politician whose personal life, not unlike that of Pericles, came under hostile scrutiny and was found wanting.

18. *The Fortunes of Nigel* was a novel published in 1822 by Sir Walter Scott (1771–1832).

19. James Stuart (1566–1625) was the Scots king who came to the English throne in 1603 at the death of his kinswoman Elizabeth Tudor (Elizabeth I).

or dilettanti, heartily and humanly. No men have appreciated more, none perhaps so much, the services which Mr. Carlyle[20] has rendered to history and biography, by giving substance and personality to names that had been mere watchwords of vague admiration or horror. Without his genius, we may, if we have battles to fight ourselves, understand a little how other men fought theirs; and the tougher and harder the fight is of the men whom we try to educate, the better they will enter into our meaning when we try to communicate it to them.

I need not speak of the value of places in giving an interest or reality to history, or of the rich store of topographical associations which the English workman, and especially the London workman, may possess, if there is any one to make him aware of his treasures. I can have no remark to make on that subject which has not been anticipated in Mr. Stanley's admirable Lecture at Exeter Hall.[21] But I would observe, in reference to the larger subject of geography, that I conceive all instruction upon it ought to start like our historical lessons from present topics and interests. If you begin with defining continents, and islands, and peninsulas, you will be falling into the Dominie Sampson method; if you take a map of the seat of the war, and comment upon it, the elements of the subject, which you may seem to have passed over, will gradually be acquired in the most satisfactory manner; and you may then go on to arrange and organize the knowledge you have communicated upon it as carefully as you will; the more order you can put into the student's mind the more grateful he will be to you.

In these last words I have indicated the rule which I should apply to all our studies, but which is specially important in reference to Ethics. What we want is not to put things into our pupils' minds, so much as to set in order what we find there, to untie knots, to disentangle complicated threads. I cannot conceive a stupider or a more useless task than that of prelecting[22] to a set of tired artisans, about the benevolent theory and the selfish theory of morals, about the Platonical ideas, and the Aristotelian mean, and the Benthamite[23] analysis of motives. But if there be in every artisan the seeds of all the theories of morals that have ever existed in the world; if you see these seeds bearing fruit in different parts of his practice; if he is the selfish man and the benevolent man, the idealist and the pursuer of compromises, the seeker of pleasure and the sufferer of pain a hundred times in the same week; then I know nothing more interesting, or that may be more useful,

---

20. Thomas Carlyle (1795–1881), perhaps best known as an essayist, social critic, and advocate of the value of work (see the introduction to his works in part 1), composed a celebrated *History of the French Revolution* (1837) as well as *Chartism* (1839) and *Past and Present* (1843); his biographical writings include various sketches worked up for *On Heroes, Hero-Worship and the Heroic in History* (1841), his edition of Oliver Cromwell's letters and speeches (1845), and, ultimately, *The History of Frederick II of Prussia called Frederick the Great* (1858–1865).

21. Arthur Penrhyn Stanley (1815–1881) was a Broadchurchman committed to the goals of Maurice's Christian Socialism, the biographer of Thomas Arnold, and a respected church historian.

Exeter Hall had served, for two decades before Maurice's founding of the Working Men's College, as a meeting place and lecture site for social reformers and philanthropists.

22. Lecturing publicly.

23. Reference to a follower of Jeremy Bentham (1748–1832), regarded as the founder of utilitarian theory.

than to follow out these different tracks to the point from which they arise and in which they terminate. The effort presumes some knowledge of what is going on in the minds of our pupils and in our own, together with a sense that it is very fragmentary, and needs to be increased by intercourse with them and with ourselves. It presumes also that we have sufficient faith in what we have hold of, to be willing that it should be subjected to all possible tests; and that we are quite certain that in no possible case shall we come at the discovery that wrong means right, and falsehood, truth. Like all efforts, it must be attended with much humiliation; but then what a reward! We shall feel, and we shall lead working men to feel, that there is a standing ground for their acts and their existence, a deeper and a firmer one than they or we had suspected. I can only repeat the hint about the text of our lessons, which I gave when I was speaking of Politics and History. It must be furnished by the topic in which we find that our students are taking the most direct interest, whatever that may be. We need care little what the occasion is, whether it seems an important or an insignificant one in our eyes. It cannot be insignificant if it is stirring the hearts of any number of people,—if it is deeply stirring the hearts of even the one or two we are conversing with. If they are attaching an extravagant consequence to some trivial point, we shall not make them think less of it, by treating them or it with scorn. We can only dispossess them of their exaggeration, by leading them from the paltry subject-matter to the principle which lies beneath it, and which really gives them their interest in it. When they have come into the daylight of a principle, they will perceive the relative magnitude of different objects which were distorted by the twilight and the morning mist. Another hint, which may serve to connect this subject with the last, is that questions concerning our relations with society commonly take stronger hold of men in our day than questions concerning individual morality, and that we therefore have a better chance of coming to ethics through politics, than to politics through ethics. I do not say which is abstractedly the best method; I do not know. That which answers its purpose best in any given time is the best for that time.

I must repeat again, because I know how much reasonable ridicule we expose ourselves to if the remark is not recollected, that in speaking of these studies, I am trying to find different channels through which we may reach different minds. I take the most general subjects first, those which may have an interest for a great number, if we do not mar them by our way of handling them. But I do not assume that all will care for political teaching, or all for ethical, or the same for both. I wish to explain how, if they should take but one, they would unawares be introduced to some of the lore which strictly appertains to the other. Lessons on Morals, I think, will be good for nothing if they are not illustrated from Biography and History; nay, if biography and history do not supply the substance of them. So also historical lessons will, in my judgment, be far less useful than they might be, if they are separated from Poetry and Painting. I should expect the plays of Shakspeare and the portraits in the National Gallery—supposing the College were in London—to supply continual suggestions to the Ethical lecturer. I should be surprised if he did not often take a play or a picture as the direct and formal subject of his lesson, and if he did not find that it served his end better than Paley or Stewart.[24] It must be clearly understood that in doing so, he would not be poaching on the manor of a teacher who undertook to give lessons on Painting or Poetry. I think there should be such lessons; they would meet a number of feelings which would be less open to the Ethical instructor. If he was jealous, he would as often have to complain of intrusions from the artists as they from him. I do not speak, of course, of direct lessons in Drawing, which are invaluable and indispensable on other grounds, but of teachings upon the principles of the art, or upon the productions of its masters. I presume also whenever the musical doctor proceeds beyond the mere practice of his art, there must be allusions to the character that chords and sounds denote, which would be in the strictest sense Ethical.

The reasons which I gave for the wonderful popularity of Abelard's[25] Lectures at Paris in the twelfth century, will be a sufficient defence for me, when I plead for offering instruction in Logic to our working classes. If I supposed I should be introducing them to a new subject, to one apart from all their previous thoughts and habits, I should be obliged, by the maxims which I have laid down, to reject it from our circle. But since the workers speak and think and reason, they are logicians in embryo: what they want in this, as in other cases, is to be taught what they are doing, to have their minds set in order about their own operations. I am far from sure that the person who undertook this task, knowing what it signified, and with a resolution to avoid pedantry, might not make his lessons popular as well as very profitable. I do not indeed anticipate a return of the middle age frenzy. I do not suppose that if Mr. Mill[26] announced a lecture on Universals at Drury Lane Theatre or Exeter Hall, there would be an instant rush for front boxes, and that tickets would be unprocurable. But the working man who has been used to vagueness often manifests such a delight in discovering lines and distinctions which were always existing, and which he had not perceived, as the student, tired of these lines and distinctions, and longing to fill them up with actual forms, cannot appreciate. Everything shows what a blessing each may be to the other.

The study of language has been *the* study of our English schools,—it has given them their name. You will feel at once that it cannot be pursued in a working College under the same conditions which we find in them. Latin and Greek can never be the *groundwork* of a mechanic's education. The love of intellectual acquisition for its own sake exists only in a few—the passion for philology only in one here and there; these generally find means of gratifying it, and are transported from the working class into the scholar class. For such cases we do not wish to provide, if we could. But does it follow that the objects which our Grammar-

24. William Paley (1743–1805) was the author of *Moral and Political Philosophy* (1785) and, more notably, *Evidences of Christianity* (1794) and *Natural Theology* (1802). Dugald Stewart (1753–1828) was Professor of Moral Philosophy at Edinburgh and the author of *Outlines of Moral Philosophy* (1793).

25. Pierre Abelard (1079–1142), more recognized by many for his famous love affair with Héloïse, was a noted rhetorician and philosopher. Maurice subsequently refers to "the [M]iddle [A]ge frenzy" to describe Abelard's popularity as a teacher which drew students to the University of Paris.

26. John Stuart Mill (1806–1873) was the famous English utilitarian philosopher and political activist. See the introductory essay to *The Subjection of Women* in part 4.

schools propose to themselves in their culture, are not objects which we should seek after, and which the working people themselves desire? The best good that any scholar gets from his Latin or Greek schooling is the reverence for words; a belief in their vitality and power; a capacity of tracing them from their roots through the different stages of their growth; a dread of the corruption which they contract both in the schools and the world; a lively pleasure in recovering them to their proper use, not only by observing that use in the best and most considerate writers, but also by listening to the speech of those who have retained some of their lost meanings in their provincialisms. All these benefits the scholar may owe to other tongues, but he turns them to the account of his own. He is not more fond of exotics, but more tenacious of the idioms, or at all events the principles, of his language, than other people. Why then can he not communicate what he has received, to those whose training must be chiefly in English? Why cannot he lead them to observe the etymologies, powers, and distinctions of the words which they are continually uttering; why may he not cultivate in them the respect for their own native speech, and the feeling of responsibility in the use of it, which he owes to his own discipline? I am far from thinking that some working men may not wish to learn another language besides their own—French, German, or Latin—and that they should not have facilities for doing so. But first of all, I would have special lessons upon words—the words which occur in the most familiar conversation, as well as on technical words; those which have the widest range and the greatest depth of signification. How much may be done in this way, is sufficiently proved by Mr. Trench's book on Words,[27] which arose out of lectures delivered to the elder boys in a parish school. The interest which the lectures excited among them, and their popularity among all classes of readers, show clearly enough that there is a demand for this kind of instruction, which might be satisfied if scholars could only do themselves the highest of all services, by consenting to become as little children.[28]

I shall have been greatly mistaken indeed, if I am supposed to undervalue physical studies because I have spoken at so much length of these human studies. Natural studies, it seems to me, have been unfairly treated in not being regarded as parts of a human discipline; as belonging, not to things only or chiefly, but to men. The highest of them all is surely that which we call, by way of eminence, Physiology; and this because it has a more direct relation to the human being than any other has. I believe there are the most obvious, practical reasons,—reasons which any benevolent man will at once recognise, why lessons on the human body should be given to working people, and should occupy a place above even those that touch most closely upon their occupations. This subject at once brings us into contact with the laws of health, with the conditions of the poor man's dwelling, therefore

27. Richard Chenevix Trench (1807–1886), friend of Maurice and archbishop of Dublin, authored *On the Study of Words* (1857); it was at Trench's prompting that the Oxford English Dictionary project was undertaken.
28. "And [Jesus] said, Verily I say unto you, Except ye be converted and become as little children, ye shall not enter into the kingdom of heaven" (Matthew 18:3).

with all those common things of which I was speaking in the last lecture. The experiences of the working man,—his bitterest sufferings,—show him the need he has of this culture; the reward of receiving it would be an admiration of the curious and wonderful frame which has been given him, and a higher sense of his own moral responsibility for the use of it. Such lessons would promote the objects which the Temperance Societies have at heart, better, perhaps, than any pledges.[29] A knowledge of the mischief and curse of drunkenness may be useful; but surely it is better for a man to know that he may be, and that all classes will help him in being, something better than an animal. For sottishness will always exist where there is despair: you will never cure it except by kindling hope.

When I was speaking of Mechanics' Institutes, I dwelt upon the necessity of teaching the class for whom they were originally designed, the laws upon which their Machines have been constructed, and which they obey; that is a way to show that the worker obeys another kind of laws himself. One cannot carry out the principle of Dr. Birkbeck[30] too far; our object should be to discover how we may make it more effectual; how we may give the mechanic a fuller and clearer impression of its truth and of its connexion with his own life. He will not lose the sense of that connexion at all, if, besides giving him the opportunity of studying practical mechanics, we offer him that instruction in the principles of mathematics, for which so many of his class have manifested a desire, and which they *have* obtained without our aid. From thence the way will be open to any even of the highest physical sciences, into which very few, perhaps, may seek a thorough initiation, but which should be within the reach of all.

I have often felt as if the phrases "manly education"—"education for men"— which I have used so often in these Lectures, must have an offensive sound, as if I were devising a teaching which should be confined to one sex. But I have adopted these phrases deliberately, being certain that by employing them, I am doing my best to vindicate a high education for women. Where the education of men is not manly—where it is effeminate—they will always be disposed to degrade their wives and sisters; they will always be suspicious of their rivalry. When it has been most masculine—as in Queen Elizabeth's days,—the culture of women has been free and noble in the same proportion. This remark is no less true of the working class, than of every other. I look forward to no result of a College with so much pleasure as to the improvement which I trust it will make in those evenings which the man spends, not there, but in his own dwelling. At the same time, I apprehend that much of the teaching I have described would be as applicable to women as to men. And I hopefully trust that if our present experiment should be at all successful, we may be able to adapt some modification of it very speedily to the use of females.

---

29. The Temperance Movement in England began in the nineteenth century. When people joined a temperance society, they were urged to take a public pledge to abstain from drinking alcoholic beverages.

30. George Birkbeck (1776–1841) was the physician who was the motivating force behind the founding, in 1824, of the London Mechanics' Institution that became the model for similar institutes throughout Britain.

There will be this great advantage in such a course, that we shall be able to claim the help of English ladies in following it out. Parts of it may, perhaps, be more advantageously managed by men. But the whole subject of domestic economy, many lessons respecting health, many respecting practical ethics, will not only come with greater force and influence from persons of their own sex, but would be, probably, full of follies and blunders, if they proceeded from ours.

I had hoped to say a few words on the subject of Amusements, which Mr. Dickens has lately obliged us all to think of;[31] but I find that I must defer this till next week, or I shall not have time to tell you what I think about the teaching of Theology. Perhaps you will be of opinion that I have anticipated the greatest difficulty on this subject, when I alluded to the doctrines of the Secularists and the Anti-Secularists, and expressed my assent to the judgment of the first, that we may teach any study whatever without insisting that any other whatever shall be taught along with it, and my entire sympathy with the second, in their professed belief that man is a spiritual being, and that all education is good only so far as it proceeds upon that supposition. But that statement would not be a sufficient justification to me, for offering specific instruction in Theology, if I had not the same reason to give for that course, which I have given for teaching Politics and Logic. Unless I felt sure that the working men were divines in embryo as well as logicians in embryo,—in other words, that they must think about Divinity, whether we speak to them of it or not; unless I believed that their vague thoughts about it interfere with the feeling that they are men and have the rights of men— and that it is possible to give their thoughts harmony, and so to do more for the freedom and the order of their minds than by any other of our lessons; I should rather avoid a subject which no man of common sense or ordinary experience hopes to handle without giving offence. Having that conviction very strongly and deeply rooted in my mind, so strongly that it must have its expression in every lesson of mine on any subject, if it did not find this direct outlet, I think it would be dishonest to the working people if I did not give them notice of it, by using a word which is likely to frighten many of them. Of course no one need take more of our instruction than he likes; but he has a right to know what sort of people they are who offer it; he has cause to complain if they sail under false colours. If I asked any one to suppress his convictions, I should feel as I were under a sort of obligation to stifle my own; but as I think all peril to truth as well as charity lies in evasions and concealments—and that there will be most safety, and most tenderness of others, when every one speaks out that which is deepest in him—I must exercise the privilege of which I count it a shame and a folly that we should deprive any. And as I make that our defence for giving a substantive place to Theology in our College course, so it is upon this principle that I should wish to see it taught. There are

---

31. In *Hard Times*, published in 1854 by Charles Dickens (1812–1870), the lisping circus manager Sleary offers to the workaholic utilitarian activist Gradgrind the simple philosophy that Gradgrind must suffer greatly in order to comprehend and accept: "People mutht be amuthed, Thquire, thomehow; they can't be alwayth a working, nor yet they can't be alwayth a learning." See part 3 for an extended excerpt from *Hard Times*.

those who suppose that if we excite any one to tell that which makes him discontented with us and our conclusions, or what he takes to be our conclusions, we must be propagating doubts and divisions. I can only say that I have tried, and I believe it to be the best method of delivering our pupils and ourselves from doubts and divisions, of leading them and us to know where we are standing, and what we have to stand upon. If I believed that Truth belonged to us and that we could settle strifes, I should think and act otherwise. Believing that Truth is of God, and that our divisions come from our narrow and partial apprehensions of it, I would ask Him to vindicate it, and to establish Unity in His own way. If I thought that we could give men Freedom or Order, I should leave the science of Theology alone; I should suppose that no such science existed. I would teach it, because I believe that God desires Freedom and Order for us, and will help us to desire them and claim them for ourselves.

ELLEN JOHNSTON

A SCOTTISH working-class poet, Ellen Johnston (1835–1873) endured considerable hardship in her brief life. When she was ten, her stepfather put her to
work in a weaving factory. Seven years later, she became a single mother with a
daughter to support. Over the years, she found factory work in Belfast, Manchester,
and Dundee. Her collected poems, originally published in weekly newspapers and
working-class magazines, were published in 1867, with a slightly expanded edition
appearing in 1869. Despite her modest literary success, Johnston died at the age of
thirty-eight in the Barony Poorhouse in Glasgow.

Written in Scots dialect, "The Working Man" celebrates the dignity and worth
of the common laborer.

The Working Man

The spring is come at last, my freens,[1] cheer up, you sons of toil,
Let the seeds of independence be sown in labour's soil,
And tho' the nipping blast of care should blight your wee bit crop,
Oh dinna[2] let your spirits sink, cling closer aye to hope.

If youth and health be on your side, you ha'e a richer boon   5
Than him that's dressed in royal robes and wears a diamond crown;
Nae widow's curse lies in your cup, you bear nae orphan's blame;
Nae guilty conscience haunts your dreams wi' visions of the slain.

1. Friends.
2. Do not.

Tho' light your purse, and worn your coat the darkest hour of night,
Is whiles[3] the very ane[4] that is before it dawns daylight;   10
And tho' your lot looks unco[5] hard, your future prospects drear,
Hope's sun may burst through sorrow's cloud, your sinking soul to cheer.

The summer's drawing near, my freens, cheer up ye sons of toil,
Let the sun of independence aye greet ye wi' a smile;
His genial beams will light your hearth when it is mirk[6] wi' care,   15
When ye ha'e little for to spend, and far less for to spare.

Let him that ne'er kent[7] labour's yoke but come to Glasgow toon,[8]
And let him take a cannie[9] walk her bonny buildings roon,[10]
And let him wi' his lady hands, his cheeks sae pale and wan,
Stand face to face, without a blush, before the Working Man.   20

But the man who wins fair fortune wi' labour's anxious pain,
He is the man who's justly earned her favour and her fame;
And may he aye keep flourishing wherever he may gang,[11]
And ne'er forget the days now gane[12] when but a Working Man.

The harvest soon will be, my freens, cheer up, you sons of toil,   25
And the fu'some hand of plenty will store your domicile;
Ye are the sons of nature's art, aye forming some new plan,
Oh what would bonny Scotland do without the Working Man?

3. Sometimes.
4. One.
5. Uncommonly.
6. Dark.
7. Knew.
8. Town.
9. Observant.
10. Round.
11. Go.
12. Gone.

ANNA JAMESON

Bᴏʀɴ ɪɴ Dᴜʙʟɪɴ, the daughter of a painter, Anna Brownell Murphy Jameson (1794–1860) became a well-known art historian and social commentator. In addition to a collection of essays on Shakespeare's heroines and a series of influential museum guides and books on art history, Jameson published several volumes devoted to the issue of employment for women, among them *Memoirs and Essays* (1846) and *Sisters of Charity* (1855). In *The Communion of Labour* (1856), from which the following representative selections are taken, she discusses opportunities for greater involvement of women in the administration of public service institutions.

Jameson chooses a biblical text as the epigraph for *The Communion of Labour:* "Nevertheless neither is the man without the woman, nor the woman without the man, in the Lord" (1 Corinthians 11:11). In the operation of hospitals, prisons, and workhouses, Jameson argues for "a due admixture of female influence and management combined with the man's government" and describes model institutions she has visited on the Continent.

From *The Communion of Labour*

The Influence of Legislation on the Morals and Happiness of Men and Women

It is now nearly a year and a half since my friends gathered round me and listened very kindly and patiently to certain suggestions relative to the social employments of women, more especially as "sɪsᴛᴇʀs ᴏꜰ ᴄʜᴀʀɪᴛʏ, at home and abroad."[1] The views I then advocated had been long in my mind: but great events, at that time recent, and coming home to all hearts, had rendered the exposition of those views more seasonable, more interesting, perhaps also more intelligible, than they would otherwise have been.

The publication of that Lecture having attracted more attention than I had reason to expect, and having given rise to some discussion, public and private, I

---

1. Jameson uses the term "Sisters of Charity" generically to refer to any sisterhood, Protestant or Roman Catholic, committed to social service. In her published lecture *Sisters of Charity* (1855), she discusses the work of Anglican and Catholic sisterhoods as well as that of Evangelical deaconesses.

have been advised, and have taken courage, once more, and probably for the last time, to recur to the same subject. It is a subject which, if it be worth any attention whatever, is worth the most serious and solemn consideration; for it concerns no transient, no partial interest, lying on the surface of life, but rather the very stuff of which life is made. Some new observations, some additional facts, I have to communicate, which, while they illustrate the principles laid down in my former Lecture, will, I hope, add force to my arguments. These observations, these facts, will not at once overcome all objections, will not in the first instance meet with anything like general acceptance; but they will perhaps open up new sources of thought; and if thought lead to inquiry, and inquiry lead to conviction—for or against—I should be content to abide that issue.

The questions as yet unsettled seem to be these:—

Whether a more enlarged sphere of social work may not be allowed to woman in perfect accordance with the truest feminine instincts? Whether there be not a possibility of her sharing practically in the responsibilities of social as well as domestic life? Whether she might not be better prepared to meet and exercise such higher responsibilities? Whether such a communion of labour might not lead to the more humane ordering of many of our public institutions; to a purer standard of morals; and to a better mutual comprehension and a finer harmony between men and women, when thus called upon to work together, and (in combining what is best in the two natures) becoming what God intended them to be, the supplement to each other? . . . .

The Communion of Labour in Sanitary, Educational, Reformatory and Penal Institutions

Work in some form or other is the appointed lot of all—divinely appointed; and, given as equal the religious responsibilities of the two sexes, might we not, in distributing the work to be done in this world, combine and use in more equal proportion the working faculties of men and women, and so find a remedy for many of those mistakes which have vitiated some of our noblest educational and charitable institutions? Is it not possible that in the apportioning of the work we may have too far sundered what in God's creation never can be sundered without pain and mischief, the masculine and the feminine influences?—lost the true balance between the element of power and the element of love? and trusted too much to mere mechanical means for carrying out high religious and moral purposes?

Hospitals

I will now proceed to illustrate my position by certain facts connected with the administration of various public institutions at home and abroad.

And, first, with regard to hospitals. . . .

One purpose of an hospital supposes the presence of the feminine nature to *minister* through love as well as the masculine intellect to *rule* through power,—the presence of those who can soothe and comfort as well as those who can heal. Now I will speak of what I have seen where this combined *régime* prevails. . . .

When I was at Vienna, I saw a small hospital belonging to the Sisters of Charity there. The beginning had been very modest, two of the Sisters having settled in a small old house. Several of the adjoining buildings were added one after the other, connected by wooden corridors: the only new part which had any appearance of being adapted to its purpose was the infirmary, in which were fifty-two patients, twenty-six men and twenty-six women, besides nine beds for cholera. There were fifty Sisters, of whom one-half were employed in the house, and the other half were going their rounds amongst the poor, or nursing the sick in private houses. There was a nursery for infants, whose mothers were at work; a day-school for one hundred and fifty girls, in which only knitting and sewing were taught; all clean, orderly, and, above all, cheerful. There was a dispensary, where two of the Sisters were employed in making up prescriptions, homeopathic and allopathic.[2] There was a large airy kitchen where three of the Sisters with two assistants were cooking. There were two priests and two physicians. So that, in fact, under this roof we had the elements on a small scale of an English workhouse;[3] but very different was the spirit which animated it.

I saw at Vienna another excellent hospital for women alone, of which the whole administration and support rested with the ladies of the Order of St. Elizabeth. These are *cloistered*, that is, not allowed to go out of their home to nurse the sick and poor; nor have they any schools; but all sick women who apply for admission are taken in without any questions asked, so long as there is room for them—cases of child-birth excepted. At the time I visited this hospital it contained ninety-two patients: about twenty were cases of cholera. There were sixteen beds in each ward, over which two Sisters presided. The dispensary, which was excellently arranged, was entirely managed by two of the ladies. The Superior told me that they have always three or more Sisters preparing for their profession under the best apothecaries; and there was a large garden principally of medicinal and kitchen herbs. Nothing could exceed the purity of the air, and the cleanliness, order, and quiet everywhere apparent. . . .

Prisons

I must now say a few words with regard to female administration in prisons. . . .

In my Lecture last year I mentioned the employment of trained Sisters of Charity in some of the prisons of Piedmont.[4]. . .

2. Homeopathic prescriptions treat disease with small doses of drugs that in a healthy person would produce symptoms similar to those of the disease being treated. Allopathic prescriptions would be substances that produce effects different from those produced by the disease.

3. The New Poor Law of 1834 eliminated outdoor relief and mandated that welfare recipients live and, if they were able, work in government-run institutions. The punitive nature of workhouses gradually changed in the second half of the century as they came to be seen as legitimate places of refuge for the orphaned, the infirm, and the aged.

4. A region in northwestern Italy. The city of Turin which Jameson mentions in subsequent paragraphs is in this part of Italy.

In the general Report on the condition of the prisons, addressed to the Minister of the Interior, I found this paragraph, which I translate from the original Italian:—

"It is an indisputable fact that the prisons which are served by the Sisters are the best ordered, the most cleanly, and in all respects the best regulated in the country; hence it is to be desired that the number should be increased; and this is the more desirable because where the Sisters are not established, the criminal women are under the charge of jailors of the other sex, which ought not to be tolerated."

To this I add the testimony of the Minister himself from a private communication. "Not only have we experienced the advantage of employing the Sisters of Charity in the prisons, in the supervision of the details, in distributing food, preparing medicines, and nursing the sick in the infirmaries; but we find that the influence of these ladies on the minds of the prisoners, when recovering from sickness, has been productive of the greatest benefit, as leading to permanent reform in many cases and a better frame of mind always: for this reason, among others, we have given them every encouragement."[5]

Reformatory Schools

If what I have said of the salutary effects of female influence in prisons carry any weight, yet more does it apply to the employment of superior women in the Reformatory schools for young criminals. Profligate boys, accustomed to see only the most coarse and depraved women (their own female relatives are in general examples of the worst class), would be especially touched and tamed by the mere presence of a better order of women. . . .

Penitentiaries and Houses of Refuge

The reformatory schools for perverted and criminal girls present many more difficulties than those for boys. . . .

When I was at Turin, I visited an institution for the redemption of "unfortunate girls" (as they call themselves,[6] poor creatures!), which appeared to me peculiarly successful. I did not consider it perfect, nor could all its details be imitated here. Yet some of the *natural* principles, recognised and carried out, appeared to me most important. . . .

The institution began on a small scale with few inmates: it now covers a large

5. Jameson's note: "In my former lecture, 'Sisters of Charity,' I have alluded to the employment of women in the prisons of Piedmont. My visit to Turin in November 1855, confirmed by personal knowledge and inquiry the testimony already received on this point."

6. Jameson's note: "If you ask a good-looking girl in an hospital, or the infirmary of a workhouse, what is her condition of life, she will perhaps answer, 'If you please, ma'am, I'm an unfortunate girl,' in a tone of languid indifference, as if it were a profession like any other. If she were to answer, 'If you please, ma'am, I'm a social evil,' it would mean the same thing, and the one denomination would be as true as the other."

space of ground, and several ranges of buildings for various departments, all connected, and yet most carefully separated. There are several distinct gardens enclosed by these buildings, and the green trees and flowers give an appearance of cheerfulness to the whole.

. . . [T]he young girls and children are kept distinct from the elder ones, and those who had lately entered from the others. I saw about twenty girls under the age of fifteen, but only a few together in one room. Only a few were tolerably handsome; many looked intelligent and kindly. In one of these rooms I found a tame thrush hopping about, and I remember a girl with a soft face crumbling some bread for it, saved from her dinner. Reading, writing, plain work,[7] and embroidery are taught, also cooking, and other domestic work. A certain number assisted by rotation in the large, lightsome kitchens, and the general service of the house, but not till they had been there some months, and had received badges for good conduct. There are three gradations of these badges of merit, earned by various terms of probation. It was quite clear to me that these badges were worn with pleasure: whenever I fixed my eyes upon the little bits of red or blue ribbon, attached to the dress, and smiled approbation, I was met by a responsive smile— sometimes by a deep, modest blush. The third and highest order of merit, which was a certificate of good conduct and steady industry during three years at least, conferred the privilege of entering an order destined to nurse the sick in the infirmary, or entrusted to keep order in the small classes. They had also a still higher privilege. And now I come to a part of the institution which excited my strongest sympathy and admiration. Appended to it is an infant hospital for the children of the very lowest orders—children born diseased or deformed, or maimed by accidents,—epileptic or crippled. In this hospital were thirty-two poor suffering infants, carefully tended by such of the penitents as had earned this privilege. . . .

Any inmate is free to leave the Refuge whenever she pleases, and may be received a second time, but not a third time.

I was told that when these girls leave the institution, after a probation of three or four years, there is no difficulty in finding them good places, as servants, cooks, washerwomen, and even nurses; but all do not leave it. Those who, after a residence of six years, preferred to remain, might do so: they were devoted to a religious and laborious life, and lived in a part of the building which had a sort of conventual sanctity and seclusion. They are styled *"les Madeleines"* (Magdalens).[8] I saw sixteen of such; and I had the opportunity of observing them. They were all superior in countenance and organisation, and belonged apparently to a better class. They were averse to reentering the world, had been disgusted and humiliated by their bitter experience of vice, and disliked or were unfitted for servile occupations. They had a manufactory of artificial flowers, were skilful embroiderers and needlewomen, and supported themselves by the produce of their work. They were

7. Plain sewing.
8. The name signifies a reformed prostitute, after Mary Magdalen, who has traditionally been identified as the New Testament woman accused of adultery, although contemporary biblical scholars note that the Gospels do not specifically identify her as such.

no longer objects of pity or dependent on charity: they had become objects of respect—and more than respect, of reverence.

Workhouses

I come now to an institution peculiar to ourselves; and truly can I affirm that if ever the combination of female with masculine supervision were imperatively needed, it is in an English parish workhouse. . . .

I have seen many workhouses and of all grades. The regulation of details varies in different parishes. Some are admirably clean, and, as far as mere machinery can go, admirably managed; some are dirty and ill ventilated; and one or two, as we learn from recent disclosures, quite in a disgraceful state: but whatever the arrangement and condition, in one thing I found all alike;—the want of a proper moral supervision. I do not say this in the grossest sense; though even in *that* sense, I have known of things I could hardly speak of. But surely I may say there is want of proper *moral* supervision where the most vulgar of human beings are set to rule over the most vulgar; where the pauper is set to manage the pauper; where the ignorant govern the ignorant; where the aged and infirm minister to the aged and infirm; where every softening and elevating influence is absent, or of rare occurrence, and every hardening and depraving influence continuous and ever at hand. Never did I visit any dungeon, any abode of crime or misery, in any country, which left the same crushing sense of sorrow, indignation, and compassion—almost despair—as some of our English workhouses. Never did I see more clearly what must be the inevitable consequences, where the feminine and religious influences are ignored; where what we call charity is worked by a stern, hard machinery; where what we mean for good is not bestowed but inflicted on others, in a spirit not pitiful nor merciful, but reluctant and adverse, if not cruel. . . .

I have not found in my limited travels any institutions exactly similar to our workhouses, that is, charitable institutions supported by enforced contributions. There are, however, two institutions at Turin which struck me as very remarkable, and which may be said, each in its way, to fulfil some of the purposes for which our workhouses were originally instituted.

One of these is a community of women called *Rosines,* from the name of their founder, Rosa Governo, who had been a servant girl. It cannot be styled a religious community, in the usual sense, as neither vows nor seclusion are required: it is a working joint-stock company, with a strong interfusion of the religious element, without which I believe it could not have held together. Here I found, wonderful to tell, nearly 400 women of all ages, from fifteen and upwards, living together in a very extensive, clean, airy building (or rather assemblage of buildings, for they had added one house to another), maintaining themselves by their united labour, and carrying on a variety of occupations, as tailoring, embroidery (especially the embroidery of military accoutrements for the army), weaving, spinning, shirt-making, lace-making—everything, in short, in which female ingenuity could be employed. They have a large, well-kept garden; a school for the poor children of the neighbourhood; an infirmary, including a ward for those whose age had exempted them from work; a capital dispensary, with a small medical library; here I found one of the women preparing some medicines, and another studying intently a French medical work.

This female community is much respected in Turin, and has flourished for more than a century. It is entirely self-supported, and the yearly revenue averages between 70,000 and 80,000 francs. . . .

Education and Training of Women for Social Employments[9]

And now, having shown what an extensive field there is for work, what are the qualifications required in the workers? It is plain that mere kindly impulses and self-confidence (so different from practical benevolence and tender, humble faith!) will not suffice. By what means are we to prepare and discipline our women for the work they may be called to perform? What has been done, what may be done, to render them fitting helpmates for energetic and benevolent men, and instruments of beneficent power? These are momentous questions, which we have now to consider.

The complaint has become threadbare; yet I must begin by noticing the mere *fact* as such. There is no adequate provision for the practical education of the middle and lower classes of girls in this country; . . .

. . . [S]uppose the necessity of a better and more sympathetic education for *all* conceded, and suppose it even already provided for by more enlightened public opinion, there remain some special and plausible objections against the training of women for active, and social, and responsible avocations, such as I have pointed out. Of these objections, which I have often had to listen to, *three* only appear to me worth a moment's attention.

And first, you hear people say, quite sententiously, "I object to anything which takes a woman out of her home, and removes her from the sphere of domestic duty." So do I! I object strongly to anything which takes a woman out of her proper sphere, out of a happy and congenial home, where her presence is delightful and her services necessary: *there* is her first duty. I object also to everything which takes away a man from *his* first duty, the protection and support of his home. Let us bear in mind that for every man who does not provide a home, there must exist a woman who must make or find a home for herself, somehow or somewhere. There seems to be no objection to taking the lower classes of women out of their homes to be domestic servants, milliners, shopwomen, factory-girls, and the better educated to be governesses; or if there be objections, they are overborne by the pressure of an

9. The need for education and training for women workers is discussed more fully in essays by Octavia Hill (at the end of part 2) and by Emily Davies and Josephine Butler (part 4). For a different view of the role of women, see the essay by Eliza Lynn Linton in part 4.

obvious necessity. Then why should the objection be urged, merely with respect to other employments, only because they are as yet rather unusual, or at least not yet recognised among us, but which are of a far more elevated kind?

Then there is much sentimental speech of women being educated to "adorn a home," to be "a good wife," "a good mother." But how many women are there who have no home, who are neither wives nor mothers, nor ever will be while they live? Will you deny to them the power to carry into a wider sphere the duties of home—the wifely, motherly, sisterly instincts, which bind them to the other half of the human race? Must these be utterly crushed; or may they not be expanded and gratified healthily, innocently, usefully? This, surely, is at least worth considering, before we allow the force of an objection which seems to consist in phrases rather than in arguments.

A second objection, which I have heard chiefly from medical men, is, that the women of the educated classes, from which our volunteers are to be taken, are in general feeble, over-refined, and excitable, apt to take fancies to individuals where their aid and attention ought to be impartial and general, too self-confident for obedience, too sensitive to be trusted. That these objections apply to many women I have no doubt: that they apply to women generally, I deny. . . .

And now for the third objection; it is thus put:—

"Would you make charity a profession?"

Why not? why should not charity be a profession in our sex, just so far *(and no farther)* as religion is a profession in yours? If a man attires himself in a black surplice, ascends a pulpit, and publicly preaches religion, are we, therefore, to suppose that his religious profession is merely a profession, instead of a holy, heartfelt vocation? If a woman puts on a grey gown, and openly takes upon herself the blessed duty of caring for the sick, the poor, the perverted, are we therefore to suppose that charity is with her merely a profession? Here we have surely a distinction without a difference! No doubt we should all be religious, whether we assume the outward garb or not; no doubt we should all be charitable, whether in white, black, or grey; but why should not charity assume functions publicly recognised—openly, yet quietly and modestly exercised? . . .

Women for Hire and Working for Love

There is no question I have heard more warmly contested, than the question of paid or unpaid female officials. I think there should be both. We should have them of two classes; those who receive direct pay, and those who do not. Consider the qualifications required. There must be force of character of no common kind; the humility which can obey, and the intelligence which can rule; great enthusiasm, great self-command, great benevolence; quickness of perception with quietness of temper; the power of dealing with the minds of others, and a surrender of the whole being to the love and service of God: without the religious spirit we can do nothing. Now, can we hope to obtain these qualifications for any pay which our jails, workhouses, or hospitals could afford?—or indeed for any pay whatever? Yet it is precisely an order of women, quite beyond the reach of any remuneration that could be afforded, which is so imperatively required in our institutions.

The idea of service without pay seems quite shocking to some minds, quite unintelligible; they quote sententiously, "The labourer is worthy of his hire."[10] True; but what shall be that hire? Must it necessarily be in coin of the realm? There are many women of small independent means, who would gladly serve their fellow-creatures, requiring nothing but the freedom and the means so to devote themselves. There are women who would prefer "laying up for themselves treasures in heaven,"[11] to coining their souls into pounds, shillings, and pence on earth; who, having nothing, ask nothing but a subsistence secured to them; and for this are willing to give the best that is in them, and work out their lives while strength is given them. I believe that such service is especially blessed. I believe that such service does not weary, is more gracious and long-suffering than any other, blessing those who give and those who receive. I believe it has a potency for good that no hired service can have. . . .

It is better than a dozen sermons on toleration, to count up the women who, during this half-century, have left the strongest and most durable impress on society—on the minds and hearts of their generation. First, there is Mrs. Fry,[12] the Quakeress, to whom we owe the cleansing of our prisons, and in part the reform of our criminal code; Caroline Chisholm,[13] the Roman Catholic, with her strong common sense, her decision and independence of character, who may be said to have reformed the system of emigration; Mary Carpenter,[14] the Dissenter, who has become an authority in all that concerns the treatment of juvenile delinquents; and Florence Nightingale,[15] who in our time has opened a new path for female charity and female energy, is understood to belong to the Anglican church. And let us remember that there is not one of these four admirable women who has not been assailed in turn by the bitterest animosity, by the most vulgar, so-called religious abuse from those who differed from them in their religious tenets, or from those who contemned them and would have put them down merely as women; not one of them who has not outlived prejudice and jealousy; not one of them who could have carried out their large and beneficent views without the aid

10. Luke 10:7.

11. Matthew 6:20.

12. Elizabeth Fry (1780–1845), a Quaker activist, was instrumental in effecting prison reforms including classification of criminals, separation of male and female prisoners, and useful employment.

13. Caroline Chisholm (1808?–1877) assisted great numbers of working-class women and families in emigrating to Australia in the 1840s and 1850s.

14. Mary Carpenter (1807–1877) devoted herself to the plight of impoverished children. Her efforts resulted in the establishment of a number of "ragged schools" and reformatories and to the passage of important protective legislation for unfortunate youth.

15. Florence Nightingale (1820–1910) was instrumental in effecting reforms in the nursing profession as well as in public health and sanitation. (See the entry on Nightingale in part 1.)

of generous and enlightened men,—men who had the nobleness of mind to accept them as fellow-workers in the cause of humanity, to admit them on equal terms into the communion of labour and the communion of charity.

I must now conclude with a few last words.

We cannot look around us without seeing that a demand has not only been created, but becomes every day increasingly urgent, for a supply of working women at once more efficient and more effective. . . .

I would place before you, this once more, ere I turn to other duties, that most indispensable yet hardly acknowledged truth, that at the core of all social reformation, as a necessary condition of health and permanency in all human institutions, lies the working of the man and the woman together, in mutual trust, love, and reverence.

I would impress it now for the last time on the hearts and the consciences of those who hear me, that there is an essential, eternal law of life, affirmed and developed by the teaching of Christ, which if you do not take into account, your fine social machinery, however ingeniously and plausibly contrived, will at last fall into corruption and ruin. Wherever men and women do not work together helpfully and harmoniously, and in accordance with the domestic relations—wherever there is not THE COMMUNION OF LOVE AND THE COMMUNION OF LABOUR—there must necessarily enter the elements of discord and decay. If men bring their conventionalities and practicabilities into conflict with the natural law of God's divine appointment, we know which must in the end succumb. Meantime I would, if possible, assist in diminishing the duration and the pain of that conflict. If anything I have now spoken carry conviction into the kind hearts around me, help! those who can and will,—and God help us all!

HARRIET MARTINEAU

THE DAUGHTER of a Norwich textile manufacturer, Harriet Martineau (1802–1876) was educated largely at home where she studied Latin and music and read widely. In 1825, Martineau's father suffered financial setbacks. He died the following year, leaving his family little on which to live. Further reversals in 1829 left them in financial ruin. Martineau supported herself by doing needlework and writing magazine articles. In 1832, she achieved instant fame upon the publication of the first of twenty-five volumes in her series of didactic stories titled *Illustrations of Political Economy*. Following a two-year tour of the United States, Martineau published two books on her impressions of the country (most notably, *Society in America*, 1837) and a novel (*Deerbrook*, 1839). She produced a steady stream of articles that appeared in such prominent journals as the *Quarterly Review, Macmillan's*, the *Edinburgh Review*, and Charles Dickens's *Household Words*. In 1852, she began contributing to the *Daily News*, a liberal paper directed at a middle-class audience. She became the leader, or editorial writer, and in that capacity, over the next four years, Martineau published more than 1,600 articles in the *News* alone. In the pages of the leading periodicals of her time, Martineau brought her support for women's rights, education, and laissez-faire economics to bear on an incredible range of specific issues, as the essays reprinted in this anthology demonstrate.

Over the course of her long and prolific career, she published adult fiction, children's stories, histories, autobiography, travel essays, and social commentary. Well-known and highly regarded, Martineau was acquainted with many of the leading intellectual and literary figures of her time, including Elizabeth Barrett Browning, Arthur Henry Hallam, Thomas Malthus, Florence Nightingale, Thomas Carlyle, and William Wordsworth.

The following article on women's work, which appeared in the *Daily News*, was written in response to a paper titled "The Market for Educated Female Labour" presented by feminist activist Bessie Rayner Parkes (1829–1925) at a meeting in Bradford of the Association for the Promotion of Social Science. Parkes's controversial paper, subsequently published in the November 1, 1859, issue of *The English Woman's Journal*, provoked widespread public debate. Parkes, referring to the necessity for thousands of middle-class women to earn a living and to the small number of professions open to them, urges fathers to provide for their daughters' futures through savings plans or life insurance or by educating them for a career. Martineau emphasizes the latter, contending that training sufficient to make women capable and independent is what is most needed. For a very different (anonymous) response to Parkes's essay, see "Queen Bees or Working Bees?" in part 4.

From the *Daily News,* November 17, 1859
[Independent Industry for Women]

For a good many years now the subject of the independent industry of women in Great Britain has come up at shorter intervals, and with a more peremptory demand on the attention of society. From the day when the *Song of the Shirt* appeared[1] there could be no doubt that the industrial condition of women would occupy attention as we see it doing now. The founding of the Governesses' Benevolent Institution,[2] the controversies about factory employment for women, the movement in favour of women and watchwork,[3] the opening of a few Schools of Design to women, and of an annual exhibition of pictures by them, and the successful footing they have established in various departments of Art,[4] have all pointed to the awakening of that wide interest in the subject which we witness now. The *Edinburgh Review* of last April contained a full narrative of the actual state of female industry in this country;[5] and at the Social Science Meeting at Bradford, a paper read by Miss Parkes excited so much interest that the discussion has been kept up, and does not seem likely to drop at present.

Discussion about what? This is an important thing to know in a case in which

1. Thomas Hood's popular poem about the plight of seamstresses, which appeared in the December 16, 1843, issue of *Punch,* is included in part 3.

2. Founded in 1843, the Governesses' Benevolent Institution assisted governesses by maintaining an employment registry and providing financial support for the incapacitated and the elderly.

3. Watchmaking, because of the delicacy of the work, was considered by some an appropriate career for women.

4. Women artists in the nineteenth century faced numerous obstacles, including the narrow range of subjects considered appropriate for female painters to treat and also restrictions on formal training, in particular prohibitions against drawing from nude models. Women were not admitted to the prestigious Royal Academy until 1860, could not draw from nude male models until 1893, and could not attend co-educational classes until 1903. While some female artists did manage to show their work at annual Royal Academy exhibitions, they received little serious critical notice or patronage. Opportunities for training and advancement gradually increased as the century advanced. For instance, in 1843 the Female School of the Government Schools of Design opened in London, and associations such as the Society of Female Artists (established in 1857) were organized to promote and exhibit works by women.

5. Martineau refers to her own article on "Female Industry," which appeared in the *Edinburgh Review* 109 (April 1859): 333.

so much sentiment is involved, and so much prejudice, and so much sense, and so much goodwill. What is the precise mischief to be taken in hand? and what is to be done to cure it?

Miss PARKES's paper was abundantly clear and definite. She tells us the truth that a multitude of the daughters of middle-class men are neither educated nor provided for like their brothers; and that if they do not marry, they must work (unprepared by education as they are) or starve. The terms demanded on behalf of women are that parents shall either educate their daughters so as to fit them for independent industry; or lay by a provision for them; or insure their own lives for the benefit of their daughters in the day which will make them fatherless. This is very simple and clear. It is also very interesting; and, as a natural consequence, we hear of sympathy, in the form of advice and suggestions, in all directions; and of various establishments, existing or proposed, with more or less of the same charitable element involved for the relief and aid of industrial women of the middle class. Under such circumstances there must be a melancholy waste of effort, unless we ascertain betimes what it is that is wanted, and how the want may be met, with something like concert and business-like faculty. Looking at the matter from a practical point of view, the conditions of the case seem to be these.

It is supposed by persons whose attention has not been particularly called to the subject, that the women of Great Britain are maintained by their fathers, husbands, or brothers. It was once so; and careless people are unaware that we have long outgrown the fit of that theory of female maintenance. It has been out at elbows at least since the war which ended with Waterloo.[6] From the last Census Report[7] we learn how things were eight years ago—before the last war which has much increased the tendency of women to maintain themselves. In Great Britain, without Ireland, there were in 1851 six millions of women above twenty years of age. More than half of these work for their living. Does this surprise our readers? If it never occurred to them before, they will be still further impressed by the fact that two millions of women, out of the six millions, are independent in their industry—are self-supporting, like men. So far is the theory of women being maintained by their male relatives from being now true. But how do these women work? and how far do they succeed in maintaining themselves? for it is universally understood that women are paid less than men for the same kind and degree of work. Society has been a good deal surprised by the disclosures in the Divorce Court[8] of the amount of effectual female industry, proved by applications for protection of earnings from bad husbands. That women should maintain themselves and their children seems a matter of course when they are unhappily married; and the revelation has caused a good many people to perceive that there is a good deal going on in middle-class life which they were unaware of. It may strike some observers that the matter has far outgrown the scope and powers of charitable societies, and that the independent industry of Englishwomen has become a

6. Napoleon Bonaparte was defeated at the Battle of Waterloo in Belgium in 1815.

7. Census Report of 1851.

8. A civil divorce court was established in London following passage of the Divorce and Matrimonial Causes Act in 1857.

fact which must be recognised by the law, and which must itself essentially modify middle-class education throughout the kingdom.

What, then, are these three millions and more of working women doing? and especially the two millions who are industrial in the same sense as men?

There were in 1851 nearly 130,000 employed in agriculture, without reckoning the farmers' wives and daughters, who usually have their hands full. This is also exclusive of the widow-farmers, who are numerous. Nearly half of the independent class of workers are dairymaids. The ores and clays of the mining districts afford occupation to 7,000, now that female labour has ceased (ostensibly) in coal-pits.[9] It does not seem to be ascertained how many women are employed in the catching, curing, and itinerant sale of fish. Jersey oysters alone maintain 1,000 women, and this may give some notion of the scores of thousands so employed all round our coasts. The country districts, however, afford the greatest number of all in the department of domestic service. Nearly two-thirds of our maid-servants are country born; and there are considerably more than half-a-million of them altogether. They constitute a fourth part of the independent workers. We employ no fewer than 400,000 maids-of-all-work. Other female servants amount to above 180,000, without reckoning the large class (about 51,000) of charwomen.

There are many thousands of shopkeepers, but they are for the most part the widows of the men who had the business before them; and it is too common a thing to see them marry their assistants in the business, from their own inability to keep the books, and manage the financial part of their concerns. The Divorce Court and the police courts, all the year round, afford evidence of this weakness and ignorance among women who have had a good business as innkeepers or shopkeepers. There are 14,000 of this class, butchers and milk merchants; 8,000 waggon or hackney-coach proprietors; 10,000 beer-shop keepers or victuallers, besides 9,000 innkeepers. These are the independent proprietors, excluding the wives, who are yet the mainstay of the industry in houses of entertainment and many branches of retail trade. With all this shopkeeping by women, there are no more than 1,742 shopwomen. This is a fact eminently worthy of consideration. The function is one which occurs first to almost everybody's mind, when female industry is discussed, as one precisely fit for women. The failure may be partly owing to the jealousy of the men, who have hitherto engrossed it, and partly to the well-known prejudice of purchasers in favour of shopmen; but it is no doubt in part ascribable to the inferiority of women in the special training required; and especially in accounts and bookkeeping.

Manufactures maintain a million and a quarter of the women of Great Britain. More than half a million are employed on dress; that is, in millinery and laundry-work, exclusive of shoemakers' wives, who amount to nearly 100,000. Losing sight of the great field of female labour, because female industry is so completely established there, we are apt to say that there is no choice for a middle-class woman who

9. Shaftesbury's Act of 1842 prohibited underground work by women and girls and by boys under the age of ten.

must work but between the needle and tuition. The milliner's workroom and the school-room, we are wont to say, afford the only alternative. Yet we find in the Census returns "Teachers, Authors, and Artists," all lumped together, their collective number being under 65,000, exclusive of nearly 2,000 set down as "miscellaneous." Independent proprietors of lands, houses, or incomes are declared to be under 173,000.

Considering these figures in relation to each other, we strive at some sort of notion of what is wanted—first, to provide for a certain proportion of women now left helpless or miserable on the death of fathers, or under the accidents of fortune; and next, to improve the quality of existing female industry, so as to render it more effective for the support of the individual, and the benefit of society. We do not conceive that any appeal to fathers to provide better for their daughters, in comparison with their sons, will be of much practical use (however just and right) till the women have established the fact of their own capability, and their will to be independent. All sorts of people have to show what they can do before obtaining free scope to do it; and, antecedently unjust as this seems, it is a fact, and to be taken into the calculation. Women need not object to this, judging by what they have lately achieved for themselves under manifold disadvantages. They have won a good position in many departments of literature and art; and there is a good prospect of their soon occupying what we have repeatedly insisted on as their proper place in the medical profession. The thing would be done at once (as it is already in the United States), if the decision rested with our wisest physicians and most enlightened heads of households.[10] We see women now entering in increasing numbers on new methods of industry, introduced by the progress of science and art. We see them in the telegraph offices and at railway stations, transmitting reports with remarkable accuracy, and selling railway tickets—if not yet in charge of the signals, like French women. The arts of design for manufactures are open to them; and this is a wide and profitable field of labour. As authors and artists there is no hindrance in their way when they can prove their capability. No doubt, the counting-house, the shop-counter, secretaryships, and indeed any trade, and the medical profession will afford them entrance, notwithstanding a good deal of jealousy and prejudice, if they can make themselves valuable enough to defy obstacles. The practical question is how to establish the fact of the capacity. The fitness which exists may be called out and put to use by such associations as those which we see proposing to register applicants for work and for workers, and to train young women to mechanical fitness for certain occupations. These efforts are good as far as they go; and we are always glad to hear of them. The educational

10. At the time, women were not admitted into medical colleges in England and the name of only one woman, Elizabeth Blackwell (1821–1901), who had earned her M.D. in the United States, was entered on the British medical register. In 1869, ten years after Blackwell, Elizabeth Garrett Anderson (1836–1917) became the second registered female doctor. The tireless efforts of a third pioneer, Sophia Julia Jex-Blake (1840–1912), led to the opening of the London School of Medicine for Women in 1874 and to the passage of legislation making it possible for women to take certification exams. See Emily Davies's "Medicine as a Profession for Women" in part 4.

preparation which is necessary to make effective workers of either men or women is a deeper and wider affair of which we must speak another day.[11] Our present object is to show that it is mere waste of time to speak for or against the industrial independence of Englishwomen—above one-third of their whole number being already established in that destiny. A smaller number of women are passing miserable lives under the wreck of the old theory that women are not self-supporting. These sufferers are not supported: they cannot support themselves, and they form the most prominent of our "uneasy classes." The old theory can never be reinstated in practice, and the question is how best to obey the natural laws of society, which now compel women to work.

The first step is to perceive that the problem is now simply an educational one. This is the point which the facts of the last Census seem to us to establish. The next step will be to provide the education specially required.

Responding to letters from Florence Nightingale in February 1865 about the need for trained nurses in London workhouse infirmaries and in Indian hospitals, Martineau wrote the following leader for the *Daily News* in which she attempts to persuade the parents of middle- and upper-class young women that nursing is an honorable and respectable profession.

From the *Daily News,* February 23, 1865
[Nurses]

There are two unhappy features in our social condition which apparently ought not to coexist: and so absurd is it that they should present themselves at the same time, that it can only be supposed that the facts of the case are not understood. We are at our wits' end to save the starving women who, with every desire to earn their bread, cannot obtain remunerative employment; and the most remunerative employment ever offered to an unlimited number of women is at the same time going

11. Martineau, in her publications, repeatedly expressed her conviction of the importance of education for women and was a strong supporter of early institutions of higher learning for women such as Queen's College (1848) and Bedford College for Women (1849).

a-begging through society. Social Science Associations[1] and sensible and benevolent persons in private life are striving, in increasing numbers and with ever-growing zeal, to open new occupations to educated women, as well as to the poor needlewomen who may be yet capable of doing something else than bad sewing; and all the while there is an occupation, more indispensable than any thus proposed, and far better paid than any of them, which seems to be seldom or never recommended by the patrons or sought by their clients. While the preachers of woman's mission are enforcing their own views, or denouncing the existing conditions of female life in society, there is a mission for women, a vocation for them, honoured, undisputed, and well rewarded, which is left so nearly unnoticed that one would suppose the champions of the sex had never heard of it. While we have an unmanageable crowd of hungry and disappointed women, poor and idle, on the one hand, we have on the other an absolute destitution of nurses of all classes—sick nurses for the household, hospital nurses, midwifery nurses, and nurses for our civil and military stations in India and elsewhere.

We are all in the habit of hearing of the private demand for trained nurses, and of the inability of such institutions (homes and schools for nursing) as there are to meet a twentieth part of the demand for the services of the members. Once having had the opportunity of knowing what the comfort is of a trained nurse in a sick house, we cannot wonder at the consideration which attends that inestimable person, nor at the terms which she can command. If this demand were all, there would be a good prospect open before not only hundreds but thousands of women, more or less educated, who can otherwise only turn to dressmaking or teaching, affording only low pay, and involving many hardships and mortifications. But this private demand is but one feature of the case. Hospital reform is proceeding, both at home and wherever we have settlements abroad; and the want most difficult to supply is that of trustworthy and capable nurses. The Sanitary Commissions in India,[2] at the outset of their prodigious task, see before them an alarming difficulty in the demand they have to make on this country for qualified nurses. For the female regimental hospitals alone, midwifery nurses and assistants are wanted in hundreds: and this is but one item in the demand created by that sanitary reform in India which is to save life and health incalculably, and obliterate the worst features of life, civil, military, and native, in our Eastern Empire. It needs no gift of prophecy to forsee that we must have trained nurses in our workhouse in infirmaries—and that immediately. We shall hear of TIMOTHY DALY[3] till this is accomplished—and of every other pauper death in which there is any room for suspicion of the quality of the nursing in the workhouse; and there will be such a

1. The National Association for the Promotion of Social Science was founded in 1857 and exerted influence on public policy for the next twenty-eight years.

2. Sanitary commissions in India were supervised by Florence Nightingale's friend Viceroy Sir John Lawrence. By the mid-1860s, Nightingale was making plans to send nurses to military hospitals in India.

3. Irish laborer who died in Holborn workhouse infirmary, apparently as a result of neglect. The *Times* covered the story in articles published on December 24, 1864, and on February 16, 1865.

peremptory demand of a system of paid nursing, skilled and effective, as will show the authorities very plainly what they must do. But, if they were ready and willing at this hour—as they probably are, after recent exposures—what could they do, so long as the nurses are actually not to be had? Let the patrons and friends of working women of all degrees consider for a moment what a body of honourable and well-paid workers we should have among us if every workhouse in the country contained its proportion. Again, there is that admirable institution of Village Hospitals stopped in its development by the difficulty which meets us everywhere. Wherever the Village Hospital has been tried it has been found such a blessing, that our rural districts generally would soon be provided with them if the indispensable presiding nurse could be had for the asking and the pay. A small house can be got, and a few beds put into it, and the kitchen be well arranged and furnished. The doctors are always favourable to the scheme, not only because it saves them great fatigue to have their surgical and fever cases at hand, and under their own eye, but because their patients have the chances all in their favour instead of against them, as they have in their own poor homes. As agricultural machinery comes more into use, accidents become commoner, and a hospital for their treatment is almost indispensable, wherever the county infirmary is some miles off. The theory is that a trained nurse is resident in the house, and that she is qualified to act as a midwifery nurse in the village when the hospital is empty. But this prime element is deficient, and while it is so we shall have to wait for our Village Hospitals, which ought already to be scattered over all our rural districts. Meantime, let the promoters of women's work consider what a body of useful, independent, well-provided women would be supported by Village Hospitals alone. The fact is they are wanted by thousands in half-a-dozen different departments of society at this hour.

What can be the reason? How can there be so plain a case of too much on the one hand and too little on the other, while the employment of women is really an interesting object to wise and good people among us? The only conceivable reason is that the women of England (and we may add their parents) do not know anything about the matter. The whole thing is perhaps still rather new; and even the high pay and the social regard may need time to operate. But still, everybody has heard of the Nightingale Fund,[4] and multitudes must have heard how it is applied in the training of nurses. If not, the particulars cannot be made known too widely. That fund provides lodging, board, washing, and some outer clothing for young women of good character, who should be from twenty-five to thirty-five years old, and who learn their business while serving as assistant nurses in St. Thomas Hospital. They receive regular instruction, and some pay at the end of each quarter, for a year, when they are considered qualified to act as hospital nurses. The demand for them is so urgent as to be perplexing to the managers, and most encouraging to themselves, and to anybody who may be disposed to follow

4. Monies contributed in honor of Nightingale's work on behalf of British soldiers in the Crimea (1854–56) were used to establish the first secular English school for nurses at St. Thomas's Hospital in London in 1861.

their choice of an occupation. The mischief is that so few know anything of the matter, or, knowing, venture to propose for themselves any plan that may be called new and strange.

Perhaps the circumstances of female life may account for the slowness that women show in such cases as this. If ladies, or clergymen, or the prosperous branch of the family will lead and persuade them, and a few companions will join in the pursuit, young women will sometimes venture to propose to become nurses; but we shall have to wait long if we wait for them to stir of their own accord. We appeal, then, to their countrywomen, to sensible and benevolent mothers, neighbours, and friends, to look out for the nursing element wherever they live, in town or country, and to do what they can to give society the benefit of it, as well as the young women themselves the respect, profit, and blessing of such an occupation. As for those champions of the sex who have most to say about a mission, we hope they will tell us what woman's mission is if it be not nursing the sick. Those who are gifted with the high female quality—the capacity for domestic administration—may find full use for it in the same department of enterprise. The lack of matrons for hospitals of all kinds is as perplexing as that of nurses. Let this fact become known to the hundreds of women who are eating the bitter bread of dependence, and we shall soon see whether some of them have not sense and spirit enough to emancipate themselves in a practical way which shall command unmingled respect, and authorise warm congratulations from their friends, and gratitude from the society in which they live.

R. ARTHUR ARNOLD

"PRISON LABOUR" was published in *Fraser's Magazine* in December 1868. The author of the article, R. Arthur Arnold, is identified in a byline as a "Late Government Inspector of Public Works."

In 1800, few prison facilities existed in England. The large number of capital offenses and the frequency with which those convicted of lesser crimes were sentenced to be transported overseas to a penal colony meant that most local and county jails were used merely as holding stations for those awaiting trial, transportation, or execution. Until mid-century as many as 70 percent of those imprisoned were secured in hulks, or prison ships. Many of the jails that did exist were privately owned and operated for profit. Over the course of the century, a drastic reduction in the number of capital crimes and the elimination of the sentence of transportation led to the construction of many new government prisons. Houses of Correction held those charged with minor offenses while those found guilty of serious crimes were sentenced to penal servitude in Convict Prisons. Efforts were made to impose uniform practices and procedures; however, not until 1877 was legislation passed placing all prisons under the central control of the Home Office and the administrative authority of the Prison Commission.

In nineteenth-century England, prison issues focused on the goals of incarceration (whether for deterrence of crime or for reformation of the individual) and on the most appropriate discipline for prisoners. The imposition of silence and separation was generally endorsed. In prisons that adhered to the silent system, prisoners lived and worked together but were forbidden to speak. In institutions that adopted the separate system, prisoners were confined in individual cells. They too worked, but their interaction with one another was limited. Although there was general consensus that inmates should work, there was considerable disagreement about the most suitable type of employment. In 1791, Utilitarian philosopher and social reformer Jeremy Bentham (1748–1832) had proposed a model prison plan, Panopticon. According to Bentham's scheme, the jailers' salary would be entirely dependent on profits of prisoners' labor. Bentham advocated not only productive employment but profitable and even pleasurable work to motivate prisoners to exert themselves and better fit them for reentry into society. Though the government at first found Bentham's plan attractive, ultimately it failed to win adoption because of high costs and the commercial component, which some lawmakers considered unsuitable. Not all reformers believed that prison labor should be productive. William Crawford (1788–1847), an early prison inspector who emphasized the need for religious reformation of convicts, contended that job training and the development of work skills were inappropriate. "It should never be forgotten," he maintained, "that a gaol is not a school for the instruction of artisans, but a place of punishment." Some of Crawford's colleagues, however, though not interested in making incarceration pleasurable, did hold that a measure of practical, public good might come of prisoners' labor. Accordingly, in 1848, the first public works convict prison opened at Portland. Developed by Sir Joshua Jebb (1793–1863), Surveyor-General of Prisons, these facilities focused on punishment through hard labor rather than on religious reformation. In Jebb's view, "the deterring elements of punishment are hard labour, hard fare, and a hard bed." Inmates were assigned tasks such as farming, quarrying, and building harbors. By 1868, when "Prison Labour" was written, three other public works convict prisons had been constructed in England: at Dartmoor, Portsmouth, and Chatham.

Hard, purposeless work as a punishment continued to find many adherents until late in the century. For example, in 1863, one of two government commissions appointed to investigate penal discipline recommended that prisoners be assigned to labor on the treadwheel, at the crank, or in the shot drill (see notes 10–12 below). The 1865 Prison Act, which grew out of the commissions' reports and applied to all English prisons, stressed deterrence and punishment of crime. Geared more toward behavior modification rather than genuine rehabilitation, the Act distinguished first-class hard labor, which was largely heavy, unproductive work, from second-class hard labor, which was less physically demanding. More than three decades passed before significant changes were effected. Widespread public opposition to unproductive prison labor in the 1890s led to passage of the 1899 Prison Rules, which stipulated that all prisoners were to be engaged in "useful industrial labor," the very position for which R. Arthur Arnold argues in the following essay.

Prison Labour

In writing upon this subject I have a double object in view,—to effect a reduction from the heavy cost of prisons, and to make the period of sentence more useful to prisoners. But, before I state and explain the plan by which, in my opinion, this may be accomplished, it is advisable to consider the capabilities of

Figure 2.5. *Female Convicts at Work during the Silent Hour in Brixton Prison.* English school. Private Collection/The Stapleton Collection. Courtesy of Bridgeman Art Library.

This engraving numbered among the illustrations to *The Criminal Prisons of London and Scenes of Prison Life,* published in 1860 by Henry Mayhew (1812–1887) and John Binny.

the persons whose liberty and labour has by misconduct become forfeited to the State for periods of differing length, and also to regard the existing system of employment in prisons.

Generally speaking, convicts do not belong to the manual labour class, a fact which suggests the wholesome moral influence of work. They are drawn for the most part from that lowest stratum of society, whose profession is crime, and from that "floating" section of the population whose physical infirmities, whose errant tastes, or whose neglected education, have left them without settled occupation, and who, for want of a better, employ their wits, often very considerable, in preying upon society. From these two classes—if I may so distinguish them—come the great majority of the criminals whose custody at present involves a very heavy charge upon the working members of the community.

A reference to the number of re-convictions, and to the educational registries of convicts during the past year, will confirm the general accuracy of this definition. In the Government Convict Prisons, where only those are removed who are sentenced to lengthened terms of penal servitude, out of 1,808 convicts—excluding those condemned for treason-felony—there were 464 males and 125 females, together 589 persons, who had previously received similar condemnation. With reference to Chatham Prison,[1] the Chaplain reports:—"Of the 758 prisoners received here during the year, 189 are noted as having been before sentenced to penal servitude once, twice, and in two instances, three times. Thirty of them had been inmates of some reformatory, and 370 had been summarily convicted for minor offences ranging from once to 28 times." These facts show how large a number of the convicts belong to the criminal class—to that portion of the population which is unacquainted with honest labour and is lowest in the order of society.

On the other hand, prison statistics will show that a large number of the convicts belong to a class possessed of much more education. In Millbank Prison,[2] out of 950 convicts confined there during the year 1867, not less than 557 could read "tolerably" and "well"; all "with profit to themselves"; while out of the 393 who were "practically unable to read," only 47 could be described as "entirely ignorant." Upon reception, 503 of these prisoners could write a letter, and only 142 were "entirely ignorant" of writing; while in arithmetic considerably more than half understood "simple addition," and nearly half comprehended the "simple rules" of the science. In Portland Prison,[3] another very large establishment, out of 661 prisoners received, 266 were "sufficiently educated to be exempted from school,"[4] and only 20 "could neither read nor write." From Portsmouth Convict Prison,[5] also a Government establishment, the Chaplain reports that, "of the 588 prisoners received in 1867, 460 were found able to read and write tolerably, 80 imperfectly, and 46 not at all."

As to the physical condition of convicts, this is generally much improved during imprisonment;[6] but what I wish to press upon this point is that improvement

1. A public works prison opened in 1856.
2. First national penitentiary, opened in London in 1816. Inmates were drawn from those who seemed most capable of reformation. As Arnold mentions below, by 1868 Millbank and Pentonville were being used as "depôt" prisons where convicts were assessed before being assigned to another penal institution.
3. A public works prison opened in 1848.
4. Instruction, often presented as a privilege, was provided in most prisons, though the extent and quality varied widely.
5. A public works prison opened in 1852.
6. Charles Dickens and Thomas Carlyle were among those critical of the relatively comfortable conditions in modern prisons such as Pentonville (see next note). In an article entitled "Pet Prisoners," which appeared in the April 28, 1850, issue of his journal *Household Words*, Dickens, a proponent of judicious prison reform, expressed outrage that convicted criminals were fed and housed better than paupers in workhouses; through the experiences of the hypocritical villains Uriah Heep

is always proportioned to the suitableness of their employment, and to the encouragement which is given them to exert themselves in their compulsory labour. The figures which I shall quote in support of this will abundantly prove that convicts live under better sanitary conditions than the average of the population, and will show that their mode of life under punishment is by no means prejudicial to health or ability for work.

In Pentonville Prison,[7] where 1,007 prisoners were admitted during 1867, there was no death in the course of the year. In Portland Prison, where the daily average number of convicts throughout the year was 1,434, there were eleven deaths, three of that number being caused by "fatal accident upon the public works." Other large prisons show a similarly low death-rate. It may be said that this test is not fair, because the sick and unhealthy convicts are sent to Woking Prison Hospital.[8] But when we find that during the last seven years the average number of invalids at Woking has been 799, and the deaths 35 annually, we have conclusive proof that convicts are not an unhealthy class, and that their treatment is not detrimental to existence. This hospital death-rate is only 43 per thousand, which is not nearly equal to twice the ordinary death-rate of Manchester or Liverpool, and is less than two thirds of the mortality which at one time, regularly and unchecked by sanitary reform, was permitted to diminish the ranks of the Anglo-Indian army.

For such a body of men, generally healthy and not destitute of education, it would seem easy to provide remunerative employment, so that their cost to the country should be much reduced, and if possible, turned to an advantage. But so great are the difficulties attending endeavours to make compulsory labour of unskilled men profitable, that this latter possibility has scarcely ever been regarded by those charged with the care of criminals but as extravagant and unattainable. That it is practically so in most of the existing prisons I have no doubt, because, for the most part, the prisoners received are without skill in any kind of labour. In a recent communication addressed to me on the subject of prison labour, the Governor of Portland Prison wrote: "Only a few mechanics are now received into this prison"; and throughout all the gaols of the kingdom, the "hard labour" undertaken is of the least remunerative character, and is frequently what may be called "idle labour," by which I mean entirely unproductive labour, a waste of strength exerted upon compulsion and with no object but the punishment of the labourer.

---

and Mr. Littimer in his 1849–50 novel *David Copperfield,* he satirized the separate system and the prospect of religious reformation.

Thomas Carlyle, who held most philanthropic projects in contempt, issued "Model Prisons" in March 1850 as the second of his eight essays collectively titled *Latter-Day Pamphlets;* in it he vented his scorn for the clean, wholesome "accommodation of the scoundrel-world" when, just beyond the walls of the "beautiful [prison] Establishment," the honest poor "toil and moil . . . amid famine, darkness, tumult, dust and desolation."

In 1863, the government-appointed Carnarvon Committee went so far as to advise that prison diet be worse than workhouse diet so paupers would not be enticed to commit crimes in order to be sent to jail.

7. A "model" prison, opened in 1842, where a strict separate system was in force. The architectural design allowed each cell door to be visible from a central location.

8. Opened in 1860 and used for invalid and mentally disturbed convicts.

In or near to every assize town, and in two or three towns of several counties, there are prisons, and all of these establishments are managed upon the same system, the average cost of the prisoners varying very much according to the number in each gaol. In Abingdon Prison, the average annual cost of each inmate is 55*l*. 12*s*. 3*d*., while in Swansea Prison, this charge is only 21*l*. 19*s*. The average annual cost of each prisoner in the borough and county gaols may be fairly assessed at the medium between these two amounts, which are taken after the deduction of any profit derived from the prisoners' labour. In Abingdon Prison, the total net profit so obtained during the year was 5*l*. 6*s*. 5*d*.; in Poole Gaol the labour of all the prisoners only produced a net profit amounting to 1*l*. 5*s*. during the twelve months; and in Cold Bath Fields Prison,[9] where there were 1,585 prisoners "employed at profitable labour," the net profit on their work for the year 1867 was considerably less than 1*l*. per head!

It seems to be a matter of great difficulty to invent prison labour, for in all the English prisons the labour adopted is of a similar and, in my opinion, equally improper character. The treadmill—which it is high time should be broken up, one specimen only being retained for the British Museum—is still in general use and, indeed, in growing favour.[10] At Cold Bath Fields there is a treadmill constructed to employ 342 convicts, the power being usually devoted to grinding wheat. This is the biggest "mill" in the kingdom, and there are comparatively few of which the power is so usefully bestowed. The most recent reports from the governors of county and borough gaols show that a majority of the treadmills at work have no other use than providing hard labour.

But prisoners may be ignorant whether the power of their tread is or is not producing flour or lifting water; degrading and unsuitable as the work is, there appears to be at least a fiction of useful labour about the treadmill which does not exist in the employment of "shot drill,"[11] with one exception the most wanton waste of human labour that ever entered the mind of a gaoler. Many of the prison yards are "arranged for shot drill," and "shot drill about to be introduced" occurs in many of the reports from the minor prisons. Thus hard labour is to be accomplished by making the convicts roll and carry round shot about a yard, the prisoners knowing all the while that their labour is wasted.

But even the shot drill does not appear to me so wicked an invention as the "hard labour machines,"[12] of which there are ten in use at the Bedford County Prison, and hundreds throughout the kingdom. Can anything be more demoralising, more devilish, than such a waste of power? Of the inhabitants of gaols, most

9. A·House of Correction.

10. Invented by Sir William Cubitt (1785–1861), a civil engineer, the treadmill (or treadwheel) was first used in Brixton Prison in 1817. Operated by a person walking on the steps of a mounted wheel, the treadmill was originally intended to supply power for grinding grain, but in some prisons was used simply as a means of punishment and served no useful purpose. In other prisons, treadmills were used to draw water or to power windmills that provided ventilation.

11. Line of prisoners compelled to lift and pass cannon balls for an hour or more.

12. Arnold may be referring to the crank, a hand-cranked iron drum, which scooped up sand and emptied it.

are there because they neglected to labour and wished to eat and drink without making payment in work. With such men, the obvious duty of the State is to teach them the honour and the worthiness of labour; the only justification for holding such men to hard labour, is to give them habits of industry, to enforce work, and by the compulsion to create a habit. If it be not this—if work be made hateful and degrading to the man who has wronged the commonwealth by neglecting to labour—how can good results be looked for from our prison system? Is not the State most false to its duty when it thus degrades labour in the eyes of prisoners? Suppose a man of the working class imprisoned and compelled to abuse the strength which has provided his family with food and clothing and many comforts—suppose such a one set to work a hard labour machine—would not this be moral prostitution of the most shameful character?

Or suppose him, with insult to the trained skill of his fingers, employed upon that very common prison labour, picking oakum,[13] at which a man, beginning with bleeding finger-ends and broken nails, may earn 3s. 6d. in a calendar month, during which time he will have picked about a hundred-weight; such a man is degraded in his own estimation far more than by his crime or his condemnation. His education, bad as it may have been, has however not left him ignorant of the value of good work: in prison he is taught that his skill cannot be better employed than in working a hard labour machine or in picking oakum. He is daily trained to idleness by this bad prison system, because without some encouragement to labour no man will fully exert his strength. And when he leaves the gaol it is more than probable that his skill in his own trade is nearly lost, and that the only career which seems open is one that will quickly return him to the treadmill and the oakum.

I well know the difficulty of providing suitable labour for unskilled men, and am quite willing to admit that it is hardly possible to abolish such degrading work while the prisoners are dispersed in so many small prisons. A part of the reform I intend to propose would be the disuse of these prisons for any persons undergoing punishment, and the concentration in every circuit of all the prisoners at one large establishment. Under the worst system, the cost of supervision is reduced by aggregation. This may be seen from the reports of two of the county prisons I have previously mentioned. In Abingdon Prison, where the average number in confinement is 10, the annual cost of each prisoner is more than 55l., and in Swansea Prison, where the average number in custody is 116, the annual cost of each prisoner does not amount to 22l. The average cost to the counties of the thousands of persons who are confined in the local gaols and prisons exceeds for each prisoner the wages of an agricultural labourer, and outside the prison, would be held to be sufficient for the maintenance of a man with his wife and family of young children!

Prisoners sentenced to penal servitude are sent to the convict depôts at Millbank and Pentonville, to be drafted off from thence to the Government establishments at Chatham, Portland, Portsmouth, or elsewhere, there to be employed

---

13. A loose hemp fiber used primarily for caulking seams in wooden ships.

upon public works; and the results of their labour in these great establishments are most satisfactory and encouraging. But men do not like compulsory work, especially when they do not receive the value of their labour. Even in these large prisons it was found impossible to get the convicts to exert their full strength without hope of reward, and lately a system of marks has been introduced by means of which the convicts earn gratuities, paid to them on their discharge, and much valued privileges within the prison. Under the same system, they are permitted by persevering labour to work off some portion of their sentences; so that, without the payment of wages, they are encouraged by rewards bearing but a very small proportion to the value of their labour, to exert themselves and lessen or entirely recompense the cost of their maintenance.

Of this mark-system, Mr. Clifton, the Governor of Portland Prison, says, "The majority of officers and prisoners understand it; the former exercise discretion in awarding the marks, and the latter appreciate their value and strive by willing industry and good conduct to earn daily the maximum number in order to reap the advantages of being promoted from the lower to the higher classes at the minimum periods, and thus be placed in possession of the additional privileges and gratuities belonging thereto."

The most signal result of this mark-system is the balance sheet of Chatham Prison for the year 1867, where, for the first time in prison history, the inmates have more than earned their food and paid the heavy cost of their clothing and supervision. The estimated expenditure of Chatham Convict Prison for the year ending March 31, 1868, was 35,315*l.* 18*s.*, of which no less than 13,382*l.* 13*s.* 3*d.* was for salaries and wages of officers, clerks, and servants. The value of the prisoners' labour, of whom there was a daily average of 990 engaged upon the works, was 40,898*l.* 7*s.* 0½*d.*, which is 5,582*l.* 8*s.* 11½*d.* in excess of the total expenditure. At Portland Prison, under the same system of labour, the result is almost equally encouraging. A daily average of 1,213 men performed work valued at 40,601*l.* 13*s.* 2*d.*, the total expenditure in reference to the prison for the year being 45,724*l.* 7*s.* 8*d.*

It does not lessen the value of these facts, nor their importance as showing what may be done with prison labour, that all this work was devoted to the construction of fortresses and the enlargement of naval and military arsenals. At Chatham, during the season, more than 17,000,000 bricks were made by the convicts, and at Portland, the work generally consisted of quarrying and dressing stone for Portsmouth and Chatham dockyards. The value of the convicts' labour was taken upon schedules approved by the Admiralty and the War Department at prices which appear to my experience fair and customary.

This mark-system is a reform in the right direction which aims at keeping hope alive in the prisoner's breast, and using that hope as the means to secure his improvement and maintenance while he is in the custody of the State. The convict from whose mind hope is excluded is beyond the reach of reform; therefore, I think this mark-system should be extended even to those under life sentence, allowing some remission of penal servitude. It has been suggested to me by a thoughtful and charitable lady, that a life sentence should be held to imply servitude only for the natural expectation of life according to authorised government tables, and I think the suggestion is well worthy of consideration as a humane endeavour to avoid the defeat of hope. It is interesting to observe how the improving moral sense of the public has practically abolished life sentences. In 1833, no less than 783 persons were sentenced to transportation for life; in 1867, there were only three persons out of a greatly increased population who received sentences of penal servitude for that indefinite period. With the year 1867, transportation has ceased after a usage of eighty years.[14] Since 1787, the English Government have shipped to Australia and Tasmania 124,201 convicts, an outlet for our criminals henceforth and for ever closed. During the past year, 451 convicts formed the conclusion of a deportation which has nearly amounted to 5,000 a year.

There is one great moral advantage in being forced to retain our "black sheep" at home, and that is in the compulsion it puts upon us to adopt a reforming system with criminals. According to the Directors of Convict Prisons, there are 24,107 male, and 3,752 female convicts "at large" in our society at the present time, and regarding the subject in the light of self-preservation only, it must be of vast importance to the community in what frame of mind, and with what fitness for employment, this army of criminals is poured from our gaols.

A great many estimable people are fearful of what they call "maudlin sentimentality" in regard to the treatment of prisoners. In advocating the extension of the mark-system and the organisation of suitable labour for all prisoners, I do not think there is any reason to fear that liberty will become less attractive by comparison with compulsory servitude. Even under the mark-system, hard work is not loved by all. Last year, in Portland Prison, R. J. No. 5,719, obtained a knife while he was in hospital and divided the *tendo achilles* of both legs, in order that he might be long kept to bed with lameness. The poor wretch succeeded in his object, and has probably lamed himself for life. Think of the horror of work this man must have had, and of his cruel resolution! Touch the thick cord-like muscle above your heel, and think what would induce you to sever, not one only, but both, before you denounce the mark-system as making the position of convicts too advantageous!

The Surgeon of Woking Invalid Prison reports concerning another prisoner whose conduct also denotes that public works, even under the mark-system, are not made too agreeable. This convict, with the same object, "nearly lost his leg by producing sores around the knee-joint, and keeping up a great degree of swelling and inflammation by means of rag and thread pushed into the wounds; that being discovered, he afterwards tried *lime,* and *again* a bandage was found firmly bound round the thigh, producing extensive swelling and lividity of the leg. A large piece of gutta percha[15] made to envelop the limb having failed to check his tampering, it

14. Legislation abolishing transportation was passed in 1857, but the practice did not officially end until a decade later.

15. A rubbery substance from various tropical trees.

was exposed outside the bedclothes day and night to the view of the officer, and soon improved."

Humane as the English system is compared with that which I have seen in Spain and other countries, where crowds of prisoners, without employment, are huddled together with little better accommodation than would be afforded to so many sheep, there will be no danger in advancing yet more in the direction of reforming prisoners by teaching them the habit and the value of useful labour. My experience with men has taught me that there is nothing the incorrigibly bad dislike more than a wholesome reformatory system. If a man can be brought in prison to perform useful labour by the promise of receiving a twentieth part of its value in money upon the expiration of his sentence, he will certainly count the weeks of his confinement with an impatience to be earning its full value, which would never have moved within him under the system of crank and treadmill labour.

If liberty had no other meaning to a convict than a pipe of tobacco when he pleased, it would have all-powerful attraction for the great majority of prisoners. The Chaplain of Millbank Prison reports that during 1867 he received no less than 109 applications from prisoners who expressed a wish to change the religion which had been registered as their creed; of these, 93 were from prisoners who on entry had been booked as Roman Catholics, and who desired to be registered as Protestants. The reverend gentleman does not ascribe these sudden and wholesale conversions to the effect of his ministrations, but to a defeated desire on the part of these prisoners to be sent to Portsmouth Prison, where, according to convict traditions, there is most probability of getting tobacco, the dockyard labour affording great facilities for obtaining the forbidden luxury from the free *employés*. It has been usual to send Roman Catholic convicts to Portsmouth, and the Chaplain of Millbank believes that prisoners frequently profess Roman Catholicism in the hope of getting sent there, and then revert to their original Protestantism when they find the design unsuccessful.

To further the progress of such a reform of prison labour as has been inaugurated at Chatham and Portland, I would propose that the smaller gaols should be used only as places of detention and not of punishment, the prisoners undergoing sentence being concentrated in large establishments where all would be employed in productive labour, the skilled hands in their own trade, and the unskilled subjected to training by a permanent staff of labour instructors. No labour should be allowed which did not admit of being valued according to printed schedules of prices. The Governor of Portland Prison, writing to me on the subject, says, "that all work performed by the convicts is done under the immediate supervision of six instructing warders, one belonging to each trade," and such a system of employment would certainly attain the double object with which I commenced:—"to effect a reduction from the heavy cost of prisons and to make the period of sentence more useful to prisoners."

In circuit gaols, each with capacity for a thousand prisoners, it would be easy to establish and maintain an organised system of labour. Whatever work could be executed for the Government with a view of reducing the cost of military, naval or other establishments, should be first taken in hand. During the summer months, gangs of convicts might be sent with tents to the shores or estuaries, where harbour and river works could be beneficially undertaken.

The Governors of the Convict Prisons report that few convicts are without at least a little knowledge of some trade or work, but even if they are quite destitute of such skill they can be profitably employed, and a month's training will make them skilful. In superintending the administration of the Cotton Famine Public Works Act,[16] I had large experience of unskilled labour. No employment could be more strange and uncongenial to prisoners than the trench-work of sewering was to the voluntary hands of the cotton operatives of Lancashire. Yet, after one month's training, more than 4,000 of such men earned good wages upon the public works, and handled their implements with such an appearance of practice, that many of them were quite the equals of the skilled men, while their health and strength were greatly improved by the change of labour.

The directors of such large prisons might engage in the production of any commodities which would be most profitable. But it would be necessary they should abandon the notion that they are restricted to the basest forms of labour. I would almost go so far as to prohibit such employment as stone-breaking, oakum picking and mat-making, which degrade most prisoners and render prison life of no use to the remainder. It is far better that a man should be engaged in abortive efforts to make a pair of shoes, than in picking oakum, an employment which might be retained as a punishment for misconduct in prison.

In the work of prisoners and the sale of their manufactures it should especially be remembered that the authorities are not encompassed by the difficulties which beset the employment of the poor by Boards of Guardians.[17] Prisoners have forfeited their claims to wages, such as would be given to working men outside the walls, and if goods of prison manufacture are sold for a third of their cost in labour, valued at the outside rate of wages, the community profits by the reduction of prison expenses and industry is not deranged; because, if proper severity of treatment is maintained within the prison, the manufacture and sale will not attract free labour.

If Boards of Guardians undertook to pay wages and to manufacture salable commodities, confusion would soon follow, because in their certain failure to manufacture at a profit, they must supplement the wages with relief from the rates. They must also, to prevent starvation, grant a minimum rate of relief alike for the idle and industrious, and by a process easily understood the earnings would exhibit a tendency to decline towards this amount, while the aggregate sum of the supplement would be always increasing, the ratepayers being taxed in order to

16. The Cotton Famine refers to conditions in England between 1862 and 1864 when the Union blockade of the South in the American Civil War cut off the cotton supply to textile manufacturers in England, resulting in mill closings and lost jobs for thousands of workers.

17. In rural regions, local officials were elected to each of the Poor Law Unions, or districts, established following the passage of the 1834 Poor Law. These Boards of Guardians were charged with distributing welfare, maintaining highways, and providing sanitation.

produce ill-made goods with the labour of persons encouraged to remain a burden upon them, until by the bankruptcy of the union the economic error was at length discovered.

Such disabilities, I repeat, do not apply to prison labour: and to employment upon the most useful and productive labour of which he is capable, every prisoner should be sentenced, this rule being accepted and made universal,—that the effect of the labour upon the prisoner is to be regarded, which cannot be good when he is deliberately taught the waste of power upon a useless treadmill or a hard labour machine, or when he is set to such work as can be better performed by steam or horses.

SAMUEL SMILES

S AMUEL SMILES (1812–1904) was, at various points in his very active life, physician, newspaper editor, political reformer, railway executive, public lecturer,
biographer, and director of the National Provident Institution. Smiles was the
grand Victorian promoter of self-reliance, the retailer of biographical sketches
wherein hard work, an enterprising spirit, and responsible thrift led individuals
to commercial and therefore social success. Self-Help Smiles, as he came to be
known, wrote a number of books that enjoyed a truly phenomenal popularity with
the British and American reading public. The most familiar of these was titled *Self-
Help;* in England, it sold over 258,000 copies and, as Smiles would proudly note in
his *Autobiography,* was also translated into at least eighteen other languages. That
Self-Help appeared in 1859 just when Darwin's *The Origin of Species* also came out
is interesting, for, as did Darwin, Smiles focused upon a struggle for existence,
economic existence in this case. For Smiles, however, there was a happy sense of
individual free will and potential progress which distinguished the struggle and
seemed to guarantee that the prudently fit and active would survive. *Self-Help* is
replete with success stories of the predictable sort; so, too, are other books by
Smiles (*The Life of George Stephenson; Lives of the Engineers; Industrial Biography;
The Huguenots; Character; Thrift; Duty; Life and Labour*). The importance and
dignity of perseverance, frugality, steady habits, delayed gratification, prudent
venturing, and, above all, hard work form the ready themes and morals throughout these books.

Although Smiles appealed to the desire of his readers for economic well-being
and social advancement, he was a moralist of the traditional sort, and, rather than
seeing acquisition and maintenance of wealth as the goal of work, he advances the
religious notion of stewardship: "For we are but as stewards, appointed to employ
the means entrusted to us for our own and for others' good." (Compare "The Use
of Money" by John Wesley in part 1.) This most famous Victorian evangelist of
work argued that the securing of material wealth was pointless unless one cultivated social benevolence in combination with personal integrity. The essential
qualities that Smiles saw in almost all whose lives he set forth as exemplary were
responsible concern for others, public-mindedness, commitment to progress, and
social justice for the entire culture. Consistently, he celebrates that resolution
which self-made men made to improve both working conditions and the well-
being of the commonwealth.

The selection below, titled "Work," is a compression of many of Smiles's often-repeated ideas concerning his favorite subject. It is the fourth chapter of *Character*, initially published in 1871. His style of argument consists in frequent quotation and reference to the thoughts of others, some his own less than famous contemporaries, but most the prominent historical and literary figures of the Western tradition with whom Smiles had a familiarity usually enjoyed only by the professional scholar. He continues the practice of sustained quotation in often lengthy footnotes that have not been included with this selection.

From *Character*

Work

"Arise therefore, and be doing, and the Lord be with thee."
—1 *Chronicles* 22:16

"Work as if thou hadst to live for aye;
Worship as if thou wert to die to-day"
—Tuscan Proverb

"C'est par le travail qu'on regne."
—Louis XIV[1]

"Blest Work! if ever thou wert curse of God,
What must His blessing be!"

—J. B. Selkirk[2]

"Let every man be *occupied,* and occupied in the highest
employment of which his nature is capable, and die with the
consciousness that he has done his best."

—Sydney Smith[3]

1. "It is by work that one rules." Louis XIV (1638–1715) was the most famous of the kings of France.
2. James Brown Selkirk (1832–1904) was the author of *Bible Truths, with Shakspearian Parallels.*
3. Sydney Smith (1771–1836), a popular essayist.

Work is one of the best educators of practical character. It evokes and disciplines obedience, self-control, attention, application, and perseverance; giving a man deftness and skill in his special calling, and aptitude and dexterity in dealing with the affairs of ordinary life.

Work is the law of our being—the living principle that carries men and nations onward. The greater number of men have to work with their hands, as a matter of necessity, in order to live; but all must work in one way or another, if they would enjoy life as it ought to be enjoyed.

Labor may be a burden and a chastisement, but it is also an honor and a glory. Without it nothing can be accomplished. All that is great in man comes through work, and civilization is its product. Were labor abolished, the race of Adam were at once stricken by moral death.

It is idleness that is the curse of man—not labor. Idleness eats the heart out of men as of nations, and consumes them as rust does iron. When Alexander[4] conquered the Persians, and had an opportunity of observing their manners, he remarked that they did not seem conscious that there could be any thing more servile than a life of pleasure, or more princely than a life of toil.

When the Emperor Severus[5] lay on his death-bed at York, whither he had been borne on a litter from the foot of the Grampians, his final watch-word to his soldiers was, *"Laboremus"* (we must work); and nothing but constant toil maintained the power and extended the authority of the Roman generals.

In describing the earlier social condition of Italy, when the ordinary occupations of rural life were considered compatible with the highest civic dignity, Pliny[6] speaks of the triumphant generals and their men returning contentedly to the plough. In those days the lands were tilled by the hands even of generals, the soil exulting beneath a ploughshare crowned with laurels, and guided by a husbandman graced with triumphs: *"Ipsorum tunc manibus imperatorum colebantur agri: ut fas est credere, gaudente terra vomere laureato et triumphali aratore."*[7] It was only after slaves became extensively employed in all departments of industry that labor came to be regarded as dishonorable and servile. And so soon as indolence and luxury became the characteristics of the ruling classes of Rome, the downfall of the empire, sooner or later, was inevitable.

There is, perhaps, no tendency of our nature that has to be more carefully guarded against than indolence. When Mr. Gurney asked an intelligent foreigner who had travelled over the greater part of the world, whether he had observed any one quality which, more than another, could be regarded as a universal characteristic of our species, his answer was, in broken English, "Me tink dat all men

---

4. Alexander the Great (356–333 B.C.E.), Macedonian king and military leader who extended his rule and Greek culture over the Eastern Mediterranean world and the Near East.

5. Lucius Septimius Severus (145–211), Roman Emperor from 193 to 211, took a major interest in stabilizing Roman rule in Britain.

6. Smiles may refer here either to Pliny the Elder (23–79) or his nephew Pliny the Younger (62–112). The former is better known as a natural historian, the latter as a prose stylist and writer of epistles.

7. As is his common practice, Smiles translates the Latin prefatory to the quotation itself.

love lazy." It is characteristic of the savage as of the despot. It is natural to men to endeavor to enjoy the products of labor without its toils. Indeed, so universal is this desire, that James Mill[8] has argued that it was to prevent its indulgence at the expense of society at large, that the expedient of Government was originally invented.

Indolence is equally degrading to individuals as to nations. Sloth never made its mark in the world, and never will. Sloth never climbed a hill, nor overcame a difficulty that it could avoid. Indolence always failed in life, and always will. It is in the nature of things that it should not succeed in any thing. It is a burden, an incumbrance, and a nuisance—always useless, complaining, melancholy, and miserable.

Burton, in his quaint and curious book—the only one, Johnson says, that ever took him out of bed two hours sooner than he wished to rise—describes the causes of Melancholy as hinging mainly on Idleness.[9] "Idleness," he says, "is the bane of body and mind, the nurse of naughtiness, the chief mother of all mischief, one of the seven deadly sins, the devil's cushion, his pillow and chief reposal. . . . An idle dog will be mangy; and how shall an idle person escape? Idleness of the mind is much worse than that of the body: wit, without employment, is a disease—the rust of the soul, a plague, a hell itself. As in a standing pool, worms and filthy creepers increase, so do evil and corrupt thoughts in an idle person; the soul is contaminated. . . . Thus much I dare boldly say: he or she that is idle, be they of what condition they will, never so rich, so well allied, fortunate, happy—let them have all things in abundance and felicity that heart can wish and desire, all contentment—so long as he, or she, or they, are idle, they shall never be pleased, never well in body or mind, but weary still, sickly still, vexed still, loathing still, weeping, sighing, grieving, suspecting, offended with the world, with every object, wishing themselves gone or dead, or else carried away with some foolish phantasie or other."

Burton says a great deal more to the same effect; the burden and lesson of his book being embodied in the pregnant sentence with which it winds up: "Only take this for a corollary and conclusion, as thou tenderest thine own welfare in this, and all other melancholy, thy good health of body and mind, observe this short precept, Give not way to solitariness and idleness. *Be not solitary—be not idle.*"

The indolent, however, are not wholly indolent. Though the body may shirk labor, the brain is not idle. If it do not grow corn, it will grow thistles, which will be found springing up all along the idle man's course in life. The ghosts of indolence rise up in the dark, ever staring the recreant in the face, and tormenting him:

> "The gods are just, and of our pleasant vices,
> Make instruments to scourge us."[10]

True happiness is never found in torpor of the faculties, but in their action and useful employment. It is indolence that exhausts, not action, in which there is life, health, and pleasure. The spirits may be exhausted and wearied by employment, but they are utterly wasted by idleness. Hence a wise physician was accustomed to regard occupation as one of his most valuable remedial measures. "Nothing is so injurious," said Dr. Marshall Hall, "as unoccupied time." An archbishop of Mayence used to say that "the human heart is like a millstone: if you put wheat under it, it grinds the wheat into flour; if you put no wheat, it grinds on, but then 'tis itself it wears away."

Indolence is usually full of excuses; and the sluggard, though unwilling to work, is often an active sophist. "There is a lion in the path;" or "The hill is hard to climb;" or "There is no use trying—I have tried, and failed, and can not do it." To the sophistries of such an excuser, Sir Samuel Romilly[11] once wrote to a young man: "My attack upon your indolence, loss of time, etc., was most serious, and I really think that it can be to nothing but your habitual want of exertion that can be ascribed your using such curious arguments as you do in your defense. Your theory is this: Every man does all the good that he can. If a particular individual does no good, it is a proof that he is incapable of doing it. That you don't write proves that you can't; and your want of inclination demonstrates your want of talents. What an admirable system!—and what beneficial effects would it be attended with if it were but universally received!"

It has been truly said that to desire to possess without being burdened with the trouble of acquiring is as much a sign of weakness, as to recognize that every thing worth having is only to be got by paying its price is the prime secret of practical strength. Even leisure can not be enjoyed unless it is won by effort. If it have not been earned by work, the price has not been paid for it.

There must be work before and work behind, with leisure to fall back upon; but the leisure, without the work, can no more be enjoyed than a surfeit. Life must needs be disgusting alike to the idle rich man as to the idle poor man, who has no work to do, or, having work, will not do it. The words found tattooed on the right arm of a sentimental beggar of forty, undergoing his eighth imprisonment in the jail of Bourges in France, might be adopted as the motto of all idlers: *"Le passé m'a trompé; le présent me tourment; l'avenir m'épouvante"* (The past has deceived me; the present torments me; the future terrifies me).

The duty of industry applies to all classes and conditions of society. All have

---

10. The words are Edgar's in Shakespeare's *King Lear,* 5.3.171–72.

11. Sir Samuel Romilly (1757–1818) was a disciple of the utilitarian Jeremy Bentham and served as legal counsel for Lady Byron in her suit to secure separation from the poet Byron. Byron despised Romilly for his actions and ridiculed him in *Don Juan,* 1.15; see also the letter to Lady Byron dated November 18, 1818, in which he regards Romilly's suicide following the death of his wife as a measure of "even-handed justice" for Romilly's part in the "blighting, branding, and exile" which Byron had undergone as a result of Lady Byron's suit.

their work to do in their respective conditions of life—the rich as well as the poor. The gentleman by birth and education, however richly he may be endowed with worldly possessions, can not but feel that he is in duty bound to contribute his quota of endeavor towards the general well-being in which he shares. He can not be satisfied with being fed, clad, and maintained by the labor of others, without making some suitable return to the society that upholds him. An honest, high-minded man would revolt at the idea of sitting down to and enjoying a feast, and then going away without paying his share of the reckoning. To be idle and useless is neither an honor nor a privilege; and though persons of small natures may be content merely to consume—*fruges consumere nati*[12]—men of average endowment, of manly aspirations, and of honest purpose, will feel such a condition to be incompatible with real honor and true dignity.

"I don't believe," said Lord Stanley (now Earl of Derby)[13] at Glasgow, "that an unemployed man, however amiable and otherwise respectable, ever was, or ever can be, really happy. As work is our life, show me what you can do, and I will show you what you are. I have spoken of love of one's work as the best preventive of merely low and vicious tastes. I will go farther, and say that it is the best preservative against petty anxieties, and the annoyances that arise out of indulged self-love. Men have thought before now that they could take refuge from trouble and vexation by sheltering themselves, as it were, in a world of their own. The experiment has often been tried, and always with one result. You can not escape from anxiety and labor—it is the destiny of humanity. . . . Those who shirk from facing trouble find that trouble comes to them. The indolent may contrive that he shall have less than his share of the world's work to do, but Nature, proportioning the instinct to the work, contrives that the little shall be much and hard to him. The man who has only himself to please finds, sooner or later, and probably sooner than later, that he has got a very hard master; and the excessive weakness which shrinks from responsibility has its own punishment too, for where great interests are excluded little matters become great, and the same wear and tear of mind that might have been at least usefully and healthfully expended on the real business of life is often wasted in petty and imaginary vexations, such as breed and multiply in the unoccupied brain."

Even on the lowest ground—that of personal enjoyment—constant useful occupation is necessary. He who labors not can not enjoy the reward of labor. "We sleep sound," said Sir Walter Scott,[14] "and our waking hours are happy, when they are employed; and a little sense of toil is necessary to the enjoyment of leisure, even when earned by study and sanctioned by the discharge of duty."

12. "Those born to consume the fruits of the earth."

13. Edward George Geoffrey Smith, Lord Stanley and Earl of Derby (1789–1869), prominent British statesman.

14. Sir Walter Scott (1771–1832) was a very popular—and very prolific—poet and novelist of the Romantic period. Smiles was particularly attracted to Scott not only because they shared a common Scots heritage but also because Scott had assumed full responsibility for the bankruptcy of a firm with which his own bookselling business was connected and had worked until his death to clear the immense debts resulting from this bankruptcy.

It is true, there are men who die of overwork; but many more die of selfishness, indulgence, and idleness. Where men break down by overwork, it is most commonly from want of duly ordering their lives, and neglect of the ordinary conditions of physical health. Lord Stanley was probably right when he said, in his address to the Glasgow students above mentioned, that he doubted whether "hard work, steadily and regularly carried on, ever yet hurt any body."

Then, again, length of *years* is no proper test of length of *life*. A man's life is to be measured by what he does in it, and what he feels in it. The more useful work the man does, and the more he thinks and feels, the more he really lives. The idle, useless man, no matter to what extent his life may be prolonged, merely vegetates.

The early teachers of Christianity ennobled the lot of toil by their example. "He that will not work," said St. Paul, "neither shall he eat";[15] and he glorified himself in that he had labored with his hands, and had not been chargeable to any man. When St. Boniface[16] landed in Britain, he came with a gospel in one hand and a carpenter's rule in the other; and from England he afterwards passed over into Germany, carrying thither the art of building. Luther[17] also, in the midst of a multitude of other employments, worked diligently for a living, earning his bread by gardening, building, turning, and even clock-making.

It was characteristic of Napoleon,[18] when visiting a work of mechanical excellence, to pay great respect to the inventor, and, on taking his leave, to salute him with a low bow. Once at St. Helena, when walking with Mrs. Balcombe, some servants came along carrying a load. The lady, in an angry tone, ordered them out of the way, on which Napoleon interposed, saying, "Respect the burden, madam." Even the drudgery of the humblest laborer contributes towards the general well-being of society; and it was a wise saying of a Chinese emperor that "if there was a man who did not work, or a woman that was idle, somebody must suffer cold or hunger in the empire."

The habit of constant useful occupation is as essential for the happiness and well-being of woman as of man. Without it women are apt to sink into a state of listless *ennui* and uselessness, accompanied by sick-headache and attacks of "nerves." Caroline Perthes[19] carefully warned her married daughter Louisa to beware of giving way to such listlessness. "I myself," she said, "when the children are gone out for a half-holiday, sometimes feel as stupid and dull as an owl by daylight; but one must not yield to this, which happens more or less to all young wives. The best relief is *work*, engaged in with interest and diligence. Work, then,

---

15. 2 Thessalonians 3:10.

16. Saint Boniface (675–754), Anglo-Saxon missionary to Germany.

17. Martin Luther (1483–1546), leader of the Protestant Reformation in Germany. In the list of Luther's occupations, Smiles refers to "turning," or the shaping of objects on a lathe.

18. Napoleon Bonaparte (1769–1821), Corsican soldier who became Emperor of France (1804–1815). Following his defeat by the British, he was exiled to the island of St. Helena.

19. Caroline Claudius Perthes (1774–1821), the wife and collaborator of Friedrich Christopher Perthes (1772–1843), who established a publishing firm in Hamburg, Germany, where he also founded a national museum. They are both celebrated in a biography of the father written by their son.

constantly and diligently, at something or other; for idleness is the devil's snare for small and great, as your grandfather says, and he says true."

Constant useful occupation is thus wholesome, not only for the body, but for the mind. While the slothful man drags himself indolently through life, and the better part of his nature sleeps a deep sleep, if not morally and spiritually dead, the energetic man is a source of activity and enjoyment to all who come within reach of his influence. Even any ordinary drudgery is better than idleness. Fuller says of Sir Francis Drake,[20] who was early sent to sea, and kept close to his work by his master, that such "pains and patience in his youth knit the joints of his soul, and made them more solid and compact." Schiller[21] used to say that he considered it a great advantage to be employed in the discharge of some daily mechanical duty— some regular routine of work, that rendered steady application necessary.

Thousands can bear testimony to the truth of the saying of Greuze,[22] the French painter, that work—employment, useful occupation—is one of the great secrets of happiness. Casaubon[23] was once induced by the entreaties of his friends to take a few days' entire rest, but he returned to his work with the remark, that it was easier to bear illness doing something than doing nothing.

When Charles Lamb[24] was released for life from his daily drudgery of desk-work at the India Office, he felt himself the happiest of men. "I would not go back to my prison," he said to a friend, "ten years longer for ten thousand pounds." He also wrote in the same ecstatic mood to Bernard Barton: "I have scarce steadiness of head to compose a letter," he said; "I am free! free as air! I will live another fifty years. . . . Would I could sell you some of my leisure! Positively the best thing a man can do is—Nothing; and next to that, perhaps, Good Works." Two years—two long and tedious years—passed; and Charles Lamb's feelings had undergone an entire change. He now discovered that official, even humdrum work—"the appointed round, the daily task"—had been good for him, though he knew it not. Time had formerly been his friend; it had now become his enemy. To Bernard Barton he again wrote: "I assure you, *no* work is worse than overwork; the mind preys on

---

20. Sir Francis Drake (1540–1596) circumnavigated the world and was knighted by Elizabeth I in 1581 for that feat. He is noted for his disruption of Spanish colonization in the New World and for taking part in the defeat of the Spanish Armada during the attempt by Philip II to invade England.

21. (Johann Cristoph) Friedrich von Schiller (1759–1805), German poet and playwright.

22. Jean-Baptiste Greuze (1725–1805), French Rococo painter whose fame has been overshadowed by that of his predecessor Antoine Watteau and his contemporary Jean-Honoré Fragonard.

23. Isaac Casaubon (1559–1614), French scholar of Huguenot background who, toward the conclusion of his life, became a naturalized British citizen. He was an indefatigable researcher and writer; his name, his absorption in arcane classical scholarship, and his failure to complete the *magnum opus* concerning church history which he had projected all helped to establish him as one model for the obsessive pedant Edward Casaubon in George Eliot's novel *Middlemarch*. Smiles had himself devoted considerable research to the success enjoyed by Huguenot émigrés, anticipating both Ernst Troeltsch (1865–1923) and Max Weber (1864–1920) in the analysis of a "Calvinist work ethic" as being bound up with the success of some individuals.

24. Charles Lamb (1775–1834), essayist and literary critic of the Romantic era who worked steadily at the East India House while publishing his writings; the best-known of his works are those published as *Essays of Elia,* first and second series.

itself—the most unwholesome of food. I have ceased to care for almost any-thing. . . . Never did the waters of heaven pour down upon a forlorner head. What I can do, and overdo, is to walk. I am a sanguinary murderer of time. But the oracle is silent."

No man could be more sensible of the practical importance of industry than Sir Walter Scott, who was himself one of the most laborious and indefatigable of men. Indeed, Lockhart[25] says of him that, taking all ages and countries together, the rare example of indefatigable energy, in union with serene self-possession of mind and manner, such as Scott's, must be sought for in the roll of great sovereigns or great captains, rather than in that of literary genius. Scott himself was most anxious to impress upon the minds of his own children the importance of industry as a means of usefulness and happiness in the world. To his son Charles, when at school, he wrote: "I can not too much impress upon your mind that *labor* is the condition which God has imposed on us in every station of life; there is nothing worth having that can be had without it, from the bread which the peasant wins with the sweat of his brow to the sports by which the rich man must get rid of his *ennui*. . . . As for knowledge, it can no more be planted in the human mind without labor than a field of wheat can be produced without the previous use of the plough. There is, indeed, this great difference, that chance or circumstances may so cause it that another shall reap what the farmer sows; but no man can be deprived, whether by accident or misfortune, of the fruits of his own studies; and the liberal and extended acquisitions of knowledge which he makes are all for his own use. Labor, therefore, my dear boy, and improve the time. In youth our steps are light, and our minds are ductile, and knowledge is easily laid up; but if we neglect our spring, our summers will be useless and contemptible, our harvest will be chaff, and the winter of our old age unrespected and desolate."

Southey[26] was as laborious a worker as Scott. Indeed, work might almost be said to form part of his religion. He was only nineteen when he wrote these words: "Nineteen years! certainly a fourth part of my life; perhaps how great a part! and yet I have been of no service to society. The clown who scares crows for twopence a day is a more useful man; he preserves the bread which I eat in idleness." And yet Southey had not been idle as a boy—on the contrary, he had been a most diligent student. He had not only read largely in English literature, but was well ac-quainted, through translations, with Tasso, Ariosto, Homer, and Ovid.[27] He felt, however, as if his life had been purposeless, and he determined to do something. He began, and from that time forward he pursued, an unremitting career of literary labor down to the close of his life—"daily progressing in learning," to use

25. John Gibson Lockhart (1794–1854), who married Scott's eldest daughter Charlotte, was a nov-elist, essayist, translator, editor, historian, and biographer. His seven-volume biography of Scott was held in high esteem by many in the nineteenth century. Smiles admired Lockhart's productivity as much as his skill as a biographer.

26. Robert Southey (1774–1843), poet, historian, and biographer who became poet laureate of England in 1813. Smiles greatly admired his prodigious literary output.

27. Torquato Tasso (1544–1595), Italian poet; Lodovica Ariosto (1474–1533), Italian poet; Ovid (43 B.C.E.–18 C.E.), Roman poet; Homer (9th century B.C.E.), Greek epic poet.

his own words—"not so learned as he is poor, not so poor as proud, not so proud as happy."

The maxims of men often reveal their character.[28] That of Sir Walter Scott was, "Never to be doing nothing." Robertson the historian, as early as his fifteenth year, adopted the maxim of *"Vita sine literis mors est"* (Life without learning is death). Voltaire's motto was, *"Toujours au travail"* (Always at work). The favorite maxim of Lacepede, the naturalist, was, *"Vivre c'est veiller"* (To live is to observe): it was also the maxim of Pliny. When Bossuet was at college, he was so distinguished by his ardor in study, that his fellow-students, playing upon his name, designated him as *Bos-suetus aratro* (the ox used to the plough). The name of *Vita-lis* (life a struggle), which the Swedish poet Sjoberg assumed, as Frederik von Hardenberg assumed that of *Nova-lis,* described the aspirations and the labors of both these men of genius.

We have spoken of work as a discipline: it is also an educator of character. Even work that produces no results, because it *is* work, is better than torpor—inasmuch as it educates faculty, and is thus preparatory to successful work. The habit of working teaches method. It compels economy of time, and the disposition of it with judicious forethought. And when the art of packing life with useful occupations is once acquired by practice, every minute will be turned to account; and leisure, when it comes, will be enjoyed with all the greater zest.

Coleridge[29] has truly observed, that "if the idle are described as killing time, the methodical man may be justly said to call it into life and moral being, while he makes it the distinct object not only of the consciousness, but of the conscience. He organizes the hours and gives them a soul; and by that, the very essence of which is to fleet and to have been, he communicates an imperishable and spiritual nature. Of the good and faithful servant, whose energies thus directed are thus methodized, it is less truly affirmed that he lives in time than that times lives in him. His days and months and years, as the stops and punctual marks in the record of duties performed, will survive the wreck of worlds, and remain extant when time itself shall be no more."

It is because application to business teaches method most effectually, that it is

---

28. Smiles especially enjoyed the practice of multiplying references and quotations. Those mentioned in this paragraph include the following:

William Robertson (1721–1793) was a scholar at Edinburgh University who wrote a number of detailed historical studies.

François-Marie Arouet (1694–1778), who assumed the name *Voltaire,* was the most famous figure of the French Enlightenment. As is the case with others whom Smiles admired, Voltaire produced a goodly amount and a goodly variety of written work.

(Bernard-Germain-)Etienne de La Ville-sur-Illon, Comte de Lacépède (1756–1825), noted French natural historian.

Jacques Benigne Bossuet (1627–1704) was a French cleric noted for his oratory.

Vitalis was the pseudonym of the Swedish Romantic poet Erik Sjoberg (1794–1828).

Friedrich Leopold von Hardenberg (1772–1801), who assumed the name *Novalis,* was a German Romantic poet.

29. Samuel Taylor Coleridge (1772–1834), English Romantic poet and essayist. It is strange that Smiles should quote Coleridge, whose life was characterized by indolence, uncompleted projects, and a general undirectedness.

so useful as an educator of character. The highest working qualities are best trained by active and sympathetic contact with others in the affairs of daily life. It does not matter whether the business relate to the management of a household or of a nation. Indeed, as we have endeavored to show in a preceding chapter, the able housewife must necessarily be an efficient woman of business. She must regulate and control the details of her home, keep her expenditure within her means, arrange every thing according to plan and system, and wisely manage and govern those subject to her rule. Efficient domestic management implies industry, application, method, moral discipline, forethought, prudence, practical ability, insight into character, and power of organization—all of which are required in the efficient management of business of whatever sort.

Business qualities have, indeed, a very large field of action. They mean aptitude for affairs, competency to deal successfully with the practical work of life—whether the spur of action lie in domestic management, in the conduct of a profession, in trade or commerce, in social organization, or in political government. And the training which gives efficiency in dealing with these various affairs is of all others the most useful in practical life. Moreover, it is the best discipline of character; for it involves the exercise of diligence, attention, self-denial, judgment, tact, knowledge of and sympathy with others.

Such a discipline is far more productive of happiness, as well as useful efficiency in life, than any amount of literary culture or meditative seclusion; for in the long run it will usually be found that practical ability carries it over intellect, and temper and habits over talent. It must, however, be added that this is a kind of culture that can only be acquired by diligent observation and carefully improved experience. "To be a good blacksmith," said General Trochu, in a recent publication, "one must have forged all his life: to be a good administrator, one should have passed his whole life in the study and practice of business."

It was characteristic of Sir Walter Scott to entertain the highest respect for able men of business; and he professed that he did not consider any amount of literary distinction as entitled to be spoken of in the same breath with the mastery in the higher departments of practical life—least of all with a first-rate captain.

The great commander leaves nothing to chance, but provides for every contingency. He condescends to apparently trivial details. Thus, when Wellington[30] was at the head of his army in Spain, he directed the precise manner in which the soldiers were to cook their provisions. When in India, he specified the exact speed at which the bullocks were to be driven; every detail in equipment was carefully arranged beforehand. And thus not only was efficiency secured, but the devotion of his men, and their boundless confidence in his command.

Like other great captains, Wellington had an almost boundless capacity for work. He drew up the heads of a Dublin Police Bill (being still the Secretary for

---

30. Arthur Wellesley (1769–1852) was made Duke of Wellington after his success in the Peninsular War against Napoleon's forces. Commander of the army that defeated Napoleon at Waterloo, he became a national hero and subsequently served as prime minister (1828–1830).

Ireland) when tossing off the mouth of the Mondego, with Junot[31] and the French army waiting for him on the shore. So Caesar, another of the greatest commanders, is said to have written an essay on Latin Rhetoric while crossing the Alps at the head of his army. And Wallenstein,[32] when at the head of 60,000 men, and in the midst of a campaign, with the enemy before him, dictated from headquarters the medical treatment of his poultry-yard.

Washington, also, was an indefatigable man of business. From his boyhood he diligently trained himself in habits of application, of study, and of methodical work. His manuscript school-books, which are still preserved, show that, as early as the age of thirteen, he occupied himself voluntarily in copying out such things as forms of receipts, notes of hand, bills of exchange, bonds, indentures, leases, land-warrants, and other dry documents, all written out with great care. And the habits which he thus early acquired were, in a great measure, the foundation of those admirable business qualities which he afterwards so successfully brought to bear in the affairs of government.

The man or woman who achieves success in the management of any great affair of business is entitled to honor—it may be, to as much as the artist who paints a picture, or the author who writes a book, or the soldier who wins a battle. Their success may have been gained in the face of as great difficulties, and after as great struggles; and where they have won their battle, it is at least a peaceful one, and there is no blood on their hands.

The idea has been entertained by some that business habits are incompatible with genius. In the Life of Richard Lovell Edgeworth,[33] it is observed of a Mr. Bicknell—a respectable but ordinary man, of whom little is known but that he married Sabrina Sidney, the *élève*[34] of Thomas Day, author of "Sandford and Merton"[35]—that "he had some of the too usual faults of a man of genius: he detested the drudgery of business." But there can not be a greater mistake. The greatest geniuses have, without exception, been the greatest workers, even to the extent of drudgery. They have not only worked harder than ordinary men, but brought to their work higher faculties and a more ardent spirit. Nothing great and durable was ever improvised. It is only by noble patience and noble labor that the masterpieces of genius have been achieved.

Power belongs only to the workers; the idlers are always powerless. It is the laborious and painstaking men who are the rulers of the world. There has not been a statesman of eminence but was a man of industry. "It is by toil," said even Louis XIV, "that kings govern." When Clarendon described Hampden,[36] he spoke of him

---

31. Andoche Junot, Duc d'Abrantes (1771–1813), one of Napoleon's most competent generals.

32. Albrecht von Wallenstein (1583–1634), Austrian nobleman and general who fought in the Thirty Years War.

33. Richard Lovell Edgeworth (1744–1817) was a member of the Irish Parliament interested in social, educational, and government reforms and father of the novelist Maria Edgeworth (1767–1849).

34. Student.

35. *The History of Sandford and Merton*, three volumes (1783–89), by Thomas Day (1748–1789) was a tremendously popular didactic children's novel.

36. Edward Hyde, Earl of Clarendon (1609–1674), was an advisor to both Charles I and Charles II,

as "of an industry and vigilance not to be tired out or wearied by the most laborious, and of parts not to be imposed on by the most subtle and sharp, and of a personal courage equal to his best parts." While in the midst of his laborious though self-imposed duties, Hampden, on one occasion, wrote to his mother: "My lyfe is nothing but toyle, and hath been for many yeares, nowe to the Commonwealth, nowe to the Kinge. . . . Not so much tyme left as to doe my dutye to my deare parents, nor to sende to them." Indeed, all the statesmen of the Commonwealth were great toilers; and Clarendon himself, whether in office or out of it, was a man of indefatigable application and industry.

The same energetic vitality, as displayed in the power of working, has distinguished all the eminent men in our own as well as in past times. During the Anti-Corn-Law[37] movement, Cobden,[38] writing to a friend, described himself as "working like a horse, with not a moment to spare." Lord Brougham[39] was a remarkable instance of the indefatigably active and laborious man; and it might be said of Lord Palmerston,[40] that he worked harder for success in his extreme old age than he had ever done in the prime of his manhood—preserving his working faculty, his good-humor and *bonhomie,* unimpaired to the end. He himself was accustomed to say that being in office, and consequently full of work, was good for his health. It rescued him from *ennui.* Helvetius[41] even held that it is man's sense of *ennui* that is the chief cause of his superiority over the brute—that it is the necessity which he feels for escaping from its intolerable suffering that forces him to employ himself actively, and is hence the greatest stimulus to human progress.

Indeed, this living principle of constant work, of abundant occupation, of practical contact with men in the affairs of life, has in all times been the best

---

having followed the latter into exile and having assumed the position of Lord Chancellor once Charles II had been restored to the throne. He wrote a history of the Civil War *(The True Historical Narrative of the Rebellion and Civil Wars in England)* in which he offers a complimentary appraisal of the staunchness of John Hampden (1594–1643), a political agitator who fought with the Parliamentary forces against Clarendon and the Royalists.

37. In nineteenth-century England, the word *corn* referred to any cereal grain. The Corn Laws placed a tariff upon imported grains, thereby guaranteeing English grain producers a stable market. However, such protectionism was strongly opposed by those who believed that this regulation made the price of bread too dear for the working classes, especially during hard times. Resistance to regulation became more pointed after 1828, when specific legislation made the Corn Laws seem still more repressive, and various anti–Corn Law associations were formed.

38. Richard Cobden (1804–1865), a successful manufacturer prominent in the anti–Corn Law lobby. He served as a member of Parliament and spoke strongly for both free trade and extension of the suffrage.

39. Henry Brougham (1778–1868), liberal Whig politician who, in 1826, helped found the Society for the Diffusion of Useful Knowledge and who also, in 1856, fostered the organization of the National Association for the Promotion of Social Science. Committed to both educational and legal reforms, Brougham was a reformer whose championing of mechanics' institutes was particularly appreciated by Smiles.

40. John Henry Temple Palmerston (1784–1865), the most prominent English politician of the first half of the nineteenth century, serving two sustained terms as prime minister and holding important positions in other ministries wherein he vigorously championed England's global interests.

41. Claude Adrien Helvetius (1715–1771), one of the better-known *philosophes* of the French Enlightenment.

ripener of the energetic vitality of strong natures. Business habits, cultivated and disciplined, are found alike useful in every pursuit—whether in politics, literature, science, or art. Thus, a great deal of the best literary work has been done by men systematically trained in business pursuits. The same industry, application, economy of time and labor, which have rendered them useful in the one sphere of employment, have been found equally available in the other.

Most of the early English writers were men of affairs, trained to business; for no literary class as yet existed, excepting it might be the priesthood. Chaucer, the father of English poetry, was first a soldier, and afterwards a comptroller of petty customs. The office was no sinecure either, for he had to write up all the records with his own hand; and when he had done his "reckonings" at the custom-house, he returned with delight to his favorite studies at home—poring over his books until his eyes were "dazed" and dull.

The great writers in the reign of Elizabeth, during which there was such a development of robust life in England, were not literary men according to the modern acceptation of the word, but men of action trained in business.[42] Spenser acted as secretary to the Lord Deputy of Ireland; Raleigh was, by turns, a courtier, soldier, sailor, and discoverer; Sydney was a politician, diplomatist, and soldier; Bacon was a laborious lawyer before he became lord keeper and lord chancellor; Sir Thomas Browne was a physician in country practice at Norwich; Hooker was the hard-working pastor of a country parish; Shakspeare was the manager of a theatre, in which he was himself but an indifferent actor, and he seems to have been even more careful of his money investments than he was of his intellectual offspring. Yet these, all men of active business habits, are among the greatest writers of any age;

---

42. Smiles refers to a number of English writers in this paragraph:

Edmund Spenser (1552–1599), in addition to the *Amoretti* sonnet sequence, *The Shepheardes Calendar,* "Astrophel" (an elegy for Sir Philip Sidney), and other poetry, historical analyses, and essays, authored the monumental but uncompleted romance epic *The Faerie Queene;* much of *The Faerie Queene* was composed while Spenser was serving as secretary to Lord Grey of Wilson, lord deputy in Ireland, and, indeed, Spenser points some of the political allegory of book 5 toward the situation in Ireland.

Sir Walter Raleigh (1554–1618), indeed, fulfilled all the roles that Smiles here sets forth; his most famous literary work is *The History of the World,* composed while he was imprisoned for a lengthy period (1603–16) on fabricated charges of treason, for which he was ultimately executed.

Sir Philip Sidney (1554–1586) was an Elizabethan courtier, soldier, and poet noted for his prose pastoral romance *The Arcadia,* his sonnet sequence *Astrophel and Stella,* and his treatise *A Defense of Poetry.*

Francis Bacon (1561–1626) was a courtier who accumulated considerable wealth as a very successful holder of political offices during the reigns of Elizabeth I and James I, eventually securing the title first Baron Verulam and Viscount St. Albans. He was also a most prolific author whose writings on philosophy, natural history, utopian thought, and political history influenced, both in style and approach to subject matter, many subsequent writers. He is generally credited with valorizing an experimental, inductive approach to understanding the natural world.

Samuel Smiles was particularly attracted to Thomas Browne (1605–1682), for, like Smiles, Browne was a medical practitioner who achieved more recognition for his literary output, in Browne's case notably three works of meditative philosophical reflection: *Religio Medici, The Garden of Cyrus,* and *Hydriotaphia or Urn Burial.*

Richard Hooker (1554–1600) was an Anglican cleric and scholar who authored *Of the Laws of Ecclesiastical Politie,* a lengthy defense of the evolution of the English Church under the rule of Elizabeth I.

the period of Elizabeth and James I standing out in the history of England as the era of its greatest literary activity and splendor.

In the reign of Charles I, Cowley[43] held various offices of trust and confidence. He acted as private secretary to several of the royalist leaders, and was afterwards engaged as private secretary to the queen, in ciphering and deciphering the correspondence which passed between her and Charles I—the work occupying all his days, and often his nights, during several years. And while Cowley was thus employed in the royal cause, Milton was employed by the Commonwealth, of which he was the Latin secretary,[44] and afterwards secretary to the lord protector.[45] Yet, in the earlier part of his life, Milton was occupied in the humble vocation of a teacher. Dr. Johnson says, "that in his school, as in every thing else which he undertook, he labored with great diligence, there is no reason for doubting." It was after the Restoration, when his official employment ceased, that Milton entered upon the principal literary work of his life; but before he undertook the writing of his great epic, he deemed it indispensable that to "industrious and select reading" he should add "steady observation," and "insight into all seemly and generous arts and affairs."

Locke[46] held office in different reigns: first under Charles II as secretary to the board of trade, and afterwards under William III as commissioner of appeals and of trade and plantations. Many literary men of eminence held office in Queen Anne's reign. Thus Addison was secretary of state; Steele, commissioner of stamps; Prior, under-secretary of state, and afterwards ambassador to France; Tickell, under-

43. Abraham Cowley (1618–1667), courtier and poet noted for introducing into English verse the Pindaric ode.

44. Latin was still, in Milton's day, the language employed in certain international communications; the position of Latin secretary was a rather important one.

45. The "lord protector" was Oliver Cromwell (1599–1658), the most powerful of the political and military leaders who deposed and executed Charles I. As it became clear in the early 1650s that Commonwealth government in England would not prove effectual, Cromwell assumed dictatorial powers and most of the trappings of monarchy. Milton continued as Latin secretary until the Restoration, but Smiles greatly exaggerates the closeness of his relationship with Cromwell.

46. In this paragraph, once again, Smiles supplies multiple references:

John Locke (1632–1704) was a physician and scholar best known for his rational empiricism evidenced in the *Essay Concerning Human Understanding* (1690) and for his conception of contractual civil polity advanced in the *Treatises of Government* (1690).

Joseph Addison (1672–1719) was a prominent Whig politician and noted prose stylist who, with Richard Steele, popularized the familiar essay in periodical publications such as *The Tatler, The Spectator,* and *The Guardian.*

Richard Steele (1672–1729) was a Whig who received various political appointments and sinecures during the reign of Queen Anne. He was the motivating force behind *The Tatler, The Spectator,* and *The Guardian,* and he helped introduce to the English stage the sentimental drama that replaced the comedy of wit and manners characteristic of Restoration drama.

Matthew Prior (1664–1721) was a satirist and poet who was also, in large measure, responsible for the terms established in the 1713 Treaty of Utrecht that concluded the longstanding war with France.

Thomas Tickell (1685–1740) was a minor poet who also served, after Addison's death, as the editor for Addison's works.

William Congreve (1670–1729) brought the Restoration comedy of wit to its most elegant refinement in such plays as *Love for Love* (1695) and *The Way of the World* (1700). He grew wealthy as a result of his political appointments, which allowed him to live well in polite society.

John Gay (1685–1732) was a poet and playwright who achieved his best success with *The Beggar's Opera* (1728) only a few years before his death.

secretary of state, and secretary to the lords justices of Ireland; Congreve secretary to Jamaica; and Gay, secretary of legation at Hanover.

Indeed, habits of business, instead of unfitting a cultivated mind for scientific or literary pursuits, are often the best training for them. Voltaire insisted with truth that the real spirit of business and literature are the same; the perfection of each being the union of energy and thoughtfulness, of cultivated intelligence and practical wisdom, of the active and contemplative essence—a union commended by Lord Bacon as the concentrated excellence of man's nature. It has been said that even the man of genius can write nothing worth reading in relation to human affairs, unless he has been in some way or other connected with the serious every-day business of life. . . .

Nor, on the other hand, have thoroughly-trained men of science and learning proved themselves inefficient as first-rate men of business. Culture of the best sort trains the habit of application and industry, disciplines the mind, supplies it with resources, and gives it freedom and vigor of action—all of which are equally requisite in the successful conduct of business. Thus, in young men, education and scholarship usually indicate steadiness of character, for they imply continuous attention, diligence, and the ability and energy necessary to master knowledge; and such persons will also usually be found possessed of more than average promptitude, address, resource, and dexterity.

Montaigne[47] has said of true philosophers that "if they were great in science, they were yet much greater in action; . . . and whenever they have been put upon the proof, they have been seen to fly to so high a pitch, as made it very well appear their souls were strangely elevated and enriched with the knowledge of things."

At the same time, it must be acknowledged that too exclusive a devotion to imaginative and philosophical literature, especially if prolonged in life until the habits become formed, does to a great extent incapacitate a man for the business of practical life. Speculative ability is one thing, and practical ability another; and the man who, in his study, or with his pen in hand, shows himself capable of forming large views of life and policy, may, in the outer world, be found altogether unfitted for carrying them into practical effect.

Speculative ability depends on vigorous thinking—practical ability on vigorous acting; and the two qualities are usually found combined in very unequal proportions. The speculative man is prone to indecision; he sees all the sides of a question, and his action becomes suspended in nicely weighing the pros and cons, which are often found pretty nearly to balance each other; whereas the practical man overleaps logical preliminaries, arrives at certain definite convictions, and proceeds forthwith to carry his policy into action. . . .

To conclude: a fair measure of work is good for mind as well as body. Man is an intelligence sustained and preserved by bodily organs, and their active exercise is

47. Michel Eyquem de Montaigne (1533–1592), a French courtier and writer whose *Essais* had considerable influence on subsequent French and English writing, especially during the latter eighteenth and the nineteenth centuries.

necessary to the enjoyment of health. It is not work, but overwork, that is hurtful; and it is not hard work that is injurious so much as monotonous work, fagging work, hopeless work. All hopeful work is healthful; and to be usefully and hopefully employed is one of the great secrets of happiness. Brain-work, in moderation, is no more wearing than any other kind of work. Duly regulated, it is as promotive of health as bodily exercise; and, where due attention is paid to the physical system, it seems difficult to put more upon a man than he can bear. Merely to eat and drink and sleep one's way idly through life is vastly more injurious. The wear-and-tear of rust is even faster than the tear-and-wear of work.

But overwork is always bad economy. It is, in fact, great waste, especially if conjoined with worry. Indeed, worry kills far more than work does. It frets, it excites, it consumes the body—as sand and grit, which occasion excessive friction, wear out the wheels of a machine. Overwork and worry have both to be guarded against. For over-brain-work is strain-work; and it is exhausting and destructive according as it is in excess of nature. And the brain-worker may exhaust and overbalance his mind by excess, just as the athlete may overstrain his muscles and break his back by attempting feats beyond the strength of his physical system.

GERARD MANLEY HOPKINS

GERARD MANLEY HOPKINS (1844–1889) was virtually unknown as a poet in his own lifetime: most of his poetry remained unpublished until 1918. As a student at Oxford, Hopkins had Walter Pater as his tutor, and from Pater he received a sense of the transcendent if ephemeral nature of physical beauty. At Oxford, he also was caught up in the High Church movement and then converted to Roman Catholicism, eventually becoming a Jesuit priest. Hopkins wrote relatively little, subordinating his own desire to compose poetry to the demands placed upon him in his work as parish priest and teacher. His own devotion to duty and work was a virtue that he needed to cultivate: he was disposed to reflection and introspection. His appreciation of the worth and the beauty of work is a feature of his poetry that often has gone unremarked.

In "Harry Ploughman," readers find the readiest example of Hopkins's celebrated emphasis upon instress and inscape. Instress he sees as the natural energy or force required to enable any element of creation to realize its ideal form or inscape. Hopkins links instress to pressure or energy in this fashion in his introductory comments on the Ignatian Spiritual Exercises: "Chance then is the *energeia,* the stress, of the intrinsic possibility which things have." In speaking about the divine stress of God's indwelling in man, Hopkins adopts analogies that reflect his conviction that some vital energy straining against boundaries is requisite for a being to realize its ideal potential: he posits that conformity to Christ "best brings out the nature of the man himself, as the lettering on a sail or device upon a flag are best seen when it fills." Inscape, then, comprises beauty, yet since instress creates a body's latent inscape, the more intense the instress the more strikingly brilliant the resulting design.

It is this intensity of instress that is best seen in the worker's body in the midst of toil, when the maximum energy necessary to that which is aesthetically sound constitutes an excruciating tautness akin to physical anguish. Hopkins intended "Harry Ploughman" as a "direct picture of a ploughman without afterthought." Hopkins directs all attention to the interplay of bone, muscle, nerve, and sinew as the man's whole being "Stand[s] at stress." There is no actual suffering in this sonnet, yet there is straining tantamount to suffering, and Hopkins feared that it might strike the reader as "intolerably violent." Harry Ploughman experiences, happily it would seem, an extremity of physical exertion which creates in him shifting inscapes of manly power, the beauty of the working body in which Hopkins delights.

Figure 2.6. Sir George Clausen, *The Mowers*. Courtesy of Lincolnshire County Council, Usher Gallery, England.

Influenced by the French Impressionists, particularly Jean François Millet (1814–1875) and Claude Monet (1840–1926), Sir George Clausen (1852–1944) produced a number of images of traditional agricultural laborers, such as *The Mowers* of 1893.

Harry Ploughman

Hard as hurdle[1] arms, with a broth of goldish flue
Breathed round; the rack of ribs; the scooped flank; lank
Rope-over thigh;[2] knee-nave; and barrelled shank—
    Head and foot, shouldér and shank—
By a grey eye's heed steered well, one crew,[3] fall to;   5
Stand at stress. Each limb's barrowy[4] brawn, his thew[5]
That onewhere curded,[6] onewhere sucked or sank—
    Soared ór sánk—,
Though as a beechbole firm, finds his,[7] as at a rollcall, rank
And features, in flesh, what deed he[8] each must do—   10
His sinew-service where do.
He leans to it, Harry bends, look. Back, elbow, and liquid waist
In him, all quáil[9] to the wallowing o' the plough. 'S[10] cheek crímsons; curls
Wag or crossbridle, in a wind lifted, windlaced—
    Wind-lilylocks-laced;   15
Churlsgrace too, chíld of Amansstrength, how it hángs or hurls
Them—broad in bluff[11] hide his frowning[12] feet lashed! raced
With, along them, cragiron under and cold furls[13]—
    With-a-fountain's shining-shot furls.

1. Wattled fences made of intertwined withes or strips of wood; the strength that derives from banded and twisted branches is descriptive of the sinewy strength Hopkins sees in Harry Ploughman.
2. Like the arms, the worker's leg has strength because it is corded, "roped" with muscle and sinew.
3. The diverse portions of the worker's body fuse in harmonious rhythm: again, Hopkins's emphasis is upon the combined strength of interwoven parts.
4. A barrow is a gelded male hog, an animal of great bulk and strength.
5. Muscle or sinew.
6. Knotted together in lumps or curds.
7. The word *his* refers to the *brawn* or *thew* of line 6.
8. The word *he* refers to the *brawn* or *thew* of line 6.
9. Curdle or coagulate: the various parts of the worker's body gather to hardness in struggling against the "wallowing of the plough."
10. His.
11. The leather of Harry Ploughman's boots.
12. Frowning as in the sense of wrinkled: within the leather or "bluff hide" of Harry Ploughman's boots, his feet, too, are tensed, creased, and ridged with the effort to move the plough.
13. Furrows. Hopkins is playing with two unrelated words: *furled*, from the Old French *ferlier*, "to tie tightly," and the Old English *fuhr*, meaning a furrow. Hopkins sometimes tried, not always with rigorous scholarship, to suggest linguistic connections between homophonic words.

WILLIAM MORRIS

F OR AN INTRODUCTION to William Morris, see "Useful Work *versus* Useless Toil" in part 1.

"The Revival of Handicraft" was originally published in the *Fortnightly Review* for November 1888. In this essay, Morris traces the decline of craftsmanship. From his perspective, the failure of modern art reflects a failure of modern society. Only when social relations are transformed will there be a true and lasting revival of handicraft.

The Revival of Handicraft

For some time past there has been a good deal of interest shown in what is called [in] our modern slang Art Workmanship, and quite recently there has been a growing feeling that this art workmanship to be of any value must have some of the workman's individuality imparted to it beside whatever of art it may have got from the design of the artist who has planned, but not executed the work. This feeling has gone so far that there is growing up a fashion for demanding handmade goods even when they are not ornamented in any way, as for instance, woollen and linen cloth spun by hand and woven without power, hand-knitted hosiery, and the like. Nay, it is not uncommon to hear regrets for the hand labour in the fields, now fast disappearing from even backward districts of civilised countries. The scythe, the sickle, and even the flail are lamented over, and many are looking forward with drooping spirits to the time when the hand plough will be as completely extinct as the quern,[1] and the rattle of the steam-engine will take the place of the whistle of the curly-headed ploughboy through all the length and breadth of the land. People interested, or who suppose that they are interested, in the details of the arts of life

1. A hand-turned grain mill.

feel a desire to revert to methods of handicraft for production in general; and it may therefore be worth considering how far this is a mere reactionary sentiment incapable of realisation, and how far it may foreshadow a real coming change in our habits of life as irresistible as the former change which has produced the system of machine production, the system against which revolt is now attempted.

In this paper I propose to confine the aforesaid consideration as much as I can to the effect of machinery *versus* handicraft upon the arts; using that latter word as widely as possible so as to include all products of labour which have any claims to be considered beautiful. I say as far as possible; for as all roads lead to Rome, so the life, habits, and aspirations of all groups and classes of the community are founded on the economical conditions under which the mass of the people live, and it is impossible to exclude socio-political questions from the consideration of æsthetics. Also, although I must avow myself a sharer in the above-mentioned reactionary regrets, I must at the outset disclaim the mere æsthetic point of view which looks upon the ploughman and his bullocks and his plough, the reaper, his work, his wife, and his dinner, as so many elements which compose a pretty tapestry hanging, fit to adorn the study of a contemplative person of cultivation, but which it is not worth while differentiating from each other except in so far as they are related to the beauty and interest of the picture. On the contrary, what I wish for is that the reaper and his wife should have themselves a due share in all the fulness of life; and I can, without any great effort, perceive the justice of their forcing me to bear part of the burden of its deficiencies, so that we may together be forced to attempt to remedy them, and have no very heavy burden to carry between us.

To return to our æsthetics: though a certain part of the cultivated classes of to-day regret the disappearance of handicraft from production, they are quite vague as to how and why it is disappearing, and as to how and why it should or may reappear. For to begin with the general public is grossly ignorant of all the methods and processes of manufacture. This is of course one result of the machine-system we are considering. Almost all goods are made apart from the life of those who use them; we are not responsible for them, our will has had no part in their production, except so far as we form a part of the market on which they can be forced for the profit of the capitalist whose money is employed in producing them. The market assumes that certain wares are wanted; it produces such wares, indeed, but their kind and quality are only adapted to the needs of the public in a very rough fashion, because the public needs are subordinated to the interest of the capitalist masters of the market, and they can force the public to put up with the less desirable article if they choose, as they generally do. The result is that in this direction our boasted individuality is a sham; and persons who wish for anything that deviates ever so little from the beaten path have either to wear away their lives in a wearisome and mostly futile contest with a stupendous organisation which disregards their wishes, or to allow those wishes to be crushed out for the sake of a quiet life.

Let us take a few trivial but undeniable examples. You want a hat, say, like that you wore last year; you go to the hatter's, and find you cannot get it there, and you have no resource but in submission. Money by itself won't buy you the hat you want; it will cost you three months' hard labour and twenty pounds to have an inch added to the brim of your wideawake;[2] for you will have to get hold of a small capitalist (of whom but few are left), and by a series of intrigues and resolute actions which would make material for a three-volume novel,[3] get him to allow you to turn one of his hands into a handicraftsman for the occasion; and a very poor handicraftsman he will be, when all is said. Again, I carry a walking-stick, and like all sensible persons like it to have a good heavy end that will swing out well before me. A year or two ago it became the fashion to pare away all walking-sticks to the shape of attenuated carrots, and I really believe I shortened my life in my attempts at getting a reasonable staff of the kind I was used to, so difficult it was. Again, you want a piece of furniture which the trade (mark the word, Trade, not Craft!) turns out, blotched over with idiotic sham ornament; you wish to dispense with this degradation, and propose it to your upholsterer, who grudgingly assents to it; and you find that you have to pay the price of two pieces of furniture for the privilege of indulging your whim of leaving out the trade finish (I decline to call it ornament) on the one you have got made for you.[4] And this is because it has been made by handicraft instead of machinery. For most people, therefore, there is a prohibitive price put upon the acquirement of the knowledge of methods and processes. We do not know how a piece of goods is made, what the difficulties are that beset its manufacture, what it ought to look like, feel like, smell like, or what it ought to cost apart from the profit of the middleman. We have lost the art of marketing, and with it the due sympathy with the life of the workshop, which would, if it existed, be such a wholesome check on the humbug of party politics.

It is a natural consequence of this ignorance of the methods of making wares, that even those who are in revolt against the tyranny of the excess of division of labour in the occupations of life, and who wish to recur more or less to handicraft, should also be ignorant of what that life of handicraft was when all wares were made by handicraft. If their revolt is to carry any hope with it, it is necessary that they should know something of this. I must assume that many or perhaps most of my readers are not acquainted with Socialist literature, and that few of them have read the admirable account of the different epochs of production given in Karl Marx' great work entitled "Capital."[5] I must ask to be excused, therefore, for stating very briefly what, chiefly owing to Marx, has become a commonplace of Socialism, but is not generally known outside it. There have been three great epochs of production since the beginning of the Middle Ages. During the first or mediæval period all production was individualistic in method; for though the

2. A low-crowned felt hat.
3. Nineteenth-century novels tended to be lengthy and were typically published in rather expensive three-volume editions.
4. Morris scorned mass-produced furnishings.
5. Karl Marx (1818–1883) published the first volume of *Capital* in 1867; volumes two and three were brought out by Friedrich Engels after Marx's death. Marx's works were little known in England until the early 1880s. Morris read a French translation of *Capital* in 1883.

workmen were combined into great associations for protection and the organisation of labour, they were so associated as citizens not as mere workmen. There was little or no division of labour, and what machinery was used was simply of the nature of a multiplied tool, a help to the workman's hand labour and not a supplanter of it. The workman worked for himself and not for any capitalistic employer, and he was accordingly master of his work and his time; this was the period of pure handicraft. When in the latter half of the sixteenth century the capitalist employer and the so-called free workman began to appear, the workmen were collected into workshops, the old tool-machines were improved, and at last a new invention, the division of labour, found its way into the workshops. The division of labour went on growing throughout the seventeenth century, and was perfected in the eighteenth, when the unit of labour became a group and not a single man; or in other words the workman became a mere part of a machine composed sometimes wholly of human beings and sometimes of human beings plus labour-saving machines, which towards the end of this period were being copiously invented; the fly-shuttle may be taken for an example of these. The latter half of the eighteenth century saw the beginning of the last epoch of production that the world has known, that of the automatic machine which supersedes hand labour, and turns the workman who was once a handicraftsman helped by tools, and next a part of a machine, into a tender of machines. And as far as we can see, the revolution in this direction as to kind is complete, though as to degree, as pointed out by Mr. David A. Wells last year (1887), the tendency is towards the displacement of ever more and more "muscular" labour, as Mr. Wells calls it.[6]

This is very briefly the history of the evolution of industry during the last five hundred years; and the question now comes: Are we justified in wishing that handicraft may in its turn supplant machinery? Or it would perhaps be better to put the question in another way: Will the period of machinery evolve itself into a fresh period of machinery more independent of human labour than anything we can conceive of now, or will it develop its contradictory in the shape of a new and improved period of production by handicraft? The second form of the question is the preferable one, because it helps us to give a reasonable answer to what people who have any interest in external beauty will certainly ask: Is the change from handicraft to machinery good or bad? And the answer to that question is to my mind that, as my friend Belfort Bax[7] has put it, statically it is bad, dynamically it is good. As a condition of life, production by machinery is altogether an evil; as an instrument for forcing on us better conditions of life it has been, and for some time yet will be, indispensable.

Having thus tried to clear myself of mere reactionary pessimism, let me attempt to show why statically handicraft is to my mind desirable, and its destruction a degradation of life. Well, first I shall not shrink from saying bluntly that produc-

---

6. David Ames Wells (1828–1898), an American economist, was a leading advocate of free trade.

7. Ernest Belfort Bax (1854–1926) was a writer who helped Morris found the Socialist League and edit *Commonweal* and with Morris wrote *Socialism, Its Growth and Outcome* (1894).

tion by machinery necessarily results in utilitarian ugliness in everything which the labour of man deals with, and that this is a serious evil and a degradation of human life. So clearly is this the fact that though few people will venture to deny the latter part of the proposition, yet in their hearts the greater part of cultivated civilised persons do not regard it as an evil, because their degradation has already gone so far that they cannot, in what concerns the sense of seeing, discriminate between beauty and ugliness: their languid assent to the desirableness of beauty is with them only a convention, a superstitious survival from the times when beauty was a necessity to all men. The first part of the proposition (that machine industry produces ugliness) I cannot argue with these persons, because they neither know, nor care for, the difference between beauty and ugliness; and with those who do understand what beauty means I need not argue it, as they are but too familiar with the fact that the produce of all modern industrialism is ugly, and that when-ever anything which is old disappears, its place is taken by something inferior to it in beauty; and that even out in the very fields and open country. The art of making beautifully all kinds of ordinary things, carts, gates, fences, boats, bowls, and so forth, let alone houses and public buildings, unconsciously and without effort has gone; when anything has to be renewed among these simple things the only question asked is how little it can be done for, so as to tide us over our respon-sibility and shift its mending on to the next generation.

It may be said, and indeed I have heard it said, that since there is some beauty still left in the world and some people who admire it, there is a certain gain in the acknowledged eclecticism of the present day, since the ugliness which is so com-mon affords a contrast whereby the beauty which is so rare, may be appreciated. This I suspect to be only another form of the maxim which is the sheet anchor of the laziest and most cowardly group of our cultivated classes, that it is good for the many to suffer for the few; but if any one puts forward in good faith the fear that we may be too happy in the possession of pleasant surroundings, so that we shall not be able to enjoy them, I must answer that this seems to me a very remote terror. Even when the tide at last turns in the direction of sweeping away modern squalor and vulgarity, we shall have, I doubt, many generations of effort in perfecting the transformation, and when it is at last complete, there will be first the triumph of our success to exalt us, and next the history of the long wade through the putrid sea of ugliness which we shall have at last escaped from. But furthermore, the proper answer to this objection lies deeper than this. It is to my mind that very consciousness of the production of beauty for beauty's sake which we want to avoid; it is just what is apt to produce affectation and effeminacy amongst the artists and their following. In the great times of art conscious effort was used to produce great works for the glory of the City, the triumph of the Church, the exaltation of the citizens, the quickening of the devotion of the faithful; even in the higher art, the record of history, the instruction of men alive and to live hereafter, was the aim rather than beauty; and the lesser art was unconscious and spontane-ous, and did not in any way interfere with the rougher business of life, while it enabled men in general to understand and sympathise with the nobler forms of art. But unconscious as these producers of ordinary beauty may be, they will not and cannot fail to receive pleasure from the exercise of their work under these conditions, and this above all things is that which influences me most in my hope for the recovery of handicraft. I have said it often enough, but I must say it once again, since it is so much a part of my case for handicraft, that so long as man allows his daily work to be mere unrelieved drudgery he will seek happiness in vain. I say further that the worst tyrants of the days of violence were but feeble tormentors compared with those Captains of Industry[8] who have taken the pleasure of work away from the workmen. Furthermore I feel absolutely certain that handicraft joined to certain other conditions, of which more presently, would produce the beauty and the pleasure in work above mentioned; and if that be so, and this double pleasure of lovely surroundings and happy work could take the place of the double torment of squalid surroundings and wretched drudgery, have we not good reason for wishing, if it might be, that handicraft should once more step into the place of machine production?

I am not blind to the tremendous change which this revolution would mean. The maxim of modern civilisation to a well-to-do man is, Avoid taking trouble! Get as many of the functions of your life as you can performed by others for you! Vicarious life is the watchword of our civilisation, and we well-to-do and cultivated people live smoothly enough while it lasts. But, in the first place, how about the vicars, who do more for us than the singing of mass for our behoof for a scanty stipend? Will they go on with it for ever? For indeed the shuffling off of responsibilities from one to the other has to stop at last, and somebody has to bear the burden in the end. But let that pass, since I am not writing politics, and let us consider another aspect of the matter. What wretched lop-sided creatures we are being made by the excess of the division of labour in the occupations of life! What on earth are we going to do with our time when we have brought the art of vicarious life to perfection, having first complicated the question by the ceaseless creation of artificial wants which we refuse to supply for ourselves? Are all of us (we of the great middle class I mean) going to turn philosophers, poets, essayists, men of genius, in a word, when we have come to look down on the ordinary functions of life with the same kind of contempt wherewith persons of good breeding look down upon a good dinner, eating it sedulously however? I shudder when I think of how we shall bore each other when we have reached that perfection. Nay, I think we have already got in all branches of culture rather more geniuses than we can comfortably bear, and that we lack, so to say, audiences rather than preachers. I must ask pardon of my readers; but our case is at once so grievous and so absurd that one can scarcely help laughing out of bitterness of soul. In the very midst of our pessimism we are boastful of our wisdom, yet we are helpless in the face of the necessities we have created, and which, in spite of our anxiety about art, are at present driving us into luxury unredeemed by beauty on

---

8. "Captains of Industry" is the title of chapter 4 in book 4 of Thomas Carlyle's *Past and Present* (1843). See the introductory essay in part 1.

the one hand, and squalor unrelieved by incident or romance on the other, and will one day drive us into mere ruin.

Yes, we do sorely need a system of production which will give us beautiful surroundings and pleasant occupation, and which will tend to make us good human animals, able to do something for ourselves, so that we may be generally intelligent instead of dividing ourselves into dull drudges or duller pleasure-seekers according to our class, on the one hand, or hapless pessimistic intellectual personages, and pretenders to that dignity, on the other. We do most certainly need happiness in our daily work, content in our daily rest; and all this cannot be if we hand over the whole responsibility of the details of our daily life to machines and their drivers. We are right to long for intelligent handicraft to come back to the world which it once made tolerable amidst war and turmoil and uncertainty of life, and which it should, one would think, make happy now we have grown so peaceful, so considerate of each other's temporal welfare.

Then comes the question, How can the change be made? And here at once we are met by the difficulty that the sickness and death of handicraft is, it seems, a natural expression of the tendency of the age. We willed the end, and therefore the means also. Since the last days of the Middle Ages the creation of an intellectual aristocracy has been, so to say, the spiritual purpose of civilisation side by side with its material purpose of supplanting the aristocracy of status by the aristocracy of wealth. Part of the price it has had to pay for its success in that purpose (and some would say it is comparatively an insignificant part) is that this new aristocracy of intellect has been compelled to forgo the lively interest in the beauty and romance of life, which was once the portion of every artificer at least, if not of every workman, and to live surrounded by an ugly vulgarity which the world amidst all its changes has not known till modern times. It is not strange that until recently it has not been conscious of this degradation; but it may seem strange to many that it has now grown partially conscious of it. It is common now to hear people say of such and such a piece of country or suburb: "Ah! it was so beautiful a year or so ago, but it has been quite spoilt by the building." Forty years back the building would have been looked on as a vast improvement; now we have grown conscious of the hideousness we are creating, and we go on creating it. We see the price we have paid for our aristocracy of intellect, and even that aristocracy itself is more than half regretful of the bargain, and would be glad if it could keep the gain and not pay the full price for it. Hence not only the empty grumbling about the continuous march of machinery over dying handicraft, but also various elegant little schemes for trying to withdraw ourselves, some of us, from the consequences (in this direction) of our being superior persons; none of which can have more than a temporary and very limited success. The great wave of commercial necessity will sweep away all these well-meant attempts to stem it, and think little of what it has done, or whither it is going.

Yet after all even these feeble manifestations of discontent with the tyranny of commerce are tokens of a revolutionary epoch, and to me it is inconceivable that machine production will develop into mere infinity of machinery, or life wholly lapse into a disregard of life as it passes. It is true indeed that powerful as the cultivated middle class is, it has not the power of re-creating the beauty and romance of life; but that will be the work of the new society which the blind progress of commercialism will create, nay, is creating. The cultivated middle class is a class of slave-holders, and its power of living according to its choice is limited by the necessity of finding constant livelihood and employment for the slaves who keep it alive. It is only a society of equals which can choose the life it will live, which can choose to forgo gross luxury and base utilitarianism[9] in return for the unwearying pleasure of tasting the fulness of life. It is my firm belief that we shall in the end realise this society of equals, and also that when it is realised it will not endure a vicarious life by means of machinery; that it will in short be the master of its machinery and not the servant, as our age is.

Meantime, since we shall have to go through a long series of social and political events before we shall be free to choose how we shall live, we should welcome even the feeble protest which is now being made against the vulgarisation of all life: first because it is one token amongst others of the sickness of modern civilisation; and next, because it may help to keep alive memories of the past which are necessary elements of the life of the future, and methods of work which no society could afford to lose. In short, it may be said that though the movement towards the revival of handicraft is contemptible on the surface in face of the gigantic fabric of commercialism; yet, taken in conjunction with the general movement towards freedom of life for all, on which we are now surely embarked, as a protest against intellectual tyranny, and a token of the change which is transforming civilisation into socialism, it is both noteworthy and encouraging.

9. Also known as Benthamism, after Jeremy Bentham (1748–1832), utilitarianism referred to the theory that humans are motivated by self-interest. Given this premise, the utilitarians argued that economic, social, and political conflicts should be resolved rationally by calculating what would produce "the greatest happiness for the greatest number" of people.

WILLIAM ERNEST HENLEY

W ILLIAM ERNEST HENLEY (1849–1903), whose hearty, declamatory personality and physical appearance served as the model for his friend Robert
Louis Stevenson's (1850–1894) characters Burly (in "Talk and Talkers") and Long
John Silver (in *Treasure Island*), was a victim of tuberculosis who had needed to
have his lower left leg amputated. In hopes of saving the other leg, he submitted in
1873 to an extended (twenty-month) hospitalization under the care of Joseph
Lister (1827–1912), celebrated for establishing practical antiseptic surgery. Two
operations overseen by Lister proved largely successful, and Henley composed a
series of poems, *In Hospital,* based upon his experiences as a long-term patient in
the Edinburgh Infirmary. Released from medical care, he entered into a vigorous
literary life as playwright, reviewer, poet, and editor. As editor of various journals
(notably the *National Observer* and the *New Review*), Henley introduced England,
in the course of fifteen years, to some of the now acclaimed but then unknown
writers of the late Victorian period: Thomas Hardy, Andrew Lang, Henry James,
William Butler Yeats, H. G. Wells, and Rudyard Kipling.

Noted for his own steady work habits, Henley offered (in *London Types* of 1898
and *In Hospital* of 1888) verse descriptions of men and women engaged in a variety
of occupations. The five selections from *In Hospital* that follow concern vocational
opportunities in the medical profession. Physicians and nurses earned increasing
respect throughout the nineteenth century in response to the growing demands
for professional preparation and conduct placed upon them. Edward H. Cohen, in
"Henley among the Nightingales" (*Nineteenth-Century Studies* 8 [1994]: 23–43),
supplies helpful commentary about the professionalization of nursing and about
the gradual realization of reforms inaugurated by Florence Nightingale (see *Cassandra* in part 1); Cohen also provides biographical backgrounds of the women
who were the original subjects of the four sonnets concerned with nurses. "House-
Surgeon," the fifth poem, suggests the substantial respectability enjoyed, in the
1870s, by the surgeon, a medical officer often somewhat looked down upon earlier
in the century.

From *In Hospital*

Scrubber[1]

She's tall and gaunt, and in her hard, sad face,
With flashes of the old fun's animation,
There lowers the fixed and peevish resignation
Bred of a past where troubles came apace.
She tells me that her husband, ere he died,   5
Saw seven of their children pass away,
And never knew the little lass at play
Out on the green, in whom he's deified.
Her kin dispersed, her friends forgot and gone,
All simple faith her honest Irish mind,   10
Scolding her spoiled young saint, she labors on:
Telling her dreams, taking her patients' part,
Trailing her coat sometimes; and you shall find
No rougher, quainter speech, nor kinder heart.

Lady-Probationer[2]

Some three, or five, or seven and thirty years;
A Roman nose; a dimpling double-chin;
Dark eyes and shy that, ignorant of sin,
Are yet acquainted, it would seem, with tears;
A comely shape; a slim, high-coloured hand,   5
Graced, rather oddly, with a signet ring;
A bashful air, becoming everything;
A well-bred silence always at command.
Her plain print gown, prim cap, and bright steel chain
Look out of place on her, and I remain   10
Absorbed in her, as in a pleasant mystery.
Quick, skilful, quiet, soft in speech and touch . . .
"Do you like nursing?" "Yes, Sir, very much."
Somehow, I rather think she has a history.

1. One of the signs of the professionalization of nursing was the establishment of a hierarchy within the ranks of women serving in hospitals. Work related to cleaning had once fallen to every nurse's lot, but, in the reformed system, such work was assigned more regularly to less well-trained individuals who came to be called "scrubbers."

2. Probationers were essentially student-nurses; often better-educated women who were financially needy, they were, in the reformed system of nursing, held to a strict professional and personal regimen, the austerity of their lives being a register of the respectability enjoyed by the new nurses.

Staff-Nurse: Old Style

The great masters of the commonplace,
Rembrandt[1] and good Sir Walter[2]—only these
Could paint her all to you: experienced ease,
And antique liveliness and ponderous grace;
The sweet old roses of her sunken face;   5
The depth and malice of her sly, gray eyes;
The broad Scots tongue that flatters, scolds, defies;
The thick Scots wit that fells you like a mace.
These thirty years has she been nursing here,
Some of them under Syme,[3] her hero still.   10
Much is she worth, and even more is made of her.
Patients and students hold her very dear.
The doctors love her, tease her, use her skill.
They say "The Chief"[4] himself is half-afraid of her.

Staff-Nurse: New Style

Blue-eyed and bright of face but waning fast
Into the sear of virginal decay,
I view her as she enters, day by day,
As a sweet sunset almost overpast.
Kindly and calm, patrician to the last,   5
Superbly falls her gown of sober gray,
And on her chignon's elegant array
The plainest cap is somehow touched with caste.
She talks Beethoven;[5] frowns disapprobation
At Balzac's[6] name, sighs it at "poor George Sand's";[7]   10
Knows that she has exceeding pretty hands;
Speaks Latin with a right accentuation;

1. Rembrandt van Rijn (1606–1669), Dutch painter celebrated for the realism of his style.
2. Sir Walter Scott (1771–1832), romantic novelist and poet noted for his intensely realized characters.
3. James Syme (1799–1870), celebrated Edinburgh diagnostician and surgeon.
4. Joseph Lister (1827–1912) inaugurated procedures for modern antiseptic surgery; he was the Director of Surgery ("The Chief") at the Edinburgh Infirmary where Henley was a patient for almost two years.
5. Ludwig van Beethoven (1770–1827), the most famous of German romantic composers; during the latter part of the century, he became increasingly popular.
6. Honoré de Balzac (1799–1850), French writer of naturalistic fiction who, in the 1870s and 1880s, was both extolled and condemned in England because in his novels he offered an aggressively non-idealistic interpretation of human nature and motivation.
7. Amandine-Aurore Lucille Dupin (1804–1876), French baroness who, in her twenties, separated from her husband, the Baron Dudevant, embarked on a career as a writer, and adopted the pseudonym of George Sand.

And gives at need (as one who understands)
Draft, counsel, diagnosis, exhortation.

House-Surgeon

Exceeding tall, but built so well his height
Half-disappears in flow of chest and limb;
Moustache and whisker trooper-like in trim;
Frank-faced, frank-eyed, frank-hearted; always bright
And always punctual—morning, noon, and night;   5
Bland as a Jesuit, sober as a hymn;
Humorous, and yet without a touch of whim;
Gentle and amiable, yet full of fight.
His piety, though fresh and true in strain,
Has not yet whitewashed up his common mood   10
To the dead blank of his particular Schism.
Sweet, unaggressive, tolerant, most humane,
Wild artists like his kindly elderhood,
And cultivate his mild Philistinism.[1]

---

1. Philistinism was a term popularized by Matthew Arnold in the essays eventually collected under the title *Culture and Anarchy;* Arnold employs the term to indicate a self-satisfied, middle-class conservatism that was hostile to genuine culture but quite well disposed to material well-being.

MAY KENDALL

MAY KENDALL (1861–?1931)—born Emma Goldworth Kendall—wrote poetry and fiction and assisted sociologist and philanthropist Seebohm Rowntree (1871–1954) in writing two studies, *How the Labourer Lives* (1913) and *The Human Needs of Labour* (1918). Around the turn of the century, Kendall largely abandoned writing to devote more time to working for social reforms and for the relief of the poor. In "Woman's Future," she speaks out boldly, urging women to free themselves from conformity and conventionality and to expand their minds and become "The poets, the sages, the seers of the land!"

Woman's Future

Complacent they tell us, hard hearts and derisive,
    In vain is our ardour: in vain are our sighs:
Our intellects, bound by a limit decisive,[1]
    To the level of Homer's may never arise.
We heed not the falsehood, the base innuendo,
    The laws of the universe, these are our friends,   5

1. In 1859, Charles Darwin (1809–1882) published *On the origin of species by means of natural selection, or preservation of favoured races in the struggle for life,* in which he posited his theory of evolution. In *The descent of man, and selection in relation to sex* (1871), Darwin reinforces notions of biologically determined male and female traits. Writing about the mental characteristics of women, he maintains, "It is generally admitted that with woman the powers of intuition, of rapid perception, and perhaps of imitation, are more strongly marked than in man; but some, at least, of these faculties are characteristic of the lower races, and therefore of a past and lower state of civilisation. The chief distinction in the intellectual powers of the two sexes is shewn by man's attaining to a higher eminence, in whatever he takes up, than can woman—whether requiring deep thought, reason, or imagination, or merely the use of the senses and hands" (part 3, chapter 19, "Difference in the Mental Powers of the two Sexes"). By contrast, Kendall suggests that the actual intellectual abilities of women have been unnaturally distorted and repressed but, in an environment free of social constraints, will manifest themselves.

Our talents shall rise in a mighty crescendo,
    We trust Evolution to make us amends!

But ah, when I ask you for food that is mental,
    My sisters, you offer me ices and tea!   10
You cherish the fleeting, the mere accidental,
    At cost of the True, the Intrinsic, the Free.
Your feelings, compressed in Society's mangle,[2]
    Are vapid and frivolous, pallid and mean.
To slander you love; but you don't care to wrangle;   15
    You bow to Decorum, and cherish Routine.

Alas, is it woolwork you take for your mission,
    Or Art that your fingers so gaily attack?
Can patchwork atone for the mind's inanition?
    Can the soul, oh my sisters, be fed on a *plaque*?   20
Is this your vocation? My goal is another,
    And empty and vain is the end you pursue.
In antimacassars[3] the world you may smother;
    But intellect marches o'er them and o'er you.

On Fashion's vagaries your energies strewing,   25
    Devoting your days to a rug or a screen,
Oh, rouse to a lifework—do something worth doing!
    Invent a new planet, a flying-machine.
Mere charms superficial, mere feminine graces,
    That fade or that flourish, no more you may prize;   30
But the knowledge of Newton[4] will beam from your faces,
    The soul of a Spencer[5] will shine in your eyes.

Envoy

Though jealous exclusion may tremble to own us,
    Oh, wait for the time when our brains shall expand!
When once we're enthroned, you shall never dethrone us—
    The poets, the sages, the seers of the land!

2. A machine for pressing clothes by feeding them through heated rollers.

3. Macassar was a brand of hair oil used by gentlemen. Antimacassar refers to a protective covering for the backs of chairs and sofas, often in the shape of doilies hand-crocheted by the ladies of the household. In lines 17–26, Kendall speaks scornfully of the decorative needlework and crafts that occupied the hours of fashionable ladies.

4. Sir Isaac Newton (1643–1727), English mathematician and physicist.

5. Herbert Spencer (1820–1903), an influential English philosopher in his own day, is considered the founder of sociology.

ANGELA BURDETT-COUTTS

A NGELA GEORGINA BURDETT (1814–1906) added her maternal grandfather's
surname to her own when, at the age of twenty-three, she inherited his vast
fortune and his partnership in the bank he had founded. For her work as a
philanthropist, she became in 1871 the first woman to be made a peer on the basis
of her own accomplishments.

Burdett-Coutts's wide-ranging charitable projects included the founding of
schools for working-class children; an orphanage; a boys' reformatory; model
apartments for the poor; and Urania Cottage, a home for "fallen" women in which
Charles Dickens took an interest. She assisted English families in emigrating, helped
revive the Irish fishing industry, financed explorer David Livingstone's (1813–1873)
trip to Zanzibar in 1858, and took an active role in the work of the Royal Society for
the Prevention of Cruelty to Animals.

In 1881, Burdett-Coutts married William Ashmead Bartlett, who was granted a
royal license to take her surname. As a member of Parliament, he was instrumental
in effecting improvements in the army's medical services and took a keen interest
in his wife's philanthropic ventures, especially those in Ireland and Turkey.

Burdett-Coutts contributed not only her financial resources but also her managerial skills to the projects she undertook, which extended far beyond the examples given above. Moreover, she helped to reshape attitudes toward the poor and
toward philanthropy, particularly among the upper classes.

In 1893, the World's Columbian Exposition opened in Chicago to celebrate the
four-hundredth anniversary of Columbus's voyage to America. For the first time at
a world's fair, women played a significant role in planning and organization, and a
Woman's Building was constructed. Women's organizations in the United States
and abroad were invited to develop exhibits demonstrating the accomplishments
of women in industry, the arts, science, and the professions, as well as in their domestic and maternal roles. As a member of the Ladies' Committee of the Royal
British Commission, Burdett-Coutts was asked to compile a report on philanthropic work undertaken by British women. Her committee solicited reports from
charitable enterprises and individual philanthropists throughout Great Britain.
Burdett-Coutts then turned to a number of women with recognized expertise in
given areas, such as Florence Nightingale in nursing and Louisa Twining in workhouse reform, and asked them to write articles summarizing and interpreting the
mass of information that had been submitted. Their articles were collected in a

volume titled *Woman's Mission* (1893), edited by Burdett-Coutts, who is also the author of two of the essays, including "Woman the Missionary of Industry," reprinted here.

From *Woman's Mission*

Woman the Missionary of Industry

"Idleness alone is without hope";[1] by useful labour the lives of the most wretched can be ennobled and rendered happy. This is the moral to be pointed by this paper on "Woman, the Missionary of Industry," and is amply confirmed by the records of the work of Mrs. Morrogh Bernard, Mrs. Rogers, and Miss Roberts among the Irish peasants, of Mrs. Arthur Hanson among the Turkish refugees at Constantinople, and by many other deeply interesting reports[2] I have had the honour, as President of the Section of the Philanthropic Work of British Women, of sending to the Chicago Exhibition. Woman, both from nature and circumstance, has been generally a silent worker for the benefit of her fellow-beings; doing good by stealth; making many a "nook of God's creation a little fruitfuller, better, more worthy of God," many "human hearts a little wiser, manfuller, and happier"; and, especially in our age, in the van among the captains of the world, battling with evil in all its multitudinous forms. But although in this great work, and this great conflict, women have borne their full share of the heat and burden of the day,[3] their services until quite recently have received but scant recognition. Even now scarcely a tithe is known of what woman has done and is doing to bring brightness and hope into the dark lives of dumb millions of toilers. It will be accounted to the honour of the American people in the future that they were the first to give a national recognition to the moral and material effects of woman's

1. Thomas Carlyle, *Past and Present,* bk. 3, chap. 2, "The Gospel of Mammonism." See other selections from *Past and Present* in part 1.

2. Burdett-Coutts includes a note referring to the entire collection of typewritten reports available for perusal by visitors to the Chicago fair: "Many other records of the beneficent results of the work of individual women in aiding the poor to help themselves, are dealt with in the papers by Mrs. Gilbert and Miss Petrie; and I would like to direct special attention to what is said respecting the work of Miss Maude among the labourers in Somersetshire, of the Duchess of Sutherland, Lady Grisell Baillie Hamilton, and Miss Ferguson in isolated country districts in Scotland."

3. Matthew 20:12, the parable of the generous employer.

work and influence for good in the world. For the first time in the records of National and International Exhibitions, an attempt has been made at Chicago to give, what I may term, a dramatic and impressive representation of what women have endeavoured to accomplish in every branch of philanthropy, literature, science, and art. "How far that little candle throws its beams"[4] will be uppermost in the minds of visitors to the Women's Building; though but a glimmer of the shining light of woman's philanthropic work is reflected there.

Of the devotion and self-sacrifice of the women who are everywhere about us labouring with unfailing patience and faith to bring light into dark places, it is impossible to speak without emotion. Theirs, in truth, is no "May game, but a battle and stern pilgrimage";[5] and only in the knowledge of the good they have wrought lies their reward. Through the efforts of Mrs. Bernard, Mrs. Rogers, Miss Roberts, and Mrs. Hanson, as well as of thousands of others, idleness has given place to industry, squalid poverty to prosperity, ignorance to enlightenment. And no feature of the single-handed work of women is more striking than the wisdom and discretion with which it is generally conducted. Inspired by a large-hearted benevolence, and warm sympathy with the poor and suffering, the majority of women workers in philanthropy have not allowed their feelings to obscure their judgment. They recognize that—

> "The truly generous is the truly wise."[6]

To enable those who would otherwise be destitute to help themselves is more truly generous than to give alms. In the one case those in distress are made self-reliant, independent, and useful members of the community; in the other degradation and demoralization are too often the result.

The difficulty of adequately representing the philanthropic work of women in the United Kingdom of Great Britain and Ireland will be best appreciated by those most intimately acquainted with the subject, and it is with the object of bringing some of the difficulties home to the minds of others that I have undertaken in this paper to give a brief outline of what four women, whose names have hitherto been comparatively unknown, have been able to accomplish by their individual efforts. The story, which shall be told as far as possible in the words of the reports kindly sent to me in response to a special request, illustrates at once the vast importance of the philanthropic work quietly carried on by thousands of individual ladies, of whose very existence the public has no idea, and the impossibility of obtaining even an approximately accurate report of what British women are doing for the welfare of humanity. Not only is the record of the work of the four ladies I have already named, deeply interesting and instructive, but, owing to exigencies of time

4. "How far that little candle throws its beams / So shines a good deed in a naughty world." Shakespeare, *The Merchant of Venice*, 5.1.90–91.

5. Thomas Carlyle, *Past and Present*, bk. 3, chap. 13, "Democracy": "Life was never a May game for men: in all times the lot of the dumb millions born to toil was defaced with manifold sufferings, injustices, heavy burdens, avoidable and unavoidable; not play at all, but hard work that made the sinews sore and the heart sore."

6. John Home (1722–1808), *Douglas*, 3.1.

and space, it must be taken as representative of the noble results achieved by thousands of other silent workers.

We all remember those gloomy days in the eighties when, by the failure of the potato harvest, thousands of Irish peasants were brought face to face with starvation.[7] It was the Duchess of Marlborough, aided chiefly by women, who organized the relief fund for holding the famine at bay. In the still more gloomy days that followed, when men were forced to sit with folded hands whilst their wives and children were lacking bread, it was women who first brought help. In every part of Ireland there are traces of their work. Many a village in which a few years ago misery and want were chronic, is now the centre of a flourishing little industrial community. Such undertakings as those of Mrs. Bernard, Mrs. Rogers, and Miss Roberts have brought fresh life and hope to Ireland; and what these ladies are doing at Foxford, at Carrick, and among the "Rosses,"[8] others are doing elsewhere, from Cape Clear to the Giant's Causeway.

Mrs. Morrogh Bernard has long done yeoman's service in the cause of philanthropy. For many years she was the Superior of a convent at Ballaghaderin; and whilst there she took a warm interest in all movements for improving the condition of the peasants. The National Schools which, as Mother Superior, she had under her direction, were models of good management. The girls she trained were as a rule bright and intelligent, and she fitted them so far as in them lay to do good work in the world. Unfortunately, for many a mile around Ballaghaderin, there were more hands to work than there was work for them to do; more mouths to be fed than there was food wherewith to feed them; for it is in the centre of one of the so-called congested districts, where a failure of the potato crop always means famine. The soil is so poor that it hardly defrays the cost of cultivation, and in those days there was no industrial employment of any kind in the neighbourhood. Thus, when their school-days were over, the peasant girls had to face a painful alternative. They either had to leave their friends and country, without having received the training necessary to render them successful emigrants, and to guard them against many privations and dangers, or they had to linger on at home in hopeless idleness, with semi-starvation for a companion. Mrs. Bernard was keenly alive to the suffering this state of things entailed on the poor among whom she lived. It was heart-breaking work for her to see the girls she had so carefully trained wasting their lives, a burden on those of whom they should have been the support. There was work enough in the world that wanted doing, she was sure, if only she could put them in the way of doing it. After much anxious thought, she resolved to try to organize a woollen mill, to provide not only profitable occupation for the

7. The potato blight of 1845–46 resulted in the Great Famine, or Great Hunger, which claimed the lives of more than 800,000 Irish between 1845 and 1851. Serious crop failures recurred periodically throughout the second half of the century as well, with another famine from 1878 to 1881, the effects of which Burdett-Coutts describes.

8. As Burdett-Coutts explains later in the essay, "Ross" in Irish means headland, or promontory, extending into a large body of water. The "Rosses" refer to the northwest of Ireland.

women and girls in the neighbourhood, but also technical training for the children under her care.

Whilst she was pondering on ways and means, it chanced that the bishop of the diocese paid her schools a visit. As he was passing through the class-room, one of the children asked him to give "handsel,"[9] and "get the Reverend Mother a hand-loom." The child added that her mother had "a grand one at home." The bishop consented, and the loom, a veritable heirloom, full of years and moth-holes, was purchased for thirty shillings. The loom was harnessed at once, and the head weaver of the Manchester Technical School devoted his Christmas holidays to teaching the nuns and their pupils how it was to be served. It was soon evident, however, that Mrs. Bernard could not put her scheme into execution at Ballaghaderin, and she felt that she would have to find some more suitable site for her mill.

One day she was at Foxford, about twenty miles from Ballaghaderin; and whilst standing on the bridge across the Moy, she noticed the tremendous force with which the torrent there comes rushing down the rock-side. Such a water power as this was the very thing she wanted; and there and then she determined to buy a piece of land close to the stream for her mill. She resigned her post as Superior of the convent, and accompanied by a little band of Sisters of Charity,[10] set out for Foxford, April 25, 1891. She was convinced that the wisest course would be to start a school for peasant children first, and then, when that was in working order, a mill. The plan was to begin with the infants in the junior school, and gradually educate them with a view of introducing them to mill life after they had acquired a knowledge of the woollen industry, in a sort of woollen kindergarten. When they had been fairly instructed in religious and secular matters, these children were to be sent to the technical mill as half-timers, at the usual standard ages, and continue to receive education and training until they could be sent out as finished mill-workers. Then they would take rank as skilled workwomen, and as such would have little difficulty in earning an honest livelihood.

On the land Mrs. Bernard bought at Foxford there was an old corn store, which she speedily had transformed into a class-room, and in it, on August 1, 1891, she opened her school with eighty-four pupils. So far her work had been comparatively easy. It was in the organization of the mill that the real difficulty lay. The woollen manufacture is a very complex business, one in which it is by no means easy, even for those specially trained for the work, to succeed. Neither Mrs. Bernard nor her companions had any technical knowledge: and we can hardly wonder, therefore, that the announcement of their project was greeted with prophecies of failure. The undertaking seemed hopeless; but the nuns, true to their motto, *Caritas Christi urget nos*,[11] never wavered in their faith that Providence would help them on their way. Mrs. Bernard and one of the Sisters set out in search of

9. A gift to express good wishes at the beginning of a new venture.
10. Numerous non-cloistered orders, the members of which are engaged in social service, especially teaching and nursing.
11. Latin: "The love of Christ impels us."

information. They visited mill after mill, bent upon learning every detail of the industry they wished to establish.

"It was a curious sight to see veiled nuns studying the various machines used in the woollen trade, and taking copious notes of the many processes through which the wool passes before it becomes finished cloth." At best it was weary work for them, for the more they went into the details of the business the more perplexing did it become. Probably they never realized all the difficulties they would have to contend against until they went on this journey. Just when things were at the darkest, however, there came a gleam of light. Nothing daunted by the discouragement she met with, though sorely troubled, Mrs. Bernard appealed for advice to Mr. J. C. Smith, the managing partner of a firm noted for the beautiful woollen fabrics it turns out. This gentleman was keenly interested by what she told him of her plans; still, he had little faith in women as organizers, and strove earnestly to persuade her to try some other and less intricate method of doing good. But when he found that, in spite of his warnings, Mrs. Bernard persisted in her project, he drew up for her the plan of the technical mill as it now stands, and gave her the full benefit of his experience in arranging how the work was to be done.

The months that followed were a great anxiety for Mrs. Bernard, for it was a serious undertaking this starting of a woollen mill in a wild district. In addition to all her other cares, she had financial difficulties to struggle against. She had but scant means at her disposal, building and machinery were a heavy expense, and she soon found herself compelled to borrow money. Even in those days, however, before it was properly started, she had the happiness of knowing that her scheme was proving a blessing to her poorer neighbours. Numbers of the peasants were kept busily employed all through the dreary winter—the first time for many a long year. "Gradually the plans were carried out; the mill-race was completed; a powerful turbine water-motor of the latest modern construction was placed in position; and in due time all the woollen machinery was ready. Mr. Burdett-Coutts, M.P., and Mr. Wrench as representative of the Congested Districts Board,[12] were present when the first start was made. It fell to the lot of Mr. Burdett-Coutts to draw forth the beautiful soft fleece from the first bag ever opened at Foxford, and as a souvenir of this little ceremony he has since had some hand-looms set up in the mill for the Sisters."

During the last two years the state of things at Foxford has been transformed. Since Mrs. Bernard began her work there, the place has quite lost the desolate look which used to distinguish it, and is now full of life and cheerful bustle. In addition to the mill she has built two large schools. In the upper school, more than a hundred girls are being carefully trained to use not only their heads but their hands; whilst in the infants' school, an equal number of children are being fitted for their future duties as half-timers at the mill. They all take delight in their work, and seem to feel real affection for the little balls of wool they are being taught to

12. Established in 1891, the Congested Districts Board was formed to provide relief and economic stimulation in the poorest districts of Ireland.

handle; and when the time comes for these two hundred girls to leave school, each one of them will have, literally at her finger-ends, a profitable calling. Already some forty girls are at work in the mill, where they lead busy, useful lives, and earn enough to keep themselves, and often their parents, too, from want.

Mrs. Rogers had done much good work in London before she began her Irish undertaking. For years she had been trying to render women financially independent by putting them in the way of earning their own livelihood. At the very time the potato famine was causing such terrible distress in Ireland, it chanced that a trading company which she had organized, received several large orders for knitted gloves. Here was work, paying work too, waiting to be done; whilst in Ireland women were starving because they had no work to do. Mrs. Rogers felt it was an opportunity which must not be lost, of giving a helping hand to people destitute through no fault of their own. She resolved to go to the famine district, and try to organize the knitting industry there on a regular basis. On the 27th of February, 1880, she set out for Donegal, taking with her a lady who was both a skilful knitter and an expert in technical teaching. Mrs. Rogers' first experiences were certainly not encouraging. When she arrived at Pettigo, sixteen miles from the town of Donegal, she found that the railway went no further. There was neither food nor lodging to be had in the village, and the only way to Donegal was by a bridle-path across mountains. To make matters worse, a violent snowstorm was raging. Even when she reached Donegal, her troubles were far from being at an end; for obstacles of all kinds were thrown in her way by local tradesmen, who were afraid she would interfere with an embroidery industry for which they were the agents. At length, after a fortnight spent in a vain endeavour to find girls to undertake the knitting, Mrs. Rogers, almost in despair, appealed for counsel to the parish priest. He warmly approved of her scheme, but advised her, instead of staying in Donegal where the people were tolerably well off, to go to Carrick, some twenty-four miles farther in the country, where the peasants were on the very verge of starvation. In consequence of his report she decided to make Carrick her head-quarters.

In those days Carrick was only a dismal, poverty-stricken little hamlet, with nothing but bog and hills for miles around. It stands just at the foot of the Sleive League Mountain, in the midst of the wildest and most picturesque scenery. To all intents and purposes it was then completely cut off from the outside world, for the nearest railway station was at Stranorlar, fully fifty miles away. At Carrick, Mrs. Rogers met with a cordial welcome from Father Kelly, who is at once the priest, lawyer, and lawgiver of the district. He had a heart-rending tale to tell of the distress amongst his parishioners. There was not a girl in the country side, he said, but would gladly do the knitting, and he undertook to have a goodly array of workers for her to choose from by the following Monday. From the altar on the Sunday he explained to his hearers what Mrs. Rogers proposed doing for them, and implored them to make the most of the chance she was giving them.

The news that there was work to be had, spread like wildfire through the district; and when, on the Monday morning, Mrs. Rogers arrived at the cottage she had hired, she found it in a state of siege. More than a thousand women were assembled, many of them wild with excitement—wild, perhaps, with hunger too. The case was one of special difficulty, for hardly one of these peasants could understand a word of English, and neither Mrs. Rogers nor her companion could speak Irish. Fortunately, just when the confusion was at its highest, and the crush was becoming dangerous, Father Kelly arrived, speedily cleared the women from the house, and mounted guard over them outside. The cottage contained four rooms, and into each one of them, when something like order was restored, twelve women were admitted, there to be initiated into the mysteries of knitting. It was soon clear that none of them had any idea even of putting stitches on the needles. The whole of the first day, therefore, was taken up teaching this very elementary process. So soon as one girl could cast the stitches, she was provided with needles and wool, and sent home to practise, whilst another took her place. But the work advanced very slowly, for all the instruction had to be given through an interpreter; and at nightfall, hundreds of women were still standing there in the cold, waiting for their first lesson. The Irish are, however, a good-natured, long-suffering race; and not a word of complaint was heard. They trudged off to their cabins on the hills again, vowing they would be amongst the first at the cottage the next morning.

Day after day the same scene was repeated. Crowds of women stood waiting from morning till night for this knitting, which was to keep the wolf from the door. Unluckily, their very eagerness for the work only increased the difficulty of showing them how to do it. They were so wild and boisterous in their ways, that the task of teaching them seemed hopeless. It is no easy thing to knit gloves; in the special kind Mrs. Rogers required, wool of three different colours had to be used, and the shaping of the thumbs and fingers was quite an elaborate business. It was work, in fact, that needed some amount of technical skill; and potato-hoeing was all these people had been accustomed to. At the end of a week of ceaseless toil, the wrist of one glove was all that had been achieved! Little wonder both teachers and taught felt inclined to despair. The former could see nothing but difficulties before them, whilst the latter were weighed down by the thought that what they were trying to learn was unlearnable. During this depressing time, when her undertaking seemed doomed, Mrs. Rogers found an invaluable auxiliary in Father Kelly, who spent his days striving to keep the women to their work by "threats, bribes, and kindly words of encouragement." Sunday after Sunday an odd little scene was enacted in the Roman Catholic Church: the priest in full canonicals stood by the altar and solemnly announced a list of prizes to be competed for. Five shillings was promised to the woman who should first knit a creditable thumb; two and six-pence for a well-shaped finger, and a whole sovereign for the first glove. Every sermon he preached, too, was an earnest exhortation to perseverance. Still it was three months before a single pair of gloves was made, and during that time Mrs. Rogers had spent £100 on her undertaking.

The first six months were certainly a terrible struggle, and then things began to look brighter; some of the girls became wonderfully deft at the work, and besides knitting gloves themselves, helped to teach their companions to knit them. Soon huge packets of goods were sent off to London, and in the course of a year £1000 was paid to the women in wages. A thousand pounds is not a large sum, but at Carrick money went far, and to those among whom it was divided it made all the difference between starvation and comfort. For two years the women were kept busily employed knitting gloves; then a change of fashion came; knitted gloves were no longer in demand, and Mrs. Rogers had to find some other occupation for her *protégées*. In the course of a very few weeks she entirely reorganized their work, and put them in the way of making knitted underclothing for children.

Carrick is now a very different place from what it was when Mrs. Rogers made her first visit there. It has developed into quite a thriving little town, with a singularly prosperous air about it. Well-built cottages have replaced many of the miserable huts which used to stand there, and even shops with plate-glass windows—an unfailing sign of material progress—have appeared of late. Though the people still retain all their simple primitive ways, few signs of real poverty are to be seen in the district.

In 1888 Sir Henry Roscoe appealed to Mrs. Rogers to do for Connemara what she had already done for Carrick. All around Carna there was terrible distress, and against it the late Father Flannery—the famous "Father Tom" of Carna, whose name will live in the hearts of his grateful people for many a long day—was fighting almost singlehanded. After some hesitation Mrs. Rogers went to his assistance, and at Carna established, notwithstanding many difficulties and discouragements, a knitting industry for the benefit of the women, on the same lines as the one she had already organized at Carrick.

Miss Dorothea Roberts, of Berry Hill, Mansfield, has founded a knitting industry which provides employment for some hundreds of poor women, in that wild north-west corner of Ireland, called locally "the Rosses." Ross, in the Irish language, means "headland." "Our Rosses," Miss Roberts writes, "stretch out into the Atlantic like the fingers of some giant hand. America, we say, is our 'next parish.' The great New World seems all the closer because there is not a family in our parish which has not some of its members living there, across the wild Atlantic billows. By that stern seaboard the harvest of the land is scanty, grown only on such washings of soil as can accumulate in cups between big, rolling, stony mountains. The harvest of the sea, rich as it is, remains ungathered for the most part, awaiting such generous help as that which has turned Baltimore, in the county of Cork, into a busy hive of industry. For half a century past the Rosses women have been excellent knitters. The late Lord George Hill, and Mr. Forster, his agent, greatly encouraged this work by industrial shows and prize-giving in the neighbouring parish of Gweedore.

"Ten years ago the excellent parish priest of the Rosses, Father B. Walker, received my first hanks of wool, which he promptly returned to me, in London, knitted into shapely stockings. The work begun by me in so small a way has grown and flourished by the kind help of sympathizers all over Great Britain. Our parish lies remote from the Donegal centres where agents give out yarns for Scottish and other hosiers. Those beneficent new railways, which I see opening up whole 'congested' districts elsewhere, can scarcely climb over our rugged mountains, or cross the long fiords which wind up amongst the cliffs of our western seaboard. The Parcel Post is our main dependence at present, both for delivery of yarns and export of goods.

"The eager, barefooted, Irish-speaking women, who crowd in from remote islands to my agent when the news of the coming of a bale of wool has spread, are quick to seize new ideas, and very quick with their fingers, too."

Miss Roberts has for ten years past been able to pay on an average £10 a month in wages; and has recently executed an order for thirteen thousand pairs of army socks. The particularly fine work done by the knitters is purchased by persons all over England from Miss Roberts, who adds, "It has been touching to me to meet with such kind help from people of all ranks, creeds, and parties, for by their means alone I have been able to keep up this work—the best help of our poor district."

We must now shift the scene to a distant but not less interesting country, where Mrs. Arthur Hanson's work at Constantinople, for the Turkish refugees, must certainly be ranked among the most remarkable and successful efforts made by individual women of this century for the welfare of their fellow-beings. Here, again, the motto adopted is, "Not alms, but work"; and seldom has the truly philanthropic desire of aiding those who would be otherwise absolutely destitute, to help themselves, been followed by greater good or more far-reaching results. No less than two thousand Turkish women and children are at the present time enabled to gain an honourable living, while, owing to the wise management of Mrs. Hanson, a fund is also maintained out of the earnings for the support of those stricken down by age or illness.

The origin of this work is peculiar and historic. Fifteen years ago Turkey had been desolated by a terrible war.[13] Before the Russian armies, advancing in a line which stretched from Varna to Sofia, the whole Turkish population of Bulgaria and Roumelia had fled from their homes in terrified haste, snatching up such scanty provisions and small household treasures as they could carry on their journey. Amidst scenes of indescribable misery and suffering, Mr. Burdett-Coutts had carried on an extended system of temporary relief in his capacity as Special Commissioner of the Turkish Compassionate Fund, which was raised in England for the special relief of the refugees, as the Stafford House Fund was for the

13. Long-standing conflict between Turkey and Russia resulted in renewed warfare in the 1870s. Despite Turkish atrocities in the Balkans that horrified many English citizens, including social activists such as William Morris, the Conservative government of Prime Minister Benjamin Disraeli (1804–1881) supported the Turks. In 1877, Burdett-Coutts supported the conservative position and urged the British to come to the aid of displaced Turkish peasants; she set the example by personally contributing £2000 to the Turkish Compassionate Fund.

wounded soldiers. As long as the Russian armies kept to the north of the Balkans, the centres of distribution were mainly in the country.

The defeat of the Turks at Orkhanié and the capture of the Schipka Pass, was the signal for a *sauve qui peut*[14] throughout the fertile provinces to the south of the Balkan range. All the roads to Constantinople were crowded with long trains of refugees. A vast number died of starvation and the cold of a bitter winter; but something like a quarter of a million reached Constantinople in a terrible condition of destitution, and were housed on the floors of the numerous mosques in Stamboul,[15] at all times a teeming and overcrowded city. There they were fed by thousands every day by the Commissioner of the Fund. The Turkish officials were also most humane in their treatment of the hapless wretches, and the higher authorities did all in their power to provide for their wants by distributing food and raiment; and as Mr. Burdett-Coutts says, "His Majesty the Sultan throughout evinced the deepest commiseration for his unhappy people, and did all in his power to assist them." But little could be done by those who with one hand had to ward off the attack of the advancing Russians, while with the other they tried to help their victims to escape from them.

Among the small possessions to which the women had clung to the last were the old embroideries of Turkey, many of which had been precious heirlooms in their families. Some of the women retained the rare art of making these embroideries. It occurred to Mrs. Arthur Hanson, one of the leading English ladies in Constantinople, that the art might be revived, the old beautiful colours reproduced, and a useful industry established among these unfortunate women, many of whom had been wealthy and comfortable. After the resources of the fund already named had been strained to their utmost in saving these refugees from starvation, a small balance still remained in hand. Upon this slender foundation, coupled with Mrs. Hanson's wonderful energy, the industry was at first built up; employment was provided for the refugee women who were skilled workers; instruction and a means of livelihood were afforded to the ignorant and young; and the new supplies of the beautiful Turkish embroideries found a ready market in the great cities of Western Europe. Portions of the money advanced for these purposes were repaid as the undertaking grew and prospered under the energetic and wise control of Mrs. Hanson; and the fund still exists, and by supplying Mrs. Hanson with working capital has been a source of incalculable benefit to thousands of the most helpless victims of a terrible war.

From the first Mrs. Hanson's work prospered. Its success is due to two causes: first, to the untiring energy, patience, great organizing, administering, business capacity, and artistic taste of Mrs. Hanson, who has devoted her life to the promotion of the moral and material welfare of the Turkish refugees; and secondly, to the superb quality of the embroideries produced. In every department of art embroideries, the products of Mrs. Hanson's frames are unrivalled. The work, as visitors to

14. Idiomatic French expression meaning "everyone for him- or herself."
15. Stamboul is the oldest section of Istanbul or Constantinople.

the Chicago Exhibition may see for themselves, is the most beautiful of modern times. In the admirable report upon the industry which has been kindly supplied to me by Miss Constance Eaglestone, and from which I have already quoted, she says, "The charm of this Turkish embroidery consists in the originality as well as the beauty of the designs. Many of these have been handed down from generation to generation in the Turkish harems, and so jealously were they guarded as heirlooms, that had not the fortunes of war brought the princesses from palaces in the Balkans down to the level of the peasant women in huts at their gates, the secret of their creation would never have been divulged. Other patterns have been copied from designs of Eighth Century work collected by Mr. Wrench, British Vice-Consul at Constantinople; some, again, are from scrolls and arabesques in early mosques of different parts of the Ottoman Empire, and among these may be specially mentioned those from the enamels of the historic Green Mosque of Broussa, to enter which, until a few decades ago, was death to any but a Mussulman.[16] Others are believed to be the exact counterpart of the embroideries alluded to in the Books of Moses[17] as covering the robes which the priests wore during the services in the Temple, and must, therefore, have come into the hands of this race from another of far greater antiquity, while the possession of them by the Osmanli[18] is easily explained by their triumphant progress through Western Asia before they established themselves on the Bosphorus in 1453. Nor has the attraction of modern art been wanting to bring this work still nearer to perfection. When the Parisian dealers saw how popular the Oriental embroidery was becoming throughout France, they made useful suggestions for the yet more artistic combination of the colours employed, and sent some of their own lovely textiles of silk and gauze to serve as a foundation, instead of the coarser fabrics which had hitherto been used." Another property of the embroideries is that they are as durable as they are beautiful. They never fade, and the gold used in them never tarnishes, not even when exposed to the damp of the English climate.

"The Ottoman race itself," Miss Eaglestone adds, "has little or no inventive power. The refugee women could bring out their woven treasures which they had concealed about their persons when they fled from their Bulgarian homes, but they can do nothing but copy from the model set before then, while orders to make even the slightest alteration in it only bewilder them. When new ideas are to be introduced, Mrs. Hanson, or her helpers, must patiently guide the willing but errant fingers, stitch by stitch, through the frame that supports the dainty mesh, until the secret has been made the worker's own. Another difficulty is, that having once learnt a new stitch the women seem to lose all power of remembering an old one. 'It is gone, gone,' they repeat hopelessly, when the enigma that they could have solved with closed eyes a week before is laid before them; thus it is a serious

16. Muslim.

17. Beginning in Exodus 25, God directs Moses in the making and furnishing of a tabernacle, or portable sanctuary. Curtains within the tabernacle as well as the holy garments for the priests were to be of richly colored cloth embellished with elaborate needlework.

18. Ottoman Turk.

undertaking to lead a skilled worker away from the design which her lithe brown fingers have made popular at every Court of Europe."

The work which this paper has described is essentially individual. In each case it has been by personal exertions, by personal thought and labour, that help and comfort have been brought to those in need and distress. There could be no more striking evidence of the far-reaching results being achieved through the wisely-directed efforts of individual women, than is furnished by the story I have briefly sketched of how these four notable industries were established in the face of overwhelming odds. It is a noble record of difficulties overcome, of circumstances conquered, of suffering relieved. Thousands of lives have been made happier, thousands of hearts have been cheered, and thousands of souls aroused to higher and nobler aspirations.

OCTAVIA HILL

OCTAVIA HILL (1838–1912) was a social reformer, especially in the area of public housing, and a founder of the National Trust for the preservation of historic places. Hill became involved in social work early on. At the age of fourteen, she was given responsibility for the children employed by the Ladies Cooperative Guild, an organization directed by her mother. In the late 1850s, she taught classes for women at F. D. Maurice's Working Men's College and, in the early 1860s, classes for poor children at a school established by her family.

In 1864, with financial assistance from John Ruskin, Hill bought three houses with the intention of creating model dwellings for the working poor. Hill maintained close contact with and supervision of her tenants. She found jobs for adults and apprenticeships for children but expected a good bit in return. Insistent on fiscal responsibility and moral rectitude, she promoted self-discipline and self-reliance.

As her housing reform project expanded, Hill trained a large number of agents to carry out her system of management. In 1869, she helped establish the Charity Organization Society, an association dedicated to centralizing and monitoring private philanthropy.

"Trained Workers for the Poor" appeared in the January 1893 issue of *The Nineteenth Century*. In this article, Hill voices many of her views on social work, in particular her impatience with the well-intentioned but misguided philanthropists who offer random assistance and her conviction that those who are to work among the poor must be carefully educated and prepared for the opportunity to serve others.

Trained Workers for the Poor

A great increase of sympathy with the poor has taken place in England during the last few years, bringing forward countless devoted and industrious volunteers in all branches of work for the people. Their sympathy, their self-sacrifice, and their zeal are of priceless value; but many circumstances point to the necessity of their being definitely trained. In old days, when our population was smaller, when parishes were more distinct from one another, when more of English life was in the country villages, district visiting was less *work* than *neighbourly kindness* taking its natural course in the flow of help to individuals who had long been known, and the inclination to do loving and serviceable acts was sufficient qualification. No inquiry was needed, all applicants for alms were known; no precedent seemed to be established by helping under given circumstances, these perhaps never repeated themselves; no huge, baseless, unreasoning hope that never could be fulfilled was called up by scattered almsgiving;[1] nor was there the great yawning gulf of London into which the agricultural population might be enticed by the squandering of ill-considered gifts, or the wholesale gratuitous supply of necessary things which most men provide for themselves. A few years ago when sanitary science, social science, educational science were in their infancy, and there were few people who had made a study of them, native common-sense was all the young worker could trust to. Now, how changed are all things! Who would not scorn to offer the uninstructed nursing which kindliness alone guides, thinking of the subtle perfections of the art which a trained nurse has? Who would dare to teach classes without preparation, knowing what is expected of the humblest infant school-teacher in the smallest, most out-of-the-way school. The advance of knowledge, and the massing of large bodies of people which absolutely demands organisation, alike point to the altered duties of those who would be really serviceable.

The problem, as it seems to me, is how to unite the fresh, loving, spontaneous, individual sympathy with the quiet, grave, sustained, and instructed spirit of the trained worker; it is, in fact, how to gain the wisdom, and increase, not lose, the love.

First, we shall need patience. All fresh workers entering the field must say to themselves, "I must be humble, and work, and wait, and prepare."

Then, secondly, we must recognise that there must be special training, and it is only the extreme boldness of the wholly ignorant which induces them to rush in, confident in their goodwill, with a temerity which it makes the more experienced tremble to see.

---

1. Hill and other members of the Charity Organization Society were outspoken in their opposition to the indiscriminate aid distributed by such nineteenth-century organizations as the Salvation Army. By contrast, the COS investigated all candidates for assistance to determine which were worthy and conducted subsequent checks to confirm that recipients remained deserving as long as they received aid.

Let us, then, suppose that a beginner is conscious of the need of preparation—how is she to obtain it? In certain departments the courses of study and procedure are too clearly laid down and known for it to be necessary even to mention them—education and nursing are now among the skilled and certificated branches of work. With regard to the others, one may lay down the general rules that time for preparation must be given; that fresh recruits should begin at the bottom and rise gradually, and that they should deliberately set themselves under those who have experience.

There will, then, arise the question whether training is best in institutions or in one's own home, and also as to what is the best point from which to work, an institution or one's own home. So far as training is concerned, it is manifest that the answer must be different in different cases. If it be true that to be under experienced teachers is essential, new volunteers must go where such are to be found, and those whose homes are inaccessible to such centres must, for a time at least, transplant themselves to other neighbourhoods during the period of their training. If, on the other hand, their own homes are within reach of leaders and teachers, and they have the will and the power to take up work among the poor, steadily, as their brothers prepare for their professions, if their home duties make them feel it right so to devote a regular, even if it be a small, part of their time, then I say, very deliberately, that in my estimation the training is best done from the natural home.

For, note, we are educating, not a mechanic to practise manual work, not a lawyer whose intellect must be developed and mind stored with facts, not a physician who must gather knowledge and dispense advice, but a worker who, though she may need a certain manual skill, and clear intellect, and knowledge, is primarily a human being who may use manual and mental power for the help and blessing of numbers of families. That being so, all will depend on what she is; unconscious as she may, and should be, of herself, her influence will radiate from her like light from a star; and we have yet to learn that there is any training for noble and gentle souls like that of family life. Besides all this, in my estimation the work most needed now is in the homes of the people; and how are we to teach and help in the family, if the sacred duties to parents, to brothers and sisters—if the old household claims—seem to us of little moment, and to be easily thrown aside for others? In my experience, those who are deeply imbued with the spirit of family life are those who best help the poor; in this spirit they meet on the great human ground, older than theories of equality, safer than our imaginings of fresh arrangements for the world, and fitter to inspire the noblest and the simplest sense of duty.

Far be it from me to generalise, or to try to lay down a law as to what is best for anyone—let each see and judge for herself;—but this I will say, that the deep honour for home-life is essential to the best kind of work for the poor now. Thrift?—yes, if you like; education?—yes, if it be good; preparing girls for service, sanitary improvement, skilled nursing, country holidays, amusements, drill, open spaces, and fifty more things, all are valuable; but one spark of honour for and love of home, and sense of duty therein, if it were granted to you to fan it into life, would be a better gift, one more far-reaching in its influence, and bearing better fruit, *without* which all the other gifts are very poor—*with* which they will bring much good.

This belief of mine will very distinctly show what I feel with regard to deaconesses,[2] settlements,[3] and other groups of trained workers living apart from their homes. They may, and in many cases probably will, excel in what we may call the technical portions of their work, and will have, in certain ways, more weight in a district, from these being as a rule carried on more continuously; they form, moreover, a centre in many large towns where the poor live far from the rich. In such institutions will naturally be found those who have taken up work for the poor as their main duty in life, among whom will be, as a rule, probably, many of the more experienced workers and leaders; but whether, with all their technical advantages, residents in them can ever give the great crowning spiritual help in the home-life of the poor will depend on why and how those residents left their own homes: whether, on the one hand, they had any lurking belief that life in a community was holier than life in a family; whether they had shrunk from the discipline and humility of fulfilling duties *laid* upon them, and preferred *chosen* duties; or whether, on the other hand, no home existing for them, they entered into joyful service of the poor, and what reflex of family and household duty life with fellow-workers opened out; or whether the daily duties of home being done by others, the devotion to out-of-the-way poor districts seemed due from them, and, still remaining in near touch with, and full reverence for, home and family life, they, as it were, kept a foothold, too, nearer the most desolate districts; or again whether they were new workers going, as to school or college, to gather knowledge, hereafter to be used when they return home.

Since, in the autumn of 1891, I brought before the public in the pages of this Review the new scheme for district visiting in connection with the Women's University Settlement in Southwark,[4] my thoughts have been turned, even more than before, to the question of training those who would work among the poor.

In the management of houses the duties are so responsible, and the knowledge needed so special, that I have always been obliged either to secure ladies with

---

2. Unlike the Anglican sisterhoods, which were revived in the 1840s and combined a social mission with communal living and the taking of vows, Evangelical deaconesses continued to live in their own homes but were engaged in active, public service.

3. The first settlements, or residential homes for social workers, were founded in the 1880s with the idea that, if workers lived among the poor, they could establish a closer connection to them and serve them more effectively.

4. Founded in 1887, the Women's University Settlement refers to the establishment supplied with social workers by the women's colleges (primarily Lady Margaret Hall and Newnham, but also Girton, Somerville, and London). Hill's concern that single women living outside their homes would substitute service to the poor for their foremost responsibilities to their own families made her initially skeptical about a settlement house for women. Nevertheless, she recognized the need for trained workers to live in closer proximity to those they assisted, as her essay "Our Dealings with the Poor" in the August 1891 number of *The Nineteenth Century* makes clear. There Hill discusses the need for co-ordinated relief efforts and the desirability of district visitors coming to know and interact with poor families in their homes.

experience, or to put those who offer help through a long and careful course of preparation. They begin by serving under leaders, and by fulfilling the easiest and simplest duties; only after considerable time are they put in positions of trust. The necessities of the case, the absolute need of special knowledge, drove me either to give good training, or to leave my volunteers as mere kindly messengers between the more experienced workers and the tenants under their charge.

But directly that, as a member of the Committee of the Women's University Settlement, I was in part instrumental in enrolling a body of visitors in the homes of the poor, I saw that they also would require definite, though different, training. Each of them would be responsible for a small group of families in a given court or street, would be pledged to care for them wisely as well as kindly; but would not have the duties to owners, to local and sanitary authorities, nor the charge of money, accounts, and repairs, which are required for the management of houses, and which have formed so valuable a means of education to my own workers. If they were to do the steady, thorough, real work they and we wished, they must have special preparation for it.

We found, as was to be expected, a certain number of women who had by steady work gained experience; but every year brings forward a fresh body of younger and ardent helpers, women of power developed by the better education now open to them, capable of becoming workers of a very high order, but absolutely without knowledge to deal with the problems they will have to face. Many of them, in their very eagerness to help, and their sense of maturity and power, are inclined to think first of being useful at once, and feel as if they had not now time to devote to preparation. This arises in great measure, however, from there being no training-place for those intending to live at home and take up work for the poor, no course of study sketched out for them by those of experience, no definite requirements demanded of those who would serve—not even of those who would earn—in such fields of work. We are, with regard to this most important and complicated matter, where we were with regard to nursing before Florence Nightingale qualified as a nurse, and before teachers were expected to pass through colleges and obtain certificates.[5]

What appeared to the Committee of the Women's University Settlement important was to set before the public a higher standard of what was requisite, and to render it possible for those who desire it to qualify themselves.

It seemed to the Committee that the Women's University Settlement was a very suitable place for such a course of training. The lady warden, Miss Sewell,[6] has shown, in an unusual degree, knowledge of the subject, combined with power of teaching. The near connection and continuous intercourse of the Settlement with the Universities to which it owes its origin, bring it into touch with those who have

---

5. Largely as a result of the efforts of physician and education reformer James Kay-Shuttleworth (1804–1877), a training and certification program for elementary school teachers was put into effect in 1846. Serious professional training for secondary and college teachers came much later, in the last quarter of the century.

6. M. A. Sewell was warden for almost ten years, until 1901.

received a university education, and who are likely to prove the most able of future workers. The situation of the Settlement in the heart of a large and poor district renders it useful to have helpers there, and they can there study questions affecting life in London, and can find ample sphere for practical effort. It is available as a teaching centre not only for residents, but for many ladies living at their own homes. The Ecclesiastical Commissioners and others having put under my charge a large number of houses for the poor in the immediate neighbourhood, I am able to train and use in them those few ladies who prove qualified for, and inclined to, that form of helpfulness. Finally, it is the place where we who are deeply impressed with the need of raising the standard of qualification are at work, and can give the necessary supervision.

We consider that our scheme should be framed so as to meet the requirements both of volunteers and of those purposing to engage in work professionally.

(1) *The Volunteers.* These include the large and ever-increasing number who desire to help wisely their poorer friends and neighbours, whether directly as district visitors, on committees of institutions, as members of district committees of the Charity Organisation Society, or indirectly in their own households and on their own estates; and also those who should be ready to come forward to undertake more definite responsibilities as poor law guardians or members of school boards.[7] There is, at present, no recognised qualified body of people to certify the training or fitness of candidates for such offices. One person tells someone else she knows Mrs.—, whom she thinks likely to do, and those who uphold women as women support her, or those who think workhouses and district schools should have at least some woman to see to the hundreds of women and children they contain, gladly support any who will come forward. It may be she is fit; it may be she is unfit; at any rate she has to learn laboriously, sometimes disastrously, what might have been taught her gradually, and under experienced leaders.

(2) *Professional workers.* The more volunteer work increases, the more need there is of a certain proportion of paid work to keep it together. As the board of guardians, or bench of magistrates, has its paid clerk; as the good Charity Committee has its paid secretary; as the choir has its choir-master; so most groups of volunteers have, and must have, their paid worker. This opens the way to a moderate income for many women who have the care of the poor as much on their hearts as any volunteer. Give them training, and they will become increasingly valuable and valued. On many a Charity Organisation Committee, attached to many a parochial organisation, as managers of houses for the poor, how eagerly would trained workers be caught up, how valuable they would be!

The Committee, therefore, determined to offer a course of training to women, resident or non-resident at the Settlement, but who are willing to prepare themselves steadily, and to pass through a given course as advised.

---

7. After the turn of the century, women more and more often held such positions. Earlier office-holders included Emily Davies (see part 4), who was elected to the London School Board in 1870. Hill herself was appointed to the Royal Commission on the Poor Law in 1905.

During the past year the visitors in the various districts have been not only doing and learning their practical duties, and growing into nearer friendship with their people, but have had opportunities of talking over with experienced workers what is best to be done with any family under their care.

With regard to theoretical study, Miss Margaret Benson has given a course of six lectures on Capital and Labour, Co-operation, Trade Unions, &c. This course has been attended by from thirty to forty ladies. Miss Sewell has also given an elementary course on the various agencies at present existing in Southwark, medical, educational, and recreative; on the Poor Law, the School Board, the Sanitary Laws, &c.; and has drawn up a list of books helpful to those intending to take up work among the poor.

The Committee recently heard that the trustees of the Pfeiffer bequest, which was left for the benefit of women and girls, had made grants to Girton, Somerville, and Newnham Colleges, available for scholarships. The Committee has, therefore, sent in an application asking whether the trustees will found two scholarships tenable at the Women's University Settlement, the value of each of which should be 50*l.* per annum, for the benefit of such women as may be selected by the Settlement Committee in conjunction with any college or representative body whom the trustees may see fit to appoint. Such scholars to hold the scholarship for one, or better still for two years, and to go through the course which may be laid down for practical and theoretical training. The Settlement is registered under the Limited Liabilities Act, as is Girton; and its constitution and by-laws have been settled by Lord Thring for the Association. It is governed by a Committee elected by the various women's colleges; and therefore, though it is only five years old, we think it might be entrusted with such scholarships.

But, if the trustees should unfortunately decide differently; if, as so often has happened before, individuals have to lead the way as pioneers who may dare to risk in order to show paths whereon the public hereafter walks securely, then we commend our scheme to the consideration of those who wish to secure sounder help for the poor, who would gladly promote this by providing the means of training for one or two of those earnest and willing of our younger workers, who, able to give their time to their poorer neighbours, and capable of forming centres of light and leading on their return to their homes, yet cannot afford to pay for a year's or two years' residence at the Settlement where they can get the needful preparation, and who, living out of London, cannot come daily.[8] Let those who can help think also of the means such scholarships would be of opening up to women one more branch of honourable and useful remunerative work, preparing them—not to do some new design in crewels, or ornamental leather, which a jaded public may be induced to buy in "charity" at a fashionable bazaar, but setting them in forlorn and desolate districts, where their wisdom and strength are urgently

---

8. In *Independent Women: Work and Community for Single Women* (University of Chicago Press, 1985), Martha Vicinus points out that no one beneath an upper-middle-class income level could have afforded to live in a settlement house. According to Vicinus, in 1901, the annual charge to the worker for room, board, and training was £60.

needed; where, ready with counsel, with clear knowledge, with trained sagacity and self-control, they may stand by the poor, having learned to render them help which shall endure; enabling such women to feel that when they draw their salary and take it back to help their own home, they have earned it by work which was really wanted. Let those who could help remember that, if they can manage for a year or two thus to arrange for training one or two workers without any paraphernalia of perpetual scholarships, they will have helped to set a standard of necessary preparation which may go far to save our poor from the degrading curse of our shiftless and unreasoning almsgiving, as well as having started willing and good women on a useful professional career.

Every year brings forward some new huge and widely advertised panacea for poverty which can only be met by steady, quiet, and wise action; every fall of snow, or suspicion of slackness, causes an outcry that some fresh remedy is necessary. Great are the temptations to politicians, to newspaper-writers, to philanthropists, to the indolent whose uneasy consciences are aroused, to rush into hasty action which ever more degrades, and induces a gambling recklessness in the miserable receivers of gifts suddenly lavished, and again suddenly withheld. Men flock in from the country to London, tempted by these huge schemes, from which they hope to receive something without due labour. Every young man fresh from college has his certain cure for social evils. Labour is paid for at a higher rate in London than elsewhere; nearly everything is cheaper here than elsewhere; a large proportion of wages goes to the public-house; dirt and neglect attract alms. Thrift hardly exists among our poor, and the self-controlled among them may well ask themselves whether it pays or not, so lavish are the scattered gifts of foolish donors. Considering all these ominous facts, one feels as if, whatever wild things the inexperienced may do, some of us must set ourselves to make our people worth more, must help them to be their best selves, to prepare their children for useful work, to use the hardly-earned wages well, to put by for the rainy day. We must try to bring all the knowledge of the present day to bear on their lives, to make their homes happy—often to learn from themselves how we can help them. All this needs preparation and experience, gained not at the cost of the poor, but side by side with experienced workers.

PART 3

Work as Oppression

"I see two classes dependent on each other in every possible way, yet each evidently regarding the interests of the other as opposed to their own; . . ."

—Margaret Hale in Elizabeth Gaskell's *North and South*

Introduction

SHORTLY BEFORE his death in 1883 at the age of thirty-one, Arnold Toynbee urged university faculty and students to live with and educate the displaced and economically oppressed; he also offered a series of talks *(Lectures on the Industrial Revolution in England)* in which he maintained that the "effects of the Industrial Revolution prove that free competition may produce wealth without producing well-being," that England's early "capitalists used all their power to oppress the labourers, and drove down wages to starvation point." His social activism gave rise to Oxford's historic commitment to settlement house projects at Toynbee Hall in London's East End; his series of lectures, in addition to popularizing the phrase "industrial revolution," prompted a still ongoing dialectic among historians about whether owners' consuming preoccupation with laissez-faire economics was the chief cause of the suffering and deprivation common to many in the working classes.

Whatever the judgments of modern analysts, traditional or revisionist, many nineteenth-century observers did conclude that overriding concern about financial profit, sanctioned by the prevailing economic theory, led to consistent exploitation of workers. Elizabeth Gaskell, in her 1855 novel *North and South,* focuses readers' attention upon the character of John Thornton, a self-made industrialist who initially reasons "as if commerce were everything and humanity nothing" but who ultimately redeems himself by becoming an employer who takes responsibility for his "stewardship" of labor. Gaskell's book was commissioned by Charles Dickens as he was finishing his own industrial novel *Hard Times,* selections from which appear in this section, a less sanguine story in which he attacks the heartlessly aggressive spirit that he saw dominating business, industry, government, and even labor unions. A tendency to repudiate or at least temper the belief that unimpeded pursuit of self-interest would lead to a widening social good informs many of the selections in this part of the anthology. It is an operating assumption behind the moral storytelling of the Chartist writer Thomas Cooper in "Seth Thompson, Stockinger," but it also forms the basis for critical assessment by those normally committed to the principles of laissez faire, such as Thomas Babington Macaulay, a thinker ordinarily opposed to government intervention in business who nonetheless felt the need for some regulation to protect workers from abuse by profit-seeking owners and entrepreneurs.

While some writers, such as Wordsworth and Coleridge, explored the ways individuals can develop a debilitating craving for busy-ness or a psychological depression associated with the burden of work, most saw the distresses of labor as social and political evils visited from the outside upon unwilling victims. Certain selections represent the egalitarian protest against basic social inequities, the sense of frustration that some who labor still go without while others who are idle arrogate to themselves the fruits of workers' efforts. The privileged poet Percy Bysshe Shelley and the impoverished artisan W. J. Linton shared assumptions about the fundamental injustices of a class system. So did Henrietta Tindal, who spoke for "the many [workers] who served the few," and the affluent William Morris, who found "incurably vicious" that division into rich and poor which Benjamin Disraeli, in 1845, described as having made of England "two nations"— those possessing wealth and exercising power and those subjected to toiling poverty and political inconsequence. Indeed, it is impossible to separate the political history of nineteenth-century England from discussions of labor, for what historian E. P. Thompson has called "the making of the English working class" was the signal phenomenon behind many of the political challenges and much of the social evolution that distinguished England in the nineteenth century.

From the time of the French Revolution, which aroused great anxiety about the international dissemination of Jacobinism, an English culture uncertain of its own identity was apprehensive about a workers' revolt. Although upper- and middle-class uneasiness probably exaggerated the danger of potential revolutionary action by artisans, factory workers, miners, and farm laborers, the workers' oppressive living conditions certainly provided a substantial basis for discontent. In the early Napoleonic era, the Despard conspiracy to establish egalitarian control of government through armed rebellion drew support from artisans and working men and was supposed to have had its greatest strength in the new industrial and commercial centers of Leeds, Birmingham, and Manchester. The much-feared coercive activities and the machine-breaking of clandestine Luddite organizations, prominent from 1811 to 1816, were in large measure a response to technological innovations in the means of production, innovations that displaced workers by rendering traditional modes of labor obsolete. The armed working-class revolt of the abortive Pentridge Uprising in 1817 had as its objective "Levelution"; and, during the economic depression following the Napoleonic wars, fear of oppressed workers' leveling sentiments underlay the militia's attack, in 1819, upon a peaceful assembly of workers at St. Peter's Field in Manchester, an appallingly brutal event that immediately became known as "Peterloo." Misgivings about labor violence extended into rural areas, also, especially in the late 1820s and the early 1830s when impoverished farm workers swore to follow "Captain Swing" (a fictitious figure, as was the "King Ludd" of the secret Luddite associations); demanding employment and improved wages, these desperate agricultural laborers burned hayricks, ruined farming implements (notably the threshing machine), maimed cattle, and ransacked the farmhouses of the wealthy.

Some historians see prominent legislation of this period as a deliberate effort to counter the disquiet and the threat posed by oppressed laborers. It may be true that Dissenting, Methodist, and (limited) Catholic participation in working-class movements had some bearing both upon the repeal, in 1828, of the Test Act that had restricted political activities of religious Nonconformists and also upon subsequent Catholic Emancipation in 1829. The Reform Act of 1832 certainly was a step toward democratization, in that it did grant parliamentary representation to some of the new industrial towns; it enfranchised the upper middle rather than the working class, however, aligning managerial with landowning interests and deliberately deferring any settlement of workers' claims to rightful participation in the electorate. That significant (yet still not full) enfranchisement of laborers did not occur until the Second Reform Act of 1867 was one of the most severe disabilities under which workers lived. As did the Reform Act of 1832, the Poor Law Amendment Act of 1834 responded, though not necessarily with humane sympathy, to complaints about the sufferings of the lower class, creating workhouses for the unemployed such as the one described by Dickens in "A Walk in a Workhouse" (included in this section) and establishing social relief at a deliberately minimal level. What followed from the 1830s forward throughout the century was a series of investigative parliamentary reports that addressed stressful, unhygienic, and dangerous working conditions in factories, mines, and farming areas. The great ambition of workers to achieve political equality became fixed in the Chartist movement of the late 1830s and the 1840s, but, amidst the most intense uneasiness concerning political revolution, it failed in 1848; the fitful yet ongoing responsiveness of Parliament to investigative reports concerning labor abuse, however, effected some genuine though limited redress of specific oppressive conditions.

Much may be learned by studying official political responses to labor unrest, the reports of various investigative commissions, and the statutes enacted. What the diverse non-governmental literature of the period imparts is a more personal understanding of the sufferings endured by oppressed workers and the chronically unemployed. Yet certain of the most moving of these documents actually include a measure of social science research and even statistical analysis. Henry Mayhew's *London Labour and the London Poor*, originally published as a series of newspaper articles, offers investigative interviews with lower-class laborers, accounts often cast as first-person narratives by the indigent workers Mayhew met. His mid-century social surveys, selections from which are included in this section, shocked his upper- and middle-class readership, revealing in the heart of London what reviewers called "an unknown country" populated by ill-fed, sometimes diseased, uneducated, often homeless, and uncared-for citizens of the wealthiest and most advanced industrial nation in the world. Over the next decades, Mayhew was followed in his journalistic exposés by others, many of whom emulated the dramatic style of his presentation. "The Fur-Pullers of South London" by Edith Hogg, included in this section, is another good example of such reporting, an exploration of how traditional cottage industry had been transferred to an urban setting and debased into a system that was physically revolting and morally appalling. Others added to their exposés an objective tone of documentary realism. Conducting comprehensive investigations and supplying fair-minded analyses were guiding principles for the most thoroughgoing and systematic report on urban working-class life, the seventeen-volume *Life and Labour of the People in London,* published just after the turn of the century by Charles Booth. Booth was a man of compelling integrity and enlightened social interest, a business leader who, with clear commercial success, rejected the appetitive principles of laissez-faire theory: "It is not in our interest," he wrote, "to get the better of either the men we buy from or those we sell to—but to do the best we can for each, subject to a modest remuneration for ourselves." Concerned to downplay sensationalism and to make his inquiry about urban workers genuinely instructive, Booth relied upon statistical analyses, tables, charts, and comparative records in his study. This scientific approach accorded well with the increasing use of photographs in the nineteenth century to portray living and working conditions as laborers actually experienced them.

Booth dealt with London urban workers, but factory operatives in the new industrial centers, miners, and domestic servants also were subjects of concern to writers of the period. Although agriculture employed, throughout the nineteenth century, more men, women, and children than any other single component of national industry, and although conditions on farms were harsh, there was less concern about abusive working situations on the varied types of agricultural estates; indeed, the experience of farm labor was often sentimentalized, set as a vanishing idyllic contrast to the mechanized and "unnatural" worlds of factory and mine. (See Elizabeth Gaskell's "Cumberland Sheep-Shearers" in part 2, "Work as Opportunity.") The centralized manufactory was the focus for many who wrote about work. While early writers celebrated the opportunities made possible by the factory system, they also shared the concern set forth by Wordsworth in *The Excursion* (excerpted in part 2) that this system could jeopardize the success and happiness of domestic life and dehumanize people by subjecting them to the insistently repetitive demands of a machine rather than to the natural and health-giving rhythms of the earth. More specific dangers, however, engaged later writers such as Richard Oastler, Thomas Babington Macaulay, and Friedrich Engels, selections from whose writings documenting dangerous factory conditions appear in this section. Persistent emphasis upon abusive conditions in factories led to gradual reforms, but owners resisted controls over industry as zealously as advocates insisted upon reforms.

With the advent of centralized factories and the development of the iron, steel, and railway industries came a marked increase in the demand for coal and a concomitant escalation in the hazards of mining. Labor in the mines, apart from fostering specific health problems such as respiratory diseases and skeletal deformities, was so physically stressful and threatening that it debilitated workers' bodies and psyches. That women were employed in mines at tasks that stripped them of essential dignity and reduced them to brutish existence was a criticism that received added emphasis; even children's author Frances Hodgson Burnett wrote a now-neglected novel titled *That Lass o' Lowry's* about the demeaning life of a pit-girl in the mines. The writings by Charlotte Elizabeth Tonna and Joseph Skipsey included in this section make evident the inhumanly harsh and often needlessly dangerous conditions of mining work as well as the need for regulatory action to address such problems.

As a growing number of middle-class families achieved financial security and self-consciously cultivated the image of well-established genteel households, the number of positions for domestic servants increased dramatically. Even as the situations of female laborers in mines and factories received frequent and angry emphasis from activists who deplored the strenuous and enervating tasks assigned to women, W. J. Linton, in the ironically titled piece "The Free-Servant" included in this section, makes clear that domestic service could be equally exhausting. Service in a home was the most common employment for women, but the occupation of seamstress regularly associated with such service was one pursued both at central work sites and at individual lodgings. The work of the seamstress (or sempstress) was almost universally depicted in terms of abusive relationships, perhaps because the contrast between the neediness and ceaseless work of the laborer and the self-indulgent idleness of the consumer of the luxury items thus produced could be readily accentuated. The victimization of the needlewoman had become so celebrated that Thomas Carlyle could deride it as overexposed (see "Occasional Discourse on the Nigger Question" in part 1), while Alfred, Lord Tennyson, in "Locksley Hall Sixty Years After," includes as a matter of course in his litany of the ills of the age "the Master scrimp[ing] his haggard sempstress of her daily bread." Thomas Hood's celebrated "The Song of the Shirt" and the sensationalist story "The Slave of the Needle" by J. P. H. are complementary pieces included in this section to represent the common portrayal of the plight of the seamstress, a subject that informs much fiction of the period and also some popular visual art. (See figures 3.2, 3.3, and 3.7.)

Reformers frequently focused their criticisms upon the treatment allotted to women, for the idealization of middle-class women as moral guardians of the home did not accord well with the demonstrable exploitation of working-class women, and this anomaly had no easy resolution. Children even more than women were the subjects of moral crusades against labor abuses. The nineteenth century had, in a curious sense, invented childhood, extolling it as a time of enchanted delight when an intuitive innocence verged on near mystical union with divinity. This almost hallowed position held by the child, like that exalted one held by woman, enabled activists to depict as not only immoral but also sacrilegious that callous mistreatment of children as laborers which, early on, had become common practice in factories and mines. William Blake, Richard Oastler, Caroline Norton, Elizabeth Barrett Browning, and Eliza Cook all lodged protests, presented in this section, against abuse of children in the workplace. Intensely emotional and keen edged, their social protest on behalf of children epitomizes the most pervasive and trenchant criticism of work as oppression—the indictment that employers were, in the selfish pursuit of profit and their own ease, deliberately ignoring the simple humanity of those over whom they held arbitrary power.

WILLIAM BLAKE

Though he received little recognition until late in his life, William Blake (1757–1827) excelled in both art and literature. He was educated at home until age ten, when he was sent to drawing school. At age fourteen, he began a seven-year apprenticeship to an engraver, during which time he read widely on his own and composed his first poems. In his short lyrics as well as in his longer prophetic and visionary poems, Blake often voices protests against injustice and inhumanity. For Blake, the solution to society's problems could be found in the transforming power of the imagination to unlock the "mind-forged manacles" and envision a radically different social order. Many of Blake's poems were accompanied by hand-colored engravings integral to the meaning of the text.

The first "Chimney Sweeper"[1] poem reprinted below comes from *Songs of Innocence* (1789). The second "Chimney Sweeper" and "London" come from the expanded collection, *Songs of Innocence and Experience,* published in 1794.

The Chimney Sweeper (1789)

> When my mother died I was very young,
> And my father sold me while yet my tongue
> Could scarcely cry " 'weep! 'weep! 'weep! 'weep!"[2]
> So your chimneys I sweep & in soot I sleep.

1. An estimated four hundred to five hundred boys were employed as chimney sweeps in London at the turn of the century. Laws to protect young chimney sweeps were passed in 1840 and 1864 but were not adequately enforced; government commissioners charged with investigating child labor reported in the 1860s that two thousand children were still working as sweeps. Effective legislation did not exist until 1875. Charles Kingsley's fantasy *The Water Babies* (1863) presents another literary exposé of the abuse of chimney sweeps.

2. The young child's attempt to articulate the street cry of "Sweep! Sweep!"

There's little Tom Dacre, who cried when his head   5
That curl'd like a lamb's back, was shav'd, so I said,
"Hush, Tom! never mind it, for when your head's bare,
You know that the soot cannot spoil your white hair."

And so he was quiet, & that very night,
As Tom was a-sleeping he had such a sight!   10
That thousands of sweepers, Dick, Joe, Ned, & Jack,
Were all of them lock'd up in coffins of black;

And by came an Angel who had a bright key,
And he open'd the coffins & set them all free;
Then down a green plain, leaping, laughing they run,   15
And wash in a river and shine in the Sun.

Then naked & white, all their bags left behind,
They rise upon clouds, and sport in the wind.
And the Angel told Tom, if he'd be a good boy,
He'd have God for his father & never want joy.   20

And so Tom awoke; and we rose in the dark
And got with our bags & our brushes to work.
Tho' the morning was cold, Tom was happy & warm;
So if all do their duty, they need not fear harm.

The Chimney Sweeper (1794)

A little black thing among the snow
Crying " 'weep, 'weep," in notes of woe!
"Where are thy father & mother? say?"
"They are both gone up to the church to pray.

"Because I was happy upon the heath,   5
And smil'd among the winter's snow;
They clothed me in the clothes of death,
And taught me to sing the notes of woe.

"And because I am happy, & dance & sing,
They think they have done me no injury,   10
And are gone to praise God & his Priest & King,
Who make up a heaven of our misery."

London

I wander thro' each charter'd[1] street,
Near where the charter'd Thames does flow,
And mark in every face I meet
Marks of weakness, marks of woe.

In every cry of every Man,   5
In every Infant's cry of fear,
In every voice, in every ban,[2]
The mind-forg'd manacles I hear:

How the Chimney-sweeper's cry
Every blackning Church appalls,   10
And the hapless Soldier's sigh
Runs in blood down Palace walls.

But most thro' midnight streets I hear
How the youthful Harlot's curse
Blasts the new-born Infant's tear,   15
And blights with plagues the Marriage hearse.[3]

1. Officially enfranchised.
2. Prohibition.
3. In referring to the marriage coach as a hearse, Blake changes the nominally life-giving sacrament of marriage into a funeral procession.

WILLIAM WORDSWORTH

See the introduction to Wordsworth in part 1.

The short selection below, "The world is too much with us; late and soon," composed in 1802 and published in *Poems in Two Volumes*, 1807, comprises Wordsworth's indignant denunciation of business as busy-ness, his complaint that, all too readily, the practice of getting and spending becomes oppressively obsessive, cutting people off from the natural sources of inspiration and consolation. As do other short verses Wordsworth composed near the turn of the century ("To My Sister," "Anecdote for Fathers," "Expostulation and Reply," "The Tables Turned"), this sonnet sets over against the active disposition associated with the ideal of work a responsive sensitivity that is not always seeking but that is receptively attuned to moral lessons that come unsought.

The world is too much with us; late and soon

The world is too much with us; late and soon,
Getting and spending, we lay waste our powers:
Little we see in Nature that is ours;
We have given our hearts away, a sordid boon!
This Sea that bares her bosom to the moon;   5
The winds that will be howling at all hours,
And are up-gathered now like sleeping flowers;
For this, for everything, we are out of tune;
It moves us not.—Great God! I'd rather be
A Pagan suckled in a creed outworn;   10
So might I, standing on this pleasant lea,

Have glimpses that would make me less forlorn;
Have sight of Proteus[1] rising from the sea;
Or hear old Triton[2] blow his wreathéd horn.

1. Proteus is the Old Man of the Sea, the sea-god who can change shapes at will: see *Odyssey* 4.385ff.
2. Triton was a minor sea-deity or merman, often represented as blowing on a conch shell; perhaps the best-known reference to Triton comes in *Aeneid* 6.176ff., when the sea god drowns the mortal trumpeter Misenus, who had challenged the gods to compete with him at creating music with the conch.

SAMUEL TAYLOR COLERIDGE

S AMUEL TAYLOR COLERIDGE (1772–1834) was the Romantic author whose career is most often summarized with the phrase "unfulfilled genius." While perhaps not altogether fair, this assessment does address Coleridge's recurring failure
(not uncommon among Romantic writers in general) to complete projects that he
had undertaken. In Coleridge's case, the habitually unrealized goals may have been
the result of chronic illness treated with laudanum as well as the expression of a
temperament easily unsettled and distracted. A gifted youngster at Christ's Hospital School and a promising student at Cambridge, he left university without taking
a degree. Early political radicalism (which both subsequently rejected) brought
Coleridge into close contact with the poet Robert Southey, with whom he developed the never-realized project of establishing an egalitarian commune in America, which Coleridge prematurely named "Pantisocracy." He also, in 1795, met
William Wordsworth (see the preceding selection), with whom he began collab-
orative work that resulted in the publication, in 1798, of *Lyrical Ballads*, a seminal
work of the Romantic movement. Toward the turn of the century, however, mari-
tal difficulties, ill health, and depression combined with his taking of laudanum to
lead Coleridge to a condition of mental disquiet and paralysis of the will that
afflicted him for the remainder of his life. He separated from his wife, had a major
falling out with Wordsworth, engaged only fitfully in literary composition, and
contemplated suicide. In the second decade of the century, he began a partial
recovery, reconverted to orthodox Christianity, and committed himself to more
sustained composition of poetry, literary and cultural criticism, and theological
essays. Through the kindness of Dr. James Gillam, he was cared for until his death,
when his reputation as a philosopher and metaphysician had eclipsed any sense of
his worth as a poet.

"Work without Hope" (published 1828) offers an introspective analysis of how
the very effort to pursue work of any sort was an impossibility for Coleridge. The
overwhelming sense of oppressive failure recorded here is, of course, personal, but
the poem aptly describes similar experiences of incapacitating ennui that befell
many nineteenth-century intellectuals who, conscious of great enterprises to be
embraced and driven by a sense of duty to work, nevertheless found themselves
emotionally impotent to commit themselves to meaningful labor.

Work without Hope
Lines Composed 21st February 1825

All Nature seems at work. Slugs leave their lair—
The bees are stirring—birds are on the wing—
And Winter slumbering in the open air,
Wears on his smiling face a dream of Spring!
And I the while, the sole unbusy thing,   5
Nor honey make, nor pair, nor build, nor sing.

Yet well I ken[1] the banks where amaranths[2] blow,
Have traced the fount whence streams of nectar[3] flow.
Bloom, O ye amaranths! bloom for whom ye may,
For me ye bloom not! Glide, rich streams, away!   10
With lips unbrightened, wreathless brow, I stroll:
And would you learn the spells that drowse my soul?
Work without Hope draws nectar in a sieve,
And Hope without an object cannot live.

1. Know.
2. Magical flowers that never fade.
3. The drink of the gods.

RICHARD OASTLER

Richard Oastler (1789–1861) succeeded his father as steward of the Fixby estates in Huddersfield in the north of England in 1820. In 1830, Oastler paid a visit to John Wood, a progressive manufacturer, who described to him the plight of child laborers in the nearby Bradford district. The same day, Oastler sent to the *Leeds Mercury* the letter that appears below. In his relentless crusade for a ten-hour work day and protection for child laborers, Oastler came to be known as "the factory king." His campaign for reform legislation led him to author countless pamphlets and articles, to travel widely delivering speeches, and to give testimony to parliamentary committees. From 1841 to 1843, he was an inmate of the Fleet Debtors' Prison. While there, Oastler composed political pamphlets written weekly as letters to his former employer, Thomas Thornhill, and published as *The Fleet Papers*.

In a prefatory column, the editors of the *Leeds Mercury* note that while Oastler writes "with undue warmth and violence," "the evil he complains of is a real one." From their perspective, however, the fault rests with lawmakers rather than with factory owners. The editors maintain that it would be more appropriate for Oastler to petition Parliament for a change in the law than to "charge a respectable class of manufacturers with hypocrisy and oppression." Despite this statement, Oastler went on to denounce employers in a series of letters that appeared in both the *Leeds Mercury* and the *Leeds Intelligencer.*

Slavery in Yorkshire
To the Editors of the *Leeds Mercury*

> "It is the pride of Britain that a Slave cannot exist on her
> soil; and if I read the genius of her constitution aright, I
> find that Slavery is most abhorrent to it—that the air
> which Britons breath[e] is free—the ground on which
> they tread is sacred to liberty."
>
> —Rev. R. W. Hamilton's *Speech at the Meeting held in the
> Cloth-hall Yard, Sept. 22d, 1830.*

GENTLEMEN,—No heart responded with truer accents to the sounds of liberty which were heard in the Leeds Cloth-hall yard, on the 22d inst.[1] than did mine, and from none could more sincere and earnest prayers arise to the throne of Heaven, that hereafter Slavery might only be known to Britain in the pages of her history.[2] One shade alone obscured my pleasure, arising not from any difference in principle, but from the want of application of the general principle *to the whole Empire.* The pious and able champions of *Negro* liberty and *Colonial* rights should, if I mistake not, have gone farther than they did; or perhaps, to speak more correctly, before they had travelled so far as the West Indies, should, at least for a few moments, have sojourned in our own immediate neighbourhood, and have directed the attention of the meeting to scenes of misery, acts of oppression and victims of Slavery, even on the threshold of our homes!

Let truth speak out, appalling as the statements may appear. The fact is true. Thousands of our fellow-creatures and fellow-subjects, both male and female, the miserable inhabitants of a *Yorkshire town;* (Yorkshire now represented in Parliament by the giant of anti-slavery principles,) are this very moment existing in a state of Slavery *more horrid* than are the victims of that hellish system— "*Colonial Slavery.*" These innocent creatures drawl[3] out unpitied their short but miserable existence, in a place famed for its profession of religious zeal, whose inhabitants are ever foremost in *professing* "Temperance" and "Reformation," and are striving to outrun their neighbours in Missionary exertions, and would fain send the Bible to the farthest corner of the globe—aye in the very place where the anti-slavery fever rages most furiously, her *apparent charity,* is not more admired on earth, than her *real cruelty* is abhorred in heaven. The very streets which receive the droppings of an "Anti-Slavery Society" are every morning wet by the tears of innocent victims at the accursed shrine of avarice, who are *compelled* (not by the

---

1. "Inst" is the abbreviation for "instant," or current month.
2. The slave trade was outlawed in 1807, and slavery was abolished in the British colonies in 1833.
3. To crawl or drag along.

cartwhip of the negro slave-driver) but by the dread of the equally appalling thong or strap of the overlooker, to hasten, half-dressed, *but not half-fed,* to those magazines[4] of British Infantile Slavery—*the Worsted Mills in the town and neighbourhood of Bradford!!!*

Would that I had Brougham's eloquence,[5] that I might rouse the hearts of the nation, and make every Briton swear "These innocents shall be free!"

Thousands of little children, both male and female, *but principally female,* from SEVEN to fourteen years of age, are daily *compelled* to *labour* from six o'clock in the morning to seven in the evening, with only—Britons blush whilst you read it!— *with only thirty minutes allowed for eating and recreation!*—Poor infants! ye are indeed sacrificed at the shrine of avarice, *without even the solace of the negro slave:*—ye are no more than he is, *free agents*—ye are compelled to work as long as the *necessity* of your needy parents may require, or the cold-blooded avarice of your worse than barbarian masters *may demand!* Ye live in the boasted land of freedom, and *feel* and mourn that *ye are Slaves,* and slaves without the only comfort which the Negro has. He knows it is his sordid mercenary master's INTEREST that he should *live,* be *strong* and *healthy. Not so with you.* Ye are doomed to labour from morn till night for one who cares not how soon your weak and tender frames are stretched to breaking! You are not mercifully valued at so much per head; this would assure you at least (even with the worst and most cruel masters), of the mercy shown to their own labouring beasts. No, no! your soft and delicate limbs are tired, and fagged,[6] and jaded at only *so much per week;* and when your joints can act no longer, your emaciated frames are cast aside, the boards on which you lately toiled and wasted life away, are instantly supplied with other victims, who in this boasted land of liberty are HIRED—not sold—as Slaves, and daily forced to *hear* that they are free. Oh! Duncombe![7] Thou hatest Slavery—I know thou dost resolve that "Yorkshire children shall no more be slaves." And Morpeth![8] who justly gloriest in the Christian faith—Oh Morpeth listen to the cries and count the tears of these poor babes, and let St. Stephen's[9] hear thee swear—"they shall no longer groan in Slavery!" And Bethell, too![10] who swears

---

4. Warehouses.

5. In September 1830 when Oastler's letter appeared, Henry Brougham (1778–1868) was a Whig M.P. for Yorkshire. Two months later, he was appointed Lord Chancellor. In addition to his commitment to the abolition of slavery and the slave trade, Brougham worked throughout his career in support of other reforms. An advocate of popular education, he founded in 1826 the Society for the Diffusion of Useful Knowledge, which published a series of inexpensive, informative books aimed at working-class readers. Brougham also was instrumental in effecting much-needed law reform.

6. Worked hard.

7. Thomas Slingsby Duncombe (1796–1861), a radical member of the House of Commons and staunch supporter of the Chartist cause.

8. Title by which George William Frederick Howard (1802–1864) was known prior to 1848, when he became the seventh Earl of Carlisle. A Whig, Morpeth was first elected to the House of Commons in 1826; in 1830, he represented Yorkshire.

9. The House of Commons met in St. Stephen's Chapel in Westminster until the chapel was destroyed by fire in 1834.

10. Probably Richard Bethell (1772–1864), a Conservative member of the House of Commons who represented the East Riding of Yorkshire in 1830 and from 1832 to 1841.

eternal hatred to the name of Slave, whene'er thy manly voice is heard in Britain's senate, assert the rights and liberty of Yorkshire Youths. And Brougham! Thou who art the chosen champion of liberty in every clime! Oh bend thy giant's mind, and listen to the sorrowing accents of these poor Yorkshire little ones, and note their tears; then let thy voice rehearse their woes, and touch the chord thou only holdest—the chord that sounds above the silvery notes in praise of heavenly liberty, and down descending at thy will, groans in the horrid caverns of the deep in unuttering sounds of misery accursed to hellish bondage; and as thou soundst these notes, let Yorkshire hear thee swear "Her *children* shall be free!" Yes, all ye four protectors of our rights, chosen by freemen to destroy oppression's rod,

> "Vow one by one, vow altogether, vow
> With heart and voice, eternal enmity
> Against oppression by your brethren's hands;
> Till man nor woman under Britain's laws,
> Nor son nor daughter born within her empire,
> Shall buy, or sell, or HIRE, or BE a Slave!"

The nation is now most resolutely determined that Negroes shall be free. Let them, however, not forget that Briton's have common rights with Afric's sons.

The blacks may be fairly compared to beasts of burden, *kept for their master's use.* The whites to those *which others keep and let for hire!* If I have succeeded in calling the attention of your readers to the horrid and abominable system on which the worsted mills in and near Bradford are conducted, I have done some good. Why should not children working in them be protected by legislative enactments, as well as those who work in cotton mills?[11] Christians should feel and act for those whom Christ so eminently loved and declared that "of such is the kingdom of heaven."[12]

Your insertion of the above in the *Leeds Mercury,* at your earliest convenience, will oblige, Gentlemen,

Your most obedient servant,

RICHARD OASTLER,

Fixby-Hall, near Huddersfield, Sept. 29th, 1830.

---

11. In 1815, Sir Robert Peel presented what came to be referred to as the first Ten Hours Bill. It was intended to apply only to children employed in the cotton mills. Oastler asks why reform should not also apply to those working in mills that manufactured "worsted," or tightly twisted woolen yarn. In his letters to the *Leeds Mercury* and the *Leeds Intelligencer,* Oastler demanded a ten-hour day for all workers under age twenty-one. Not until 1833, three years after Oastler's first letter on child labor appeared, did Parliament pass a bill, restricted to textile mills, which prohibited the employment of children under age nine and which limited to eight hours a day the employment of those between the ages of nine and thirteen.

12. Matthew 19:14: "but Jesus said, 'Let the children come to me, and do not hinder them; for to such belongs the Kingdom of Heaven.'"

CAROLINE NORTON

CAROLINE SHERIDAN NORTON (1808–1877), granddaughter of the playwright Richard Brinsley Sheridan (1751–1816), was the popular author of over one hundred works of poetry, fiction, drama, and nonfiction. Praised for her wit and beauty, Norton moved in fashionable circles. Nevertheless, in her writing she addressed a variety of serious social issues, some of which affected her own life. When her unhappy marriage dissolved, Norton's husband denied her a divorce and refused to allow her to see their three young sons. Thereafter, despite her resistance to radical, organized feminism, she devoted herself to obtaining legal rights to divorce, property ownership, and child custody for women. In the course of her crusade, she wrote a number of influential pamphlets, including *English Laws for Women in the Nineteenth Century* (1854) and *A Letter to the Queen on Lord Chancellor Cranworth's Marriage and Divorce Bill* (1855), which contributed to the passage of the 1857 Divorce and Matrimonial Causes Act. Norton also authored pamphlets and poems that called for other wide-ranging social reforms, for instance, for improvements in education and in the prison system as well as for relief of the misery of child laborers.

Appearing anonymously in 1836, *A Voice from the Factories* was one of the earliest poems to address factory reform. For five years, Parliament had debated the merits of a bill introduced in 1831 by Michael Sadler (1780–1835), proposing a shorter work day and restrictions on the employment of children in factories. Sadler, a Tory member of the House of Commons with commercial interests, was an outspoken critic of child labor abuses. His bill called for prohibiting labor for children under age nine and limiting the working hours of those between nine and eighteen to ten hours each weekday and eight hours on Saturday. In response, the House appointed a Select Committee to investigate child labor in textile factories. Chaired by Sadler, the committee conducted extensive interviews and presented its disturbing findings in 1832. Throughout the 1830s and 1840s, Parliament commissioned a number of official studies, the results of which stirred controversy and promoted activism.

A Voice from the Factories
In Serious Verse

Dedicated to the Right Honourable Lord Ashley

> The abuses even, of such a business, must be cautiously
> dealt with; lest, in eradicating them, we shake or disorder
> the whole fabric. We admit, however, that the case of
> CHILDREN employed in the Cotton Factories is one of
> those that call fairly for legislative regulation.
>
> —McCulloch[1]

TO

THE RIGHT HONOURABLE
LORD ASHLEY[2]

My Lord,

An anonymous Author, whose own name could give no importance to this ephemeral production, ventures to claim the aid of yours; as one not only noble, but intimately connected with the subject of his[3] verse.

To the just-minded, the opinions of *no* individual, however obscure, should be utterly indifferent; since each man undoubtedly represents the opinions of a certain number of his fellow-men. It is the conviction of this, and the belief, that to abstain from giving our views on any point because we fear due attention will not be paid us, savours rather of vanity than humility, which have induced me to intrude at this time on your Lordship and the Public.

For the *mode* in which I have done so, some apology is perhaps necessary; since the application of serious poetry to the passing events of the day has fallen into disuse, and is, if not absolutely contemned, at least much discouraged.

---

1. John Ramsay McCulloch (1789–1864), an influential political economist who contended that England's prosperity depended upon the division of labor and the development of industrial enterprise.

2. *A Voice from the Factories* is dedicated to Lord Ashley—Anthony Ashley Cooper (1801–1885), who became the seventh earl of Shaftesbury in 1851. A prominent Evangelical, Ashley was elected a Tory member of Parliament in 1826 and established a reputation as a reformer when he promptly took on a number of social causes, prompting investigations into lunatic asylums, child labor conditions, and urban sanitation. When Michael Sadler was defeated in his bid for reelection by Thomas Babington Macaulay (see "The Ten Hours Bill" later in this section), Ashley took over the campaign to improve working conditions and submitted a Ten Hours Bill in 1833. At the time, most factory employees worked twelve hours a day, though in some mills laborers worked thirteen and a half hours a day. A weakened version of Ashley's bill passed in 1833. Its provisions were restricted to textile mills. Children under age nine were prohibited from labor; those between the ages of nine and thirteen were limited to eight hours a day, six days a week and were required to attend school in the factory two hours each day. Most important, the bill provided for enforcement through official government inspections.

3. Although *A Voice from the Factories* was published anonymously, the dedication implies that the author of the poem is male.

Doubtless there are those to whose tastes and understandings, dry and forcible arguments are more welcome than reasonings dressed in the garb of poetry. Yet as poetry is the language of feeling, it should be the language of the multitude; since all men can feel, while comparatively few can reason acutely, and still fewer reduce their reasoning theories to practicable schemes of improvement.

My Lord, I confess myself anxious to be *heard*, even though unable to convince. It is the misfortune of the time, that subjects of great and pressing interest are so numerous, that many questions which affect the lives and happiness of hundreds, become, as it were, comparatively unimportant; and are thrust aside by others of greater actual moment. Such, as it appears to me, is the present condition of the Factory Question: and although I am conscious that it requires but an inferior understanding to *perceive* an existing evil, while the combined efforts of many superior minds are necessary to its remedy; yet I cannot but think it incumbent on all who feel, as I do, that there *is* an evil which it behoves Christian lawgivers to remove,—to endeavour to obtain such a portion of public attention as may be granted to the expression of their conviction.

My Lord, my ambition extends so far, and no farther. I publish this little Poem with the avowed hope of obtaining that attention; I publish it *anonymously*, because I have no right to expect that my personal opinion would carry more weight with it than that of any other individual. The inspiriting cheer of triumph, and the startling yell of disapprobation, are alike composed of a number of voices, each in itself insignificant, but in their union most powerful. I desire, therefore, only to *join* my voice to that of wiser and better men, in behalf of those who suffer; and if the matter or the manner of my work be imperfect, allowance will, I trust, be made for its imperfection, since it pretends to so little.

I will only add, that I have in *no* instance overcharged or exaggerated, by poetical fictions, the picture drawn by the Commissioners appointed to inquire into this subject. I have strictly adhered to the printed Reports;[4] to that which I believe to be the melancholy truth; and that which I have, in some instances, myself had an opportunity of witnessing.

I earnestly hope I shall live to see this evil abolished. There will be delay—there will be opposition: such has ever been the case with all questions involving conflicting interests, and more especially where the preponderating interest has been on the side of the existing abuse. Yet, as the noble-hearted and compassionate Howard[5] became immortally connected with the removal of the abuses which for centuries disgraced our prison discipline; as the perseverance of Wilberforce[6]

4. Norton maintains that "the melancholy truth" presented in *A Voice from the Factories* is based on the printed reports prepared by government officials. Parliamentary reports were widely disseminated and the texts used as the basis for a number of literary treatments of social issues. See Elizabeth Barrett Browning's *The Cry of the Children* and selections from Charlotte Elizabeth Tonna's *The Perils of the Nation* and Friedrich Engels's *The Condition of the Working Class in England* later in part 3.

5. In 1777, following four years of intensive investigation of the conditions in penal institutions, John Howard (1726?–1790) published *The State of Prisons*, a work whose shocking revelations led to gradual prison reform.

6. William Wilberforce (1759–1833) led a tireless campaign that succeeded in effecting the abolition of the slave trade in 1807 and the abolition of slavery in the British colonies in 1833.

created the dawn of the long-delayed emancipation of the negroes;—so, my Lord, I trust to see *your* name enrolled with the names of these great and good men, as the Liberator and Defender of those helpless beings, on whom are inflicted many of the evils both of slavery and imprisonment, without the odium of either.

I remain, my Lord,

Your Lordship's

Obedient Servant,

The Author

London, October, 1836

A Voice from the Factories

I

When fallen man from Paradise was driven
Forth to a world of labour, death, and care;
Still, of his native Eden, bounteous Heaven
Resolved one brief memorial to spare,
And gave his offspring an imperfect share   5
Of that lost happiness, amid decay;
Making their first *approach* to life seem fair,
And giving, for the Eden past away,
CHILDHOOD, the weary life's long happy holyday.[7]

II

Sacred to heavenly peace, those years remain!   10
And when with clouds their dawn is overcast,
Unnatural seem the sorrow and the pain
(Which rosy joy flies forth to banish fast,
Because that season's sadness may not last).
Light is their grief! a word of fondness cheers   15
The unhaunted heart; the shadow glideth past;
Unknown to them the weight of boding fears,
And soft as dew on flowers their bright, ungrieving tears.

III

See the Stage-Wonder (taught to earn its bread
By the exertion of an infant skill),   20
Forsake the wholesome slumbers of its bed,
And mime, obedient to the public will.
Where is the heart so cold it does not thrill
With a vexatious sympathy, to see

7. "Holiday" comes from the Old English *halig daeg* or holy day.

That child prepare to play its part, and still   25
  With simulated airs of gaiety
Rise to the dangerous rope, and bend the supple knee?

IV

Painted and spangled, trembling there it stands,
  Glances below for friend or father's face,
Then lifts its small round arms and feeble hands   30
  With the taught movements of an artist's grace:
  Leaves its uncertain gilded resting-place—
Springs lightly as the elastic cord gives way—
  And runs along with scarce perceptible pace—
Like a bright bird upon a waving spray,   35
Fluttering and sinking still, whene'er the branches play.

V

Now watch! a joyless and distorted smile
  Its innocent lips assume; (the dancer's leer!)
Conquering its terror for a little while:
  Then lets the TRUTH OF INFANCY appear,   40
  And with a stare of numbed and childish fear
Looks sadly towards the audience come to gaze
  On the unwonted skill which costs so dear,
While still the applauding crowd, with pleased amaze,
Ring through its dizzy ears unwelcome shouts of praise.   45

VI

What is it makes us feel relieved to see
  That hapless little dancer reach the ground;
With its whole spirit's elasticity
  Thrown into one glad, safe, triumphant bound?
Why are we sad, when, as it gazes round   50
  At that wide sea of paint, and gauze, and plumes,
  (Once more awake to sense, and sight, and sound,)
The nature of its age it re-assumes,
And one spontaneous smile at length its face illumes?

VII

Because we feel, for Childhood's years and strength,   55
  Unnatural and hard the task hath been;—
Because our sickened souls revolt at length,
  And ask what infant-innocence may mean,
  Thus toiling through the artificial scene;—
Because at that word, CHILDHOOD, start to birth   60

All dreams of hope and happiness serene—
All thoughts of innocent joy that visit earth—
Prayer—slumber—fondness—smiles—and hours of rosy mirth.

VIII

And therefore when we hear the shrill faint cries
Which mark the wanderings of the little sweep;[8]   65
Or when, with glittering teeth and sunny eyes,
The boy-Italian's voice, so soft and deep,
Asks alms for his poor marmoset[9] asleep;
They fill our hearts with pitying regret,
Those little vagrants doomed so soon to weep—   70
As though a term of joy for all was set,
And that *their* share of Life's long suffering was not yet.

IX

Ever a toiling *child* doth make us sad:
'T is an unnatural and mournful sight,
Because we feel their smiles should be so glad,   75
Because we know their eyes should be so bright.
What is it, then, when, tasked beyond their might,
They labour all day long for others' gain,—
Nay, trespass on the still and pleasant night,
While uncompleted hours of toil remain?   80
Poor little FACTORY SLAVES—for YOU these lines complain!

X

Beyond all sorrow which the wanderer knows,
Is that these little pent-up wretches feel;
Where the air thick and close and stagnant grows,
And the low whirring of the incessant wheel   85
Dizzies the head, and makes the senses reel:
There, shut for ever from the gladdening sky,
Vice[10] premature and Care's corroding seal
Stamp on each sallow cheek their hateful die,
Line the smooth open brow, and sink the saddened eye.[11]   90

---

8. The "little sweep" refers to a chimney sweeper. See "The Chimney Sweeper" poems of 1789 and 1794 by William Blake, the opening selections in this section. Although regulatory legislation concerning chimney sweepers was passed in 1840 and 1864, it was not until 1875 that effective laws were enacted.

9. A small monkey used for street performances.

10. Politicians and government reports often cited evidence of the deleterious effect of labor conditions on morality, especially that of women and children. (See the excerpt from Friedrich Engels, *The Condition of the Working Class in England,* later in this section.) More recently, social historians have argued that morals were more determined by economic class than by employment.

11. Andrew Ure (1778–1857), a well-known physician and economist, was a staunch supporter of

XI

For them the fervid summer only brings
A double curse of stifling withering heat;
For them no flowers spring up, no wild bird sings,
No moss-grown walks refresh their weary feet;—
No river's murmuring sound;—no wood-walk, sweet   95
With many a flower the learned slight and pass;—
Nor meadow, with pale cowslips thickly set
Amid the soft leaves of its tufted grass,—
Lure *them* a childish stock of treasures to amass.

XII

Have we forgotten our own infancy,   100
That joys so simple are to them denied?—
Our boyhood's hopes—our wanderings far and free,
Where yellow gorse-bush left the common wide
And open to the breeze?—The active pride
Which made each obstacle a pleasure seem;   105
When, rashly glad, all danger we defied,
Dashed through the brook by twilight's fading gleam,
Or scorned the tottering plank, and leapt the narrow stream?

XIII

In lieu of this,—from short and bitter night,
Sullen and sad the infant labourer creeps;   110
He joys not in the glow of morning's light,
But with an idle yearning stands and weeps,
Envying the babe that in its cradle sleeps:
And ever as he slowly journeys on,
His listless tongue unbidden silence keeps;   115
His fellow-labourers (playmates hath he none)
Walk by, as sad as he, nor hail the morning sun.

XIV

Mark the result. Unnaturally debarred
All nature's fresh and innocent delights,
While yet each germing energy strives hard,   120
And pristine good with pristine evil fights;

---

laissez faire and the factory system. Ure contended that children did not suffer unduly from the effects of factory labor. On the contrary, factory work taught young people the value of self-discipline and self-support. The countryside, which Norton presents as an idyllic natural playground for innocent children, was, according to Ure, overrun with idle, dissolute youths who would inevitably grow up to be a burden on the parish. In *The Philosophy of Manufactures* (1835), Ure goes so far as to claim, "It is, in fact, in the factory districts alone that the demoralizing agency of pauperism has been effectually resisted, and a noble spirit of industry, enterprise, and intelligence called forth."

When every passing dream the heart excites,
And makes even *guarded* virtue insecure;
Untaught, unchecked, they yield as vice invites:
With all around them cramped, confined, impure,   125
Fast spreads the moral plague which nothing new shall cure.

XV

Yes, this reproach is added; (infamous
In realms which own a Christian monarch's sway!)
Not suffering *only* is their portion, thus
Compelled to toil their youthful lives away: 130
Excessive labour works the SOUL's decay—
Quenches the intellectual light within—
Crushes with iron weight the mind's free play—
Steals from us LEISURE purer thoughts to win—
And leaves us sunk and lost in dull and native sin.   135

XVI

Yet in the British Senate men rise up,
(The freeborn and the fathers of our land!)
And while these drink the dregs of Sorrow's cup,
Deny the sufferings of the pining band.[12]
With nice-drawn calculations at command,   140
They prove—rebut—explain—and reason long;
Proud of each shallow argument they stand,
And prostitute their utmost powers of tongue
Feebly to justify this great and glaring wrong.

XVII

So rose, with such a plausible defence   145
Of the unalienable RIGHT OF GAIN,
Those who against Truth's brightest eloquence
Upheld the cause of torture and of pain:
And fear of Property's Decrease made vain,
For years, the hope of Christian Charity   150
To lift the curse from SLAVERY's dark domain,
And send across the wide Atlantic sea
The watchword of brave men—the thrilling shout, "BE FREE!"

---

12. W. Cooke Taylor's chapter on "Infant Labour" in *Factories and the Factory System* (1844), in part 2 of this anthology, presents some of the same arguments advanced by politicians. Taylor insists, as does Ure in *The Philosophy of Manufactures,* that the abuse of child workers has been greatly exaggerated: their labor is not demanding; their hours are not excessively long; they are protected from dangerous machinery. Both point out that factory work is much less oppressive than work in mines or cottage industries, a claim corroborated by twentieth-century social historians.

XVIII

What is it to be a slave? Is't not to spend
A life bowed down beneath a grinding ill?—   155
To labour on to serve another's end,—
To give up leisure, health, and strength, and skill—
And give up each of these *against your will*?
Hark to the angry answer:—"Theirs is not
A life of slavery; if they labour,—still   160
We *pay* their toil. Free service is their lot;
And what their labour yields, by us is fairly got."

XIX

Oh Men! blaspheme not Freedom! Are they free
Who toil until the body's strength gives way?
Who may not set a term for Liberty,   165
Who have no time for food, or rest, or play,
But struggle through the long unwelcome day
Without the leisure to be good or glad?
Such is their service—call it what you may.
Poor little creatures, overtasked and sad,   170
Your Slavery hath no name,—yet is its Curse as bad![13]

XX

Again an answer. "'T is their parents' choice.
By *some* employ the poor man's child must earn
Its daily bread; and infants have no voice
In what the allotted task shall be: they learn   175
What answers best, or suits the parents' turn."
Mournful reply! Do not your hearts inquire
Who tempts the parents' penury? They yearn
Toward their offspring with a strong desire,
But those who starve *will* sell, even what they most require.[14]   180

XXI

We grant their class must labour—young and old;[15]
We grant the child the needy parents' tool:

13. See Richard Oastler's editorial, "Slavery in Yorkshire," in this section, for a similar argument and Taylor's chapter on "Infant Labour" in part 2 for a different perspective.

14. Norton echoes Michael Sadler who, in his March 1832 address to the House of Commons, scornfully rejected the notion that the masses of poor people freely chose to send their children to work in the factories.

15. Norton refers to the arguments of politicians and authors who contended that government interference with working hours and wages would result in the failure of British enterprises and the triumph of foreign competitors. Those who subscribed to laissez-faire economic policies never hesitated to point out that, if domestic industry failed, the poor would suffer most by being out of work altogether. See chapters from Taylor in part 2.

But still our hearts a better plan behold;
No bright Utopia of some dreaming fool,
But rationally just, and good by rule.   185
Not against Toil, but Toil's Excess we pray,
(Else were we nursed in Folly's simplest school);
That so our country's hardy children may
Learn not to loathe, but bless, the well apportioned day.

XXII

One more reply! The *last* reply—the great   190
Answer to all that sense or feeling shows,
To which all others are subordinate:—
"The Masters of the Factories must lose
By the abridgment of these infant woes.
Show us the remedy which shall combine   195
Our equal gain with their increased repose—
Which shall not make our trading class repine,
But to the proffered boon its strong effects confine."

XXIII

Oh! shall it then be said that Tyrant acts
Are those which cause our country's looms to thrive?   200
That Merchant England's prosperous trade exacts
This bitter sacrifice, [ere] she derive
That profit due, for which the feeble strive?
Is her commercial avarice so keen,
That in her busy multitudinous hive   205
Hundreds must die like insects, scarcely seen,
While the thick-thronged survivors work where they have been?

XXIV

Forbid it, Spirit of the glorious Past
Which gained our Isle the surname of 'The Free,'
And made our shores a refuge at the last   210
To all who would not bend the servile knee,
The vainly-vanquished sons of Liberty!
Here ever came the injured, the opprest,
Compelled from the Oppressor's face to flee—
And found a home of shelter and of rest   215
In the warm generous heart that beat in England's breast.

XXV

Here came the Slave, who straightway burst his chain,[16]
And knew that none could ever bind him more;

16. See note 6 above.

Here came the melancholy sons of Spain;[17]
And here, more buoyant Gaul's illustrious poor[18]   220
Waited the same bright day that shone before.
Here rests the Enthusiast Pole![19] and views afar
With dreaming hope, from this protecting shore,
The trembling rays of Liberty's pale star
Shine forth in vain to light the too-unequal war!   225

XXVI

And shall REPROACH cling darkly to the name
Which every memory so much endears?
Shall *we,* too, tyrannise,—and tardy Fame
Revoke the glory of our former years,
And stain Britannia's flag with children's tears?   230
So shall the mercy of the English throne
Become a by-word in the Nations' ears,
As one who pitying heard the stranger's groan,
But to these nearer woes was cold and deaf as stone.

XXVII

Are there not changes made which grind the Poor?   235
Are there not losses every day sustained,—
Deep grievances, which make the spirit sore?
And what the answer, when *these* have complained?
"For crying evils there hath been ordained
The REMEDY OF CHANGE; to obey its call   240
Some individual loss must be disdained,
And pass as unavoidable and small,
Weighed with the broad result of general good to all."

XXVIII

Oh! such an evil *now* doth cry aloud!
And CHANGE should be by generous hearts begun,   245
Though slower gain attend the prosperous crowd,
Lessening the fortunes for their children won.
Why should it grieve a father, that his son

17. In 1820, revolution broke out in Spain against the repressive government of Ferdinand VII. Ferdinand was deposed but restored to the throne in 1823 with the aid of French forces.

18. Gaul is the ancient name for the region roughly comprising modern France and Belgium. In 1830, French liberals revolted against the restored Bourbon monarchy. When Charles X abdicated, the liberals rejected a Bourbon successor to the throne and chose instead the Duke of Orleans, who became King Louis-Philippe I. The 1830 French revolution sparked revolts throughout Europe; Belgium that year declared its independence from the Netherlands and subsequently established a constitutional monarchy.

19. Provisions of the 1815 Congress of Vienna made the Tsar of Russia also the King of Poland. An 1830–31 uprising by the Poles was crushed by the Russians in 1832, causing thousands of Poles to flee to Western nations.

Plain competence must moderately bless?
That he must trade, even as his sire has done,   250
Not born to independent idleness,
Though honestly above all probable distress?

XXIX

Rejoice! Thou hast not left enough of gold
From the lined heavy ledger, to entice
His drunken hand, irresolutely bold,   255
To squander it in haggard haunts of vice:—
The hollow rattling of the uncertain dice
Eats not the portion which thy love bestowed;—
Unable to afford that PLEASURE's price,
Far off he slumbers in his calm abode,   260
And leaves the Idle Rich to follow Ruin's road.

XXX

Happy his lot! For him there shall not be
The cold temptation given by vacant time;
Leaving his young and uncurbed spirit free
To wander thro' the feverish paths of crime!   265
For *him* the Sabbath bell's returning chime
Not vainly ushers in God's day of rest;
No night of riot clouds the morning's prime:
Alert and glad, not languid and opprest,
He wakes, and with calm soul is the Creator blest.   270

XXXI

Ye save for children! Fathers, is there not
A plaintive magic in the name of child,
Which makes you feel compassion for *their* lot
On whom Prosperity hath never smiled?
When with your OWN an hour hath been beguiled   275
(For whom you hoard the still increasing store),
Surely, against the face of Pity mild,
Heart-hardening Custom vainly bars the door,
For that less favoured race—THE CHILDREN OF THE POOR.

XXXII

"The happy homes of England!"—they have been   280
A source of triumph, and a theme for song;
And surely if there be a hope serene
And beautiful, which may to Earth belong,
'T is when (shut out the world's associate throng,

And closed the busy day's fatiguing hum),   285
Still waited for with expectation strong,
Welcomed with joy, and overjoyed to come,
The good man goes to seek the twilight rest of home.

XXXIII

There sits his gentle Wife, who with him knelt
Long years ago at God's pure altar-place;   290
Still beautiful,—though all that she hath felt
Hath calmed the glory of her radiant face,
And given her brow a holier, softer grace.
Mother of SOULS IMMORTAL, she doth feel
A glow from Heaven her earthly love replace;   295
Prayer to her lip more often now doth steal,
And meditative hope her serious eyes reveal.

XXXIV

Fondly familiar is the look she gives
As he returns, who forth so lately went,—
For they *together* pass their happy lives;   300
And many a tranquil evening have they spent
Since, blushing, ignorantly innocent,
She vowed, with downcast eyes and changeful hue,
To love Him only. Love fulfilled, hath lent
Its deep repose; and when he meets her view,   305
Her soft look only says,—"I trust—and I am true."

XXXV

Scattered like flowers, the rosy children play—
Or round her chair a busy crowd they press;
But, at the FATHER'S coming, start away,
With playful struggle for his loved caress,   310
And jealous of the one he first may bless.
To each, a welcoming word is fondly said;
He bends and kisses some; lifts up the less;
Admires the little cheek, so round and red,
Or smooths with tender hand the curled and shining head.   315

XXXVI

Oh! let us pause, and gaze upon them now.
Is there not one—beloved and lovely boy!
With Mirth's bright seal upon his open brow,
And sweet fond eyes, brimful of love and joy?
He, whom no measure of delight can cloy,   320

The daring and the darling of the set;
He who, though pleased with every passing toy,
Thoughtless and buoyant to excess, could yet
Never a gentle word or kindly deed forget?

XXXVII

And one, more fragile than the rest, for whom—   325
As for the weak bird in a crowded nest—
Are needed all the fostering care of home
And the soft comfort of the brooding breast:
One, who hath oft the couch of sickness prest!
On whom the Mother looks, as it goes by,   330
With tenderness intense, and fear supprest,
While the soft patience of her anxious eye
Blends with "God's will be done,"—"God grant thou may'st not die!"

XXXVIII

And is there not the elder of the band?
She with the gentle smile and smooth bright hair,   335
Waiting, some paces back,—content to stand
Till these of Love's caresses have their share;
Knowing how soon his fond paternal care
Shall seek his violet in her shady nook,—
Patient she stands—demure, and brightly fair—   340
Copying the meekness of her Mother's look,
And clasping in her hand the favourite story-book.

XXXIX

Wake, dreamer!—Choose;—to labour Life away,
Which of these little precious ones shall go
(Debarred of summer-light and cheerful play)   345
To that receptacle for dreary woe,
The Factory Mill?—Shall He, in whom the glow
Of Life shines bright, whose free limbs' vigorous tread
Warns us how much of beauty that we know
Would fade, when *he* became dispirited,   350
And pined with sickened heart, and bowed his fainting head?

XL

Or shall the little quiet one, whose voice
So rarely mingles in their sounds of glee,
Whose life can bid no living thing rejoice,
But rather is a long anxiety;—   355
Shall he go forth to toil? and keep the free

Frank boy, whose merry shouts and restless grace
Would leave all eyes that used his face to see,
Wistfully gazing towards that vacant space
Which makes their fireside seem a lone and dreary place?   360

XLI

Or, sparing these, send Her whose simplest words
Have power to charm,—whose warbled, childish song,
Fluent and clear and bird-like, strikes the chords
Of sympathy among the listening throng,—
Whose spirits light, and steps that dance along,   365
Instinctive modesty and grace restrain:
The fair young innocent who knows no wrong,—
Whose slender wrists scarce hold the silken skein
Which the glad Mother winds;—shall *She* endure this pain?

XLII

Away! The thought—the *thought* alone brings tears!   370
THEY labour—*they,* the darlings of our lives!
The flowers and sunbeams of our fleeting years;
From whom alone our happiness derives
A lasting strength, which every shock survives;
The green young trees beneath whose arching boughs   375
(When failing Energy no longer strives,)
Our wearied age shall find a cool repose;—
THEY toil in torture!—No—the painful picture close.

XLIII

Ye shudder,—nor behold the vision more!
Oh, Fathers! is there then one law for these,   380
And one for the pale children of the Poor,—
That to their agony your hearts can freeze;
Deny their pain, their toil, their slow disease;
And deem with false complaining they encroach
Upon your time and thought? Is yours the Ease   385
Which misery vainly struggles to approach,
Whirling unthinking by, in Luxury's gilded coach?

XLIV

Examine and decide. Watch through his day
One of these little ones. The sun hath shone
An hour, and by the ruddy morning's ray,   390
The last and least, he saunters on alone.
See where, still pausing on the threshold stone,

He stands, as loth to lose the bracing wind;
With wistful wandering glances backward thrown
On all the light and glory left behind,   395
And sighs to think that HE must darkly be confined!

XLV

Enter with him. The stranger who surveys
The little natives of that dreary place
(Where squalid suffering meets his shrinking gaze),
Used to the glory of a young child's face,   400
Its changeful light, its coloured sparkling grace,
(Gleams of Heaven's sunshine on our shadowed earth!)
Starts at each visage wan, and bold, and base,
Whose smiles have neither innocence nor mirth,—
And comprehends the Sin original from birth.   405

XLVI

There the pale Orphan,[20] whose unequal strength
Loathes the incessant toil it *must* pursue,
Pines for the cool sweet evening's twilight length,
The sunny play-hour, and the morning's dew:
Worn with its cheerless life's monotonous hue,   410
Bowed down, and faint, and stupified it stands,
Each half-seen object reeling in its view—
While its hot, trembling, languid little hands
Mechanically heed the Task-master's commands.[21]

XLVII

There, sounds of wailing grief and painful blows   415
Offend the ear, and startle it from rest;[22]
(While the lungs gasp what air the place bestows;)

20. The New Poor Law of 1834 stipulated that orphans, as well as paupers' children, would reside in Poor Law schools and could be sent out to work or be apprenticed by the overseers of the schools. Charles Dickens's Oliver Twist is subjected to such a fate.

21. Peter Gaskell, a surgeon and the author of *The Manufacturing Population of England* (1833), described the physical traits of factory operatives thus: "Any man who has stood at twelve o'clock at the single narrow door-way, which serves as the place of exit for the hands employed in the great cotton-mills, must acknowledge, that an uglier set of men and women, of boys and girls, taking them in the mass, it would be impossible to congregate in a smaller compass. Their complexion is sallow and pallid—with a peculiar flatness of feature. . . . Their stature low. . . . Their limbs slender, and playing badly and ungracefully." See also the selection from Engels in this section for similar testimony from other medical men. Ure, on the other hand, refutes these findings and cites corroborating reports by a number of colleagues. See *The Philosophy of Manufactures,* chapter 2: "Health of Factory Inmates."

22. Addressing the House of Commons on March 16, 1832, Michael Sadler maintained that "in order to keep the children awake, and to stimulate their exertions," they "are beaten with thongs prepared for the purpose. Yes, the females of this country, no matter whether children or grown up,—I hardly know which is the more disgusting outrage—are beaten upon the face, arms, and bosom—beaten in your 'free market of labour,' as you term it, like slaves!"

Or misery's joyless vice, the ribald jest,
Breaks the sick silence: staring at the guest
Who comes to view their labour, they beguile   420
The unwatched moment; whispers half supprest
And mutterings low, their faded lips defile,—
While gleams from face to face a strange and sullen smile.

XLVIII

These then are his Companions: he, too young
To share their base and saddening merriment,   425
Sits by: his little head in silence hung;
His limbs cramped up; his body weakly bent;
Toiling obedient, till long hours so spent
Produce Exhaustion's slumber, dull and deep.
The Watcher's stroke,—bold—sudden—violent,—   430
Urges him from that lethargy of sleep,
And bids him wake to Life,—to labour and to weep!

XLIX

But the day hath its End. Forth then he hies
With jaded, faltering step, and brow of pain;
Creeps to that shed,—his HOME,—where happy lies   435
The sleeping babe that cannot toil for Gain;
Where his remorseful Mother tempts in vain
With the best portion of their frugal fare:
Too sick to eat—too weary to complain—
He turns him idly from the untasted share,   440
Slumbering sinks down unfed, and mocks her useless care.

L

Weeping she lifts, and lays his heavy head
(With all a woman's grieving tenderness)
On the hard surface of his narrow bed;
Bends down to give a sad unfelt caress,   445
And turns away;—willing her God to bless,
That, weary as he is, he need not fight
Against that long-enduring bitterness,
The VOLUNTARY LABOUR of the Night,
But sweetly slumber on till day's returning light.   450

LI

Vain hope! Alas! unable to forget
The anxious task's long, heavy agonies,
In broken sleep the victim labours yet!

Waiting the boding stroke that bids him rise,
He marks in restless fear each hour that flies—   455
Anticipates the unwelcome morning prime—
And murmuring feebly, with unwakened eyes,
"Mother! Oh Mother! is it yet THE TIME?"—
Starts at the moon's pale ray—or clock's far distant chime.

LII

Such is *his* day and night! Now then return   460
Where your OWN slumber in protected ease;
They whom no blast may pierce, no sun may burn;
The lovely, on whose cheeks the wandering breeze
Hath left the rose's hue. Ah! not like these
Does the pale infant-labourer ask to be: 465
He craves no tempting food—no toys to please—
Not Idleness,—but less of agony;
Not Wealth,—but comfort, rest, CONTENTED POVERTY.

LIII

There is, among all men, in every clime,
A difference instinctive and unschooled: 470
God made the MIND unequal. From all time
By fierceness conquered, or by cunning fooled,
The World hath had its Rulers and its Ruled:—
Yea—uncompelled—men abdicate free choice,
Fear their own rashness, and, by thinking cooled,   475
Follow the counsel of some trusted voice;—
A self-elected sway, wherein their souls rejoice.

LIV

Thus, for the most part, willing to obey,
Men rarely set Authority at naught:
Albeit a weaker or a worse than they   480
May hold the rule with such importance fraught:
And thus the peasant, from his cradle taught
That some must *own*, while some must *till* the land,
Rebels not—murmurs not—even in his thought.
Born to his lot, he bows to high command,   485
And guides the furrowing plough with a contented hand.

LV

But, if the weight which habit renders light
Is made to gall the Serf who bends below—

The dog that watched and fawned, prepares to bite!
Too rashly strained, the cord snaps from the bow—   490
Too tightly curbed, the steeds their riders throw—
And so, (at first contented his fair state
Of customary servitude to know,)
Too harshly ruled, the poor man learns to hate
And curse the oppressive law that bids him serve the Great.[23]   495

LVI

THEN first he asks his gloomy soul the CAUSE
Of his discomfort; suddenly compares—
Reflects—and with an angry Spirit draws
The envious line between his lot and theirs,
Questioning the JUSTICE of the unequal shares.   500
And from the gathering of this discontent,
Where there is strength, REVOLT his standard rears;
Where there is weakness, evermore finds vent
The sharp annoying cry of sorrowful complaint.

LVII

Therefore should Mercy, gentle and serene,   505
Sit by the Ruler's side, and share his Throne:—
Watch with unerring eye the passing scene,
And bend her ear to mark the feeblest groan;
Lest due Authority be overthrown,
And they that ruled perceive (too late confest!)   510
Permitted Power might still have been their own,
Had they but watched that none should be opprest—
No just complaint despised—no WRONG left unredrest.

LVIII

Nor should we, Christians in a Christian land,
Forget who smiled on helpless infancy,   515
And blest them with divinely gentle hand.—
"Suffer that little children come to me":[24]
Such were His words to whom we bow the knee!
These to our care the Saviour did commend;
And shall we HIS bequest treat carelessly,   520
Who yet our full protection would extend
To the lone Orphan child left by an Earthly Friend?

23. Thomas Carlyle in *Past and Present* and John Ruskin in *The Stones of Venice* present the same argument. See part 1.
24. Matthew 19:14.

LIX

No! rather what the Inspired Law imparts
To guide our ways, and make our path more sure;
Blending with Pity (native to our hearts),   525
Let us to these, who patiently endure
Neglect, and penury, and toil, secure
The innocent hopes that to their age belong:
So, honouring Him, the Merciful and Pure,
Who watches when the Oppressor's arm grows strong,—   530
And helpeth them to right—the Weak—who suffer wrong!

THE PEOPLE'S CHARTER

A T THE DIRECTION of the London Working Men's Association, William Lovett (1800–1877) and Francis Place (1771–1854) assumed major responsibility for drawing up The People's Charter. The Charter had six main points, most of which hardly seem revolutionary to a contemporary audience. Yet when presented to Parliament as a petition, The Charter was voted down on three separate occasions (1839, 1842, 1848). What perhaps, then, needs some explanation is the cultural context that made the document and the general Chartist movement seem so threatening not only to the more conservative but also to the fairly liberal among English intellectuals.

The Reform Bill of 1832 extended the franchise to a number of propertied individuals who had previously been unable to vote in parliamentary elections; the act did not, however, extend voting rights to the lower middle classes or to the working classes. Throughout the later 1830s and 1840s, therefore, residual enthusiasm for more representative government combined with labor unrest and general depressive economic conditions to fuel a somewhat inchoate yet sustained working-class movement ultimately termed Chartism. Calls for egalitarian democracy, in themselves disquieting to some, were readily associated with what many perceived as the much more threatening political agendas of a thoroughgoing socialist or communist movement. Specters of the French Revolution and more recent continental political unrest as well as rhetorical excesses of certain Chartist leaders led those in power to conceive of Chartist goals as a prelude to violent class antagonism, the abolition of property rights, and social anarchy.

Uneasiness prompted by revolutions on the continent in 1848 may have had something to do with the final defeat of The People's Charter in April of that year. As a political movement, Chartism was effectively dead by mid-century, yet the direction and spirit that it had given to political discourse endured. Anxiety about the dissatisfactions of the working classes as well as genuine concern about their welfare informed the thinking of many activists in the early 1850s, particularly men such as F. D. Maurice, Thomas Hughes, and Charles Kingsley, all of whom devoted considerable energy to bridging the chasm that separated what Benjamin Disraeli, in the subtitle of his 1845 novel *Sybil*, had called "The Two Nations"—the Rich and the Poor. (See selections by Maurice and Hughes in parts 2 and 1, respectively.) Within little more than a generation, essential political goals of the Chartists had been met through the passage of reforms in 1858, 1867, and 1884. The specific working-class orientation of The People's Charter may be seen in points 2,

3, and 4, all concerned with the rights of the working man freely to vote and also to serve in Parliament.

The Six Points of The People's Charter

1. A VOTE for every man twenty-one years of age, of sound mind, and not undergoing punishment for crime.
2. THE BALLOT.[1]—To protect the elector in the exercise of his vote.
3. NO PROPERTY QUALIFICATION for Members of Parliament—thus enabling the constituencies to return the man of their choice, be he rich or poor.
4. PAYMENT OF MEMBERS, thus enabling an honest tradesman, working man, or other person, to serve a constituency, when taken from his business to attend to the interests of the Country.
5. EQUAL CONSTITUENCIES, securing the same amount of representation for the same number of electors, instead of allowing small constituencies to swamp the votes of large ones.[2]
6. ANNUAL PARLIAMENTS, thus presenting the most effectual check to bribery and intimidation, since though a constituency might be bought once in seven years (even with the ballot), no purse could buy a constituency (under a system of universal suffrage) in each ensuing twelve-month; and since members, when elected for a year only, would not be able to defy and betray their constituents as now.

1. The call here is for a secret ballot. Until the secret ballot was secured, employers could know how a laborer voted and could discharge him if they found his political action at odds with their own wishes.
2. During the early nineteenth century, electoral districts that had become largely depopulated often enjoyed parliamentary representation equal to or greater than that of newly developed manufacturing areas. Workers in the burgeoning industrial centers especially resented such "rotten boroughs," as they were called.

PERCY BYSSHE SHELLEY

POET AND ESSAYIST Percy Bysshe Shelley (1792–1822) early on rebelled against the traditions and values cherished by the privileged family into which he was born. Shelley was educated at Eton and went on to Oxford but was expelled after only six months for writing and distributing a pamphlet on atheism. For several decades following the French Revolution (1789), agitation for radical social reform in England met with repressive measures, including censorship of the press, prohibitions against public assembly, and suspension of *habeas corpus*. Shelley joined other Romantic writers in promoting the cause of individual rights and condemning tyranny and oppression. His crusade ended prematurely when, at the age of thirty, he drowned in a boating accident in Italy.

"A Song: 'Men of England'" was prompted, in part, by Shelley's outrage over the tragedy that came to be referred to as the Peterloo Massacre. In 1819, the Manchester militia assaulted a crowd of sixty thousand peaceably assembled in St. Peter's Fields, killing at least nine people and injuring hundreds more. Yet of even greater concern to Shelley than the brutal violence at Manchester was the routine exploitation of the working classes by the "ungrateful drones" of the managerial and upper classes who appropriated the "forced produce of [the workers'] toil." The incendiary tone of Shelley's "Song" led his friends to advise him against publication during his lifetime. The poem first appeared in the collected edition of his works prepared by his second wife, Mary Wollstonecraft Shelley, in 1839.

A Song: "Men of England"

Men of England, wherefore plough
For the lords who lay ye low?
Wherefore weave with toil and care
The rich robes your tyrants wear?

Wherefore feed and clothe and save   5
From the cradle to the grave
Those ungrateful drones who would
Drain your sweat—nay, drink your blood?

Wherefore, Bees of England, forge
Many a weapon, chain, and scourge,   10
That these stingless drones may spoil
The forced produce of your toil?

Have ye leisure, comfort, calm,
Shelter, food, love's gentle balm?
Or what is it ye buy so dear   15
With your pain and with your fear?

The seed ye sow, another reaps,
The wealth ye find, another keeps;
The robes ye weave, another wears;
The arms ye forge, another bears.   20

Sow seed—but let no tyrant reap:
Find wealth—let no impostor heap:
Weave robes—let not the idle wear:
Forge arms—in your defence to bear.

Shrink to your cellars, holes, and cells—   25
In halls ye deck another dwells.
Why shake the chains ye wrought? Ye see
The steel ye tempered glance on ye.

With plough and spade and hoe and loom
Trace your grave and build your tomb   30
And weave your winding-sheet—till fair
England be your Sepulchre.

WILLIAM JAMES LINTON

W ILLIAM JAMES LINTON (1812–1897) was trained as a wood engraver. Apprenticed to George Wilmot Bonner at age sixteen, Linton was exposed to radical politics as he learned the trade. Even as he established a reputation as a talented engraver, he also earned a name as a journalist, author, and Chartist. Linton married the novelist and journalist Eliza Lynn in 1858 (author of "What Is Women's Work" in part 4); however, the two separated six years later. In 1866, Linton emigrated to the United States, where he continued to develop his craft and engage in political activism.

"The Free-Servant," a moral fable, first appeared in W. J. Linton's journal, the *National,* in 1839. In the story, Linton exposes the abuse of servants, especially those at the bottom of the hierarchy who were hired as "maids of all work." Their duties typically included all those assigned to Jane Stephens in the story: cooking, cleaning, and child care for the employer's family as well as for lodgers. In addition to long hours (a domestic servant was always on call), hard manual labor, and abusive treatment, the majority of servants, like other working-class laborers, received such miserable wages that they had no opportunity to put aside funds to care for themselves in the event of sickness or upon retirement. Jane Stephens, whose employers are thoughtless rather than cruel, works diligently but declines physically and, as a consequence, falls ill. Linton leaves Jane's story unfinished, with a series of dire conjectures about her possible fate.

In the nineteenth century, more women and girls were employed as domestic servants than in any other capacity. Not until the end of the century, when a wider range of occupations opened to working-class people and made servants more difficult to find and keep, were those who took positions in service able to negotiate better salaries and working conditions.

The Free-Servant

"Next to governesses, the largest class of female patients
in lunatic asylums is Maids of All Work."

—Harriet Martineau[1]

"Britons never will be slaves!"

—National Song[2]

Jane Stephens was the daughter of a ploughman. The Legislature, in its benevolent wisdom, had decided it was for the good of the community that Richard
Stephens should be condemned to hard labour without hope of improvement, for
the term of his natural life; and Sir Thomas Jenkins, who drew large rents from the
produce of the fields on which Stephens and others laboured, was decidedly of the
Legislature's opinion. Indeed, Sir Thomas was one of the "collective wisdom" or
House of *Commons,* and as such had voted that it was just and necessary that one
in ten of these condemned labourers should be shot or cut in pieces to preserve
this beautiful constitution of society. Stephens only thought there was no beauty in
slavery: but what mattered what a ploughman thought when the landlord and
government, and of course the clergy, chose otherwise?—but my business is with
the ploughman's daughter. Jane was the eldest of a large family. She was soon
useful: nursed the baby, took her father his dinner, kept the house in order, and
was both the assistant and companion of her mother. She was a fine healthy girl—
would have been called beautiful, had she been born "a lady"; good-tempered and
loving; industrious and ever ready to help any who were in need. When she was
about fifteen, her father not being allowed to support his family, it became necessary that she should go to *service.* It was a hard thing to part from home and all
who were loved and loving, to go among strangers, to be alone—for her mistress
allowed no "followers," thinking servants had not the same affections as others, or,
if they did wish to see their friends, there was no time; and to work like a mill-
horse—but that she did not think of—in fact, to sell herself for five pounds a year.
But then, she would be helping her mother; and anything was to be endured for
that:—so, with a cheerful countenance Jane engaged herself to a *mistress*; and
exchanged the old cottage in the fields for a dirty house in a narrow street in
London, nearly two hundred miles from her native place. Here for three years she
laboured as under-housemaid to an arrogant woman who had "no idea of being

1. Harriet Martineau (1802–1876) was a prolific author whose works addressed a number of social
and economic issues. (See selections by Martineau in part 2.)
2. The national song from which the second epigraph is taken is Thomas Augustine Arne's (1710–
1778) "Rule, Britannia."

Figure 3.1. Frederick D. Hardy, *After the Party.* Courtesy of The Forbes Magazine Collection, New York. © All rights reserved.

Frederick D. Hardy (1826–1911) was best known for his amusing genre paintings. This image of 1876 titled *After the Party* presents a more somber scene of a young maid being gently roused by a fellow servant at dawn. Charged with tidying the ballroom, she is discovered the morning after the party in a chair where she has collapsed from weariness. The older maid, and the butler who can be seen in the mirror, seem sympathetic and prepared to assist.

spoken to by *a servant*"; one who wondered servants' instincts did not teach them how to adopt immediately the habits of every new place, how to humour the ever-varying caprices of possibly a fretful mistress:—but I must pass to her next situation, as maid of all work, procured solely on account of her excellent character from her last place.

And maid of all work she was. Her master was the owner of a manufactory and, consequently, from home the greater part of the day, coming home for his meals. His family consisted of himself, his wife, a son and daughter nearly grown up, a boy eleven years old, a girl rather younger, and an infant in arms. The house was let out to lodgers. An artist had the first floor; an actor had one room on the second floor; and three noisy and not very clean Germans shared the remainder of the second floor and an attic; the family occupied the other attic, the ground floor, and the kitchen. At this time I was acquainted with Jane's master. He was a worthy man, good-hearted, and very kind to Jane. His wife was, I think, as well-meaning a body, but rather warm, and a little bit hasty; and poor Jane seldom passed a day without some opportunity of understanding her mistress's disposition. The son worked at his father's business. The daughter assisted in the light work, but left the laborious part to her mother and the maid. To do Mrs. Simpson justice, *she* was never idle: always working, and muddling as she worked, so that Jane often wished her mistress wouldn't help her. The children were not much less troublesome.

Soon after Jane went to them, Mrs. Simpson was laid up with a bad bilious attack. The daughter had enough to do, nursing her mother, even with some assistance from Jane, on whom the work of the house entirely devolved. She had to scrub and sweep the house, to make the beds, to cook for the family, and the first-floor lodger (who sometimes had company), to wait upon all the lodgers, to answer the door (the knocker had just discovered the perpetual motion), to run errands—marketing &c., to look after the children, and, in her leisure time, to wean the baby. Amid all this, for which she received eight pounds a year, Jane was assiduous and good tempered; and though not happy—for she had not forgotten her home, and pined for the green fields and old country friendliness—still she never neglected her work. At length, her health gave way: she was obliged to leave her place; and a long illness was the result of the over-tasking of her strength. Slowly she recovered, to find herself in the desert of London without friends or money, almost without clothes—having been compelled to part with them during her illness.

From this time I lost sight of her. God knows what became, or will become of her. Perhaps she was reduced to beg her bread in our very Christian streets; or perhaps—for she was beautiful—destitution and despair may have conspired with villainy to force her into that lowest deep of degradation, the life—Oh, no! not the life, the horrible wretchedness of prostitution; or perhaps she may have been fortunate enough to procure another situation: fortunate enough! Is it good fortune to be worked to death, either without or with kindness? (The Simpsons were kind: the rigours of her servitude there arose more from ignorance, which renders people careless of others' sufferings, than from any wilful cruelty.) But, even if she were *fortunate* enough to get another place, what must be the result? Continual toil, unbefriended and without hope, till at length, too old for service, she is compelled to seek a precarious subsistence as sempstress or char-woman,[3] hardly living in some miserable garret; and when that last fortune fails her, she may die of cold and starvation in the streets, "a natural death"; (How dare men so lie? Well-fed jurymen, reconsider your verdict!) or she may have the comforts of a work-house[4] hospital. Oh! there are but too many who bear this doom. What has become of girlhood's hope and gaiety; of the woman's beauty and lovingness? Did not they deserve a better destiny? Domestic service, indeed!—domestic slavery! Respectable philanthropists! can you not prescribe any remedy?

Now I am well to do in the world: but I keep no servant. My wife and children wait upon me, and I help them. We know nothing of command and obedience: for we take a pleasure in serving those we love:—and I would recommend rich folk

3. Person hired to clean a large building.
4. Institution where paupers with no other recourse resided. The able-bodied were required to work.

and gentlemen, if it be only on account of their own comfort, to discharge all their servants, and be served by those who love them, taking their turn in the work most fit for them. But, even if they are not wise enough to study their own good, let them be just to others, and not condemn their betters (perhaps) to slavery, merely because their laziness or pride—I don't care which: they may settle it between themselves—will not condescend to *menial* offices. Nothing is menial to Love.

"But what shall we do without servants?" says the fine Lady. Do what honester folks do—wait upon yourself! Why should other people be sacrificed to your selfishness?—Poor Jane Stephens! there are many such as thou wert; as worthy of good, and as ill-used:—I can write no more. It is too horrible to think of.

THOMAS HOOD

Author and editor Thomas Hood (1799–1845) suffered from poor health and the threat of financial ruin for much of his life. Primarily known for his poetry, which ranges from the comic and satiric to the humanitarian, Hood also held editorial posts for journals including the *London Magazine* and *New Monthly Magazine* and edited several publications of his own.

Hood was moved to write his enormously popular poem "The Song of the Shirt" following the arrest on October 25, 1843, of a seamstress named Biddell, who was accused of pawning some of her employers' possessions. Court testimony revealed that Biddell was attempting to support herself and her two young children by sewing trousers for seven shillings a week. Articles in the *Times* on October 27 and in *Punch* the following week brought the case to the attention of the general public, and Hood's poem, which appeared anonymously in the Christmas issue of *Punch* on December 16, further roused the social conscience. Widely known and often quoted, the poem inspired a number of paintings, among them Richard Redgrave's *The Seamstress* of 1844 (figure 3.2) and George Frederic Watts's *The Song of the Shirt* of ca. 1850 (figure 3.3). A public monument erected at Hood's grave in Kensal Green Cemetery in 1854, more than a decade after his poem appeared, bore the inscription "He sang the Song of the Shirt."

Official reports of government commissions and social documentaries such as those compiled by Henry Mayhew (*The Morning Chronicle* for November 16, 20, and 23, 1849) and Charles Booth (*Life and Labour of the People in London*, First Series, vol. 4, 1904) confirmed that Biddell's situation was not uncommon. Though considered a promising, respectable profession for ambitious working-class girls and for lower-middle-class women compelled to support themselves, needlework often required excessively long hours in poorly-lit and inadequately ventilated rooms in exchange for starvation wages. Attention was repeatedly drawn to the contrast between the wretched seamstresses and the demanding, self-indulgent socialites for whom they toiled. See John Leech's cartoons "Needle Money" and "Pin Money" (figure 3.7), which appeared in *Punch* in 1849.

Literary treatments of the plight of women employed in the clothing trade abounded. Examples include the sensationalist story "The Slave of the Needle," another selection in this section; Charlotte Elizabeth Tonna's account of "Milliners and Dressmakers" in *The Wrongs of Women* (1852); and novels such as Elizabeth Gaskell's *Mary Barton* (1848) and *Ruth* (1853) and Charles Dickens's *Nicholas Nick-*

leby (1838–39). In *Alton Locke* (1850), Charles Kingsley exposed comparable abuse of male workers in tailoring sweatshops.

The Song of the Shirt

With fingers weary and worn,
    With eyelids heavy and red,
A woman sat in unwomanly rags,
    Plying her needle and thread—
    Stitch! stitch! stitch!   5
In poverty, hunger, and dirt,
    And still with a voice of dolorous pitch
She sang the "Song of the Shirt!"

"Work! work! work!
While the cock is crowing aloof!   10
    And work—work—work,
Till the stars shine through the roof!
It's Oh! to be a slave
    Along with the barbarous Turk,
Where woman has never a soul to save,   15
    If this is Christian work!

"Work—work—work
Till the brain begins to swim;
    Work—work—work
Till the eyes are heavy and dim!   20
Seam, and gusset, and band,
    Band, and gusset, and seam,
    Till over the buttons I fall asleep,
    And sew them on in a dream!

"O, Men, with Sisters dear!   25
    O, Men! with Mothers and Wives!

Figure 3.2. Richard Redgrave, *The Seamstress*. Courtesy of The Forbes Magazine Collection, New York. © All rights reserved.

Painter, designer, art historian, and art school official, Richard Redgrave (1804–1888) exhibited a series of pictures at the Royal Academy between 1840 and 1847 representing distressed working women.

Redgrave completed the original of *The Seamstress* in 1844; this version is from 1846. The setting is a small, scantily furnished attic room where a solitary young woman continues her work far into the night (as the late hour on the clock reveals). Inspired by Thomas Hood's "The Song of the Shirt" (reprinted here), the picture was accompanied at its original showing by the following lines from the poem:

Oh! men with sisters dear,

Oh! men with mothers and wives,

It is not linen you're wearing out,

But fellow creatures' lives.

Fellow artist Paul Falconer Poole (1807–1879) found the painting very moving. He wrote to Redgrave, "Believe me, I think it is the most powerful for truth and touching from its pathos of any picture I have ever seen. Who can help exclaiming, 'Poor soul: God help her?' If any circumstances could make me wage war against the present social arrangements, and make us go down shirtless to our graves, it is the contemplation of this truthful and wonderful picture."

Figure 3.3. George Frederic Watts, *The Seamstress or The Song of the Shirt* (oil on canvas). Courtesy of the Trustees of the Watts Gallery, Surrey, UK / Bridgeman Art Library, London/New York.

George Frederic Watts (1817–1904) was considered by many to be the greatest English painter of his day. He too was inspired by Thomas Hood's poem "The Song of the Shirt," but he presents an even grimmer image in his representation of *The Seamstress* (ca. 1850) than that produced by Richard Redgrave (see figure 3.2).

It is not linen you're wearing out,
    But human creatures' lives!
    Stitch—stitch—stitch,
    In poverty, hunger, and dirt,   30
Sewing at once, with a double thread,
    A Shroud as well as a Shirt.

"But why do I talk of Death?
    That Phantom of grisly bone,
I hardly fear his terrible shape,   35
    It seems so like my own—
    It seems so like my own,
    Because of the fasts I keep,
Oh, God! that bread should be so dear,
    And flesh and blood so cheap!   40

"Work—work—work!
    My labour never flags;
And what are its wages? A bed of straw,
    A crust of bread—and rags.
That shatter'd roof—and this naked floor—   45
    A table—a broken chair—
And a wall so blank, my shadow I thank
    For sometimes falling there!

"Work—work—work!
From weary chime to chime,   50
    Work—work—work—
As prisoners work for crime!
    Band, and gusset, and seam,
    Seam, and gusset, and band,
Till the heart is sick, and the brain benumb'd,   55
    As well as the weary hand.

"Work—work—work,
In the dull December light,
    And work—work—work,
When the weather is warm and bright—   60
While underneath the eaves
    The brooding swallows cling
As if to show me their sunny backs
    And twit me with the spring.

"Oh! but to breathe the breath 65
Of the cowslip and primrose sweet—
　　With the sky above my head,
And the grass beneath my feet,
For only one short hour
　　To feel as I used to feel, 70
Before I knew the woes of want
　　And the walk that costs a meal!

"Oh but for one short hour!
　　A respite however brief!
No blessed leisure for Love or Hope,
　　But only time for Grief! 75
A little weeping would ease my heart,
　　But in their briny bed
My tears must stop, for every drop
　　Hinders needle and thread!" 80

With fingers weary and worn,
　　With eyelids heavy and red,
A Woman sat in unwomanly rags,
　　Plying her needle and thread—
　　Stitch! stitch! stitch! 85
　　In poverty, hunger, and dirt,
And still with a voice of dolorous pitch,
Would that its tone could reach the Rich!
　　She sang this "Song of the Shirt!"

ELIZABETH BARRETT BROWNING

E LIZABETH BARRETT BROWNING (1806–1861) was the eldest of eleven children in a well-to-do family. She began writing poetry as a child, saw her poems published in prominent literary magazines when she was in her teens, and published several volumes in her twenties. Her reputation was established with the publication of *Poems* in 1844.

In the following year, she began to correspond with Robert Browning, whose own work had received little notice at that time. Against her father's wishes, she secretly married in 1846 and, a few days later, moved with her husband to Florence, Italy, where she lived until her death fifteen years later.

"The Cry of the Children" was first published in *Blackwood's Magazine* in August 1843. Barrett Browning never visited a mine or factory and, therefore, had no firsthand knowledge of labor conditions. Her poem is entirely based on the report submitted by her friend R. H. Horne (1803–1884), an assistant commissioner investigating the employment of children in mines and factories. Eliza Cook's poem "Our Father!" reprinted later in this section, is also based on Horne's report. See the introduction and notes to Caroline Norton's *A Voice from the Factories*, earlier in this section, for details on the controversy surrounding child labor.

The Cry of the Children

I

Do ye hear the children weeping, O my brothers,
    Ere the sorrow comes with years?
They are leaning their young heads against their mothers,
    And *that* cannot stop their tears.
The young lambs are bleating in the meadows,   5
    The young birds are chirping in the nest,

The young fawns are playing with the shadows,
 The young flowers are blowing toward the west—
But the young, young children, O my brothers,
 They are weeping bitterly!   10
They are weeping in the playtime of the others,
 In the country of the free.

II

Do you question the young children in the sorrow
 Why their tears are falling so?
The old man may weep for his to-morrow   15
 Which is lost in Long Ago;
The old tree is leafless in the forest,
 The old year is ending in the frost,
The old wound, if stricken, is the sorest,
 The old hope is hardest to be lost.   20
But the young, young children, O my brothers,
 Do you ask them why they stand
Weeping sore before the bosoms of their mothers,
 In our happy Fatherland?

III

They look up with their pale and sunken faces,   25
 And their looks are sad to see,
For the man's hoary anguish draws and presses
 Down the cheeks of infancy.
"Your old earth," they say, "is very dreary;
 Our young feet," they say, "are very weak!   30
Few paces have we taken, yet are weary—
 Our grave-rest is very far to seek.
Ask the aged why they weep, and not the children,
 For the outside earth is cold;
And we young ones stand without, in our bewildering, 35
 And the graves are for the old."

IV

"True," say the children, "it may happen
 That we die before our time:

Little Alice died last year, her grave is shapen
  Like a snowball, in the rime.[1]   40
We looked into the pit prepared to take her:
  Was no room for any work in the close clay!
From the sleep wherein she lieth none will wake her,
  Crying, 'Get up, little Alice! it is day.'
If you listen by that grave, in sun and shower,   45
  With your ear down, little Alice never cries;
Could we see her face, be sure we should not know her,
  For the smile has time for growing in her eyes:
And merry go her moments, lulled and stilled in
  The shroud by the kirk-chime.[2]   50
It is good when it happens," say the children,
  "That we die before our time."

V

Alas, alas, the children! they are seeking
  Death in life, as best to have;
They are binding up their hearts away from breaking, 55
  With a cerement[3] from the grave.
Go out, children, from the mine and from the city,
  Sing out, children, as the little thrushes do;
Pluck you handfuls of the meadow-cowslips pretty,
  Laugh aloud, to feel your fingers let them through! 60
But they answer, "Are your cowslips of the meadows
  Like our weeds anear the mine?
Leave us quiet in the dark of the coal-shadows,
  From your pleasures fair and fine!

VI

"For oh," say the children, "we are weary,   65
  And we cannot run or leap;
If we cared for any meadows, it were merely
  To drop down in them and sleep.
Our knees tremble sorely in the stooping,
  We fall upon our faces, trying to go;   70

1. Frost covering the ground.
2. A kirk is a church.
3. Cloth coated with wax, used for wrapping a corpse.

And, underneath our heavy eyelids drooping,
    The reddest flower would look as pale as snow;
For, all day, we drag our burden tiring
    Through the coal-dark, underground—
Or, all day, we drive the wheels of iron   75
    In the factories, round and round.

VII

"For all day, the wheels are droning, turning;
    Their wind comes in our faces,—
Till our hearts turn,—our heads with pulses burning,
    And the walls turn in their places: 80
Turns the sky in the high window blank and reeling,
    Turns the long light that drops adown the wall,
Turn the black flies that crawl along the ceiling:
    All are turning, all the day, and we with all.
And all day, the iron wheels are droning,   85
    And sometimes we could pray,
'O ye wheels,' (breaking out in a mad moaning)
    'Stop! be silent for to-day!' "

VIII

Aye, be silent! Let them hear each other breathing
    For a moment, mouth to mouth!   90
Let them touch each other's hands, in a fresh wreathing
    Of their tender human youth!
Let them feel that this cold metallic motion
    Is not all the life God fashions or reveals:
Let them prove their living souls against the notion   95
    That they live in you, or under you, O wheels!—
Still, all day, the iron wheels go onward,
    Grinding life down from its mark;
And the children's souls, which God is calling sunward,
    Spin on blindly in the dark.   100

IX

Now tell the poor young children, O my brothers,
    To look up to Him and pray;

So the blessed One who blesseth all the others,
    Will bless them another day.
They answer, "Who is God that He should hear us,   105
    While the rushing of the iron wheels is stirred?
When we sob aloud, the human creatures near us
    Pass by, hearing not, or answer not a word.
And *we* hear not (for the wheels in their resounding)
    Strangers speaking at the door: 110
Is it likely God, with angels singing round Him,
    Hears our weeping any more?

X

"Two words, indeed, of praying we remember,
    And at midnight's hour of harm,[4]
'Our Father,'[5] looking upward in the chamber,   115
    We say softly for a charm.
We know no other words except 'Our Father'
    And we think that, in some pause of angels' song,
God may pluck them with the silence sweet to gather,
    And hold both within His right hand which is strong.   120
'Our Father!' If He heard us, He would surely
    (For they call Him good and mild)
Answer, smiling down the steep world very purely,
    'Come and rest with me, my child.'

XI

"But no!" say the children, weeping faster,   125
    "He is speechless as a stone:
And they tell us, of His image is the master
    Who commands us to work on.
Go to!" say the children—"up in heaven,
    Dark, wheel-like, turning clouds are all we find.   130
Do not mock us; grief has made us unbelieving—
    We look up for God, but tears have made us blind."
Do you hear the children weeping and disproving,
    O my brothers, what ye preach?

4. The "witching hour" when the powers of evil are most potent.
5. According to Horne, many of the working children interviewed claimed to say the prayer "Our Father" each night before going to sleep. Horne came to realize in the course of further questioning that the children meant this literally; these were the only two words of the Lord's Prayer that most of them knew.

For God's possible is taught by His world's loving,   135
    And the children doubt of each.

XII

And well may the children weep before you!
    They are weary ere they run;
They have never seen the sunshine, nor the glory
    Which is brighter than the sun.   140
They know the grief of man, without its wisdom;
    They sink in man's despair, without its calm;
Are slaves, without the liberty in Christdom,
    Are martyrs, by the pang without the palm,—[6]
Are worn as if with age, yet unretrievingly   145
    The harvest of its memories cannot reap,—
Are orphans of the earthly love and heavenly.
    Let them weep! let them weep!

XIII

They look up with their pale and sunken faces,
    And their look is dread to see,   150
For they mind you of their angels in high places,
    With eyes turned on Deity!—
"How long," they say, "how long, O cruel nation,
    Will you stand, to move the world, on a child's heart,—
Stifle down with a mailed heel its palpitation,   155
    And tread onward to your throne amid the mart?
Our blood splashes upward, O gold-heaper,
    And your purple shows your path!
But the child's sob in the silence curses deeper
    Than the strong man in his wrath."   160

6. Martyrs are often depicted as carrying a branch of palm to signify their spiritual victory.

CHARLOTTE ELIZABETH TONNA

T HE DAUGHTER OF a clergyman, Charlotte Elizabeth Tonna (1790–1846) pursued an evangelical mission of her own through her writing. A widely read
author of religious tracts, poems, stories, and novels and the editor of several periodicals, including the *Christian Lady's Magazine,* she is best known for her thoroughly documented social problem novels and stories. The most popular was
Helen Fleetwood (1841), a book endorsing the Ten Hours Movement. (See Thomas
Babington Macaulay's speech, "The Ten Hours Bill," in this section.)

In 1842, Tonna accepted an invitation from the Christian Influence Society to
write a book on the condition of the working class. Drawing heavily on parliamentary reports and summaries of private investigations, Tonna produced *The Perils of
the Nation: An Appeal to the Legislature, the Clergy, and the Higher and Middle
Classes,* published anonymously in 1843. As in the majority of her other works,
Tonna concentrates on the oppression of women and children and reminds her
privileged Christian readers of their duty to their less fortunate brothers and
sisters. Chapter 4, "Mining Poor," is reprinted here.

In 1840, Parliament appointed a commission to investigate the child labor in
mines and manufacturing firms. In May 1842, the commission submitted its first
report on mines, complete with illustrations. Tonna's description of conditions in
the mines is entirely consistent with that presented in the government report. Her
article may be compared with Friedrich Engels's even more detailed account of
"The Mining Proletariat," chapter 9 of *The Condition of the Working Class in
England.*

From *The Perils of the Nation*

Chapter 4
Mining Poor

The horrors of this department have, like their sable treasuries, be[en] long hidden from the light of day. Now, drawn from the depths, they have kindled a twofold fire; on the one part of vehement indignation, on the other of angry resentment; aloof from both of which stands a third party, who, having no immediate interest at stake, or being imperfectly informed on the subject, is neither shocked at the disclosures, nor angry with those who have made them. By recent legislative enactments,[1] some of the worst features of the system will be removed within a short time; but, looking at things as they have been for a long series of years, and as at this day they still are, we cannot speak prospectively. The intended removal of females from this sphere of labour is a matter of great thankfulness; and we shall best excite that thankful feeling, by giving a true, though brief and feeble sketch of what is, at this time, still in full operation underground, and against the possible continuance of which it behoves the country most vigilantly to guard. It is no new page in our history that we are about to consider, though newly opened to the public eye; and truly it is a page that needs all the authentication we can give it, to vindicate it from the character of a horrible and a libellous romance.

I. The position of a miner is inevitably one of unnatural gloom, discomfort, and imminent peril. The interior of a coal-mine, as described by those who, without any other object in view than the gratification of natural or scientific curiosity, have explored one, is a region of darkness and fear, sufficient to daunt the boldest spirit, and to sadden the most mirthful. The usual descent is by a perpendicular shaft, varying of course in depth, but from the bottom of which the wide mouth, with daylight above it, is described as resembling in size the palm of a man's hand. The manner of descending shall, by-and-by, be noticed; at present, we speak only of the place itself. At certain depths, passages, or galleries, branch off, intersecting each other like streets in a city, but often exceedingly low-roofed, hewn out in the solid bed, of which immense masses are here and there left, like huge misshapen pillars, to support the roof, which would otherwise be liable to break in and ruin the whole work. Connected with these main and permanent thoroughfares are others,—excavations from whence the coal is taken, for conveyance to the surface; and these vary in size according to the thickness of the seam; but if they be very narrow and low, it is evident that the acts of detaching and or carrying the coal, must be performed in positions painfully cramping and unnatural. Some of these

---

1. A month after the government report was published, Lord Ashley (1801–1885) introduced legislation to end the worst abuses. Women and girls as well as boys under age ten were prohibited from engaging in underground work.

seams are ten yards in thickness; others ten inches; and in many of the mines now working, the roads or passages do not exceed *eighteen inches in height!*

The closeness of the place would speedily produce suffocation, were it not ventilated from above: this can only be done effectually by the sinking of two shafts; a large fire being kept burning at the foot of one, and the air which descends the other being by this means constantly borne upwards, after traversing the various passages—through which it is forced, by means of a suitable arrangement of doors and partitions—a supply of fresh atmospheric air is ensured; dependent of course on the pains bestowed in constructing, and the care taken in working, the necessary apparatus. The heat of these subterranean workshops varies so considerably, that the difference of temperature, in the main road and in the workings, often ranges to twenty degrees; the latter being of course the highest. If the ventilation be imperfect, the heat in the workings becomes most offensive; and the character of the gases combined, the moisture, where the drainage is not very complete, and animal effluvia,[2] render it the most noisome,—most horrible atmosphere that man's lungs can inhale. The drainage of a coal-mine is, indeed, only secondary in immediate importance to its ventilation; and when it is considered that not only the ground beneath the feet, but the roof overhead, frequently assumes the character of a wet sponge, and that the almost naked bodies toiling therein are constantly bathed in the perspiration which severe muscular exertion and a close-pent passage of heated air combine to produce, we may form some estimate of the sufferings undergone from these continual risings and drippings of a damp the most chill and sepulchral that can be conceived. Even the horses are sometimes covered with waxed cloths, to protect them from the descending streams, while the water, thickened with coal-dust, often rises so high, that, except the labourers employed, all who pass are obliged to use a carriage, drawn through this compound to the depth of a man's knee. Such, in very brief outline, is for the most part the scene of a miner's labour; with the addition of all being wrapped in primeval darkness, save as the glimmer of candles, and the still more contracted gleam of the lantern, serve to make that darkness visible:[3] no ray of natural light, no breath of unfettered air, no sound from among the many that gladden man's heart, as he mingles in the daylight haunts of his fellow-men, or crosses the sunshiny meadow, ever visit the miner's place of work; but perils[4] fearful to contemplate impend over him, requiring above almost any other predicament of human life, that his way amid the bowels of the earth should be cleared of all unavoidable enticements to transgression, and the solemn truth allowed to bear with full force upon his conscience, that "there is but a step between him and death." The more common dangers to which they all are generally exposed, are precipitation down the shaft, to a depth, perhaps, of some hundred feet, by the

---

2. Horses and donkeys were sometimes used to cart ore, and their excreted wastes ("effluvia") were simply left in the mine passages.

3. In *Paradise Lost,* John Milton describes the fires of Hell: "yet from those flames / No light, but rather darkness visible. . . ." 1.62–63.

4. See Joseph Skipsey's poem, "The Hartley Calamity," in this section.

breaking of a rope, or other damage to machinery employed in the descent and ascent, or from a false step, giddiness, or overbalancing; being drawn over the pulley, through carelessness in the hand employed to turn it, and so flung back into the shaft; crushing, by the fall of stones, or other heavy material, down the shafts or in the mines; drowning in the pits of water; explosions of gas or of gunpowder, from which no degree of precaution can always guard the miner; suffocation by choke-damp[5] always apt to accumulate; and being run down by the team-waggons in their rapid descent, with a load of coal sufficient to crush the human frame to a jelly. Of these it would naturally be supposed that the latter class of perils,—the explosions, damps, and crushings,—were more generally destructive; but the returns show that a greater extent of mortality results from the unguarded state of the pit's mouth, and utter recklessness of those who superintend the pulleys, and from the neglect of drainage below, than from any other cause. So little do the lives of our fellow-creatures sometimes weigh in the balance against the procurement of some extra indulgence brought within reach by the augmented produce of their toil, that few are found to expend in fencing the mouth of a coal-pit, or paying an adult for attending to the apparatus usually committed to a young child,[6] the sum available for modernizing after the newest pattern, the furniture of a boudoir; or to care for the perfect drainage of a damp mine, in preference to the immediate beautifying of a domain, the purchase of its sable wealth. How far this neglect operates, we shall see under another head. Hitherto we have spoken principally of coal-mines: there are others, namely, iron-stone, tin, copper, lead, and zinc. The iron-stone mines nearly resemble the coal, being worked in a very similar manner; with this difference, that the beds are rarely more than three feet in thickness, consequently the space for the movements of the workers is more painfully confined; and neither horses nor asses can assist in bringing the iron-stone to the foot of the shaft. Its great weight renders the carriage exceedingly laborious; and these mines being usually much more wet and cold than the coal-mines, neither can they be so effectually ventilated. The other mines are worked in a dissimilar manner, their productions being principally imbedded in solid rock; and the veins of metal not lying in horizontal beds, their course must be followed by boring, and by continual blasting with gunpowder. It is also obvious, that due ventilation cannot be supplied through such shafts and galleries as compose these works; in fact, after the first blasting in the morning, they are generally filled with smoke for the day, so dense, that sometimes the miner can scarcely see his hand. Steam-engines, and various kinds of machinery, are requisite for removing the broken rocks, and raising the continual gushes of water to the surface. There are instances, as in Alston Moor, where the labourer's place of work is at the end of a passage *five miles* in length from the level by which he entered; no

5. Atmospheric condition in a mine caused by very low levels of oxygen and high levels of carbon dioxide, which leads to choking.

6. The commissioners' 1842 report condemned "the almost universal practice of intrusting the closing of the air-doors to very young Children [i.e., the trappers]" and the practice in some mines "of employing boys at the steam-engines for letting down and drawing up the workpeople."

atmospheric air reaching him, but such as slowly winds its way, unassisted by any current, to that distance. In such instances, the expense of sinking an extra shaft, or otherwise forming a current, is often considered more than the mine is worth: the proprietor would rather abandon it: but men and boys are found so pressed by hunger, as to subject themselves to every extremity of suffering inseparable from such fearful exclusion of the vital element, to earn a morsel of food. Falls and explosions are the principal causes of injury in these mines: the descent and ascent are generally by ladders; a very toilsome exertion where the depth is great. Having thus briefly noticed the points of variation between different descriptions of mines, we will return to those, (the coal-mines,) by far the most numerous and extensive, with which we set out, and which open a scene to the eye of man, from which the eye of God is never withdrawn: though into all the abominations that are naked and open to Him, we cannot enter. The work would be liable to a prosecution by the Society for discountenancing vice,[7] that should only touch upon certain features of those pandemoniums,[8] to which some of the noblest and wealthiest of the land have long consigned the wives and daughters of their brethren, for the sake of the few paltry trinkets which may for a season sparkle on their own.

II. The nature of the ordinary employment in coal-mines, is to the stout heart of man appalling, to his vigorous intellect debilitating, to his sinewy frame in its full maturity exhausting. But of man we will not now speak, except to individualize one, the head of a family, which he is bound to provide with the necessaries of life: we will fix our gaze on the only means left within his reach for so providing them, in a mining district; where what he, by the utmost efforts of willing labour, can earn, is often utterly insufficient: whence it follows that ere his wife and babes can eat, they must be immersed in the untold horrors of those subterranean hells: ere they can be so clad as to meet either the breeze of heaven, or the daylight-gaze, they must labour almost naked in those abodes of darkness and of the shadow of death.[9] Or, yet worse than from necessity, men whose natural selfishness has been fostered in this school of hardening profligacy, and their blunted feelings brought to crave the perpetual excitement of strong drink and other gross indulgencies, avail themselves of the inducements held out to barter there the health, the morals, the lives, the souls of their wretched partners and offspring, that they may themselves revel above ground on the wages of their cruel sufferings below. Even where humane proprietors, made acquainted for the first time with the extent of these atrocities, desire to abate them, and would willingly alter the system; an obstacle exists in the interested cruelty of such men, on whom nothing short of a compulsory law will operate, to rescue their helpless dependents from the slavery of the coal-pits.

7. The Society for the Suppression of Vice was established in 1802 by William Wilberforce (1759–1833), best known for his effective leadership of the anti-slavery campaign.

8. Pandemonium is the name Milton coined for "the high capital / Of Satan and his peers." It literally means All-Demons. *Paradise Lost* 1.756–57.

9. Psalm 23:4.

The coal having been broken off by men, who are often obliged to lie along on their backs, and in that position to knock it away, it must be collected and carried to the bottom of the shafts. To get the skips[10] or vehicles along, various plans are adopted, where the narrowness of the seam, or road, renders it impracticable to introduce any four-footed beast of burden; and, among these, the girdle and chain prevail, the former being fastened round the loins; the latter, attached to it, passed between the legs, and hooked on the carriage, or corve,[11] which is thus drawn along; the woman, girl, or boy, going on all-fours, in a position of which it is hard to say, whether the pain or the degradation is the greater. A loaded corve, perhaps above eight hundred weight, is usually drawn on an average from three to nine miles a day: that is to say, twenty journeys are taken upon a line, it may be of 150, it may be 400 yards in length, of which some portion is generally very much inclined: how terrible the exertion must be to a delicate girl, or to a woman, often compelled to continue her toil till within a few hours of giving birth to a child, may be partially conceived; but the reality can be understood only by such as suffer it. And this in darkness, in damp, in extreme cold and extreme heat alternating, under the control of men whose discontent and discomfort can vent themselves in any measure of cruelty on the poor harnessed slave who works at their beck! A variety is sometimes introduced in the mode of working, particularly when it is up-hill: instead of dragging the corve, the guide, or hurrier, pushes it forward by great force, resting the head and hand against it; while either upon the carriage, or in the front of the hurrier's cap, a bit of candle is stuck, to light the otherwise rayless path. It is no unusual thing for a girl of fifteen or less to lift a single coal of an hundred weight from the ground to the top of a corve, three feet high, preparatory to moving on with her burden. The dress of these young labourers of both sexes is the same: from seven or eight years of age to twenty and upwards they may be seen, naked to the waist, and having a loose pair of ragged trowsers, frequently torn to tatters by the constant friction of the chain. When the passage is sufficiently high to admit of it, the hurrier faces the front of the corve, and, by violent effort, pulls it along, proceeding backwards. In some mines, there are rails laid down, and long narrow waggons, placed on small wheels, convey the coal; two or three children are required to move them at the customary speed; one with girdle and chain drags on all-fours; two others, with their heads and the palms of their hands pressed against the back, thrust it forward, their bodies being very nearly horizontal, the roof very low, and the velocity of the waggon rendering it necessary: for, if not bent to within a few inches of the ground, their heads would be smashed against the rugged surface above.

One of the carriages used is an oblong tub, without wheels, containing three hundred weight of coals, which is dragged by a woman on a rough ground, frequently over a considerable ascent. Where this road is very steep, they usually have

10. Buckets or cages used for lowering and raising workers or materials in a mine or quarry.

11. Large baskets, later tubs, used for conveying ore. The conditions Tonna describes are depicted in the *Punch* cartoon *Capital and Labour* and the woodcut *Child-Labour in Coal-Mines of the 'Forties.* See figures 3.4 and 3.5.

a rope lying loosely on the ground, to cling to, the position being a very painful stoop, and the whole weight drawn on by means of a chain passing between the legs. A candle, stuck upon the black wall, here and there, by a bit of wet clay, throws a sickly glimmer on the drawer's path, and a young boy or girl, called a thrutcher, pushes along the tub.

Coal-bearing is another branch of labour assigned to women, girls, and boys, and practised where no carriage could ascend. This is so very peculiar an exercise, that it deserves a little closer description. A female is provided with a basket, shaped somewhat like a cockle-shell, filled with coals, and which a man can some-times scarcely lift to her back, where it is fastened by passing two straps across her forehead, while she bends her body as nearly to a semicircular form as possible. Large pieces of coal are then heaped about the top of the basket, till the weight, in the case of a stout girl, has reached a hundred, or a hundred and a half; when she hangs her bit of candle to the cloth that crosses her head, and begins her journey. She first has to walk on level ground eighty-four feet, then to ascend a ladder eighteen feet high; then to proceed along a road, or passage, between three feet and a half, and four feet and a half high: then another ladder, another road, and so on, till she has traversed a distance equal to the height of St. Paul's Cathedral.[12] There she casts her load into the tub, and returns for another. This work is continued, in the case referred to, from two in the morning to one or two in the afternoon. In the east of Scotland the Commissioner found one little girl, a beautiful child of only *six years old,* whose daily task was to carry loads of half a cwt.[13] of coal, making with such a load, fourteen of these long journeys per day!

It frequently happens that the large pieces of coal heaped loosely upon the bearer's neck, fall off; and occasionally the band across the forehead breaks; in either case the falling weight descends upon the person next behind. Sometimes, in trying to save or recover the burden, the bearer loses her footing, and slips from the ladder into the depth below. The bearing, hurrying, and drawing, are practised by girls, young women, and the mothers of large families, up to the very hour when they find it necessary to hasten home to give birth to a child, probably dead, through the mother's previous sufferings; and within the week after, or at latest in ten or twelve days, they are again hurried to their post of slavery, and its subterra-nean horrors.

But one more branch of the mining occupation remains to be noticed: it has been stated that the ventilation of mines is effected by judiciously arranging pas-sages, and closing them up at proper points, to prevent a current sweeping along the narrow roads, to the exclusion of branches that require an equal supply. Through these doors it is necessary that the laden carriages, corves, waggons, tubs, &c. should pass, but they must be instantly closed again. A string is therefore fixed to the door, and a helper, called a trapper, placed behind it; who, on hearing the

12. London cathedral designed by Sir Christopher Wren (1632–1723) and built between 1675 and 1710; its dome is 365 feet high.
13. Hundredweight.

Figure 3.4. *Child-Labour in Coal-Mines of the 'Forties—a little "trapper" opening an air-door for a truck to pass through.* B/W photo courtesy of *The Illustrated London News* Picture Library, London, UK/Bridgeman Art Library.

This woodcut, originally accompanying an article in *The Cyclopedia of Useful Arts* (1840–45) and typical of the woodcuts that illustrated the reports of official government commissions appointed to investigate working conditions in the mines, was reproduced in *The Illustrated London News,* June 26, 1926, p. 1130.

vehicle approach, pulls the string, holds the door open while the carriage goes through, and lets it close again directly. For this work little creatures of eight, five, yea, four years are chosen, whose fathers carry them down to the pit even in their night-gowns, as the evidence has shown, place each poor babe behind a door, and leave it, crying with cold and terror, in total darkness for twelve or fourteen hours; with no one variation of its wretched employment, so long as a corve is at work in the mine. This is the practice in England, Wales, Scotland, (not in Ireland, to the eternal honour of her race be it recorded:) this, in the land of infant education, the land of light and liberty! This has been done by Christian parents, with the complaisant acquiescence of Christian gentlemen, noblemen, legislators, and in fact of the whole country, and we challenge the universe to outdo it in point of cold-blooded barbarity! It was shown on evidence, that if the poor babe, exhausted by fretting, and pining for the rest so absolutely needful for infancy, should fall asleep in the still darkness of its frightful prison, a beating would be the consequence; and a little experience of the weight of a man's fist soon teaches the trembling creatures to devise means for remaining awake.[14] Sometimes they beg a small end of candle from a compassionate hurrier as he passes, and that gives them a few moments of comparative cheerfulness. Some of the older children, who may have learned their letters, will take a little book, perhaps; but it is only when a few drops of tallow are bestowed, that it can be looked into. A little girl said to the Commissioners, "I have to trap without a light, and I'm scared. I go at four, and sometimes half-past three in the morning, and come out at five and half-past. I never go to sleep. Sometimes I sing when I've light, but not in the dark; I dare not

14. According to the commissioners' report, in many mines children suffered abuse from adult colliers rather than from "persons in authority."

sing then."[15] In the Cumberland collieries, the expenditure is submitted to of providing a small candle for the poor little trapper at his monotonous post; but this is not the case in other quarters: and it is enough to appal man's spirit, to think on the impartial eye that beholds without an intervening obstruction, the poor man's solitary child immured in ebon darkness, suffering what the hardened felon in his cell is not condemned to endure; and the blaze of light that falls on the jewelled assembly, luxuriating in the drawing-room of that poor child's enriched employer. That such things should have been laid before the British public, printed by order of Parliament, and made known, through our public press, in every corner of the civilized globe, is a humiliating thought; and when viewed in con-nexion with our high privileges of light and knowledge, and the profession of a pure faith, it becomes the more alarming; because we cannot expect that He who ruleth over all, will permit such deeds to come before the world as though they consisted with that religion, of which the golden rule is, "Whatsoever ye would that men should do unto you, that do ye likewise unto them."[16]

III. But we have now to enquire into the moral state of the mining population, necessarily resulting from their mode of life; and here a scene of deepened gloom opens upon us, but faintly cheered by approaching amelioration: for the evil has existed so long and so widely in full vigour, that a generation must pass away ere the frightfully demoralizing effects of what may be discontinued, but cannot be recalled, can cease to operate. Indeed, the transfer to the surface, of a body of females so utterly hardened in the gross depravities of the mines, must, for a time, spread contamination on all sides. This is the deadly consequence of sin: it pro-duces its own punishment, as naturally as the tree bears its own fruit. We may cease to connive at the fearful oppression that has, in this department, ground down our female poor; but we cannot remove the sable stain from their minds, by ceasing to smear their bodies with the filth of our coal-pits; nor remove the fetter of sin from their souls, while unloosing from their loins the degrading chain that yokes them to the corve. Individual repentance alone can stay this flood of iniq-uity, thus to be turned into a different channel; and only national repentance can avert the issue, as regards the reckless desperation of tens of thousands, steeled in habitual guilt, loving the wages of iniquity, and exasperated by the withdrawal at once of the gains acquired by the unnatural toil of their own female dependants, and the criminal gratifications constantly afforded them by the presence of their neighbours' wives and daughters in this pandemonium of licentiousness. It is easy to corrupt a people; but to restore to the way of righteousness such as have utterly fallen from it, or to bring into the good paths those whom we have prevented from seeking them early, and led or driven into the very midst of the strongest tempta-tions, is hard indeed!

In reference to this distressing branch of the subject, we have shown that the persons employed are of both sexes and all ages; that a great proportion of them

15. Testimony given by Sarah Gooder, age eight, included in the 1842 commission report.
16. Matthew 7:12.

Figure 3.5. *Capital and Labour.* Courtesy Mansell/Time Inc.

Capital and Labour appeared in the periodical *Punch* in 1843 in reaction to the government report of 1842 that exposed the working conditions in the mines. "Labour" is shown in the bottom panel of the cartoon in the shape of deformed and wretched figures under the watchful eye of a fat, indolent overlooker while "Capital," symbolically at the top of the drawing, is represented by members of the wealthy leisure class who are surrounded by servants in silk and brocade and pampered pet dogs reclining on satin pillows. Connecting the two groups, pictorially as well as literally, is a network of mine tunnels where scantily clad workers lie on their backs digging a deeper shaft or crawl on their hands and knees lugging coal carts. They are pictured in the cartoon just as they were in the drawings that accompanied official government reports (see figure 3.4).

work almost entirely naked, the one ragged garment they wear not being available even for purposes of decency; and that the place of their labour is of wide extent, divided into low narrow passages and cells; all utterly dark, save where a candle at long intervals glimmers against the black walls, or is attached to their own headgear, or to the carriage they draw. The coal-getters, and some other classes of workers must be men; a large proportion of the hurriers, drawers, and bearers, who wait on them, are females; and these again are promiscuously mixed in their field of labour with lads and youths. No circumstances can possibly be conceived more inevitably tending to general profligacy; and that the most abandoned vice does reign in the mines, transforming the female character into something so depraved that their language and conduct are described as being far worse than the men's, is but too well attested. No visitor can pass among them, without being shocked by the obscenity of their discourse, and the indecency of their appearance; and even the men, whose worst passions are continually excited and gratified by their presence, are often known, in sober moments, to express a wish that females were excluded from the pits. Added to the powerful influence of constant persuasion to sin, is the total absence of all restraining principle. Commencing in infancy the miner's career, they cannot have enjoyed even a glimpse of decent education. Many are carried down before they can speak plainly, and not a few have passed years without seeing daylight except on the sabbath. In some districts, no doubt, Sunday and Adult Schools are provided;[17] but even if compelled to attend them, what degree of application to the dull contents of a spelling-book, can be expected from persons to whom the very light that streams through the window is a dazzling novelty, and every passing object seen under its beam a rare attraction? The testimony of all engaged in the enquiry, goes to establish the fact, that wretchedness in some of its most degrading forms characterizes the mining population; and a harvest must be reaped from what is already sown, before we can prepare the ground to yield a different crop.

IV. In reference to the effects on children, of mining occupations, there are a few points which remain to be noticed. The Act recently passed provides for the rescue of all girls, and of boys under ten years old. But at that age the latter may be apprenticed, and for eight years; and the fate to which the greater part of them are doomed is dreadful indeed. They are principally taken from the most helpless and pitiable class, the orphan or deserted pauper-children, sheltered in workhouses;[18] who have not, upon earth, a friend to defend their cause, or to succour them when oppressed. These are bound to the men permanently employed in mines, and whatever the selfish indolence, caprice or savage ill-temper of their owners may see fit to inflict upon them, that they must bear. Frightful outrages are common, where these defenceless boys are found unequal to the stretch of laborious exertion required of them. A very common mode of punishment is by flinging a large coal at the offender, the weight of which, and its sharp, jagged, angular edges, may inflict at one blow bruises and cuts sufficient to torture him for many a day; the latter especially, being irritated by the perpetual admission of coal-dust into the wounds. Extreme barbarity is a too frequent feature in the dispositions of those who, having outgrown alike their own turn of similar suffering, and every kindly impulse cherished beneath the light of day, and in the social circle, have only two propensities to satisfy in those dreary dens of midnight gloom—the rage of licen-

17. The Sunday school movement began in the late eighteenth century with the aim of inculcating in working-class children basic Christian values and teaching them how to read. By mid-century there were more than 23,000 Sunday schools in England. Early in the nineteenth century, adult Sunday school classes were started by Evangelicals, and self-help groups were established by radical workers to provide a fundamental education for working-class adults. By mid-century, evening schools with more advanced courses had been added. See F. D. Maurice's "The Studies in a Working College" in part 2.

18. Institution where paupers with no other recourse were housed. The able-bodied were required to work.

tiousness and the rage of tyranny. It may be expected, that the removal of what now gratifies the one, will render the other more pitiless in its exactions; and many a gust of fury must the poor little fellows encounter. Common humanity pleads their cause within our bosoms; but there is a voice much nearer to us all, even that of self-preservation, which demands attention to their case: for the God of heaven is bound, by His own immutable word, to show Himself the avenger of such.[19] No being, however obscure or insignificant, is hidden from His view; "Are not two sparrows sold for a farthing?" said the Lord Jesus, "and one of them shall not fall to the ground without your Father."[20] How much more valuable than many sparrows, must be an heir of immortality, in the sight of Him who breathed into man's nostrils the breath of life![21] If there be to Him any difference between the infant cradled in down and pillowed on satin, and the babe that moans out its unheeded wants from a truss of mouldy straw, it surely arises from the tender compassion with which He, who shed his own blood for the sin of the world, regards the inheritor alike of Adam's iniquity, and of the original doom pronounced upon the culprit—one who must eat bread in the sweat of his face, in labour also and in sorrow all the days of his life.[22] There is a perpetual testimony against us going up from this neglected and afflicted class of sufferers: a class which might be trained to become a social and national blessing; who, having no acknowledged ties to divide their affection, would attach themselves closely to the benevolent guides and guardians of their helpless years; and, on that principle, would prove loyal, faithful subjects; instead of growing up, as now they do, the most degraded of slaves, to become the most reckless of insurgents, and the fiercest of tyrants.

We have done with this department; not that the subject is exhausted, for in truth we have not fairly entered into it; but because, unhappily, a multitude of rival topics press upon us. As in the case of the manufacturing poor, it is freely admitted that there are exceptions to the account we have given; nay, that whole counties are comparatively free from some of the worst features of the system. Still, the picture we have drawn is faithfully copied from the official reports of the government commissioners; and the abuses we have detailed have both a real and a very extensive existence.

19. God's law and His role as avenger are prescribed in a number of biblical passages. See Romans 12, for example.

20. Matthew 10:29–31.

21. Genesis 2:7.

22. Genesis 3:19, 17.

FRIEDRICH ENGELS

F RIEDRICH ENGELS (1820–1895) was born in Barmen, Germany, the eldest of eight children of a well-to-do manufacturer of thread. Engels enjoyed school as a boy but was required by his enterprising father to abandon his formal education at age sixteen in order to learn the family business. Nevertheless, he continued to read widely on his own. His exposure to the ideas of the German theologians and philosophers David Friedrich Strauss (1808–1874), Friedrich Schleiermacher (1768–1834), and Georg Wilhelm Friedrich Hegel (1770–1831) led to his abandonment of the religious fundamentalism of his father. At age seventeen, Engels moved to Bremen where he worked for over two years. While there, he began to publish anonymously in the *Telegraph für Deutschland* a series of articles exploring social conditions under the title *Letters from the Wupper Valley.* In 1842 in Cologne, he met the German political philosophers Moses Hess (1812–1875), who introduced him to an early version of Communism, and Karl Marx (1818–1883), with whom he would later co-author *The German Ideology* (1846) and *The Communist Manifesto* (1848).

Engels spent the next two years working in his father's firm in Manchester, England. He devoted considerable time to investigating working-class labor and living conditions, involving himself in politics, and getting to know working-class people—one in particular, Mary Burns, an illiterate Irish servant girl with whom he lived off and on for twenty years. Engels wrote *The Condition of the Working Class in England* between the fall of 1844 and the spring of 1845 after he returned to Barmen. It received considerable attention upon its publication in German in 1846. An English translation was published in the United States in 1887 and in England in 1892.

In *The Condition of the Working Class,* Engels examines the impact of the Industrial Revolution on the workers. He opens with a discussion of pre-industrial working conditions, traces the rise of industrialization, and explores the effects on the living conditions, family relationships, health, and morality of the laborers. Drawing heavily from contemporary publications, Engels provides abundant evidence from official documents, eyewitness accounts, and statistics to support his argument that those who must work for others (the proletariat) have been effectively enslaved by the materialistic middle-class employers (the bourgeoisie). In the letter addressed to "Working Men" that introduces the book, Engels describes his efforts to distance himself from his middle-class associations and to acquire accurate information:

I have lived long enough admidst you to know something about your circumstances; I have devoted to their knowledge my most serious attention, I have studied the various official and non-official documents as far as I was able to get hold of them—I have not been satisfied with this, I wanted more than a mere *abstract* knowledge of my subject, I wanted to see you in your own homes, to observe you in your everyday life, to chat with you on your condition and grievances, to witness your struggles against the social and political power of your oppressors. I have done so: I forsook the company and the dinner-parties, the port wine and champagne of the middle classes, and devoted my leisure hours almost exclusively to the intercourse with plain Working Men; I am both glad and proud of having done so.

From the outset, Engels makes plain his contempt for the bourgeoisie and his allegiance to "the cause of Humanity" for which he urges the proletariat to continue to fight:

Having, at the same time, ample opportunity to watch the middle classes, your opponents, I soon came to the conclusion that you are right, perfectly right in expecting no support whatever from them. Their interest is diametrically opposed to yours, though they always will try to maintain the contrary and to make you believe in their most hearty sympathy with your fates. Their doings give them the lie. I hope to have collected more than sufficient evidence of the fact that—be their words what they please—the middle classes intend in reality nothing else but to enrich themselves by your labour while they can sell its produce, and to abandon you to starvation as soon as they cannot make a profit by this indirect trade in human flesh. What have they done to prove their professed goodwill towards you? Have they ever paid any serious attention to your grievances? Have they done more than paying the expenses of half a dozen commissions of inquiry, whose voluminous reports are damned to everlasting slumber among heaps of waste paper on the shelves of the Home Office? Have they even done as much as to compile from those rotting Blue Books[1] a single readable book from which everybody might easily get some information on the condition of the great majority of "free-born Britons"? Not they indeed, those are things they do not like to speak of—they have left it to a foreigner to inform the civilized world of the degrading situation you have to live in.

The sixth chapter, which focuses on the textile industry, is reprinted here.

---

1. Blue Books, so called because they were typically bound in blue paper covers, were the official reports generated by government-appointed commissions.

From *The Condition of the Working Class in England*

Single Branches of Industry: Factory-Hands

In dealing now with the more important branches of the English manufacturing proletariat, we shall begin, according to the principle already laid down, with the factory-workers, i.e. those who are comprised under the Factory Act.[2] This law regulates the length of the working day in mills in which wool, silk, cotton, and flax are spun or woven by means of water or steam-power and embraces, therefore, the more important branches of English manufacture. The class employed by them is the most intelligent and energetic of all the English workers, and, therefore, the most restless and most hated by the bourgeoisie. It stands as a whole, and the cotton-workers pre-eminently stand, at the head of the labour movement, as their masters the manufacturers, especially those of Lancashire, take the lead of the bourgeois agitation.

We have already seen in the introduction how the population employed in working up the textile materials were first torn from their former way of life.[3] It is, therefore, not surprising that the progress of mechanical invention in later years also affected precisely these workers most deeply and permanently. The history of cotton manufacture as related by Ure,[4] Baines,[5] and others is the story of improvements in every direction, most of which have become domesticated in the other branches of industry as well. Hand-work is superseded by machine-work almost universally, nearly all manipulations are conducted by the aid of steam or water, and every year is bringing further improvements.

In a well-ordered state of society, such improvements could only be a source of rejoicing; in a war of all against all, individuals seize the benefit for themselves, and so deprive the majority of the means of subsistence. Every improvement in machinery throws workers out of employment, and the greater the advance, the more numerous the unemployed; each great improvement produces, therefore, upon a number of workers the effect of a commercial crisis, creates want, wretchedness, and crime. Take a few examples. The very first invention, the jenny,[6] worked by one man, produced at least sixfold what the spinning-wheel had yielded in the same

2. The 1833 Factory Act prohibited the employment in textile mills of children under age nine and limited to eight hours a day, six days a week the employment of those between the ages of nine and thirteen. In 1844, Parliament passed additional legislation lowering the allowable age of child workers to eight but limiting their daily hours to six and a half and restricting women to a twelve-hour workday.

3. Engels refers to the fact that spinning and weaving were cottage industries prior to the development of machinery.

4. Engels's note: "Dr A. Ure, *The Cotton Manufacture of Great Britain* (1836)." Andrew Ure (1778–1857) was an economist and physician who, in this and other books, voiced enthusiastic support for the factory system.

5. Engels's note: "E[dward] Baines, *History of the Cotton Manufacture of Great Britain* (1835)."

6. The spinning jenny, a hand-operated spinning machine, was invented by James Hargreaves (d. 1778), in 1764.

time; thus every new jenny threw five spinners out of employment. The throstle,[7] which, in turn, produced much more than the jenny, and like it, was worked by one man, threw still more people out of employment. The mule,[8] which required yet fewer hands in proportion to the product, had the same effect, and every improvement in the mule, every multiplication of its spindles, diminished still further the number of workers employed. But this increase of the number of spindles in the mule is so great that whole armies of workers have been thrown out of employment by it. For, whereas one spinner, with a couple of children for piecers, formerly set 600 spindles in motion, he could now manage 1,400 to 2,000 spindles upon two mules, so that two adult spinners and a part of the piecers whom they employed were thrown out. And since self-acting[9] mules have been introduced into a very large number of spinning-mills, the spinners' work is wholly performed by the machine. There lies before me a book from the pen of James Leach,[10] one of the recognized leaders of the Chartists in Manchester. The author has worked for years in various branches of industry, in mills and coal-mines, and is known to me personally as an honest, trustworthy, and capable man. In consequence of his political position, he had at command extensive detailed information as to the different factories, collected by the workers themselves, and he publishes tables from which it is clear that in 1841, in 35 factories, 1,060 fewer mule spinners were employed than in 1829, though the number of spindles in these 35 factories had increased by 99,239. He cites five factories in which no spinners whatever are employed, self-actors only being used. While the number of spindles increased by 10 per cent, the number of spinners diminished more than 60 per cent. And Leach adds that since 1841, so many improvements have been introduced by double-decking[11] and other means, that in some of the factories named, half the operatives have been discharged. In one factory alone, where eighty spinners were employed a short time ago, there are now but twenty left; the others having been discharged or set at children's work for children's wages. Of Stockport Leach tells a similar story, that in 1835, 800 spinners were employed, and in 1843 but 140, though the manufacture of Stockport has greatly increased during the last eight or nine years. Similar improvements have now been made in carding-frames,[12] by which one-half the operatives have been thrown out of employment. In one factory improved frames have been set up, which have thrown four hands out of eight out of work, besides

---

7. Sir Richard Arkwright (1732–1792) invented the spinning throstle or "water frame" in 1867. It had several hundred spindles and, therefore, could be used only in large mills. The throstle spun coarse thread that had to be re-spun on jennies.

8. Invented in 1785 by Samuel Crompton (1753–1827), the mule combined the techniques of the jenny and the throstle.

9. Capable of operating automatically.

10. Engels's note: "W. Rashleigh, MP, *Stubborn Facts from the Factories by a Manchester Operative.* Published and dedicated to the working classes. (London, 1844), 28ff." According to Engels, the "Manchester Operative" is James Leach, a factory worker and Chartist organizer, who later became a printer. See, in this section, the introduction to "The People's Charter" for a discussion of the Chartist movement.

11. Installing two rows of spindles.

12. A machine with rows of wire teeth, used to untangle fibers prior to spinning.

which the employer reduced the wages of the four retained from 8s. to 7s. The same process has gone on in the weaving industry; the power-loom[13] has taken possession of one branch of hand-weaving after another, and since it produces much more than the hand-loom, while one weaver can work two looms, it has superseded a multitude of working-people. And in all sorts of manufacture, in flax- and wool-spinning, in silk-twisting, the case is the same. The power-loom, too, is beginning to appropriate one branch after another of wool- and linen-weaving; in Rochdale alone, there are more power- than hand-looms in flannel and other wool-weaving branches. The bourgeoisie usually replies to this, that improvements in machinery, by decreasing the cost of production, supply finished goods at lower prices, and that these reduced prices cause such an increase in consumption that the unemployed operatives soon find full employment in newly founded factories.[14] The bourgeoisie is so far correct that under certain conditions favourable for the general development of manufacture, every reduction in price of goods *in which the raw material is cheap*, greatly increases consumption, and gives rise to the building of new factories; but every further word of the assertion is a lie. The bourgeoisie ignores the fact that it takes years for these results of the decrease in price to follow and for new factories to be built; it is silent upon the point that every improvement in machinery throws the real work, the expenditure of force, more and more upon the machine, and so transforms the work of full-grown men into mere supervision, which a feeble woman or even a child can do quite as well, and does for half or even one-third the wages; that, therefore, grown men are constantly more and more supplanted and *not re-employed* by the increase in manufacture; it conceals the fact that whole branches of industry fall away, or are so changed that they must be learned afresh; and it takes good care not to confess what it usually harps upon, whenever the question of forbidding the work of children is broached, that factory-work must be learned in earliest youth in order to be learned properly. It does not mention the fact that the process of improvement goes steadily on, and that as soon as the operative has succeeded in making himself at home in a new branch, if he actually does succeed in so doing, this, too, is taken from him, and with it the last remnant of security which remained to him for winning his bread. But the bourgeoisie gets the benefit of the improvements in machinery; it has a capital opportunity for piling up money during the first years while many old machines are still in use, and the improvement not yet universally introduced; and it would be too much to ask that it should have an open eye for the disadvantages inseparable from these improvements.

The fact that improved machinery reduces wages has also been as violently disputed by the bourgeoisie, as it is constantly reiterated by the working men. The bourgeoisie insists that although the price of piece-work has been reduced, yet the total of wages for the week's work has rather risen than fallen, and the condition of

---

13. The power loom, patented in the 1780s by a clergyman, Edmund Cartwright (1743–1823), was sufficiently perfected by 1815 to be in widespread use.

14. Engels's note: "Compare Factories' Inquiry Commission's Report." Engels refers to the report of the Royal Commission appointed to study the employment of children in factories, 1833–1834.

the operatives rather improved than deteriorated. It is hard to get to the bottom of the matter, for the operatives usually dwell upon the price of piece-work. But it is certain that the weekly wage, also, has, in many branches of work, been reduced by the improvement of machinery. The so-called fine spinners (who spin fine mule yarn), for instance, do receive high wages, 30–40s. a week, because they have a powerful association for keeping wages up, and their craft requires long training; but the coarse spinners who have to compete against self-actors (which are not as yet adapted for fine spinning), and whose association was broken down by the introduction of these machines, receive very low wages. A mule spinner told me that he does not earn more than 14s. a week, and his statement agrees with that of Leach, that in various factories the coarse spinners earn less than 16s. 6d. a week, and that a spinner, who three years ago earned 30s., can now hardly scrape up 12s. 6d., and had not earned more on an average in the past year. The wages of women and children may perhaps have fallen less, but only because they were not high from the beginning. I know several women, widows with children, who have trouble enough to earn 8–9s. a week; and that they and their families cannot live decently upon that sum, everyone must admit who knows the price of the barest necessaries of life in England. That wages in general have been reduced by the improvement of machinery is the unanimous testimony of the operatives. The bourgeois assertion that the condition of the working class has been improved by machinery is most vigorously proclaimed a falsehood in every meeting of working men in the factory districts. And even if it were true that the relative wage, the price of piece-work only, has fallen, while the absolute wage, the sum to be earned in the week, remained unchanged, what would follow? That the operatives have had quietly to look on while the manufacturers filled their purses from every improvement without giving the hands the smallest share in the gain. The bourgeois forgets, in fighting the working man, the most ordinary principles of his own Political Economy. He who at other times swears by Malthus,[15] cries out in his anxiety before the workers: "Where could the millions by which the population of England has increased find work, without the improvements in machinery?"[16] As though the bourgeois did not know well enough that without machinery and the expansion of industry which it produced, these "millions" would never have been brought into the world and grown up! The service which machinery has rendered the workers is simply this: that it has brought home to their minds the necessity of a social reform by means of which machinery shall no longer work against but for them. Let the wise bourgeois ask the people who sweep the streets in Manchester and elsewhere (though even this is past now, since machines for the purpose have

---

15. Thomas Malthus (1766–1834), a clergyman, argued in *Essay on the Principle of Population* (1798) that since the population increases much more rapidly than the food supply, it is inevitable that a good number of people are destined to suffer from want and disease. Malthus's theory is the basis of "political economy," the nineteenth-century term for fixed, indisputable economic laws propounded by the Utilitarians.

16. Engels's note: "J. Symons, in *Arts and Artisans*." Engels's paraphrase of a question posed by journalist Jelinger Symons (1809–1860) in *Arts and Artisans at Home and Abroad* (1839).

been invented and introduced),[17] or sell salt, matches, oranges, and shoe-strings on the streets, or even beg, what they were formerly, and he will see how many will answer: "Mill-hands thrown out of work by machinery." The consequences of improvement in machinery under our present social conditions are, for the working man, solely injurious, and often in the highest degree oppressive. Every new advance brings with it loss of employment, want, and suffering, and in a country like England where, without that, there is usually a "surplus population"[18] to be discharged from work is the worst that can befall the operative. And what a dispiriting, unnerving influence this uncertainty of his position in life, consequent upon the unceasing progress of machinery, must exercise upon the worker, whose lot is precarious enough without it! To escape despair, there are but two ways open to him; either inward and outward revolt against the bourgeoisie or drunkenness and general demoralization. And the English operatives are accustomed to take refuge in both. The history of the English proletariat relates hundreds of uprisings against machinery and the bourgeoisie; we have already spoken of the moral dissolution which, in itself, is only another form of despair.

The worst situation is that of those workers who have to compete against a machine that is making its way. The price of the goods which they produce adapts itself to the price of the kindred product of the machine, and as the latter works more cheaply, its human competitor has but the lowest wages. The same thing happens to every operative employed upon an old machine in competition with later improvements. And who else is there to bear the hardship? The manufacturer will not throw out his old apparatus, nor will he sustain the loss upon it; out of the dead mechanism he can make nothing, so he fastens upon the living worker, the universal scapegoat of society. Of all the workers in competition with machinery, the most ill-used are the hand-loom cotton weavers. They receive the most trifling wages, and, with full work, are not in a position to earn more than 10s. a week. One class of woven goods after another is annexed by the power-loom, and hand-weaving is the last refuge of workers thrown out of employment in other branches, so that the trade is always overcrowded. Hence it comes that, in average seasons, the hand-weaver counts himself fortunate if he can earn 6s. or 7s. a week, while to reach this sum he must sit at his loom fourteen to eighteen hours a day. Most woven goods require moreover a damp weaving-room, to keep the weft from snapping, and in part, for this reason, in part because of their poverty, which prevents them from paying for better dwellings, the workrooms of these weavers are usually without wooden or paved floors. I have been in many dwellings of such weavers, in remote, vile courts and alleys, usually in cellars. Often half a dozen of

17. An automatic street sweeper was used in Manchester between 1842 and 1848 but was ultimately rejected because hand sweeping was found to be more effective and cost-efficient.

18. Allusion to Charles Dickens's A Christmas Carol (1843). When two gentlemen approach Ebenezer Scrooge at Christmas soliciting a contribution to alleviate the sufferings of the poor, Scrooge replies he will give nothing, that through his taxes he already supports the prisons and workhouses. The gentlemen protest that many would rather die than go to the workhouse, to which Scrooge responds, "If they would rather die, they had better do it, and decrease the surplus population."

these handloom weavers, several of them married, live together in a cottage with one or two workrooms, and one large sleeping-room. Their food consists almost exclusively of potatoes, with perhaps oatmeal porridge, rarely milk, and scarcely ever meat. Great numbers of them are Irish or of Irish descent.[19] And these poor hand-loom weavers, first to suffer from every crisis, and last to be relieved from it, must serve the bourgeoisie as a handle in meeting attacks upon the factory system. "See," cries the bourgeois, triumphantly, "see how these poor creatures must famish, while the mill operatives are thriving, and *then* judge the factory system!"[20] As though it were not precisely the factory system and the machinery belonging to it which had so shamefully crushed the hand-loom weavers, and as though the bourgeoisie did not know this quite as well as ourselves! But the bourgeoisie has interests at stake, and so a falsehood or two and a bit of hypocrisy won't matter much.

Let us examine somewhat more closely the fact that machinery more and more supersedes the work of men. The human labour, involved in both spinning and weaving, consists chiefly in piecing broken threads, as the machine does all the rest. This work requires no muscular strength, but only flexibility of finger. Men are, therefore, not only not needed for it, but actually, by reason of the greater muscular development of the hand, less fit for it than women and children, and are, therefore, naturally almost superseded by them. Hence, the more the use of the arms, the expenditure of strength, can be transferred to steam or water-power, the fewer men need be employed; and as women and children work more cheaply, and in these branches better than men, they take their places. In the spinning-mills women and girls are to be found in almost exclusive possession of the throstles; among the mules one man, an adult spinner (with self-actors, he, too, becomes superfluous), and several piecers for tying the threads, usually children or women, sometimes young men of from 18 to 20 years, here and there an old spinner[21] thrown out of other employment. At the power-looms women, from 15 to 20 years, are chiefly employed, and a few men; these, however, rarely remain at this trade after their twenty-first year. Among the preparatory machinery, too, women alone are to be found, with here and there a man to clean and sharpen the carding-frames. Besides all these, the factories employ numbers of children—doffers—for mounting and taking down bobbins, and a few men as overlookers, a mechanic and an engineer for the steam-engines, carpenters, porters, etc.; but the actual work of the mills is done by women and children. This the manufacturers deny.

19. Large-scale emigration resulted from widespread poverty in Ireland, particularly in the first half of the century. Repeated crop failures in the 1820s and 1830s culminated in the Irish famine in 1845. Irish immigrants, forced to accept the worst jobs for the lowest wages, were abused by employers and resented by English workers.

20. Engels's note: "See Dr Ure in the *Philosophy of Manufactures*."

21. Engels's note: "Report of Factory Inspector, L[eonard] Horner [1785–1864], October 1844: 'The state of things in the matter of wages is greatly perverted in certain branches of cotton manufacture in Lancashire; there are hundreds of young men, between twenty and thirty, employed as piecers and otherwise, who do not get more than 8 or 9 shillings a week, while children under thirteen years, working under the same roof, earn 5 shillings and young girls, from sixteen to twenty years, 10–12 shillings per week.' "

They published last year elaborate tables to prove that machinery does not supersede adult male operatives. According to these tables, rather more than half of all the factory-workers employed, viz. 52 per cent, were females and 48 per cent males, and of these operatives more than half were over 18 years old. So far, so good. But the manufacturers are very careful not to tell us, how many of the adults were men and how many women. And this is just the point. Besides this, they have evidently counted the mechanics, engineers, carpenters, all the men employed in any way in the factories, perhaps even the clerks, and still they have not the courage to tell the whole truth. These publications teem generally with falsehoods, perversions, crooked statements, with calculations of averages, that prove a great deal for the uninitiated reader and nothing for the initiated, and with suppressions of facts bearing on the most important points; and they prove only the selfish blindness and want of uprightness of the manufacturers concerned. Let us take some of the statements of a speech with which Lord Ashley introduced the Ten Hours Bill,[22] on 15 March 1844, into the House of Commons. Here he gives some data as to the relations of sex and age of the operatives, not yet refuted by the manufacturers, whose statements, as quoted above, cover moreover only a part of the manufacturing industry of England. Of 419,560 factory operatives of the British Empire in 1839, 192,887, or nearly half, were under 18 years of age, and 242,296 of the female sex, of whom 112,192 were less than 18 years old. There remain, therefore, 80,695 male operatives under 18 years, and 96,569 adult male operatives, *or not one full quarter* of the whole number. In the cotton factories, 56.5 per cent; in the woollen mills, 69.5 per cent; in the silk mills, 70.5 per cent; in the flax-spinning mills, 70.5 per cent of all operatives are of the female sex. These numbers suffice to prove the crowding out of adult males. But you have only to go into the nearest mill to see the fact confirmed. Hence follows of necessity that inversion of the existing social order which, being forced upon them, has the most ruinous consequences for the workers. The employment of women at once breaks up the family; for when the wife spends twelve or thirteen hours every day in the mill, and the husband works the same length of time there or elsewhere, what becomes of the children? They grow up like wild weeds; they are put out to nurse for a shilling or eighteenpence a week,[23] and how they are treated may be imagined. Hence the accidents to which little children fall victims multiply in the factory districts to a terrible extent. The lists of the Coroner of Manchester[24] showed for nine months: 69 deaths from

22. Anthony Ashley Cooper (1801–1885) became the seventh earl of Shaftesbury in 1851. Ashley was elected a Tory member of Parliament in 1826 and quickly made a name for himself as a social reformer. He submitted a Ten Hours Bill for textile mill workers in 1833. A weaker version of the bill which became law did restrict the ages of child laborers and limit the number of hours they could work. Another bill passed in 1844 further limited the number of hours children could work and restricted women to a twelve-hour workday. It was not until 1847 that the working hours for women and youth (and therefore, necessarily, for the men who relied on their assistance as well) were reduced to ten.

23. Engels refers to the practice by working mothers of hiring wet-nurses who were typically underprivileged and often undernourished women themselves.

24. Engels's note: "Report of Factories' Inquiry Commission. Testimony of Dr Hawkins, p. 3." Francis Hawkins (1796–1894) was a physician and journalist.

burning, 56 from drowning, 23 from falling, 77 from other causes, or a total of 225[25] deaths from accidents, while in non-manufacturing Liverpool during twelve months there were but 146 fatal accidents. The mining accidents are excluded in both cases; and since the Coroner of Manchester has no authority in Salford, the population of both places mentioned in the comparison is about the same. The *Manchester Guardian* reports one or more deaths by burning in almost every number. That the general mortality among young children must be increased by the employment of the mothers is self-evident, and is placed beyond all doubt by notorious facts. Women often return to the mill three or four days after confinement, leaving the baby, of course; in the dinner-hour they must hurry home to feed the child and eat something, and what sort of suckling that can be is also evident. Lord Ashley repeats the testimony of several workwomen:

> "M. H., twenty years old, has two children, the youngest a baby, that is tended by the other, a little older. The mother goes to the mill shortly after five o'clock in the morning, and comes home at eight at night; all day the milk pours from her breasts, so that her clothing drips with it." "H. W. has three children, goes away Monday morning at five o'clock, and comes back Saturday evening; has so much to do for the children then that she cannot get to bed before three o'clock in the morning; often wet through to the skin, and obliged to work in that state." She said: "My breasts have given me the most frightful pain, and I have been dripping wet with milk."

The use of narcotics to keep the children still is fostered by this infamous system, and has reached a great extent in the factory districts. Dr Johns, Registrar-in-Chief for Manchester, is of opinion that this custom is the chief source of the many deaths from convulsions.[26] The employment of the wife dissolves the family utterly and of necessity, and this dissolution, in our present society, which is based upon the family, brings the most demoralizing consequences for parents as well as children. A mother who has no time to trouble herself about her child, to perform the most ordinary loving services for it during its first year, who scarcely indeed sees it, can be no real mother to the child, must inevitably grow indifferent to it, treat it unlovingly like a stranger. The children who grow up under such conditions are utterly ruined for later family life, can never feel at home in the family which they themselves found, because they have always been accustomed to isolation, and they contribute therefore to the already general undermining of the family in the working class. A similar dissolution of the family is brought about by the employment of the children. When they get on far enough to earn more than they cost their parents from week to week, they begin to pay the parents a fixed sum for board and lodging, and keep the rest for themselves. This often happens

---

25. Engels's note: "In 1842, among the accidents brought to the Infirmary in Manchester, 189 were from burning."

26. Dr. William Johns, a physician, published "Report upon the working of the Registration and Marriage Acts during the two years 1837–38 and 1838–39 in the registration district of Manchester" in the *Journal of the Statistical Society of London* 3 (1840): 191–205. The practice of giving fretful children narcotics (often opium) to quiet them was quite widespread.

from the fourteenth or fifteenth year.[27] In a word, the children emancipate them-selves, and regard the paternal dwelling as a lodging-house, which they often exchange for another, as suits them.

In many cases the family is not wholly dissolved by the employment of the wife, but turned upside down. The wife supports the family, the husband sits at home, tends the children, sweeps the room and cooks. This case happens very frequently; in Manchester alone, many hundred such men could be cited, condemned to domestic occupations. It is easy to imagine the wrath aroused among the working men by this reversal of all relations within the family, while the other social condi-tions remain unchanged. There lies before me a letter from an English working man, Robert Pounder, Baron's Buildings, Woodhouse, Moorside, in Leeds (the bourgeoisie may hunt him up there; I give the exact address for the purpose), writ-ten by him to Oastler.[28]

He relates how another working man, being on tramp, came to St Helens, in Lancashire, and there looked up an old friend.

> He found him in a miserable, damp cellar, scarcely furnished; and when my poor friend went in, there sat poor Jack near the fire, and what did he, think you? why he sat and mended his wife's stockings with the bodkin; and as soon as he saw his old friend at the doorpost, he tried to hide them. But Joe, that is my friend's name, had seen it, and said: "Jack, what the devil art thou doing? Where is the missus? Why, is that thy work?" and poor Jack was ashamed, and said: "No, I know this is not my work, but my poor missus is i' th' factory; she has to leave at half-past five and works till eight at night, and then she is so knocked up that she cannot do aught when she gets home, so I have to do everything for her what I can, for I have no work, nor had any for more nor three years, and I shall never have any more work while I live"; and then he wept a big tear. Jack again said: "There is work enough for women folks and childer hereabouts, but none for men; thou mayest sooner find a hundred pound on the road than work for men—but I should never have believed that either thou or any one else would have seen me mending my wife's stockings, for it is bad work. But she can hardly stand on her feet; I am afraid she will be laid up, and then I don't know what is to become of us, for it's a good bit that she has been the man in the house and I the woman; it is bad work, Joe"; and he cried bitterly, and said, "It has not been always so." "No," said Joe; "but when thou hadn't no work, how hast thou not shifted?" "I'll tell thee, Joe, as well as I can, but it was bad enough; thou knowest when I got married I had work plenty, and thou knows I was not lazy." "No, that thou wert not." "And we had a good furnished house, and Mary need not go to work. I could work for the two of us; but now the world is upside down. Mary has to work and I have to stop at home, mind the childer, sweep and wash, bake and mend;

27. Engels's note: "Factories' Inquiry Commission's Report, Power's Report on Leeds, *passim;* Tufnell Report on Manchester, p. 17, etc." Edward C. Tufnell was a member of the Commission.

28. "This letter is re-translated from the German, no attempt being made to reproduce either the spelling or the original Yorkshire dialect." Richard Oastler (1789–1861) was a political activist. See his "Slavery in Yorkshire" earlier in this section. The letter to which Engels refers originally appeared in Oastler's *The Fleet Papers* 4 (August 31, 1844): 486–88. Oastler was imprisoned in the Fleet Debtors' Prison from 1841 to 1843; from there he produced weekly pamphlets written as letters to Thomas Thornhill, his former employer.

and, when the poor woman comes home at night, she is knocked up. Thou knows, Joe, it's hard for one that was used different." "Yes, boy, it is hard." And then Jack began to cry again, and he wished he had never married, and that he had never been born; but he had never thought, when he wed Mary, that it would come to this. "I have often cried over it," said Jack. Now when Joe heard this, he told me that he had cursed and damned the factories, and the masters, and the Government, with all the curses that he had learned while he was in the factory from a child.

Can any one imagine a more insane state of things than that described in this letter? And yet this condition, which unsexes the man and takes from the woman all womanliness without being able to bestow upon the man true womanliness, or the woman true manliness—this condition which degrades, in the most shameful way, both sexes, and, through them, Humanity, is the last result of our much-praised civilization, the final achievement of all the efforts and struggles of hundreds of generations to improve their own situation and that of their posterity. We must either despair of mankind, and its aims and efforts, when we see all our labour and toil result in such a mockery, or we must admit that human society has hitherto sought salvation in a false direction; we must admit that so total a reversal of the position of the sexes can have come to pass only because the sexes have been placed in a false position from the beginning. If the reign of the wife over the husband, as inevitably brought about by the factory system, is inhuman, the pristine rule of the husband over the wife must have been inhuman too. If the wife can now base her supremacy upon the fact that she supplies the greater part, nay, the whole of the common possession, the necessary inference is that this community of possession is no true and rational one, since one member of the family boasts offensively of contributing the greater share. If the family of our present society is being thus dissolved, this dissolution merely shows that, at bottom, the binding tie of this family was not family affection, but private interest lurking under the cloak of a pretended community of possessions. The same relation exists on the part of those children who support unemployed parents[29] when they do not directly pay board as already referred to. Dr Hawkins testified in the Factories' Inquiry Commission's Report that this relation is common enough, and in Manchester it is notorious. In this case the children are the masters in the house, as the wife was in the former case, and Lord Ashley gives an example of this in his speech:[30] A man berated his two daughters for going to the public house, and they answered that they were tired of being ordered about, saying, "Damn you, we have to keep you!" Determined to keep the proceeds of their work for themselves, they left the family dwelling, and abandoned their parents to their fate.

The unmarried women, who have grown up in mills, are no better off than the married ones. It is self-evident that a girl who has worked in a mill from her ninth

29. Engels's note: "How numerous married women are in the factories is seen from information furnished by a manufacturer: In 412 factories in Lancashire, 10,721 of them were employed; of the husbands of these women, but 5,314 were also employed in the factories, 3,927 were otherwise employed, 821 were unemployed, and information was wanting as to 659; or two, if not three men for each factory, are supported by the work of their wives."

30. Engels's note: "House of Commons, 15th Mar. 1844."

year is in no position to understand domestic work, whence it follows that female operatives prove wholly inexperienced and unfit as housekeepers. They cannot knit or sew, cook or wash, are unacquainted with the most ordinary duties of a housekeeper, and when they have young children to take care of, have not the vaguest idea how to set about it. The Factories' Inquiry Commission's Report gives dozens of examples of this, and Dr Hawkins, Commissioner for Lancashire, expresses his opinion as follows:[31]

> The girls marry early and recklessly; they have neither means, time, nor opportunity to learn the ordinary duties of household life; but if they had them all, they would find no time in married life for the performance of these duties. The mother is more than twelve hours away from her child daily; the baby is cared for by a young girl or an old woman, to whom it is given to nurse. Besides this, the dwelling of the mill-hands is too often no home but a cellar, which contains no cooking or washing utensils, no sewing or mending materials, nothing which makes life agreeable and civilised, or the domestic hearth attractive. For these and other reasons, and especially for the sake of the better chances of life for the little children, I can but wish and hope that a time may come in which married women will be shut out of the factories.[32]

But that is the least of the evil. The moral consequences of the employment of women in factories are even worse. The collecting of persons of both sexes and all ages in a single workroom, the inevitable contact, the crowding into a small space of people, to whom neither mental nor moral education has been given, is not calculated for the favourable development of the female character. The manufacturer, if he pays any attention to the matter, can interfere only when something scandalous actually happens; the permanent, less conspicuous influence of persons of dissolute character, upon the more moral, and especially upon the younger ones, he cannot ascertain, and consequently cannot prevent. But precisely this influence is the most injurious. The language used in the mills is characterized by many witnesses in the report of 1833, as "indecent," "bad," "filthy," etc.[33] It is the same process upon a small scale which we have already witnessed upon a large one in the great cities. The centralization of population has the same influence upon the same persons, whether it affects them in a great city or a small factory. The smaller the mill the closer the packing, and the more unavoidable the contact; and the consequences are not wanting. A witness in Leicester said that he would rather let his daughter beg than go into a factory; that they are perfect gates of hell; that most of the prostitutes of the town had their employment in the mills to thank for their present situation.[34] Another, in Manchester, "did not hesitate to assert that three-fourths of the young factory employees, from fourteen to twenty years of

31. Engels's note: "Factories' Inquiry Commission's Report, p. 4."
32. Engels's note: "For further examples and information compare Factories' Inquiry Commission's Report, Cowell Evidence, pp. 37, 38, 39, 72, 77, 82; Tufnell Evidence, pp. 9, 15, 45, 54, etc." John Cowell was a member of the Commission.
33. Engels's note: "Cowell Evidence, pp. 35, 37, and elsewhere."
34. Engels's note: "Power Evidence, p. 8." A. Power was a member of the Commission.

age, were unchaste."[35] Commissioner Cowell expresses it as his opinion, that the morality of the factory operatives is somewhat below the average of that of the working class in general.[36] And Dr Hawkins says:[37]

> An estimate of sexual morality cannot readily be reduced to figures; but if I may trust my own observations and the general opinion of those with whom I have spoken, as well as the whole tenor of the testimony furnished me, the aspect of the influence of factory life upon the morality of the youthful female population is most depressing.

It is, besides, a matter of course that factory servitude, like any other, and to an even higher degree, confers the *jus primae noctis*[38] upon the master. In this respect also the employer is sovereign over the persons and charms of his employees. The threat of discharge suffices to overcome all resistance in nine cases out of ten, if not in ninety-nine out of a hundred, in girls who, in any case, have no strong inducements to chastity. If the master is mean enough, and the official report mentions several such cases, his mill is also his harem; and the fact that not all manufacturers use their power, does not in the least change the position of the girls. In the beginning of manufacturing industry, when most of the employers were upstarts without education or consideration for the hypocrisy of society, they let nothing interfere with the exercise of their vested rights.

To form a correct judgement of the influence of factory-work upon the health of the female sex, it is necessary first to consider the work of children, and then the nature of the work itself. From the beginning of manufacturing industry, children have been employed in mills, at first almost exclusively by reason of the smallness of the machines, which were later enlarged. Even children from the workhouses were employed in multitudes, being rented out for a number of years to the manufacturers as apprentices. They were lodged, fed, and clothed in common, and were, of course, completely the slaves of their masters, by whom they were treated with the utmost recklessness and barbarity. As early as 1796, the public objection to this revolting system found such vigorous expression through Dr Percival and Sir Robert Peel (father of the Cabinet Minister, and himself a cotton manufacturer), that in 1802 Parliament passed an Apprentices' Bill, by which the most crying evils were removed.[39] Gradually the increasing competition of free work-people crowded out the whole apprentice system; factories were built in cities, machinery was constructed on a larger scale, and workrooms were made more airy and wholesome; gradually, too, more work was found for adults and young

35. Engels's note: "Cowell Evidence, p. 57."
36. Engels's note: "Ibid 82."
37. Engels's note: "Factories' Inquiry Commission's Report, p. 4, Hawkins."
38. Literally, "right of the first night." A reference to the right of a medieval lord to sleep with his vassal's bride on the wedding night.
39. Tory statesman Sir Robert Peel (1750–1830), supported by physician Thomas Percival (1740–1804), introduced the first factory legislation, the Health and Morals of Apprentices Act, to Parliament in 1802. The bill applied to pauper children apprenticed under provisions of the Poor Law and limited their work to twelve hours a day, required that they be educated, and controlled their working conditions.

persons. The number of children in the mills diminished somewhat, and the age at which they began to work rose a little; few children under 8 or 9 years were now employed. Later, as we shall see, the power of the State intervened several times to protect them from the money-greed of the bourgeoisie.

The great mortality among children of the working class, and especially among those of the factory operatives, is proof enough of the unwholesome conditions under which they pass their first years. These influences are at work, of course, among the children who survive, but not quite so powerfully as upon those who succumb. The result in the most favourable case is a tendency to disease, or some check in development, and consequent less than normal vigour of the constitution. A 9-year-old child of a factory operative that has grown up in want, privation, and changing conditions, in cold and damp, with insufficient clothing and unwholesome dwellings, is far from having the working force of a child brought up under healthier conditions. At 9 years of age it is sent into the mill to work 6½ hours (formerly 8, earlier still, 12 to 14, even 16 hours) daily, until the thirteenth year; then twelve hours until the eighteenth year. The old enfeebling influences continue, while the work is added to them. It is not to be denied that a child of 9 years, even an operative's child, can hold out through 6½ hours' daily work, without anyone being able to trace visible bad results in its development directly to this cause; but in no case can its presence in the damp, heavy air of the factory, often at once warm and wet, contribute to good health; and, in any case, it is unpardonable to sacrifice to the greed of an unfeeling bourgeoisie the time of children which should be devoted solely to their physical and mental development, withdraw them from school and the fresh air, in order to wear them out for the benefit of the manufacturers. The bourgeoisie says: "If we do not employ the children in the mills, they only remain under conditions unfavourable to their development"; and this is true on the whole.[40] But what does this mean if it is not a confession that the bourgeoisie first places the children of the working class under unfavourable conditions, and then exploits these bad conditions for its own benefit, appeals to that which is as much its own fault as the factory system, excuses the sin of today with the sin of yesterday? And if the Factory Act did not in some measure fetter their hands, how this "humane," this "benevolent" bourgeoisie, which has built its factories solely for the good of the working class, would take care of the interests of these workers! Let us hear how they acted before the factory inspector was at their heels. Their own admitted testimony shall convict them in the report of the Factories' Inquiry Commission of 1833.

The report of the Central Commission relates that the manufacturers began to employ children rarely of 5 years, often of 6, very often of 7, usually of 8 to 9 years; that the working day often lasted fourteen to sixteen hours, exclusive of meals and intervals; that the manufacturers permitted overlookers to flog and maltreat children, and often took an active part in so doing themselves. One case is related of a

---

40. W. Cooke Taylor presents this argument in *Factories and the Factory System from Parliamentary Documents and Personal Examination* (1844). See "Infant Labour" in part 2.

Scots manufacturer, who rode after a 16-year-old runaway, forced him to return, running after the employer as fast as the master's horse trotted, and beat him the whole way with a long whip.[41] In the large towns where the operatives resisted more vigorously, such things naturally happened less often. But even this long working day failed to satisfy the greed of the capitalists. Their aim was to make the capital invested in the building and machinery produce the highest return, by every available means, to make it work as actively as possible. Hence the manufacturers introduced the shameful system of night-work. Some of them employed two sets of operatives, each numerous enough to fill the whole mill, and let one set work the twelve hours of the day, and the other the twelve hours of the night. It is needless to picture the effect upon the frames of young children, and even upon the health of young persons and adults, produced by permanent loss of sleep at night, which cannot be made good by any amount of sleep during the day. Irritation of the whole nervous system, with general lassitude and enfeeblement of the entire frame, were the inevitable results, with the fostering of temptation to drunkenness and unbridled sexual indulgence. One manufacturer testifies[42] that during the two years in which night-work was carried on in his factory, the number of illegitimate children born was doubled, and such general demoralization prevailed that he was obliged to give up night-work. Other manufacturers were yet more barbarous, requiring many hands to work thirty to forty hours at a stretch, several times a week, letting them get a couple of hours sleep only, because the night-shift was not complete, but calculated to replace a part of the operatives only.

The reports of the Commission touching this barbarism surpass everything that is known to me in this line. Such infamies, as are here related, are nowhere else to be found—yet we shall see that the bourgeoisie constantly appeals to the testimony of the Commission as being in its own favour. The consequences of these cruelties became evident quickly enough. The Commissioners mention a crowd of cripples who appeared before them, who clearly owed their distortion to the long working hours. This distortion usually consists of a curving of the spinal column and legs, and is described as follows by Francis Sharp, MRCS, of Leeds:[43]

> I never saw the peculiar bending of the lower ends of the thigh bones before I came to Leeds. At first I thought it was rachitis,[44] but I was soon led to change my opinion in consequence of the mass of patients who presented themselves at the hospital, and the appearances of the disease at an age (from eight to fourteen) in which children are usually not subject to rachitis, as well as by the circumstance that the malady had first appeared after children began to work in the mills. Thus far I have seen about a hundred such cases, and can, most decidedly, express the opinion that

41. Engels's note: "Stuart Evidence, p. 35." Evidence submitted by James Stuart (1775–1849), a physician and author. The worker was a twenty-two-year-old named John Ross who related an incident that had happened to him "some years" before.

42. Engels's note: "Tufnell Evidence, p. 91." Evidence given by Aaron Lees about a factory owned by his father at the turn of the century.

43. Engels's note: "Dr Loudon Evidence, pp. 12, 13." Charles Loudon (1801–1844) was a physician. The evidence was taken from another physician, Francis Sharp.

44. Inflammation of the spine.

they are the consequences of overwork. So far as I know they were all mill children, and themselves attributed the evil to this cause. The number of cases of curvature of the spine which have fallen under my observation, and which were evidently consequent upon too protracted standing, was not less than three hundred.

Precisely similar is the testimony of Dr Hey, for eighteen years physician in the hospital in Leeds:[45]

Malformations of the spine are very frequent among mill-hands; some of them consequent upon mere overwork, others the effect of long work upon constitutions originally feeble, or weakened by bad food. Deformities seem even more frequent than these diseases; the knees were bent inward, the ligaments very often relaxed and enfeebled, and the long bones of the legs bent. The thick ends of these long bones were especially apt to be bent and disproportionately developed, and these patients came from the factories in which long work-hours were of frequent occurrence.

Surgeons Beaumont[46] and Sharp, of Bradford, bear the same testimony. The reports of Drinkwater, Power, and Dr Loudon contain a multitude of examples of such distortions, and those of Tufnell and Sir David Barry,[47] which are less directed to this point, give single examples.[48] The Commissioners for Lancashire, Cowell, Tufnell, and Hawkins, have almost wholly neglected this aspect of the physiological results of the factory system, though this district rivals Yorkshire in the number of cripples. I have seldom traversed Manchester without meeting three or four of them, suffering from precisely the same distortions of the spinal columns and legs as that described, and I have often been able to observe them closely. I know one personally who corresponds exactly with the foregoing description of Dr Hey, and who got into this condition in Mr Douglas's factory in Pendleton, an establishment which enjoys an unenviable notoriety among the operatives by reason of the former long working periods continued night after night. It is evident, at a glance, whence the distortions of these cripples come, they all look exactly alike. The knees are bent inward and backwards, the ankles deformed and thick, and the spinal column often bent forwards or to one side. But the crown belongs to the philanthropic manufacturers of the Macclesfield silk district. They employed the youngest children of all, even from 5 to 6 years of age. In the supplementary testimony of Commissioner Tufnell, I find the statement of a certain factory manager Wright,[49] both of whose sisters were most shamefully crippled, and who had once counted the cripples in several streets, some of them the cleanest and neatest streets of Macclesfield. He found in Townley Street ten, George Street five, Charlotte Street

45. Engels's note: "Dr Loudon Evidence, p. 16." Evidence taken from another medical man, William Hey (1772–1844), surgeon to the Leeds Infirmary.

46. Thomas Beaumont, surgeon.

47. Sir David Barry (1780–1835) was a physiologist.

48. Engel's note: "Drinkwater Evidence, pp. 72, 80, 146, 148, 150 (two brothers); 69 (two brothers); 155, and many others. [From John Drinkwater, a Commission member.] Power Evidence, pp. 63, 66, 67 (two cases); 68 (three cases); 69 (two cases); in Leeds, pp. 29, 31, 40, 43, 53 ff. Loudon Evidence, pp. 4, 7 (four cases); 8 (several cases), etc. Sir D. Barry Evidence, pp. 6, 8, 13, 21, 22, 44, 55 (three cases), etc. Tufnell Evidence, pp. 5, 6, 16, etc."

49. John Wright, manager of the silk factory of Brinsley and Shatwell, Macclesfield.

four, Watercots fifteen, Bank Top three, Lord Street seven, Mill Lane twelve, Great George Street two, in the workhouse two, Park Green one, Peckford Street two, whose families all unanimously declared that the cripples had become such in consequence of overwork in the silk-twisting mills. One boy is mentioned so crippled as not to be able to go upstairs, and girls deformed in back and hips.

Other deformities also have proceeded from this overwork, especially flattening of the foot, which Sir D. Barry[50] frequently observed, as did the physicians and surgeons in Leeds.[51] In cases, in which a stronger constitution, better food, and other more favourable circumstances enabled the young operative to resist this effect of a barbarous exploitation, we find, at least, pain in the back, hips, and legs, swollen joints, varicose veins, and large, persistent ulcers in the thighs and calves. These affections are almost universal among the operatives. The reports of Stuart, Mackintosh,[52] and Sir D. Barry contain hundreds of examples; indeed, they know almost no operative who did not suffer from some of these affections; and in the remaining reports, the occurrence of the same phenomena is attested by many physicians. The reports covering Scotland place it beyond all doubt, that a working day of thirteen hours, even for men and women from 18 to 22 years of age, produces at least these consequences, both in the flax-spinning mills of Dundee and Dunfermline, and in the cotton mills of Glasgow and Lanark.

All these affections are easily explained by the nature of factory-work, which is, as the manufacturers say, very "light," and precisely by reason of its lightness, more enervating than any other. The operatives have little to do, but must stand the whole time. Any one who sits down, say upon a window-ledge or a basket, is fined, and this perpetual upright position, this constant mechanical pressure of the upper portions of the body upon spinal column, hips, and legs, inevitably produces the results mentioned. This standing is not required by the work itself, and at Nottingham chairs have been introduced, with the result that these affections disappeared, and the operatives ceased to object to the length of the working day. But in a factory where the operative works solely for the bourgeois, and has small interest in doing his work well, he would probably use the seats more than would be agreeable and profitable to the manufacturer; and in order that somewhat less raw material may be spoiled for the bourgeois, the operative must sacrifice health and strength.[53] This long protracted upright position, with the bad atmosphere prevalent in the mills, entails, besides the deformities mentioned, a marked relaxation of all vital energies, and, in consequence, all sorts of other affections general rather than local. The atmosphere of the factories is, as a rule, at once damp and warm, unusually warmer than is necessary, and, when the ventilation is not *very* good, impure, heavy, deficient in oxygen, filled with dust and the smell of the machine oil, which almost everywhere smears the floor, sinks into it, and becomes

50. Engels's note: "Factories' Inquiry Commission's Report, 1833, Sir D. Barry Evidence, p. 21 (two cases)."

51. Engels's note: "Factories' Inquiry Commission's Report, 1833, Loudon Evidence, pp. 13, 16, etc."

52. Robert Mackintosh was a member of the Commission.

53. Engels's note: "In the spinning-room of a mill at Leeds, too, chairs had been introduced. Drinkwater Evidence, p. 85."

rancid. The operatives are lightly clad by reason of the warmth, and would readily take cold in case of irregularity of the temperature; a draught is distasteful to them, the general enervation which gradually takes possession of all the physical functions diminishes the animal warmth: this must be replaced from without, and nothing is therefore more agreeable to the operative than to have all the doors and windows closed, and to stay in his warm factory-air. Then comes the sudden change of temperature on going out into the cold and wet or frosty atmosphere, without the means of protection from the rain, or of changing wet clothing for dry, a circumstance which perpetually produces colds. And when one reflects that, with all this, not one single muscle of the body is really exercised, really called into activity, except perhaps those of the legs; that nothing whatsoever counteracts the enervating, relaxing tendency of all these conditions; that every influence is wanting which might give the muscles strength, the fibres elasticity and consistency; that from youth up, the operative is deprived of all fresh air recreation, it is impossible to wonder at the almost unanimous testimony of the physicians in the Factories' Report, that they find a great lack of ability to resist disease, a general depression in vital activity, a constant relaxation of the mental and physical powers. Let us hear Sir D. Barry first:[54]

> The unfavourable influences of mill-work upon the hands are the following: (1) The inevitable necessity of forcing their mental and bodily effort to keep pace with a machine moved by a uniform and unceasing motive power. (2) Continuance in an upright position during unnaturally long and quickly recurring periods. (3) Loss of sleep in consequence of too long working-hours, pain in the legs, and general physical derangement. To these are often added low, crowded, dusty, or damp workrooms, impure air, a high temperature, and constant perspiration. Hence the boys especially very soon and with but few exceptions, lose the rosy freshness of childhood, and become paler and thinner than other boys. Even the hand-weaver's bound boy, who sits before his loom with his bare feet resting upon the clay-floor, retains a fresher appearance, because he occasionally goes into the fresh air for a time. But the mill child has not a moment free except for meals, and never goes into the fresh air except on its way to them. All adult male spinners are pale and thin, suffer from capricious appetite and indigestion; and as they are all trained in the mills from their youth up, and there are very few tall, athletic men among them, the conclusion is justified that their occupation is very unfavourable for the development of the male constitution; females bear this work far better. [Very naturally. But we shall see that they have their own diseases.]

So, too, Power:[55]

> I can bear witness that the factory system in Bradford has engendered a multitude of cripples, and that the effect of long continued labour upon the physique is apparent not alone in actual deformity, but also, and much more generally, in stunted growth, relaxation of the muscles, and delicacy of whole frame.

54. Engels's note: "General report by Sir D. Barry."
55. Engels's note: "Power Report, p. 74."

So, too, F. Sharp, in Leeds, the surgeon already quoted:[56]

When I moved from Scarborough to Leeds, I was at once struck by the fact that the general appearance of the children was much paler, and their fibre less vigorous here than in Scarborough and its environs. I saw, too, that many children were exceptionally small for their age. I have met with numberless cases of scrofula,[57] lung trouble, mesenteric affections,[58] and indigestion, concerning which I, as a medical man, have no doubt that they arose from mill-work. I believe that the nervous energy of the body is weakened by the long hours, and the foundation of many diseases laid. If people from the country were not constantly coming in, the race of mill-hands would soon be wholly degenerate.

So, too, Beaumont, surgeon in Bradford:

To my thinking, the system, according to which work is done in the mills here, produces a peculiar relaxation of the whole organism, and thereby makes children in the highest degree susceptible to epidemic, as well as to incidental illness. I regard the absence of all appropriate regulations for ventilation and cleanliness in the mills very decidedly as the chief cause of that peculiar tendency or susceptibility to morbid affections which I have so frequently met in my practice.

Similar testimony is borne by Dr Kay:[59]

(1) I have had opportunity of observing the effects of the factory system upon the health of children under the most favourable circumstances [in Wood's mill, in Bradford, the best arranged of the district, in which he was factory surgeon]. (2) These effects are decidedly, and to a very great extent, injurious, even under these most favourable circumstances. (3) In the year 1842, three-fifths of all the children employed in Wood's mill were treated by me. (4) The worst effect is not the predominance of deformities, but of enfeebled and morbid constitutions. (5) All this is greatly improved since the working-hours of children have been reduced at Wood's to ten.

The Commissioner, Dr Loudon himself, who cites these witnesses, says:

In conclusion, I think it has been clearly proved that children have been worked a most unreasonable and cruel length of time daily, and that even adults have been expected to do a certain quantity of labour which scarcely any human being is able to endure. The consequence is that many have died prematurely, and others are afflicted for life with defective constitutions, and the fear of a posterity enfeebled by the shattered constitution of the survivors is but too well founded, from a physiological point of view.

56. Engels's note: "The surgeons in England are scientifically educated as well as the physicians, and have, in general, medical as well as surgical practice. They are, in general, for various reasons, preferred to the physicians."

57. A constitutional condition characterized by a predisposition to tuberculosis.

58. Pertaining to the mesentery, any of several folds of membrane that connect the intestines to the abdominal wall.

59. Physician Sir James Kay (1804–1877).

And, finally, Dr Hawkins, in speaking of Manchester:

I believe that most travellers are struck by the lowness of stature, the leanness and the paleness which present themselves so commonly to the eye at Manchester, and above all, among the factory classes. I have never been in any town in Great Britain, nor in Europe, in which degeneracy of form and colour from the national standard has been so obvious. Among the married women all the characteristic peculiarities of the English wife are conspicuously wanting. I must confess that all the boys and girls brought before me from the Manchester mills had a depressed appearance, and were very pale. In the expression of their faces lay nothing of the usual mobility, liveliness, and cheeriness of youth. Many of them told me that they felt not the slightest inclination to play out of doors on Saturday and Sunday, but preferred to be quiet at home.

I add, at once, another passage of Hawkins's report, which only half belongs here, but may be quoted here as well as anywhere else:

Intemperance, excess, and want of providence are the chief faults of the factory population, and these evils may be readily traced to the habits which are formed under the present system, and almost inevitably arise from it. It is universally admitted that indigestion, hypochondria, and general debility affect this class to a very great extent. After twelve hours of monotonous toil, it is but natural to look about for a stimulant of one sort or another; but when the above-mentioned diseased conditions are added to the customary weariness, people will quickly and repeatedly take refuge in spirituous liquors.

For all this testimony of the physicians and commissioners, the report itself offers hundreds of cases of proof. That the growth of young operatives is stunted, by their work, hundreds of statements testify; among others, Cowell gives the weight of 46 youths of 17 years of age, from one Sunday school,[60] of whom 26 employed in mills, averaged 104.5 pounds, and 20 not employed in mills, 117.7 pounds. One of the largest manufacturers of Manchester, leader of the opposition against the working men, I think Robert Hyde Greg[61] himself, said, on one occasion, that if things went on as at present, the operatives of Lancashire would soon be a race of pigmies.[62] A recruiting officer[63] testified that operatives are little adapted for military service, looked thin and nervous, and were frequently rejected by the surgeons as unfit. In Manchester he could hardly get men of 5 feet 8 inches; they were usually only 5 feet 6 to 7, whereas in the agricultural districts, most of the recruits were 5 feet 8.

The men wear out very early in consequence of the conditions under which they live and work. Most of them are unfit for work at 40 years, a few hold out to

60. The Sunday School movement was inaugurated in the late eighteenth century as part of the Evangelical movement. The aim was to teach working class children Christian precepts and basic reading skills.
61. Robert Hyde Greg (1795–1875).
62. Engels's note: "This statement is not taken from the report."
63. Engels's note: "Tufnell, p. 59."

45, almost none to 50 years of age. This is caused not only by the general enfeeblement of the frame, but also very often by a failure of the sight, which is a result of mule-spinning, in which the operative is obliged to fix his gaze upon a long row of fine, parallel threads, and so greatly to strain the sight.

Of 1,600 operatives employed in several factories in Harpur and Lanark, but ten were over 45 years of age; of 22,094 operatives in diverse factories in Stockport and Manchester, but 143 were over 45 years old. Of these 143, sixteen were retained as a special favour, and one was doing the work of a child. A list of 131 spinners contained but seven over 45 years, and yet the whole 131 were rejected by the manufacturers, to whom they applied for work, as "too old." Of fifty worked-out spinners in Bolton only two were over 50 and the rest did not yet average 40 and all were without means of support by reason of old age! Mr Ashworth,[64] a large manufacturer, admits in a letter to Lord Ashley, that, towards the fortieth year, the spinners can no longer prepare the required quantity of yarn, and are therefore "sometimes" discharged; he calls operatives 40 years of age "old people"![65] Commissioner Mackintosh expresses himself in the same way in the report of 1833: "Although I was prepared for it from the way the children are employed, I still found it difficult to believe the statements of the older hands as to their ages; they age so very early."

Surgeon Smellie of Glasgow, who treated operatives chiefly, says that 40 years is old age for them.[66] And similar evidence may be found elsewhere.[67] In Manchester, this premature old age among the operatives is so universal that almost every man of 40 would be taken for ten to fifteen years older, while the prosperous classes, men as well as women, preserve their appearance exceedingly well if they do not drink too heavily.

The influence of factory-work upon the female physique also is marked and peculiar. The deformities entailed by long hours of work are much more serious among women. Protracted work frequently causes deformities of the pelvis, partly in the shape of abnormal position and development of the hip bones, partly of malformation of the lower portion of the spinal column. "Although," says Dr Loudon, in his report, "no example of malformation of the pelvis and of some other affections came under my notice, these things are nevertheless so common, that every physician must regard them as probable consequences of such working-hours, and as vouched for besides by men of the highest medical credibility."

That factory operatives undergo more difficult confinement than other women is testified to by several midwives and accoucheurs,[68] and also that they are more liable to miscarriage.[69] Moreover, they suffer from the general enfeeblement common

---

64. Edmund Ashworth (1801–1881).

65. Engels's note: "All taken from Lord Ashley's speech (sitting of Lower House, 15 Mar. 1844). *(Note in the German edition.)*"

66. Engels's note: "Stuart Evidence, p. 101." Taken from James Smellie.

67. Engels's note: "Tufnell Evidence, pp. 3, 9, 15; Hawkins Report, p. 4; Evidence, p. 11 etc., etc."

68. People who assist during childbirth.

69. Engels's note: "Hawkins Evidence, pp. 11, 13."

to all operatives, and, when pregnant, continue to work in the factory up to the hour of delivery, because otherwise they lose their wages and are made to fear that they may be replaced if they stop away too soon. It frequently happens that women are at work one evening and delivered the next morning, and the case is none too rare of their being delivered in the factory among the machinery. And if the gentlemen of the bourgeoisie find nothing particularly shocking in this, their wives will perhaps admit that it is a piece of cruelty, an infamous act of barbarism, indirectly to force a pregnant woman to work twelve or thirteen hours daily (formerly still longer), up to the day of her delivery, in a standing position, with frequent stoopings. But this is not all. If these women are not obliged to resume work within two weeks, they are thankful, and count themselves fortunate. Many come back to the factory after eight, and even after three to four days, to resume full work. I once heard a manufacturer ask an overlooker: "Is so and so not back yet?" "No." "How long since she was confined?" "A week." "She might surely have been back long ago. That one over there only stays three days." Naturally, fear of being discharged, dread of starvation drives her to the factory in spite of her weakness, in defiance of her pain. The interest of the manufacturer will not brook that his employees stay at home by reason of illness; they must not be ill, they must not venture to lie still through a long confinement, or he must stop his machinery or trouble his supreme head with a temporary change of arrangements; and rather than do this, he discharges his people when they begin to be ill. Listen:[70] "A girl feels very ill, can scarcely do her work. Why does she not ask permission to go home? Ah! the master is very particular, and if we are away a quarter of a day, we risk being sent away altogether." Or Sir D. Barry:[71] "Thomas McDurt, workman, has slight fever. Cannot stay at home longer four days, because he would fear of losing his place."

And so it goes on in almost all the factories. The employment of young girls produces all sorts of irregularities during the period of development. In some, especially those who are better fed, the heat of the factories hastens this process, so that in single cases, girls of 13 and 14 are wholly mature. Roberton, whom I have already cited (mentioned in the Factories' Inquiry Commission's Report as the "eminent" gynaecologist of Manchester), relates in the North of England *Medical and Surgical Journal*,[72] that he had seen a girl of 11 years who was not only a wholly developed woman, but pregnant, and that it was by no means rare in Manchester for women to be confined at 15 years of age. In such cases, the influence of the warmth of the factories is the same as that of a tropical climate, and, as in such climates, the abnormally early development revenges itself by correspondingly premature age and debility. On the other hand, retarded development of the female constitution occurs, the breasts mature late or not at all.[73] Menstruation

70. Engels's note: "Cowell Evidence, p. 77."
71. Engels's note: "Sir D. Barry Evidence, p. 44."
72. John Roberton was the author of "An Inquiry respecting the period of puberty in women," *North of England Medical and Surgical Journal* 1 (August 1830–May 1831): 69–85; 179–191.
73. Engels's note: "Cowell, p. 35."

first appears in the seventeenth or eighteenth, sometimes in the twentieth year, and is often wholly wanting.[74] Irregular menstruation, coupled with great pain and numerous affections, especially with anaemia, is very frequent, as the medical reports unanimously state.

Children of such mothers, particularly of those who are obliged to work during pregnancy, cannot be vigorous. They are, on the contrary, described in the report, especially in Manchester, as very feeble; and Barry alone asserts that they are healthy, but says further, that in Scotland, where his inspection lay, almost no married women worked in factories. Moreover, most of the factories there are in the country (with the exception of Glasgow), a circumstance which contributes greatly to the invigoration of the children. The operatives' children in the neighbourhood of Manchester are nearly all thriving and rosy, while those within the city look pale and scrofulous; but with the ninth year the colour vanishes suddenly, because all are then sent into the factories, when it soon becomes impossible to distinguish the country from the city children.

But besides all this, there are some branches of factory-work which have an especially injurious effect. In many rooms of the cotton- and flax-spinning mills, the air is filled with fibrous dust, which produces chest affections, especially among workers in the carding- and combing-rooms. Some constitutions can bear it, some cannot; but the operative has no choice. He must take the room in which he finds work, whether his chest is sound or not. The most common effects of this breathing of dust are bloodspitting, hard, noisy breathing, pains in the chest, coughs, sleeplessness—in short, all the symptoms of asthma ending in the worst cases in consumption.[75] Especially unwholesome is the wet spinning of linen-yarn which is carried on by young girls and boys. The water spirts over them from the spindle so that the front of their clothing is constantly wet through to the skin; and there is always water standing on the floor. This is the case to a less degree in the doubling-rooms[76] of the cotton mills, and the result is a constant succession of colds and affections of the chest. A hoarse, rough voice is common to all operatives, but especially to wet spinners and doublers. Stuart, Mackintosh, and Sir D. Barry express themselves in the most vigorous terms as to the unwholesomeness of this work, and the small consideration shown by most of the manufacturers for the health of the girls who do it. Another effect of flax-spinning is a peculiar deformity of the shoulder, especially a projection of the right shoulderblade, consequent upon the nature of the work. This sort of spinning and the throstle-spinning of cotton frequently produce diseases of the knee-pan, which is used to check the spindle during the joining of broken threads. The frequent stooping and the bending to the low machines common to both these branches of

74. Engels's note: "Dr Hawkins Evidence, p. 11; Dr Loudon, p. 14, etc.; Sir D. Barry, p. 5, etc."

75. Engels's note: "Compare Stuart, pp. 13, 70, 101; Mackintosh, p. 24, etc.; Power Report on Nottingham, on Leeds; Cowell, p. 33, etc.; Barry, p. 12 (five cases in one factory), pp. 17, 44, 52, 60, etc.; Loudon, p. 13."

76. Doubling is a term for the process of laying two or more filaments together and compressing them into one.

work have, in general, a stunting effect upon the growth of the operative. In the throstle-room of the cotton mill at Manchester, in which I was employed, I do not remember to have seen one single tall, well-built girl; they were all short, dumpy, and badly formed, decidedly ugly in the whole development of the figure. But apart from all these diseases and malformations, the limbs of the operatives suffer in still another way. The work between the machinery gives rise to multitudes of accidents of more or less serious nature, which have for the operative the secondary effect of unfitting him for his work more or less completely. The most common accident is the squeezing off of a single joint of a finger, somewhat less common the loss of the whole finger, half or a whole hand, an arm, etc., in the machinery. Lockjaw[77] very often follows, even upon the lesser among these injuries, and brings death with it. Besides the deformed persons, a great number of maimed ones may be seen going about in Manchester; this one has lost an arm or a part of one, that one a foot, the third half a leg; it is like living in the midst of an army just returned from a campaign. But the most dangerous portion of the machinery is the strapping which conveys motive power from the shaft to the separate machines, especially if it contains buckles which, however, are rarely used now. Whoever is seized by the strap is carried up with lightning speed, thrown against the ceiling above and floor below with such force that there is rarely a whole bone left in the body, and death follows instantly. Between 12 June and 3 August 1843, the *Manchester Guardian* reported the following serious accidents (the trifling ones it does not notice): 12 June, a boy died in Manchester of lockjaw, caused by his hand being crushed between wheels. 16 June, a youth in Saddleworth seized by a wheel and carried away with it; died, utterly mangled. 29 June, a young man at Green Acres Moor, near Manchester, at work in a machine shop, fell under the grindstone, which broke two of his ribs and lacerated him terribly. 24 July, a girl in Oldham died, carried around fifty times by a strap; no bone unbroken. 27 July, a girl in Manchester seized by the blower (the first machine that receives the raw cotton), and died of injuries received. 3 August, a bobbins turner died in Dukenfield, caught in a strap, every rib broken. In the year 1843, the Manchester Infirmary treated 962 cases of wounds and mutilations caused by machinery, while the number of all other accidents within the district of the hospital was 2,426, so that for five accidents from all other causes, two were caused by machinery. The accidents which happened in Salford are not included here, nor those treated by surgeons in private practice. In such cases, whether or not the accident unfits the victim for further work, the employer, at best, pays the doctor, or, in very exceptional cases, he may pay wages during treatment; what becomes of the operative afterwards, in case he cannot work, is no concern of the employer.

The Factory Report says on this subject, that employers must be made responsible for all cases, since children cannot take care, and adults will take care in their own interest. But the gentlemen who write the report are bourgeois, and so they must contradict themselves and bring up later all sorts of bosh on the subject of the culpable temerity of the operatives.

77. Tetanus.

The state of the case is this: If children cannot take care, the employment of children must be forbidden. If adults are reckless, they must be mere overgrown children on a plane of intelligence which does not enable them to appreciate the danger in its full scope and who is to blame for this but the bourgeoisie which keeps them in a condition in which their intelligence cannot develop? Or the machinery is ill-arranged, and must be surrounded with fencing, to supply which falls to the share of the bourgeoisie. Or the operative is under inducements which outweigh the threatened danger; he must work rapidly to earn his wage, has no time to take care, and for this, too, the bourgeoisie is to blame. Many accidents happen, for instance, while the operatives are cleaning machinery in motion. Why? Because the bourgeois would otherwise oblige the worker to clean the machinery during the free hours while it is not going, and the worker naturally is not disposed to sacrifice any part of his free time. Every free hour is so precious to the worker that he often risks his life twice a week rather than sacrifice one of them to the bourgeois. Let the employer take from working hours the time required for cleaning the machinery, and it will never again occur to an operative to clean machinery in motion. In short, from whatever point of view, the blame falls ultimately on the manufacturer, and of him should be required at the very least, lifelong support of the incapacitated operative, and support of the victim's family in case death follows the accident. In the earliest period of manufacture, the accidents were much more numerous in proportion than now, for the machinery was inferior, smaller, more crowded, and almost never fenced. But the number is still large enough, as the foregoing cases prove, to arouse the grave question as to a state of things which permits so many deformities and mutilations for the benefit of a single class, and plunges so many industrious working people into want and starvation by reason of injuries undergone in the service and through the fault of the bourgeoisie.

A pretty list of diseases engendered purely by the hateful money-greed of the manufacturers! Women made unfit for childbearing, children deformed, men enfeebled, limbs crushed, whole generations wrecked, afflicted with disease and infirmity, purely to fill the purses of the bourgeoisie. And when one reads of the barbarism of single cases, how children are seized naked in bed by the overlookers, and driven with blows and kicks to the factory, their clothing over their arms,[78] how their sleepiness is driven off with blows, how they fall asleep over their work nevertheless, how one poor child sprang up, still asleep, at the call of the overlooker, and mechanically went through the operations of its work after its machine was stopped; when one reads how children, too tired to go home, hide away in the wool in the drying-room to sleep there, and could only be driven out of the factory with straps; how many hundreds came home so tired every night, that they could eat no supper for sleepiness and want of appetite, that their parents found them kneeling by the bedside, where they had fallen asleep during their prayers; when one reads all this and a hundred other villainies and infamies in this one report, all testified to on oath, confirmed by several witnesses, deposed by men whom the

78. Engels's note: "Stuart, p. 39."

commissioners themselves declare trustworthy; when one reflects that this is a Liberal report, a bourgeois report, made for the purpose of reversing the previous Tory report, and rehabilitating the pureness of heart of the manufacturers, that the commissioners themselves are on the side of the bourgeoisie, and report all these things against their own will, how can one be otherwise than filled with wrath and resentment against a class which boasts of philanthropy and self-sacrifice, while its one object is to fill its purse *à tout prix*?[79] Meanwhile, let us listen to the bourgeoisie speaking through the mouth of its chosen apostle, Dr Ure, who relates in his *Philosophy of Manufactures*[80] that the workers have been told that their wages bore no proportion to their sacrifices, the good understanding between masters and men being thus disturbed. Instead of this, the working men should have striven to recommend themselves by attention and industry, and should have rejoiced in the prosperity of their masters. They would then become overseers, superintendents, and finally partners, and would thus—(Oh! Wisdom, thou speakest as the dove!)—"have increased at the same time the demand for their companions' labour in the market!" "Had it not been for the violent collisions and interruptions resulting from erroneous views among the operatives, the factory system would have been developed still more rapidly and beneficially."[81] Hereupon follows a long Jeremiad[82] upon the spirit of resistance of the operatives, and on the occasion of a strike of the best paid workers, the fine spinners, the following naïve observation:[83] "In fact, it was their high wages which enabled them to maintain a stipendiary committee in affluence, and to pamper themselves into nervous ailments, by a diet too rich and exciting for their indoor employments."

Let us hear how the bourgeois describes the work of children:[84]

> I have visited many factories, both in Manchester and in the surrounding districts, during a period of several months, entering the spinning-rooms unexpectedly, and often alone, at different times of the day, and I never saw a single instance of corporal chastisement inflicted on a child; nor, indeed, did I ever see children in ill-humour. They seemed to be always cheerful and alert; taking pleasure in the light play of their muscles, enjoying the mobility natural to their age. The scene of industry, so far from exciting sad emotions, in my mind, was always exhilarating. It was delightful to observe the nimbleness with which they pieced broken ends, as the mule carriage began to recede from the fixed roller beam, and to see them at leisure, after a few seconds' exercise of their tiny fingers, to amuse themselves in any attitude they chose, till the stretch and winding on were once more completed. The work of these lively elves seemed to resemble a sport, in which habit gave them a pleasing dexterity. Conscious of their skill, they were delighted to show it off to any stranger. As to exhaustion by the day's work, they evinced no trace of it on emerging from the

79. At any cost.
80. Engels's note: "Dr Andrew Ure, *Philosophy of Manufactures*, 277 ff."
81. Engels's note: "Ibid. 277."
82. A prolonged complaint, a reference to Jeremiah, a prophet of the sixth and seventh centuries B.C.E.
83. Engels's note: "Ibid. 298."
84. Engels's note: "Ibid. 301."

mill in the evening; for they immediately began to skip about any neighbouring playground, and to commence their little games with the same alacrity as boys issuing from a school.

Naturally! As though the immediate movement of every muscle were not an urgent necessity for frames grown at once stiff and relaxed! But Ure should have waited to see whether this momentary excitement had not subsided after a couple of minutes. And besides, Ure could see this whole performance only in the afternoon after five or six hours' work, but not in the evening! As to the health of the operatives, the bourgeois has the boundless impudence to cite the report of 1833 just quoted in a thousand places, as testimony for the excellent health of these people; to try to prove by detached and garbled quotations that no trace of scrofula can be found among them, and what is quite true, that the factory system frees them from all acute diseases (that they have every variety of chronic affection instead he naturally conceals). To explain the impudence with which our friend Ure palms off the grossest falsehoods upon the English public, it must be known that the report consists of three large folio volumes, which it never occurs to a well-fed English bourgeois to study through. Let us hear further how he expresses himself as to the Factory Act of 1834,[85] passed by the Liberal bourgeoisie, and imposing only the most meagre limitations upon the manufacturers, as we shall see. This law, especially its compulsory education clause, he calls an absurd and despotic measure directed against the manufacturers, through which all children under 12 years of age have been thrown out of employment; and with what results? The children thus discharged from their light and useful occupation receive no education whatsoever; cast out from the warm spinning-room into a cold world, they subsist only by begging and stealing, a life in sad contrast with their steadily improving condition in the factory and in Sunday school. Under the mask of philanthropy, this law intensifies the sufferings of the poor, and will greatly restrict the conscientious manufacturer in his useful work, if, indeed, it does not wholly stop him.[86]

The ruinous influence of the factory system began at an early day to attract general attention. We have already alluded to the Apprentices' Act of 1802. Later, towards 1817, Robert Owen,[87] then a manufacturer in New Lanark, in Scotland, afterwards founder of English Socialism, began to call the attention of the Government, by memorials and petitions, to the necessity of legislative guarantees for the health of the operatives, and especially of children. The late Sir Robert Peel and other philanthropists united with him, and gradually secured the Factory Acts of 1819, 1825,[88] and 1831, of which the first two were never enforced, and the last only

85. Incorrect date given. The Act was actually passed in 1833.
86. Engels's note: "Ure, *Philosophy of Manufactures*, 405, 406 ff."
87. The Socialist Robert Owen (1771–1858) established a model factory at New Lanark. See the entry on Owen in part 2.
88. The Factory Act of 1819 applied only to cotton mills. It prohibited the employment of children under age nine and required that those under sixteen be employed no more than twelve hours a day. An amending act was approved shortly after the passage of the 1819 Factory Act which allowed over-

here and there. This law of 1831, based upon the motion of Sir J. C. Hobhouse, provided that in cotton mills no one under 21 should be employed between half-past seven at night and half-past five in the morning; and that in all factories young persons under 18 should work no longer than twelve hours daily, and nine hours on Saturday. But since operatives could not testify against their masters without being discharged, this law helped matters very little. In the great cities, where the operatives were more restive, the larger manufacturers came to an agreement among themselves to obey the law; but even there, there were many who, like the employers in the country, did not trouble themselves about it. Meanwhile, the demand for a ten hours' law had become lively among the operatives; that is, for a law which should forbid all operatives under 18 years of age to work longer than ten hours daily; the Trade Unions, by their agitation, made this demand general throughout manufacturing population; the philanthropic section of the Tory party, then led by Michael Sadler,[89] seized upon the plan, and brought it before Parliament. Sadler obtained a parliamentary committee for the investigation of the factory system, and this committee reported in 1832. Its report was emphatically partisan, composed by strong enemies of the factory system, for party ends. Sadler permitted himself to be betrayed by his noble enthusiasm into the most distorted and erroneous statements, drew from his witnesses by the very form of his questions, answers which contained the truth, but truth in a perverted form. The manufacturers themselves, incensed at a report which represented them as monsters, now demanded an official investigation; they knew that an exact report must, in this case, be advantageous to them; they knew that Whigs, genuine bourgeois, were at the helm, with whom they were upon good terms, whose principles were opposed to any restriction upon manufacture. They obtained a commission, in due order, composed of Liberal bourgeois, whose report I have so often cited. This comes somewhat nearer the truth than Sadler's, but its deviations therefrom are in the opposite direction. On every page it betrays sympathy with the manufacturers, distrust of the Sadler report, repugnance to the working men agitating independently and the supporters of the Ten Hours Bill. It nowhere recognizes the right of the working man to a life worthy of a human being, to independent activity, and opinions of his own. It reproaches the operatives that in sustaining the Ten Hours Bill they thought, not of the children only, but of themselves as well; it calls the working men engaged in the agitation demagogues, ill-intentioned, malicious, etc., is written, in short, on the side of the bourgeoisie; and still it cannot whitewash the manufacturers, and still it leaves such a mass of infamies upon the shoulders of the employers, that even after this report, the agitation for the Ten Hours

---

time or night work in the event of an accident that resulted in lost time during the day. It also permitted employers to schedule the dinner break anytime between 11:00 and 4:00. In 1825, Sir John Cam Hobhouse (1786–1869) introduced another amending bill which resulted in only minor improvements, scheduling the dinner hour at a more reasonable time and limiting work on Saturdays to nine hours.

89. Michael Sadler (1780–1835), an economist and politician, was an impassioned advocate of work reform.

Bill, the hatred against the manufacturers, and the committee's severest epithets applied to them are all fully justified. But there was the one difference, that whereas the Sadler report accuses the manufacturers of open, undisguised brutality, it now became evident that this brutality was chiefly carried on under the mask of civilization and humanity. Yet Dr Hawkins, the medical commissioner for Lancashire, expresses himself decidedly in favour of the Ten Hours Bill in the opening lines of his report, and Commissioner Mackintosh explains that his own report does not contain the whole truth, because it is very difficult to induce the operatives to testify against their employers, and because the manufacturers, besides being forced into greater concessions towards their operatives by the excitement among the latter, are often prepared for the inspection of the factories, have them swept, the speed of the machinery reduced, etc. In Lancashire especially they resorted to the device of bringing the overlookers of workrooms before the commissioners, and letting them testify as working men to the humanity of the employers, the wholesome effects of the work, and the indifference, if not the hostility of the operatives, towards the Ten Hours Bill. But these are not genuine working men; they are deserters from their class, who have entered the service of the bourgeoisie for better pay, and fight in the interests of the capitalists against the workers. Their interest is that of the capitalists, and they are, therefore, almost more hated by the workers than the manufacturers themselves.

And yet this report suffices wholly to exhibit the most shameful recklessness of the manufacturing bourgeoisie towards its employees, the whole infamy of the industrial exploiting system in its full inhumanity. Nothing is more revolting than to compare the long register of diseases and deformities engendered by overwork, in this report, with the cold, calculating political economy of the manufacturers, by which they try to prove that they, and with them all England, must go to ruin, if they should be forbidden to cripple so and so many children every year.[90] The language of Dr Ure alone, which I have quoted, would be yet more revolting if it were not so preposterous.

The result of this report was the Factory Act of 1834, which forbade the employment of children under 9 years of age (except in silk mills), limited the working hours of children between 9 and 13 years to forty-eight per week, or nine hours in any one day at the utmost; that of young persons from 14 to 18 years of age to sixty-nine per week, or twelve on any one day as the maximum, provided for an hour and a half as the minimum interval for meals, and repeated the total prohibition of night-work for persons under 18 years of age. Compulsory school attendance two hours daily was prescribed for all children under 14 years, and the manufacturer declared punishable in case of employing children without a certificate of age from the factory surgeon, and a certificate of school attendance from the teacher. As recompense, the employer was permitted to withdraw one penny from the child's weekly earnings to pay the teacher. Further, surgeons and inspectors were appointed to visit the factories at all times, take testimony of operatives on oath, and

90. See W. Cooke Taylor, "Infant Labour" (in part 2), for this very argument.

enforce the law by prosecution before a Justice of the Peace. This is the law against which Dr Ure inveighs in such unmeasured terms!

The consequence of this law, and especially of the appointment of inspectors, was the reduction of working hours to an average of twelve to thirteen, and the superseding of children as far as possible. Hereupon some of the most crying evils disappeared almost wholly. Deformities arose now only in cases of weak constitution, and the effects of overwork became much less conspicuous. Nevertheless, enough testimony remains to be found in the Factory Report, that the lesser evils, swelling of the ankles, weakness and pain in the legs, hips, and back, varicose veins, ulcers on the lower extremities, general weakness, especially of the pelvic region, nausea, want of appetite alternating with unnatural hunger, indigestion, hypochondria, affections of the chest in consequence of the dust and foul atmosphere of the factories, etc., etc., all occur among employees subject to the provisions of Sir J. C. Hobhouse's Law (of 1831), which prescribes twelve to thirteen hours as the maximum. The reports from Glasgow and Manchester are especially worthy of attention in this respect. These evils remained too, after the law of 1834, and continue to undermine the health of the working class to this day. Care has been taken to give the brutal profit-greed of the bourgeoisie a hypocritical, civilized form, to restrain the manufacturers through the arm of the law from too conspicuous villainies, and thus to give them a pretext for self-complacently parading their sham philanthropy. That is all. If a new commission were appointed today, it would find things pretty much as before. As to the extemporized compulsory attendance at school, it remained wholly a dead letter, since the Government failed to provide good schools. The manufacturers employed as teachers worn-out operatives, to whom they sent the children two hours daily, thus complying with the letter of the law; but the children learned nothing. And even the reports of the factory inspectors, which are limited to the scope of the inspector's duties, i.e. the enforcement of the Factory Act, give data enough to justify the conclusion that the old evils inevitably remain. Inspectors Horner and Saunders,[91] in their reports for October and December 1843, state that, in a number of branches in which the employment of children can be dispensed with or superseded by that of adults, the working day is still fourteen to sixteen hours, or even longer. Among the operatives in these branches they found numbers of young people who had just outgrown the provisions of the law. Many employers disregard the law, shorten the meal times, work children longer than is permitted, and risk prosecution, knowing that the possible fines are trifling in comparison with the certain profits derivable from the offence. Just at present especially, while business is exceptionally brisk, they are under great temptation in this respect.

Meanwhile the agitation for the Ten Hours Bill by no means died out among the operatives; in 1839 it was under full headway once more, and Sadler's place, he having died, was filled in the House of Commons by Lord Ashley[92] and Richard

---

91. Leonard Horner (1785–1864) and Robert Saunders were factory inspectors.
92. Engels's note: "Afterwards Earl of Shaftesbury, died 1885."

Oastler, both Tories. Oastler especially, who carried on a constant agitation in the factory districts, and had been active in the same way during Sadler's life, was the particular favourite of the working men. They called him their "good old king," "the king of the factory children," and there is not a child in the factory districts that does not know and revere him, that does not join the procession which moves to welcome him when he enters a town. Oastler vigorously opposed the New Poor Law[93] also, and was therefore imprisoned for debt by a Mr Thornhill, on whose estate he was employed as agent, and to whom he owed money. The Whigs offered repeatedly to pay his debt and confer other favours upon him if he would only give up his agitation against the Poor Law. But in vain; he remained in prison, whence he published his Fleet Papers against the factory system and the Poor Law.

The Tory Government of 1841 turned its attention once more to the Factory Acts. The Home Secretary, Sir James Graham,[94] proposed, in 1843, a bill restricting the working hours of children to six and one-half, and making the enactments for compulsory school attendance more effective, the principal point in this connection being a provision for better schools. This bill was, however, wrecked by the jealousy of the dissenters; for, although compulsory religious instruction was not extended to the children of dissenters,[95] the schools provided for were to be placed under the general supervision of the Established Church, and the Bible made the general reading-book, religion being thus made the foundation of all instruction, whence the dissenters felt themselves threatened. The manufacturers and the Liberals generally united with them; the working men were divided by the Church question, and therefore inactive. The opponents of the bill, though outweighed in the great manufacturing towns, such as Salford and Stockport, and able in others, such as Manchester, to attack certain of its points only, for fear of the working men, collected nevertheless nearly two million signatures for a petition against it, and Graham allowed himself to be so far intimidated as to withdraw the whole bill. The next year he omitted the school clauses, and proposed that, instead of the previous provisions, children between 8 and 13 years should be restricted to six and one-half hours, and so employed as to have either the whole morning or the whole afternoon free; that young people between 13 and 18 years, and all females, should be limited to twelve hours; and that the hitherto frequent evasions of the law should be prevented. Hardly had he proposed this bill, when the ten hours' agitation was begun again more vigorously than ever. Oastler had just then regained his liberty; a number of his friends and a collection among the workers had paid his debt, and he threw himself into the movement with all his might. The defenders of the Ten Hours Bill in the House of Commons had increased in numbers, the masses of petitions supporting it which poured in from all sides brought them allies, and on 19 March 1844 Lord Ashley carried, with a majority of 179 to 170, a

---

93. The New Poor Law aimed to eliminate outdoor relief and to require all able-bodied paupers to reside and work in government-established workhouses. See note 28 for further discussion of Oastler and Thornhill.

94. Sir James Graham (1792–1861) was a Tory politician.

95. Dissenters were Protestants who had left the Anglican (or "Established") Church.

resolution that the word "Night" in the Factory Act should express the time from six at night to six in the morning, whereby the prohibition of night-work came to mean the limitation of working hours to twelve, including free hours, or ten hours of actual work a day. But the ministry did not agree to this. Sir James Graham began to threaten resignation from the Cabinet, and at the next vote on the bill the House rejected by a small majority both ten and twelve hours! Graham and Peel now announced that they should introduce a new bill, and that if this failed to pass they should resign. The new bill was exactly the old Twelve Hours Bill with some changes of form, and the same House of Commons which had rejected the principal points of this bill in March, now swallowed it whole. The reason of this was that most of the supporters of the Ten Hours Bill were Tories who let fall the bill rather than the ministry; but be the motives what they may, the House of Commons by its votes upon this subject, each vote reversing the last, has brought itself into the greatest contempt among all the workers, and proved most brilliantly the Chartists' assertion of the necessity of its reform. Three members, who had formerly voted against the ministry, afterwards voted for it and rescued it. In all the divisions, the bulk of the opposition voted *for* and the bulk of its own party *against* the ministry.[96] The foregoing propositions of Graham touching the employment of children six and one-half and of all other operatives twelve hours are now legislative provisions, and by them and by the limitation of overwork for making up time lost through breakdown of machinery or insufficient water-power by reason of frost or drought, a working day of more than twelve hours has been made well-nigh impossible. There remains, however, no doubt that, in a very short time, the Ten Hours Bill will really be adopted.[97] The manufacturers are naturally all against it; there are perhaps not ten who are for it; they have used every honourable and dishonourable means against this dreaded measure, but with no other result than that of drawing down upon them the ever-deepening hatred of the working men. The bill will pass. What the working men will do they can do, and that they will have this bill they proved last spring. The economic arguments of the manufacturers that a Ten Hours Bill would increase the cost of production and incapacitate the English producers for competition in foreign markets, and that wages must fall, are all *half* true; but they prove nothing except this, that the industrial greatness of England can be maintained only through the barbarous treatment of the operatives, the destruction of their health, the social, physical, and mental decay of whole generations. Naturally, if the Ten Hours Bill were a final measure, it must ruin England; but since it must inevitably bring with it other measures which must draw England into a path wholly different from that hitherto followed, it can only prove an advance.

96. Engels's note: "It is notorious that the House of Commons made itself ridiculous a second time in the same session in the same way on the Sugar Question [a plan to lower taxes on sugar imported from the West Indies], when it first voted against the ministry and then for it, after an application of the ministerial whip."

97. See the next selection for Thomas Babington Macaulay's 1846 speech to the House of Commons in favor of the Ten Hours Bill. The bill passed in 1847.

Let us turn to another side of the factory system which cannot be remedied by legislative provisions so easily as the diseases now engendered by it. We have already alluded in a general way to the nature of the employment, and enough in detail to be able to draw certain inferences from the facts given. The supervision of machinery, the joining of broken threads, is no activity which claims the operative's thinking powers, yet it is of a sort which prevents him from occupying his mind with other things. We have seen, too, that this work affords the muscles no opportunity for physical activity. Thus it is, properly speaking, not work, but tedium, the most deadening, wearing process conceivable. The operative is condemned to let his physical and mental powers decay in this utter monotony, it is his mission to be bored every day and all day long from his eighth year. Moreover, he must not take a moment's rest; the engine moves unceasingly; the wheels, the straps, the spindles hum and rattle in his ears without a pause, and if he tries to snatch one instant, there is the overlooker at his back with the book of fines. This condemnation to be buried alive in the mill, to give constant attention to the tireless machine is felt as the keenest torture by the operatives, and its action upon mind and body is in the long run stunting in the highest degree. There is no better means of inducing stupefaction than a period of factory-work, and if the operatives have, nevertheless, not only rescued their intelligence, but cultivated and sharpened it more than other working men, they have found this possible only in rebellion against their fate and against the bourgeoisie, the sole subject on which under all circumstances they can think and feel while at work. Or, if this indignation against the bourgeoisie does not become the supreme passion of the working man, the inevitable consequence is drunkenness and all that is generally called demoralization. The physical enervation and the sickness, universal in consequence of the factory system, were enough to induce Commissioner Hawkins to attribute this demoralization thereto as inevitable; how much more when mental lassitude is added to them, and when the influences already mentioned which tempt every working man to demoralization, make themselves felt here too! There is no cause for surprise, therefore, that in the manufacturing towns especially, drunkenness and sexual excesses have reached the pitch which I have already described.[98]

Further, the slavery in which the bourgeoisie holds the proletariat chained, is nowhere more conspicuous than in the factory system. Here ends all freedom in

---

98. Engels's note: "Let us hear another competent judge: 'If we consider the example of the Irish in connection with the ceaseless toil of the cotton operative class, we shall wonder less at their terrible demoralization. Continuous exhausting toil, day after day, year after year, is not calculated to develop the intellectual and moral capabilities of the human being. The wearisome routine of endless drudgery, in which the same mechanical process is ever repeated, is like the torture of Sisyphus; the burden of toil, like the rock, is ever falling back upon the worn-out drudge. The mind attains neither knowledge nor the power of thought from the eternal employment of the same muscles. The intellect dozes off in dull indolence, but the coarser part of our nature reaches a luxuriant development. To condemn a human being to such work is to cultivate the animal quality in him. He grows indifferent, he scorns the impulses and customs which distinguish his kind. He neglects the conveniences and finer pleasures of life, lives in filthy poverty with scanty nourishment, and squanders the rest of his earnings in debauchery.'—Dr J. Kay."

law and in fact. The operative must be in the mill at half-past five in the morning; if he comes a couple of minutes too late, he is fined; if he comes ten minutes too late, he is not let in until breakfast is over, and a quarter of the day's wages is withheld, though he loses only two and one-half hours' work out of twelve. He must eat, drink, and sleep at command. For satisfying the most imperative needs, he is vouchsafed the least possible time absolutely required by them. Whether his dwelling is a half-hour or a whole one removed from the factory does not concern his employer. The despotic bell calls him from his bed, his breakfast, his dinner.

What a time he has of it, too, inside the factory! Here the employer is absolute law-giver; he makes regulations at will, changes and adds to his codex[99] at pleasure, and even, if he inserts the craziest stuff, the courts say to the working man: "You were your own master, no one forced you to agree to such a contract if you did not wish to; but now, when you have freely entered into it, you must be bound by it." And so the working man only gets into the bargain the mockery of the Justice of the Peace who is a bourgeois himself, and of the law which is made by the bourgeoisie. Such decisions have been given often enough. In October 1844 the operatives of Kennedy's mill, in Manchester, struck. Kennedy prosecuted them on the strength of a regulation placarded in the mill, that at no time more than two operatives in one room may quit work at once. And the court decided in his favour, giving the working men the explanation cited above.[100] And such rules as these usually are! For instance: (1) The doors are closed ten minutes after work begins, and thereafter no one is admitted until the breakfast hour; whoever is absent during this time forfeits 3d. per loom. (2) Every power-loom weaver detected absenting himself at another time, while the machinery is in motion, forfeits for each hour and each loom, 3d. Every person who leaves the room during working hours, without obtaining permission from the overlooker, forfeits 3d. (3) Weavers who fail to supply themselves with scissors forfeit, per day, 1d. (4) All broken shuttles, brushes, oil-cans, wheels, window-panes, etc., must be paid for by the weaver. (5) No weaver to stop work without giving a week's notice. The manufacturer may dismiss any employee without notice for bad work or improper behaviour. (6) Every operative detected speaking to another, singing or whistling, will be fined 6d.; for leaving his place during working hours, 6d.[101] Another copy of factory regulations lies before me, according to which every operative who comes three minutes too late forfeits the wages for a quarter of an hour, and every one who comes twenty minutes too late, for a quarter of a day. Every one who remains absent until breakfast forfeits 1s. on Monday, and 6d. every other day of the week, etc., etc. This last is the regulation of the Phoenix Works in Jersey Street, Manchester. It may be said that such rules are necessary in a great, complicated factory, in order to insure the harmonious working of the different parts; it may be asserted that such a severe discipline is as necessary here as in an army. This may be so, but what sort of a social order is it which cannot be maintained without such shameful tyranny?

99. Book of statutes or rules.
100. Engels's note: "*Manchester Guardian*, 30 Oct."
101. Engels's note: "*Stubborn Facts*, 9 ff."

Either the end sanctifies the means, or the inference of the badness of the end from the badness of the means is justified. Everyone who has served as a soldier knows what it is to be subjected even for a short time to military discipline. But these operatives are condemned from their ninth year to their death to live under the sword, physically and mentally. They are worse slaves than the Negroes in America, for they are more sharply watched, and yet it is demanded of them that they shall live like human beings, shall think and feel like men! Verily, this they can do only under glowing hatred towards their oppressors, and towards that order of things which places them in such a position, which degrades them to machines. But it is far more shameful yet, that according to the universal testimony of the operatives, numbers of manufacturers collect the fines imposed upon the operatives with the most heartless severity, and for the purpose of piling up extra profits out of the farthings thus extorted from the impoverished proletarians. Leach asserts, too, that the operatives often find the factory clock moved forward a quarter of an hour and the doors shut, while the clerk moves about with the fines-book inside, noting the many names of the absentees. Leach claims to have counted ninety-five operatives thus shut out, standing before a factory, whose clock was a quarter of an hour slower than the town clocks at night, and a quarter of an hour faster in the morning. The Factory Report relates similar facts. In one factory the clock was set back during working hours, so that the operatives worked overtime without extra pay; in another, a whole quarter of an hour overtime was worked; in a third, there were two clocks, an ordinary one and a machine clock, which registered the revolutions of the main shaft; if the machinery went slowly, working hours were measured by the machine clock until the number of revolutions due in twelve hours was reached; if work went well, so that the number was reached before the usual working hours were ended, the operatives were forced to toil on to the end of the twelfth hour. The witness adds that he had known girls who had good work, and who had worked overtime, who, nevertheless, betook themselves to a life of prostitution rather than submit to this tyranny.[102] To return to the fines, Leach relates having repeatedly seen women in the last period of pregnancy fined 6*d.* for the offence of sitting down a moment to rest. Fines for bad work are wholly arbitrary; the goods are examined in the wareroom, and the supervisor charges the fines upon a list without even summoning the operative, who only learns that he has been fined when the overlooker pays his wages, and the goods have perhaps been sold, or certainly been placed beyond his reach. Leach has in his possession such a fines list, ten feet long, and amounting to £35 17*s.* 10*d.* He relates that in the factory where this list was made, a new supervisor was dismissed for fining too little, and so bringing in £5 too little weekly.[103] And I repeat that I know Leach to be a thoroughly trustworthy man incapable of a falsehood.

But the operative is his employer's slave in still other respects. If his wife or daughter finds favour in the eyes of the master, a command, a hint suffices, and she

102. Engels's note: "Drinkwater Evidence, p. 80."
103. Engels's note: "*Stubborn Facts,* 13–17."

must place herself at his disposal. When the employer wishes to supply with signatures a petition in favour of bourgeois interests, he need only send it to his mill. If he wishes to decide a parliamentary election he sends his enfranchised operatives in rank and file to the polls, and they vote for the bourgeois candidate whether they will or no. If he desires a majority in a public meeting, he dismisses them half an hour earlier than usual, and secures them places close to the platform, where he can watch them to his satisfaction.

Two further arrangements contribute especially to force the operative under the dominion of the manufacturer; the Truck system and the Cottage system. The truck system, the payment of the operatives in goods, was formerly universal in England. The manufacturer opens a shop, "for the convenience of the operatives, and to protect them from the high prices of the petty dealers." Here goods of all sorts are sold to them on credit; and to keep the operatives from going to the shops where they could get their goods more cheaply—the "Tommy shops"[104] usually charging 25 to 30 per cent more than others—wages are paid in requisitions on the shop instead of money. The general indignation against this infamous system led to the passage of the Truck Act in 1831, by which, for most employees, payment in truck orders was declared void and illegal, and was made punishable by fine; but, like most other English laws, this has been enforced only here and there. In the towns it is carried out comparatively efficiently; but in the country, the truck system, disguised or undisguised, flourishes. In the town of Leicester, too, it is very common. There lie before me nearly a dozen convictions for this offence, dating from the period between November 1843, and June 1844, and reported, in part, in the *Manchester Guardian* and, in part, in the *Northern Star*. The system is, of course, less openly carried on at present; wages are usually paid in cash, but the employer still has means enough at command to force him to purchase his wares in the truck shop and nowhere else. Hence it is difficult to combat the truck system, because it can now be carried on under cover of the law, provided only that the operative receives his wages in money. The *Northern Star* of 27 April 1844 publishes a letter from an operative of Holmfirth, near Huddersfield, in Yorkshire, which refers to a manufacturer of the name of Bowers, as follows (retranslated from the German):

> It is very strange to think that the accursed truck system should exist to such an extent as it does in Holmfirth, and nobody be found who has the pluck to make the manufacturer stop it. There are here a great many honest hand-weavers suffering through this damned system; here is one sample from a good many out of the noble-hearted Free Trade Clique. There is a manufacturer who has upon himself the curses of the whole district on account of his infamous conduct towards his poor weavers; if they have got a piece ready which comes to 34 or 36 shillings, he gives them 20s. in money and the rest in cloth or goods, and 40 to 50 per cent dearer than at the other shops, and often enough the goods are rotten into the bargain. But,

104. In the so-called truck system, employers would often provide a tommy shop. Rather than pay wages, the employers would provide food and other goods (referred to generally as "tommy") which workers could "purchase" based on the number of hours they had worked.

what says the Free Trade *Mercury*, the *Leeds Mercury*?[105] They are not bound to take them; they can please themselves. Oh, yes, but they must take them or else starve. If they ask for another 20s. in money, they must wait eight or fourteen days for a warp;[106] but if they take the 20s. and the goods, then there is always a warp ready for them. And that is Free Trade. Lord Brougham said we ought to put by something in our young days, so that we need not go to the parish when we are old. Well, are we to put by the rotten goods? If this did not come from a lord, one would say his brains were as rotten as the goods that our work is paid in. When the unstamped papers came out "illegally", there was a lot of them to report it to the police in Holmfirth, the Blythes, the Edwards, etc.; but where are they now? But this is different. Our truck manufacturer belongs to the pious Free Trade lot; he goes to church twice every Sunday, and repeats devotedly after the parson: "We have left undone the things we ought to have done, and we have done the things we ought not to have done, and there is no good in us; but, good Lord, deliver us."[107] Yes, deliver us till tomorrow, and we will pay our weavers again in rotten goods.

The cottage system looks much more innocent and arose in a much more harmless way, though it has the same enslaving influence upon the employee. In the neighbourhood of the mills in the country, there is often a lack of dwelling accommodation for the operatives. The manufacturer is frequently obliged to build such dwellings and does so gladly, as they yield great advantages, besides the interest upon the capital invested. If any owner of working-men's dwellings averages about 6 per cent on his invested capital, it is safe to calculate that the manufacturer's cottages yield twice this rate; for so long as his factory does not stand perfectly idle he is sure of occupants, and of occupants who pay punctually. He is therefore spared the two chief disadvantages under which other house-owners labour; his cottages never stand empty, and he runs no risk. But the rent of the cottages is as high as though these disadvantages were in full force, and by obtaining the same rent as the ordinary house-owner, the manufacturer, at cost of the operatives, makes a brilliant investment at 12 to 14 per cent. For it is clearly unjust that he should make twice as much profit as other competing house-owners, who at the same time are excluded from competing with him. But it implies a double wrong, when he draws his fixed profit from the pockets of the non-possessing class, which must consider the expenditure of every penny. He is used to that, however, he whose whole wealth is gained at the cost of his employees. But this injustice becomes an infamy when the manufacturer, as often happens, forces his operatives, who must occupy his houses on pain of dismissal, to pay a higher rent than the ordinary one, or even to pay rent for houses in which they do not live! The *Halifax Guardian*, quoted by the Liberal *Sun*,[108] asserts that hundreds of operatives in Ashton-under-Lyne, Oldham, and Rochdale, etc., are forced by their employers to pay house-rent whether they occupy the house or not. The cottage system is universal in the country districts; it has created whole villages, and the manufacturer

---

105. Engels's note: "*Leeds Mercury*: a radical bourgeois newspaper. *(Note in the German edition.)*"
106. A set of threads or yarns placed lengthwise in a loom.
107. From the General Confession in the *Book of Common Prayer*; adapted from Romans 7:19.
108. Engels's note: "*Sun*, a London daily; end of Nov. 1844."

usually has little or no competition against his houses, so that he can fix his price regardless of any market rate, indeed at his pleasure. And what power does the cottage system give the employer over his operatives in disagreements between master and men? If the latter strike, he need only give them notice to quit his premises, and the notice need only be a week; after that time the operative is not only without bread but without a shelter, a vagabond at the mercy of the law which sends him, without fail, to the treadmill.[109]

Such is the factory system sketched as fully as my space permits, and with as little partisan spirit as the heroic deeds of the bourgeoisie against the defenceless workers permit—deeds towards which it is impossible to remain indifferent, towards which indifference were a crime. Let us compare the condition of the free Englishman of 1845 with the Saxon serf under the lash of the Norman barons of 1145. The serf was *glebae adscriptus,*[110] bound to the soil, so is the free working man through the cottage system. The serf owed his master the *jus primae noctis,* the right of the first night—the free working man must, on demand, surrender to his master not only that, but the right of every night. The serf could acquire no property; everything that he gained, his master could take from him; the free working man has no property, can gain none by reason of the pressure of competition, and what even the Norman baron did not do, the modern manufacturer does. Through the truck system, he assumes every day the administration in detail of the things which the worker requires for his immediate necessities. The relation of the lord of the soil to the serf was regulated by the prevailing customs and bylaws which were obeyed, because they corresponded to them. The free workingman's relation to his master is regulated by laws which are *not* obeyed, because they correspond neither with the interests of the employer nor with the prevailing customs. The lord of the soil could not separate the serf from the land, nor sell him apart from it, and since almost all the land was fief[111] and there was no capital, practically could not sell him at all. The modern bourgeois forces the working man to sell himself. The serf was the slave of the piece of land on which he was born, the working man is the slave of his own necessaries of life and of the money with which he has to buy them—both are *slaves of a thing.* The serf had a guarantee for the means of subsistence in the feudal order of society in which every member had his own place. The free working man has no guarantee whatsoever, because he has a place in society only when the bourgeoisie can make use of him; in all other cases he is ignored, treated as non-existent. The serf sacrificed himself for his master in war, the factory operative in peace. The lord of the serf was a barbarian who regarded his villein[112] as a head of cattle; the employer of operatives is civilized and

109. A machine powered by people or animals walking on a set of moving steps or a beltway. Prison workers were often put to work on a treadmill. See R. Arthur Arnold, "Prison Labour," in part 2.

110. A Latinism meaning, "attached to the soil," the phrase refers to someone bound to an estate or to a lord.

111. Something over which one has rights.

112. In the feudal system, a villein was someone who was a serf in relationship only to his lord; in his relationships with all others, he had the rights of a free man.

regards his "hand" as a machine. In short, the position of the two is not far from equal, and if either is at a disadvantage, it is the free working man. Slaves they both are, with the single difference that the slavery of the one is undissembled, open, honest; that of the other cunning, sly, disguised, deceitfully concealed from himself and everyone else, a hypocritical servitude worse than the old. The philanthropic Tories were right when they gave the operatives the name white slaves.[113] But the hypocritical disguised slavery recognizes the right to freedom, at least in outward form; bows before a freedom-loving public opinion, and herein lies the historic progress as compared with the old servitude, that the *principle* of freedom is affirmed, and the oppressed will one day see to it that this principle is carried out.

At the close a few stanzas of a poem which voices the sentiments of the workers themselves about the factory system. Written by Edward P. Mead of Birmingham, it is a correct expression of the views prevailing among them.

THE STEAM KING[114]

There is a King, and a ruthless King,
Not a King of the poet's dream;
But a tyrant fell, white slaves know well,
And that ruthless King is Steam.
   He hath an arm, an iron arm,
   And tho' he hath but one,
   In that mighty arm there is a charm,
   That millions hath undone.
Like the ancient Moloch[115] grim, his sire
In Himmon's vale that stood,
His bowels are of living fire,
And children are his food.
   His priesthood are a hungry band,
   Blood-thirsty, proud, and bold;
   'Tis they direct his giant hand,
   In turning blood to gold.
For filthy gain in their servile chain
All nature's rights they bind;
They mock at lovely woman's pain,
And to manly tears are blind.
   The sighs and groans of Labour's sons
   Are music in their ear,
   And the skeleton shades of lads and maids,
   In the Steam King's Hells appear.
Those hells upon earth, since the Steam King's birth,
Have scatter'd around despair;

113. The term "white slave" was first used in the 1830s.
114. Mead's poem appeared in the *Northern Star* in February 1843.
115. The word actually means "king." Moloch was a Canaanite god associated with child sacrifice.

> For the human mind for Heav'n design'd,
> With the body, is murdered there.
>   Then down with the King, the Moloch King,
>   Ye working millions all;
>   O chain his hand, or our native land
>   Is destin'd by him to fall.
> And his Satraps[116] abhor'd, each proud Mill Lord,
>   Now gorg'd with gold and blood,
>   Must be put down by the nation's frown,
>   As well as their monster God.[117]

116. Subordinate, often despotic, ruler.

117. Engels's note:

I have neither time nor space to deal in detail with the replies of the manufacturers to the charges made against them for twelve years past. These men will not learn because their supposed interest blinds them. As, moreover, many of their objections have been met in the foregoing, the following is all that it is necessary for me to add:

You come to Manchester, you wish to make yourself acquainted with the state of affairs in England. You naturally have good introductions to respectable people. You drop a remark or two as to the condition of the workers. You are made acquainted with a couple of the first Liberal manufacturers, Robert Hyde Greg [1795–1875], perhaps, Edmund Ashworth [1801–1881], Thomas Ashton, or others. They are told of your wishes. The manufacturer understands you, knows what he has to do. He accompanies you to his factory in the country; Mr Greg to Quarrybank in Cheshire, Mr Ashworth to Turton near Bolton, Mr Ashton to Hyde. He leads you through a superb, admirably arranged building, perhaps supplied with ventilators, he calls your attention to the lofty, airy rooms, the fine machinery, here and there a healthy looking operative. He gives you an excellent lunch, and proposes to you to visit the operatives' homes; he conducts you to the cottages, which look new, clean, and neat, and goes with you into this one and that one, naturally only to overlookers, mechanics, etc., so that you may see "families who live wholly from the factory." Among other families you might find that only wife and children work, and the husband darns stockings. The presence of the employer keeps you from asking indiscreet questions; you find every one well paid, comfortable, comparatively healthy by reason of the country air; you begin to be converted from your exaggerated ideas of misery and starvation. But, that the cottage system makes slaves of the operatives, that there may be a truck shop in the neighbourhood, that the people hate the manufacturer, this they do not point out to you, because he is present. He has built a school, church, reading-room, etc. That he uses the school to train children to subordination, that he tolerates in the reading-room such prints only as represent the interests of the bourgeoisie, that he dismisses his employees if they read Chartist or Socialist papers or books, this is all concealed from you. You see an easy, patriarchal relation, you see the life of the overlookers, you see what the bourgeoisie *promises* the workers if they become its slaves, mentally and morally. This "country manufacture" has always been what the employers like to show, because in it the disadvantages of the factory system, especially from the point of view of health, are, in part, done away with by the free air and surroundings, and because the patriarchal servitude of the workers can here be longest maintained. Dr Ure sings a dithyramb [an impassioned choric song] upon the theme. But woe to the operatives to whom it occurs to think for themselves and become Chartists! For them the paternal affection of the manufacturer comes to a sudden end. Further, if you should wish to be accompanied through the working-people's quarters of Manchester, if you should desire to see the development of the factory system in a factory town, you may wait long before these rich bourgeoisie will help you! These gentlemen do not know in what condition their employees are nor what they want, and they dare not know things which would make them uneasy or even oblige them to act in opposition to their own interests. But, fortunately, that is of no consequence: what the working men have to carry out, they carry out for themselves.

In the 1830s and early 1840s, W. Cooke Taylor (see part 2) and Andrew Ure visited the mills Engels names at the beginning of this note.

THOMAS BABINGTON MACAULAY

Thomas Babington Macaulay (1800–1859) attended Trinity College, Cambridge, and was elected a fellow in 1824. He authored best-selling essays, poems, and a five-volume history of England. During his distinguished and influential political career, he served several terms as a Whig, or Liberal, in the House of Commons, crafted a criminal code for India during a three-and-a-half year assignment in that country, and was appointed Minister at War in Lord Melbourne's cabinet. In 1857, he was made a peer and took the title of Baron Macaulay of Rothley. When he died two years later, he was buried in the Poet's Corner of Westminster Abbey.

Macaulay spoke in the House of Commons on May 22, 1846, in support of the Ten Hours Bill, a bill to restrict the working hours of women and children. Macaulay, as a Whig, generally endorsed laissez-faire economic policies and opposed protective legislation; yet, in this speech, he argues that there are higher laws than economic or commercial ones. "[W]here the public morality is concerned," he declares, "it may be the duty of the State to interfere." Despite the power of Macaulay's rhetoric, the bill failed by a vote of 203 to 193. It finally won approval the following year.

The Ten Hours Bill
May 22, 1846

On the twenty-ninth of April, 1846, Mr. Fielden, Member for Oldham, moved the second reading of a bill for limiting the labor of young persons in factories to ten hours a day. The debate was adjourned, and was repeatedly resumed at long intervals. At length on the twenty-second of May the bill was rejected by 203 votes to 193. On that day the following Speech was made.

It is impossible, Sir, that I can remain silent after the appeal which has been made to me in so pointed a manner by my honourable friend the Member for Sheffield.[1] And even if that appeal had not been made to me, I should have been very desirous to have an opportunity of explaining the grounds on which I shall vote for the second reading of this bill.

It is, I hope, unnecessary for me to assure my honourable friend that I utterly disapprove of those aspersions which have, both in this House and out of it, been thrown on the owners of factories. For that valuable class of men I have no feeling but respect and good will. I am convinced that with their interests the interests of the whole community, and especially of the labouring classes, are inseparably bound up. I can also with perfect sincerity declare that the vote which I shall give to-night will not be a factious vote. In no circumstances indeed should I think that the laws of political hostility warranted me in treating this question as a party question. But at the present moment I would much rather strengthen than weaken the hands of Her Majesty's Ministers.[2] It is by no means pleasant to me to be under the necessity of opposing them. I assure them, I assure my friends on this side of the House with whom I am so unfortunate as to differ, and especially my honourable friend, the Member for Sheffield, who spoke, I must say, in rather too plaintive a tone, that I have no desire to obtain credit for humanity at their expense. I fully believe that their feeling towards the labouring people is quite as kind as mine. There is no difference between us as to ends: there is an honest difference of opinion as to means: and we surely ought to be able to discuss the points on which we differ without one angry emotion or one acrimonious word.

The details of the bill, Sir, will be more conveniently and more regularly discussed when we consider it in Committee. Our business at present is with the principle: and the principle, we are told by many gentlemen of great authority, is unsound. In their opinion, neither this bill, nor any other bill regulating the hours of labour, can be defended. This, they say, is one of those matters about which we ought not to legislate at all: one of those matters which settle themselves far better than any government can settle them. Now, it is most important that this point should be fully cleared up. We certainly ought not to usurp functions which do not properly belong to us: but, on the other hand, we ought not to abdicate functions which do properly belong to us. I hardly know which is the greater pest to society, a paternal government, that is to say a prying, meddlesome government, which intrudes itself into every part of human life, and which thinks that it can do everything for everybody better than anybody can do anything for himself; or a careless, lounging government, which suffers grievances, such as it could at once remove, to grow and multiply, and which to all complaint and remonstrance has

1. Identified in early published editions of the speech as Mr. Ward: Sir Henry George Ward (1797–1860).

2. Robert Peel was the Conservative Prime Minister from 1834 to 1835 and again from August 1841 to June 1846. Threat of famine in Ireland in 1846 led Peel's administration to suspend temporarily the Corn Laws, which levied a tariff on imported grain. The controversy that ensued led to division in the Conservative party and to Peel's resignation. Macaulay was strongly opposed to the Corn Laws.

only one answer: "We must let things alone: we must let things take their course: we must let things find their level." There is no more important problem in politics than to ascertain the just mean between these two most pernicious extremes, to draw correctly the line which divides those cases in which it is the duty of the state to interfere from those cases in which it is the duty of the state to abstain from interference. In old times the besetting sin of rulers was undoubtedly an inordinate disposition to meddle. The lawgiver was always telling people how to keep their shops, how to till their fields, how to educate their children, how many dishes to have on their tables, how much a yard to give for the cloth which made their coats. He was always trying to remedy some evil which did not properly fall within his province; and the consequence was that he increased the evils which he attempted to remedy. He was so much shocked by the distress inseparable from scarcity that he made statutes against forestalling and regrating,[3] and so turned the scarcity into a famine. He was so much shocked by the cunning and hard-heartedness of money lenders, that he made laws against usury; and the consequence was that the bor- rower, who, if he had been left unprotected, would have got money at ten per cent, could hardly, when protected, get it at fifteen per cent. Some eminent political philosophers of the last century exposed with great ability the folly of such legisla- tion, and, by doing so, rendered a great service to mankind. There has been a reaction, a reaction which has doubtless produced much good, but which, like most reactions, has not been without evils and dangers. Our statesmen cannot now be accused of being busybodies. But I am afraid that there is, even in some of the ablest and most upright among them, a tendency to the opposite fault. I will give an instance of what I mean. Fifteen years ago it became evident that railroads[4] would soon, in every part of the kingdom, supersede to a great extent the old highways. The tracing of the new routes which were to join all the chief cities, ports, and naval arsenals of the island was a matter of the highest national impor- tance. But unfortunately, those who should have acted for the nation refused to interfere. Consequently, numerous questions which were really public, questions which concerned the public convenience, the public prosperity, the public se- curity, were treated as private questions. That the whole society was interested in having a good system of internal communication seemed to be forgotten. The speculator who wanted a large dividend on his shares, the landowner who wanted a large price for his acres, obtained a full hearing. But nobody applied to be heard on behalf of the community. The effects of that great error we feel, and we shall not soon cease to feel. Unless I am greatly mistaken, we are in danger of committing to-night an error of the same kind. The honourable Member for Montrose[5] and my honourable friend, the Member for Sheffield, think that the question before us

3. To forestall is to interfere with normal trading by buying goods on their way to market with the plan to resell at a higher price. To regrate is to buy goods at a market with the plan to resell near the same location at a profit.

4. English railways (from ca. 1825) were designed, constructed, and operated by private investors with little government interference.

5. Joseph Hume (1777–1855), a leading radical politician.

is merely a question between the old and the new theories of commerce. They cannot understand how any friend of free trade can wish the Legislature to interfere between the capitalist and the labourer. They say, "You do not make a law to settle the price of gloves, or the texture of gloves, or the length of credit which the glover shall give. You leave it to him to determine whether he will charge high or low prices, whether he will use strong or flimsy materials, whether he will trust or insist on ready money. You acknowledge that these are matters which he ought to be left to settle with his customers, and that we ought not to interfere. It is possible that he may manage his shop ill. But it is certain that we shall manage it ill. On the same grounds on which you leave the seller of gloves and the buyer of gloves to make their own contract, you ought to leave the seller of labour and the buyer of labour to make their own contract."

I have a great respect, Sir, for those who reason thus: but I cannot see this matter in the light in which it appears to them; and, though I may distrust my own judgment, I must be guided by it. I am, I believe, as strongly attached as any member of this House to the principle of free trade, rightly understood. Trade, considered merely as trade, considered merely with reference to the pecuniary interest of the contracting parties, can hardly be too free. But there is a great deal of trade which cannot be considered merely as trade, and which affects higher than pecuniary interests. And to say that government never ought to regulate such trade is a monstrous proposition, a proposition at which Adam Smith[6] would have stood aghast. We impose some restrictions on trade for purposes of police. Thus, we do not suffer everybody who has a cab and a horse to ply for passengers in the streets of London. We do not leave the fare to be determined by the supply and the demand. We do not permit a driver to extort a guinea for going half a mile on a rainy day when there is no other vehicle on the stand. We impose some restrictions on trade for the sake of revenue. Thus, we forbid a farmer to cultivate tobacco on his own ground. We impose some restrictions on trade for the sake of national defence. Thus, we compel a man who would rather be ploughing or weaving to go into the militia; and we fix the amount of pay which he shall receive without asking his consent. Nor is there in all this anything inconsistent with the soundest political economy. For the science of political economy teaches us only that we ought not on commercial grounds to interfere with the liberty of commerce; and we, in the cases which I have put, interfere with the liberty of commerce on higher than commercial grounds.

And now, Sir, to come closer to the case with which we have to deal, I say, first, that where the health of the community is concerned, it may be the duty of the state to interfere with the contracts of individuals; and to this proposition I am quite sure that Her Majesty's Government will cordially assent. I have just read a very interesting report signed by two members of that Government, the Duke of

6. Adam Smith (1723–1790) was a Scots philosopher and author of *The Wealth of Nations* (1776), a book in which he argued that free pursuit of self-interest, the motivating force for each individual, will inevitably benefit society as a whole.

Buccleuch, and the noble earl who was lately Chief Commissioner of the Woods and Forests, and who is now Secretary for Ireland; and, since that report was laid before the House, the noble earl himself has, with the sanction of the Cabinet, brought in a bill for the protection of the public health. By this bill it is provided that no man shall be permitted to build a house on his own land in any great town without giving notice to certain Commissioners. No man is to sink a cellar without the consent of these Commissioners. The house must not be of less than a prescribed width. No new house must be built without a drain. If an old house has no drain, the Commissioners may order the owner to make a drain. If he refuses, they make a drain for him, and send him the bill. They may order him to whitewash his house. If he refuses, they may send people with pails and brushes to whitewash it for him, at his charge. Now, suppose that some proprietor of houses at Leeds or Manchester were to expostulate with the Government in the language in which the Government has expostulated with the supporters of this bill for the regulation of factories. Suppose that he were to say to the noble earl, "Your lordship professes to be a friend to free trade. Your lordship's doctrine is that everybody ought to be at liberty to buy cheap and to sell dear. Why then may not I run up a house as cheap as I can, and let my rooms as dear as I can? Your lordship does not like houses without drains. Do not take one of mine then. You think my bedrooms filthy. Nobody forces you to sleep in them. Use your own liberty: but do not restrain that of your neighbors. I can find many a family willing to pay a shilling a week for leave to live in what you call a hovel. And why am not I to take the shilling which they are willing to give me? And why are not they to have such shelter as, for that shilling, I can afford them? Why did you send a man without my consent to clean my house, and then force me to pay for what I never ordered? My tenants thought the house clean enough for them; or they would not have been my tenants; and, if they and I were satisfied, why did you, in direct defiance of all the principles of free trade, interfere between us?" This reasoning, Sir, is exactly of a piece with the reasoning of the honourable Member for Montrose, and of my honourable friend, the Member for Sheffield. If the noble earl will allow me to make a defence for him, I believe that he would answer the objection thus: "I hold," he would say, "the sound doctrine of free trade. But your doctrine of free trade is an exaggeration, a caricature of the sound doctrine; and by exhibiting such a caricature you bring discredit on the sound doctrine. We should have nothing to do with the contracts between you and your tenants, if those contracts affected only pecuniary interests. But higher than pecuniary interests are at stake. It concerns the commonwealth that the great body of the people should not live in a way which makes life wretched and short, which enfeebles the body and pollutes the mind. If, by living in houses which resemble hogstyes, great numbers of our countrymen have contracted the tastes of hogs, if they have become so familiar with filth and stench and contagion, that they burrow without reluctance in holes which would turn the stomach of any man of cleanly habits, that is only an additional proof that we have too long neglected our duties, and an additional reason for our now performing them."

Secondly, I say that where the public morality is concerned it may be the duty of the state to interfere with the contracts of individuals. Take the traffic in licentious books and pictures. Will anybody deny that the state may, with propriety, interdict that traffic? Or take the case of lotteries. I have, we will suppose, an estate for which I wish to get twenty thousand pounds. I announce my intention to issue a thousand tickets at twenty pounds each. The holder of the number which is first drawn is to have the estate. But the magistrate interferes; the contract between me and the purchasers of my tickets is annulled; and I am forced to pay a heavy penalty for having made such a contract. I appeal to the principle of free trade, as expounded by the honourable gentlemen, the Members for Montrose and Sheffield. I say to you, the legislators who have restricted my liberty, "What business have you to interfere between a buyer and a seller? If you think the speculation a bad one, do not take tickets. But do not interdict other people from judging for themselves." Surely you would answer, "You would be right if this were a mere question of trade: but it is a question of morality. We prohibit you from disposing of your property in this particular mode, because it is a mode which tends to encourage a most pernicious habit of mind, a habit of mind incompatible with all the qualities on which the well-being of individuals and of nations depends."

It must then, I think, be admitted that where health is concerned, and where morality is concerned, the State is justified in interfering with the contracts of individuals. And, if this be admitted, it follows that the case with which we now have to do is a case for interference.

Will it be denied that the health of a large part of the rising generation may be seriously affected by the contracts which this bill is intended to regulate? Can any man who has read the evidence which is before us, can any man who has ever observed young people, can any man who remembers his own sensations when he was young, doubt that twelve hours a day of labor in a factory is too much for a lad of thirteen?

Or will it be denied that this is a question in which public morality is concerned? Can any one doubt—none, I am sure, of my friends around me doubts— that education is a matter of the highest importance to the virtue and happiness of a people? Now we know that there can be no education without leisure. It is evident that, after deducting from the day twelve hours for labor in a factory, and the additional hours necessary for exercise, refreshment, and repose, there will not remain time enough for education.

I have now, I think, shown that this bill is not in principle objectionable; and yet I have not touched the strongest part of our case. I hold that, where public health is concerned, and where public morality is concerned, the State may be justified in regulating even the contracts of adults. But we propose to regulate only the contracts of infants. Now was there ever a civilised society in which the contracts of infants were not under some regulation? Is there a single member of this House who will say that a wealthy minor of thirteen ought to be at perfect liberty to execute a conveyance of his estate, or to give a bond for fifty thousand pounds? If anybody were so absurd as to say, "What has the Legislature to do with the matter? Why cannot you leave trade free? Why do you pretend to understand the boy's interest better than he understands it?"—you would answer: "When he grows up, he may squander his fortune away if he likes; but at present the State is his guardian; and he shall not ruin himself till he is old enough to know what he is about." The minors whom we wish to protect have not indeed large property to throw away: but they are not the less our wards. Their only inheritance, the only fund to which they must look for their subsistence through life, is the sound mind in the sound body. And is it not our duty to prevent them from wasting that most precious wealth before they know its value?

But, it is said, this bill, though it directly limits only the labour of infants, will, by an indirect operation, limit also the labour of adults. Now, Sir, though I am not prepared to vote for a bill directly limiting the labour of adults, I will plainly say that I do not think that the limitations of the labour of adults would necessarily produce all those frightful consequences which we have heard predicted. You cheer me in very triumphant tones, as if I had uttered some monstrous paradox. Pray, does it not occur to any of you that the labour of adults is now limited in this country? Are you not aware that you are living in a society in which the labour of adults is limited to six days in seven? It is you, not I, who maintain a paradox opposed to the opinions and the practices of all nations and ages. Did you ever hear of a single civilised State since the beginning of the world in which a certain portion of time was not set apart for the rest and recreation of adults by public authority? In general, this arrangement has been sanctioned by religion. The Egyptians, the Jews, the Greeks, the Romans, had their holidays: the Hindoo has his holidays: the Mussulman[7] has his holidays: there are holidays in the Greek Church, holidays in the Church of Rome, holidays in the Church of England. Is it not amusing to hear a gentleman pronounce with confidence that any legislation which limits the labour of adults must produce consequences fatal to society, without once reflecting that in the society in which he lives, and in every other society that exists, or ever has existed, there has been such legislation without any evil consequence? It is true that a Puritan Government in England,[8] and an Atheistical Government in France,[9] abolished the old holidays as superstitious. But those governments felt it to be absolutely necessary to institute new holidays. Civil festivals were substituted for religious festivals. You will find among the ordinances of the Long Parliament[10] a law providing that, in exchange for the days of rest and amusement which the people had been used to enjoy at Easter, Whitsuntide, and Christmas, the second Tuesday of every month should be given to the working man, and that any apprentice who was forced to work on the second Tuesday of any month might have his master up before a magistrate. The French Jacobins

7. Muslim.

8. A reference to the Commonwealth and Protectorate governments of the Puritan soldier and statesman Oliver Cromwell and, very briefly, his son Richard (1649–1660).

9. Following the Revolution in 1789—a goal of which was to eliminate the oppression of church and state—the radical Jacobin government abolished the practice of Christianity in France on October 5, 1793.

10. Convened by King Charles I in 1640; stripped of royalist and opposition members in subsequent years and disbanded by Oliver Cromwell in 1649.

decreed that the Sunday should no longer be a day of rest; but they instituted another day of rest, the Decade.[11] They swept away the holidays of the Roman Catholic Church; but they instituted another set of holidays, the Sansculottides,[12] one sacred to Genius, one to Industry, one to Opinion, and so on. I say, therefore, that the practice of limiting by law the time of the labour of adults, is so far from being, as some gentlemen seem to think, an unheard of and monstrous practice, that it is a practice as universal as cookery, as the wearing of clothes, as the use of domestic animals.

And has this practice been proved by experience to be pernicious? Let us take the instance with which we are most familiar. Let us inquire what has been the effect of those laws which, in our own country, limit the labour of adults to six days in every seven. It is quite unnecessary to discuss the question whether Christians be or be not bound by a divine command to observe the Sunday. For it is evident that, whether our weekly holiday be of divine or of human institution, the effect on the temporal interests of society will be exactly the same. Now, is there a single argument in the whole Speech of my honourable friend, the Member for Sheffield, which does not tell just as strongly against the laws which enjoin the observance of the Sunday as against the bill on our table? Surely, if his reasoning is good for hours, it must be equally good for days.

He says, "If this limitation be good for the working people, rely on it that they will find it out, and that they will themselves establish it without any law." Why not reason in the same way about the Sunday? Why not say, "If it be a good thing for the people of London to shut their shops one day in seven, they will find it out, and will shut their shops without a law"? Sir, the answer is obvious. I have no doubt that, if you were to poll the shopkeepers of London, you would find an immense majority, probably a hundred to one, in favour of closing shops on the Sunday; and yet it is absolutely necessary to give to the wish of the majority the sanction of a law; for, if there were no such law, the minority, by opening their shops, would soon force the majority to do the same.

But, says my honourable friend, you cannot limit the labour of adults unless you fix wages. This proposition he lays down repeatedly, assures us that it is incontrovertible, and indeed seems to think it self-evident; for he has not taken the trouble to prove it. Sir, my answer shall be very short. We have, during many centuries, limited the labour of adults to six days in seven; and yet we have not fixed the rate of wages.

But, it is said, you cannot legislate for all trades; and therefore you had better

11. The Jacobins replaced the traditional Gregorian Calendar with a Revolutionary Calendar, use of which was officially decreed in 1793 and not discontinued until January 1, 1806. The Revolutionary Calendar divided the year into twelve months of thirty days each. Each month was divided into three ten-day weeks, known as *decades*. The tenth day of each decade, the *décadi*, was to be the one day of rest in each week.

12. Five days (six in leap year) were left over to balance the Revolutionary Calendar of twelve thirty-day months. These days, the Sansculottides, were to be celebrated as national holidays and were named in honor of the *sans-culottes* (i.e., without breeches), the radical republicans who wore trousers rather than the knee breeches of pre-revolutionary aristocrats.

not legislate for any. Look at the poor sempstress. She works far longer and harder than the factory child. She sometimes plies her needle fifteen, sixteen hours in the twenty-four. See how the housemaid works, up at six every morning, and toiling up stairs and down stairs till near midnight. You own that you cannot do anything for the sempstress and the housemaid.[13] Why then trouble yourself about the factory child? Take care that by protecting one class you do not aggravate the hardships endured by the classes which you cannot protect. Why, Sir, might not all this be said, word for word, against the laws which enjoin the observance of the Sunday? There are classes of people whom you cannot prevent from working on the Sunday. There are classes of people whom, if you could, you ought not to prevent from working on the Sunday. Take the sempstress of whom so much has been said. You cannot keep her from sewing and hemming all Sunday in her garret. But you do not think that a reason for suffering Covent Garden Market, and Leadenhall Market, and Smithfield Market, and all the shops from Mile End to Hyde Park to be open all Sunday. Nay, these factories about which we are debating,—does anybody propose that they shall be allowed to work all Sunday? See then how inconsistent you are. You think it unjust to limit the labour of the factory child to ten hours a day, because you cannot limit the labour of the sempstress. And yet you see no injustice in limiting the labour of the factory child, aye, and of the factory man, to six days in the week, though you cannot limit the labour of the sempstress.

But, you say, by protecting one class we shall aggravate the sufferings of all the classes which we cannot protect. You say this; but you do not prove it; and all experience proves the contrary. We interfere on the Sunday to close the shops. We do not interfere with the labour of the housemaid. But are the housemaids of London more severely worked on the Sunday than on other days? The fact notoriously is the reverse. For your legislation keeps the public feeling in a right state, and thus protects indirectly those whom it cannot protect directly.

Will my honourable friend, the Member for Sheffield, maintain that the law which limits the number of working days has been injurious to the working population? I am certain that he will not. How then can he expect me to believe that a law which limits the number of working hours must necessarily be injurious to the working population? Yet he and those who agree with him seem to wonder at our dullness because we do not at once admit the truth of the doctrine which they propound on this subject. They reason thus: We cannot reduce the number of hours of labour in factories without reducing the amount of production. We cannot reduce the amount of production without reducing the remuneration of the laborer. Meanwhile, foreigners, who are at liberty to work till they drop down dead at their looms, will soon beat us out of all the markets in the world. Wages

---

13. The first factory acts applied only to the textile industry. Over the course of the next few decades, regulations were gradually imposed on other industries. On the plight of seamstresses, see the story "The Slave of the Needle" and Thomas Hood's poem "The Song of the Shirt," both in this section. On the condition of domestic servants, see W. J. Linton's story "The Free-Servant," also reprinted in this section.

will go down fast. The condition of our working people will be far worse than it is; and our unwise interference will, like the unwise interference of our ancestors with the dealings of the corn factor and the money lender, increase the distress of the very class which we wish to relieve.

Now, Sir, I fully admit that there might be such a limitation of the hours of labor as would produce the evil consequences with which we are threatened: and this, no doubt, is a very good reason for legislating with great caution, for feeling our way, for looking well to all the details of this bill. But it is certainly not true that every limitation of the hours of labour must produce these consequences. And I am, I must say, surprised when I hear men of eminent ability and knowledge lay down the proposition that a diminution of the time of labour must be followed by a diminution of the wages of labour, as a proposition universally true, as a proposition capable of being strictly demonstrated, as a proposition about which there can be no more doubt than about any theorem in Euclid.[14] Sir, I deny the truth of the proposition; and for this plain reason. We have already, by law, greatly reduced the time of labour in factories. Thirty years ago, the late Sir Robert Peel[15] told the House that it was a common practice to make children of eight years of age toil in mills fifteen hours a day. A law has since been made which prohibits persons under eighteen years of age from working in mills more than twelve hours a day. That law was opposed on exactly the same grounds on which the bill before us is opposed. Parliament was told then, as it is told now, that with the time of labour the quantity of production would decrease, that with the quantity of production the wages would decrease, that our manufacturers would be unable to contend with foreign manufacturers, and that the condition of the labouring population instead of being made better by the interference of the Legislature would be made worse. Read over those debates; and you may imagine that you are reading the debate of this evening. Parliament disregarded these prophecies. The time of labour was limited. Have wages fallen? Has the cotton trade left Manchester for France or Germany? Has the condition of the working people become more miserable? Is it not universally acknowledged that the evils which were so confidently predicted have not come to pass? Let me be understood. I am not arguing that, because a law which reduced the hours of daily labour from fifteen to twelve did not reduce wages, a law reducing those hours from twelve to ten or eleven cannot possibly reduce wages. That would be very inconclusive reasoning. What I say is this, that, since a law which reduced the hours of daily labour from fifteen to twelve has not reduced wages, the proposition that every reduction of the hours of labour must necessarily reduce wages is a false proposition. There is evidently some flaw in that demonstration which my honourable friend thinks so complete; and what the flaw is we may perhaps discover if we look at the analogous case to which I have so often referred.

14. Third-century B.C.E. Greek mathematician and physicist.
15. Sir Robert Peel (1750–1830), father of the Prime Minister, introduced to Parliament in 1802 the first factory legislation, the Health and Morals of Apprentices Act. The bill applied to pauper children apprenticed under provisions of the Poor Law, limiting their work to twelve hours a day, requiring that they be educated, and controlling their working conditions.

Sir, exactly three hundred years ago, great religious changes were taking place in England.[16] Much was said and written, in that inquiring and innovating age, about the question whether Christians were under a religious obligation to rest from labour on one day in the week; and it is well known that the chief Reformers, both here and on the continent, denied the existence of any such obligation.[17] Suppose then that, in 1546, Parliament had made a law that there should thenceforth be no distinction between the Sunday and any other day. Now, Sir, our opponents, if they are consistent with themselves, must hold that such a law would have immensely increased the wealth of the country and the remuneration of the working man. What an effect, if their principles be sound, must have been produced by the addition of one sixth to the time of labour! What an increase of production! What a rise of wages! How utterly unable must the foreign artisan, who still had his days of festivity and of repose, have found himself to maintain a competition with a people whose shops were open, whose markets were crowded, whose spades, and axes, and planes, and hods, and anvils, and looms were at work from morning till night on three hundred and sixty-five days a year! The Sundays of three hundred years make up fifty years of our working days. We know what the industry of fifty years can do. We know what marvels the industry of the last fifty years has wrought. The arguments of my honourable friend irresistibly lead us to this conclusion, that if, during the last three centuries, the Sunday had not been observed as a day of rest, we should have been a far richer, a far more highly civilised people than we now are, and that the labouring class especially would have been far better off than at present. But does he, does any Member of the House, seriously believe that this would have been the case? For my own part, I have not the smallest doubt that, if we and our ancestors had, during the last three centuries, worked just as hard on the Sundays as on the week days, we should have been at this moment a poorer people and a less civilised people than we are; that there would have been less production than there has been; that the wages of the labourer would have been lower than they are, and that some other nation would have been now making cotton stuffs and woollen stuffs and cutlery for the whole world.

Of course, Sir, I do not mean to say that a man will not produce more in a week by working seven days than by working six days. But I very much doubt whether, at the end of a year, he will generally have produced more by working seven days a week than by working six days a week; and I firmly believe that, at the end of twenty years, he will have produced much less by working seven days a week than by working six days a week. In the same manner I do not deny that a factory child will produce more, in a single day, by working twelve hours than by working ten hours, and by working fifteen hours than by working twelve hours. But I do deny that a great society in which children work fifteen, or even twelve hours a day, will, in the lifetime of a generation, produce as much as if those children had worked

16. Following the refusal of the Roman Catholic Church to grant him a divorce from Catherine of Aragon, King Henry VIII in 1534 declared himself Supreme Head of the English Church.

17. The Protestant Reformation grew out of Martin Luther's revolt in 1517 against the Roman Catholic Church. He responded to his subsequent excommunication by establishing his own church.

less. If we consider man merely in a commercial point of view, if we consider him merely as a machine for the production of worsted and calico, let us not forget what a piece of mechanism he is, how fearfully and wonderfully made.[18] We do not treat a fine horse or a sagacious dog exactly as we treat a spinning jenny. Nor will any slaveholder, who has sense enough to know his own interest, treat his human chattels exactly as he treats his horses and his dogs. And would you treat the free labourer of England like a mere wheel or pulley? Rely on it that intense labour, beginning too early in life, continued too long every day, stunting the growth of the body, stunting the growth of the mind, leaving no time for healthful exercise, leaving no time for intellectual culture, must impair all those high qualities which have made our country great. Your overworked boys will become a feeble and ignoble race of men, the parents of a more feeble and more ignoble progeny; nor will it be long before the deterioration of the labourer will injuriously affect those very interests to which his physical and moral energies have been sacrificed. On the other hand, a day of rest recurring in every week, two or three hours of leisure, exercise, innocent amusement, or useful study, recurring every day, must improve the whole man, physically, morally, intellectually; and the improvement of the man will improve all that the man produces. Why is it, Sir, that the Hindoo cotton manufacturer, close to whose door the cotton grows, cannot, in the bazaar of his own town, maintain a competition with the English cotton manufacturer, who has to send thousands of miles for the raw material, and who has then to send the wrought material thousands of miles to market? You will say that it is owing to the excellence of our machinery. And to what is the excellence of our machinery owing? How many of the improvements which have been made in our machinery do we owe to the ingenuity and patient thought of working men? Adam Smith tells us in the first chapter of his great work, that you can hardly go to a factory without seeing some very pretty machine—that is his expression—devised by some labouring man. Hargraves, the inventor of the spinning jenny, was a common artisan.[19] Crompton, the inventor of the mule jenny, was a working man.[20] How many hours of the labour of children would do so much for our manufactures as one of these improvements has done? And in what sort of society are such improvements most likely to be made? Surely in a society in which the faculties of the working people are developed by education. How long will you wait before any negro, working under the lash in Louisiana, will contrive a better machinery for squeezing the sugar canes? My honourable friend seems to me, in all his reasonings about the commercial prosperity of nations, to overlook entirely the chief cause on which that prosperity depends. What is it, Sir, that makes the great difference between country and country? Not the exuberance of soil; not the mildness of climate; not mines, nor havens, nor rivers. These things are indeed valuable when put to their

18. Psalms 139:14.

19. James Hargreaves (sometimes spelled Hargraves, d. 1778) was the English inventor of the spinning jenny, a hand-operated machine that could spin several threads simultaneously.

20. Samuel Crompton (1753–1827), an Englishman, invented the spinning mule, a machine that made possible large-scale production of high-quality thread and yarn.

proper use by human intelligence: but human intelligence can do much without them; and they without human intelligence can do nothing. They exist in the highest degree in regions of which the inhabitants are few, and squalid, and barbarous, and naked, and starving; while on sterile rocks, amidst unwholesome marshes, and under inclement skies, may be found immense populations, well fed, well lodged, well clad, well governed. Nature meant Egypt and Sicily to be the gardens of the world. They once were so. Is it anything in the earth or in the air that makes Scotland more prosperous than Egypt, that makes Holland more prosperous than Sicily? No; it was the Scotchman that made Scotland; it was the Dutchman that made Holland. Look at North America. Two centuries ago the sites on which now arise mills, and hotels, and banks, and colleges, and churches, and the Senate Houses of flourishing commonwealths, were deserts abandoned to the panther and the bear. What has made the change? Was it the rich mould, or the redundant rivers? No: the prairies were as fertile, the Ohio and the Hudson were as broad and as full then as now. Was the improvement the effect of some great transfer of capital from the old world to the new? No: the emigrants generally carried out with them no more than a pittance; but they carried out the English heart, and head, and arm; and the English heart and head and arm turned the wilderness into cornfield and orchard, and the huge trees of the primeval forest into cities and fleets. Man, man is the great instrument that produces wealth. The natural difference between Campania[21] and Spitzbergen[22] is trifling when compared with the difference between a country inhabited by men full of bodily and mental vigour, and a country inhabited by men sunk in bodily and mental decrepitude. Therefore, it is that we are not poorer but richer, because we have, through many ages, rested from our labour one day in seven. That day is not lost. While industry is suspended, while the plough lies in the furrow, while the Exchange is silent, while no smoke ascends from the factory, a process is going on quite as important to the wealth of nations as any process which is performed on more busy days. Man, the machine of machines, the machine compared with which all the contrivances of the Watts[23] and the Arkwrights[24] are worthless, is repairing and winding up, so that he returns to his labours on the Monday with clearer intellect, with livelier spirits, with renewed corporal vigour. Never will I believe that what makes a population stronger, and healthier, and wiser, and better, can ultimately make it poorer. You try to frighten us by telling us that, in some German factories, the young work seventeen hours in the twenty-four; that they work so hard that among thousands there is not one who grows to such a stature that he can be admitted into the army; and you ask whether, if we pass this bill, we can possibly hold our own against such competition as this? Sir, I laugh at the thought of such

21. A region of southern Italy on the Tyrrhenian Sea.
22. Norwegian archipelago in the Arctic Ocean.
23. James Watt (1763–1819), a Scots engineer, invented the steam engine.
24. Sir Richard Arkwright (1732–1792), an English manufacturer, invented the spinning frame, a water-powered machine that had a much larger capacity than the jenny but could spin only coarse thread.

competition. If ever we are forced to yield the foremost place among commercial nations, we shall yield it, not to a race of degenerate dwarfs, but to some people preëminently vigorous in body and in mind.

For these reasons, Sir, I approve of the principle of this bill, and shall, without hesitation, vote for the second reading. To what extent we ought to reduce the hours of labour is a question of more difficulty. I think that we are in the situation of a physician who has satisfied himself that there is a disease, and that there is a specific medicine for the disease, but who is not certain what quantity of that medicine the patient's constitution will bear. Such a physician would probably administer his remedy by small doses, and carefully watch its operation. I cannot help thinking that, by at once reducing the hours of labour from twelve to ten, we should hazard too much. The change is great, and ought to be cautiously and gradually made. Suppose that there should be an immediate fall of wages, which is not impossible. Might there not be a violent reaction? Might not the public take up a notion that our legislation had been erroneous in principle, though, in truth, our error would have been an error, not of principle, but merely of degree? Might not Parliament be induced to retrace its steps? Might we not find it difficult to maintain even the present limitation? The wisest course would, in my opinion, be to reduce the hours of labour from twelve to eleven, to observe the effect of that experiment, and if, as I hope and believe, the result should be satisfactory, then to make a further reduction from eleven to ten.[25] This is a question, however, which will be with more advantage considered when we are in Committee.

One word, Sir, before I sit down, in answer to my noble friend near me.[26] He seems to think that this bill is ill timed. I own that I cannot agree with him. We carried up on Monday last to the bar of the Lords a bill which will remove the most hateful and pernicious restriction that ever was laid on trade.[27] Nothing can be more proper than to apply, in the same week, a remedy to a great evil of a directly opposite kind. As lawgivers, we have two great faults to confess and to repair. We have done that which we ought not to have done; we have left undone that which we ought to have done.[28] We have regulated that which we should have left to regulate itself. We have left unregulated that which we were bound to regulate. We have given to some branches of industry a protection which has proved their bane. We have withheld from public health and public morals the protection which was their due. We have prevented the labourer from buying his loaf where he could get it cheapest; but we have not prevented him from ruining his body and mind by premature and immoderate toil. I hope that we have seen the last both of a vicious system of interference and of a vicious system of noninterference, and that our poorer countrymen will no longer have reason to attribute their sufferings either to our meddling or to our neglect.

25. The proposal outlined by Macaulay for gradually reducing the number of working hours was the one actually adopted. In 1847, the working hours were reduced to eleven and, in 1848, to ten.

26. Identified in early editions as Lord Morpeth: George William Howard (1802–1864).

27. The Corn Laws were permanently abolished in 1849.

28. From "A General Confession" from the Order for Morning Prayer in the *Book of Common Prayer* of the Anglican Church.

THOMAS COOPER

B orn into a working-class family, Thomas Cooper (1805–1892) nevertheless obtained a broad, classical education, mostly through his own efforts. He worked by turns as a shoemaker, teacher, journalist, author, and preacher. Cooper joined the Chartists (see the entry on "The People's Charter") in 1840 when he discovered the extent of the workers' misery in the course of writing a story for the *Leicestershire Mercury*. He supported the cause in rousing speeches and songs and in his role as the editor of the *Midland Counties Illuminator*, a Chartist paper. He spent two years in prison, from 1843 to 1845, on a charge of sedition resulting from his promotion of mass strikes. While there, he wrote stories and an epic-length political poem, *The Purgatory of Suicides*, that received considerable critical notice. Cooper abandoned Chartism in 1845 following a quarrel with the Chartist leader Feargus O'Connor (1794–1855). Ten years later, he renewed his commitment to Christianity and became a Baptist minister. Thomas Cooper is the basis for the hero of Charles Kingsley's 1850 novel, *Alton Locke*, about a self-educated poet-tailor who takes up the Chartist cause.

"Seth Thompson, the Stockinger" was written while Cooper was in prison; it was published in 1845 in a collection of stories titled *Wise Saws and Modern Instances*. Typical of working-class fiction, the story revolves around a model worker, stereotypically orphaned at a young age and oppressed by the masters. Despite his best efforts, Seth is ultimately forced to leave his homeland and seek his fortune elsewhere.

Seth Thompson, the Stockinger[1]
or,
"When Things Are at the Worst They Begin to Mend"

Leicestershire stockingers call that a false proverb. "People have said so all our lives," say they; "but, although we have each and all agreed, every day, that things were at the worst, they never begun to mend yet!" This was not their language sixty years ago, but it is their daily language *now*; and the story that follows is but, as it were, of yesterday.

Seth Thompson was the only child of a widow, by the time that he was six years old, and became a "winding boy," in a shop of half-starved framework-knitters at Hinckley,—a kindred lot with hundreds of children of the same age, in Leicester-shire. Seth's mother was a tender mother to her child; but he met tenderness in no other quarter. He was weakly, and since that rendered him unable to get on with his winding of the yarn as fast as stronger children, he was abused and beaten by the journeymen, while the master stockinger, for every slight flaw in his work,—though it always resulted from a failure of strength rather than carelessness,—unfeelingly took the opportunity to "dock" his paltry wages.

Since her child could seldom add more than a shilling or fifteen-pence to the three, or, at most, four shillings, she was able to earn herself,—and she had to pay a heavy weekly rent for their humble home,—it will readily be understood that neither widow Thompson nor Seth were acquainted with the meaning of the word "luxury," either in food or habits. A scanty allowance of oatmeal and water formed their breakfast, potatoes and salt their dinner, and a limited portion of bread, with a wretchedly diluted something called "tea" as an accompaniment, constituted their late afternoon, or evening meal; and they knew no variety for years, winter or summer. The widow's child went shoeless in the warm season, and the cast-off substitutes he wore in winter, together with lack of warmth in his poor mother's home, and repulses from the shop fire by the master and men while at work, subjected him, through nearly the whole of every winter, to chilblains and other diseases of the feet. Rags were his familiar acquaintances, and, boy-like, he felt none of the aching shame and sorrow experienced by his mother when she beheld his destitute covering, and reflected that her regrets would not enable her to amend his tattered condition.

Seth's mother died when he reached fifteen, and expressed thankfulness, on her death-bed, that she was about to quit a world of misery, after being permitted to live till her child was in some measure able to struggle for himself. In spite of hard

---

1. Stockingers are hosiery workers.

usage and starvation, Seth grew up a strong lad, compared with puny youngsters that form the majority of the junior population in manufacturing districts. He was quick-witted, too, and had gathered a knowledge of letters and syllables, amidst the references to cheap newspapers and hourly conversation on politics by starving and naturally discontented stockingers. From a winding-boy, Seth was advanced to the frame, and, by the time he had reached seventeen, was not only able to earn as much as any other stockinger in Hinckley, when he could get work, but, with the usually improvident haste of the miserable and degraded, married a poor "seamer," who was two years younger than himself.

Seth Thompson at twenty-one, with a wife who was but nineteen, had become the parent of four children; and since he had never been able to bring home to his family more than seven shillings in one week, when the usual villainous deductions were made by master and manufacturer, in the shape of "frame-rent" and other "charges,"—since he had often had but *half*-work, with the usual deduction of *whole* charges, and had been utterly without work for six several periods, of from five to nine weeks each, during the four years of his married life,—the following hasty sketch of the picture which this "home of an Englishman" presented one noon, when a stranger knocked at the door, and it was opened by Seth himself, will scarcely be thought overdrawn:—

Except a grey deal table, there was not a single article within the walls which could be called "furniture," by the least propriety of language. This stood at the farther side of the room, and held a few soiled books and papers, Seth's torn and embrowned hat, and the mother's tattered straw bonnet. The mother sat on a three-legged stool, beside an osier cradle,[2] and was suckling her youngest child while she was eating potatoes and salt from an earthen dish upon her knee. Seth's dish of the same food stood on a seat formed of a board nailed roughly across the frame of a broken chair; while, in the centre of the floor, where the broken bricks had disappeared and left the earth bare, the three elder babes sat squatted round a board whereon boiled potatoes in their skins were piled,—a meal they were devouring greedily, squeezing the inside of the root into their mouths with their tiny hands, after the mode said to be practised in an Irish cabin. An empty iron pot stood near the low expiring fire, and three rude logs of wood lay near it,—the children's usual seats when they had partaken their meal. A description of the children's filthy and bedaubed appearance with the potato starch, and of the "looped and windowed" rags[3] that formed their covering, could only produce pain to the reader. Seth's clothing was not much superior to that of his offspring; but the clean cap and coloured cotton handkerchief of the mother, with her own really beautiful but delicate face and form, gave some relief to the melancholy picture.

Seth blushed, as he took up his dish of potatoes, and offered the stranger his fragment of a seat. And the stranger blushed, too, but refused the seat with a look

2. Cradle made from willow twigs.
3. Shakespeare, *King Lear* 3.4.31.

of so much benevolence that Seth's heart glowed to behold it; and his wife set down her porringer, and hushed the children that the stranger might deliver his errand with the greater ease.

"Your name is Thompson, I understand," said the stranger; "pray, do you know what was your mother's maiden name?"

"Greenwood,—Martha Greenwood was my poor mother's maiden name, sir," replied Seth, with the tears starting to his eyes.

The stranger seemed to have some difficulty in restraining similar feelings; and gazed, sadly, round upon the room and its squalid appearance, for a few moments, in silence.

Seth looked hard at his visitor, and thought of one whom his mother had often talked of; but did not like to put an abrupt question, though he imagined the stranger's features strongly resembled his parent's.

"Are working people in Leicestershire usually so uncomfortably situated as you appear to be?" asked the stranger, in a tone of deep commiseration which he appeared to be unable to control.

Seth Thompson and his wife looked uneasily at each other, and then fixed their gaze on the floor.

"Why, sir," replied Seth, blushing more deeply than before, "we married very betime, and our family, you see, has grown very fast; we hope things will mend a little with us when some o' the children are old enough to earn a little. We've only been badly off as yet, but you'd find a many not much better off, sir, I assure you, in Hinckley and elsewhere."

The stranger paused again, and the working of his features manifested strong inward feeling.

"I see nothing but potatoes," he resumed; "I hope your meal is unusually poor to-day, and that you and your family generally have a little meat at dinner."

"Meat, sir!" exclaimed Seth; "we have not known what it is to set a bit of meat before our children more than three times since the first was born; we usually had a little for our Sunday dinner when we were first married, but we can't afford it now!"

"Good God!" cried the stranger, with a look that demonstrated his agony of grief and indignation, "is this England,—the happy England, that I have heard the blacks in the West Indies talk of as a Paradise?"

"Are you my mother's brother? Is your name Elijah Greenwood?" asked Seth Thompson, unable longer to restrain the question.

"Yes," replied the visitor, and sat down upon Seth's rude seat, to recover his self-possession.

That was a happy visit for poor Seth Thompson and his wife and children. His mother had often talked of her only brother who went for a sailor when a boy, and was reported to be settled in some respectable situation in the West Indies, but concerning whom she never received any certain information. Elijah Greenwood had suddenly become rich, by the death of a childless old planter, whom he had faithfully served, and who had left him his entire estate. England was Elijah's first thought, when this circumstance took place; and, as soon as he could settle his new possession under some careful and trusty superintendent till his return, he had taken ship, and come to his native country and shire. By inquiry at the inn, he had learnt the afflictive fact of his sister's death, but had been guided to the poverty-stricken habitation of her son.

That was the last night that Seth Thompson and his children slept on their hard straw sacks on the floor,—the last day that they wore rags and tatters, and dined upon potatoes and salt. Seth's uncle placed him in a comfortable cottage, bought him suitable furniture, gave him a purse of 50*l.* for ready money, and promised him a half-yearly remittance from Jamaica, for the remainder of his, the uncle's life, with a certainty of a considerable sum at his death.

Seth and his wife could not listen, for a moment, to a proposal for leaving England, although they had experienced little but misery in it, their whole lives. The uncle, however, obtained from them a promise that they would not restrain any of their children from going out to Jamaica; and did not leave them till he had seen them fairly and comfortably settled, and beheld what he thought a prospect of comfort for them, in the future. Indeed, on the very morning succeeding that in which Seth's new fortune became known, the hitherto despised stockinger was sent for by the principal manufacturer of hosen,[4] in Hinckley, and offered "a shop of frames," in the language of the working men; that is, he was invited to become a "master," or one who receives the "stuff" from the capitalist or manufacturer, and holds of him, likewise, a given number of frames,—varying from half-a-dozen to a score or thirty, or even more; and thus becomes a profit-sharing middleman between the manufacturer and the labouring framework-knitters. Seth accepted the offer, for it seemed most natural to him to continue in the line of manufacture to which he had been brought up; and his uncle, with pleasurable hopes for his prosperity, bade him farewell!—

"Well, my dear," said Seth to his wife, as they sat down to a plentiful dinner, surrounded with their neatly-dressed and happy children, the day after the uncle's departure, "we used to say we should never prove the truth of the old proverb, but we have proved it at last: times came to the worst with us, and began to mend."

"Thank God! we have proved it, my love," replied the wife; "and I wish our poor neighbours could prove it as well."

Seth sighed,—and was silent.—

Some years rolled over, and Seth Thompson had become a well-informed, and deep-thinking man, but one in whom was no longer to be found that passionate attachment to his native country which he once felt. The manufacturer under whom he exercised the office of "master," had borrowed the greater part of Seth's uncle's remittances, as regularly as they arrived; and as Seth received due interest for these loans, and confided that the manufacturer's wealth was real, he believed he was taking a prudent way of laying up enough for the maintenance of his old age, or for meeting the misfortunes of sickness, should they come. But the manufacturer

4. Plural of "hose."

broke; and away went all that Seth had placed in his hands. Every week failures became more frequent,—employ grew scantier, for trade was said to decrease, though machinery increased,—discontent glowered on every brow,—and the following sketch of what was said at a meeting of starving framework-knitters held in Seth Thompson's shop but a month before he quitted England for ever, may serve to show what were his own reflections, and those of the suffering beings around him.

About twenty working men had assembled, and stood in three or four groups,—no "chairman" having been, as yet, chosen, since a greater number of attendants was expected.

"I wish thou would throw that ugly thing away, Timothy!" said a pale, intellectual looking workman, to one whose appearance was rendered filthy, in addition to his ragged destitution, by a dirty pipe stuck in his teeth, and so short that the head scarcely projected beyond his nose.

"I know it's ugly, Robert," replied the other, in a tone between self-accusation and despair,—"but it helps to pass away time. I've thrown it away twice,—but I couldn't help taking to it again last week, when I had nought to do. I think I should have hanged myself if I had not smoked a bit o' 'bacco."

"Well, I'm resolute that I'll neither smoke nor drink any more," said a third; "the tyrants can do what they like with us, as long as we feed their vices by paying taxes. If all men would be o' my mind there would soon be an end of their extravagance,—for they would have nothing to support it."

"Indeed, James," replied the smoker, "I don't feel so sure about your plan as you seem to be, yourself: you'll never persuade all working-men to give up a sup of ale or a pipe, if they can get hold of either; but, not to talk of that, what's to hinder the great rascals from inventing other taxes if these fail?"

"They couldn't easily be hindered, unless we had all votes," said the first speaker, "we're all well aware of that; but it would put 'em about, and render the party more unpopular that wanted to put on a new tax."

"I don't think that's so certain, either," replied the smoker; "depend on't, neither Whigs nor Tories will run back from the support of taxes. D'ye ever read of either party agreeing to 'stop the supplies,' as they call it, or join in any measure to prevent taxes from being collected till grievances are redressed?"

"No, indeed, not we," chimed another, lighting his short pipe by the help of his neighbour's, and folding his arms, with a look of something like mock bravery; "and, for my part, I don't think they ever will be redressed till we redress 'em ourselves!"

"Ah, Joseph!" said the pale-looking man, shaking his head, "depend upon it that's all a dream! How are poor starvelings like us, who have neither the means of buying a musket, nor strength to march and use it, if he had it,—how are we to overthrow thousands of disciplined troops with all their endless resources of ammunition?—It's all a dream, Joseph! depend on't."

"Then what are we to do,—lie down and die?" asked the other; but looked as if he were aware he had spoken foolishly, under the impulse of despair.

"I'm sure I often wish to die," said another, joining the conversation in a doleful tone; "I've buried my two youngest, and the oldest lad's going fast after his poor mother; one can't get bread enough to keep body and soul together!"

"Well, if it hadn't been for Seth Thompson's kindness," said another, "I believe I should have been dead by this time. I never felt so near putting an end to my life as I did last Sunday morning. I've been out o' work, now, nine weeks; and last Saturday I never put a crumb in my mouth, for I couldn't get it, and I caught up a raw potato in the street last Sunday morning, and ate if for sheer hunger. Seth Thompson saw me, and—God bless his heart!—he called me in and gave me a cup of warm coffee and some toast, and slipped a shilling into my hand." And the man turned aside to dash away his tears.

"Ay, depend upon it, we shall miss Seth, when he leaves us," said several voices together.

"It's many a year since there was a master in Hinckley like him," said the man with the short black pipe, "and, I fear, when he is gone, the whole grinding crew will be more barefaced than ever with their extortions and oppressions of poor men. Seth knew what it was to be nipped himself when he was younger; that's the reason that he can feel for others that suffer."

"It isn't always the case, though," said another; "look at skin-flint Jimps, the glove-master; I remember him when he was as ragged as an ass's colt: and where is there such another grinding villain as Jimps, now he is so well off?"

"The more's the shame for a man that preaches and professes to be religious," said the smoker.

"It was but last Saturday forenoon," resumed the man who had mentioned Jimps, the glove-master, "that he docked us two-pence a dozen, again: and when I asked him if his conscience wouldn't reproach him when he went to chapel, he looked like a fiend, and said, 'Bob! I knew what it was to be ground once; but it[']s my turn to grind now!'"

"And they call that religion, do they?" said the smoker, with an imprecation.

"It won't mend it to swear, my lad," said the intellectual-looking man; "we know one thing—that whatever such a fellow as this may do that professes religion, he doesn't imitate the conduct of his Master."

"I believe religion's all a bag of moonshine," said the smoker, "or else they that profess it would not act as they do."

"Don't talk so rashly, Tim," rejoined the other; "we always repent when we speak in ill-temper. Religion can't cure hypocrites, man, though it can turn drunkards and thieves into sober and honest men: it does not prove that religion is all a bag of moonshine, because some scoundrels make a handle of it. Truth's truth, in spite of all the scandal that falsehood and deceit brings upon it."

"Isn't it time we got to business?" said one of the group.

"I don't think it will be of any use to wait longer," said another; "there will not be more with us, if we wait another hour; the truth is, that men dare not attend a meeting like this, for fear of being turned off, and so being starved outright;—there's scarcely any spirit left in Hinckley."

"I propose that Seth Thompson takes the chair," said another, taking off his ragged hat, and speaking aloud.

A faint clapping of hands followed, and Seth took a seat upon a raised part of one of the frames at the end of the shop, and opened the meeting according to the simple but business-like form, which working men are wont to observe in similar meetings, in the manufacturing districts.

"I feel it would scarcely become me to say much, my friends," he said, "since I am about to leave you. I thought, at one time, that nothing could have ever inclined me to leave old England; but it seems like folly to me, now, to harbour an attachment to a country where one sees nothing but misery, nor any chance of improvement. I would not wish to damp your spirits; but if I were to tell you how much uneasiness I have endured for some years past, even while you have seen me apparently well off and comfortable, you would not wonder that I am resolved to quit this country, since I have the offer of ease and plenty, though in a foreign clime. I tell you, working men, that I had power over Mr. _____, by the moneys I had lent him, or I should have been turned out of this shop years ago. Week by week have we quarrelled, because I would not practise the tyrannies and extortions upon working men that he recommended and urged. It is but a hateful employ to a man of any feeling,—is that of a master-stockinger under an avaricious and inhuman hosier. But, if the master's situation be so far from being a happy one, I need not tell you that I know well, by experience, how much more miserable is that of the starved and degraded working man. Indeed, indeed,—I see no hope for you, my friends,—yet, I repeat, I would not wish to damp your spirits. Perhaps things may mend yet; but I confess I see no likelihood of it, till the poor are represented as well as the rich."

It might produce weariness to go through all the topics that were touched upon by Seth and others. They were such as are familiarly handled, daily, in the manufacturing districts; ay, and with a degree of mental force and sound reasoning,—if not with polish of words,—that would make some gentlefolk stare, if they were to hear the sounds proceeding from the haggard figures in rags who often utter them. The "deceit" of the Reform Bill,[5] as it is usually termed by manufacturing "operatives"; the trickery of the Whigs; the corruption and tyranny of the Tories; the heartlessness of the manufacturers and "the League";[6] and the right of every sane Englishman of one and twenty years of age to a vote in the election of those who have to govern him, were each and all broadly, and unshrinkingly, and yet not intemperately, asserted.

5. The First Reform Bill, passed by Parliament in 1832, extended the franchise to a greater number of middle-class men. Lower-middle-class and working-class men had agitated for the legislation, thinking that they too would receive the vote. One of the six points of "The People's Charter" called for universal manhood suffrage (see "The People's Charter" in this section).

6. The Anti-Corn Law League (1838–1846) was an organization led by Manchester manufacturers Richard Cobden (1804–1865) and John Bright (1811–1889). The League espoused free trade and laissez-faire economic policies and opposed protectionist legislation, in particular the Corn Laws, which levied a tariff on imported grain to safeguard English agricultural interests. The League was instrumental in effecting the repeal of the Corn Laws in 1846.

One or two, in an under-tone, ventured to suggest that it might be advantageous to try, once more, to act with the Anti-Corn Law men, since many of the members of the League professed democracy; and, if that were done, working men would not fear to attend a meeting such as that they were then holding. But this was scouted by the majority; and a proposal was, at length, made, in a written form, and seconded,—"That a branch of an association of working men, similar to one that was stated to have been just established at Leicester, should be formed." The motion was put and carried,—a committee, and secretary, and treasurer, were chosen,—and the men seemed to put off their dejection, and grow energetic in their resolution to attempt their own deliverance from misery, in the only way that they conceived it could ever be substantially effected: but their purpose came to the ears of the manufacturers on the following day, threats of loss of work were issued, and no association was established!

Seth Thompson took his family to the West Indies, pursuant to the many and urgent requests contained in his uncle's letters, and soon entered upon the enjoyment of the plenty in store for him. Hinckley stockingers remain in their misery still; and, perhaps, there is scarcely a place in England where starving working men have so little hope,—although "things," they say, "have come to the worst,"—that "they" will ever "begin to mend."

CHARLES DICKENS

NOVELIST AND JOURNALIST Charles Dickens (1812–1870) was the son of an improvident navy pay clerk. When his father was imprisoned for debt, Dickens, then age twelve, was sent to work in a warehouse pasting labels on bottles of shoe blacking. Though he was rescued after a few months by his father's timely inheritance of a sum sufficient to settle his debts, Dickens never forgot the sense of degradation and humiliation he had suffered. As a young man, he taught himself shorthand and worked as a parliamentary recorder while submitting articles to newspapers and journals. From the publication of his first novel, *Pickwick Papers,* in 1836–37, Dickens enjoyed extraordinary popularity. When he chose, therefore, to expose social and political ills such as the plight of destitute orphans (*Oliver Twist,* 1837–38), the maddening inefficiency of the legal system (*Bleak House,* 1852–53), or the narrowness and sterility of utilitarianism and the dispiriting and debilitating effects of factory labor (*Hard Times,* 1854), he drew popular attention to the problems addressed. The two journals he edited, *Household Words* (1850–59) and *All the Year Round* (1859–70), offered yet another forum for his exposés on social issues ranging from the rehabilitation of fallen women to the reform of prisons.

The following essay, "A Walk in a Workhouse," appeared in the May 25, 1850, issue of *Household Words.* Upon the passage of the New Poor Law of 1834, which was designed to deter the able-bodied poor from seeking welfare, the government opened a system of workhouses where paupers were housed and, if mentally and physically fit, put to work. In the first half of the century, workhouses, commonly known as Poor Law Bastilles, were harsh, forbidding institutions where families were separated; physically demanding but useless work was assigned; and food, sleeping accommodations, and medical attention were inadequate. Although the prospect of entering the workhouse inspired fear in many paupers, no more than one-third of the able-bodied poor were ever institutionalized; most of those who found "refuge" there were—like the inmates Dickens meets—orphaned, elderly, ill, or infirm. For other accounts of the workhouse, see Henry Mayhew's interviews (from *London Labour and the London Poor,* included in this section) with the crippled seller of nutmeg-graters and with the elderly woman who collects "pure."

A Walk in a Workhouse

A few Sundays ago, I formed one of the congregation assembled in the chapel of a large metropolitan Workhouse. With the exception of the clergyman and clerk, and a very few officials, there were none but paupers present. The children sat in the galleries; the women in the body of the chapel, and in one of the side aisles; the men in the remaining aisle. The service was decorously performed, though the sermon might have been much better adapted to the comprehension and to the circumstances of the hearers. The usual supplications were offered, with more than the usual significancy in such a place, for the fatherless children and widows, for all sick persons and young children, for all that were desolate and oppressed, for the comforting and helping of the weak-hearted, for the raising-up of them that had fallen; for all that were in danger, necessity, and tribulation. The prayers of the congregation were desired "for several persons in the various wards, dangerously ill"; and others who were recovering returned their thanks to Heaven.

Among this congregation, were some evil-looking young women, and beetle-browed young men; but not many—perhaps that kind of characters kept away. Generally, the faces (those of the children excepted) were depressed and subdued, and wanted colour. Aged people were there, in every variety. Mumbling, blear-eyed, spectacled, stupid, deaf, lame; vacantly winking in the gleams of sun that now and then crept in through the open doors, from the paved yard; shading their listening ears, or blinking eyes, with their withered hands; poring over their books, leering at nothing, going to sleep, crouching and drooping in corners. There were weird old women, all skeleton within, all bonnet and cloak without, continually wiping their eyes with dirty dusters of pocket-handkerchiefs; and there were ugly old crones, both male and female, with a ghastly kind of contentment upon them which was not at all comforting to see. Upon the whole, it was the dragon, Pauperism, in a very weak and impotent condition; toothless, fangless, drawing his breath heavily enough, and hardly worth chaining up.

When the service was over, I walked with the humane and conscientious gentleman whose duty it was to take that walk, that Sunday morning, through the little world of poverty enclosed within the workhouse walls. It was inhabited by a population of some fifteen hundred or two thousand paupers, ranging from the infant newly born or not yet come into the pauper world, to the old man dying on his bed.

In a room opening from a squalid yard, where a number of listless women were lounging to and fro, trying to get warm in the ineffectual sunshine of the tardy May morning—in the "Itch Ward,"[1] not to compromise the truth—a woman such

---

1. The "itch" was a slang term for scabies, a contagious skin disease caused by a mite.

as Hogarth[2] has often drawn was hurriedly getting on her gown, before a dusty fire. She was the nurse, or wardswoman, of that insalubrious department—herself a pauper—flabby, raw-boned, untidy—unpromising and coarse of aspect as need be. But, on being spoken to about the patients whom she had in charge, she turned round, with her shabby gown half on, half off, and fell a crying with all her might. Not for show, not querulously, not in any mawkish sentiment, but in the deep grief and affliction of her heart; turning away her dishevelled head: sobbing most bitterly, wringing her hands, and letting fall abundance of great tears, that choked her utterance. What was the matter with the nurse of the itch-ward? Oh, "the dropped child"[3] was dead! Oh, the child that was found in the street, and she had brought up ever since, had died an hour ago, and see where the little creature lay, beneath this cloth! The dear, the pretty dear!

The dropped child seemed too small and poor a thing for Death to be in earnest with, but Death had taken it; and already its diminutive form was neatly washed, composed, and stretched as if in sleep upon a box. I thought I heard a voice from Heaven saying, It shall be well for thee, O nurse of the itch-ward, when some less gentle pauper does those offices to thy cold form, that such as the dropped child are the angels who behold my Father's face!

In another room, were several ugly old women crouching, witch-like, round a hearth, and chattering and nodding, after the manner of the monkeys. "All well here? And enough to eat?" A general chattering and chuckling; at last an answer from a volunteer. "Oh yes gentleman! Bless you gentleman! Lord bless the parish of St. So-and-So! It feed the hungry, Sir, and give drink to the thirsty, and it warm them which is cold, so it do, and good luck to the parish of St. So-and-So, and thankee gentleman!" Elsewhere, a party of pauper nurses were at dinner. "How do *you* get on?" "Oh pretty well Sir! We works hard, and we lives hard—like the sodgers!"[4]

In another room, a kind of purgatory or place of transition, six or eight noisy madwomen were gathered together, under the superintendence of one sane attendant. Among them was a girl of two or three and twenty, very prettily dressed, of most respectable appearance, and good manners, who had been brought in from the house where she had lived as domestic servant (having, I suppose, no friends), on account of being subject to epileptic fits, and requiring to be removed under the influence of a very bad one. She was by no means of the same stuff, or the same breeding, or the same experience, or in the same state of mind, as those by whom she was surrounded; and she pathetically complained, that the daily association and the nightly noise made her worse, and was driving her mad—which was perfectly evident. The case was noted for enquiry and redress, but she said she had already been there for some weeks.

2. Artist William Hogarth (1697–1764) excelled in portrait painting and in engraving series of pictures that "told" stories of the seamy side of eighteenth-century English life such as *Marriage à la Mode* and *The Harlot's Progress.*
3. The Oxford English Dictionary gives "abandoned" as one meaning of "dropped."
4. Soldiers.

If this girl had stolen her mistress's watch, I do not hesitate to say she would, in all probability, have been infinitely better off. Bearing in mind, in the present brief description of this walk, not only the facts already stated in this Journal, in reference to the Model Prison at Pentonville,[5] but the general treatment of convicted prisoners under the associated silent system too, it must be once more distinctly set before the reader, that we have come to this absurd, this dangerous, this monstrous pass, that the dishonest felon is, in respect of cleanliness, order, diet, and accommodation, better provided for, and taken care of, than the honest pauper.

And this conveys no special imputation on the workhouse of the parish of St. So-and-So, where, on the contrary, I saw many things to commend. It was very agreeable, recollecting that most infamous and atrocious enormity committed at Tooting[6]—an enormity which, a hundred years hence, will still be vividly remembered in the bye-ways of English life, and which has done more to engender a gloomy discontent and suspicion among many thousands of the people than all the Chartist[7] leaders could have done in all their lives—to find the pauper children in this workhouse looking robust and well, and apparently the objects of very great care. In the Infant School—a large, light, airy room at the top of the building—the little creatures, being at dinner, and eating their potatoes heartily, were not cowed by the presence of strange visitors, but stretched out their small hands to be shaken, with a very pleasant confidence. And it was comfortable to see two mangy pauper rocking-horses rampant in a corner. In the girls' school, where the dinner was also in progress, everything bore a cheerful and healthy aspect. The meal was over, in the boys' school, by the time of our arrival there, and the room was not yet quite re-arranged; but the boys were roaming unrestrained about a large and airy yard, as any other school-boys might have done. Some of them had been drawing large ships upon the schoolroom wall; and if they had a mast with shrouds and stays set up for practice (as they have in the Middlesex House of Correction[8]), it would be so much the better. At present, if a boy should feel a strong impulse upon

5. At Pentonville, opened as a "model" prison in 1842, a strict separate system was in force, with each prisoner housed in an individual cell. Other prisons imposed a silent system, allowing prisoners to live and work together but forbidding them to speak to one another. Charles Dickens was highly critical of the living conditions in modern prisons such as Pentonville. In an article titled "Pet Prisoners," which appeared in the April 28, 1850, issue of *Household Words,* Dickens expressed outrage that convicted criminals were fed and housed better than paupers in workhouses. Moreover, he satirized the model prison through the experiences of two incarcerated villains, Uriah Heep and Mr. Littimer, in his novel *David Copperfield* (1849–50).

6. In 1848, an outbreak of cholera took the lives of a number of children at Drouet's baby farm at Tooting, where 1,400 foster children were kept in appalling, overcrowded conditions. Dickens wrote two articles for the *Examiner* on the tragedy, assigning blame to the London Board of Guardians, who sent children to the farm, and to the Poor Law Authority.

7. Supporter of the working-class political movement of the 1830s and 1840s that presented to Parliament, on three separate occasions, a document known as The People's Charter. The Charter called for six reforms: universal manhood suffrage, a secret ballot, payment for service in Parliament, the elimination of the property qualification for members of Parliament, equal electoral districts, and annual elections. For the specific wording of this document, see "The People's Charter" in this section.

8. Houses of Correction held individuals charged with minor offenses while those found guilty of serious crimes were sentenced to convict prisons.

him to learn the art of going aloft, he could only gratify it, I presume, as the men and women paupers gratify their aspirations after better board and lodging, by smashing as many workhouse windows as possible, and being promoted to prison.

In one place, the Newgate[9] of the workhouse, a company of boys and youths were locked up in a yard alone; their day-room being a kind of kennel where the casual poor[10] used formerly to be littered down at night. Divers of them had been there some long time. "Are they never going away?" was the natural enquiry. "Most of them are crippled, in some form or other," said the Wardsman, "and not fit for anything." They slunk about, like dispirited wolves or hyaenas; and made a pounce at their food when it was served out, much as those animals do. The big-headed idiot shuffling his feet along the pavement, in the sunlight outside, was a more agreeable object everyway.

Groves of babies in arms; groves of mothers and other sick women in bed; groves of lunatics; jungles of men in stone-paved downstairs day-rooms, waiting for their dinners; longer and longer groves of old people, in upstairs Infirmary wards, wearing out life, God knows how—this was the scenery through which the walk lay, for two hours. In some of these latter chambers, there were pictures stuck against the wall, and a neat display of crockery and pewter on a kind of sideboard; now and then it was a treat to see a plant or two; in almost every ward, there was a cat.

In all of these Long Walks of aged and infirm, some old people were bed-ridden, and had been for a long time; some were sitting on their beds half-naked; some dying in their beds; some out of bed, and sitting at a table near the fire. A sullen or lethargic indifference to what was asked, a blunted sensibility to every-thing but warmth and food, a moody absence of complaint as being of no use, a dogged silence and resentful desire to be left alone again, I thought were generally apparent. On our walking into the midst of one of these dreary perspectives of old men, nearly the following little dialogue took place, the nurse not being imme-diately at hand:

"All well here?"

No answer. An old man in a Scotch cap sitting among others on a form at the table, eating out of a tin porringer, pushes back his cap a little to look at us, claps it down on his forehead again with the palm of his hand, and goes on eating.

"All well here?" (repeated.)

No answer. Another old man sitting on his bed, paralytically peeling a boiled potato, lifts his head, and stares.

"Enough to eat?"

No answer. Another old man, in bed, turns himself and coughs.

"How are *you* to day?" To the last old man.

That old man says nothing; but another old man, a tall old man of a very good address, speaking with perfect correctness, comes forward from somewhere, and volunteers an answer. The reply almost always proceeds from a volunteer, and not from the person looked at or spoken to.

9. A London prison used exclusively for felons awaiting execution.
10. Those who received temporary welfare relief.

"We are very old, Sir," in a mild, distinct voice. "We can't expect to be well, most of us."

"Are you comfortable?"

"I have no complaint to make, Sir." With a half shake of his head, a half shrug of his shoulders, and a kind of apologetic smile.

"Enough to eat?"

"Why, Sir, I have but a poor appetite," with the same air as before; "and yet I get through my allowance very easily."

"But," showing a porringer with a Sunday dinner in it; "here is a portion of mutton, and three potatoes. You can't starve on that?"

"Oh dear no, Sir," with the same apologetic air. "Not starve."

"What do you want?"

"We have very little bread, Sir. It's an exceedingly small quantity of bread."

The nurse, who is now rubbing her hands at the questioner's elbow, interferes with, "It ain't much raly, Sir. You see they've only six ounces a day, and when they've took their breakfast, there *can* only be a little left for night, Sir."

Another old man, hitherto invisible, rises out of his bedclothes, as out of a grave, and looks on.

"You have tea at night?" The questioner is still addressing the well-spoken old man.

"Yes, Sir, we have tea at night."

"And you save what bread you can from the morning, to eat with it?"

"Yes, Sir—if we can save any."

"And you want more to eat with it?"

"Yes, Sir." With a very anxious face.

The questioner, in the kindness of his heart, appears a little discomposed, and changes the subject.

"What has become of the old man who used to lie in that bed in the corner?"

The nurse don't remember what old man is referred to. There has been such a many old men. The well-spoken old man is doubtful. The spectral old man who has come to life in bed says, "Billy Stevens." Another old man who has previously had his head in the fireplace pipes out, "Charley Walters."

Something like a feeble interest is awakened. I suppose Charley Walters had conversation in him.

"He's dead!" says the piping old man.

Another old man, with one eye screwed up, hastily displaces the piping old man, and says:

"Yes! Charley Walters died in that bed, and—and—"

"Billy Stevens," persists the spectral old man.

"No, no! and Johnny Rogers died in that bed, and—and—they're both on 'em dead—and Sam'l Bowyer," this seems very extraordinary to him, "he went out!"

With this he subsides, and all the old men (having had quite enough of it) subside, and the spectral old man goes into his grave again, and takes the shade of Billy Stevens with him.

As we turn to go out at the door, another previously invisible old man, a hoarse old man in a flannel gown, is standing there, as if he had just come up through the floor.

"I beg your pardon, Sir, could I take the liberty of saying a word?"

"Yes; what is it?"

"I am greatly better in my health, Sir; but what I want, to get me quite round," with his hand on his throat, "is a little fresh air, Sir. It has always done my complaint so much good, Sir. The regular leave for going out, comes round so seldom, that if the gentlemen, next Friday, would give me leave to go out walking, now and then—for only an hour or so, Sir!—"

Who could wonder, looking through those weary vistas of bed and infirmity, that it should do him good to meet with some other scenes, and assure himself that there was something else on earth? Who could help wondering why the old men lived on as they did; what grasp they had on life; what crumbs of interest or occupation they could pick up from its bare board; whether Charley Walters had ever described to them the days when he kept company with some old pauper woman in the bud, or Billy Stevens ever told them of the time when he was a dweller in the far-off foreign land called Home!

The morsel of burnt child, lying in another room, so patiently, in bed, wrapped in lint, and looking steadfastly at us with his bright quiet eyes when we spoke to him kindly, looked as if the knowledge of these things, and of all the tender things there are to think about, might have been in his mind—as if he thought, with us, that there was a fellow-feeling in the pauper nurses which appeared to make them more kind to their charges than the race of common nurses in the hospitals—as if he mused upon the Future of some older children lying around him in the same place, and thought it best, perhaps, all things considered, that he should die—as if he knew, without fear, of those many coffins, made and unmade, piled up in the store below—and of his unknown friend, "the dropped child," calm upon the box-lid covered with a cloth. But there was something wistful and appealing, too, in his tiny face, as if, in the midst of all the hard necessities and incongruities he pondered on, he pleaded, in behalf of the helpless and the aged poor, for a little more liberty—and a little more bread.

Published in 1854, *Hard Times* is one of Dickens's most brief and least happy novels. Setting the action in the fictional Coketown, modeled on the industrial towns of Manchester and Preston, Dickens addresses, among other concerns, the plight of factory operatives caught between two forces struggling for domination: exploitative owners or masters who refer to employees, by a reductive synecdoche, only as "hands" and manipulative labor organizers who use workers to secure political ends not clearly beneficial to the working class. In language that reflects the ideas and moral indignation of Thomas Carlyle, to whom *Hard Times* is dedicated (see part 1), Dickens portrays laissez-faire economics as altogether dehumanizing, and he establishes with lucidity and force just how bleak were the living conditions with which workers needed to contend.

> It was a town of red brick, or of brick that would have been red if the smoke and ashes had allowed it; but as matters stood it was a town of unnatural red and black like the painted face of a savage. It was a town of machinery and tall chimneys, out of which interminable serpents of smoke trailed themselves for ever and ever, and never got uncoiled. It had a black canal in it, and a river that ran purple with ill-smelling dye, and vast piles of building full of windows where there was a rattling and a trembling all day long, and where the piston of the steam engine worked monotonously up and down like the head of an elephant in a state of melancholy madness. It contained several large streets all very like one another, and many small streets still more like one another, inhabited by people equally like one another, who all went in and out at the same hours, with the same sound upon the same pavements, to do the same work, and to whom every day was the same as yesterday and to-morrow, and every year the counterpart of the last and the next.

The description of the dreariness and monotony that characterize Coketown is typical of complaints lodged by many against the desperately grim world of the working classes. Unlike some other commentators, however, Dickens is insistent that oppression derives not alone from employers but also from fellow workers who, driven by the extremity of their own situations and by their belief in "naturally" competitive and antagonistic labor relations, act as unfeelingly as do their masters.

Dickens focuses upon the struggles of Stephen Blackpool, a guileless Coketown worker employed by Mr. Bounderby, a brutally self-interested, aggressive individual who purports to be a self-made man. Stephen has given a solemn promise that he will take no part in labor agitation, and, accordingly, he refuses to join the union organizers with his coworkers. The upshot of his refusal is that Slackbridge, the union agent who arrives as an outsider unfamiliar with Coketown, convinces Stephen's comrades to make him a social pariah alienated from his fellows, who will no longer speak with or even acknowledge him. Dickens based his portrayal of owner and union tensions upon his own observations of a developing strike in Preston, about which he wrote a probing editorial titled "On Strike" (*Household Words,* February 11, 1854). He published *Hard Times* in serial installments in his weekly periodical *Household Words,* and he made a point of following its serialization with *North and South* by Elizabeth Gaskell, another novel about labor relations, which developed further his own portrayal of the harshly divisive actions of the unionists as well as of the stubborn clinging by owners to predatory relations with workers. Angered by the conditions that working men and women faced, Dickens was nonetheless suspicious that regulatory organizations such as unions would, in the effort to secure workers' rights, ignore the personal well-being of the individual worker.

The first of the three excerpts from *Hard Times* is taken from Dickens's introductory description of Stephen Blackpool in book 1 of the novel. The subsequent selections comprise two entire chapters from book 2 in which Stephen finds himself estranged from his comrades and then discharged and blacklisted by his employer for resolutely defending the very men who have so unjustly disclaimed his solidarity with them.

From *Hard Times*
Book the First

Chapter X
Stephen Blackpool

I entertain a weak idea that the English people are as hard-worked as any people upon whom the sun shines. I acknowledge to this ridiculous idiosyncrasy, as a reason why I would give them a little more play.

In the hardest working part of Coketown; in the innermost fortifications of that ugly citadel, where Nature was as strongly bricked out as killing airs and gases were bricked in; at the heart of the labyrinth of narrow courts upon courts, and close streets upon streets, which had come into existence piecemeal, every piece in a violent hurry for some one man's purpose, and the whole an unnatural family, shouldering, and trampling, and pressing one another to death;[1] in the last close nook of this great exhausted receiver, where the chimneys, for want of air to make a draught, were built in an immense variety of stunted and crooked shapes, as though every house put out a sign of the kind of people who might be expected to be born in it; among the multitude of Coketown, generically called "the Hands,"— a race who would have found more favour with some people, if Providence had seen fit to make them only hands, or, like the lower creatures of the seashore, only hands and stomachs—lived a certain Stephen Blackpool, forty years of age.

Stephen looked older, but he had had a hard life. It is said that every life has its roses and thorns; there seemed, however, to have been a misadventure or mistake in Stephen's case, whereby somebody else had become possessed of his roses, and he had become possessed of the same somebody else's thorns in addition to his

---

1. In his portrayal of the streets and houses as non-communal, "piecemeal" units, engaged in a precipitously violent competition with one another for survival, Dickens makes Coketown the embodiment of the laissez-faire business ethic that, he maintains, creates of humankind "an unnatural family" indeed.

own. He had known, to use his words, a peck of trouble. He was usually called Old Stephen, in a kind of rough homage to the fact.

A rather stooping man, with a knitted brow, a pondering expression of face, and a hard-looking head sufficiently capacious, on which his iron-grey hair lay long and thin, Old Stephen might have passed for a particularly intelligent man in his condition. Yet he was not. He took no place among those remarkable "Hands," who, piecing together their broken intervals of leisure through many years, had mastered difficult sciences, and acquired a knowledge of most unlikely things. He held no station among the Hands who could make speeches and carry on debates. Thousands of his compeers could talk much better than he, at any time. He was a good power-loom weaver, and a man of perfect integrity. What more he was, or what else he had in him, if anything, let him show for himself.

Book the Second

Chapter IV
Men and Brothers

"Oh my friends, the down-trodden operatives of Coketown! Oh my friends and fellow-countrymen, the slaves of an iron-handed and a grinding despotism! Oh my friends and fellow-sufferers, and fellow-workmen, and fellow-men! I tell you that the hour is come, when we must rally round one another as One united power, and crumble into dust the oppressors that too long have battened upon the plunder of our families, upon the sweat of our brows, upon the labour of our hands, upon the strength of our sinews, upon the God-created glorious rights of Humanity, and upon the holy and eternal privileges of Brotherhood!"

"Good!" "Hear, hear, hear!" "Hurrah!" and other cries, arose in many voices from various parts of the densely crowded and suffocatingly close Hall, in which the orator, perched on a stage, delivered himself of this and what other froth and fume he had in him. He had declaimed himself into a violent heat, and was as hoarse as he was hot. By dint of roaring at the top of his voice under a flaring gaslight, clenching his fists, knitting his brows, setting his teeth, and pounding with his arms, he had taken so much out of himself by this time, that he was brought to a stop, and called for a glass of water.

As he stood there, trying to quench his fiery face with his drink of water, the comparison between the orator and the crowd of attentive faces turned towards him, was extremely to his disadvantage. Judging him by Nature's evidence, he was above the mass in very little but the stage on which he stood. In many great respects he was essentially below them. He was not so honest, he was not so manly, he was not so good-humoured; he substituted cunning for their simplicity, and

Figure 3.6. Sir Hubert von Herkomer, *On Strike*. Courtesy of Royal Academy of Arts, London, UK/Bridgeman Art Library.

Bavarian immigrant Hubert von Herkomer (1849–1914) developed a reputation in the 1870s as the contributor of pictures of working-class life to *The Graphic*, a weekly newspaper that attracted a wide readership. In later years, Herkomer produced portraits, rural scenes, and pictures such as the one shown here that were marked by their social realism. *On Strike*, c. 1891, shows a working man torn between his obligation to support his coworkers and his responsibility to provide for his family.

passion for their safe solid sense. An ill-made, high-shouldered man, with lowering brows, and his features crushed into an habitually sour expression, he contrasted most unfavourably, even in his mongrel dress, with the great body of his hearers in their plain working clothes. Strange as it always is to consider any assembly in the act of submissively resigning itself to the dreariness of some complacent person, lord or commoner, whom three-fourths of it could, by no human means, raise out of the slough[2] of inanity to their own intellectual level, it was particularly strange, and it was even particularly affecting, to see this crowd of earnest faces, whose honesty in the main no competent observer free from bias could doubt, so agitated by such a leader.

2. A stagnant hollow in which one might become mired.

Good! Hear, hear! Hurrah! The eagerness both of attention and intention, exhibited in all the countenances, made them a most impressive sight. There was no carelessness, no languor, no idle curiosity; none of the many shades of indifference to be seen in all other assemblies, visible for one moment there. That every man felt his condition to be, somehow or other, worse than it might be; that every man considered it incumbent on him to join the rest, towards the making of it better; that every man felt his only hope to be in his allying himself to the comrades by whom he was surrounded; and that in this belief, right or wrong (unhappily wrong then), the whole of that crowd were gravely, deeply, faithfully in earnest; must have been as plain to any one who chose to see what was there, as the bare beams of the roof and the whitened brick walls. Nor could any such spectator fail to know in his own breast, that these men, through their very delusions, showed great qualities, susceptible of being turned to the happiest and best account; and that to pretend (on the strength of sweeping axioms, howsoever cut and dried) that they went astray wholly without cause, and of their own irrational wills, was to pretend that there could be smoke without fire, death without birth, harvest without seed, anything or everything produced from nothing.

The orator having refreshed himself, wiped his corrugated forehead from left to right several times with his handkerchief folded into a pad, and concentrated all his revived forces, in a sneer of great disdain and bitterness.

"But, oh my friends and brothers! Oh men and Englishmen, the down-trodden operatives of Coketown! What shall we say of that man—that working man, that I should find it necessary so to libel the glorious name—who, being practically and well acquainted with the grievances and wrongs of you, the injured pith and marrow[3] of this land, and having heard you, with a noble and majestic unanimity that will make Tyrants tremble, resolve for to subscribe to the funds of the United Aggregate Tribunal, and to abide by the injunctions issued by that body for your benefit, whatever they may be—what, I ask you, will you say of that working-man, since such I must acknowledge him to be, who, at such a time, deserts his post, and sells his flag; who, at such a time, turns a traitor and a craven and a recreant; who, at such a time, is not ashamed to make to you the dastardly and humiliating avowal that he will hold himself aloof, and will *not* be one of those associated in the gallant stand for Freedom and for Right?"

The assembly was divided at this point. There were some groans and hisses, but the general sense of honour was much too strong for the condemnation of a man unheard. "Be sure you're right, Slackbridge!" "Put him up!" "Let's hear him!" Such things were said on many sides. Finally, one strong voice called out, "Is the man heer? If the man's heer, Slackbridge, let's hear the man himseln, 'stead o' yo." Which was received with a round of applause.

Slackbridge, the orator, looked about him with a withering smile; and, holding out his right hand at arm's length (as the manner of all Slackbridges is), to still the thundering sea, waited until there was a profound silence.

3. The most central and significant elements.

"Oh my friends and fellow-men!" said Slackbridge then, shaking his head with violent scorn, "I do not wonder that you, the prostrate sons of labour, are incredulous of the existence of such a man. But he who sold his birthright for a mess of pottage existed, and Judas Iscariot existed, and Castlereagh existed,[4] and this man exists!"

Here, a brief press and confusion near the stage, ended in the man himself standing at the orator's side before the concourse. He was pale and a little moved in the face—his lips especially showed it; but he stood quiet, with his left hand at his chin, waiting to be heard. There was a chairman to regulate the proceedings, and this functionary now took the case into his own hands.

"My friends," said he, "by virtue o' my office as your president, I askes o' our friend Slackbridge, who may be a little over hetter[5] in this business, to take his seat, whiles this man Stephen Blackpool is heern. You all know this man Stephen Blackpool. You know him awlung o'[6] his misfort'ns, and his good name."

With that, the chairman shook him frankly by the hand, and sat down again. Slackbridge likewise sat down, wiping his hot forehead—always from left to right, and never the reverse way.

"My friends," Stephen began, in the midst of a dead calm; "I ha' hed[7] what's been spok'n o' me, and 'tis lickly that I shan't mend it. But I'd liefer[8] you'd hearn the truth concernin myseln, fro my lips than fro onny other man's, though I never cud'n speak afore so monny, wi'out bein moydert[9] and muddled."[10]

Slackbridge shook his head as if he would shake it off, in his bitterness.

"I'm th' one single Hand in Bounderby's mill, o' a' the men theer, as don't coom in wi' th' proposed reg'lations. I canna' coom in wi' 'em. My friends, I doubt their doin' yo onny good. Licker they'll do yo hurt."

Slackbridge laughed, folded his arms, and frowned sarcastically.

"But 't an't sommuch for that as I stands out. If that were aw, I'd coom in wi' th' rest. But I ha' my reasons—mine, yo see—for being hindered; not on'y now, but awlus—awlus—life long!"[11]

---

4. Esau betrays his heritage, for, when he was near to starvation, he sold his birthright to his twin brother Jacob for a meal of bread and red pottage of lentils: see Genesis 25:29–34. Judas Iscariot was the disciple who betrayed Jesus: see Luke 22. Viscount Robert Stewart Castlereagh, Marquis of Londonderry (1769–1822), was blamed for the "Peterloo Massacre" in Manchester in 1819 when at least nine people were killed and several hundred were injured by an armed but ill-directed militia who charged a crowd gathered at St. Peter's Field to protest working conditions.

5. Heated, angrily disposed.

6. Because of.

7. Heard.

8. Rather; prefer.

9. Timidly reticent and disordered.

10. Troublingly confused. *Muddle* and *muddled* are the terms Stephen consistently employs to describe the social and moral chaos that threatens humane relations in his world of work; his culminating assessment of the world is that it is "aw a muddle! Fro first to last, a muddle!"

11. As Stephen subsequently tells Bounderby, he will not join with the other workers because he has "passed a promess." Readers of the full novel, however, remain unenlightened about the nature of this promise. In a manuscript version, Dickens had included a brief interchange between Stephen and his beloved companion Rachael in which Stephen does vow to refrain from active labor protest, but this passage was never included in published versions of the novel.

Slackbridge jumped up and stood beside him, gnashing and tearing. "Oh my friends, what but this did I tell you? Oh my fellow-countrymen, what warning but this did I give you? And how shows this recreant conduct in a man on whom unequal laws are known to have fallen heavy? Oh you Englishmen, I ask you how does this subornation show in one of yourselves, who is thus consenting to his own undoing and to yours, and to your children's and your children's children's?"

There was some applause, and some crying of Shame upon the man; but the greater part of the audience were quiet. They looked at Stephen's worn face, rendered more pathetic by the homely emotions it evinced; and, in the kindness of their nature, they were more sorry than indignant.

" 'Tis this Delegate's trade for t' speak," said Stephen, "an' he's paid for 't, an' he knows his work. Let him keep to 't. Let him give no heed to what I ha' had'n to bear. That's not for him. That's not for nobbody but me."

There was a propriety, not to say a dignity in these words, that made the hearers yet more quiet and attentive. The same strong voice called out, "Slackbridge, let the man be heern, and howd thee tongue!" Then the place was wonderfully still.

"My brothers," said Stephen, whose low voice was distinctly heard, "and my fellow-workmen—for that yo are to me, though not, as I knows on, to this delegate here—I ha' but a word to sen, and I could sen nommore if I was to speak till Strike o' day. I know weel, aw what's afore me. I know weel that yo aw resolve to ha' nommore ado wi' a man who is not wi' yo in this matther. I know weel that if I was a lyin parisht i' th' road, yo'd feel it right to pass me by, as a forrenner and stranger. What I ha' getn, I mun mak th' best on.'"

"Stephen Blackpool," said the chairman, rising, "think on 't agen. Think on 't once agen, lad, afore thou'rt shunned by aw owd friends."

There was an universal murmur to the same effect, though no man articulated a word. Every eye was fixed on Stephen's face. To repent of his determination, would be to take a load from all their minds. He looked around him, and knew that it was so. Not a grain of anger with them was in his heart; he knew them, far below their surface weaknesses and misconceptions, as no one but their fellow-labourer could.

"I ha' thowt on 't, above a bit, Sir. I simply canna coom in. I mun go th' way as lays afore me. I mun tak my leave o' aw heer."

He made a sort of reverence to them by holding up his arms, and stood for the moment in that attitude; not speaking until they slowly dropped at his sides.

"Monny's the pleasant word as soom heer has spok'n wi' me; monny's the face I see heer, as I first seen when I were yoong and lighter heart'n than now. I ha' never had no fratch[12] afore, sin ever I were born, wi' any o' my like; Gonnows[13] I ha' none now that's o' my makin'. Yo'll ca' me traitor and that—yo I mean t' say," addressing Slackbridge, "but 'tis easier to ca' than mak' out. So let be."

He had moved away a pace or two to come down from the platform, when he remembered something he had not said, and returned again.

"Haply," he said, turning his furrowed face slowly about, that he might as it

12. Harsh quarrel.
13. God knows.

were individually address the whole audience, those both near and distant; "haply, when this question has been tak'n up and discoosed, there'll be a threat to turn out if I'm let to work among yo. I hope I shall die ere ever such a time cooms, and I shall work solitary among yo unless it cooms—truly, I mun do 't, my friends; not to brave yo, but to live. I ha' nobbut[14] work to live by; and wheerever can I go, I who ha' worked sin I were no heighth at aw, in Coketown heer? I mak' no complaints o' bein turned to the wa',[15] o' being outcasten and overlooken fro this time forrard, but hope I shall be let to work. If there is any right for me at aw, my friends, I think 'tis that."

Not a word was spoken. Not a sound was audible in the building, but the slight rustle of men moving a little apart, all along the centre of the room, to open a means of passing out, to the man with whom they had all bound themselves to renounce companionship. Looking at no one, and going his way with a lowly steadiness upon him that asserted nothing and sought nothing, Old Stephen, with all his troubles on his head, left the scene.

Then Slackbridge, who had kept his oratorical arm extended during the going out, as if he were repressing with infinite solicitude and by a wonderful moral power the vehement passions of the multitude, applied himself to raising their spirits. Had not the Roman Brutus, oh my British countrymen, condemned his son to death; and had not the Spartan mothers,[16] oh my soon to be victorious friends, driven their flying children on the points of their enemies' swords? Then was it not the sacred duty of the men of Coketown, with forefathers before them, an admiring world in company with them, and a posterity to come after them, to hurl out traitors from the tents they had pitched in a sacred and a Godlike cause? The winds of heaven answered Yes; and bore Yes, east, west, north, and south. And consequently three cheers for the United Aggregate Tribunal!

Slackbridge acted as fugleman,[17] and gave the time. The multitude of doubtful faces (a little conscience-stricken) brightened at the sound, and took it up. Private feeling must yield to the common cause. Hurrah! The roof yet vibrated with the cheering, when the assembly dispersed.

Thus easily did Stephen Blackpool fall into the loneliest of lives, the life of solitude among a familiar crowd. The stranger in the land who looks into ten thousand faces for some answering look and never finds it, is in cheering society as compared with him who passes ten averted faces daily, that were once the countenances of friends. Such experience was to be Stephen's now, in every waking moment of his life; at his work, on his way to it and from it, at his door, at his window, everywhere. By general consent, they even avoided that side of the street on which he habitually walked; and left it, of all the working men, to him only.

14. Nothing but.
15. Wall.
16. Lucius Junius Brutus was, in Roman historical legend, the leader who exemplified self-sacrificing concern for the larger civic good: he ordered his own sons to be executed for attempting to restore the Tarquins to control of Rome. Spartan mothers, too, were noted for putting the larger community above family interest: their traditional farewell to sons going off to war was to succeed or die but not to surrender, to "return with your shield or on it."
17. An exemplary soldier leading others to follow his example.

He had been for many years, a quiet silent man, associating but little with other men, and used to companionship with his own thoughts. He had never known before the strength of the want in his heart for the frequent recognition of a nod, a look, a word; or the immense amount of relief that had been poured into it by drops through such small means. It was even harder than he could have believed possible, to separate in his own conscience his abandonment by all his fellows from a baseless sense of shame and disgrace.

The first four days of his endurance were days so long and heavy, that he began to be appalled by the prospect before him. Not only did he see no Rachael all the time, but he avoided every chance of seeing her; for, although he knew that the prohibition did not yet formally extend to the women working in the factories, he found that some of them with whom he was acquainted were changed to him, and he feared to try others, and dreaded that Rachael might be even singled out from the rest if she were seen in his company. So, he had been quite alone during the four days, and had spoken to no one, when, as he was leaving his work at night, a young man of a very light complexion accosted him in the street.

"Your name's Blackpool, ain't it?" said the young man.

Stephen coloured to find himself with his hat in his hand, in his gratitude for being spoken to, or in the suddenness of it, or both. He made a feint of adjusting the lining, and said, "Yes."

"You are the Hand they have sent to Coventry,[18] I mean?" said Bitzer, the very light young man in question.

Stephen answered "Yes," again.

"I supposed so, from their all appearing to keep away from you. Mr. Bounderby wants to speak to you. You know his house, don't you?"

Stephen said "Yes," again.

"Then go straight up there, will you?" said Bitzer. "You're expected, and have only to tell the servant it's you. I belong to the Bank; so, if you go straight up without me (I was sent to fetch you), you'll save me a walk."

Stephen, whose way had been in the contrary direction, turned about, and betook himself as in duty bound, to the red brick castle of the giant Bounderby.

Chapter V
Men and Masters

"Well, Stephen," said Bounderby, in his windy manner, "what's this I hear? What have these pests of the earth been doing to *you*? Come in, and speak up."

It was into the drawing-room that he was thus bidden. A tea-table was set out; and Mr. Bounderby's young wife, and her brother, and a great gentleman from London, were present. To whom Stephen made his obeisance, closing the door and standing near it, with his hat in his hand.

"This is the man I was telling you about, Harthouse," said Mr. Bounderby. The

18. The phrase means shaming someone by excluding him or her from acceptance in the community.

gentleman he addressed, who was talking to Mrs. Bounderby on the sofa, got up, saying in an indolent way, "Oh really?" and dawdled to the hearthrug where Mr. Bounderby stood.

"Now," said Bounderby, "speak up!"

After the four days he had passed, this address fell rudely and discordantly on Stephen's ear. Besides being a rough handling of his wounded mind, it seemed to assume that he really was the self-interested deserter he had been called.

"What were it, Sir," said Stephen, "as yo were pleased to want wi' me?"

"Why, I have told you," returned Bounderby. "Speak up like a man, since you are a man, and tell us about yourself and this Combination."[19]

"Wi' yor pardon, Sir," said Stephen Blackpool, "I ha' nowt to sen about it."

Mr. Bounderby, who was always more or less like a Wind, finding something in his way here, began to blow at it directly.

"Now, look here, Harthouse," said he, "here's a specimen of 'em. When this man was here once before, I warned this man against the mischievous strangers who are always about—and who ought to be hanged wherever they are found—and I told this man that he was going in the wrong direction. Now, would you believe it, that although they have put this mark upon him, he is such a slave to them still, that he's afraid to open his lips about them?"

"I sed as I had nowt to sen, Sir; not as I was fearfo' o' openin' my lips."

"You said. Ah! *I* know what you said; more than that, I know what you mean, you see. Not always the same thing, by the Lord Harry![20] Quite different things. You had better tell us at once, that that fellow Slackbridge is not in the town, stirring up the people to mutiny; and that he is not a regular qualified leader of the people: that is, a most confounded scoundrel. You had better tell us so at once; you can't deceive me. You want to tell us so. Why don't you?"

"I'm as sooary as yo, Sir, when the people's leaders is bad," said Stephen, shaking his head. "They taks such as offers. Haply 'tis na' the sma'est o' their misfortuns when they can get no better."

The wind began to get boisterous.

"Now, you'll think this pretty well, Harthouse," said Mr. Bounderby. "You'll think this tolerably strong. You'll say, upon my soul this is a tidy specimen of what my friends have to deal with; but this is nothing, Sir! You shall hear me ask this man a question. Pray, Mr. Blackpool"—wind springing up very fast—"may I take the liberty of asking you how it happens that you refused to be in this Combination?"

"How 't happens?"

"Ah!" said Mr. Bounderby, with his thumbs in the arms of his coat, and jerking his head and shutting his eyes in confidence with the opposite wall: "how it happens."

"I'd leefer[21] not coom to 't, Sir; but sin you put th' question—an' not want'n t' be ill-manner'n—I'll answer. I ha' passed a promess."

---

19. The association of united workmen, Slackbridge's United Aggregate Tribunal.
20. By the devil.
21. Rather.

"Not to me, you know," said Bounderby. (Gusty weather with deceitful calms. One now prevailing.)

"O no, Sir. Not to yo."

"As for me, any consideration for me has had just nothing at all to do with it," said Bounderby, still in confidence with the wall. "If only Josiah Bounderby of Coketown had been in question, you would have joined and made no bones about it?"

"Why yes, Sir. 'Tis true."

"Though he knows," said Mr. Bounderby, now blowing a gale, "that there are a set of rascals and rebels whom transportation[22] is too good for! Now, Mr. Harthouse, you have been knocking about in the world some time. Did you ever meet with anything like that man out of this blessed country?" And Mr. Bounderby pointed him out for inspection, with an angry finger.

"Nay, ma'am," said Stephen Blackpool, staunchly protesting against the words that had been used, and instinctively addressing himself to Louisa,[23] after glancing at her face. "Not rebels, nor yet rascals. Nowt o' th' kind, ma'am, nowt o' th' kind. They've not doon me a kindness, ma'am, as I know and feel. But there's not a dozen men amoong 'em, ma'am—a dozen? Not six—but what believes as he has doon his duty by the rest and by himseln. God forbid as I, that ha' known, and had'n experience o' these men aw my life—I, that ha' ett'n an' droonken wi' 'em, an' seet'n wi' 'em, and toil'n wi' 'em, and lov'n 'em, should fail fur to stan by 'em wi' the truth, let 'em ha' doon to me what they may!"

He spoke with the rugged earnestness of his place and character—deepened perhaps by a proud consciousness that he was faithful to his class under all their mistrust; but he fully remembered where he was, and did not even raise his voice.

"No, ma'am, no. They're true to one another, faithfo' to one another, fectionate to one another, e'en to death. Be poor amoong 'em, be sick amoong 'em, grieve amoong 'em for onny o' th' monny causes that carries grief to the poor man's door, an' they'll be tender wi' yo, gentle wi' yo, comfortable wi' yo, Chrisen wi' yo. Be sure o' that, ma'am. They'd be riven to bits, ere ever they'd be different."

"In short," said Mr. Bounderby, "it's because they are so full of virtues that they have turned you adrift. Go through with it while you are about it. Out with it."

"How 'tis, ma'am," resumed Stephen, appearing still to find his natural refuge in Louisa's face, "that what is best in us fok, seems to turn us most to trouble an' misfort'n an' mistake, I dunno. But 'tis so. I know 'tis, as I know the heavens is over me ahint the smoke. We're patient too, an' wants in general to do right. An' I canna think the fawt[24] is aw wi' us."

22. Transportation was the punishment of being exiled from England to penal colonies, the most notable of which in Dickens's time was Australia. Bounderby subsequently threatens to have Slackbridge and his like "shipped off to penal settlements." In *Great Expectations* (1860), Dickens deals more fully with transportation, which was discontinued as a penal option three years after he had published *Hard Times*.

23. Louisa is Mrs. Bounderby, a young woman who, as is Stephen, is victimized by the ruthlessly self-interested actions of those who should be most concerned about her well-being.

24. Fault.

"Now, my friend," said Mr. Bounderby, whom he could not have exasperated more, quite unconscious of it though he was, than by seeming to appeal to any one else, "if you will favour me with your attention for half a minute, I should like to have a word or two with you. You said just now, that you had nothing to tell us about this business. You are quite sure of that before we go any further."

"Sir, I am sure on 't."

"Here's a gentleman from London present," Mr. Bounderby made a back-handed point at Mr. James Harthouse with his thumb, "a Parliament gentleman. I should like him to hear a short bit of dialogue between you and me, instead of taking the substance of it—for I know precious well, beforehand, what it will be; nobody knows better than I do, take notice!—instead of receiving it on trust from my mouth."

Stephen bent his head to the gentleman from London, and showed a rather more troubled mind than usual. He turned his eyes involuntarily to his former refuge, but at a look from that quarter (expressive though instantaneous) he settled them on Mr. Bounderby's face.

"Now, what do you complain of?" asked Mr. Bounderby.

"I ha' not coom here, Sir," Stephen reminded him, "to complain. I coom for that I were sent for."

"What," repeated Mr. Bounderby, folding his arms, "do you people, in a general way, complain of?"

Stephen looked at him with some little irresolution for a moment, and then seemed to make up his mind.

"Sir, I were never good at showin o' 't, though I ha' had'n my share in feeling o' 't. 'Deed we are in a muddle, Sir. Look round town—so rich as 'tis—and see the numbers o' people as has been broughten into bein heer, fur to weave, an' to card,[25] an' to piece out a livin', aw the same one way, somehows, 'twixt their cradles and their graves. Look how we live, an' wheer we live, an' in what numbers, an' by what chances, and wi' what sameness; and look how the mills is awlus a goin, and how they never works us no nigher to onny dis'ant object—ceptin awlus, Death. Look how you considers of us, and writes of us, and talks of us, and goes up wi' yor deputations to Secretaries o' State 'bout us, and how yo are awlus right, and how we are awlus wrong, and never had'n no reason in us sin ever we were born. Look how this ha' growen an' growen, Sir, bigger an' bigger, broader an' broader, harder an' harder, fro year to year, fro generation unto generation. Who can look on 't, Sir, and fairly tell a man 'tis not a muddle?"

"Of course," said Mr. Bounderby. "Now perhaps you'll let the gentleman know, how you would set this muddle (as you're so fond of calling it) to rights."

"I donno, Sir. I canna be expecten to 't. 'Tis not me as should be looken to for that, Sir. 'Tis them as is put ower me, and ower aw the rest of us. What do they tak upon themseln, Sir, if not to do 't?"

"I'll tell you something towards it, at any rate," returned Mr. Bounderby. "We

25. To comb or open fibers in preparation for spinning.

will make an example of half-a-dozen Slackbridges. We'll indict the blackguards for felony, and get 'em shipped off to penal settlements."

Stephen gravely shook his head.

"Don't tell me we won't, man," said Mr. Bounderby, by this time blowing a hurricane, "because we will, I tell you!"

"Sir," returned Stephen, with the quiet confidence of absolute certainty, "if yo was t' tak a hundred Slackbridges—aw as there is, and aw the number ten times towd—an' was t' sew 'em up in separate sacks, an' sink 'em in the deepest ocean as were made ere ever dry land coom to be, yo'd leave the muddle just wheer 'tis. Mischeevous strangers!" said Stephen, with an anxious smile; "when ha' we not heern, I am sure, sin ever we can call to mind, o' th' mischeevous strangers! 'Tis not by *them* the trouble's made, Sir. 'Tis not wi' *them* 't commences. I ha' no favour for 'em—I ha' no reason to favour 'em—but 'tis hopeless and useless to dream o' takin them fro their trade, 'stead o' takin their trade fro them! Aw that's now about me in this room were heer afore I coom, an' will be heer when I am gone. Put that clock aboard a ship an' pack it off to Norfolk Island,[26] an' the time will go on just the same. So 'tis wi' Slackbridge every bit."

Reverting for a moment to his former refuge, he observed a cautionary movement of her eyes towards the door. Stepping back, he put his hand upon the lock. But he had not spoken out of his own will and desire; and he felt it in his heart a noble return for his late injurious treatment to be faithful to the last to those who had repudiated him. He stayed to finish what was in his mind.

"Sir, I canna, wi' my little learning an' my common way, tell the genelman what will better aw this—though some working men o' this town could, above my powers—but I can tell him what I know will never do 't. The strong hand will never do 't. Vict'ry and triumph will never do 't. Agreeing fur to mak one side unnat'rally awlus and for ever right, and toother side unnat'rally awlus and for ever wrong, will never, never do 't. Nor yet lettin alone[27] will never do 't. Let thousands upon thousands alone, aw leading the like lives and aw faw'en into the like muddle, and they will be as one, and yo will be as anoother, wi' a black unpassable world betwixt yo, just as long or short a time as sitch-like misery can last. Not drawin nigh to fok, wi' kindness and patience an' cheery ways, that so draws nigh to one another in their monny troubles, and so cherishes one another in their distresses wi' what they need themseln—like, I humbly believe, as no people the genelman ha' seen in aw his travels can beat—will never do 't till th' Sun turns t' ice. Most o' aw, rating 'em as so much Power, and reg'latin 'em as if they was figures in a soom, or machines: wi'out loves and likens, wi'out memories and inclinations, wi'out souls to weary and souls to hope—when aw goes quiet, draggin on wi' 'em as if they'd nowt[28] o' th' kind, and when aw goes onquiet, reproachin 'em for their want

---

26. An island in the Pacific used as one of the penal settlements to which Bounderby has referred. See note 22.

27. A translation of the French *laissez faire*, the phrase was a rallying cry of industrialists who wanted no government regulation of industry.

28. Nought; nothing.

o' sitch humanly feelins in their dealins wi' yo—this will never do 't, Sir, till God's work is onmade."

Stephen stood with the open door in his hand, waiting to know if anything more were expected of him.

"Just stop a moment," said Mr. Bounderby, excessively red in the face. "I told you, the last time you were here with a grievance, that you had better turn about and come out of that. And I also told you, if you remember, that I was up to the gold spoon look-out."[29]

"I were not up to 't myseln, Sir; I do assure yo."

"Now it's clear to me," said Mr. Bounderby, "that you are one of those chaps who have always got a grievance. And you go about, sowing it and raising crops. That's the business of *your* life, my friend."

Stephen shook his head, mutely protesting that indeed he had other business to do for his life.

"You are such a waspish, raspish, ill-conditioned chap, you see," said Mr. Bounderby, "that even your own Union, the men who know you best, will have nothing to do with you. I never thought those fellows could be right in anything; but I tell you what! I so far go along with them for a novelty, that *I'll* have nothing to do with you either."

Stephen raised his eyes quickly to his face.

"You can finish off what you're at," said Mr. Bounderby, with a meaning nod, "and then go elsewhere."

"Sir, yo know weel," said Stephen expressively, "that if I canna get work wi' yo, I canna get it elsewheer."[30]

The reply was, "What I know, I know; and what you know, you know. I have no more to say about it."

Stephen glanced at Louisa again, but her eyes were raised to his no more; therefore, with a sigh, and saying, barely above his breath, "Heaven help us aw in this world!" he departed.

29. Earlier, when Stephen had sought advice from him concerning how legally to deal with an alcoholic and abusive wife, Bounderby had congratulated Stephen upon having a work history untroubled by dissension and protest, being unlike his fellows: " 'we have never had any difficulty with you, and you have never been one of the unreasonable ones. You don't expect to be set up in a coach and six, and to be fed on turtle soup and venison, with a gold spoon, as a good many of 'em do!' Mr. Bounderby always represented this to be the sole, immediate, and direct object of any Hand who was not entirely satisfied."

30. Stephen anticipates what will happen to him: discharged by Bounderby, he will also be blacklisted by him. Owners would circulate among themselves lists of "troublesome" workers who would, as a result of such listing, never be hired anywhere.

J. P. H.

"THE SLAVE OF the Needle" was serialized in the *London Journal* from mid-February to mid-March in 1850. The author of the story, identified only by the initials J. P. H., contributed a number of stories to the *Journal*. In the 1840s and 1850s, the *London Journal* (1845–1912) shared the largest English readership with the *Family Magazine* (1842–1939). Both were family publications directed at lower-middle-class readers. They featured advice columns, informative articles, commentary on contemporary social or economic issues, and sensational fiction. The sentimental, melodramatic depiction of the young seamstress in "The Slave of the Needle" is characteristic of popular Victorian narrative.

The Slave of the Needle

The world we live in is a bright and glorious one; and kindly feelings, pure desires, and holy passions march with us to our inevitable and inscrutable destiny. Heaven's hallowed sunshine falls on all alike; but there are those with bruised hearts, who walk amidst its beams unmindful of their beauty, and insensible to the warmth they afford. Creatures fashioned after the image of the Great Eternal turn their haggard faces imploringly to the sky, and see only one vast blue depth, in which they can read nothing but the vague hope, the doubtful though half-smiling promise of something better hereafter; and then they look at the stately buildings, the pomp and insignia of wealth, the regal magnificence of power, landscapes glittering in their almost garden beauty, waving fields of God's food, pastures dotted with sleek and stately cattle; and then they gaze at what they see in and around themselves, and with a sigh, oftentimes a groan, they exclaim that there is a world within that which meets the dazzled eye of prosperity, of which no one knows aught save those whom capricious fortune has doomed to be its inhabitants. This world, as typified in the vigorous language of poetry is

> "That frozen continent,
> Dark and wild, beat with perpetual storms
> Of whirlwind and dire hail"[1]

wherein the tossed and troubled soul bewails the hour of its birth in the bitter language of despair. Those born in more genial social climes know nothing of this dreary existence. They never felt the pang that corrodes the heart, or the bitter woe that fires the brain as with a red-hot iron, or had to deplore the loss of a knowledge of the pure or true, or struggle with a life made up of fretful anguish, wounded delicacy, bruised sentiment, and that gnawing and unceasing, though hopeless, craving for those blessings which the human mind, in its lowest degradation, instinctively feels to be its heritage on earth.

There are shadows deep and long on the ground we tread; and the children of success, when they pursue their thousand different ways, are too apt to forget they are treading on the funeral pall of a multitude whose hearts were never made to beat only to the dirge of their own sorrows and miseries—to the wild sad notes breathing eloquent reproach, sent up from every corner of the land. This is a condition of existence as dreadful as the fabled one of Tantalus;[2] and every feature of its wretchedness, every variety of which it is so susceptible, claims from us all that consideration and respectful attention which are based on the best, the warmest, and the holiest feelings.

The participators in the dreadful suffering under which England groans are ranged in classes, and their grievances start up in the gloom like "a forest huge of spears"[3] tipped with dark red fire. Among them is one which flickers dimly in the rear, but the light from it is sufficient to disclose a fair wan face and wasted form, with attenuated hand cramped and stiffened with body-and-mind-destroying toil. That is the slave of the needle; and to leave the language of metaphor, let us introduce her in the garb and under the circumstances which are as common and as well known in this huge wilderness of bricks and mortar as the ebbs and flows of its queenly river.

It was morning, and the old Father Frost and his cousin, the Snow-fiend, had been very busy during the night, for the streets were whitened, and the icicles, like pendant drops, hung from the house-tops, window-sills, and lamp-posts, in a very glistening but by no means comfort-inspiring manner. The air of the streets was "nipping and eager,"[4] and every now and then cold blasts swept through them to a very dismal and freezy tune. It was such a morning as makes the nose, ears, fingers, and toes tingle, and produces throughout the frame a chilliness, a sensation of

1. Description of Hell from Milton's *Paradise Lost* 2.587–89.
2. Tantalus, a mortal son of Zeus, had his only son Pelops killed, cooked, and served to the gods when they came to dine with him. He was punished by being placed in a pool of water which receded whenever he tried to drink and by being surrounded by fruit which hung just beyond his reach.
3. Milton, *Paradise Lost* 1.547.
4. Shakespeare, *Hamlet* 1.4.2.

Figure 3.7. John Leech, *Needle Money* and *Pin Money*. Courtesy Mansell/Time Inc.

John Leech (1817–1864) was a book illustrator and the principal caricaturist for the enormously popular comic journal, *Punch*. In his companion engravings, *Needle Money* and *Pin Money* (1849), Leech renders the contrast between the lives of Victorian needlewomen and those of the wealthy women for whom they sewed.

Pin money is another term for an allowance, money to spend on trinkets such as the symbolic jeweled snake that the young woman in the second drawing is admiring.

coldness, which leaves an individual in doubt whether he ought much longer to expose himself to its congealing influence. The hour was that singularly unsettled one, nine o'clock; and streams of well-shod and cosily muffled up pedestrians were hurrying down the hill of Holborn to that great centre of the world's commerce, the city of London. Amid the throng was a thinly-clad and delicate-looking girl, who timidly threaded her way, with a package in her hands. Her costume was neat, but scanty. Her cotton frock, fitting tightly across her well-developed bosom, fell in folds around her person; and as the wind drove mercilessly against it, disclosed to the observing eye the whole outline of her slender but elegant figure. The undergarments must have been very limited in number; for as her little feet, encased in fragile, papery-looking slippers, paddled in the snow, her frame shivered, and she hurried on at increased speed. In the crowd she escaped notice, but there was that in her gait and mien which bespoke of poverty and affliction borne with meekness. Her little black bonnet, which only just fitted her head, was faded; it had a melancholy rustiness about it, as if it had frequently been beaded with tears; and the crown was slightly, very slightly indented. It suggested sad thoughts; for no one capable of feeling acutely could look upon that humble little bonnet without sighting and conjuring up in his mind a whole host of grave reflections. It spoke of trials, tribulations and self-denials imposed by cruel depression, and increased in their severity by contrast with those upon whom the demon had not breathed his spell. It told of contention with a degree of adversity too cruel to permit the slightest gratification of female vanity, and forcibly appealed to that keen sympathy which rarely deserts the human breast, however apathetic it may be in its practical appreciation of the distresses of others. Poor girl! she was friendless, and was soon to be alone, with no other support and monitor than her own pure upright heart.

The shop to which she was wending her way was one with a dashing exterior, an imposing array of goods, and half a score of good-looking assistants. It was a noted cheap ready-made shirt mart, and the conductor of the establishment held a kind of levée every morning before the business of the day commenced. His audiences generally consisted of some half-score wretched creatures who had toiled through the previous day and night to earn the scanty pittances doled out for their most killing labour. Annie Lee stood in the crowd, and, like the rest, was exposed to the ribald remarks and bald attempts at wit of the young gentlemen who were dusting the counter, arranging goods for the day's display, and doing a multitude of little things with a vast deal of bustle and noise. Presently the great man arrived, and the trembling slaves of the needle opened their little bundles for his inspection. And now ensued one of those sickening scenes which it is wonderful how any thing in the shape of a man [can] endure. It was a perfect haggling between the women and man who appeared to be responsible for the quality of the work he admitted into the establishment. The women implored to be paid, not an increased sum, but the bare amount previously bargained for and allowed; but the man found so many faults with this collar and that collar, this band and that band—the seams were crooked, the necks awry—and so many faults were pointed out, that many of the poor creatures became frightened, and, to escape from such a place, gladly took what was offered them. Others, more obstinate, insisted upon their lawful demands, and were paid and discharged with a coarse rebuke. Annie was the last to present her package, which consisted of two shirts, the produce of her own and her mother's exertions since the preceding evening, and she did it with fear and trembling.

Now we should mention that Annie was remarkably pretty. Her face, of classic proportions, was as fair as an angel's and her two eyes, of deepest blue, fringed by long lashes, reflected a quiet subdued light that fell upon the gazer as softly as the mild rays of the young moon. Her nostril was delicately chiselled, and her two lips, from which the carnation had not been banished, were slightly parted, and disclosed teeth of dazzling brightness. Her light auburn hair was arranged in braids on each side of her pale cheeks; and as she extended her little hand to receive what might be offered to her, and modestly kept her eyes fixed on the counter, she looked no inapt representation of humility in rags, appealing to insolence and tyranny in tawdry finery.

The fellow, whose name was Watkins, attempted to catch Annie's eye, but in vain; she knew that he was looking at her, and her repugnance at the undisguised assurance of his manner prevented her even attempting to meet his gaze. Her claim was paid without cavil or deduction, and as some more work was handed to her,

Watkins in a silky whisper said to her, "To-morrow evening, if you please, Miss Lee. I shall be here; don't fail, my dear."

Annie hurried away; for, although she knew not why, she was afraid of that man. He had ever been civil to her, and paid her death-wages in full; but she was afraid of him, he shocked the extreme purity and delicacy that were interwoven with her nature, and whenever she left his presence she was inexpressibly relieved. On the present occasion she carried with her ninepence; yes, one tiny sixpence, and three heavy ugly penny pieces—the price paid for making two shirts, with showy linen fronts and an elaborate display of wristbands, with their countless stitches, so neat and delicate that the eye could scarcely detect them.

> "O! men, with sisters dear!
> O! men, with mothers and wives!
> It is not linen you're wearing out,
> But human creatures' lives!"[5]

Annie, however, thought not of the hardship of her lot; she had a helpless hungry parent at home, and she traversed the wet pavement of the streets with the lightness of the fawn. Upon arriving in the squalid locality where she resided, the investment of her little stock became to her an object of much concern, and after no small amount of consideration she devised upon the number of purchases she would make. She entered the chandler's shop where she was accustomed to deal, and the following were the items of her expenditure:—

	d.
Half-a-quartern loaf	3
Two ounces of butter	1¾
Quarter of an ounce of tea	1
Seven pounds of coals	1
One bundle of wood	0
	6¾

The balance, being twopence-farthing, was reserved for rent; and here we may observe that the earnings of herself and mother, when in full work, never exceeded six shillings and ninepence per week, and for that they would have between them to make eighteen shirts of the description which the labels in the shop windows term "fine"; Annie did twelve, her ailing parent six, and to accomplish this Annie often worked eighteen hours out of the twenty-four, and her mother, when nature would allow her, sixteen. Out of the six shillings and ninepence they had to pay two shillings for the apartment in which they lived, and thus had only four shillings and ninepence left for their subsistence during one whole week of work sufficient to prostrate the strongest constitution.

With this four shillings and ninepence per week two human beings—women pure as light—copies of that fair and gentle gift placed by Providence under the protection of him whose "fair large front and eye sublime declared absolute

5. Thomas Hood, "The Song of the Shirt," 25–28.

rule"[6]—were obliged to provide themselves with food and raiment. Sickness, accident, a diminished demand, a host of casualties might destroy even this miserable supply—but what matter? they were only women; and their complaining cries would be drowned in the roar of the multitude, whose bellowings they could hear like distant thunder in the crow's-nest-like place in which they were perched.

Such worse than pauper allowance made them thin and wan, and they pined like birds in a cage, and starved in the midst of wealth and luxury greater than ever was created before—yes, starved, lacked the bread of life in London, the capital of the world, than which

> "Not Babylon,
> Nor great Alcairo, such magnificence
> Equall'd in all their glories."[7]

But let us describe the habitation of these two poor deserted and friendless creatures. It was situated in the topmost story of a house lying in one of those narrow filthy alleys from which the pure air of heaven is most sedulously excluded. The neighbourhood was rank and foetid with abominations; and the people, who leaned idly from out of some of the windows, seemed scarcely human. The alley itself was a mass of ricketty houses, tenanted by the poorest of the poor. The occupants manifested no absolute depravity, but there was something in their aspect which repelled, instead of attracted, sympathy. It was, in the men, neither ferocity nor brutality, but something of a lean, gin-and-water character, which scowled from out its drunken eyes. In the women it was filth, dishevelled hair, unwashed faces, and disordered garments, that prevented near approach; and when a beholder looked at both sexes, he fancied that he beheld before him wretches whom casual hunger had starved into a reckless indifference to all the decencies of life. The house in which Annie and her mother resided was one of the least inviting in the place; it manifested a decided inclination to embrace its neighbour opposite, but several strong beams interposed, and, as if indignant at being de-barred one of the pleasures it sought, it became sulky, and had departed upwards of a foot from its original upright position.

The room which Annie and her parent occupied was, as we have stated, in the storey next to the sky, and upon entering it, the first object that attracted attention was its cleanliness, but there was a desolation in its aspect which struck a chill to the heart; it looked empty, just like a newly-washed room totally devoid of furniture. There was a coldness about it, a clamminess and dampness, which benumbed and deadened all feeling. The contents were two broken chairs, an old round table, a palliass[8] of slender pretensions, rolled up and placed in a corner, a plate-shelf, on which were a few cups and saucers, two or three knives and forks, a tin tea-pot, and a fragment of looking-glass. The fire-place was more like a hole in the wall than anything else, but it was large enough for the grate, and that kindly accommodated

---

6. Description of Adam from Milton's *Paradise Lost* 4.300–301.

7. Milton, *Paradise Lost* 1.717–19.

8. A paillasse or palliasse is a straw mattress.

itself to the coals it had to consume. The latter threw out, with no small amount of blowing and puffing, heat just sufficient to boil water in a very ancestral-looking little kettle, and that was the only work it had to do, if we except the occasional bits of heat it afforded to the cramped fingers that were held before it in the "dead waist and middle of the night."[9] The window of this room was very small, but clean; and the panes that were broken were not stuffed with dirty cloths or remnants, like their neighbours', but had their holes neatly pasted over with brown paper. Before it

> "A woman sat, in unwomanly rags,
> Plying her needle and thread."[10]

Chapter II

> No friends, no hope! no kindred weep for me!
> Almost no grave allow'd me! like the lily
> That once was mistress of the field, and flourish'd,
> I'll hang my head, and perish.
>
> —*Henry VIII*[11]

We have stated that before the broken but paper-mended window of the almost empty room in which Annie Lee and her mother resided the latter sat stitching. Let us describe the fragile creature upon whom the world had rained its heavy afflictions of rags and destitution, and buried in a living grave of cold and hunger. Traces of former beauty lingered on her features, but they were darkened by the shadows of lines which gathered round her eyes and mouth, and fastened themselves remorselessly on the dead white of cheeks where roses had once bloomed as in a fair garden. Her hair, of mingled auburn and grey, was thin, and hanging in disorder over her sunken brows, imparted to her appearance a wild sorrow, which a pair of dull, glassy, deeply-sunken eyes painfully heightened. Beneath all this sad desolation, a long neck, white as snow, tapered gracefully down to a bosom flat and shrivelled like a crumpled sheet of unstained paper. One of her breasts, once a fountain of life to the babe born to her in her days of prosperity, half-peeped out of a rent in her garment, and although shrunken, looked in that dismal apartment like that early white flower which decks the last days of winter. Yes, it was a snowdrop, glistening amid waste and ruin, and a purer one never reared its modest head. But it told a sad tale; for while a beholder might dream of the beauty of which it formerly made up a portion, he had only to look before him and see its shattered and wasting remnants.

The dress of this victim to our present social arrangements was so scanty, albeit

9. Shakespeare, *Hamlet* 1.2.198.
10. Thomas Hood, "The Song of the Shirt," 3–4.
11. Shakespeare, *Henry VIII* 3.1.150–53. Queen Katharine is bemoaning the loss of Henry's love.

patched with care and neatness, that it disclosed the whole outline of her form. Her fleshless bones were distinctly traced out, and her knees, like two sharp points, almost seemed to be bursting through the frail covering that could not conceal their worn and hungry leanness. Flesh or muscle on her body there was none; and there she sat, with stockingless feet, shivering and shaking in the cold of a winter's morning, without fire, without food, without one ray of hope to warm her frozen sympathies with the world outside.

But she plied the bright and sparkling symbol of her slavery in unrepining silence; and all that was heard in that chilling room was the click of her needle and thimble. Click, click, click, they went, like a watch, keeping time, and wearing itself out; and as the faint shadow of her fast-moving scraggy hand fell on the wall opposite, it looked like a soul darkened by wrong, trembling on the brink of eternity. And the woman, dulled, spell-bound under the curse of her fate never lifted her eyes, but went swiftly on, expending her reel of cotton and her fast ebbing life, until her daughter burst into the room with something like the joyous bound of youth and then a faint smile spread over her haggard face and she whispered, "My child!" It was all she could do, and as her daughter hastily busied herself about the morning meal *their* providence had allotted them, click, click, sounded her needle and thimble.

"Mother," said Annie, putting her arm gently round her parent's neck. Click, click, click, was the only response. "Mother"—the pressure of the rounded arm increased—"come and see how nicely I have made breakfast." Click, click, click. "Mother! dear mother!" exclaimed the alarmed girl, tightly clasping the skeleton frame she embraced, and with tears in her eyes turning her young face up to the one that had withered ere it had looked upon forty years.

Click, click, went the needle and thimble, and then ceased their horrid notes, as with a shriek the mother looked up and clasped her only joy to her prematurely aged bosom.

Her morning dream was over, but its reminiscences swept across her brain like lightning streaks over a dun sky.

"My child—my darling child!" was the stifled, agonising cry, as she wound her bony arms round all that had been left her to love on earth. That grasp was an agonising one; it endured but a few seconds, but to both it was an age.

"I am awake now—oh, yes, awake—but I have been dreaming. Oh, Father in heaven! such a dream!" and she strained her daughter to her heart as if she would hide her there for ever.

Annie, terrified at the unwonted energy displayed by her mother, sobbed, and the more deeply because she knew not why. Poor untutored child of misery! she felt a presentiment—heard a wailing in her soul—but could not recognise the features of a fast approaching evil. She tried to speak, but the grief suddenly excited in her delicate organisation choked her utterance.

"Hush!" said the mother, her eyes brightening as she spoke; "what I should tell you had better be told now. I often thought of it over my work, but this morning it came upon me like memories of the past, and then I slumbered in fancy, and phantoms—things of the earth—slimy creeping things troubled me; and I saw one—oh! merciful God! hear a mother's prayer and let it be but a dream!" A shudder almost convulsed her emaciated frame, but an idea as frightful as it was bold and vivid seemed to endow her with renewed strength. "Listen, my child," said she; "twenty years ago I was rich, young, and as beautiful, they told me, as you are now. I had home, friends, and all that a happy girl could desire, until I loved, and then I married, and was happy for many many months, until the demon poverty withered the roses that gladdened our sweet cottage, and your father died of a broken heart, and I lived because you nestled at my bosom. A wretch persecuted me with odious offers. I fled from him and came to this great town, and after many vicissitudes came to be a needlewoman. Yes, I have stitched my life away, and the last threads are in my hands. I shall not be here much longer."

Annie screamed with agony as this gloomy anticipation flashed across her mind in all its terrible reality.

"Hush, my darling," said her mother; "all is in the hands of Him who has permitted all this suffering to prepare me for happiness hereafter. But listen. When I am gone, think of me, and pray, when evil men cross your path, and evil thoughts crawl like serpents into your mind, pray, my child, or your beauty will be your curse. Pray—pray!" she wildly exclaimed, "for this is an awful town, and sin stalks unblushingly through every street. Pray, or hush if you must fall. Oh! no, no! You are too good—too pure—too holy to be a victim. Listen! If you should or must— but no—when the temptation comes, whether it be gentle as the lamb or as savage as the tiger, think of me, and," here her voice sunk to a whisper, "*die first.*"

She fixed her eyes firmly on the face of her daughter, and in one greedy look saw its beauty and stainless purity; and then as the future and one dark spot came upon the mirror of innocence before her, she uttered a groan, and fell back insensible. She had fainted. This was no novelty to the afflicted daughter; for the poor creature, whose temples she bathed with her trembling hands, had often fallen from her seat through sheer exhaustion. On this occasion she revived but slowly; and when she did, it was only to discover that the last blow had been struck—she was paralysed, and never spoke again. Annie shrieked so loud and piercingly, that an old hag-like figure hobbled into the room, and, in squeaking notes, demanded to know the reason for so great an outcry.

"My mother!—look at my mother, Tibby, and save her!" exclaimed Annie.

"Save her?" said the crone, feeling the pulse of the dying woman with her brown and bony fingers. "She's got her billy-do[12] this time, any how. Yes, young woman, it's a clay-box case this; but a drop of something short might bring the tongue back to bless you. Have you any gin?" (Annie shook her head); "nor money? Must call in the parish. But ah!" (here her eye fell on the shirts, in the various stages of preparation) "we can raise something on these. Shall I step over with them to Simkins's? Don't stand shilly-shally, or your mother may die before she opens her mouth!"

---

12. Billet-doux: love letter.

Annie, prostrate by the terrible affliction before her, offered no opposition. She neither meditated nor formed the slightest conception of wrong; and the old woman bore off the embryo cheap shirts to that grave of a poor man's independence, the pawn-shop. She soon returned with a bottle of gin in her hand, and the change, but the sacrifice had been a useless one. The mouth of the sufferer was too rigidly closed to admit of any liquid being poured down her throat; and all that could be done for her was to place her tenderly on her humble bed, and send for such assistance as the miserable can obtain. The parish doctor came, but his services were not required—it was too late; and the slave of the needle was left to die under the spell of an awful silence. The old woman crouched at the foot of the bed like a cat, and every now and then raised the bottle to her lips; while Annie, on her knees, prayed as only those who have been smitten by Providence can. Hours passed away, and the potations of the witch-like figure on the floor had so affected her senses, that she began to mutter and indulge in execrations.

"They all goes this way," said she; "they gets thinner and thinner, and then hops away like a light dancing on the wall; and they never says a blessed word again them as brought 'em to it. That cuts me to the heart. If they'd only curse—just leave one curse to them that did it—I'd be satisfied. But no; they gets into the par-leyticks,[13] or whimpers about their bright young days, and all is over; and the men that did it all goes on as smiling as ever. May they drink poison, the brutes! And people goes to them—what dirt the fools get for their pains!—and buys cheap shirts; and never thinks of the garret or the attic where God never comes—no, never! No happy face has been here these forty years, that I'll swear to; but there's a rod in pickle[14] for them all."

There appeared to be some consolation in the latter idea, for very soon after indulging in it she dozed off to sleep. Annie kept her position at her parent's head, and when day departed she was the only watcher at that awful death-bed. On the third night, about nine o'clock, Annie, wearied and harassed, slept; and her mother lay looking at her with glazed and watery eyes. We have said that her features were remarkably delicate, but in the state of repose in which they were then, although the cheek was worn, they were enchanting. There was a loveliness in their expression which to the imagination was like a dream of beauty. There was nothing of the earth about them; calm, pure, and holy, they spoke to the heart; and the soul of a beholder who had untainted instincts, as he gazed at them in their classic purity, would have felt elevated—it would have thrilled the presence of so much excellence; and he would have almost deemed it profanity to have left even one soft kiss on that snowy brow. The mother, as she dwelt upon them, was transported to the past, and in fancy she saw herself as in her days of maidenhood with a light heart and a bounding step. She drew from their airy cells sweet memories, and inhaled the perfume of the flowers that grew around her when the world to her wore a smile, and in her own guileless, trusting fondness, she believed it had a heart.

13. Politics.
14. The phrase refers to the practice of soaking birch whipping rods in brine to keep the twigs pliable.

Old associations, like jewels well preserved, nestled at her heart; and worn and withered as she was, she clung to them with a warmth that gave her life, even at the brink of the grave. Wan and wasted, as she lay on the floor of her wretched dwelling, she had still a love for the bright and beautiful; and although her body had been the sport of the fiend Starvation, she could feel that there is an ecstasy in goodness—a delicious reward in the treasured-up reminiscences of an unspotted life—which neither hunger nor oppression can destroy. She was happier in that last hour of thought than the most favoured daughter of fortune; for reproach, with its rankling barb, stood not at the bar of her judgement.

At length a dimness came upon her mental vision, and the voice of the past, in her fond ear, melted away. Her daughter at that moment looked up from her slumber, and her first act was to imprint a kiss on the cold cheek of her now half-blind parent. With the near approach of death came almost renewed strength, and Annie was pressed passionately to her mother's heart.

Poor girl! she considered the embrace as a symptom of amendment, and to soothe the sufferer, in a low but distinct and sweet tone, sung that affecting melody, "Home, sweet home." Tears gathered in the mother's eyes, and, with a gentle sigh, she fell asleep, and never awoke more.

The daughter, jaded and worn, nodded her head, and was soon in the land of dreams. The candle, burnt down to its last fragment, flickered and trembled for a moment, and then all was darkness.

"Annie," whispered the old woman, who had crept into the room, "did she curse?—asleep—well, well, the doom is upon you, and will soon put you in the black pit, where the toads hiss and dance their wicked pastimes; so sleep on, and be as rich in fancy as the Queen. I hope she cursed the monster before she died; I do daily, but I want the curse of a good heart to blight them."

And, thus muttering, she kept swaying her body to and fro like a pendulum, and waited for the wakening of the desolate girl, whose soft breathings came and went like the sighing of a summer's wind.

Chapter III

"Nor long did her life for this sphere seem intended,
For pale was her cheek with the spirit-like hue,
Which comes when the day of this world is nigh ended,
And light from another already shines through"

—*Moore*[15]

It is sad to be alone, to be in the world and yet not of it; to think only, to dream with the eyes open, and the senses painfully acute; to be a stranger in the midst of buxom life, and yet have no sympathy with a single one of the myriads of beings who throng the highways and bye-ways of this bustling world. There is a dirge-like

15. Thomas Moore (1779–1852), "The Stranger," lines 17–20.

melancholy inseparable from an involuntary and undeserved seclusion from the busy scenes of earth, which saddens the heart and brings the tears of sorrow unbidden to the eye. It seems as if the soul in its affliction would, in despite of the assistance of fortitude or the support of pride, mourn over its isolation and in silence reproach the evil fortune that condemned it to a cruel expatriation, while the blossoms of hope and love shed their fragrance over the most favoured children of Providence. Many of the sons and daughters of mankind upon whom Nature has lavishly smiled—who revel in her choice gifts of health and beauty—are condemned to this hopeless solitude, this crushing and sad despair; and the voices of their complaints are never heard amid the din, of the sonorous notes of prosperity. They fall in the thick atmosphere of despair, and are lost ere they reach the roar in the light outside.

Of this class of unfortunates was Annie Lee, after the death of her surviving parent. She had no sooner seen her poor mother's body consigned by rude hands to a pauper grave, than she felt a desolation—an awful sense of loneliness creep upon her, which made her, young and untutored as she was, shudder with an undefinable creeping sensation of terror. As the few clods allowed by the stringent poor-degrading regulations[16] fell on the unsightly plateless coffin, she felt that every one of the hollow sounds made by them had an echo in her own heart. For days afterwards she moped about like one in a hideous dream, and only awoke to a consciousness of the reality of the destitution by which she was surrounded on every side, when assailed by the keen pangs of hunger. Youth struggled with grief, and in a measure triumphed, for she began to think how she could procure a meal. Every thing in her miserable room of any value at all, even the ragged and slender palliass on which her mother had died, had been disposed of; and as she glanced round and saw nothing on which her eye could rest with any degree of promise of realising something, a feeling of callous despair began to wind itself in serpent folds round her heart. Her little hands became clenched, her delicate nostril quivered, and a cold moisture gathered like dew on her almost transparent brows.

She had formed no distinct idea of what she either could or would do, but a dark shadow fell upon her and it only required a sufficiently tempting motive to induce her to plunge into the grave or dishonour. Her gentle impulses were subdued, and her high moral nature so untuned, that she would at that moment have voluntarily sought relief in the excitement most readily at hand. It was in this mood that she was discovered by Watkins, the overseer and junior partner in the firm in whose service her mother had yielded up her life. He had kept her in view ever since she failed to return at the stipulated time with the work given to her previous to her mother's death—had heard all the particulars of that, by him, long expected event—and, with the ingenuity of the most practised police spy, had ascertained the fact of the pawning of the goods entrusted to her to make up into shirts to adorn the stomachs of gentlemen who never dream, when they look clean

16. The "poor-degrading regulations" refer to the cheap paupers' coffins and shallow graves provided by the parish for those who died destitute.

and respectable, that they do so at the expense of the toil of the most abused and trampled upon portion of that sex to whose favours they aspire most arrogantly.

Annie was sitting on the only chair, or rather apology for one, the room contained; and as it was mid-day, just sufficient light was admitted through the window to disclose the whole of her thinly clad figure with its exquisite proportions and face "wan and thin," but beautiful, surpassingly beautiful in its pale and contracted earnestness of expression.

Watkins approached her with the air and attitude of a ruffian, who intended to intimidate with a threat of exposure and punishment; but he no sooner caught a glimpse of her features, lovely in their deep sorrow, than he hesitated, looked again, paused, and was subdued. There is something touching in female sorrow, it reaches the rudest disposition, and brings up its good from the lowest depths. It was so on this occasion. Watkins was a man of exceedingly coarse tastes, repulsive morals, and habits of the vilest profligacy. He uniformly selected his victims from among the slaves of the needle, over whom he exercised despotic sway, and was frequently truly diabolical in the refined villany with which he treated them. Many familiar with the features of vice, and others hardened into recklessness by horrible privations, had yielded to his solicitations without much resistance, and he formed an estimate of the character of the whole sex from the conduct displayed by the least courageous and resisting. All were poor, and he thought all were alike. Annie he had long before "booked" as an addition to the number of his dark iniquities, and no cat ever watched a mouse-hole with more vigilance than he did for an opportunity to accomplish his object. Now that the mother was dead, and the girl had been reduced to the degradation of subsisting on the charity of her half-starved fellow-lodgers, he deemed, in his awful indifference to the value of chastity, that he would find her ready to embrace any proposal he should make to her. But, as we have stated, her attitude disarmed the wretch of half his purpose. The demoniac part of his nature was not invincible; but compassion from such a source to a hungry heart-broken girl was more dangerous than brutal violence, and Annie had to undergo the dreadful trial; and surely the angels, who hover round innocence, must have trembled when that man's honeyed sentences fell upon the ear of the solitary mourner of that cold gloomy garret like

"Silvery sounds, so soft, so dear,"

that the listener, charmed out of her repugnance, held up her head, and, while the tears trembled in her eyes, essayed to speak. She was unable; and Watkins, rightly divining the cause of her emotion, had some refreshments, including wine, procured from a neighbouring tavern, and persuaded her to partake heartily of them. A week's dietary of one scanty meal of dry bread and weak tea per day is a wonderful sharpener of the appetite, and Annie ate of the food before her without reluctance, little dreaming that in driving away the famine-fiend, she was giving audience to one of swarthier hue. But so it is, danger ever dogs the steps of poverty, and the removal of one calamity frequently provokes a still harsher one. With women this is especially so; if poor, and fair, and fascinating, she becomes poor indeed, she listens too attentively to the oily phrases that fall seductively upon her flattered ear, or perhaps in a moment of passion yields with ungoverned impulse to the warm prompting of her loving nature.

Watkins, although uniformly successful, was but a coarse wooer; he trusted more to bribes and coercion, and that species of persuasion which prevails with those untrained instincts and inferior moral organisations. Still he was dangerous even to the habitually correct in thought, for there are moments when the appetites, like ravenous beasts of prey, break the laws imposed by religion and social morality, and drag those they torture through the mire, which only deep and earnest repentance can remove, when once it has soiled the human temple. There are moments when the sentinels of the soul sleep, and then evil, with its magic, makes the brain giddy, and the animal within us all fierce in its thirst for gratification.

Annie, sheltered under the wing of a fond parent, knew little of mankind, and, in her simplicity, thought all that glittered was pure gold; but she was soon to be undeceived. The wine she had drank infused warmth into her frame, and imparted a liveliness to her spirits, which induced her to tell her tale of grief to the scoundrel, who was observing her every action with a degree of pleasure perfectly horrible to imagine. He had great faith in the wine and gin bottle, and on this occasion, as the glow deepened on the girl's cheeks, and an animation sparkled in her winning eyes, he anticipated an easier triumph than he had expected upon entering the room. Affecting to be charmed with her candour and the confidence she had reposed in him, he promised her his friendship and countenance whenever it should be required to promote her views. Annie, flushed and excited, answered him in broken accents, and, like a reed, bent to the storm that wicked man had raised in her bosom. She was under a spell, and in the very excess of her innocence stood on the brink of ruin. Had an impure thought ever darkened her mind, she would have had a defence—a monitor to warn her of the outrage that was contemplated by the sensualist who stood gloating over her person with the undisguised effrontery of the terrible temperament to which he belonged. He had drawn closer to her side, and had one of her hands clasped in his large, but soft and greasy one.

"This is no place for you to dwell in, my pretty Annie," said Watkins, peeping into her face with his bold and impudent one; "let us go to where you will be comfortable, and be dressed like a lady."

Annie looked up surprised; she was too guileless to understand the nature of the proposition.

"Yes," continued the fellow—"to where you will be your own mistress, and forget that you ever were in want of a friend."

And so saying, with increasing confidence he began to sing the first verse of the hackneyed song, "Come, dwell with me," and had flung his arm round her waist, and was proceeding to snatch a kiss, when he suddenly started, and, not without some trepidation, kept his eyes fixed in the direction of the doorway. The object that saluted his vision there was the old woman we formerly mentioned, and who, by the way, was held in a species of reverence in the establishment as being a sort of witch, or wise woman. Certainly her appearance qualified her for the former title, for her clothes were ragged and dirty, and her flesh had accommodated itself to the dead brown colour that prevailed all over the neighbourhood.

"A! aha!" hissed the woman through her toothless gums, and fastening her cold glittering eyes on the face of the seducer, "come at last, have you, to sing to my pretty bird, eh? and take her away, and ride in a coachey poachey, eh? and have a horsey porsey, and be a *lady*, eh?"

The manner in which the last words were uttered was as powerful as the sneer of an evil spirit, and their effect was not lost on the, when tried, not over-valorous Mr. Watkins.

"Who is this person?" demanded he from Annie, at the same time releasing his hold of her.

"Who am I!" shrieked the old woman, hobbling into the room, and placing herself before Annie; "I'll tell you—poor, weak old woman; but strong enough to drive *you* hence with the curse of a heart turned to stone by wrong and oppression. Begone! I know your purpose—your vile, ungodly thought. Away! or I'll call those as will soon put the everlasting gloom upon you. Away, monster! and leave us one flower in this little hell for us to gaze at, and think of youth and innocence once again before we die. Away! and may your slumbers be haunted by the ghosts of the dead—of the girls with Thames mud dripping from their hairs! Aha! you tremble at the thought of seeing them again; but they'll come and curse you, shake you about, and drive you mad—ay, mad—and you will beg in vain for that which even wealth cannot buy—for any thing that will bring ease to the burning head of the woman slayer. Away! or I'll call those who will hurl you into the street."

Watkins, amazed and half frightened at this attack, requested Annie to call at the shop on the following day, and bidding her a hurried good-bye, left the room, and descend[ed] the rotten stairs out-side with marvellous rapidity.

Annie began to feel giddy; the wine and the excitement had been too potent for her reduced frame, and she began to stagger and reel. The old woman watched her attentively, and laying her finger on her shoulder, said, "Do you know what that man wanted with you?"

"Work—work. Kind to me. I mean to work for him," replied Annie confusedly.

"Work!" sneered the old woman; "do you remember what your mother told you on the day she died—what she whispered in your ear, and bade you think of when the dark hour came? That man and the warning go together. Think, and remember your mother."

Slowly, but surely, the truth flashed across the mind of the poor slave of the needle; and, as it broke upon her in all its hideous reality, a shiver crept through her body, and with a piteous sigh she sank senseless to the floor.

"Oh that Heaven in its mercy would take her way, for the worst has yet to come," muttered the old woman, as she sat on the floor and placed Annie's head in her lap.

Chapter IV

The tale that I would unfold to-day
No fiction is, but from the records pure
Of truth has been obtained.

—Renaldo, the Visionary

The bleak wind of March
Made her tremble and shiver;
But not the dark arch
Or black flowing river
Mad from life's history,
Glad to death's mystery
Swift to be hurled—
Anywhere, anywhere
Out of this world.
In she plunged boldly,
No matter how coldly
The rough river ran;
Over the brink of it,
Picture it—think of it,
Dissolute man!
Lave in it, drink of it,
Then, if you can!

—The Bridge of Sighs[17]

The sorrows of the poor have not yet found their true chronicler; and when they have, the pen of the writer must have been dipped into the fire that dries up the warm blood of the heart, and worms its destructive way into the system like a flame noiselessly creeping from chamber to chamber in a fair tenement.

And this dreadful chapter, whenever it shall appear, will be sadly defective if it does not portray the anguish and despair, which are the heritage on earth of myriads of forlorn creatures, in colours which shall not only startle and amaze by their vividness, but be everlasting witnesses against the wrongs matured in the bosom of a social dispensation which crush and mangle the dearest feelings, sully the holiest impulses, and hurry the fair, the loving, the manly, and the pure in purpose to one common dark and howling desolation. It is not that people are indifferent to all this that it exists; the magnitude of the calamity, its almost universal presence, prevents its being so striking to the eye as the painful features of individual cases. Nevertheless, the admission has been made that it is not a creature of the imagination, and the acknowledgement gathers force as time rolls on into deep, unfathomable eternity.

17. From the Thomas Hood poem about a ruined girl who has committed suicide.

A warm, new feeling on the subject has sprung into existence, and its sympathy promises to be as boundless as practical. But while the heart is in training for its holy mission of redemption, thousands are falling into the dreadful sleep of crime and despair. Women fashioned after the most delicate and beautiful models— gentle creatures whom we sing and write about—form a mighty mass of this al- most super-human amount of woe; and not the least appalling feature of the mis- ery to which they are so mercilessly subjected is the fiendish cruelty with which they are delivered over to the tiger-passion that seduces man to trample on those he is commanded by his instincts and high intellectual powers to love and cherish. For a woman once fallen there is no hope—the gates of the hell into which she has been coaxed by fraud and artifice are closed upon her for ever, and she never sees the bright sun and pleasant flowers that cheered and gladdened her heart in her days of innocence. Sneered and jeered at by men, and avoided as a contamination by the [un]fallen of her own sex, she falls into the darkness of her own sad despair, and withers away like a weed plucked from a fair garden and flung indignantly away. Oppressed and trampled upon, she sinks deeper and deeper into the mire of her degradation, and society hails her disappearance as a blessing. But the day of retribution, however long it may be postponed, comes at last, and man's inhu- manity to woman is sure to be terribly avenged. The wailing of a broken heart *will* find its way into the most obdurate disposition some day or another, and although the whispers of conscience for a season may be broken and divided, retribution, like a shadow, follows the footsteps of guilt, and deepens as age advances. Nature punishes the delinquencies of her children in themselves, and in this life, however careless or reckless the individual may be, the lash, even in the hours of indulgence, falls heavily on his shoulders, and he feels the pang and the agony which bad deeds fix indelibly in the human system. Remorse, aggravated by decayed faculties, bounds him on to the fate he never attempted to avoid, and the wail of the ruined woman is drowned in the shriek of the destroyer as he tumbles headlong over the precipice on the brink of which he has sported with such blind confidence and daring assurance. In the blaze of his noon he was no better than a toad spitting venom "in the blind cave of eternal night," and in his death a miserable compensa- tion to society for the outrages it had sustained at his hands.

It was not within the scope of our intention to have demonstrated how this wonderful compensatory power might have been developed in the instance before us; we rather intended to have aimed at depicting a few scenes in the life of a fragile creature slain in the murderous war of avarice and brutal passion; and the subject of our sketch is no coinage of the brain,[18] or exaggerated creation of a false and sickly sentiment, but the copy of a living being walking daily in the midst of us, having feelings, instincts, and appetites like our own, and above all those

"Dreams treasured up from early days"[19]

---

18. Queen Gertrude speaking in *Hamlet* 3.4.138.
19. William Wordsworth, "Yarrow Revisited," 79.

which sweeten and breathe a fragrance over the imagination, even in the direst and most wretched hours of poverty.

The girl we have selected to typify the class to which she belonged was not, like the heroines of wire-drawn[20] romances, sheathed in the triple mail of a well-trained and refined sense of virtue. Her sense of delicacy, from long association with the features of misery, was more instinctive than otherwise; she had an innate appreciation of the pure and beautiful, a yearning after the tender and true, but no indomitable power to resist temptation in the shape of honeyed persuasion, supported by the supply of the means of subsistence, and a few articles of luxury to which she had previously been a total stranger. Her instincts revolted at wrong, but her necessities, like so many fiends, tugged at her natural modesty and weakened its power of resistance. She fell, as many others have done, in the maze and whirl of disordered sense, flushed sensibility, and physical obedience to an idea which insult and fierce unscrupulous effrontery had implanted in her jaded and fevered imagination. In the abstract, between herself and her Maker, she was as spotless as a finely polished mirror; but to her fellow-creatures—men careful of their families, and women proud of their unblemished chastity, those prosperous beings who are privileged to be critics in morals by their education and auspicious circumstances—she was fallen and degraded—a lost spirit driven from the paradise of hope to wander as an outcast in a world where every thing to her, of all others, was cold and repelling. Poor defenceless girl; she only knew the priceless value of the jewel she had parted with in a moment of aberration from the dreadful certainty of its loss. The wretch who had marked her out for his prey succeeded in effecting his infamous purpose, and she was soon to learn that there is but one step from honour to the lowest infamy. To use a commercial phrase, she had never been rated very high, even as a slave of the needle; but now that she had, as her betrayer considered, become a burden to him, she began to experience that cold and cutting neglect, that heartless behaviour which, while it repudiates the intimacy, seeks to hold up its victim to the censure of her own judgement and the scoffs and scorns of those who think of her rather as she is than what she might and could have been had she been allowed to have followed the dictates of her unoffending impulses. Her last appearance in the mart of cheap-clothing was painful and harrowing in the last degree.

It was, as before, morning, and Annie, like the rest stood awaiting the high behests of the slave driver. He was, if possible, more stern and insolent than ever, but his eye wandered and there was a restlessness in his manner which did not much flatter his strength of nerve. Hardened as he was, he was not wholly insensible to the reproach which beamed from the mild blue eyes of his latest victim. The shop was beginning to look very gay, for the arrangement of the goods had almost been completed, and the young gentlemen were practising every variety of smile, from the plain simper to the whole bunch of deluding contortions, for the purpose of entering with spirit into the arduous business of the day. Everyone felt himself

20. Lengthy, excessively detailed, overly refined.

to be a species of general officer in his own particular way, and thought that when accoutred and ready for action it would be no idle waste of ammunition to bestow a few leering glances upon the youngest and prettiest of the slaves of the needle. Annie, being unquestionably the most attractive in the throng—for she was well and neatly dressed—had the largest share of these equivocal attentions awarded to her, but heeded them not; for with the shirts—every one of them more accursed than that worn by Hercules[21]—pressed timidly to her bosom she had her eyes fixed firmly on the floor, and tremulously expected the now unkind salutation of the man who had abused her so cruelly.

"Well, now, what for you?" said the fellow, rudely addressing Annie, but looking in another direction.

The work was presented and paid for, but the poor girl was so shocked at the undisguised ruffianism of his manner, that she trembled, and her wages rolled on the floor. Few in that miserable throng knew her story, and she was too beautiful to be pitied, so found little sympathy with any one of them. Their hearts were frozen, and hunger, rags and filth had dried up in them the fountain of feeling.

Hastily picking up the few coins she had dropped, she hurried from the shop to her home. Guilt had made her a little more sagacious, and she saw that her influence with her seducer was at an end.

The circumstance did not cause her any uneasiness, for disgust had already weakened the little attachment she ever bore him, but she felt a sinking of the spirits, a nervous dread of approaching evil, which drew the bitter tears from her eyes. She was stained and sinful she knew but too well, and without hope or promise of something better she hardly dared to pray. A horrible future was before her, and as she toiled on from day to day, and got thinner and thinner, horrid creatures of her own sex poured vile suggestions into her ears, and men, things disguised in the fair proportions of nature's choicest production, mocked and wounded her bruised and broken spirit. At length she became ill, and she could not perform her work as regularly as formerly; the pretext was seized, and she was dismissed from all connection with the establishment in which she had ruined her health and perilled her soul. For weeks she toiled on in vain expectation of winning a crust of bread and a drop of water. Other shops were glad of her devotion to the needle—she worked well and neatly, and accepted the wages of slavery in such meek silence, that she was rather a favourite than otherwise. But all would not do; work as much as possible, she could not earn the means of subsistence, and starved—wanted bread in the spring of her beauty. The temptation came—drink lured her on, and like a mad creature she leaped into the wild abyss of dark and fearful suffering. She struggled through the world in a dream of guilt—it was to her the grave of the good she once possessed; and one night, when the stars shone and the moon showered down its silver light, she took a mute farewell of them all, and

21. Hercules, a mortal son of Zeus, was the strongest man on earth. His wife, Deianira, put what she believed to be a love charm on Hercules's robe to ensure his devotion to her. The effect was agonizing pain for him which ended only when he killed himself.

without a pang of regret went to her Maker. As she lay in her pauper shroud, without a solitary mourner near her, it was dreadful

> "To see that white face in its stillness there
> Proving how much she suffered ere she slept
> The dreadful sleep of crime and despair."

A reminiscence might sweep across the brain, and a shudder pass over the heart, but the corpse was there in its ghastly reality, and when hurried to the "blind cave of eternal night," would soon be forgotten by the few who had deigned to bestow a glance on the slave of the needle.

ELIZA COOK

T HE YOUNGEST of eleven children in a working-class family, Eliza Cook (1818–1889) was self educated. Cook began writing poetry when she was quite young; her first volume of poems, *Lays of a Wild Harp,* appeared in 1835. She became a regular contributor of poems to London periodicals and enjoyed considerable popularity, especially in the 1830s and 1840s.

In addition to writing poetry, Cook founded, edited, and wrote most of the text for a successful periodical called *Eliza Cook's Journal,* which was aimed at working-class readers and appeared weekly from 1849 to 1854. She focused on social issues affecting women and children but also published didactic articles, stories, book reviews, and biographical sketches. Moreover, many of Cook's poems initially appeared or were reissued in her *Journal.* "Our Father," for example, was published in the August 11, 1849, issue.

Cook's poems tend to celebrate home and hearth, natural beauty, friendship, and love and consistently endorse middle-class virtues and values. Even her literary attempts to raise social consciousness about the plight of the poor were couched in terms that her readers would not have found unduly disturbing.

"Our Father," like Elizabeth Barrett Browning's "The Cry of the Children" (also reprinted in this section), was based on a report prepared by R. H. Horne (1803–1884) as assistant commissioner on the employment of children in mines and factories. Along with Barrett Browning and Caroline Norton (see *A Voice from the Factories* in this section), Cook emphasizes the miserable bondage of young laborers, but she tempers her criticism with a lesson on piety rather than with a demand that the sufferings of working children be alleviated.

In "The Poor Man to His Son," a father insists that all work is honorable and urges his boy to strive diligently and accept his place in life. Echoing Carlylean principles, the father tells his son to be satisfied if he can but earn remuneration sufficient to keep on working.

Cook idealizes rural labor in "Song of the City Artisan" (published in *Poems, Second Series,* 1845) through the voice of a weaver who complains about neither hard work nor his lowly position; he asks only that he be allowed to earn his bread under the "open sky."

"Our Father!"

"Many of the children told me they always said their
prayers at night, and the prayer they said was 'Our
Father.' I naturally thought they meant that they repeated
the Lord's Prayer, but I soon found that few of them
knew it. They only repeated the first two words; they
knew no more than 'Our Father.' These poor children,
after their laborious day's work (nail-making, japanning,
screw-making), lying down to sleep with this simple
appeal, seemed to me inexpressibly affecting."

—*Report of the Commissioners on the Employment of*
  Children; Evidence of R. H. Horne,
  Town of Wolverhampton

Pale, struggling blossoms of mankind,
    Born only to endure,
White, helpless slaves whom Christians bind,
    Sad children of the poor!
Ye walk in rags, ye breathe in dust,   5
    With souls too dead to ask
For aught beyond a scanty crust,
    And Labour's grinding task.
Ye ne'er have heard the code of love,
    Of Hope's eternal light;   10
Ye are not led to look above
    The clouds of earthly night;
And yet 'mid Ignorance and Toil,
    Your lips, that ne'er have known
The "milk and honey" of the soil,   15
    Sleep not before they own
                "Our Father!"

Unheeded workers in the marts
    Of England's boasted wealth,
Ye, who may carry ulcered hearts,   20
    If hands but keep their health;
Ye, whose young eyes have never watched
    June's roses come and go,
Whose hard-worn fingers ne'er have snatched
    The spring flowers as they blow;   25

Who slave beneath the summer sun,
    With dull and torpid brain,
Ye, who lie down when work is done,
    To rise and work again;
Oh! even ye, poor, joyless things;   30
    Rest not, before you pray;
Striving to mount on fettered wings
    To Him who hears you say,
            "Our Father!"

Proud, easy tenants of the earth,   35
    Ye who have fairer lots;
Who live with Plenty, Love, and Mirth,
    On Fortune's golden spots;
Ye, who but eat, laugh, drink, and sleep,
    Who walk 'mid Eden's bloom,   40
Who know not what it is to weep
    O'er Poverty's cold gloom;
Oh, turn one moment from your way,
    And learn what these can teach.
Deign in your rosy path to stay,   45
    And hear the "untaught" preach.
Then to your homes so bright and fair,
    And think it good to pray;
Since the sad children of Despair
    Can kneel in thanks, and say,
            "Our Father!"   50

The Poor Man to His Son

Work, work, my boy, be not afraid,
    Look Labor boldly in the face;
Take up the hammer or the spade,
    And blush not for your humble place.

Earth was first conquered by the power 5
    Of daily sweat and peasant toil;
And where would kings have found their dower
    If poor men had not trod the soil?

Hold up your brow in honest pride,
    Though rough and swarth[1] your hands may be: 10
Such hands are sap-veins that provide
    The life-blood of the Nation's tree.

There's honor in the toiling part,
    That finds us in the furrowed fields;
It stamps a crest upon the heart 15
    Worth more than all your quartered shields.[2]

There's glory in the shuttle's song,
    There's triumph in the anvil's stroke:
There's merit in the brave and strong,
    Who dig the mine or fell the oak. 20

Work, work, my boy, and murmur not,
    The fustian[3] garb betrays no shame;
The grime of forge-soot leaves no blot;
    And labor gilds the meanest name.

There's duty for all those, my son, 25
    Who act their earthly part aright;
The spider's home-threads must be spun,
    The bee sucks on 'twixt flowers and light.

The hungry bird his food must seek,
    The ant must pile his winter fare; 30
The seed drops not into the beak;
    The store is only gained by care.

The wind disturbs the sleeping lake,
    And bids it ripple pure and fresh;
It moves the green boughs till they make 35
    Grand music in their leafy mesh.

And so the active breath of life
    Should stir our dull and sluggard wills;

1. Dark.
2. Coats of arms.
3. Coarse, sturdy cloth made of cotton and flax.

For are we not created rife
    With health that stagnant torpor kills?   40

I doubt if he who lolls his head
    Where Idleness and Plenty meet,
Enjoys his pillow or his bread
    As those who *earn* the meals they eat.

And man is never half so blest   45
    As when the busy day is spent
So as to make his evening rest
    A holiday of glad content.

God grant thee but a due reward,
    A guerdon[4] portion fair and just;   50
And then ne'er think thy station hard,
    But work, my boy, work, hope, and trust!

Song of the City Artisan

I never murmur at the lot
    That dooms me as the rich man's slave;
His wealthy ease I covet not—
    No power I seek, no wealth I crave.

Labor is good, my strong right hand   5
    Is ever ready to endure;
Though meanly born, I bless my land,
    Content to be among its poor.

But look upon this forehead pale,
    This tintless cheek, this rayless eye;   10
What do they ask?—the mountain gale,
    The dewy turf, and open sky.

4. Reward.

I read of high and grassy hills,
    Of balmy dells and tangled woods;
Of lily-cups where dew distils,
    Of hawthorns where the ringdove broods.

I hear of bright and perfumed flowers,
    That spring to kiss the wanderer's feet;
Of forests where the young fawn cowers,
    Of streamlets rippling, cool and sweet.

They tell of waving fields of grain,
    Of purple fruit and shining leaves;
Of scattered seed and laden wain,[5]
    Of furrowed glebe[6] and rustling sheaves.

They speak of Nature, fresh and free,
    Lighting the dullest eyes that look;
Bards sing its glory,—but to me
    It is a sealed and hidden book.

The radiant summer beams may fall,
    But fail to break my cheerless gloom:
They cannot pierce the dusty wall
    Where pallid fingers ply the loom.

No warbler sings his grateful joys,
    No laden bee goes humming by;
Nought breaks the shifting shuttle's noise
    But angry oath or suffering sigh.

Pent with the crowd, oppressed and faint,
    My brow is damp, my breath is thick;
And though my spirit yield no plaint,
    My pining heart is deadly sick.

Give me a spade to delve the soil
    From early dawn to closing night;
The plough, the flail,[7] or any toil
    That will not shut me from the light.

I often dream of an old tree,
    With violets round it, growing wild;

15

20

25

30

35

40

45

5. Large open wagon.
6. Archaic term for soil or earth.
7. A traditional agricultural tool used for threshing.

I know that happy dream must be
  Of where I played, a tiny child:

A dog-rose hedge, a cottage door,
  Still linger in my wearied brain;   50
I feel my soul yearn more and more
  To see that hedgerow once again.

Double the labor of my task,
  Lessen my poor and scanty fare!
But give, oh! give me what I ask—   55
  The sunlight and the mountain air.

HENRY MAYHEW

B EST KNOWN as a journalist and social historian, Henry Mayhew (1812–1887) was one of seventeen children born to Joshua Dorset Joseph Mayhew, a prominent London solicitor. Henry studied law with his father for a time but abandoned legal pursuits to devote himself to writing. He began his career producing farces for the theater and articles for popular periodicals and was one of the four founders of the satirical journal *Punch*. In 1849–50, Mayhew made a name for himself when he published seventy-six interviews with low-income workers in the *Morning Chronicle*'s series *Labour and the Poor*. Over the next two years, he conducted scores more interviews, which were ultimately collected into four volumes and published in 1861–62 as *London Labour and the London Poor*. Although scholars have pointed out that he left many ambitious projects, including this one, unfinished, and have questioned the accuracy of his accounts, Mayhew has been consistently recognized for his contribution to social history. Following the appearance of his articles in the *Chronicle*, a number of other journalists turned their attention to the poor, producing articles and books such as T. Beames's *The Rookeries of London* (1851), J. Ewing Ritchie's *Night Side of London* (1857), and James Greenwood's *Seven Curses of London* (1869).

London Labour and the London Poor is notable for Mayhew's sympathetic representation of the working class and for his ability to capture and reproduce the distinctive voices of the individuals he met. Mayhew himself spoke of the work as "the first attempt to publish the history of a people, from the lips of the people themselves—giving a literal description of their labour, their earnings, their trials, and their sufferings, in their own unvarnished language...." From rat catchers and ham sandwich sellers to street clowns, omnibus conductors, and crossing sweeps, Mayhew introduces his readers to an incredible range of people and professions. The five interviews reprinted here are representative. In many—such as the interviews with the watercress girl and the coster-lad—Mayhew provides little commentary, electing instead to allow the workers to tell their own stories. At times, however, as is the case with the account of the pure-finders, Mayhew offers an overview of the profession, highlighted by workers' narratives. The result is a remarkable portrait of nineteenth-century working-class life.

From *London Labour and the London Poor*

From A Watercress Girl

The little watercress girl who gave me the following statement, although only eight years of age, had entirely lost all childish ways, and was, indeed, in thoughts and manner, a woman. There was something cruelly pathetic in hearing this infant, so young that her features had scarcely formed themselves, talking of the bitterest struggles of life, with the calm earnestness of one who had endured them all. I did not know how to talk with her. At first I treated her as a child, speaking on childish subjects; so that I might, by being familiar with her, remove all shyness, and get her to narrate her life freely. I asked her about her toys and her games with her companions; but the look of amazement that answered me soon put an end to any attempt at fun on my part. I then talked to her about the parks, and whether she ever went to them. "The parks!" she replied in wonder, "where are they?" I explained to her, telling her that they were large open places with green grass and tall trees, where beautiful carriages drove about, and people walked for pleasure, and children played. Her eyes brightened up a little as I spoke; and she asked, half doubtingly, "Would they let such as me go there—just to look?" All her knowledge seemed to begin and end with watercresses, and what they fetched. She knew no more of London than that part she had seen on her rounds, and believed that no quarter of the town was handsomer or pleasanter than it was at Farringdon-market or at Clerkenwell, where she lived. Her little face, pale and thin with privation, was wrinkled where the dimples ought to have been, and she would sigh frequently. When some hot dinner was offered to her, she would not touch it, because, if she eat too much, "it made her sick," she said; "and she wasn't used to meat, only on a Sunday."

The poor child, although the weather was severe, was dressed in a thin cotton gown, with a threadbare shawl wrapped round her shoulders. She wore no covering to her head, and the long rusty hair stood out in all directions. When she walked she shuffled along, for fear that the large carpet slippers that served her for shoes should slip off her feet.

"I go about the streets with water-creases, crying, 'Four bunches a penny, water-creases.' I am just eight years old—that's all, and I've a big sister, and a brother and a sister younger than I am. On and off, I've been very near a twelve-month in the streets. Before that, I had to take care of a baby for my aunt. No, it wasn't heavy—it was only two months old; but I minded it for ever such a time—till it could walk. It was a very nice little baby, not a very pretty one; but, if I touched it under the chin, it would laugh. Before I had the baby, I used to help mother, who was in the fur trade; and, if there was any slits in the fur, I'd sew them up. My mother learned me to needle-work and to knit when I was about five. I used to go to school, too; but I wasn't there long. I've forgot all about it now, it's such a time ago; and mother took me away because the master whacked me, though the missus use'n't to never touch me. I didn't like him at all. What do you think? he hit me three times, ever so hard, across the face with his cane, and made me go dancing downstairs; and when mother saw the marks on my cheek, she went to blow him up, but she couldn't see him—he was afraid. That's why I left school.

"The creases is so bad now, that I haven't been out with 'em for three days. They're so cold, people won't buy 'em; for when I goes up to them, they say, 'They'll freeze our bellies.' Besides, in the market, they won't sell a ha'penny handful now—they're ris to a penny and tuppence.[1] In summer there's lots, and 'most as cheap as dirt, but I have to be down at Farringdon-market between four and five, or else I can't get any creases, because every one almost—especially the Irish—is selling them, and they're picked up so quick. . . . We children never play down there, 'cos we're thinking of our living. No; people never pities me in the street—excepting one gentleman, and he says, says he, 'What do you do out so soon in the morning?' but he gave me nothink—he only walked away.

"It's very cold before winter comes on reg'lar—specially getting up of a morning. I gets up in the dark by the light of the lamp in the court. When the snow is on the ground, there's no creases. I bears the cold—you must; so I puts my hands under my shawl, though it hurts 'em to take hold of the creases, especially when we takes 'em to the pump to wash 'em. No; I never see any children crying—it's no use.

"Sometimes I make a great deal of money. One day I took 1s. 6d.,[2] and the creases cost 6d.; but it isn't often I get such luck as that. I oftener makes 3d. or 4d. than 1s.; and then I'm at work, crying 'Creases, four bunches a penny, creases!' from six in the morning to about ten. . . .

"I always give mother my money, she's so very good to me. She don't often beat me; but, when she do, she don't play with me. She's very poor, and goes out cleaning rooms sometimes, now she don't work at the fur. I ain't got no father, he's a father-in-law. No; mother ain't married again—he's a father-in-law. He grinds scissors, and he's very good to me. No; I don't mean by that that he says kind things to me, for he never hardly speaks. When I gets home, after selling creases, I stops at home. I puts the room to rights: mother don't make me do it, I does it myself. I cleans the chairs, though there's only two to clean. I takes a tub and scrubbing-brush and flannel, and scrubs the floor—that's what I do three or four time a week.

"I don't have no dinner. Mother gives me two slices of bread-and-butter and a cup of tea for breakfast, and then I go till tea, and has the same. We has meat of a Sunday, and, of course, I should like to have it every day. Mother has just the same to eat as we has, but she takes more tea—three cups, sometimes. No; I never has no sweet-stuff; I never buy none—I don't like it. . . . I knows a good many games, but I don't play at 'em 'cos going out with creases tires me. On a Friday night, too, I

---

1. Halfpenny, a British coin issued from the time of Edward I. Tuppence refers to the twopence coin.
2. British currency: "*s*" stands for shilling, a coin equivalent to twelve pence; "*d*" stands for pence.

goes to a Jew's house till eleven o'clock on Saturday night. All I has to do is to snuff the candles and poke the fire. You see they keep their Sabbath then, and they won't touch anything; so they gives me my wittals and 1½*d.*, and I does it for 'em. I have a reg'lar good lot to eat. Supper of Friday night, and tea after that, and fried fish of a Saturday morning, and meat for dinner, and tea, and supper, and I like it very well.

"Oh, yes; I've got some toys at home. I've a fire-place, and a box of toys, and a knife and fork, and two little chairs. The Jews gave 'em to me where I go to on a Friday, and that's why I said they was very kind to me. I never had no doll; but I misses little sister—she's only two years old. . . .

"I am a capital hand at bargaining—but only at buying water-creases. They can't take me in. If the woman tries to give me a small handful of creases, I says, 'I ain't a goin' to have that for a ha'porth,'[3] and I go to the next basket, and so on, all round. . . . I can't read or write, but I knows how many pennies goes to a shilling, why, twelve, of course, but I don't know how many ha'pence there is, though there's two to a penny. When I've bought 3*d.* of creases, I ties 'em up into as many little bundles as I can. They must look biggish, or the people won't buy them, some puffs them out as much as they'll go. All my money I earns I puts in a club[4] and draws it out to buy clothes with. It's better than spending it in sweet-stuff, for them as has a living to earn. Besides it's like a child to care for sugar-sticks, and not like one who's got a living and vittals to earn. I ain't a child, and I shan't be a woman till I'm twenty, but I'm past eight, I am. I don't know nothing about what I earns during the year, I only know how many pennies goes to a shilling, and two ha'pence goes to a penny, and four fardens[5] goes to a penny. I knows, too, how many fardens goes to tuppence—eight. That's as much as I wants to know for the markets."

The Life of a Coster-Lad[6]

One lad that I spoke to gave me as much of his history as he could remember. He was a tall stout boy, about sixteen years old, with a face utterly vacant. His two heavy lead-coloured eyes stared unmeaningly at me, and, beyond a constant anxiety to keep his front lock curled on his cheek, he did not exhibit the slightest trace of feeling. He sank into his seat heavily and of a heap, and when once settled down he remained motionless, with his mouth open and his hands on his knees—almost as if paralyzed. He was dressed in all the slang beauty of his class, with a bright red handkerchief and unexceptionable boots.

"My father" he told me in a thick unimpassioned voice, "was a waggoner, and worked the country roads. There was two on us at home with mother, and we used to play along with the boys of our court, in Golding-lane, at buttons and marbles. I recollects nothing more than this—only the big boys used to cheat like bricks and

---

3. Halfpennyworth.
4. A savings club.
5. Dialectal variation of "farthing," a British coin worth one-fourth of a penny.
6. Coster is short for costermonger, a seller of fruit or vegetables from a street stand.

Figure 3.8. O. G. Rejlander, *Crossing Sweeper.* Courtesy of the Gernsheim Collection, Harry Ransom Humanities Research Center.

Swedish-born Oscar G. Rejlander (1813–1875) began his career as a painter and lithographer. By the mid-1840s, he had settled in England and started taking photographs in the 1850s. Rejlander specialized in portraits and genre pictures. In the 1850s and 1860s, he took a number of sentimental photographs of ragged children, using hired models who were carefully posed. *Crossing Sweeper* of about 1860 is a typical example. Although the young crossing sweep has no shoes and his clothes are tattered, he nevertheless appears healthy. His broad smile and cheerful salute belie the actual conditions in which many such children lived and present a charming image to a public that often found street urchins simultaneously troubling and troublesome.

thump us if we grumbled—that's all I recollects of my infancy, as you calls it. Father I've heard tell died when I was three and brother only a year old. It was worse luck for us!—Mother was so easy with us. I once went to school for a couple of weeks, but the cove[7] used to fetch me a wipe over the knuckles with his stick, and as I wasn't going to stand that there, why you see I ain't no great schollard. We did as we liked with mother, she was so precious easy, and I never learned anything but playing buttons and making leaden 'bonces,'[8] that's all," (here the youth laughed

7. Slang term for a man or fellow.
8. Bonce refers to a large marble or the game played with such marbles.

slightly). "Mother used to be up and out very early washing in families—anything for a living. She was a good mother to us. We was left at home with the key of the room and some bread and butter for dinner. Afore she got into work—and it was a goodish long time—we was shocking hard up, and she pawned nigh everything. Sometimes, when we hadn't no grub at all, the other lads, perhaps, would give us some of their bread and butter, but often our stomachs used to ache with the hunger, and we would cry when we was werry far gone. She used to be at work from six in the morning till ten o'clock at night, which was a long time for a child's belly to hold out again, and when it was dark we would go and lie down on the bed and try and sleep until she came home with the food. I was eight year old then.

"A man as know'd mother, said to her, 'Your boy's got nothing to do, let him come along with me and yarn a few ha'pence,' and so I became a coster. He gave me 4*d.* a morning and my breakfast. I worked with him about three year, until I learnt the markets, and then I and brother got baskets of our own, and used to keep mother. One day with another, the two on us together could make 2*s.* 6*d.* by selling greens of a morning, and going round to the publics[9] with nuts of an evening, till about ten o'clock at night. Mother used to have a bit of fried meat or a stew ready for us when we got home, and by using up the stock as we couldn't sell, we used to manage pretty tidy. When I was fourteen I took up with a girl. She lived in the same house as we did, and I used to walk out of a night with her and give her half-pints of beer at the publics. She were about thirteen, and used to dress werry nice, though she weren't above middling pretty. Now I'm working for another man as gives me a shilling a week, victuals, washing, and lodging, just as if I was one of the family.

"On a Sunday I goes out selling, and all I yarns I keeps. As for going to church, why, I can't afford it,—besides, to tell the truth, I don't like it well enough. Plays, too, ain't in my line much; I'd sooner go to a dance—it's more livelier. The 'penny gaffs'[10] is rather more in my style; the songs are out and out, and makes our gals laugh. The smuttier the better, I thinks; bless you! the gals likes it as much as we do. If we lads ever has a quarrel, why, we fights for it. If I was to let a cove off once, he'd do it again; but I never give a lad a chance, so long as I can get anigh him. I never heard about Christianity, but if a cove was to fetch me a lick of the head, I'd give it him again, whether he was a big 'un or a little 'un. I'd precious soon see a henemy of mine shot afore I'd forgive him,—where's the use? Do I understand what behaving to your neighbour is?—In coorse I do. If a feller as lives next me wanted a basket of mine as I wasn't using, why, he might have it; if I was working it though, I'd see him further! I can understand that all as lives in a court is neighbours; but as for policemen,[11] they're nothing to me, and I should like to pay 'em all off well. No; I never heerd about this here creation you speaks about. In coorse God Almighty made the world, and the poor bricklayers' labourers built the houses arterwards—

9. Public houses or taverns.
10. Cheap amusement spots such as music halls.
11. The Metropolitan Police Act of 1829 established municipal police forces.

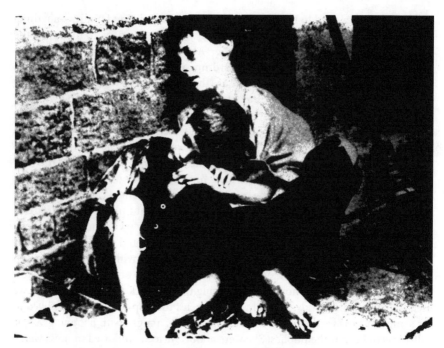

Figure 3.9. Crossing Sweepers. Present location unknown.
   Landscapes and portraits provided the subjects for the majority of early photographs. However, in the second half of the century, photographers began to document
social conditions such as the plight of young crossing sweeps. This picture presents a
striking contrast to the lighthearted image captured by O. G. Rejlander's camera (see
figure 3.8).

that's *my* opinion; but I can't say, for I've never been in no schools, only always
hard at work, and knows nothing about it. I have heerd a little about our Saviour,—
they seem to say he were a goodish kind of a man; but if he says as how a cove's to
forgive a feller as hits you, I should say he know'd nothing about it. In coarse the
gals the lads goes and lives with thinks our walloping 'em wery cruel of us, but we
don't. Why don't we?—why, because we don't. Before father died, I used sometimes
to say my prayers, but after that mother was too busy getting a living to mind
about my praying. Yes, I knows!—in the Lord's prayer they says, 'Forgive us our
trespasses, as we forgives them as trespasses agin us.' It's a very good thing, in
coarse, but no costers can't do it."

Statement of a Prostitute

   The narrative which follows—that of a prostitute, sleeping in the low lodging-
houses, where boys and girls are all huddled promiscuously together, discloses a

system of depravity, atrocity, and enormity, which certainly cannot be paralleled in any nation, however barbarous, nor in any age, however "dark." The facts detailed, it will be seen, are gross enough to make us all blush for the land in which such scenes can be daily perpetrated. The circumstances, which it is impossible to publish, are of the most loathsome and revolting nature.

A good looking girl of sixteen gave me the following awful statement:—

"I am an orphan. When I was ten I was sent to service as maid of all-work,[12] in a small tradesman's family. It was a hard place, and my mistress used me very cruelly, beating me often. When I had been in place three weeks, my mother died; my father having died twelve years before. I stood my mistress's ill-treatment for about six months. She beat me with sticks as well as with her hands. I was black and blue, and at last I ran away. I got to Mrs. ____, a low lodging-house. I didn't know before that there was such a place. I heard of it from some girls at the Glasshouse (baths and washhouses), where I went for shelter. I went with them to have a halfpenny worth of coffee, and they took me to the lodging-house. I then had three shillings, and stayed about a month, and did nothing wrong, living on the three shillings and what I pawned my clothes for, as I got some pretty good things away with me. In the lodging-house I saw nothing but what was bad, and heard nothing but what was bad. I was laughed at, and was told to swear. They said, 'Look at her for a d____ modest fool'—sometimes worse than that, until by degrees I got to be as bad as they were. During this time I used to see boys and girls from ten and twelve years old sleeping together, but understood nothing wrong. I had never heard of such places before I ran away. I can neither read nor write. My mother was a good woman, and I wish I'd had her to run away to. I saw things between almost children that I can't describe to you—very often I saw them, and that shocked me. At the month's end, when I was beat out, I met with a young man of fifteen—I myself was going on to twelve years old—and he persuaded me to take up with him. I stayed with him three months in the same lodging-house, living with him as his wife, though we were mere children, and being true to him. At the three months' end he was taken up for picking pockets, and got six months. I was sorry, for he was kind to me; though I was made ill through him; so I broke some windows in St. Paul's-churchyard to get into prison to get cured. I had a month in the Compter,[13] and came out well. I was scolded very much in the Compter, on account of the state I was in, being so young. I had 2*s*. 6*d*. given to me when I came out, and was forced to go into the streets for a living. I continued walking the streets for three years, sometimes making a good deal of money, sometimes none, feasting one day and starving the next. The bigger girls could persuade me to do anything they liked with my money. I was never happy all the time, but I could get no character and could not get out of the life. I lodged all this time at a lodging-house in Kent-street. They were all thieves and bad girls. I have known between

---

12. A maid-of-all-work was one of the lowest ranking servants. She was responsible for a wide range of duties, including cleaning, cooking, and childcare. See the story by W. J. Linton, "The Free-Servant," in this section.
    13. London debtors' prison.

three and four dozen boys and girls sleep in one room. The beds were horrid filthy and full of vermin. There was very wicked carryings on. The boys, if any difference, was the worst. We lay packed on a full night, a dozen boys and girls squeedged into one bed. That was very often the case—some at the foot and some at the top—boys and girls all mixed. I can't go into all the particulars, but whatever could take place in words or acts between boys and girls did take place, and in the midst of the others. I am sorry to say I took part in these bad ways myself, but I wasn't so bad as some of the others. There was only a candle burning all night, but in summer it was light great part of the night. Some boys and girls slept without any clothes, and would dance about the room that way. I have seen them, and, wicked as I was, felt ashamed. I have seen two dozen capering about the room that way; some mere children, the boys generally the youngest.* * * *

"There were no men or women present. There were often fights. The deputy never interfered. This is carried on just the same as ever to this day, and is the same every night. I have heard young girls shout out to one another how often they had been obliged to go to the hospital, or the infirmary, or the workhouse.[14] There was a great deal of boasting about what the boys and girls had stolen during the day. I have known boys and girls change their 'partners,' just for a night. At three years' end I stole a piece of beef from a butcher. I did it to get into prison. I was sick of the life I was leading, and didn't know how to get out of it. I had a month for stealing. When I got out I passed two days and a night in the streets doing nothing wrong, and then went and threatened to break Messrs. _____ windows again. I did that to get into prison again; for when I lay quiet of a night in prison I thought things over, and considered what a shocking life I was leading, and how my health might be ruined completely, and I thought I would stick to prison rather than go back to such a life. I got six months for threatening. When I got out I broke a lamp next morning for the same purpose, and had a fortnight. That was the last time I was in prison. I have since been leading the same life as I told you of for the three years, and lodging at the same houses, and seeing the same goings on. I hate such a life now more than ever. I am willing to do any work that I can in washing and cleaning. I can do a little at my needle. I could do hard work, for I have good health. I used to wash and clean in prison, and always behaved myself there. At the house where I am it is 3d. a night; but at Mrs. _____'s it is 1d. and 2d. a night, and just the same goings on. Many a girl—nearly all of them—goes out into the streets from this penny and twopenny house, to get money for their favourite boys by prostitution. If the girl cannot get money she must steal something, or will be beaten by her 'chap' when she comes home. I have seen them beaten, often kicked and beaten until they were blind from bloodshot, and their teeth knocked out with kicks from boots as the girl lays on the ground. The boys, in their turn, are out thieving all day, and the lodging-house keeper will buy any stolen provisions of them, and sell them to the lodgers. I never saw the police in the house. If a boy

14. Government-run institutions for the destitute who were expected to work in exchange for food and lodging.

comes to the house on a night without money or sawney,[15] or something to sell to the lodgers, a handkerchief or something of that kind, he is not admitted, but told very plainly, 'Go thieve it, then.' Girls are treated just the same. Any body may call in the daytime at this house and have a halfpennyworth of coffee and sit any length of time until evening. I have seen three dozen sitting there that way, all thieves and bad girls. There are no chairs, and only one form[16] in front of the fire, on which a dozen can sit. The others sit on the floor all about the room, as near the fire as they can. Bad language goes on during the day, as I have told you it did during the night, and indecencies too, but nothing like so bad as at night. They talk about where there is good places to go and thieve. The missioners call sometimes, but they're laughed at often when they're talking, and always before the door's closed on them. If a decent girl goes there to get a ha'porth of coffee, seeing the board over the door, she is always shocked. Many a poor girl has been ruined in this house since I was, and boys have boasted about it. I never knew boy or girl do good, once get used there. Get used there, indeed, and you are life-ruined. I was an only child, and haven't a friend in the world. I have heard several girls say how they would like to get out of the life, and out of the place. From those I know, I think that cruel parents and mistresses cause many to be driven there. One lodging-house keeper, Mrs. ____, goes out dressed respectable, and pawns any stolen property, or sells it at public-houses."

As a corroboration of the girl's statement, a wretched-looking boy, only thirteen years of age, gave me the following additional information. He had a few rags hanging about him, and no shirt—indeed, he was hardly covered enough for purposes of decency, his skin being exposed through the rents in his jacket and trowsers. He had a stepfather, who treated him very cruelly. The stepfather and the child's mother went "across the country," begging and stealing. Before the mother died, an elder brother ran away on account of being beaten:—

"Sometimes (I give his own words) he (the stepfather) wouldn't give us a bit to eat, telling us to go and thieve for it. My brother had been a month gone (he's now a soldier in Gilbralter) when I ran away to join him. I knew where to find him, as we met sometimes. We lived by thieving, and I do still—by pulling flesh (stealing meat). I got to lodge at Mrs. ____, and have been there this eight months. I can read and write a little." [This boy then confirmed what the young girl had told me of the grossest acts night by night among the boys and girls, the language, &c., and continued]—"I always sleep on the floor for 1*d*. and pay a ½*d*. besides for coke.[17] At this lodging-house cats and kittens are melted down, sometimes twenty a day. A quart pot is a cat, and pints and half pints are kittens. A kitten (pint) brings 3*d*. from the rag shops, and a cat 6*d*. There's convenience to melt them down at the lodging-house. We can't sell clothes in the house, except any lodger wants them; and clothes nearly all goes to the Jews in Petticoat-lane.[18] Mrs. ____ buys the

---

15. Slang term for bacon.
16. A bench.
17. Coal.
18. Petticoat Lane was a street in London dominated by secondhand garment sellers.

sawney of us; so much for the lump, 2d. a pound about; she sells it again for twice what she gives, and more. Perhaps 30 lb. of meat every day is sold to her. I have been in prison six times, and have had three dozen;[19] each time I came out harder. If I left Mrs. _____'s house I don't know how I could get my living. Lots of boys would get away if they could. I never drink, I don't like it. Very few of us boys drink. I don't like thieving, and often go about singing; but I can't live by singing, and I don't know how I could live honestly. If I had money enough to buy a stock of oranges I think I could be honest."

The above facts require no comment from me.

The Crippled Street-seller of Nutmeg-graters

I now give an example of one of the classes *driven* to the streets by utter inability to labour. I have already spoken of the sterling independence of some of these men possessing the strongest claims to our sympathy and charity, and yet preferring to *sell* rather than *beg*. As I said before, many ingrained beggars certainly use the street *trade* as a cloak for alms-seeking, but as certainly many more, with every title to our assistance, use it as a means of redemption from beggary. That the nutmeg-grater seller is a noble example of the latter class, I have not the least doubt. I have made all due inquiries to satisfy myself as to his worthiness, and I feel convinced that when the reader looks at the portrait here given, and observes how utterly helpless the poor fellow is, and then reads the following plain unvarnished tale, he will marvel like me, not only at the fortitude which could sustain him under all his heavy afflictions, but at the resignation (not to say philosophy) with which he bears them every one. His struggles to earn his own living (notwithstanding his physical incapacity even to put the victuals to his mouth after he has earned them), are instances of a nobility of pride that are I believe without a parallel. The poor creature's legs and arms are completely withered; indeed he is scarcely more than head and trunk. His thigh is hardly thicker than a child's wrist. His hands are bent inward from contraction of the sinews, the fingers being curled up and almost as thin as the claws of a bird's foot. He is unable even to stand, and cannot move from place to place but on his knees, which are shod with leather caps, like the heels of a clog,[20] strapped round the joint; the soles of his boots are on the *upper* leathers, that being the part always turned towards the ground while he is crawling along. His countenance is rather handsome than otherwise; the intelligence indicated by his ample forehead is fully borne out by the testimony as to his sagacity in his business, and the mild expression of his eye by the statements as to his feeling for all others in affliction.

"I sell nutmeg-graters and funnels," said the cripple to me; "I sell them at 1d. and 1½d. a piece. I get mine of the man in whose house I live. He is a tinman, and makes for the street-trade and shops and all. I pay 7d. a dozen for them, and I get

19. Number of lashes administered as punishment.
20. Heavy shoe with a thick sole.

12*d*. or 18*d*. a dozen, if I can when I sell them, but I mostly get only a penny a piece—it's quite a chance if I have a customer at 1½*d*. Some days I sell only three—some days not one—though I'm out from ten o'clock till six. The most I ever took was 3*s*. 6*d*. in a day. Some weeks I hardly clear my expenses—and they're between 7*s*. and 8*s*. a week; for not being able to dress and ondress myself, I'm obligated to pay some one to do it for me—I think I don't clear more than 7*s*. a week take one week with another. When I don't make that much, I go without—sometimes friends who are kind to me give me a trifle, or else I should starve. As near as I can judge, I *take* about 15*s*. a week, and out of that I clear about 6*s*. or 7*s*. I pay for my meals as I have them—3*d*. or 4*d*. a meal. I pay every night for my lodging as I go in, if I can; but if not my landlady lets it run a night or two. I give her 1*s*. a week for my washing and looking after me, and 1*s*. 6*d*. for my lodging. When I do very well I have three meals a day, but it's oftener only two—breakfast and supper—unless of Sunday. On a wet day when I can't get out, I often go without food. I may have a bit of bread and butter give me, but that's all—then I lie a-bed. I feel miserable enough when I see the rain come down of a week day, I can tell you. Ah, it *is* very miserable indeed lying in bed all day, and in a lonely room, without perhaps a person to come near one—helpless as I am—and hear the rain beat against the windows, and all that without nothing to put in your lips. I've done *that* over and over again where I lived before; but where I am now I'm more comfortable like. My breakfast is mostly bread and butter and tea; and my supper, bread and butter and tea with a bit of fish, or a small bit of meat. What my landlord and landlady has I share with them. I never break my fast from the time I go out in the morning till I come home—unless it is a halfpenny orange I buy in the street; I do that when I feel faint. I have only been selling in the streets since this last winter. I was in the workhouse with a fever all the summer. I was destitute afterwards, and obliged to begin selling in the streets. The Guardians[21] gave me 5*s*. to get stock. I had always dealt in tin ware, so I knew where to go to buy my things. It's very hard work indeed is street-selling for such as me. I can't walk no distance. I suffer a great deal of pains in my back and knees. Sometimes I go in a barrow, when I'm travelling any great way. When I go only a short way I crawl along on my knees and toes. The most I've ever crawled is two miles. When I get home afterwards, I'm in great pain. My knees swell dreadfully, and they're all covered with blisters, and my toes ache awful. I've corns all on top of them.

"Often after I've been walking, my limbs and back ache so badly that I can get no sleep. Across my lines[22] it feels as if I'd got some great weight, and my knees are in a heat, and throb, and feel as if a knife was running into them. When I go up-stairs I have to crawl upon the back of my hands and my knees. I can't lift nothing to my mouth. The sinews of my hands is all contracted. I am obliged to have things held to my lips for me to drink, like a child. I *can* use a knife and fork by leaning my

21. The 1834 Poor Law provided for a Central Poor Law Commission and regional Poor Law Unions directed by locally elected Guardians.
22. Loins.

arm on the table and then stooping my head to it. I can't wash nor ondress myself. Sometimes I think of my helplessness a great deal. The thoughts of it used to throw me into fits at one time—very bad. It's the Almighty's will that I am so, and I must abide by it. People says, as they passes me in the streets, 'Poor fellow, it's a shocking thing'; but very seldom they does any more than pity me; some lays out a half-penny or a penny with me, but the most of 'em goes on about their business. Persons looks at me a good bit when I go into a strange place. I *do* feel it very much, that I haven't the power to get my living or to do a thing for myself, but I never begged for nothing. I'd sooner starve than I'd do that. I never thought that people whom God had given the power to help theirselves ought to help me. I *have* thought that I'm as I am—obliged to go on my hands and knees, from no fault of my own. Often I've done that, and I've over and over again laid in bed and wondered why the Almighty should send me into the world in such a state; often I've done that on a wet day, with nothing to eat, and no friend to come a-nigh me. When I've gone along the streets, too, and been in pain, I've thought, as I've seen the people pass straight up, with all the use of their limbs, and some of them the biggest blackguards, cussing and swearing, I've thought, Why should I be deprived of the use of mine? and I've felt angry like, and perhaps at that moment I couldn't bring my mind to believe the Almighty was so good and merciful as I'd heard say; but then in a minute or two afterwards I've prayed to Him to make me better and happier in the next world. I've always been led to think He's afflicted me as He has for some wise purpose or another that I can't see. I think as mine is so hard a life in this world, I shall be better off in the next. Often when I couldn't afford to pay a boy, I've not had my boots off for four or five nights and days, nor my clothes neither. Give me the world I couldn't take them off myself, and then my feet has swollen to that degree that I've been nearly mad with pain, and I've been shivering and faint, but still I was obliged to go out with my things; if I hadn't I should have starved. Such as I am can't afford to be ill—it's only rich folks as can lay up, not we; for us to take to our beds is to go without food altogether. When I was without never a boy, I used to tie the wet towel round the back of one of the chairs, and wash myself by rubbing my face up against it. I've been two days without a bit of anything passing between my lips. I couldn't go and beg for victuals—I'd rather go without. Then I used to feel faint, and my head used to ache dreadful. I used then to drink a plenty of water. The women sex is mostly more kinder to me than the men. Some of the men fancies, as I goes along, that I can walk. They often says to me, "Why, the sole of your boot is as muddy as mine"; and one on 'em is, because I always rests myself on that foot—the other sole, you see, is as clean as when it was first made. The women never seem frightened on me. My trade is to sell brooms and brushes, and all kinds of cutlery and tin-ware. I learnt it myself. I never was brought up to nothing, because I couldn't use my hands. Mother was a cook in a nobleman's family when I were born. They say as I was a love-child. I was not brought up by mother, but by one of her fellow-servants. Mother's intellects was so weak, that she couldn't have me with her. She used to fret a great deal about me, so her fellow-servant took me when she got married. After I were born, mother married a farmer in middling circumstances. They tell me as my mother was frightened afore I was born. I never knew my father. He went over to Buonos Ayres, and kept an hotel there—I've heard mother say as much. No mother couldn't love a child more than mine did me, but her feelings was such she couldn't bear to see me. I never went to mother's to live, but was brought up by the fellow-servant as I've told you of. Mother allowed her 30*l.* a-year. I was with her till two years back. She was always very kind to me—treated me like one of her own. Mother used to come and see me about once a-year—sometimes not so often: she was very kind to me then. Oh, yes; I used to like to see her very much. Whatever I wished for she'd let me have; if I wrote to her, she always sent me what I wanted. I was very comfortably then. Mother died four years ago; and when I lost her I fell into a fit— I was told of it all of a sudden. She and the party as I was brought up with was the only friends as I had in the world—the only persons as cared anything about a creature like me. I was in a fit for hours, and when I came to, I thought what would become of me: I knew I could do nothing for myself, and the only friend as I had as could keep me was gone. The person as brought me up was very good, and said, while she'd got a home I should never want; but two years after mother's death, she was seized with the cholera, and then I hadn't a friend left in the world. When she died I felt ready to kill myself; I was all alone then, and what could I do—cripple as I was? She thought her sons and daughters as I'd been brought up with—like brothers and sisters—would look after me; but it was not in their power—they was only hard-working people. My mother used to allow so much a year for my schooling, and I can read and write pretty well." (He wrote his name in my presence kneeling at the table; holding the pen almost as one might fancy a bird would, and placing the paper sideways instead of straight before him.) "While mother was alive, I was always foraging about to learn something unbeknown to her. I wanted to do so, in case mother should leave me without the means of getting a living. I used to buy old bedsteads, and take them to a man, and get him to repair them, and then I'd put the sacking on myself; I can hold a hammer somehow in my right hand. I used to polish them on my knees. I made a bench to my height out of two old chairs. I used to know what I should get for the bedsteads, and so could tell what I could afford to give the man to do up the parts as I couldn't manage. It was so I got to learn something like a business for myself. When the person died as had brought me up, I *could* do a little; I had then got the means. Before her death I had opened a kind of shop for things in the general line; I sold tin-ware, and brass-work, and candlesticks, and fire-irons, and all old furniture, and gown-prints as well. I went into the tally business,[23] and that ruined me altogether. I couldn't get my money in; there's a good deal owing to me now. Me and a boy used to manage the whole. I used to make all my account-books and everything. My lodgers didn't pay me my rent, so I had to move from the house, and live on what stock I had. In my new lodging I went on as well as I could for a little while; but about eighteen months ago I could hold on no longer. Then I

---

23. Business operated on credit.

borrowed a little, and went hawking tin-ware and brushes in the country. I sold baking-dishes, Dutch ovens, roasting-jacks,[24] skewers and gridirons, teapots, and saucepans, and combs. I used to exchange sometimes for old clothes. I had a barrow and a boy with me; I used to keep him, and give him 1s. a week. I managed to get just a living that way. When the winter came on I gave it up; it was too cold. After that I was took bad with a fever; my stock had been all gone a little while before, and the boy had left because I couldn't keep him, and I had to do all for myself. All my friends was dead, and I had no one to help me, so I was obliged to lay about all night in my things, for I couldn't get them off alone; and that and want of food brought on a fever. Then I was took into the workhouse, and there I stopped all the summer, as I told you. I can't say they treated me bad, but they certainly didn't use me well. If I could have worked after I got better, I could have had tea; but 'cause I couldn't do nothing, they gave me that beastly gruel morning and night. I had meat three times a week. They would have kept me there till now, but I would die in the streets rather than be a pauper. So I told them, if they would give me the means of getting a stock, I would try and get a living for myself. After refusing many times to let me have 10s., they agreed to give me 5s. Then I came out, but I had no home, and so I crawled about till I met with the people where I am now, and they let me sit up there till I got a room of my own. Then some of my friends collected for me about 15s. altogether, and I did pretty well for a little while. I went to live close by the Blackfriars-road, but the people where I lodged treated me very bad. There was a number of girls of the town in the same street, but they was too fond of their selves and their drink to give nothing. They used to buy things of me and never pay me. They never made game of me, nor played me any tricks, and if they saw the boys doing it they would protect me. They never offered to give me no victuals; indeed, I shouldn't have liked to have eaten the food they got. After that I couldn't pay my lodgings, and the parties where I lodged turned me out, and I had to crawl about the streets for four days and nights. This was only a month back. I was fit to die with pain all that time. If I could get a penny I used to go into a coffee-shop for half-a-pint of coffee, and sit there till they drove me out, and then I'd crawl about till it was time for me to go out selling. Oh! dreadful, dreadful, it was to be all them hours—day and night—on my knees. I couldn't get along at all, I was forced to sit down every minute, and then I used to fall asleep with my things in my hand, and be woke up by the police to be pushed about and druv on by them. It seemed like as if I was walking on the bare bones of my knees. The pain in them was like the cramp, only much worse. At last I could bear it no longer, so I went afore Mr. Secker, the magistrate, at Union Hall, and told him I was destitute, and that the parties where I had been living kept my bed and the few things I had, for 2s. 6d. rent, that I owed them. He said he couldn't believe that anybody would force me to crawl about the streets, for four days and nights, cripple as I was, for such a sum. One of the officers told him I was a honest and striving man, and the magistrate sent the officer, with the money, to get my things,

---

24. A jack is a contrivance for turning a spit.

but the landlady wouldn't give them till the officer compelled her, and then she chucked my bed out into the middle of the street. A neighbour took it in for me and took care of it till I found out the tinman who had before let me sit up in his house. I should have gone to him at first, but he lived farther than I could walk. I am stopping with him now, and he is very kind to me. I have still some relations living, and they are well to do, but, being a cripple, they despise me. My aunt, my mother's sister, is married to a builder, in Petersham, near Richmond, and they are rich people—having some houses of their own besides a good business. I have got a boy to wheel me down on a barrow to them, and asked assistance of them, but they will have nothing to do with me. They won't look at me for my affliction. Six months ago they gave me half-a-crown. I had no lodgings nor victuals then; and *that* I shouldn't have had from them had I not said I was starving and must go to the parish. This winter I went to them, and they shut the door in my face. After leaving my aunt's, I went down to Ham Common, where my father-in-law[25] lives, and there his daughter's husband sent for a policeman to drive me away from the place. I told the husband I had no money nor food; but he advised me to go begging, and said I shouldn't have a penny of them. My father-in-law was ill upstairs at the time, but I don't think he would have treated me a bit better—and all this they do because the Almighty has made me a cripple. I can, indeed, solemnly say, that there is nothing else against me, and that I strive hard and crawl about till my limbs ache enough to drive me mad, to get an honest livelihood. With a couple of pounds I could, I think, manage to shift very well for myself. I'd get a stock, and go into the country with a barrow, and buy old metal, and exchange tin ware for old clothes, and, with that, I'm almost sure I could get a decent living. I'm accounted a very good dealer."

In answer to my inquiries concerning the character of this man, I received the following written communication:

"I have known C____ A____ twelve years; the last six years he has dealt with me for tinware. I have found him honest in all his dealings with me, sober and industrious.

C____ H____, Tinman."

From the writer of the above testimonial I received the following account of the poor cripple:—

"He is a man of generous disposition, and very sensitive for the afflictions of others. One day while passing down the Borough he saw a man afflicted with St. Vitus's dance[26] shaking from head to foot, and leaning on the arm of a woman who appeared to be his wife." The cripple told my informant that he should never forget what he felt when he beheld that poor man. "I thought," he said, "what a blessing it is I am not like him." Nor is the cripple, I am told, less independent than he is generous. In all his sufferings and privations he never pleads poverty to

---

25. Step-father.
26. St. Vitus was a third-century Christian child martyr. St. Vitus is called on by the sufferers of chorea, various nervous disorders marked by involuntary, uncontrollable movements.

others; but bears up under the trials of life with the greatest patience and fortitude. When in better circumstances he was more independent than at present, having since, through illness and poverty, been much humbled.

"His privations have been great," adds my informant. "Only two months back, being in a state of utter destitution and quite worn out with fatigue, he called at the house of a person (where my informant occupied a room) about ten o'clock at night, and begged them to let him rest himself for a short while, but the inhuman landlady and her son laid hold of the wretched man, the one taking him by the arms and the other by the legs, and literally hurled him into the street. The next morning," my informant continued, "I saw the poor creature leaning against a lamp-post, shivering with the cold, and my heart bled for him; and since that he has been living with me."

Of the "Pure"-Finders

Dogs'-dung is called "Pure," from its cleansing and purifying properties.

The name of "Pure-finders," however, has been applied to the men engaged in collecting dogs'-dung from the public streets only, within the last 20 or 30 years. Previous to this period there appears to have been no men engaged in the business, old women alone gathered the substance, and they were known by the name of "bunters," which signifies properly gatherers of rags; and thus plainly intimates that the rag-gatherers originally added the collecting of "Pure" to their original and proper vocation. Hence it appears that the bone-grubbers, rag-gatherers,[27] and pure-finders, constituted formerly but one class of people, and even now they have, as I have stated, kindred characteristics.

The pure-finders meet with a ready market for all the dogs'-dung they are able to collect, at the numerous tanyards in Bermondsey, where they sell it by the stable-bucket full, and get from 8d. to 10d. per bucket, and sometimes 1s. and 1s. 2d. for it, according to its quality. The "dry limy-looking sort" fetches the highest price at some yards, as it is found to possess more of the alkaline, or purifying properties; but others are found to prefer the dark moist quality. Strange as it may appear, the preference for a particular kind has suggested to the finders of Pure the idea of adulterating it to a very considerable extent; this is effected by means of mortar broken away from old walls, and mixed up with the whole mass, which it closely resembles; in some cases, however, the mortar is rolled into small balls similar to those found. Hence it would appear, that there is no business or trade, however insignificant or contemptible, without its own peculiar and appropriate tricks.

The pure-finders are in their habits and mode of proceeding nearly similar to the bone-grubbers. Many of the pure-finders are, however, better in circumstances, the men especially, as they earn more money. They are also, to a certain extent, a better educated class. Some of the regular collectors of this substance have been mechanics, and others small tradesmen, who have been reduced. Those pure-

27. Those who collect trash (such as rags, bones, and bottles) to sell.

finders who have "a good connection," and have been granted permission to cleanse some kennels, obtain a very fair living at the business, earning from 10s. to 15s. a week. These, however, are very few; the majority have to seek the article in the streets, and by such means they can obtain only from 6s. to 10s. a week. The average weekly earnings of this class are thought to be about 7s. 6d.

From all the inquiries I have made on this subject, I have found that there cannot be less than from 200 to 300 persons constantly engaged solely in this business. There are about 30 tanyards large and small in Bermondsey, and these all have their regular Pure collectors from whom they obtain the article. Leomont and Roberts's, Bavingtons', Beech's, Murrell's, Cheeseman's, Powell's, Jones's, Jourdans', Kent's, Moorcroft's, and Davis's, are among the largest establishments, and some idea of the amount of business done in some of these yards may be formed from the fact, that the proprietors severally employ from 300 to 500 tanners. At Leomont and Roberts's there are 23 regular street-finders, who supply them with pure, but this is a large establishment, and the number supplying them is considered far beyond the average quantity; moreover, Messrs. Leomont and Roberts do more business in the particular branch of tanning in which the article is principally used, viz., in dressing the leather for book-covers, kid-gloves, and a variety of other articles. Some of the other tanyards, especially the smaller ones, take the substance only as they happen to want it, and others again employ but a limited number of hands. If, therefore, we strike an average, and reduce the number supplying each of the several yards to eight, we shall have 240 persons regularly engaged in the business: besides these, it may be said that numbers of the starving and destitute Irish have taken to picking up the material, but not knowing where to sell it, or how to dispose of it, they part with it for 2d. or 3d. the pail-full to the regular purveyors of it to the tanyards, who of course make a considerable profit by the transaction. The children of the poor Irish are usually employed in this manner, but they also pick up rags and bones, and anything else which may fall in their way.

I have stated that some of the pure-finders, especially the men, earn a considerable sum of money per week; their gains are sometimes as much as 15s.; indeed I am assured that seven years ago, when they got from 3s. to 4s. per pail for the pure, that many of them would not exchange their position with that of the best paid mechanic in London. Now, however, the case is altered, for there are twenty now at the business for every one who followed it then; hence each collects so much the less in quantity, and, moreover, from the competition gets so much less for the article. Some of the collectors at present do not earn 3s. per week, but these are mostly old women who are feeble and unable to get over the ground quickly; others make 5s. and 6s. in the course of the week, while the most active and those who clean out the kennels of the dog fanciers may occasionally make 9s. and 10s. and even 15s. a week still, but this is of very rare occurrence. Allowing the finders, one with the other, to earn on an average 5s. per week, it would give the annual earnings of each to be 13l., while the income of the whole 200 would amount to 50l. a week, or 2,600l. per annum. The kennel "pure" is not much valued, indeed many of the tanners will not even buy it, the reason is that the dogs of the "fanciers" are fed on almost anything, to save expense; the kennel cleaners consequently take the precaution of mixing it with what is found in the street, previous to offering it for sale.

The pure-finder may at once be distinguished from the bone-grubber and rag-gatherer; the latter, as I have before mentioned, carries a bag, and usually a stick armed with a spike, while he is most frequently to be met with in back streets, narrow lanes, yards and other places, where dust and rubbish are likely to be thrown out from the adjacent houses. The pure-finder, on the contrary, is often found in the open streets, as dogs wander where they like. The pure-finders always carry a handle basket, generally with a cover, to hide the contents, and have their right hand covered with a black leather glove; many of them, however, dispense with the glove, as they say it is much easier to wash their hands than to keep the glove fit for use. The women generally have a large pocket for the reception of such rags as they may chance to fall in with, but they pick up those only of the very best quality, and will not go out of their way to search even for them. Thus equipped they may be seen pursuing their avocation in almost every street in and about London, excepting those streets as are now cleansed by the "street orderlies,"[28] of whom the pure-finders grievously complain, as being an unwarrantable interference with the privileges of their class.

The pure collected is used by leather-dressers and tanners, and more especially by those engaged in the manufacture of morocco and kid leather from the skins of old and young goats, of which skins great numbers are imported, and of the roans[29] and lambskins which are the sham morocco and kids of the "slop" leather trade, and are used by the better class of shoemakers, book-binders, and glovers, for the inferior requirements of their business. Pure is also used by tanners, as is pigeon's dung, for the tanning of the thinner kinds of leather, such as calf-skins, for which purpose it is placed in pits with an admixture of lime and bark.

In the manufacture of moroccos and roans the pure is rubbed by the hands of the workman into the skin he is dressing. This is done to "purify" the leather, I was told by an intelligent leather-dresser, and from that term the word "pure" has originated. The dung has astringent as well as highly alkaline, or, to use the expression of my informant, "scouring," qualities. When the pure has been rubbed into the flesh and grain of the skin (the "flesh" being originally the interior, and the "grain" the exterior part of the cuticle), and the skin, thus purified, has been hung up to be dried, the dung removes, as it were, all such moisture as, if allowed to remain, would tend to make the leather unsound or imperfectly dressed. This imperfect dressing, moreover, gives a disagreeable smell to the leather—and leather-buyers often use both nose and tongue in making their purchases—and would consequently prevent that agreeable odour being imparted to the skin which is found in some kinds of morocco and kid. The peculiar odour of the Russia leather,

---

28. Sanitation workers.

29. Morocco is a pebble-grained leather originally made in Morocco from goatskins. Kid refers to leather made from the skin of a young goat while roan is soft sheepskin leather often made to resemble morocco and used to bind books.

so agreeable in the libraries of the rich, is derived from the bark of young birch trees. It is now manufactured in Bermondsey.

Among the morocco manufacturers, especially among the old operatives, there is often a scarcity of employment, and they then dress a few roans, which they hawk to the cheap warehouses, or sell to the wholesale shoemakers on their own account. These men usually reside in small garrets in the poorer parts of Bermondsey, and carry on their trade in their own rooms, using and keeping the pure there; hence the "homes" of these poor men are peculiarly uncomfortable, if not unhealthy. Some of these poor fellows or their wives collect the pure themselves, often starting at daylight for the purpose; they more frequently, however, buy it of a regular finder.

The number of pure-finders I heard estimated, by a man well acquainted with the tanning and other departments of the leather trade, at from 200 to 250. The finders, I was informed by the same person, collected about a pail-full a day, clearing 6s. a week in the summer—1s. and 1s. 2d. being the charge for a pail-full; in the short days of winter, however, and in bad weather, they could not collect five pail-fulls in a week.

In the wretched locality already referred to as lying between the Docks and Rosemary-lane, redolent of filth and pregnant with pestilential diseases, and whither all the outcasts of the metropolitan population seem to be drawn, either in the hope of finding fitting associates and companions in their wretchedness (for there is doubtlessly something attractive and agreeable to them in such companionship), or else for the purpose of hiding themselves and their shifts and struggles for existence from the world,—in this dismal quarter, and branching from one of the many narrow lanes which interlace it, there is a little court with about half-a-dozen houses of the very smallest dimensions, consisting of merely two rooms, one over the other. Here in one of the upper rooms (the lower one of the same house being occupied by another family and apparently *filled* with little ragged children), I discerned, after considerable difficulty, an old woman, a Pure-finder. When I opened the door the little light that struggled through the small window, the many broken panes of which were stuffed with old rags, was not sufficient to enable me to perceive who or what was in the room. After a short time, however, I began to make out an old chair standing near the fire-place, and then to discover a poor old woman resembling a bundle of rags and filth stretched on some dirty straw in the corner of the apartment. The place was bare and almost naked. There was nothing in it except a couple of old tin kettles and a basket, and some broken crockeryware in the recess of the window. To my astonishment I found this wretched creature to be, to a certain extent, a "superior" woman; she could read and write well, spoke correctly, and appeared to have been a person of natural good sense, though broken up with age, want, and infirmity, so that she was characterized by all that dull and hardened stupidity of manner which I have noticed in the class. She made the following statement:—

"I am about 60 years of age. My father was a milkman, and very well off; he had a barn and a great many cows. I was kept at school till I was thirteen or fourteen years of age; about that time my father died, and then I was taken home to help my mother in the business. After a while things went wrong; the cows began to die, and mother, alleging she could not manage the business herself, married again. I soon found out the difference. Glad to get away, anywhere out of the house, I married a sailor, and was very comfortable with him for some years; as he made short voyages, and was often at home, and always left me half his pay. At last he was pressed,[30] when at home with me, and sent away; I forget now where he was sent to, but I never saw him from that day to this. The only thing I know is that some sailors came to me four or five years after, and told me that he deserted from the ship in which he had gone out, and got on board the *Neptune*, East Indiaman, bound for Bombay, where he acted as boatswain's mate; some little time afterwards, he had got intoxicated while the ship was lying in harbour, and, going down the side to get into a bumboat,[31] and buy more drink, he had fallen overboard and was drowned. I got some money that was due to him from the India House,[32] and, after that was all gone, I went into service, in the Mile-end Road. There I stayed for several years, till I met my second husband, who was bred to the water, too, but as a waterman on the river. We did very well together for a long time, till he lost his health. He became paralyzed like, and was deprived of the use of all one side, and nearly lost the sight of one of his eyes; this was not very conspicuous at first, but when we came to get pinched,[33] and to be badly off, then any one might have seen that there was something the matter with his eye. Then we parted with everything we had in the world; and, at last, when we had no other means of living left, we were advised to take to gathering 'Pure.' At first I couldn't endure the business; I couldn't bear to eat a morsel, and I was obliged to discontinue it for a long time. My husband kept at it though, for he could do *that* well enough, only he couldn't walk as fast as he ought. He couldn't lift his hands as high as his head, but he managed to work under him, and so put the Pure in the basket. When I saw that he, poor fellow, couldn't make enough to keep us both, I took heart and went out again, and used to gather more than he did; that's fifteen years ago now; the times were good then, and we used to do very well. If we only gathered a pail-full in the day, we could live very well; but we could do much more than that, for there wasn't near so many at the business then, and the Pure was easier to be had. For my part I can't tell where all the poor creatures have come from of late years; the world seems growing worse and worse every day. They have pulled down the price of Pure, that's certain; but the poor things must do something, they can't starve while there's anything to be got. Why, no later than six or seven years ago, it was as high as 3*s.* 6*d.* and 4*s.* a pail-full, and a ready sale for as much of it as you could get; but now you can only get 1*s.* and in some places 1*s.* 2*d.* a pail-full; and, as I said before,

---

30. Impressment was the practice of seizing men for public service. The practice was largely accepted until military recruitment reform began in the 1850s.

31. A boat that brings goods to a larger boat either in port or off shore.

32. The East India Company was the company chartered by the British government in 1600 to trade in the East Indies; it was dissolved in 1874.

33. To experience financial hardship.

there are so many at it, that there is not much left for a poor old creature like me to find. The men that are strong and smart get the most, of course, and some of them do very well, at least they manage to live. Six years ago, my husband complained that he was ill, in the evening, and lay down in the bed—we lived in Whitechapel then—he took a fit of coughing, and was smothered in his own blood. O dear" (the poor old soul here ejaculated), "what troubles I have gone through! I had eight children at one time, and there is not one of them alive now. My daughter lived to 30 years of age, and then she died in childbirth, and, since then, I have had nobody in the wide world to care for me—none but myself, all alone as I am. After my husband's death I couldn't do much, and all my things went away, one by one, until I've nothing but bare walls, and that's the reason why I was vexed at first at your coming in, sir. I was yesterday out all day, and went round Aldgate, Whitechapel, St. George's East, Stepney, Bow, and Bromley, and then came home; after that, I went over to Bermondsey, and there I got only 6*d.* for my pains. To-day I wasn't out at all; I wasn't well; I had a bad headache, and I'm so much afraid of the fevers that are all about here—though I don't know why I should be afraid of them—I was lying down, when you came, to get rid of my pains. There's such a dizziness in my head now, I feel as if it didn't belong to me. No, I have earned no money to-day. I have had a piece of dried bread that I steeped in water to eat. I haven't eat anything else to-day; but, pray, sir, don't tell anybody of it. I could never bear the thought of going into the 'great house' [workhouse]; I'm so used to the air, that I'd sooner die in the street, as many I know have done. I've known several of our people, who have sat down in the street with their basket alongside them, and died. I knew one not long ago, who took ill just as she was stooping down to gather up the Pure, and fell on her face; she was taken to the London Hospital, and died at three o'clock in the morning. I'd sooner die like them than be deprived of my liberty, and be prevented from going about where I liked. No, I'll never go into the workhouse; my master is kind to me" [the tanner whom she supplies]. "When I'm ill, he sometimes gives me a sixpence; but there's one gentleman has done us great harm, by forcing so many into the business. He's a poor-law guardian, and when any poor person applies for relief, he tells them to go and gather Pure, and that he'll buy it of them (for he's in the line), and so the parish, you see, don't have to give anything, and that's one way that so many have come into the trade of late, that the likes of me can do little or no good at it. Almost every one I've ever known engaged at Pure-finding were people who were better off once. I knew a man who went by the name of Brown, who picked up Pure for years before I went to it; he was a very quiet man; he used to lodge in Blue Anchor-yard, and seldom used to speak to anybody. We two used to talk together sometimes, but never much. One morning he was found dead in his bed; it was of a Tuesday morning, and he was buried about 12 o'clock on the Friday following. About 6 o'clock on that after-noon, three or four gentlemen came searching all through this place, looking for a man named Brown, and offering a reward to any who would find him out; there was a whole crowd about them when I came up. One of the gentlemen said that the man they wanted had lost the first finger of his right hand, and then I knew that it was the man that had been buried only that morning. Would you believe it, Mr. Brown was a real gentleman all the time, and had a large estate, of I don't know how many thousand pounds, just left him, and the lawyers had advertised and searched everywhere for him, but never found him, you may say, till he was dead. We discovered that his name was not Brown; he had only taken that name to hide his real one, which, of course, he did not want any one to know. I've often thought of him, poor man, and all the misery he might have been spared, if the good news had only come a year or two sooner."

Another informant, a Pure-collector, was originally in the Manchester cotton trade, and held a lucrative situation in a large country establishment. His salary one year exceeded 250*l.*, and his regular income was 150*l.* "This," he says, "I lost through drink and neglect. My master was exceedingly kind to me, and has even assisted me since I left his employ. He bore with me patiently for many years, but the love of drink was so strong upon me that it was impossible for him to keep me any longer." He has often been drunk, he tells me, for three months together; and he is now so reduced that he is ashamed to be seen. When at his master's it was his duty to carve and help the other assistants belonging to the establishment, and his hand used to shake so violently that he has been ashamed to lift the gravy spoon.

At breakfast he has frequently waited till all the young men had left the table before he ventured to taste his tea; and immediately, when he was alone, he has bent his head down to his cup to drink, being utterly incapable of raising it to his lips. He says he is a living example of the degrading influence of drink. All his friends have deserted him. He has suffered enough, he tells me, to make him give it up. He earned the week before I saw him 5*s.* 2*d.*; and the week before that, 6*s.*

Before leaving me I prevailed upon the man to "take the pledge."[34] This is now eighteen months ago, and I have not seen him since.

34. The promise, promoted by the temperance movement, to abstain from drinking alcoholic beverages.

MATTHEW ARNOLD

F OR BIOGRAPHICAL information, see the introduction to Matthew Arnold
("Rugby Chapel") in part 1.

Matthew Arnold's paired sonnets "East London" and "West London," published
in 1867, explore the ironies of poverty and want.

East London

'Twas August, and the fierce sun overhead
Smote on the squalid streets of Bethnal Green,[1]
And the pale weaver, through his windows seen
In Spitalfields,[2] looked thrice dispirited.
I met a preacher there I knew, and said: 5
"Ill and o'erworked, how fare you in this scene?"—
"Bravely!" said he; "for I of late have been
Much cheered with thoughts of Christ, *the living bread.*"
O human soul! as long as thou canst so
Set up a mark of everlasting light,   10
Above the howling senses' ebb and flow,
To cheer thee, and to right thee if thou roam—
Not with lost toil thou laborest through the night!
Thou mak'st the heaven thou hop'st indeed thy home.

1. One of the poorer sections of London.
2. The notorious London district where the silk-weavers lived and labored.

West London

Crouched on the pavement, close by Belgrave Square,[3]
A tramp I saw, ill, moody, and tongue-tied.
A babe was in her arms, and at her side
A girl; their clothes were rags, their feet were bare.
Some laboring men, whose work lay somewhere there,   5
Passed opposite; she touched her girl, who hied
Across, and begged, and came back satisfied.
The rich she had let pass with frozen stare.
Thought I: "Above her state this spirit towers;
She will not ask of aliens, but of friends,   10
Of sharers in a common human fate.
She turns from that cold succour, which attends
The unknown little from the unknowing great,
And points us to a better time than ours."

3. A wealthy, fashionable residential area.

JOSEPH SKIPSEY

J OSEPH SKIPSEY (1832–1903), a coal miner for over forty years, entered the pits
as a trapper (or worker responsible for opening and closing passage doors)
when he was seven years old. Self-taught, Skipsey began as a boy reading widely and
writing poems. He published his first volume of verse in 1859 and a half dozen more
volumes over the next few decades. His works received favorable reactions from
critics and from other writers such as Dante Gabriel Rossetti and Oscar Wilde. He
also edited and wrote introductions to the works of five authors in the *Canterbury
Poets* series: Blake, Shelley, Coleridge, Poe, and Burns. For two years (1889–91)
Skipsey and his wife were the custodians of Shakespeare's birthplace at Stratford-
upon-Avon.

"The Hartley Calamity" is based on the true story of an accident at the Hartley Colliery in January 1862, as a result of which over two hundred miners lost
their lives.

The Hartley Calamity

The Hartley men are noble, and
   Ye'll hear a tale of woe;
I'll tell the doom of the Hartley men—
   The year of Sixty-two.

'Twas on a Thursday morning, on   5
   The first month of the year,
When there befell the thing that well
   May rend the heart to hear.

Ere chanticleer[1] with music rare
    Awakes the old homestead,   10
The Hartley men are up and off
    To earn their daily bread.

On, on they toil; with heat they broil,
    And streams of sweat still glue
The stour[2] unto their skins, till they   15
    Are black as the coal they hew.

Now to and fro the putters[3] go,
    The waggons to and fro,
And clang on clang of wheel and hoof
    Ring in the mine below.   20

The din and strife of human life
    Awake in "wall" and "board,"
When, lo! a shock is felt which makes
    Each human heart-beat heard.

Each bosom thuds, as each his duds[4]   25
    Then snatches and away,
And to the distant shaft he flees
    With all the speed he may.

Each, all, they flee—by two—by three
    They seek the shaft, to seek   30
An answer in each other's face,
    To what they may not speak.

"Are we entombed?" they seem to ask,
    For the shaft is closed, and no
Escape have they to God's bright day   35
    From out the night below.

So stand in pain the Hartley men,
    And swiftly o'er them comes
The memory of home, nay, all
    That links us to our homes.   40

1. A rooster. The word is from Old French, a reference to Chantecler, a rooster in the *Roman de Renart.*
    2. Chiefly Scottish: dust, powder.
    3. Coal mining term for those employed as haulers.
    4. Belongings.

Despair at length renews their strength,
    And they the shaft must clear,
And soon the sound of mall[5] and pick,
    Half drowns the voice of fear.

And hark! to the blow of the mall below   45
    Do sounds above reply?
Hurra, hurra, for the Hartley men,
    For now their rescue's nigh.

Their rescue nigh? The sounds of joy
    And hope have ceased, and ere   50
A breath is drawn a rumble's heard
    Re-drives them to despair.

Together, now behold them bow;
    Their burden'd souls unload
In cries that never rise in vain   55
    Unto the living God.

Whilst yet they kneel, again they feel
    Their strength renew'd—again
The swing and the ring of the mall attest
    The might of the Hartley men.   60

And hark! to the blow of the mall below
    Do sounds above reply?
Hurra, hurra, for the Hartley men,
    For now their rescue's nigh.

But lo! yon light, erewhile so bright,   65
    No longer lights the scene;
A cloud of mist yon light hath kiss'd,
    And shorn it of its sheen.

A cloud of mist yon light hath kiss'd,
    And see! along must crawl,   70
Till one by one the lights are smote,
    And darkness covers all.

"O, father, till the shaft is cleared,
    Close, close beside me keep;

5. Variation of "maul," a heavy hammer used for driving wedges.

My eye-lids are together glued,
  And I—and I—must sleep."   75

"Sleep, darling, sleep, and I will keep
  Close by—heigh-ho!"—To keep
Himself awake the father strives—
  But he—he too—must sleep.   80

"O, brother, till the shaft is cleared,
  Close, close beside me keep;
My eye-lids are together glued,
  And I—and I—must sleep."

"Sleep, brother, sleep, and I will keep
  Close by—heigh-ho!"—To keep   85
Himself awake the brother strives—
  But he—he too—must sleep.

"O, mother dear! wert, wert thou near
  Whilst sleep!"—The orphan slept;   90
And all night long by the black pit-heap
  The mother a dumb watch kept.

And fathers, and mothers, and sisters, and brothers—
  The lover and the new-made bride—
A vigil kept for those who slept,   95
  From eve to morning tide.

But they slept—still sleep—in silence dread,
  Two hundred old and young,
To awake when heaven and earth have sped,
  And the last dread trumpet rung.   100

HENRIETTA TINDAL

H ENRIETTA TINDAL (1818–1879), the daughter of a vicar, authored two collections of poems and one novel. Her friend, popular novelist and playwright Mary Russell Mitford (1787–1855), helped find publishers for her poetry. "The Cry of the Oppressed" gives voice to the sufferings of the working poor.

The Cry of the Oppressed

Bondmen, and helots,¹ and serfs were we,
Slaves in plantation and stifling mill,
Pauper and 'prentice: from sea to sea,
Our bands are rising and gathering still.

We are the many who served the few;   5
We made their glory, and strength, and gain;
We passed as sand, when the west wind blew,
As the myriad drops of the autumn rain;

We sank at night off the surge-beat strand,—
The rotting bark and its living freight,   10
The o'erflowing swarm of a straitened land,
Who went forth bravely to seek their fate.

For a trader's gain our lives were sold—
The blooming mother, the maiden bright,

1. Unlike most slaves in ancient Greek culture, who were foreign to the city-states, a helot was an indigenous person subjected to the rule of the citizen families.

The vigorous father, the stripling bold,   15
With the rough and wrong of life to fight.

We are the souls who were pent within
The narrow street and the valley dim;
Bred in the darkness of want and sin,
We peopled the hulks[2] and the prisons grim.   20

The blazing gas on the night was shed,
To lure our lips to the liquid flame;[3]
And bitter upon our hard-earned bread
The poisonous fraud of the dealer came.

We breathed the heated and noisome air   25
In crowded chambers of daily toil;
And the green, slow, slimy drain was there,
Creeping below on the black wet soil.[4]

Ha! we have blunted the hungry tooth
Of ev'ry plague[5] that hath stalked the land;   30
It took our beauty, and strength, and youth,
Father, mother, and household band!

Yes! we have parched in the fever's fire,
Till madness throbbed in the whirling brain,
When fancy feasted the vain desire,   35
The suff'rer rose o'er his want and pain!

Mercy! for those we have left to die
Beyond your hearing, walled out from sight,
In the black close lane to the palace nigh—
For the body, food—for the spirit, light!   40

We ask no weary life of leisure,
That robs your joy of its bloom and zest—
Give us God's just and righteous measure,
The worth of labour, the hours of rest.

2. Old ships anchored offshore and used as prisons.
3. In other words, the gas lamps lure the people out at night to bars and taverns.
4. Edwin Chadwick's (1800–1890) *Report on the Sanitary Condition of the Labouring Population* (1842) described in comprehensive and graphic detail the appalling environment in which the poor lived and prompted serious sanitation reform measures.
5. The urban poor were particularly vulnerable to the epidemics of typhus, cholera, smallpox, scarlet fever, and other deadly contagious diseases that swept through England periodically throughout the nineteenth century.

Ye lack emotions who live at ease   45
In bright warm chambers of prosp'rous life;
Ye tales of terror and sorrow please—
Look out around ye, they're rife, aye,—rife,

As berries in autumn, as leaves in May,
Seek! ye will find in the neighbouring street   50
Tragedies acted before the day,
That stir the heart to a quicker beat,
And draw the tear from its deepest seat.

WILLIAM MORRIS

SEE THE INTRODUCTION to William Morris ("Useful Labour *versus* Useless Toil") in part 1. "The Voice of Toil" was published in 1884.

The Voice of Toil

I heard men saying, Leave hope and praying,
All days shall be as all have been;
Today and tomorrow bring fear and sorrow,
The never ending toil between.

When Earth was younger mid toil and hunger,   5
In hope we strove, and our hands were strong;
Then great men led us, with words they fed us,
And bade us right the earthly wrong.

Go read in story their deeds and glory,
Their names amidst the nameless dead;   10
Turn then from lying to us slow-dying
In that good world to which they led;

Where fast and faster our iron master,
The thing we made, forever drives,
Bids us grind treasure and fashion pleasure   15
For other hopes and other lives.

Where home is a hovel and dull we grovel,
Forgetting that the world is fair;
Where no babe we cherish, lest its very soul perish;
Where mirth is crime, and love a snare.   20

Who now shall lead us, what god shall heed us
As we lie in the hell our hands have won?
For us are no rulers but fools and befoolers;
The great are fallen, the wise men gone.

I heard men saying, Leave tears and praying,   25
The sharp knife heedeth not the sheep;
Are we not stronger than the rich and the wronger,
When day breaks over dreams and sleep?

Come, shoulder to shoulder, ere the world grows older!
Help lies in naught but thee and me;   30
Hope is before us, the long years that bore us
Bore leaders more than men may be.

Let dead hearts tarry and trade and marry,
And trembling nurse their dreams of mirth,
While we the living our lives are giving   35
To bring the bright new world to birth.[1]

Come, shoulder to shoulder, ere earth grows older!
The cause spreads over land and sea;
Now the world shaketh, and fear awaketh,
And joy at last for thee and me.   40

1. In a letter of 1883, Morris declared, "I believe that the whole basis of Society, with its contrasts of rich and poor, is incurably vicious." In his view, the only hope lay in the overthrow of capitalism and the creation of a socialist order.

EDITH NESBIT

EDITH NESBIT (1858–1924) wrote poetry and fiction but is best known for her children's books, of which the most widely read has been *The Railway Children* (1906). Unorthodox in her appearance, bohemian in her lifestyle, and radical in her politics, Nesbit became a charter member of the socialist Fabian Society in 1884. In "A Great Industrial Centre," Nesbit expresses the same message that William Morris—another, more famous English socialist—presents in "The Voice of Toil" (see preceding entry) and "Useful Work *versus* Useless Toil" (see part 1).

A Great Industrial Centre

Squalid street after squalid street,
    Endless rows of them, each the same,
Black dust under your weary feet,
Dust upon every face you meet,
Dust in their hearts, too—or so it seems—   5
    Dust in the place of dreams.

Spring in her beauty thrills and thrives,
    Here men hardly have heard her name.
Work is the end and aim of their lives—
Work, work, work! for children and wives;   10
Work for a life which, when it is won,
    Is the saddest under the sun!

Work—one dark and unending round
    In black dull workshops, out of the light;

Work that others' ease may abound,   15
Work that delight for them may be found,
Work without hope, without pause, without peace,
    That only in death can cease.

Brothers, who live glad lives in the sun,
    What of these men, at work in the night?   20
God will ask you what you have done;
Their lives be required of you—every one—[1]
Ye, who were glad and who liked life well,
    While they did your work—in hell!

1. According to Matthew 25:31–46, the nations will be judged according to their treatment of the needy.

JOHN DAVIDSON

J OHN DAVIDSON (1857–1909), the son of a Scots Evangelical minister, worked variously as a chemical analyst in a sugar refinery, as a schoolteacher, and as a journalist but struggled against poverty in his own life. The author of plays, fiction, and poetry, he abandoned his writing in the early 1900s to preach. Impoverished and suffering from poor health, he drowned himself in 1909. "Thirty Bob a Week" was published in 1894.

Thirty Bob[1] a Week

I couldn't touch a stop[2] and turn a screw,
    And set the blooming world a-work for me,
Like such as cut their teeth—I hope, like you—
    On the handle of a skeleton gold key;
I cut mine on a leek, which I eat it every week;   5
    I'm a clerk at thirty bob, as you can see.

But I don't allow it's luck and all a toss;
    There's no such thing as being starred and crossed;
It's just the power of some to be a boss,
    And the bally[3] power of others to be bossed.   10
I face the music, sir; you bet I ain't a cur;
    Strike me lucky if I don't believe I'm lost!

1. Shilling. Twenty shillings equal a pound.
2. A part of a machine that stops or controls movement.
3. An intensifying adjective.

For like a mole I journey in the dark,
    A-traveling along the underground[4]
From my Pillared Halls and broad Suburban Park,   15
    To come the daily dull official round;
And home again at night with my pipe all alight,
    A-scheming how to count ten bob a pound.

And it's often very cold and wet,
    And my missis stitches towels for a hunks;[5]   20
And the Pillared Halls is half of it to let—
    Three rooms about the size of traveling trunks.
And we cough, my wife and I, to dislocate a sigh,
    When the noisy little kids are in their bunks.

But you never hear her do a growl or whine,   25
    For she's made of flint and roses, very odd;
And I've got to cut my meaning rather fine,
    Or I'd blubber, for I'm made of greens and sod.
So p'r'aps we are in Hell for all that I can tell,
    And lost and damned and served up hot to God.   30

I ain't blaspheming, Mr. Silver-tongue;
    I'm saying things a bit beyond your art.
Of all the rummy[6] starts you ever sprung,
    Thirty bob a week's the rummiest start!
With your science and your books and your the'ries about spooks,   35
    Did you ever hear of looking in your heart?

I didn't mean your pocket, Mr., no—
    I mean that having children and a wife,
With thirty bob on which to come and go,
    Isn't dancing to the tabor and the fife;   40
When it doesn't make you drink, by Heaven! it makes you think,
    And notice curious items about life.

I step into my heart and there I meet
    A god-almighty devil singing small,
Who would like to shout and whistle in the street,   45
    And squelch the passers flat against the wall;
If the whole world was a cake he had the power to take,
    He would take it, ask for more, and eat it all.

4. The first completely underground London railway line was built in 1890.
5. A miser.
6. Odd, peculiar.

And I meet a sort of simpleton beside,
  The kind that life is always giving beans;
With thirty bob a week to keep a bride
  He fell in love and married in his teens.
At thirty bob he stuck; but he knows it isn't luck;
  He knows the seas are deeper than tureens.

And the god-almighty devil and the fool
  That meet me in the High Street on the strike,
When I walk about my heart a-gathering wool,
  Are my good and evil angels if you like.
And both of them together in every kind of weather
  Ride me like a double-seated bike.

That's rough a bit and needs its meaning curled.
  But I have a high old hot un in my mind—
A most engrugious[7] notion of the world,
  That leaves your lightning 'rithmetic behind:
I give it at a glance when I say "There ain't no chance,
  Nor nothing of the lucky-lottery kind."

And it's this way that I make it out to be:
  No fathers, mothers, countries, climates—none;
Not Adam was responsible for me,
  Nor society, nor systems, nary one;
A little sleeping seed, I woke—I did, indeed—
  A million years before the blooming sun.[8]

I woke because I thought the time had come;
  Beyond my will there was no other cause;
And everywhere I found myself at home,
  Because I chose to be the thing I was;
And in whatever shape of mollusc or of ape
  I always went according to the laws.

I was the love that chose my mother out;
  I joined two lives and from the union burst;
My weakness and my strength without a doubt
  Are mine alone forever from the first;
It's just the very same with a difference in the name
  As "Thy will be done." You say it if you durst!

7. Egregious.
8. Davidson applied evolutionary theory to society.

They say it daily up and down the land
    As easy as you take a drink, it's true;
But the difficultest go to understand,
    And the difficultest job a man can do,
Is to come it brave and meek with thirty bob a week,
    And feel that that's the proper thing for you.

It's a naked child against a hungry wolf;
    It's playing bowls[9] upon a splitting wreck;
It's walking on a string across a gulf
    With millstones fore-and-aft about your neck;
But the thing is daily done by many and many a one;
    And we fall, face forward, fighting, on the deck.

9. Bowls: lawn bowling.

EDITH F. HOGG

E DITH F. HOGG wrote articles concerning child labor, education in Ireland, and oppressive working conditions faced by women. "The Fur-Pullers of South London," published in *The Nineteenth Century* in November 1897, is a particularly graphic exposé of abusive labor practices that were almost impossible to regulate because work was carried on in home-dwellings and because those being exploited were so fearful of losing employment that they were the ones most strongly opposed to regulatory codes. While Hogg does not refrain from advancing a strongly emotional appeal that working conditions be improved, she relies for the effectiveness of her presentation more on the straightforward description of the situations of the fur-pullers themselves. Even the most melodramatic narrative ploy—the attractive, defiant woman's saying, "Miss, I wish I had your life"—is made more forceful by Hogg's decision not to comment further but simply to let the woman's words conclude one distinct episode of the general narrative.

The Fur-Pullers of South London

Among the "dangerous trades" dealt with in the recently issued report of the Royal Commission is included one, of the very nature of which the vast majority of the public are totally ignorant. The fur-pullers of South London are the subject of the following article. The facts here related were obtained by personal investigation—forming a part of a general inquiry into the conditions of women's "homework" in South London; and truly, if it is well that light should be thrown on the dark places of the earth, there is no spot to be found where such light is more needed.

The employment of fur-pulling finds its slaves—there is no other word—only among those whose conception of life is strictly limited to keeping body and soul together; to whom a wage of ten shillings a week is wealth unattainable; to whom an eight-hour day is unimaginable. They belong one and all to that most pitiful, most helpless, most hopeless class which is produced by modern industrial conditions—those who acquiesce in starvation of body and soul as the state of life in which they were born, out of which they can never rise, in which they are doomed to die. To them, want and filth and disease are the normal inevitable conditions of existence, against which they lack the will as well as the power to rebel. Mr. Booth[1] has said that they are the despair of those who work among them, "not so much because they are bad as because their standard is hopelessly low." They are "not to be roused to better things, or else the right way to rouse them has not yet been found."

Of the fur-pullers working in factories we shall have something to say in the latter part of this paper; it is with the home workers, however, that we shall have chiefly to deal.

The area within which our investigation was carried on is a small one: from Union Street on the north to the New Kent Road on the south; from Blackfriars Road on the west to Long Lane on the east. This district is the last refuge of the casual worker.[2] Among the inhabitants, the few who have regular employment find it chiefly in that mysterious El Dorado[3] which is always spoken of as "the other side of the water"; but for the vast mass of the people on that grey south side, the broad sweeping bend of the river forms a moral no less than a physical barrier, shutting them off from every hope and every aspiration beyond the unending struggle somehow to keep alive.

This perpetually shifting population is as perpetually recruited from the larger pitiful army of the helpless and inefficient. The flotsam and jetsam from other quarters and other classes who come to merge their individual failure in the general failure of the invertebrate mass where room seems somehow to be made for all who drift into it. Hopelessly excluded by their own incompetence from a secure position in the labour market, with a natural abhorrence and incapacity for the discipline of regular employment, the men, for the most part, pick up odds and ends of jobs at the riverside or in the streets; working two or three days a week and loafing for the remaining four or five. Under these circumstances it is the women who must, perforce, become the staple breadwinners, and accordingly we find them working with far greater regularity than the men, rising in the early dawn, toiling through the long weary day, and snatching a few brief hours of sleep as the exigencies of their trade allow.

A few find employment in factories and workshops; others—and it is with these that we are dealing—take work given out at the factories to be done in their own

---

1. Charles Booth (1840–1916) was a reformer and social analyst whose monumental seventeen-volume *Life and Labour of the People in London* provides some of the most helpful information concerning working people, their conduct, their responses to poverty, and their attitudes toward religion. For selections from his work, see the final entry in this section.

2. A worker who is irregularly employed.

3. A fabled South American city of gold.

Figure 3.10. *Matchbox Makers at Bow.* Courtesy Mansell/Time Inc.
Despite the indictments of industrialization by Friedrich Engels, William Morris, and others, those who toiled at home often fared little better than factory workers. This engraving of matchbox makers at Bow, East London, 1871, shows the grim reality of much cottage industry.

homes. This work is, to an exceptional extent, fluctuating and casual; it demands little specialised skill or intelligence, and offers the maximum of long hours with the minimum of pay. There are, among these women, isolated cases of flower makers, tailoresses, machinists, sack makers, paper-bag makers, &c.; but a close investigation shows the main industries to be three, *i.e.* fur-pulling, box-making, and brush-drawing. Whole streets are given up to these, and in almost every room of some of the wretched tenement dwellings are inert, exhausted women plying one or other of these trades, and using up life and strength in a hard, unavailing struggle to keep the wolf from the door.

The inquirer who turns aside out of that historic street from which one April day there started long ago a famous and jocund company of pilgrims[4]—where to-day a sadder stream of humanity ceaselessly ebbs and flows—and who plunges under one of the narrow archways on its western side, will find himself at once face to face with the lowest depths to which the toil of women can be dragged. Here, in an endless network of pestilential courts and alleys, into which can penetrate no

4. Geoffrey Chaucer's Canterbury Pilgrims, described in the *General Prologue* to the *Canterbury Tales* as setting out from "Southwerk," the borough just south of London Bridge, the very area of Hogg's investigative report.

pure, purging breath of heaven, where the plants languish and die in the heavy air, and the very flies seem to lose the power of flight and creep and crawl in sickly, loathsome adhesion to mouldering walls and ceilings—here, without one glimpse of the beauty of God's fair world, or of the worth and dignity of that human nature made after the image of the Divine, we find the miserable poverty-stricken rooms of the fur-pullers.

To apply the word "homes" to dens such as these is cruel mockery. There are no "kindred points" between them and heaven.[5]

Of all these home-workers the fur-pullers are the hardest to find. Whether it is from some strange sense of the degradation of their work, some faint glimmer of the divine spark of self-respect, which makes them seek to hide from prying eyes; or whether it is merely from a vague terror lest discovery by the mysterious higher powers should deprive them of their last means of buying a crust of bread, the fact remains that they hide themselves away with a curious persistence. If you want to find them, the surest and quickest method is to inquire of the swarms of neglected unwashed children who are always to be found playing on the greasy pavements "where the lady lives who does fur-pulling." A dozen names will be instantly shouted out, with graphic descriptions of the owners and their abodes. Changes of residence are too much an affair of every day for either parents or children in these parts to burden themselves with remembering the numbers even of the houses in which they themselves are lodged for the time being.

It is the business of the fur-puller, broadly speaking, to remove the long coarse hairs from rabbit skins; the skins and the collected hairs having each their further uses. Accordingly, as we approach the first of those tenement dwellings to which the inquiry is directed, the countless miscellaneous odours of the alley are absorbed in one which overpowers the rest—the sickly unmistakable smell of uncleaned skins. On entering the house the air becomes thick with the millions of almost impalpable hairs which float in it. They force their way through every chink and crevice, clinging to everything they touch, and lying piled in layers of horrible dust on the dilapidated and dirty staircase.

Groping your way upwards, avoiding as carefully as possible all contact with the walls and low ceilings, and guided by the ever-increasing density of the "fluff," you enter a back attic in which two of the fur-pullers are at work.

The room is barely eight feet square, even less, because of its accumulation of dirt; and it has to serve for day and night alike. Pushed into one corner is the bed, a dirty pallet tied together with string, upon which is piled a black heap of bedclothes. On one half of the table are the remains of breakfast—a crust of bread, a piece of butter, and a cracked cup, all thickly coated with the all-pervading hairs. The other half is covered with pulled skins, waiting to be taken into "shop." The window is tightly closed, because such air as can find its way in from the stifling

---

5. The reference is to William Wordsworth's poem "To a Sky-Lark" (composed 1825, published 1827), wherein the skylark is celebrated as a "Type of the wise who soar, but never roam; / True to the kindred points of Heaven and Home."

court below would force the hairs into the noses and eyes and lungs of the workers, and make life more intolerable for them than it is already. To the visitor, indeed, the choking sensation caused by the passage of the hairs into the throat, and the nausea from the smell of the skins, is at first almost too overpowering for speech.

The two prematurely aged women—whose unkempt matted hair is almost hidden under a thick covering of fluff, and whose clothing is of the scantiest, seeming to consist of bits of sacking fashioned into some semblance of garments—are sitting on low stools before a roughly made deal trough,[6] into which they throw the long upper hairs of the skin, reducing them to the fine, silky down growing next to the skin itself, which is afterwards to be manufactured into felt halts. The heaps of skins by their side are dried, but uncleaned, and still covered with congealed blood.

At first the women are suspicious. They imagine that you are an emissary of the London County Council[7]—in their eyes, the embodiment of unlimited and tyrannical power. The County Council and the law are their standing dread; for, if these take it upon them to interfere and deprive the fur-puller of her employment, there is nothing left but starvation. The idea of interference for the fur puller's benefit has never presented itself. But once they are satisfied that you have nothing to do with the law or the County Council, they become friendly and communicative, ready to tell you all about themselves and their work.

"Yes, it stuffs your chest up," they admit—they can hardly deny it while you stand choking before them, and a tearing cough is racking them as they talk—"but you gets used to it when you've been at it all your life." Even so, according to the proverb, eels get used to skinning.

What do they get for it? They say each of them can pull "a turn and a half," working twelve hours. A "turn" means sixty skins; and the rate of pay is 11d. per turn—1s. 4½ d. for the twelve hours. That is when they are supplied with "English" skins. "Furriners"—$i.e.$ Australian and New Zealand skins—take longer; but the rate per turn is 1s. 1d. or 1s. 2d. From the point of view of wages, the English skins are preferred; but "furriners" have one great point of superiority, due to the necessities of packing. They are properly cleaned, and the skins as white as parchment, a marked contrast to the repulsive state in which the English skins are given out to the workers.

The women provide their own plucking knives and the shields for their hands. The knives cost 8d. and last some time; but the shields, which cost 3d., wear out quickly. Another 2d. a week usually goes in knife-grinding. The pulled-out hair is carefully collected, and weighed at the shop, a turn being supposed to yield two pounds. If the return is deficient in quantity, the value is, at some factories, deducted from the price of the work. These arbitrary deductions are, in the hands

6. A trough made of deal, or yellow pine wood, cut in wide, thick planks.

7. Local Government Acts passed in 1888 and 1894 created sixty-one county boroughs in England and established district councils, one of whose principal responsibilities was sanitation. Women voted in local elections and were elected to local government positions in the 1890s; thus the author is open to the suspicion of being an "emissary" of the Council.

of tyrannous foremen, often made a means of grievous oppression to the half-starved creatures, who are only too well aware that if they resist there are plenty of others ready enough to step into their shoes, and to take the work at any price that is offered for it.

In another room of the same house was an elderly woman, almost breathless from asthma, but working doggedly on to finish her "turn" before closing time at the factory. Her hand was strained and swollen from the perpetual grasping of the knife, and she said that her skins, which were "furriners," were tough and hard to pull. She was paid 1s. 1d. a turn, but could make more in a day at English skins at a lower rate of pay. Sometimes her daughter pulled too, and then they made 2s. 2d. between them, working till eight o'clock or thereabouts. She had been left an orphan at ten years old, and had done the pulling ever since. Her husband was a waterside labourer, never in regular work, and his earnings did no more than pay the rent. Out of a family of eight she had "buried" five, but did not apparently see any connection between this and the pulling, though it was "dreadful unhealthy work." When her son lived at home, they were able to have another room for the pulling; but it spoilt his clothes, and when "a suit of black he bought for his grandfather"[8] got spoilt with the dust he moved to pleasanter quarters elsewhere, leaving the old folks to do the best they could. "And that's bad enough," she added; "for now I can't hardly do a turn a day, and that's the truth."

In a small landing-room of the next house, choked up with fluff, and intolerable from the smell, was one of the many deserted wives with whom the poorer quarters of London abound. Doubtless she was better off without the husband, who never did a good day's work in his life. At any rate, it did not occur to her to attempt to find him, though she had heard of him no farther off than the Minories.[9]

She kept herself and her child, a stunted, half-starved girl of nine, making, as it appeared from her wage book, an average of 7s. 6d. a week, working all day. The foreman had often promised her a place "inside," and the realisation of this was the height to which her ambition was able to soar; "for the shop was a beautiful place, more like the 'orspital than a shop." The child went to and fro with the work, wrangled with the costermongers of every description who supply the scanty needs of the street, did such intermittent cleaning as seemed good in her eyes, prepared the poor food hastily snatched in the intervals of work, and evaded the School Board officer with all the ingenuity of the true slum child. The mother had not left the house for weeks. When the day's work was over, she threw herself on the bed, too tired even to get "a bit of victuals."

In a kitchen of this house were three women, one lying ill in the bed, and two others working at the trough in front of the tightly closed window. One of these was old and garrulous, the other still young, as age is reckoned by years, and with

8. The phrasing would suggest a suit of mourning purchased by the son to wear to his grandfather's funeral.

9. A street near Aldgate, a section of London just across the Thames to the northeast of the section where the fur-pullers lived and worked.

traces of what had once been great beauty. In marked contrast to the apathetic endurance of the other workers, her worn, defiant face was arresting, as the central figure in Walker's picture of "The Vagrants,"[10] in its expression of fierce, unavailing protest against the cruelty of fate. Not even the dusty coating of fur could wholly conceal the beauty of the dark hair lying softly on the low, wide forehead, nor the symmetry of the large bowed figure in its coarse repulsive rags. She scarcely even glanced round as the door opened, and the harsh voices of the other women did not seem to reach her ears; but there was no submission in her utter immobility; every feature of her face told its story of fierce rebellion, not yet crushed into despair. She pulled on in the same oppressive silence until farewells were being exchanged. Then, lifting her great sombre eyes for an instant from her work, she said, with a tragic simplicity, "*Miss, I wish I had your life.*"

Further down the court was a woman snipping the hair from the tails and ears and corners of the skins which cannot be passed through the shearing machines at the fitting factories. Her hands were cut in several places by the shears she was using, and she mentioned, as an incident of little or no importance, that the acid in the fur made the wounds sore. Compared with the pulling, her work made little dust, and she looked clean and tidy. She had two rooms, using the kitchen for her work. She was paid 1s. a pound for corners, and 6d. for tails, and made about 8s. a week. "Some can do pretty well at it; but if you want to make 10s. a week you can't mind the house as well."

Her next-door neighbour, a paper-bag maker, was working long hours to complete an order for bags for hot cross buns. It may be incidently mentioned that the rate of pay for these bags is ¾d. per gross. The woman—a widow—and her four children, who all helped out of school hours—and in them too when there was pressure of work—earned an average of 2s. 4d. a day, "much less than could be earned in the shop." The guv'nor employed eighty inside hands. She was sure he didn't even know the addresses of his out-workers, much less keep a register.

Next came an attic belonging to a fur-puller, a woman with six children, whose work was done in the one indescribably dirty bedroom, the boards black with grease from the skins. The factory at which she was employed had no inside pulling-rooms. All the work was given out.

And so on, through one close little street after another. Everywhere the same dead level of squalor, of joyless days and months and years passed in ceaseless and repulsive toil, with the reward of starvation wages, almost invariably supplemented by Poor Law relief.[11] Everywhere these "homes" in which leisure is unknown, or if it comes as the rarest of visitors, it comes as a curse. In them, these mothers with no time to rejoice in their motherhood, to give or receive love and sympathy and care from those for whom they are responsible; and children, who, from the time they are first launched into their troubled sea of life, must be a law

10. *The Vagrants* (1869) was one of the most famous paintings by Frederick Walker (1840–1875), whose productions during the 1860s were very popular.
11. Institutionalized charitable assistance.

unto themselves, who are born and nurtured in life's darkest places, "like plants in mines that never see the sun."[12] Everywhere the cry of the city going up to heaven, not in the "still sad music of humanity,"[13] but in a sadder discord of sorrow, in a babel of oaths and curses and foul jests, and in the horrible hoarse laughter more piteous far than tears.

This life of the "home" workers is sufficiently ghastly, though no words can adequately present its utter sickening repulsiveness. It must be seen and breathed in to be realised. Yet any attempt at remedying it by direct means involves enormous difficulties. Within the factory, however, the Government inspector can make his presence felt. Nevertheless, here too there is a general reluctance to admit visitors, an apparent fear of "revelations," a defensive attitude in speaking of the women and the work, which points to a lively dread of the possible effects of publicity, and a lively consciousness that improvement may be demanded.

To show that in fact little, very little, has been done to remove even the worst elements of the work, we may take the case of one workshop, said to be the best of its kind in South London, and employing large numbers both of in- and out-workers.

The process of treatment commences in a room where the smell of the skins is peculiarly overpowering. Here stands a large tank in which they are steamed and softened before being "opened." This opening is considered by the women to be the lowest work they can take. Those engaged on it, many of whom are only girls, will not take it up unless driven to do so by desperate straits. After the opening comes the drying process, done in large racks heated by stoves on the floor beneath. When dried the skins are brushed on the hairy side, with a solution of nitric acid, by machinery, tied up in "turns" for "pulling," and given out. After the pulling (*i.e.* the removal of the longer and coarser hairs) the skins are again dried, put through an hydraulic press, and packed in bales, to be despatched to the great felt-manufacturing centres of Stockport and Macclesfield, or to America, where the felting process is largely carried on. There the soft fur is converted into felt, the actual skin being boiled down for fine glue and size.[14] Skins of tame rabbits which are less valuable for felt, are made up into cheap muffs and linings for cloaks, and into the article of wearing apparel known as "electric sealskin."[15]

The "fluff" plucked by the fur pullers is collected and sold for cheap bedding, largely used by miners in the north of England. It may here be remarked that the report above mentioned is emphatic in condemning the foul condition of rags and other materials used for a similar purpose. It is all bought by weight, and it is no unusual thing for 40 per cent of the weight to be lost in the process of washing. "It

---

12. Robert Browning, *Paracelsus* (1835), part 5, line 882.

13. The reference is to "Tintern Abbey," one of the most famous poems by William Wordsworth: "For I have learned / To look on nature, not as in the hour / Of thoughtless youth; but hearing oftentimes / The still, sad music of humanity, / Nor harsh nor grating, though of ample power / To chasten and subdue."

14. Size is a glutinous substance used to fill the pores of cloth or paper.

15. "Electric sealskin" was the name given to rabbit fur clipped and dyed to resemble sealskin.

is therefore obvious," says the report, "that an upholsterer who is content to use the lowest sample of flock can purchase enough to stuff two beds for about the same money as another upholsterer, willing to use only the best flock, has to pay for sufficient to stuff one bed, even apart from the cost of washing." Any one who has seen the conditions under which the fur-pullers' "fluff" is collected will probably judge that the percentage of foul matter accompanying it is particularly high.

Within our workshop every available inch of space, from the large tunneled cellars to the storage rooms of the roof, is filled with rabbit skins. They are stacked in racks reaching to the ceiling; lying in heaps around the rooms; tied up in "turns" ready for the home workers, or in great bales of 5,000 for sending away. The stench arising from them is noisome; yet, except in the manager's rooms, where disinfectants are freely used, no attempt is made to minimise it. Moreover, though the atmosphere of the whole building is absolutely befogged with hair; yet, while the managers and foremen are careful to wear linen overalls, not only are the women unprovided with anything of the sort, but their outdoor garments are actually allowed to remain all day long hung up *in* one of the pulling-rooms. Of course the effect is that the women carry with them into their homes the sickly smell with which these clothes have become saturated, and the abominable fluff which sticks to them with the pertinacity of an Old Man of the Sea.[16]

Worse still, in total disregard of all factory regulations, the women actually cook and eat food in the pulling-room *at the same time* as others are at work at a table not three yards distant.

Although fur-pulling is not yet included in the list of "dangerous" trades, it is evident from the chronic bronchial catarrh from which so large a percentage of the workers suffer, the attacks of fever to which young unseasoned workers are liable, and the enormously high rate of infant mortality among the home-workers, that it is a trade which stands in urgent need of further regulation.

The report of the Royal Commission (to which allusion has already been made) in connection with those diseases to which workers in hair of every form are peculiarly liable, contains recommendations which, if they were strictly enforced, would do much to lessen the sufferings of this class of workers in the factories. It is suggested (1) that the ventilation should be so arranged as to carry the fluff away from the worker by means of powerful extracting fans with a down-draught, such as are already in use in rag mills and other factories where the material carried away is of value in manufacturing processes; (2) that the wearing of overalls and caps made to exclude dust should be compulsory; (3) that a prohibition to take meals in workrooms or other places to which noxious dust may penetrate should be strictly enforced.

Within the factories and workshops the strict application of these rules would have a beneficial effect. But hitherto the new factory regulations as to air and space have had one result which was by no means desired: they have tended to drive a

---

16. The Old Man of the Sea, sometimes called Proteus, would, when caught, change shapes repeatedly, assuming the form of a lion, a serpent, a leopard, a boar, or even water. Only one who could hold him tight through all these changes could compel him to give prophetic answers to significant questions. See *Odyssey* 4:399–570.

large quantity of the work from the factories to the home-workers. Now if the condition of things in the factories is bad, in the rooms of the home-workers it is many degrees worse; and it is exceedingly difficult to see how legislation is to interfere effectively in such places.

The report, having remarked that "any old dilapidated buildings are considered good enough for the accommodation of the fur-pullers," proceeds with suggestions—viz. that the Secretary of State should license every building in which the trade is carried on, that health registers should be kept, and periodical visits be paid by the certifying surgeons. But this would apply only to the factories. With the host of isolated workers, constantly changing and moving, the difficulty of efficient registration seems almost insuperable. To extend the rule effectively to home-workers, power would have to be given to factory inspectors to enforce sanitary regulations of a similar character and standard to those required in the factory; a license being granted only after the house had been visited and certified as a place where the work could be done without injury to those working there. Whereas, as the law now stands, the factory inspector, though empowered to demand from the employer a list of his out-workers and to visit them in their homes, has no authority to remedy any of the evils he may find there; and the sanitary authorities, who alone have power to act, can only do so in cases where complaints are made of a public nuisance. Moreover, every home-worker who can plead irregularity of employment—and *all* home-work is irregular—can thereby claim exemption from all the provisions of the Act.

It does not, in short, seem practicable to make the worker responsible. To prohibit home-work altogether is equally impracticable. But what does seem practicable is to throw the responsibility on to the employer. It is not beyond his power to ensure that the "homes" to which work is given out answer to the necessary conditions. Moreover, the adoption of this principle would have one very marked advantage. In order to avoid the trouble of attending to the condition of the home-workers, the employer would find a strong inducement to get as much work as possible done in the factory or workshop proper. A tendency would set in, working towards the gradual extinction of home-work; and the effect of that would be infinitely more satisfactory than any system of registration, inspection, or regulation of actual home-work that can be devised.

The evils of both subcontracting and home-work in all departments have become so thoroughly realised in the United States that a Bill was last year introduced by Mr. Sulzer which certainly had the effect of annihilating home-work entirely. It provides that, when a wholesaler gives out work to be done not by his own employés but by a contractor, the wholesaler must prepay a tax of 300 dollars. If the contractor in turn sublets a part of his contract, he also must pay the same tax for each subcontractor. And if the subcontractor divides his work among home-workers and others not in his own direct employment, he must pay the same tax for each one of those home-workers. It is tolerably obvious that if the employer has to pay a tax of 60*l.* per head for every home-worker, he will give up employing home-workers.

For the legislative extinction of home-work by such drastic measures, neither the public nor the workers are probably at present prepared. The public, unaware of the conditions under which home-work—at least in such trades as these—must be carried on; deluded also to some extent by a vague idea that family ties, parental influence, and family affection are preserved by it; are either indifferent or adverse to any such measures. The workers would see in them not the opportunity of work under healthier conditions, but the loss of employment. But a system which gradually and automatically turned home-work into factory work would excite no serious opposition; the end accomplished would have the approval of every competent observer who knows what such home-work means.

An important conference on the subject of home-work, called by the Women's Industrial Council, will meet in November in London, under the presidency of Mrs. Creighton. The condition of the fur-pullers will be under discussion. It is earnestly to be desired that the problems in connection with the subject will have received full and careful consideration, and that practical suggestions duly weighed and thought out may be laid before the conference, for giving effect to the recommendations of the report, and for appreciably ameliorating the lot of the fur-pullers. Heaven knows, they need it!

CHARLES BOOTH

C HARLES BOOTH (1840–1916) is best known as the editor of a massive seventeen-volume study titled *Life and Labour of the People in London,* published between 1891 and 1903. Booth was born in Liverpool and attended school there. He took a job in a shipowner's office when he finished his education and, at age twenty-five, he and his brother opened their own shipping company.

Interested throughout his life in social reform, Booth undertook in 1886 to determine the working and living conditions of members of the various social classes in London. The team of investigators he organized and financed conducted countless personal interviews and collated their findings with those drawn from census reports and other official documents. The voluminous reports they published—featuring copious charts, graphs, maps, and figures—provided a major contribution to social science. Booth was recognized for his work by being awarded honorary doctorates by Liverpool, Oxford, and Cambridge Universities and by being appointed a privy councillor and a fellow of the Royal Society.

The two selections reprinted here are from the volumes on "Industry"; one describes the work of London cow-keepers and milk-sellers while the other describes the work of the London police.

Figure 3.11. John Thomson, *London Cabmen*. Woodbury Type. Courtesy of the Victoria and Albert Museum, London, UK/Bridgeman Art Library.

John Thomson (1837–1921) took many of his published photographs during his travels in the Far East and eventually became a fashionable portrait photographer; however, he is best known for *Street Life in London*, a series of thirty-seven documentary pictures with written commentary by Adolphe Smith on the individuals photographed and their occupations. Initially published in twelve monthly installments in 1877–78 and avowedly influenced by Henry Mayhew's *London Labour and the London Poor* (see selections earlier in part 3), *Street Life in London* was intended to present an accurate picture of working-class life. *London Cabmen* is taken from this collection. In the essay accompanying the photograph, Smith reports that in London "there are 4142 Hansom cabs [like the one pictured], and 4120 Clarence, or four-wheel cabs." He asserts, "Despite the traditional hoarse voice, rough appearance, and quarrelsome tone, cab-drivers are as a rule reliable and honest men, who can boast of having fought the battle of life in an earnest, persevering, and creditable manner."

From *Life and Labour of the People in London*

(*from* Second Series—Industry, Vol. 3)

Milk-Sellers

Cow-Keepers

Before the railway era,[1] the milk consumed in London was of necessity obtained from cows kept either in the town or its immediate neighbourhood, and London dairymen were almost without exception cow-keepers. That the universal combination of the two businesses would long have survived the advent of railways is not likely; but the inevitable change was greatly accelerated by the dreadful disease known to cow-keepers as the rinderpest,[2] which constantly visited the London cow-sheds between the years 1840 and 1870, killing the cattle by hundreds, and in many cases clearing the sheds of the whole of the stock at one visitation. This dire pestilence forced London dairymen to look to the country for their supplies. At first the trade in country milk was insignificant, and was chiefly in the hands of the lower class of shops; a prejudice, probably to some extent justifiable, existed against railway-borne milk; no means were used to cool it before it was despatched; the train service was slow and unpunctual; the railway companies made no special arrangements for carriage of milk, which no doubt seldom reached London in good condition, and compared unfavourably with that derived from the town-fed cows. However, the last and most fatal visitation of the plague, between 1860 and 1870, compelled even the best dairymen to look elsewhere for their supply, and with a growing trade in country milk the railways gradually improved their arrangements for delivery; the invention of the milk-cooler—an appliance consisting of tubes filled with cold water over which the milk trickles, and is thereby reduced in temperature by about thirty degrees—enabled it to be delivered in good condition; and by 1870 the trade was fairly started on its present lines. Since that date the cow-keepers have been a rapidly decreasing body; the trade has yearly fallen more and more into the hands of large companies, who look entirely to country farms for their supply, and now town-fed cows provide but a drop in the great ocean of milk which is daily consumed by Londoners. No doubt other causes besides rapid railway communication and the rinderpest have contributed to this result. Those cow-keepers who have struggled on in spite of discouragement have been for the most part small men of poor education, and

1. The success of the steam-powered Liverpool and Manchester Railway (1830) led to considerable railway construction in the 1830s and to the "mania" of the 1840s. The miles of track increased from 6,621 in 1850 to 15,195 in 1900. As the century progressed, Victorians came to rely heavily on trains to transport freight as well as passengers.
2. A contagious viral disease in cattle.

often with insufficient capital; even if they could afford to do so they have scarcely kept up with the times; their cows, in many cases, have not been properly fed, and they have failed to recognize the necessity of using the cooling apparatus; the result is that their milk has, as a whole, been inferior in quality to that derived from the country. That this is so there seems to be little difference of opinion; even the cow-keepers themselves, when they have to supplement their supply, find that the milk which they purchase is usually sweeter than that obtained from their own cows; but there is some doubt as to how far the general inferiority of milk from London sheds is due to causes under the cow-keeper's control. The largest cow-keeper in London, whose dairy we have visited, has built up his reputation by making a special feature of milk direct from his own sheds; his success would seem to show that with scientific feeding, good sanitary arrangements, and the use of appliances for keeping the milk in proper condition, London sheds can send out milk equal to the best which the country can supply. On one point, at all events, London has the advantage; it is easier there to insure a pure water supply, and the cows have no opportunity of drinking from stagnant ponds, a habit to which they are said to be addicted. The truth of the matter probably is, that good milk can be produced in the country more easily and with less expense, and that the London cow-keeper can only hope to compete with the farmer by working on a large scale, and with the most perfect business methods.

Of quite recent years the cow-keeper has had yet another cross to bear. The London County Council[3] have enforced with increased, though not undue, severity their regulations as to ventilation, air space, lighting, water supply, and drainage. In many cases they have insisted on structural alterations in the sheds, which have put the occupier to considerable expense, while some of the weaker members of the trade have been forced out by inability to comply with their requirements. How far the very rapid decrease of cow-keepers during the last five years has been due to this cause, how far to other causes working in the same direction, we are unable to say, but the figures in the Council's yearly reports seem to show that the effect of this increased stringency must have been considerable. At the beginning of 1891 the number of licensed cow-houses was 673; by the close of 1894 they were reduced to 491.

As a result of these various causes the cow-keeper has fallen on evil days, and it seems unlikely that he will be able to stem the tide of depression. That his numbers have not been reduced far more rapidly is probably due to the fact that the vast majority of those who follow the trade belong to the thrifty race of Welshmen. Throughout the London milk trade generally the proportion of Welsh masters is very large, how large we shall to some extent be able to show when considering dairymen; but there are no reliable figures which will enable us to determine the exact proportion of Welsh cow-keepers. However, common report and our own observation lead us to suppose that they number considerably over 50 per cent of

3. Local Government Acts passed in 1888 and 1894 created sixty-one county boroughs in England and established district councils, one of whose principal responsibilities was sanitation.

the trade. As to the cause of this preponderance of Welshmen there seems little doubt; they alone among the inhabitants of the United Kingdom can make cow-keeping in London pay; or rather, perhaps they alone are content to accept the conditions under which the cow-keeper is forced to work in order to make a living. Without exception, these men seem to be the sons or near relations of small Welsh farmers; they are, for the most part, poorly educated; they speak English very imperfectly, and come to London unfit for any other occupation than that to which they have been brought up in their own country. They are thrifty and self-denying; prepared to live in rough surroundings; and content to work exceedingly hard, and for abnormally long hours, with a very small return. Even accepting these conditions, most of them now have a hard struggle for existence. It is the smaller businesses in poor neighbourhoods that they most affect, and the part of London where they are most thickly planted is Whitechapel. This is probably due to the demand for Kosher milk[4] among the Jews, a demand which seems to necessitate perpetually the keeping of cows in this neighbourhood.

The cow-keeper, if he is in a fairly large way of business, employs cowmen exclusively to milk and tend the cows, and clean the sheds; in the smaller businesses, where only two or three cows are kept, some of the men will probably tend the cows and deliver milk. We will deal here with the cowman only, leaving the milk-carrier and his position to be considered under the head of dairymen. The most important of the cowman's duties, and the only one which requires skill, is milking. The yield of milk from a cow, and even its quality, depend to some extent upon the way in which she is milked. The chief requisites in good milking are quickness and gentleness, and of the two quickness is the more important—slowness not only reduces the quantity of the milk, but actually, we are told, leads to a considerable decrease in the yield of butter fat. The cowman therefore is, or ought to be, a skilled workman; there are, however, complaints as to the difficulty of getting good milkers, with the result that milking machines have been invented, which seem likely in time to deprive the cowman of his chief duty. Whether he is classed as skilled or unskilled, the cowman is certainly not highly paid for his work. His wages vary from 20s to 26s[5] a week; the usual wage in the very best firms seems to be 24s a week, but in small businesses, which are much more common, they are certainly lower, and it is doubtful if the average exceeds 22s a week. In some cases the man is allowed, in addition, a pint of milk a day, and when he is not entitled to it probably helps himself to that or some other quantity. Though his fixed wage is little smaller, the earnings of the cowman are much less than those of the milk-carrier, and yet his duties are equally important, his hours are longer, and the conditions under which he works less favourable to health and comfort. The comparative smallness of his wage is no doubt due in some degree to the fact that he comes as a rule from the agricultural labourer class; slender as are his earnings

---

4. Prepared in accordance with Jewish dietary laws. Booth's note: "This should be milked by a Jew, but at any rate must be milked direct into a jug or vessel, and not mixed with other milk."

5. British currency: "*s*" stands for shilling, a coin equivalent to twelve pence; "*d*" stands for pence.

in London, they have probably been a good deal smaller in the country, and at all events, when he first comes to the great city, he looks upon his new position as a rise in the world.

The cowman's hours of labour are long. He has to begin work seldom later than 4 A.M., and will work on, with short intervals for meals, till about 5 P.M.

He has naturally suffered much from the decay of the trade, and each year finds it increasingly difficult to get work, but is reluctant to return to the country, where the outlook is no better.

Dairymen

From cow-keepers we pass to dairymen, or the purveyors of milk. The first point that strikes one is the extent to which the business has fallen into the hands of large firms with a number of branches. The managing directors or heads of these firms are nearly always English, but among the smaller masters we again find an extraordinary proportion of Welshmen. In Kelly's London Directory for 1895, 1450 dairymen are enumerated, of whom, judging by their names, not less than 529 are of Welsh extraction. The name Jones appears in the list 103 times, Davies or Davis 83, Evans 63, Williams 38, Morgan 36, Jenkins 30, Edwards 29, Lewis 22 times, and so on through Griffiths, Hughes, Lloyd, Owen, Price, Rees, Thomas, &c. Among these numerous Welshmen there are to be found only 10 Smiths, 9 Browns, and 2 Robinsons, and of these one is named David. That the proportion of Welshmen in the trade has grown enormously in the last twenty-five years is proved by a reference to Kelly for 1870, when of 1465 dairymen only 178 appear to be Welsh; in that year there were 40 Jones's and 30 Smiths. It is clear, therefore, that in the small businesses the Welsh have gradually been ousting the English, while of Scotch and Irish, we are told on the best authority, there are none in the trade. In addition to the fact that he is well suited to the business, the advent of the Welshman has no doubt been accelerated by the circumstance noted in Volume III, that when one member of a family has established himself in London, he very frequently sends for some of his relations to join him, or even lends them money to set up for themselves. The Welsh are a clannish people, and no doubt their numbers in the milk trade have been greatly swelled by the immigration of the friends and relations of the original founders of businesses.

Earnings.—Of the men employed in London dairies, the vast proportion are milk-carriers, though in large businesses there are in addition managers of branches, foremen of rounds, and a few men employed in making butter.

Managers are paid from 30s to 60s a week, with a house or rooms rent free. In most cases they have, in addition, milk, eggs, and butter for their own consumption.

Round foremen receive from 30s to 35s a week, and as a rule get a commission on each new customer they obtain.

Milk carriers in the wholesale trade are paid fixed wages of from 20s to 24s a week, with a commission on sales. Their earnings from the two sources would seldom exceed 35s a week, and would average about 30s. They have less opportunity than carriers in the retail trade of adding to their wages by methods legitimate or illegitimate, though possibly they get something from their customers, to whom a punctual service is of the utmost importance.

The fixed wages of carriers in the retail trade range from 20s to 26s a week. Those who drive a cart are usually paid 1s more than those who wheel a "pram"; their duties, however, are somewhat harder, as they generally have to attend to their horse and cart. In addition to the fixed wage, a commission is always paid of from 2s to 4s for each new customer who takes a quart a day. In many dairies a further commission is given of ½d on each pound of butter, ½d on each shillingsworth of eggs, and ½d on each quart of milk, to other than regular customers. Wages and commission, however, seldom represent the whole earnings of the milk-carrier; there is no doubt that by sundry illegitimate methods he too often helps himself. So notorious is the fact, and so difficult if not impossible is it found to prevent the objectionable practices, that masters, with rare exceptions, have found it necessary to wink at them, and to insist only that each man shall pay in full money for the milk which he takes out. In one way and another the earnings of the carriers average 33s a week; those who are abnormally dishonest make more for a time, but their career is likely to be short, for there is a point no doubt beyond which dishonesty is not the best policy. Short measure, or an unusual excess of water in the milk, is likely in the end to rouse the anger of a long-suffering public, and to lead to complaints to the master, who in his own interest as well as that of the customer will dismiss the peccant[6] carrier.

Hours of Work.—In the wholesale trade work begins habitually at 4 o'clock. The first round is completed from 8 to 9 o'clock; the men then go home to breakfast, and return to work about 10:30 A.M. The second round, during which they dine when and where they please, ought to be finished not later than 5 P.M.

In the retail trade work begins an hour later, and lasts with intervals till 6 or 7 o'clock. In most businesses each man has to do three rounds, the second round—when eggs and butter are taken as well as milk—being called "the pudding round."

Both in wholesale and retail trade, the actual hours of work vary to some extent for each man. It is obviously impossible to make all the rounds of exactly equal size, and even if they were, much depends on the speed of a man's horse, or on his walking power; while an even more powerful cause of difference in the hours worked is the characters of the men themselves. When once they leave the dairy they are almost free from supervision, and can, within certain limits, get through their work as fast or as slowly as they please; one man will spend a good deal of time in gossiping, another, perhaps, cannot resist the temptation of an occasional halt for liquid refreshment. That the hours can be curtailed when the men wish it is proved by the fact that on Bank Holidays[7] and other special occasions, they manage to get home about two hours earlier than usual. This, no doubt, involves working at high pressure, and in the interests of neither master nor men is it desirable that the work should be done in other than a leisurely fashion; the carrier

6. Sinful.
7. Instituted in 1871 by the banking industry, these holidays were observed by workers of all professions within a few years.

who is in a hurry cannot look about for new customers, nor can he serve his regular customers with the politeness and attention which are so requisite.

The most essential virtue for a milk carrier is punctuality in the morning, and in nearly all large businesses it is enforced by a system of fines. In some cases the fines may go to swell the master's profits, but as a rule they are returned to the men. Occasionally they are used for a sick fund, and the surplus shared equally at Christmas. Sometimes they are divided at short intervals of three weeks or a month; any man whose fines for that period exceed a certain amount forfeiting his share. This method of punishment is, we suppose, illegal, but it seems to be preferred to the only other alternative—instant dismissal for unpunctuality.

The great grievance of carriers and cowmen is the necessity for working every day in the year. There is hardly any other trade in which the work is so continuous; even omnibus and tram drivers and conductors can, by forfeiting a day's pay, take a holiday when they choose; but the cowman must do his milking every day, and the carrier must work his round, at least twice a day, from one year's end to another. In small dairies a holiday of any sort is certainly a rare occurrence, either for master or men; but in the large dairies it is necessary to keep reserve men, and each carrier may get a day off occasionally. In such dairies, too, it is now usual to give each man a holiday, not exceeding a week, once a year. The necessity for seven days' labour every week from year's end to year's end makes the trade unpopular, and is evidently much regretted by the masters, but the grievance is not an easy one to remedy. The best-intentioned cow can only yield a certain quantity at each milking, and, even were it possible to forestall the supplies so as to send out in the morning the whole of the milk required for the day, a double quantity could not well be delivered in one round. That the public would ever consent to curtail their supply, though but for one day in the week, is not at all likely. In no trade, perhaps, is the demand of the consumer more imperative. Man's wants may be disregarded, but in this case it is the women and children who are to be considered, and above all, the voice of the baby, which would make itself heard.

Regularity.—Both very hot and very cold weather increase the consumption of milk; in hot weather it is largely used as a beverage, both alone and in combination with soda-water; in cold weather there is an increase in the desire for tea, coffee, cocoa, and porridge. In one quarter we have been told that the sale falls off when fruit is cheap and plentiful. In the West End,[8] and to some extent in most districts, less milk is sold during the summer exodus from town. But, except in so far as it may lessen their commissions or "makings," a diminished sale does not affect the men; it is the masters who suffer. Everywhere some milk consumer is left, and, though the house which in May is taking a gallon a day may in September require only a pint, practically the same labour is required to deliver either quantity, with the result that for about two months in the year the West End dairyman works at a heavy loss.[9]

8. The wealthy, fashionable section of London.

9. Booth's note: "In no other trade probably is the cost of delivery so great; it is estimated by the large companies at 1¼*d* per imperial gallon." Imperial weights and measures are those conforming to the nonmetric standards legally set in Great Britain.

Health.—The work of the carrier is certainly healthy; it is neither arduous nor exhausting. A large part of the day is spent in the open air, and the necessity for early rising prevents the spending of a long evening in the public-house. The cowman works under less favourable conditions; in spite of the efforts of the County Council to improve matters, the sheds are often deficient in ventilation, and even at their best they are necessarily filled with unsavoury exhalations.

With the desire of ensuring punctuality, masters prefer that men should live near their work, and some of the large companies have built model dwellings for their employees.

There seems no reason why a trade which requires little stamina should not be recruited to an unusual degree from Londoners, but masters, with few exceptions, tell us that the majority of their men are countrymen, and that they much prefer them to Londoners.

General Condition of the Trade.—The trade of the dairyman, as apart from that of the cow-keeper, seems to be in a fairly prosperous condition, though the fall in the dividends of the large companies during recent years shows that profits are generally smaller than they were. The sale of milk has increased, and is increasing quite out of proportion to the growth of population; but, as in other trades, the cutting of the price[10] has made it difficult for the dairyman to earn a profit unless he works on a large scale, or adopts methods of trading which, when not actually dishonest, are not such as his customers would be likely to approve. The practice of "washing" or watering the milk, though still very prevalent, is less common than it was. At one time certain members of the trade boasted of their ability to make one churn do the work of three. Those "good old days" are gone; inspectors are more numerous and more active than they were, and the risk of prosecution for selling watered milk is very great, a risk which no respectable dairyman can run without great injury to his trade. But though "washing" has declined, the dairyman is able to effect the same purpose in another way, and still to keep within the law; thousands of gallons are sold daily as pure milk, which have undergone a great deterioration in their progress from the cow to the consumer. The practice of abstracting some portion of the cream, or of mixing separated with whole milk is increasingly prevalent, with the result that the dairyman who does not resort to it is placed at a serious disadvantage, and has to compete with his rivals on unequal terms. So widespread is the custom that the great question which is now (1895) agitating the trade is the advisability of fixing a legal standard for milk. Great difficulties surround the question, for the cow, whom one would suppose to be the least guileful of animals, lends herself to the deception. It seems that in milk of average quality the total solids amount to about 12.90 per cent, of which about 3.99 per cent is fat. Not only, however, does the composition of milk vary enormously in different cows, but in the same cow it will vary at different seasons of the year, and even from day to day under altered conditions of health or weather. To fix a high

---

10. Booth's note: "A remarkable instance of the vigour of the English aristocracy in these democratic days is found in the fact that the men who are chiefly complained of as the pioneers of 'cutting,' are certain noble lords who have entered the trade."

standard might therefore lead to much injustice, while if it were fixed too low the temptation to adulteration of whole with separated milk would seem to be increased. Whatever be the end of the "battle of the standard," it seems only right that the honest dairyman should be protected from this unfair competition, and that the sellers of milk which is not "whole" should, if possible, be forced to notify the fact to the public.

Another objectionable custom not unknown in the trade is the colouring of milk. The public, or some portion of them, prefer a yellow liquid. As the vast majority of cows persist in yielding white milk, the dairyman has been obliged to call in art to remedy the deficiencies of nature. The added matter is said as a rule to be anatto, a harmless vegetable substance.[11]

Few retail traders are now content with the profits to be derived from their nominal business, or rather perhaps the profits of one business are so small that each man is compelled to encroach upon his neighbour's province. The dairyman has not altogether escaped this tendency; he sells bread in large quantities, and in many cases does a small trade in refreshments, especially in temperance drinks. We are told that his efforts thus to add to his takings have not been altogether successful, and that his profits are still almost entirely derived from the three staple articles of his trade—milk, butter, and new laid eggs.

The dairyman has no doubt suffered for many years from the sale of cheap foreign butter and margarine, but until quite lately he has not been troubled by the competition of foreign milk. However, within the last three years milk has been imported from the Continent in large quantities; in 1894 over 93,000 gallons were imported from Sweden, and more than 67,000 gallons from Holland. A great deal of this milk is frozen or chilled to near freezing point before exportation; to that which is not frozen preservatives, such as salicylic acid, are added; but whatever the means adopted for preserving, it does not at present seem probable that it can reach London in a satisfactory condition.

Trade Organization

There is an entire absence of organization among the men employed in the milk trade. Masters are associated in the Metropolitan Dairymen's Society, the two main objects of which are stated to be—(1) "The advancement of the interests of the milk trade, especially by taking every possible means to prevent the adulteration of milk"; and (2) "The formation of a Benevolent Fund for deserving, aged, or infirm members of the milk trade." In close connection with this society is the Metropolitan Dairymen's Benevolent Institution, the purpose of which is "to relieve the deserving members of the trade and their widows in old age and infirmities by pensions or otherwise, and the orphans of annuitants by gratuities." The benefits of this institution were originally open only to "any subscriber to the Metropolitan Dairymen's Benevolent Institution or Member of the Metropolitan Dairymen's

---

11. A yellowish-red dye obtained from the seeds of the tropical American annato tree.

Society who shall have paid his subscription for five successive years, being sixty years of age, and having carried on the business of a dairyman within the Metropolitan Postal District upon his own account ten years"; but in 1894, owing to the increase in the number of dairies carried on by managers, the benefits were extended to include any who had "acted as manager of a dairy in the said district for a corresponding period." There is, further, the Dairy Trade and Can Protection Society, which acts as a can exchange and clearing house, and endeavours to prevent the adulteration of milk.

Wages Statistics

In 1891, according to the census, 4503 adult males were employed in this trade; our wages' returns are very unsatisfactory, but such as they are we give them. We have returns for 179 men, employed by six firms. Their earnings in an average week are as follows:—

Below 20s	5,	or	3	per cent	
20s to 25s	133	"	75	"	Under 30s, 90½ per cent
25s " 30s	23	"	12½	"	
30s " 35s	12	"	6½	"	
35s " 40s		"		"	
40s " 45s	3	"	1½	"	Over 30s, 9½ per cent.
45s and upward	3	"	1½	"	
	179	"	100	"	

Quite apart from the fact that, owing to the circumstances already mentioned, they do not represent all the earnings of the men, too much reliance must not be placed on these figures, as they are not drawn from a sufficiently wide field. Masters, knowing that a statement of the sums paid by them to their men would give a false impression as to the true state of affairs, have for the most part refused to give us exact details as to wages, and have confined themselves to general statements. But unreliable as the figures are, it is certain that an enormous proportion of the men do not legitimately earn over 30s a week, and we doubt if the proportion shown is much too high.

Social Condition

Of the 4503 adult males employed, about 2860 come under social classification as heads of families. It will be seen from the table that follows that 30 per cent are living under crowded conditions with two or more persons to a room; that 33 per cent live one or two persons in room; and that there are 37 per cent of the central classes.

The table is interesting as showing that in a trade where the nominal wages are small the standard of comfort is above the average of the industrial classes. This is, however, partly accounted for by the considerable proportion who are returned as "neither employer nor employed," and who are probably the keepers of small milkshops:—

Classification of Population according to Style of Life
(Milksellers)

3 or more in each room	1750 or	9 per cent	}	Crowded 30%
2 to 3　　　　"	3900　"	21　　"		
1 " 2　　　　"	6150　"	33　　"	}	
Less than 1　　"				Not Crowded 70%
More than 4 rooms	6700　"	37　　"		
4 or more persons to a servant				
	18,500　"	100　　"		
Families of employers, servants, &c	7050			
	25,550			

(*from* Second Series—Industry, Vol. 4)

Police and Prisons

Police and Prison Service

The Metropolitan police force was established in 1829, as was also the City police. These two organizations divide the London area between them. The City police, numbering 1018, are responsible for the City "and its liberties"; and the Metropolitan police, with 15,216 men, undertakes the surrounding district within a radius of fifteen miles from Charing Cross, thus including not only suburban London, but places as detached and populous as Bromley, Croydon, Kingston-on-Thames, Enfield, Walthamstow, and West Ham. The force has also since 1860 provided constables for special duties at Royal palaces, dockyards, and Government establishments outside of the Metropolitan area. Deducting these men, and adding in the City police, we have in all 14,500 men available for ordinary police duties in an area of nearly seven hundred square miles with a rateable yearly value of more than £42,000,000. Of London itself the annual rateable value is about £34,000,000, with an area of 118 square miles, and the proportion of police employed in this smaller district is about 11,500, or including the men detailed for special service something over 12,000 all told.[12]

A policeman is liable to duty at any time in the twenty-four hours, but the time spent regularly on his beat is only eight hours out of the twenty-four, being either two watches of four hours in the daytime, between 6 A.M. and 10 P.M., or one period of eight hours in the night, between 10 P.M. and 6 A.M. Night and day duty

---

12. Booth's note: "Of the twenty-three Metropolitan police divisions, eleven, with a strength of 5849 men, are entirely within the London boundary, while the districts of the other twelve, with 8413 men, are partly within and partly without the area."

are shared in rotation. The hours on beat do not by any means include all the time ordinarily occupied, as a constable has to attend the court as required, and is expected to work up his cases, and on extraordinary occasions, when a larger force than usual is needed in the streets, he may be kept on duty for many extra hours. Otherwise it would appear as a general rule that one-third of the whole force is on, and two-thirds off, duty at any one time. This, however, is not exactly the case, as a certain number of constables are detailed for special duties as "patrols," who are out from 5 P.M. to 1 A.M. or 6 P.M. to 2 A.M., or as "point" police (being men stationed at convenient places ready to respond to calls from the public or the men on the adjacent beats) whose work falls also in the evening hours, finishing alternately at 9 P.M. and 1 A.M. The result of this arrangement is to provide extra force during the evening and midnight hours, when the ordinary day's work being over, and the population on pleasure bent, order is most liable to be disturbed. This applies principally to the Metropolitan police. In the City it is different, as there the day work is the heaviest, and a number of men are specially employed to direct the traffic.

The policeman's work varies greatly according to the district in which he is stationed. In a suburban neighbourhood, except for occasional disturbances, the duties are not heavy, but tedious, and the prolonged walking, even at the regulation pace, is wearying to the feet. The ordinary policeman must constantly perambulate his beat, visiting every street and entry. At night he examines the fastenings of windows and doors, marks entrances so that he can tell whether they have been visited in the intervals of his round, and walking silently in the shadows of the houses comes upon the belated pedestrian with startling suddenness. In busy neighbourhoods the strain is greater, especially upon those engaged in regulating vehicular traffic, for whom special reliefs are found necessary. "When in doubt ask a policeman" is a rule largely adopted by visitors to the Metropolis, and, bombarded by a series of not always coherent questions, the London constable almost invariably succeeds in giving courteous replies. In spite of an occasional pomposity of manner, he compares favourably with the police of some other cities.

In addition to their primary duties—the prevention of crime and the detection of offenders—the police have been charged with the enforcement of special laws and other obligations for which their wide-spread organization and exact local knowledge fit them. They deliver magistrates' orders and serve summonses. In 1894 the Metropolitan police served 87,783 summonses applied for by private individuals, and 14,371 taken out officially. The Licensing department examines and licenses hackney carriages, omnibuses, and tramcars, and issues the licences to the drivers and conductors. Nearly 30,000 articles left in these vehicles during 1894 were dealt with by the Lost Property Office. By the Army Act (1881) the police act as billet-masters and provide billets for soldiers when called upon by the military authorities, while the Army Enlistment Act requires them to serve within their districts all notices relating to the Reserve Forces when desired to do so by the Secretary of State. They have to see that public-houses are properly conducted during the day and closed during the prohibited hours; that bicycle lamps are lighted at the proper time and kept alight; they have to look after stray and unmuzzled dogs, and to assist sheriffs' officers and county court bailiffs. Additional duties are imposed under the Public Health Act, the Explosives Act, the Pedlars, the Gun Licence, the Contagious Diseases (Animals), the Vagrancy, and other statutes too numerous to mention.

Neither Sundays nor other public holidays are times of rest for the police, but on Sundays the number of men on duty is reduced. One day off in fourteen is allowed, and this should fall on a Sunday once in four weeks, and after twelve months' service in the Metropolitan and eighteen months' in the City police, sergeants and constables have a week or ten days, and inspectors two or three weeks' leave annually.

The scale of pay is higher in the City than with the Metropolitan police and was raised for both forces in 1890. In the City the pay for constables begins at 25s and rises gradually till it reaches 36s 3d at the end of six years. Sergeants commence with 41s 5d and rise to 45s 3d. For inspectors 57s 6d is the minimum. In the Metropolitan force the pay at first is 24s and rises to 32s in eight years. Sergeants start at 34s and rise to 40s. Station sergeants begin at 45s. Inspectors begin at 56s.[13] Compared with the old scale these rates show an advance for the constables of 4s 9d on the maximum in the City, and 2s on the maximum in the Metropolitan force. At nearly every stage towards the maximum rather more is paid than formerly.

Particulars of the number of men of each rank, with the proportion at each rate of wages, are given below:[14]

Weekly Rate			Inspectors	Sergeants	Constables	Total	Per cent
75s and over			74	—	—	74	.4
70s and under		75s	111	—	—	111	.7
65s	"	70s	10	—	—	10	.1
60s	"	65s	190	—	—	190	1.2
55s	"	60s	167	15	—	182	1.1
50s	"	55s	1	32	—	33	.2
45s	"	50s	44	379	—	423	2.6
40s	"	45s	25	609	—	634	4.0
35s	"	40s	13	697	353	1,063	6.6
30s	"	35s	5	162	7,656	7,823	48.9
25s	"	30s	—	—	4,595	4,595	28.3
24s			—	—	946	946	5.9
			640	1,894	13,550	16,084	100

13. Booth's note: "There is one curious exception. The Act of Parliament does not give police officers of lower rank than inspector authority to board vessels. Consequently in the Thames division 'inspectors' are provided for each police boat. The pay of these men is the same as that of sergeants in any other division, and 27 per cent of the force are inspectors in place of 4 per cent elsewhere."

14. Booth's note: "Compiled from information kindly furnished by the Commissioner of City police, and from the annual statement of accounts for the Metropolitan police (1894–5)."

The effect of the revised rates of pay upon the men's earnings is shown by the fact that of the 14,696 men composing the two forces in 1886, 6945, or 47 per cent, earned under 27s 6d, compared with 22½ per cent in 1895, while 5833, or 40 per cent, earned 27s 6d and under 32s 6d, compared with 58½ per cent in 1895.

In addition to their nominal wages, various allowances increase the real earnings of the police. All are supplied with uniform clothing and boots, or a money allowance instead. Men living in the stations receive a small allowance of coals, and other men 3½d or 4d a week as an equivalent. Special duties also carry extra pay. Men employed at public buildings, &c., receive about 1s a day and those engaged in regulating the street traffic 1s to 2s 6d a week in addition to their regular money. The reserve men, a selected body in each division, wearing the letter R on their collars, receive 1s 6d extra a week. Superannuation also must be counted as a benefit, for the deduction of (at most) 2½ per cent from the wages does not nearly provide the pension of two-thirds pay to which the men are entitled after twenty-six years' service.

Other legitimate though unrecognized emoluments come in return for occasional small services rendered, as for instance that of calling workmen in the morning. That there may be some illegitimate sources of profit of which a few of the men do not scruple to avail themselves, is we fear indisputable, but we have no right or reason to suppose that such practices are widespread, and in considering the average earnings of policemen, we do not take them into account. As a rule the men are now satisfied with their lot; the policeman's position, if indeed "not a happy one,"[15] is equal to that of most skilled workmen, and the proportion of voluntary resignations is less than 1 per cent per annum.

The following table shows the length of service of the men employed in the Metropolitan force, December 31st, 1894:—

	Super-intendents	Inspectors and sub-inspectors	Sergeants	Constables	Total
Over 30 years	12	6	5	7	30
20 years and under 30	19	319	388	1,290	2,016
10 " " 20	—	255	1,243	3,887	5,385
5 " " 10	—	8	173	3,252	3,433
Under 5 years	—	—	5	4,250	4,255
Total.	31	588	1,814	12,686	15,119

This table indicates clearly the course of promotion from grade to grade, length of service being an important element in a man's chances. An officer is seldom advanced into a higher grade until he has reached the maximum pay of the preceding class. General ability, however, tells, and a strict record is kept of each man's career, with the result that every breach of regulations, or other fault,

15. The quotation is from the Gilbert and Sullivan operetta *The Pirates of Penzance* (1879). The song "When a felon's not engaged in his employment" is sung by a sergeant and a chorus of police.

remains in evidence and retards advancement. To obtain the rank of sergeant in the Metropolitan police, a constable must pass the police board and also the civil service commissioners, being examined on general attainments as well as knowledge of police duties, and a further civil service examination is requisite for inspectors, as well as technical examinations for each minor step.

Candidates must be under twenty-seven years of age, and, if married, must not have more than two children when joining. The standard of height is 5 ft. 9 in., and the medical test very strict; more than half the applicants failing to pass the doctor. Accepted candidates are trained in police duties and receive systematic instruction at a candidates' class. The army provides a good proportion of the men. During the six years ending 1894, 14 per cent of recruits had been soldiers. The age limit is extended in favour of retired soldiers, but the number of London police liable to be called out for service, in the army reserve, is limited to 550. The bulk of police recruits, however, are countrymen, straight from rural employment, to whom the wages offered appear wealth, and it is probable that Londoners of equally good character and physique could obtain higher wages for other work.

Except as regards the City, where the rule does not apply, policemen have to live in the district they serve, and are obliged to find respectable quarters as best they can, paying often dearly. A few of the married men live at the stations, and most of the single ones are accommodated in what are called "section houses," otherwise, in the more crowded parts of London, the choice is almost limited to the better class of block dwellings.[16] This no doubt accounts for the high percentage of crowding shown by the statistics, when compared to the known earnings of the men. Another noticeable result is that married men prefer the suburban districts and the unmarried the more lively central parts.

Section houses are attached to the principal London stations, at which the men pay a small sum weekly for lodging, and find their own food. These houses frequently form part of the station itself, but in other cases consist of a separate block of buildings. They vary in size according to the space available, the largest of them having accommodation for 164 men. All contain dormitories, a kitchen, and a mess-room. The larger houses have reading and recreation rooms, and are supplied with a library and even billiard tables. In all cases there is also a cloak room, in which the men keep their uniforms, and a drying room for wet clothes. In the older houses the beds are ranged along the walls of the dormitories, but in the newer ones separate cubicles are provided. Dinner is prepared by the cooks, and the men are divided into three messes according to the hours of work, the meal being served from 1 to 2 and 7 to 8, before going on beat, and from 2 to 3 on coming off. Their other meals the men take when they please and prepare for themselves, but often with assistance from the cook if she is not otherwise occupied. In some cases there is a canteen where food and drink can be obtained at

16. Booth's note: "In central London a large block of dwellings not far from Charing Cross was found to contain 156 families with children, and of the heads of these families forty-eight were police officers, and thirty-three were commissionaires."

low rates. The accommodation is rather better than that provided for soldiers in barracks. Everything necessary for vigorous physical existence is provided, but refinements are lacking.

Health.—In 1894 the daily average sick list was equal to 2.86 per cent of the whole force; in 1893 it had been 3.34 and in 1892 3.58 per cent. Besides diseases resulting from exposure, such as bronchitis and rheumatism, their occupation renders the police exceptionally liable to accidents and malicious injuries. There were in all 8644 cases of absence from duty for illness or accident in 1894, representing 6946 separate individuals (besides 645 cases carried forward from 1893). Of these cases 1274 were due to injuries, of which 882 happened while the men were on duty. In addition to injuries serious enough to keep the men from their work, there were nearly two thousand slighter cases. One shilling a day (or one-fifth of the pay for long periods) is deducted in case of absence from duty owing to sickness, and the amount credited to the pension fund, as also are fines, both those incurred by the police for breach of regulations and those imposed for assaults on the men. In receiving about four-fifths of their pay when disabled by sickness, policemen are better off (and rightly so, considering the risks they run) than the rank and file of the working classes. There is no deduction from pay in case of absence due to injury while on duty.

PART 4

(Separate) Spheres of Work

We are foolish, and without excuse foolish, in speaking
of the "superiority" of one sex to the other, as if they
could be compared in similar things. Each has what the
other has not: each completes the other, and is
completed by the other: they are in nothing alike, and
the happiness and perfection of both depends on each
asking and receiving from the other what the other only
can give.

—John Ruskin, "Lilies: Of Queens' Gardens"

Introduction

B Y THE MIDDLE of the nineteenth century, women had demonstrated that they could excel in a wide range of occupations. Florence Nightingale was effecting far-reaching reforms in the nursing profession; Elizabeth Barrett Browning was recognized as one of England's foremost poets; Anna Jameson had earned a reputation as a noted art critic; and Angela Burdett-Coutts, with her wealth and her administrative talents, had established schools for paupers, reformatories, an orphanage, and an emigration "service." Others had founded organizations and sisterhoods to work among the poor and institutions of higher education for women. Louisa Twining (1820–1912) had begun the Workhouse Visiting Society, Lydia Sellon (1821–1876) had formed a Devonport sisterhood to minister to cholera victims, and Elizabeth Reid had established Bedford College for Women.

Despite their achievements, however, and despite the fact that women constituted one-third of the labor force, prejudice persisted against women's working outside the home, especially middle- and upper-class "ladies." While most women of the classes below the aristocracy worked hard within the home, managing the household and raising children, work for pay was generally condemned as making a woman less feminine, distracting her from her more important domestic duties, and demonstrating the failure of her father or husband as a provider. The notion persisted throughout the century that every woman's career *should be* that of homemaker. Mrs. John Sandford (d. 1853), in *Woman in Her Social and Domestic Character* (1833), reminded her readers that women should "be content with a quiet fulfillment of duties which bring them no notoriety." A woman's "heart must be at home," says Sandford. "She must not be on the look-out for excitement of any kind, but must find her pleasure as well as her occupation in the sphere which is assigned to her," in other words, in her role as devoted, self-sacrificing wife and mother. Sarah Stickney Ellis (1799–1882) offered similar advice in *The Women of England: Their Social Duties, and Domestic Habits* (1838) and conveyed her hope that the education of women would fit them to fill "the stations appointed them by Providence" and content them with "seeking [their] own happiness only in the happiness of others." Lecturing in Manchester in 1864, John Ruskin likewise justified distinctive roles for men and women on the basis of inherent, God-given male and female capabilities. "The man's power," Ruskin proclaimed,

> is active, progressive, defensive. He is eminently the doer, the creator, the discoverer, the defender. His intellect is for speculation and invention; his energy for adventure,

for war, and for conquest. . . . But the woman's power is for rule, not for battle,—and her intellect is not for invention or creation, but for sweet ordering, arrangement, and decision. She sees the qualities of things, their claims, and their places. Her great function is Praise. . . . ("Lilies: Of Queens' Gardens")

Traditional views were not always so politely and delicately expressed. In 1859, a writer for the *Saturday Review* bluntly announced, "Married life is woman's profession and to this her life training—that of dependence—is modelled. Of course by not getting a husband, or losing him, she may find that she is without resources. All that can be said of her is, she has failed in business, and no social reform can prevent such failures" (see "Queen Bees or Working Bees?" in this section).

At the same time, social and political leaders began to accept the reality that not all women were married or would be married. In 1862, businessman and essayist William Rathbone Greg (1809–1881) published an influential article in the *National Review* titled "Why Are Women Redundant?" Using figures from the 1851 census, Greg calculated that the number of females over age twenty exceeded the number of males by six percent. To Greg, this "disproportionate and quite abnormal" number of single women was "indicative of an unwholesome social state." It meant that "in place of completing, sweetening, and embellishing the existence of others," these "redundant" women would be "compelled to lead an independent and incomplete existence of their own." Strongly opposed to expanding employment opportunities, which he believed would have the effect of discouraging even more women from marrying and fulfilling their pre-ordained roles, Greg endorsed large-scale female emigration programs instead. To other commentators, the same census figures suggested different courses of action. For the remainder of the century, the Woman Question, as the issue of women's roles came to be called, provoked lively debate in the periodical press, the pulpit, and the lecture hall.

Of course, in reality, the debate focused on a small percentage of the female population, ironically on the smallest percentage of those obliged to work for wages. Whereas the majority of journalistic, artistic, and literary treatments of the topic addressed the plight of middle-class women who found themselves in "reduced circumstances," a much greater number of women born into much worse circumstances received much less attention. The masses of women who belonged to the lower socio-economic classes had always worked, in the home and outside it: in cottage industry (such as sewing, laundering, or lace-, nail-, or box-making), as domestic servants, in the fields and coal mines, and, when all else failed, as prostitutes.

Early parliamentary investigations of factories and collieries brought attention to the miserable conditions in which the working classes toiled, with the plight of women arousing almost as much horror and outrage as that of children. Here, too, concerns focused on the removal of women from their proper sphere. In addition to reporting on long hours and unsafe workplaces, government officials voiced concern over the threat posed to the social order when women of any rank detached themselves from their homes to undertake paid work. Friedrich Engels claimed that "The employment of women at once breaks up the family"; if girls spend most of their lives working outside the home, they never learn to sew or cook or care for children. And he addressed the "moral consequences" of men and women working together in close proximity. Even among working-class families, the ideal was for married women to remain at home occupied with domestic and maternal duties. The Trades Union Congress of 1877 proclaimed that one of the goals of unions was "to bring about a condition . . . where wives should be in their proper sphere at home." As the century advanced and wages increased, this goal was more often realized.

Nevertheless, a significant number of women remained in the workforce. Because so many women "failed in [the] business" of marriage and were forced to work, because a certain percentage of men failed to provide adequately for their families, and because more and more women failed to find fulfillment at home and actually expressed a desire for meaningful employment beyond the domestic sphere, labor reforms did occur. For much of the century, middle-class women who ventured outside the home to earn a living found only three respectable occupations open to them: governess, companion, or seamstress. However, through the concerted efforts of feminists such as Barbara Bodichon (1827–1891) and Bessie Parkes (1829–1925), women moved gradually into other fields, increasingly finding employment as shop assistants, office clerks, and civil servants. In 1858, Bodichon and Parkes founded the *English Woman's Journal,* a periodical dedicated to advancing women's work opportunities, and, in the following year, they established the Society for the Promotion of the Employment of Women. Led by energetic reformers such as Emily Davies, women slowly gained access to higher education and assumed better-paid, more responsible positions. Opportunities for women within the professions—artistic, scientific, and commercial—developed slowly but fairly steadily. According to T. R. Gourvish, "By 1901 there were 3700 female artists in England and Wales (27 per cent of the total), 6400 actresses (52 per cent), and 22,600 musicians (also 52 per cent). Elsewhere, representation was very much that of a few pioneers: 212 physicians and surgeons, 140 in dentistry, 6 architects, 2 accountants and 3 vets." Still, he observes, "many male preserves remained unbreached. There were as yet no female barristers, solicitors, engineers or surveyors" ("The Rise of Professions" in *Later Victorian Britain, 1867–1900,* ed. T. R. Gourvish and Alan O'Day [New York: St. Martin's, 1988], 23).

The rate of progress remained slow because, with few exceptions, social commentators emphasized the primacy of domestic duties for women. Even feminist writers, including Emily Davies and Josephine Butler, most often directed their campaigns for female employment at unwed women and expressed misgivings about the appropriateness of wives pursuing careers. Nevertheless, public opinion about working women did shift as the century advanced. In *The Subjection of Women,* published in 1869, John Stuart Mill had unsettled the majority of his readers when he asked,

Is there so great a superfluity of men fit for high duties, that society can afford to reject the service of any competent person? Are we so certain of always finding a man made to our hands for any duty or function of social importance which falls vacant, that we lose nothing by putting a ban upon one-half of mankind, and refusing beforehand to make their faculties available, however distinguished they may be? And even if we could do without them, would it be consistent with justice to refuse to them their fair share of honor and distinction?

By the end of Victoria's reign, a much larger audience was willing to give serious consideration to such questions. Attitudes toward working women and the nature of work available to them had changed dramatically.

ALFRED, LORD TENNYSON

S EE THE INTRODUCTION to Tennyson (*Idylls of the King*) in part 1.
Tennyson began composition of *The Princess* in the late 1830s and devoted much energy to it in the mid-1840s when there was heated debate about women's roles in society and about the education they should receive in order to fulfill their roles. Already underway as Tennyson composed the poem were plans to establish Queen's College, London, for the better education of governesses; and the controversy concerning "woman's mission," "separate spheres," and "innate womanliness" was a major concern of the day.

The central plot of *The Princess* involves a Prince and a Princess of adjacent kingdoms who have been betrothed from infancy. As a young woman, Princess Ida forswears the company of men, withdraws from the court, and establishes a college for women from which men are barred; no man may enter its precincts without forfeit of his life. The Prince and two friends disguise themselves as women, enroll in the university, and subsequently are discovered and driven out. The Prince's father then urges his son to prosecute his suit by force of arms; reluctant at first to do so, the Prince finally responds to the challenge of a tournament when Ida's brother proposes an arranged battle between fifty champions of his sister's cause and fifty followers of the Prince. In this battle, the Prince's forces are defeated, and the Prince himself is wounded in what is feared to be a fatal fashion. Ida then converts her college into a hospital to tend to the needs of those seriously injured and takes upon herself the care of the Prince. Through the crisis of his illness and his subsequent recovery, Ida comes to reassess her general attitude and her specific actions, and she recognizes in the Prince a companion who respects her insistence upon women's abilities but who rejects the notion that women and men should be isolated from each other. The Prince renews his suit from his sickbed, winning the love he had previously been unable to secure.

The full title of the poem is *The Princess: A Medley,* and the subtitle suggests that the poem offers expression to a number of viewpoints concerning woman's position in society. In its own time, the poem was, of course, read in its entirety, and Tennyson's contemporaries had a narrative context for any segment singled out for attention. Because, today, excerpts only are generally offered, it is important that contemporary readers know which character speaks the lines quoted.

In the initial passage presented here (II.153–64), the speaker is Lady Psyche, one of Ida's friends and colleagues, who has offered at the university a lecture concerning women's history and who concludes this presentation with an enthusiastic projection of a future in which men and women work together without division into separate spheres. Tennyson presents her as a sympathetic figure: a young widow with a baby girl, Psyche proves reluctant to expose to the capital penalty the Prince and his two companions through whose feminine disguises she sees, and whose intrusion into the women's college she conceals. The aspirations she expresses anticipate, in some measure, that hope of harmonious collaboration between man and woman which the Prince extends to Ida and which Ida ultimately accepts.

The second passage (V.434–56) comprises what seems an endorsement of the propriety of separate spheres of work and life, but Tennyson has it offered by his least sympathetic character, "the hard old king" who is father to the Prince. Irascible, violent, insensitive, the King is an embarrassment to his son, who resists his control and repudiates his precepts.

The third passage (VII.242–90) would appear, in the "medley," as a response to the King's assertion that separate spheres for men and women are necessary to prevent "All else" from becoming "confusion." The words are addressed to Ida by the Prince as he proposes to her, urging her to "work no more alone" but to accept the complementarity of manly and womanly nature. In the vision of collaboration offered, he dismisses unhelpful language of "equal" and "unequal" in favor of a devotion to a common mission and common work in which individuality is preserved but isolation is rejected. Ida accepts the Prince's challenge to "walk this world, / Yoked in all exercise of noble end" (VII.339–40), and the central narrative of *The Princess* comes to conclusion.

From *The Princess*

From II

At last
She rose upon a wind of prophecy
Dilating on the future; "everywhere   155
Two heads in council, two beside the hearth,
Two in the tangled business of the world,
Two in the liberal offices of life,
Two plummets dropt for one to sound the abyss
Of science, and the secrets of the mind: 160

Musician, painter, sculptor, critic, more:
And everywhere the broad and bounteous Earth
Should bear a double growth of those rare souls,
Poets,[1] whose thoughts enrich the blood of the world."

From V

"When the man wants weight, the woman takes it up,
And topples down the scales; but this is fixt   435
As are the roots of earth and base of all;
Man for the field and woman for the hearth:
Man for the sword and for the needle she:
Man with the head and woman with the heart:
Man to command and woman to obey;   440
All else confusion. Look you! the gray mare[2]
Is ill to live with, when her whinny shrills
From tile to scullery, and her small goodman[3]
Shrinks in his arm-chair while the fires of Hell
Mix with his hearth: but you—she's yet a colt—   445
Take, break her: strongly groomed and straitly curbed
She might not rank with those detestable
That let the bantling[4] scald at home, and brawl
Their rights or wrongs like potherbs[5] in the street.
They say she's comely; there's the fairer chance: 450
I like her none the less for rating at her!
Besides, the woman wed is not as we,

---

1. The most celebrated woman poet of the period was Elizabeth Barrett Browning. In early 1846, she had written to her husband Robert that Tennyson had finished the second book of *The Princess,* from which this passage is taken, and she remarked, "I don't know what to think—it makes me open my eyes" (quoted in *The Poems of Tennyson,* ed. Christopher Ricks [London: Longman, Green, 1969], 741).

2. Tennyson has the King repeatedly employ animal parallels to human relationships. In an earlier reprimand to the Prince, he construes woman as the "game" whom man the hunter pursues for his own gratification and, curiously enough, for her satisfaction, too:
>   "Look you, Sir!
> Man is the hunter; woman is his game:
> The sleek and shining creatures of the chase,
> We hunt them for the beauty of their skins;
> They love us for it, and we ride them down."
>   (V.146–50)

That Tennyson does not advance the King's views as normative should be evident not only from the Prince's rejection of them and the coarse extremism of the animal comparisons in these passages but also from earlier portrayals of the King as intemperate and from previous speeches of the King's which are distinguished by immoderation and crudeness.

3. Husband.

4. Disparaging term for a young child. The reference is to negligent mothers who would allow a child to be scalded.

5. Cooked herbs.

But suffers change of frame. A lusty brace
Of twins may weed her of her folly. Boy,
The bearing and the training of a child   455
Is woman's wisdom."
      Thus the hard old king. . . .

From VII

"Henceforth thou hast a helper, me, that know
The woman's cause is man's: they rise or sink
Together, dwarfed or godlike, bond or free:[6]
For she that out of Lethe[7] scales with man   245
The shining steps of Nature, shares with man
His nights, his days, moves with him to one goal,
Stays all the fair young planet in her hands—
If she be small, slight-natured, miserable,
How shall men grow? but work no more alone!   250
Our place is much; as far as in us lies
We two will serve them both in aiding her—
Will clear away the parasitic forms
That seem to keep her up but drag her down—
Will leave her space to burgeon out of all   255
Within her—let her make herself her own
To give or keep, to live and learn and be
All that not harms distinctive womanhood.
For woman is not undevelopt man,
But diverse: could we make her as the man,   260
Sweet Love were slain: his dearest bond is this,
Not like to like, but like in difference.
Yet in the long years liker must they grow;
The man be more of woman, she of man;
He gain in sweetness and in moral height,   265
Nor lose the wrestling thews[8] that throw the world;
She mental breadth, nor fail in childward care,
Nor lose the childlike in the larger mind;
Till at the last she set herself to man,

---

6. 1 Corinthians 12:13 has the particular phrasing "bond or free," but the larger context in which this phrasing is situated proves instructive. In 1 Corinthians 12:4–31, Paul articulates his conception of the mystical body of Christ in which all members employ a diversity of gifts to work toward a common goal, doing so without concern for precedence or superiority. The synergy that Paul describes is very much akin to that ideal cooperation that the Prince advocates wherein both woman and man remain "Distinct in individualities" and "each fulfils / Defect in each."

7. Legendary river in the classical underworld whose water caused forgetfulness.

8. Muscles.

Like perfect music unto noble words;   270
And so these twain, upon the skirts of Time,
Sit side by side, full-summed in all their powers,
Dispensing harvest, sowing the To-be,
Self-reverent each and reverencing each,
Distinct in individualities,   275
But like each other even as those who love.
Then comes the statelier Eden back to men:
Then reign the world's great bridals, chaste and calm:
Then springs the crowning race of humankind.
May these things be!"
                        Sighing she spoke "I fear   280
They will not."
                    "Dear, but let us type⁹ them now
In our own lives, and this proud watchword rest
Of equal; seeing either sex alone
Is half itself, and in true marriage lies
Nor equal, nor unequal: each fulfils   285
Defect in each, and always thought in thought,
Purpose in purpose, will in will, they grow,
The single pure and perfect animal,
The two-celled heart beating, with one full stroke,
Life."   290

9. Tennyson recurred in the concluding segments of *In Memoriam* to this notion of "typing" within individual lives a dynamic of progressive development. Also important in crucial passages of *In Memoriam* is the concept of "the crowning race" touched on in line 279 of *The Princess* as well as the repeated images of sowing and harvesting, as in line 273. See *In Memoriam* 118.7–28 and "Epilogue," 123–44; the phrase "the crowning race" occurs in line 128 of the "Epilogue" to *In Memoriam*; it probably derives from Robert Chambers, who in *The Vestiges of Creation* posited the idea that the human race might be but the inauguration of "the grand crowning type."

DINAH MULOCK CRAIK

D INAH MARIA MULOCK CRAIK (1826–1887) published her first poems at age
fifteen but went on to establish a reputation as a journalist, children's writer,
and novelist as well. Her most famous novel is *John Halifax, Gentleman* (1856). In
1857, Craik published *A Woman's Thoughts about Women*, in which she proposed a
conservative answer to the "Woman Question." Though she disapproved of public
activism and unladylike conduct, Craik argued that all women, single and married, need to be well-educated, "self-dependent," and self-reliant, a message that
runs throughout her writing. Craik points out in chapter 3, "Female Professions,"
that as one who has been a working woman all her life, she is qualified to address the topic. When her mother died in 1845, Craik's father, a Nonconformist
preacher, refused to support Dinah and her two younger brothers. Craik did not
marry until 1865 and in the intervening years supported herself with her pen.

A Woman's Thoughts about Women appeared anonymously in *Chambers' Edinburgh Journal* from May 2 to December 19, 1857, and was issued in book form the
following year.

From *A Woman's Thoughts about Women*

Chapter II
Self-dependence

"If you want a thing done, go yourself; if not, send."

This pithy axiom, of which most men know the full value, is by no means so
well appreciated by women. One of the very last things we learn, often through a
course of miserable helplessness, heart-burnings, difficulties, contumelies,[1] and
pain, is the lesson, taught to boys from their school-days, of self-dependence.

1. Humiliating insults.

Figure 4.1. Emily Mary Osborn, *Nameless and Friendless.* Courtesy of the Courtauld Institute of Art. Private Collection.

One of the few successful female artists of nineteenth-century England, Emily Mary Osborn (1834–after 1913) was inspired by Mary Brunton's novel *Self Control* (1810) to paint *Nameless and Friendless* (1857), a picture showing the prejudices against women painters. A meek young widow, thrown on her own resources, visits a gallery in the company of her son but shrinks before the stares of male patrons and the critical gaze of the haughty art dealer who examines her work.

Its opposite, either plainly or impliedly, has been preached to us all our lives. "An independent young lady"—"a woman who can take care of herself"—and such-like phrases, have become tacitly suggestive of hoydenishness,[2] coarseness, strong-mindedness, down to the lowest depth of bloomerism,[3] cigarette-smoking,[4] and talking slang.

And there are many good reasons, ingrained in the very tenderest core of woman's nature, why this should be. We are "the weaker vessel"—whether acknowledging it or not, most of us feel this: it becomes man's duty and delight to show us honour accordingly. And this honour, dear as it may be to him to give, is still dearer to us to receive.

2. Tomboyishness.

3. Amelia Jenks Bloomer (1818–1894), an American, advocated more sensible dress for women. Bloomers, loose trousers gathered at the ankles, appeared in 1851.

4. Smoking cigarettes, which became available after mid-century, was not considered ladylike.

Dependence is in itself an easy and pleasant thing: dependence upon one we love being perhaps the very sweetest thing in the world. To resign one's self totally and contentedly into the hands of another; to have no longer any need of asserting one's rights or one's personality, knowing that both are as precious to that other as they ever were to ourselves; to cease taking thought about one's self at all, and rest safe, at ease, assured that in great things and small we shall be guided and cherished, guarded and helped—in fact, thoroughly "taken care of"—how delicious is all this! So delicious, that it seems granted to very few of us, and to fewer still as a permanent condition of being.

Were it our ordinary lot, were every woman living to have either father, brother, or husband, to watch over and protect her, then, indeed, the harsh but salutary doctrine of self-dependence need never be heard of. But it is not so. In spite of the pretty ideals of poets, the easy taken-for-granted truths of old-fashioned educators of female youth, this fact remains patent to any person of common sense and experience, that in the present day, whether voluntarily or not, one-half of our women are *obliged* to take care of themselves—obliged to look solely to themselves for maintenance, position, occupation, amusement, reputation, life.

Of course I refer to the large class for which these Thoughts are meant—the single women; who, while most needing the exercise of self-dependence, are usually the very last in whom it is inculcated, or even permitted. From babyhood they are given to understand that helplessness is feminine and beautiful; helpfulness,— except in certain received forms of manifestation—unwomanly and ugly. The boys may do a thousand things which are "not proper for little girls."

And herein, I think, lies the great mistake at the root of most women's education, that the law of their existence is held to be, not Right, but Propriety; a certain received notion of womanhood, which has descended from certain excellent great-grandmothers, admirably suited for some sorts of their descendants, but totally ignoring the fact that each sex is composed of individuals, differing in character almost as much from one another as from the opposite sex. For do we not continually find womanish men and masculine women? and some of the finest types of character we have known among both sexes, are they not often those who combine the qualities of both? Therefore, there must be somewhere a standard of abstract right, including manhood and womanhood, and yet superior to either. One of the first of its common laws, or common duties, is this of self-dependence.

We women are, no less than men, each of us a distinct existence. In two out of the three great facts of our life[5] we are certainly independent agents, and all our life long we are accountable only, in the highest sense, to our own souls, and the Maker of them. Is it natural, is it right even, that we should be expected—and be ready enough, too, for it is much the easiest way—to hang our consciences, duties, actions, opinions, upon some one else—some individual, or some aggregate of individuals yclept[6] Society? Is this Society to draw up a code of regulations as to

5. Birth, marriage, and death.
6. Archaic word meaning called.

what is proper for us to do, and what not? Which latter is supposed to be done for us; if not done, or there happens to be no one to do it, is it to be left undone? Alack, most frequently, whether or not it ought to be, it is!

Every one's experience may furnish dozens of cases of poor women suddenly thrown adrift—widows with families, orphan girls, reduced gentlewomen—clinging helplessly to every male relative or friend they have, year after year, sinking deeper in poverty or debt, eating the bitter bread of charity, or compelled to bow an honest pride to the cruellest humiliations, every one of which might have been spared them by the early practice of self-dependence.

I once heard a lady say—a tenderly-reared and tender-hearted woman—that if her riches made themselves wings, as in these times riches will, she did not know anything in the world that she could turn her hand to, to keep herself from starving. A more pitiable, and, in some sense, humbling confession, could hardly have been made; yet it is that not of hundreds, but of thousands, in England.

Sometimes exceptions arise: here is one:—

Two young women, well educated and refined, were left orphans, their father dying just when his business promised to realise a handsome provision for his family. It was essentially a man's business—in many points of view, decidedly an unpleasant one. Of course friends thought "the girls" must give it up, go out as governesses, depend on relatives, or live in what genteel poverty the sale of the good-will might allow. But the "girls" were wiser. They argued: "If we had been boys, it would have been all right; we should have carried on the business, and provided for our mother and the whole family. Being women, we'll try it still. It is nothing wrong; it is simply disagreeable. It needs common sense, activity, diligence, and self-dependence. We have all these; and what we have not, we will learn." So these sensible and well-educated young women laid aside their pretty uselessness and pleasant idleness, and set to work. Happily, the trade was one that required no personal publicity; but they had to keep the books, manage the stock, choose and superintend fit agents—to do things difficult, not to say distasteful, to most women, and resign enjoyments that, to women of their refinement, must have cost daily self-denial. Yet they did it; they filled their father's place, sustained their delicate mother in ease and luxury, never once compromising their womanhood by their work, but rather ennobling the work by their doing of it.

Another case—different, and yet alike. A young girl, an elder sister, had to receive for step-mother a woman who ought never to have been any honest man's wife. Not waiting to be turned out of her father's house, she did a most daring and "improper" thing—she left it, taking with her the brothers and sisters, whom by this means only she believed she could save from harm. She settled them in a London lodging, and worked for them as a daily governess. "Heaven helps those who help themselves." From that day this girl never was dependent upon any human being; while during a long life she has helped and protected more than I could count—pupils and pupils' children, friends and their children, besides brothers and sisters-in-law, nephews and nieces, down to the slenderest tie of blood, or even mere strangers. And yet she has never been anything but a poor governess, always independent, always able to assist others—because she never was and never will be indebted to any one, except for love while she lives, and for a grave when she dies. May she long possess the one and want the other!

And herein is answered the "*cui bono?*"[7] of self-dependence, that its advantages end not with the original possessor. In this much-suffering world, a woman who can take care of herself can always take care of other people. She not only ceases to be an unprotected female, a nuisance and a drag upon society, but her working-value therein is doubled and trebled, and society respects her accordingly. Even her kindly male friends, no longer afraid that when the charm to their vanity of "being of use to a lady" has died out, they shall be saddled with a perpetual claimant for all manner of advice and assistance; the first not always followed, and the second often accepted without gratitude—even they yield an involuntary consideration to a lady who gives them no more trouble than she can avoid, and is always capable of thinking and acting for herself, so far as the natural restrictions and decorums of her sex allow. True, these have their limits, which it would be folly, if not worse, for her to attempt to pass; but a certain fine instinct, which, we flatter ourselves, is native to us women, will generally indicate the division between brave self-reliance and bold assumption.

Perhaps the line is most easily drawn, as in most difficulties, at that point where duty ends and pleasure begins. Thus, we should respect one who, on a mission of mercy or necessity, went through the lowest portions of St. Giles' or the Gallowgate;[8] we should be rather disgusted if she did it for mere amusement or bravado. All honour to the poor sempstress or governess who traverses London streets alone, at all hours of day or night, unguarded except by her own modesty; but the strong-minded female who would venture on a solitary expedition to investigate the humours of Cremorne Gardens or Greenwich fair,[9] though perfectly "respectable," would be an exceedingly condemnable sort of personage. There are many things at which, as mere pleasures, a woman has a right to hesitate; there is no single duty, whether or not it lies in the ordinary line of her sex, from which she ought to shrink, if it be plainly set before her.

Those who are the strongest advocates for the passive character of our sex, its claims, proprieties, and restrictions, are, I have often noticed, if the most sensitive, not always the justest or most generous. I have seen ladies, no longer either young or pretty, shocked at the idea of traversing a street's length at night, yet never hesitate at being "fetched" by some female servant, who was both young and pretty, and to whom the danger of the expedition, or of the late return alone, was by far the greater of the two. I have known anxious mothers, who would not for worlds be guilty of the indecorum of sending their daughters unchaperoned to the theatre or a ball—and very right, too!—yet send out some other woman's young daughter, at eleven P.M., to the stand for a cab, or to the public-house for a supply

7. Latin: "to whose benefit?"
8. Among the worst of nineteenth-century London slums.
9. London slums near the Thames.

for beer. It never strikes them that the doctrine of female dependence extends beyond themselves, whom it suits so easily, and to whom it saves so much trouble; that either every woman, be she servant or mistress, sempstress or fine lady, should receive the "protection" suitable to her degree; or that each ought to be educated into equal self-dependence. Let us, at least, hold the balance of justice even, nor allow an over-consideration for the delicacy of one woman to trench[10] on the rights, conveniences, and honest feelings of another.

We *must* help ourselves. In this curious phase of social history, when marriage is apparently ceasing to become the common lot, and a happy marriage the most uncommon lot of all, we must educate our maidens into what is far better than any blind clamour for ill-defined "rights"—into what ought always to be the foundation of rights—duties. And there is one, the silent practice of which will secure to them almost every right they can fairly need—the duty of self-dependence. Not after any Amazonian fashion; no mutilating of fair womanhood in order to assume the unnatural armour of men;[11] but simply by the full exercise of every faculty, physical, moral, and intellectual, with which Heaven has endowed us all, severally and collectively, in different degrees; allowing no one to rust or lie idle, merely because their owner is a woman. And, above all, let us lay the foundation of all real womanliness by teaching our girls from their cradle that the priceless pearl of decorous beauty, chastity of mind as well as body, exists in themselves alone; that a single-hearted and pure-minded woman may go through the world, like Spenser's Una,[12] suffering, indeed, but never defenceless; foot-sore and smirched, but never tainted; exposed, doubtless, to many trials, yet never either degraded or humiliated, unless by her own act she humiliates herself.

For heaven's sake—for the sake of "woman-hede,"[13] the most heavenly thing next angelhood, (as men tell us when they are courting us, and which it depends upon ourselves to make them believe in all their lives)—young girls, trust yourselves; rely on yourselves! Be assured that no outward circumstances will harm you while you keep the jewel of purity in your bosom, and are ever ready with the steadfast, clean right hand, of which, till you use it, you never know the strength, though it be only a woman's hand.

Fear not the world: it is often juster to us than we are to ourselves. If in its harsh jostlings the "weaker goes to the wall"[14]—as so many allege is sure to happen to a woman—you will almost always find that this is not merely because of her sex, but from some inherent qualities in herself, which, existing either in woman or man, would produce just the same result, pitiful and blameable, but usually more pitiful than blameable. The world is hard enough, for two-thirds of it are struggling for

10. Infringe.

11. According to legend, Amazons cut off their right breasts to make themselves more effective archers.

12. A character who represents truth and true religion in book 1 of *The Faerie Queene* by Edmund Spenser (1552–1599).

13. Middle English form for womanhood.

14. Shakespeare, *Romeo and Juliet* 1.1.20: "Women, being the weaker vessels, are ever thrust to the wall."

the dear life—"each for himself, and de'il tak the hindmost"; but it has a rough sense of moral justice after all. And whosoever denies that, spite of all hindrances from individual wickedness, *the right* shall not ultimately prevail, impugns not alone human justice, but the justice of God.

The age of chivalry, with all its benefits and harmfulnesses, is gone by, for us women. We cannot now have men for our knights-errant, expending blood and life for our sake, while we have nothing to do but sit idle on balconies, and drop flowers on half-dead victors at tilt and tourney. Nor, on the other hand, are we dressed-up dolls, pretty playthings, to be fought and scrambled for—petted, caressed, or flung out of window, as our several lords and masters may please. Life is much more equally divided between us and them. We are neither goddesses nor slaves; they are neither heroes nor semi-demons: we just plod on together, men and women alike, on the same road, where daily experience illustrates Hudibras's[15] keen truth, that

> "The value of a thing
> Is just as much as it will bring."

And our value is—exactly what we choose to make it.

Perhaps at no age since Eve's were women rated so exclusively at their own personal worth, apart from poetic flattery or tyrannical depreciation; at no time in the world's history judged so entirely by their individual merits, and respected according to the respect which they earn for themselves. And shall we value ourselves so meanly as to consider this unjust? Shall we not rather accept our position, difficult indeed, and requiring from us more than the world ever required before, but from its very difficulty rendered the more honourable?

Let us not be afraid of men; for that, I suppose, lies at the root of all these amiable hesitations. "Gentlemen don't like such and such things." "Gentlemen fancy so and so unfeminine." My dear little foolish cowards, do you think a man— a *good* man, in any relation of life, ever loves a woman the more for reverencing her the less? or likes her better for transferring all her burdens to his shoulders, and pinning her conscience to his sleeve? Or, even supposing he did like it, is a woman's divinity to be man—or God?

And here, piercing to the Foundation of all truth—I think we may find the truth concerning self-dependence, which is only real and only valuable when its root is not in self at all; when its strength is drawn not from man, but from that Higher and Diviner Source whence every individual soul proceeds, and to which alone it is accountable. As soon as any woman, old or young, once feels *that*, not as a vague sentimental belief, but as a tangible, practical law of life, all weakness ends, all doubt departs: she recognises the glory, honour, and beauty of her existence; she is no longer afraid of its pains; she desires not to shift one atom of its responsibilities to another. She is content to take it just as it is, from the hands of the All-Father; her only care being so to fulfil it, that while the world at large may recognise and

---

15. Title character of a political and religious satire in verse by Samuel Butler (1612–1680), published in three parts between 1663 and 1678.

profit by her self-dependence, she herself, knowing that the utmost strength lies in the deepest humility, recognises, solely and above all, her dependence upon God.

Chapter III
Female Professions

Granted the necessity of something to do, and the self-dependence required for its achievement, we may go on to the very obvious question—*what* is a woman to do?

A question more easily asked than answered; and the numerous replies to which, now current in book, pamphlet, newspaper, and review, suggesting everything possible and impossible, from compulsory wifehood in Australia[16] to voluntary watchmaking at home, do at present rather confuse the matter than otherwise. No doubt, out of these "many words," which "darken speech,"[17] some plain word or two will one day take shape in action, so as to evolve a practical good. In the meantime, it does no harm to have the muddy pond stirred up a little; any disturbance is better than stagnation.

These Thoughts—however desultory and unsatisfactory, seeing the great need there is for deeds rather than words—are those of a "working" woman, who has been such all her life, having opportunities of comparing the experience of other working women with her own: she, therefore, at least escapes the folly of talking of what she knows nothing about.

Female professions, as distinct from what may be termed female handicrafts, which merit separate classification and discussion, may, I think, be thus divided: the instruction of youth; painting or art; literature; and the vocation of public entertainment—including actresses, singers, musicians, and the like.

The first of these, being a calling universally wanted, and the easiest in which to win, at all events, daily bread, is the great chasm into which the helpless and penniless of our sex generally plunge; and this indiscriminate Quintus Curtius-ism,[18] so far from filling up the gulf, widens it every hour. It must be so, while young women of all classes and all degrees of capability rush into governessing, as many young men enter the church,—because they think it a "respectable" profession to get on in, and are fit for nothing else. Thus the most important of ours, and the highest of all men's vocations, are both degraded—in so far as they can be degraded—by the unworthiness and incompetency of their professors.

If, in the most solemn sense, not one woman in five thousand is fit to be a mother, we may safely say that not two out of that number are fit to be governesses.

16. In the 1840s, two organizations, Caroline Chisholm's Family Colonization Loan Society and Sidney Herbert's Fund for Promoting Female Emigration, assisted women in emigrating to one of the British colonies. In 1859, two years after *A Woman's Thoughts about Women* was published, the Society for the Promotion of the Employment of Women was established.

17. Job 38:1–2. "Then the Lord answered Job out of the whirlwind: 'Who is this that darkens counsel by words without knowledge?'"

18. In Roman legend, there is a story that in order to close a chasm that had opened in the Forum, a Roman soldier named *Marcus* Curtius rode his horse into the opening.

Consider all that the office implies: very many of a mother's duties, with the addition of considerable mental attainments, firmness of character, good sense, good temper, good breeding; patience, gentleness, loving-kindness. In short, every quality that goes to make a perfect woman, is required of her who presumes to undertake the education of one single little child.

Does any one pause to reflect what a "little child" is? Not sentimentally, as a creature to be philosophised upon, painted and poetised; nor selfishly, as a kissable, scoldable, sugar-plum-feedable plaything; but as a human soul and body, to be moulded, instructed, and influenced, in order that it in its turn may mould, instruct, and influence unborn generations. And yet, in face of this awful responsibility, wherein each deed and word of hers may bear fruit, good or ill, to indefinite ages, does nearly every educated gentlewoman thrown upon her own resources, nearly every half-educated "young person" who wishes by that means to step out of her own sphere into the one above it, enter upon the vocation of a governess.

Whether it really is her vocation, she never stops to think; and yet, perhaps, in no calling is a personal bias more indispensable. For knowledge, and the power of imparting it intelligibly, are two distinct and often opposite qualities; the best student by no means necessarily makes the best teacher: nay, when both faculties are combined, they are sometimes neutralised by some fault of disposition, such as want of temper or of will. And allowing all these, granting every possible intellectual and practical competency, there remains still doubtful the moral influence, which, according to the source from which it springs, may ennoble or corrupt a child for life.

All these are facts so trite and so patent, that one would almost feel it superfluous to state them, did we not see how utterly they are ignored day by day by even sensible people; how parents go on lavishing expense on their house, dress, and entertainments—everything but the education of their children; sending their boys to cheap boarding-schools, and engaging for their daughters governesses at 20*l.* a year, or daily tuition at sixpence an hour; and how, as a natural result, thousands of incapable girls, and ill-informed, unscrupulous women, go on professing to teach everything under the sun, adding lie upon lie, and meanness upon meanness—often through no voluntary wickedness, but sheer helplessness, because they must either do that or starve!

Yet, all the while we expect our rising generation to turn out perfection; instead of which we find it—what?

I do solemnly aver, having seen more than one generation of young girls grow up into womanhood—that the fairest and best specimens of our sex that I have ever known have been among those who have never gone to school, or scarcely ever had a regular governess.

Surely such a fact as this—I put it to general experience, whether it is not a fact?—indicates some great flaw in the carrying out of this large branch of women's work. How is it to be remedied? I believe, like all reformations, it must begin at the root—with the governesses themselves.

Unless a woman has a decided pleasure and facility in teaching, an honest knowledge of everything she professes to impart, a liking for children, and above all, a strong moral sense of her responsibility towards them, for her to attempt to enrol herself in the scholastic order is absolute profanation. Better turn shop-woman, needlewoman, lady's-maid—even become a decent housemaid, and learn how to sweep a floor, than belie her own soul, and peril many other souls, by entering upon what is, or ought to be, a female "ministry," unconsecrated for, and incapable of the work.

"But," say they, "work we must have. Competition is so great, that if we did not profess to do everything, it would be supposed we could do nothing: and so we should starve."

Yet, what is competition? A number of people attempting to do what most of them can only half do, and some cannot do at all—thereby "cutting one another's throats," as the saying is, so long as their incapacity is concealed; when it is found out, starving. There may be exceptions from exceeding misfortune and the like—but in the long run, I believe it will be found that few women, really competent to do what they undertake, be it small or great, starve for want of work to do. So, in this case, no influence is so deeply felt in a house, or so anxiously retained, if only from self-interest, as the influence of a good governess over the children; among the innumerable throng of teachers, there is nothing more difficult to find—or more valuable when found, to judge by the high terms asked and obtained by many professors—than a lady who can teach only a single thing, solidly, conscientiously, and well.

In this, as in most social questions, where to theorise is easy and to practise very difficult, it will often be found that the silent undermining of an evil is safer than the loud outcry against it. If every governess, so far as her power extends, would strive to elevate the character of her profession by elevating its members, many of the unquestionable wrongs and miseries of governess-ship would gradually right themselves. A higher standard of capability would weed out much cumbersome mediocrity; and, competition lessened, the value of labour would rise. I say "the value of labour," because, when we women do work, we must learn to rate ourselves at no ideal and picturesque value, but simply as *labourers*—fair and honest competitors in the field of the world; and our wares as mere merchandise, where money's worth alone brings money, or has any right to expect it.

This applies equally to the two next professions, art and literature. I put art first, as being the most difficult—perhaps, in its highest form, almost impossible to women. There are many reasons for this; in the course of education necessary for a painter, in the not unnatural repugnance that is felt to women's drawing from "the life,"[19] attending anatomical dissections, and so on—all which studies are indispensable to one who would plumb the depths and scale the heights of the most

19. Women artists, even in their own academies (such as the Female School of Art established in 1851) were not allowed to study nude models until 1893. See Susan Casteras, *Images of Victorian Womanhood in English Art* (Fairleigh Dickinson University Press, 1987) and Pamela Gerrish Nunn, *Victorian Women Artists* (The Women's Press, 1987).

arduous of the liberal arts. Whether any woman will ever do this, remains yet to be proved. Meantime, many lower and yet honourable positions are open to female handlers of the brush.

But in literature we own no such boundaries; there we meet men on level ground—and, shall I say it?—we do often beat them in their own field. We are acute and accurate historians, clear explanators of science, especially successful in imaginative works, and within the last year *Aurora Leigh*,[20] has proved that we can write as great a poem as any man among them all. Any publisher's list, any handful of weekly or monthly periodicals, can testify to our power of entering boldly on the literary profession, and pursuing it wholly, self-devotedly, and self-reliantly, thwarted by no hardships, and content with no height short of the highest.

So much for the best of us—women whose work will float down the ages, safe and sure; there is no need to speak of it or them. But there is another secondary class among us, neither "geniuses" nor ordinary women—aspiring to both destinies, and usually achieving neither: of these it is necessary to say a word.

In any profession, there is nothing, short of being absolutely evil, which is so injurious, so fatal, as mediocrity. To the amateur who writes "sweetly" or paints "prettily," her work is mere recreation; and though it may be less improving for the mind to do small things on your own account, than to be satisfied with appreciating the greater doings of other people, still, it is harmless enough, if it stops there. But all who leave domestic criticism to plunge into the open arena of art—I use the word in its widest sense—must abide by art's severest canons. One of these is, that every person who paints a common-place picture, or writes a mediocre book, contributes temporarily—happily, only temporarily—to lower the standard of public taste, fills unworthily some better competitor's place, and without achieving any private good, does a positive wrong to the community at large.

One is often tempted to believe, in the great influx of small talents which now deluges us, that if half the books written, and pictures painted, were made into one great bonfire, it would be their shortest, easiest, and safest way of illuminating the world.

Therefore, let men do as they will—and truly they are often ten times vainer and more ambitious than we!—but I would advise every woman to examine herself and judge herself, morally and intellectually, by the sharpest tests of criticism, before she attempts art or literature, either for abstract fame or as a means of livelihood.[21] Let her take to heart, humbly, the telling truth, that

"Fools rush in where angels fear to tread,"[22]

and be satisfied that the smallest perfect achievement is nobler than the grandest failure. But having, after mature deliberation, chosen her calling, and consci-

---

20. Epic-length poem published by Elizabeth Barrett Browning in 1856 (though dated 1857). See the following excerpts.

21. A number of popular Victorian women writers originally picked up a pen to support themselves and their families: Craik herself, as mentioned above, as well as Margaret Oliphant (1828–1897) and Frances Trollope (1779–1863), to name two other noteworthy examples.

22. From line 625 of *An Essay on Criticism* (1711), a poem by Alexander Pope (1688–1744).

entiously believing it is her calling—that in which she shall do most good, and best carry out the aim of her existence—let her fulfil to the last iota its solemn requirements.

These entail more, much more, than flighty young genius or easily-satisfied mediocrity ever dreams of; labour incessant, courage inexhaustible, sustained under difficulties, misfortunes, and rebuffs of every conceivable kind—added thereto, not unfrequently, the temperament to which these things come hardest. *Le génie c'est la patience*;[23] and though there is a truth beyond it—since all the patience in the world will not serve as a substitute for genius,—still, never was a truer saying than this of old Buffon's.[24] Especially as applied to women, when engaged in a profession which demands from them, no less than from men, the fervent application, and sometimes the total devotion of a lifetime.

For, high as the calling is, it is not always, in the human sense, a happy one; it often results in, if it does not spring from, great sacrifices; and is full of a thousand misconstructions, annoyances, and temptations. Nay, since ambition is a quality far oftener deficient in us than in the other sex, its very successes are less sweet to women than to men. Many a "celebrated authoress" or "exquisite paintress" must have felt the heart-truth in *Aurora Leigh*:

> "I might have been a common woman, now,
> And happier, less known and less left alone,
> Perhaps a better woman after all—
> With chubby children hanging round my neck,
> To keep me low and wise. Ah me! the vines
> That bear such fruit are proud to stoop with it—
> The palm stands upright in a realm of sand."[25]

And, setting aside both these opposite poles of the female character and lot, it remains yet doubtful whether the maiden-aunt who goes from house to house, perpetually busy and useful—the maiden house-mother, who keeps together an orphan family, having all the cares, and only half the joys of maternity or mistress-ship—even the active, bustling "old maid," determined on setting everybody to rights, and having a finger in every pie that needs her, and a few that don't—I question whether each of these women has not a more natural, and therefore, probably, a happier existence, than any "woman of genius" that ever enlightened the world.

But happiness is not the first nor the only thing on earth. Whosoever has entered upon this vocation in the right spirit, let her keep to it, neither afraid nor ashamed. The days of blue-stockings are over:[26] it is a notable fact, that the best housekeepers, the neatest needlewomen, the most discreet managers of their own and others' affairs, are ladies whose names the world cons over in library lists and

---

23. Genius is patience.
24. Georges de Buffon (1707–1788), French naturalist.
25. *Aurora Leigh* 2.513–19.
26. Reference to an eighteenth-century women's literary club. The term is used to designate pedantic women.

exhibition catalogues. I could give them now—except that the world has no possible business with them, except to read their books and look at their pictures. It must imply something deficient in the women themselves, if the rude curiosity of this said well-meaning but often impertinent public is ever allowed to break in upon that dearest right of every woman—the inviolable sanctity of her home.

Without—in these books and by these pictures—let it always be a fair fight, and no quarter. To exact consideration merely on account of her sex, is in any woman the poorest cowardice. She has entered the neutral realm of pure intellect—has donned brain-armour, and must carry on with lawful, consecrated weapons a combat, of which the least reward in her eyes, in which she never can freeze up or burn out either the woman-tears or woman-smiles, will be that public acknowledgement called Fame.

This fame, as gained in art or literature, is certainly of a purer and safer kind than that which falls to the lot of the female *artiste*.[27]

Most people will grant that no great gift is given to be hid under a bushel; that a Sarah Siddons, a Rachel, or a Jenny Lind,[28] being created, was certainly not created for nothing. There seems no reason why a great actress or vocalist should not exercise her talents to the utmost for the world's benefit, and her own; nor that any genius, boiling and bursting up to find expression, should be pent down, cruelly and dangerously, because it refuses to run in the ordinary channel of feminine development. But the last profession of the four which I have enumerated as the only paths at present open to women, is the one which is the most full of perils and difficulties, on account of the personality involved in its exercise.

We may paint scores of pictures, write shelvesful of books—the errant children of our brain may be familiar half over the known world, and yet we ourselves sit as quiet by our chimney-corner, live a life as simple and peaceful as any happy "common woman" of them all. But with the *artiste* it is very different; she needs to be constantly before the public, not only mentally, but physically: the general eye becomes familiar, not merely with her genius, but her corporeality; and every comment of admiration or blame awarded to her, is necessarily an immediate personal criticism. This of itself is a position contrary to the instinctive something—call it reticence, modesty, shyness, what you will—which is inherent in every one of Eve's daughters. Any young girl, standing before a large party in her first *tableau vivant*[29]—any singing-pupil at a public examination—any boy-lover of some adorable actress, at the moment when he first thinks of that goddess as *his wife*, will understand what I mean.

But that is by no means the chief objection; for the feeling of personal shyness

27. Craik adheres to modern practice in using the word *artiste* to refer to a public performer such as a singer, actor, or dancer, as opposed to an *artist*, who practices one of the arts such as painting, sculpting, or composing.

28. Sarah Siddons (1775–1831), English actress; Elisa Felix or Rachel (1820–1858), French actress; Jenny Lind (1820–1887), Swedish singer.

29. Popular entertainment at evening parties. Silent, motionless actors in costume pose to recreate a well-known scene from art or literature.

dies out, and in the true *artiste* becomes altogether merged in the love and inspiration of her art—the inexplicable fascination of which turns the many-eyed gazing mass into a mere "public," of whose individuality the performer is no more conscious than was the Pythoness[30] of her curled and scented Greek audience, when she felt on her tripod the afflatus of the unconquerable, inevitable god. The saddest phase of artiste-life—which is, doubtless, the natural result of this constant appearance before the public eye, this incessant struggle for the public's personal verdict—is its intense involuntary egotism.

No one can have seen anything of theatrical or musical circles without noticing this—the incessant recurrence to "*my* part," "*my* song," "what the public think of *me*." In the hand-to-hand struggle for the capricious public's favour, this sad selfishness is apparently inevitable. "Each for himself" seems implanted in masculine nature, for its own preservation; but when it comes to "each for *herself*"— when you see the fairest Shakspeare heroines turn red or pale at the mention of a rival impersonator—when Miss This cannot be asked to a party for fear of meeting Madame That, or if they do meet, through all their smiling civility you perceive their backs are up, like two strange cats meeting at a parlour-door—I say, this is the most lamentable of all results, not absolutely vicious, which the world, and the necessity of working in it, effect on women.

And for this reason the profession of public entertainment, in all its gradation, from the inspired *tragédienne* to the poor chorus-singer, is, above any profession I know, to be marked with a spiritual Humane Society's pole, "Dangerous." Not after the vulgar notion: we have among us too many chaste, matronly actresses, and charming maiden-vocalists, to enter now into the old question about the "respectability" of the stage; but on account of the great danger to temperament, character, and mode of thought, to which such a life peculiarly exposes its followers.

But, if a woman has chosen it—I repeat in this as in any other—let her not forego it; for in every occupation the worthiness, like the "readiness," "is all."[31] Never let her be moulded by her calling, but mould her calling to herself; being, as every woman ought to be, the woman first, the *artiste* afterwards. And, doubtless, so are many; doubtless one could find, not only among the higher ranks of this profession, where genius itself acts as a purifying and refining fire, but in its lower degrees, many who, under the glare of the footlights and the din of popular applause, have kept their freshness and singleness of character unfaded to the end. Ay, even among poor ballet-dancers, capering with set rouged smiles and leaden hearts—coarse screaming concert-singers, doing sham pathos at a guinea a-night—flaunting actresses-of-all-work, firmly believing themselves the best *Juliet* or *Lady Macbeth* extant, and yet condescending to take ever so small a part—even the big-headed "*princess*" of an Easter extravaganza, for the sake of the old parents, or the fiddler-husband and the sickly babies at home. No doubt, many of them live—let us rather say, endure—a life as pure, as patient, as self-denying, as that of hundreds of timid,

30. Priestess/prophetess of Apollo at Delphi who sat on a tripod.
31. *Hamlet* 5.2.223.

daintily protected girls, and would-be correct matrons, who shrink in safe privacy from the very thought of these. But Heaven counts and cares for all.

Therefore, in this perilous road, double honour be unto those who walk upright, double pity unto those who fall!

Conning over again this desultory chapter, it seems to me it all comes to neither more nor less than this: that since a woman, by choosing a definite profession, must necessarily quit the kindly shelter and safe negativeness of a private life, and assume a substantive position, it is her duty not hastily to decide, and before deciding, in every way to count the cost. But having chosen, let her fulfil her lot. Let there be no hesitations, no regrets, no compromises—they are at once cowardly and vain. She may have missed or foregone much;—I repeat, our natural and happiest life is when we lose ourselves in the exquisite absorption of home, the delicious retirement of dependent love; but what she has, she has, and nothing can ever take it from her. Nor is it, after all, a small thing for any woman—be she governess, painter, author, or *artiste*—to feel that, higher or lower, according to her degree, she ranks among that crowned band who, whether or not they are the happy ones, are elected to the heaven-given honour of being the Workers of the world.

ELIZABETH BARRETT BROWNING

SEE THE INTRODUCTION to Elizabeth Barrett Browning ("The Cry of the Children") in part 3.

In the Dedication of her "novel-poem" *Aurora Leigh,* published in 1857, Barrett Browning described the book as "the most mature of my works, and the one into which my highest convictions upon Life and Art have entered." In the poem, Aurora Leigh tells the story of her development as a woman and as a poet. An orphan raised by a dour maiden aunt, she proves rebellious when confronted with the constricting activities and especially the mindless busywork of her girl's education, and she repudiates her aunt's traditional understanding of what comprises the distinctively feminine nature and mission; the initial brief passage below (1.415–65) encapsulates what Barrett Browning presents as the frustration that many a well-to-do young woman of the period must have endured: see, in this regard, Florence Nightingale's autobiographical essay *Cassandra* in part 1.

On her twentieth birthday, Aurora rejects the marriage proposal of her cousin Romney Leigh, a social activist who calls upon her to join him in his mission to serve and elevate the lower classes; acknowledging the worthiness of his vocation, she claims the right to pursue her own particular calling to become a poet and dedicates herself to this end. The major selection below details Romney's proposal and her refusal. The passage is significant in part because of Aurora's passionate defense of a woman's right to a career and her assertion of the value of poetry. It is also instructive because of Romney's pronouncement that the special mission and necessary vocation of the age consists in the bridging of the gulf that separates the privileged wealthy from the poor who need their help.

That the work of artistic creation should come at the expense of dedication to social mission is an impasse that Barrett Browning does not leave unresolved, however. After years in which each pursues individual goals, Aurora somewhat more successfully than Romney, they are reunited. Romney has come to understand the importance of the artist's vision in leading others to "comprehend / Humanity and so work humanly" (9.851–52), while Aurora has been led to acknowledge that she has taken too little care to assist Romney in his "dedication to the human need" (9.793). Ultimately, she realizes that, without great love, her life and art are incomplete: "Art is much, but love is more," she concludes (9.656). Both personal and social love are linked to that future shared work which they envision together, as Romney's concluding exhortation to Aurora makes clear:

> The world waits
> For help. Beloved, let us love so well,
> Our work shall still be better for our love,
> And still our love be sweeter for our work,
> And both commended, for the sake of each,
> By all true workers and true lovers born.
>
> (9.923–28)

From *Aurora Leigh*

[*From* Book 1]

I learnt much music—such as would have been   415
As quite impossible in Johnson's[1] day
As still it might be wished—fine sleights of hand
And unimagined fingering, shuffling off
The hearer's soul through hurricanes of notes
To a noisy Tophet;[2] and I drew . . . costumes   420
From French engravings, nereids[3] neatly draped
(With smirks of simmering godship)—I washed in
Landscapes from nature (rather say, washed out).
I danced the polka and Cellarius,[4]
Spun glass, stuffed birds, and modelled flowers in wax,   425
Because she[5] liked accomplishments in girls.
I read a score of books on womanhood
To prove, if women do not think at all,
They may teach thinking (to a maiden-aunt
Or else the author)—books that boldly assert   430
Their right of comprehending husband's talk

1. Samuel Johnson (1709–1784) was the most famous English literary figure of the latter eighteenth century. He was a lexicographer, poet, biographer, and essayist who was known for his curmudgeonly witticisms and epigrammic pronouncements offered on a variety of subjects. Scholars have identified in these lines a specific reference to Johnson's acerbic comment about the alleged difficulty of a performance that he had heard by a noted musician: "I would it had been impossible."

2. Tophet and Gehenna are Old Testament sites associated with idol worship and human sacrifice; in subsequent Christian literature, the words are used as substitutes for Hell.

3. Daughters of the sea god Nereus.

4. A particular form of the waltz.

5. Aurora's maiden aunt.

When not too deep, and even of answering
With pretty "may it please you," or "so it is"—
Their rapid insight and fine aptitude,
Particular worth and general missionariness,   435
As long as they keep quiet by the fire
And never say "no" when the world says "ay,"
For that is fatal—their angelic reach
Of virtue, chiefly used to sit and darn,
And fatten household sinners—their, in brief,   440
Potential faculty in everything
Of abdicating power in it: she owned
She liked a woman to be womanly,
And English women, she thanked God and sighed
(Some people always sigh in thanking God),   445
Were models to the universe. And last
I learnt cross-stitch, because she did not like
To see me wear the night with empty hands
A-doing nothing. So, my shepherdess
Was something after all (the pastoral saints   450
Be praised for 't), leaning lovelorn with pink eyes
To match her shoes, when I mistook the silks;
Her head uncrushed by that round weight of hat
So strangely similar to the tortoise-shell
Which slew the tragic poet.[6]
                    By the way,   455
The works of women are symbolical.
We sew, sew, prick our fingers, dull our sight,
Producing what? A pair of slippers, sir,
To put on when you're weary—or a stool
To stumble over and vex you . . . "curse that stool!"   460
Or else at best, a cushion, where you lean
And sleep, and dream of something we are not
But would be for your sake. Alas, alas!
This hurts most, this—that, after all, we are paid
The worth of our work, perhaps.   465

[*From* Book 2]

"Aurora,[7] let's be serious, and throw by
This game of head and heart. Life means, be sure,   130
Both heart and head—both active, both complete,

6. The fifth-century Greek tragedian Aeschylus was said to have died as the result of an eagle's having dropped a tortoise on his head.
7. The speaker is Romney Leigh, Aurora Leigh's cousin.

And both in earnest. Men and women make
The world, as head and heart make human life.[8]
Work man, work woman, since there's work to do
In this beleaguered earth, for head and heart,   135
And thought can never do the work of love:
But work for ends, I mean for uses, not
For such sleek fringes (do you call them ends,
Still less God's glory?) as we sew ourselves
Upon the velvet of those baldaquins[9]   140
Held 'twixt us and the sun. That book of yours,
I have not read a page of; but I toss
A rose up—it falls calyx[10] down, you see!
The chances are that, being a woman, young
And pure, with such a pair of large, calm eyes,   145
You write as well . . . and ill . . . upon the whole,
As other women. If as well, what then?
If even a little better . . . still, what then?
We want the Best in art now, or no art.
The time is done for facile settings up   150
Of minnow gods, nymphs here and tritons there;
The polytheists have gone out in God,
That unity of Bests. No best, no God!
And so with art, we say. Give art's divine,
Direct, indubitable, real as grief,   155
Or leave us to the grief we grow ourselves
Divine by overcoming with mere hope
And most prosaic patience. You, you are young
As Eve with nature's daybreak on her face,
But this same world you are come to, dearest coz,   160
Has done with keeping birthdays, saves her wreaths[11]

---

8. Compare the traditionally gendered roles that Tennyson has "the hard old king" of *The Princess* propound:

> but this is fixt
> As are the roots of earth and base of all;
> Man for the field and woman for the hearth:
> Man for the sword and for the needle she;
> *Man with the head and woman with the heart:*
> Man to command and woman to obey;
> All else confusion. (5.435–41) [Emphasis added]

That women had a more refined emotional sensitivity and greater capacity for love was as commonplace a nineteenth-century assumption as the belief that men were intellectually superior to women; compare Romney's subsequent assertion that woman is "nobler than the man" "in the use / And comprehension of what love is" (2.421–23).

9. Baldaquins (or baldachins) were canopies traditionally carried over important dignitaries or placed over altars or thrones.

10. The leafy outer covering of the flower.

11. Romney has found Aurora in the estate gardens on the morning of her twentieth birthday; he has come upon her as she is fashioning a poet's wreath for herself out of ivy leaves.

Figure 4.2. *Useless Embroidery*

The photograph *Useless Embroidery*, c. 1860, presents a telling image of the empty lives of many privileged women and offers a striking contrast to the misery of distressed needlewomen (see figures 3.2, 3.3, and 3.7).

> To hang upon her ruins—and forgets
> To rhyme the cry with which she still beats back
> Those savage, hungry dogs that hunt her down
> To the empty grave of Christ. The world's hard pressed;   165
> The sweat of labour in the early curse[12]
> Has (turning acrid in six thousand years)[13]
> Become the sweat of torture. Who has time,

12. That man should find labor difficult is the punishment pronounced by God upon Adam for man's sin; see Genesis 3:17–19. Many years later, when Aurora is finally reunited with him, Romney will define work as a privilege rather than as a curse:

> He cried, "True. After Adam, work was curse;
> The natural creature labours, sweats, and frets.
> But, after Christ, work turns to privilege,
> And henceforth, one with our humanity,
> The Six-day Worker working still in us
> Has called us freely to work on with Him
> In high companionship. So, happiest!
> I count that Heaven itself is only work
> To a surer issue. (8.717–25)

13. That the age of the earth was approximately six thousand years was a well-established tradition. Many Victorian readers accepted as valid the calculations of the seventeenth-century theologian Bishop James Ussher that the world was created in six days in 4004 B.C.E., some even believing in the more specific determination of one of Ussher's followers that it was during the morning of October 23, 4004 B.C.E., that the earth was made.

An hour's time . . . think!—to sit upon a bank
And hear the cymbal tinkle in white hands?   170
When Egypt's slain, I say, let Miriam sing!—
Before—where's Moses?"[14]

          "Ah, exactly that.
Where's Moses?—is a Moses to be found?
You'll seek him vainly in the bulrushes,[15]
While I in vain touch cymbals. Yet concede,   175
Such sounding brass[16] has done some actual good
(The application in a woman's hand,
If that were credible, being scarcely spoilt)
In colonising beehives."

          "There it is!—
You play beside a death-bed like a child,   180
Yet measure to yourself a prophet's place
To teach the living. None of all these things,
Can women understand. You generalise[17]
Oh, nothing—not even grief! Your quick-breathed hearts,
So sympathetic to the personal pang,   185
Close on each separate knife-stroke, yielding up
A whole life at each wound, incapable
Of deepening, widening a large lap of life
To hold the world-full woe. The human race
To you means, such a child, or such a man,   190
You saw one morning waiting in the cold,
Beside that gate, perhaps. You gather up
A few such cases, and when strong sometimes

14. Miriam was the sister of Moses and a prophetess; when Pharaoh and his soldiers, in pursuing the Israelites of the exodus, had drowned in the sea, Miriam took a timbrel and danced in celebration. Moses had earlier assumed the unwelcome and dangerous task of demanding that Pharaoh let the Israelites leave Egypt, and Moses had heroically led the people forth. See Exodus 7 through 15, especially 15. Romney suggests that poets may be acceptable to celebrate heroic labor *after* the struggle has been won but that, before such victory, a worker and leader rather than a poet is needed.

15. See Exodus 2.

16. For "sounding brass" as well as the cymbals of lines 170 and 175, see 1 Corinthians 13:1–2.

17. The inadequacy of personal compassionate response to individual suffering and the need for large-scale programs to redress pervasive social ills are the considerations that drive Romney's anger here. Romney would seem to anticipate the concerns that social historian Gertrude Himmelfarb, in her thoroughgoing study *Poverty and Compassion: The Moral Imagination of the Late Victorians,* finds distinctive of the activists of the latter part of the century:

    The driving mission of most of the late-Victorian reformers, philanthropists, and social critics was precisely to infuse a sense of proportion into the sentiments of compassion, to make compassion proportionate to and compatible with the proper ends of social policy. This is what Charles Booth most notably did in his survey of the London poor, when he insisted upon the importance of "proportion" in calculating the "arithmetic of woe"—the proportion of the "very poor" to the "poor" and the "comfortable" and the ratio of "misery" to "happiness" in the daily lives of the poor (5).

See the introduction to the selections from Charles Booth at the end of section 3.

Will write of factories and of slaves, as if
Your father were a negro, and your son   195
A spinner in the mills.[18] All's yours and you,
All, coloured with your blood, or otherwise
Just nothing to you. Why, I call you hard
To general suffering. Here's the world half blind
With intellectual light, half brutalised   200
With civilisation, having caught the plague
In silks from Tarsus, shrieking east and west
Along a thousand railroads, mad with pain
And sin too! . . . does one woman of you all
(You who weep easily) grow pale to see   205
This tiger shake his cage?—does one of you
Stand still from dancing, stop from stringing pearls,
And pine and die because of the great sum
Of universal anguish?—Show me a tear
Wet as Cordelia's,[19] in eyes bright as yours,   210
Because the world is mad. You cannot count,
That you should weep for this account, not you!
You weep for what you know. A red-haired child
Sick in a fever, if you touch him once,
Though but so little as with a finger-tip,   215
Will set you weeping; but a million sick . . .
You could as soon weep for the rule of three
Or compound fractions. Therefore, this same world
Uncomprehended by you, must remain
Uninfluenced by you.—Women as you are,   220
Mere women, personal and passionate,
You give us doting mothers, and perfect wives,
Sublime Madonnas, and enduring saints!
We get no Christ from you—and verily
We shall not get a poet, in my mind."   225

"With which conclusion you conclude" . . .
                                             "But this:
That you, Aurora, with the large live brow

___

18. Barrett Browning had written about both slavery and oppressive working conditions in factories. See the introduction to "The Cry of the Children" in part 2. The autobiographical elements in
Barrett Browning's depiction of Aurora are numerous, but it would be a misunderstanding to construe the heroine simply as a self-projection of the author.

19. In Shakespeare's *The Tragedy of King Lear,* Cordelia is the faithful, youngest daughter of Lear,
who foolishly disowns her and gives over the kingdom to her cruel sisters; when he subsequently is rejected by these other daughters and driven out to wander on the heath, he becomes mad. Rescued by
the attendants of a Cordelia newly returned to England, he lapses into unconsciousness, awakes to
find Cordelia weeping over him, and asks, "Be your tears wet? Yes, faith. I pray weep not" (4.7.70).

And steady eyelids, cannot condescend
To play at art, as children play at swords,
To show a pretty spirit, chiefly admired   230
Because true action is impossible.
You never can be satisfied with praise
Which men give women when they judge a book
Not as mere work but as mere woman's work,
Expressing the comparative respect   235
Which means the absolute scorn. 'Oh, excellent!
What grace, what facile turns, what fluent sweeps,
What delicate discernment . . . almost thought!
The book does honour to the sex, we hold.
Among our female authors we make room   240
For this fair writer, and congratulate
The country that produces in these times
Such women, competent to' . . . spell."
                                    "Stop there,"
I answered, burning through his thread of talk
With a quick flame of emotion—"You have read   245
My soul, if not my book, and argue well
I would not condescend . . . we will not say
To such a kind of praise (a worthless end
Is praise of all kinds) but to such a use
Of holy art and golden life. I am young,   250
And peradventure weak—you tell me so—
Through being a woman. And, for all the rest,
Take thanks for justice. I would rather dance
At fairs on tight-rope, till the babies dropped
Their gingerbread for joy—than shift the types   255
For tolerable verse, intolerable
To men who act and suffer. Better far
Pursue a frivolous trade by serious means,
Than a sublime art frivolously."
                                    "You,
Choose nobler work than either, O moist eyes   260
And hurrying lips and heaving heart! We are young
Aurora, you and I. The world—look round—
The world, we're come to late, is swollen hard
With perished generations and their sins:
The civiliser's spade grinds horribly   265
On dead men's bones, and cannot turn up soil
That's otherwise than fetid. All success
Proves partial failure; all advance implies
What's left behind; all triumph, something crushed
At the chariot-wheels; all government, some wrong: 270

And rich men make the poor, who curse the rich,
Who agonise together, rich and poor,
Under and over, in the social spasm
And crisis of the ages. Here's an age
That makes its own vocation! here we have stepped   275
Across the bounds of time! here's nought to see,
But just the rich man and just Lazarus,[20]
And both in torments, with a mediate gulf,
Though not a hint of Abraham's bosom. Who
Being man, Aurora, can stand calmly by   280
And view these things, and never tease his soul
For some great cure? No physic for this grief,
In all the earth and heavens too?"
                              "You believe
In God, for your part?—ay? that He who makes,
Can make good things from ill things, best from worst,   285
As men plant tulips upon dunghills when
They wish them finest?"
                              "True. A death-heat is
The same as life-heat, to be accurate,
And in all nature is no death at all,
As men account of death, so long as God   290
Stands witnessing for life perpetually,
By being just God. That's abstract truth, I know,
Philosophy, or sympathy with God:
But I, I sympathise with man, not God
(I think I was a man for chiefly this),   295
And when I stand beside a dying bed,
'Tis death to me. Observe—it had not much
Consoled the race of mastodons to know,
Before they went to fossil, that anon
Their place would quicken with the elephant: 300
They were not elephants but mastodons;
And I, a man, as men are now and not
As men may be hereafter, feel with men
In the agonizing present."
                              "Is it so,"
I said, "my cousin? is the world so bad,   305
While I hear nothing of it through the trees?
The world was always evil—but so bad?"

---

20. The story of the wealthy man and the abjectly poor Lazarus whom he ignores is told in Luke 16:19–31. Both men die, the wealthy man going to hell and Lazarus to "Abraham's bosom" (line 279). In these distinct afterworlds, the wealthy man can repent but not undo his hardness of heart, and Lazarus can offer no relief to the suffering the wealthy man undergoes.

"So bad, Aurora. Dear, my soul is gray
With poring over the long sum of ill;
So much for vice, so much for discontent,   310
So much for the necessities of power,
So much for the connivances of fear,
Coherent in statistical despairs
With such a total of distracted life . . .
To see it down in figures on a page,   315
Plain, silent, clear, as God sees through the earth
The sense of all the graves—that's terrible
For one who is not God, and cannot right
The wrong he looks on. May I choose indeed
But vow away my years, my means, my aims,   320
Among the helpers, if there's any help
In such a social strait? The common blood
That swings along my veins, is strong enough
To draw me to this duty."
               Then I spoke.
"I have not stood long on the strand of life,   325
And these salt waters have had scarcely time
To creep so high up as to wet my feet:
I cannot judge these tides—I shall, perhaps.
A woman's always younger than a man
At equal years, because she is disallowed   330
Maturing by the outdoor sun and air,
And kept in long clothes[21] past the age to walk.
Ah well, I know you men judge otherwise!
You think a woman ripens as a peach,
In the cheeks, chiefly. Pass it to me now;   335
I'm young in age, and younger still, I think,
As a woman. But a child may say amen
To a bishop's prayer and feel the way it goes,
And I, incapable to loose the knot
Of social questions, can approve, applaud   340
August compassion, Christian thoughts that shoot
Beyond the vulgar white[22] of personal aims.
Accept my reverence."
              There he glowed on me
With all his face and eyes. "No other help?"

21. Until they were well able to walk, both boys and girls wore, in the nineteenth century, long, dress-like apparel. Aurora suggests that, different from boys, girls and young women continue to be constrained by clothing that prevents their exerting themselves and exploring the world.

22. Different from certain common archery targets today, nineteenth-century targets had as their center a white rather than a dark circle.

Said he—"no more than so?"
                       "What help?" I asked.   345
"You'd scorn my help—as Nature's self, you say,
Has scorned to put her music in my mouth
Because a woman's. Do you now turn round
And ask for what a woman cannot give?"

"For what she only can, I turn and ask,"   350
He answered, catching up my hands in his,
And dropping on me from his high-eaved brow
The full weight of his soul—"I ask for love,
And that, she can; for life in fellowship
Through bitter duties—that, I know she can;   355
For wifehood—will she?"
                    "Now," I said, "may God
Be witness 'twixt us two!" and with the word,
Meseemed I floated into a sudden light
Above his stature—"am I proved too weak
To stand alone, yet strong enough to bear   360
Such leaners on my shoulder? poor to think,
Yet rich enough to sympathize with thought?
Incompetent to sing, as blackbirds can,
Yet competent to love, like HIM?"[23]
                         I paused;
Perhaps I darkened, as the lighthouse will   365
That turns upon the sea. "It's always so.
Anything does for a wife."
                      "Aurora, dear,
And dearly honoured,"—he pressed in at once
With eager utterance—"you translate me ill.
I do not contradict my thought of you   370
Which is most reverent, with another thought
Found less so. If your sex is weak for art
(And I who said so, did but honour you
By using truth in courtship), it is strong
For life and duty. Place your fecund heart   375
In mine, and let us blossom for the world
That wants love's colour in the gray of time.
My talk, meanwhile, is arid to you, ay,
Since all my talk can only set you where
You look down coldly on the arena-heaps   380
Of headless bodies, shapeless, indistinct!

23. God.

The Judgment-Angel[24] scarce would find his way
Through such a heap of generalised distress
To the individual man with lips and eyes,
Much less Aurora. Ah my sweet, come down,   385
And hand in hand we'll go where yours shall touch
These victims, one by one! till, one by one,
The formless, nameless trunk of every man
Shall seem to wear a head with hair you know,
And every woman catch your mother's face   390
To melt you into passion."[25]
                          "I am a girl,"
I answered slowly; "you do well to name
My mother's face. Though far too early, alas,
God's hand did interpose 'twixt it and me,
I know so much of love as used to shine   395
In that face and another.[26] Just so much;
No more indeed at all. I have not seen
So much love since, I pray you pardon me,
As answers even to make a marriage with
In this cold land of England. What you love,   400
Is not a woman, Romney, but a cause:
You want a helpmate, not a mistress, sir,
A wife to help your ends—in her no end!
Your cause is noble, your ends excellent,
But I, being most unworthy of these and that,   405
Do otherwise conceive of love. Farewell."

"Farewell, Aurora? you reject me thus?"
He said.
          "Sir, you were married long ago.
You have a wife already whom you love,
Your social history. Bless you both, I say.   410
For my part, I am scarcely meek enough
To be the handmaid of a lawful spouse.
Do I look a Hagar,[27] think you?"
                          "So you jest."

24. See Revelations 20:1–6.

25. Compare Romney's complaint that women fail to sympathize when they cannot conceive of suffering in personal terms: 2.179–225.

26. The face of Aurora's father. Both of Aurora's parents have died, her mother when Aurora was quite young, her father as she entered her teens.

27. Hagar was the handmaid of Sarah, Abraham's wife. Because she was so long childless, Sarah gave Hagar to Abraham to bear him children. After Hagar had given birth to a son, Ishmael, Sarah conceived and gave birth to her own son Isaac. At the time of Isaac's weaning, Abraham acquiesced to Sarah's demand that both Hagar and Ishmael be banished. See Genesis 16:1–16; 17:15–21; 21:1–21.

"Nay, so, I speak in earnest," I replied.
"You treat of marriage too much like, at least,   415
A chief apostle: you would bear with you
A wife . . . a sister . . . shall we speak it out?
A sister of charity."
                    "Then, must it be
Indeed farewell? And was I so far wrong
In hope and in illusion, when I took   420
The woman to be nobler than the man,
Yourself the noblest woman, in the use
And comprehension of what love is—love,
That generates the likeness of itself
Through all heroic duties? so far wrong,   425
In saying bluntly, venturing truth on love,
'Come, human creature, love and work with me'—
Instead of, 'Lady, thou art wondrous fair,
And, where the Graces walk before, the Muse
Will follow at the lightning of their eyes,   430
And where the Muse walks, lovers need to creep:
Turn round and love me, or I die of love.'"

With quiet indignation I broke in.
"You misconceive the question like a man,
Who sees a woman as the complement   435
Of his sex merely. You forget too much
That every creature, female as the male,
Stands single in responsible act and thought
As also in birth and death. Whoever says
To a loyal woman, 'Love and work with me,'   440
Will get fair answers if the work and love,
Being good themselves, are good for her—the best
She was born for. Women of a softer mood,
Surprised by men when scarcely awake to life,
Will sometimes only hear the first word, love,   445
And catch up with it any kind of work,
Indifferent, so that dear love go with it.
I do not blame such women, though, for love,
They pick much oakum;[28] earth's fanatics make
Too frequently heaven's saints. But *me* your work   450
Is not the best for—nor your love the best,
Nor able to commend the kind of work

---

28. Oakum is the term for the fiber that, picked from old ropes and mixed with tar or pitch, was used for caulking ships. Those who sought shelter in the workhouse, the "poor man's Bastille," were sometimes employed in picking oakum.

For love's sake merely. Ah, you force me, sir,
To be overbold in speaking of myself:
I too have my vocation—work to do,   455
The heavens and earth have set me since I changed
My father's face for theirs, and, though your world
Were twice as wretched as you represent,
Most serious work, most necessary work
As any of the economists'. Reform,   460
Make trade a Christian possibility,
And individual right no general wrong;
Wipe out earth's furrows of the Thine and Mine,
And leave one green for men to play at bowls,[29]
With innings for them all! . . . what then, indeed,   465
If mortals are not greater by the head
Than any of their prosperities? what then,
Unless the artist keep up open roads
Betwixt the seen and unseen—bursting through
The best of your conventions with his best,   470
The speakable, imaginable best
God bids him speak, to prove what lies beyond
Both speech and imagination? A starved man
Exceeds a fat beast: we'll not barter, sir,
The beautiful for barley.—And, even so,   475
I hold you will not compass your poor ends
Of barley-feeding and material ease,
Without a poet's individualism
To work your universal. It takes a soul,
To move a body: it takes a high-souled man,   480
To move the masses, even to a cleaner sty:
It takes the ideal, to blow a hair's-breadth off
The dust of the actual.—Ah, your Fouriers[30] failed,
Because not poets enough to understand
That life develops from within.—For me,   485
Perhaps I am not worthy, as you say,
Of work like this: perhaps a woman's soul
Aspires, and not creates: yet we aspire,
And yet I'll try out your perhapses, sir,
And if I fail . . . why, burn me up my straw   490
Like other false works—I'll not ask for grace;
Your scorn is better, cousin Romney. I

29. A term for either bowling or cricket, the latter game involving innings.
30. Charles Fourier (1772–1837) was a French socialist reformer who advocated regulated working communes as a remedy for the evils generated by uncontrolled economic competition.

Who love my art, would never wish it lower
To suit my stature. I may love my art.
You'll grant that even a woman may love art,   495
Seeing that to waste true love on anything
Is womanly, past question."
                          I retain
The very last word which I said that day,
As you the creaking of the door, years past,
Which let upon you such disabling news   500
You ever after have been graver. He,
His eyes, the motions in his silent mouth,
Were fiery points on which my words were caught,
Transfixed for ever in my memory
For his sake, not their own. And yet I know   505
I did not love him . . . nor he me . . . that's sure . . .
And what I said, is unrepented of,
As truth is always. Yet . . . a princely man!—
If hard to me, heroic for himself!
He bears down on me through the slanting years,   510
The stronger for the distance. If he had loved,
Ay, loved me, with that retributive face . . .
I might have been a common woman now
And happier, less known and less left alone,
Perhaps a better woman after all,   515
With chubby children hanging on my neck
To keep me low and wise.[31] Ah me, the vines
That bear such fruit, are proud to stoop with it.
The palm stands upright in a realm of sand.

---

31. There is the echo here of Raphael's advice to Adam to "be lowlie wise" (*Paradise Lost* 8.173), but more pertinent may be the evocation of Milton in Wordsworth's "Ode to Duty": "Give unto me, made lowly wise, / The spirit of self-sacrifice." When, many years later, Aurora and Romney are reunited, she upbraids herself for having been arrogant in her dismissal of his proposal and wrongheaded in her self-willed insistence upon her career as a poet (9.601–714).

This article appeared in the *Saturday Review* for November 12, 1859, in response to a paper by Bessie Rayner Parkes (1829–1925) titled "The Market for Educated Female Labour" published in *The English Woman's Journal* on November 1. In her essay, originally delivered at a meeting of the National Association for the Promotion of Social Science, Parkes, a well-known leader of the women's rights movement, analyzed the situation of the thousands of middle-class women forced to earn a living who had turned to teaching as the most respectable profession open to them. She observed that, since so few jobs were available to women, the teaching field had become overcrowded and salaries had remained low. To demonstrate the extent of the problem, Parkes cited figures and case histories from reports of the Governesses' Benevolent Institution (founded in 1843). Parkes argued that rather than naively assuming that their daughters will be provided for permanently through marriage, middle-class fathers should invest in their daughters' futures through savings plans or life insurance or by educating them to pursue a career other than teaching. Parkes suggested such positions as telegraph clerks, bookkeepers, business women, and social workers. No doubt many readers of the *Saturday Review* would have sided with the author of the following unsigned essay whose alternately condescending and stern tone reveals contempt for new answers to the "Woman Question."

Queen Bees or Working Bees?

Miss Bessie Parkes, in a paper read before the Social Science Congress,[1] and since published in the *Englishwoman's Journal*—and subsequently recommended

---

1. Parkes was one of the first women to speak before the National Association for the Promotion of Social Science, an organization which exerted considerable influence on public policy and social reform from 1857 to 1885.

by the same authority which has also adopted Dr. Cumming and the so-called School of the Prophets[2]—has, either consciously or unconsciously, committed an ordinary argumentative fallacy. She has mixed up two or three subjects between which not the slightest connexion subsists; and she suggests that the arguments for the one position support the others, only because she chooses to place them together. The point which it has been the labour of her life to establish is that which she places first in her recent argument—viz., that it is the duty of middle-class parents to train their daughters to some useful art, however humble. She argues, secondly, that they ought not to consider tuition more genteel than any other honest calling; and, thirdly, that it is their duty to insure their lives for the benefit of their daughters. Now, we might urge, and not unreasonably, that this last duty makes the first superfluous. If all women in the reformed social state are to be self-supporting (which is Miss Parkes' first position), the motive and duty in parents to provide for them after death (which is her third) ceases. Given, all women trained to a useful art and capable of exercising it successfully, we cannot imagine any state of things which would more reasonably release parents from all solicitude as to their daughters. The very notion of life insurance implies making a provision for those who have no visible means or hopes of supporting themselves. The very notion of all women being trained to work implies that they have means, and hopes elevated to a certainty, of independence. And be it observed that Miss Parkes does not urge that these duties are alternative, but correlative.[3] Make your daughters watchmakers and clerks, *and* leave them a provision out of your savings. She says that both duties are equally imperative and both equally neglected by parents.

We do not dispute the obligation of life insurance. We only say that this consideration has nothing to do with Miss Parkes' main subject; though, were it worth while, we should join issue here on the matter of fact. Had Miss Parkes merely urged that life insurance might with advantage be more generally used, we should not object to the propriety of such a hint. But we do say that, in point of fact, life insurance is largely adopted, and, in nine cases out of ten, in order to insure provision for those very parties whom Miss Parkes complains—or else why her homily?—that fathers systematically neglect. For one case in which a middle-class man effects a life insurance for his sons, there are ninety-and-nine in which he makes this provision solely and exclusively for those widows and female orphans whose hard estate Miss Parkes bewails.

Then as to her second point—that governesses are badly paid, and often get into difficulties—this is only an indirect mode of urging the proposition, which nobody disputes, that female education is very bad. Governesses get little, because the

2. Clergyman John Cumming (1807–1881) was best known for his published interpretations of prophecy. He wrote a number of letters to the *Times*, signing himself "Beemaster," a reference to his hobby of beekeeping.

3. Contrary to what her critic maintains, Parkes does not contend that parents should educate their daughters *and* make them financially secure, but she does declare that parents are "sacredly and morally bound" to do "one or the other." At the close of her essay, she plainly states, "Let each father consider how he can best provide, whether by giving her a special training, by saving money, or by insurance."

wares they sell are worthless. This is a mere matter of political economy, and it requires no social lecturess to urge the need of improving the education of girls. If governesses had a better education to impart, they would get a better price for it.[4] Their pay is next to nothing, because their services are next to nothing. This journal has not been very backward in urging the deficiencies of female educators; though we certainly are not eager for extending the Oxford middle-class system of examinations so as to include lady candidates for the degree of certificated associate—a plan which Miss Parkes recommends as a remedy for an evil which we admit to the full.[5] To have better governesses, however, they need not be fewer, which is Miss Parkes' suggestion; but if all governesses were better, all would get better stipends, of which Miss Parkes does not seem to be aware. She seeks to raise the average standard of skill by limiting the number of workmen—an economical fallacy which she shares with the trades now on strike. For it comes to much the same thing whether, with the bricklayers, you say no man shall be skilful beyond a certain point, or whether, with Miss Parkes, you say you must only employ trained workwomen. In either case, the thing sought is to limit the amount of competing labour; and it would be a just application of Miss Parkes' argument to urge that there ought to be none but the best trained masons and engineers, and that the inferior hands should turn to agriculture and soldiering. Miss Parkes is perfectly right in saying that improved female education would be a great social gain; but, having stumbled on a truth, she misses its value. Its value would be to raise the governesses' wages—not, as she thinks, to diminish the numbers of governesses. Female education wants great and substantial improvements; but to admit this is no step whatever towards Miss Parkes' real conclusion, that every woman should be taught a trade.

She argues thus:—If every woman could marry, it might perhaps be best to leave the bread-winning department to the man, and to submit to the conclusion to which even Tennyson's Princess[6] was driven, that woman's sphere is to be provided for, and not to provide. But, as things are, there are a vast number of women who never get husbands, or who lose them without jointures or life insurances; and what is to be done for them? Miss Parkes' answer is—Educate every woman on the assumption that she will never get a husband. Now, it would be quite enough to dispose of the whole question by reducing it to this very elementary conception. Our answer is summary, therefore—that, as the chances

4. See articles elsewhere in this anthology by Dinah Mulock Craik, Emily Davies, and Josephine Butler, who make a similar point about the poor qualifications of many women to be governesses and who, consequently, argue for improved education for girls. Queen's College, established in 1848, and Bedford College for Women, 1849, focused on preparing teachers.

5. While, around mid-century, Parkes and other feminists recommended opening examinations to women, it was Emily Davies, who founded Girton College at Cambridge in 1869, who led the aggressive campaign to permit women to take examinations and receive university degrees. Not until 1881 were women formally admitted to examinations at Cambridge (some took them informally beginning in the 1860s) and not until 1884 at Oxford. Some institutions (Manchester New College, St. Andrew's, and London University) granted degrees to women beginning in the 1870s; the two major universities, however, delayed awarding degrees to women until the twentieth century.

6. Ida, the feminist heroine of Tennyson's 1847 poem, *The Princess*. See excerpts in this section.

are very much in favour of every woman getting a husband,[7] there is really no call upon us even to entertain the other hypothesis. But we say much more than this. We say that the greatest of social and political duties is to encourage marriage. The interest of a State is to get as many of its citizens married as possible. The equality of the sexes demonstrates this to be a law of nature. And we add that man, in European communities, has deliberately adopted the view that, as much as possible, women should be relieved from the necessity of self-support. The measure of civilization is the maximum at which this end is attained in any given community or nation. Women labourers are a proof of a barbarous and imperfect civilization. We should be retrograding in the art and science of civilization were more women encouraged to be self-supporters. And the reason of this is plain enough. Wherever women are self-supporters, marriage is, *ipso facto,* discouraged. The factory population is proof of this. In the manufacturing districts women make worse wives and worse helpmates than where they are altogether dependent on the man.[8] And where there are fewer marriages there is more vice. Miss Parkes says, make your women, as a rule, capable to support themselves—"teach every daughter some useful art." The prevailing theory is, let as many women as possible be dependent on marriage. Let woman be trained to this as the end of her being. And though it is not seldom more roughly expressed, there is the highest social wisdom in it. Distressed governesses and distressed workwomen are social anomalies, but the social fabric is for the greatest happiness of the greatest number.[9] And this is attained by making marriage the rule. In a community where all the women were clerks, telegraph-workers, watchmakers, and book-keepers, the inducements to marriage would be lessened on either side. Men do not like, and would not seek, to mate with an independent factor, who at any time could quit—or who at all times would be tempted to neglect—the tedious duties of training and bringing up children, and keeping the tradesmen's bills, and mending the linen, for the more lucrative returns of the desk or counter. It is not the interest of States, and it is not therefore true social policy, to encourage the existence, as a rule, of women who are other than entirely dependent on man as well for subsistence as for protection and love.

Possibly Miss Parkes may reply with the old story of the man and the lion. All our laws are man-made laws, and our social theories are of the male manufacture. This is no reason why it should be so, she and the Women's Rights conventions[10]

---

7. This optimistic statement runs counter to contemporary statistics. According to the 1851 census, women outnumbered men by half a million in Great Britain, and one million women were unmarried. Later in the paragraph, when the writer mentions the "equality of the sexes," the reference is to the roughly equivalent numbers of men and women, not to social or political equality.

8. A nearly universal claim made in government reports and social commentaries; see selections from Friedrich Engels in part 3.

9. The author here refers to the Utilitarian philosophy which promoted the use of reason to determine what would produce the greatest practical good, or utility, for the greatest number of people.

10. Perhaps the writer has in mind the campaigns for social, legal, and political reform organized by Bessie Rayner Parkes, Emily Davies, Barbara Bodichon (1827–1891), and other feminists who came to be known as the Langham Place Circle, in reference to the location of the offices of the *English Woman's Journal,* which they established.

would reply. It is not, we admit; but—and it really comes to this after all—Miss Parkes' grievance lies deeper, and her complaint is with human nature. Lady Psyche[11] found the same fault; and the remedy is the same. The answer to these theories is, fall in love and get a husband. It is a prosaic way of putting it; but this, according to the Apostle,[12] common sense, and the verdict of mankind, is the long and short of it. "Let them marry." "But they can't." More's the pity, we say; but we are not disposed to innovate on society, and to make that more difficult which already is too difficult. Miss Parkes not only argues as though every woman were a possible old maid and a contingent widow, but contends that her education is to be framed to meet this, which is only an accident of life. Married life is woman's profession; and to this life her training—that of dependence—is modelled. Of course by not getting a husband, or losing him, she may find that she is without resources. All that can be said of her is, she has failed in business; and no social reform can prevent such failures. The mischance of the distressed governess and unprovided widow, is that of every insolvent tradesman. He is to be pitied; but all the Social Congresses in the world will not prevent the possibility of a mischance in the shape of broken-down tradesmen, old maids, or widows. Each and all are frequently left without resources; and each and all always will be left without resources; but it would be just as reasonable to demand that every boy should be taught two or three professions because he may fail in one, as it is to argue that all our social habits should be changed because one woman in fifty—or whatever the statistics are—is a spinster or widow without any resources. We fear we are driven, in spite of Miss Parkes and a writer in the *Times*, to the old-fashioned view, that it is better for all parties—men and women, for the State and for society—that women should not, as a rule, be taught some useful art, and so be rendered independent of the chances of life. We do not want our women to be androgynous. We had rather do what we can for the Governesses' Institution, and, if need be, subscribe to a dozen more such institutions, than realize Miss Parkes' Utopia of every middle-class girl taught some useful art.

> For woman is not undevelopt man,
> But diverse: could we make her as the man,
> Sweet love were slain: his dearest bond is this,
> Not like to like, but like in difference.[13]

11. Psyche was the classical goddess of the soul. As a mortal, Psyche suffers as a result of overwhelming curiosity and disobedience, but ultimately she becomes the wife of Cupid and is granted immortality by Jupiter. The Lady Psyche to whom the writer of the article refers is the young widow who, in Tennyson's *The Princess*, delivers to students of Princess Ida's academy of women a lecture concerning the history of male domination in culture and politics.

12. Paul gives directions concerning marriage in 1 Corinthians 7.

13. Tennyson, *The Princess* 7.259–62. See excerpts from *The Princess* in this section.

EMILY DAVIES

E MILY DAVIES (1830–1921) became interested in promoting the rights of women early in her life. Davies's efforts on behalf of the advancement of women included establishment of a women's employment agency, support of Elizabeth Garrett Anderson's efforts to become a physician, the editing of *The English Woman's Journal,* and delivery to John Stuart Mill of the first women's suffrage petition for presentation to Parliament. Davies did much to improve the education of girls at all levels and, in 1869, founded Girton, the first women's college at Cambridge. Davies's most significant publications include *The Higher Education of Women* (1866) and *Thoughts on Some Questions Relating to Women, 1860–1908* (1910), from which the following two selections are taken.

In "Letters Addressed to a Daily Paper at Newcastle-upon-Tyne, 1860," Davies addresses the general issue of women's work. The first letter is concerned with the evils of idleness, the second with a discussion of worthwhile professions that might be opened to women, the third with answers to the arguments against women's working.

From *Thoughts on Some Questions Relating to Women, 1860–1908*

Letters addressed to a Daily Paper at Newcastle-upon-Tyne, 1860

I

In a recent charge to the Grand Jury of Hull, the Recorder, Mr. S. Warren, expressed himself as follows:—"Human ingenuity could hardly more admirably occupy itself, than in discovering and devising new and creditable modes of occupation for females, especially the younger ones, of the middle classes. The sufferings and exposure to dangers of the worst kind—the griefs and anxieties of overburdened families, which might thus be averted, would richly reward a persevering philanthropist." In these words Mr. Warren gave utterance to thoughts that are at this time occupying the minds of many; and yet probably, few of us have considered so seriously as the question deserves, what young women are actually doing. We take for granted in a general way that they are doing something, or might be, if they liked, but we really do not know what. The fact is, that those who are not compelled by necessity to labour for their maintenance, are discouraged—partly by conventional prejudices, and partly by the difficulty of finding employment suited to their powers—from applying themselves to settled work of any kind. Take the case of a young girl just entering, or rather who should be just entering, upon the business of life. She has spent a few years at school, has learnt the rudiments of French, can play on the piano, and is tolerably skilful with her needle. She can read and write—whether she can also spell, and work a sum correctly and quickly, is doubtful, as too many parents are more anxious for proficiency in what are called accomplishments than in these fundamentals which make no show. She is released from the wholesome discipline of school, and thrown suddenly upon her own resources. Her mother probably expects her to help a little in household matters, which occupy her for, perhaps, two hours of the day, and the rest of her time is thrown upon her hands, to spend as she likes. Can we wonder that her days are passed in laborious trifling, and her nights in dissipation? Far be it from me to say that she does nothing. She would probably tell you that she is so busy she really does not know what to do first. There are notes that *must* be written, calls that *must* be returned, visits that *must* be paid, and a hundred other *musts*, all of which would vanish in a moment before the breath of a real necessity. And so the months go round. If she marries, the arrangement answers tolerably well—not too well, for such a life of busy idleness is not the best preparation for the cares and responsibilities of a wife and mother. But if she does not marry? Or if, through misfortune or by the sickness, or death, or misconduct, of her husband, the duty of providing for herself and her children devolves upon her, what can she do? Relations and kind friends take counsel together, and after much deliberation it is decided that Miss or Mrs. ____ must either find a situation as governess, or keep a school. She is not fond of teaching, it is true, and she has had no training for it, and the little she once knew she has forgotten; but, after all, people must adapt themselves to their circumstances, and if her terms are low enough she will get pupils. Of the laborious days with scanty earnings, implied in such a decision, it is not necessary here to speak; the hardships of governess-life are proverbial. But there is another aspect of the question which has, I think, received less attention than it deserves. I refer to the injury done to children by putting their education into unskilful hands. It seems to be taken for granted that anybody can educate, and so the honourable office of training the young comes to be looked upon as a mere money-getting speculation, in which puffing, canvassing, and other tricks of trade, are unblushingly practised. The few who take a higher view of their duties, who look upon their office as a sacred calling, not to be lightly dealt with, are confounded with the ignorant and unfit, and our children suffer. And this, not because people are unwilling to pay for the education of their children, but because women who have no vocation for teaching are forced by necessity into a profession for which they are unsuited. It may be fairly objected, indeed, that parents have the matter in their own hands, and are not obliged to give their children into the charge of persons whom they consider incompetent. But if a reasonable discrimination were at all commonly practised, how deplorable would be the condition of many governesses! Their one resource would be taken from them, and beggary or starvation would be their only alternative.

The case of unmarried women "not obliged to do anything," is, at first sight, and in many respects, far less urgent and distressing. But in one point of view, those who are compelled to work have the advantage. The spur of hard necessity, at least, brings out some energy, and awakens some activity, while those whose daily bread is brought to them, without a thought on their part, having no pressing motive to exertion, and being unable to "discover or devise" any "new and credit-able mode of occupation for females," in too many cases merely fill up their time as best they may, in the practice of the various arts known under the general name of fancy-work. The labourers are standing idle in the market-place, because no man hath hired them.[1] I am aware that I shall here be met with the objection, that in a community like our own, and in most large towns, the difficulty is not to find work, but to find labourers; that there is abundant employment for all, in visiting the poor, in the management of schools, and in other works of charity. In answer to this, I beg leave to submit, that all women are not made to be philanthropists. It would be considered unreasonable to expect that all men should take Holy Orders, or enrol themselves as town missionaries, and it is equally unreasonable to expect that all women should engage in similar work. Indeed, as a general rule, young unmarried women are not the best fitted for the office of counselling their neigh-bours, and it is by this class that the discipline of some steady work is most needed. I do not say that they are always conscious of the want. People in general, I fancy, do pretty much what is expected of them, and so long as it is the theory of society, that the whole duty of woman is to "go gracefully idle," it is not likely that ordinary women will disturb the peace of their neighbours by passionate appeals for work. But the want is not the less pressing where it is not felt, and society cannot afford to disregard it. It is usual to treat this as a mere woman's question, and we hear now and then of women's rights and women's wrongs. I believe the best women think more of duties and responsibilities than of rights and wrongs, and care com-paratively little for any "right" but that of giving their best in the service of God and humanity, by the free development of whatever capacities of usefulness they possess; and if, by our narrow conventional notions and social prejudices, we deny this just claim, it is not women only who are wronged. They may indeed suffer

1. Matthew 20:1–16.

from what Coleridge calls "the obscure trouble of a baffled instinct,"[2] but they do not suffer alone. That which God hath joined, man cannot put asunder:

> "The woman's cause is man's; they rise or sink
> Together, dwarf'd or godlike, bond or free;
> For she that out of Lethe scales with man
> The shining steps of Nature, shares with man
> His nights, his days, moves with him to one goal,
> Stays all the fair young planet in her hands—
> If she be small, slight-natured, miserable,
> How shall men grow?"[3]

Frivolity is not harmless. So far as its influence extends, it works for evil, and the absence of any definite settled occupation, about which it is not a mere matter of choice from hour to hour whether to do it or leave it undone, is in itself calculated to encourage a trifling habit of mind, injurious not only to the women who indulge in it, but to every one with whom they have to do. To bring about a more healthy state of things is surely an object worth trying for. The means by which we may hope to attain it, will make the subject of a future letter.

II

In considering the various means by which the present condition of women may be improved, the most obvious is that of extending the range of occupations open to them. It is manifestly necessary, however, to make at the same time some change in the mode of their education, as they are unable, under the system at present pursued, to accept a position, even when offered, in which special preparatory training is required. These two operations must, so to speak, dovetail together, and, this being the case, it is clear that the task must be accomplished by the general public, not by any particular class alone. It has been said, indeed, that women have the matter in their own hands; and I have little doubt that if a large number of women were to unite in an energetic demand for an enlarged sphere of work, backing up their claim with satisfactory evidence of fitness, they would meet with ready attention, and their admission into many offices from which they are now excluded would be a question only of time. The superior cheapness of their labour would recommend them to employers uninfluenced by any higher motive. But it seems to be forgotten, that women are, happily, not a class apart. They are acted upon by all the influences which give an impress to public opinion, and *young* women are especially bound by the conventional usages of society. It is, therefore, as unlikely as it would be undesirable, that women should unite in a separate movement, even for the attainment of an object in which they are the

2. Samuel Taylor Coleridge (1772–1834) was a Romantic poet and essayist. The phrase is taken from *The Friend*, vol. 3, essay 11 (1818).

3. Tennyson, *The Princess* 7.243–50. See the selections from the poem in this section.

parties more immediately interested.[4] I say immediately, for, as has been before remarked, the whole community is concerned, more or less directly, in the solution of this question. There is one class, however, with whom rests the largest share of the power, as well as of the responsibility. I refer to the parents of daughters, and to them I would appeal. Let them well understand, once for all, that their daughters, as they grow up, will have faculties to be developed, understandings to be cultivated and turned to account, and that it is the duty of parents to help and guide them in the choice of a field for the useful exercise of their talents. Let them pass under review the various departments of labour hitherto unoccupied by women, and carefully weigh the advantages and disadvantages of each particular sphere of exertion, always bearing in mind, that, in choosing a trade or profession for a girl, there is to be considered not only what she is able to do, but what will be most useful to her hereafter, should she be called upon to fulfil the duties of a wife and mother. The guidance of a family is a calling which will never become obsolete, and whose importance should never be overlooked. Let us consider whether there are not some occupations, the training for which would help women to do their duty in any state of life, be it married or single, into which it should please God to call them.

In Mr. Ward's Trades' Directory for Newcastle I find enumerated no less than 320 different trades and professions. Of these, many are manifestly unsuited to women; others are equally inappropriate to men. There remains a considerable proportion which might with propriety be pursued by both sexes.

To begin with what may be looked upon as the highest class in the social scale—that of owners of landed property. Not many women are to be found in this category, and among the few, still fewer retain the management of their affairs in their own hands. It is generally confided to a brother or uncle, or in default of any male relation, an agent is employed. Sometimes the deputy does his work well, sometimes not. In either case, the really responsible person is kept idle, forfeiting the benefit of the moral and intellectual education which the possession of property ought to imply, out of deference to the received idea that women "do not understand business." It is indeed true that many women do not, but is it also true that they cannot understand business? In the few instances in which the experiment has been tried, experience seems to prove the contrary. One instance will doubtless occur to many of your readers, of a lady in our own locality, of high rank and noble birth, who, being in the order of Providence left a widow in the possession of large estates, including some of the most extensive collieries in the North of England, thought it no shame to accept the responsibilities thus devolving upon her, and who has discharged the duties of her stewardship with a zeal and perseverance, and a conscientious regard to the best interests of those connected with her, well worthy of imitation, as those who have the best opportunities of knowing can testify. Other examples on a smaller scale might be adduced—all tending to

---

4. John Stuart Mill makes a similar point about the pressure exerted on women by tradition and popular opinion. See selections from *The Subjection of Women* in this section.

prove that women have no natural incapacity for business, provided only that they have been trained to habits of accuracy and order—habits which can never be useless in any condition of life.

Among the learned professions, that of medicine might be advantageously practised by both men and women. It is an art for which many women have a marked natural predilection, showing itself in their eagerness to prescribe for their friends and neighbours. They seem determined to be doctors, whether we will or no, and the only question to be decided is, Shall they be ignorant empirics or thoroughly-educated practitioners? We laugh at their fancy for doctoring, as a harmless weakness: is it not rather a divinely implanted instinct which we should do well to cultivate and improve? I believe that in imparting to a young woman a sound scientific medical education we should be bestowing a gift which would be of infinite value, whatever might be her lot in life. If she should marry, such a knowledge of medicine would enable her to prescribe wisely for her children and servants; if she should remain single, she would be free to exercise her talent for the benefit of women and children in general. There is no doubt that, as a rule, women would prefer the services of physicians of their own sex; and a well-qualified practitioner would have plenty of patients. But there are at present great and almost insuperable difficulties in the way of obtaining the necessary education in England. It is a fact, I believe, that the only female physician legally registered in this country—Elizabeth Blackwell, M.D.—was obliged to obtain the greater part of her instruction elsewhere, and, though herself an Englishwoman, she is indebted to an American college for her degree.[5] There is reason to hope, however, that the prejudices of medical authorities are gradually giving way, and that ere long they will be prepared to aid women in the acquirement of a thorough knowledge of a science which, as mothers and nurses, they are already so frequently called upon to practise.

In passing from the professions to the counting-house and manufactory, we find that the question, Have women a place here—has already been solved in individual cases. Large concerns have prospered under the direction of women, and it may be considered as proved by experience that it is possible for a woman to manage a business without injury to her "distinctive womanhood."[6] It is certainly not easy to see why it should be unfeminine for a girl to sit in her father's office, under his immediate eye (and protection if needed), gradually acquiring experience which may, in process of time, when she arrives at years of discretion, enable her to take his place and relieve him of the anxiety which so often presses upon loving fathers, who feel themselves growing old with a family inadequately provided for. Nor would her time have been thrown away, looked upon as a preparation for married life. Though as a wife she would cease to work in the counting-house, the habit of work and the experience in business would make her more able to admin-

5. Elizabeth Blackwell received her medical degree from Geneva College in New York in 1849. See introduction to "Medicine as a profession for women" immediately following.
6. Tennyson, *The Princess* 7.258.

ister the affairs of her household, and would keep her from being a helpless burden in case of misfortune or widowhood. It ought to be understood, however, that a daughter should be paid for her services, like any other clerk, according to their value. A mere dilettante "helping papa a little with his accounts," would be no discipline; it would be only one more added to the many expedients already in use for killing a girl's time.

The trades may be divided into two departments, that of production and that of retail. It would be difficult to mention any trade in which a woman could not sell as well as a man, provided she has the necessary knowledge of book-keeping, and a capacity, to be acquired by experience, of judging of the quality of her goods. The employment of shop-women is becoming more common every day, and it is probable that before many years elapse, women will also be admitted to the management of shops, especially of some which seem to be their peculiar province, such as those of drapers, hosiers, &c. But the manufacturing department is much less accessible. It is scarcely credible, though I am afraid true, that at this moment it would be useless to ask a respectable hairdresser to take a female apprentice. And yet, surely, of all arts, that of cutting and curling ladies' hair, and manufacturing frizettes,[7] is the least masculine. I believe that, with a few exceptions, there would be a similar reluctance on the part of chemists and druggists to initiate a female apprentice into the mysteries of their craft, though as a sort of scientific cookery, if I may be allowed the expression, it would not seem out of place in female hands.[8] The experiment of a printing office, entirely managed by women, has been tried in London, and is thoroughly successful.[9] Carving and gilding, enamelling, and other arts in which manual skill is chiefly required, have also been proposed. It would occupy too much space to enumerate all the branches of manufacture which might occupy the hands and brains of women, and it is unnecessary to pursue this part of the subject farther. I am aware that many objections, reasonable and unreasonable, may be urged against the carrying out of the foregoing suggestions. I have purposely avoided referring to these objections in passing, feeling that they are too numerous and too serious to be dismissed with a casual notice. I therefore propose to consider them separately in a final communication.

III

The arguments brought forward against the employment of women in fields of labour hitherto closed against them, are so various, and in some instances, so confused and mutually contradictory, that it is somewhat difficult to state them fairly. I believe, however, that almost all the current objections are based upon one

7. A curled fringe of hair, usually worn on the forehead.

8. In "The Education and Employment of Women" (1868), reprinted in this section, Josephine Butler discusses continued opposition to female apothecaries.

9. The Victoria Press, founded in 1860 by feminist Emily Faithfull (1835–1895), printed the *English Woman's Journal* and the *Transactions* of the National Association for the Promotion of Social Science. Queen Victoria ultimately made Faithfull the Printer and Publisher in Ordinary to Her Majesty.

or other of these two assumptions: either, that the proposed changes are undesirable in an economical point of view; or, that they are objectionable on moral and social grounds. To begin with the first class. It is said that the labour market is already amply supplied, and that by the introduction of more workers, the rate of wages would be lowered, by which the whole community would suffer. If this were so, it would at least be fair that all should suffer alike, and not that, as now, the heaviest share of the burden should be borne by the weaker sex. But is not the whole argument based upon a fallacy? It seems to be forgotten that whether women work or not, they must exist, and if they are not allowed to labour with their hands the thing that is good, they must be burdensome to society. Nothing is saved by keeping them inactive, and the produce of their labour is lost. No man in his senses would keep two or three of his sons doing nothing, in order to give the rest a better chance of getting on; yet this would be as reasonable as to refuse work to women lest there should not be enough left for men. If the labour market should become overstocked, it would be necessary to seek fresh outlets; and it seems likely that the colonies will supply openings for both men and women during many years to come. I do not think, however, that the admission of women into certain trades and professions, from which they are now excluded, would perceptibly affect the general rate of wages. It should be borne in mind that female workers would be continually drafted off by marriage, and that consequently the number of additional competitors would not be very formidable.

This brings me to another argument, which is so reasonable that I am anxious to give it full consideration. It is urged that as, in the great majority of cases, women would give up their business on entering upon that other business of marriage, it is not worth while to throw away upon them an expensive preparation for anything else. I reply, that the training of clerks is not expensive. They learn by experience, for which they do not pay in money. Capital is no doubt required to set up in trade, but even that expenditure could scarcely be looked upon as thrown away, as it is generally easy to dispose of a business, supposing there is no other member of the family to succeed to it. The money spent in preparing for the medical profession is sunk, but a few years of practice would probably repay the actual cost, and to the mother of a family it would, to a great extent, be made up by saving the expense of a family doctor. The Rev. Charles Simeon[10] is reported to have said to a friend, "If you have a thousand pounds to give your son, put it in his head rather than in his pocket." The advice is equally applicable to the case of daughters. Give them an education which in case of need they can turn to some profitable account, rather than invest the savings destined for their use in the Funds,[11] or in joint-stock banks, those attractive but dangerous concerns, whose downfall from time to time brings ruin on hundreds of helpless women.

The objectors to an extension of the sphere of women, on moral and social grounds, take a different line of argument. It is contended by some that a certain

10. Associated with the "Low Church" movement within the Anglican faith at Cambridge University, Rev. Charles Simeon (1759–1836) urged the training of Evangelical clergymen.

11. Davies is probably referring to the Consolidated Fund, a mutual fund that from 1751 owned the bonds of the national debt. This Fund was actually a very secure investment.

degree of helplessness in women is not only becoming but useful, as a stimulus to exertion in men. This is scarcely a fair argument, unless it could be proved that it is also good for women to sit with folded hands admiring the activity of men. I believe, however, that it is in itself without foundation. Single men do not feel stimulated by the vague knowledge that there are a good many women in the world requiring to be supported, and married men would in any case have their families to provide for. A fear has indeed been expressed that, if women had any- thing else to do, they would be unwilling to marry, and a diminution in the number of marriages (justly regarded as a serious evil), would ensue.[12] But those who entertain such an apprehension must surely look upon matrimony as a very unhappy estate. If women can only be driven into it by *ennui*, or as a means of earning a livelihood, how is it that men are willing to marry? Are the advantages all on their side? The experience of happy wives and mothers forbids such a supposi- tion. It is likely, on the contrary, that, by making women more capable, the number of marriages would be increased, as many men would be glad to marry, who are now deterred from doing so by prudential considerations.

There remains one more objection, which, I believe, lies at the root of all. It is averred that "public life" is injurious to women; that they are meant for the do- mestic circle; and that, though we are bound to sympathise with, and relieve to the extent of our ability, cases of individual suffering, we must on no account interfere with the law of nature, which has made home, and home only, woman's sphere. It is most true that no advantages, real or apparent, to be gained in public life would compensate for the loss of the domestic virtues; but does it necessarily follow that, if women took a more active part in the business of the world, they would there- fore cease to care for home? Let us look at this bugbear—this *bête-noire*[13] called "public life"—fairly in the face. What is it we mean by it? Is there any woman living who does not go more or less into public; and what is it that makes the difference between justifiable and unjustifiable publicity? Probably no woman in the three kingdoms leads a more public life than the Queen, yet it may be questioned whether a more admirable wife and mother is to be found among her subjects.[14] The work of a medical practitioner is scarcely more public than that of a district visitor;[15] the head of a manufacturing firm may lead as private a life as the head of a millinery establishment; the business of a chemist and druggist is no more public

12. Davies addresses the widely held belief that independent women would be reluctant to marry. For strong statements of the view she challenges, see "Queen Bees or Working Bees?" immediately preceding in this section and Florence Nightingale's *Cassandra* in part 1.

13. From the French "bête," or beast, and "noire," or black, the phrase refers to someone or some- thing one strongly dislikes.

14. Victoria (1819–1901) reigned from 1837 to 1901. The Queen is a curious figure for Davies to mention, for, while it is true that in her relationship to her husband, Prince Albert (1819–1861), and their nine children, she presented the image of an "admirable wife and mother," it is also true that she held conventional views about gender roles and opposed the higher education and enfranchisement of women. Moreover, the year after Davies's letters appeared in print, Prince Albert died, and, con- trary to Davies's point about the Queen's public character, Victoria appeared infrequently after her husband's death.

15. A lay member of a church who assumed responsibility for paying visits to those in the parish, especially the ill and the infirm.

than that of a confectioner. The fact is, that "to us, the fools of habit,"[16] what is new is dangerous; what we have long been accustomed to, is proper and becoming. Fathers who would shake their heads at the idea of taking their daughters into their own counting-houses, allow them to stand behind a stall at a bazaar, or to lead off at a charity ball—far more public scenes, and where, indeed, publicity is essential to success. And if we really hold the doctrine that it is improper for a woman to follow any calling which cannot be pursued at her own fireside, how is it that we flock to hear public singers? It is idle to say that we would not allow our own daughters or sisters to perform in public. We have no right to sanction by our presence, and to derive enjoyment from the exercise of, a profession which in theory we condemn as unfeminine and, if so, of a demoralising tendency.

In conclusion, I may be permitted to say a few words to those liberal-minded persons who are favourable to the movement now in progress, but who content themselves with standing aside and wishing it God-speed, under the impression that that is all they can do. You can—nay, you must—either help this movement forward, or, in a greater or less degree, retard it. If you are a medical man, you can throw the weight of your influence into the scale in favour of extending to women the educational advantages you have yourself enjoyed; if you are a merchant or a banker, you may be able to make such arrangements in your office as would render it practicable to employ female clerks and cashiers; if you are a master-tradesman, you can make known your willingness to receive female apprentices; if you take part in the government of hospitals, prisons, &c., you can encourage the increased employment of women as officers in these and kindred institutions. Whoever and whatever you are, you can testify against the notion that indolence is feminine and refined; and that if a lady may, in certain cases, be permitted to work, her labour must at any rate be unpaid. You can assist in breaking down those false notions of propriety by which women are hampered in so many directions. And so you may help them to exchange a condition of labour without profit, and leisure without ease, for a life of wholesome activity, and the repose that comes with fruitful toil.

"Medicine as a profession for women," the second selection from Emily Davies's collection *Thoughts on Some Questions Relating to Women*, was originally read in 1862 at the Annual Meeting of the National Association for the Promotion of Social Science. At that time, women were not accepted into medical colleges in England, and the name of only one woman was entered on the British medical register. Elizabeth Blackwell (1821–1901), a native of England whose family emigrated to the United States when she was a child, earned her medical degree from Geneva College in New York in 1849. In 1858 she returned to England to conduct a lecture tour urging women to study medicine and succeeded in having her name added to the register in 1859. A decade later, she made England her permanent

---

16. Tennyson, *In Memoriam* 10.11–12.

home and continued to advance the cause of medical education for women through her work as a teacher, lecturer, and writer.

Inspired by Blackwell, Elizabeth Garrett Anderson (1836–1917), who received her M.D. from the Sorbonne, became the second woman registered in England in 1869. Two years later, Anderson married and subsequently had three children but continued to practice medicine and to teach at the London Medical College for Women, thereby calling into question the Victorian assumption that a woman could not combine a family with a career outside her home.

The individual most responsible for advances made in medical education for British women was Sophia Julia Jex-Blake (1840–1912), whose relentless efforts led to the establishment of the London School of Medicine for Women in 1874, the passage of legislation that made it possible for women to take certification exams, and the expansion of medical practice and education for women in England.

Because of pioneers such as Blackwell, Anderson, and Jex-Blake, the names of 264 women appeared on the medical register by 1895. Despite this improvement, the issues raised by Davies in her 1862 lecture still would have been pertinent when *Thoughts* was published in 1910.

Medicine as a profession for women

[*Read at the Annual Meeting of the National Association for the promotion of Social Science, 1862*]

In speaking of Medicine as a profession for women, it is not my intention to enter upon the general question of the employment of women. I may be allowed, however, in passing, to protest against a notion which seems to have taken possession of many minds, that those who are endeavouring to extend the range of women's labour, are desirous of adding to the severity of their toil. Women already work hard, and it ought scarcely to be said that we wish to increase the aggregate amount of their labour. What we are striving for is rather a re-adjustment of the burden, a somewhat different apportionment of mental and physical labour as relatively distributed between men and women. We desire to see such a condition of society as is described by Coleridge, who in picturing an imagined golden age, speaks of it as a time "when labour was a sweet name for the activity of sane minds in healthful bodies."[1] It is not too much to say that the great mass of women are much less healthy, both in mind and body, than they might be if they had a fair chance of physical and mental development. Many ladies are sickly and hysterical, not, strictly speaking, from want of work, but from want of some steady occupation, sufficiently interesting and important to take them out of themselves. The very poor, on the other hand, are worn down by an amount and a kind of physical toil for which their frames were never intended, their minds being utterly unculti-

1. *The Friend*, vol. 1, essay 1 (1818).

vated, while their earnings are so small that it is impossible for them to maintain themselves in decency and comfort.[2] Of neither of these classes can it be fairly said that they are in that state of life into which it has pleased God to call them. Some other agency must be at work, some disturbing cause, hindering them from filling their appropriate positions. It is to help them to find their place, and to occupy it when found, that our efforts are directed.

If it be true, as the most experienced persons tell us, that what women want in the way of employment is something which gives room for the exercise of their mental activities, without excessive physical toil, we are led to inquire in what professions and occupations these conditions can be obtained. For ladies, it is also requisite that the occupation should not involve the forfeiture of social position. A parent may reasonably say, "I feel that my daughter would be better and happier with some definite work, but what can I bring her up to?" The practice of Medicine among women and children, as being to all appearance essentially a woman's work, naturally occurs first, and we have now to consider whether it fulfils the before-mentioned conditions. As to the first—no one doubts that the study and practice of Medicine afford ample scope for the use of the mental powers. Some persons have indeed expressed a fear that, the minds of women being naturally inferior, the strain on their faculties would be too great. There seems little reason, however, to apprehend danger on this score, as a little observation proves that the most highly cultivated women, whose mental energies are at least as much in use as those of the average doctors, are not less healthy-minded than others, but rather the reverse. With regard to bodily exertion, there is no doubt that a physician in full practice goes through a very considerable amount of work. But after all, walking, and riding, and driving about, are among the recognised means of gaining health, and even the night work, of which some share falls to the lot of all doctors, is perhaps not much more trying to the constitution than the night work habitually performed by ladies of all ages, in heated rooms, and under other unfavourable circumstances. It should be understood throughout that in making these comparisons, I speak of the general run of doctors all over the country, not of a few picked men at the head of their profession, on whose energies the demand must be extraordinarily great, and with whom it would not be necessary for ladies to compete.

The last-named condition—that the profession should not involve the sacrifice of social position—is the one which marks out Medicine as eminently suitable for women of the middle-class. We are constantly told that women are made to be nurses, and that a better class of nurses is urgently required. But it seems to be forgotten that though a few philanthropic ladies may undertake nursing in hospitals, or among the poor, as a work of charity, without loss of social rank, the business of a hired nurse cannot be looked upon as a profession for a lady. The salary of a hospital nurse is less than the wages of a butler or a groom, and even

2. Davies's note: "Those who have come into immediate contact, as I have, with the female workers in glass-houses, paper-mills, brick-yards, &c., will confess that this is no exaggerated statement."

supposing that superior women would command higher remuneration, the position of a nurse is in every way too nearly allied to that of an upper servant, to be in the least appropriate for the daughters and sisters of the mercantile and professional classes.

Apart from the foregoing considerations, which apply chiefly to the want of some outlet for the mental energies of women, there is another aspect of the question, which ought not to be overlooked. I refer to the want of women in the medical profession. The existence of this want is not generally admitted by medical men, but I submit that they are not likely to be the best judges. It is an unquestionable fact—and here I speak, not from hearsay or conjecture but from personal knowledge obtained by extended inquiry—that women of all ranks, do earnestly desire the attendance of physicians of their own sex. The want is most strongly felt by those who cannot command the services of the higher class of medical men. It is equally unquestionable, and here again I speak from authority, that women wish to enter the profession. Is not the mere existence of these two corresponding facts a sufficient reason for giving leave to try the experiment? If we fail, we fail, and having fairly tried, we shall be content to abide by the result. That an innovation *is* an innovation, is not a sufficient ground for opposing it. The opponents of a change are bound to give reasons for their resistance. In the case under consideration I am ready to admit that they have done so freely. Some of the objections seem indeed to cancel each other. For instance, one asks, "Where are your lady students to come from?" while another complains, "What is to become of the men, if women crowd into this already overstocked profession?" At one time women are ordered to keep their place, while at another they are assured that their place is at the bedside of the sick. Those who are most anxious to see women waiting upon male patients as nurses, consider it an outrage upon propriety that they should attend their own sex as physicians.

There are, however, more serious difficulties than these thoughtless cavils. It cannot be denied that there are grave objections to the study of medicine by male and female students in mixed schools, and although a few exceptional women might be willing, for the sake of others, to go through the medical course, even under existing arrangements, it is evident that for female students generally, some modification of these arrangements would be necessary. Such a modification might easily be effected, if the demand for it were clearly made out. Separate classes might be formed for lady students in connexion with the existing schools. There would be no difficulty in obtaining the services of eminent medical men as teachers. Some of those who most strongly object to the admission of ladies into the schools for men, have expressed their willingness to give separate instruction. The examination must, of course, be the same for both sexes, as a security that the standard of proficiency should not be lowered for women, but to that there can be no objection. The difficulty of the case arises, neither from a want of aptitude on the part of women, to whom the practice of Medicine seems to come more naturally than to men, nor from opposition of the medical authorities, many of whom have shown marked liberality and freedom from prejudice. The real obstacles are the unwillingness of young women to incur the reproach of singularity and self-sufficiency, and the less excusable unwillingness of their parents and friends to aid them in overcoming difficulties which they cannot conquer alone. The medical course ought to be begun early in life, and young women cannot be expected to force themselves into a profession against the wishes of those to whom they have learnt to look up for advice and guidance. At the same time, it should be remembered that no class are more sensitively alive to the influence of public opinion than the parents of daughters. Many people who would be favourable to women-physicians in the abstract, would shrink from giving the least encouragement to their own daughters to take a single step out of the beaten path. And it is here that we can all do something. We can at least refrain from joining in the thoughtless cry of horror and astonishment at the idea of women-physicians. Ladies may help much by simply making known in the proper quarters their wish for medical attendance of women. By so doing they would encourage ladies to offer themselves as students, and would afford to them a moral support which they much need. We cannot, indeed, save them from the prominence which must be the lot of the pioneers in any movement, a prominence which has little attraction for those thoughtful women, who, feeling the responsibilities of life more strongly than others, are more earnest in desiring to take their modest share in the work of the world. A certain amount of notoriety is unavoidable, but it rests with the public to decide whether it shall be an unmerited stigma or an honourable distinction.

JOHN RUSKIN

S EE THE INTRODUCTION to John Ruskin (*The Stones of Venice*) in part 1. "Lilies: Of Queens' Gardens" is one of two lectures published together in 1865 under the title *Sesame and Lilies*. These lectures were delivered a week apart in December of 1864, the first ("Sesame: Of Kings' Treasuries") being directed toward young men and the second toward young women. Ostensibly concerned with what reading boys and girls might find most profitable, the lectures comprise Ruskin's analysis of the duties that both men and women must be ready to assume. Prime among those duties is the responsibility to work diligently for the common good. In the preface to a new edition (1871) of *Sesame and Lilies*, Ruskin offers to any young "girl who had enough confidence in me to believe what I told her" the following instruction:

> If there is any one point which, in six thousand years of thinking about right and wrong, wise and good men have agreed upon, or successively by experience discovered, it is that God dislikes idle and cruel people more than any others; that His first order is, "Work while you have light"; and His second, "Be merciful while you have mercy."

The sermonizing that echoes Thomas Carlyle so directly becomes the burden of the concluding paragraphs to "Lilies: Of Queens' Gardens" presented below. Concerned to insist that a woman's work differs from a man's, Ruskin does not exclude woman from the public sphere but does define her work within that sphere as distinguished by the power "to guide, and to guard." Her obligation lies in service to others, fulfilling what, echoing John Wesley (see the introduction to "The Use of Money" in part 1), Ruskin subsequently defined as the duties that all must discharge:

> And, whatever our station in life may be, at this crisis, those of us who mean to fulfill our duty ought, first, to live on as little as we can; and, secondly, to do all the wholesome work for it we can, and to spend all we can spare in doing all the sure good we can.
>
> And sure good is first in feeding people, then in dressing people, then in lodging people, and lastly in rightly pleasing people, with arts, or sciences, or any subject of thought. ("The Mystery of Life and Its Arts")

Such corporal and spiritual works of mercy Ruskin saw as every person's responsibility, but he saw women as specially disposed to carry forward such good works.

From Lecture II—Lilies: Of Queens' Gardens

> "Be thou glad, oh thirsting Desert; let the desert be made
> cheerful, and bloom as the lily; and the barren places of
> Jordan shall run wild with wood."
>
> —Isaiah XXXV, I. (Septuagint.)

. . .

We cannot determine what the queenly power of women should be, until we are agreed what their ordinary power should be. We cannot consider how education may fit them for any widely extending duty, until we are agreed what is their true constant duty. And there never was a time when wilder words were spoken, or more vain imagination permitted, respecting this question—quite vital to all social happiness. The relations of the womanly to the manly nature, their different capacities of intellect or of virtue, seem never to have been yet estimated with entire consent. We hear of the "mission" and of the "rights" of Woman, as if these could ever be separate from the mission and the rights of Man;—as if she and her lord were creatures of independent kind, and of irreconcilable claim. This, at least, is wrong. And not less wrong—perhaps even more foolishly wrong (for I will anticipate thus far what I hope to prove)—is the idea that woman is only the shadow and attendant image of her lord, owing him a thoughtless and servile obedience, and supported altogether in her weakness by the pre-eminence of his fortitude.

This, I say, is the most foolish of all errors respecting her who was made to be the helpmate[1] of man. As if he could be helped effectively by a shadow, or worthily by a slave!

Let us try, then, whether we cannot get at some clear and harmonious idea (it must be harmonious if it is true) of what womanly mind and virtue are in power and office, with respect to man's; and how their relations, rightly accepted, aid, and increase, the vigor, and honor, and authority of both. . . .[2]

But how, you will ask, is the idea of this guiding function of the woman reconcilable with a true wifely subjection? Simply in that it is a *guiding*, not a determining, function. Let me try to show you briefly how these powers seem to be rightly distinguishable.

We are foolish, and without excuse foolish, in speaking of the "superiority" of

---

1. The phrase "helpmate" used as a synonym for "wife" derives from Genesis 2:18: "And the Lord God said, It is not good that man should be alone; I will make an helpmeet for him."

2. Following this introductory comment, Ruskin gives extended attention to the conceptions of active feminine virtue advanced by various authors, notably Shakespeare, suggesting that girls, by reading such literature, might learn about their own potential for working productively. In the paragraphs that follow in this abridgement, Ruskin returns directly to the concern with women's special office.

Figure 4.3. George Elgar Hicks, *Woman's Mission: Companion to Manhood.* Courtesy of the Tate Gallery, London, 1999.

George Elgar Hicks (1824–1914) earned a respectable living as a painter of genre pictures, or scenes of everyday experience. *Woman's Mission: Companion to Manhood* was the second image in a triptych exhibited at the Royal Academy in 1863. The first picture, *Guide of Childhood,* celebrates motherhood while the third, *Comfort of Old Age,* features a woman in her role as dutiful daughter. In *Woman's Mission,* a devoted wife clings to her distraught husband, sharing the anguish he is feeling after reading the ominously black-bordered letter in his hand.

one sex to the other, as if they could be compared in similar things. Each has what the other has not: each completes the other, and is completed by the other: they are in nothing alike, and the happiness and perfection of both depends on each asking and receiving from the other what the other only can give.

Now their separate characters are briefly these: The man's power is active, progressive, defensive. He is eminently the doer, the creator, the discoverer, the defender. His intellect is for speculation and invention; his energy for adventure, for war, and for conquest, wherever war is just, wherever conquest necessary. But the woman's power is for rule, not for battle,—and her intellect is not for invention or creation, but for sweet ordering, arrangement, and decision. She sees the qualities of things, their claims, and their places. Her great function is Praise: she enters into no contest, but infallibly judges the crown of contest. By her office, and place, she is protected from all danger and temptation. The man, in his rough work in open world, must encounter all peril and trial: to him, therefore, must be the failure, the offense, the inevitable error: often he must be wounded, or subdued; often misled; and *always* hardened. But he guards the woman from all this; within his house, as ruled by her, unless she herself has sought it, need enter no danger, no temptation, no cause of error or offense. This is the true nature of home—it is the place of Peace; the shelter, not only from all injury, but from all terror, doubt, and division. In so far as it is not this, it is not home: so far as the anxieties of the outer life penetrate into it, and the inconsistently-minded, unknown, unloved, or hostile society of the outer world is allowed by either husband or wife to cross the threshold, it ceases to be home; it is then only a part of that outer world which you have roofed over, and lighted fire in. But so far as it is a sacred place, a vestal temple, a temple of the hearth watched over by Household Gods, before whose faces none may come but those whom they can receive with love,—so far as it is this, and roof and fire are types only of a nobler shade and light,—shade as of the rock in a weary land, and light as of the Pharos[3] in the stormy sea,—so far it vindicates the name, and fulfills the praise, of home.

And wherever a true wife comes, this home is always round her. The stars only may be over her head; the glowworm in the night-cold grass may be the only fire at her foot: but home is yet wherever she is; and for a noble woman it stretches far round her, better than ceiled with cedar, or painted with vermilion, shedding its quiet light far, for those who else were homeless.

This, then, I believe to be,—will you not admit it to be,—the woman's true place and power? But do not you see that to fulfill this, she must—as far as one can use such terms of a human creature—be incapable of error? So far as she rules, all must be right, or nothing is. She must be enduringly, incorruptibly good; instinctively, infallibly wise—wise, not for self-development, but for self-renunciation: wise, not that she may set herself above her husband, but that she may never fail from his side: wise, not with the narrowness of insolent and loveless pride, but with the passionate gentleness of an infinitely variable, because infinitely applicable, modesty of service—the true changefulness of woman.[4] In that great sense—"La donna è mobile,"[5] not "Qual piùm' al vento";[6] no, nor yet "Variable as the shade, by the

3. Famous lighthouse built by Sostratus Cnidius on the island of Pharos near the Egyptian port of Alexandria.

4. The specific wording associated with the tradition of woman's changefulness comes from the *Aeneid* of Virgil (70–19 B.C.E.). The god Mercury appears to Aeneas in a dream and instructs him to flee immediately from the vengeful anger of the Carthaginian Queen Dido, warning Aeneas that "varium et mutabile semper / femina": woman is ever a variable and changeful thing (4.469–70). Ruskin endeavors to provide a positive way of reading a clearly misogynist tradition.

5. Italian for "The woman is adaptable."

6. Italian for "A feather in the wind."

light quivering aspen made";[7] but variable as the *light*, manifold in fair and serene division, that it may take the color of all that it falls upon, and exalt it. . . .

Thus far, then, of the nature, thus far of the teaching, of woman, and thus of her household office, and queenliness. We come now to our last, our widest question,—What is her queenly office with respect to the state?

Generally we are under an impression that a man's duties are public, and a woman's private. But this is not altogether so. A man has a personal work or duty, relating to his own home, and a public work or duty, which is the expansion of the other, relating to the state. So a woman has a personal work or duty, relating to her own home, and a public work or duty, which is also the expansion of that.

Now the man's work for his own home is, as has been said, to secure its maintenance, progress, and defense; the woman's to secure its order, comfort, and loveliness.

Expand both these functions. The man's duty, as a member of a commonwealth, is to assist in the maintenance, in the advance, in the defense of the state. The woman's duty, as a member of the commonwealth, is to assist in the ordering, in the comforting, and in the beautiful adornment of the state.

What the man is at his own gate, defending it, if need be, against insult and spoil, that also, not in a less, but in a more devoted measure, he is to be at the gate of his country, leaving his home, if need be, even to the spoiler, to do his more incumbent work there.

And, in like manner, what the woman is to be within her gates, as the center of order, the balm of distress, and the mirror of beauty; that she is also to be without her gates, where order is more difficult, distress more imminent, loveliness more rare.

And as within the human heart there is always set an instinct for all its real duties,—an instinct which you cannot quench, but only warp and corrupt if you withdraw it from its true purpose;—as there is the intense instinct of love, which, rightly disciplined, maintains all the sanctities of life, and, misdirected, undermines them; and *must* do either the one or the other;—so there is in the human heart an inextinguishable instinct, the love of power, which, rightly directed, maintains all the majesty of law and life, and, misdirected, wrecks them.

Deep-rooted in the innermost life of the heart of man, and of the heart of woman, God set it there, and God keeps it there. Vainly, as falsely, you blame or rebuke the desire of power!—For Heaven's sake, and for Man's sake, desire it all you can. But *what* power? That is all the question. Power to destroy? the lion's limb, and the dragon's breath? Not so. Power to heal, to redeem, to guide, and to guard. Power of the scepter and shield; the power of the royal hand that heals in touching,—that binds the fiend and looses the captive; the throne that is founded on the rock of Justice, and descended from only by steps of mercy. Will you not covet such power as this, and seek such throne as this, and be no more housewives, but queens?

7. A description of woman taken from *Marmion* by Sir Walter Scott (1771–1832): canto 6, stanza 30.

It is now long since the women of England arrogated, universally, a title which once belonged to nobility only, and, having once been in the habit of accepting the simple title of gentlewoman, as correspondent to that of gentleman, insisted on the privilege of assuming the title of "Lady,"[8] which properly corresponds only to the title of "Lord."

I do not blame them for this; but only for their narrow motive in this. I would have them desire and claim the title of Lady, provided they claim, not merely the title, but the office and duty signified by it. Lady means "bread-giver" or "loaf-giver," and Lord means "maintainer of laws," and both titles have reference, not to the law which is maintained in the house, nor to the bread which is given to the household, but to law maintained for the multitude and to bread broken among the multitude. So that a Lord has legal claim only to his title in so far as he is the maintainer of the justice of the Lord of Lords; and a Lady has legal claim to her title only so far as she communicates that help to the poor representatives of her Master, which women once, ministering to Him of their substance, were permitted to extend to that Master Himself; and when she is known, as He Himself once was, in breaking of bread.

And this beneficent and legal dominion, this power of the Dominus,[9] or House-Lord, and of the Domina,[10] or House-Lady, is great and venerable, not in the number of those through whom it has lineally descended, but in the number of those whom it grasps within its sway; it is always regarded with reverent worship wherever its dynasty is founded on its duty, and its ambition co-relative with its beneficence. Your fancy is pleased with the thought of being noble ladies, with a train of vassals. Be it so: you cannot be too noble, and your train cannot be too great; but see to it that your train is of vassals whom you serve and feed, not merely of slaves who serve and feed *you*; and that the multitude which obeys you is of those whom you have comforted, not oppressed,—whom you have redeemed, not led into captivity.

And this, which is true of the lower or household dominion, is equally true of the queenly dominion;—that highest dignity is open to you, if you will also accept that highest duty. Rex et Regina—Roi et Reine—"*Right*-doers"; they differ but from the Lady and Lord, in that their power is supreme over the mind as over the person—that they not only feed and clothe, but direct and teach. And whether consciously or not, you must be, in many a heart, enthroned: there is no putting by that crown; queens you must always be; queens to your lovers; queens to your husbands and your sons; queens of higher mystery to the world beyond, which

---

8. Ruskin's note: "I wish there were a true order of chivalry instituted for our English youth of certain ranks, in which both boy and girl should receive, at a given age, their knighthood and ladyhood by true title; attainable only by certain probation and trial both of character and accomplishment; and to be forfeited, on conviction, by their peers, of any dishonorable act. Such an institution would be entirely, and with all noble results, possible, in a nation which loved honor. That it would not be possible among us is not to the discredit of the scheme."

9. Latin for "lord" or "master."

10. Latin for "lady" or "mistress."

bows itself, and will forever bow, before the myrtle crown, and the stainless scepter, of womanhood. But, alas! you are too often idle and careless queens, grasping at majesty in the least things, while you abdicate it in the greatest; and leaving misrule and violence to work their will among men, in defiance of the power which, holding straight in gift from the Prince of all Peace, the wicked among you betray, and the good forget.

"Prince of Peace." Note that name. When kings rule in that name, and nobles, and the judges of the earth, they also, in their narrow place, and mortal measure, receive the power of it. There are no other rulers than they: other rule than theirs is but *mis*rule; they who govern verily "Dei gratiâ"[11] are all princes, yes, or princesses, of peace. There is not a war in the world, no, nor an injustice, but you women are answerable for it; not in that you have provoked, but in that you have not hindered. Men, by their nature, are prone to fight; they will fight for any cause, or for none. It is for you to choose their cause for them, and to forbid them when there is no cause. There is no suffering, no injustice, no misery in the earth, but the guilt of it lies with you. Men can bear the sight of it, but you should not be able to bear it. Men may tread it down without sympathy in their own struggle; but men are feeble in sympathy, and contracted in hope; it is you only who can feel the depths of pain; and conceive the way of its healing. Instead of trying to do this, you turn away from it; you shut yourselves within your park walls and garden gates; and you are content to know that there is beyond them a whole world in wilderness—a world of secrets which you dare not penetrate; and of suffering which you dare not conceive.

I tell you that this is to me quite the most amazing among the phenomena of humanity. I am surprised at no depths to which, when once warped from its honor, that humanity can be degraded. I do not wonder at the miser's death, with his hands, as they relax, dropping gold. I do not wonder at the sensualist's life, with the shroud wrapped about his feet. I do not wonder at the single-handed murder of a single victim, done by the assassin in the darkness of the railway, or reed-shadow of the marsh. I do not even wonder at the myriad-handed murder of multitudes, done boastfully in the daylight, by the frenzy of nations, and the immeasurable, unimaginable guilt, heaped up from hell to heaven, of their priests and kings. But this is wonderful to me—oh, how wonderful!—to see the tender and delicate woman among you, with her child at her breast, and a power, if she would wield it, over it, and over its father, purer than the air of heaven, and stronger than the seas of earth—nay, a magnitude of blessing which her husband would not part with for all that earth itself, though it were made of one entire and perfect chrysolite:—to see her abdicate this majesty to play at precedence with her next-door neighbor! This is wonderful—oh, wonderful!—to see her, with every innocent feeling fresh within her, go out in the morning into her garden to play with the fringes of its guarded flowers, and lift their heads when they are drooping, with her happy smile upon her

11. Latin for "by the grace of God."

face, and no cloud upon her brow, because there is a little wall around her place of peace: and yet she knows, in her heart, if she would only look for its knowledge, that, outside of that little rose-covered wall, the wild grass, to the horizon, is torn up by the agony of men, and beat level by the drift of their life-blood.

Have you ever considered what a deep under meaning there lies, or at least may be read, if we choose, in our custom of strewing flowers before those whom we think most happy? Do you suppose it is merely to deceive them into the hope that happiness is always to fall thus in showers at their feet?—that wherever they pass they will tread on the herbs of sweet scent, and that the rough ground will be made smooth for them by depth of roses? So surely as they believe that, they will have, instead, to walk on bitter herbs and thorns; and the only softness to their feet will be of snow. But it is not thus intended they should believe; there is a better meaning in that old custom. The path of a good woman is indeed strewn with flowers: but they rise behind her steps, not before them. "Her feet have touched the meadows, and left the daisies rosy."[12]

You think that only a lover's fancy;—false and vain! How if it could be true? You think this also, perhaps, only a poet's fancy—

> "Even the light harebell raised its head
> Elastic from her airy tread."[13]

But it is little to say of a woman, that she only does not destroy where she passes. She should revive; the harebells should bloom, not stoop, as she passes. You think I am rushing into wild hyperbole? Pardon me, not a whit—I mean what I say in calm English, spoken in resolute truth. You have heard it said—(and I believe there is more than fancy even in that saying, but let it pass for a fanciful one)—that flowers only flourish rightly in the garden of some one who loves them. I know you would like that to be true; you would think it a pleasant magic if you could flush your flowers into brighter bloom by a kind look upon them: nay, more, if your look had the power, not only to cheer, but to guard;—if you could bid the black blight turn away and the knotted caterpillar spare—if you could bid the dew fall upon them in the drought, and say to the south wind, in frost—"Come, thou south, and breathe upon my garden, that the spices of it may flow out." This you would think a great thing? And do you think it not a greater thing, that all this (and how much more than this!) you *can* do for fairer flowers than these—flowers that could bless you for having blessed them, and will love you for having loved them;— flowers that have thoughts like yours, and lives like yours; which, once saved, you save forever? Is this only a little power? Far among the moorlands and the rocks,— far in the darkness of the terrible streets,—these feeble florets are lying, with all their fresh leaves torn, and their stems broken—will you never go down to them, nor set them in order in their little fragrant beds, nor fence them in their trem-

---

12. From Tennyson's *Maud* 1.12.434–35.
13. From Sir Walter Scott's *The Lady of the Lake*: canto 1, stanza 18.

bling, from the fierce wind? Shall morning follow morning, for you, but not for them; and the dawn rise to watch, far away, those frantic Dances of Death, but no dawn rise to breathe upon these living banks of wild violet, and woodbine, and rose; nor call to you, through your casement,—call (not giving you the name of the English poet's lady, but the name of Dante's great Matilda,[14] who, on the edge of happy Lethe, stood wreathing flowers with flowers), saying:—

> "Come into the garden, Maud,
> For the black bat, night, has flown,
> And the woodbine spices are wafted abroad
> And the musk of the roses blown"?[15]

Will you not go down among them?—among those sweet living things, whose new courage, sprung from the earth with the deep color of heaven upon it, is starting up in strength of goodly spire; and whose purity, washed from the dust, is opening, bud by bud, into the flower of promise;—and still they turn to you, and for you, "The Larkspur listens—I hear, I hear! And the Lily whispers—I wait."[16]

Did you notice that I missed two lines when I read you that first stanza; and think that I had forgotten them? Hear them now:—

> "Come into the garden, Maud,
> For the black bat, night, has flown.
> Come into the garden, Maud,
> I am here at the gate, alone."[17]

Who is it, think you, who stands at the gate of this sweeter garden, alone, waiting for you? Did you ever hear, not of a Maud, but a Madeleine, who went down to her garden in the dawn and found One waiting at the gate, whom she supposed to be the gardener?[18] Have you not sought Him often;—sought Him in vain, all through the night;—sought Him in vain at the gate of that old garden where the fiery sword is set?[19] He is never there; but at the gate of *this* garden He is waiting always—waiting to take your hand—ready to go down to see the fruits of the valley, to see whether the vine has flourished, and the pomegranate budded. There you shall see with Him the little tendrils of the vines that His hand is guiding—there you shall see the pomegranate springing where His hand cast the

14. In *The Divine Comedy* by Dante Alighieri (1265–1321), as he moves toward the river Lethe which separates him from the Earthly Paradise at the top of Purgatory, Dante encounters the beautiful Matilda (who represents the active life), the counterpart to Beatrice (who represents the contemplative life). He sees Matilda gathering flowers and wreathing them and, subsequently, she informs him that the Highest Good has made humankind both to be and to do good, an expression of Ruskin's ideal for women to act benevolently to others through work and service. See *Purgatorio,* 28.34–92.

15. From Tennyson's *Maud* 1.22.850–51; 854–55.

16. From Tennyson's *Maud* 1.22.914–15.

17. From Tennyson's *Maud* 1.22.850–53.

18. See John 20:1–18 for the story of Mary Magdalene's first finding the sepulchre of the Savior empty and then seeing the risen Christ but mistaking him initially for the gardener.

19. The reference is to the Garden of Eden. Following the expulsion of Adam and Eve, God sets cherubim and a flaming sword at the east of the garden to keep humankind from re-entering Paradise.

sanguine seed;—more: you shall see the troops of the angel keepers that, with their wings, wave away the hungry birds from the pathsides where He has sown, and call to each other between the vineyard rows, "Take us the foxes, the little foxes, that spoil the vines, for our vines have tender grapes."[20] Oh—you queens—you queens; among the hills and happy greenwood of this land of yours, shall the foxes have holes, and the birds of the air have nests; and in your cities, shall the stones cry out against you,[21] that they are the only pillows where the Son of Man can lay His head?[22]

20. Solomon 2:15.
21. Luke 19:40.
22. Luke 9:58.

ELIZA LYNN LINTON

E LIZA LYNN LINTON (1822–1898) was one of several successful professional women in nineteenth-century England who consistently (and virulently) spoke against changes in women's traditional roles. Well established in a career as a journalist and writer of popular fiction, in her mid-thirties she married the engraver and Chartist advocate William James Linton, who published the radical *English Republic;* the marriage was short-lived, and, publishing under the name E. Lynn Linton whenever she did not publish anonymously, she continued with her journalism following their separation in 1864 and William Linton's emigration to America in 1866. (W. J. Linton's "The Free-Servant," included in part 2, "Work as Oppression," provides a good example of the short sentimental narratives characteristic of the Chartist press.)

"Saturday Mornings," a series of E. Lynn Linton's unsigned essays commissioned for the *Saturday Review,* offered stringent criticism not only of women's concern for fashion and social recognition but also of women's efforts to redefine their political and economic status. This series, especially the inflammatory piece "The Girl of the Period," attracted national attention; when, in 1883, Linton subsequently published these bimonthly essays together and affixed her name to the collection, she confirmed her reputation as an articulate critic resistant to most challenges to cultural norms. Significant tensions informed Linton's life as an independent woman who achieved prominence in a "man's profession" and who left her husband and her adopted children but who staunchly advocated that women in general should be submissive to men and commit their energies to a separate domestic sphere.

In "What Is Woman's Work?" which first appeared in the February 15, 1868, issue of the *Saturday Review,* Linton dismisses as "another part of the subject" those who, in the latter half of the century, constituted a growing population of so-termed redundant women—women who, of necessity, were committed to "professional self-support" because they had "no men to work for them." Focusing instead upon financially secure upper middle-class women, Linton addresses the complaint voiced by Florence Nightingale in *Cassandra* (see part 1 of this anthology) that women suffered from the absence of meaningful work. Unlike Nightingale, however, she insists that women should seek happiness through the active fulfillment of those familial and household duties that she conceives as natural to their sex.

What Is Woman's Work?

This is a question which one half the world is at this moment asking the other half; with very wild answers as the result. Woman's work seems to be in these days everything that it was not in times past, and nothing that it was. Professions are undertaken and careers invaded which were formerly held sacred to men; while things are left undone which, for all the generations that the world has lasted, have been naturally and instinctively assigned to women to do. From the savage squaw gathering fuel or drawing water for the wigwam, to the lady giving up the keys to her housekeeper, housekeeping has been considered one of the primary functions of women. The man to provide—the woman to dispense; the man to do the rough initial work of bread-winning, whether as a half-naked barbarian hunting live meat or as a City clerk painfully scoring lines of rugged figures—the woman to cook the meat when got, and to lay out to the best advantage for the family the quarter's salary gained by casting up ledgers and writing advices and bills of lading. Take human society in any phase we like, we must come down to these radical conditions; and any system which ignores this division of labour, and confounds these separate functions, is of necessity imperfect and wrong. We have nothing whatever to say against the professional self-support of women who have no men to work for them, and who must therefore work for themselves in order to live.[1] In what direction soever they can best make their way, let them take it. Brains and intellectual gifts are of no sex and no condition, and it is far more important that good work should be done than that it should be done by this or that particular set of workers. But we are speaking of the home duties of married women, and of those girls who have no need to earn their daily bread, and who are not so specially gifted as to be driven afield by the irrepressible power of genius. We are speaking of women who cannot help in the family income, but who might both save and improve in the home; women whose lives are one long day of idleness, *ennui* and vagrant imagination, because they despise the activities into which they were born, while seeking outlets for their energies impossible to them both by functional and social restrictions.

It is strange to see into what unreasonable disrepute active housekeeping—woman's first social duty—has fallen in England. Take a family with four or five hundred a year—and we know how small a sum that is for "genteel humanity" in these days—the wife who is an active housekeeper, even with such an income, is an exception to the rule; and the daughters who are anything more than drawing-

---

1. In "The Modern Revolt," a December 1870 article for *Macmillan's,* Linton returned to the issue of redundant women somewhat more directly, noting that there simply were more women than men in England and that many women, therefore, would need to support themselves. Here again, however, she urged that such women would best serve within the labor force by undertaking work related to home and families.

room dolls waiting for husbands to transfer them to a home of their own, where they may be as useless as they are now, are rarer still. For things are getting worse, not better, and our young women are less useful even than were their mothers; while these last do not, as a rule, come near the housekeeping ladies of olden times, who knew every secret of domestic economy and made a wise and pleasant "distribution of bread"[2] their grand point of honour. The usual method of London housekeeping, even in the second ranks of the middle-classes, is for the mistress to give her orders in the kitchen in the morning, leaving the cook to pass them on to the tradespeople when they call. If she be not very indolent, and if she have a due regard for neatness and cleanliness, she may supplement her kitchen commands by going up stairs through some of the bedrooms; but after a kind word of advice to the housemaid if she be sweet-tempered, or a harsh note of censure if she be of the cross-grained type, her work in that department will be done, and her duties for the day are at an end. There is none of the clever marketing by which fifty per cent is saved in the outlay, if a woman knows what she is about and how to buy; none of that personal superintendence, so encouraging to servants when genially performed, which renders slighted work impossible; none of that "seeing to things" herself, or doing the finer parts of the work with her own hands, which used to form part of a woman's unquestioned duty. She gives her orders, weighs out her supplies, then leaves the maids to do the best they know or the worst they will, according to the degree in which they are supplied with faculty or conscience. Many women boast that their housekeeping takes them perhaps an hour, perhaps half an hour in the morning, and no more; and they think themselves clever and commendable in proportion to the small amount of time given to their largest family duty. This is all very well where the income is such as to secure first-class servants—professors of certain specialties of knowledge and far in advance of the mistress; but how about the comfort of the house under this hasty generalship, when the maids are mere scrubs who ought to go through years of training if they are ever to be worth their salt? It may be very well too in large households governed by general system, and not by individual ruling; but where the service is scant and poor, it is a stupid, uncomfortable, as well as wasteful way of housekeeping. It is analogous to English cookery—a revolting poverty of result with flaring prodigality of means; all the pompous paraphernalia of tradespeople and their carts and their red-books for orders, with nothing worth the trouble of booking; and everything of less quantity and lower quality than would be if personal pains were taken—which is always the best economy.

What is there in practical housekeeping less honourable than the ordinary work of middle-class gentlewomen? and why should women shrink from doing for utility, and for the general comfort of the family, what they would do at any time for vanity or idleness? No one need go into extremes, and wish our middle-class

---

2. Linton refers here to the etymology of the word "lady" as "loaf-giver," distributor of bread. John Ruskin offers extended comment about this etymology in "Lilies: Of Queens' Gardens" (see previous selection).

gentlewomen to become exaggerated Marthas occupied only with much serving, Nausicaas washing linen, or "wise Penelopes"[3] spending their lives in needlework alone. But, without undertaking anything unpleasant to her senses or degrading to her condition, a lady might do hundreds of things which are now left undone in a house, or are given up to the coarse handling of servants; and domestic life would gain in consequence. What degradation, for instance, is there in cookery? and how much more home happiness would there not be if wives would take in hand that great cold-mutton question? But women are both selfish and small on this point. Born for the most part with feebly-developed gustativeness, they affect to despise the stronger instinct in men, and think it low and sensual if they are expected to give special attention to the meals of the man who provides the meat. This contempt for good cooking is one cause of the ignorance there is among them of how to secure good living. Those horrible traditions of "plain roast and boiled" cling about them as articles of culinary faith; and because they have reached no higher knowledge for themselves, they decide that no one else shall go beyond them. For one middle-class gentlewoman who understands anything about cookery, or who really cares for it as a scientific art or domestic necessity, there are ten thousand who do not; yet our mothers and grandmothers were not ashamed to be known as deft professors, and homes were happier in proportion to the respect paid to the stewpan and the stockpot. And cookery is more interesting now than it was then, because more advanced, more scientific, and with improved appliances; and, at the same time, it is of confessedly more importance.

It may seem humiliating, to those who go in for spirit pure and simple, to speak of the condition of the soul as in any way determined by beef and cabbage; but it is so, nevertheless; the connexion between food and virtue, food and thought, being a very close one. And the sooner wives recognize this connexion the better for them and for their husbands. The clumsy savagery of a plain cook, or the vile messes of a fourth-rate confectioner, are absolute sins in a house where a woman has all her senses, and can, if she will, attend personally to the cooking. Many things pass for crimes which are really not so bad as this. But how seldom do we find a house where the lady does look after the food of the family; where clean hands and educated brains are put to active service for the good of others! The trouble would be too great in our fine-lady days, even if there were the requisite ability; but there is as little ability as there is energy, and the plain cook with her savagery and the fourth-rate confectioner with his rancid pastry, have it all their own way, according as the election is for economy or ostentation. If by chance we stumble on a

3. When Jesus visits the home of Martha and Mary, Martha is "cumbered about much serving" and complains that her sister Mary sits and listens to Jesus but does not work. Jesus admonishes Martha that she is "troubled about many things"—excessively caught up with work (Luke 10:38–42). When he is shipwrecked on the island of the Phaiakians, Odysseus encounters the king's daughter Nausicaa, who is superintending the laundering of the family's garments. She welcomes Odysseus and instructs him how best to petition her parents for help; see *Odyssey* 6. Wise Penelope is the faithful wife of Odysseus who is consistently associated with spinning, sewing, and weaving, tending to her "own work, / the loom and the distaff." (*Odyssey* 1.356–57).

household where the woman does not disdain housewifely work, and specially does not disdain the practical superintendence of the kitchen, there we are sure to find cheerfulness and content.

There seems to be something in the life of a practical housekeeper that answers to the needs of a woman's best nature, and that makes her pleasant and good-humoured. Perhaps it is the consciousness that she is doing her duty—of itself a wonderful sweetener of the temper; perhaps the greater amount of bodily exercise keeps her liver in good case; whatever the cause, sure it is that the homes of the active housekeepers are more harmonious than those of the feckless and do-nothing sort. Yet the snobbish half of the middle-classes holds housewifely work as degrading, save in the trumpery pretentiousness of "giving orders." A woman may sit in a dirty drawing-room which the slipshod maid has not had time to clean, but she must not take a duster in her hands and polish the legs of the chairs:—there is no disgrace in the dirt, only in the duster. She may do fancy-work of no earthly use, but she must not be caught making a gown. Indeed very few women could make one, and as few will do plain needlework. They will braid and embroider, "cut holes, and sew them up again," and spend any amount of time and money on beads and wools for messy draperies which no one wants. The end, being finery, sanctions the toil and refines it. But they will not do things of practical use; or, if they are compelled by the exigencies of circumstances, they think themselves martyrs and badly used by the Fates.

The whole scheme of woman's life at this present time is untenable and unfair. She wants to have all the pleasures and none of the disagreeables. Her husband goes to the City and does monotonous and unpleasant work there; but his wife thinks herself very hardly dealt with if asked to do monotonous housework at home. Yet she does nothing more elevating nor more advantageous. Novel-reading, fancy-work, visiting and letter-writing, sum up her ordinary occupations; and she considers these more to the point than practical housekeeping. In fact it becomes a serious question what women think themselves sent into the world for—what they hold themselves designed by God to be or to do. They grumble at having children and at the toil and anxiety which a family entails; they think themselves degraded to the level of servants if they have to do any practical house-work whatever; they assert their equality with man, and express their envy of his life, yet show themselves incapable of learning the first lesson set to men—that of doing what they do not like to do. What, then, do they want? What do they hold themselves made for? Certainly some of the more benevolent sort carry their energies out of doors, and leave such prosaic matters as savoury dinners and fast shirt-buttons for committees and charities, where they get excitement and *kudos*[4] together. Others give themselves to what they call keeping up society, which means being more at home in every person's house than their own; and some do a little

---

4. *Kudos* is a classical Greek term for glory or renown. *Kudos* is recognition granted to a mortal by a god and is usually associated with success in *athloi*, contests or struggles.

weak art, and others a little feeble literature; but there are very few indeed who honestly buckle to the natural duties of their position, and who bear with the tedium of home-work as men bear with the tedium of office-work.

The little royalty of home is the last place where a woman cares to shine, and the most uninteresting of all the domains she seeks to govern. Fancy a high-souled creature, capable of aesthetics, giving her mind to soup or the right proportion of chutnee for the curry! Fancy, too, a brilliant creature foregoing an evening's conversational glory abroad for the sake of a prosaic husband's more prosaic dinner! He comes home tired from work, and desperately in need of a good dinner as a restorative; but the plain cook gives him cold meat and pickles, or an abomination which she calls hash, and the brilliant creature, full of mind, thinks the desire for anything else rank sensuality. It seems a little hard, certainly, on the unhappy fellow who works at the mill for such a return; but women believe that men are made only to work at the mill that they may receive the grist accruing, and be kept in idleness and uselessness all their lives. They have no idea of lightening the labour of that mill-round by doing their own natural work cheerfully and diligently. They will do everything but what they ought to do. They will make themselves doctors, committee-women, printers, what not; but they will not learn cooking, and they will not keep their own houses. There never was a time when women were less the helpmates of men than they are at present; when there was such a wide division between the interests and the sympathies of the sexes coincident with the endeavour, on the one side, to approximate their pursuits.

A great demand is being made now for more work for woman and wider fields for her labour. We confess we should feel a deeper interest in the question if we saw more energy and conscience put into the work lying to her hand at home; and we hold that she ought to perfectly perform the duties which we may call instinctive to her sex before claiming those hitherto held remote from her natural condition. Much of this demand springs from restlessness and dissatisfaction; little, if any, from higher aspirations or nobler energies unused. Indeed, the nobler the woman the more thoroughly she will do her own proper work, in the spirit of old George Herbert's well-worn line;[5] and the less she will feel herself above that work. It is only the weak who cannot raise their circumstances to the level of their thoughts; only the poor in spirit who cannot enrich their deeds by their motives.

That very much of this demand for more power of work comes from necessity and the absolute need of bread, we know; and that the demand will grow louder as marriage becomes scarcer, and there are more women adrift in the world without

---

5. George Herbert (1593–1633) was an Anglican cleric and religious poet who advocated subordination of individual will to the will of God; no poem of Herbert's, however, has the phrase that Linton here singles out. It is possible that she was recalling the concluding lines of "The Collar," Herbert's most celebrated poem, in which the restive persona, having rebelled against a situation perceived as constricting, finally accepts duty and direction by God:

> But as I raved and grew more fierce and wild
>   At every word
> Me thoughts I heard one calling, *Child:*
>   And I replied, *My Lord.*

the protection and help of men, we also know. But this belongs to another part of the subject. What we want to insist on now is the pitiable ignorance and shiftless indolence of most middle-class housekeepers; and what we would urge on woman is the value of a better system of life at home before laying claim to the discharge of extra-domestic duties abroad.

JOSEPHINE ELIZABETH BUTLER

JOHN AND HANNAH GREY instilled in their daughter Josephine (1828–1906) strong religious and ethical values which became the foundation of her social reform work as an adult. In 1852, she married George Butler, an Anglican clergyman who supported her efforts to improve the status of women. As an outgrowth of her work with prostitutes in Liverpool, she established the House of Rest, a home for destitute women, in 1866. Butler also campaigned tirelessly to have the Contagious Diseases Acts of 1864, 1866, and 1869 repealed. These laws, enacted to curb the spread of venereal disease especially around military posts and ports, were particularly repugnant to women's rights activists as they required any woman suspected of being a prostitute to be examined for venereal disease, but made no provision for the examination of men. Harriet Martineau and Florence Nightingale numbered among those who opposed the legislation, which was finally overturned in 1886.

In addition to her work on behalf of indigent women, Butler promoted better education and employment opportunities for middle-class women. In 1868, she published "The Education and Employment of Women," an essay in which she combines appeals to justice with telling statistics, affecting first-person accounts, and biblical precepts to argue for viable options for women to fulfill their God-given potential and to make a significant contribution to society.

The Education and Employment of Women

The economical position of women is one of those subjects on which there exists a "conspiracy of silence." While most people, perhaps, imagine that nearly all women marry and are supported by their husbands, those who know better how women live, or die, have rarely anything to say on the subject. Such social problems as this are certainly painful; they may or may not be insoluble; they must not be ignored.

The phrase "to become a governess" is sometimes used as if it were a satisfactory outlet for any unsupported woman above the rank of housemaid. When we see advertisements in the newspapers, offering "a comfortable home," with no salary, as a sufficient reward for accomplishments of the most varied character, we sometimes wonder at the audacity of employers; but when we learn that such an advertisement, offering the situation of nursery governess, *unpaid*, was answered by *three hundred women*, our surprise has in it something of despair.

The truth is, that the facts of society have changed more rapidly than its conventions. Formerly muscles did the business of the world, and the weak were protected by the strong; now brains do the business of the world, and the weak are protected by law. The industrial disabilities of women, unavoidable under the earlier *régime*, have become cruel under the later. There is neither the old necessity of shelter, nor the old certainty of support.

The census of 1861 gave nearly six millions of adult English women, distributed as follows:—

Wives	3,488,952
Widows	756,717
Spinsters over 20	1,537,314
	5,782,983

The census also gives the numbers of women who work for their own subsistence, as follows:—

Wives	838,856
Widows	487,575
Spinsters (above or under 20)	2,110,318
	3,436,749

In the first place, then, it appears that marriage, as a means of subsistence (to say nothing of the indecorum of looking forward to it in this light) is exceedingly precarious in two ways. The proportion of wives to widows and spinsters in 1861 was just about three to two, while of these wives themselves nearly one in four was occupied in other than domestic duties, either as her husband's coadjutor, as in farm-houses and shops, or, of necessity, as his substitute in cases of his desertion, or helplessness, or vice. In the second place, the number of widows and spinsters supporting themselves, which in 1851 was two millions, had increased in 1861 to more than two millions and a half. The rapidity of the increase of this class is painfully significant. Two and a half millions of Englishwomen without husbands, and working for their own subsistence! This is not an accident, it is a new order of things. Of the three and a half millions of women—wives, widows, and spinsters—engaged in other than domestic occupations, it is probable that scarcely a thousand make, without capital, and by their own exertions, one hundred pounds a year. The best paid are housekeepers in large establishments, a few finishing governesses,

Figure 4.4. Richard Redgrave, *The Governess.* Courtesy of the Victoria and Albert Museum, London, UK / Bridgeman Art Library, London/New York.

Inspired by the experiences of his sister Jane, who worked as a governess until she contracted and died of typhoid, Redgrave painted four different versions of *The Governess,* which was originally exhibited at the Royal Academy in 1843. In this one, from 1844, a young woman is pictured in her schoolroom. She has turned away from the piano, on which rests the sheet music for "Home Sweet Home," to read the unpleasant tidings of a black-bordered letter. Redgrave creates a striking contrast between her loneliness and pensive melancholy and the gaiety of the girls nearby.

and professed cooks. 43,964 women are returned as outdoor agricultural labourers—a fact worthy of remembrance when it is said that women are too weak to serve in haberdashers' shops. Women, refused admission to such shops on the pretext that they are not strong enough to lift bales of goods, have been afterwards traced to the occupations of dock porters and coal-heavers. In practice the employments of women are not determined by their lightness, but by their low pay. One newspaper still scoffs at the desire of women to be self-supporting: but starvation is a sufficient answer to sneers. As a favourable symptom of the last few years, I may add that 1822 women are returned as employed by the Post-office. 213 women are returned as telegraph-clerks. It is instructive to note the way in which the salary of these women telegraph-clerks has fallen. When the telegraph companies were first formed, the pay of a female clerk was eight shillings a week, to be increased by a shilling yearly, until it reached fourteen shillings a week. So great, however, has been the competition of women for these situations, that the pay has been reduced to five shillings a week, a sum on which a woman can scarcely live unassisted. In France the women telegraph-clerks have met with a worse fate. The government took the management of the telegraphs, and dismissed the women, because they had no votes to bestow on the government candidates. The exclusion of women from the suffrage[1] has been called a harmless injustice; but there is no injustice which is not liable to become an injury.

At present the principal employments open to women are teaching, domestic service, and sewing. I come to consider the remuneration of the highest profession open to women.

In 1861 there were 80,017 female teachers in England, of whom the majority were governesses in private families. It is difficult to ascertain the average salary of governesses, because the Governesses' Institutions[2] in London and Manchester, which are the chief sources of information on the subject, refuse to register the applications of governesses who accept salaries of less than £25 a year. The number of this lowest class may be guessed from the fact that for a situation as nursery governess, with a salary of £20 a year, advertised in a newspaper, there were five hundred applicants; as I have already stated, three hundred applied for a similar place with no salary at all. To return to the higher class. The register of the last six months at the Manchester Governesses' Institution shows an entry of—

54 governesses who asked for £30				and under, per annum.		
20	"	"	"	40	"	"
19	"	"	"	50	"	"
17	"	"	"	60	"	"
10	"	"	"	70	and upwards	"

These sums, it must be remembered, are expressions of what governesses wish to receive.[3] Taking nursery governesses into the account, and remembering that the above statistics refer only to the higher ranks of the profession, it is probably not too much to say that from 0 to £50 a year is the salary of nine governesses in ten. Situations offering more than £50 are the prizes of the profession, but are generally such as to compel a serious outlay on dress and personal expenditure. It is difficult

1. By mid-century, the campaign for women's suffrage in England was becoming organized. In 1867, the year before the publication of this essay, John Stuart Mill presented to Parliament an amendment to the Second Reform Bill calling for the enfranchisement of women, but the amendment was soundly defeated. Nevertheless, the campaign continued. By 1888, women were permitted to vote in municipal and county elections. Yet it was not until 1918 that women, and even then only those over age thirty, had the right to vote in national elections; women of twenty-one and over won the vote in 1928.

2. The Governesses' Benevolent Institution was founded in 1843 to provide assistance to governesses by maintaining a job list and, later in the century, by providing charity to the elderly and the incapacitated.

3. Butler's note: "Miss Strongitharm states in respect of the Governesses' Institution at Manchester—'Remember that those who register here are the favourable specimens of the class, the governesses who accept salaries under £20,—and their name is Legion,—being excluded by the Rules of the Institution, and that the salaries asked by no means represent, in most cases, the salaries obtained—a governess being often too glad to get a home on almost any terms.'"

to imagine how the majority of governesses manage to scramble through life, when we remember that their position involves several journeys in the year, that they must sometimes provide for themselves during holiday seasons, and that they must always dress as ladies. Miserable must be their means of providing for old age or sickness, to say nothing of claims of affection or of charity throughout life, or the means required for self-culture.[4]

Probably there are few portions of society in which more of silent suffering and misery is endured than among female teachers, and in the class which supplies them. Charitable people who have opened little "Homes" for decayed governesses can tell histories of struggling lives and crushed hopes which it saddens one to hear. The reports of Bethlehem Hospital[5] and other lunatic asylums prove that not a few poor governesses find their way thither. Some are found in Penitentiaries among the fallen. Inquiry shows that insufficient food while out of situations, added to the mental trials of an unloved and isolated being, have driven some of these governesses to opium or to strong drink, until, penniless and degraded, they have sought a refuge among penitents where there was nothing to pay. "Her funds are exhausted, and she earnestly seeks a re-engagement"; words such as these, taken from an advertisement in the *Times*, headed—"To the benevolent," are no unfrequent symptom of a deep and wide distress. Some determined women there are who have devoted to self-culture as much of their pittance as could be spared from the barest needs of life, and of whom it is known that, night after night when they went to bed, they have tied a band round their waist to keep down the gnawings of hunger. One such I know who has risen by her force of character to almost as high a place as it is at present possible for a *woman* to occupy in the educational world, but who is not yet free from sufferings entailed by years of mental anxiety and bodily privations. An insufficiency of the necessaries of life is not the bitterest complaint of many of these sufferers, who by their lives protest that man does not live by bread alone.[6] "Worse than bodily privations or pains" (I quote the words of one of them) "are these *aches and pangs of ignorance*, this unquenched thirst for knowledge, these unassisted and disappointed efforts to obtain it, this sight of bread enough and to spare, but locked away from *us*, this depressing sense of a miserable waste of powers bestowed on us by God, and which we know we could have used for the lessening of evil and the increase of the happiness of our fellow-creatures."

The desire for education which is widely felt by English women, and which has begun to find its expression in many practical ways, is a desire which springs from no conceit of cleverness, from no ambition of the prizes of intellectual success, as is sometimes falsely imagined, but from the conviction that for many women to get knowledge is the only way to get bread, and still more from that instinctive craving

---

4. Butler's note: "The condition of governesses in schools is, on the whole, better than in private families; they have more companionship and independence, and, except in the very poor schools, are better paid."

5. First official hospital for the insane in England. Often referred to as Bedlam.

6. Matthew 4:4.

for light which in many is stronger than the craving for bread. "Amongst the wealthier classes,"—I give the words of one who has much knowledge of that of which she speaks—"women are better provided for materially, though even here they are often left to the mercy of the chances of life, indulged and petted whilst fortune smiles, left helpless to face the storm of adverse circumstances; but here, more often than elsewhere, one meets with those sad, dreary lives, that have always seemed to me amongst the worst permitted evils of earth,—

> 'A wall so blank
> My shadow I thank
> For sometimes falling there'—[7]

is true of many a life. Even sharp misfortune is sometimes a blessing in a life of this sort; something to do, and leave to do it. I do not say that any possible education, any freedom of career, any high training of faculty, would spare *all* this waste; some part of it is of that sad mystery of life which we cannot explain, and for the unveiling of which we can only wait and pray. But I am quite sure that much of it is altogether needless, and comes from the shutting up in artificial channels of those good gifts of God which were meant to flow forth freely and bless the world. If I could only tell, as I have felt it in my own life, and in the lives of other women whom I have loved, how wearily one strains the eyes for light, which often comes not at all!

"God knows it all, and if men do not know it, it is because they have been, I will not say they are, cruelly and criminally thoughtless. I wish some of those men who talk as if they imagined our life a delightful one, could but be women for one little year, and could feel the dreariness I speak of, feel too the intense longing to be up and doing, helping in the world's work which is God's work, and know the depressing effect of that inaptitude, which is the want, not of capacity or of faculty, but of training. The serious work of life needs all the help that women as well as men can bring to it,[8] and for helpfulness something more than goodwill is needed. Always have my own ignorance and helplessness been the hindrances to that for which I would have freely given my life; and I know that other women feel in just the same way: I have heard and known too much of thoughtful women not to be sure of this. Confessions of this kind, the simplest and frankest confessions of ignorance, and of why that ignorance is painful, have been made to me many a time by women whom the world pleases to think clever, but who are too true-hearted to believe the world.

"It is not as luxury that we crave knowledge, but as bread of life for ourselves and others. We want it that we may distribute it to others, with helpful hands and words of blessing. We want it as the lever by which we may help to raise the world. If we thought only of gratifying vanity, there are easier and shorter ways to that end. Whilst men are a little too apt to depreciate the intelligence of women as a

---

7. Thomas Hood, "The Song of the Shirt," lines 47–48. See part 3 of this anthology.

8. In *The Subjection of Women*, John Stuart Mill presents a similar argument that society cannot afford to dispense with the talents of one-half of the population. See the following selection.

class, they are apt to over-rate the intelligence of individual women whom they may happen to know and esteem. Many a woman is credited with power merely because she has never been brought to the test of performance."

For the amelioration of the condition of female teachers two things are necessary: the first is to raise the intellectual status of qualified teachers, and to accord a juster social recognition to their profession; the second is, to find other occupations for those who are unfit to teach, and only take to teaching because they can do nothing else.

The first of these objects will be materially advanced—

1st—By the establishment of places for a higher education than schools can offer, such as the projected College for women.[9] Mr. Bryce,[10] in his interesting "Report on Schools in Lancashire," says, "The teachers cannot be greatly blamed for this" (i.e. inefficient teaching), "since it is the result of the inadequate provision now made in this country for the instruction of women. Conceive what schoolmasters would be, if there were in England no Universities, or any foundation schools either of the higher or the lower grade, and if the private schools, by which alone education would then be supplied, were to lose the reflex influence and the stimulating rivalry of these public institutions. This is exactly what the state of the teachers of girls is now."

2ndly—By the accordance of University certificates to women, provided always that these University certificates possess intrinsic value, declare a due amount of knowledge and of capacity to teach, and are given "with scrupulous care to none but deserving persons."

Governesses would, I hope, not be the only women who would avail themselves of these privileges. Everything is good which tends to break down the line of social demarcation which still, to a great extent, separates governesses from other ladies, as once it separated school-masters from other gentlemen; and it is greatly to be desired that women with a real talent for teaching, whatever their social position, should actually teach for a few years, and raise the profession of governesses, as the profession of schoolmasters has been raised, by an infusion of disinterested zeal and the energy of voluntary choice.

Any effort in the cause of governesses is important, not only as it affects individuals at this moment engaged in the profession, but still more in its bearing upon the future of all English girls and women, through the prospect which it holds out of an improved education for the daughters of the middle classes, who, more and more, will have to maintain themselves. And if we think how much honour and dignity ought to attach to the office of a teacher (rightly understood) we should, from the highest motives, be anxious to raise the character and social

9. Queen's College was established in London in 1848 to provide better education for governesses, and Bedford College for Women was founded the following year. Girton, the first women's college at Cambridge, was established by Emily Davies in 1869, the year following the publication of Butler's essay. It, therefore, is most likely the one to which Butler refers. Not until 1878 did the first women's college at Oxford, Lady Margaret Hall, open its doors.

10. Probably the Scotsman James Bryce (1838–1922).

standing of those who seek that office. For this question of woman's education is far from being one of intellectual progress merely; it is a question of deep moral import, and enters far into the heart of society, affecting the best interests of men as well as those of women. Mr. Francis Newman[11] says, "the increased influence of women" (through education chiefly) "will keep in check the liquor traffic, and other abominations which men too readily excuse." The connection of this question of woman's education with some of the most grievous of social problems is closer than might be supposed. De Tocqueville[12] asked an American gentleman why open immorality, such as England has to shew, was so rare in New England: the answer was, "because of the greater respect which men have for women, the women who are their equals in society." It will not be for themselves alone that enlightened and educated women will demand respect; they will claim it also for poor women, whom it is too often deemed a light matter to injure in the worst way, and even for the fallen, who through the voice of their happier sisters shall yet demand, not only compassion, but the respect due to every human being, however clouded with misery and sin.

When, on the other hand, we consider the best means of relieving the profession of Governesses by drafting its incompetent members into other occupations, the whole question of the employment of women rises before us, a painful and even a terrible problem. Three principal obstacles stand in the way of such an enlargement of woman's opportunities. These are—

(1.) Prejudice of employers and of the public.

(2.) Combinations among workmen to exclude women from their trades.

(3.) Defective education and training of the women themselves.

I will consider these in order—

(1.) Prejudice is slowly dying out, but indifference remains. Educated men who can help, who *would* help if they knew the need, have not yet learnt that need. I do not blame them with any bitterness. There has been enough already of bitterness on the one side and of levity on the other. But an acknowledgment of past error lies at the base of every true reform. Let that be acknowledged here, which every thoughtful observer must see, that through all ages of the world's history the more powerful sex have been liable to use their power carelessly, not for protection only, but for pain. So comes it that at this day just and chivalrous men find themselves, (as Lord Palmerston[13] said of the Emperor of Russia), "born to a heritage of wrong and oppression." They cannot, if they would, at once alter the structure of the society around them. But even of these just men I complain that they *do not see.* If

---

11. Francis Newman (1805–1897), brother of Cardinal John Henry Newman, was a respected scholar and author of works on religion and social and political issues. He supported women's rights, including suffrage.

12. Alexis de Tocqueville (1805–1859), French political scientist, historian, and politician, is best remembered as the author of such works as *Democracy in America* (1835–1840), a four-volume analysis of early nineteenth-century American political and social life.

13. The Irish peer, Henry John Temple 1784–1865), third Viscount Palmerston, served as Secretary of State for Foreign Affairs off and on from 1830 to 1851 and was twice prime minister.

they saw, they would act; and ought they not to see? Our best men too often know nothing of the lives of any women except those with whom they are immediately connected, and whom they guard in comfort and ease. They do not think of those who sit in cold and want outside. Many a tender-hearted but not large-hearted man, on hearing some hint of hardships among women outside his own circle, thanks God that *his* dear wife or daughter is exempted from them, and so dismisses the subject. When once such men are brought to see and to feel, we invariably find them *more* indignant than women themselves, who are well schooled in patience. Much of this misery is strange and unknown to men, and was certainly never designed by them. The old social order has changed, giving place to the new, but women have fallen out of line with the onward movement, fettered by their own cowardice and the careless selfishness of men. Custom and use press heavily on women, they endure long before they dare to think whether the system under which they suffer is a right or a wrong one, whether their burdens be removable or no,—whether, in short, they have fallen into the hands of God or man. Even when they are fully persuaded that their burdens are removable, they have no voice to raise. They are unrepresented, and the interests of the unrepresented always tend to be overlooked.

(2.) The exclusion of women from trades is in most cases notoriously based upon a coarse selfishness. Take the instance of the china painters at Worcester. "It appears that both men and women are employed in this art, but that the women having excited the jealousy of the men by surpassing them in skilful execution, and consequently earning better wages, were by them forcibly deprived of the maulsticks on which it is necessary to rest the wrist while painting. Thus the women are at once rendered incapable of any fine work, and can only be employed in the coarser kinds of painting. The masters submit to this tyranny, though to their own disadvantage, being probably afraid of a strike or riot if they resist, and the women are forced to yield from the fear of personal violence from their less skilful but heavier-fisted rivals. This story appeared in the *Edinburgh Review* for 1859,[14] and it is surprising that it did not excite more general indignation." The conduct of the Apothecaries' Company is worse than that of the china painters, inasmuch as doctors have not the excuse of indigence to justify their exclusiveness. The *Daily News*, in a recent article, concludes an account of some of the proceedings of that body with these words:—"We recommend these facts to the good people who think that coercion, restriction, and the tyranny of combination are peculiar to any one class of society. It will be a great day in England when the right of every individual to make the most of the ability which God has given him, free from interested interference, is recognised, and to that goal we are surely advancing; but our progress is slow, and it is very clear that it is not only in the lower ranks of the community that the obstructive trades' union spirit is energetically operating."

The chivalry, or the justice of educated men could scarcely be brought to bear upon a subject where chivalry and justice are needed more. In this matter, of the

14. *Edinburgh Review* 109 (April 1859): 293–336.

bad effects of trades' unions,[15] much may be hoped for from the known character of working men themselves, as a class. They are not wanting in justice, in tenderness of heart, and in a shrewd perception of right and wrong when they are placed before them: but they need enlightenment and instruction,—and they wait for it,—from those who are their superiors in education and trained intelligence. Untold good might be done, and much future misery averted, if those among our leading men who have the ear and the confidence of working-men would (themselves first instructed) bring before them fairly and patiently, such subjects as these. Economics lie at the very root of practical morality, and it is to be hoped that men of influence, and genius, and experience of life, will address themselves gravely to the task of instructing the working classes on this most grave subject.

The common objection brought before the Society for Promoting the Employment of Women,[16] is that a risk would be thus incurred of decreasing the employment of men. Now, in the first place, this is by no means certain. No one proposes to interfere with the men at present working at any trade; but while the demand for young men at high wages in the colonies continues practically unlimited, it may be questioned whether the admission to a sedentary employment at home is not a pitfall as often as an advantage. Many a young man would be healthier and happier at some manly trade in Canada or Australia, than in standing behind an English counter or plaiting straw. To take only the trades connected with women's dress and such matters, the census of 1861[17] gives the following numbers of *men* employed in trades, some of which would seem as distinctly appropriate to the one sex, as soldiering and sailoring to the other.

	Males
Mercers, Drapers, and Linen Drapers	45,660
Hair Dressers and Wig Makers	10,652
Haberdashers and Hosiers	4,327
Straw Hat and Bonnet Makers	1,687
Washermen and Laundry Keepers	1,165
Stay and Corset Makers	884
Milliners and Dress Makers	803
Artificial Flower Makers	761
Berlin Wool Dealers	63
Artists in Hair—Hair Workers	42
Baby Linen Makers	13
	66,057

15. In response to the efforts of a number of trade unions dominated by men to limit the employment of women, Emma Paterson (1848–1886) helped to establish a number of women's unions and the Women's Protective and Provident League (1874).

16. The Society for Promoting the Employment of Women was established in 1859 by a group of female activists, known as the Langham Place Circle. Prominent members included Bessie Rayner Parkes (1829–1925), Barbara Bodichon (1827–1891), and Emily Faithfull (1835–1895).

17. Butler's note: "Census for England and Wales. Vol. ii. Occupation of the people: summary tables."

Disabilities of sex are parallel to disabilities of creed, and the economical results are likely to be the same. Silk weaving was driven *into* England by the revocation of the Edict of Nantes,[18] and I believe that now several light trades are being driven *out of* England by the industrial proscription of women. "But supposing," says Miss Boucherett,[19] "that the competition for employment were so great that whatever was added to the prosperity of one sex must be deducted from that of the other, is it just that the whole of the suffering thus caused should be laid upon the weaker half of humanity? How great a contrast is there between the spirit of Christianity, and the course of conduct too frequently pursued in this our country!"

"Be just before you are chivalrous," many a woman is tempted to exclaim, when she finds every door through which she might pass to a subsistence, closed in her face with expressions of deference. Signs have not been wanting which have justified the saying "that a selfish disregard of the interests of women, and indifference to their sufferings, is the great national sin of England,—and all national sins, if unrepented, meet with their punishment sooner or later."

(3.) The defective training of the women themselves is the most serious of all the hindrances which I have been considering. Here it is that the vicious circle returns upon itself. These women cannot teach, because they are so ill educated, and again, they are so ill educated that they can do nothing *but* teach.[20] Many a woman rejected from the shop-till or housekeeper's room for ignorance and inefficiency, is compelled to offer herself among the lowest class of nursery governesses, or, failing all, to embrace the career,[21] the avenues to which stand ever wide open, yawning like the gates of hell, when all other doors are closed.

The fault of this defective training lies mainly with the middle-class parents who, as the Endowed Schools Commissioners[22] say plainly enough, educate their daughters to get husbands, and for nothing else.

Education was what the slave-owners most dreaded for their slaves, for they knew it to be the sure road to emancipation. It is to education that we must first look for the emancipation of women from the industrial restrictions of a bye gone age. In the meantime I may surely say that no lover of his country, of justice or of God, can

18. In 1598, Henry IV of France issued the Edict of Nantes, which granted considerable religious liberty to French Protestants (the Huguenots). The Edict was revoked in 1685 by Louis XIV, causing more than 400,000 Huguenots, France's major industrial class, to emigrate to England, Holland, and America.

19. Author and activist, Jessie Boucherett (1825–1905), became editor of the financially-troubled *English Woman's Journal* in 1866 and changed the title to the *Englishwoman's Review of Social and Industrial Questions* (1866–1910).

20. Butler's note: " 'In one of Jerrold's sketches, Mr. Isaac Cheek is asked, "What can you do?" Now, as Isaac had not dined for three days, he thought himself justified in saying—"*Anything.*" Hunger thus conferred the cheap diploma of omnipotence: why not of omniscience too? In a bitter moment I have been tempted to say that a governess is too often a poor lady who knows nothing, and teaches everything for nothing.'—*Dr. Hodgson.*" Douglas William Jerrold (1803–1857) was a popular playwright and contributor to the satiric journal *Punch*.

21. Prostitution.

22. The Endowed Schools Act was passed in 1869 and led to broadening the curriculum in some existing schools and to financing new schools.

see this misery unmoved. "He looked for judgment, but behold oppression, for righteousness, but behold a cry."[23]

I sometimes hear it said "I am weary of this question of the rights, or the wrongs, of women." Undoubtedly there are many who are quickly weary of any thought which is perplexing or painful: nevertheless the facts remain the same— that women constitute one half of the human race, that whatever affects them, for good or evil, affects not one half, but the whole of the human race, and that the *primary* education of all generations of men rests in the hands of women.

There are two classes of advocates of the improvement of the education and condition of women. The one class urge everything from the domestic point of view. They argue in favour of all which is likely to make women better mothers, or better companions for men,[24] but they seem incapable of judging of a woman as a human being by herself, and superstitiously afraid of anything which might strengthen her to stand alone, prepared, singlehanded, to serve her God and her country. When it is urged upon them that the women who do and must stand alone are counted by millions, they are perplexed, but only fall back on expressions of a fear lest a masculine race of women should be produced, if we admit any theories respecting them apart from conjugal and maternal relationships.

On the other hand, there are advocates who speak with some slight contempt of maternity, in whose advocacy there appears to me little evidence of depth of thought, or tenderness, or wisdom, and which bespeaks a dry, hard, unimaginative conception of human life. They appear to have no higher ideal for a woman than that of a *man* who has been "tripos'ed,"[25] and is going to "get on in the world," either in the way of making money or acquiring fame. They speak of women as if it were a compliment to them, or in any way true, to say that they are like men. Now it appears to me that both these sets of advocates have failed to see something which is very true, and that their ears are deaf to some of the subtle harmonies

23. Isaiah 5:7.

24. Butler has in mind advice books for women such as those written by the best-selling author, Sarah Stickney Ellis (1799–1882). For instance, in *The Women of England, Their Social Duties, and Domestic Habits* (1838), Ellis proposes that a woman should say to herself at the start of the day

"... if nothing extraordinary occurs to claim my attention, I will meet the family with a consciousness that, being the least engaged of any member of it, I am consequently the most at liberty to devote myself to the general good of the whole, by cultivating cheerful conversation, adapting myself to the prevailing tone of feeling, and leading those who are least happy, to think and speak of what will make them more so."

Discussing the education of women, Ellis concludes:

I still cling fondly to the hope, that, ere long, some system of female instruction will be discovered, by which the young women of England may be sent home from school prepared for the stations appointed them by Providence to fill in after life, and prepared to fill them well. Then indeed may this favoured country boast of her privileges, when her young women return to their homes and their parents, habituated to be on the watch for every opportunity of doing good to others; making it the first and the last inquiry of every day, "What can I do to make my parents, my brothers, or my sisters, more happy? I am but a feeble instrument in the hands of Providence, to work out any of his benevolent designs; but as he will give me strength, I hope to pursue the plan to which I have been accustomed, of seeking my own happiness only in the happiness of others."

25. Tripos refers to a final honors examination.

which exist in God's creation—harmonies sometimes evolved from discords—and which we are much hindered from hearing by the noise of the world, and by our own discordant utterances.

The first class of advocates do not know how strong Nature is, how true she is for the most part, and how deeply the maternal character is rooted in almost all women, married or unmarried: they are not, therefore, likely to see that when a better education is secured to women, when permission is granted them not only to win bread for themselves, but to use for the good of society, every gift bestowed on them by God, we may expect to find, (as certainly we shall find,) that they will become the *more* and not the *less* womanly. Every good quality, every virtue which we regard as distinctively feminine, will, under conditions of greater freedom, develop more freely, like plants brought out into the light from a cellar in which they languished, dwarfed and blanched, without sun or air. The woman is strong in almost every woman; and it may be called an infidelity against God and against the truth of nature to suppose that the removal of unjust restrictions, and room given to breathe freely, and to do her work in life without depression and without bitterness, will cause her to cast off her nature. It will always be in her nature to foster, to cherish, to take the part of the weak, to train, to guide, to have a care for individuals, to discern the small seeds of a great future, to warm and cherish those seeds into fulness of life. "I serve," will always be one of her favourite mottos, even should the utmost freedom be accorded her in the choice of vocation; for she, more readily perhaps than men do, recognises the wisdom and majesty of Him who said—"I am among you as he that serveth."[26] In Him,—"in Christ Jesus," says the apostle, "there is neither Jew nor Greek, there is neither bond nor free; there is neither male nor female."[27] It has been the tendency of Christianity, gradually and slowly, to break down all unfriendly barriers between races, and to extinguish slavery; and last of all it will—this is our hope—remove disabilities imposed by the stronger portion of society upon the weaker.

What do we lose by the abandonment of national exclusiveness? Is labour demoralized because slaves are free? Does *service* cease when servitude is at an end? Common sense alone, without the help of historical knowledge, might lead us to suppose that women will not do their *special* work in the world worse, but better, when justice shall be done them.[28] It is in the name of *Christ* that the removal of burdens and disabilities is preached: much wisdom might be learned regarding some of these matters if people would look more closely at this, and note that this

26. Luke 22:27.
27. Galatians 3:28.
28. Butler's note: " 'I have preached,' says Theodore Parker, 'the equivalency of man and woman— that each in some particulars is inferior to the other, but, on the whole, mankind and womankind, though so diverse, are yet equal in their natural faculties; and have set forth the evils which come to both from her present inferior position. . . . But I have thought she will generally prefer domestic to public functions, and have found no philosophic or historic argument for thinking she will ever incline much to the rough works of man, or take any considerable part in Republican politics.' " Theodore Parker (1810–1860) was a United States Unitarian theologian, pastor, and social reformer.

is the Person in whom all virtues which are considered essentially womanly, as well as those which are considered essentially manly, found their perfect development. A little meditation on this double truth—that in Christ all distinctions are done away, and that in Him, nevertheless, were exhibited in perfect beauty the distinctive virtues of the feminine character—would suggest some lessons which the world has been very slow to learn, would tend to remove groundless fears regarding the consequences of the abandonment of many unreasonable and unchristian theories which prevail, and to counteract the materialistic doctrine which has sunk too deep into the heart of our so-called Christian community, a doctrine which amounts to this, that "the weaker races, classes, persons must struggle on unaided, and if they are trampled down and die out, the fact proves that it is better for the world that they should perish, so only a stronger and higher stock will remain";[29] a doctrine of which we see the fruits in our wickednesses in Asia, &c.,[30] and which takes its stand on a supposed "law of nature" that the weak must go down.

The tone in which certain foolish popular writers speak of unmarried and childless women betrays both coarseness of feeling and ignorance. They speak of these women as having altogether missed their vocation,[31] and as necessarily dwarfed in affection and motive, because they have not performed certain physical functions. We are all mothers or foster-mothers. The few exceptions to this rule,— the cases in which the maternal feelings are weak or wanting,—are to be found among mothers of families as well as among childless women. I have known many unmarried women in whom all the best characteristics of maternity are stronger than in some who are actually mothers. It would be wise of the State to avail itself of this abundance of generous womanliness, of tender and wise motherliness which lives in the hearts of thousands of women who are free to bring their capacities to bear where they are most needed. The country counts by tens of thousands its orphan and outcast children, in workhouses,[32] and in the streets of our great cities. These orphans have lately been called "the children of the State": for the care of these children of the State alone, mothers and nurses of the State are needed, women who must be free to some extent from domestic ties of their own. These workhouse children are not likely to grow up to be useful to the country or

29. Butler's note: "F. Newman." See note 11 above.

30. Conservative Britons, particularly in the years following the Indian Mutiny of 1857, accepted the imperialistic notion of Indians as culturally and intellectually inferior and, therefore, in need of British rule. The same attitude applied to Africans. See Kipling's "The White Man's Burden" and Carlyle's "The Nigger Question" in part 1.

31. The anonymous author of an 1859 article for the *Saturday Review* put it bluntly: "Married life is woman's profession; and to this life her training—that of dependence—is modelled. Of course by not getting a husband, or losing him, she may find that she is without resources. All that can be said of her is, she has failed in business; and no social reform can prevent such failures." See "Queen Bees or Working Bees?" in this section.

32. Under the provisions of the New Poor Law of 1834, the government established workhouses where paupers lived and, if able, labored. Children between the ages of five and fourteen who were orphans or whose parents were paupers were housed separately in Poor Law schools and could be put to work or apprenticed.

other than dangerous classes, while they are left wholly to the mercy of vulgar, uneducated people.[33]

Leon Fauchat exclaimed, when told of crimes committed in our country against children,—"Est-il possible que ces choses soient permises par une nation qui a des entrailles!"[34] "Take heed that ye offend not one of these little ones,"[35] are words of most solemn import: when women begin to deserve and acquire more weight in the community, the warning contained in them will be better understood. The interests of children will not remain unrepresented any longer than women remain so. I say this with certainty, knowing the nature of woman. It will not be left to an indignant father, or philanthropist, or to an impassioned poetess, at long intervals to translate in the ears of the public the inarticulate cry of the children:

> "They are weeping in the playtime of the others,
>   In the country of the free,
>
> . . . .
>
> For the man's grief abhorrent, draws and presses
>   Down the cheeks of infancy.
>
> . . . .
>
> "They look up with their pale and sunken faces,
>   And their look is dread to see,
> For they mind you of their Angels in their places,
>   With eyes meant for Deity:
> 'How long,' they say, 'how long, O cruel nation,
> Will you stand, to move the world, on a child's heart,
>   Stifle down with a mailed heel its palpitation,
> And tread onward to your throne amid the mart?
> Our blood splashes upwards, O our tyrants,
>   And your purple shows your path;
> *But the child's sob curseth deeper in the silence*
>   *Than the strong man in his wrath.'* "[36]

33. Butler's note: "I have spoken of the incompetency of a vast number of teachers, an incompetency sometimes natural, more often the effect of want of training. But I believe it is widely acknowledged that women generally have a great aptitude for teaching boys as well as girls. Mr. Bryce, in his Report, says, 'The bright point in this otherwise gloomy landscape is that women are naturally skilful teachers, and that they are, as far as my observation goes, zealous and conscientious teachers. Whenever I happened to hear the teaching of a lady of good ability who had herself been thoroughly educated, its merits struck me as at least equal, and probably superior, to those which would be found in the teaching of a man of the same general capacity and education. Women seem to have more patience as teachers, more quickness in seeing whether the pupil understands, more skill in adapting their explanations to the peculiarities of the pupils' minds, and certainly a nicer discernment of his or her character. They are quite as clear in exposition as men are, and, when well trained, quite as capable of making their teaching philosophical. I must confess myself to have been also impressed by the interest which they so often took in their pupils, and their genuine ardour to do their best for them.' "

34. "Is it possible that such things as these are allowed by a nation which has feelings?" Léon Faucher (1804–1854) was a French journalist, economist, and politician who published *d'Etudes sur l'Angleterre* in 1837.

35. Matthew 18:10.

36. Elizabeth Barrett Browning, "The Cry of the Children," lines 11–12, 27–28, 149–60. See part 3 for the complete poem.

The ears of my reader would not endure to hear what I could tell, what my eyes have seen, of outraged innocence, of horrors and miseries endured among the children of the poor. I am not unmindful of the benevolent enterprise there is in our country, the orphanages, schools and homes springing up everywhere. God be thanked for these! but they do not yet meet the evil; and we must remember that stone walls do not shut out crime, nor regulations confer blessing; these institutions themselves fail in their purpose unless the compassionate motive which originated them be sustained in a constant and abundant flow. The histories of many charities in foreign countries and at home prove that institutions devised by loving hearts for protection and blessing, have become, for lack of the constancy of the internal impulse, neither more nor less than "habitations of cruelty." What I here complain of is the thriftless waste of good feelings, of emotion,—emotion which on the one hand is ill trained, and consequently takes a false or unreal direction, and on the other is wearing itself out, unclaimed. Tears shed over sentimental works of fiction or some imaginative woe might well be bestowed on the realities around us. Surely there is room enough among *them* for the promptings of a mighty compassion! Surely there is cause enough *here* for tears! "Mine eye runneth down with rivers of water for the destruction of the daughter of my people."[37]

And there is other work on every side waiting to be done by women,—the work of healers, preachers, physicians, artists, organizers of labour, captains of industry,[38] &c., while on the other hand women are waiting to be prepared for service, and ready to bridge over, as they alone can, many a gulf between class and class which now presents a grave obstacle to social and political progress.[39]

The second kind of advocacy of the rights of women, of which I spoke, may be said to be simply a reaction against the first. It is chiefly held by a few women of superior intellect who feel keenly the disadvantages of their class, their feebleness, through want of education, against public opinion, which is taken advantage of by base people, their inability, through want of representation, to defend their weaker members, and the dwarfing of the faculties of the ablest and best among them. These women have associated little with men, or at best, know very little of their inner life, and do not therefore see as clearly as they see their own loss, the equal loss that it is to men, and the injury it involves to their characters, to live dissociated from women: they therefore look forth from their isolation with something of an excusable envy on the freer and happier lot, which includes, they believe, a greater power to do good, and imagine that the only hope for themselves is to push into the ranks of men, to demand the same education, the same opportunities, in order that they may compete with them on their own ground. They have lost the conception of the noblest development possible for both men and women; for assuredly that which men, for the most part, aim at, is not the noblest, and yet that is what such women appear to wish to imitate; they have lost sight of the truth, too,

37. Lamentations 3:48.
38. "Captains of Industry" is the title of the fourth chapter of the fourth book of *Past and Present* by Thomas Carlyle. See part 1 for selections from *Past and Present.*
39. See Octavia Hill's "Trained Workers for the Poor," in part 2, for a similar argument.

that men and women were made equal indeed, but not alike, and were meant to supplement one another, and that in so doing,—each supplying force which the other lacks,—they are attracted with a far greater amount of impulse to a common centre. When St. Chrysostom[40] preached in Constantinople, that "men ought to be pure, and women courageous," he was treated as a dangerous innovator, a perverter of the facts of nature, a changer of customs. I hope that many such innovators will arise, who will shew forth in practice the possibility of the attainment of a common standard of excellence for man and woman, not by usurpation on either hand, nor by servile imitation, but by the action of each upon each, by mutual teaching and help. The above misconception, like many other errors, results from men and women living so dissociated as they do in our country; hence comes also all that reserve, and incapacity for understanding each other which has existed between the sexes for so many generations, those false notions about women which are entertained in society, and great injury to the work, and happiness, and dignity of man and woman alike: for it may be truly said that many of the most serious evils in England are but the bitter and various fruit of the sacrilegious disjoining of that which God had joined together, the disunion of men and women, theoretically and practically, in all the graver work of life.

The following account of the School of Art, in Newman Street, London, is interesting, as affording some illustration of this subject. Mrs. Heatherley writes, "This School was begun on the separate principle, about twenty-three years ago, by Mr. James Mathews Leigh.[41] I first knew the place in 1848, when I studied as an amateur. Mr. Leigh, whilst agreeing to the idea of mixed classes as a theory, always declared that the men's conduct and conversation would render it impossible for any lady to come amongst them, and they were certainly very rough in manner when, after Mr. Leigh's death, we took the school. We were warned that we should be ruined by introducing the mixed system. Very soon both parties found the convenience of studying in the Gallery every day, instead of having to take their places on alternate days. Finding it succeed, at the end of 1861 we admitted ladies to the evening school: there are about two hundred students in the course of the year. Great individual freedom is allowed, and a most friendly feeling exists amongst the students. Every one who knew the place before the admission of women agrees that there has been great improvement; quite another tone prevails. We have never had to dismiss anyone for conduct that was disapproved. From here went the first ladies to the Royal Academy,[42] one of whom, a girl of about twenty-one, gained the gold medal, last December, for the best historical picture. As a general rule, where there are equal facilities, the women are the most successful. The Academy ceased

40. St. John Chrysostom (ca. 347–407), an early church father recognized as a great preacher, who became Archbishop of Constantinople in 398.

41. James Mathews Leigh (1808–1860), a painter and teacher of drawing, established a popular London art school.

42. Laura Herford was the first female artist to be admitted to the prestigious Royal Academy school in 1860 when she signed only her initials to her entry. No woman was elected to full membership in the Academy in the nineteenth century.

to admit them when their numbers reached about twelve, and now takes them in only when the time of studentship of others expires. They made this change at the end of two years, without giving any notice here or at any other school, to the great disappointment of a number of girls. This I think is an act of hardship, as there has been shown positively that no incompetence exists. Unless there be chances offered to women of being able to follow a profession, parents will invest in consols,[43] as a general rule, rather than in a superior education. The mention of our school may be useful, because there are doubts in many minds as to the expediency of free intercourse between young people, and facts are better than theories. The more that is done to bring young men and women together in a rational manner, the sooner we may hope to arrive at a social state less immoral than the present."

I am persuaded that anyone who will candidly and carefully consider the histories of separate communities of men or women, for educational or other purposes, must see that the evils attendant on such a system as they represent outweigh its conveniences. The arrangement is for a given period, but not so the evils which accompany it, for they,—and of this men are not ignorant,—too often leave their effects, I may say their curse, throughout life. The objection rises at once of the difficulty of adopting any other arrangement than the present, which may be called an unnatural one. This objection will be more effectually met by facts than by reasoning, and in time facts will speak for themselves, while up to the present they attest that whenever the experiment of a different system has been tried, the difficulties have been found to be very much less than it was believed they would be, before the trial was made.

To conclude this part of my subject, although I grant that too much stress cannot be laid upon the improvement of the education of women who will be actually the mothers of a future generation, yet I wish, on the one hand, that persons who only look at it from this point of view would take more into account the valuable service our country might command if it but understood the truth about the condition and feelings of its unmarried women, and that a more generous trust were felt in the strength of woman's nature, and the probable direction of its development when granted more expansion, while on the other hand I should like to see a truer conception of the highest possibilities for women than is implied in the attempt to imitate men, and a deeper reverence for the God of nature, whose wisdom is more manifested in variety than in uniformity. It cannot be denied that a just cause has sometimes been advocated by women in a spirit of bitterness. Energy impeded in one direction, will burst forth in another; hence the defiant and sometimes grotesque expression which the lives and acts of some few women have been of the injustice done to them by society. This will cease, and while it lasts, it ought to excite our pity rather than our anger. It must be remembered that it is but a symptom of a long endured servitude, a protest against a state of things which we hope will give place to a better. It is folly to regard it as the

---

43. Consols refer to the Consolidated Fund, a mutual fund that from 1751 owned the bonds of the national debt and was an exceptionally secure investment.

natural fruit of that of which we have scarcely seen the beginning. Acts of violence on the part of a long oppressed nation are not the offspring of dawning liberties, but of a doomed tyranny. Again, no important reform can be carried without a measure of attendant confusion. Evil agencies are the most vigilant for destruction at the beginning of a great and good work, and many lives have to be consumed in its inauguration. Any evils which may at first attend a social reform ought not to alarm us: they are transient; they are but the breakers on the bar which must be crossed before we launch into deep waters, but the "noise and dust of the wagon which brings the harvest home."

There is a near future and there is a far future; there are plans for the near future and plans for the far future. The world is full of plans for the near future; not so of plans for the far future. There are people who do just what comes first to their hand to do, there are others who do all for a near future, others again who do all for a far off end. The first and the last have much in common; it is the second aim, which when exclusively pursued, misleads. Plans and schemes for the near future gain and obtain with most people; not unfrequently they wither away like untimely fruit: those who look afar off prevail, yet not they, but rather He prevails in them, who taught them to stretch their vision to the distant horizon, and enables them to bear with composure the disappointment of present hopes.

Some say, "in order to insure success for this or that movement, you must have a scheme beforehand, a well-planned system, a fixed principle of action, else you will be blown hither and thither." Without offering any opposition to such a theory, there are others to whom there appears but one principle of action,—to fix the eyes on the far future, and to do to-day the work of to-day; each day to undo the heavy burdens as they come to their hand, each day to break some link of the chains which bind, and to let some who are now oppressed go free, God guiding these efforts to the desired end.[44] They have more faith in that which grows from within than in that which is planned from without, and built according to the preconceived plan. Such plans or schemes as must be adopted by them are made as elastic as possible, so that the builders can avail themselves, at each step, of experience gained, and be ready to correct or undo any part of the work without sacrificing the whole; they are content with the light which falls on the path immediately at their feet, and with the fairer light in the distance. Perhaps it is by such a principle of action that we can best supply "the needs of the times," and it is the possibility of adopting such a principle in times of need that alone can ensure permanence in usefulness for the venerable institutions of the country. What such institutions generally do is to resist all movement, or if they admit any change, it is only to crystallize anew in an altered form. Almost all true help is special; and crystallized institutions seldom have help to give for great and special necessities. But there are times when an impulse, having its origin in the *hearts* of men, is

44. Butler's note: " 'Is not this the fast that I have chosen? to loose the bands of wickedness, to undo the heavy burdens, and to let the oppressed go free, and that ye break every yoke; is it not to deal thy bread to the hungry, and that thou bring the poor that are cast out to thy house?'—Isaiah lviii.6,7."

found to be stronger than custom and use; if it cannot work within the established bounds, or by existing machinery, it will work without them. Somehow or other difficulties vanish before such an impulse, and much is accomplished which before was held to be impossible.

I cannot conclude these remarks without expressing the gladness and gratitude with which I am filled when I see the earnest spirit in which some of the best and most thoughtful men are beginning to consider these matters; and I venture especially to acknowledge the kindness of men in high educational positions themselves, whose sympathies have lately been enlisted on behalf of the women-teachers whose struggles, and sorrows, and social disadvantages I have tried to indicate. Mr. Maurice[45] says, very truly, "Whenever in trade or in any department of human activity, restrictions tending to the advantage of one class and the injury of others have been removed, there a divine power has been at work counteracting not only the selfish calculations, but often the apparently sagacious reasonings of their defenders." If we were not assured that there is indeed a divine power at work in all these things which some of us have so deeply at heart, we should lack the only stimulus which enables us to work on, to live and to die for that which we hold to be right and true; for "except the Lord build the house, their labour is but vain that build it."[46]

45. Frederick Denison Maurice (1805–1872), was an educator and theologian and one of the founders, along with Charles Kingsley (1819–1875) and John Malcolm Ludlow (1812–1911), of the Christian Socialist Movement, which stressed the Christian imperative of working for social salvation. See part 2 for an essay by Maurice.

46. Psalms 127:1.

JOHN STUART MILL

ONE OF THE leading intellectuals of the nineteenth century, John Stuart Mill (1806–1873) was the eldest son of James Mill, a historian and dedicated friend and follower of the social, political, and economic reformer Jeremy Bentham. Bentham's disciples subscribed to the philosophy of Utilitarianism (also called Benthamism), which relied on the use of reason to determine what would produce the greatest practical good, or utility, for the greatest number of individuals.

John Stuart Mill was instructed at home by his father, who applied Utilitarian principles in an intensive educational experiment. At age three, John studied Greek and was reading Plato by age seven; at age eight, he began Latin, studied geometry and calculus, and assumed the responsibility of teaching his younger sister. His father introduced the study of logic when Mill was twelve, challenging him to determine the fallacies in arguments. Mill wrote years later in his *Autobiography*, "I know of nothing, in my education, to which I am more indebted for whatever capacity of thinking I have attained." Demanding as the curriculum was, it never degenerated into rote memorization. Mill credited his father with continually emphasizing comprehension.

In 1823, at age seventeen, Mill accepted employment with the East India Company and published his first articles in the *Westminster Review*, an influential Utilitarian journal. In 1830, he met and fell in love with Harriet Taylor, a married woman, whom he wed in 1851, two years after her husband died. The anonymous author of "The Enfranchisement of Women," an 1851 essay that appeared in the *Westminster Review*, Harriet was also said by Mill to be the co-author of much of his best work.

In addition to holding a responsible position with the East India Company throughout his adult life, Mill managed to produce a significant volume of analytic work on logic, economics, and politics. His *System of Logic* (1843) and *Principles of Political Economy* (1848) were assigned as university textbooks throughout the nineteenth century. Other influential and widely read works include *On Liberty* (1859), *The Subjection of Women* (1869), and his *Autobiography* (published posthumously in 1873).

Mill was elected to Parliament as a Liberal in 1865, but his unpopular support for such controversial issues as women's suffrage and government reform resulted in his serving for only three years. In 1867, his amendment to the Second Reform Bill calling for the enfranchisement of women was soundly defeated. His book, *The Subjection of Women*, written six years earlier, was not published until 1869, when it met with damning reviews labeling Mill as insane and depraved. In actuality, Mill brings to the subject of women's rights and women's roles the thorough, carefully reasoned analysis characteristic of all his prose. In his examination of social, legal, and moral issues, he counters the traditional male argument that female equality is "unnatural" by pointing out that it is only "uncustomary," and, from his perspective, unsound. Mill's book is devoted to providing a more rational and enlightened answer to the "Woman Question."

From *The Subjection of Women*

From Chapter I

Even the preliminary knowledge, what the differences between the sexes now are, apart from all question as to how they are made what they are, is still in the crudest and most incomplete state.[1] Medical practitioners and physiologists have ascertained, to some extent, the differences in bodily constitution; and this is an important element to the psychologist; but hardly any medical practitioner is a psychologist. Respecting the mental characteristics of women, their observations are of no more worth than those of common men. It is a subject on which nothing

1. Scientific and medical treatises addressing sexual differences became more common in the nineteenth century; most reinforced traditional views of gender roles. For instance, in *The Functions and Disorders of the Re-productive Organs in Childhood, Youth, Adult Age, and Advanced Life Considered in Their Physiological, Social, and Moral Relations* (1857), Dr. William Acton (1813–1875) presents the domestic role as natural for women: "The best mothers, wives, and managers of households, know little or nothing of sexual indulgences. Love of home, children, and domestic duties, are the only passions they feel." Charles Darwin (1809–1882), in *On the Origin of Species by Means of Natural Selection* (1859), and more explicitly in *The Descent of Man, and Selection in Relation to Sex* (1871), advanced the notion of biologically determined characteristics, both physical and mental: "It is generally admitted," he claims in *The Descent of Man*, "that with woman the powers of intuition, of rapid perception, and perhaps of imitation, are more strongly marked than in man; but some, at least, of these faculties are characteristic of the lower races, and therefore of a past and lower state of civilisation." In 1874, five years after the publication of *The Subjection of Women*, the *Fortnightly Review* published Henry Maudsley's "Sex in Mind and in Education," an essay that presented long-standing, widely held beliefs in forceful terms. Maudsley expressed doubts about the advisability of higher education for young women. Since "the development of puberty does draw heavily upon the vital resources of the female constitution," the reproductive system would be weakened if energy were directed toward intellectual pursuits. Reasoning that "When Nature spends in one direction, she must economise in another direction," Maudsley reminded women of their patriotic duty to produce strong sons of England: ". . . it would be an ill thing, if it should so happen, that we got the advantages of a quantity of female intellectual work at the price of a puny, enfeebled, and sickly race."

final can be known, so long as those who alone can really know it, women themselves, have given but little testimony, and that little, mostly suborned. It is easy to know stupid women. Stupidity is much the same all the world over. A stupid person's notions and feelings may confidently be inferred from those which prevail in the circle by which the person is surrounded. Not so with those whose opinions and feelings are an emanation from their own nature and faculties. It is only a man here and there who has any tolerable knowledge of the character even of the women of his own family. I do not mean, of their capabilities; these nobody knows, not even themselves, because most of them have never been called out. I mean their actually existing thoughts and feelings. . . .

One thing we may be certain of,—that what is contrary to women's nature to do, they never will be made to do by simply giving their nature free play. The anxiety of mankind to interfere in behalf of nature, for fear lest nature should not succeed in effecting its purpose, is an altogether unnecessary solicitude. What women by nature cannot do, it is quite superfluous to forbid them from doing. What they can do, but not so well as the men who are their competitors, competition suffices to exclude them from; since nobody asks for protective duties and bounties in favor of women; it is only asked that the present bounties and protective duties in favor of men should be recalled. If women have a greater natural inclination for some things than for others, there is no need of laws or social inculcation to make the majority of them do the former in preference to the latter. Whatever women's services are most wanted for, the free play of competition will hold out the strongest inducements to them to undertake. And, as the words imply, they are most wanted for the things for which they are most fit; by the apportionment of which to them, the collective faculties of the two sexes can be applied on the whole with the greatest sum of valuable result.

The general opinion of men is supposed to be, that the natural vocation of a woman is that of a wife and mother. I say, is supposed to be, because, judging from acts—from the whole of the present constitution of society—one might infer that their opinion was the direct contrary. They might be supposed to think that the alleged natural vocation of women was of all things the most repugnant to their nature; insomuch that if they are free to do anything else—if any other means of living, or occupation of their time and faculties, is open, which has any chance of appearing desirable to them—there will not be enough of them who will be willing to accept the condition said to be natural to them. If this is the real opinion of men in general it would be well that it should be spoken out. I should like to hear somebody openly enunciating the doctrine (it is already implied in much that is written on the subject)—"It is necessary to society that women should marry and produce children. They will not do so unless they are compelled. Therefore it is necessary to compel them." The merits of the case would then be clearly defined. It would be exactly that of the slave-holders of South Carolina and Louisiana. "It is necessary that cotton and sugar should be grown. White men cannot produce them. Negroes will not, for any wages which we choose to give them. *Ergo* they must be compelled." An illustration still closer to the point is that of impressment.[2] Sailors must absolutely be had to defend the country. It often happens that they will not voluntarily enlist. Therefore there must be the power of forcing them. How often has this logic been used! and, but for one flaw in it, without doubt it would have been successful up to this day. But it is open to the retort—First pay the sailors the honest value of their labor. When you have made it as well worth their while to serve you, as to work for other employers, you will have no more difficulty than others have in obtaining their services. To this there is no logical answer except "I will not": and as people are now not only ashamed, but are not desirous, to rob the laborer of his hire,[3] impressment is no longer advocated. Those who attempt to force women into marriage by closing all other doors against them, lay themselves open to a similar retort. If they mean what they say, their opinion must evidently be, that men do not render the married condition so desirable to women, as to induce them to accept it for its own recommendations. . . .

From Chapter III

On the other point which is involved in the just equality of women, their admissibility to all the functions and occupations hitherto retained as the monopoly of the stronger sex, I should anticipate no difficulty in convincing anyone who has gone with me on the subject of the equality of women in the family. I believe that their disabilities elsewhere are only clung to in order to maintain their subordination in domestic life; because the generality of the male sex cannot yet tolerate the idea of living with an equal. Were it not for that, I think that almost everyone, in the existing state of opinion in politics and political economy, would admit the injustice of excluding half the human race from the greater number of lucrative occupations, and from almost all high social functions; ordaining from their birth either that they are not, and cannot by any possibility become, fit for employments which are legally open to the stupidest and basest of the other sex, or else that however fit they may be, those employments shall be interdicted to them, in order to be preserved for the exclusive benefit of males. In the last two centuries, when (which was seldom the case) any reason beyond the mere existence of the fact was thought to be required to justify the disabilities of women, people seldom assigned as a reason their inferior mental capacity; which, in times when there was a real trial of personal faculties (from which all women were not excluded) in the struggles of public life, no one really believed in. The reason given in those days was not women's unfitness, but the interest of society, by which was meant the interest of men: just as the *raison d'état*, meaning the convenience of the government, and the support of existing authority, was deemed a sufficient explanation and excuse for

2. Impressment refers to seizing men for public service. The practice was largely accepted until military recruitment reform began in the 1850s.

3. Luke 10:7.

the most flagitious[4] crimes. In the present day, power holds a smoother language, and whomsoever it oppresses, always pretends to do so for their own good: accordingly, when anything is forbidden to women, it is thought necessary to say, and desirable to believe, that they are incapable of doing it, and that they depart from their real path of success and happiness when they aspire to it. But to make this reason plausible (I do not say valid), those by whom it is urged must be prepared to carry it to a much greater length than anyone ventures to do in the face of present experience. It is not sufficient to maintain that women on the average are less gifted than men on the average, with certain of the higher mental faculties, or that a smaller number of women than of men are fit for occupations and functions of the highest intellectual character. It is necessary to maintain that no women at all are fit for them, and that the most eminent women are inferior in mental faculties to the most mediocre of the men on whom those functions at present devolve. For if the performance of the function is decided either by competition, or by any mode of choice which secures regard to the public interest, there needs be no apprehension that any important employments will fall into the hands of women inferior to average men, or to the average of their male competitors. The only result would be that there would be fewer women than men in such employments; a result certain to happen in any case, if only from the preference always likely to be felt by the majority of women for the one vocation in which there is nobody to compete with them. Now, the most determined depreciator of women will not venture to deny, that when we add the experience of recent times to that of ages past, women, and not a few merely, but many women, have proved themselves capable of everything, perhaps without a single exception, which is done by men, and of doing it successfully and creditably. The utmost that can be said is, that there are many things which none of them have succeeded in doing as well as they have been done by some men—many in which they have not reached the very highest rank. But there are extremely few, dependent only on mental faculties, in which they have not attained the rank next to the highest. Is not this enough, and much more than enough, to make it a tyranny to them, and a detriment to society, that they should not be allowed to compete with men for the exercise of these functions? Is it not a mere truism to say, that such functions are often filled by men far less fit for them than numbers of women, and who would be beaten by women in any fair field of competition? What difference does it make that there may be men somewhere, fully employed about other things, who may be still better qualified for the things in question than these women? Does not this take place in all competitions? Is there so great a superfluity of men fit for high duties, that society can afford to reject the service of any competent person? Are we so certain of always finding a man made to our hands for any duty or function of social importance which falls vacant, that we lose nothing by putting a ban upon one-half of mankind, and refusing beforehand to make their faculties available, however distinguished they may be? And even if we could do without them, would

4. Vicious.

it be consistent with justice to refuse to them their fair share of honor and distinction, or to deny to them the equal moral right of all human beings to choose their occupation (short of injury to others) according to their own preferences, at their own risk? Nor is the injustice confined to them: it is shared by those who are in a position to benefit by their services. To ordain that any kind of persons shall not be physicians, or shall not be advocates, or shall not be members of Parliament,[5] is to injure not them only, but all who employ physicians or advocates, or elect members of Parliament, and who are deprived of the stimulating effect of greater competition on the exertions of the competitors, as well as restricted to a narrower range of individual choice. . . .

I have said that it cannot now be known how much of the existing mental differences between men and women is natural, and how much artificial; whether there are any natural differences at all; or, supposing all artificial causes of difference to be withdrawn, what natural character would be revealed. I am not about to attempt what I have pronounced impossible; but doubt does not forbid conjecture, and where certainty is unattainable, there may yet be the means of arriving at some degree of probability. The first point, the origin of the differences actually observed, is the one most accessible to speculation; and I shall attempt to approach it, by the only path at which it can be reached; by tracing the mental consequences of external influences. We cannot isolate a human being from the circumstances of his condition, so as to ascertain experimentally what he would have been by nature; but we can consider what he is, and what his circumstances have been, and whether the one would have been capable of producing the other.

Let us take, then, the only marked case which observation affords, of apparent inferiority of women to men, if we except the merely physical one of bodily strength. No production in philosophy, science, or art, entitled to the first rank, has been the work of a woman. Is there any mode of accounting for this, without supposing that women are naturally incapable of producing them?

In the first place we may fairly question whether experience has afforded sufficient grounds for an induction. It is scarcely three generations since women, saving very rare exceptions, have begun to try their capacity in philosophy, science, or art.[6] It is only in the present generation that their attempts have been at all

5. Parliamentary seats were out of the question for nineteenth-century women, who were ineligible to vote. Women aged thirty or over won the vote in 1918; the voting age for women was lowered to twenty-one in 1928. Entry into the legal profession was also belated for women because it required a university education, which women were denied until late in the century (see note 6). An Englishwoman, Elizabeth Blackwell (1821–1901), who received her medical training in the United States, became the first female physician to have her name added to the British medical register in 1859; however, she had few nineteenth-century successors due to the exclusion of women from medical education and certification exams until the last quarter of the century. See Emily Davies's 1862 speech, "Medicine as a Profession for Women" in this section.

6. Women stood little chance of entering fields such as philosophy, science, and art as long as a university education and membership in learned and professional organizations remained closed to them. Women's colleges were established at Cambridge in 1869 and at Oxford in 1879; however, women were not permitted to take degrees from these venerable institutions until 1920–21. Women were denied membership in scientific societies such as the Linnaean Society (natural history), the

numerous; and they are even now extremely few, everywhere but in England and France. It is a relevant question, whether a mind possessing the requisites of first-rate eminence in speculation or creative art could have been expected, on the mere calculation of chances, to turn up during that lapse of time, among the women whose tastes and personal position admitted of their devoting themselves to these pursuits. In all things which there has yet been time for—in all but the very highest grades in the scale of excellence, especially in the department in which they have been longest engaged, literature (both prose and poetry)—women have done quite as much, have obtained fully as high prizes and as many of them, as could be expected from the length of time and the number of competitors. . . .

There are other reasons, besides those which we have now given, that help to explain why women remain behind men, even in the pursuits which are open to both. For one thing, very few women have time for them. This may seem a paradox; it is an undoubted social fact. The time and thoughts of every woman have to satisfy great previous demands on them for things practical. There is, first, the superintendence of the family and the domestic expenditure, which occupies at least one woman in every family, generally the one of mature years and acquired experience; unless the family is so rich as to admit of delegating that task to hired agency, and submitting to all the waste and malversation[7] inseparable from that mode of conducting it. The superintendence of a household, even when not in other respects laborious, is extremely onerous to the thoughts; it requires incessant vigilance, an eye which no detail escapes, and presents questions for consideration and solution, foreseen and unforeseen, at every hour of the day, from which the person responsible for them can hardly ever shake herself free. If a woman is of a rank and circumstances which relieve her in a measure from these cares, she has still devolving on her the management for the whole family of its intercourse with others—of what is called society, and the less the call made on her by the former duty, the greater is always the development of the latter; the dinner parties, concerts, evening parties, morning visits, letter writing, and all that goes with them. All this is over and above the engrossing duty which society imposes exclusively on women, of making themselves charming. A clever woman of the higher ranks finds nearly a sufficient employment of her talents in cultivating the graces of manner and the arts of conversation. To look only at the outward side of the subject: the great and continual exercise of thought which all women who attach any value to dressing well (I do not mean expensively, but with taste, and perception of natural and of artificial *convenance*[8]) must bestow upon their own dress, perhaps also upon that of their daughters, would alone go a great way towards achieving respectable results in art, or science, or literature, and does actually exhaust much

---

Geological Society, the Zoological Society, and the Royal Society of London. Similarly, women were excluded from the schools of the Royal Academy, the most prestigious British art institute, until 1860 and from full membership in the Academy until 1936.

7. Misconduct.

8. Convention; agreement.

of the time and mental power they might have to spare for either.[9] If it were possible that all this number of little practical interests (which are made great to them) should leave them either much leisure, or much energy and freedom of mind, to be devoted to art or speculation, they must have a much greater original supply of active faculty than the vast majority of men. But this is not all. Independently of the regular offices of life which devolve upon a woman, she is expected to have her time and faculties always at the disposal of everybody. If a man has not a profession to exempt him from such demands, still, if he has a pursuit, he offends nobody by devoting his time to it; occupation is received as a valid excuse for his not answering to every casual demand which may be made on him. Are a woman's occupations, especially her chosen and voluntary ones, ever regarded as excusing her from any of what are termed the calls of society? Scarcely are her most necessary and recognized duties allowed as an exemption. It requires an illness in the family, or something else out of the common way, to entitle her to give her own business the precedence over other people's amusement. She must always be at the beck and call of somebody, generally of everybody. If she has a study or a pursuit, she must snatch any short interval which accidentally occurs to be employed in it. . . .

From Chapter IV

There remains a question, not of less importance than those already discussed, and which will be asked the most importunately by those opponents whose conviction is somewhat shaken on the main point. What good are we to expect from the changes proposed in our customs and institutions? Would mankind be at all better off if women were free? If not, why disturb their minds, and attempt to make a social revolution in the name of an abstract right? . . .

To which let me first answer, the advantage of having the most universal and pervading of all human relations regulated by justice instead of injustice. . . .

The second benefit to be expected from giving to women the free use of their faculties, by leaving them the free choice of their employments, and opening to them the same field of occupation and the same prizes and encouragements as to other human beings, would be that of doubling the mass of mental faculties available for the higher service of humanity. Where there is now one person qualified to benefit mankind and promote the general improvement, as a public

---

9. Mill's note: " 'It appears to be the same right turn of mind which enables a man to acquire the *truth*, or the just idea of what is right, in the ornaments, as in the more stable principles of art. It has still the same center of perfection, though it is the center of a smaller circle. To illustrate this by the fashion of dress, in which there is allowed to be a good or bad taste. The component parts of dress are continually changing from great to little, from short to long; but the general form still remains: it is still the same general dress which is comparatively fixed, though on a very slender foundation; but it is on this which fashion must rest. He who invents with the most success, or dresses in the best taste, would probably, from the same sagacity employed to greater purposes, have discovered equal skill, or have formed the same correct taste, in the highest labors of art.'—*Sir Joshua Reynolds' Discourses*, Disc. vii."

teacher, or an administrator of some branch of public or social affairs, there would then be a chance of two. Mental superiority of any kind is at present everywhere so much below the demand; there is such a deficiency of persons competent to do excellently anything which it requires any considerable amount of ability to do; that the loss to the world, by refusing to make use of one-half of the whole quantity of talent it possesses, is extremely serious. It is true that this amount of mental power is not totally lost. Much of it is employed, and would in any case be employed, in domestic management, and in the few other occupations open to women; and from the remainder indirect benefit is in many individual cases obtained, through the personal influence of individual women over individual men. But these benefits are partial; their range is extremely circumscribed; and if they must be admitted, on the one hand, as a deduction from the amount of fresh social power that would be acquired by giving freedom to one-half of the whole sum of human intellect, there must be added, on the other, the benefit of the stimulus that would be given to the intellect of men by the competition; or (to use a more true expression) by the necessity that would be imposed on them of deserving precedency before they could expect to obtain it.

This great accession to the intellectual power of the species, and to the amount of intellect available for the good management of its affairs, would be obtained, partly, through the better and more complete intellectual education of women, which would then improve *pari passu*[10] with that of men. Women in general would be brought up equally capable of understanding business, public affairs, and the higher matters of speculation, with men in the same class of society; and the select few of the one as well as of the other sex, who were qualified not only to comprehend what is done or thought by others, but to think or do something considerable themselves, would meet with the same facilities for improving and training their capacities in the one sex as in the other. In this way, the widening of the sphere of action for women would operate for good, by raising their education to the level of that of men, and making the one participate in all improvements made in the other. But independently of this, the mere breaking down of the barrier would of itself have an educational virtue of the highest worth. The mere getting rid of the idea that all the wider subjects of thought and action, all the things which are of general and not solely of private interest, are men's business, from which women are to be warned off—positively interdicted from most of it, coldly tolerated in the little which is allowed them—the mere consciousness a woman would then have of being a human being like any other, entitled to choose her pursuits, urged or invited by the same inducements as anyone else to interest herself in whatever is interesting to human beings, entitled to exert the share of influence on all human concerns which belongs to an individual opinion, whether she attempted actual participation in them or not—these alone would effect an immense expansion of the faculties of women, as well as enlargement of the range of their moral sentiments. . . .

10. At the same pace.

But it is not only through the sentiment of personal dignity, that the free direction and disposal of their own faculties is a source of individual happiness, and to be fettered and restricted in it, a source of unhappiness, to human beings, and not least to women. There is nothing, after disease, indigence, and guilt, so fatal to the pleasurable enjoyment of life as the want of a worthy outlet for the active faculties. Women who have the cares of a family, and while they have the cares of a family, have this outlet, and it generally suffices for them: but what of the greatly increasing number of women who have had no opportunity of exercising the vocation which they are mocked by telling them is their proper one? What of the women whose children have been lost to them by death or distance, or have grown up, married, and formed homes of their own? There are abundant examples of men who, after a life engrossed by business, retire with a competency to the enjoyment, as they hope, of rest, but to whom, as they are unable to acquire new interests and excitements that can replace the old, the change to a life of inactivity brings ennui, melancholy, and premature death. Yet no one thinks of the parallel case of so many worthy and devoted women, who, having paid what they are told is their debt to society—having brought up a family blamelessly to manhood and womanhood—having kept a house as long as they had a house needing to be kept—are deserted by the sole occupation for which they have fitted themselves; and remain with undiminished activity but with no employment for it, unless perhaps a daughter or daughter-in-law is willing to abdicate in their favor the discharge of the same functions in her younger household. Surely a hard lot for the old age of those who have worthily discharged, as long as it was given to them to discharge, what the world accounts their only social duty. Of such women, and of those others to whom this duty has not been committed at all—many of whom pine through life with the consciousness of thwarted vocations, and activities which are not suffered to expand—the only resources, speaking generally, are religion and charity. But their religion, though it may be one of feeling, and of ceremonial observance, cannot be a religion of action, unless in the form of charity. For charity many of them are by nature admirably fitted; but to practice it usefully, or even without doing mischief, requires the education, the manifold preparation, the knowledge and the thinking powers, of a skilful administrator.[11] There are a few of the administrative functions of government for which a person would not be fit, who is fit to bestow charity usefully. In this as in other cases (pre-eminently in that of the education of children), the duties permitted to women cannot be performed properly, without their being trained for duties which, to the great loss of society, are not permitted to them. . . .

The injudiciousness of parents, a youth's own inexperience, or the absence of external opportunities for the congenial vocation, and their presence for an uncongenial, condemn numbers of men to pass their lives in doing one thing reluctantly and ill, when there are other things which they could have done well and happily.

11. Octavia Hill presents a similar argument in "Trained Workers for the Poor"; see part 2 of this anthology

But on women this sentence is imposed by actual law, and by customs equivalent to law. What, in unenlightened societies, color, race, religion, or in the case of a conquered country, nationality, are to some men, sex is to all women; a peremptory exclusion from almost all honorable occupations, but either such as cannot be fulfilled by others, or such as those others do not think worthy of their acceptance. Sufferings arising from causes of this nature usually meet with so little sympathy, that few persons are aware of the great amount of unhappiness even now produced by the feeling of a wasted life. The case will be even more frequent, as increased cultivation creates a greater and greater disproportion between the ideas and faculties of women, and the scope which society allows to their activity.

When we consider the positive evil caused to the disqualified half of the human race by their disqualification—first in the loss of the most inspiriting and elevating kind of personal enjoyment, and next in the weariness, disappointment, and profound dissatisfaction with life, which are so often the substitute for it—one feels that among all the lessons which men require for carrying on the struggle against the inevitable imperfections of their lot on earth, there is no lesson which they more need, than not to add to the evils which nature inflicts, by their jealous and prejudiced restrictions on one another. Their vain fears only substitute other and worse evils for those which they are idly apprehensive of: while every restraint on the freedom of conduct of any of their human fellow-creatures (otherwise than by making them responsible for any evil actually caused by it), dries up *pro tanto*[12] the principal fountain of human happiness, and leaves the species less rich, to an inappreciable degree, in all that makes life valuable to the individual human being.

12. To that extent.

ARTHUR SYMONS

ARTHUR W. SYMONS (1865–1945) was, with the exception of Bernard Shaw, the longest lived of the late-Victorian intellectuals whose lives and writings helped define the colorful and aesthetic nineties. Born to a Cornish father whose Methodist ministry led him to serve in Wales, Symons chose, early on, to forsake both his religious background and his Welsh surroundings; moving to London, he associated with William Butler Yeats, Oscar Wilde, George Moore, and others, deliberately cultivating an identity as a polished, urbane writer and critic. Both as essayist and as editor of *The Savoy,* he championed what came to be called the decadent movement; as poet, he produced quite good minor verse, focusing upon responses to experience which celebrated that sensitivity to evanescent moods and perceptions which the critic Walter Pater (1839–1894) had advocated in his influential and controversial conclusion to *Studies in the History of the Renaissance* (1873).

"The Old Women" and "The Unloved," both published in 1900, are two poems in which Symons explores the situation of the older, unattached ("redundant") woman. The first concerns the fate of the demi-mondaine who, having aged and lost her beauty, is reduced to selling cachets and matches to the young men whose fathers she would have known. That women of the stage and others of similar dubious character were reduced to supporting themselves in this fashion was a fact that became a cliché in the literature of the period; Symons's portrayal is fully sympathetic yet redeemed from sentimentality by his descriptive clarity in presenting the impoverished and homeless woman as nothing more than "a vague thing of bones / And draggled hair." The second poem deals with women of a higher class who, perhaps not falling into the category of economically "distressed gentlewomen," nonetheless have not found that expected vocation of wives and mothers for which they are presented as wistfully yearning. These putatively natural roles having been frustrated, "the women whom no man has loved" occupy themselves with ornamental stitchwork and with "The telling of a patient rosary": physical and emotional busywork that Symons presents as palliating but not remedying the painful apprehension of meaninglessness that threatens those lacking truly purposeful work and activity.

The Old Women

They pass upon their old, tremulous feet,
Creeping with little satchels down the street,
And they remember, many years ago,
Passing that way in silks. They wander, slow
And solitary, through the city ways,   5
And they alone remember those old days
Men have forgotten. In their shaking heads
A dancer of old carnivals yet treads
The measure of past waltzes, and they see
The candles lit again, the patchouli[1]   10
Sweeten the air, and the warm cloud of musk
Enchant the passing of the passionate dusk.
Then you will see a light begin to creep
Under the earthen eyelids, dimmed with sleep,
And a new tremor, happy and uncouth,   15
Jerking about the corners of the mouth.
Then the old head drops down again, and shakes,
Muttering.
Sometimes, when the swift gaslight wakes
The dreams and fever of the sleepless town,   20
A shaking huddled thing in a black gown
Will steal at midnight, carrying with her
Violet little bags of lavender,
Into the tap-room full of noisy light;
Or, at the crowded earlier hour of night,   25
Sidle, with matches, up to some who stand
About a stage-door, and, with furtive hand,
Appealing: "I too was a dancer, when
Your fathers would have been young gentlemen!"
And sometimes, out of some lean ancient throat,   30
A broken voice, with here and there a note
Of unspoilt crystal, suddenly will arise
Into the night, while a cracked fiddle cries
Pantingly after; and you know she sings
The passing of light, famous, passing things,   35
And sometimes, in the hours past midnight, reels
Out of an alley upon staggering heels,

1. Patchouli is an oil with a very heavy scent; the mint-like perfume was much in vogue during the
1880s and 1890s.

Or into the dark keeping of the stones
About a doorway, a vague thing of bones
And draggled hair.   40

And all these have been loved.
And not one ruinous body has not moved
The heart of man's desire, nor has not seemed
Immortal in the eyes of one who dreamed
The dream that men call love. This is the end   45
Of much fair flesh; it is for this you tend
Your delicate bodies many careful years,
To be this thing of laughter and of tears,
To be this living judgment of the dead,
An old gray woman with a shaking head.   50

The Unloved

These are the women whom no man has loved.
Year after year, day after day has moved
These hearts with many longings, and with tears,
And with content; they have received the years
With empty hands, expecting no good thing;   5
Life has passed by their doors, not entering.
In solitude, and without vain desire,
They have warmed themselves beside a lonely fire;
And, without scorn, beheld as in a glass
The blown and painted leaves of Beauty pass.   10
Their souls have been made fragrant with the spice
Of costly virtues lit for sacrifice;
They have accepted Life, the unpaid debt,
And looked for no vain day of reckoning.

Yet   15
They too in certain windless summer hours
Have felt the stir of dreams, and dreamed the powers
And the exemptions and the miracles
And the cruelty of Beauty. Citadels
Of many-walled and deeply-moated hearts   20
Have suddenly surrendered to the arts

Of so compelling magic; entering,
They have esteemed it but a little thing
To have won so great a conquest; and with haste
They have cast down, and utterly laid waste,   25
Tower upon tower, and sapped their roots with flame;
And passed on that eternity of shame
Which is the way of Beauty on the earth.
And they have shaken laughter from its mirth,
To be a sound of trumpets and of horns   30
Crying the battle-cry of those red morns
Against a sky of triumph.

On some nights
Of delicate Springtide, when the hesitant lights
Begin to fade, and glimmer, and grow warm,   35
And all the softening air is quick with storm,
And the ardors of the young year, entering in,
Flush the gray earth with buds; when the trees begin
To feel a trouble mounting from their roots,
And all their green life blossoming into shoots,   40
They too, in some obscure, unblossoming strife,
Have felt the stirring of the sap of life.
And they have wept, with bowed head; in the street
They hear the twittering of little feet,
The rocking of the cradles in their hearts.   45

This is a mood, and, as a mood, departs
With the dried tears; and they resume the tale
Of the dropt stitches; these must never fail
For a dream's sake; nor, for a memory,
The telling of a patient rosary.   50

BERNARD SHAW

Bernard Shaw (1856–1950) wrote about work, as, indeed, he wrote about every other subject, with authority and conviction. Initially an author of reviews and political tracts, he is best known as a playwright who used the stage as a means to promote what he considered radical political views and socialist analyses of contemporary economic and cultural ills. Shaw had joined the Fabian Society in the early days of its existence, and his plays reflect certain of the socialist ideas circulated within that reformist group. He is more concerned with the iconoclastic than with the doctrinaire, however, and, while sermonic in tone, his plays revolve around moral incongruities and paradoxes in which public reformers find themselves: in many of his dramas, the agents of social change find themselves caught up in contradictions that link them to the very institutions that they wish to eliminate or, at the very least, reform.

Mrs Warren's Profession was banned from production in 1894 by the Lord Chamberlain, who thereby gave Shaw the immense satisfaction of being designated a subversive and radical. Shaw protested the censorship, eventually saw the play into print in 1898, and organized a private performance (at a dramatic club rather than at a commercial theater) in 1902. The play was not performed at a public theater until 1926.

The subject of the play, prostitution, was less the direct cause of the banning than was Shaw's linking of prostitution to establishment power structures: national church, the aristocracy, and, most pointedly, capitalist entrepreneurs. In a preface written eight years after the Lord Chamberlain's action, Shaw asserted that *Mrs Warren's Profession* was written in 1894

> to draw attention to the truth that prostitution is caused, not by female depravity and male licentiousness, but simply by underpaying, undervaluing, and overworking women so shamefully that the poorest of them are forced to resort to prostitution to keep body and soul together. Indeed all attractive unpropertied women lose money by being infallibly virtuous or contracting marriages that are not more or less venal. If on the large social scale we get what we call vice instead of what we call virtue it is simply because we are paying more for it. No normal woman would be a professional prostitute if she could better herself by being respectable, nor marry for money if she could afford to marry for love. Also, I desired to expose the fact that prostitution is not only carried on without organization by individual enterprise in the lodgings of solitary women, each her own mistress as well as every customer's mistress, but organized and exploited as a big international commerce for the profit

of capitalists like any other commerce, and very lucrative to great city estates, including Church estates, through the rents of the houses in which it is practised.

Shaw's analysis of prostitution in terms of economic need was not novel, but, in the impassioned defense by Mrs Warren of her decision to work as a prostitute and brothel-keeper (act 2), he gave powerful expression to this interpretation of the social problem, and he remained convinced that this explanation of prostitution was the truth that evoked opposition to the play from established social and economic interests.

There is more to the play, however, than social protest. In both Mrs Warren and her daughter Vivie, one of the most distinctive incarnations of the 1890s "new woman," Shaw portrays the personality compulsively driven to derive from work a sense of individual self-worth. Neither woman can rest from or find satisfaction apart from work, and Shaw seems deliberately to have cultivated for both of them a decidedly anti-romantic view of the worth of labor, a view that stands at odds with a more traditional Carlylean attitude. Mrs Warren's relentless determination to continue in her profession seems designed both to dismay and repel, while Vivie's own concluding obsession with vocation leaves playgoers with an equally disquieting alternative to the self-indulgent social parasitism of Vivie's suitor Frank or the traditional idealism of the aesthetic Praed. The view of work with which the play concludes is perversely perplexing, as Shaw, who wanted always to appear enigmatic, no doubt wished it to be.

Mrs Warren's Profession

Act I

Summer afternoon in a cottage garden on the eastern slope of a hill a little south of Haslemere in Surrey. Looking up the hill, the cottage is seen in the left hand corner of the garden, with its thatched roof and porch, and a large latticed window to the left of the porch. A paling¹ completely shuts in the garden, except for a gate on the right. The common rises uphill beyond the paling to the sky line. Some folded canvas garden chairs are leaning against the side bench in the porch. A lady's bicycle is propped against the wall, under the window. A little to the right of the porch a hammock is

---

1. A fence.

slung from two posts. A big canvas umbrella, stuck in the ground, keeps the sun off the hammock, in which a young lady lies reading and making notes, her head towards the cottage and her feet towards the gate. In front of the hammock, and within reach of her hand, is a common kitchen chair, with a pile of serious-looking books and a supply of writing paper on it.

A gentleman walking on the common comes into sight from behind the cottage. He is hardly past middle age, with something of the artist about him, unconventionally but carefully dressed, and clean-shaven except for a moustache, with an eager susceptible face and very amiable and considerate manners. He has silky black hair, with waves of grey and white in it. His eyebrows are white, his moustache black. He seems not certain of his way. He looks over the paling; takes stock of the place; and sees the young lady.

THE GENTLEMAN [*taking off his hat*] I beg your pardon. Can you direct me to Hindhead View—Mrs Alison's?

THE YOUNG LADY [*glancing up from her book*] This is Mrs Alison's. [*She resumes her work*].

THE GENTLEMAN. Indeed! Perhaps—may I ask are you Miss Vivie Warren?

THE YOUNG LADY [*sharply, as she turns on her elbow to get a good look at him*] Yes.

THE GENTLEMAN [*daunted and conciliatory*] I'm afraid I appear intrusive. My name is Praed. [*Vivie at once throws her books upon the chair, and gets out of the hammock*]. Oh, pray dont let me disturb you.

VIVIE [*striding to the gate and opening it for him*] Come in, Mr Praed. [*He comes in*]. Glad to see you. [*She proffers her hand and takes his with a resolute and hearty grip. She is an attractive specimen of the sensible, able, highly-educated young middle-class Englishwoman. Age 22. Prompt, strong, confident, self-possessed. Plain business-like dress, but not dowdy. She wears a chatelaine² at her belt, with a fountain pen and a paper knife among its pendants*].

PRAED. Very kind of you indeed, Miss Warren. [*She shuts the gate with a vigorous slam. He passes in to the middle of the garden, exercising his fingers, which are slightly numbed by her greeting*]. Has your mother arrived?

VIVIE [*quickly, evidently scenting aggression*] Is she coming?

PRAED [*surprised*] Didnt you expect us?

VIVIE. No.

PRAED. Now, goodness me, I hope Ive not mistaken the day. That would be just like me, you know. Your mother arranged that she was to come down from London and that I was to come over from Horsham to be introduced to you.

VIVIE [*not at all pleased*] Did she? Hm! My mother has rather a trick of taking me by surprise—to see how I behave myself when she's away, I suppose. I fancy I shall take my mother very much by surprise one of these days, if she makes arrangements that concern me without consulting me beforehand. She hasnt come.

PRAED [*embarrassed*] I'm really very sorry.

---

2. A clasp from which keys or small items are suspended.

VIVIE [*throwing off her displeasure*] It's not your fault, Mr Praed, is it? And I'm very glad youve come. You are the only one of my mother's friends I have ever asked her to bring to see me.

PRAED [*relieved and delighted*] Oh, now this is really very good of you, Miss Warren!

VIVIE. Will you come indoors; or would you rather sit out here and talk?

PRAED. It will be nicer out here, dont you think?

VIVIE. Then I'll go and get you a chair. [*She goes to the porch for a garden chair*].

PRAED [*following her*] Oh, pray, pray! Allow me. [*He lays hands on the chair*].

VIVIE [*letting him take it*] Take care of your fingers: theyre rather dodgy things, those chairs. [*She goes across to the chair with the books on it; pitches them into the hammock; and brings the chair forward with one swing*].

PRAED [*who has just unfolded his chair*] Oh, now d o let me take that hard chair. I like hard chairs.

VIVIE. So do I. Sit down, Mr Praed. [*This invitation she gives with genial peremptoriness, his anxiety to please her clearly striking her as a sign of weakness of character on his part. But he does not immediately obey*].

PRAED. By the way, though, hadnt we better go to the station to meet your mother?

VIVIE [*coolly*] Why? She knows the way.

PRAED [*disconcerted*] Er—I suppose she does [*he sits down*].

VIVIE. Do you know, you are just like what I expected. I hope you are disposed to be friends with me.

PRAED [*again beaming*] Thank you, my d e a r Miss Warren: thank you. Dear me! I'm so glad your mother hasnt spoilt you!

VIVIE. How?

PRAED. Well, in making you too conventional. You know, my dear Miss Warren, I am a born anarchist. I hate authority. It spoils the relations between parent and child: even between mother and daughter. Now I was always afraid that your mother would strain her authority to make you very conventional. It's such a relief to find that she hasnt.

VIVIE. Oh! have I been behaving unconventionally?

PRAED. Oh no: oh dear no. At least not conventionally unconventionally, you understand. [*She nods and sits down. He goes on, with a cordial outburst*] But it was so charming of you to say that you were disposed to be friends with me! You modern young ladies are splendid: perfectly splendid!

VIVIE [*dubiously*] Eh? [*watching him with dawning disappointment as to the quality of his brains and character*].

PRAED. When I was your age, young men and women were afraid of each other: there was no good fellowship. Nothing real. Only gallantry copied out of novels, and as vulgar and affected as it could be. Maidenly reserve! gentlemanly chivalry! always saying no when you meant yes! simple purgatory for shy and sincere souls.

VIVIE. Yes, I imagine there must have been a frightful waste of time. Especially women's time.

PRAED. Oh, waste of life, waste of everything. But things are improving. Do you know, I have been in a positive state of excitement about meeting you ever since your magnificent achievements at Cambridge: a thing unheard of in my day. It was perfectly splendid, your tieing with the third wrangler.[3] Just the right place, you know. The first wrangler is always a dreamy, morbid fellow, in whom the thing is pushed to the length of a disease.

VIVIE. It doesnt pay. I wouldnt do it again for the same money!

PRAED [*aghast*] The same money!

VIVIE. I did it for £50.

PRAED. Fifty pounds!

VIVIE. Yes. Fifty pounds. Perhaps you dont know how it was. Mrs. Latham my tutor at Newnham,[4] told my mother that I could distinguish myself in the mathematical tripos[5] if I went in for it in earnest. The papers were full just then of Phillipa Summers beating the senior wrangler. You remember about it, of course.

PRAED [*shakes his head energetically*]!!!

VIVIE. Well anyhow she did: and nothing would please my mother but that I should do the same thing. I said flatly it was not worth my while to face the grind since I was not going in for teaching; but I offered to try for fourth wrangler or thereabouts for £50. She closed with me at that, after a little grumbling; and I was better than my bargain. But I wouldnt do it again for that. £200 would have been nearer the mark.

PRAED [*much damped*] Lord bless me! Thats a very practical way of looking at it.

VIVIE. Did you expect to find me an unpractical person?

PRAED. But surely it's practical to consider not only the work these honors cost, but also the culture they bring.

VIVIE. Culture! My dear Mr Praed: do you know what the mathematical tripos means? It means grind, grind, grind for six to eight hours a day at mathematics, and nothing but mathematics. I'm supposed to know something about science; but I know nothing except the mathematics it involves. I can make calculations for engineers, electricians, insurance companies, and so on; but I know next to nothing about engineering or electricity or insurance. I dont even know arithmetic well. Outside mathematics, lawn-tennis, eating, sleeping, cycling, and walking, I'm a more ignorant barbarian than any woman could possibly be who hadnt gone in for the tripos.

PRAED [*revolted*] What a monstrous, wicked, rascally system! I knew it! I felt at once that it meant destroying all that makes womanhood beautiful.

VIVIE. I dont object to it on that score in the least. I shall turn it to very good account, I assure you.

---

3. Wranglers are candidates who have been placed in the first class in the mathematical tripos or competition for honors at Cambridge University.

4. Newnham and Girton were the colleges for women at Cambridge University; Newnham was established in 1871, Girton having been established in 1869.

5. An examination for honors in the bachelor's degree at Cambridge University.

PRAED. Pooh! in what way?

VIVIE. I shall set up in chambers in the City, and work at actuarial calculations and conveyancing.[6] Under cover of that I shall do some law, with one eye on the Stock Exchange all the time. Ive come down here by myself to read law: not for a holiday, as my mother imagines. I hate holidays.

PRAED. You make my blood run cold. Are you to have no romance, no beauty in your life?

VIVIE. I dont care for either, I assure you.

PRAED. You cant mean that.

VIVIE. Oh yes I do. I like working and getting paid for it. When I'm tired of working, I like a comfortable chair, a cigar, a little whisky, and a novel with a good detective story in it.

PRAED [rising in a frenzy of repudiation] I dont believe it. I am an artist; and I cant believe it: I refuse to believe it. It's only that you havnt discovered yet what a wonderful world art can open up to you.

VIVIE. Yes I have. Last May I spent six weeks in London with Honoria Fraser. Mamma thought we were doing a round of sightseeing together; but I was really at Honoria's chambers in Chancery Lane every day, working away at actuarial calculations for her, and helping her as well as a greenhorn[7] could. In the evenings we smoked and talked, and never dreamt of going out except for exercise. And I never enjoyed myself more in my life. I cleared all my expenses, and got initiated into the business without a fee into the bargain.

PRAED. But bless my heart and soul, Miss Warren, do you call that discovering art?

VIVIE. Wait a bit. That wasnt the beginning. I went up to town on an invitation from some artistic people in Fitzjohn's Avenue: one of the girls was a Newnham chum. They took me to the National Gallery—

PRAED [approving] Ah!! [He sits down, much relieved].

VIVIE [continuing] —to the Opera—

PRAED [still more pleased] Good!

VIVIE.—and to a concert where the band played all the evening: Beethoven and Wagner and so on. I wouldnt go through that experience again for anything you could offer me. I held out for civility's sake until the third day; and then I said, plump out, that I couldnt stand any more of it, and went off to Chancery Lane. Now you know the sort of perfectly splendid modern young lady I am. How do you think I shall get on with my mother?

PRAED [startled] Well, I hope—er—

VIVIE. It's not so much what you hope as what you believe, that I want to know.

PRAED. Well, frankly, I am afraid your mother will be a little disappointed. Not from any shortcoming on your part, you know: I dont mean that. But you are so different from her ideal.

---

6. Actuarial calculations are those made by insurance companies in order to determine risks and estimate premiums; conveyancing is the legal transfer of real estate from one person to another.

7. A novice.

VIVIE. Her what?!

PRAED. Her ideal.

VIVIE. Do you mean her ideal of ME?

PRAED. Yes.

VIVIE. What on earth is it like?

PRAED. Well, you must have observed, Miss Warren, that people who are dissatisfied with their own bringing-up generally think that the world would be all
right if everybody were to be brought up quite differently. Now your mother's
life has been—er—I suppose you know—

VIVIE. Dont suppose anything, Mr Praed. I hardly know my mother. Since I was a
child I have lived in England, at school or college, or with people paid to take
charge of me. I have been boarded out all my life. My mother has lived in Brussels or Vienna and never let me go to her. I only see her when she visits England
for a few days. I dont complain: it's been very pleasant; for people have been
very good to me; and there has always been plenty of money to make things
smooth. But dont imagine I know anything about my mother. I know far less
that you do.

PRAED [*very ill at ease*] In that case—[*He stops, quite at a loss. Then, with a forced
attempt at gaiety*] But what nonsense we are talking! Of course you and your
mother will get on capitally. [*He rises, and looks abroad at the view*]. What a
charming little place you have here!

VIVIE [*unmoved*] Rather a violent change of subject, Mr Praed. Why wont my
mother's life bear being talked about?

PRAED. Oh, you really mustnt say that. Isnt it natural that I should have a certain
delicacy in talking to my old friend's daughter about her behind her back? You
and she will have plenty of opportunity of talking about it when she comes.

VIVIE. No: she wont talk about it either. [*Rising*] However, I daresay you have good
reasons for telling me nothing. Only, mind this, Mr Praed. I expect there will be
a battle royal when my mother hears of my Chancery Lane project.

PRAED [*ruefully*] I'm afraid there will.

VIVIE. Well, I shall win, because I want nothing but my fare to London to start
there to-morrow earning my own living by devilling[8] for Honoria. Besides, I
have no mysteries to keep up; and it seems she has. I shall use that advantage
over her if necessary.

PRAED [*greatly shocked*] Oh no! No, pray. Youd not do such a thing.

VIVIE. Then tell me why not.

PRAED. I really cannot. I appeal to your good feeling. [*She smiles at his sentimentality*]. Besides, you may be too bold. Your mother is not to be trifled with when
she's angry.

VIVIE. You cant frighten me, Mr Praed. In that month at Chancery Lane I had opportunities of taking the measure of one or two women v e r y like my mother.
You may back me to win. But if I hit harder in my ignorance than I need,

8. Serving as an apprentice.

remember that it is you who refuse to enlighten me. Now, let us drop the subject. [*She takes her chair and replaces it near the hammock with the same vigorous swing as before*].

PRAED [*taking a desperate resolution*] One word, Miss Warren. I had better tell you. It's very difficult; but—

Mrs Warren and Sir George Crofts arrive at the gate. Mrs Warren is between 40 and 50, formerly pretty, showily dressed in a brilliant hat and a gay blouse fitting tightly over her bust and flanked by fashionable sleeves. Rather spoilt and domineering, and decidedly vulgar, but, on the whole, a genial and fairly presentable old blackguard of a woman.

Crofts is a tall powerfully-built man of about 50, fashionably dressed in the style of a young man. Nasal voice, reedier than might be expected from his strong frame. Clean-shaven bulldog jaws, large flat ears, and thick neck: gentlemanly combination of the most brutal types of city man, sporting man, and man about town.

VIVIE. Here they are. [*Coming to them as they enter the garden*] How do, mater? Mr Praed's been here this half hour waiting for you.

MRS WARREN. Well, if youve been waiting, Praddy, it's your own fault: I thought youd have the gumption[9] to know I was coming by the 3.10 train. Vivie: put your hat on, dear: youll get sunburnt. Oh, I forgot to introduce you. Sir George Crofts: my little Vivie.

Crofts advances to Vivie with his most courtly manner. She nods, but makes no motion to shake hands.

CROFTS. May I shake hands with a young lady whom I have known by reputation very long as the daughter of one of my oldest friends?

VIVIE [*who has been looking him up and down sharply*] If you like. [*She takes his tenderly proffered hand and gives it a squeeze that makes him open his eyes; then turns away and says to her mother*] Will you come in, or shall I get a couple more chairs? [*She goes into the porch for the chairs*].

MRS WARREN. Well, George, what do you think of her?

CROFTS [*ruefully*] She has a powerful fist. Did you shake hands with her, Praed?

PRAED. Yes: it will pass off presently.

CROFTS. I hope so. [*Vivie reappears with two more chairs. He hurries to her assistance*]. Allow me.

MRS WARREN [*patronizingly*] Let Sir George help you with the chairs, dear.

VIVIE [*pitching them into his arms*] Here you are. [*She dusts her hands and turns to Mrs Warren*]. Youd like some tea, wouldnt you?

MRS WARREN [*sitting in Praed's chair and fanning herself*] I'm dying for a drop to drink.

VIVIE. I'll see about it. [*She goes into the cottage*].

Sir George has by this time managed to unfold a chair and plant it beside Mrs Warren, on her left. He throws the other on the grass and sits down, looking de-

9. Common sense.

jected and rather foolish, with the handle of his stick in his mouth. Praed, still very uneasy, fidgets about the garden on their right.

MRS WARREN [*to Praed, looking at Crofts*] Just look at him, Praddy: he looks cheerful, dont he? He's been worrying my life out these three years to have that little girl of mine shewn to him; and now that Ive done it, he's quite out of countenance. [*Briskly*] Come! sit up, George; and take your stick out of your mouth. [*Crofts sulkily obeys*].

PRAED. I think, you know—if you dont mind my saying so—that we had better get out of the habit of thinking of her as a little girl. You see she has really distinguished herself; and I'm not sure, from what I have seen of her, that she is not older than any of us.

MRS WARREN [*greatly amused*] Only listen to him, George! Older than any of us! Well, she has been stuffing you nicely with her importance.

PRAED. But young people are particularly sensitive about being treated in that way.

MRS WARREN. Yes; and young people have to get all that nonsense taken out of them, and a good deal more besides. Dont you interfere, Praddy: I know how to treat my own child as well as you do. [*Praed, with a grave shake of his head, walks up the garden with his hands behind his back. Mrs Warren pretends to laugh, but looks after him with perceptible concern. Then she whispers to Crofts*] Whats the matter with him? What does he take it like that for?

CROFTS [*morosely*] Youre afraid of Praed.

MRS WARREN. What! Me! Afraid of dear old Praddy! Why, a fly wouldnt be afraid of him.

CROFTS. Y o u r e afraid of him.

MRS WARREN [*angry*] I'll trouble you to mind your own business, and not try any of your sulks on me. I'm not afraid of you, anyhow. If you cant make yourself agreeable, youd better go home. [*She gets up, and turning her back on him, finds herself face to face with Praed*]. Come, Praddy, I know it was only your tender-heartedness. Youre afraid I'll bully her.

PRAED. My dear Kitty: you think I'm offended. Dont imagine that: pray dont. But you know I often notice things that escape you; and though you never take my advice, you sometimes admit afterwards that you ought to have taken it.

MRS WARREN. Well, what do you notice now?

PRAED. Only that Vivie is a grown woman. Pray, Kitty, treat her with every respect.

MRS WARREN [*with genuine amazement*] Respect! Treat my own daughter with respect! What next, pray!

VIVIE [*appearing at the cottage door and calling to Mrs Warren*] Mother: will you come to my room before tea?

MRS WARREN. Yes, dearie. [*She laughs indulgently at Praed's gravity, and pats him on the cheek as she passes him on her way to the porch*]. Dont be cross, Praddy. [*She follows Vivie in to the cottage*].

CROFTS [*furtively*] I say, Praed.

PRAED. Yes.

CROFTS. I want to ask you a rather particular question.

PRAED. Certainly. [*He takes Mrs Warren's chair and sits close to Crofts*].

CROFTS. Thats right: they might hear us from the window. Look here: did Kitty ever tell you who that girl's father is?

PRAED. Never.

CROFTS. Have you any suspicion of who it might be?

PRAED. None.

CROFTS [*not believing him*] I know, of course, that you perhaps might feel bound not to tell if she had said anything to you. But it's very awkward to be uncertain about it now that we shall be meeting the girl every day. We wont exactly know how we ought to feel towards her.

PRAED. What difference can that make? We take her on her own merits. What does it matter who her father was?

CROFTS [*suspiciously*] Then you know who he was?

PRAED [*with a touch of temper*] I said no just now. Did you not hear me?

CROFTS. Look here, Praed. I ask you as a particular favor. If you d o know [*movement of protest from Praed*]—I only say, if you know you might at least set my mind at rest about her. The fact is, I feel attracted.

PRAED [*sternly*] What do you mean?

CROFTS. Oh, dont be alarmed: it's quite an innocent feeling. Thats what puzzles me about it. Why, for all I know, *I* might be her father.

PRAED. You! Impossible!

CROFTS [*catching him up cunningly*] You know for certain that I'm not?

PRAED. I know nothing about it, I tell you, any more than you. But really, Crofts— oh no, it's out of the question. Theres not the least resemblance.

CROFTS. As to that, theres no resemblance between her and her mother that I can see. I suppose she's not y o u r daughter, is she?

PRAED [*rising indignantly*] Really, Crofts—!

CROFTS. No offence, Praed. Quite allowable as between two men of the world.

PRAED [*recovering himself with an effort and speaking gently and gravely*] Now listen to me, my dear Crofts. [*He sits down again*]. I have nothing to do with that side of Mrs Warren's life, and never had. She has never spoken to me about it; and of course I have never spoken to her about it. Your delicacy will tell you that a handsome woman needs some friends who are not—well, not on that footing with her. The effect of her own beauty would become a torment to her if she could not escape from it occasionally. You are probably on much more confidential terms with Kitty than I am. Surely you can ask her the question yourself.

CROFTS. I have asked her, often enough. But she's so determined to keep the child all to herself that she would deny that it ever had a father if she could. [*Rising*] I'm thoroughly uncomfortable about it, Praed.

PRAED [*rising also*] Well, as you are, at all events, old enough to be her father, I dont mind agreeing that we both regard Miss Vivie in a parental way, as a young girl whom we are bound to protect and help. What do you say?

CROFTS [*aggressively*] I'm no older than you, if you come to that.

PRAED. Yes you are, my dear fellow: you were born old. I was born a boy: Ive never been able to feel the assurance of a grown-up man in my life. [*He folds his chair and carries it to the porch*].

MRS WARREN [*calling from within the cottage*] Prad-dee! George! Tea-ea-ea-ea!

CROFTS [*hastily*] She's calling us. [*He hurries in*].

Praed shakes his head bodingly, and is following Crofts when he is hailed by a young gentleman who has just appeared on the common, and is making for the gate. He is pleasant, pretty, smartly dressed, cleverly good-for-nothing, not long turned 20, with a charming voice and agreeably disrespectful manners. He carries a light sporting magazine rifle.

THE YOUNG GENTLEMAN. Hallo! Praed!

PRAED. Why, Frank Gardner! [*Frank comes in and shakes hands cordially*]. What on earth are you doing here?

FRANK. Staying with my father.

PRAED. The Roman father?[10]

FRANK. He's rector here. I'm living with my people this autumn for the sake of economy. Things came to a crisis in July: the Roman father had to pay my debts. He's stony broke in consequence; and so am I. What are you up to in these parts? Do you know the people here?

PRAED. Yes: I'm spending the day with a Miss Warren.

FRANK [*enthusiastically*] What! Do you know Vivie? Isnt she a jolly girl? I'm teaching her to shoot with this [*putting down the rifle*]. I'm so glad she knows you: youre just the sort of fellow she ought to know. [*He smiles, and raises the charming voice almost to a singing tone as he exclaims*] It's e v e r so jolly to find you here, Praed.

PRAED. I'm an old friend of her mother. Mrs Warren brought me over to make her daughter's acquaintance.

FRANK. The mother! Is s h e here?

PRAED. Yes: inside, at tea.

MRS WARREN [*calling from within*] Prad-dee-ee-ee-eee! The tea-cake'll be cold.

PRAED [*calling*] Yes, Mrs Warren. In a moment. Ive just met a friend here.

MRS WARREN. A what?

PRAED [*louder*] A friend.

MRS WARREN. Bring him in.

PRAED. All right. [*To Frank*] Will you accept the invitation?

FRANK [*incredulous, but immensely amused*] Is that Vivie's mother?

PRAED. Yes.

FRANK. By jove! What a lark! Do you think she'll like me?

PRAED. Ive no doubt youll make yourself popular, as usual. Come in and try [*moving towards the house*].

10. The Roman qualities of the father, ironically attributed to the Reverend Samuel Gardner, would have included absolute authority within the family as well as an austere integrity of the sort associated with the elder Cato, who became the model of traditional Roman values, or Lucius Junius Brutus, who reputedly gave his sons over to capital punishment for their disloyalty to Rome.

FRANK. Stop a bit. [*Seriously*] I want to take you into my confidence.

PRAED. Pray dont. It's only some fresh folly, like the barmaid at Redhill.

FRANK. It's ever so much more serious than that. You say youve only just met Vivie for the first time?

PRAED. Yes.

FRANK [*rhapsodically*] Then you can have no idea what a girl she is. Such character! Such sense! And her cleverness! Oh, my eye, Praed, but I can tell you she is clever! And—need I add?—she loves me.

CROFTS [*putting his head out of the window*] I say, Praed: what are you about? Do come along. [*He disappears*].

FRANK. Hallo! Sort of chap that would take a prize at a dog show, aint he? Who's he?

PRAED. Sir George Crofts, an old friend of Mrs Warren's. I think we had better come in.

> On their way to the porch they are interrupted by a call from the gate. Turning, they see an elderly clergyman looking over it.

THE CLERGYMAN [*calling*] Frank!

FRANK. Hallo! [*To Praed*] The Roman father. [*To the clergyman*] Yes, gov'nor: all right: presently. [*To Praed*] Look here, Praed: youd better go in to tea. I'll join you directly.

PRAED. Very good. [*He goes into the cottage*].

> The clergyman remains outside the gate, with his hands on the top of it. The Rev. Samuel Gardner, a beneficed clergyman[11] of the Established Church, is over 50. Externally he is pretentious, booming, noisy, important. Really he is that obsolescent social phenomenon the fool of the family dumped on the Church by his father the patron, clamorously asserting himself as father and clergyman without being able to command respect in either capacity.

REV. S. Well, sir. Who are your friends here, if I may ask?

FRANK. Oh, it's all right, gov'nor! Come in.

REV. S. No, sir; not until I know whose garden I am entering.

FRANK. It's all right. It's Miss Warren's.

REV. S. I have not seen her at church since she came.

FRANK. Of course not: she's a third wrangler. Ever so intellectual. Took a higher degree than you did; so why should she go to hear you preach?

REV. S. Dont be disrespectful, sir.

FRANK. Oh, it dont matter: nobody hears us. Come in. [*He opens the gate, unceremoniously pulling his father with it into the garden*]. I want to introduce you to her. Do you remember the advice you gave me last July, gov'nor?

REV. S. [*severely*] Yes. I advised you to conquer your idleness and flippancy, and to work your way into an honorable profession and live on it and not upon me.

FRANK. No: thats what you thought of afterwards. What you actually said was that since I had neither brains nor money, I'd better turn my good looks to account

---

11. A beneficed clergyman received the interest from an endowed position within the Church of England; the amount of a benefice varied, some being substantial and others meager.

by marrying somebody with both. Well, look here. Miss Warren has brains: you cant deny that.

REV. S. Brains are not everything.

FRANK. No, of course not: theres the money—

REV. S. [*interrupting him austerely*] I was not thinking of money sir. I was speaking of higher things. Social position, for instance.

FRANK. I dont care a rap about that.

REV. S. But I do, sir.

FRANK. Well, nobody wants you to marry her. Anyhow she has what amounts to a high Cambridge degree; and she seems to have as much money as she wants.

REV. S. [*sinking into a feeble vein of humor*] I greatly doubt whether she has as much money as y o u will want.

FRANK. Oh, come: I havnt been so very extravagant. I live ever so quietly; I dont drink; I dont bet much; and I never go regularly on the razzle-dazzle as you did when you were my age.

REV. S. [*booming hollowly*] Silence, sir.

FRANK. Well, you told me yourself, when I was making ever such an ass of myself about the barmaid at Redhill, that you once offered a woman £50 for the letters you wrote to her when—

REV. S. [*terrified*] Sh-sh-sh, Frank, for Heaven's sake! [*He looks round apprehensively. Seeing no one within earshot he plucks up courage to boom again, but more subduedly*]. You are taking an ungentlemanly advantage of what I confided to you for your own good, to save you from an error you would have repented all your life long. Take warning by your father's follies, sir; and dont make them an excuse for your own.

FRANK. Did you ever hear the story of the Duke of Wellington and his letters?

REV. S. No, sir; and I dont want to hear it.

FRANK. The old Iron Duke didnt throw away £50: not he. He just wrote: "Dear Jenny: publish and be damned! Yours affectionately, Wellington."[12] Thats what you should have done.

REV. S. [*piteously*] Frank, my boy: when I wrote those letters I put myself into that woman's power. When I told you about them I put myself, to some extent, I am sorry to say, in your power. She refused my money with these words, which I shall never forget. 'Knowledge is power,' she said; 'and I never sell power'. Thats more than twenty years ago; and she has never made use of her power or caused me a moment's uneasiness. You are behaving worse to me than she did, Frank.

FRANK. Oh yes I dare say! Did you ever preach at her the way you preach at me every day?

REV. S. [*wounded almost to tears*] I leave you sir. You are incorrigible. [*He turns towards the gate*].

---

12. "Publish and be damned" is reputed to have been the response of Arthur Wellesley, the Duke of Wellington (1769–1852), military hero and statesman, when the publisher of the *Memoirs* of the infamous courtesan Harriette Wilson attempted to blackmail him.

FRANK [*utterly unmoved*] Tell them I shant be home to tea, will you, gov'nor, like a good fellow? [*He moves towards the cottage door and is met by Praed and Vivie coming out*].

VIVIE [*to Frank*] Is that your father, Frank? I do so want to meet him.

FRANK. Certainly. [*Calling after his father*] Gov'nor. Youre wanted. [*The parson turns at the gate, fumbling nervously at his hat. Praed crosses the garden to the opposite side, beaming in anticipation of civilities*]. My father: Miss Warren.

VIVIE [*going to the clergyman and shaking his hand*] Very glad to see you here, Mr Gardner. [*Calling to the cottage*] Mother: come along: youre wanted.

    Mrs Warren appears on the threshold, and is immediately transfixed recognizing the clergyman.

VIVIE [*continuing*] Let me introduce—

MRS WARREN [*swooping on the Reverend Samuel*] Why, it's Sam Gardner, gone into the Church! Well, I never! Dont you know us, Sam? This is George Crofts, as large as life and twice as natural. Dont you remember me?

REV. S. [*very red*] I really—er—

MRS WARREN. Of course you do. Why, I have a whole album of your letters still: I came across them only the other day.

REV. S. [*miserably confused*] Miss Vavasour, I believe.

MRS WARREN [*correcting him quickly in a loud whisper*] Tch! Nonsense! Mrs Warren: dont you see my daughter there?

Act II

Inside the cottage after nightfall. Looking eastward from within instead of westward from without, the latticed window, with its curtains drawn, is now seen in the middle of the front wall of the cottage, with the porch door to the left of it. In the left-hand side wall is the door leading to the kitchen. Farther back against the same wall is a dresser with a candle and matches on it, and Frank's rifle standing beside them, with the barrel resting in the plate-rack. In the centre a table stands with a lighted lamp on it. Vivie's books and writing materials are on a table to the right of the window, against the wall. The fireplace is on the right, with a settle: there is no fire. Two of the chairs are set right and left of the table.

    The cottage door opens, shewing a fine starlit night without; and Mrs Warren, her shoulders wrapped in a shawl borrowed from Vivie, enters, followed by Frank, who throws his cap on the window seat. She has had enough of walking, and gives a gasp of relief as she unpins her hat; takes it off; sticks the pin through the crown; and puts it on the table.

MRS WARREN. O Lord! I dont know which is the worst of the country, the walking or the sitting at home with nothing to do. I could do with a whisky and soda now very well, if only they had such a thing in this place.

FRANK. Perhaps Vivie's got some.

MRS WARREN. Nonsense! What would a young girl like her be doing with such things! Never mind: it dont matter. I wonder how she passes her time here! I'd a good deal rather be in Vienna.

FRANK. Let me take you there. [*He helps her to take off her shawl, gallantly giving her shoulders a very perceptible squeeze as he does so*].

MRS WARREN. Ah! would you? I'm beginning to think youre a chip of the old block.

FRANK. Like the gov'nor, eh? [*He hangs the shawl on the nearest chair and sits down*].

MRS WARREN. Never you mind. What do you know about such things? Youre only a boy. [*She goes to the hearth, to be farther from temptation*].

FRANK. Do come to Vienna with me? It'd be ever such larks.

MRS WARREN. No, thank you. Vienna is no place for you—at least not until youre a little older. [*She nods at him to emphasize this piece of advice. He makes a mock-piteous face, belied by his laughing eyes. She looks at him; then comes back to him*]. Now, look here, little boy [*taking his face in her hands and turning it up to her*]: I know you through and through by your likeness to your father, better than you know yourself. Dont you go taking any silly ideas into your head about me. Do you hear?

FRANK [*gallantly wooing her with his voice*] Cant help it, my dear Mrs Warren: it runs in the family.

   She pretends to box his ears; then looks at the pretty laughing upturned face for a moment, tempted. At last she kisses him, and immediately turns away, out of patience with herself.

MRS WARREN. There! I shouldnt have done that. I am wicked. Never mind, my dear: it's only a motherly kiss. Go and make love[13] to Vivie.

FRANK. So I have.

MRS WARREN [*turning on him with a sharp note of alarm in her voice*] What!

FRANK. Vivie and I are ever such chums.

MRS WARREN. What do you mean? Now see here: I wont have any young scamp tampering with my little girl. Do you hear? I wont have it.

FRANK [*quite unabashed*] My dear Mrs Warren: dont you be alarmed. My intentions are honorable: ever so honorable; and your little girl is jolly well able to take care of herself. She dont need looking after half so much as her mother. She aint so handsome, you know.

MRS WARREN [*taken aback by his assurance*] Well, you have got a nice healthy two inches thick of cheek all over you. I dont know where you got it. Not from your father, anyhow.

CROFTS [*in the garden*] The gipsies, I suppose?

REV. S. [*replying*] The broomsquires[14] are far worse.

---

13. In the nineteenth century, the phrase "to make love" meant "to court" or "to flirt with."
14. Landed gentry with insubstantial holdings.

MRS WARREN [*To Frank*] S-sh! Remember! youve had your warning.

Crofts and the Reverend Samuel come in from the garden, the clergyman continuing his conversation as he enters.

REV. S. The perjury at the Winchester assizes[15] is deplorable.

MRS WARREN. Well? what became of you two? And wheres Praddy and Vivie?

CROFTS [*putting his hat on the settle and his stick in the chimney corner*] They went up the hill. We went to the village. I wanted a drink. [*He sits down on the settle, putting his legs up along the seat*].

MRS WARREN. Well, she oughtnt go off like that without telling me. [*To Frank*] Get your father a chair, Frank: where are your manners? [*Frank springs up and gracefully offers his father his chair; then takes another from the wall and sits down at the table, in the middle, with his father on his right and Mrs Warren on his left*]. George: where are you going to stay tonight? You cant stay here. And whats Praddy going to do?

CROFTS. Gardner'll put me up.

MRS WARREN. Oh, no doubt youve taken care of yourself! But what about Praddy?

CROFTS. Dont know. I suppose he can sleep at the inn.

MRS WARREN. Havnt you room for him, Sam?

REV. S. Well—er—you see, as rector here, I am not free to do as I like. Er—what is Mr Praed's social position?

MRS WARREN. Oh, he's all right: he's an architect. What an old stick-in-the-mud you are, Sam!

FRANK. Yes, it's all right, gov'nor. He built that place down in Wales for the Duke. Caernarvon Castle[16] they call it. You must have heard of it. [*He winks with lightning smartness at Mrs Warren, and regards his father blandly*].

REV. S. Oh, in that case, of course we shall only be too happy. I suppose he knows the Duke personally.

FRANK. Oh, ever so intimately! We can stick him in Georgina's old room.

MRS WARREN. Well, thats settled. Now if those two would only come in and let us have supper. Theyve no right to stay out after dark like this.

CROFTS [*aggressively*] What harm are they doing you?

MRS WARREN. Well, harm or not, I dont like it.

FRANK. Better not wait for them, Mrs Warren. Praed will stay out as long as possible. He has never known before what it is to stray over the heath on a summer night with my Vivie.

CROFTS [*sitting up in some consternation*] I say, you know! Come!

---

15. The assizes were sessions of superior county courts held on a seasonal basis; both civil and criminal cases were tried at the assizes.

16. Caernarvon Castle is a thirteenth-century castle in northwest Wales. The well-known tradition is that the English King Edward I (1239–1307), having defeated Welsh rebel princes, promised the Welsh people "a native prince—one who could not speak a word of English"; he then presented to them his infant son (Edward II), who had just been born at Caernarvon Castle, as the first "Prince of Wales." That the Reverend Sam Gardner could accept Caernarvon Castle as of recent construction is another indication of his ignorance and of the shallowness of the university and ecclesiastical systems that had nurtured him.

REV. S. [*rising, startled out of his professional manner into real force and sincerity*] Frank, once for all, it's out of the question. Mrs Warren will tell you that it's not to be thought of.

CROFTS. Of course not.

FRANK [*with enchanting placidity*] Is that so, Mrs Warren?

MRS WARREN [*reflectively*] Well, Sam, I dont know. If the girl wants to get married, no good can come of keeping her unmarried.

REV. S. [*astounded*] But married to him!—your daughter to my son! Only think: it's impossible.

CROFTS. Of course it's impossible. Dont be a fool, Kitty.

MRS WARREN [*nettled*] Why not? Isnt my daughter good enough for your son?

REV. S. But surely, my dear Mrs Warren, you know the reasons—

MRS WARREN [*defiantly*] I know no reasons. If you know any, you can tell them to the lad, or to the girl, or to your congregation, if you like.

REV. S. [*collapsing helplessly into his chair*] You know very well that I couldnt tell anyone the reasons. But my boy will believe me when I tell him there are reasons.

FRANK. Quite right, Dad: he will. But has your boy's conduct ever been influenced by your reasons?

CROFTS. You cant marry her; and thats all about it. [*He gets up and stands on the hearth, with his back to the fireplace, frowning determinedly*].

MRS WARREN [*turning on him sharply*] What have you got to do with it, pray?

FRANK [*with his prettiest lyrical cadence*] Precisely what I was going to ask myself, in my own graceful fashion.

CROFTS [*to Mrs Warren*] I suppose you dont want to marry the girl to a man younger than herself and without either a profession or twopence to keep her on. Ask Sam, if you dont believe me. [*To the parson*] How much more money are you going to give him?

REV. S. Not another penny. He has had his patrimony and he spent the last of it in July. [*Mrs Warren's face falls*].

CROFTS [*watching her*] There! I told you. [*He resumes his place on the settle and puts up his legs on the seat again, as if the matter were finally disposed of*].

FRANK [*plaintively*] This is ever so mercenary. Do you suppose Miss Warren's going to marry for money? If we love one another—

MRS WARREN. Thank you. Your love's a pretty cheap commodity, my lad. If you have no means of keeping a wife, that settles it: you cant have Vivie.

FRANK [*much amused*] What do y o u say, gov'nor, eh?

REV. S. I agree with Mrs Warren.

FRANK. And good old Crofts has already expressed his opinion.

CROFTS [*turning angrily on his elbow*] Look here: I want none of y o u r cheek.

FRANK [*pointedly*] I'm ever so sorry to surprise you, Crofts, but you allowed yourself the liberty of speaking to me like a father a moment ago. One father is enough, thank you.

CROFTS [*contemptuously*] Yah! [*He turns away again*].

FRANK [*rising*] Mrs Warren: I cannot give my Vivie up, even for your sake.

MRS WARREN [*muttering*] Young scamp!

FRANK [*continuing*] And as you no doubt intend to hold out other prospects to her, I shall lose no time in placing my case before her. [*They stare at him, and he begins to declaim gracefully*]

> He either fears his fate too much,
> Or his deserts are small,
> That dares not put it to the touch
> To gain or lose it all.[17]

The cottage door opens whilst he is reciting; and Vivie and Praed come in. He breaks off. Praed puts his hat on the dresser. There is an immediate improvement in the company's behavior. Crofts takes down his legs from the settle and pulls himself together as Praed joins him at the fireplace. Mrs Warren loses her ease of manner and takes refuge in querulousness.

MRS WARREN. Wherever have you been, Vivie?

VIVIE [*taking off her hat and throwing it carelessly on the table*] On the hill.

MRS WARREN. Well, you shouldnt go off like that without letting me know. How could I tell what had become of you? And night coming on too!

VIVIE [*going to the door of the kitchen and opening it, ignoring her mother*] Now, about supper? [*All rise except Mrs Warren*]. We shall be rather crowded in here, I'm afraid.

MRS WARREN. Did you hear what I said, Vivie?

VIVIE [*quietly*] Yes, mother. [*Reverting to the supper difficulty*] How many are we? [*Counting*] One, two, three, four, five, six. Well, two will have to wait until the rest are done: Mrs Alison has only plates and knives for four.

PRAED. Oh, it doesnt matter about me. I—

VIVIE. You have had a long walk and are hungry, Mr Praed: you shall have your supper at once. I can wait myself. I want one person to wait with me. Frank: are you hungry?

FRANK. Not the least in the world. Completely off my peck, in fact.

MRS WARREN [*to Crofts*] Neither are you, George. You can wait.

CROFTS. Oh, hang it, Ive eaten nothing since tea-time. Cant Sam do it?

FRANK. Would you starve my poor father?

REV. S. [*testily*] Allow me to speak for myself, sir. I am perfectly willing to wait.

VIVIE [*decisively*] Theres no need. Only two are wanted. [*She opens the door of the kitchen*]. Will you take my mother in, Mr Gardner. [*The parson takes Mrs Warren; and they pass into the kitchen. Praed and Crofts follow. All except Praed clearly disapprove of the arrangement, but do not know how to resist it. Vivie stands at the door looking in at them*]. Can you squeeze past to that corner, Mr

17. From the poem "I'll Never Love Thee More" (also known as "My Dear and Only Love"), lines 13–16, by James Graham, the first Marquis of Montrose (1612–1650), English general, stateman, and poet.

Praed: it's rather a tight fit. Take care of your coat against the white-wash: thats right. Now, are you all comfortable?

PRAED [*within*] Quite, thank you.

MRS WARREN [*within*] Leave the door open, dearie. [*Vivie frowns; but Frank checks her with a gesture, and steals to the cottage door, which he softly sets wide open*]. Oh Lor, what a draught! Youd better shut it, dear.

> Vivie shuts it with a slam, and then, noting with disgust that her mother's hat and shawl are lying about, takes them tidily to the window seat, whilst Frank noiselessly shuts the cottage door.

FRANK [*exulting*] Aha! Got rid of em. Well, Vivvums: what do you think of my governor?

VIVIE [*preoccupied and serious*] Ive hardly spoken to him. He doesnt strike me as as being a particularly able person.

FRANK. Well, you know, the old man is not altogether such a fool as he looks. You see, he was shoved into the Church rather; and in trying to live up to it he makes a much bigger ass of himself than he really is. I dont dislike him as much as you might expect. He means well. How do you think youll get on with him?

VIVIE [*rather grimly*] I dont think my future life will be much concerned with him, or with any of that old circle of my mother's, except perhaps Praed. [*She sits down on the settle*]. What do you think of my mother?

FRANK. Really and truly?

VIVIE. Yes, really and truly.

FRANK. Well, she's ever so jolly. But she's rather a caution, isnt she? And Crofts! oh my eye, Crofts! [*He sits beside her*].

VIVIE. What a lot, Frank!

FRANK. What a crew!

VIVIE [*with intense contempt for them*] If I thought that *I* was like that—that I was going to be a waster, shifting along from one meal to another with no purpose, and no character, and no grit in me, I'd open an artery and bleed to death without one moment's hesitation.

FRANK. Oh no, you wouldnt. Why should they take any grind when they can afford not to? I wish I had their luck. No: what I object to is their form. It isnt the thing: it's slovenly, ever so slovenly.

VIVIE. Do you think your form will be any better when youre as old as Crofts, if you dont work?

FRANK. Of course I do. Ever so much better. Vivvums mustnt lecture: her little boy's incorrigible. [*He attempts to take her face caressingly in his hands*].

VIVIE [*striking his hands down sharply*] Off with you: Vivvums is not in a humor for petting her little boy this evening. [*She rises and comes forward to the other side of the room*].

FRANK [*following her*] How unkind!

VIVIE [*stamping at him*] Be serious. I'm serious.

FRANK. Good. Let us talk learnedly. Miss Warren: do you know that all the most advanced thinkers are agreed that half the diseases of modern civilization are due to starvation of the affections in the young. Now, I—

VIVIE [*cutting him short*] You are very tiresome. [*She opens the inner door*]. Have you room for Frank there? He's complaining of starvation.

MRS WARREN [*within*] Of course there is [*clatter of knives and glasses as she moves the things on the table*]. Here! theres room now beside me. Come along, Mr Frank.

FRANK. Her little boy will be ever so even with his Vivvums for this. [*He passes into the kitchen*].

MRS WARREN [*within*] Here, Vivie: come on you too, child. You must be famished. [*She enters, followed by Crofts, who holds the door open for Vivie with marked deference. She goes out without looking at him; and shuts the door after her*]. Why, George, you cant be done: youve eaten nothing. Is there anything wrong with you?

CROFTS. Oh, all I wanted was a drink. [*He thrusts his hands in his pockets, and begins prowling about the room, restless and sulky*].

MRS WARREN. Well, I like enough to eat. But a little of that cold beef and cheese and lettuce goes a long way. [*With a sigh of only half repletion she sits down lazily on the settle*].

CROFTS. What do you go encouraging that young pup for?

MRS WARREN [*on the alert at once*] Now see here, George: what are you up to about that girl? Ive been watching your way of looking at her. Remember: I know you and what your looks mean.

CROFTS. Theres no harm in looking at her, is there?

MRS WARREN. I'd put you out and pack you back to London pretty soon if I saw any of your nonsense. My girl's little finger is more to me than your whole body and soul. [*Crofts receives this with a sneering grin. Mrs Warren, flushing a little at her failure to impose on him in the character of a theatrically devoted mother, adds in a lower key*] Make your mind easy: the young pup has no more chance than you have.

CROFTS. Maynt a man take an interest in a girl?

MRS WARREN. Not a man like you.

CROFTS. How old is she?

MRS WARREN. Never you mind how old she is.

CROFTS. Why do you make such a secret of it?

MRS WARREN. Because I choose.

CROFTS. Well, I'm not fifty yet; and my property is as good as ever it was—

MRS WARREN [*interrupting him*] Yes; because youre as stingy as youre vicious.

CROFTS [*continuing*] And a baronet[18] isnt to be picked up every day. No other man in my position would put up with you for a mother-in-law. Why shouldnt she marry me?

MRS WARREN. You!

18. A baronet, ranking above a knight, held a title that could be inherited.

CROFTS. We three could live together quite comfortably: I'd die before her and leave her a bouncing widow with plenty of money. Why not? It's been growing in my mind all the time Ive been walking with that fool inside there.

MRS WARREN [*revolted*] Yes: it's the sort of thing that would grow in your mind.

He halts in his prowling; and the two look at one another, she steadfastly, with a sort of awe behind her contemptuous disgust: he stealthily, with a carnal gleam in his eye and a loose grin.

CROFTS [*suddenly becoming anxious and urgent as he sees no sign of sympathy in her*] Look here, Kitty: youre a sensible woman: you neednt put on any moral airs. I'll ask no more questions; and you need answer none. I'll settle the whole property on her; and if you want a cheque for yourself on the wedding day, you can name any figure you like—in reason.

MRS WARREN. So it's come to that with you, George, like all the other worn-out old creatures!

CROFTS [*savagely*] Damn you!

Before she can retort the door of the kitchen is opened; and the voices of the others are heard returning. Crofts, unable to recover his presence of mind, hurries out of the cottage. The clergyman appears at the kitchen door.

REV. S. [*looking around*] Where is Sir George?

MRS WARREN. Gone out to have a pipe. [*The clergyman takes his hat from the table, and joins Mrs Warren at the fireside. Meanwhile Vivie comes in, followed by Frank, who collapses into the nearest chair with an air of extreme exhaustion. Mrs Warren looks round at Vivie and says, with her affectation of maternal patronage even more forced than usual*] Well, dearie: have you had a good supper?

VIVIE. You know what Mrs Alison's suppers are. [*She turns to Frank and pets him*]. Poor Frank! was all the beef gone? did it get nothing but bread and cheese and ginger beer? [*Seriously, as if she had done quite enough trifling for one evening*] Her butter is really awful. I must get some down from the stores.

FRANK. Do, in Heaven's name!

Vivie goes to the writing-table and makes a memorandum to order the butter. Praed comes in from the kitchen, putting up his handkerchief, which he has been using as a napkin.

REV. S. Frank, my boy: it is time for us to be thinking of home. Your mother does not know yet that we have visitors.

PRAED. I'm afraid we're giving trouble.

FRANK [*rising*] Not the least in the world: my mother will be delighted to see you. She's a genuinely intellectual artistic woman; and she sees nobody here from one year's end to another except the gov'nor; so you can imagine how jolly dull it pans out for her. [*To his father*] Y o u r e not intellectual or artistic: are you, pater? So take Praed home at once; and I'll stay here and entertain Mrs Warren. Youll pick up Crofts in the garden. He'll be excellent company for the bull-pup.

PRAED [*taking his hat from the dresser, and coming close to Frank*] Come with us, Frank. Mrs Warren has not seen Miss Vivie for a long time; and we have prevented them from having a moment together yet.

FRANK [*quite softened and looking at Praed with romantic admiration*] Of course. I forgot. Ever so thanks for reminding me. Perfect gentleman, Praddy. Always were. My ideal through life. [*He rises to go, but pauses a moment between the two older men, and puts his hand on Praed's shoulder*]. Ah, if you had only been my father instead of this unworthy old man! [*He puts his other hand on his father's shoulder*].

REV. S. [*blustering*] Silence, sir, silence: you are profane.

MRS WARREN [*laughing heartily*] You should keep him in better order, Sam. Goodnight. Here: take George his hat and stick with my compliments.

REV. S. [*taking them*] Goodnight. [*They shake hands. As he passes Vivie he shakes hands with her also and bids her goodnight. Then, in booming command, to Frank*] Come along, sir, at once. [*He goes out*].

MRS WARREN. Byebye, Praddy.

PRAED. Byebye, Kitty.

They shake hands affectionately and go out together, she accompanying him to the garden gate.

FRANK [*to Vivie*] Kissums?

VIVIE [*fiercely*] No. I hate you. [*She takes a couple of books and some paper from the writing-table, and sits down with them at the middle table, at the end next the fireplace*].

FRANK [*grimacing*] Sorry. [*He goes for his cap and rifle. Mrs Warren returns. He takes her hand*] Goodnight, d e a r Mrs Warren. [*He kisses her hand. She snatches it away, her lips tightening, and looks more than half disposed to box his ears. He laughs mischievously and runs off, clapping-to the door behind him*].

MRS WARREN [*resigning herself to an evening of boredom now that the men are gone*] Did you ever in your life hear anyone rattle on so? Isnt he a tease? [*She sits at the table*]. Now that I think of it, dearie, dont you go encouraging him. I'm sure he's a regular good-for-nothing.

VIVIE [*rising to fetch more books*] I'm afraid so. Poor Frank! I shall have to get rid of him; but I shall feel sorry for him, though he's not worth it. That man Crofts does not seem to me to be good for much either: is he? [*She throws the books on the table rather roughly*].

MRS WARREN [*galled by Vivie's indifference*] What do you know of men, child, to talk that way about them? Youll have to make up your mind to see a good deal of Sir George Crofts, as he's a friend of mine.

VIVIE [*quite unmoved*] Why? [*She sits down and opens a book*]. Do you expect that we shall be much together? You and I, I mean?

MRS WARREN [*staring at her*] Of course: until youre married. Youre not going back to college again.

VIVIE. Do you think my way of life would suit you? I doubt it.

MRS WARREN. Y o u r way of life! What do you mean?

VIVIE [*cutting a page of her book with the paper knife on her chatelaine*] Has it really never occurred to you, mother, that I have a way of life like other people?

MRS WARREN. What nonsense is this youre trying to talk? Do you want to shew your independence, now that youre a great little person at school? Dont be a fool, child.

VIVIE [*indulgently*] Thats all you have to say on the subject, is it, mother?

MRS WARREN [*puzzled, then angry*] Dont you keep on asking me questions like that. [*Violently*] Hold your tongue. [*Vivie works on, losing no time, and saying nothing*]. You and your way of life, indeed! What next? [*She looks at Vivie again. No reply*]. Your way of life will be what I please, so it will. [*Another pause*]. Ive been noticing these airs in you ever since you got that tripos or whatever you call it. If you think I'm going to put up with them youre mistaken; and the sooner you find it out, the better. [*Muttering*] All I have to say on the subject, indeed! [*Again raising her voice angrily*] Do you know who youre speaking to, Miss?

VIVIE [*looking across at her without raising her head from her book*] No. Who are you? What are you?

MRS WARREN [*rising breathless*] You young imp!

VIVIE. Everybody knows my reputation, my social standing, and the profession I intend to pursue. I know nothing about you. What is that way of life which you invite me to share with you and Sir George Crofts, pray?

MRS WARREN. Take care. I shall do something I'll be sorry for after, and you too.

VIVIE [*putting aside her books with cool decision*] Well, let us drop the subject until you are better able to face it. [*Looking critically at her mother*] You want some good walks and a little lawn tennis to set you up. You are shockingly out of condition: you were not able to manage twenty yards uphill today without stopping to pant; and your wrists are mere rolls of fat. Look at mine. [*She holds out her wrists*].

MRS WARREN [*after looking at her helplessly, begins to whimper*] Vivie—

VIVIE [*springing up sharply*] Now pray dont begin to cry. Anything but that. I really cannot stand whimpering. I will go out of the room if you do.

MRS WARREN [*piteously*] Oh, my darling, how can you be so hard on me? Have I no rights over you as your mother?

VIVIE. Are you my mother?

MRS WARREN [*appalled*] Am I your mother! Oh, Vivie!

VIVIE. Then where are our relatives? my father? our family friends? You claim the rights of a mother: the right to call me fool and child; to speak to me as no woman in authority over me at college dare speak to me; to dictate my way of life; and to force on me the acquaintance of a brute whom anyone can see to be the most vicious sort of London man about town. Before I give myself the trouble to resist such claims, I may as well find out whether they have any real existence.

MRS WARREN [*distracted, throwing herself on her knees*] Oh no, no. Stop, stop. I am your mother: I swear it. Oh, you cant mean to turn on me—my own child! it's not natural. You believe me, dont you? Say you believe me.

VIVIE. Who was my father?

MRS WARREN. You dont know what youre asking. I cant tell you.

VIVIE [*determinedly*] Oh yes you can, if you like. I have a right to know; and you know very well that I have that right. You can refuse to tell me, if you please; but if you do, you will see the last of me tomorrow morning.

MRS WARREN. Oh, it's too horrible to hear you talk like that. You wouldnt—you c o u l d n t leave me.

VIVIE [*ruthlessly*] Yes, without a moment's hesitation, if you trifle with me about this. [*Shivering with disgust*] How can I feel sure that I may not have the contaminated blood of that brutal waster in my veins?

MRS WARREN. No, no. On my oath it's not he, nor any of the rest that you have ever met. I'm certain of that, at least.

Vivie's eyes fasten sternly on her mother as the significance of this flashes on her.

VIVIE [*slowly*] You are certain of that, at l e a s t. Ah! You mean that that is all you are certain of. [*Thoughtfully*] I see. [*Mrs Warren buries her face in her hands*]. Dont do that, mother: you know you dont feel it a bit. [*Mrs Warren takes down her hands and looks up deplorably at Vivie, who takes out her watch and says*] Well, that is enough for tonight. At what hour would you like breakfast? Is half-past eight too early for you?

MRS WARREN [*wildly*] My God, what sort of woman are you?

VIVIE [*coolly*] The sort the world is mostly made of, I should hope. Otherwise I dont understand how it gets its business done. Come [*taking her mother by the wrist, and pulling her up pretty resolutely*]: pull yourself together. Thats right.

MRS WARREN [*querulously*] Youre very rough with me, Vivie.

VIVIE. Nonsense. What about bed? It's past ten.

MRS WARREN [*passionately*] Whats the use of my going to bed? Do you think I could sleep?

VIVIE. Why not? I shall.

MRS WARREN. You! youve no heart. [*She suddenly breaks out vehemently in her natural tongue—the dialect of a woman of the people—with all her affectations of maternal authority and conventional manners gone, and an overwhelming inspiration of true conviction and scorn in her*]. Oh, I wont bear it: I wont put up with the injustice of it. What right have you to set yourself up above me like this? You boast of what you are to me—to me, who gave you the chance of being what you are. What chance had I? Shame on you for a bad daughter and a stuck-up prude!

VIVIE [*sitting down with a shrug, no longer confident; for her replies, which have sounded sensible and strong to her so far, now begin to ring rather woodenly and even priggishly against the new tone of her mother*] Dont think for a moment I set myself above you in any way. You attacked me with the conventional authority of a mother: I defended myself with the conventional superiority of a respectable woman. Frankly, I am not going to stand any of your nonsense; and when you drop it I shall not expect you to stand any of mine. I shall always respect your right to your own opinions and your own way of life.

MRS WARREN. My own opinions and my own way of life! Listen to her talking! Do you think I was brought up like you? able to pick and choose my own way of life? Do you think I did what I did because I liked it, or thought it right, or wouldnt rather have gone to college and been a lady if I'd had the chance?

VIVIE. Everybody has some choice, mother. The poorest girl alive may not be able to choose between being Queen of England or Principal of Newnham; but she can choose between ragpicking and flowerselling, according to her taste. People are always blaming their circumstances for what they are. I dont believe in circumstances. The people who get on in this world are the people who get up and look for the circumstances they want, and, if they cant find them, make them.

MRS WARREN. Oh, it's easy to talk, very easy, isnt it? Here! would you like to know what my circumstances were?

VIVIE. Yes: you had better tell me. Wont you sit down?

MRS WARREN. Oh, I'll sit down: dont you be afraid. [*She plants her chair farther forward with brazen energy, and sits down. Vivie is impressed in spite of herself*]. D'you know what your gran'mother was?

VIVIE. No.

MRS WARREN. No, you dont. I do. She called herself a widow and had a fried-fish shop down by the Mint, and kept herself and four daughters out of it. Two of us were sisters: that was me and Liz; and we were both good-looking and well made. I suppose our father was a well-fed man: mother pretended he was a gentleman; but I dont know. The other two were only half sisters: undersized, ugly, starved looking, hard working, honest poor creatures: Liz and I would have half-murdered them if mother hadnt half-murdered u s to keep our hands off them. They were the respectable ones. Well, what did they get by their respectability? I'll tell you. One of them worked in a whitelead factory[19] twelve hours a day for nine shillings a week until she died of lead poisoning. She only expected to get her hands a little paralyzed; but she died. The other was always held up to us as a model because she married a Government laborer in the Deptford victualling yard,[20] and kept his room and the three children neat and tidy on eighteen shillings a week—until he took to drink. That was worth being respectable for, wasnt it?

VIVIE [*now thoughtfully attentive*] Did you and your sister think so?

MRS WARREN. Liz didnt, I can tell you: she had more spirit. We both went to a church school—that was part of the ladylike airs we gave ourselves to be superior to the children that knew nothing and went nowhere—and we stayed there until Liz went out one night and never came back. I know the schoolmistress thought I'd soon follow her example; for the clergyman was always warning me that Lizzie'd end by jumping off Waterloo Bridge.[21] Poor fool: that was all he

19. Whitelead was a poisonous lead carbonate compound used in the making of paints.
20. "Victualling" refers to the official supplying of provisions for the British navy.
21. The end that the clergyman foresees for Lizzie had become a cliche in both visual and literary portrayals of prostitutes in nineteenth-century culture. The melodrama of such moralizing portrayals was part of what Shaw saw as the cant that he needed to expose and repudiate in *Mrs Warren's Profession*.

knew about it! But I was more afraid of the whitelead factory than I was of the river; and so would you have been in my place. That clergyman got me a situation as scullery maid in a temperance restaurant where they sent out for anything you liked. Then I was waitress; and then I went to the bar at Waterloo station: fourteen hours a day serving drinks and washing glasses for four shillings a week and my board. That was considered a great promotion for me. Well, one cold, wretched night, when I was so tired I could hardly keep myself awake, who should come up for a half of Scotch but Lizzie, in a long fur cloak, elegant and comfortable, with a lot of sovereigns in her purse.

VIVIE [*grimly*] My aunt Lizzie!

MRS WARREN. Yes; and a very good aunt to have, too. She's living down at Winchester now, close to the cathedral, one of the most respectable ladies there. Chaperones girls at the county ball, if you please. No river for Liz, thank you! You remind me of Liz a little: she was a first-rate business woman—saved money from the beginning—never let herself look too like what she was—never lost her head or threw away a chance. When she saw I'd grown up good-looking she said to me across the bar 'What are you doing there, you little fool? wearing out your health and your appearance for other people's profit!' Liz was saving money then to take a house for herself in Brussels; and she thought we two could save faster than one. So she lent me some money and gave me a start; and I saved steadily and first paid her back, and then went into business with her as her partner. Why shouldnt I have done it? The house in Brussels was real high class: a much better place for a woman to be in than the factory where Anne Jane got poisoned. None of our girls were ever treated as I was treated in the scullery of that temperance place, or at the Waterloo bar, or at home. Would you have had me stay in them and become a worn out old drudge before I was forty?

VIVIE [*intensely interested by this time*] No; but why did you choose that business? Saving money and good management will succeed in any business.

MRS WARREN. Yes, saving money. But where can a woman get the money to save in any other business? Could y o u save out of four shillings a week and keep yourself dressed as well? Not you. Of course, if youre a plain woman and cant earn anything more; or if you have a turn for music, or the stage, or newspaper-writing: thats different. But neither Liz nor I had any turn for such things: all we had was our appearance and our turn for pleasing men. Do you think we were such fools as to let other people trade in our good looks by employing us as shopgirls, or barmaids, or waitresses, when we could trade in them ourselves and get all the profits instead of starvation wages? Not likely.

VIVIE. You were certainly quite justified—from the business point of view.

MRS WARREN. Yes; or any other point of view. What is any respectable girl brought up to do but to catch some rich man's fancy and get the benefit of his money by marrying him?—as if a marriage ceremony could make any difference in the right or wrong of the thing! Oh! the hypocrisy of the world makes me sick! Liz and I had to work and save and calculate just like other people; elseways we should be as poor as any good-for-nothing drunken waster of a woman that thinks her luck will last for ever. [*With great energy*] I despise such people: theyve no character; and if theres a thing I hate in a woman, it's want of character.

VIVIE. Come now, mother: frankly! Isnt it part of what you call character in a woman that she should greatly dislike such a way of making money?

MRS WARREN. Why, of course. Everybody dislikes having to work and make money; but they have to do it all the same. I'm sure Ive often pitied a poor girl, tired out and in low spirits, having to try to please some man that she doesnt care two straws for—some half-drunken fool that thinks he's making himself agreeable when he's teasing and worrying and disgusting a woman so that hardly any money could pay her for putting up with it. But she has to bear with disagreeables and take the rough with the smooth, just like a nurse in a hospital or anyone else. It's not work that any woman would do for pleasure, goodness knows; though to hear the pious people talk you would suppose it was a bed of roses.

VIVIE. Still, you consider it worth while. It pays.

MRS WARREN. Of course it's worth while to a poor girl, if she can resist temptation and is good-looking and well conducted and sensible. It's far better than any other employment open to her. I always thought that oughtnt to be. It cant be right, Vivie, that there shouldnt be better opportunities for women. I stick to that: it's wrong. But it's so, right or wrong; and a girl must make the best of it. But of course it's not worth while for a lady. If you took to it youd be a fool; but I should have been a fool if I'd taken to anything else.

VIVIE [*more and more deeply moved*] Mother: suppose we were both as poor as you were in those wretched old days, are you quite sure that you wouldnt advise me to try the Waterloo bar, or marry a laborer, or even go into the factory?

MRS WARREN [*indignantly*] Of course not. What sort of mother do you take me for! How could you keep your self-respect in such starvation and slavery? And whats a woman worth? whats life worth? without self-respect! Why am I independent and able to give my daughter a first-rate education, when other women that had just as good opportunities are in the gutter? Because I always knew how to respect myself and control myself. Why is Liz looked up to in a cathedral town? The same reason. Where would we be now if we'd minded the clergyman's foolishness? Scrubbing floors for one and sixpence a day and nothing to look forward to but the workhouse infirmary. Dont you be led astray by people who dont know the world, my girl. The only way for a woman to provide for herself decently is for her to be good to some man that can afford to be good to her. If she's in his own station of life, let her make him marry her; but if she's far beneath him she cant expect it: why should she? it wouldnt be for her own happiness. Ask any lady in London society that has daughters; and she'll tell you the same, except that I tell you straight and she'll tell you crooked. Thats all the difference.

VIVIE [*fascinated, gazing at her*] My dear mother: you are a wonderful woman:

you are stronger than all England. And are you really and truly not one wee bit doubtful—or—or—ashamed?

MRS WARREN. Well, of course, dearie, it's only good manners to be ashamed of it: it's expected from a woman. Women have to pretend to feel a great deal that they dont feel. Liz used to be angry with me for plumping out the truth about it. She used to say that when every woman could learn enough from what was going on in the world before her eyes, there was no need to talk about it to her. But then Liz was such a perfect lady! She had the true instinct of it; while I was always a bit of a vulgarian. I used to be so pleased when you sent me your photos to see that you were growing up like Liz: youve just her ladylike, determined way. But I cant stand saying one thing when everyone knows I mean another. Whats the use in such hypocrisy? If people arrange the world that way for women, theres no good pretending it's arranged the other way. No: I never was a bit ashamed really. I consider I had a right to be proud of how we managed everything so respectably, and never had a word against us, and how the girls were so well taken care of. Some of them did very well: one of them married an ambassador. But of course now I darent talk about such things: whatever would they think of us! [She yawns]. Oh dear! I do believe I'm getting sleepy after all. [She stretches herself lazily, thoroughly relieved by her explosion, and placidly ready for her night's rest].

VIVIE. I believe it is I who will not be able to sleep now. [She goes to the dresser and lights the candle. Then she extinguishes the lamp, darkening the room a good deal]. Better let in some fresh air before locking up. [She opens the cottage door, and finds that it is broad moonlight]. What a beautiful night! Look! [She draws aside the curtains of the window. The landscape is seen bathed in the radiance of the harvest moon rising over Blackdown].

MRS WARREN [with a perfunctory glance at the scene] Yes, dear; but take care you dont catch your death of cold from the night air.

VIVIE [contemptuously] Nonsense.

MRS WARREN [querulously] Oh yes: everything I say is nonsense, according to you.

VIVIE [turning to her quickly] No: really that is not so, mother. You have got completely the better of me tonight, though I intended it to be the other way. Let us be good friends now.

MRS WARREN [shaking her head a little ruefully] So it h a s been the other way. But I suppose I must give in to it. I always got the worst of it from Liz; and now I suppose it'll be the same with you.

VIVIE. Well, never mind. Come: goodnight, dear old mother. [She takes her mother in her arms].

MRS WARREN [fondly] I brought you up well, didnt I, dearie?

VIVIE. You did.

MRS WARREN. And youll be good to your poor old mother for it, wont you?

VIVIE. I will, dear. [Kissing her] Goodnight.

MRS WARREN [with unction] Blessings on my own dearie darling! a mother's blessing!

She embraces her daughter protectingly, instinctively looking upward for divine sanction.

Act III

In the Rectory garden next morning, with the sun shining from a cloudless sky. The garden wall has a five-barred wooden gate, wide enough to admit a carriage, in the middle. Beside the gate hangs a bell on a coiled spring, communicating with a pull outside. The carriage drive comes down the middle of the garden and then swerves to its left, where it ends in a little gravelled circus opposite the Rectory porch. Beyond the gate is seen the dusty high road, parallel with the wall, bounded on the farther side by a strip of turf and an unfenced pine wood. On the lawn, between the house and the drive, is a clipped yew tree, with a garden bench in its shade. On the opposite side the garden is shut in by a box hedge; and there is a sundial on the turf, with an iron chair near it. A little path leads off through the box hedge, behind the sundial.

Frank, seated on the chair near the sundial, on which he has placed the morning papers, is reading The Standard. His father comes from the house, red-eyed and shivery, and meets Frank's eye with misgiving.

FRANK [*looking at his watch*] Half-past eleven. Nice hour for a rector to come down to breakfast!

REV. S. Dont mock, Frank: dont mock. I am a little—er—[*Shivering*]—

FRANK. Off color?

REV. S. [*repudiating the expression*] No, sir: u n w e l l this morning. Wheres your mother?

FRANK. Dont be alarmed: she's not here. Gone to town by the 11.13 with Bessie. She left several messages for you. Do you feel equal to receiving them now, or shall I wait til youve breakfasted?

REV. S. I h a v e breakfasted, sir. I am surprised at your mother going to town when we have people staying with us. Theyll think it very strange.

FRANK. Possibly she has considered that. At all events, if Crofts is going to stay here, and you are going to sit up every night with him until four, recalling the incidents of your fiery youth, it is clearly my mother's duty, as a prudent house-keeper, to go up to the stores and order a barrel of whisky and a few hundred siphons.

REV. S. I did not observe that Sir George drank excessively.

FRANK. You were not in a condition to, gov'nor.

REV. S. Do you mean to say that I—?

FRANK [*calmly*] I never saw a beneficed clergyman less sober. The anecdotes you told about your past career were so awful that I really dont think Praed would have passed the night under your roof if it hadnt been for the way my mother and he took to one another.

REV. S. Nonsense, sir. I am Sir George Crofts' host. I must talk to him about something; and he has only one subject. Where is Mr Praed now?

FRANK. He is driving my mother and Bessie to the station.

REV. S. Is Crofts up yet?

FRANK. Oh, long ago. He hasnt turned a hair: he's in much better practice than you. He has kept it up ever since, probably. He's taken himself off somewhere to smoke.

> Frank resumes his paper. The parson turns disconsolately towards the gate; then comes back irresolutely.

REV. S. Er—Frank.

FRANK. Yes.

REV. S. Do you think the Warrens will expect to be asked here after yesterday afternoon?

FRANK. They've been asked already.

REV. S. [appalled] What ! ! !

FRANK. Crofts informed us at breakfast that you told him to bring Mrs Warren and Vivie over here today, and to invite them to make this house their home. My mother then found she must go to town by the 11.13 train.

REV. S. [with despairing vehemence] I never gave any such invitation. I never thought of such a thing.

FRANK [compassionately] How do you know, gov'nor, what you said and thought last night?

PRAED [coming in through the hedge] Good morning.

REV. S. Good morning. I must apologise for not having met you at breakfast. I have a touch of—of—

FRANK. Clergyman's sore throat, Praed. Fortunately not chronic.

PRAED [changing the subject] Well, I must say your house is in a charming spot here. Really most charming.

REV. S. Yes: it is indeed. Frank will take you for a walk, Mr Praed, if you like. I'll ask you to excuse me: I must take the opportunity to write my sermon while Mrs Gardner is away and you are all amusing yourselves. You wont mind, will you?

PRAED. Certainly not. Dont stand on the slightest ceremony with me.

REV. S. Thank you. I'll—er—er—[He stammers his way to the porch and vanishes into the house].

PRAED. Curious thing it must be writing a sermon every week.

FRANK. Ever so curious, if h e did it. He buys em. He's gone for some soda water.

PRAED. My dear boy: I wish you would be more respectful to your father. You know you can be so nice when you like.

FRANK. My dear Praddy: you forget that I have to live with the governor. When two people live together—it dont matter whether theyre father and son or husband and wife or brother and sister—they cant keep up the polite humbug thats so easy for ten minutes on an afternoon call. Now the governor, who unites to many admirable domestic qualities the irresoluteness of a sheep and the pompousness and aggressiveness of a jackass—

PRAED. No, pray, pray, my dear Frank, remember! He is your father.

FRANK. I give him due credit for that. [Rising and flinging down his paper] But just imagine his telling Crofts to bring the Warrens over here! He must have been ever so drunk. You know, my dear Praddy, my mother wouldnt stand Mrs Warren for a moment. Vivie mustnt come here until she's gone back to town.

PRAED. But your mother doesnt know anything about Mrs Warren, does she? [*He picks up the paper and sits down to read it*].

FRANK. I dont know. Her journey to town looks as if she did. Not that my mother would mind in the ordinary way: she has stuck like a brick to lots of women who had got into trouble. But they were all nice women. Thats what makes the real difference. Mrs Warren, no doubt, has her merits; but she's ever so rowdy; and my mother simply wouldnt put up with her. So—hallo! [*This exclamation is provoked by the reappearance of the clergyman, who comes out of the house in haste and dismay*].

REV. S. Frank: Mrs Warren and her daughter are coming across the heath with Crofts: I saw them from the study windows. What a m I to say about your mother?

FRANK. Stick on your hat and go out and say how delighted you are to see them; and that Frank's in the garden; and that mother and Bessie have been called to the bedside of a sick relative, and were ever so sorry they couldnt stop; and that you hope Mrs Warren slept well; and—and—say any blessed thing except the truth, and leave the rest to Providence.

REV. S. But how are we to get rid of them afterwards?

FRANK. There's no time to think of that now. Here! [*He bounds into the house*].

REV. S. He's so impetuous. I dont know what to do with him, Mr Praed.

FRANK [*returning with a clerical felt hat, which he claps on his father's head*] Now: off with you. [*Rushing him through the gate*]. Praed and I'll wait here, to give the thing an unpremeditated air. [*The clergyman, dazed but obedient, hurries off*].

FRANK. We must get the old girl back to town somehow, Praed. Come! Honestly, dear Praddy, do you like seeing them together?

PRAED. Oh, why not?

FRANK [*his teeth on edge*] Dont it make your flesh creep ever so little? that wicked old devil, up to every villainy under the sun, I'll swear, and Vivie—ugh!

PRAED. Hush, pray. Theyre coming.

    The clergyman and Crofts are seen coming along the road, followed by Mrs Warren and Vivie walking affectionately together.

FRANK. Look: she actually has her arm round the old woman's waist. It's her right arm: she began it. She's gone sentimental, by God! Ugh! ugh! Now do you feel the creeps? [*The clergyman opens the gate; and Mrs Warren and Vivie pass him and stand in the middle of the garden looking at the house. Frank, in an ecstasy of dissimulation, turns gaily to Mrs Warren, exclaiming*] Ever so delighted to see you, Mrs Warren. This quiet old rectory garden becomes you perfectly.

MRS WARREN. Well, I never! Did you hear that, George? He says I look well in a quiet old rectory garden.

REV. S. [*still holding the gate for Crofts, who loafs through it, heavily bored*] You look well everywhere, Mrs Warren.

FRANK. Bravo, gov'nor! Now look here: lets have a treat before lunch. First lets see the church. Everyone has to do that. It's a regular old thirteenth century church, you know: the gov'nor's ever so fond of it, because he got up a restoration fund and had it completely rebuilt six years ago. Praed will be able to shew its points.

PRAED [*rising*] Certainly, if the restoration has left any to shew.

REV. S. [*mooning hospitably at them*] I shall be pleased, I'm sure, if Sir George and Mrs Warren really care about it.

MRS WARREN. Oh, come along and get it over.

CROFTS [*turning back towards the gate*] Ive no objection.

REV. S. Not that way. We go through the fields, if you dont mind. Round here. [*He leads the way by the little path through the box hedge*].

CROFTS. Oh, all right. [*He goes with the parson*].

   Praed follows with Mrs Warren. Vivie does not stir: she watches them until they have gone, with all the lines of purpose in her face marking it strongly.

FRANK. Aint you coming?

VIVIE. No. I want to give you a warning, Frank. You were making fun of my mother just now when you said that about the rectory garden. That is barred in future. Please treat my mother with as much respect as you treat your own.

FRANK. My dear Viv: she wouldnt appreciate it: the two cases require different treatment. But what on earth has happened to you? Last night we were perfectly agreed as to your mother and her set. This morning I find you attitudinizing sentimentally with your arm round your parent's waist.

VIVIE [*flushing*] Attitudinizing!

FRANK. That was how it struck me. First time I ever saw you do a second-rate thing.

VIVIE [*controlling herself*] Yes, Frank: there has been a change; but I dont think it a change for the worse. Yesterday I was a little prig.

FRANK. And today?

VIVIE [*wincing; then looking at him steadily*] Today I know my mother better than you do.

FRANK. Heaven forbid!

VIVIE. What do you mean?

FRANK. Viv: theres a freemasonry among thoroughly immoral people that you know nothing of. Youve too much character. T h a t s the bond between your mother and me: thats why I know her better than youll ever know her.

VIVIE. You are wrong: you know nothing about her. If you knew the circumstances against which my mother had to struggle—

FRANK [*adroitly finishing the sentence for her*] I should know why she is what she is, shouldnt I? What difference would that make? Circumstances or no circumstances, Viv, you wont be able to stand your mother.

VIVIE [*very angrily*] Why not?

FRANK. Because she's an old wretch, Viv. If you ever put your arm round her waist in my presence again, I'll shoot myself there and then as a protest against an exhibition which revolts me.

VIVIE. Must I choose between dropping your acquaintance and dropping my mother's?

FRANK [*gracefully*] That would put the old lady at ever such a disadvantage. No, Viv; your infatuated little boy will have to stick to you in any case. But he's all the more anxious that you shouldnt make mistakes. It's no use, Viv: your mother's impossible. She may be a good sort; but she's a bad lot, a very bad lot.

VIVIE [*hotly*] Frank—! [*He stands his ground. She turns away and sits down on the bench under the yew tree, struggling to recover her self-command. Then she says*] Is she to be deserted by all the world because she's what you call a bad lot? Has she no right to live?

FRANK. No fear of that, Viv: s h e wont ever be deserted. [*He sits on the bench beside her*].

VIVIE. But I am to desert her, I suppose.

FRANK [*babyishly, lulling her and making love to her with his voice*] Mustnt go live with her. Little family group of mother and daughter wouldn't be a success. Spoil our little group.

VIVIE [*falling under the spell*] What little group?

FRANK. The babes in the wood:[22] Vivie and little Frank. [*He nestles against her like a weary child*]. Lets go and get covered up with leaves.

VIVIE [*rhythmically, rocking him like a nurse*] Fast asleep, hand in hand, under the trees.

FRANK. The wise little girl with her silly little boy.

VIVIE. The dear little boy with his dowdy little girl.

FRANK. Ever so peaceful, and relieved from the imbecility of the little boy's father and the questionableness of the little girl's—

VIVIE [*smothering the word against her breast*] Sh-sh-sh-sh! little girl wants to forget all about her mother. [*They are silent for some moments, rocking one another. Then Vivie wakes up with a shock, exclaiming*] What a pair of fools we are! Come: sit up. Gracious! your hair. [*She smooths it*]. I wonder do all grown up people play in that childish way when nobody is looking. I never did it when I was a child.

FRANK. Neither did I. You are my first playmate. [*He catches her hand to kiss it, but checks himself to look round first. Very unexpectedly, he sees Crofts emerging from the box hedge*]. Oh damn!

VIVIE. Why damn, dear?

FRANK [*whispering*] Sh! Heres this brute Crofts. [*He sits farther away from her with an unconcerned air*].

CROFTS. Could I have a few words with you, Miss Vivie?

22. The children in the wood is the subject of an old ballad included in *Percy's 'Reliques'* (1765) by Thomas Percy (1729–1811). The story concerns a dying gentleman who bequeaths his estate to his young son and daughter whom he leaves in the care of his brother. The wicked brother hires two assassins to take the children to the woods and kill them. One of the assassins cannot bring himself to murder the children. He kills the other assassin instead and abandons the children in the forest. They perish and are covered with leaves by a robin.

VIVIE. Certainly.

CROFTS [*to Frank*] Youll excuse me, Gardner. Theyre waiting for you in the church, if you dont mind.

FRANK [*rising*] Anything to oblige you, Crofts—except church. If you should happen to want me, Vivvums, ring the gate bell. [*He goes into the house with unruffled suavity*].

CROFTS [*watching him with a crafty air as he disappears, and speaking to Vivie with an assumption of being on privileged terms with her*] Pleasant young fellow that, Miss Vivie. Pity he has no money, isnt it?

VIVIE. Do you think so?

CROFTS. Well, whats he to do? No profession. No property. Whats he good for?

VIVIE. I realize his disadvantages, Sir George.

CROFTS [*a little taken aback at being so precisely interpreted*] Oh, it's not that. But while we're in this world we're in it; and money's money. [*Vivie does not answer*]. Nice day, isnt it?

VIVIE [*with scarcely veiled contempt for this effort at conversation*] Very.

CROFTS [*with brutal good humor, as if he liked her pluck*] Well, thats not what I came to say. [*Sitting down beside her*] Now listen, Miss Vivie. I'm quite aware that I'm not a young lady's man.

VIVIE. Indeed, Sir George?

CROFTS. No; and to tell you the honest truth I dont want to be either. But when I say a thing I mean it; when I feel a sentiment I feel it in earnest; and what I value I pay hard money for. Thats the sort of man I am.

VIVIE. It does you great credit, I'm sure.

CROFTS. Oh, I dont mean to praise myself. I have my faults, Heaven knows: no man is more sensible of that than I am. I know I'm not perfect; thats one of the advantages of being a middle-aged man; for I'm not a young man, and I know it. But my code is a simple one, and, I think, a good one. Honor between man and man; fidelity between man and woman; and no cant about this religion or that religion, but an honest belief that things are making for good on the whole.

VIVIE [*with biting irony*] 'A power, not ourselves, that makes for righteousness', eh?[23]

CROFTS [*taking her seriously*] Oh certainly. Not ourselves, of course. Y o u understand what I mean. Well, now as to practical matters. You may have an idea that Ive flung my money about; but I havnt: I'm richer today than when I first came into the property. Ive used my knowledge of the world to invest my money in ways that other men have overlooked; and whatever else I may be, I'm a safe man from the money point of view.

VIVIE. It's very kind of you to tell me all this.

---

23. Vivie quotes here the definition of God that Matthew Arnold advanced in chapter one of *Literature and Dogma* (1873), a defintion that had become so well known (and often criticized) in late Victorian culture that Shaw could play with it and off it.

CROFTS. Oh well, come, Miss Vivie: you neednt pretend you dont see what I'm driving at. I want to settle down with a Lady Crofts. I suppose you think me very blunt, eh?

VIVIE. Not at all: I am much obliged to you for being so definite and business-like. I quite appreciate the offer: the money, the position, L a d y   C r o f t s, and so on. But I think I will say no, if you don't mind. I'd rather not. [*She rises, and strolls across to the sundial to get out of his immediate neighborhood*].

CROFTS [*not at all discouraged, and taking advantage of the additional room left him on the seat to spread himself comfortably, as if a few preliminary refusals were part of the inevitable routine of courtship*] I'm in no hurry. It was only just to let you know in case young Gardner should try to trap you. Leave the question open.

VIVIE [*sharply*] My no is final. I wont go back from it.

   Crofts is not impressed. He grins; leans forward with his elbows on his knees to prod with his stick at some unfortunate insect in the grass; and looks cunningly at her. She turns away impatiently.

CROFTS. I'm a good deal older than you. Twenty-five years: quarter of a century. I shant live for ever; and I'll take care that you shall be well off when I'm gone.

VIVIE. I am proof against even that inducement, Sir George. Dont you think youd better take your answer? There is not the slightest chance of my altering it.

CROFTS [*rising, after a final slash at a daisy, and coming nearer to her*] Well, no matter. I could tell you some things that would change your mind fast enough; but I wont, because I'd rather win you by honest affection. I was a good friend to your mother: ask her whether I wasnt. She'd never have made the money that paid for your education if it hadnt been for my advice and help, not to mention the money I advanced her. There are not many men would have stood by her as I have. I put not less than £40,000 into it, from first to last.

VIVIE [*staring at him*] Do you mean to say you were my mother's business partner?

CROFTS. Yes. Now just think of all the trouble and the explanations it would save if we were to keep the whole thing in the family, so to speak. Ask your mother whether she'd like to have to explain all her affairs to a perfect stranger.

VIVIE. I see no difficulty, since I understand that the business is wound up, and the money invested.

CROFTS [*stopping short, amazed*] Wound up! Wind up a business thats paying 35 per cent in the worst years! Not likely. Who told you that?

VIVIE [*her color quite gone*] Do you mean that it is still—? [*She stops abruptly, and puts her hand on the sundial to support herself. Then she gets quickly to the iron chair and sits down*]. What business are you talking about?

CROFTS. Well, the fact is it's not what would be considered exactly a high-class business in my set—the county set, you know—o u r set it will be if you think better of my offer. Not that theres any mystery about it: dont think that. Of course you know by your mother's being in it that it's perfectly straight and honest. Ive known her for many years; and I can say of her that she'd cut off her hands sooner than touch anything that was not what it ought to be. I'll tell you all about it if you like. I dont know whether youve found in travelling how hard it is to find a really comfortable private hotel.

VIVIE [*sickened, averting her face*] Yes: go on.

CROFTS. Well, thats all it is. Your mother has a genius for managing such things. Weve got two in Brussels, one in Ostend, one in Vienna, and two in Budapest. Of course there are others besides ourselves in it: but we hold most of the capital; and your mother's indispensable as managing director. Youve noticed, I daresay, that she travels a good deal. But you see you cant mention such things in society. Once let out the word hotel and everybody says you keep a public-house. You wouldnt like people to say that of your mother, would you? Thats why we're so reserved about it. By the way, youll keep it to yourself, wont you? Since it's been a secret so long, it had better remain so.

VIVIE. And this is the business you invite me to join you in?

CROFTS. Oh no. My wife shant be troubled with business. Youll not be in it more than youve always been.

VIVIE. *I* always been! What do you mean?

CROFTS. Only that youve always lived on it. It paid for your education and the dress you have on your back. Dont turn up your nose at business, Miss Vivie; where would your Newnhams and Girtons be without it?

VIVIE [*rising, almost beside herself*] Take care. I know what this business is.

CROFTS [*starting, with a suppressed oath*] Who told you?

VIVIE. Your partner. My mother.

CROFTS [*black with rage*] The old—

VIVIE. Just so.

He swallows the epithet and stands for a moment swearing and raging foully to himself. But he knows that his cue is to be sympathetic. He takes refuge in generous indignation.

CROFTS. She ought to have had more consideration for you. *I*'d never have told you.

VIVIE. I think you would probably have told me when we were married: it would have been a convenient weapon to break me in with.

CROFTS [*quite sincerely*] I never intended that. On my word as a gentleman I didnt.

Vivie wonders at him. Her sense of the irony of his protest cools and braces her. She replies with contemptuous self-possession.

VIVIE. It does not matter. I suppose you understand that when we leave here today our acquaintance ceases.

CROFTS. Why? Is it for helping your mother?

VIVIE. My mother was a very poor woman who had no reasonable choice but to do as she did. You were a rich gentleman; and you did the same for the sake of 35 per cent. You are a pretty common sort of scoundrel, I think. That is my opinion of you.

CROFTS [*after a stare: not at all displeased, and much more at his ease on these frank terms than on their former ceremonious ones*] Ha! ha! ha! ha! Go it, little missie, go it; it doesnt hurt me and it amuses you. Why the devil shouldnt I invest my money that way? I take the interest on my capital like other people: I hope you dont think I dirty my own hands with the work. Come! you wouldnt refuse the acquaintance of my mother's cousin the Duke of Belgravia because some of the rents he gets are earned in queer ways. You wouldnt cut the Archbishop of Canterbury, I suppose, because the Ecclesiastical Commissioners have a few publicans and sinners among their tenants. Do you remember your Crofts scholarship at Newnham? Well, that was founded by my brother the M.P. He gets his 22 per cent out of a factory with 600 girls in it, and not one of them getting wages enough to live on. How d'ye suppose they manage when they have no family to fall back on? Ask your mother. And do you expect me to turn my back on 35 per cent when all the rest are pocketing what they can, like sensible men? No such fool! If youre going to pick and choose your acquaintances on moral principles, youd better clear out of this country, unless you want to cut yourself out of all decent society.

VIVIE [*conscience stricken*] You might go on to point out that I myself never asked where the money I spent came from. I believe I am just as bad as you.

CROFTS [*greatly reassured*] Of course you are; and a very good thing too! What harm does it do after all? [*Rallying her jocularly*] So you dont think me such a scoundrel now you come to think it over. Eh?

VIVIE. I have shared profits with you; and I admitted you just now to the familiarity of knowing what I think of you.

CROFTS [*with serious friendliness*] To be sure you did. You wont find me a bad sort: I dont go in for being superfine intellectually: but Ive plenty of honest human feeling; and the old Crofts breed comes out in a sort of instinctive hatred of anything low, in which I'm sure youll sympathize with me. Believe me, Miss Vivie, the world isnt such a bad place as the croakers make out. As long as you dont fly openly in the face of society, society doesnt ask any inconvenient questions; and it makes precious short work of the cads who do. There are no secrets better kept than the secrets everybody guesses. In the class of people I can introduce you to, no lady or gentleman would so far forget themselves as to discuss my business affairs or your mother's. No man can offer you a safer position.

VIVIE [*studying him curiously*] I suppose you really think youre getting on famously with me.

CROFTS. Well, I hope I may flatter myself that you think better of me than you did at first.

VIVIE [*quietly*] I hardly find you worth thinking about at all now. When I think of the society that tolerates you, and the laws that protect you! when I think of how helpless nine out of ten young girls would be in the hands of you and my mother! the unmentionable woman and her capitalist bully—

CROFTS [*livid*] Damn you!

VIVIE. You need not. I feel among the damned already.

She raises the latch of the gate to open it and go out. He follows her and puts his hand heavily on the top bar to prevent its opening.

CROFTS [*panting with fury*] Do you think I'll put up with this from you, you young devil?

VIVIE [*unmoved*] Be quiet. Some one will answer the bell. [*Without flinching a step she strikes the bell with the back of her hand. It clangs harshly; and he starts back involuntarily. Almost immediately Frank appears at the porch with his rifle*].

FRANK [*with cheerful politeness*] Will you have the rifle, Viv; or shall I operate?

VIVIE. Frank: have you been listening?

FRANK [*coming down into the garden*] Only for the bell, I assure you; so that you shouldnt have to wait. I think I shewed great insight into your character, Crofts.

CROFTS. For two pins I'd take that gun from you and break it across your head.

FRANK [*stalking him cautiously*] Pray dont. I'm ever so careless in handling fire-arms. Sure to be a fatal accident, with a reprimand from the coroner's jury for my negligence.

VIVIE. Put the rifle away, Frank; it's quite unnecessary.

FRANK. Quite right, Viv. Much more sportsmanlike to catch him in a trap. [*Crofts, understanding the insult, makes a threatening movement*]. Crofts: there are fifteen cartridges in the magazine here; and I am a dead shot at the present distance and at an object of your size.

CROFTS. Oh, you neednt be afraid. I'm not going to touch you.

FRANK. Ever so magnanimous of you under the circumstances! Thank you!

CROFTS. I'll just tell you this before I go. It may interest you, since youre so fond of one another. Allow me, Mister Frank, to introduce you to your half-sister, the eldest daughter of the Reverend Samuel Gardner. Miss Vivie: your half-brother. Good morning. [*He goes out through the gate and along the road*].

FRANK [*after a pause of stupefaction, raising the rifle*] Youll testify before the coroner that it's an accident, Viv. [*He takes aim at the retreating figure of Crofts. Vivie seizes the muzzle and pulls it round against her breast*].

VIVIE. Fire now. You may.

FRANK [*dropping his end of the rifle hastily*] Stop! take care. [*She lets it go. It falls on the turf*]. Oh, youve given your little boy such a turn. Suppose it had gone off! ugh! [*He sinks on the garden seat overcome*].

VIVIE. Suppose it had: do you think it would not have been a relief to have some sharp physical pain tearing through me?

FRANK [*coaxingly*] Take it ever so easy, dear Viv. Remember: even if the rifle scared that fellow into telling the truth for the first time in his life, that only makes us the babes in the wood in earnest.[24] [*He holds out his arms to her*]. Come and be covered up with leaves again.

VIVIE [*with a cry of disgust*] Ah, not that, not that. You make all my flesh creep.

FRANK. Why, whats the matter?

VIVIE. Goodbye. [*She makes for the gate*].

---

24. Frank refers to the fact that, if Crofts's statement is true, then he and Vivie, like the fabled babes in the woods, are brother and sister. See note 22.

FRANK [*jumping up*] Hallo! Stop! Viv! Viv! [*She turns in the gateway*] Where are you going to? Where shall we find you?

VIVIE. At Honoria Fraser's chambers, 67 Chancery Lane, for the rest of my life. [*She goes off quickly in the opposite direction to that taken by Crofts*].

FRANK. But I say—wait—dash it! [*He runs after her*].

Act IV

Honoria Fraser's chambers in Chancery Lane. An office at the top of New Stone Buildings, with a plate-glass window, distempered walls,[25] *electric light, and a patent stove. Saturday afternoon. The chimneys of Lincoln's Inn and the western sky beyond are seen through the window. There is a double writing table in the middle of the room, with a cigar box, ash pans, and a portable electric reading lamp almost snowed up in heaps of papers and books. This table has knee holes and chairs right and left and is very untidy. The clerk's desk, closed and tidy, with its high stool, is against the wall, near a door communicating with the inner rooms. In the opposite wall is the door leading to the public corridor. Its upper panel is of opaque glass, lettered in black on the outside,* FRASER AND WARREN. *A baize screen hides the corner between this door and the window.*

Frank, in a fashionable light-colored coaching suit, with his stick, gloves, and white hat in his hands, is pacing up and down the office. Somebody tries the door with a key.

FRANK [*calling*] Come in. It's not locked.

Vivie comes in, in her hat and jacket. She stops and stares at him.

VIVIE [*sternly*] What are you doing here?

FRANK. Waiting to see you. Ive been here for hours. Is this the way you attend to your business? [*He puts his hat and stick on the table, and perches himself with a vault on the clerk's stool looking at her with every appearance of being in a specially restless, teasing, flippant mood*].

VIVIE. Ive been away exactly twenty minutes for a cup of tea. [*She takes off her hat and jacket and hangs them up behind the screen*]. How did you get in?

FRANK. The staff had not left when I arrived. He's gone to play cricket on Primrose Hill. Why dont you employ a woman, and give your sex a chance?

VIVIE. What have you come for?

FRANK [*springing off the stool and coming close to her*] Viv: lets go and enjoy the Saturday half-holiday somewhere, like the staff. What do you say to Richmond, and then a music hall, and a jolly supper?

VIVIE. Cant afford it. I shall put in another six hours work before I go to bed.

FRANK. Cant afford it, cant we? Aha! Look here. [*He takes out a handful of sovereigns and makes them chink*]. Gold, Viv: gold!

VIVIE. Where did you get it?

25. Walls on which a mixture of paint and a more glutinous substance has been applied to a plaster surface.

FRANK. Gambling, Viv: gambling. Poker.

VIVIE. Pah! It's meaner than stealing it. No: I'm not coming. [*She sits down to work at the table, with her back to the glass door, and begins turning over the papers*].

FRANK [*remonstrating piteously*] But, my dear Viv, I want to talk to you ever so seriously.

VIVIE. Very well: sit down in Honoria's chair and talk here. I like ten minutes chat after tea. [*He murmurs*]. No use groaning: I'm inexorable. [*He takes the opposite seat disconsolately*]. Pass that cigar box, will you?

FRANK [*pushing the cigar box across*] Nasty womanly habit. Nice men dont do it any longer.

VIVIE. Yes: they object to the smell in the office; and weve had to take to cigarets. See! [*She opens the box and takes out a cigaret, which she lights. She offers him one; but he shakes his head with a wry face. She settles herself comfortably in her chair, smoking*]. Go ahead.

FRANK. Well, I want to know what youve done—what arrangements youve made.

VIVIE. Everything was settled twenty minutes after I arrived here. Honoria has found the business too much for her this year; and she was on the point of sending for me and proposing a partnership when I walked in and told her I hadnt a farthing in the world. So I installed myself and packed her off for a fortnight's holiday. What happened at Haslemere when I left?

FRANK. Nothing at all. I said youd gone to town on particular business.

VIVIE. Well?

FRANK. Well, either they were too flabbergasted to say anything, or else Crofts had prepared your mother. Anyhow, she didnt say anything; and Crofts didnt say anything; and Praddy only stared. After tea they got up and went; and Ive not seen them since.

VIVIE [*nodding placidly with one eye on a wreath of smoke*] Thats all right.

FRANK [*looking round disparagingly*] Do you intend to stick in this confounded place?

VIVIE [*blowing the wreath decisively away, and sitting straight up*] Yes. These two days have given me back all my strength and self-possession. I will never take a holiday again as long as I live.

FRANK [*with a very wry face*] Mps! You look quite happy. And as hard as nails.

VIVIE [*grimly*] Well for me that I am!

FRANK [*rising*] Look here, Viv: we must have an explanation. We parted the other day under a complete misunderstanding. [*He sits on the table, close to her*].

VIVIE [*putting away the cigaret*] Well: clear it up.

FRANK. You remember what Crofts said?

VIVIE. Yes.

FRANK. That revelation was supposed to bring about a complete change in the nature of our feeling for one another. It placed us on the footing of brother and sister.

VIVIE. Yes.

FRANK. Have you ever had a brother?

VIVIE. No.

FRANK. Then you dont know what being brother and sister feels like? Now I have lots of sisters; and the fraternal feeling is quite familiar to me. I assure you my feeling for you is not the least in the world like it. The girls will go their way; I will go mine; and we shant care if we never see one another again. Thats brother and sister. But as to you, I cant be easy if I have to pass a week without seeing you. Thats not brother and sister. It's exactly what I felt an hour before Crofts made his revelation. In short, dear Viv, it's love's young dream.

VIVIE [*bitingly*] The same feeling, Frank, that brought your father to my mother's feet. Is that it?

FRANK [*so revolted that he slips off the table for a moment*] I very strongly object, Viv, to have my feelings compared to any which the Reverend Samuel is capable of harboring; and I object still more to a comparison of you to your mother. [*Resuming his perch*]. Besides, I dont believe the story. I have taxed my father with it, and obtained from him what I consider tantamount to a denial.

VIVIE. What did he say?

FRANK. He said he was sure there must be some mistake.

VIVIE. Do you believe him?

FRANK. I am prepared to take his word as against Crofts'.

VIVIE. Does it make any difference? I mean in your imagination or conscience; for of course it makes no real difference.

FRANK [*shaking his head*] None whatever to me.

VIVIE. Nor to me.

FRANK [*staring*] But this is ever so surprising! [*He goes back to his chair*]. I thought our whole relations were altered in your imagination and conscience, as you put it, the moment those words were out of that brute's muzzle.

VIVIE. No: it was not that. I didnt believe him. I only wish I could.

FRANK. Eh?

VIVIE. I think brother and sister would be a very suitable relation for us.

FRANK. You really mean that?

VIVIE. Yes. It's the only relation I care for, even if we could afford any other. I mean that.

FRANK [*raising his eyebrows like one on whom a new light has dawned, and rising with quite an effusion of chivalrous sentiment*] My dear Viv: why didnt you say so before? I am ever so sorry for persecuting you. I understand, of course.

VIVIE [*puzzled*] Understand what?

FRANK. Oh, I'm not a fool in the ordinary sense: only in the Scriptural sense of doing all the things the wise man declared to be folly, after trying them himself on the most extensive scale.[26] I see I am no longer Vivvum's little boy. Dont be alarmed: I shall never call you Vivvums again—at least unless you get tired of your new little boy, however he may be.

26. Frank refers here to the speaker in Ecclesiastes who "gave [his] heart to seek and search out by wisdom concerning all *things* that are done under heaven" before he concluded that "all *is* vanity and vexation of spirit" (Ecclesiastes 1:11, 14). See chapter 2 of Ecclesiastes for a description of the speaker's experiences.

VIVIE. My new little boy!

FRANK [*with conviction*] Must be a new little boy. Always happens that way. No other way, in fact.

VIVIE. None that you know of, fortunately for you.

    Someone knocks at the door.

FRANK. My curse upon yon caller, whoe'er he be!

VIVIE. It's Praed. He's going to Italy and wants to say goodbye. I asked him to call this afternoon. Go and let him in.

FRANK. We can continue our conversation after his departure for Italy. I'll stay him out. [*He goes to the door and opens it*]. How are you, Praddy? Delighted to see you. Come in.

    Praed, dressed for travelling, comes in, in high spirits.

PRAED. How do you do, Miss Warren? [*She presses his hand cordially, though a certain sentimentality in his high spirits jars on her*]. I start in an hour from Holborn Viaduct. I wish I could persuade you to try Italy.

VIVIE. What for?

PRAED. Why, to saturate yourself with beauty and romance, of course.

    Vivie, with a shudder, turns her chair to the table, as if the work waiting for her there were a support to her. Praed sits opposite to her. Frank places a chair near Vivie, and drops lazily and carelessly into it, talking at her over his shoulder.

FRANK. No use, Praddy. Viv is a little Philistine.[27] She is indifferent to my romance, and insensible to my beauty.

VIVIE. Mr Praed: once for all, there is no beauty and no romance in life for me. Life is what it is; and I am prepared to take it as it is.

PRAED [*enthusiastically*] You will not say that if you come with me to Verona and on to Venice. You will cry with delight at living in such a beautiful world.

FRANK. This is most eloquent, Praddy. Keep it up.

PRAED. Oh, I assure you *I* have cried—I shall cry again, I hope—at fifty! At your age, Miss Warren, you would not need to go so far as Verona. Your spirits would absolutely fly up at the mere sight of Ostend. You would be charmed with the gaiety, the vivacity, the happy air of Brussels.

VIVIE [*springing up with an exclamation of loathing*] Agh!

PRAED [*rising*] Whats the matter?

FRANK [*rising*] Hallo, Viv!

VIVIE [*to Praed, with deep reproach*] Can you find no better example of your beauty and romance than Brussels to talk to me about?

PRAED [*puzzled*] Of course it's very different from Verona. I dont suggest for a moment that—

VIVIE [*bitterly*] Probably the beauty and romance come to much the same in both places.

---

27. Name for the materialistic, self-satisfied middle class, a word made popular by Matthew Arnold in his influential cultural critique, *Culture and Anarchy* (1867–68).

PRAED [*completely sobered and much concerned*] My dear Miss Warren: I—[*looking inquiringly at Frank*] Is anything the matter?

FRANK. She thinks your enthusiasm frivolous, Praddy. She's had ever such a serious call.

VIVIE [*sharply*] Hold your tongue, Frank. Dont be silly.

FRANK [*sitting down*] Do you call this good manners, Praed?

PRAED [*anxious and considerate*] Shall I take him away, Miss Warren? I feel sure we have disturbed you at your work.

VIVIE. Sit down: I'm not ready to go back to work yet. [*Praed sits*]. You both think I have an attack of nerves. Not a bit of it. But there are two subjects I want dropped, if you dont mind. One of them [*to Frank*] is love's young dream in any shape or form: the other [*to Praed*] is the romance and beauty of life, especially Ostend and the gaiety of Brussels. You are welcome to any illusions you may have left on these subjects: I have none. If we three are to remain friends, I must be treated as a woman of business, permanently single [*to Frank*] and permanently unromantic [*to Praed*].

FRANK. I also shall remain permanently single until you change your mind. Praddy: change the subject. Be eloquent about something else.

PRAED [*diffidently*] I'm afraid theres nothing else in the world that I c a n talk about. The Gospel of Art is the only one I can preach. I know Miss Warren is a great devotee of the Gospel of Getting on; but we cant discuss that without hurting your feelings, Frank, since you are determined not to get on.

FRANK. Oh, dont mind my feelings. Give me some improving advice by all means: it does me ever so much good. Have another try to make a successful man of me, Viv. Come: lets have it all: energy, thrift, foresight, self-respect, character. Dont you hate people who have no character, Viv?

VIVIE [*wincing*] Oh, stop, stop: let us have no more of that horrible cant. Mr Praed: if there are really only those two gospels in the world, we had better all kill ourselves; for the same taint is in both, through and through.

FRANK [*looking critically at her*] There is a touch of poetry about you today, Viv, which has hitherto been lacking.

PRAED [*remonstrating*] My dear Frank: arnt you a little unsympathetic?

VIVIE [*merciless to herself*] No: it's good for me. It keeps me from being sentimental.

FRANK [*bantering her*] Checks your strong natural propensity that way, dont it?

VIVIE [*almost hysterically*] Oh yes: go on: dont spare me. I was sentimental for one moment in my life—beautifully sentimental—by moonlight; and now—

FRANK [*quickly*] I say, Viv: take care. Dont give yourself away.

VIVIE. Oh, do you think Mr Praed does not know all about my mother? [*Turning on Praed*] You had better have told me that morning, Mr Praed. You are very old fashioned in your delicacies, after all.

PRAED. Surely it is you who are a little old fashioned in your prejudices, Miss Warren. I feel bound to tell you, speaking as an artist, and believing that the most intimate human relationships are far beyond and above the scope of the law, that though I know that your mother is an unmarried woman, I do not respect her the less on that account. I respect her more.

FRANK [*airily*] Hear! Hear!

VIVIE [*staring at him*] Is that a l l you know?

PRAED. Certainly that is all.

VIVIE. Then you neither of you know anything. Your guesses are innocence itself compared to the truth.

PRAED [*rising, startled and indignant, and preserving his politeness with an effort*] I hope not. [*More emphatically*] I hope not, Miss Warren.

FRANK [*whistles*] Whew!

VIVIE. You are not making it easy for me to tell you, Mr Praed.

PRAED [*his chivalry drooping before their conviction*] If there is anything worse— that is, anything else—are you sure you are right to tell us, Miss Warren?

VIVIE. I am sure that if I had the courage I should spend the rest of my life in telling everybody—stamping and branding it into them until they all felt their part in its abomination as I feel mine. There is nothing I despise more than the wicked convention that protects these things by forbidding a woman to mention them. And yet I cant tell you. The two infamous words[28] that describe what my mother is are ringing in my ears and struggling on my tongue; but I cant utter them: the shame of them is too horrible for me. [*She buries her face in her hands. The two men, astonished, stare at one another and then at her. She raises her head again desperately and snatches a sheet of paper and a pen*]. Here: let me draft you a prospectus.

FRANK. Oh, she's mad. Do you hear, Viv? mad. Come! pull yourself together.

VIVIE. You shall see. [*She writes*]. 'Paid up capital: not less than £40,000 standing in the name of Sir George Crofts, Baronet, the chief shareholder. Premises at Brussels, Ostend, Vienna and Budapest. Managing director: Mrs Warren'; and now dont let us forget h e r qualifications: the two words. [*She writes the words and pushes the paper to them*]. There! Oh no: dont read it: don't! [*She snatches it back and tears it to pieces; then seizes her head in her hands and hides her face on the table*].

    Frank, who has watched the writing over her shoulder, and opened his eyes very widely at it, takes a card from his pocket; scribbles the two words on it; and silently hands it to Praed, who reads it with amazement, and hides it hastily in his pocket.

FRANK [*whispering tenderly*] Viv, dear: thats all right. I read what you wrote: so did Praddy. We understand. And we remain, as this leaves us at present, yours ever so devotedly.

PRAED. We do indeed, Miss Warren. I declare you are the most splendidly courageous woman I ever met.

---

28. What the two words are is not absolutely clear, but "white slaver" would seem a good possibility. In his Preface to the play, Shaw had used the phrase "white slave traffic" as a synonym for Mrs Warren's profession, another way of describing the activities of those who dealt in organized prostitution by exploiting young women.

This sentimental compliment braces Vivie. She throws it away from her with an impatient shake, and forces herself to stand up, though not without some support from the table.

FRANK. Dont stir, Viv, if you dont want to. Take it easy.

VIVIE. Thank you. You can always depend on me for two things: not to cry and not to faint. [*She moves a few steps towards the door of the inner room, and stops close to Praed to say*] I shall need much more courage than that when I tell my mother that we have come to the parting of the ways. Now I must go into the next room for a moment to make myself neat again, if you dont mind.

PRAED. Shall we go away?

VIVIE. No: I'll be back presently. Only for a moment. [*She goes into the other room, Praed opening the door for her*].

PRAED. What an amazing revelation! I'm extremely disappointed in Crofts: I am indeed.

FRANK. I'm not in the least. I feel he's perfectly accounted for at last. But what a facer for me, Praddy! I cant marry her now.

PRAED [*sternly*] Frank! [*The two look at one another, Frank unruffled, Praed deeply indignant*] Let me tell you, Gardner, that if you desert her now you will behave very despicably.

FRANK. Good old Praddy! Ever chivalrous! But you mistake: it's not the moral aspect of the case: it's the money aspect. I really cant bring myself to touch the old woman's money now.

PRAED. And was that what you were going to marry on?

FRANK. What else? *I* havnt any money, not the smallest turn for making it. If I married Viv now she would have to support me; and I should cost her more than I am worth.

PRAED. But surely a clever bright fellow like you can make something by your own brains.

FRANK. Oh yes, a little [*He takes out his money again*]. I made all that yesterday in an hour and a half. But I made it in a highly speculative business. No, dear Praddy: even if Bessie and Georgina marry millionaires and the governor dies after cutting them off with a shilling, I shall have only four hundred a year. And he wont die until he's three score and ten: he hasnt originality enough. I shall be on short allowance for the next twenty years. No short allowance for Viv, if I can help it. I withdraw gracefully and leave the field to the gilded youth of England. So thats settled. I shant worry her about it: I'll just send her a little note after we're gone. She'll understand.

PRAED [*grasping his hand*] Good fellow, Frank! I heartily beg your pardon. But must you never see her again?

FRANK. Never see her again! Hang it all, be reasonable. I shall come along as often as possible, and be her brother. I can not understand the absurd consequences you romantic people expect from the most ordinary transactions. [*A knock at the door*]. I wonder who this is. Would you mind opening the door? If it's a client it will look more respectable than if I appeared.

PRAED. Certainly. [*He goes to the door and opens it. Frank sits down in Vivie's chair to scribble a note*]. My dear Kitty: come in: come in.

Mrs Warren comes in, looking apprehensively round for Vivie. She has done her best to make herself matronly and dignified. The brilliant hat is replaced by a sober bonnet, and the gay blouse covered by a costly black silk mantle. She is pitiably anxious and ill at ease: evidently panic-stricken.

MRS WARREN. [*to Frank*] What! Y o u r e here, are you?

FRANK [*turning in his chair from his writing, but not rising*] Here, and charmed to see you. You come like a breath of spring.

MRS WARREN. Oh, get out with your nonsense. [*In a low voice*] Where's Vivie?

Frank points expressively to the door of the inner room, but says nothing.

MRS WARREN [*sitting down suddenly and almost beginning to cry*] Praddy: wont she see me, dont you think?

PRAED. My dear Kitty: dont distress yourself. Why should she not?

MRS WARREN. Oh, you never can see why not: youre too innocent. Mr Frank: did she say anything to you?

FRANK [*folding his note*] She m u s t see you, i f [*very expressively*] you wait til she comes in.

MRS WARREN [*frightened*] Why shouldnt I wait?

Frank looks quizzically at her; puts his note carefully on the inkbottle, so that Vivie cannot fail to find it when next she dips her pen; then rises and devotes his attention to her.

FRANK. My dear Mrs Warren: suppose you were a sparrow—ever so tiny and pretty a sparrow hopping in the roadway—and you saw a steam roller coming in your direction, would you wait for it?

MRS WARREN. Oh, dont bother me with your sparrows. What did she run away from Haslemere like that for?

FRANK. I'm afraid she'll tell you if you rashly await her return.

MRS WARREN. Do you want me to go away?

FRANK. No: I always want you to stay. But I a d v i s e you to go away.

MRS WARREN. What! And never see her again!

FRANK. Precisely.

MRS WARREN [*crying again*] Praddy: dont let him be cruel to me. [*she hastily checks her tears and wipes her eyes*]. She'll be so angry if she sees Ive been crying.

FRANK [*with a touch of real compassion in his airy tenderness*] You know that Praddy is the soul of kindness, Mrs Warren. Praddy: what do you say? Go or stay?

PRAED [*to Mrs Warren*] I really should be very sorry to cause you unnecessary pain; but I think perhaps you had better not wait. The fact is—[*Vivie is heard at the inner door*].

FRANK. Sh! Too late. She's coming.

MRS WARREN. Dont tell her I was crying. [*Vivie comes in. She stops gravely on seeing Mrs Warren, who greets her with hysterical cheerfulness*]. Well, dearie. So here you are at last.

VIVIE. I am glad you have come: I want to speak to you. You said you were going, Frank, I think.

FRANK. Yes. Will you come with me, Mrs Warren? What do you say to a trip to Richmond, and the theatre in the evening? There is safety in Richmond. No steam roller there.

VIVIE. Nonsense, Frank. My mother will stay here.

MRS WARREN [*scared*] I dont know: perhaps I'd better go. We're disturbing you at your work.

VIVIE [*with quiet decision*] Mr Praed: please take Frank away. Sit down, mother. [*Mrs Warren obeys helplessly*].

PRAED. Come, Frank. Goodbye, Miss Vivie.

VIVIE [*shaking hands*] Goodbye. A pleasant trip.

PRAED. Thank you: thank you. I hope so.

FRANK [*to Mrs Warren*] Goodbye: youd ever so much better have taken my advice. [*He shakes hands with her. Then airily to Vivie*] Byebye, Viv.

VIVIE. Goodbye. [*He goes out gaily without shaking hands with her*].

PRAED [*sadly*] Goodbye, Kitty.

MRS WARREN [*snivelling*]—oodbye!

> *Praed goes. Vivie, composed and extremely grave, sits down in Honoria's chair, and waits for her mother to speak. Mrs Warren, dreading a pause, loses no time in beginning.*

MRS WARREN. Well, Vivie, what did you go away like that for without saying a word to me? How could you do such a thing! And what have you done to poor George? I wanted him to come with me; but he shuffled out of it. I could see that he was quite afraid of you. Only fancy: he wanted me not to come. As if [*trembling*] I should be afraid of you, dearie. [*Vivie's gravity deepens*]. But of course I told him it was all settled and comfortable between us, and that we were on the best of terms. [*She breaks down*]. Vivie: whats the meaning of this? [*She produces a commercial envelope, and fumbles at the enclosure with trembling fingers*]. I got it from the bank this morning.

VIVIE. It is my month's allowance. They sent it to me as usual the other day. I simply sent it back to be placed to your credit, and asked them to send you the lodgment receipt. In future I shall support myself.

MRS WARREN [*not daring to understand*] Wasnt it enough? Why didnt you tell me? [*With a cunning gleam in her eye*] I'll double it: I was intending to double it. Only let me know how much you want.

VIVIE. You know very well that that has nothing to do with it. From this time I go my own way in my own business and among my own friends. And you will go yours. [*She rises*]. Goodbye.

MRS WARREN [*rising, appalled*] Goodbye?

VIVIE. Yes: Goodbye. Come: dont let us make a useless scene: you understand perfectly well. Sir George Crofts has told me the whole business.

MRS WARREN [*angrily*] Silly old—[*She swallows an epithet, and turns white at the narrowness of her escape from uttering it*].

VIVIE. Just so.

MRS WARREN. He ought to have his tongue cut out. But I thought it was ended: you said you didnt mind.

VIVIE [*steadfastly*] Excuse me: I d o mind.

MRS WARREN. But I explained—

VIVIE. You explained how it came about. You did not tell me that it is still going on. [*She sits*].

> Mrs Warren, silenced for a moment, looks forlornly at Vivie, who waits, secretly hoping that the combat is over. But the cunning expression comes back into Mrs Warren's face; and she bends across the table, sly and urgent, half whispering.

MRS WARREN. Vivie: do you know how rich I am?

VIVIE. I have no doubt you are very rich.

MRS WARREN. But you dont know all that that means: youre too young. It means a new dress every day; it means theatres and balls every night; it means having the pick of all the gentlemen in Europe at your feet; it means a lovely house and plenty of servants; it means the choicest of eating and drinking; it means everything you like, everything you want, everything you can think of. And what are you here? A mere drudge, toiling and moiling early and late for your bare living and two cheap dresses a year. Think over it. [*Soothingly*] Youre shocked, I know. I can enter into your feelings; and I think they do you credit; but trust me, nobody will blame you: you may take my word for that. I know what young girls are; and I know youll think better of it when youve turned it over in your mind.

VIVIE. So thats how it's done, is it? You must have said all that to many a woman, mother, to have it so pat.

MRS WARREN [*passionately*] What harm am I asking you to do? [*Vivie turns away contemptuously. Mrs Warren continues desperately*]. Vivie: listen to me: you dont understand: youve been taught wrong on purpose: you dont know what the world is really like.

VIVIE [*arrested*] Taught wrong on purpose! What do you mean?

MRS WARREN. I mean that youre throwing away all your chances for nothing. You think that people are what they pretend to be: that the way you were taught at school and college to think right and proper is the way things really are. But it's not: it's all only a pretence, to keep the cowardly slavish common run of people quiet. Do you want to find that out, like other women, at forty, when youve thrown yourself away and lost your chances; or wont you take it in good time now from your own mother, that loves you and swears to you that it's truth: gospel truth? [*Urgently*] Vivie: the big people, the clever people, the managing people, all know it. They do as I do, and think what I think. I know plenty of them. I know them to speak to, to introduce you to, to make friends of for you. I dont mean anything wrong: thats what you dont understand: your head is full of ignorant ideas about me. What do the people that taught you know about life or about people like me? When did they ever meet me, or speak to me, or let anyone tell them about me? the fools! Would they ever have done anything for you if I hadnt paid them? Havnt I told you that I want you to be respectable? Havnt I brought you up to be respectable? And how can you keep it up without my money and my influence and Lizzie's friends? Cant you see that youre cutting your own throat as well as breaking my heart in turning your back on me?

VIVIE. I recognize the Crofts philosophy of life, mother. I heard it all from him that day at the Gardners'.

MRS WARREN. You think I want to force that played-out old sot on you! I dont, Vivie: on my oath I dont.

VIVIE. It would not matter if you did: you would not succeed. [*Mrs Warren winces, deeply hurt by the implied indifference towards her affectionate intention. Vivie, neither understanding this nor concerning herself about it, goes on calmly*]. Mother: you dont at all know the sort of person I am. I dont object to Crofts more than to any other coarsely built man of his class. To tell you the truth, I rather admire him for being strongminded enough to enjoy himself in his own way and make plenty of money instead of living the usual shooting, hunting, dining-out, tailoring, loafing life of his set merely because all the rest do it. And I'm perfectly aware that if I'd been in the same circumstances as my aunt Liz, I'd have done exactly what she did. I dont think I'm more prejudiced or straitlaced than you: I think I'm less. I'm certain I'm less sentimental. I know very well that fashionable morality is all a pretence, and that if I took your money and devoted the rest of my life to spending it fashionably, I might be as worthless and vicious as the silliest woman could possibly want to be without having a word said to me about it. But I dont want to be worthless. I shouldnt enjoy trotting about the park to advertise my dressmaker and carriage builder, or being bored at the opera to shew off a shopwindowful of diamonds.

MRS WARREN [*bewildered*] But—

VIVIE. Wait a moment: Ive not done. Tell me why you continue your business now that you are independent of it. Your sister, you told me, has left all that behind her. Why dont you do the same?

MRS WARREN. Oh, it's all very easy for Liz: she likes good society, and has the air of being a lady. Imagine me in a cathedral town! Why, the very rooks in the trees would find me out even if I could stand the dulness of it. I must have work and excitement, or I should go melancholy mad. And what else is there for me to do? The life suits me: I'm fit for it and not for anything else. If I didnt do it somebody else would; so I dont do any real harm by it. And then it brings in money; and I like making money. No: it's no use: I cant give it up—not for anybody. But what need you know about it? I'll never mention it. I'll keep Crofts away. I'll not trouble you much: you see I have to be constantly running about from one place to another. Youll be quit of me altogether when I die.

VIVIE. No: I am my mother's daughter. I am like you: I must have work, and must make more money than I spend. But my work is not your work, and my way not your way.[29] We must part. It will not make much difference to us: instead of meeting one another for perhaps a few months in twenty years, we shall never meet: thats all.

MRS WARREN [*her voice stifled in tears*] Vivie: I meant to have been more with you: I did indeed.

VIVIE. It's no use, mother: I am not to be changed by a few cheap tears and entreaties any more than you are, I daresay.

MRS WARREN [*wildly*] Oh, you call a mother's tears cheap.

VIVIE. They cost you nothing; and you ask me to give you the peace and quietness of my whole life in exchange for them. What use would my company be to you if you could get it? What have we two in common that could make either of us happy together?

MRS WARREN [*lapsing recklessly into her dialect*] We're mother and daughter. I want my daughter. Ive a right to you. Who is to care for me when I'm old? Plenty of girls have taken to me like daughters and cried at leaving me; but I let them all go because I had you to look forward to. I kept myself lonely for you. Youve no right to turn on me now and refuse to do your duty as a daughter.

VIVIE [*jarred and antagonized by the echo of the slums in her mother's voice*] My duty as a daughter! I thought we should come to that presently. Now once for all, mother, you want a daughter and Frank wants a wife. I dont want a mother; and I dont want a husband. I have spared neither Frank nor myself in sending him about his business. Do you think I will spare you?

MRS WARREN [*violently*] Oh, I know the sort you are: no mercy for yourself or anyone else. *I* know. My experience has done that for me anyhow: I can tell the pious, canting, hard, selfish woman when I meet her. Well, keep yourself to yourself: *I* dont want you. But listen to this. Do you know what I would do with you if you were a baby again? aye, as sure as theres a Heaven above us.

VIVIE. Strangle me, perhaps.

MRS WARREN. No: I'd bring you up to be a real daughter to me, and not what you are now, with your pride and your prejudices and the college education you stole from me: yes, stole: deny it if you can: what was it but stealing? I'd bring you up in my own house, I would.

VIVIE [*quietly*] In one of your own houses.

MRS WARREN [*screaming*] Listen to her! listen to how she spits on her mother's grey hairs! Oh, may you live to have your own daughter tear and trample on you as you have trampled on me. And you will: you will. No woman ever had luck with a mother's curse on her.

VIVIE. I wish you wouldnt rant, mother. It only hardens me. Come: I suppose I am the only young woman you ever had in your power that you did good to. Dont spoil it all now.

MRS WARREN. Yes, Heaven forgive me, it's true; and you are the only one that ever

---

29. Vivie's words here seem a deliberate yet negative echo of Ruth's well-known promise to her mother-in-law Naomi: see Ruth 1:15–17.

turned on me. Oh, the injustice of it! the injustice! the injustice! I always wanted to be a good woman. I tried honest work; and I was slave-driven until I cursed the day I ever heard of honest work. I was a good mother; and because I made my daughter a good woman she turns me out as if I was a leper. Oh, if I only had my life to live over again! I'd talk to that lying clergyman in the school. From this time forth, so help me Heaven in my last hour, I'll do wrong and nothing but wrong. And I'll prosper on it.

VIVIE. Yes: it's better to choose your line and go through with it. If I had been you, mother, I might have done as you did: but I should not have lived one life and believed in another. You are a conventional woman at heart. That is why I am bidding you goodbye now. I am right, am I not?

MRS WARREN [*taken aback*] Right to throw away all my money?

VIVIE. No: right to get rid of you! I should be a fool not to! Isnt that so?

MRS WARREN [*sulkily*] Oh well, yes, if you come to that, I suppose you are. But Lord help the world if everybody took to doing the right thing! And now I'd better go than stay where I'm not wanted. [*She turns to the door*].

VIVIE [*kindly*] Wont you shake hands?

MRS WARREN [*after looking at her fiercely for a moment with a savage impulse to strike her*] No, thank you. Goodbye.

VIVIE [*matter-of-factly*] Goodbye. [*Mrs Warren goes out, slamming the door behind her. The strain on Vivie's face relaxes; her grave expression breaks up into one of joyous content; her breath goes out in a half sob, half laugh of intense relief. She goes buoyantly to her place at the writing-table; pushes the electric lamp out of the way; pulls over a great sheaf of papers; and is in the act of dipping her pen in the ink when she finds Frank's note. She opens it unconcernedly and reads it quickly, giving a little laugh at some quaint turn of expression in it*]. And goodbye, Frank. [*She tears the note up and tosses the pieces into the wastepaper basket without a second thought. Then she goes at her work with a plunge, and soon becomes absorbed in its figures*].

Author and Title Index

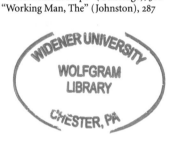